KU-639-789

To my wife, Debby,

for her love and devotion:

This book is for you.

THE ENCYCLOPEDIA OF ANIMATED CARTOONS

SECOND EDITION

JEFF LENBURG
FOREWORD BY JUNE FORAY

Checkmark Books™

An imprint of Facts On File, Inc.

THE ENCYCLOPEDIA OF ANIMATED CARTOONS, SECOND EDITION

Copyright © 1999 by Jeff Lenburg

All rights reserved. No part of this book may be reproduced or utilized in any form or by any means, electronic or mechanical, including photocopying, recording, or by any information storage or retrieval system, without permission in writing from the publisher. For information contact:

Checkmark Books
An Imprint of Facts On File, Inc.
11 Penn Plaza
New York, NY 10001

Library of Congress Cataloging-in-Publication Data

Lenburg, Jeff.
The encyclopedia of animated cartoons / by Jeff Lenburg ; foreword by June Foray.—2nd ed.
p. cm.
Includes bibliographical references and index.
ISBN 0-8160-3831-7 (hc : alk. paper).—ISBN 0-8160-3832-5 (pbk. : alk. paper)
1. Animated films—United States—History and criticism.
I. Title.
NC1766.U5L46 1999
791.43'3—dc21 98-46100

Checkmark Books are available at special discounts when purchased in bulk quantities for businesses, associations, institutions or sales promotions. Please call our Special Sales Department in New York at (212) 967-8800 or (800) 322-8755.

You can find Facts On File on the World Wide Web at http://www.factsonfile.com

Color insert designed by Sandra Watanabe
Text design by Cathy Rincon
Cover design by Sandra Watanabe

Illustration Credits: page iii, page 1: Bugs Bunny © Warner Bros., Inc.; page 18: Felix the Cat © Joe Oriolo Productions; page 160: Casper the Friendly Ghost © Harvey Cartoons; page 215: The Little Drummer Boy © Rankin-Bass Productions; page 353: Yogi Bear and Boo-Boo © Hanna-Barbera Productions; page 553: Woody Woodpecker © Walter Lantz Productions

Printed in the United States of America

VB Hermitage 10 9 8 7 6 5 4 3 2 1
(Pbk) 10 9 8 7 6 5 4 3 2 1

This book is printed on acid-free paper.

CONTENTS

FOREWORD

Way back in the 1950s I became aware of the significance and my love of animation, which insinuates itself into all our lives, not only in the United States, but in every country in the world that produces this art form.

When Jeff Lenburg asked me to write this foreword to his remarkable history of animation, I seriously examined the impact of moving cartoons since the work of French animator Georges Méliès, in 1896, and American animator Winsor McCay, in the early 1900s with his *Gertie the Dinosaur* graced our screens and entered our consciousness through their frame-by-frame animated films. Print cartoons are still alive and well in newspapers and magazines, but think of all those cartoons that have been and still are transferred as living images on movie screens in theaters and on television sets around the world. What a remarkable history they have had.

Becoming a professional radio actor at the age of 15, I never entertained the idea of being a voice-over artist in animation—in fact, it never occurred to me. Bugs Bunny and Mickey Mouse were just amusing characters in movies, nothing more.

Of course, today it's hard for me to imagine what my life would have been like if I had never entered the world of cartoons. What magic moments I have experienced: working under contract at Capitol Records; recording children's albums with Mel Blanc, Stan Freberg and Daws Butler (with original stories written by then A&R man and legendary music composer Alan Livingston); then being called to do my first cartoon voice-over as Lucifer the cat in Disney's 1950 full-length animated feature, *Cinderella*, my first introduction to an animation studio. Then followed the metamorphosis of my persona into the hand-drawn Indian woman in *Peter Pan*, the comically evil Witch Hazel, Goofy's wife and assorted characters in sundry Disney theatrical cartoon shorts in the 1940s and 1950s, not to mention working and becoming closely acquainted with directors, storyboarders, animators and writers and realizing that hand-drawn sketches on paper and cels could move us to laughter and tears. What magic moments indeed.

The Disney experience propelled me toward a lifelong profession that I learned to enjoy even more when legendary Warner Bros. animator Chuck Jones, intrigued by my voice of Disney's Witch Hazel, hired me to perform his version of the crusty old witch in Warner Bros. cartoons. What a joy it was working alongside Chuck (who didn't forget me when he left Warners for MGM and used me in many of his productions), and later another Warner Bros. cartoon legend, Friz Freleng, who cast me for the voice of Sylvester and Tweety's Granny for his theatrical shorts (Forty years later I'm still doing Granny on the *Sylvester and Tweety Mysteries* on the WB Network—can you believe it?), Miss Prissy (in the *Foghorn Leghorn* cartoons), Alice in *The Honey-mousers* (a spoof of TV's *The Honeymooners* directed by Warner Bros. cartoon great Robert McKimson) and so many other wonderful characters.

I've been lucky to work with the true greats in the biz, including famed screwball animator Tex Avery, during his stopover at MGM after he left Warner Bros., providing voices for his cartoons (*One Cab's Family* and *Cars of Tomorrow*, which I narrated), and Bill Hanna and Joe Barbera, legends in their own right at MGM and seven-time Oscar winners for their outrageous *Tom and Jerry* cartoon shorts. (Wouldn't you know? They also loved Witch Hazel, so I became a witch again in their MGM cartoon short, *Flying Sorceress*.) And dear old Walter Lantz even hired me to do voices for numerous characters (Knothead and Splinter, to name a few) on his wildly funny *Woody Woodpecker* cartoon shorts.

What fun! And the explosion of animation on television brought many new and exciting roles. I was chosen by the wonderfully talented Jay Ward to do the voice of Rocky the flying squirrel and the evil Pottsylvanian spy Natale Fatale, and later Nell Fenwick, girlfriend of that dum-dum mountie Dudley Do-Right (in the eponymous cartoons). Later I lent my voice to Brooklyn princesses, loud-mouthed fairy godmothers and witches—again in the silly *Fractured Fairytales*—as well as to the long-suffering Ursula, wife of George of the Jungle, and Marigold, girlfriend of that not-so-slick racecar driver Tom Slick. For that matter, voices of assorted other characters then and since on many other programs, such as Ross Bagdasarian Sr.'s *The Alvin Show, Calvin and the Colonel* (with the voices of the radio's original *Amos 'n' Andy*, Freeman Gosden and Charles Correll), and *The Lone Ranger*, not to forget Grammi Gummi, Jokey Smurf (from TV's *The Smurfs*), Ma Beagle and Magica De Spell. I've also filled steady parts on *Spider-Man and His Amazing Friends, Teen Wolf* and many recently produced shows. (Just check the credits and you'll see my name.)

It's been a rewarding experience, to say the least. From my involvement in the 1960s in forming the first American chapter of the International Animated Film Society (ASIPA), made up of animators, writers, actors and editors worldwide; attending festivals in Annecy, Zagreb, Moscow, Bucharest, London, Ottawa and Hiroshima in tribute to other great animators in the world—from John Halas to Bruno Bozzetto to Chiro Kawamoto, many of whom have received Oscars; honoring every segment of animation with the start of ASIFA's annual Annie Awards in 1972; and representing animated short films on the Board of Governors of the Academy of Motion Pictures Arts and Science (since 1977). It has all only increased my zealousness for the encouragement, promotion and preservation of this dazzling art form.

Thank you, Jeff Lenburg, for the privilege of writing a perhaps self-indulgent foreword to your encyclopedia and for your efforts not only to preserve and document the great history of our industry but to affirm that animation is resplendent and inspiring to us all.

S'wunnerful! Take it from a flying squirrel.

June Foray

PREFACE

⊚ ⊚ ⊚ ⊚ ⊚

Eighteen years ago I penned what was intended to be the most complete book on animated cartoon series ever, *The Encyclopedia of Animated Cartoon Series*. The book was born out of the dream that there be a major reference on animated cartoons. This volume became the first to document hundreds of cartoon series—silent cartoons, theatrical cartoons and television cartoons.

In 1991, on the 10th anniversary of the original edition, Facts On File published my updated and expanded version of the former, retitled *The Encyclopedia of Animated Cartoons*. Unlike my first encyclopedia, this one was more definitive in scope, chronicling the history of every silent cartoon series, theatrical cartoon series, animated feature, animated television special and animated television series.

In my relentless pursuit to fully document the history of this subject, *The Encyclopedia of Animated Cartoons, Second Edition* again delivers the most comprehensive, authoritative volume on cartoons ever imagined. Designed as the ultimate cartoon fan's guide, it features detailed information on every animated cartoon production, series or program exhibited theatrically or broadcast on television (on major commercial networks and cable networks, now expanded to cover cartoon programs broadcast on Animal Planet, Arts & Entertainment Network, Black Entertainment Television, The Cartoon Network, Comedy Central, The Disney Channel, The Family Channel, The Fox Network, HBO, The History Channel, MTV, Nickelodeon, PBS, Sci-Fi Channel, Showtime, The Learning Channel, TBS, TNT, UPN, USA Network, VH1 and the WB Network) in the United States (foreign cartoon imports from Japan, Canada and elsewhere are included) from 1911 to April 1998—roughly 87 years' worth of 'toons!

Every attempt has been made to provide the most complete account possible of each cartoon production listed, culling the information from studio production records, motion picture trade paper listings, television program guides,

movie and television reviews, film vaults and movie warehouses and, in many cases, from credits listed on the films themselves. This information was then cross-referenced with countless reliable sources to ensure its accuracy.

The book is divided into six sections: silent cartoon series, theatrical sound cartoon series, full-length animated features, animated television specials, television cartoon series (including Saturday-morning, syndicated and cable-produced programs), and Academy Award and Emmy Award listings, featuring winners and nominees in the area of cartoon animation since the honors first began.

For easy reference, each entry provides the following: series history, voice credits (except silent cartoons, of course) and year produced or broadcast, and complete filmographes (except in the case of animated television specials and animated television series).

Silent cartoon entries include a complete historical account of each series and, where available, director and producer credits, and release dates (month, day and year) of each cartoon in the series. For theatrical sound cartoon series, director credits (overall and for each cartoon), voice credits, release dates (month, day and year), reissue dates (abbreviated as "re"), working titles (original titles of cartoons before they were changed for release), episode costars (example: with Porky Pig), Academy Award nominations (listed as A.A. nominee or A.A. winner) and special film format (i.e., Cinecolor, CinemaScope, Technicolor, etc.) are listed under the respective series.

In the full-length animated feature section, complete summaries have been provided for each entry, as well as technical credits and side notes about the production (listed under "PN," for "production notes"). The section contains only feature films that received wide distribution in this country, whether produced domestically or overseas.

For animated television specials and animated television series, program overviews, primary voice credits, premiere dates and rebroadcast dates (in most cases, only primary rebroadcast dates are noted, due to space limitations) have been included wherever possible. In many cases, background information and reminiscences of the animators or producers have been incorporated into the entries to paint a vivid picture of the production and its characters and to provide insights into the filmmaking process. In order to add hundreds of new animated specials and animated cartoon series for television to this second edition, additional voice credits and episode title listings, featured in the past two editions, are not included. (Please consult the Facts On File first edition for this information.)

The following common abbreviations have been used to identify the corresponding networks when listing broadcast dates for television specials and television series entries:

A&E: Arts & Entertainment Network
ABC: American Broadcasting Company
AP: Animal Planet
BET: Black Entertainment Television
CAR: The Cartoon Network
CBS: Columbia Broadcasting Company
COM: Comedy Central
DIS: The Disney Channel

FAM: The Family Channel
FOX: Fox Television Network
HBO: Home Box Office
HIS: The History Channel
MTV: Music Television
NBC: National Broadcasting Company
NIK: Nickelodeon
SHO: Showtime
TLC: The Learning Channel
TBS: Turner Broadcasting System
TNT: Turner Network Television
UPN: United Paramount Network
USA: USA Network
VH1: VH1
WB: The WB Television Network

In addition, the book has been carefully indexed for each of the following areas of interest: general subject references, voice actors, producers and directors, and animated characters.

Enjoy!

Jeff Lenburg
Rancho Mirage, California

ACKNOWLEDGMENTS

Few people could imagine the man-hours involved in compiling a definitive reference with one single purpose: to offer the most informative, nostalgic reference on nearly every animated cartoon since humans first invented the art.

Well, the truth of the matter is that most of the information contained in this volume took more years than I would personally like to remember to research, write and cross-check in order to present the most accurate account possible for each production listed. Studios, distributors, directors, producers, animators, cartoon collectors and even curators of film vaults were consulted in the course of compiling this book. The result was hundreds of letters, phone calls, faxes, emails and other means of correspondence in the United States and abroad to corroborate facts and acquire information necessary to make this wonderful celebration of animated cartoons as complete as possible.

Fortunately, a great many people shared my belief in the importance of documenting the history of this popular medium, and all were willing to offer one more bit of information or render a few more minutes of their precious time to make this "dream book" a reality.

First and foremost, I would like to thank the many producers, directors, animators and voice artists—many of whom I have admired for their ingenuity and talent—who, over the years, supplied information, materials and their personal support to this project. They include Joe Barbera, Jules Bass, Joy Batchelor, Dick Brown, Daws Butler, Fred Calvert, Bob Clampett, Shamus Culhane, David H. DePatie, Friz Freleng, June Foray, John Halas, Bill Hanna, Faith Hubley, Bill Hurtz, Chuck Jones, Fred Ladd, Walter Lantz, Norman Maurer, Bill Melendez, Don Messick, Joe Oriolo, Arthur Rankin, Joe Ruby, Lou Scheimer, Hal Seeger, Ken Spears, Jay Ward and Rudy Zamora.

Much of the information featured in this volume would not have been possible without the generous support of many production companies and their staffs. In this instance, I would like to extend my personal thanks to David R. Smith and Paula Sigman, Walt Disney Archives; Derek Westervelt, Nancy Battele and Nan Kelinson, Walt Disney Productions; Joanna Coletta and Leo Moran, Bill Melendez Productions; William Ruiz, Eric Stein and George Robertson, DIC Enterprises; Trudi Takamatsu, Murakami-Wolf-Swenson Films; Melani Tandon, Nelvana Limited; Steven Gold, Klasky Csupo, Inc.; Henry Saperstein, United Productions of America (UPA); Jim Graziano, Kelly Irwin and Star Kaplan, Marvel Productions; Stanley Stunell and Jacki Yaro, Lone Ranger Television; Ken Snyder and Tish Gainey, Ken Snyder Productions; Victoria McCollom, Collette Sunderman, Michael Diaz, Hanna-Barbera Productions; Janie Fields and Jan Albright, DePatie-Freleng Enterprises; Dave Bennett, Rick Reinert Pictures; and Jeff Cooke, Ruby-Spears Productions.

I would also like to acknowledge Joanne McQueen, Rankin-Bass Productions; Robert Miller, Walter Lantz Productions; Herbert A. Nusbaum, Metro-Goldwyn-Mayer; Quan Phung, Tod Roberts and Sari DeCesare, National Broadcasting Company (NBC); Jenny Trias and Joyce Loeb, Filmation; Suzy Missirlani, Film Roman Productions; Gloria Foster, ZIV International; Lee Polk and Laurie Tritini, King Features Entertainment; Leon Harvey and Evelyn Johnson, Harvey Films; William Weiss, Charles Tolep, Terrytoons Productions; Ann Pulley, Royal Productions; Deborah Fine LucasFilm; Janis Diamond, Farmhouse Films; James Stabile and Lee Orgel, Metromedia Producers Corporation; Elizabeth Shaw, MCA; Bart Farber, Virginia Brown and Maury Oken, United Artists; Hal Geer, Ahuva Rabani and Edward A. Hoffman, Warner Brothers; Robert L. Rosen, RLR Associates; Laura Ramsay, Bob Keeshan Enterprises; Loretta Petersohn, Thea Flaum Productions; Dana Booton, Gledye Newman, Amber Santilli and C.J. Grant, Saban International; Stephen Worth, Bagdasarian Productions; Jody Zucker and Howard Barton, Paramount Pictures; Rosalind Goldberg, Larry

Harmon Pictures; and Michael Hack, TMS Entertainment.

I would further like to thank Anthony Gentile Sr., Abrams/Gentile Entertainment; Jennifer Thieroff and Julie Hildebrand, Britt Alcroft Incorporated; Marija Miletic Dail, Animation Cottage; Dionne Nosek and Terry Weiss, Children's Television Workshop; Caroline Faucher, Cinar Films; Bob Higgins, Rita Johnstone and Michelle Beber, Columbia/TriStar Television; Ralph Edwards, Ralph Edwards Films; Scott Taylor and Russell P. Marleau, Hyperion Animation; Cary Silver, MGM Animation; Becky Mancuso-Winding, Lois Kramer and Dana Coccara, Sony Wonder; Christina Rundbaken and Robin Alcock, Sunbow Productions; Barbara Beasley, Don Barrett, Nest Entertainment, Jerry Reynolds, Perennial Pictures; Liz Topazzio, Active Entertainment; Paola Fantini, Hallmark Entertainment; Jan Nagel, Calico Creations; Michael Sporn and Christine O'Neill, Michael Sporn Animation; Rick Pack, Kookanooga Toons; Teresa Frisani, Paragon Entertainment (formerly Lacewood Productions); Jay Poynor, AniMagic Entertainment; Paul Marshal, O Entertainment; John Sinclair and Eadie Morley, Playmate Toys; and Sam McKendry, PorchLight Entertainment.

The support of the following individuals and companies was also most appreciated: Tiffany Fegley, Hearst Entertainment; Pam Bobbitt-Daniel, Lightyear Entertainment; Valerie Delafoy, Parafrance Communication; Adrian Woolery, Playhouse Pictures; Keven Reher, Premavision; Liz Foster and Claire Wilmut, Evergreen Productions; Steven Melnick and Joyce Irby, 20th Century-Fox Television; Peggy Ray, Republic Pictures Corporation; Vicki Lowry and Anita Kelso, World Events Productions; Leslie Maryon-LaRose, Scholastic Productions; Allan Migram, Marvel Comics Group; Riaya Aboul Ela, Prism Entertainment; Sallie Smith, Vicki Greenleaf, Family Home Entertainment; Robert Kanner, Buena Vista Home Video; Carol Paskewitz, Just for Kids Home Video; Alex Drosin, Golden Book Home Video; Andy Stern, Celebrity Just For Kids Video; Amy Sprecher, Polygram Home Video, Dirk Van Tilborg, SSA Public Relations; Jeryl Reitzer, Summit Media Group; Linda LePage-Chown, Telegenic; Karen Samfilippo, Jeff Fink and Cindy Anderson, Live Entertainment; Paul J. Newman, Columbia/TriStar Home Video; Aaron Severson, BKN Kids Network (formerly Bohbot Entertainment); and Jennifer Erskine, Santa Ventura Studios.

Television networks, local television stations and television program distributors also played significant roles in contributing material to this book. Among those who helped were Jerry Westfeldt, TV Cinema Sales; Sandy Frank, Sandy Frank Film Syndication; Lonnie D. Halouska, Rex Waggoner and Phyllis Kirk, National Telefilm Associates (NTA); Sandra R. Mueller and Tom Hatten, KTLA-TV; Tim McGowan, KCAL-Channel 9; Carol Martz, KCOP-Channel 13; Casey Garvey, KCET-TV; Lisa Mateas, Dick Connell, Michelle Couch and Walt Ward, Turner Network Television; Mike Lazzo, Frederika Brooksfield and Paul Siefken, The Cartoon Network; Peter DeJong, A&E Television Networks; Lee Nash, Worldvision; Barry Kluger, March 5; Caroline Ansell, Viacom International; Robert Ferson, The Right Stuf; Donita J. Delzer, Evangelical Lutheran Church in America; Ann B. Cody, Westchester Films; Nancy Allen, Thames Taffner; Priscilla French, Harmony Gold; Joe Adelman and Elise Sugar, Color Systems Technology; and Bob Mittenthal, Heather Morgan, Christopher Adams, Kat Fair, Donna Smith, Lisa Schiraldi and Fran Brochstein, Nickelodeon.

Also Holly Grieve, MG Perin, Inc.; Amy Sauertieg, SFM Entertainment; Daniel Mulholland, Muller Media, Inc.; Yolanda Cortez, Alice Communications; Claudia Cooper, ABC Children's Programming; Carol Rosen, Katherine Pongracz, Jody Stahl, Lisa Fishkind, Mara Mellin, Sara Fitzsimmons, HBO; Carolyn Ceslik and Joyce Nishihira, CBS Entertainment; Farrell Meisel, WWOR-TV; Jefferi K. Lee and Cindy Mahmoud, Black Entertainment Television; Carol Sussman, The Disney Channel; Carol Monroe, Amanda Gumbs and Erik Aronson, Fox Kids Network; Jennifer Gershon, Barry Kluger and Merle Becker, MTV/VH1; Alice Cahn, PBS; David Schwartz, USA Network; Carolyn Miller, Wayne Baker, The Family Channel; Barry Schulman, The Sci-Fi Channel; Leisa Rivosecchi and Ken Preister, Italtoons Corporation; Andrea Roy, Cambium Releasing; Sally Thoun and Jean Flores, Warner Brothers International; and William Cayton, Radio and Television Packagers.

Many historians, cartoon collectors and buffs (some of them experts in their own field of interest) provided information critical to the successful completion of numerous entries in this book. I would like to pay special tribute to Joe Adamson, Al Bigley, Eric Bolden, Dan Brown, John Cawley, Karl Cohen, Jeff Cook, Greg Duffel, Mark Evanier, James Gauthier, Aaron Handy III, Ronnie James, Mark Kausler, Ken Layton, Mike Lefebvre, Greg Lenburg, Bob Miller, David Moore, Quinn Norman, Brian Pearce, Doug Ranney, Randy Skretvedt, Anthony Specian Jr. and Charles Wagner.

In the area of Japanese cartoons, perhaps the most difficult to document, I would like to thank the following for their time in furnishing vital information and materials to me for the many entries listed: Barbara Edmunds, Meg Evans, Tom Hamilton, James Long, Frederick Patten, Lorraine Savage and Scott Wheeler.

Naturally, I cannot forget the tremendous support that I received from the following libraries and their staffs in tracking down background information, reviews, production listings, special collections and illustrations to make this project as authoritative as possible. They are: Kristine Krueger and Howard H. Prouty, The Academy of Motion

Pictures Arts and Sciences Library; The Museum of Modern Art; Alan Braun, The Louis B. Mayer Library of The American Film Institute; The Cerritos Public Library; The Anaheim Public Library; The College of the Desert Library and The Rancho Mirage Public Library.

Much of the information contained in this book was dependent on not only studio records and private collections but also on material culled from the pages of a number of major Hollywood motion picture and television journals. To this end, I would like to offer my personal thanks to the men and women of the following publications, whose diligence in recording weekly productions logs and other technical information made this book what it is today: *Box Office, Daily Variety, Hollywood Reporter, Motion Picture Herald* and *Motion Picture News*. Also, the following publications were invaluable resources for facts and information contained in this book: *American Film, Animania* (formerly *Mindrot*), *Animation Magazine, Broadcast Information Bureau—TV Series Source Book, Broadcasting Magazine, The Los Angeles Times, Millimeter Magazine, The New York Times, Radio/TV Age, TV Guide* and *USA Today*.

I would further like to tip my hat to other devotees of animation who through their own personal interest and commitment have provided the basis for research on various cartoon characters, their films or programs through their own labors of love, including Jerry Beck, Will Friedwald, Leonard Maltin, George Woolery, Joe Adamson, Donald Crafton and Hal Erickson.

Last but not least, I want to thank God for providing me with the patience and fortitude to cope with the challenges that greeted me at every turn—especially in typing the nearly 2,300-page manuscript—and to complete the task at hand. And, of course, to my wife, Debby, for her love and encouragement every step of the way.

A Nutshell History of the American Animated Cartoon

For more than 90 years, the animated cartoon has been entertaining people, young and old, in movie theaters and on television with countless works of art and a virtual calvacade of cartoon characters that have captured the hearts and imaginations of fans in every corner of the globe. This legion of animated heroes and vast array of cartoon productions still produces wild cheers and uncontrollable laughter, whether it is through television reruns of old favorites or the debut of new, original characters who create enchanting and memorable moments that endure forever.

Why this long–running love affair with cartoons? Why do so many people still watch their favorite cartoon characters in countless television reruns? And why do new characters and new ideas still turn on audiences today? The reason for this amazing phenomenon is simple: Animated cartoons are the embodiment of a fantasy world worth treasuring, worth enjoying and, most of all, worth remembering over and over again, no matter what place in time or what changes have occurred in the real world around it.

It is funny, in a strange sort of way, but animated cartoons were not always held in such high esteem. In the days of silent cartoons, the industry experienced a tremendous backlash of criticism from film critics, movie fans and even studio executives who felt the new medium lacked congruent stories and consistent animation quality to be taken seriously in the world of entertainment. Maybe so. But, like any untested product, it was just a matter of time before the technique of animation would be mastered, creating a visually perfect running machine with plenty of mileage still ahead.

The beginning was 1906, with the debut of the first animated film in this country, *Humorous Phases of Funny Faces*. Released by Vitagraph, cartoonist James Stuart Blackton, who sold his first cartoon to the *New York World* and cofounded Vitagraph, entered the animation business with this first effort six years after his nonanimated triumph, *The Enchanted Drawing*, a short Edison film based on the newspaper cartoonist's "chalk–talk" vaudeville act.

By today's standards of animation, Blackton's *Humorous Phases of Funny Faces* is rudimentary at best. The film is composed of a series of scenes featuring letters, words and faces drawn by an "unseen" hand. For the era in which it was made, the simplistically styled one–reel short was an important first step.

The concept of animated cartoons in this country ultimately took root thanks to two other foresighted pioneers: French cartoonist Emil Cohl and American newspaper cartoonist Winsor McCay.

Cohl followed Blackton with a stick–figure animated short presented in a series of comic vignettes entitled *Drame Chez Les Fantoches* (1908). The film was everything that an animated cartoon was supposed to be—funny, sophisticated and well conceived. McCay surpassed even Cohl's landmark effort with his first entry, *Little Nemo*, the first fully animated cartoon. Based on his own beloved *New York Herald* strip *Little Nemo in Slumberland*, McCay reportedly spent four years animating the production.

While the films of all three men were important to the growth of the cartoon industry, McCay may have done more for the art of animation than his predecessors when he created what many historians consider to be the first genuine American cartoon star in *Gertie the Dinosaur* (1914). The first film to feature frame-by-frame animation and fluid, sophisticated movement, it took McCay approximately 10,000 drawings to animate the five–minute production. The one-reel short was animated on six-by-eight-inch sheets of translucent rice paper, with the drawings lightly penciled first and then detailed in Higgins black ink.

It was a tremendous technical achievement, but surprisingly most critics felt the production lost audiences with its story line. In the film, the animator (McCay) is seen drawing the cartoon, in live action, slowly bringing Gertie into existence and into the real world to then try to tame the beast.

Audiences did not share critics' opinions. Reportedly they were awed by the dinosaur's lifelike movements, unaware that what they had seen would change the course of animation's young history for the better.

The late Paul Terry, the father of Terrytoons, often credited McCay for arousing his and others' interest in animated cartoons, at a time when most people did not fully grasp the potential of the medium. As he once said, "Together with more than a hundred other artists, I attended a dinner in 1914 at which McCay spoke. He showed us his cartoon *Gertie, the Dinosaur*. It was the first animated cartoon we had ever seen, and as McCay told us his ideas about animation as a great coming medium of expression, we really hardly knew what he was talking about, he was so far ahead of his time."

McCay's imprint on the cartoon industry was widespread, but another early pioneer was responsible for improving the consistency of animation and the health of the industry overall. John Randolph ("J.R.") Bray was perhaps the country's most prolific producer of cartoon shorts. In 1913, following a career as an American newspaper cartoonist, Bray produced his first animated short, *The Artist's Dream* (or *The Dachsund and the Sausage*), which quickly established him in the medium.

Bray followed this celluloid feat with his first of many successful cartoon series, *Colonel Heeza Liar,* based on the tale-spinning adventures of Baron Munchausen. (Walter Lantz, the father of Woody Woodpecker, was one of the series' chief animators.) The series spawned other successes for Bray, among them *Bobby Bumps* (1915), *Otto Luck* (1915), *Police Dog* (1915) and *Quacky Doodles* (1917). By 1916 his studio was so successful that he began producing one cartoon per week.

In 1914 Bray revolutionized the business of animation with his patented invention of a labor–saving animation process in which backgrounds were printed on translucent paper to facilitate the positioning of moving objects in successive drawings. (This economy of drawings is evident in many of Bray's early cartoons, including "Colonel Heeza Liar, Hobo" (1916), which used only a few more than 100 basic arrangements of the cels in 1,600 frames of footage.) During the next year he would patent two other methods to enhance the quality of animation. The first was a technique that enabled animators to affix solid cutouts to the back of drawings so they were visible from the front of the drawing; the second, a process of cutout animation.

Other pioneer animators followed Bray with patented techniques of their own. Earl Hurd patented the first cel animation process, probably one of the most significant of the early animation patents, while Max and Dave Fleischer, of Ko-Ko the Clown and later Betty Boop fame, developed a fascinating process called Rotoscope, which enabled animators to trace figures seen on projected film.

During the teens, Bray was not the only major cartoon studio producing animated films. Two others came into existence: Raoul Barre and Hearst International. Barre was an established cartoonist whose caricatures of Indians and the lifestyle of French Canadian women were published as *En Rolant Ma Boule.* Turning his energies to animation, he produced several noteworthy animated series. His first was *Animated Grouch Chasers* (1915–16), an intriguing use of live-action openings and animated segues that won him widespread acclaim. He went on to develop one of the most successful comic-strip cartoon adaptations, *Mutt and Jeff* (1918), based on Bud Fisher's popular strip characters.

In 1916 newspaper mogul William Randolph Hearst realized the promise of animation by opening his own studio, International Film Service. Hearst hired talented animators Gregory LaCava, Frank Moser and Bill Nolan away from Raoul Barre's studio to bring many of his newspaper syndicate's cartoon properties to the screen. In short order, Hearst's company produced animated versions of such comic–page favorites as *Krazy Kat* (1916), *The Katzenjammer Kids* (1916) and *Happy Hooligan* (1917).

Other comicstrip artists brought their strip creations to the screen to capitalize on the success of the new medium. Henry ("Hy") Mayer, a prolific illustrator, drew comics on the screen for the Universal Weekly newsreel in 1913. He ultimately produced a series of screen magazines known as *Travelaughs.* Rube Goldberg briefly pursued a career in animation by signing up with Pathé Films to produce a newsreel spoof called *Boob Weekly.* Other animated versions of popular strips included George McManus's *Bringing Up Father* (1918), Walter Hoban's *Jerry on the Job* (1917), Jimmy Swinnerton's *Little Jimmy* (1916) and Tom E. Powers's *Phables* (1916).

Paul Terry, who first started working as an animator for Bray in 1916–17, also became an important figure during this period. After he opened his own studio, Terry became the first to prefigure the visual style of the Hollywood cartoons of the 1930s and 1940s by giving characters more depth and dimension, as is evident in a handful of early titles, including *Farmer Al Falfa's Catastrophe* (1916) and *Farmer Al Falfa's Wayward Pup* (1917).

In general, production staffs for most of these studios were minimal at best. On the average, producers turned out one new cartoon short a week, which was often animated by one person. (Hearst was known to enlist the services of well-known artists who sketched strips for his syndicate to contribute animate ideas to his weekly newsreel.) In most cases the cartoonist was the animator, director, gagman and artist. Toward week's end, the animator's sketchings were collected, photographed and wound onto a single reel before being distributed to theaters throughout the country.

In some cases, the final product was inferior because of such streamlined operations, prompting critics to denounce animated works. As one film critic stated, the major problem inherent in the cartoons was that "the artist was merely sketching his ideas on film."

Walter Lantz, who wrote and directed many cartoons for J.R. Bray, discussed the story-line difficulties he and other animators encountered. "We had a makeshift studio on the top floor of a loft building in Fordham, New York," he recalled. "There weren't enough people in the organization to make the story department of a cartoon studio today. But we didn't bother with stories. Our only object was to turn out 500 to 600 feet of film!"

Because animators overlooked story transitions, the films often confused theater audiences. (Some confusion was due to the inconsistent use of cartoon balloons over the subject's head to describe dialogue or action.) Sometimes when studios churned out 500 to 600 feet of cartoon film, that's exactly what the audience got—just film, with no real story. "Most audiences would rather flee from the theater than sit through a screening of these cartoons," commented one reviewer.

Dick Huemer, who animated *Mutt and Jeff*, had this to say about the reaction of moviegoers to silent cartoons: "They didn't get it. I swear, they didn't get what we were doing. For one thing, our timing was way off or nonexistent. And we didn't have sound. Sound was the great savior of the animated cartoon."

There were at this same time, however, several animators who set new standards for the industry through their unique storytelling ability. Among them were Max and Dave Fleischer, Walt Disney and Walter Lantz. All four men blazed new trails in animation and achieved great success through instinct and imagination, as evidenced their work.

The Fleischers turned heads with their inventive series, *Out of the Inkwell* (1916), which combined live action and animation and featured the antics of Koko the Clown (later hyphenated as Ko-Ko). The films are technical marvels—beautifully blending animation and live scenes of the animator (Max) bringing Koko to life as well as the entire story on the drawing board at the animator's table. This feat was equaled by Disney and Lantz, who employed the process of live action/animation in similar fashion with successful results. Disney mastered the art with his series of cartoon

The farmer's true identity is unmasked in this scene from Aesop's *"Amateur Night on the Ark"* (1923). (COURTESY: BLACKHAWK FILMS)

fables, *Alice Comedies* (1924), shot in Los Angeles at various outdoor locations. The films starred a young girl—played mostly by billboard star–turned–child actor Virginia Davis—who was joined by animated characters in telling each story. The films were extremely popular vehicles, as was Lantz's *Dinky Doodle* (1924), which he wrote and directed for Bray.

Lantz starred as the comic straight man in these films alongside his cartoon counterparts Dinky, a young boy, and his faithful dog, Weakheart, in comical exploits that were often as funny as the best of the era's silent film comedies. (Lantz admitted his source of inspiration was the work of several silent films comedians, including Charlie Chaplin, Harry Langdon and Chester Conklin.)

One reason for Lantz's success may have been his understanding of his role as an animator. In an interview he defined his job thusly: "An animator is like an actor going before the camera, only he has to act out his feelings and interpret the scene with that pencil. Also he has to know

Model sheet for Max and Dave Fleischer's Ko-Ko the Clown.

Animator Walter Lantz looks on as cartoon star Colonel Heeza Liar takes on a menacing bull in a studio publicity still to promote the classic silent cartoon series. (COURTESY: WALTER LANTZ)

how to space characters because the spacing of their movements determines the tempo; he must know expression; he must know feeling; he has to know the character, and make him walk with a funny action."

The ardent process of sound changed the whole method of making animated cartoons and, if anything, enabled the industry to prosper at a time when the silent film industry was stagnating. The first sound cartoons were produced in 1924 by the Fleischers. *Song Car-Tunes*, a series of "bouncing ball singalongs," were synchronized to popular music by a revolutionary DeForest Phonofilm system. One major disadvantage prevented the concept from flourishing: Many of the theaters were "unwired" and thus were unable to project the films accompanied by 18-piece orchestrations.

The first "talking" motion picture, Al Jolson's musical feature *The Jazz Singer* (1927), helped popularize the use of sound in the film industry and inspired theaters to accommodate this innovation.

Walt Disney introduced the first widely distributed synchronized sound cartoon in 1928, Mickey Mouse's *Steamboat Willie*. With this creation began another chapter in animation history. Sound gave cartoons a dimension that was not possible in silent form. It enabled animators to create better

stories, more lifelike characters and fuller animation. The process did not come cheaply, however. Production costs skyrocketed from the normal $6,000 budgets for silent cartoons, yet the all-around quality improved and was worth the price.

Mickey Mouse starred in the first synchronized sound cartoon, "Steamboat Willie" (1928). © Walt Disney Productions

4

During the 1930s, as animators explored the virtues of sound, many new characters burst onto the screen in productions featuring popular musical tunes of the day. Warner Bros. introduced several cartoon stars, many of them influenced by vaudeville and radio. The studio's first real star was Bosko, a Black Sambo–type character, who spoke for the first time in 1930's *Sinkin' in the Bathtub.* Created by former Disney animators Hugh Harman and Rudolf Ising, Bosko became enormously popular and was soon joined by a handful of other characters in the studio's *Looney Tunes* series, among them Foxy, Piggy and Goopy Geer.

Meanwhile, Metro-Goldwyn-Mayer (MGM) contributed its own series of musical cartoons, *Happy Harmonies,* directed by Harman and Ising, who left Warners to open the Metro's cartoon department. Walt Disney continued making his Oscar-winning *Silly Symphony* (1928) series, the forerunner to the musical cartoon concept, while Ub Iwerks, Disney's former protégé, set up shop to produce his musically inclined *Flip the Frog* (1931) series. Van Beuren Studios also joined the competition with its popular *Aesop's Fables* (1928) series, initially released by Pathé and then RKO Radio Pictures.

While many of the early sound cartoons had merit, most of these productions—outside a few that had name stars—lacked distinguishable personalities and featured a myriad of characters appearing in a single setting.

More than any individual, Warner Bros. director Chuck Jones credits Walt Disney for establishing the concept of cartoon "personalities" and inspiring the rest of the industry to develop their own unique characters. As Jones explained: "Anybody who knows anything about animation knows that the things that happened at Disney Studio were the backbone that upheld everything else. Disney created a climate that enabled us all to exist. Everyone in animation considered themselves behind Disney. We all did. Strange thing: That was probably healthy for us all. Perhaps the biggest thing Disney contributed was that he established the idea of individual personality. We would look at his stuff and say 'No matter what we do, Disney is going to be a little ahead of us, particularly in technique.' He created the idea that you could make an animated cartoon character who had personality and wasn't just leaping in the air like *Terrytoons.* So without thinking he forced us into evolving our own style."

Thus, from the mid-1930s on, animators began to develop the sound cartoon era's first bona fide stars—characters with heart and soul and mass appeal. Many of the characters people remember today emerged during this period. Walt Disney added to his stable of stars the likes of Donald Duck (1934) and Goofy (1932), while studio rival Warner Bros. introduced several "superstars": Porky Pig (1936), Daffy Duck (1938), and Bugs Bunny (1940). MGM's famed cat-and-mouse tandem Tom and Jerry (1940) won over audiences, as did Walter Lantz's Andy Panda (1940) and Woody Woodpecker (1941). Meanwhile, Paul

Terry, of *Terrytoons* fame, unveiled his most promising creations, Dinky Duck (1939) and Mighty Mouse (1942).

These solidly constructed characterizations together with tightly written scripts captured in animated form the crazy appeal of Laurel and Hardy, the Marx Brothers, Buster Keaton, Abbott and Costello, and Charlie Chaplin, and became important factors in the success of sound cartoons.

One other important element in their success was physical action. Unlike silent cartoons, sound cartoons were fast-paced, full of slapstick and punctuated by violence. Combined, these qualities generated a terrific response from moviegoers whose sides often arched from fits of laughter before the main feature was even introduced. (Cartoons, newsreels and live-action shorts were shown prior to the feature-length attraction, appropriately called "curtain-raisers" in their day.)

"We found that you can get terrific laughs out of someone just getting demolished, as long as you clean up and bring him back to life again," the late Tex Avery told biographer Joe Adamson. "It's exaggeration to the point where we hope it's funny."

The successful cartoon formula of transitions, action and sound was further improved in 1932 when Walt Disney produced the first true Technicolor cartoon, a *Silly Symphony* short called "Flowers And Trees." (The production cost $27,500 to make, two-thirds more than black-and-white cartoons.) Disney was not the first to experiment with color by any means. Others toyed with the process as far back as the early 1920s by "tinting" the films. (In 1930 Walter Lantz animated the first two-color Technicolor cartoon, a four-minute opening segment for Paul Whiteman's *King of*

In 1932 Walt Disney introduced the first three-strip Technicolor cartoon, "Flowers and Trees," which won an Academy Award.
© *Walt Disney Productions*

Jazz.) Disney's introduction of color to animated cartoons brought a whole new dimension to the screen that had never before been realized. It was a gamble that paid off not only for his studio; it took the cartoon industry into a whole new era of filmmaking.

In the beginning, because of Disney's exclusive contract to use the Technicolor process, several studios were forced to use a less effective two-strip color method, Cinecolor. The results were not as vivid as the three-strip color process, but that did not prevent several rival studios from competing.

Ub Iwerks was among the first to use Cinecolor for his 1933 *ComiColor* cartoon, "Jack and the Beanstalk." Warner Bros. offered two Cinecolor releases in the 1934–35 season, "Honeymoon Hotel" and "Beauty and the Beast," both *Merrie Melodies*. Walter Lantz countered with "The Jolly Elves" (1933), which received an Oscar nomination the same year Disney's "Flowers and Trees" (1932) won Best Short Subject honors. Max Fleischer also employed the Cinecolor technique in his *Color Classics* series, beginning with "Poor Cinderella" (1934).

Max Fleischer's attempt to compete with Walt Disney by producing full-length features ended with the release of his second feature Mister Bug Goes to Town *(1940).* (COURTESY: REPUBLIC PICTURES)

Sexy screen star Betty Boop is joined by sidekicks Bimbo and Ko-Ko the Clown in 1932's "A Hunting We Will Go," produced by Max Fleischer.

The most spectacular use of color was yet to come, however. In 1937 Walt Disney again paved the way when he produced the first full-length feature, *Snow White and the Seven Dwarfs.* It was a monumental undertaking for his studio, costing a tiny fortune to produce (six times more than its original budget of $250,000). Fortunately, it was well worth the price as the film became a tremendous box-office hit, earning $8 million in revenue following its release. With this newfound success, Disney opened many animators' eyes to the full potential of color to animated cartoons, no matter what their length.

Max Fleischer shared the same vision as Disney. He gave Disney perhaps his strongest competition in the feature-film arena when he produced his studio's first fully animated feature, *Gulliver's Travels* (1939), two years after Disney's Technicolor extravaganza. While the film did compare in quality to Disney's full-length production, unfortunately it never produced the same financial and critical success.

Nonetheless, Fleischer would produce one more feature, *Mister Bug Goes to Town* (1941), before abandoning the idea of producing cartoon features altogether and leaving the field to his contemporary, Walt Disney, who became the sole producer of feature-length cartoons for the next two decades.

The outbreak of World War II unified the cartoon industry in a patriotic sort of way. Studios showed their allegiance by producing propaganda training films and cartoons satirizing the war, with obvious anti-German and anti-Japanese overtones, to boost the public's morale.

The effort resulted in a number of flag-waving sendups that are still funny today, among them Donald Duck's "Der Fuehrer's Face" (Disney, 1943), an Oscar-winning short subject; Tex Avery's "Blitz Wolf" (MGM, 1942); and "Daffy's Draftee" (Warner, 1944). Warner Bros. also produced a topical war bond short, "Bugs Bunny's Bond Rally" (1943), with Bugs Bunny, Daffy Duck and Porky Pig urging Americans to buy war bonds, as well as its own share of animated training films, namely *Private Snafu*, first directed by Frank Tashlin, the noted comedy film director, and *Hook*, which dealt with the misadventures of a navy sailor.

While the war proved to be a timely subject, Hollywood animators continued to display their affection for the actors, actresses and comedians of Hollywood's Golden Age. Caricatured versions of many celebrities have made their way to the screen in one cartoon or another since the early 1930s. Some of the most notable appearances by movie stars in animated form include "Hollywood Steps Out" (Warner, 1941), featuring Clark Gable, Harpo Marx, Buster Keaton, Joan Crawford, the Three Stooges and others; "A Tale of Two Mice" (Warner, 1942), depicting Abbott and Costello as mice (*Babbit and Catstello*); "Bacall to Arms" (Warner, 1946), with Humphrey Bogart and Lauren Bacall as cartoon characters; and "Popeye's 25th Anniversary" (Paramount, 1948), with Dean Martin and Jerry Lewis, Bob Hope and Jimmy Durante.

The measure of success that cartoons had attained in the 1930s and 1940s continued into the 1950s. During this decade the cartoon industry experienced several important achievements. In 1953, with 3-D becoming the rage, several studios began turning out three-dimensional feature films and short subjects, to the delight of moviegoing audiences. The technique was used in cartoons as well. In 1953 Paramount's Famous Studios created two three-dimensional cartoons, "Popeye, The Ace of Space" and "Boo Man," starring Casper the Friendly Ghost. The following year Warner Bros. added its own 3-D favorite, "Lumber Jack Rabbit" (1954), starring Bugs Bunny.

Lobby card from Bob Clampett's 1938 Looney Tunes cartoon, "Porky's Poppa." © Warner Bros.

Perhaps more important than 3-D was the unveiling of a new style of animation four years earlier, which used fewer cartoon cels to tell a complete story. The method—called "limited animation"—was the brainchild of United Productions of America (UPA), producers of Mr. Magoo and Gerald McBoing Boing cartoons. The concept presented an economical way for producers to animate cartoons while still achieving a wide range of motion and believability on screen. Bill Scott, a former UPA animator, recalls the new process "proved that cartoonists could use fewer drawings and still do an excellent job telling their story."

Economically, the new system of animation made sense, as the cost to produce fully animated cartoons had become more and more prohibitive. As costs rose, many of the major cartoon producers would adopt this method of animation. (Television cartoon producers later employed the same style of animation.) Only through limited animation could theatrical cartoons stay economically feasible.

For years it was believed that television brought about the demise of the animated cartoon short. This is true to some extent. But what actually killed the cartoon short was a 1949 U.S. Supreme Court ruling forcing studios to abandon "block bookings." Under this method, theater owners were offered hit feature films as long as they agreed to book a cartoon, newsreel or live-action short as part of the package. Usually a percentage of the rental fee helped finance the cartoon production.

After this ruling, theater owners refused to pay more than nominal fees for cartoons. As a result, the animated short couldn't earn back its production costs on its initial release. It often took several rereleases before most cartoons turned a profit, if any. The impact of this ruling and the birth of television ultimately resulted in many Hollywood cartoon studios closing their doors during the late 1950s

Opening title sequence from Ub Iwerks's ComiColor cartoon, "Jack Frost" (1934). (COURTESY: BLACKHAWK FILMS)

BULL FIGHT
PROD. # 185
DIRECTED BY
TEX AVERY

177

Senor Droopy

"HAPPY HOUND"

KEEP TAIL LIMP AND INACTIVE

NO PADS ON FEET

HOLD HAT ANGLES THUS

NEVER HOLD THIS ANGLE OF HAT

BOTTOM

OR THUS

COLOR SEPARATION

MGM *animators used this cartoon model sheet as a guide when drawing Tex Avery's Droopy in "Senor Droopy" (1949).* © *Turner Entertainment*

and early 1960s. Walter Lantz, who was the last to stop production in 1972, said, "We didn't stop producing cartoons because their popularity died out, it was because we couldn't afford to make them."

In essence, television replaced movie theaters as a place to showcase animated productions. The growth of this medium clearly undermined the success of movie theaters in this country, as witnessed in a strong decline in box-office receipts. (The number of television sets in use in 1950 jumped from 1 million at the beginning of the year to 4 million by the end of the year.) With many programs accessible on the "tube" for free, American moviegoers had little incentive to go to the theater.

"People began to care less about going to the movies," remarked Norm Prescott, cofounder of Filmation Studios. "As a consequence, it took four or five years for studios to recoup their cartoon costs."

Viewing television as fertile ground, several film distributors of vintage cartoons kept in well-guarded film vaults took advantage of this new and thriving medium by syndicating the films to local television stations. The first cartoons to appear were black-and-white treasures made by Van Beuren

Studios in the 1930s, seen on DuMont's WABD-TV, New York, in 1947 on *Movies for Small Fry*. The program was broadcast Tuesday evenings and inspired *The Small Fry Club*,

An electrified musician rings out vibrant new sounds on his old harp for the onlooking conductor in a scene from Hugh Harman's "Mad Maestro" (1939). © *Turner Entertainment*

Popeye gets the best of Bluto in the first Popeye two-reeler, "Popeye the Sailor Meets Sinbad the Sailor" (1936).

Daffy Duck meets up with Sherlock Holmes in a scene from Bob Clampett's 1946 cartoon "The Great Piggy Bank Robbery." © Warner Bros., Inc. (COURTESY: BOB CLAMPETT ANIMATION ART)

a network continuation of the show in January 1948, hosted by Big Brother Bob Emery. The latter continued through the 1950–51 season, screening Van Beuren's Cubby cartoon series and several early Walter Lantz cartoons before the program was canceled. (The Van Beuren films also appeared on *TV Tots Time* on WENR, Chicago, and on the ABC network between 1950 and 1952.)

This did not mark the first time cartoons were used on television. Chad Grothkopf, a Disney employee in his 20s, went East in 1938 to work for NBC on "the very first animated show on the network." Only 50 television sets were in use at the time when Grothkopf produced "Willie the Worm," a low-budget, eight-minute black-and-white cartoon that aired in April 1938. The film was full of cutout animation, plus a small amount of cel animation, to illustrate the popular children's poem ("Willie Worm has taken a wife, to live and to love the rest of his life").

One year later, in May 1939, when NBC presented its first full schedule of evening programming on experimental station W2XBS (now WNBC), New York, the station previewed Walt Disney's Donald Duck cartoon, "Donald's Cousin," for viewers.

In the early 1950s many classic cartoons that previously had been released to theaters made their way to the tiny screen, shown almost exclusively on children's shows hosted by local television station personalities. Cartoons were the cornerstone of such popular programs as the *Captain Bob Show*, Buffalo, New York; *Uncle Willie's Cartoon Show*, Beaumont, Texas; and scores of others.

In 1953, 20 to 25 stations were regularly broadcasting cartoons throughout the country, garnering high ratings from their predominantly juvenile audience. And by January 1955 more than 400 television stations were programming animated cartoons.

The increase in the number of stations that aired cartoons was due largely to a high number of cartoon packages that became available for the first time. Warner Bros.,

Paramount-Fleischer-Famous Studios and Terrytoons all released cartoons to television, joined by MGM's *Tom and Jerry* package and spot broadcasts of various Walt Disney cartoons on ABC's *Disneyland.*

With the availability of new films, television stations throughout the country launched their own afternoon children's shows hosted by a virtual army of "sea captains, space commanders, Western sodbusters and neighborhood policemen." Office Joe Bolton hosted cartoons and comedy short subjects in New York. In Los Angeles Tom Hatten

Early animated cartoon broadcasts occurred on afternoon children's programs hosted by local television station personalities. Tom Hatten (in sailor outfit) introduced Popeye cartoons on his weekday show, Pier 5 Club, for Los Angeles' KTLA-TV. (COURTESY: TOM HATTEN)

entertained youngsters with Popeye cartoons in his *Pier 5 Club* on KTLA-TV Channel 5.

Other stations devised clever titles to inform children when "cartoon time" aired on their local station. Philadelphia's WFIL added *Funny Flickers*, while WGRB in Schenectady ran *Kartoon Karnival* to attract young viewers with large doses of cartoon entertainment. CBS was the first network to join the cartoon craze. In 1953, the network added *Barker Bill's Cartoon Show* to its daytime schedule, featuring early Terrytoon cartoons. Three years later, CBS again segmented an assortment of Terrytoons cartoons on *The CBS Cartoon Theatre*, a three-month-long prime-time series hosted by newcomer comedian Dick Van Dyke.

These programs only whetted viewers' appetites, however. What was missing from television logs was newly produced cartoon programs to keep viewers interested. Since producers could not afford to produce fully animated, theatrical style cartoons, the medium had to settle for a less expensive process.

"Full animation was very, very expensive," recalled Norm Prescott. "Television, in turn, could not support full animation. The economics just wouldn't jibe unless somebody could come up with a way of doing animation with fewer drawings."

The UPA-style of animation thus came to television. Early animated fare reflected this cost-efficient, or "cookie-cutter," method. The process enabled producers to use a variety of angles, cuts and camera moves to imply motion, while using the fewest number of cels possible to tell their story. For television, the format fit like a glove and audiences never noticed the difference.

The technique was officially introduced to viewers in the first made-for-television series, the cliff-hanging, serialized adventures of *Crusader Rabbit*, co-invented by Rocky and Bullwinkle creator Jay Ward. The series was test marketed in 1949 and made its debut one year later. Ward produced the program expressly for television, animating the series out of his makeshift studio in San Francisco and sending his sketches to Hollywood film producer Jerry Fairbanks to film, edit and add soundtracks to complete each story for broadcast.

"When Jay did *Crusader Rabbit*, it was still axiomatic that no one could produce a cartoon series for television," remembered Bill Scott, who created UPA's Gerald McBoing Boing and was the voice of Bullwinkle J. Moose. "Jay refused to believe that."

As was the case with other cartoon programs that followed, the cost of the *Crusader Rabbit* series is what made it attractive for television sales. One complete 19 1/2-minute story cost approximately $2,500 to produce. "We would simply plan a story so we reused some of the animation with a different background," series producer Jerry Fairbanks recalled.

Ward was followed into the television arena by two veteran animators who were most responsible for giving limited animation its biggest boost: Bill Hanna and Joe Barbera. They perpetuated the art form in a number of highly successful series for television. The seven-time Academy Award–winning directors, who invented the hilarious hijinks of MGM's Tom and Jerry, entered television's animated age eight years after Ward with *Ruff and Reddy* (NBC, 1957), the first hosted cartoon series for Saturday morning. (Between 1958 and 1963, with their package of Huckleberry Hound, Quick Draw McGraw and Yogi Bear cartoons, they were the first to introduce the half-hour all-cartoon program.) The series used only 12,000 cels to animate 30 minutes of cartoon entertainment (in this case, roughly three cartoons per show).

For television, this style of animation seemed most effective. "When we first started limited animation, it disturbed me," Hanna admitted in an interview. "Then when I saw some of the old cartoons on TV, I saw that actually limited animation came off better on the dimly lit television screen than the old fully animated things."

For Barbera, the biggest adjustment was not conforming to the new style of animation but to the low prices television paid for his and Hanna's animated productions. "We received about $2,700 (per show) and that was after great negotiating and pleading," he once said.

To retain a tidy profit, Hanna and Barbera effectively did away with production items that usually resulted in higher costs. They trimmed most schedule-delaying procedures, eliminated many preliminary sketches and recorded soundtracks in one sitting.

By producing cartoons at such rock-bottom prices, the marketplace for made-for-television cartoons blossomed overnight. In 1959 Jay Ward returned to television with a new series, the misadventures of a moose and a flying squir-

Walter Lantz reviews the storyboard to a cartoon that is under production. (COURTESY: CITIZEN-NEWS)

A studio one-sheet from the 1947 Mighty Mouse cartoon "Dead End Cats." © 20th Century-Fox

Japanese cartoon producers also began to import fully animated fantasy/adventure series that were reedited and redubbed in English for broadcast. Many have cult followings today. Some popular titles were *Astro Boy* (1964), *Eighth Man* (1965), *Gigantor* (1966) and *Speed Racer* (1967).

Many of television's earliest concepts for animated shows were derived from successful characters or formats that worked well in many popular live-action shows. *The Flintstones* (ABC, 1960), featuring television's "modern stone-age family," was actually based on the classic television sitcom *The Honeymooners*. *Top Cat* (ABC, 1961), another Hanna-Barbera Production, mirrored the antics of Sergeant Bilko and his platoon of misfits from *The Phil Silvers Show*. *Calvin and the Colonel* (ABC, 1961), patterned after radio's *Amos 'n' Andy*, featured the voices of the original radio team, Freeman Gosden and Charles Correll, who created the animated spin-off. Like television sitcoms, several programs even featured studio-recorded laugh tracks to provoke laughter in the home.

Producers later turned to other bankable properties to attract viewers. Comic strips and comics gave television characters with built-in followings. Chester Gould's *Dick Tracy* (1961), caricatured in a series of cheaply produced

One of the most popular cartoon shows to appear on prime-time television was The Flintstones. The series was a cartoon version of the classic sitcom The Honeymooners. © Hanna-Barbera Productions, Inc.

rel, better known as *Rocky and His Friends*. (Ward originated the characters years earlier for a never-produced series entitled *The Frostbite Falls Follies*.) Pat Sullivan produced a new litter of *Felix the Cat* cartoons, bearing the trademark limited animation style that had become so suitable for television. (Animator Chuck Jones often has called this style of animation "illustrated radio" because it's like "a radio script with a minimum of drawings in front of it, and if you turn off the picture, you can still tell what's happening because you hear it.")

Consequently, during the next 10 years, the syndicated marketplace would be deluged with other all-cartoon series, aimed at attracting adults and children with characters and situations that appealed to both segments of the population. Other characters to barnstorm the "tube" during its early days of animation included Quick Draw McGraw (1959), Spunky and Tadpole (1960), Q.T. Hush (1960), Lippy the Lion (1962), Wally Gator (1962) and Magilla Gorilla (1964).

five-minute cartoons, headed a legion of renowned comic characters in cartoon versions for television. Superheroes were included in this menagerie, flying onto television screens in countless action/adventure shows like *Marvel Superheroes* (1966), featuring the extraordinary feats of Spider-Man, The Incredible Hulk, Captain America and The Mighty Thor; *The New Adventures of Superman* (CBS, 1966) was the first fully animated network show based on a superhero character.

Motion picture and recording stars were also naturals for animated cartoons. Hanna-Barbera was the first to get into the act by producing cartoon versions of Abbott and Costello (1965), featuring the voice of straight man Bud Abbott, and Laurel and Hardy (1966). The Three Stooges (Moe Howard, Larry Fine and Curly Joe DeRita) brought their zany brand of slapstick to animation in *The New Three Stooges*, a live-action/animated series for syndication. Musical artists who gave animation a new beat in cartoon form included Ross Bagdasarian's Alvin and the Chipmunks in *The Alvin Show* (CBS, 1961) and Liverpool's Fab Four in *The Beatles* (ABC, 1965), the last musical group to be given animated life until Motown's *The Jackson 5ive* (ABC, 1971) and teenage rock sensations *The Osmonds* (ABC, 1972) burst onto the musical scene.

With so many programs eventually flooding the market, however, even film and television critics wondered just how long cartoons could last in the medium. In reviewing television animation, Charles Champlin, *Los Angeles Times* critic, wrote: "Operating on the adage 'if it works, copy it,' networks went so cartoon happy there was talk of animating the *Huntley-Brinkley Report*."

One recurring criticism of television animation was that the work often appeared rushed, thus dramatically undermining the quality. Animators had little control over the quality because "the pressures of television are greater than the pressures of producing films for theatres," Bill Hanna noted. "Back when we made the MGM cartoons, we worked at a more leisurely, almost relaxed pace. There was definitely more care put into the drawing, timing, sound effects and the recording of the music. Much more time was taken to discuss stories and to design characters; pictures were reviewed in pencil test form, and changes were made before they were inked and painted. It was an elaborate process. Every phase of production was handled much more carefully than it is today. We just don't have the time today to put in all that effort."

Friz Freleng, who created several successful cartoon series for television for his company, DePatie-Freleng Enterprises, offered his own perspective of television cartoons. "I used to turn out 11 or 12 theatrical cartoons a year. At six minutes per cartoon, that was a little over an hour's worth. Here, in one week, they'll turn out four shows. They do at least one and a half hours of new animation a week," he said. "The networks go for the numbers (or viewers). They don't care

what the quality of the show is—I don't think they even watch the shows. As long as it's got high numbers, it doesn't matter whether the show is good or not."

Former Disney animator Don Bluth, the genius behind such full-length cartoon treasures as *The Secret of NIMH* (1982), *Land Before Time* (1988) and *Anastasia* (1997), shared Freleng's frustration. "They cut corners on Saturday-morning animation and when they cut corners, they kill the product," he said. "The networks say, 'A kid will watch cartoons that cost $90,000 a half hour, so why spend $300,000?'"

While the quality of most cartoons was suspect, most viewers welcomed the glut of animated cartoon fare that infiltrated Saturday mornings and prime-time television. Long before *The Simpsons*, cartoon programs demonstrated they could attract nighttime audiences.

In 1958 CBS pioneered the concept of airing the all-cartoon show in prime-time for the very first time. The network reran that summer *The Gerald McBoing Boing Show*, featuring the first-ever newly produced cartoons for network television. (The series actually debuted two years earlier.)

Networks did not fully pick up on the idea of slotting fully animated cartoons during the family viewing hour until the turn of the decade. ABC did the most with cartoons in prime time. In September 1960 it began airing *The Flintstones* on its nighttime schedule, followed by *The Bugs Bunny Show* one month later. In 1962 the network also spotted *The Jetsons* on Sunday evenings, with *The Adventures of Johnny Quest* (1964) to make it debut in prime time two years later, also on ABC. CBS ran a distant second in the prime-time cartoon derby. During the 1961–62 season, it aired *Alvin and the Chipmunks* during the evening hours as well as *Calvin and the Colonel*.

In 1962, after networks won big ratings with prime-time cartoon programs, NBC aired the first made-for-television special, sponsored by Timex, *Mr. Magoo's Christmas Carol*, starring the nearsighted codger of theatrical cartoon fame. The program, which was also the first animated television musical, was an hour-long adaptation of Charles Dickens's classic holiday story. This program marked the illustrious beginning of the prime-time holiday special and the animated special in general.

Although this charming animated rendering produced explosive ratings, it took three years before television viewers were treated to their second prime-time special, *A Charlie Brown Christmas* (CBS, 1965), based on Charles M. Schulz's beloved *Peanuts* comic-strip characters. (The special remained on the shelf for one year, with no takers, before Coca-Cola agreed to sponsor the show.) The thirty-minute program generated a huge audience—nearly half of the nation's television viewers.

Due to the show's impressive performance, CBS made *Peanuts* an annual attraction on the network; it has since become the longest-running series of cartoon specials in tele-

Charlie Brown (left), Lucy and Linus dance around their beagle-topped tree in A Charlie Brown Christmas (1965), *the first prime-time animated special based on Charles Schulz's popular comic strip.*
(COURTESY: CBS)

Attracting national sponsors like Kellogg's and General Mills, the network's new Saturday-morning lineup included the new *Tennessee Tuxedo and His Tales, Quick Draw McGraw,* which had previously premiered in syndication, and network returnees *The Alvin Show* and *Mighty Mouse Playhouse.* (In the following two seasons, CBS expanded the schedule by another hour, adding *Linus the Lionhearted* and *The Tom and Jerry Show.*

CBS daytime programmer Fred Silverman, who was only 26 years old, was responsible for the new Saturday-morning programming. He recognized that adults, like children, love animated cartoons and that cartoons could attract a larger viewing audience. Silverman's assumption proved correct. Ratings skyrocketed and by the 1966–67 season, after restructuring Saturday morning with nine back-to-back half-hour cartoon shows, CBS rocketed into first place in that time slot's ratings derby.

Taking notice of CBS's success, runners-up NBC and ABC soon began their own Saturday-morning cartoon scheduling in earnest. ABC followed CBS in 1964 by adding cartoons to its Saturday-morning schedule, while NBC did the same in 1965. In the late 1960s, Saturday morning became known as "a jungle of competition," and rightfully so. New cartoons were delivering the largest network audience ever, and network bidding for programs became intensely competitive. The average price for a half-hour cartoon show ranged from $48,000 to $62,000, climbing to $70,000 to $100,000 by the 1970s. Financially, these figures were nothing compared to the revenues Saturday-morning cartoons generated. By 1970 the combined network take was $66.8 million in advertising revenue from their respective Saturday-morning lineups.

vision history. Runner-up Dr. Seuss inspired the first of several specials beginning with 1966's *Dr. Seuss' How The Grinch Stole Christmas,* produced by Chuck Jones and children's book author Ted Geisel. The show also premiered on CBS.

During the 1960s, many other made-for-television cartoon specials were produced, most notably by television innovators Arthur Rankin Jr. and Jules Bass, who presented a string of perennial cartoon classics in prime time. They created such memorable shows as *Rudolph, The Red-Nosed Reindeer* (NBC, 1964); *The Ballad of Smokey the Bear* (NBC, 1964), narrated by James Cagney; *Frosty the Snowman* (CBS, 1969); and *The Little Drummer Boy* (ABC, 1968). The pair's first prime-time entry was the hour-long animated special *Return to Oz,* which debuted on NBC in February 1964.

Not all of these shows used conventional animation, however. Many were filmed using a lifelike stop-motion puppet process created by Rankin and Bass called "Animagic," a technique they initiated in their 1961 children's series, *Tales of the Wizard of Oz.*

Until 1963 the Saturday-morning lineup on all three networks was mostly composed of reruns of theatrical cartoons and popular children's programs, including *My Friend Flicka, Sky King* and others. For the 1963–64 season, CBS took the first step toward creating an all-cartoon Saturday-morning schedule by offering a two-hour block of cartoons.

Holiday themes became a popular forum for animated network specials in the 1960s. Here Frosty leads a merry parade in a scene from the animated musical special Frosty the Snowman.
© *Rankin-Bass Productions*

By 1968, however, the success of television cartoons was somewhat diminished by one factor: the public outcry against television violence. The aftermath of the shocking assasinations of Dr. Martin Luther King and Senator Robert Kennedy brought about tremendous unrest among the public when it came to violence, whether in their neighborhood streets or on television.

In a survey *The Christian Science Monitor* recorded 162 threats or acts of violence on Saturday morning, the majority occurring between 7:30 and 9:30 A.M. when an estimated 26.7 million children, ages 2 to 17, were tuned in. The issue of violence on television was seconded by a report prepared by the National Commission on the Causes and Prevention of Violence (Kerner Commission), which ultimately forced networks to make changes in policy with respect to children's programming.

Network censors were hired to sit in on script meetings, approve storyboards and veto subject matter right up to airtime in an effort to control the violent or suggestive content of cartoons. The policy remains in force today.

In addition to instituting in-house control, the three major networks removed most of the shows and characters that were the subject of parental protests. Action-adventure shows were thus replaced by comedy series that deemphasized violence. The new aim of children's programming would be to "entertain, stimulate and educate." However, not all animators agreed that censorship was the right thing.

"Cartoon characters never die—they never bleed," remarked veteran animator Walter Lantz. "They get blown up or run over and the next scene there they are, hale and hearty. That's part of their magic, their fantasy. These so-called critics say kids can't separate fantasy from reality. They're looking at things they, as adults, consider harmful to the child. The critics don't look at cartoons through the eyes of a child. I always considered our type of humor as being slapstick, not violent."

Japanese cartoon offerings were staples of 1960s' television. One syndicated favorite was Kimba, the White Lion. (COURTESY: NBC)

Director Friz Freleng, of Warner Bros. fame, supported Lantz's theory that home audiences would rather be watching slapstick comedies. "The adult audience today has been robbed of a certain amount of entertainment," he said. "Kids keep getting it [cartoons] on TV, but you won't find an adult sitting down and watching a kid's show. I believe they miss it, and I believe there's a neglected audience."

Freleng and others had their reason to be concerned. In many instances, the network's decisions on what to censor were questionable. Lou Scheimer, cartoon producer for Filmation Studios, related that he had run into trouble when he was animating *Superboy*. One sequence called for Superboy to stop an oncoming train with his hands. "It was thought that it might tempt kids to try the same," Scheimer said. The scene was changed.

In one episode of CBS's *Josie and the Pussycats* (CBS, 1970), a script called for one of the pussycats to escape from a science-fiction menace by taking refuge in a dish of spaghetti. Former producer and comic-book artist Norman Maurer, who wrote the scene, once recalled, "CBS disallowed it. They said, 'Kids will put their cats in spaghetti.' I was told to rewrite the scene."

Also frustrating for most animators during this time was the audience response to early screenings of the fall shows. In the late 1970s, during a screening of Filmation's *Fat Albert* and *Space Academy* shows at a Hollywood preview house, more than half the audience walked out, prompting producer Joe Barbera, who was on hand to measure the audience response to his own Hanna-Barbera cartoons, to remark that he yearned for a return to the old days so that "when a cat chases a mouse, he doesn't have to stop and teach him how to blow glass or weave a basket. My wish for

Model sheet from Pat Sullivan's syndicated cartoon series Felix the Cat. *Pictured: Rock Bottom, the Professor, Felix and Poindexter.* © *Joe Oriolo Productions*

Christmas is they would leave education to the schools and entertainment to us."

While many animators might disagree, network censorship, in its earliest form, brought forth stronger values that were necessary in cartoons. The action/adventure shows had their place in history, as much as their replacements, teenage mystery and rock 'n' roll group programs, which served to educate and entertain children in a manner that reflected new attitudes in society and the world.

In the theatrical cartoon marketplace, it was a completely different story. Producers trod forbidden turf by producing animated works that were aimed largely at adults. One principal reason for this was the increase of grown-ups and young adults lining up to see cartoon features.

The one film that changed the visual and commercial style of the cartoon feature more than any single production was *Yellow Submarine* (1968), an animated odyssey featuring The Beatles (John, Paul, George and Ringo) that incorporated images and stylized movement. Audiences were most receptive to the film, proving there was indeed room for animated films that were less Disneyesque.

Another film that revolutionized the cartoon feature industry was Ralph Bakshi's *Fritz the Cat* (1971), the first X-rated full-length cartoon based on Robert Crumb's underground comic strip. Like *Yellow Submarine*, this departure from mainstream animation was full of topical statements—this time about life in the 1960s, including the decade's sexual and political revolution.

The landmark accomplishments of both films marked a new beginning for the animated feature film business that for several years had been stifled by the lack of other innovators in the field taking chances with full-length cartoons in this high-risk area. As a result, more feature-length cartoons were produced than ever before, and, for the first time in years, Disney actually had to compete in an ever-crowded marketplace.

Some of the new and original concepts, from here and abroad, that followed included *A Boy Named Charlie Brown* (1969), *Charlotte's Web* (1972), *Fantastic Planet* (1973), *Hugo the Hippo* (1976), *Raggedy Ann and Andy* (1977) and *Watership Down* (1978).

In the 1980s the success of the animated feature continued, spawning new ideas to meet the increased demand of baby-boomer families. While most of the films' characters were based on greeting-card and action-toy figures (this was also true in television animation), one film renewed hope in the animation business that original characters and stories still sold audiences: *Who Framed Roger Rabbit* (1988), a splendidly conceived comedy/mystery produced by Walt Disney whose style harkened back to Hollywood's golden age of animation. The blockbuster film, which grossed more than $100 million, renewed interest in creating quality animated films for adults and children and pumped new life into the cartoon industry.

Throughout the 1990s, animated feature films became enduring profit machines, led by Disney with a series of blockbusters: *The Little Mermaid* (1989), *Beauty and the Beast* (1991), *Aladdin* (1992), *The Lion King* (1994, the top-grossing animated feature of all time), *Toy Story* (1995, the first fully computer-animated feature), *Pocahontas* (1995) and *The Hunchback of Notre Dame* (1996). Other Hollywood studios rushed onto the scene eager to make animated features. Universal (notably Steven Spielberg's "Amblimation" studios), Warner Bros., Paramount and 20th Century-Fox jumped in to compete with Disney, producing animated features aimed at the family market. Few came close to having the same box-office success as Disney.

As a ripple effect, theaters witnessed the return of the theatrical cartoon short, absent as a regular program feature in the cinema for almost 20 years. Disney's release of the 1989 Roger Rabbit cartoon short, "Tummy Trouble," ushered in a new era for animated theatrical shorts. The studio began producing new cartoon shorts for theaters, including the first new Mickey Mouse cartoon in 37 years, *The Prince and the Pauper*, a 35-minute featurette released to theaters. In 1990 Warner Bros. produced its first new cartoon short since closing down its animation department in the 1960s: *Box Office Bunny*, starring Bugs Bunny. More new *Looney Tunes* followed, featuring Bugs and his Looney Tunes pals, and in 1994 legendary animator Chuck Jones returned to Warner Bros. to produce and direct a series of new *Looney Tunes*, beginning with the Road Runner and Coyote cartoon, "Chariots of Fur."

With animation short subjects back in favor with studios to a degree not seen perhaps since animation's heyday, other studios, such Hanna-Barbera, MGM and MCA/Universal got into the act. In 1995 Hanna-Barbera, which had become active in producing cartoon shorts for the Cartoon Network's *World Premiere Toons* program, released several cartoon shorts to movie theaters overseas. That same year MGM issued an all-new Pink Panther cartoon, while Universal distributed its first theatrical cartoon starring Earthworm Jim, star of the popular series of the same name on the WB Network. *The Ren & Stimpy Show* creator John Kricfalusi tried to join the already crowded field by producing a series of "Brik Blastoff" and "Jimmy the Idiot Boy" cartoon shorts for theaters, but the films were never released theatrically. In 1997 Kricfalusi instead released them on the Internet under his Spumco company Web page under the series title *The Goddamn George Liquor Program*, becoming the first Internet-produced cartoon series.

Television experienced the largest growth and expansion of cartoon programming in its long and illustrious history. In 1990 the Fox Kids Network premiered, changing the face of kids' TV forever, while Disney unveiled *The Disney Afternoon Block*, a two-hour daily programming service featuring original made-for-syndication cartoon series. The Fox Kids Network, headed by Margaret Loesch, became a force with which to reckon, producing fresh, original and highly rated cartoon series following the network's launching, including *Bobby's World*, *Tiny Toon Adventures* and *Taz-Mania*. Not to be outdone, media mogul Ted Turner launched another network two years later: The Cartoon Network, the first cable network to feature cartoons exclusively around the clock. Turner started the network—his company's fifth—after acquiring the Hanna-Barbera cartoon library for $320 million. Combined with his company's existing stockpile of MGM, Paramount and Warner Bros. cartoons, The Cartoon Network—whose audience would be adults and children—had a backlog of 8,500 cartoon titles to broadcast.

Once again the Fox Network took a revolutionary approach in programming, and in 1990 it debuted a cartoon series that would become the single most popular animated program of the decade: *The Simpsons*, which matured into a megahit for the network. The success of *The Simpsons* marked the returned of animated cartoons to prime time, and other networks attempted to capitalize on Fox's good fortune.

In 1991 MTV aired the first animated series created for a cable broadcaster, *Liquid Television*, featuring the work of independent animators, including Mike Judge, whose "Beavis and Butt-Head" attracted immediate attention and premiered as its own series in 1993. Meanwhile, Nickelodeon entered the animation business, introducing three original cartoon series on the network (under the name of "Nicktoons"): *Rugrats*, *Ren and Stimpy* and *Doug*, each major hits for the network.

The major networks soon followed with their own prime-time fare. In 1992 ABC added as a midseason replacement, *Capitol Critters*, produced by Steven Bocho and Hanna-Barbera, while CBS premiered another prime-time cartoon

series, *Fish Police*, also produced by Hanna-Barbera. Neither was a ratings success, and both were quickly canceled. Other series premiered in prime time but didn't fare any better. Steven Spielberg's long-awaited *Family Dog* was launched on CBS in 1993, but poor reviews and bad ratings brought a swift end to the show. In 1994 ABC tried to succeed where CBS failed by unveiling *The Critic*, an animated spoof of Hollywood and the movies hosted by cable-TV movie critic Jay Sherman (voiced by *Saturday Night Live's* Jon Lovitz). Despite the program's biting satire of the movie business, the show did not generate ratings to stay in prime time on ABC. It was revived on the Fox Network but its run was short.

In general, cable networks outshined the competition in the prime-time cartoon derby. The same year *The Critic* premiered, USA Network launched its first prime-time cartoon show, *Duckman*, the adventures of an irritable, web-footed detective. The series, starring the voice of Jason Alexander of TV's *Seinfeld*, proceeded to become USA's signature show, much as *The Simpsons* did for Fox. The Cartoon Network also debuted its first series of original programs: in 1994, *Space Ghost Coast to Coast*, the first talk show hosted by an animated cartoon superhero, and in 1995 *What a Cartoon!* a joint project with Hanna-Barbera featuring 48 cartoon shorts created by a pool of well-known cartoon directors. Comedy Central joined the growing list of networks to produce prime-time cartoon series, introducing *Dr. Katz: Professional Therapist*, presented in a process called "Squigglevision."

As in the past, children's advocates turned up the heat over the level of violence in cartoons on television. Networks found themselves on the losing end as Congress ordered an inquiry to determine whether stations had in fact been complying with the Children's Television Act of 1990, a law that limits advertising time in children's programming and requires stations to make a serious effort to serve kids' educational and informational needs. In three years since the law passed, little had changed. Faced with threats from Washington lawmakers, in the fall of 1994 networks unveiled their fall lineups, offering a variety of educational and informational shows, including *Beakman's World*, *The Spacewatch Club*, *Mad Scientist Toon Club* and *Real News for Kids*.

For a variety of reasons, economic and otherwise, NBC became the first major network to drop animated cartoons from its Saturday morning lineup. The network's new lineup would feature educational and informational shows for kids instead. NBC's decision to bow out left ABC, CBS and Fox to compete for the $300 million-plus in kids advertising.

Beginning in the fall of 1997, the Federal Communications Commission made it mandatory that television stations air three hours a week of educational programming for children. ABC endorsed the concept and worked with educators, who read scripts for upcoming shows and made sug-

Characters with built-in appeal were given animated series of their own. NBC's hit television sitcom Alf *inspired an animated spinoff that proved highly successful on Saturday mornings.* © Alien Productions
(COURTESY: DIC ENTERPRISES)

The dark comedy feature Beetlejuice *made its way to television as a hit Saturday-morning series in 1989.* © Warner Bros., Inc.

(COURTESY: NELVANA LIMITED)

gestions to producers. CBS bowed out altogether, joining NBC in its decision to drop animated cartoons from its Saturday morning lineup and replace them with live-action shows, such as *Wheel of Fortune 2000* and *Sports Illustrated for Kids*.

Strengthening NBC's and later CBS's decision was Disney's $19 billion acquisition of ABC/Capital Cities and the emergence of the Kids' WB Network in 1995. Disney revitalized ABC's Saturday morning programming, turning it into a powerhouse once again, while the Kids' WB Network would find its own niche with original programming—some of which first began on Fox—attracting a mix of adults and children as viewers.

Throughout the decade, animation's boom times resulted in a merchandise explosion of epic proportions. Baby boomers principally fueled the growth in cartoon merchandise that for the first time in history saw total licensing revenue top the $100 million mark. The home video market enjoyed record sales and rentals of cartoon videos, capturing lovers of cartoons, young and old. Celebrations of Hollywood's glory days of animation were held the world over. Film festivals honored legendary animators from animation's "golden age"—Warner Bros. animators Chuck Jones, Friz Freleng, and Tex Avery as well as former MGM greats Bill Hanna and Joe Barbera.

With such high interest in animation, the future of animated cartoons is bright. As it heads into the next century, the force behind animation's success will be the same underlying element as in the past: its commitment to quality. That said, the animated cartoon will last as long as people thirst for the flicker of action, the ingenious blend of characers and well-conceived original stories that only cartoons can offer. If this holds true, the next 90 years should be worth watching.

SILENT CARTOON SERIES

◎ ABIE THE AGENT

Based on the popular comic strip by Harry Hershfield. *Directed by Gregory La Cava. An International Film Service Production.*

1917: "Iska Worreh" (Aug. 5); and "Abie Kabibble Outwitting His Rival" (Sept. 23).

◎ AESOP'S FABLES

After forming his own studio near the end of World War I, pioneer animator Paul Terry brought this series of popular fables to the screen in 1921, using animal characters in the roles of humans to depict their improprieties without offending audiences. (The series was also known simply as *Fables.*) The series concluded with an Aesop-type moral at the end of each picture. While most of the films were enacted by animals, other starred Farmer Al Falfa, Terry's best-known character at the time.

During the first eight years of the series' run, Terry's staff wrote, animated and produced one complete Aesop's cartoon a week. Five director-animators shared the workload—men like Frank Moser, Harry Bailey, John Foster, Fred Anderson and Jerry Shields each were instrumental in the series' success. Mannie Davis and Bill Tytla, two other animation veterans, joined Terry's team of director-animators in the late 1920s.

Terry devised the basic stories for most of the films, borrowing many of his "morals" from a short-subject series entitled "Topics of the Day," in addition to others he dreamed up himself.

The Keith-Albee Theatre circuit, one of the largest vaudeville/movie theater chains in the country, bankrolled the series, setting up Terry in business as Fable Pictures Inc. (The name was later changed to Fables Studio.) His deal with Keith-Albee guaranteed that his cartoons played in each of the chain's theaters throughout the country, earning him the distinction of becoming "the first [animator] to really make money in the business," as animator Dick Huemer, who worked on the rival *Mutt and Jeff* series, remarked.

In 1928, following the arrival of sound, Fable Studios was taken over by Amadee J. Van Beuren, who purchased the studio from Keith-Albee. As Van Beuren Productions, the company successfully revived the series by adding soundtracks. Van Beuren had actually served as president of Fables Studios prior to buying the studio, so he was already familiar with the series. Terry went on to start his famed Terrytoons studio, where he created such cartoon notables as Mighty Mouse and Heckle and Jeckle. *A Paul Terry Production released by Pathe Film Exchange, Inc.*

1921: "The Cat and the Canary" (May 13); "The Country Mouse and City Mouse" (May 13); "The Donkey in Lion's Skin" (May 13); "The Fashionable Fox" (May 13); "The Fox and the Crow" (May 13); "The Fox and the Goat" (May 13); "The Goose That Laid the Golden Egg" (May 13); "The Hare and Frogs" (May 13); "The Hare and the Tortoise" (May 13); "The Hermit and the Bear" (May 13); "The Lioness and the Bugs" (May 13); "Mice at War" (May 13); "Mice in Council" (May 13); "The Wolf and the Crane" (May 13); "The Rooster and the Eagle" (May 13); "Cats at Law" (May 13); "The Cat and the Monkey" (Oct. 15); "The Dog and the Bone" (Oct 15); "The Frog and the Ox" (Oct. 15); "The Fly and the Ant" (Oct. 15); "The Owl and the Grasshopper" (Nov 13); "Venus and the Cat" (Nov. 15); "The Woman and the Hen" (Nov. 20); "The Frogs

The farmer conspires to rid himself of a pesky cat in a scene from the Aesop's Fable "The Farmer and His Cat" (1922). (COURTESY: BLACKHAWK FILMS)

That Wanted a King" (Nov. 27); "The Conceited Donkey" (Dec. 6); "The Wolf and the Kid" (Dec. 6); "The Wayward Dog" (Dec. 10); "The Cat and the Mice" (Dec. 13); and "The Dog and the Flea" (Dec. 31).

1922: "The Bear and the Bees" (Jan. 26); "The Miller and His Donkey" (Jan. 26); "The Tiger and the Donkey" (Jan. 26); "The Cat and the Swordfish" (Jan. 26); "The Dog and the Thief" (Jan. 26); "The Fox and the Grapes" (Jan. 26); "The Spendthrift" (Jan. 26); "The Villain in Disguise" (Jan. 26); "The Farmer and the Ostrich" (Jan. 26); "The Dissatisfied Cobbler" (Feb. 8); "The Lion and the Mouse" (Feb. 21); "The Rich Cat and the Poor Cat" (Feb. 21); "The Wicked Cat" (Mar. 4); "The Wolf in Sheep's Clothing" (Mar. 4); "The Boy and the Dog" (Apr. 3); "The Eternal Triangle" (Apr. 3); "The Model Diary" (Apr. 11); "Love at First Sight" (Apr. 11); "The Hunter and His Dog" (Apr. 27); "The Dog and the Wolves" (Apr. 27); "The Maid and the Millionaire" (Apr. 27); "The Farmer and His Cat" (May 17); "The Cat and the Pig" (May 17); "Crime in a Big City" (May 29); "The Country Mouse and City Cat" (June 22); "The Brewing Trouble" (June 22); "The Boastful Cat" (June 22); "The Dog and the Fish" (June 22); "The Mischievous Cat" (June 22); "The Worm That Turned" (June 22); "The Farmer and the Mice" (June 26); "The Fearless Fido" (July 20); "The Mechanical Horse" (Aug. 9); "The Dog and the Mosquito" (Aug. 12); "The Two Explorers" (Aug. 12); "The Two Slick Traders" (Aug. 12); "The Henpecked Henry" (Sept. 27); "The Hated Rivals" (Sept. 27); "The Romantic Mouse" (Sept. 27); "The Elephant's Trunk" (Sept. 27); "The Two of a Trade" (Sept. 27); "The Enchanted Fiddle" (Sept. 27); "The Rolling Stone" (Oct. 9); "Friday the Thirteenth" (Nov. 11); "Henry's Busted Romance" (Nov. 11); "The Fortune Hunters" (Nov. 11); "The Man Who

Laughs" (Nov. 11); "The Frog and the Catfish" (Dec. 1); "Two Trappers" (Dec. 1); "The Dog's Paradise" (Dec. 1); "A Stone Age Romeo" (Dec. 14); and "Cheating the Cheaters" (Dec. 14).

1923: "A Fisherman's Jinx" (Feb. 17); "A Raisin and a Cake" (Feb. 17); "The Alley Cat" (Feb. 17); "Troubles on the Ark" (Feb. 17); "The Gliders" (Feb. 17); "The Mysterious Hat" (Feb. 17); "The Sheik" (Feb. 17); "The Spider and the Fly" (Feb. 17); "The Traveling Salesman" (Feb. 17); "Day by Day in Every Day" (Mar. 22); "One Hard Pull" (Mar. 22); "The Jolly Rounders" (Mar. 22); "Pharaoh's Tomb" (Mar. 22); "The Gamblers" (Mar. 22); "The Mouse Catcher" (Apr. 27); "Amateur Night on the Ark" (Apr. 27); "A Fishy Story" (Apr. 27); "Spooks" (Apr. 27); "The Stork's Mistake" (May 12); "Springtime" (May 12); "The Burglar Alarm" (June 6); "The Beauty Parlor" (June 6); "The Covered Pushcart" (June 6); "Do Women Pay?" (June 7); "The Pace That Kills" (June 7); "The Great Explorers" (July 19); "The Bad Bandit" (July 19); "The Marathon Dancers" (July 19); "Mysteries of the Seas" (July 19); "The Pearl Divers" (July 19); "The Nine of Spades" (Aug. 2); "The Cat That Failed" (Aug. 7); "The Cat's Revenge" (Aug. 11); "The Walrus Hunters" (Aug. 11); "Love in a Cottage" (Sept. 1); "Derby Day" (Sept. 1); "The Cat's Whiskers" (Sept. 1); "Aged in the Wood" (Sept. 29); "The High Flyers" (Sept. 29); "The Circus" (Sept. 29); "Thoroughbred" (Sept. 29); "The Best Man Wins" (Nov. 9); "Happy Go Luckies" (Nov. 9); "The Five Fifteen" (Nov. 9); "A Dark Horse" (Nov. 9); "Farmer Al Falfa's Pet Cat" (Nov. 9); "The Cat That Came Back" (Nov. 16); "The Morning After" (Nov. 16); "The Animals' Fair" (Dec. 14); "Five Orphans of the Storm" (Dec. 22); and "Good Old Days" (Dec. 24).

1924: "The Black Sheep" (Jan. 9); "Good Old College Days" (Jan. 26); "The Rat's Revenge" (Jan. 26); "A Rural Romance" (Jan. 26); "The All-Star Cast" (Feb. 20); "Captain Kidder" (Feb. 20); "From Rags to Riches" (Feb. 20); "Herman the Great Mouse" (Feb. 20); "Why Mice Leave Home" (Feb. 20); "The Champion" (Mar. 20); "Runnin' Wild" (Mar. 20); "Homeless Pups" (Apr. 22); "An Ideal Farm" (Apr. 22); "If Noah Lived Today" (Apr. 22); "The Jealous Fisherman" (Apr. 22); "A Trip to the Pole" (Apr. 22); "When Winter Comes" (Apr. 22); "The Jolly Jail Bird" (May 12); "The Organ Grinder" (May 29); "That Old Can of Mine" (June 14); "Home Talent" (June 28); "One Good Turn" (June 30); "The Body in the Bag" (July 5); "Desert Sheiks" (July 12); "A Woman's Honor" (July 19); "The Sport of the Kings" (July 26); "Amelia Comes Back" (Aug. 2); "Flying Fever" (Aug. 2); "The Prodigal Pup" (Aug. 2); "House Cleaning" (Aug. 2); "The Barnyard Olympics" (Sept. 5); "A Message from the Sea" (Sept. 5); "In the Good Old Summer Time" (Sept. 13); "The Mouse That Turned" (Sept. 20); "A Lighthouse by the Sea" (Sept.

25); "Hawks of the Sea" (Sept. 25); "Noah's Outing" (Sept. 25); "Black Magic" (Oct. 29); "The Cat and the Magnet" (Oct. 29); "Monkey Business" (Oct. 29); "She Knew Her Man" (Oct. 29); "Good Old Circus Days" (Nov. 22); "Lumber Jacks" (Nov. 22); "Sharp Shooters" (Dec. 3); "She's in Again" (Dec. 3); "On the Ice" (Dec. 3); "Mysteries of Old Chinatown" (Dec. 3); "Down on the Farm" (Dec. 3); "African Huntsmen" (Dec. 11); "One Game Pup" (Dec. 11); "Hold That Thought" (Dec. 26); and "Biting the Dust" (Dec. 31).

1925: "Bigger and Better Jails" (Jan. 19); "Fisherman's Luck" (Jan. 19); "Transatlantic Flight" (Jan. 19); "Clean Up Week" (Feb. 19); "In Dutch" (Feb. 13); "Jungle Bike Riders" (Feb. 13); "The Pie Man" (Feb. 13); "At the Zoo" (Mar. 5); "Housing Shortage" (Mar. 26); "S.O.S." (Mar. 26); "The Adventures of Adenoid" (Apr. 10); "Permanent Waves" (Apr. 10); "Darkest Africa" (May 4); "Runaway Balloon" (May 8); "When Men Were Men" (May 18); "Wine, Women and Song" (May 18); "Bugville Field Day" (June 11); "Office Help" (June 11); "Over the Plate" (June 23); "Bubbles" (July 6); "Yarn About Yarn" (July 6); "Barnyard Follies" (July 20); "Deep Stuff" (Aug. 10); "Hungry Hounds" (Aug. 28); "The Lion and the Monkey" (Aug. 28); "Nuts And Squirrels" (Aug. 28); "Ugly Duckling" (Aug. 28); "Air-Cooled" (Sept. 28); "Closer Than a Brother" (Sept. 28); "The Hero Wins" (Sept. 28); "The Honor System" (Sept. 28); "Wild Cats of Paris" (Sept. 28); "Laundry Man" (Oct. 26); "The Great Open Spaces" (Nov. 6); "On the Links" (Nov. 10); "The Bonehead Age" (Dec. 17); "Day's Outing" (Dec. 17); "The English Channel Swim" (Dec. 17); "The Haunted House" (Dec. 17); "More Mice Than Brains" (Dec. 17); and "Noah Had His Troubles" (Dec. 17).

1926: "Hunting in 1950" (Jan. 23); "The June Bride" (Jan. 23); "Lighter Than Air" (Jan. 23) "Little Brown Jug" (Jan. 23); "Three Blind Mice" (Jan. 23); "Wicked City" (Jan. 23); "The Wind Jammers" (Jan. 23); "The Mail Coach" (Feb. 6); "The Merry Blacksmith" (Mar. 2); "Fire Fighters" (Mar. 26); "Big Hearted Fish" (Apr. 20); "Hearts and Showers" (Apr. 20); "Rough and Ready Romeo" (Apr. 20); "Farm Hands" (Apr. 20); "The Shootin' Fool" (Apr. 20); "An Alpine Flapper" (May 16); "Liquid Dynamite" (May 17); "A Bumper Crop" (May 26); "Chop Suey and Noodle" (July 6); "Jungle Sports" (July 6); "The Land Boom" (July 6); "Plumber's Life" (July 6); "Pirates Gold" (July 22); "The Last Ha Ha" (July 26); "Little Parade" (July 26); "A Knight Out" (Sept. 17); "Pests" (Sept. 17); "Scrambled Eggs" (Sept. 17); "Charleston Queen" (Sept. 17); "Phoney Express" (Oct. 22); "Buck Fever" (Oct. 26); "Hitting the Rails" (Oct. 26); "Home Sweet Home" (Oct. 26); "In Vaudeville" (Oct. 26); "Radio Controlled" (Oct. 26); "Thru Thick and Thin" (Oct. 26); "Bars and Stripes" (Dec. 31); "Musical Parrot" (Dec. 31); "School Days" (Dec. 31); and "Where Friendship Ceases" (Dec. 31).

1927: "Chasing Rainbows" (Jan. 13); "Plow Boy's Revenge" (Jan. 13); "Tit for Tat" (Jan. 13); "The Mail Pilot" (Feb. 14); "All For a Bride" (Mar. 4); "Cracked Ice" (Mar. 4); "Taking the Air" (Mar. 4); "The Honor Man" (Apr. 1); "Bubbling Over" (May 6); "When Snow Flies" (May 6); "A Fair Exchange" (May 6); "Pie-Eyed Piper" (May 6); "Horses, Horses, Horses" (May 10); "Big Reward" (May 12); "Crawl Stroke Kid" (May 12); "Died in the Wool" (May 12); "Digging For Gold" (May 12); "A Dog's Day" (May 12); "One Man Dog" (May 12); "Hard Cider" (May 12); "Riding High" (May 12); "Ant Life as It Isn't" (June 20); "Red Hot Sands" (July 8); "Cutting a Melon" (July 22); "Line and Sinker" (July 22); "The Small-Town Sheriff" (July 22); "All Bull and Yard Wide" (Aug. 16); "Human Fly" (Aug. 16); "In Again, Out Again" (Aug. 16); "River of Doubt" (Aug. 16); "The Big Tent" (Sept. 2); "Lindy's Cat" (Sept. 2); "Brave Heart" (Sept. 17); "The Fox Hunt" (Oct. 13); "Saved by a Keyhole" (Oct. 13); and "Flying Hunters" (Oct. 26).

1928: "Flying Age" (Terry, Foster/Apr. 20); "War Bride" (Terry, Bailey/Apr. 20); "Alaska Or Bust" (Terry, Moser/Aug. 16); "Static" (Aug. 4); "Sunday on the Farm" (Terry, Foster/Aug. 16); "Monkey Love" (Terry, Davis/Sept. 24); "Big Game" (Terry, Bailey/Oct. 2); "Laundry Man" (Oct. 26); "On the Links" (Nov. 10); "Day Off" (Terry, Foster/Nov. 24); "Barnyard Politics" (Terry, Shields/Nov. 26); "Flying Hoofs" (Terry, Bailey/Dec. 3); "Gridiron Demons" (Terry, Moser/Dec. 4); "Mail Man" (Terry, Davis/Dec. 12); "White Elephant" (Terry, Shields/Dec. 27); and "Land O' Cotton" (Terry, Moser/Dec. 28).

1929: "Break of the Day" (Terry, Davis/Jan. 2); "Snapping the Whip" (Terry, Moser/Jan. 6); "Wooden Money" (Terry, Foster/Jan. 6); "Sweet Adeline" (Terry, Moser/Jan. 8); "Queen Bee" (Terry, Shields/Jan. 30); "Grandma's House" (Terry/Feb. 11); "Back to the Soil" (Terry/Feb. 12); "Lad and His Lamp" (Mar. 2); "Underdog" (Mar. 13); "Fight Game" (Apr. 26); "Homeless Cats" (Apr. 26); "Little Game Hunter" (May 5); "Custard Pies" (May 9); "Ball Park" (May 19); "Fish Day" (May 26); "Skating Hounds" (May 27); "Polo Match" (June 2); "Snow Birds" (June 3); "Kidnapped" (June 23); "In His Cups" (June 30); "The Cold Steel" (July 7); "House Cleaning Time" (July 21); "A Midsummer's Day" (July 28); "Farmer's Goat" (July 29); "3 Game Guys" (Aug. 4); "Enchanted Flute" (Aug. 11); "Fruitful Farm" (Aug. 22); and "The Cabaret" (Aug. 25).

⊚ ALICE COMEDIES

Walt Disney produced this series featuring animated characters and a live-action girl, employing techniques similar to those popularized earlier by Max Fleischer in his *Out of the Inkwell* series. Alice was portrayed by several girls, primarily Virginia Davis and Margie Gay, who interacted with animated friends on screen in various episodes.

Distributor M.J. Winkler financed the series, which was Disney's second, and enabled the mustached animator to establish a studio in Los Angeles (near the corner of Vermont and Hollywood Boulevard) to animate these imaginative productions. Along with animators Ub Iwerks, Rudolf Ising and Hugh Harman, Disney turned out these films at a rate of one every two or three weeks. For the era in which these were made, the productions were clearly ingenious, with the interplay between the live and cartoon figures proving to be magical on screen.

"We'd film in a vacant lot," said Virginia "Gini" McGhee, formerly Virginia Davis, who remembered her days playing Alice with fondness. "Walt would drape a white tarpaulin over the back of a billboard and along the ground, and I'd have to work in pantomime. They would add the animation around me later. It was such fun. Kids in the neighborhood would act as extras, and Walt paid them fifty cents apiece."

As Disney's first star, Davis appeared in 14 Alice shorts, featured in roles ranging from cowgirl to big-game hunter. Disney brought Davis with him from Kansas to star in the pictures. He selected her for the part after spotting her face on a billboard advertisement for Warneker's bread.

How Disney got the series off the ground is noteworthy. When a bankrupt distributor forced him to shut down his Laugh-O-Grams studio, laying off his entire staff, he raised fare to travel to Los Angeles and, with the financial support of brother Roy, finished the sample reel for what became the series pilot. After relentless attempts to find a distributor, he nearly gave up until noted film distributor M.J. Winkler offered him $1,500 a reel to produce the Alice series. (The venture became quite profitable for Walt since the first film cost him only $750.)

In 1927 Disney dropped the series when his distributor encouraged him to start a new series. It starred a floppy-eared character, dubbed Oswald the Rabbit, which was immediately successful with moviegoing audiences. *Directed by Walt Disney. A Walt Disney Production released by M.J. Winkler.*

1924: "Alice's Day at Sea" (Mar. 1); "Alice's Spooky Adventure" (Apr. 1); "Alice's Wild West Show" (May 1); "Alice's Fishy Story" (June 1); "Alice and the Dog Catcher" (July 1); "Alice the Peacemaker" (Aug. 1); "Alice Gets in Dutch" (Nov. 1); "Alice Hunting in Africa" (Nov. 15); "Alice and the Three Bears" (Dec. 1); and "Alice the Piper" (Dec. 15).

1925: "Alice Cans the Cannibals" (Jan. 1); "Alice the Toreador" (Jan. 15); "Alice Gets Stung" (Feb. 1); "Alice Solves the Puzzle" (Feb. 15); "Alice's Egg Plant," "Alice Loses Out," "Alice Stage Struck," "Alice Wins the Derby," "Alice Picks the Champ," "Alice's Tin Pony," "Alice Chops the Suey," "Alice the Jail Bird" (Sept. 15); "Alice Plays Cupid" (Oct. 15); "Alice Rattled by Rats" (Nov. 15); and "Alice in the Jungle" (Dec. 15).

1926: "Alice on the Farm" (Jan. 1); "Alice's Balloon Race" (Jan. 15); "Alice's Ornery Orphan," "Alice's Little Parade" (Feb. 1); "Alice's Mysterious Mystery" (Feb. 15); "Alice Charms the Fish" (Sept. 6); "Alice's Monkey Business" (Sept. 20); "Alice in the Wooly West" (Oct. 4); "Alice the Fire Fighter" (Oct. 18); "Alice Cuts the Ice" (Nov. 1); "Alice Helps the Romance" (Nov. 15); "Alice's Spanish Guitar" (Nov. 29); "Alice's Brown Derby" (Dec. 13); and "Alice the Lumber Jack" (Dec. 27).

1927: "Alice the Golf Bug" (Jan. 10); "Alice Foils the Pirates" (Jan. 24); "Alice at the Carnival" (Feb. 7); "Alice at the Rodeo" (Feb. 21/originally "Alice's Rodeo"); "Alice the Collegiate" (Mar. 7); "Alice in the Alps" (Mar. 21); "Alice's Auto Race" (Apr. 4); "Alice's Circus Daze" (Apr 18); "Alice's Knaughty Knight" (May 2); "Alice's Three Bad Eggs" (May 16); "Alice's Picnic" (May 30); "Alice's Channel Swim" (June 13); "Alice in the Klondike" (June 27); "Alice's Medicine Show" (July 11); "Alice the Whaler" (July 25); "Alice the Beach Nut" (Aug. 8); and "Alice in the Big League" (Aug. 22).

ANIMATED GROUCH CHASERS

French Canadian cartoonist Raoul Barré produced this series of thematically related films for Edison Company in New York. Employing the technique of animation on paper, the films featured a burlesque introduction by live actors followed by a comic book title, *The Grouch Chasers*, signaling the beginning of the animation program.

The series starred a group of insects—the most notable being Ferdinand the fly and his "flyancee"—and three of Barré's other prized creations: Kid Kelly and his larcenous sidekick dog, Jip; Hercule Hicks, a henpecked little man who escaped his overbearing wife by means of dreaming; and Silas Bunkum, a potbellied teller of tales. *A Gaumount Studios release.*

1915: "The Animated Grouch Chaser" (Mar. 4); "Cartoons in the Kitchen" (Apr. 21); "Cartoons in the Barber Shop" (May 22); "Cartoons in the Parlor" (June 5); "Cartoons in the Hotel" (June 21); "Cartoons in the Laundry" (July 8); "Cartoons on Tour" (Aug. 6); "Cartoons on the Beach" (Aug. 25); "Cartoons in a Seminary" (Sept. 9); "Cartoons in the Country" (Oct. 9); "Cartoons on a Yacht" (Oct. 29); "Cartoons in a Sanitarium" (Nov. 12); and "Black's Mysterious Box and Hicks in Nightmareland" (Dec. 4).

ANIMATED HAIR

Celebrity caricatures evolved (out of "a strand of hair") in this series of line-drawn cartoons by noted caricaturist Marcus, a former *Life* magazine cartoonist. The series ran from November 1924 to 1925 and was distributed by Max

Fleischer's distribution company, Red Seal Pictures. *A Red Seal Pictures release.*

B.D.F. CARTOONS

Paul Fenton produced, directed and animated this series of advertising cartoons. *A B.D.F. Film Company Production.*

1918: "Old Tire Man Diamond Cartoon Film" (July 13).

1919: "Re-Blazing the '49 Trail in a Motor Car Train" (Sept. 10); "Tire Injury" (Sept. 13); and "Paradental Anesthesia" (Sept. 13).

1921: "A Movie Trip Through Film Land" (Dec. 17).

1922: "For Any Occasion" (Nov. 20) and "In Hot Weather" (Nov. 20).

1923: "The Champion" (Sept. 30) and "Land of the Unborn Children" (Nov. 1).

1924: "Some Impressions on the Subject of Thrift."

1925: "Live and Help Live" (May 22).

1926: "The Carriage Awaits" (June 15); "Family Album" (June 15); "What Price Noise" (June 16); and "For Dear Life" (Dec. 30).

BERTLEVYETTES

This series combined live action and animation and was produced and written by Bert Levy and directed by Sidney Olcott. *A World Film Corporation Production.*

1915: "Great Americans Past and Present" (Jan. 4); "Famous Men of Today" (Jan. 11); "Famous Rulers of the World" (Jan. 18); and "New York and Its People" (Jan. 25).

BOBBY BUMPS

Pioneer animator Earl Hurd created this mischievous little boy, inspired by R.F. Outcault's well-known comic strip character Buster Brown. (Like Buster, Bobby was given a bulldog companion, only named Fido.) These humorous and delightfully sympathetic adventures of a boy's life were first produced in 1915 by J.R. Bray's studio following the success of his *Colonel Heeza Liar* series. The idea of producing a figure "out of the inkwell" was a key element in the films—Bumps was introduced by Hurd's hand—foreshadowing Max Fleischer's technique by several years. Early stories were shaped around Bobby's pranks, often played on his parents or friends. *Directed by Earl Hurd. A Bray Production released by Paramount Pictures.*

1915: "Bobby Bumps Gets Pa's Goat" (July 3) and "Bobby Bumps' Adventures."

1916: "Bobby Bumps and His Pointer Pup" (Feb. 24); "Bobby Bumps Gets a Substitute" (Mar. 30); "Bobby Bumps and His Goatmobile" (Apr. 30); "Bobby Bumps Goes Fishing" (June 1); "Bobby Bumps' Fly Swatter" (June 29); "Bobby Bumps and the Detective Story" (July 27); "Bobby Bumps Loses His Pup" (Aug. 17); "Bobby Bumps and the Stork" (Sept. 7); "Bobby Bumps Starts a Lodge" (Sept. 28); "Bobby Bumps Helps Out a Book Agent" (Oct. 23); "Bobby Bumps Queers a Choir" (Oct. 26); and "Bobby Bumps at the Circus" (Nov. 11).

1917: "Bobby Bumps in the Great Divide" (Feb. 5); "Bobby Bumps Adopts a Turtle" (Mar. 5); "Bobby Bumps, Office Boy" (Mar. 26); "Bobby Bumps Outwits the Dognatcher" (Apr. 16); "Bobby Bumps Volunteers" (May 7); "Bobby Bumps Daylight Camper" (May 28); "Bobby Bumps Submarine Chaser" (June 18); "Bobby Bumps' Fourth" (July 9); "Bobby Bumps' Amusement Park" (Aug. 6); "Bobby Bumps, Surf Rider" (Aug. 27); "Bobby Bumps Starts for School" (Sept. 17); "Bobby Bumps' World Serious" (Oct. 8); "Bobby Bumps, Chef" (Oct. 29); "Bobby Bumps Fido's Birthday" (Nov. 18); "Bobby Bumps Early Shopper" (Dec. 9); and "Bobby Bumps' Tank" (Dec. 30).

1918: "Bobby Bumps' Disappearing Gun" (Jan. 21); "Bobby Bumps at the Dentist" (Feb. 25); "Bobby Bumps' Fight" (Mar. 25); "Bobby Bumps on the Road" (Apr. 15); "Bobby Bumps Caught in the Jamb" (May 13); "Bobby Bumps Out West" (June 10); "Bobby Bumps Films a Fire" (June 24); "Bobby Bumps Becomes an Ace" (July 15); "Bobby Bumps on the Doughnut Trail" (Aug. 19); "Bobby Bumps and the Speckled Death" (Sept. 30); "Bobby Bumps Incubator" (Oct. 8); "Bobby Bumps in Before and After" (Nov. 20); and "Bobby Bumps Puts a Beanery on the Bum" (Dec. 4).

1919: "Bobby Bumps' Last Smoke" (Jan. 24); "Bobby Bumps' Lucky Day" (Mar. 19); "Bobby Bumps' Night Out with Some Night Owls" (Apr. 16); "Bobby Bumps' Pup Gets the Flea-enza" (Apr. 23); "Bobby Bumps Eel-ectric Launch" (Apr. 30); "Bobby Bumps and the Sand Lizard" (May 21); "Bobby Bumps and the Hypnotic Eye" (June 25); and "Bobby Bumps Throwing the Bull" (July 16).

Paramount Magazine

1920: "Bobby Bumps the Cave Man" (Aug. 8); and "Bobby Bumps' Orchestra" (Dec 19).

1921: "Bobby Bumps Checkmated" (Mar. 20).

Paramount Cartoons

1921: "Bobby Bumps Working on an Idea" (May 8); "Bobby Bumps in Shadow Boxing" (July 9); and "Bobby Bumps in Hunting and Fishing" (Aug. 21).

1922: "Bobby Bumps at School" (Dec. 16/*Bray Magazine*); and "Railroading" (Dec. 2/Earl Hurd Comedies).

1923: "The Movie Daredevil" (Apr. 1/Earl Hurd Comedies); and "Their Love Growed Cold" (June 2/Earl Hurd Comedies).

Educational Pictures release

1925: "Bobby Bumps and Company" (Sept. 22/Pen and Ink Vaudeville).

◎ THE BOOB WEEKLY

Rube Goldberg wrote and directed this series of newsreel spoofs, which were animated by George Stallings at Barré Studios in 1916. Goldberg was actually contracted by Pathé Films to produce the series as part of a lucrative contract that netted him $75,000 a year for his efforts. *A Rube Goldberg/Barré Studios Production released by Pathé Films.*

1916: "The Boob Weekly" (May 8); "Leap Year" (May 22); "The Fatal Pie" (June 5); "From Kitchen Mechanic to Movie Star" (June 19); "Nutty News" (July 3); "Home Sweet Home" (July 17); and "Losing Weight" (July 31).

◎ BOOMER BILL

Along with his series of Felix the Cat and Charlie Chaplin cartoons, pioneer animator Pat Sullivan also produced and directed this series of comic misadventures. Unfortunately, no records could be found to describe the character or the films at length. *A Pat Sullivan Cartoon released through Universal Pictures.*

1917: "Boomer Bill's Awakening" (Jan. 3); and "Boomer Bill Goes to Sea" (Mar. 31).

◎ BOX CAR BILL

Following his widely acclaimed two-reel comic short, "Twenty Thousand Laughs Under the Sea," a spoof of Jules Verne's classic novel *Twenty Thousand Leagues Under the Sea,* Pat Sullivan produced and directed this short-lived series for Universal in 1917. Little else is known about the production and content of the films. *A Pat Sullivan Cartoon released through Universal.*

1917: "Box Car Bill Falls in Luck" (July 10).

◎ BRINGING UP FATHER

Most early silent cartoon series were comic-strip adaptations. This series was based on a long-running weekly strip, featuring henpecked Jiggs and his society wife, Maggie, created by cartoonist George McManus in 1912. *An International Films Production released by Pathé Film Exchange.*

1916: "Father Gets into the Movies" (Nov. 21); and "Just Like a Woman" (Dec. 14).

1917: "The Great Hansom Cab Mystery" (Apr. 26); "A Hot Time in the Gym" (Apr. 26); "Music Hath Charms" (June 7); and "He Tries His Hand at Hypnotism" (Aug. 8).

1918: "Second, The Stimulating Mrs. Barton" (Apr. 16); "Second, Father's Close Shave" (May 16); and "Third, Jiggs and the Social Lion" (June 27).

◎ BUD AND SUSIE

Frank Moser, who supervised George McManus's *Bringing Up Father* series, animated this series of husband-and-wife stories shaped around the madcap adventures of henpecked husband, Bud, and his overbearing wife, Susie. The films were released by Paramount in 1919, the year they were produced. *A Bray Production released by Paramount.*

(Filmography lists known titles only.)

1920: "Handy Mandy's Goat" (Mar. 21); "The Kids Find Candy's Catching" (Apr. 11); "Bud Takes the Cake" (May 2); "The New Cook's Debut" (May 23); "Mice and Money" (June 13); "Down the Mississippi" (July 25); "Play Ball" (Aug. 15); "Romance and Rheumatism" (Aug. 29); "Bud and Tommy Take a Day Off" (Sept. 5); "The North Pole" (Oct. 3); "The Great Clean Up" (Oct. 31); "Bud and Susie Join the Tecs" (Nov. 28); and "Fifty-Fifty" (Dec. 5).

1921: "Getting Theirs" (Jan. 2); "Ma's Wipe Your Feet Campaign" (Feb. 27); "Circumstantial Evidence" (Apr. 3); "By the Sea" (May 29); "$10,000 Under a Pillow" (June 26); "Dashing North" (July 31); "Kitchen, Bedroom and Bath" (Aug. 28); and "The Wars of Mice and Men" (Sept.).

◎ CANIMATED NOOZ PICTORIAL

Wallace A. Carlson, of *Goodrich Dirt* fame, unveiled this innovative series of caricatured drawings described as "photographic heads on pen and ink bodies." Premiering in 1916, Carlson produced and directed the series for Essanay Pictures until mid-1917, when he left the studio to pursue other interests. *An Essanay Pictures release.*

◎ CHARLIE CARTOONS

Comedian Charlie Chaplin's Little Tramp character inspired several animated cartoon series based on his comical film exploits. As early as 1915, European filmgoers were treated to animated adventures released by Gaumont. In July of that year, Kinema Exchange launched its own series of Chaplin cartoons—known as *Charlot*—which supposedly were authorized by the great comedian himself. Otto Messmer, who animated *Felix the Cat,* animated another series, *Charlie et l'elephant blanc,* for Beaumont Films.

One year after these series were made, Pat Sullivan contracted with Chaplin to produce a new animated series simply titled *Charlie.* In all, 12 films were made in 1916, each drawing ideas from films and photographs supplied by Chaplin. *A Gaumont/Kinema Exchange/Pat Sullivan release.*

(Following titles are from the Pat Sullivan series.)

1916: "Charlie in Carmen" (May 15); "Charlie's White Elephant"; "Charlie Has Some Wonderful Adventures in India"; "Charlie in Cuckoo Land"; "Charlie the Blacksmith"; "Charlie's Busted Romance"; "Charlie Across the Rio Grande"; "The Rooster's Nightmare"; "Charlie's Barnyard Pets"; and "Charlie Throws the Bull."

◎ CINEMA LUKE

This live-action and animated series was produced for the *Universal Screen Magazine*. Leslie Elton served as writer, animator and director of the series, which Carl Laemmle produced. *A Universal Pictures Production.*

1919: "Cinema Luke" (Dec. 6).

1920: "Cinema Luke" (Mar. 11); and "Cinema Luke" (May 28).

◎ COLONEL HEEZA LIAR

After working on Mutt and Jeff at Barré/Bowers Studios for a year, Walter Lantz joined the J.R. Bray Studios. His first assignment was to animate this series of misadventures starring a short, middle-age, fibbing army colonel created by J.R. Bray himself.

Bray had created the character 10 years earlier to illustrate gags in magazines. The colonel is said to have been a lampoon of Teddy Roosevelt, noted for telling stories that seemed like "tall tales." (The character also was modeled after Baron von Munchausen, another teller of tales.)

As with most Bray cartoons, the early *Colonel Heeza Liar* films illustrate a remarkable sense of economy in both animation and production values. Only 100 basic arrangements of cels were used for each film, so animation was quite limited. In several episodes, the colonel's small stature was played for laughs, pitting him against his domineering wife, who was three times his size!

In the 1920s Bray assigned Vernon Stallings to direct the series. *A Bray Company Production released by Pathé Film Exchange and Hodkinson and Selznick Pictures.*

1913: "Col. Heeza Liar In Africa" (Nov. 29).

1914: "Col. Heeza Liar's African Hunt" (Jan. 10); "Col. Heeza Liar Shipwrecked" (Mar. 14); "Col. Heeza Liar in Mexico" (Apr. 18); "Col. Heeza Liar, Farmer" (May 18); "Col. Heeza Liar, Explorer" (Aug. 15); "Col. Heeza Liar in the Wilderness" (Sept. 26); and "Col. Heeza Liar, Naturalist" (Oct. 24).

1915: "Col. Heeza Liar, Ghost Breaker" (Feb. 6); "Col. Heeza Liar in the Haunted Castle" (Feb. 20); "Col. Heeza

Producer J.R. Bray and animator Walter Lantz introduced the accomplished liar Colonel Heeza Liar in 1915. (COURTESY: THE MUSEUM OF MODERN ART/FILM STILLS ARCHIVE)

Liar Runs the Blockade" (Mar. 20); "Col. Heeza Liar and the Torpedo" (Apr. 3); "Col. Heeza Liar and the Zeppelin" (Apr. 10); "Col. Heeza Liar Signs the Pledge" (May 8); "Col. Heeza Liar in the Trenches" (May 13); "Col. Heeza Liar at the Front" (May 16); "Col. Heeza Liar, Aviator" (May 22); "Col. Heeza Liar Invents a New King of Shell" (June 5); "Col. Heeza Liar, Dog Fancier" (July 10); "Col. Heeza Liar Foils the Enemy" (July 31); "Col. Heeza Liar, War Dog" (Aug. 21); "Col. Heeza Liar at the Bat" (Sept. 4); "Col. Heeza Liar, Nature Faker" (Dec. 28).

1916: "Col. Heeza Liar's Waterloo" (Jan. 6); "Col. Heeza Liar and the Pirates" (Mar. 5); "Col. Heeza Liar Wins the Pennant" (Apr. 27); "Col. Heeza Liar Captures Villa" (May 25); "Col. Heeza Liar and the Bandits" (June 22); "Col. Heeza Liar's Courtship" (July 20); "Col. Heeza Liar on Strike" (Aug. 17); "Col. Heeza Liar Plays Hamlet" (Aug. 24); "Col. Heeza Liar Bachelor Quarters" (Sept. 14); "Col. Heeza Liar Gets Married" (Oct. 11); "Col. Heeza Liar, Hobo" (Nov. 15); and "Col. Heeza Liar at the Vaudeville Show" (Dec. 21).

1917: "Col. Heeza Liar on the Jump" (Feb. 4); "Col. Heeza Liar, Detective" (Feb. 25); "Col. Heeza Liar, Spy Dodger" (Mar. 19); and "Col. Heeza Liar's Temperance Lecture" (Aug. 20).

1922: "Colonel Heeza Liar's Treasure Island" (Stallings/Dec. 17).

1923: "Colonel Heeza Liar and the Ghost" (Stallings/Jan. 14); "Colonel Heeza Liar, Detective" (Stallings/Feb. 1); "Colonel Heeza Liar's Burglar" (Stallings/Mar. 11); "Col. Heeza Liar in the African Jungles" (Stallings/June 3); "Col. Heeza Liar in Uncle Tom's Cabin" (July 8); "Col. Heeza Liar's Vacation" (Aug. 5); "Col. Heeza Liar's Forbidden Fruit" (Nov. 1); and "Col. Heeza Liar, Strikebreaker" (Dec. 1).

Selznick Pictures

1924: "Col. Heeza Liar, Nature Faker" (Jan. 1); "Col. Heeza Liar's Mysterious Case" (Feb. 1); "Col. Heeza Liar's Ancestors" (Mar. 1); "Col. Heeza Liar's Knighthood" (Apr. 1); "Col. Heeza Liar, Sky Pilot" (May 1); "Col. Heeza Liar, Daredevil" (June 1); "Col. Heeza Liar's Horseplay" (July 1); "Col. Heeza Liar, Cave Man" (Aug. 1); "Col. Heeza Liar, Bull Thrower" (Sept. 1); "Col. Heeza Liar the Lyin' Tamer" (Oct. 1); and "Col. Heeza Liar's Romance" (Nov. 1).

⊚ DINKY DOODLE

Walter Lantz, best known for creating Woody Woodpecker, was writer, animator and director of this live-action/animated series for J.R. Bray Studios featuring the adventures of a young button-eyed boy named Dinky and his faithful dog, Weakheart.

Like Max Fleischer's *Out of the Inkwell* series, this production placed a live character (Lantz) in situations with the animated stars. However, several differences existed between the two series. Lantz used an entirely different process from that of Fleischer to blend the live-action sequences with animation.

After filming the scenes, he took the negative and made 8-by-10 stills of every frame—3,000 to 4,000 of them. The stills were then punched like animation paper and rephotographed with each cel of character animation overlapping the live-action scenes. (Character drawings were done on onionskin paper then inked and painted on cels before being shot in combination with the live-action enlargements).

Lantz's job of acting in the live-action scenes was difficult; he had to act without knowing how the characters were going to appear opposite him in each scene. "If Walt was supposed to duel a cartoon villain, he would first duel a live person, like Clyde Geronimi, one of his chief animators," recalled James "Shamus" Culhane, an assistant on the series. "The cartoon characters were added later and the final result was Walt dueling merrily with an animated cartoon."

Lantz took many of his live-action sequences outside the studio to be filmed in a variety of locations, unlike Fleischer, who always opened his Inkwell cartoons seated behind an animator's table. "We never opened a cartoon with the same setting," Lantz remembered in an interview. "We went outside to do our stories. We went to a large field, or to the beach or to Buckhill Falls in upstate New York. We went all over."

As the live actor in these films, Lantz's aim wasn't to upstage his cartoon contemporaries. "I was short and not especially funny looking, so I imitated Harold Lloyd's prop eyeglasses. All the comedians in those days used something—Chaplin had his tramp outfit; Conklin a walrus mustache; Langdon that ill-fitting peaked cap. The glasses weren't too good of a trademark for me, but then I wasn't aiming to be a full-time comedian."

Even so, Lantz's comic moments placed heavy emphasis on chase scenes, and he had to do more than merely resemble a comedian to make the segments work in each cartoon.

Incredibly, Lantz completed a cartoon for release about every two weeks, at a cost of $1,800 apiece for 700 feet of live-action and animated film. "I had no idea what the cartoons were costing," he admitted, "so this figure didn't frighten me."

Most stories were based on classic fairy tales and standard everyday situations. For Lantz, his personal series favorites were "Cinderella" and "Little Red Riding Hood," both based on popular children's fairy tales. Unfortunately, few examples of this great series remain; most of the films were destroyed in a warehouse fire.

In addition to Lantz, the series' chief animators were Clyde Geronimi and David Hand, who both became key animators at Walt Disney Studios in the 1930s. *A Bray Production and Standard Cinema Corporation release.*

1924: "The Magic Lamp" (Sept. 15); "The Giant Killer" (Oct. 15); and "The Pied Piper" (Dec. 1).

1925: "Little Red Riding Hood" (Jan. 4); "The House That Dinky Built" (Feb. 1); "Cinderella" (Mar. 1); "Peter Pan Handled" (Apr. 26); "Magic Carpet" (May 24); "Robinson Crusoe" (June 21); "Three Bears" (July 19); "Just Spooks" (Sept. 13); "Dinky Doodle and the Bad Man" (Sept. 20); "Dinky Doodle in the Hunt" (Nov. 1); "Dinky Doodle in the Circus" (Nov. 29); and "Dinky Doodle in the Restaurant" (Dec. 27).

1926: "Dinky Doodle in Lost and Found" (Feb. 19); "Dinky Doodle in Uncle Tom's Cabin" (Feb. 21); "Dinky Doodle in the Arctic" (Mar. 21); "Dinky Doodle in Egypt" (Apr. 8); "Dinky Doodle in the Wild West" (May 12); "Dinky

Animator Walter Lantz is joined at the animator's table by cartoon stars Dinky Doodle and Weakheart the Dog. (COURTESY: WALTER LANTZ)

Doodle's Bed Time Story" (June 6); "Dinky Doodle and the Little Orphan" (July 4); and "Dinky Doodle in the Army" (Aug. 29).

◉ DOC YAK

Created by newspaper cartoonist Sidney Smith, Doc Yak originally ran as a regular strip in the *Chicago Herald* and *New York Daily News* newspapers. Like so many other cartoonists, Smith adapted this middle-age character to the screen in a series of cartoon calamities. Smith produced a few experimental reels that were released by Selig-Polyscope in July 1913. In May 1914 he launched a second series, which was as successful as the first. *A Sidney Smith Production released by Selig-Polyscope.*

1913: "Old Doc Yak" (July 11); "Old Doc Yak and the Artist's Dream" (Oct. 29); and "Old Doc Yak's Christmas" (Dec. 30).

1914: "Doc Yak, Moving Picture Artist" (Jan. 22); "Doc Yak Cartoonist" (Mar. 14); "Doc Yak the Poultryman" (Apr. 11); "Doc Yak's Temperance Lecture" (May 2); "Doc Yak the Marksman" (May 9); "Doc Yak Bowling" (May 23); "Doc Yak's Zoo" (May 30); "Doc Yak and the Limited Train" (June 6); "Doc Yak's Wishes" (June 11); "Doc Yak's Bottle" (Sept. 16); "Doc Yak's Cats" (Oct. 15); "Doc Yak Plays Golf" (Oct. 24); and "Doc Yak and Santa Claus" (Dec. 8).

Chicago Tribune Animated Weekly

1915: "Doc in the Ring" (Sept. 18); and "Doc the Ham Actor" (Oct. 16).

◉ DREAMS OF A RAREBIT FIEND

Winsor McCay wrote, produced, directed and co-animated this series based on his popular comic strip. *A Rialto Production.*

1921: "Bug Vaudeville" (Sept. 26); "The Pet" (Sept. 26); "The Flying House" (Sept. 26); "The Centaurs;" "Flip's Circus"; and "Gertie on Tour."

◉ DREAMY DUD

Essanay Studios commissioned renowned animator Wallace A. Carlson to direct and animate this series of tall tales starring a Walter Mittyish lad whose daydreams—often a result of boredom and loneliness—lead him into trouble. Carlson projected Dreamy into all kinds of heroic situations and other feats of valor that often included his loyal dog, Wag. *An Essanay Pictures release.*

1915: "A Visit to the Zoo" (May 15); "An Alley Romance" (May 15); "Lost in the Jungle" (June 1); "Dreamy Dud in the Swim" (June 7); "Dreamy Dud Resolves Not to Smoke" (June

22); "Dreamy Dud in King Koo Koo's Kingdom" (June 30); "He Goes Bear Hunting" (July 17); "A Visit to Uncle Dudley's Farm" (July 26); "Dreamy Dud Sees Charlie Chaplin" (Aug. 9); "Dreamy Dud Cowboy" (Aug. 31); "Dreamy Dud at the Old Swimmin' Hole" (Sept. 17); "Dreamy Dud in the Air" (Oct. 14); and "Dreamy Dud in Love" (Nov. 29).

1916: "Dreamy Dud Lost at Sea" (Jan. 22); "Dreamy Dud Has a Laugh on the Boss" (Sept. 20); "Dreamy Dud in the African War Zone" (Oct. 13); and "Dreamy Dud Joyriding with Princess Zlim" (Nov. 21).

◉ EBENEZER EBONY

A Sering D. Wilson & Company Production.

1925: "The Flying Elephant" (Apr. 22); "An Ice Boy" (May 22); "Gypping the Gypsies" (June 22); "Fire in a Brimstone" (July 1); "High Moon" (Aug. 1); "Love Honor and Oh Boy" (Sept. 1); "Foam Sweet Foam" (Oct. 1); and "Fisherman's Luck" (Oct. 31).

◉ ECLAIR JOURNAL

Pioneer animator Emile Cohl wrote, directed and animated this series of animated cartoon items for a weekly newsreel. *A Eclair Company Production.*

1913: "War in Turkey" (Jan.); "Castro in New York" (Jan.); "Rockefeller" (Jan.); "Confidence" (Jan.); "Milk" (Feb.); "Coal" (Feb.); "The Subway" (Feb.); "Graft" (Feb.); "The Two Presidents" (Mar.); "The Auto" (Mar.); "Wilson and the Broom" (Mar.); "The Police Women" (Mar.); "Wilson and the Hats" (Mar.); "Poker" (Mar.); "Gaynor and the Night Clubs" (Mar.); "Universal Trade Marks" (Mar.); "Wilson and the Tariffs" (Apr.); "The Masquerade" (Apr.); "The Brand of California" (Apr.); "The Safety Pin" (May); "The Two Suffragettes" (May); "The Mosquito" (May); "The Red Balloons" (May); "The Cubists" (June); "Uncle Sam and His Suit" (June); "The Polo Boat" (June); "The Artist" (June); "Wilson's Row Row" (July); "The Hat" (Aug.); "Thaw and the Lasso" (Aug.); "Bryant and the Speeches" (Aug.); "Thaw and the Spider" (Sept.); "Exhibition of Caricatures" (Nov.); and "Pickup Is a Sportsman" (Dec.).

1914: "The Bath" (Jan.); "The Future Revealed by the Lines of the Feet" (Jan.); "The Social Group" (Nov.); "The Greedy Neighbor"; "What They Eat"; "The Anti-Neurasthenic Trumpet"; "His Ancestors"; "Serbia's Card"; and "The Terrible Scrap of Paper."

◉ FARMER AL FALFA

Animator Paul Terry developed this bald, white-bearded farmer shortly after becoming a staff animator for J.R. Bray

Studios and first brought him to the screen in 1916. Most of the early films cast this popular hayseed in barnyard skirmishes with animals. The series later focused on his attempts to make "modern improvements" to the farm.

After being inducted into the army in 1917, Terry had to interrupt work on the series briefly. At the end of the war, he returned to New York and formed a company with fellow animators Earl Hurd, Frank Moser, Hugh (Jerry) Shields, Leighton Budd and brother John Terry, but it lasted only for a short time. He continued making Farmer Al Falfa cartoons for release through Paramount until 1923, and later revived the character when sound was introduced. *Paul Terry produced and directed the series. A Paul Terry cartoon released by J.R. Bray, Thomas Edison Inc. and Pathé Film Exchange.*

1916: "Farmer Al Falfa's Catastrophe" (Feb. 3); "Farmer Al Falfa Invents a New Kite" (Mar 12); "Farmer Al Falfa's Scientific Diary" (Apr. 14); "Farmer Al Falfa and His Tentless Circus" (June 3); "Farmer Al Falfa's Watermelon Patch" (June 29); "Farmer Al Falfa's Egg-Citement" (Aug. 4); "Farmer Al Falfa's Revenge" (Aug. 25); "Farmer Al Falfa's Wolfhound" (Sept. 16); "Farmer Al Falfa Sees New York" (Oct. 9); "Farmer Al Falfa's Prune Plantation" (Nov. 3); and "Farmer Al Falfa's Blind Pig" (Dec. 1).

Thomas Edison, Inc.

1917: "Farmer Al Falfa's Wayward Pup" (May 7).

Paramount Magazine

1920: "The Bone Of Contention" (Mar. 14).

Pathé Film Exchange

1922: "The Farmer and the Ostrich" (Jan. 26); and "The Farmer and His Cat" (May 17).

1923: "Farmer Al Falfa's Bride" (Feb. 23); and "Farmer Al Falfa's Pet Cat" (Nov. 9).

⊚ FELIX THE CAT

The public loved this clever feline long before the 1960s syndicated cartoon revival. Australian-born artist Pat Sullivan (b. 1888; d. February 5, 1963) originated the character for the silent screen. The devil-eared cat headlined in more than 80 one-reel cartoon shorts. He had no bag of tricks as in the television-made cartoons, but through intelligent, spontaneous gags he overcame obstacles and awkward situations. In these early cartoons Felix was known to transform his "tail" into assorted objects to help him out of jams.

The origin of Felix's name came from the word "felicity," meaning "great happiness," and he was made black for practical reasons. "It saves making a lot of outlines, and the solid

black moves better," explained pioneer animator Otto Messmer, who brought Sullivan's character to life on screen.

Oddly, Felix was more popular overseas than in the United States, resulting in assorted merchandise bearing his name. In this country, adoration of the character took a different form. In 1922 Felix appeared as the New York Yankees' lucky mascot. Three years later a song was written in his honor called "Felix Kept Walking." By 1927 a Felix doll became Charles Lindbergh's companion on his famed flight across the Atlantic. The following year he became the first image ever to appear on television when the first experimental television broadcast took place, the subject being a Felix doll. To this day in the United Kingdom a popular pet food is affectionately named after the sly cat.

Sullivan refused to add sound to his pictures following the birth of "talkies." Consequently, series revenue fell off dramatically, and he was forced to lay off his staff. In 1936 Felix was revived in a short-lived series of sound cartoons produced by RKO-Van Beuren. *Directed by Pat Sullivan. A Pat Sullivan Production released by Pathé Film Exchange Inc. and M.J. Winkler.*

(Note: The early 1920s' cartoons had no titles but were simply referred to as "Felix" in trade paper listings. The 1921

Otto Messmer created Pat Sullivan's malicious, inventive adventures of Felix the Cat. The character was one of the most popular cartoon stars of the silent film era. (COURTESY: THE MUSEUM OF MODERN ART/FILM STILLS ARCHIVE)

and 1924 filmography contains only those that were given titles.)

Paramount Magazine

1920: "Feline Follies" (Mar. 28); "Felix the Landlord" (Oct. 24); and "My Hero" (Dec. 26).

1921: "The Hypnotist" (Mar. 13); "Free Lunch" (Apr. 17); "Felix Goes on Strike" (May 15); "Felix in the Love Punch" (June 5); "Felix Out of Luck" (July 3); "Felix Left at Home" (July 17); and "Felix the Gay Dog" (Oct. 30).

Winkler Productions

1922: "Felix Saves the Day" (Jan. 22); "Felix at the Fair" (Feb.); "Felix Makes Good" (Mar.); "Felix All at Sea" (Apr.); "Felix in Love" (May); "Felix in the Swim" (June); and "Felix Wakes Up" (Nov. 25).

1923: "Felix Turns the Tide" (Jan. 1); "Felix on the Trail" (Jan. 15); "Felix Lends a Hand" (Feb. 1); "Felix in the Bone Age" (Mar. 1); "Felix the Ghost Breaker" (Mar. 15); "Felix Wins Out" (Apr. 1); "Felix Tries for Treasure" (Apr. 15); "Felix Revolts" (May 1); "Felix Calms His Conscience" (May 15); "Felix the Globe Trotter" (June 1); "Felix Gets Broadcasted" (Sept. 1); "Felix Strikes It Rich" (Sept. 15); "Felix in Hollywood" (Oct. 1); "Felix in Fairyland" (Oct. 15); "Felix Laughs Last" (Nov. 1); "Felix Fills a Shortage" (Nov. 15); "Felix the Goat Getter" (Dec. 1); and "Felix Goes a-Hunting" (Dec. 15).

1924: "Felix Out of Luck" (Jan. 1); "Felix Loses Out" (Jan. 15); "Felix Hypes the Hippo" (Feb. 1); "Felix Crosses the Crooks" (Feb 15); "Felix Tries to Rest" (Apr. 1); "Felix Baffled by Banjos" (Aug. 15); "Felix Pinches the Pole" (Sept. 15); "Felix Puts It Over" (Oct 1); and "Felix a Friend in Need" (Oct. 15).

1925: "Felix Wins and Loses" (Jan. 1); "Felix All Puzzled" (Jan. 15); "Felix Follows the Swallows" (Feb. 1); "Felix Rests in Peace" (Feb. 15); "Felix Gets His Fill" (Mar. 1); "Felix Full of Fight" (Apr. 13); "Felix Outwits Cupid" (Apr. 27); "Felix Monkeys with Magic" (May 8); "Felix Cops the Prize" (May 25); and "Felix Gets the Can" (June 8).

Pat Sullivan Productions

1925: "Felix Uses His Head" (July 13); "Felix Trifles with Time" (Aug. 23); "Felix Busts into the Business" (Sept. 6); "Felix Trips Thru Toyland" (Sept. 20); "Felix on the Farm" (Oct. 4); "Felix on the Job" (Oct. 18); "Felix in the Cold Rush" (Nov. 1); "Felix in Eats Are West" (Nov. 15); "Felix Tries the Trades" (Nov. 29); "Felix at Rainbow's End" (Dec. 13); and "Felix Kept on Walking" (Dec. 27).

1926: "Felix Spots the Spook" (Jan. 30); "Felix Flirts with Fate" (Mar. 2); "Felix in Blunderland" (Mar. 7); "Felix Fans the Flames" (Mar. 20); "Felix Laughs It Off" (Mar. 20); "Felix Weathers the Weather" (Mar. 20); "Felix Misses the Cue" (May 8); "Felix Braves the Briny" (June 12); "Felix in a Tale of Two Kitties" (June 26); "Felix Scoots Thru Scotland" (July 3); "Felix Rings the Ringer" (July 17); "Felix in Gym Gems" (Aug. 8); "Felix Seeks Solitude" (Aug. 8); "Felix in Two-Lip Time" (Aug. 22); "Felix Misses His Swiss" (Aug. 28); "Felix in Scrambled Yeggs" (Sept. 5); "Felix Shatters the Shriek" (Sept. 19); "Felix Hunts the Hunter" (Nov. 8); "Felix in Reverse English" (Nov 14); "Felix in Land O'Fancy" (Nov. 19); "Felix Trumps the Ace" (Nov. 28); "Felix Butts a Bubble" (Nov. 30); "Felix Collars in the Button" (Dec. 12); and "Felix in Zoo Logic" (Dec. 26).

1927: "Felix Dines and Pines" (Jan. 18); "Felix in Icy Eyes" (Feb. 2); "Felix in Pedigreedy" (Feb. 8); "Felix Stars in Stripes" (Feb. 20); "Felix Sees 'Em in Season" (Mar. 6); "Felix in Barn Yarns" (Mar. 20); "Felix in Germ Mania" (Apr. 4); "Felix in Sax Appeal" (Apr. 17); "Felix In Eye Jinks" (May 1); "Felix as Roameow" (May 15); "Felix Ducks His Duty" (May 29); "Felix in Dough Nutty" (June 12); "Felix in Loco Motive" (June 26); "Felix in Art for Heart's Sake" (July 27); "Felix in the Travel-Hog" (Aug. 10); "Felix in Jack from All Trades" (Aug. 17); "Felix in Non-Stop Fright" (Sept. 20); "Felix in Flim Flam Films" (Nov. 3); "Felix Switches Witches" (Nov. 7); "Felix in No Fuelin'" (Nov 16); "Felix in Daze And Knights" (Nov. 28); "Felix in Uncle Tom's Crabbin" (Nov. 28); "Felix Behind in Front" (Dec. 12); "Felix Hits the Deck" (Dec. 19); and "Felix in Whys and Other-Whys" (Dec. 27).

1928: "Felix in the Smoke Screen" (Jan. 8); "Felix in Draggin' the Dragon" (Jan. 22); "Felix in the Oily Bird" (Feb. 5); "Felix in Ohm Sweet Ohm" (Feb. 19); "Felix in Japanicky" (Mar. 14); "Felix in Polly-tics" (Mar. 18); "Felix in Sure Locked Homes" (Apr. 15); "Felix in Eskimotive" (Apr. 29); "Felix in Comicalamities" (May 7); "Felix in Arabianatics" (May 13); "Felix in In and Outlaws" (May 27); "Felix in Outdoor Indore" (June 10); "Felix in Futuritzy" (June 24); "Felix in Astronomeows" (July 8); "Felix in Jungle Bungles" (July 22); and "Felix in the Last Life" (Aug. 5).

◎ FULLER PEP

Pat Powers introduced this series of animated films about a benign farmer, Fuller Pep, similar to Paul Terry's Farmer Al Falfa character. It was drawn by F.M. Follett in 1916–17. The series was listed in some Hollywood trade paper listings as "Mr. Fuller Pep." *A Pat Powers Production released through Universal.*

1916: "He Tries Mesmerism" (May 11); "He Dabbles in the Pond" (May 17); and "He Breaks for the Beach" (May 31).

1917: "He Celebrates His Wedding Anniversary" (Jan. 14); "He Goes to the Country" (Jan. 21); "He Wife Goes for a Rest" (Feb. 4); "He Does Some Quick Moving" (Feb. 18); "An Old Bird Pays Him a Visit" (Mar. 14); and "His Day of Rest" (Mar. 11).

◉ FUN FROM THE PRESS

In 1923 Max Fleischer produced this series of animated sequences adapted from *The Literary Digest*. The series was directed by Max's brother, Dave Fleischer. *An Out of the Inkwell Films Production*.

◉ GAUMONT REEL LIFE

This series of technical cartoons appeared in weekly magazine film series in 1917. *A Gaumont Company Production*.

1917: "A One Man Submarine" (Apr. 5); "A Flying Torpedo" (Apr. 12); "Cargo Boats of Tomorrow" (Apr. 26); and "The Liberty Loan" (June 7).

◉ GLACKENS CARTOONS

Famed painter/illustrator W.L. Glackens animated and directed this series of beautifully executed humorous drawings comparing modern customs with those of bygone days. *A Bray Production*.

1916: "Stone Age Roost Robber"; "My, How Times Have Changed"; "Yes, Times Have Changed"; "When Knights Were Bold"; and "A Stone Age Adventure."

◉ GOODRICH DIRT

In the tradition of legendary film tramp Charlie Chaplin, Wallace A. Carlson animated these skillfully drawn adventures of a cheerful hobo and his optimistic dog in pursuit of a good meal or a dishonest buck. Carlson, who started in animation in 1915, ended the series two years after its debut. He went on to direct an animated version of *The Gumps*. *A Bray Production released by Paramount*.

1917: "Goodrich Dirt at the Seashore" (Sept. 3); "Goodrich Dirt Lunch Detective" (Oct. 1); "Goodrich Dirt at the Training Camp" (Nov. 5); "Goodrich Dirt's Amateur Night" (Dec. 2); and "Goodrich Dirt and the $1000 Reward" (Dec. 23).

1918: "Goodrich Dirt and the Duke De Whatanob" (Jan. 6); "Goodrich Dirt's Bear Hunt" (Feb. 11); "Goodrich Dirt in the Barber Business" (Mar. 18); "Goodrich Dirt Mat Artist" (Apr. 6); "Goodrich Dirt Bad Man Tamer" (May 6); "Goodrich Dirt in Darkest Africa" (May 27); "Goodrich Dirt King of Spades" (June 17); "Goodrich Dirt the Cop" (July 8); "Goodrich Dirt in the Dark and Stormy Knight" (Aug. 5);

"Goodrich Dirt Coin Collector" (Aug. 26); "Goodrich Dirt Millionaire" (Sept. 30); "Goodrich Dirt When Wishes Come True" (Oct. 29); and "Goodrich Dirt Cowpuncher" (Dec. 4).

1919: "Goodrich Dirt in Spot Goes Romeoing" (Jan. 6); "Goodrich Dirt in a Difficult Delivery" (Jan. 22); and "Gooodrich Dirt Hypnotist" (Feb. 26).

◉ THE GUMPS

Harry Grossman of Celebrated Players contracted this series of 13 episodes based on cartoonist Sidney Smith's nationally syndicated strip. Mostly composed of live action, the films also featured animated sequences by Wallace Carlson, who previously animated and directed the *Dreamy Dud* series for Essanay. *A Celebrated Film Players Corp. release*.

1920: "Andy's Dancing Lesson" (June 5); "Flat Hunting" (June 5); "Andy Visits His Mamma-in-Law" (June 5); "Andy Spends a Quiet Day at Home" (June 26); "Andy Plays Golf" (June 26); "Andy's Wash Day" (June 26); "Andy on Skates" (June 26); "Andy's Mother-in-Law Pays Him a Visit" (June 26); "Andy on a Diet" (July 3); "Andy's Night Out" (July 3); "Andy and Min at the Theatre" (Aug. 14); "Andy Visits the Osteopath" (Aug. 14); "Andy's Inter-Ruben Guest" (Oct. 23); "Andy Redcorates His Flat" (Oct. 23); "Andy the Model" (Oct. 23); "Accidents Will Happen" (Oct. 23); "Andy Fights the High Cost of Living" (Oct. 23); "Militant Min" (Oct. 23); "Ice Box Episodes" (Oct. 23); "Wim and Wigor" (Oct. 23); "Equestrian Andy" (Oct. 23); "Andy the Hero" (Oct. 23); "Andy's Picnic" (Oct. 23); "Andy the Chicken Farmer" (Oct. 23); "Andy the Actor" (Oct. 23); "Andy at Shady Rest" (Oct. 23); "Andy on the Beach" (Oct. 23); "Andy on Pleasure Bent" (Oct. 23); "Howdy Partner" (Oct. 23); "There's a Reason" (Nov. 27); "Ship Ahoy" (Nov. 27); "The Toreador" (Nov. 27); "The Broilers" (Nov. 27); "Flicker Flicker Little Star" (Nov. 27); "Mixing Business with Pleasure" (Nov. 27); "Up She Goes" (Nov. 27); "A-Hunting We Will Go" (Nov. 27); and "Get to Work" (Nov. 27).

1921: "The Best of Luck" (Feb. 12); "The Promoters" (Feb. 12); "The Masked Ball" (Feb. 12); "Giver 'er the Gas" (Feb. 12); "Chester's Cat" (Feb. 12); "Rolling Around" (Feb. 12); "Andy's Holiday" (Feb. 12); "Andy Has a Caller" (Feb. 12); "Le Cuspidoree" (Feb. 12); "Andy's Cow" (Feb. 26); "Jilted and Jolted" (Mar. 19); "A Terrible Time" (Mar. 19); "A Quiet Little Game" (May 14); "Andy's Dog Day" (May 14); "Fatherly Love" (June); and "The Chicken Thief" (June).

◉ HAPPY HOOLIGAN

Once a week the Hearst newspaper syndicate produced new installments of its ever popular Hearst-Vitagraph News

Pictorial, which highlighted the week's news and were screened before the main feature at movie theaters across the country. At the end of each production were alternating adventures based on many of Hearst's comic-strip favorites: Judge Rummy, Maud the Mule, Jerry on the Job, the Katzenjammer Kids and Tad's Daffydils.

Happy Hooligan was another Hearst strip to gain national exposure via these weekly productions. Like the strip, Jiggs and Miggs appeared as supporting characters in the film series. Episodes generally ran three minutes in length.

Gregory La Cava, who later graduated to the rank of feature film director, directed the series until William C. Nolan and Ben Sharpsteen assumed this responsibility in the 1920s. *An International Film Service Production released by Educational Film Corp. and Goldwyn-Bray.*

1916: "He Tries the Movies Again" (Oct. 9).

1917: "Ananias Has Nothing on Hooligan" (Jan. 20); "Happy Hooligan, Double-Cross Nurse" (Mar. 25); "The New Recruit" (Apr. 8); "Three Strikes You're Out" (Apr. 26); "Around the World in Half an Hour" (June 9); "The Great Offensive" (July 1); "The White Hope" (July 29); "Happy Gets the Razoo" (Sept. 2); "Happy Hooligan in the Zoo" (Sept. 9); "The Tanks" (Sept. 16); "Happy Hooligan in Soft" (Oct. 7); "Happy Hooligan at the Picnic" (Oct. 16); "The Tale of a Fish" (Oct. 16); "The Tale of a Monkey" (Nov. 25); "Happy Hooligan at the Circus" (Dec. 8); and "Bullets and Bull" (Dec. 16).

1918: "Hearts and Horses" (Jan. 13); and "All for the Ladies" (Feb. 10).

Educational Film Corp.

1918: "Doing His Bit" (Apr. 19); "Throwing the Bull" (June 17); "Mopping Up a Million" (July 22); "His Dark Past" (Aug. 5); "Tramp Tramp Tramp (Aug. 12); "A Bold Bad Man" (Sept.); "The Latest in Underwear" (Oct.); and "Where Are the Papers" (Dec.).

1919: "Der Wash on Der Line" (Jan.); "Knocking the 'H' Out of Heinie" (Feb.); "A Smash-Up in China" (Mar. 22); "The Tale of a Shirt" (June 22); "A Wee Bit o' Scotch" (June 29); "Transatlantic Flight" (July 20); "The Great Handicap" (Aug. 24); "Jungle Jumble" (Sept. 7); "After the Ball" (Sept. 28); and "Business Is Business" (Nov. 23).

Goldwyn-Bray Comic

1920: "The Great Umbrella Mystery" (Apr. 17); "Turn to the Right Leg" (June 2); "All for the Love of a Girl" (June 18); "His Country Cousin" (July 3); "Cupid's Advice" (Aug.); "Happy Hooldini" (Sept. 11); "Apollo" (Sept. 18); "A Doity Deed" (Nolan/Oct. 25); "The Village Blacksmith" (Sharpsteen/Oct. 27); "A Romance of '76" (Nov. 22); "Dr. Jekyll and Mr. Zip" (Dec. 8); and "Happy Hooligan in Oil" (Nolan/Dec. 23).

1921: "Fatherly Love" (Nolan/Jan. 3); "Roll Your Own" (Jan. 3); and "A Close Shave" (Apr. 29).

◎ HARDROCK DOME

Assorted calamities were the end result for this eccentric detective, who appeared briefly in this series produced by J.R. Bray. *Directed by Pat Sullivan. A Bray Production.*

1917: "Hardrock Dome, The Great Detective (Jan. 29); "Episode 2" (Feb. 5); "Episode 3" (Feb. 12); and "Origin of the Shinny."

◎ HESANUT

A Kalem Company Production.

1914: "Hesanut Hunts Wild Game" (Sept. 25); "Hesanut Buys an Auto" (Oct. 10); "Hesanut Builds a Skyscraper" (Nov.); and "Hesanut at a Vaudeville Show" (Dec.).

1915: "A Night in New Jersey" (Jan. 16).

◎ HISTORICAL CARTOONS

This timely, short-lived series propagandized World War I through related stories that were both topical and political in nature. *Produced by J.R. Bray. A Bray Production.*

1917–18: "The Bronco Buster"; "Stung!"; "Awakening of America"; "Evolution of the Dachsund"; "Sic 'Em Cat"; "Uncle Sam's Dinner Party"; "Peril of Prussiaism"; "Putting Friz on the Water Wagon"; "Von Loon's 25,000-Mile Gun"; "Kaiser's "Surprise Party"; "The Watched Pot"; "Von Loon's Non-Capturable Gun"; "The Greased Pole"; "Long Arm of Law and Order"; "A German Trick That Failed"; "Uncle Sam's Coming Problem"; "Pictures in the Fire"; and "Private Bass: His Pass."

◎ HISTORIETS

A series of animated cartoons in color. *A Reel Colors Inc. Production.*

1924: "The Teapot Dome" (May); "Famous Sayings of Famous Americans" (May); "Witty Sayings of Witty Frenchmen" (May); and "Witty Naughty Thoughts" (May).

◎ HODGE PODGE

No main characters starred in this series of animated sequences based on specific themes, such as pioneering the movie business, which was distributed with live-action magazine films. *Produced by Lyman H. Howe. A Lyman H. Howe Films Company Production released by Educational Films Corporation.*

1922: "King Winter" (Oct. 8); "Sea Elephants" (Nov. 1); and "The Garden of Geysers" (Dec. 8).

1923: "Hot Shots" (Jan. 23); "Mrs. Hippo" (Jan. 6); "Fishing for Tarpon" (Mar. 14); "Speed Demons" (May 2); "Shooting the Earth" (May 17); "A Flivver Elopement" (July 18); "The Cat and the Fiddle" (July 18); "Dipping in the Deep" (Aug. 11); "Why the Globe Trotter Trots" (Sept. 29); "Speedville" (Oct. 16); "The Bottom of the Sea" (Nov. 19); and "Liquid Love" (Dec. 17).

1924: "A Sailor's Life" (Jan. 16); "Movie Pioneer" (Feb. 9); "Jumping Jacks" (Mar. 13); "The Realm of Sport" (Apr. 19); "A Tiny Tour of the U.S.A." (May 1); "Snapshots of the Universe" (June 12); "Frozen Water" (July 26); "Hazardous Hunting" (Aug. 29); "A Crazy Quilt of Travel" (Sept. 18); "Whirligigs" (Oct. 16); "Earth's Oddities" (Nov. 28); and "Hi-Flyers" (Dec. 28).

1925: "Topsy Turvy Travel" (Jan. 25); "Lots of Knots" (Feb. 16); "Movie Morsels" (Mar. 27); "The Village School" (Apr. 19); "Earth's Other Half" (May 26); "Mexican Melody" (June 16); "Travel Treasures" (June 30); "Pictorial Proverbs" (Aug. 1); "The Story Teller" (Aug. 22); "Knicknacks of Knowledge" (Oct. 18); "Magical Movies" (Nov. 16); and "A Mythical Monster" (Dec. 21).

1926: "Mother Goose's Movies" (Jan. 20); "Criss Cross Cruise" (Feb. 16); "Congress of Celebrities" (Mar. 20); "Neptune's Domain" (Apr. 12); "From A to Z Thru Filmdom" (May 23); "Peeking at the Planets" (June 22); "Chips off the Old Block" (July 25); "Alligator's Paradise" (Aug. 22); "A Merrygoround of Travel" (Sept. 19); "Figures of Fancy" (Nov. 28); and "Movie Medley" (Dec. 26).

1927: "A Cluster of Kings" (Jan. 6); "The Wise Old Owl" (Feb. 13); "Climbing into Cloudland" (Mar. 13); "A Bird of Flight" (Apr. 17); "A Scenic Treasure Chest" (May 22); "Tales of a Traveler" (June 16); "Capers of a Camera" (July 17); "Bubbles of Geography" (Aug. 8); "Delving into the Dictionary" (Aug. 30); "Here and there in Travel Land" (Oct. 16); "Models in Mud" (Nov. 13); and "A Whirl of Activity" (Dec. 11).

1928: "Recollections of a Rover" (Jan. 8); "Star Shots" (Jan. 28); "How to Please the Public" (Mar. 31); "Nicknames" (Apr. 8); "The Wandering Toy" (May 19); "Pictorial Tidbits" (June 19); "Conquering the Colorado" (July 3); "The Peep Show" (Aug. 7); "On the Move" (Sept. 28); "Glorious Adventure" (Nov. 2); and "A Patchwork of Pictures" (Nov. 30).

1929: "Shifting Scenes" (Jan. 11); "Question Marks" (Jan. 25); and "A Dominion of Diversity" (Mar. 15).

◎ INKLINGS

Max Fleischer produced this series featuring different types of animation between 1924 and 1925. The films were not released until three years later. *Directed by Dave Fleischer. A Red Seal Pictures Production.*

◎ INK-RAVINGS

Milt Gross wrote, animated and directed this brief series of cartoons for the *Bray Magazine*. *A Bray Production.*

1922: "Scrap Hangers" (Dec. 16); and "Taxes" (Dec. 30).

1923: "If We Reversed" (Jan.).

◎ INKWELL IMPS

Ko-Ko the Clown, who first starred in Max Fleischer's *Out of the Inkwell* series, reappeared in this 1927 Paramount series produced by Alfred Weiss and Out of the Inkwell Films. Weiss was removed from the role of producer after his company went bankrupt and Paramount contracted the Fleischer Studios to take over production of the series. (Due to copyright changes, the character's name was hyphenated for the series.) In 1929 the series was converted to sound and became known as *Talkartoons*. *An Out of the Inkwell Films, Inc. and Fleischer Studios Production released by Paramount Pictures.*

1927: (Dates listed are copyright dates.) "Ko-Ko Makes 'Em Laugh"; "Ko-Ko Plays Pool" (Aug. 6); "Ko-Ko's Kane" (Aug. 20); "Ko-Ko the Knight" (Sept. 3); "Ko-Ko Hops Off" (Sept. 17); "Ko-Ko the Kop" (Oct. 1); "Ko-Ko Explores" (Oct. 15); "Ko-Ko Chops Suey" (Oct. 29); "Ko-Ko's Klock" (Nov. 26); "Ko-Ko's Quest" (Dec. 10); "Ko-Ko the Kid" (Dec. 24); "Ko-Ko Back Tracks"; and "Ko-Ko Needles The Boss."

1928: "Ko-Ko's Kink" (Jan. 7); "Ko-Ko's Kozy Korner" (Jan. 21); "Ko-Ko's Germ Jam" (Feb. 4); "Ko-Ko's Bawth" (Feb. 18); "Ko-Ko Smokes" (Mar. 3); "Ko-Ko's Tattoo" (Mar. 17); "Ko-Ko's Earth Control" (Mar. 31); "Ko-Ko's

Max and Dave Fleischer's most popular silent cartoon character, Ko-Ko the Clown, ardently watches his musical note-eating friend co-orchestrate the melody in "In the Good Old Summertime" (1929).
(COURTESY: BLACKHAWK FILMS)

Hot Dog" (Apr. 14); "Ko-Ko's Haunted House" (Apr. 28); "Ko-Ko's Lamps Aladdin" (May 12); Ko-Ko Squeals" (May 26); "KoKo's Field Daze" (June 9); "Ko-Ko Goes Over" (June 23); "Ko-Ko's Catch" (July 7); "Ko-Ko's War Dogs" (July 21); "Ko-Ko's Chase" (Aug. 11); "Ko-Ko Heaves Ho" (Aug. 25); "Ko-Ko's Big Pull" (Sept. 7); "Ko-Ko Cleans Up" (Sept. 21); "Ko-Ko's Parade" (Oct. 8); "Ko-Ko's Dog Gone" (Oct. 22); "Ko-Ko in the Rough" (Nov. 3); "Ko-Ko's Magic" (Nov. 16); "Ko-Ko on the Track" (Dec. 4); "Ko-Ko's Act" (Dec. 17); and "Ko-Ko's Courtship" (Dec. 28).

1929: "No Eyes Today" (Jan. 11); "Noise Annoys Ko-Ko" (Jan. 25); "Ko-Ko Beats Time" (Feb. 8); "Ko-Ko's Reward" (Feb. 23); "Ko-Ko's Hot Ink" (Mar. 8); "Ko-Ko's Crib" (Mar. 23); "Ko-Ko's Saxophonies" (Apr. 5); "Ko-Ko's Knock Down" (Apr. 19); "Ko-Ko's Signals" (May 3); "Ko-Ko's Conquest" (May 31); "Ko-Ko's Focus" (May 17); "Ko-Ko's Harem Scarum" (June 14); "Ko-Ko's Big Sale" (June 28); "Ko-Ko's Hypnotism" (July 12); and "Chemical Ko-Ko" (July 26).

JERRY ON THE JOB

At the ripe age of 18, Walter Lantz was assigned to animate this series, spotlighting the adventures of a diminutive but exceedingly active and resourceful office boy named Jerry. Created by Walter Hoban, *Jerry on the Job* originated as a daily strip in the *New York Journal*. Like other Hearst cartoons, this animated version appeared at the tail end of weekly Hearst-Vitagraph News Pictorials.

In the animated episodes, stories often revolved around Jerry's ineptitude. (In one film, his attempt to soothe his boss's aching tooth results in his successfully uprooting the tooth—and the train station after stringing the tooth to the outbound train.) Two supporting characters rounded out the series: Fred Blink, a young rival for Jerry's job, and his younger brother, Herman. *Directed by Vernon Stallings and Gregory La Cava. A Bray Production released by International Film Service.*

1916: "Jerry Ships a Circus" (Nov. 13); and "On the Cannibal Isle" (Dec. 18).

1917: "A Tankless Job" (Jan. 21); "Jerry Saves the Navy" (Feb. 18); "Quinine" (May 20); "Love and Lunch" (July 5); and "On the Border" (Aug. 19).

Goldwyn-Bray Pictographs

1919: "Where Has My Little Coal Bin" (La Cava/Sept. 6); "Pigs in Clover" (La Cava/Nov. 10); "How Could William Tell" (La Cava/Nov. 26); "Sauce for the Goose" (Stallings/Dec. 9); and "Sufficiency" (Stallings/Dec. 23).

1920: "The Chinese Question" (Jan. 6); "A Warm Reception" (Feb. 10); "The Wrong Track" (Feb. 27); "The Tale of a Wag" (Mar. 9); "A Very Busy Day" (La Cava/Mar. 23); "Spring Fever" (La Cava/Apr. 21); "Swinging His Vacation" (La Cava/May 29); "A Punk Piper" (Stallings/June 12); "A Quick Change" (Stallings/July 16); "The Trained Horse" (Stallings/July 27); "Dots and Dashes" (Stallings/Aug. 26); "Water Water Everywhere" (Stallings/Sept. 14); "Jerry and the Five Fifteen Train" (Stallings/Oct. 2); "Beated by a Hare" (Stallings/Oct. 7); "A Tough Pull" (Stallings/Oct. 7); "The Bomb Idea" (Stallings/Nov. 6); "A Thrilling Drill" (Stallings/Dec. 14); and "Without Coal" (Stallings/Dec. 28).

JOE BOKO

Wallace Carlson wrote, produced and directed this short-lived series. *A Historic Feature Film Co./Essanay Film/Powers-Universal release.*

1914: "Joe Boko Breaking into the Big League" (Oct. 10).

1915: "Joe Boko in a Close Shave" (June 1); and "Joe Boko in Saved by Gasoline" (Aug. 27).

1916: "Joe Boko" (Apr. 4/Canimated Nooz Pictorial); and "Joe Boko's Adventures" (Feb. 9).

JOYS AND GLOOM

Controversial series covering topical news events in a satirical manner based on the newspaper strip by Tom E. Powers. *Directed by Gregory La Cava. An International Film Service Production.*

1916: "Bang Go the Rifles" (Jan. 4); "Old Doc Gloom" (Feb. 11); and "The Joys Elope" (Mar. 1).

1916–17: "Adventures of Mr. Nobody Holme"; "Cooks Versus Chefs"; "Feet Is Feet"; "Never Again"; "A Newlywed Phable"; "Parcel Post Pete: Not All His Troubles Are Little Ones"; "Parcel Post Pete's Nightmare"; "Phable of a Busted Romance"; "Phable of a Phat Woman"; "Phable of Sam and Bill"; "'Twas But a Dream"; and "Who Said They Never Come Back?"

JUDGE RUMMY

Created as a Hearst comic strip by Tad Dorgan, orginator of the term *hot dog*, this series featured the misadventures of a dog court justice, whose passion for upholding the law was equaled by his love for cigars. The series was one of several to utilize strip characters originally syndicated by the Hearst newspaper syndicate and transformed into animated series. *Directed by Gregory La Cava, Jack King, Burt Gillett and Grim Natwick. An International Film Service Production released by Goldwyn-Bray.*

1918: "Judge Rummy's Off Day" (Aug. 19); "Hash and Hypnotism" (Oct.); and "Twinkle Twinkle" (Dec.).

1919: "Snappy Cheese" (Mar. 22); "The Sawdust Trail" (June 22); "The Breath of a Nation" (June 29); "Good Night Nurse" (Aug. 24); "Judge Rummy's Miscue" (Sept.); "Rubbing It In" (Oct.); and "A Sweet Pickle" (Nov.).

Goldwyn-Bray Comic

1920: "Shimmie Shivers" (Apr. 21); "A Fitting Gift" (May 7); "His Last Legs" (May 25); "Smokey Smokes" (La Cava/June 6); "Doctors Should Have Patience" (June 19); "A Fish Story" (July 3); "The Last Rose of Summer" (July 17); "The Fly Guy" (Aug. 26); "Shedding the Profiteer" (Sept. 5); "The Sponge Man" (Sept. 22); and "The Prize Dance" (Oct. 3).

International Cartoons

1920: "Hypnotice Hooch" (Oct. 26); "The Hooch Ball" (Nov. 3); "Kiss Me" (King/Nov. 3); "Snap Judgement" (Gillett/Nov. 22); "Why Change Your Husband" (King/Nov. 22); "Bear Facts" (La Cava/Dec. 10); and "Yes Dear" (Natwick/Dec. 12).

1921: "Too Much Pep" (King/Jan. 4); "The Chicken Thief" (Natwick/Jan. 17); and "The Skating Fool" (Mar. 15).

🎬 JUDGE'S CROSSWORD PUZZLES

John Colman Terry produced, directed and animated this series of animated crossword puzzles for Educational Pictures. *A Crossword Film Company Production released by Educational Pictures Corporation.*

1925: "No. 1" (Jan. 31); "No. 2" (Mar. 8); "No. 3" (Mar. 15); "No. 4" (Mar. 22); "No. 5" (Mar. 29); "No. 6" (Apr. 5); "No. 7" (Apr. 12); "No. 8" (Apr. 19); "No. 9" (Apr. 26); and "No. 10" (May 3).

🎬 KARTOON KOMICS

This series of animated creations was produced, written and directed by Harry S. Palmer. *A Gaumont Company Production released by Mutual Pictures.*

1916: "Our National Vaudeville" (Mar. 4); "The Trials of Thoughtless Thaddeus" (Mar. 12); "Signs of Spring" (Mar. 26); "Nosey Ned" (Apr. 2); "The Greatest Show on Earth" (Apr. 5); "Watchful Waiting" (Apr. 12); "Nosey Ned" (Apr. 26); "Estelle and the Movie Hero" (May 3); "The Escapes of Estelle" (May 10); "As an Umpire Nosey Ned Is an Onion" (May 17); "Nosey Ned and His New Straw Lid" (May 24); "The Gnat Gets Estelle's Goat' (May 31); "The Escapades of Estelle" (June 7); "Johnny's Stepmother and the Cat" (June 14); "Johnny's Romeo" (June 28); "Scrambled Events" (July 5); "Weary's Dog Dream" (July 12); "Old Pfool Pfancy at the Beach" (July 26); "Music as a Hair Restorer" (Aug. 2); "Kuring Korpulent Karrie" (Aug. 16); "Mr. Jocko from Jungletown" (Aug. 23); "The Tale of a Whale" (Sept. 6); "Nosey Ned Commandeers an Army Mule" (Sept. 13); "Pigs" (Sept. 20); "Golf" (Sept. 27); "Abraham and the Oppossum" (Oct. 4); "Babbling Bess" (Oct. 11); "Inspiration" (Oct. 18); "I'm Insured" (Oct. 25); "Babbling Bess" (Nov. 8); "Haystack Horace" (Nov. 15); "What's Home Without a Dog" (Nov. 22); "Diary of a Murderer" (Nov. 29); "Our Forefathers" (Dec. 6); "Curfew Shall Not Ring" (Dec. 13); "Twas Ever Thus" (Dec. 20); and "Mr. Bonehead Gets Wrecked" (Dec. 27).

1917: "Miss Catnip Goes to the Movies" (Jan. 3); "The Gourmand" (Jan. 1); "Mr. Common Peepful Investigates" (Jan. 17); "Absent Minded Willie" (Jan. 24); "Never Again" (Jan. 31); "The Old Roue Visualizes" (Feb. 7); "Taming Tony" (Feb. 14); "Polly's Day at Home" (Feb. 21); "The Elusive Idea" (Feb. 28); "Ratus Runs Amuck" (Mar. 7); and "They Say Pigs Is Pigs" (July 14).

🎬 THE KATZENJAMMER KIDS

Cartoonist Rudolph Dirk first developed this well-known newspaper strip about the life of a German family in 1897, later adapting it into an animated cartoon series of its own. Spaghetti-bearded Captain, who spoke broken English, commanded this cartoon troupe comprised of the Inspector, Mamma and squat, wavy-haired sons, Hans and Fritz.

Filmmaker Gregory LaCava produced and directed the series under the International Film Service banner. Production was halted because of anti-German feelings that spread throughout the United States during World War I. The series was later revived in sound shorts at MGM in 1938 but renamed *The Captain and the Kids. An International Film Service Production released by Pathé Film Exchange Inc. and Educational Pictures.*

Pathé Film Exchange

1916: "The Captain Goes 'A-Swimming" (Dec. 11).

1917: "Der Great Bear Hunt" (Jan. 8); "Der Captain Is Examined for Insurance" (Feb. 11); "Der Captain Goets A-Flivvering" (Apr. 1); "Robbers and Thieves" (Apr. 12); "Sharks Is Sharks" (Apr. 26); "Down Where the Limburger Blows" (June 9); "20,000 Legs Under the Sea" (June 9); "Der Captain Discovers the North Pole" (July 8); "Der Captain's Valet" (Aug. 25); "Der End of Der Limit" (Oct. 14); "By the Sad Sea Waves" (Oct. 16); "The Mysterious Yarn" (Nov. 11); "Der Last Straw" (Nov. 18); "A Tempest in a Paint Pot" (Dec. 8); "Fast and Furious" (Dec. 23); and "Peace And Quiet" (Dec. 30).

1918: "Der Captain's Birthday" (Jan. 6); "Rub-a-Dud-Dud" (Jan. 20); "Rheumatics" (Jan. 27); "Policy and Pie" (Feb. 10); "Burglars" (Feb. 24); "Too Many Cooks" (Mar. 3); and "Spirits" (Mar. 10).

Educational Pictures

1918: "Vanity and Vengeance" (Apr. 22); "The Two Twins" (May 6); "His Last Will" (May 13); "Der Black Mitt" (May 20); "Fisherman's Luck" (May 27); "Up in the Air" (June 3); "Swat the Fly" (June 10); "The Best Man Loses" (June 24); "Crabs Is Crabs" (July 1); "A Picnic for Two" (July 8); "A Heathen Benefit" (July 15); "Pep" (July 19); and "War Gardens" (Aug.).

◉ KEEN CARTOONS

Henry W. Zippy and Jerry McDub were central characters in this animated series written, animated and directed by Charles F. Howell, Lee Connor and H.M. Freck. *A Keen Cartoon Corporation Production.*

1916: "Henry W. Zippy Buys A Motor Boat" (Howell/Oct.); "Slinky the Yegg" (Connor/Oct.); "Jerry McDub Collects Some Accidental Insurance" (Freck/Oct.); "Henry W. Zippy Buys a Pet Pup" (Howell/Dec.); and "Dr. Zippy Opens a Sanatorium" (Howell/Dec.)

1917: "Mose Is Cured" (Jan. 1); "The Old Forty-niner" (Jan. 8); "Jeb Jenkins the Village Genius" (Jan. 15); "Zoo-illogical Studies" (Feb. 5); "A Dangerous Girl" (Feb. 12); "The Fighting Blood of Jerry McDub" (Freck/Feb. 28); "Mr. Coon" (Mar.); and "When Does a Hen Lay" (Howell/May 9).

◉ KEEPING UP WITH THE JONESES

A series of cartoons based on the comic strip by Arthur "Pop" Momand. *Directed by Harry S. Palmer. A Gaumont Company Production.*

1915: "The Dancing Lesson" (Sept. 13); "The Reelem Moving Picture Co." (Oct. 6); "The Family Adopt a Camel" (Oct. 13); "Pa Feigns Sickness" (Oct. 20); "The Family's Taste in Modern Furniture" (Oct. 27); "Moving Day" (Nov. 3); "The Family in Mexico" (Nov. 10); "Pa Takes a Flier in Stocks" (Nov. 17); "Pa Buys a Flivver" (Nov. 24); "Pa Lectures on the War" (Dec. 1); "The Skating Craze" (Dec. 7); "Pa Sees Some New Styles" (Dec. 14); "Ma Tries To Reduce" (Dec. 21); and "Pa Dreams He Wins the War" (Dec. 28).

1916: "The Pet Parrot" (Jan. 4); "Ma Drives a Car" (Jan. 11); "The Family Visits Florida" (Jan. 23); "Pa Fishes in an Alligator Pond" (Jan. 30); "Pa Tries to Write" (Feb. 6); "Pa Dreams He Is Lost" (Feb. 13); "Pa and Ma Have Their Fortunes Told" (Feb. 20); and "Pa Rides a Goat" (Feb. 27).

◉ KRAZY KAT

Originally conceived as a daily syndicated Hearst newspaper strip, lovesick Krazy Kat and pesky Ignatz the Mouse headlined their own animated series under the guidance of their creator, George Herriman. Like Pat Sullivan's Felix the Cat, Krazy's onscreen trials and tribulations centered around intellectual fantasies.

In transferring the strip to the screen, however, the Hearst animators were not completely faithful to its original concept. Krazy Kat bore no resemblance to Herriman's drawing, and Offisa Bull Pup, a primary character in the comic panel, was rarely used. Even the humor was diluted. Animator James "Shamus" Culhane, a series inker, once wrote: "The stories were heavy-handed chases and primitive acting. Every gag was automatically repeated three times."

Small budgets played a major factor in the poor production values of these cartoons. Most films were ground out at a cost of $900, so "the animation department was obliged to bat out animation footage at breakneck speed . . . time only for breathing," noted series animator I. Klein.

The series might have benefited greatly if Herriman had been more involved. He nominally supervised the series, and instead the animation was chiefly produced by Klein, Leon Searl, William C. Nolan, Bert Green, Frank Moser, Art Davis, Al Rose and Sid Marcus, all top-notch animators, with little creative input from him. As a result, the series was given a different direction by directors H.E. Hancock, William C. Nolan, Manny Gould and Ben Harrison, who supervised the cartoons.

Initial production of the series was performed in conjunction with Hearst's International Film Service. After a short-lived association with International, the series was later distributed by R-C Pictures and the Paramount-Famous Lasky Corporation. *An International Film Service/Bray Productions/Winkler Pictures Production.*

The Hearst-Vitagraph News Pictorial

1916: "Introducing Krazy Kat and Ignatz Mouse" (Feb. 18); "Krazy Kat and Ignatz Mouse Believe in Signs" (Feb. 21); "Krazy Kat and Ignatz Mouse Discuss the Letter G" (Feb. 25); "Krazy Goes a-Wooing" (Feb. 29); "Krazy Kat and Ignatz Mouse: A Duet, He Made Me Love Him" (Mar. 3); "Krazy Kat and Ignatz Mouse in Their One-Act Tragedy, The Tale of the Nude Tail" (Mar. 6); "Krazy Kat, Bugologist" (Mar. 13); "Krazy Kat and Ignatz Mouse at the Circus" (Mar. 17); "Krazy Kat Demi-Tasse" (Mar. 21); "Krazy Kat to the Rescue' (Mar. 24); "Krazy Kat Invalid" (Mar. 27); "Krazy Kat at the Switchboard" (Apr. 3); "Krazy Kat the Hero" (Apr. 7); and "A Tale That Is Knot" (Apr. 14).

International Film Service Cartoons:

1916: "Krazy Kat at Looney Park" (June 17); "A Tempest in a Paint Pot" (July 3); "A Grid-Iron Hero" (Oct. 9); "The Missing One" (Nov. 27); and "Krazy Kat Takes Little Katrina for an Airing" (Dec. 23).

1917: "Throwing The Bull" (Feb. 4); "Roses and Thorns" (Mar. 11); "Robbers and Thieves" (Apr. 12); "The Cook"

(Apr. 29); "Moving Day" (May 27); "All Is Not Gold That Glitters" (June 24); and "A Krazy Katastrophe" (Aug. 5).

Bray Productions

1920: "The Great Cheese Robbery" (Jan. 16); "Love's Labor Lost" (Stallings/Jan. 30); "The Best Mouse Loses" (Stallings/Mar. 3); "A Tax from the Rear" (Stallings/Apr. 14); "Kats Is Kats" (Stallings/June 4); "The Chinese Honeymoon" (July 3); and "A Family Affair" (Oct. 25).

1921: "The Hinges on the Bar Room Door" (Stallings/Jan. 8); "How I Became Krazy" (Stallings/Jan. 26); "The Awful Spook" (Jan. 21); "Scrambled Eagles" (Stallings/Jan. 28); and "The Wireless Wire-Walkers" (Stallings/Feb. 26).

Winkler Pictures (released by R-C Pictures Corp.)

1925: "Hot Dogs" (Oct. 1); "The Smoke Eater" (Oct. 15); "A Uke-Calamity" (Nov. 1); "The Flight That Failed" (Nov. 15); "Hair Raiser" (Nov. 15); "The New Champ" (Nov. 30); "James and Gems" (Dec. 1); and "Monkey Business" (Dec. 15).

1926: "Battling for Barleycorn" (Jan. 1); "A Picked Romance" (Jan. 15); "The Ghost Fakir" (Feb. 1); "Sucker Game" (Feb. 15); "Back to Backing" (Mar. 1); "Double Crossed" (Mar. 15); "Invalid" (Mar. 28); "Scents and Nonsense" (Apr. 1); "Feather Pushers" (Apr. 15); "Cops Suey" (May 1); "The Chicken Chaser" (Nolan/Sept. 2); "East Is Best" (Nolan/Sept. 22); "Shore Enough" (Nolan/Oct. 11); "Watery Gravey" (Nolan/Oct. 25); "Cheese It" (Nov. 8); "Dots and Dashes" (Nov. 22); and "Gold Struck" (Dec. 10).

1927: "Horse Play" (Jan. 3); "Busy Birds" (Jan. 17); "Sharp Flats" (Jan. 31); "Kiss Crossed" (Feb. 14); "A Fool's Errand" (Feb. 28); "Stomach Trouble" (Mar. 14); "The Rug Fiend" (Mar. 28); "Hire a Hall" (Apr. 11); "Don Go On" (Apr. 23); "Burnt Up" (May 9); "Night Owl" (May 23); "On the Trail" (June 6); "Passing the Hat" (June 20); "Best Wishes" (July 4); "Black and White" (July 10); and "Wild Rivals" (July 18).

Paramount-Famous-Lasky

1927: "Sealing Whacks" (Aug. 1); "Tired Wheels" (Aug. 13); "Bee Cause" (Aug. 15); "Web Feet" (Aug. 27); "Skinny" (Aug. 29); "School Daze" (Sept. 10); "Rail Rode" (Sept. 24); "Aero Nuts" (Oct. 8); "Topsy Turvy" (Oct. 22); "Pie Curs" (Nov. 5); "For Crime's Sake" (Harrison, Gould/Nov. 19); "Milk Made" (Dec. 3); "Stork Exchange" (Dec. 17); and "Grid Ironed" (Harrison, Gould/Dec. 31).

1928: "Pig Styles" (Jan. 14); "Shadow Theory" (Jan. 28); "Ice Boxed" (Feb. 11); "A Hunger Stroke" (Feb. 25); "Wire and Fired" (Mar. 10); "Love Sunk" (Mar. 24); "Tong Tied" (Apr. 7); "A Bum Steer" (Apr. 21); "Gold Bricks" (May 5);

"The Long Count" (May 19); "The Patent Medicine Kid" (June 2); "Stage Coached" (June 16); "The Rain Dropper" (June 30); "A Companionate Mirage" (July 14); "News Reeling" (Aug. 4); "Baby Feud" (Aug. 16); "Sea Sword" (Sept. 5); "The Show Vote" (Sept. 15); "The Phantom Trail" (Sept. 29); "Come Easy, Go Slow" (Oct. 15); "Beaches and Scream" (Oct. 29); "Nicked Nags" (Nov. 9); "Liar Bird" (Nov. 23); "Still Waters" (Dec. 7); and "Night Owls" (Dec. 22).

1929: "Cow Belles" (Jan. 5); "Hospitalities" (Jan. 18); "Reduced Weights" (Feb. 1); "Flying Yeast" (Feb. 15); "Vanishing Screams" (Mar. 1); "A Joint Affair" (Mar. 15); "Sheep Skinned" (Mar. 19); "The Lone Shark" (Apr. 12); "Golf Socks" (May 10); "Petting Larceny" (May 24); "Hat Aches" (June 7); "A Fur Peace" (June 22); "Auto Suggestion" (July 6); and "Sleepy Holler" (July 19).

⊚ KRITERION KOMIC KARTOONS

Harry S. Palmer wrote, produced, directed and animated this series of comic drawn cartoons. A *Pyramid Film Company Production.*

1915: "No. 1" (Taft Playing Golf/Feb. 12); "No. 2" (Professor Dabbler/Feb. 15); "No. 3" (Hotel de Gink/Feb. 26); "No. 4" (Industrial Investigation/Mar. 5); "No. 5" (Mar. 19); and "No. 6" (Mar. 26).

⊚ LAMPOONS

Burt Gillett animated and directed this series of joke cartoons redrawn from the magazines of *Judge* and *Leslie's Weekly* for producer J.R. Bray. A *Bray Production released by Goldwyn Pictures.*

⊚ LAUGH-O-GRAMS

Walt Disney, at age 18, produced a series of short films satirizing topics of the day. Subjects ranged from police corruption to ladies' fashions.

The first batch of cartoons were made while Disney worked days for the Kansas City Film Ad Company, which produced advertisements for local businesses that were shown in motion picture theaters in the area. The animation was primitive and crude in its style—figures were cut out of paper and animated—yet the short films were so successful that local theater owners clamored for more.

Disney sold the series to the owner of the Newman Theatre, located in town. (The series was appropriately renamed *Newman Laugh-O-Grams.*) Figuring demand for commercials was great enough in the Kansas City area, he then quit his job and set up his own company, Laugh-O-Grams Films, retaining the series' original name.

After raising enough capital, Disney proceeded to animate six cartoons, each modernized versions of standard fairy tales. In the process, he expanded his staff to include several animators, namely Hugh Harman and Walker Harman, Rudolf Ising and Max Maxwell, in addition to Ub Iwerks, who served as Disney's partner on the early ad company Laugh-O-Grams.

While the first *Newman Laugh-O-Grams* were produced in 1920, when Walt was a member of the Kansas City Film Ad Company, titles and release dates of these cartoons do not exist. Only titles are available for films made after 1922. *Directed by Walt Disney. A Walt Disney cartoon.*

1922: "The Four Musicians of Bremen"; "Little Red Riding Hood"; "Puss in Boots"; "Jack and the Beanstalk"; "Goldie Locks and the Three Bears"; and "Cinderella."

(Note: Non–fairy-tale cartoons made during the same period were "Tommy Tucker's Tooth" and, in 1923: "Martha" (A Song-O-Reel) and "Alice's Wonderland," a pilot for the Alice Comedies.)

◎ LEAVES FROM LIFE

This series featured cartoons from *Life* magazine produced as animated sequences for magazine film series. *A Gaumont Company Production.*

1917: "No. 62" (July 5); "No. 63" (July 12/A Hasty Pudding); "No. 64" (July 19); "No. 65" (July 26); "No. 66" (Aug. 2); "No. 67" (Aug. 9/Not a Shadow of Doubt); "No. 68" (Aug. 16/The Absent Minded Dentist); "No. 69" (Aug. 23); "No. 70" (Aug. 30/The March of Science); "No. 71"; (Sept. 6/Fresh Advances); "No. 73" (Sept. 20/When a Big Car Goes By); "No. 74" (Sept. 27/So Easy); "No. 75" (Oct. 4); "No. 77" (Oct. 18); "No. 78" (Oct. 25); "No. 79" (Oct. 31/Had Your Missing Stock Panned Out); and "No. 80" (Nov. 8/It Was Not the Colic).

◎ LEDERER CARTOONS

Carl Francis Lederer wrote, produced, directed and animated this short-lived series of cartoons. *A Lubin/Vitagraph release.*

A scene from the Walt Disney Laugh-O-Grams adventures "Puss in Boots" (1922). (COURTESY: BLACKHAWK FILMS)

1915: "Bunny In Bunnyland" (May 1); "When They Were 21"; (May 27); "Ping Pong Woo" (June 26); and "Wandering Bill" (Sept. 9).

◎ LIFE CARTOON COMEDIES

Technical credits and production information could not be found for this series. *A Sherwood-Wadsworth Pictures Production released by Educational Pictures.*

1926: "Red Hot Rails" (Sept. 18); "Flaming Ice" (Sept. 25); "Missing Links" (Sept. 25); "The Yellow Pirate" (Oct. 5); "Cut Price Glory" (Oct. 11); "The Mighty Smithy" (Nov. 7); "Barnum Was Right" (Nov. 21); "Balloon Tried" (Dec. 5); and "Why Women Pay" (Dec. 16).

1927: "The Peaceful City" (Jan. 2); "Mike Wins a Medal" (Jan. 18); "Soft Soap" (Jan. 30); "A Heavy Date" (Feb. 8); "Hitting the Trail" (Feb. 23); "Local Talent" (Mar. 8); "Ruling the Rooster" (Mar. 27); "The Prince of Whales" (Apr. 10); "Racing Fever" (Apr. 24); and "North of Nowhere" (May 8).

◎ LITTLE EBONY

An L.B. Cornwell Inc. Production.

1925: "Ebony Cleans Up" (Oct. 15); "The Stowaway" (Nov. 1); and "A Drop in the Bucket" (Dec. 30).

◎ LITTLE JIMMY

Since its inception in mid-December 1915, Hearst's International Film Service planned to produce animated subjects for its weekly newsreel, the Hearst-Vitagraph News Pictorial. Animated cartoons based on Tom Powers's and George Herriman's characters were featured until April 1916, when other comic-strip artists joined the studio's line-up. One of the new faces who later joined the roster was star cartoonist Jimmy Swinnerton, who contributed this animated series shaped around the comic misadventures of a mischievous little boy. The series was based on Swinnerton's popular weekday strip, which he developed in 1905. *An International Films Production.*

◎ MACDONO CARTOONS

J.J. MacManus and R.E. Donahue served as producers, directors, animators and writers of this animated series. *A MacDono Cartoons Inc. Production released by Affiliated Distributors.*

Affiliated Distributors

1921: "Mr. Ima Jonah's Home Brew" (June 4); and "Skipping the Pen" (June 4).

Mastodon Films

1922: "Burr's Novelty Review No. 1" (Mar. 1); "Burr's Novelty Review No. 2" (Apr. 1); "Burr's Novelty Review No. 3" (May 1); "Burr's Novelty Review No. 4" (June 1); "Burr's Novelty Review No. 5" (July 1); and "Burr's Novelty Review No. 6" (Aug. 1).

⦿ MAUD THE MULE

William Randolph Hearst produced this series based on the comic strip *And Her Name Was Maud* by Frederick Burr Opper. *Directed by Gregory La Cava. An International Film Service Production.*

1916: "Poor Si Keeler" (Feb. 4); "A Quiet Day in the Country" (June 5); "Maud the Educated Mule" (July 3); and "Round and Round Again" (Oct. 2).

⦿ MERKEL CARTOONS

Topical issues of the day were turned into animated commentaries in this series produced by Arno Merkel. Kenneth M. Anderson wrote, directed and animated the series. *A Merkel Film Company Production.*

1918: "Me and Gott" (Feb.); "Power Pro and Con" (Feb.); "The Girth of a Nation" (Apr.); "Truths on the War in Slang" (Apr.); "Oh What a Beautiful Dream" (Apr.); and "Hocking the Kaiser" (Apr.).

⦿ MILE-A-MINUTE MONTY

Animator Leon Searl wrote, produced and directed this series. *A Lubin Company/Essanay release.*

1915: "Mile-a-Minute Monty" (Aug. 25); "Monty the Missionary" (Sept. 14); and "Mile-a-Minute Monty" (Dec. 22).

⦿ MILT GROSS

Along with George McManus and Sidney Smith, Milt Gross was another famous comic-strip artist who tried his hand at animation. In 1920, following his stint at Barré-Bowers Studios, where he animated the *Mutt and Jeff* series, Gross animated this short-lived series for J.R. Bray. The films burlesqued the foibles and frailties of people. *A Bray Production.*

1920: "We'll Say They Do"; "Tumult in Toy Town"; "Frenchy Discovers America"; "Ginger Snaps'; and "The Cow Milker."

⦿ M-IN-A CARTOONS

This series of cartoons featuring different themes was written, animated and directed by Harry S. Palmer and produced by David S. Horley. *An M-in-A Films (Made in America Films) Production.*

1915: "The Siege of Liege" (Jan. 9); "Great Americans" (Feb. 6); "The Dove of Peace" (Mar. 6); and "Doctor Monko" (May 29).

⦿ MISS NANNY GOAT

An overzealous goat starred in this series produced by J.R. Bray. *A J.R. Bray Production released by Paramount.*

1916: "Miss Nanny Goat Becomes an Aviator" (Feb. 17); and "Miss Nanny Goat on the Rampage" (May 14).

1917: "Miss Nanny Goat at the Circus" (Apr. 6).

⦿ MUTT AND JEFF

Archibald J. Mutt was first sketched by newspaper cartoonist Bud Fisher in 1907. Within a year partner Edgar Horace Jeff appeared. Mutt, a tall, lanky, mustachioed man, and Jeff, his short, wide-bristle–mustachioed, bald-headed partner replete with tuxedo hat and attire, entered films in 1916.

The series reached the screen thanks in part to Raoul Barré, a French Canadian artist who turned to animation following a successful career as a newspaper cartoonist. Barré joined forces with another cartoonist, Charles Bowers, who had acquired the screen rights to the Mutt and Jeff strip. Bowers was in charge of the Mutt and Jeff Company, which Fisher launched to handle production of the cartoon shorts. Distribution of these early films was handled by Fox Films.

Oddly, neither Barré's nor Bowers's name was ever mentioned in the screen credits of these films. Fisher denied them credit, wanting only his name to appear in connection with the characters.

World War I served as a primary backdrop for early series' story lines, pairing off the characters in spy invasions and other entanglements with the Germans. Additional stories dealt with typical daily situations—working as hospital orderlies to running a pawn shop—but with catastrophic results.

Staff animators completed these films at a rate of one a week. So, consequently, not every cartoon made its mark. Animator Dick Huemer remarked in an interview: "Very often they [theater managers] didn't even run the cartoons. If the exhibitor hated them, he didn't run them. That's how interested they were."

Gag development suffered with cartoons being cranked out so quickly. "We used to look at our own work and laugh like hell. We thought it was great. But in the theaters they didn't," said Huemer.

In 1921, production of the series was continued under the Jefferson Film Corporation banner, headed by animator Dick

Friel. The series flourished through 1926, ending production two years before the arrival of sound. *Directed by Bud Fisher. A Pathé Freres/Mutt and Jeff Films/Bud Fisher Film Corporation Production released by Pathé Film Exchange, Celebrated Players, Fox Film Corporation and Short Film Syndicate.*

Pathé Film Exchange

1913: "Mutt and Jeff" (Feb. 10); "Mutt and Jeff" (Feb. 17); "Mutt and Jeff" (Feb. 24); "Mutt and Jeff at Sea" (Part 1) (Mar. 3); "Mutt and Jeff at Sea" (Part 2) (Mar. 10); "Mutt and Jeff in Constantinople" (Mar. 17); "The Matrimonial Agency" (Mar. 24); "Mutt and Jeff in Turkey" (Mar. 31); "Mutt's Moneymaking Scheme" (Apr. 7); "The Sultan's Harem" (Apr. 14); "Mutt and Jeff in Mexico" (Apr. 21); "The Sandstorm" (Apr. 28); "Mutt Puts One Over" (May 5); "Mutt and Jeff" (May 12); "Mutt and Jeff" (May 19); "Pickaninni's G-String" (May 26); "Mutt and Jeff" (June 2); "Baseball" (June 9); "The California Alien Land Law" (June 23); "The Merry Milkmaid" (June 30); "The Ball Game" (July 7); "Mutt and Jeff" (July 24); "Mutt's Marriage" (Aug. 4); "Johnny Reb's Wooden Leg" (Aug. 11); "A Substitute for Peroxide" (Aug. 18); "Mutt and Jeff" (Aug. 25); "The Hypnotist" (Sept. 1); "The Mexican Problem" (Sept. 8); "Mutt and Jeff" (Sept. 29); "Mutt and Jeff" (Oct. 13); "Mutt and Jeff" (Oct. 20); "Mutt and Jeff" (Oct. 27); "Mutt and Jeff" (Oct. 30); "Mutt and Jeff" (Nov. 13); "Whadya Mean You're Contended" (Nov. 20); and "Mutt and Jeff" (Dec. 4).

Celebrated Players

1916: "Jeff's Toothache" (Apr. 1); "Mutt and Jeff in the Submarine" (Apr. 8); "The Indestructible Hats" (Aug. 12); "Cramps"; "The Promoters"; "Two for Hire"; "The Dog Pound"; "The Hock Shop"; and "Wall Street."

1917: "The Submarine Chasers" (July 9); "The Cheese Tamers"; "Cows and Caws"; "The Janitors"; "A Chemical Calamity"; "The Prospectors"; "The Bell Hops"; "In the Theatrical Business"; "The Boarding House"; "The Chamber of Horrors"; "A Day in Camp"; "A Dog's Life"; "The Interpreters"; "Preparedness"; and "Revenge Is Sweet."

Fox Film Corporation

1918: "The Decoy" (Mar. 24); "Back to the Balkans" (Mar. 31); "The Leak" (Apr. 7); "Freight Investigation" (Apr. 14); "On Ice" (Apr. 21); "Helping McAdoo" (Apr. 28); "A Fisherless Cartoon" (May 5); "Occultism" (May 12); "Superintendents'" (May 19); "Tonsorial Artists" (May 26); "The Tale of a Pig" (June 2); "Hospital Orderlies" (June 9); "Life Savers" (June 16); "Meeting Theda Bara" (June 23); "The Seventy-Mile Gun" (June 30); "The Burglar Alarm" (July 7); "The Extra-Quick Lunch" (July 14); "Hunting the U-Boats" (July 21); "Hotel De Mutt" (July 28); "Joining the Tanks" (Aug. 4); "An Ace and a Joker" (Aug. 11); "Landing a Spy" (Aug. 18); "Efficiency" (Aug. 25); "The Accident Attorney" (Sept. 1); "At the Front" (Sept. 8); "To the Rescue" (Sept. 15); "The Kaiser's New Dentist" (Sept. 22); "Bulling the Bolshevik" (Sept. 29); "Our Four Days in Germany" (Oct. 6); "The Side Show" (Oct. 13); "A Lot of Bull" (Nov. 10); "The Doughboy" (Nov. 17); "Around the World in Nine Minutes" (Nov. 24); "Pot Luck in the Army" (Dec. 1); "Hitting the High Sports" (Dec. 15); "The Draft Board" (Dec. 22); and "Throwing the Bull" (Dec. 29).

1919: "The Lion Tamers" (Jan. 5); "Here and There" (Jan. 19); "The Hula Hula Cabaret" (Jan. 19); "Dog-Gone Tough Luck" (Jan. 26); "Landing an Heiress" (Feb. 2); "The Bearded Lady" (Feb. 9); "500 Miles on a Gallon of Gas" (Feb. 16); "The Pousse Cafe" (Feb. 25); "Fireman Save My Child" (Mar. 2); "Wild Waves and Angry Woman" (Mar. 9); "William Hohenzollern Sausage Maker" (Mar. 16); "Out an' in Again" (Mar. 23); "The Cow's Husband" (Mar. 30); "Mutt the Mutt Trainer" (Apr. 6); "Subbing for Tom Mix" (Apr. 13); "Pigtails and Peaches" (Apr. 20); "Seeing Things" (Apr. 27); "The Cave Man's Bride" (May 4); "Sir Sidney" (May 11); "Left at the Post" (May 18); "The Shell Game" (May 25); "Oh Teacher" (June 1); "Hands Up" (June 15); "Sweet Papa" (June 15); "Pets and Pests" (June 22); "A Prize Fight" (June 29); "Look Pleasant Please" (July 6); "Downstairs and Up" (July 13); "A Tropical Eggs-pedition" (July 20); "West Is East" (July 27); "Sound Your 'A'" (Aug. 24); "Hard Lions" (Aug. 31); "Mutt and Jeff in Paris" (Sept. 7); "Mutt and Jeff in Switzerland" (Sept. 7); "All That Glitters Is Not Goldfish" (Sept. 14); "Everybody's Doing It" (Sept. 21); "Mutt and Jeff in Spain" (Sept. 28); "The Honest Book Agent" (Oct. 5); "Bound in Spaghetti" (Oct. 19); "In the Money" (Oct. 26); "The Window Cleaners" (Nov. 2); "Confessions of a Telephone Girl" (Nov. 9); "The Plumbers" (Nov. 16); "The Chambermaid's Revenge" (Nov. 23); "Why Mutt Left the Village" (Nov. 30); "Cutting Out His Nonsense" (Dec. 7); "For Bitter or for Verse" (Dec. 14); "He Ain't Done Right by Our Nell" (Dec. 21); and "Another Man's Wife" (Dec. 28).

1920: "A Glutton for Punishment" (Jan.); "His Musical Soup" (Jan.); "A Rose by Any Other Name" (Jan.); "Mutt and Jeff in Iceland" (Jan.); "Fisherman's Luck" (Jan.); "The Latest in Underwear" (Jan.); "On Strike" (Jan.); "Shaking the Shimmy" (Jan.); "The Rum Runners" (Jan.); "The Berth of a Nation" (Jan.); "Mutt And Jeff's Nooze Weekly" (Jan.); "Pretzel Farming" (Jan.); "I'm Ringing Your Party" (Feb.); "Fishing" (Feb.); "Dead Eye Jeff" (Feb.); "The Soul Violin" (Feb.); "The Mint Spy" (Feb.); "The Pawnbrokers" (Feb.); "The Chemists" (Feb.); "Putting on the Dog" (Feb.); "The Plumbers" (Feb.); "The Great Pickle Robbery" (Mar.); "The Price of a Good Sneeze" (Mar.); "The Chewing Gum Industry" (Mar.); "Hula Hula Town" (Mar.); "The Beautiful

Model" (Mar.); "The Honest Jockey" (Mar.); "The Bicycle Race" (Apr.); "The Bowling Alley" (Apr.); "Nothing But Girls" (Apr.); "The Private Detectives" (Apr.); "The Wrestlers" (Apr.); "The Paper Hangers" (Apr.); "The Toy Makers" (May); "The Tango Dancers" (May); "One Round Jeff" (May); "A Trip to Mars" (May); "Three Raisins and a Cake of Yeast" (June); "Departed Spirits" (June); "The Mystery of Galvanized Iron Ash Can" (June); "The Breakfast Food Industry" (June); "The Bare Idea" (July); "The Merry Cafe" (Aug.); "In Wrong" (Aug.); "Hot Dogs" (Aug.); "The Politicians" (Aug.); "The Yacht Race" (Aug.); "The Cowpunchers" (Sept.); "Home Sweet Home" (Sept.); "Napoleon" (Sept.); "The Song Birds" (Sept.); "The Tailor Shop" (Oct.); "The Brave Toreador" (Oct.); "The High Cost of Living" (Oct.); "Flapjacks" (Oct.); "The League of Nations" (Oct.); "A Tightrope Romance" (Oct.); "Farm Efficiency" (Nov.); "The Medicine Man" (Nov.); "Home Brew" (Nov.); "Gum Shoe Work" (Nov.); "A Hard Luck Santa Claus" (Nov.); "All Stuck Up" (Nov.); "Sherlock Hawkshaw and Company" (Dec.); "The North Woods" (Dec.); "On the Hop" (Dec.); "The Papoose" (Dec.); "The Hypnotist" (Dec.); "Cleopatra" (Dec.); and "The Parlor Bolshevist" (Dec.).

1921: "The Lion Hunters" (Feb. 26); "The Ventriloquist" (Feb. 27); "Dr. Killjoy" (Mar. 18); "Factory to Consumer" (Mar. 20); "A Crazy Idea" (Apr.); "The Naturalists" (Apr. 17); "Mademoiselle Fifi" (May 7); "Gathering Coconuts" (May 7); "It's a Bear" (May 7); "The Far North" (May 7); "The Vacuum Cleaner" (May 7); "A Hard Shell Game" (May 14); "A Rare Bird" (May 21); "Flivvering" (May 21); "The Lion Hunters" (June 11); "The Glue Factory" (June 11); "Cold Tea" (June 11); "The Gusher" (June 12); "Watering the Elephants" (June 26); "A Crazy Idea" (July); "The Far East" (July); "Training Woodpeckers" (Aug.); "A Shocking Idea" (Aug.); "Touring" (Aug.); "Darkest Africa" (Sept. 17); "Not Wedded But A Wife" (Sept. 17); "Crows and Scarecrows" (Sept. 17); "The Painter's Frolic" (Sept. 17); "The Stampede" (Sept. 17); "The Tong Sandwich" (Sept. 17); "Shadowed" (Oct. 18); "The Turkish Bath" (Oct. 18); "The Village Cutups" (Nov. 26); "A Messy Christmas" (Nov. 26); "Fast Freight" (Nov. 26); "The Stolen Snooze" (Dec. 11); "Getting Ahead" (Dec. 18); and "Bony Parts" (Dec. 25).

1922: "A Ghostly Wallop" (Jan.); "Beside the Cider" (Jan.); "Long Live the King" (Jan.); "The Last Laugh" (Jan.); "The Hole Cheese" (Feb.); "The Phoney Focus" (Feb.); "The Crystal Gazer" (Feb.); "Stuck in the Mud" (Feb.); "The Last Shot" (Feb. 27); "The Cashier" (Mar.); "Any Ice Today" (Mar.); "Too Much Soap" (Mar. 12); "Hoot Mon" (Apr.); "Golfing" (Apr.); "Tin Foiled" (Apr.); "Around the Pyramids" (Apr.); "Getting Even" (Apr.); "Hop, Skip and Jump" (May 15); "Modern Fishing" (May); "Hither and Thither" (May); "Court Plastered" (Aug.);

"Falls Ahead" (Aug.); "Riding the Goat" (Sept. 17); "The Fallen Archers" (Oct. 1); "Cold Turkey" (Oct. 8); "The Wishing Duck" (Nov. 12); "Bumps and Things" (Nov. 26); "Nearing the End" (Dec. 10); "The Chewing Gum Industry" (Dec. 23); and "Gym Jams" (Dec. 30).

1923: "Down in Dixie" (Feb. 4).

Short Film Syndicate

1925: "Accidents Won't Happen" (Aug.); "Soda Clerks" (Aug.); "Invisible Revenge" (Sept.); "Where Am I?" (Sept.); "The Bear Facts" (Oct.); "Mixing in Mexico" (Oct. 17); "All at Sea" (Nov. 14); "Oceans of Trouble" (Nov.); "Thou Shalt Not Pass" (Dec. 5); and "A Link Missing" (Dec. 12).

1926: "Bombs and Boobs" (Jan.); "On Thin Ice" (Feb. 20); "When Hell Froze Over" (Mar. 6); "Westward Whoa" (Apr.); "Slick Sleuths" (Aug. 1); "Ups and Downs" (Aug. 15); "Playing with Fire" (Sept. 1); "Dog Gone" (Sept. 15); "The Big Swim" (Oct. 1); "Mummy o' Mine" (Oct. 15); "A Roman Scandal" (Nov. 1); "Alona of the South Seas" (Nov. 15); and "The Globe Trotters" (Dec. 1).

◉ NERVY NAT

Animator Pat Sullivan, who created Felix the Cat, produced and animated this 1916 screen adaptation of James Montgomery Flagg's bulbous-nosed tramp who first appeared as a comic strip in national magazines. Not as innocent as Happy Hooligan or Charlie Chaplin, Nat's adventures involved frequent encounters with the law and others who fell prey to his well-planned schemes. A *Pat Sullivan Cartoon release*.

◉ THE NEWLYWEDS

Emile Cohl animated and directed this series based on the comic strip by George McManus. *An Eclair Films Production*.

1913: "When He Wants a Dog He Wants a Dog" (Jan. 18); "Business Must Not Interfere" (Mar. 15); "He Wants What He Wants When He Wants It" (Mar. 29); "Poor Little Chap He Was Only Dreaming" (Apr. 20); "He Loves to Watch the Flight of Time" (May 18); "He Ruins His Family's Reputation" (June 1); "He Slept Well" (June 15); "He Was Not Ill Only Unhappy" (June 19); "It Is Hard to Please Him But It Is Worth It" (July 13); and "He Poses for His Portrait" (July 27).

◉ NEWSLAFFS

William C. Nolan, who was head animator of the *Felix the Cat* series, wrote, produced, directed and animated this series of humorous news commentaries between 1927 and 1928. *A Film Booking Offices release.*

1927: "No. 1"; (Sept. 4); "No. 2" (Sept. 18); "No. 3" (Oct. 16); "No. 5" (Oct. 30); "No. 6" (Nov. 13); "No. 7" (Nov. 27); "No. 8" (Dec. 11); and "No. 9" (Dec. 25).

1928: "No. 10" (Jan. 8); "No. 11" (Jan.); "No. 12" (Feb. 5); "No. 13" (Feb. 19); "No. 14" (Mar. 2); "No. 15" (Mar. 2); "No. 16" (Mar. 5); "No. 17" (Apr. 17); "No. 18" (Apr. 30); "No. 19" (May 14); "No. 20" (May 28); "No. 21"; (June 11); "No. 22" (June 25); "No. 23" (July 9); and "No. 24" (July 23).

◎ NORBIG CARTOONS

Joseph Cammer served as producer and animator of this series, which premiered in 1915. *A Norbig Company Production released by Powers-Universal.*

1915: "Professor Wiseguy's Trip to the Moon" (June 6).

◎ OSWALD THE LUCKY RABBIT

The floppy-eared rabbit resembled Walt Disney's Mickey Mouse in attire, wearing short pants. Disney took on the series when his distributor suggested dropping the Alice series and launching something new instead.

The Oswald series became an immediate success, with producer Charles Mintz and his brother-in-law, George Winkler, releasing the cartoons through Universal. The films paid big dividends for Disney too. He earned as much as $2,500 a short.

Ub Iwerks assisted Walt on the animation, along with several other young animation stalwarts, including Isadore "Friz" Freleng, who replaced Rollin "Ham" Hamilton, later a prominent Warner Bros. animator. Story ideas were derived from "bull sessions" convened by Disney, during which time members of his animation staff made suggestions for gags and ideas to integrate into story lines.

After the second year of production, Disney felt certain he could negotiate a raise during contract negotiations with Mintz. Much to his surprise, Mintz had something else in mind. He wanted to reduce Disney's box-office share from each short to $1,800 a reel! He too realized the tremendous profit potential of the series and was determined to keep a larger percentage for himself. As it turned out, Disney found Mintz's offer completely unacceptable and rejected the proposal even though Mintz threatened to take the series away from him.

Mintz kept his word. He eventually hired animator Walter Lantz to supervise a new Oswald series. Dejected, Disney returned with an even bigger hit—a cartoon series featuring a lovable mouse named Mickey. *Directed by Walt Disney. A Walt Disney Production released by Universal Pictures.*

Walt Disney's Oswald the Rabbit (right) gallops ahead in a scene from "Ride 'Em Plow Boy" (1928). © Walt Disney Productions

1927: "Trolley Troubles" (Sept. 5); "Oh, Teacher!" (Sept. 19); "The Mechanical Cow" (Oct. 3); "Great Guns" (Oct. 17); "All Wet" (Oct. 31); "The Ocean Hop" (Nov. 14); "The Banker's Daughter" (Nov. 28); "Empty Socks" (Dec. 12); and "Rickety Gin" (Dec. 26).

1928: "Harem Scarem" (Jan. 9); "Neck 'n Neck" (Jan. 23); "Ol' Swimmin' 'Ole" (Feb. 6); "Africa Before Dark" (Feb. 20); "Rival Romeos" (Mar. 5); "Bright Lights" (Mar. 19); "Sagebrush Sadie" (Apr. 2); "Ride 'Em Plow Boy" (Apr. 16); "Ozzie of the Mounted" (Apr. 30); "Hungry Hoboes" (May 14); "Oh, What a Knight" (May 28); "Poor Papa" (June 11); "The Fox Chase" (June 25); "Tall Timber" (July 9); "Sleigh Bells" (July 23); "Hot Dogs" (Aug. 20); and "Sky Scrappers" (Sept. 3).

◎ OTTO LUCK

J.R. Bray produced this short-lived series following the adventures of a romantic young man who persistently creates the impression that there is a screw loose in his mental machinery. *Written, directed and animated by Wallace A. Carlson. A Bray Production released by Paramount.*

1915: "Otto Luck in the Movies" (June 4); "Otto Luck to the Rescue" (June 25); "Otto Luck and the Ruby of Razmataz" (July 16); and "Otto Luck's Flivvered Romance" (Aug. 13).

◎ OUT OF THE INKWELL

Animator Max Fleischer created this series starring Koko the Clown (the name was not hyphenated at this time), one of the first to combine live action and animation. The technique was accomplished through a process called

Rotoscope, which Max and brother Dave Fleischer developed for the screen.

The Fleischers invented the technique after being unsatisfied with the results of other cartoonists' animated films. They first employed this new technical marvel in the pilot film that launched the series. Rotoscope was simply a drawing board and film projector combined, enabling animators to retrace frame by frame projected film images of human characters to achieve lifelike animation.

The pilot resulted in the birth of Koko, actually Dave Fleischer dressed in a puffy-sleeved clown suit with large white buttons. He performed somersaults and other acrobatics before the camera, then exaggerated them in the final animation.

This initial film, appropriately called *Out of the Inkwell*, was so well received that Max Fleischer decided to produce additional films right away. He sold cartoon magnate J.R. Bray on the idea of handling distribution, and he animated one Inkwell cartoon a month. The films appeared as part of Bray's *Paramount Pictograph* screen magazine.

Response to the cartoons was overwhelming to say the least. As one critic for the *New York Times* noted: "One's first reflection after seeing this bit of work is, 'Why doesn't Mr. Fleischer do more?'"

Such raves were not uncommon for the series. Koko enthralled audiences with his fluid movement, and the novelty of blending live footage with animation saved these films. The stock opening had Koko materialize out of a cartoonist's inkwell or pen point, only to harrass the animator before being placed in some type of animated situation. The animator seen in the opening sequence was Max Fleischer, who played both KoKo's master and nemesis.

By 1923 Max Fleischer stopped animating the series and brother Dave took over the series direction. Some of the animators who worked on the series included Burt Gillett, Dick Huemer, Mannie Davis, Ben Sharpensteen and Roland "Doc" Crandall. Between Inkwell films, Koko also starred in sing-a-long cartoons called *Koko Songs*, animated versions using a bouncing ball set to popular tunes of the day. "My Bonnie September" was the first production under this series banner in 1925. *A Bray and Out of the Inkwell Films Production released by Warner Bros., Paramount, Rodner Productions, Winkler Pictures and Red Seal Pictures.*

Paramount-Bray Pictographs

1916: "Out of the Inkwell."

1918: "Experiment No. 1 (June 10)."

Goldwyn-Bray Pictographs

1919: "Experiment No. 2" (Mar. 5); "Experiment No. 3" (Apr. 2); "The Clown's Pup" (Aug. 30); "The Tantalizing Fly" (Oct. 4); and "Slides" (Dec. 3).

1920: "The Boxing Kangaroo" (Feb. 2); "The Chinaman" (Mar. 19); "The Circus" (May 6); "The Ouija Board" (June 4); "The Clown's Little Brother" (July 6); "Poker" (Oct. 2); "Perpetual Motion" (Oct. 2); and "The Restaurant" (Nov. 6).

1921: "Cartoonland" (Feb. 2); and "The Automobile Ride" (June 20).

Out of the Inkwell Films Inc.

1921: "Modelling" (Oct.); "Fishing" (Nov. 21); and "Invisible Ink" (Dec. 3).

1922: (released by Warner Brothers); "The Fish" (Jan. 7); "The Dresden Doll" (Feb. 7); and "The Mosquito" (Mar. 6).

Animator Dave Fleischer, dressed in a clown suit, was actually Koko the Clown, filmed live and transposed into animated sketchings for the Fleisher's Out of the Inkwell series.

1922: (released by Winkler Pictures): "Bubbles" (Apr. 20); "Flies" (May); "Pay Day" (July 8); "The Hypnotist" (July 26); "The Challenge" (Aug. 29); "The Show" (Sept. 21); "The Reunion" (Oct. 27); "The Birthday" (Nov. 4); and "Jumping Beans" (Dec. 15).

1923: (released by Rodner Productions): "Modeling" (Feb. 3); "Surprise" (Mar. 15); "The Puzzle" (Apr. 15); "Trapped" (May 15); "The Battle" (July 1); "False Alarm" (Aug. 1); "Balloons" (Sept. 1); "The Fortune Teller" (Oct. 1); "Shadows" (Nov. 1); and "Bed Time" (Dec. 1).

1924: (released by Red Seal Pictures): "The Laundry" (Jan. 1); "Masquerade" (Feb. 1); "The Cartoon Factory" (Feb. 21); "Mother Gooseland" (Mar. 21); "A Trip to Mars" (Apr. 1); "A Stitch in Time" (May 1); "Clay Town" (May 28); "The Runaway" (June 25); "Vacation" (July 23); "Vaudeville" (Aug. 20); "League of Nations" (Sept. 17); "Sparring Partners" (Oct.); and "The Cure" (Dec. 13).

1925: "Koko the Hot Shot" (Jan.); "Koko the Barber" (Feb. 25); "Big Chief Koko" (Mar. 2); "The Storm" (Mar. 21); "Koko Trains 'Em" (May 9); "Koko Sees Spooks" (June 13); "Koko Celebrates the Fourth" (July 4); "Koko Nuts" (Sept. 5); "Koko on the Run" (Sept. 26); "Koko Packs 'Em" (Oct. 17); "Koko Eats" (Nov. 15); "Koko's Thanksgiving" (Nov. 21); "Koko Steps Out" (Nov. 21); and "Koko in Toyland" (Dec. 12).

1926: "Koko's Paradise" (Feb. 27); "Koko Baffles the Bulls" (Mar. 6); "It's the Cats" (May 1); "Koko at the Circus" (May 1); "Toot Toot" (June 5); "Koko Hot After It" (June 12); "The Fadeaway" (Sept. 1); "Koko's Queen" (Oct. 1); "Koko Kidnapped" (Oct.); "Koko the Convict" (Nov. 1); and "Koko Gets Egg-Cited" (Dec. 1).

1927: "Koko Back Tracks" (Jan. 1); "Koko Makes 'em Laugh" (Feb. 10); "Koko in 1999" (Mar. 10); "Koko the Kavalier" (Apr. 10); and "Koko Needles the Boss" (May 10).

◎ PEANUT COMEDIES

Produced as part of the *Paramount Magazine*, this series combined live action and animation. The series was produced, directed, written and animated by Harry D. Leonard. A *Paramount Pictures release*.

1920: "One Hundred Per Cent Proof" (Nov. 21).

1921: "Some Sayings of Benjamin Franklin" (Jan. 9); and "The Sheriff" (Mar. 20).

1921: "Spaghetti for Two" (May 15); "In Old Madrid" (June 5); and "School Days" (Aug. 8).

◎ PEN AND INK VAUDEVILLE

These absurd cartoons feature an animator on a vaudeville stage sketching various outlandish drawings and editorial cartoons that miraculously come to life onscreen. *An Earl Hurd Production released by Educational Film Corp.*

1924: "Boneyard Blues" (Aug. 31); "The Hoboken Nightingale" (Oct. 5); "The Sawmill Four" (Nov. 2); "The Artist's Model" (Nov. 15); and "Broadcasting" (Dec. 20).

1925: "He Who Gets Socked" (Feb. 7); "Two Cats and a Bird" (Mar. 7); "The Mellow Quartette" (Apr. 4); "Monkey Business" (May 2); "Two Poor Fish" (May 30); "Props' Dash for Cash" (June 20); "Bobby Bumps and Company" (July 4); and "Props and the Spirits" (Sept. 5).

◎ PETE THE PUP

This series starred one of Walter Lantz's last silent cartoon characters, a lovable but pesky pup and his jocular tramp sidekick. Each cartoon was shaped around live segments of Lantz at his animator's table, à la Max Fleischer's *Out of the Inkwell*, while his star characters looked on. The series was also billed as *Hot Dog Cartoons*, for obvious reasons.

Lantz animated and directed the series. It lasted two years. *A Bray Production released by Pathe Film Exchange Inc.*

1926: "For the Love o' Pete" (Oct. 2); "Pete's Haunted House" (Oct. 5); and "Pete's Party" (Oct. 26).

1927: "Dog Gone It" (Jan. 4); "Along Came Fido" (Jan. 31); "The Puppy Express" (Feb. 4); "Petering Out" (Feb. 16); "S'matter, Pete?" (Mar. 15); "Lunch Hound" (Apr. 8); "Jingle Bells" (Apr. 26); "Bone Dry" (May 14); and "The Farm Hand" (May 27).

◎ PHABLES

Raoul Barré, who was associated with William Randolph Hearst's International Film Service, produced this series of films based on Tom E. Powers's clever comic drawings, which featured witty social commentary using sticklike figures. Barré quit after making only seven films to accept an offer to adapt the *Mutt and Jeff* strip into a series. *An International Film Service Production.*

1915: "The Phable of Sam And Bill" (Dec. 17); "The Phable of a Busted Romance" (Dec. 24); and "Feet Is Feet: A Phable" (Dec. 31).

1916: "A Newlywed Phable" (Jan. 7); "The Phable of a Phat Woman" (Jan. 14); and "Cooks Vs. Chefs: The Phable of Olaf and Louie" (Jan. 21).

◎ POLICE DOG

Extremely funny stories of the amazing achievements of a friendly and most precocious dog who has attached himself to the policeman on the beat. Drawn by gifted comic-strip artist Carl Anderson (who also directed), it was one of three animal series to emerge from the J.R. Bray Studios. *A Bray Production released by Pathe Film Exchange.*

1914: "The Police Dog" (Nov. 21).

1915: "The Police Dog Gets Piffles in Bad" (July 24); and "The Police Dog to the Rescue" (Sept. 25).

1916: "Police Dog on the Wire" (Jan. 27); "Police Dog Turns Nurse" (Apr. 2); "Police Dog in the Park" (May 7); and "Working Out with the Police Dog" (June 6).

◉ POPULAR SONG PARODIES

Like Max Fleischer's *Song Car-Tunes* series, this series used popular music as the basis for story lines. *Produced by Louis Weiss. An Artclass Pictures Production released by Film Booking Offices.*

1926: "Alexander's Ragtime Band" (May); "Annie Laurie"; "The Sheik of Araby"; "In My Harem"; "When I Lost You"; "Margie"; "When That Midnight Choochoo Leaves for Alabam"; "Oh What a Pal Was Mary"; "Everybody's Doing It"; "My Wife's Gone to the Country"; "Oh How I Hate to Get Up in the Morning"; "Just Try to Picture Me"; "I Love to Fall Asleep"; "For Me and My Gal"; "Yak-a-Hula-Hick-a-Doola"; "My Sweetie"; "Old Pal"; "Tumbledown Shack in Athlone"; "The Rocky Road to Dublin"; "When I Leave This World Behind"; "Finiculee Finicula"; "When the Angelus Was Ringing"; "Beautiful Eyes"; "Call Me Up Some Rainy Afternoon"; "Micky"; and "Oh I Wish I Was in Michigan."

◉ QUACKY DOODLES

Cartoonist Johnny B. Gruelle, founder of the *Raggedy Ann* comic strip among others, created this series showcasing a family of ducks: Quacky Doodles, the mother; Danny Doodles, the father; and the little Doodles. They appeared at regular intervals with J.R. Bray's Colonel Heeza Liar, Bobby Bumps and his dog Fido as part of Bray's weekly *Paramount Pictograph* screen magazine. *A Bray Production released by Paramount Pictures.*

1917: "Quacky Doodles Picnic" (Feb. 18); "Quacky Doodles' Food Crisis" (Mar. 12); "Quacky Doodles The Early Bird" (Apr. 1); "Quacky Doodles Soldiering for Fair" (Apr. 23); "Quacky Doodles Sings the Pledge" (Sept. 10); and "Quacky Doodles the Cheater" (Oct. 15).

◉ RED HEAD COMEDIES

This series of cartoons, which spoofed noted figures in world history, was produced in color. The series was written, produced, directed and animated by Frank A. Nankivell, Richard M. Friel, "Hutch" and W.E. Stark. *A Lee-Bradford Corporation Production.*

1923: "Robinson Crusoe Returns on Friday" (Sept.); "Cleopatra and Her Easy Mark" (Sept.); "Napoleon Not So Great" (Sept.); "Kidding Captain Kidd" (Sept.); "Rip Without a Wink" (Sept.); "Columbus Discovers a New Whirl" (Sept.); "Why Sitting Bull Stood Up" (Dec.); "What Did William Tell" (Dec.); "A Whale of a Story" (Dec.); "How Troy Was Collared" (Dec.); and "The Jones Boys' Sister" (Dec.).

◉ RHYME REELS

Walt Mason wrote, produced and directed this series, which combined live action with animated sequences. *A Filmcraft Corporation Production.*

1917: "Bunked and Paid For" (Aug. 18); "The Dipper" (Aug. 18); "True Love and Fake Money" (Aug.); and "Hash" (Aug.).

◉ ROVING THOMAS

This series of adventures, featuring a cat named Roving Thomas, combined live action and animation. *Produced by Charles Urban. A Kineto Films Production released by Vitagraph.*

1922: Roving Thomas Sees New York" (Sept. 17); "Roving Thomas on an Aeroplane" (Oct. 22); and "Roving Thomas on a Fishing Trip" (Dec. 10).

1923: "Roving Thomas at the Winter Carnival" (Feb.); and "Roving Thomas in Chicago" (Oct. 27).

◉ SAMMIE JOHNSIN

Inheriting the rights to comic strips penned by the great William F. Marriner, Pat Sullivan turned one of them, *Sambo and his Funny Noses*, into an animated cartoon series in 1916 called, *Sammie Johnsin.* The films centered around the adventures of this Little Black Sambo character. Sullivan reportedly photographed the films at Univeral's studio in Fort Lee, New Jersey. *A Pat Sullivan Cartoon released through Powers-Universal Pictures.*

1916: "Sammie Johnsin Hunter" (Jan. 19); "Sammie Johnsin Strong Man" (Mar. 3); "Sammie Johnsin Magician" (June 20); "Sammie Johnsin Gets a Job" (July 3); "Sammie Johnsin in Mexico" (Aug. 10); "Sammie Johnsin Minds the Baby" (Oct. 23); "Sammie Johnsin at the Seaside" (Nov. 18); "Sammie Johnsin's Love Affair" (Nov. 24); "Sammie Johnsin and His Wonderful Lamp" (Dec. 8); and "Sammie Johnsin Slumbers Not" (Dec. 21).

◉ SCAT CAT

The success of Pat Sullivan's Felix the Cat inspired several other animators to create cat characters of their own. Frank Moser's series followed the exploits of Scat Cat, which alternated with Sullivan's Felix the Cat on Paramount's *Paramount Magazine* newsreel. The series was produced in 1920. *A Paramount Pictures release.*

◎ SCENIC SKETCHOGRAPHS
Following the success of his *Travelaughs* series, Henry "Hy" Mayer wrote, produced, directed and animated this series for Pathé Exchange. *A Mayer Production released by Pathé Exchange.*

1926: "The Family Album" (July 26); "Tripping the Rhine" (July 26); "A Pup's Tale" (July 26); and "Nurenberg the Toy City" (July 26).

◎ SCREEN FOLLIES
Animators Luis Seel and F.A. Dahne wrote, produced, directed and animated this series for which little else is known. *A Capital Film Company.*

1920: "No. 1" (Jan. 4); and "No. 2" (Jan. 4).

◎ THE SHENANIGAN KIDS
Based on the comic strip by Rudolph Dirks, this series continued the adventures of Dirks's *The Katzenjammer Kids.* Directed by Gregory La Cava, Burt Gillett and Grim Natwick. *An International Film Service/Goldwyn-Bray Comic Production.*

1920: "Knock on the Window, The Door is a Jamb" (Apr. 17); "One Good Turn Deserves Another" (June 17); "The Dummy" (June 27); "The Rotisserie Brothers" (Natwick/July 24); and "Hunting Big Game" (Gillett/Oct. 9).

◎ SILHOUETTE FANTASIES
In the mid-1900s, movie-shadow plays were part of popular entertainment. J.R. Bray teamed up with his associate C. Allan Gilbert to produce a series of animated films based on this archaic art form. The films turned out to be "serious" adaptations of Greek myths, staged in art nouveau arabesque tableaux. Bray had plans to create a five-reel feature using the same technique. However, Gilbert left the studio in 1916 and the series was abandoned. *A Bray-Gilbert Films Production released by Paramount Pictures.*

1916: "Inbad the Sailor" (Jan. 20); "Haunts for Rent" (Feb. 10); "The Chess Queen" (Mar. 7); "In the Shadows" (Mar. 15); "Inbad the Sailor Gets into Deep Water" (Apr. 8); and "The Toyland Paper Chase" (May 10).

◎ SILLIETTES
Issued as part of film magazine series, this series consisted of animated silhouettes to tell a story. *Herbert M. Dawly pro-*

duced, directed and animated the series. *A Herbert M. Dawley Production released by Pathé Exchange.*

1923: "Silliettes" (Mar. 24); "The Lobster Nightmare" (Apr. 7); "The Absent Minded Poet" (June 9); and "The Classic Centaur" (July 7).

1924: "Pan the Piper" (Feb. 9); "Thumbelina" (Sept. 27); "Jack and the Beanstalk"; "Cinderella"; "Sleeping Beauty"; "Tattercoats"; and "Aladdin and the Wonderful Lamp."

1925: "Jack the Giant Killer" (May 9).

◎ SKETCHOGRAFS
Social and topical issues were among the themes covered in this series, which was included in weekly magazine film series. It was written, produced, directed and animated by Julian Ollendorff. *An Ollendorff Production released by Educational Pictures and Pathé Exchange.*

Educational Pictures
1921: "Play Ball" (Aug. 7); "Just for Fun" (Sept. 16); "Eve's Leaves" (Oct.); "Seeing Greenwich Village" (Nov.); and "What's the Limit" (Dec. 24).

Pathé Exchange
1921: "Jiggin' on the Old Sod" (Sept. 18).

Educational Pictures
1922: "Famous Men" (Oct. 21); "Athletics and Women" (Oct. 28); "Champions" (Nov. 4); "Animals and Humans" (Nov. 11); "Mackerel Fishing" (Dec. 2); and "The Coastguard" (Dec. 16).

1923: "Family Album" (Jan. 8).

Cranfield and Clarke
1926: "Beauty and the Beach" (Sept. 1); "Everybody Rides" (Sept. 15); "Fair Weather" (Oct. 1); "The Big Show" (Oct. 15); "Watch Your Step" (Nov. 1); "Revolution of the Sexes" (Nov. 15); and "Tin Pan Alley" (Dec. 1).

◎ SONG CAR-TUNES
Before the advent of sound, theaters were known to project song slides onto the movie screen showing lyrics of well-known tunes, often accompanied by a live singer or musician, to commit audiences into singing along. Animator Max Fleischer took this simple concept and illustrated lyrics with drawings and live-action footage in a series of cartoons, first shown in 1924, called, *Song Car-Tunes.*

In the beginning of most films, on-camera talent—usually a Fleischer employee—highlighted the lyrics using a long stick with a luminescent white ball at the end. Films then often cut away to Fleischer cartoon stars—Koko the Clown, Fritz the dog and others—in ingenious visual gags to lead the second or third chorus of the song.

Some sing-a-long cartoons were synchronized using Dr. Lee DeForest's Phonofilm sound process, but theaters were ill-equipped to project these musical novelties employing what was then a revolutionary technique. *An Out of the Inkwell Film Production released by Arrow Film Corp. and Red Seal Pictures.*

Arrow Film Corp.

1924: "Mother Pin a Rose on Me" (Mar. 9/released in sound in June); "Come Take a Trip in My Airship" (Mar. 9/released in sound in June); and "Goodbye My Lady Love" (Mar. 9/released with sound in June).

Red Seal Pictures

1925: "Come Take a Trip in My Airship" (Jan. 15); "The Old Folks at Home" (Feb. 1); "Mother, Mother Pin a Rose on Me" (Mar. 1); "I Love a Lassie" (Mar. 20); "The Swanee River" (Apr. 25); "Daisy Bell" (May 30); "Nutcracker Suite" (Sept./unconfirmed title); "My Bonnie Lies Over the Ocean" (Sept. 15/first "bouncing ball" cartoon); "Ta-Ra-Ra-Boom-De-A" (Oct. 15); "Dixie" (Nov. 15); and "Sailing, Sailing" (Dec. 15).

1926: "Dolly Gray" (Feb. 6); "Has Anybody Here Seen Kelly" (Feb. 21/released with sound); "My Old Kentucky Home" (Mar. 13/released with sound); "Sweet Adeline" (May 1); "Tramp, Tramp, Tramp the Boys Are Marching" (May 8); "Goodbye My Lady Love" (May 22); "Coming Through the Rye" (June 1); "Pack Up Your Troubles" (July 17); "The Trail of the Lonesome Pine" (July 17/released with sound); "By the Light of the Silvery Moon" (Aug. 21/released with sound); "In the Good Old Summer Time" (Sept./released with sound); "Oh You Beautiful Doll" (Sept./released with sound); and "Old Black Joe" (Nov. 1/released with sound).

1927: "Jingle Bells" (Apr. 1); "Waiting for the Robert E. Lee" (Apr. 15); and "Old Black Joe" (July/released with sound).

1924–1926: (Following are undated titles from the series): "Dear Old Pal"; "When the Midnight Choo-Choo Comes to Alabama"; "Yaka-Hula-Hickla-Ooola"; "When I Lost You"; "Oh, Suzanna"; "My Wife's Gone to the Country"; "Margie"; "Annie Laurie"; "Oh, How I Hate to Get Up in the Morning"; and "East Side, West Side."

◎ SUCH IS LIFE

Henry "Hy" Mayer created—he also wrote, produced, directed and animated—this series of humorous perspectives on life in New York and in Europe. *A Hy Mayer Production released by Pathé Exchange, R.C. Pictures and Film Booking Offices.*

Pathé Exchange

1920: "Such Is Life Among the Dogs" (Oct. 2); "Such Is Life at the Zoo" (Oct. 16); "Such Is Life at Coney Island" (Nov. 6); "Such Is Sporting Life" (Nov. 13); "Such Is Life in Greenwich Village" (Dec. 4); and "Such Is Life in East Side New York."

1921: "Such Is Life in the Land of Fancy" (Jan. 30); "Such Is Life at a County Fair" (Feb. 19); "Such Is Life in Summer" (Mar. 12); "Such Is Life in Ramblerville" (Apr. 10); "Such Is Life at the Race Track" (July 3); "Such Is Life at the Zoo" (July 17); and "Such Is Life in New York" (Nov. 20).

1922: "Such Is Life" (Feb. 27).

R.C. Pictures/Film Booking Offices

1922: "Such Is Life in London's West End" (Apr. 15); "Such Is Life in Vollendam" (May 7); "Such Is Life in Monte Carlo" (May 31); "Such Is Life in Mon Petit Paris" (June 4); "Such Is Life Among the Children of France" (June 18); "Such Is Life in Munich" (July 22); "Such Is Life in Montemartre" (July 22); "Such Is Life on the Riviera" (Aug. 12); "Such Is Life Among the Paris Shoppers" (Aug. 12); "Such Is Life Near London" (Aug. 19); "Such Is Life in Amsterdam and Alkmaar" (Aug. 27); "Such Is Life Among the Idlers of Paris" (Oct.); "Such Is Life in Busy London" (Nov. 4); "Such Is Life in a Dutch County Fair" (Nov.); and "Such Is Life in Italy" (Dec.).

◎ TAD'S CAT

In 1919 two films may have been made for this Universal cartoon series, produced and animated by popular American newspaper cartoonist Tad Dorgan. The films starred a tall, lanky cat whose creation was spurred by the success of Pat Sullivan's own cat series, *Felix the Cat*. *A Universal Picture release.*

◎ TECHNICAL ROMANCES

Produced by J.R. Bray, this series was written, directed and animated by J.A. Norling, Ashley Miller and F. Lyle Goldman. *A Bray Production released by Hodkinson.*

1922: "The Mystery Box" (Nov. 25); and "The Sky Splitter" (Dec. 9).

1923: "Gambling with the Gulf Stream" (Feb. 4); "The Romance of Life" (Mar. 1); "The Immortal Voice" (June 10); and "Black Sunlight" (Dec. 1).

☺ TERRY FEATURE BURLESQUES

Paul Terry wrote, produced and directed this series of witty satires. *A Paul Terry Production released by A. Kay Company.*

1917: "20,000 Feats Under the Sea" (Apr. 23); "Golden Spoon Mary" (Apr. 30); "Some Barrier" (July); and "His Trial" (July).

☺ TERRY HUMAN INTEREST REELS

This series shaped story lines around human characteristics. *Produced and directed by Paul Terry. A Paul Terry Production released by A. Kay Company.*

1917: "Character as Revealed by the Nose" (June); "Character as Revealed by the Eye" (July); "Character as Revealed by the Mouth" (Aug.); and "Character as Revealed by the Ear" (Sept.).

☺ TOM AND JERRY

No information could be found for this series—its starring characters or production staff. *An Arrow Film Corporation Production.*

1923: "The Gasoline Trail" (Aug. 1); and "Tom's First Flivver" (Sept. 1).

☺ TONY SARG'S ALMANAC

Famed illustrator Tony Sarg, who toured vaudeville with a marionette routine, wrote and animated this series of animated marionette sequences (called *Shadowgraphs*). The series was cowritten and co-animated by Herbert M. Dawley, who also produced. *A Herbert M. Dawley Production released by Rialto Productions and Educational Pictures.*

Rialto Productions

1921: "The First Circus" (May 21); "The First Dentist" (June); "Why They Love Cave Men" (July 2); "When the Whale Was Jonahed" (Aug. 20); and "Fireman Save My Child" (Sept. 10).

1922: "The Original Golfer" (Jan. 7); "Why Adam Walked the Floor" (Feb. 5); "The Original Movie" (Apr. 9); "The First Earful" (May 29); and "Noah Put the Cat Out" (July 9).

Educational Pictures

1922: "The First Flivver" (July 29); "The First Degree" (July 29); "The First Barber" (Aug. 19); "Baron Bragg and the Devilish Dragon" (Sept. 9); "The Ogling Ogre" (Nov. 19) and "Baron Bragg and the Haunted Castle" (Dec. 17).

1923: "The Terrible Tree" (Jan. 6).

☺ TOYLAND

This series featured animated dolls and toys and was produced by the team of R.F Taylor and W.W. Wheatley. *Directed by Horace Taylor. A Taylor and Wheatley Production released by Powers.*

1916: "A Romance of Toyland" (Mar. 9); "A Toyland Mystery" (Mar. 15); "The Toyland Villain" (Apr. 12); and "A Toyland Robbery" (May 10).

☺ TRAVELAUGHS

Henry "Hy" Mayer, a prolific caricaturist and illustrator, was the mastermind behind this series of tastefully done satires on travelogues, combining drawings with live footage. Films appeared as part of screen magazines and were distributed to theaters nationwide. Otto Messmer, who later animated *Felix the Cat*, served as Mayer's assistant on the series. In 1920, the series shifted to Pathé. Episodes that appear in the filmography are the only titles available through research. *A Keen Cartoon Production released by Universal Pictures.*

1915: "To 'Frisco by the Cartoon Route" (Aug. 9).

1916: "Globe Trotting with Hy Mayer" (Apr. 14); "Such Is Life in China" (June 22); "Pen and Inklings in and Around Jerusalem" (Oct. 5); "High Life on a Farm" (Nov. 9); "A Pen Trip to Palestine" (Nov. 9); and "Such Is Life in Alaska" (Dec. 19).

1917: "Such Is Life in South Algeria" (Apr. 28); "China Awakened" (June 26); "Seeing Ceylon with Hy Mayer" (Aug. 6); and "Seeing New York with Hy Mayer" (Oct. 15).

1918: "New York by Heck" (May 1).

Pathé Review

1921: "Behind the Scenes of the Circus" (Jan. 15); "Water Stuff" (Mar. 5); "Spring Hats" (Mar. 26); "All the Merry Bow-Wows" (Apr. 30); "In the Silly Summertime" (May 29); "The Door That Has No Lock" (June 26); "A Ramble Through Provincetown" (July 31); "The Little City of Dreams" (Sept. 4); "Day Dreams" (Sept. 18); "Down to the Fair" (Oct. 2); "Summer Scenes" (Oct. 16); "All Aboard" (Oct. 30); and "Puppies" (Dec. 25).

1922: "How It Feels" (Sept. 24); "In the Dear Old Summertime" (Oct. 14); and "Sporting Scenes" (Nov. 25).

1923: "Faces" (Jan. 6).

☺ THE TRICK KIDS

J.R. Bray produced this series of films, consisting of animated dolls and toys, for the *Paramount Pictographs*. *A Bray Studios Production released by Paramount Pictures.*

1916: "The Birth of the Trick Kids" (Feb. 20); "The Strange Adventures of the Lamb's Tail" (Mar. 12); "Happifat's New Playmate" (Mar. 19); "The Magic Pail" (Apr. 19); "Happifat Does Some Spring Planting" (Apr. 23); "Happifat and Flossy Fisher's Unexpected Buggy Ride" (Apr. 30); "Happifat's Fishing Trip" (May 7); "Happifat's Interrupted Meal" (May 21); "Happifat Becomes an Artist and Draws a Bear" (May 28); and "Everybody's Uncle Sam" (June).

◎ UN-NATURAL HISTORY

In true Aesopian style, Walter Lantz introduced this series of outlandish history fables, his fourth series for J.R. Bray Studios. Beginning in 1925, the series alternated with *Dinky Doodles* and was distributed by FBO until September 1926, at which time Bray resumed distribution of the series himself.

Two former Disney directors, Dave Hand and Clyde Geronimi, later supervised and helped animate the series, which used child actors to play opposite animal characters in stories that told some deep moral. Actress Anita Louis, later a contract player at 20th Century-Fox, was one of the actors to appear in the series.

Like earlier productions, Lantz's staff was limited to seven people—including the inker, painter, background artist and cameraman—to produce each new installment. He therefore wrote, directed and animated almost every cartoon. Along with *Pete the Pup*, the series marked the end for the Bray Studios, which closed its doors in 1927. *A Bray Production released by Standard Cinema Corporation and Film Booking Offices.*

1925: "How the Elephant Got His Trunk" (Lantz/Oct. 4); "How the Bear Got His Short Tail" (Lantz/Oct. 18); "How the Camel Got His Hump" (Geronimi/Nov. 15); and "The Leopard's Spots" (Dec. 13).

1926: "The Goat's Whiskers" (Jan. 10); "How the Giraffe Got His Long Neck" (Feb. 7); "The Stork Brought It" (Mar. 7); "The King of the Beasts" (Apr. 4); "The Ostrich's Plumes" (Apr. 19); "The Pelican's Bill" (Lantz/May 30); "The Cat's Whiskers" (Lantz/June 20); "The Mule's Disposition" (Lantz/July 18); "The Pig's Curly Tail" (Lantz/Aug. 15); and "The Tail of the Monkey" (Lantz, Hand/Dec. 29).

1927: "The Cat's Nine Lives" (Lantz, Hand, Geronimi/Jan. 15); and "The Hyena's Laugh" (Lantz, Geronimi/Jan. 18).

◎ US FELLERS

Cartoonist Wallace A. Carlson wrote and directed these cartoon reminiscences seen through the eyes of a young lad who dreams about events and mishaps of his boyhood days. *A Bray Production released by Paramount Pictures.*

Paramount-Bray Pictographs

1919: "Dud Perkins Gets Mortified" (Apr. 12); "The Parson" (Apr. 26); "Wounded by the Beauty" (Apr. 26); "Dud the Circus Performer" (May 29); "Dud's Greatest Circus on Earth" (June 21); and "At the "Ol' Swimmin' Hole" (Aug. 7).

Goldwyn-Bray Pictographs

1919: "Dud's Home Run" (Sept. 23); "Dud Leaves Home" (Oct. 9); "Dud's Geography Lesson" (Nov. 17); and "A Chip Off the Old Block" (Dec. 31).

1920: "Dud's Haircut" (Feb. 16); and "Dud the Lion Tamer" (Sept. 9).

◎ VERNON HOWE BAILEY'S SKETCHBOOK

This sketchbook travel series was written, produced and directed by Vernon Howe Bailey. *An Essanay Film Production.*

1915: "Vernon Howe Bailey's Sketchbook" (Nov. 13).

1916: ". . . Of Chicago" (Jan. 29); ". . . Of London" (Mar. 1); ". . . Of Philadelphia" (Mar. 14); ". . . Of Paris" (Mar. 27); ". . . Of Boston" (Apr. 14); ". . . Of Rome" (Apr. 26); ". . . Of San Francisco" (May 20); ". . . Of Berlin" (June 9); ". . . Of St. Louis" (June 19); ". . . Of New Orleans" (July 10); ". . . Of Petrograd" (July 27); and ". . . Of Washington."

◎ VINCENT WHITMAN CARTOONS

Vincent Whitman served as writer, director and animator of this animated series. *Produced by Sigmund Lubin. A Lubin Manufacturing Company Production.*

1914: "A Trip to the Moon" (Mar. 14); "The Bottom of the Sea" (Mar. 21); "A Strenuous Ride" (Apr. 11); "Another Tale" (Apr. 25); "A Hunting Absurdity" (Oct. 3); "An Interrupted Nap" (Oct. 23); and "The Troublesome Cat" (Dec. 15).

1915: "Curses Jack Dalton" (Apr. 24); "A Hot Time in Punkville" (May 3); "His Pipe Dreams" (May 21); "Studies in Clay" (July 6); "A Barnyard Mixup" (July 12); "An African Hunt" (July 15); "A One Reel Feature" (July 26); "Relentless Dalton" (Aug. 2); and "The Victorious Jockey" (Aug. 16).

◎ THE WHOZIT WEEKLY

This series of burlesque cartoon items was produced for the *Universal Screen Magazine*, written, directed and animated by Leslie Elton. *Produced by Carl Laemmle. A Universal Pictures Production.*

Winsor McCay's Gertie the Dinosaur *(1914). Only 10,000 pencil sketches were used to produce the action.* (COURTESY: THE MUSEUM OF MODERN ART/FILM STILLS ARCHIVE)

1919: "No. 115" (Mar. 23); "No. 123" (May 18); "No. 124" (May 25); "No. 126" (June 8); "No. 129" (June 29); "No. 131" (July 13); "No. 134" (Aug. 3); "No. 137" (Aug. 24); "No. 143" (Oct. 4); and "No. 144" (Oct. 11).

1920: "No. 164" (Feb. 28).

◎ WINSOR McCAY

A superb storyteller and cartoonist, Winsor McCay is often credited with producing the first animated cartoon in history. Actually, he is one of several pioneers who helped shape the industry during its formative years.

McCay honed his talent as an artist and illustrator for the *Cincinnati Commercial Tribune* in 1897 before finding fame with a weekly comic strip, *Little Nemo in Slumberland,* appearing in the *New York Herald* and other newspapers in 1905. He became interested in making animated films when his son picked up several "flip books" and brought them home to him. The tiny books produced an illusion of movement when flipping the pages. McCay became so intrigued with this technique that he decided to utilize the same concept using animated characters.

It has been said that McCay's first cartoon resulted from a friendly bet with cartoonist-cronies George McManus, Tad Dorgan and Tom Powers. As part of the wager, he claimed he would produce enough line drawings to sustain a four- or five-minute cartoon, making the film a special feature of his already popular vaudeville act. (He traveled the circuit giving what he called "chalk talks.")

In 1911 McCay released his first animated cartoon based on his popular syndicated strip. The film was masterful in more ways than style and craftsmanship. It did so much with so little, using only 4,000 penciled drawings to animate five minutes of film. In recalling his work, the famed animator once stated, "Not until I drew Gertie the Dinosaur did the audience understand that I was making drawings move."

McCay finally achieved real success in 1914 with "Gertie the Dinosaur" (also called "Gertie the Trained Dinosaur"), generally regarded as the first "cartoon star." The cartoon became quite a novelty for McCay, who built on this success and continued making animated films for seven more years. *A Winsor McCay Production released by Vitagraph Film Corp., Box Office Attractions and Jewel Productions/Universal.*

1911: "Little Nemo" (first in a series).

1912: "The Story of a Mosquito" (Jan.).

1914: "Gertie the Dinosaur" (Sept. 15).

1916: "Bug Vaudeville"; "The Pet"; and "Winsor McCay and His Jersey Skeeters."

1917: "Gertie on Tour" (second in a series); and "The Adventures of Rarebit Eater" (first in a series).

1918: "The Sinking of the Lusitania" (May 18).

1920: "The Flying House."

THEATRICAL SOUND CARTOON SERIES

⊚ AESOP'S FABLES

After Walt Disney released the first synchronized sound cartoon in 1928, Paul Terry made the conversion to sound with his *Aesop's Fables* series, first popular during the silent era.

Terry directed the series for his new boss, Amadee J. Van Beuren of Van Beuren Productions. The series was announced November 1928. The first sound release was "Dinner Time," featuring synchronized soundtracks—music but no voices—added to the silent product.

Terry directed most of the films until 1929, when he left Van Beuren to form his own studio. Other animators directed the series from then on: John Foster, Harry Bailey, J.J. McManus, George Stallings and George Rufle.

In 1945, under the *Terrytoons* banner, Terry produced his first new *Aesop's Fables* in 12 years: "Aesop Fables: The Mosquito" starring *Terrytoons* star Gandy Goose. The cartoon was the first in a new series of Aesop's produced by Terry. *Series directors were Terrytoons veterans Connie Rasinski and Eddie Donnelly. Black-and-white. Technicolor. CinemaScope. A Pathé Film released by RKO Van Beuren and RKO Pathe Film Exchange. A Terrytoons Production released by 20th Century-Fox.*

RKO Van Beuren releases
(Copyright dates are marked by ©.)

1928: "Dinner Time" (Terry/©Dec. 17).

1929: "The Faithful Pup" (Terry/May 4); "Concentrate" (Terry/May 4); "The Jail Breakers" (Terry/May 6); "Woodchoppers" (Terry/May 9); "Presto Chango" (Terry/May 20); "Skating Hounds" (Terry/May 27); "Stage Struck" (Terry/June 25); "House Cleaning Time" (Foster/July 23); "A Stone Age Romance" (Aug. 1); "The Big Scare" (Terry/Aug. 15); "Jungle Fool" (Foster, Davis/Sept. 15); "Fly's Bride" (Foster/Sept. 21); "Summer Time" (Foster/Oct. 11); "Mill Pond" (Foster/Oct. 18); "Barnyard Melody" (Foster/Nov. 1); "Tuning In" (Nov. 7); "Night Club" (Foster, Davis/Dec. 1); and "Close Call" (Bailey/Dec. 1).

1930: "The Iron Man" (Foster/Jan. 4); "Ship Ahoy" (Foster/Jan. 7); "Singing Saps" (Foster, Davis/Feb. 7); "Sky Skippers" (Foster, Bailey/Feb. 14); "Good Old Schooldays" (Foster, Davis/Mar. 7); "Foolish Follies" (Foster, Bailey/Mar. 7); "Dixie Days" (Foster, Davis/Apr. 8); "Western Whoopee" (Foster, Bailey/Apr. 10); "The Haunted Ship" (Foster, Davis/Apr. 27); "Noah Knew His Ark" (Foster, Davis/May 25); "Oom Pah Pah" (Foster, Bailey/May 30); "A Romeo Robin" (Foster, Davis/June 22); "Jungle Jazz" (Foster, Bailey/July 6); "Snow Time" (Foster, Davis/July 20); "Hot Tamale" (Foster/Aug. 3); "Laundry Blues" (Foster, Davis/Aug. 17); "Frozen Frolics" (Foster, Bailey/Aug. 31); "Farm Foolery" (Foster/Sept. 14); "Circus Capers" (Foster, Bailey/Sept. 28); "Midnight" (Foster, Davis/Oct. 12); "The Big Cheeze" (Foster/Oct. 26); "Gypped in Egypt" (Foster, Davis/Nov. 9); "The Office Boy" (Foster, Bailey/Nov. 23); "Stone Age Stunts" (Foster/Dec. 7); and "King of the Bugs" (Foster, Bailey/Dec. 21).

RKO Pathé Film Exchange releases

1931: "Toy Town Tales" (Foster, Davis/Jan. 4/a.k.a. "Toyland Adventure"); "Red Riding Hood" (Foster, Bailey/ Jan. 18); "The Animal Fair" (Foster, Davis/Feb. 1);

"Cowboy Blues" (Foster, Bailey/Feb. 15); "Radio Racket" (Foster/Mar. 1); "College Capers" (Foster, Bailey/Mar. 15); "Old Hokum Bucket" (Mar. 29); "Cinderella Blues" (Foster, Bailey/Apr. 12); "Mad Melody" (Foster, Davis/Apr. 26); "The Fly Guy" (Foster, Bailey/May 10); "Play Ball" (Foster, Davis/May 24); "Fisherman's Luck" (Foster, Bailey/June 13); "Pale Face Pup" (Foster, Davis/June 22); "Making 'em Move" (Foster, Bailey/July 5/a.k.a. "In A Cartoon Studio"); "Fun on the Ice" (Foster, Davis/July 19); "Big Game" (Aug. 3); "Love in a Pond" (Foster, Davis/Aug. 17); "Fly Hi" (Foster, Bailey/Aug. 31); "The Family Shoe" (Foster, Davis/Sept. 14); "Fairyland Follies" (Foster, Bailey/Sept. 28). "Horse Cops" (Foster, McManus/Oct. 12); "Cowboy Cabaret" (Foster, Davis/Oct. 26); "In Dutch" (Foster, Bailey/Nov. 9); and "The Last Dance" (Nov. 23).

1932: "Toy Time" (Foster, Bailey/Jan. 27); "A Romeo Monk" (Foster, Davis/Feb. 20); "Fly Frolic" (Foster, Bailey/Mar. 5); "The Cat's Canary" (Foster, Davis/Mar. 26); "Magic Art" (Foster, Bailey/Apr. 25); "Happy Polo" (May 14); "Spring Antics" (Foster, Davis/May 21); "Farmerette" (June 11); "Circus Romance" (Foster, Bailey/June 25); "Stone Age Error" (Foster, Davis/July 9); "Chinese Jinks" (Foster, Davis/July 23); "The Ball Game" (Foster, Rufle/July 30); "Wild Goose Chase" (Foster, Davis/Aug. 12); "Nursery Scandal" (Foster, Bailey/Aug. 26); "Bring 'em Back Half-Shot" (Foster, Davis/Sept. 9); "Down in Dixie" (Foster, Bailey/Sept. 23); "Catfish Romance" (Foster, Davis/Oct. 7); "Feathered Follies" (Oct. 21); "Venice Vamp" (Foster, Davis/Nov. 4); "Hokum Hotel" (Foster, Bailey/Nov. 18); "Pickaninny Blues" (Foster, Davis/© Dec. 12); "A Yarn of Wool" (Foster, Bailey/© Dec. 16); and "Bugs and Books" (Foster, Davis/© Dec. 30).

1933: "Silvery Moon" (Foster, Davis/© Jan. 13); "A.M. to P.M." (© Jan. 20); "Tumble Down Town" (Foster, Bailey/© Jan. 27); "Love's Labor Won" (Foster, Davis/© Mar. 10); "A Dizzy Day" (Bailey/© May 5); "Barking Dogs" (Davis/© May 18); "The Bully's End" (Bailey/© June 16); "Indian Whoopee" (Davis/© July 7); "Fresh Ham" (© July 12); and "Rough on Rats" (Bailey/© July 14).

20th Century-Fox Releases

1945: "Aesop Fables: The Mosquito" (with Gandy Goose/Davis/June 29/Terrytoons cartoons).

1950: "Aesop's Fables: Foiling The Fox" (Raskinski/Apr./ Terrytoons cartoon).

1951: "Aesop's Fables: Golden Egg Goosie" (Donnelly/ Aug./Terrytoons cartoon).

1952: "Happy Valley" (Donnelly/Sept./Aesop's Fables cartoon).

1953: "Sparky the Firefly" (Rasinski/Sept./Aesop's Fables cartoon).

1955: "The First Flying Fish" (Rasinski/Feb./Aesop's Fables cartoon).

1960: "Aesop's Fables: The Tiger King" (Rasinski/Mar./ CinemaScope).

AMOS 'N' ANDY

Van Beuren Studios, creators of the Little King and Cubby cartoon series, attempt to bolster its roster of stars by signing actors Freeman Gosden and Charles Correll to reprise the roles of Amos Jones and Andy Brown, characters from their popular radio program, in a series of cartoon shorts. Unfortunately, the series never caught on with moviegoers. *Directed by George Stallings. Black-and-white. An RKO Van Beuren Corporation release.*

Voices
Amos: Freeman Gosden; **Andy:** Charles Correll

1934: "The Rasslin' Match" (Jan. 5); and "The Lion Tamer" (Feb. 2).

ANDY PANDA

Created by Walter Lantz, the cuddly cartoon panda made his film debut in 1939 and proved so successful that Lantz contracted for four or five one-reelers a year. Lantz originated the idea for the character following a national news story he read about a panda being donated to the Chicago Zoo. The series opener was called "Life Begins with Andy Panda," a play on words on the title of a popular Andy Hardy feature of the same name. Three cartoons later Andy Panda marked another historical event in his young career—the first appearance of Lantz's wood-beating bird, Woody Woodpecker, in "Knock Knock" (1940). During the character's 11-year run on the screen, two cartoons in which he appeared were nominated for Academy Awards under the "Best Short Subject" category: 1944's "Fish Fry," directed by James Culhane, and "The Poet and Peasant," a 1946 "Musical Miniature" directed by Dick Lundy.

Sarah Berner, who was better known as the switchboard operator on the Jack Benny radio program, was the second actor to voice the character until Bernice Hansen assumed that role for the balance of the series. Directors were Walter Lantz, Dick Lundy, Alex Lovy and James "Shamus" Culhane. *Technicolor. A Walter Lantz Production released through Universal Pictures.*

Voices
Andy Panda: Bernice Hansen, Sarah Berner, Walter Tetley

1939: "Life Begins with Andy Panda" (Lovy/Sept. 9).

1940: "Andy Panda Goes Fishing" (Gillett/Jan. 22); "100 Pigmies and Andy Panda" (Lovy/Apr. 22); "Crazy House"

(Lantz/Sept. 2); and "Knock Knock" (Woody Woodpecker's debut/Lantz/Nov. 25).

1941: "Mouse Trappers" (Lantz/Jan. 27); "Dizzy Kitty" (Lantz/May 26); and "Andy Panda's Pop" (Lantz/July 28).

1942: "Under the Spreading Blacksmith Shop" (Lovy/Jan. 12); "Goodbye Mr. Moth" (Lantz/May 11); "Nutty Pine Cabin" (Lovy/June 1); and "Andy Panda's Victory (Lovy/Sept. 7).

1943: "Meatless Tuesday" (Culhane/Oct. 25).

1944: "Fish Fry" (Culhane/June 19/A.A. nominee); and "The Painter and the Pointer" (Culhane/Dec. 18).

1945: "Crow Crazy" (Lundy/July 9).

1946: "The Poet and Peasant" (Lundy/Mar. 18/Musical Miniature/A.A. nominee); "Mousie Come Home" (Culhane/Apr. 15); "Apple Andy" (Lundy/May 20); and "The Wacky Weed" (Lundy/Dec. 16).

1947: "Musical Moments from Chopin" (with Woody Woodpecker/Lundy/Feb. 24/Musical Miniature/A.A. nominee); and "The Band Master" (Lundy/Dec.).

1948: "Banquet Busters" (with Woody Woodpecker/Lundy/Mar. 2); "Playful Pelican" (Lundy/Oct. 8); and "Dog Tax Dodgers" (Lundy/Nov. 19).

1949: "Scrappy's Birthday" (Lundy/Feb. 11).

◎ ANIMANIACS

Known for their trademark style of zany, physical comedy, nonstop wordplay and rousing music, television's Animaniacs—Yakko, Wakko and Dot, the Warner brothers and sister—jumped to the big screen in 1994 with their first theatrical cartoon, "I'm Mad," which opened nationwide with Don Bluth's full-length animated feature, *Thumbelina*, based on the classic Hans Christian Andersen fairy tale. The success of their weekday television series—which premiered on the Fox Network in 1993—sparked a desire on the part of executive producer Steven Spielberg, senior producer Tom Ruegger and executive in charge of production Jean MacCurdy to bring the characters to a wider audience by featuring them in a series of theatrical cartoons shorts. *Directed by Rich Arons, Audu Paden and Dave Marshall. An Amblin Entertainment/Warner Brothers Animation Production released by Warner Bros. Technicolor.*

Voices
Yakko Warner: Rob Paulsen; **Wakko Warner:** Jess Harnell; **Dot Warner:** Tress MacNeille

1994: "I'm Mad" (March 30).

◎ ANIMATED ANTICS

This series evolved from Max Fleischer's *Gulliver's Travels* (1939). testing various supporting characters from the clas-

sic animated feature in a new animated series. Films spotlighted character favorites, such as Twinkletoes and Sneak, Snoop and Snith, in animated adventures. *Director and voice credits unknown. Black-and-white. A Fleischer Studios Production released through Paramount Pictures.*

1940: "The Dandy Lion" (Sept. 20); "Sneak, Snoop and Snitch" (Oct. 25); "Mommy Loves Puppy" (Nov. 29); and "Bring Himself Back Alive" (Dec. 20).

1941: (Copyright dates are marked by a ©.) "Zero, the Hound" (© Feb. 14); "Twinkletoes Gets the Bird" (Mar. 14); "Sneak, Snoop and Snitch in Triple Trouble" (May 9); "Twinkletoes—Where He Goes Nobody Knows" (June 27); "Copy Cat" (July 18); "The Wizard of Ants" (Aug. 8); and "Twinkletoes in Hat Stuff" (Aug. 29).

◎ THE ANT AND THE AARDVARK

The misadventures of a purple, vacuumed-nosed aardvark in pursuit of his meal: a tiny red ant. In his ill-fated attempts to sniff out the ant, the aardvark instead picks up gunpowder, tacks, dynamite and virtually every object imaginable during its prowl. Episodes were later featured as part of the television series, *The New Pink Panther Show. Directors were Gerry Chiniquy, Art Davis, George Gordon and Hawley Pratt. Technicolor. A Mirisch-DePatie-Freleng Production released through United Artists.*

Voices
The Ant/The Aardvark: John Byner.

Additional Voices
Athena Lorde and Marvin Miller.

1969: "The Ant and the Aardvark" (Chiniquy/Mar. 5); "Hasty But Tasty" (Chiniquy/Mar. 6); "The Ant from Uncle" (Gordon/Apr. 2); "I've Got Ants in My Plans" (Chiniquy/May 14); "Technology Phooey" (Chiniquy/June 25); "Never Bug an Ant" (Chiniquy/Sept.); "Dune Bug" (Davis/Oct. 29); and "Isle of Caprice" (Chiniquy/Dec. 18).

1970: "Scratch a Tiger" (Pratt/Jan. 28); "Odd Ant Out" (Chiniquy/Apr. 29); "Ants in the Pantry" (Pratt/June 10); "Science Friction" (Chiniquy/June 28); "Mumbo Jumbo" (Davis/Sept. 27); "The Froze Nose Knows" (Chiniquy/Nov. 18); and "Don't Hustle an Ant with Muscle" (Davis/Dec. 27).

1971: "Rough Brunch" (Davis/Jan. 3); and "From Bed to Worse" (Davis/May 16).

◎ ASTRONUT

This friendly, outer-space gremlin first appeared in a *Deputy Dawg* episode before starring in a theatrical series of his own. Each adventure followed Astronut's frolics across Earth with his friend and companion, Oscar Mild. *Directors were Connie Rasinski, Dave Tendlar, Arthur Bartsch and Cosmo Anzilotti. Technicolor. A Terrytoons Production released through 20th Century-Fox.*

Voices
Astronut: Dayton Allen, Lionel Wilson, Bob McFadden; **Oscar:** Bob McFadden

1964: "Brother from Outer Space" (Rasinski/Mar.); "Kisser Plant" (Rasinski/June); "Outer Galaxy Gazette" (Rasinski/Sept.); and "Molecular Mixup" (Tendlar/Dec.).

1965: "The Sky's the Limit" (Tendlar/Feb.); "Weather Magic" (Anzilotti/May); "Robots in Toyland" (Rasinski/Aug.); and "Twinkle, Twinkle Little Telestar" (Bartsch/Nov.).

1966: "Gems from Gemini" (Tendlar/Jan.); and "Haunted Housecleaning" (Rasinski/May).

1969: "Space Pet" (Mar.); "Scientific Sideshow" (June); and "Balloon Snatcher" (Sept.).

1970: "Going Ape" (Jan.); and "Martian Moochers" (May).

1971: "Oscar's Birthday Present" (Jan.); "Oscar's Thinking Cap" (May); and "No Space Like Home" (Oct.).

◉ BABBIT AND CATSTELLO
Bob Clampett created this pair of loquacious cats based on the antics of the movie comedy greats Abbott and Costello. Originally designed as one-shot characters. the funny felines first appeared in 1942's "A Tale of Two Kitties," which marked the debut of Tweety Bird (who was unofficially called Orson in the cartoon). They later returned in two more cartoons before the studio retired them. *Directed by Bob Clampett, Frank Tashlin and Robert McKimson. Technicolor. A Warner Bros. release.*

Voices
Babbit: Ted Pierce; **Catstello:** Mel Blanc

Merrie Melodies

1942: "A Tale of Two Kitties" (with Tweety/Clampett/Nov. 21).

1946: "The Mouse-Merized Cat" (McKimson/Oct. 19).

Looney Tunes

1945: "A Tale of Two Mice" (Tashlin/June 30).

◉ BABY FACE MOUSE
In the late 1930s, Walter Lantz introduced a flurry of new characters to the screen in one-shot cartoons and potential

Comedians Abbott and Costello inspired a series of cartoons produced by Warner Bros. As Babbit and Catstello, the pair appeared in several cartoon shorts. From "A Tale of Two Mice" (1945). © Warner Bros., Inc.

series. Baby Face Mouse was among the lot, featured in a short-lived series of his own, who bore some resemblance to Warner Bros.' Sniffles the Mouse and was introduced to moviegoers that same year (1938). *Directed by Alex Lovy and Les Kline. Black-and-white. A Walter Lantz Production released through Universal Pictures.*

1938: "Cheese Nappers" (Lovy/July 14); "The Big Cat and the Little Mousie" (Aug. 15); "The Cat and the Bell" (Oct. 3); "The Sailor Mouse" (Lovy/Nov. 7); and "Disobedient Mouse" (Kline/Nov. 28).

◉ BABY HUEY
Baby Huey was the inspiration of Paramount/Famous Studios, which also brought the likes of Casper the Friendly Ghost, Little Audrey and Herman and Katnip to the screen. The studio was formed in 1942, following Paramount's removal of Max and Dave Fleischer from control of its animation studio; thereafter it was renamed and staffed with new personnel.

Like those of his cohorts, Baby Huey's cartoons can be best described as "formula" with little room for imagination. The premise: a husky, strong baby duck whose complete naivete makes him a prime target for one hungry fox that is repeatedly thwarted by Huey's immense strength, rendering him virtually indestructible in a clumsy sort of way. Comedian Syd Raymond, who created the voice of Katnip, also provided the voice characterization for Huey.

In the fall of 1995, the five-foot-tall, 250-pound baby duck with a heart of gold returned, this time to the small screen in a new syndicated animated television series, *The*

Baby Huey Show. Directed by Isadore Sparber, Seymour Kneitel and Dave Tendlar. Technicolor. A Famous Studios Production released through Paramount Pictures.

Voices
Baby Huey: Syd Raymond

1951: (Each listed title was from the *Noveltoons* series): "One Quack Mind" (Sparber/Jan. 12); "Party Smarty" (Kneitel/Aug. 3); and "Scout Fellow" (Kneitel/Dec. 21).

1952: "Clown on the Farm" (Kneitel/Aug. 22).

1953: "Starting from Hatch" (Kneitel/Mar. 6); and "Huey's Ducky Daddy" (Sparber/Nov. 20).

1955: "Git Along Li'l Duckie" (Tendlar/Mar. 25).

1956: "Swab The Duck" (Tendlar/May 11).

1957: "Pest Pupil" (Tendlar/Jan. 25); and "Jumping with Toy" (Tendlar/Oct. 4).

1959: "Huey's Father's Day" (Kneitel/May 8).

⊚ BARNEY BEAR

MGM developed several promising animated film stars, one of which was the lumbering but lovable Barney Bear, whose slow-burn reactions, sympathetic nature and vocal patterns were reminiscent of actor Wallace Beery, who, incidentally, was an MGM star in the 1930s.

The character was redesigned in the late 1940s by animators Preston Blair and Michael Lah, the latter an understudy of director Tex Avery. Lah also directed the series following Rudolf Ising's departure in 1943. The fourth cartoon in the series, 1941's "Rookie Bear," was nominated for an Academy Award for "Best Short Subject" but lost that year to Walt Disney's Pluto cartoon, "Lend a Paw." *Directed by Preston Blair, George Gordon, Rudolf Ising, Dick Lundy and Michael Lah. Technicolor. A Metro-Goldwyn-Mayer release.*

Voices
Barney Bear: Billy Bletcher, Rudolf Ising, Paul Frees

1939: "The Bear That Couldn't Sleep" (Ising/June 10).

1940: "The Fishing Bear" (Ising/Jan. 20).

1941: "The Prospecting Bear" (Ising/Mar. 8); "Rookie Bear" (Ising/May 17/A.A. nominee); and "The Flying Bear" (Ising/Nov. 1).

1942: "The Bear and the Beavers" (Ising/Mar. 28); "Wild Honey" (Ising/Nov. 7/working title: "How to Get Along Without a Ration Book"); and "Barney Bear's Victory Garden" (Ising/Dec. 26).

1943: "Bah Wilderness" (Ising/Feb. 13); and "The Uninvited Pest" (Ising/July/re: Apr. 29. 1950).

Barney Bear looks disgusted over his "big" catch in scene from MGM's "The Fishing Bear" (1949). © Turner Entertainment

1944: "Bear Raid Warden" (Gordon/Sept. 9); and "Barney Bear's Polar Pest" (Gordon/Dec. 30/working title: "Bedtime for Barney").

1945: "Unwelcome Guest" (Gordon/Feb. 17/working title: "Skunk Story").

1948: "The Bear and the Bean" (Lah, Blair/Jan. 31); and "The Bear and the Hare" (Lah, Blair/June 26/working title: "Snowshoe Baby").

1949: "Goggle Fishing Bear" (Blair, Lah/Jan. 15/working title: "Goggle Fishing").

1952: "Little Wise Quacker" (Lundy/Nov. 8); and "Busybody Bear" (Lundy/Dec. 20).

1953: "Barney's Hungry Cousin" (Lundy/Jan. 31); "Cobs and Robbers" (Lundy/Mar. 14); "Heir Bear" (Lundy/May 30); "Wee Willie Wildcat" (Lundy/June 20); and "Half-Pint Palomino" (Lundy/Sept. 26).

1954: "Impossible Possum" (Lundy/Mar. 28); "Sleepy-Time Squirrel" (Lundy/June 19); and "Bird-Brain Bird Dog" (Lundy/July 30).

⊚ BARNEY GOOGLE

Producer Charles Mintz, who wanted another established star in Columbia Pictures' cartoon stable, brought this popular comic-strip character to the screen by special arrangement with its creator, Billy DeBeck. The character appeared in only four films before the series was abandoned. *Director and voice credits unknown. Technicolor. A Columbia Pictures release.*

1935: "Tetched in the Head" (Oct. 24); and "Patch Mah Britches" (Dec. 19).

1936: "Spark Plug" (Apr. 12); and "Major Google" (May 24).

☺ BEAKY BUZZARD

Bob Clampett dreamed up this misfit buzzard who was as stupid as he looked. Beaky, a shy, Mortimer Snerd type (who was also known as the Snerd Bird), first appeared in 1942's "Bugs Bunny Gets the Boid," which Clampett directed. He reappeared three years later in 1945's "The Bashful Buzzard." The character was voiced in these earlier adventures by an actor named Kent Rogers. After Clampett left Warner Bros. in 1946, Beaky was resurrected four years later in "The Lion's Busy." By then Mel Blanc replaced Rogers as the voice as the voice of Beaky. *Directed by Bob Clampett, Friz Freleng and Robert McKimson. Technicolor. A Warner Bros. release.*

Voice
Beaky Buzzard: Kent Rogers, Mel Blanc

Looney Tunes

1945: "The Bashful Buzzard" (Clampett/Sept. 5).

1950: "The Lion's Busy" (Freleng/Feb. 18); and "Strife with Father" (McKimson/Apr. 1).

Merrie Melodies

1942: "Bugs Bunny Gets the Boid" (Clampett/July 11).

☺ BEANS

One of Warner Bros. earliest cartoon stars, this mischievous black cat was used primarily as a supporting character in *Looney Tunes* cartoons produced in the mid-1930s. Created by Bob Clampett, Beans's first appearance was in the 1935 *Merrie Melodies* cartoon, "I Haven't Got a Hat," which also marked the debut of Porky Pig. *Directed by Jack King, Tex Avery and Friz Freleng. Black-and-white. A Warner Bros. release.*

Looney Tunes

1935: "A Cartoonist's Nightmare" (King/Sept. 21); and "Hollywood Capers" (King/Oct. 19).

1936: "Gold Diggers of '49" (with Porky/Avery/Jan. 6); "The Phantom Ship" (with Ham and Ex/King/Feb. 1); "Boom Boom" (with Porky/King/Feb. 29); "Alpine Antics" (King/Mar. 9); "The Fire Alarm" (with Ham and Ex/King/Mar. 9); and "Westward Whoa" (with Porky/King/Apr. 25).

Merrie Melodies

1935: "I Haven't Got a Hat" (with Porky/Freleng/Mar. 9).

☺ THE BEARY FAMILY

Modern cave-life situations run amuck when father Charlie, children Junior and Suzy and wife Bessie battle everyday problems of a bear's life. The series was inspired by TV's *Life of Riley* starring William Bendix, and lasted nine years. *Former Disney director Jack Hannah and veteran Lantz animator Paul J. Smith directed the series. Technicolor. A Walter Lantz Production released through Universal Pictures.*

Voices
Charlie Beary: Paul Frees; **Bessie Beary:** Grace Stafford; **Junior:** Paul Frees; **Suzy:** Grace Stafford

1962: "Fowled-Up Birthday" (Hannah/Mar. 27); and "Mother's Little Helper" (Hannah/June 12).

1963: "Charlie's Mother-in-Law" (Smith/Apr. 16); "Goose in the Rough" (Smith/July 30); and "The Goose Is Wild" (Smith/Nov. 12).

1964: "Rah, Rah, Ruckus" (Smith/May 5); and "Rooftop Razzle Dazzle" (Smith/Sept. 29).

1965: "Guest Who?" (Smith/Feb. 1); and "Davey Cricket" (Smith/May).

1966: "Foot Brawl" (Smith/Jan. 1).

1967: "Window Pains" (Smith/Jan. 1); and "Mouse on the House" (Smith/Apr. 1).

1968: "Jerkey Turkey" (Smith); "Paste Makes Waste" (Smith); and "Bugged by a Rug" (Smith).

1969: "Gopher Broke" (Smith); "Charlie's Campout" (Smith); and "Cool It, Charlie" (Smith).

1970: "Charlie in Hot Water" (Smith); "Charlie's Golf Classic" (Smith); and "The Unhandy Man" (Smith).

1971: "Charlie the Rainmaker" (Smith); "The Bungling Builder" (Smith); and "Moochin' Pooch" (Smith).

1972: "Let Charlie Do It" (Smith); "A Fish Story" (Smith); "Rain Rain, Go Away" (Smith) and "Unlucky Potluck" (Smith).

☺ BETTY BOOP

In "Dizzy Dishes," the sixth cartoon of Max Fleischer's *Talkartoon* series, this bubbling beauty of the cartoon world was first introduced. Initially she was nothing like the femme fatale who later seduced a nation of filmgoers with her cute button nose, wide-sparkling eyes, flapper-style dress and saucy "Boop-Boop-a-Doop" tag line.

Grim Natwick, who later animated for Ub Iwerks and Walt Disney, fashioned Betty after singer/actress Helen Kane, who happened to be a Paramount star. (The Betty Boop cartoons were released by the same studio.) Natwick based Betty's looks on Kane, after seeing the singer's face on a song sheet cover. He took Kane's own physical features and blended them with a French poodle. Thus, in her screen debut, Betty looks more like a hybrid of a dog, sporting long floppy ears and other characteristics that were more doglike in manner.

By 1932 Betty's character was completely modified and she returned with her new look in a number of cartoons under the *Talkartoon* banner. She was actually without a name until her appearance in "Stopping the Show," billed as the first official *Betty Boop* cartoon, that same year.

Dave Fleischer, Max Fleischer's brother, was responsible for standardizing Betty's appearance, making her feminine. She exhibited the true Betty Boop personality for the first time in "Minnie the Moocher," featuring Cab Calloway and his orchestra. (Calloway was Rotoscoped as a ghost walrus who dances to the sounds of the orchestra.)

The films' sexual themes ultimately became the series' downfall. By the mid-1930s, with stricter censorship laws enforced against cartoons, Betty underwent substantial changes again. Her garter, short skirt and decolletage were soon gone, undermining her appeal. Cast members Bimbo and Ko-Ko the Clown, who had come out of retirement, were given pink slips as well.

National Television Associates (NTA) bought the package of *Betty Boop* one-reelers in the late 1950s to distribute the series to television. *Directed by Dave Fleischer. Black-and-white. A Fleischer Studios Production released through Paramount Pictures.*

Voices

Betty Boop: Mae Questel, Ann Rothschild, Margie Heinz, Kate Wright, Bonnie Poe

1930: "Dizzy Dishes" (Aug. 9/*Talkartoon*).

1931: "Silly Scandals" (May 23/*Talkartoon*); "Bimbo's Initiation" (July 24/*Talkartoon*); "Bimbo's Express" (Aug. 22/*Talkartoon*); "Minding the Baby" (Sept. 26/*Talkartoon*); "Mask-a-Raid" (Nov. 7/*Talkartoon*); "Jack and the Beanstalk" (Nov. 21/*Talkartoon*); and "Dizzy Red Riding Hood" (Dec. 12).

1932: "Any Rags" (Jan. 2/*Talkartoon*); "Boop-Oop-a-Doop" (Jan. 16/*Talkartoon*); "Minnie the Moocher" (with Cab Calloway/Mar. 1); "Swim Or Sink" (Mar. 11/*Talkartoon*); "Crazy Town" (Mar. 25/*Talkartoon*); "The Dancing Fool" (Apr. 18/*Talkartoon*); "A Hunting We Will Go" (Apr. 28); "Admission Free" (June 10/*Talkartoon*); "The Betty Boop Limited" (July 1/*Talkartoon*); "Rudy Vallee Melodies" (Aug. 5/*Screen Song*); "Stopping The Show" (Aug. 12); "Betty Boop Bizzy Bee" (Aug. 19); "Betty Boop, M.D." (Sept. 2); "Betty Boop's Bamboo Isle" (with Royal Samoans with Miri/Sept. 23); "Betty Boop's Ups and Downs" (Oct. 14); "Betty Boop for President" (Nov. 4); "I'll

Beloved "boop-boop-a-doop" girl Betty Boop and sidekick Bimbo in a promotional still for the popular Max Fleischer cartoon series.

Be Glad When You're Dead You Rascal You" (with Louis Armstrong/Nov. 25); and "Betty Boop's Museum" (Dec. 16).

1933: "Betty Boop's Ker-Choo" (Jan. 6); "Betty Boop's Crazy Inventions" (Jan. 27); "Is My Palm Read" (Feb. 17); "Betty Boop's Penthouse" (Mar. 10); "Snow White" (Mar. 31); "Betty Boop's Birthday Party" (Apr. 21); "Betty Boop's May Party" (May 12); "Betty Boop's Big Boss" (June 2); "Mother Goose Land" (June 23); "Popeye the Sailor" (Popeye's debut/July 14); "The Old Man of the Mountain" (with Cab Calloway/Aug. 4); "I Heard" (with Don Redman/Sept. 1); "Morning, Noon and Night" (with Rubinoff/Oct. 6); "Betty Boop's Halloween Party" (Nov. 3); and "Parade of the Wooden Soldiers" (with Rubinoff/Dec. 1).

1934: "She Wrong Him Right" (Jan. 5); "Red Hot Mama" (Feb. 2); "Ha! Ha! Ha!" (Mar. 2); "Betty in Blunderland"

(Apr. 6); "Betty Boop's Rise to Fame" (May 18); "Betty Boop's Trial" (June 15); "Betty Boop's Life Guard" (July 13); "There's Something About a Soldier" (Aug. 17); "Betty Boop's Little Pal" (Sept. 21); "Betty Boop's Prize Show" (Oct. 19); "Keep in Style" (Nov. 16); and "When My Ship Comes In" (Dec. 21).

1935: "Baby Be Good" (Jan. 18); "Taking the Blame" (Feb. 15); "Stop That Noise" (Mar. 15); "Swat the Fly" (Apr. 19); "No! No! A Thousand Times No!" (May 24); "A Little Soap and Water" (June 21); "A Language All My Own" (July 19); "Betty Boop and Grampy" (Aug. 16); "Judge for a Day" (Sept. 20); "Making Stars" (Oct. 18); "Betty Boop, with Henry, The Funniest Living American" (Nov. 22); and "Little Nobody" (Dec. 27).

1936: "Betty Boop and the Little King" (Jan. 31); "Not Now" (Feb. 28); "Betty Boop and Little Jimmy" (Mar. 27); "We Did It" (Apr. 24); "A Song a Day" (May 22); "More Pep" (June 19); "You're Not Built That Way" (July 17); "Happy You and Merry Me" (Aug. 21); "Training Pigeons" (Sept. 18); "Grampy's Indoor Outing" (Oct. 16); "Be Human" (Nov. 20); and "Making Friends" (Dec. 18).

1937: "House Cleaning Blues" (Jan. 15); "Whoops! I'm a Cowboy" (Feb. 12); "The Hot Air Salesman" (Mar. 12); "Pudgy Takes a Bow-Wow" (Apr. 19); "Pudgy Picks a Fight" (May 14); "The Impractical Joker" (June 18); "Ding Dong Doggie" (July 23); "The Candid Candidate" (Aug. 27); "Service with a Smile" (Sept. 23); "The New Deal Show" (Oct. 22); "The Foxy Hunter" (Nov. 26); and "Zula Hula" (Dec. 24).

1938: "Riding the Rails" (Jan. 28); "Be Up to Date" (Feb. 25); "Honest Love and True" (Mar. 25); "Out of the Inkwell" (Apr. 22); "Swing School" (May 27); "Pudgy and the Lost Kitten" (June 24); "Buzzy Boop" (July 29); "Pudgy the Watchman" (Aug. 12); "Buzzy Boop at the Concert" (Sept. 16); "Sally Swing" (Oct. 14); "On with the New" (Dec. 2); and "Pudgy in Thrills and Chills" (Dec. 23).

1939: "My Friend the Monkey" (Jan. 27); "So Does an Automobile" (Mar. 31); "Musical Mountaineers" (May 12); "The Scared Crows" (June 9); "Rhythm on the Reservation" (July 7); and "Yip, Yip, Yippy" (Aug. 11/officially released as a *Betty Boop* cartoon even though she does not appear).

◉ BLACKIE THE LAMB

Innocent-looking Blackie the Lamb was always the target of a lamb-hungry Wolf, whose level of frustration mounted every time his attempt to capture the wool-skinned creature failed in this series of cartoon shorts released under the *Nooletoons* banner. The director of the first cartoon in the series is unknown. *Directed by Isadore Sparber. Technicolor. A Famous Studios Production released by Paramount Pictures.*

1943: "No Mutton for Nuttin'" (Nov. 26).

1945: "A Lamb in a Jam" (Sparber/May 4).

1946: "Sheep Shape" (Sparber/June 28).

1947: "Much Ado About Mutton" (Sparber/July 18).

◉ THE BLUE RACER

In the tradition of the Road Runner and Coyote cartoons, this series followed a similar "chase" premise in each episode, with the fast-moving sissy blue snake (self-billed as "the fastest little ol' snake west of the pecos") pursuing the ever-elusive Japanese beetle, a self-proclaimed black belt karate champion who is always one step ahead in outwitting the sly reptile. *Series directors included Art Davis. Technicolor. A DePatie-Freleng/Mirisch Cinema Company Production released through United Artists.*

Voices
The Blue Racer: Larry D. Mann; **Japanese Beetle:** Tom Holland

1972: "Hiss and Hers" (July 3); "Support Your Local Serpent" (July 9); "Punch and Judo" (Davis/July 23); "Love

A blue rattler is known as "the fastest little snake west of the Pecos" in the DePatie-Freleng theatrical cartoon series The Blue Racer. © *DePatie-Freleng Enterprises*

and Hisses" (Aug. 3); "Camera Bug" (Aug. 6); "Yokahama Mamma" (Dec. 24); and "Blue Racer Blues" (Dec. 31).

1973: "The Boa Friend" (Feb. 11); "Wham and Eggs" (Feb. 18); "Blue Aces Wild" (May 16); "Fowl Play" (June 1); "Freeze a Jolly Good Fellow" (June 1); "Aches and Snakes" (Aug. 10); and "Snake Preview" (Aug. 10).

1974: "Little Boa Peep" (Jan. 16).

◉ BOBO

Bobo, a sorrowful-looking, usually nontalking baby pink elephant, finds success in the big city in this short-lived *Looney Tunes* series. *Directed by Robert McKimson. Technicolor. A Warner Bros. release.*

Voices
Mel Blanc

Looney Tunes

1947: "Hobo Bobo" (May 17).

1954: "Gone Batty" (Sept. 4).

◉ BOOBIE BABOON

This klutzy baboon was one of several incidental starring cartoon characters brought to the screen in Paramount's *Modern Madcaps* of the 1960s. Boobie starred in only two cartoons, his first being "Solitary Refinement," produced in 1965. The series was written by newspaper cartoonist Jack Mendelsohn, who also directed another short-lived series for Paramount, *Jacky's Whacky World. Directed by Howard Post. Technicolor. Voices credits unknown. A Famous Studios Production released through Paramount Pictures.*

1965: "Solitary Refinement" (Sept./*Modern Madcap*); and "The Outside Dope" (Nov./*Modern Madcap*).

◉ BOSKO

In 1929 former Disney animators Hugh Harman and Rudolf Ising, who turned to animating independent productions, completed a three-minute pilot starring a black minstrel character they hoped to develop into a series. Called Bosko the Talkink Kid, the film's lead character resembled a humanized Mickey Mouse who favored a derby and spoke in a Southern Negro dialect.

Animator Friz Freleng cartooned the pilot one-reeler, with animator Hugh Harman making the first drawing of Bosko, who he had "behave like a little boy." The film was previewed for several distributors but no offers were made to distribute it.

Leon Schlesinger, president of Pacific Arts and Titles, had a different opinion. He later viewed the film and used his connections at Warner Bros. to have the series contracted by the studio, with the three men coproducing it. The first *Bosko* cartoon for Warners was also the first *Looney Tunes* cartoon, called "Sinking in the Bathtub." (The title was a play on the popular song title introduced in a Warner feature, *The Show of Shows.*

The film was so well received that Bosko became a mainstay at Warner Bros. for several years. His costars were Honey, Bosko's girlfriend (a thinly disguised Minnie Mouse); and Pluto, their dog (Harman and Ising's version of Pluto). The films were populated by visual puns and other exaggerations set to popular tunes of the day, recorded by the studio's orchestra. (Abe Lyman Brunswick Record Orchestra played on several of the first releases before relinquishing his duties.)

In 1932 Ising, the idea man of the two, left the series to work on the studio's fledgling *Merrie Melodies* cartoons. The *Bosko* series was never the same. A year later he and Harman departed Warner for good, taking *Bosko* with them to MGM, where they revived the series two years later but with little success.

Besides Freleng, the series' animators included Rollin Hamilton, Paul J. Smith and Carmen Maxwell, who also supplied the voice of Bosko. *Directed by Hugh Harman, Rudolf Ising and Friz Freleng. Black-and-white. A Vitaphone Production released through Warner Bros.*

Voices
Bosko: Carmen Maxwell; **Honey, his girlfriend:** Rochelle Hudson

1930: "Sinkin' in the Bathtub" (with Honey/Harman, Ising/Sept.); "Congo Jazz" (Harman, Ising/Oct.); "Hold Anything" (with Honey/Harman, Ising/Nov.); and "The Booze Hangs High" (Harman, Ising/Dec.).

1931: "Box Car Blues" (Harman, Ising/Jan.); "Big Man from the North" (Harman, Ising/Feb.); "Ain't Nature Grand?" (Harman, Ising/Mar.); "Ups 'n Downs" (Harman, Ising); "Dumb Patrol" (Harman, Ising/May); "Yodelling Yokels" (Harman, Ising/June); "Bosko's Holiday" (Harman, Ising/July); "The Tree's Knees" (Harman, Ising/Aug.); "Bosko Shipwrecked" (Harman/Sept. 19); "Bosko The Doughboy" (Harman/Oct. 17); "Bosko's Soda Fountain" (with Honey/Harman/Nov. 14); and "Bosko's Fox Hunt" (Harman/Dec. 12).

1932: "Bosko at the Zoo" (with Honey/Harman/Jan. 9); "Battling Bosko" (with Honey/Harman/Feb. 6); "Big-Hearted Bosko" (with Bruno/Harman, Ising/Mar. 5/originally "Bosko's Orphans"); "Bosko's Party" (with Honey/Harman/Apr. 2); "Bosko And Bruno" (with Bruno/Harman/Apr. 30); "Bosko's Dog Race" (Harman/June 25); "Bosko at the Beach" (Harman/July 23); "Bosko's Store" (Harman/Aug. 13); and "Bosko the Lumberjack" (with Honey/Harman/Sept. 3).

1933: "Ride Him, Bosko!" (Harman/Jan. 16); "Bosko's Dizzy Date" (with Honey/Harman/Feb. 6/uses footage from the unreleased "Bosko and Honey"); "Bosko the Drawback" (Harman/Feb. 24); "Bosko the Speed King" (with Honey/Harman/Mar. 22); "Bosko's Woodland Daze" (Harman/Mar. 22); "Bosko in Dutch" (with Honey, Goopy Geer/Freleng/Mar. 22/Note: Goopy Geer makes an unbilled appearance); "Bosko in Person" (with Honey/Freleng/Apr. 10); "Bosko's Knight-Mare" (Harman/June 8); "Bosko the Sheep-Herder" (Harman/June 14); "Beau Bosko" (Freleng/July 1); "Bosko the Musketeer" (with Honey/Harman/Sept. 16); "Bosko's Picture Show" (Freleng/Sept. 18); and "Bosko's Mechanical Man" (Harman/Sept. 27).

MGM Bosko cartoons released as Happy Harmonies

1934: (in Technicolor): "Bosko's Parlor Pranks" (Harman/Nov. 24).

1935: "Hey, Hey Fever" (Harman/Jan. 9); and "Run, Sheep, Run" (Harman/Dec. 14).

1936: "The Old House" (Harman/May 2).

1937: "Circus Daze" (Harman/Jan. 16); "Bosko's Easter Eggs" (Harman/Mar. 17); "Bosko and the Pirates" (Harman/May 1); and "Bosko and the Cannibals" (Harman/Aug. 28).

1938: "Bosko in Bagdad" (Harman/Jan. 1).

◎ BUDDY

As a replacement for Bosko, producer Leon Schlesinger unveiled Buddy, a nondescript, wide-eyed boy, as the new lead in the *Looney Tunes* series. A pale imitation at best, Buddy was "Bosko in whiteface" and had little impact on moviegoers, proving to be "a nothing," recalled Bob Clampett, a series animator.

The Disney influence was apparent again in this series, the third for Warner Bros.' young animation studio. Like Bosko, Buddy had Disneyish costars: a flapper girlfriend, Cookie (Minnie Mouse in costume) and, later, a dog named Towser (yet another Pluto-like clone).

Chuck Jones, a young in-betweener at the time, graduated to animator on the series and as he recalled, "Nothing in the way of bad animation could make Buddy worse than he was anyway."

Surprisingly, with such internal unrest over the character, Buddy lasted two years in 23 cartoon adventures released from 1933 to 1935. *Series direction was handled by Earl Duvall, Ben Hardaway, Friz Freleng, Tom Palmer and Jack King. Black-and-white. A Vitaphone Production released through Warner Bros.*

Voices
Buddy: Jack Carr

1933: "Buddy's Day Out" (Palmer/Sept. 9); "Buddy's Beer Garden" (Duvall/Nov. 11); and "Buddy's Show Boat" (Duvall/Dec. 9).

1934: "Buddy the Gob" (Freleng/Jan. 13); "Buddy and Towser" (Freleng/Feb. 24); "Buddy's Garage" (Duvall/Apr. 14); "Buddy's Trolley Trouble" (Freleng/May 5); "Buddy of the Apes" (Hardaway/May 26); "Buddy's Bearcats" (King/June 23); "Buddy the Detective" (King/Oct. 17); "Buddy the Woodsman" (with Cookie/King/Oct. 20); "Buddy's Circus" (King/Nov. 8); and "Viva Buddy" (King/Dec. 12).

1935: "Buddy's Adventures" (with Cookie/Hardaway/Mar. 5); "Buddy the Dentist" (Hardaway/Mar. 5); "Buddy's Pony Express" (Hardaway/Mar. 9); "Buddy's Theatre" (Hardaway/Apr. 1); "Buddy of the Legion" (Hardaway/Apr. 4); "Buddy's Lost World" (King/May 18); "Buddy's Bug Hunt" (King/June 22); "Buddy in Africa" (Hardaway/July 6); "Buddy Steps Out" (King/July 20); and "Buddy the Gee Man" (King/Aug. 24).

◎ BUGS BUNNY

Long a staple of the Warner Bros. cartoon roster, Bugs Bunny still remains one of the most popular cartoon characters in animation history. The long-eared, screwy rabbit who chomped on carrots and uttered in Brooklynese the famous words of "Eh, What's up, Doc?" starred in 150 cartoons during his 25 years on screen, the most of any character in Warner Bros. cartoon history.

First appearing in cartoons in a formative stage between 1938–39, Bugs's characterization became the basis for ridiculous situations that were offbeat and outrageously funny. Often the humor was more pointed and self-serving, with the brunt of the situational gags taken by a handful of supporting characters, including Elmer Fudd, Daffy Duck, Yosemite Sam and others.

The story behind Bugs's origin has gone through several versions over the years, mostly due to several animators' attempts to claim credit for his creation. For a long time the most accepted version was that Ben "Bugs" Hardaway, who was directing a second rabbit picture, enlisted a fellow by the name of Charlie Thorson to make a drawing of a crazy rabbit like Woody Woodpecker. When Thorson sent the drawing back to Hardaway, he labeled the corner of the page "Bugs' bunny"—and that's how Bugs supposedly got his name.

New research has revealed otherwise. Bugs did not receive his name until two years after the first model sheet was drawn. He first appeared as an "unnamed rabbit" in three cartoons "Porky's Hare Hunt" (1938), "Prest-O Change-O" (1939) and "Hare-Um Scare-Um" (1939).

Bob Clampett wrote the story for the first cartoon, "Porky's Hare Hunt," using some leftover gags from "Porky's Duck Hunt" and reshaping them for the rabbit. In this first appearance, several key aspects of Bugs's character emerged: chomping on a carrot; the fake dying act ("You got me!"); and the Groucho Marx line of "Of course, you know this means war!" When Clampett's story timed short, Hardaway added a few other touches, like having Bugs bounce across the scene à la studio contemporary Daffy Duck. (By the second cartoon, Bugs was portrayed as more high strung in the fashion of Woody Woodpecker in both voice and actions.)

Bugs's creation initially stirred some controversy, however. Some people at Walt Disney Studios cried foul as he resembled Disney's own rabbit character, Max Hare, who made his cartoon debut in "The Tortoise and the Hare" (1935), which won an Academy Award.

Ah, yes—the name. In 1940 animator Tex Avery took over the series. He directed the first official Bugs Bunny cartoon and also helped the studio, which was getting nervous since the rascally rabbit was fast becoming a rising star, decide on what to call him. It was before producing "A Wild Hare" that the studio opened discussions on naming the character.

Tex wanted to call the character Jack Rabbit, but the idea didn't stick. Finally it was suggested that he be named Bugsy after the famed West Coast mobster Bugsy Siegel, but producer Leon Schlesinger nixed that idea. Another round of discussions ensued before the issue was settled. The name that won out over all the others was Bugs Bunny.

During production of this first Bugs Bunny cartoon, Avery created the character's trademark phrase, "What's up, Doc?" partly inspired by an idea given to him by Bob Clampett, Tex's key gag man from the Termite Terrace days, who suggested the line of "What's up, Duke?" (used in the screwball comedy My Man Godfrey) and from Avery's own recollection of expressions used in his native Texas—"Hey, Doc? Whaddya know?" and "How ya been today, Doc?"

Introduced during the cartoon's first confrontation between Bugs and Elmer Fudd, the befuddled hunter ("I'm hunting wabbit! Heh-heh-heh-heh-heh!"), Avery believes the phrase was the key to Bugs's success while giving audiences something they never expected.

"We decided he [Bugs] was going to be a smart-aleck rabbit, but casual about it. That opening line of 'Eh, What's up, Doc?' in the very first picture floored them [the audience]," Avery told biographer Joe Adamson. "They expected the rabbit to scream, or anything but make a casual remark. For here's a guy pointing a gun in his face! It got such a laugh that we said, 'Boy, we'll do that every chance we get.'"

Besides his long-running feud with Elmer Fudd, Bugs developed several other rivalries with his costars Yosemite Sam, a pint-size Westerner (his classic line, "I'm the roughest, toughest, meanest hombre ever to terrorize the West") and Daffy Duck, the ever-malevolent wise quacker who was

Hollywood trade paper advertisement for Warner Bros.' "new" Bugs Bunny cartoon series. © Warner Bros. Inc.

always jealous of Bugs stealing the spotlight from him. (The most popular gag between both characters was "Duck Season! Rabbit Season!" instrumented by Chuck Jones in several cartoons.)

Bugs's final cartoon appearance was in 1964, a year after Warner Bros. closed its animation department and made special arrangements with Friz Freleng's new company, DePatie-Freleng Enterprises, to produce a series of new Looney Tunes and Merrie Melodies. (Warner reopened its department in 1967, hiring a new staff to head its productions.)

In 1990 Bugs returned to the screen in an all-new theatrical short, "Box Office Bunny," the studio's first Bugs Bunny cartoon in 26 years. The film opened nationwide with the Warner Bros. feature "The Neverending Story II: The Next Chapter." Jeff Bergman took over as the voice of Bugs Bunny and his costars Elmer Fudd and Daffy Duck, succeeding Mel Blanc, who died that year. Produced by Kathleen Helppie-Shipley and directed by Darrell Van Citters, the short was created to mark the 50th anniversary of Bugs's cartoon debut. The studio starred Bugs in a follow-up cartoon, "Invasion of the Bunny Snatchers" (a spoof of the 1950s' sci-fi classic Invasion of the Body Snatchers, in which Bugs's pals are replaced by alien look-alikes), directed by Greg Ford and Terry Lennon, but the film was never released to theaters.

Bugs marked another milestone in 1992 with the debut of the much-talked-about "Hare Jordan" television commercial for Nike, broadcast during the Super Bowl. In the $1 million spot, Bugs outsmarted basketball superstar Michael Jordan, along with a host of other Warner Bros. characters, marking the beginning of a surge of television commercials that mixed live action with animated cartoon characters. Four years later Bugs and company would team up with Jordan to star in the blockbluster live-action/animated feature Space Jam.

In 1995 two new Bugs Bunny cartoons were produced. Bugs starred in "Carrotblanca," a cartoon parody of the classic 1942 Warner Bros. feature *Casablanca*, produced by Warner Bros. Classic Animation division. Douglas McCarthy served as director. Legendary animator Chuck Jones produced and directed a handful of new cartoon shorts for Warner Bros. beginning in 1994 (under the auspices of Chuck Jones Film Productions, a new animation unit located on the Warner Bros. lot), including the 1995 Bugs Bunny–Yosemite Sam pairing, "From Hare to Eternity," dedicated to fellow animator Friz Freleng, who died in May of that year. Unfortunately, the cartoon was never released to theaters. (It was later released on home video.) Greg Burson provided the voice of Bugs Bunny; veteran comedian Frank Gorshin (who played The Riddler in the *Batman* television series starring Adam West) voiced Yosemite Sam.

Jones formed the new animation unit to supply theatrical cartoons for Warner Bros. and to re-create the spirit of Termite Terrace, the nickname of the old Warner Bros. animation headquarters during the studio's heyday when his colleagues included Tex Avery, Bob Clampett, Friz Freleng, Frank Tashlin, Robert McKimson and others. In April of 1997, after producing only six new cartoon shorts for the studio, Jones's animation unit closed its doors, leaving Warner Bros. Classic Animation Division as the studio's sole producer of theatrical cartoon shorts. *Series directors included Friz Freleng, Ben Hardaway, Robert McKimson, Bob Clampett, Frank Tashlin, Charles "Chuck" M. Jones, Abe Levitow, Dave Detiege, Tex Avery, Gerry Chiniquy, Cal Dalton, Art Davis, Ken Harris, Maurice Noble, Hawley Pratt, Darrel Van Citters, Greg Ford, Terry Lennon and Douglas McCarthy. Black-and-white. Technicolor. A Warner Bros. release.*

Voices
Bugs Bunny: Mel Blanc, Jeff Bergman, Greg Burson

Looney Tunes

1938: "Porky's Hare Hunt" (with Porky Pig/Hardaway/Apr. 30).

1940: "Patient Porky" (with Porky Pig/Clampett/Aug. 24/Porky Pig cartoon/Note: Bugs Bunny makes a cameo appearance).

1943: "Porky Pig's Feat" (with Porky Pig, Daffy Duck/Tashlin/July 17/Porky Pig cartoon).

1944: "Buckaroo Bugs" (Clampett/Aug. 26).

1945: "Hare Conditioned" (Jones/Aug. 11); and "Hare Tonic" (with Elmer Fudd/Jones/Nov. 10).

1946: "Baseball Bugs" (Freleng/Feb. 2); "Hair-Raising Hare" (Jones/May 25); "Acrobatty Bunny" (McKimson/June 29); "Racketeer Rabbit" (with Edward G. Robinson, Peter Lorre characters/Freleng/Sept. 14); and "The Big Snooze" (with Elmer Fudd/Clampett/Oct. 5).

1947: "Easter Yeggs" (with Elmer Fudd/McKimson/June 28).

1948: "Gorilla My Dreams" (McKimson/Jan. 3); "A Feather in His Hare" (Jones/Feb. 7); "Buccaneer Bunny" (with Yosemite Sam/Freleng/May 8); "Haredevil Hare" (with Marvin Martian/Jones/July 24); and "A-Lad-in His Lamp" (McKimson/Oct. 23).

1949: "Mississippi Hare" (Jones/Feb. 26); "High Diving Hare" (with Yosemite Sam/Freleng/Apr. 30); "Long-Haired Hare" (Jones/June 25); "The Grey-Hounded Hare" (McKimson/Aug. 6); and "The Windblown Hare" (McKimson/Aug. 27).

1950: "Mutiny on the Bunny" (with Yosemite Sam/Freleng/Feb. 11); "Big House Bunny" (with Yosemite Sam/Freleng/Apr. 22); "What's Up, Doc?" (with Elmer Fudd/McKimson/June 17); "8 Ball Bunny" (with Penguin, Bogart/Jones/July 8); "Bushy Hare" (McKimson/Nov. 11); and "The Rabbit of Seville" (with Elmer Fudd/Jones/Dec. 16).

1951: "Rabbit Every Monday" (with Yosemite Sam/Freleng/Feb. 10); "The Fair Haired Hare" (with Yosemite Sam/Freleng/Apr. 4); "Rabbit Fire" (with Daffy Duck, Elmer Fudd/Jones/May 19); and "His Hare Raising Tale" (with Clyde Rabbit, Bugs's nephew/Freleng/Aug. 11).

1952: "Operation: Rabbit" (with Wile E. Coyote/Jones/Jan. 19); "14 Carrot Rabbit" (with Yosemite Sam/Freleng/Feb. 16); "Water, Water Every Hare" (Jones/Apr. 19); "The Hasty Hare" (with Marvin Martian/Jones/June 7); and "Hare Lift" (with Yosemite Sam/Freleng/Dec. 20).

1953: "Forward March Hare" (Jones/Feb. 4); "Bully for Bugs" (Jones/Aug. 8); "Robot Rabbit" (with Elmer Fudd/Freleng/Dec. 12); and "Punch Trunk" (Jones/Dec. 19).

1954: "Captain Hareblower" (with Yosemite Sam/Freleng/Feb. 16); "Bugs and Thugs" (with Rocky, Mugsy/McKimson/Mar. 2); "No Parking Hare" (McKimson/May 1); "Dr. Jekyll's Hide" (with Spike and Chester/Freleng/May 8); "Devil May Hare" (with Tasmanian Devil/McKimson/June 19); "Bewitched Bunny" (with Witch Hazel/Jones/July 24); "Yankee Doodle Bugs" (with Clyde/Freleng/Aug. 28); and "Lumberjack Rabbit" (Jones/Nov. 13/released in 3-D; Warner Bros.' only cartoon produced in 3-D).

1955: "Sahara Hare" (with Yosemite Sam/Freleng/Mar. 26); "Hare Brush" (with Elmer Fudd/Freleng/May 7); "Rabbit Rampage" (Jones/June 11); "Hyde And Hare" (Freleng/Aug. 27); and "Roman Legion Hare" (with Yosemite Sam/Freleng/Nov. 12).

1956: "Broom-Stick Bunny" (with Witch Hazel/Jones/Feb. 25); "Rabbitson Crusoe" (with Yosemite Sam/Freleng/Apr. 28); "Barbary Coast Bunny" (Jones/July 21); and "A Star Is Bored" (with Daffy Duck, Elmer Fudd and Yosemite Sam/Freleng/Sept. 15).

1957: "Piker's Peak" (with Yosemite Sam/Freleng/May 25); "Bugsy and Mugsy" (with Rocky and Mugsy/Freleng/Aug. 31); and "Show Biz Bugs" (with Daffy Duck/Freleng/Nov. 2).

1958: "Hare-Way to the Stars" (with Marvin Martian/Jones/Mar. 29); "Now Hare This" (McKimson/May 31); "Knighty-Knight Bugs" (with Yosemite Sam/Freleng/Aug. 23/A.A. winner); and "Pre-Hysterical Hare" (with Elmer Fudd/McKimson/Nov. 1).

1959: "Baton Bunny" (Jones, Levitow/Jan. 10); "Wild And Wooly Hare" (with Yosemite Sam/Freleng/Aug. 1); and "A Witch's Tangled Hare" (with Witch Hazel/Levitow/Oct. 31).

1960: "Horse Hare" (with Yosemite Sam/Freleng/Feb. 13); and "Rabbit's Feat" (with Wile E. Coyote/Jones/June 4).

1961: "Prince Violent" (with Yosemite Sam/Freleng, Pratt/Sept. 2).

1962: "Wet Hare" (McKimson/Jan. 20).

1963: "The Million Hare" (McKimson/Apr. 6); and "Hare-Breadth Hurry" (with Wile E. Coyote/Jones, Noble/June 8).

DePatie-Freleng Enterprises releases

1964: "Dumb Patrol" (with Yosemite Sam, Porky Pig/Chiniquy/Jan. 18); and "False Hare" (McKimson/July 16).

1990: "Box Office Bunny" (with Daffy Duck, Elmer Fudd/Van Citters/Nov.).

1995: "Carrotblanca" (with Daffy Duck, Yosemite Sam, Sylvester, Tweety, Pepe Le Pew, Foghorn Leghorn, Penelope/McCarthy/Aug. 25).

Merrie Melodies

1939: "Prest-O Change-O" (with formative Bugs Bunny/Jones/Mar. 25); and "Hare-Um Scare-Um" (with formative Bugs Bunny/Hardaway, Dalton/Aug. 12).

1940: "Elmer's Candid Camera" (with Elmer Fudd/Jones/Mar. 2/first Elmer Fudd cartoon); and "A Wild Hare" (with Elmer Fudd/Avery/July 27/A.A. nominee/first official Bugs Bunny cartoon).

1941: "Elmer's Pet Rabbit" (with Elmer Fudd/Jones/Jan. 4); "Tortoise Beats Hare" (Avery/Mar. 15); "Hiawatha's Rabbit Hunt" (Freleng/June 7/A. A. nominee); "The Heckling Hare" (Avery/July 5); "All This and Rabbit Stew" (Avery/Sept. 13); and "Wabbit Twouble" (with Elmer Fudd/Clampett/Dec. 20/Note: Bob Clampett is credited as director under the name of "Wobert Clampett").

1942: "The Wabbit Who Came to Supper" (with Elmer Fudd/Freleng/Mar. 28); "The Wacky Wabbit" (with Elmer Fudd/Clampett/May 2); "Hold the Lion, Please!" (Jones/June 13); "Bugs Bunny Gets the Boid" (with Beaky Buzzard/Clampett/June 11); "Fresh Hare" (with Elmer Fudd/Freleng/Aug. 22); "The Hare-Brained Hypnotist" (with Elmer Fudd/Freleng/Oct. 31); and "Case of the Missing Hare" (Jones/Dec. 22).

1943: "Tortoise Wins by a Hare" (Clampett/Feb. 20); "Super Rabbit" (Jones/Apr. 3); "Jack-Wabbit and the Beanstalk" (Freleng/June 12); "Wackiki Wabbit" (Jones/July 3); "A Corny Concerto" (with Elmer Fudd, Porky Pig/Clampett/Sept. 18); and "Falling Hare" (with Gremlin/Clampett/Oct. 30).

1944: "Little Red Riding Rabbit" (Freleng/Jan. 4); "What's Cookin' Doc?" (Clampett/Jan. 8); "Bugs Bunny and the Three Bears" (with The Three Bears/Jones/Feb. 26); "Bugs Bunny Nips the Nips" (Freleng/Apr. 22); "Hare Ribbin'" (Clampett/June 24); "Hare Force" (Freleng/July 22); "The Old Grey Hare" (with Elmer Fudd/Clampett/Oct. 28); and "Stage Door Cartoon" (with Elmer/Freleng/Dec. 30).

1945: "Herr Meets Hare" (Freleng/Jan. 13); "The Unruly Hare" (with Elmer Fudd/Tashlin/Feb. 10); and "Hare Trigger" (with Yosemite Sam/Freleng/May 5).

1946: "Hare Remover" (with Elmer Fudd/Tashlin/Mar. 23); and "Rhapsody Rabbit" (Freleng/Nov. 9).

1947: "Rabbit Transit" (Freleng/May 10); "A Hare Grows in Manhattan" (Freleng/May 22); and "Slick Hare" (with Elmer Fudd/Freleng/Nov. 1).

1948: "Rabbit Punch" (Jones/Apr. 10); "Bugs Bunny Rides Again" (with Yosemite Sam/Freleng/June 12); "Hot Cross Bunny" (McKimson/Aug. 21); "Hare Splitter" (Freleng/Sept. 25); and "My Bunny Lies Over the Sea" (Jones/Dec. 14).

1949: "Hare Do" (with Elmer/Freleng/Jan. 15); "Rebel Rabbit" (McKimson/Apr. 9); "Bowery Bugs" (Davis/June 4); "Knights Must Fall" (Freleng/July 16); "Frigid Hare" (Jones/Oct. 7); and "Rabbit Hood" (Jones/Dec. 24).

1950: "Hurdy Gurdy Hare" (McKimson/Jan. 21); "Homeless Hare" (Jones/Mar. 11); "Hillbilly Hare" (McKimson/Aug. 12); and "Bunker Hill Bunny" (with Yosemite Sam/Freleng/Sept. 23).

1951: "Hare We Go" (McKimson/Jan. 6); "Bunny Hugged" (Jones/Mar. 10); "French Rarebit" (McKimson/June 30); "Ballot Box Bunny" (with Yosemite Sam/Freleng/Oct. 6); and "Big Top Bunny" (McKimson/Dec. 12).

1952: "Foxy by Proxy" (Freleng/Feb. 23); "Oily Hare" (McKimson/July 26); "Rabbit Seasoning" (with Daffy Duck, Elmer Fudd/Jones/Sept. 20); and "Rabbit's Kin" (McKimson/Nov. 15).

1953: "Upswept Hare" (with Elmer Fudd/McKimson/Mar. 14); "Southern Fried Rabbit" (with Yosemite Sam/Freleng/

UNIVERSITY OF HERTFORDSHIRE LRC

May 2); "Hare Trimmed" (with Yosemite Sam/Freleng/June 20); and "Duck! Rabbit! Duck!" (with Daffy Duck, Elmer Fudd/Jones/Oct. 3).

1954: "Baby Buggy Bunny" (Jones/Dec. 18).

1955: "Beanstalk Bunny" (with Daffy Duck, Elmer Fudd/Jones/Feb. 12); "This Is a Life?" (with Daffy Duck, Elmer Fudd, Yosemite Sam/Freleng/July 9); and "Knight-Mare Hare" (Jones/Oct. 1).

1956: "Bugs Bonnets" (with Elmer Fudd/Jones/Jan. 14); "Napoleon Bunny-Part" (Freleng/June 16); "Half Fare Hare" (McKimson/Aug. 18); "Wideo Wabbit" (with Elmer Fudd/McKimson/Oct. 27); and "To Hare Is Human" (with Wile E. Coyote/Jones/Dec. 15).

1957: "Ali Baba Bunny" (with Daffy Duck/Jones/Feb. 9); "Bedeviled Rabbit" (with Tasmanian Devil/Jones/Apr. 13); "What's Opera, Doc?" (with Elmer Fudd/Jones/July 6); and "Rabbit Romeo" (with Elmer Fudd/McKimson/Dec. 14).

1958: "Hare-Less Wolf" (Freleng/Feb. 1).

1959: "Hare-Abian Nights" (with Yosemite Sam/Harris/Feb. 28); "Apes of Wrath" (Freleng/Apr. 18); "Backwoods Bunny" (McKimson/June 13); "Bonanza Bunny" (McKimson/Sept. 5); and "People Are Bunny" (with Daffy Duck/McKimson/Dec. 19).

1960: "Person to Bunny" (with Daffy Duck, Elmer Fudd/Freleng/Apr. 1); "From Hare to Heir" (with Yosemite Sam/Freleng/Sept. 3); and "Lighter Than Hare" (with Yosemite Sam/Freleng/Dec. 17).

1961: "Compressed Hare" (with Wile E. Coyote/Jones/July 29).

1962: "Bill of Hare" (with Tasmanian Devil/McKimson/June 9).

1963: "Devil's Feud Cake" (with Yosemite Sam/Freleng/Feb. 9); "The Unmentionables" (with Rocky, Mugsy/Freleng/Sept. 7); "Mad as a Mars Hare" (with Marvin Martian/Jones, Noble/Oct. 19); and "Transylvania 6-500" (Jones, Noble/Nov. 30).

DePatie-Freleng Enterprises releases

1964: "Dr. Devil and Mr. Hare" (with Tasmanian Devil/McKimson/Mar. 28).

☺ BUNNY AND CLAUDE

One of Warner Bros.' last cartoon series, this one featured two outlaw rabbits, Bunny and Claude, who steal carrots for a living, hotly pursued by a mean redneck sheriff in comical misadventures inspired by the hit Warner feature *Bonnie and Clyde. Directed by Robert McKimson. Technicolor. A Warner Bros. release.*

Voices
Bunny: Pat Wodell; **Claude:** Mel Blanc; **Sheriff:** Mel Blanc

1968: "Bunny and Claude (We Rob Carrot Patches)" (Nov. 9/*Merrie Melodies*).

1969: "The Great Carrot Train Robbery" (Jan. 25/*Merrie Melodies*).

☺ BUZZY THE CROW

Buzzy the Crow was the star of several *Noveltoons* cartoons in which his wise-cracking, fast-talking ways enabled him to successfully outsmart his feline enemies in a series of comic misadventures. *Directed by Seymour Kneitel and Isadore Sparber. Technicolor. A Famous Studios Production released by Paramount Pictures.*

1947: "Stupidstitious Cat" (Kneitel/Apr. 25).

1950: "Sock-a-Bye Kitty" (with Katnip/Kneitel/Dec. 2).

1951: "As the Crow Lies" (Kneitel/June 1/re: Sept. 28, 1956); and "Cat-Choo" (with Katnip/Kneitel/Oct. 12).

1952: "The Awful Tooth" (Kneitel/May 2).

1953: "Better Bait Than Never" (Kneitel/June 5).

1954: "Hair Today, Gone Tomorrow" (Kneitel/Apr. 16); and "No If's, Ands or Butts" (Sparber/Dec. 17).

☺ CAPTAIN AND THE KIDS

United Features Syndicate and MGM reached an agreement in the late 1930s to coproduce a sound cartoon series of Rudolf Dirks's famous *Katzenjammer Kids* comic strip, retitling the series and featuring most of the same cast of characters as the silent version.

Fred Quimby, MGM's cartoon studio head, produced the series, while former Warner Bros. director Friz Freleng joined forces with the studio to help direct. Freleng, who broke his contract with Warner (it ran out in October of that year), accepted Quimby's offer based on the understanding that "I could could hire anyone I wanted, that money was no object, and I could use any character I saw fit."

Once he arrived at MGM, Freleng found out differently. Quimby and the studio's board of directors had already struck a deal to produce the *Captain and the Kids* series, eliminating his opportunity to invent something original. (This was what attracted Freleng to MGM in the first place.)

"I went over to MGM because they offered me a lot more money than I was making at Warners," remembered Freleng. "But I knew the Katzenjammer Kids wouldn't sell. They were humanoid characters. Humanoids were not selling, only animal pairs like Tom and Jerry were."

As Freleng feared, the series failed. The budgets were much larger than the Warner Bros. cartoons', but "it didn't help much since the audience didn't recognize that."

Freleng returned to Warner Bros. the same year of the series demise, while codirectors William Hanna, of Hanna and Barbera fame, and Robert Allen remained. Most cartoons in the series were filmed in black and white and released in "sepiatone," and only one cartoon was shot in full Technicolor: 1938's "The Captain's Christmas." *Black-and-white and Technicolor. A Metro-Goldwyn-Mayer release.*

Voices
Captain: Billy Bletcher

1938: "Cleaning House" (Allen/Feb. 19/Sepiatone); "Blue Monday" (Hanna/Apr. 2/Sepiatone); "Poultry Pirates" (Freleng/Apr. 16/Sepiatone); "Captain's Pup" (Allen/Apr. 30/Sepiatone); "A Day at the Beach" (Freleng/June 25/Sepiatone); "What a Lion!" (Hanna/July 16/Sepiatone); "The Pygmy Hunt" (Freleng/Aug. 6/Sepiatone); "Old Smokey" (Hanna/Sept. 3/Sepiatone); "Buried Treasure" (Allen/Sept. 17/Sepiatone/formerly "Treasure Hunt"); "The Winning Ticket" (Oct. 1/Sepiatone); "Honduras Hurricane" (Oct. 15/Sepiatone/formerly "He Couldn't Say No"); and "The Captain's Christmas" (Dec. 17/formerly "The Short Cut"/Technicolor).

1939: "Petunia National Park" (Jan. 14); "Seal Skinners" (Jan. 28/Sepiatone); and "Mamma's New Hat" (Feb. 11/Sepiatone).

⊚ CASPER, THE FRIENDLY GHOST

His appearance frequently met by shrieks of "It's a g-g-ghost!" Casper, the Friendly Ghost, became a huge money-maker for Paramount Pictures' Famous Studio, the same studio responsible for cartoon stalwarts like Baby Huey and others. Producer/animator Joseph Oriolo, who later revived Felix the Cat on television, created the friendly ghost, who in each adventure wished he had "someone to play with me." (Oriolo colloborated with Sy Reit on the character's conception.)

Oriolo lost out on millions of dollars in revenue the studio earned in merchandise and other licensed products, including a long-running comic-book series based on the character. He was paid by Paramount Pictures the paltry sum of $175 for the initial pilot in 1945, never making another dime.

"It's a shame that I never held onto the Casper series," explained Oriolo, "for Paramount and the Harvey people have made literally millions of dollars from the series from which I made mere pennies."

Since then several animators have claimed credit for masterminding Casper, but the first story, "The Friendly Ghost," was actually drafted by Seymour Wright. The char-

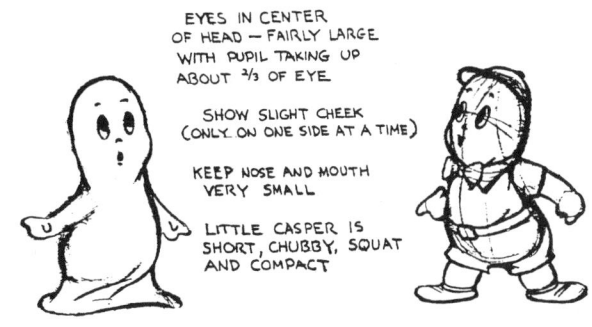

EYES IN CENTER OF HEAD — FAIRLY LARGE WITH PUPIL TAKING UP ABOUT 2/3 OF EYE

SHOW SLIGHT CHEEK (ONLY ON ONE SIDE AT A TIME)

KEEP NOSE AND MOUTH VERY SMALL

LITTLE CASPER IS SHORT, CHUBBY, SQUAT AND COMPACT

Original concept drawing for the popular friendly ghost, Casper, co-created by producer Joseph Oriolo. © Harvey Cartoons

acter did not appear again on screen until 1948, and after the 1949 cartoon, "A-Haunting We Will Go," he was finally given his name.

Made into a regular series in 1950, Casper scored a bigger hit on television in the 1960s, when a new series of films were commissioned, aimed strictly at children. Like the theatrical series, the new cartoons were built around the same premise: Casper's eternal search for a friend.

In 1995 Casper returned to the screen after a 36-year absence in an all-new live action/animated feature, *Casper,* for Universal Pictures. The movie was a smash hit with adults and children and spawned a made-for-video sequel. *Series directors were Isadore Sparber, Bill Tytla and Seymour Kneitel. A Famous Studios Production released through Paramount Pictures.*

Voices
Casper: Mae Questel, Norma McMillan, Gwen Davies, Cecil Roy

1945: "The Friendly Ghost" (Sparber/Nov. 16/*Noveltoon*).

1948: "There's Good Boos Tonight" (Sparber/Apr. 23/*Noveltoon*).

1949: "A Haunting We Will Go" (Kneitel/May 13/*Noveltoon*/narrator: Frank Gallop).

1950: "Casper's Spree Under the Sea" (Tytla/Oct. 13); and "Once Upon a Rhyme" (Sparber/Dec. 20).

1951: "Boo-Hoo Baby" (Kneitel/Mar. 30); "To Boo or Not to Boo" (Kneitel/June 8); "Boo Scout" (Sparber/July 27); "Casper Comes to Clown" (Sparber/Aug. 10); and "Casper Takes a Bow-Wow" (Sparber/Dec. 7).

1952: "The Deep Boo Sea" (Kneitel/Feb. 15); "Ghost of the Town" (Sparber/Apr. 11); "Spunky Skunky" (Sparber/May 30); "Cage Fright" (Kneitel/Aug. 8); "Pig-a-Boo" (Sparber/Sept. 12); and "True Boo" (Sparber/Oct. 24).

1953: "Frightday the 13th" (Sparber/Feb. 13/released on Friday, February 13, 1953); "Spook No Evil" (Kneitel/Mar.

13); "North Pal" (Sparber/May 29); "By the Old Mill Scream" (Kneitel/July 3); "Little Boo Peep" (Kneitel/Aug. 28); "Do or Diet" (Sparber/Oct. 16); and "Boos and Saddles" (Sparber/Dec. 25).

1954: "Boo Moon" (Kneitel, Sparber/Jan. 1/first released in 3-D; re-released in flat prints on Mar. 5); "Zero the Hero" (Kneitel/Mar. 26); "Casper Genie" (Kneitel/May 28); "Puss 'n' Boos" (Kneitel/July 16); "Boos and Arrows" (Kneitel/Oct. 15); and "Boo Ribbon Winner" (Sparber/Dec. 3).

1955: "Hide and Shriek" (Kneitel/Jan. 28); "Keep Your Grin Up" (Sparber/Mar. 4); "Spooking with a Brogue" (Kneitel/May 27); "Bull Fright" (Kneitel/July 15); "Red, White and Boo" (Sparber/Oct. 21); and "Boo Kind to Animals" (Sparber/Dec. 23).

1956: "Ground Hog Play" (Kneitel/Feb. 10); "Dutch Treat" (Sparber/Apr. 20); "Penguin for Your Thoughts" (Kneitel/June 15); "Line of Screammage" (Kneitel/Aug. 17); and "Fright from Wrong" (Kneitel/Nov. 2).

1957: "Spooking About Africa" (Kneitel/Jan. 4); "Hooky Spooky" (Kneitel/Mar. 1); "Peek-a-Boo" (Kneitel/May 24); "Ghost of Honor" (Sparber/July 19); "Ice Scream" (Kneitel/Aug. 30); and "Boo Bop" (Kneitel/Nov. 11).

1958: "Heir Restorer" (Sparber/Jan. 24); "Spook and Span" (Kneitel/Feb. 28); "Ghost Writers" (Kneitel/Apr. 25); "Which Is Witch" (Kneitel/May 2); and "Good Scream Fun" (Kneitel/Sept. 12).

1959: "Doing What's Fright" (Kneitel/Jan. 16); "Down to Mirth" (Kneitel/Mar. 20); "Not Ghoulty" (Kneitel/June 5); and "Casper's Birthday Party" (Kneitel/July 31).

◎ THE CAT

This series features a feline British supersleuth whose voice is patterned after Cary Grant's. Each time the cat escapes trouble he happily sings, "When you're wearing a new kind of hat." *Directed by Seymour Kneitel. Technicolor. A Famous Studios Production released through Paramount Pictures.*

Voices
The Cat: Dayton Allen

1960: "Top Cat" (July); and "Shootin' Stars" (Aug./Modern Madcap).

1961: "Cool Cat Blues" (Jan.); "Bopin' Hood" (Aug. 15/Modern Madcap); and "Cane And Able" (Oct. 1).

◎ CHARLIE DOG

Chuck Jones invented this wise-guy, orphan dog in stories shaped around his relentless search for a new master. Charlie was introduced to moviegoers in 1947's "Little Orphan Airedale," starring Porky Pig. The character appeared opposite Porky Pig in three cartoons before he was cast in a short-lived cartoon series of his own, beginning with 1950's "Dog Gone South." *Directed by Chuck Jones. Technicolor. A Warner Bros. release.*

Voices
Charlie Dog: Mel Blanc

Looney Tunes

1947: "Little Orphan Airedale" (with Porky Pig/Oct. 4).

1949: "Often an Orphan" (with Porky Pig/Aug. 13).

1951: "A Hound for Trouble" (Apr. 28).

Merrie Melodies

1949: "Awful Orphan" (with Porky Pig/Jan. 29).

1950: "Dog Gone South" (Aug. 26/first Charlie Dog cartoon).

◎ CHILLY WILLY

Chilly Willy, a mute penguin, was one of Walter Lantz's most productive film characters next to Woody Woodpecker. The character was Chaplinesque in nature, scooting around corners using Chaplin's famed one-legged stand, to elude his enemies in sticky situations. The series was initiated in 1953 in a film bearing the character's own name.

Unfortunately, Chilly was not well received, and Lantz brought in Tex Avery, of Warner Bros. and MGM fame, to redesign the character, which he was determined to make into a star. As Avery told biographer Joe Adamson: "The penguin wasn't funny. There was nothing to it, no personality, no nothing."

In 1954 Avery's direction of Chilly Willy in "I'm Cold" made a splash with critics and theatergoers alike. The film even earned an Academy Award nomination for Best Short Subject of that year.

Avery remained on the series only for a short time, however. He left over a salary dispute in 1955, at which time Alex Lovy took over as the series' director. The series was terminated in 1960, having amassed 35 cartoons during its lifetime. *Directed by Paul J. Smith, Alex Lovy, Jack Hannah, Tex Avery and Sid Marcus. Technicolor. A Walter Lantz Production released through Universal Pictures.*

Voices
Chilly Willy: Daws Butler

1953: "Chilly Willy" (Smith/Dec. 21).

1954: "I'm Cold" (Avery/Nov. 29/A.A. nominee/a.k.a. "Some Like It Not").

© 1977 *Walter Lantz*

Mute penguin Chilly Willy, who displayed Charlie Chaplin's famous stiff-legged walk, outwitted his adversaries in a host of Walter Lantz cartoons. © Walter Lantz Productions

1955: "The Legend of Rock-a-Bye Point" (Avery/Apr. 11/a.k.a. "Rockabye Legend"); and "Hot and Cold Penguin" (Lovy/Oct. 24).

1956: "Room and Wrath" (Lovy/June 4); and "Hold That Rock" (Lovy/July 30).

1957: "Operation Cold Feet" (Lovy/May 6); "The Big Snooze" (Lovy/Aug. 30); and "Swiss Miss-Fit" (Lovy/Dec. 2).

1958: "Polar Pests" (Lovy/May 19); "A Chilly Reception" (Lovy/June 16); and "Little Tellevillain" (Lovy/Dec. 8).

1959: "Robinson Gruesome" (Smith/Feb. 2); and "Yukon Have It" (Lovy/Mar. 30).

1960: "Fish Hooked" (Smith/Aug. 10).

1961: "Clash and Carry" (Hannah/Apr. 25); "St. Moritz Blitz" (Smith/May 16); and "Tricky Trout" (Smith/Sept. 5).

1962: "Mackerel Moocher" (Hannah/Apr. 10).

1963: "Fish and Chips" (Hannah/Jan. 8); "Salmon Loafer" (Marcus/May 28); and "Pesky Pelican" (Marcus/Sept. 24).

1964: "Deep-Freeze Squeeze" (Marcus/Mar.).

1965: "Fractured Friendship" (Marcus/Mar.); "Half-Baked Alaska" (Marcus/Apr.); and "Pesty Guest" (Marcus/June).

1966: "Snow Place Like Home" (Smith/Feb.); "South Pole Pals" (Smith/Mar.); "Polar Fright" (Smith/Apr.); and "Teeny Weeny Meany" (Marcus/May).

1967: "Operation Shanghai" (Smith/Jan.); "Vicious Viking" (Smith/Feb.); "Hot Time on Ice" (Smith/Mar.); "Chilly and the Woodchopper" (Smith/May); and "Chilly Chums" (Smith/June).

1968: "Undersea Dogs" (Smith); "Hiway Hecklers" (Smith/Sept. 1); and "Chiller Dillers" (Smith).

1969: "Project Reject" (Smith/May); "Chilly and Looney Gooney" (Smith/July); and "Sleepytime Bear" (Smith/Dec.).

1970: "Gooney's Goofy Landing" (Smith/Mar.); "Chilly's Ice Folly" (Smith/June); and "Chilly's Cold War" (Smith/Nov.).

1971: "A Gooney Is Born" (Smith/Jan.); "Airlift a La Carte" (Smith); and "Chilly's Hide-Away" (Smith).

1972: "The Rude Intruder" (Smith).

⊚ CHIP AN' DALE

These two pesty, buck-toothed chipmunks were mainly supporting characters in cartoons for Walt Disney, usually a source of irritation to the irascible Donald Duck. Formative versions of the characters first appeared in 1943's "Private Pluto" and "Squatter's Rights," also with Pluto, which was nominated for an Academy Award. The squeaky-voiced duo were given their rightful names in the Donald Duck cartoon, "Chip An' Dale," in 1947. They appeared in several more Donald Duck one-reelers before the studio featured the characters in their own series. The first series entry was 1951's "Chicken in the Rough." *Directed by Jack Hannah and Jack Kinney. Technicolor. A Walt Disney Production.*

Voices
Chip/Dale: Dessie Miller; Helen Silbert

(Cartoons listed are from the *Chip An' Dale* series only).

1951: "Chicken in the Rough" (Hannah/Jan. 19).

1952: "Two Chips and a Miss" (Hannah/Mar. 21).

1954: "The Lone Chipmunks" (Kinney/Apr. 7).

⊚ CHUCK JONES MGM CARTOONS

Director Chuck Jones's prolific career was footnoted at Warner Bros. for his direction of cartoon stars Bugs Bunny, Pepe Lew Pew and the Road Runner. In the 1960s he coproduced MGM's *Tom and Jerry* cartoons, besides directing several miscellaneous one-reelers for the studio, one of which won an Academy Award. *Technicolor. A Metro-Goldwyn-Mayer release.*

1965: "The Dot and the Line" (Dec. 31/A.A. winner).

1967: "The Bear That Wasn't" (Dec. 31).

◎ CLAUDE CAT

Created by Chuck Jones, this paranoid yellow cat was usually menaced by wise-guy mice, Hubie and Bertie, in a series of Warner Bros. cartoons. Claude first appeared in 1949's "Mouse Wreckers," which was nominated for an Academy Award. A year later Jones cast Claude opposite a new adversary: a floppy-eared, hyperactive pup named Frisky Puppy. The pair wreaked havoc on the screen in three cartoons, beginning with 1950's "Two's a Crowd." *Directed by Chuck Jones. Technicolor. A Warner Bros. release.*

Voices
Claude Cat: Mel Blanc

Looney Tunes

1949: "Mouse Wreckers" (with Hubie and Bertie/Apr. 23/A.A. nominee).

1950: "Two's a Crowd" (with Frisky Puppy/Dec. 30).

1952: "Mouse Warming" (with Hubie and Bertie/Sept. 8).

1954: "Feline Frame-Up" (with Marc Antony, Pussyfoot/Feb. 13).

Merrie Melodies

1950: "The Hypo-Condri-Cat" (with Hubie and Bertie/Jones/Apr. 15).

1951: "Cheese Chasers" (with Hubie and Bertie/McKimson/Aug. 28).

1952: "Terrier Stricken" (with Frisky Puppy/Jones/Nov. 29).

1954: "No Barking" (with Frisky Puppy/Feb. 27).

◎ CLINT CLOBBER

Fully named DeWitt Clinton Clobber, this bombastic superintendent and sanitary engineer of the Flamboyant Arms Apartments was reminiscent of comedian Jackie Gleason, especially the famed comedian's gruff demeanor. The series was one of several new Terrytoons creations made during the reign of the studio's creative director Gene Deitch from 1956 to 1958.

Initially, *Terrytoons* cameraman Doug Moye, previously the voice of the father Terry Bears character, was the voice of Clint Clobber. Moye did not last long in the role, however. "Doug was not quite up to the acting ability we needed for Clobber, who was a more complex character," recalled Gene Deitch. "So we went with another actor."

Longtime voice actor Allen Swift replaced Moye as the voice of Clint Clobber for the remainder of the series. *Directed by Connie Rasinski and Dave Tendlar. Technicolor and CinemaScope. A Terrytoons Production released through 20th Century-Fox.*

Voices
Clint Clobber: Allen Swift, Doug Moye

1957: "Clint Clobber's Cat" (Rasinski/July).

1958: "Springtime for Clobber" (Rasinski/Jan.); "Camp Clobber" (Tendlar/July); "Old Mother Clobber" (Rasinski/Sept.); and "Signed, Sealed and Clobbered" (Rasinski/Nov.).

1959: "Clobber's Ballet Ache" (Rasinski/Jan.); and "The Flamboyant Arms" (Rasinski/Apr.).

◎ COLOR CLASSICS

Max Fleischer followed Walt Disney into the color cartoon arena with this series of charming fables produced in Cinecolor and two-strip and then three-strip Technicolor. The series was initially filmed in Cinecolor and two-strip Technicolor because Walt Disney had exclusive rights to three-strip Technicolor. Fleischer began filming the series in full-blown Technicolor in 1936, beginning with "Somewhere in Dreamland." Betty Boop was featured in the series opener, a fairy-tale spoof called "Poor Cinderella," released in 1934. *Directed by Dave Fleischer. Cinecolor and Technicolor. A Fleischer Studios Production released through Paramount Pictures.*

1934: "Poor Cinderella" (with Betty Boop/Aug. 3/Cinecolor); "Little Dutch Mill" (Oct. 26/Cinecolor); and "An Elephant Never Forgets" (Dec. 28).

1935: "The Song of the Birds" (Mar. 1 /two-color Technicolor); "The Kids in the Shoe" (May 19/two-color Technicolor); "Dancing on the Moon" (July 12/two-color Technicolor); "Time for Love" (Sept. 6/two-color Technicolor); and "Musical Memories" (Nov. 8/two-color Technicolor).

All cartoons listed below were filmed in three-color Technicolor.

1936: "Somewhere in Dreamland" (Jan. 17); "The Little Stranger" (Mar. 13); "The Cobweb Hotel" (May 15); "Greedy Humpty Dumpty" (July 10); "Hawaiian Birds" (Aug. 28); "Play Safe" (Oct. 16); and "Christmas Comes But Once a Year" (Dec. 4).

1937: "Bunny Mooning" (Feb. 12); "Chicken a La King" (Apr. 16); "A Car-Tune Portrait" (June 26); "Peeping Penguins" (Aug. 26); "Educated Fish" (Oct. 29); and "Little Lamby" (Dec. 31).

1938: "The Tears of an Onion" (Feb. 26); "Hold It!" (Apr. 29); "Hunky and Spunky" (June 24); "All's Fair at the Fair" (Aug. 26); and "The Playful Polar Bears" (Oct. 28).

1939: "Always Kickin'" (Jan. 26); "Small Fry" (Apr. 21); "Barnyard Brat" (June 30); and "The Fresh Vegetable Mystery" (Sept. 29).

1940: (Copyright dates are marked by a ©.) "Little Lambkin" (© Feb. 2); "Ants in the Plants" (Mar. 15); "A Kick in Time" (May 17/Note: Animator Shamus Culhane credits himself as director, even though Dave Fleischer is given credit); "Snubbed by a Snob" (July 19); and "You Can't Shoe a Horsefly" (Aug. 23).

◉ COLOR RHAPSODIES

In an effort to emulate Walt Disney's *Silly Symphonies*, Columbia Pictures cartoon division created a similar fairy-tale series using the same commercial format of storyboarding music, children's tales and various cartoon calamities. The cartoons were initially produced using a two-strip color process over the three-strip Technicolor, for which Disney had exclusive rights at the time. (Later full Technicolor films were produced after Disney lost his exclusivity.)

The series remained popular until Columbia's animation department closed in 1948. *Produced by Charles Mintz, Dave Fleischer and Ray Katz. Directed by Ub Iwerks, Ben Harrison, Art Davis, Sid Marcus, Paul Fennell, Frank Tashlin, Alec Geiss, Bob Wickersham, Paul Sommer, John Hubley, Dun Roman, Howard Swift and Alex Lovy. Technicolor. A Columbia Pictures release.*

1934: "Holiday Land" (with Scrappy/Nov. 9/A.A. nominee); and "Babes at Sea" (Nov. 30).

1935: "The Shoemaker and the Elves" (Jan. 20); "The Make-Believe Revue" (Mar. 22); "A Cat, a Mouse, and a Bell" (May 10); "Little Rover" (June 28); "Neighbors" (Aug. 15); "Monkey Love" (Sept. 12); and "Bon Bon Parade" (Oct. 10).

1936: "Doctor Bluebird" (Feb. 5); "Football Bugs" (Apr. 29); "Glee Worms" (June 24); "The Untrained Seal" (July 26); "The Novelty Shop" (Aug. 15); "In My Gondola" (with Scrappy/Sept. 3); "Merry Mutineers" (Oct. 2); "Birds in Love" (Oct. 28); "Two Lazy Crows" (Iwerks/Nov. 26); and "A Boy And His Dog" (Dec. 23).

1937: "Gifts from the Air" (Jan. 1); "Skeleton Frolic" (Iwerks/Jan. 29); "Merry Mannequins" (Iwerks/Mar. 19); "Let's Go" (Apr. 10); "Mother Hen's Holiday" (May 7); "The Foxy Pup" (Iwerks/May 21); "The Stork Takes a Holiday" (June 11); "Indian Serenade" (July 16); "Spring Festival" (Aug. 6); "Scary Crows" (Aug. 20); "Swing Monkey Swing" (Sept. 10); "The Air Hostess" (Oct. 22); "The Little Match Girl" (Nov. 5); and "Hollywood Panic" (Dec. 18).

1938: "Bluebird's Baby" (Jan. 21); "The Horse on the Merry-Go-Round" (Iwerks/Feb. 17); "The Foolish Bunny" (Davis/Mar. 26); "Showtime" (Iwerks/Apr. 14); "The Big Birdcast" (May 13); "Window Shopping" (Marcus/June 3); "Poor Little Butterfly" (Harrison/July 4); "Poor Elmer" (Marcus/July 22); "The Frog Pond" (Iwerks/Aug. 12);

"Hollywood Graduation" (Davis/Aug. 26); "Animal Cracker Circus" (Harrison/Sept. 23); "Little Moth's Big Flame" (Marcus/Nov. 3); "Midnight Frolics" (Iwerks/Nov. 24); and "The Kangaroo Kid" (Harrison/Dec. 23).

1939: "Peaceful Neighbors" (Marcus/Jan. 26); "The Gorilla Hunt" (Iwerks/Feb. 24); "Happy Tots" (Harrison/Mar. 31); "The House That Jack Built" (Marcus/Apr. 14); "Lucky Pigs" (Harrison/May 26); "Nell's Yells" (Iwerks/June 30); "Hollywood Sweepstakes" (Harrison/July 28); "Jitterbug Knights" (Marcus/Aug. 11); "Crop Chasers" (Iwerks/Sept. 22); "Dreams on Ice" (Marcus/Oct. 20); "Mountain Ears" (Gould/Nov. 3); and "Mother Goose in Swingtime" (Gould/Dec. 18).

1940: "A Boy, a Gun and Birds" (Harrison/Jan. 12); "Happy Tots' Expedition" (Harrison/Feb. 9); "Blackboard Revue" (Iwerks/Mar. 15); "The Greyhound and the Rabbit" (Marcus/Apr. 19); "The Egg Hunt" (Iwerks/May 31); "Ye Old Swap Shoppe" (Iwerks/June 28); "The Timid Pup" (Harrison/Aug. 1); "Tangled Television" (Marcus/Aug. 30); "Mr. Elephant Goes to Town" (Davis/Oct. 4); "The Mad Hatter" (Marcus/Nov. 3); and "Wise Owl" (Iwerks/Dec. 6).

1941: "A Helping Paw" (Marcus/Jan. 7); "Way of All Pests" (Davis/Feb. 28); "The Carpenters" (Fennell/Mar. 14); "The Land of Fun" (Marcus/Apr. 18); "Tom Thumb's Brother" (Marcus/June 12); "The Cuckoo I.Q." (Marcus/July 24); "Who's Zoo in Hollywood" (Davis/Nov. 15); "The Fox and the Grapes" (with Fox and the Crow/Tashlin/Dec. 5); and "Red Riding Hood Rides Again" (Marcus/Dec. 5).

1942: "A Hollywood Detour" (Tashlin/Jan. 23); "Wacky Wigwams" (Geiss/Feb. 22); "Concerto in B-Flat Minor" (Tashlin/Mar. 20); "Cinderella Goes to a Party" (Tashlin/May 3); "Woodman Spare That Tree" (Wickersham/June 19); "Song of Victory" (Wickersham/Sept. 4); "Tito's Guitar" (with Tito/Wickersham/Oct. 30); "Toll Bridge Troubles" (with Fox and the Crow/Wickersham/Nov. 27); and "King Midas Junior" (Sommer, Hubley/Dec. 18).

1943: "Slay It with Flowers" (with Fox and the Crow/Wickersham/Jan. 8); "There's Something About a Soldier" (Geiss/Feb. 26); "Professor Small and Mister Tall" (Sommer, Hubley/Mar. 26); "Plenty Below Zero" (with Fox and the Crow/Wickersham/May 14); "Tree for Two" (with Fox and the Crow/Wickersham/June 21); "He Can't Make It Stick" (Sommer, Hubley/June 11); "A Hunting We Won't Go" (with Fox and the Crow/Wickersham/Aug. 23); "The Rocky Road to Ruin" (Sommer/Sept. 16); "Imagination" (Wickersham/Oct. 29/A.A. nominee); and "The Herring Murder Mystery" (Roman/Dec. 30).

1944: "Disillusioned Bluebird" (Swift/May 26).

1945: "Dog, Cat and Canary" (with Flippy/Swift/Jan. 5); "Fiesta Time" (with Tito/Wickersham/Apr. 4); "Rippling Romance" (Wickersham/June 21); "Hot Foot Lights"

(Swift/Aug. 2); "Carnival Courage" (with Willoughby Wren/Swift/Sept. 6); and "River Ribber" (with Professor Small and Mr. Tall/Sommer/Oct. 4).

1946: "Polar Playmates" (Swift/Apr. 25); "Picnic Panic" (Wickersham/June 20); and "Cagey Bird" (with Flippy/ Swift/July 18).

1947: "Loco Lobo" (Swift/Jan. 9); "Cockatoos for Two" (Wickersham/Feb. 13); "Big House" (with Flippy/Swift/Mar. 6); "Mother Hubba-Hubba Hubbard" (Wickersham/May 29); "Up 'n' Atom" (Marcus/July 10); "Swiss Tease" (Marcus/Sept. 1); and "Boston Beany" (Marcus/Dec. 4).

1948: "Flora" (Lovy/Mar. 18); "Pickled Puss" (Swift/Sept. 2); and "Lo, the Poor Buffalo" (Lovy/Nov. 14).

1949: "Grape Nutty" (with Fox and the Crow/Lovy/Apr. 14); and "Cat-Tastrophy" (Marcus/June 30).

◎ COMIC KINGS

The series starred the kings of Sunday comic strips, from Beetle Bailey to Krazy Kat, in madcap animated adventures simultaneously released to theaters and television. (Entries from the theatrical cartoon series, with the exception of *Little Lulu*, became part of the *King Features Trilogy*, featuring 50 episodic films of each character, broadcast in syndication.) The first entry in the theatrical series was a new *Little Lulu* cartoon, "Frog's Legs," coproduced by Lulu's creator, Marjorie H. Buell. Al Brodax, who produced a series of *Popeye* cartoons for television as well as the syndicated *King Features Trilogy*, was the executive producer of the theatrical series (except for the *Little Lulu* cartoon). *Directed by Seymour Kneitel and Gene Deitch. Technicolor. A Famous Studios Production released through Paramount Pictures.*

Voices
Private Beetle Bailey: Howard Morris; **Sgt. Orville Snorkel, General Halftrack:** Allan Melvin; **Cookie, Beetle Bailey's girlfriend:** June Foray; **Snuffy Smith:** Howard Morris; **Barney Google:** Allan Melvin; **Krazy Kat:** Penny Phillips; **Ignatz Mouse:** Paul Frees

1962: "Frog's Legs" (with Little Lulu/Kneitel/Jan. 1); "Home Sweet Swampy" (Beetle Bailey/Kneitel/May); "Hero's Reward" (with Beetle Bailey/Kneitel/May); "Psychological Testing" (with Beetle Bailey/Kneitel/June); "Snuffy's Song" (with Snuffy Smith/Kneitel/June); "The Hat" (with Snuffy Smith/Kneitel/July); "Et Tu Otto" (with Beetle Bailey/Kneitel/Sept.); "A Tree Is a Tree Is a Tree?" (with Beetle Bailey/Kneitel/Oct.); "The Method and the Maw" (with Snuffy Smith/Kneitel/Oct.); "Take Me to Your Gen'rul" (with Snuffy Smith, Barney Google/Kneitel/Oct.); "Keepin Up with Krazy" (Deitch/Oct.); and "Mouse Blanche" (with Krazy Kat/Kneitel/Nov. 1).

◎ COMICOLOR CARTOONS

Veteran animator Ub Iwerks, a former Disney protégé, directed these cartoon fables from 1933 to 1936. They were formula-type adventures using music and fanciful story lines in the Disney mold. The films were produced in Cinecolor, a two-color process combining red and blue hues, which was the forerunner to three-strip Technicolor.

The series' first entry, "Jack and the Beanstalk," premiered in 1933. In 1934 Iwerks broadened the scope of these films by adding his most prestigious invention: multiplane animation, a technique Max Fleischer later used in Paramount's two-reel Popeye cartoons.

Iwerks unveiled the process in "The Headless Horseman," based on Washington Irving's "The Legend of Sleepy Hollow." The technique added a three-dimensional foreground and background to cartoons by using a multiplane camera, capable of shooting through layers of animated background, moving either forward or backward, to project on film elaborate backgrounds and a greater feeling of depth. Not all *Comi-Color* cartoons were produced using the multiplane camera, but all had the highest quality animation and stories.

The last cartoon of the series, "Happy Days" (1936), was also the pilot for a new series Iwerks wanted to animate based on Gene Byrnes's widely syndicated strip, *Reg'lar Fellers*. Plans for the series, scheduled for the 1936–37 season, never materialized.

Musical director Carl Stalling, long at Warner Bros., scored the *ComiColor* series. *Directed by Ub Iwerks. Cinecolor. A Celebrity Pictures release.*

1933: "Jack and the Beanstalk" (Nov. 30).

1934: "The Little Red Hen" (Feb. 16); "The Brave Tin Soldier" (Apr. 7); "Puss in Boots" (May 17); "The Queen of Hearts" (June 25); "Aladdin and the Wonderful Lamp" (Aug. 10); "The Headless Horseman" (Oct. 1); "The Valiant Tailor" (Oct. 29); "Don Quixote" (Nov. 26); and "Jack Frost" (Dec. 24).

1935: "Little Black Sambo" (Feb. 6); "Bremen Town Musicians" (Mar. 6); "Old Mother Hubbard" (Apr. 3); "Mary's Little Lamb" (May 1); "Summertime" (June 15/originally "In the Good Ol' Summertime"); "Sinbad the Sailor" (July 30); "The Three Bears" (Aug. 30); "Balloonland" (Sept. 30/a.k.a.: "The Pincushion Man"); "Simple Simon" (Nov. 15); and "Humpty Dumpty" (Dec. 30).

1936: "Ali Baba" (Jan. 30); "Tom Thumb" (Mar. 30); "Dick Whittington's Cat" (May 30); "Little Boy Blue" (July 30); and "Happy Days" (Sept. 30).

◎ CONRAD CAT

Dimwitted Conrad Cat was created for the screen by Warner Brothers veteran Chuck Jones and was loosely based on rubber-limbed comedian Ben Blue, who coninci-dentally starred in several comedy short subjects at Warner Brothers. The character first starred as an errand boy for the Arctic Palm Company in "The Bird Came C.O.D.," a *Merrie Melodies* cartoon. Pinto Colvig, of Walt Disney voice fame (best known as the voice of Goofy), provided the voice of Conrad. *Directed by Chuck Jones. Technicolor. A Warner Bros. release.*

Voices
Conrad Cat: Pinto Colvig

Merrie Melodies

1942: "The Bird Came C.O.D." (Jan. 17); and "Conrad the Sailor" (with Daffy Duck/Feb. 28).

◎ COOL CAT

This series, one of the last at Warner Bros. starred a hip kind of tiger created by Alex Lovy, who was hired in 1967 to direct a new series of Speedy Gonzales and Daffy Duck cartoons for the studio's newly formed animation department. Actor Larry Storch of TV's *F Troop* provided the character's "co-o-ol" voice. *Directed by Alex Lovy and Robert McKimson. Technicolor. A Warner Bros. release.*

Voices
Cool Cat: Larry Storch

1967: "Cool Cat" (Lovy/Oct. 14/*Looney Tunes*/song: "He's Just a Cool Cat," sung by The Clingers).

1968: "Big Game Haunt" (Lovy/Feb. 10/*Merrie Melodies*); "Hippydrome Tiger" (Lovy/Mar. 30/*Looney Tunes*); and "3 Ring Wing Ding" (Lovy/July 13/*Looney Tunes*).

1969: "Bugged by a Bee" (McKimson/July 26/*Looney Tunes*).

◎ CUBBY THE BEAR

In 1933 George Stallings was appointed director of Van Beuren's animation department. Studio chief Amadee J. Van Beuren's first request was for Stallings to develop a lead character that brought life to the studio's sagging cartoon productions.

Animator Mannie Davis suggested a portly bear with round ears and an impish grin, animated in the same style as Mickey Mouse. Davis submitted a sketch to Stallings for consideration. Named Cubby, the character won immediate approval and Davis directed the series opener, "Opening Night," released in February of that year.

Unfortunately, the series never caught on, so in 1934 Van Beuren laid off personnel and to save costs subcontracted the production company of animators Rudolf Ising

and Hugh Harman to animate three cartoons for the series: "Cubby's World Flight," "Gay Gaucho" and "Mischievous Mice." "Mischievous Mice" was never released because Van Beuren broke off relations with the famed animators after its completion. *Directed by Eddie Donnelly, Steve Muffati, George Stallings, Mannie Davis, Rollin Hamilton, Tom McKimson, Rudolf Ising and Hugh Harman. Black-and-white. A Van Beuren Production released through RKO-Radio Pictures. (Copyright dates are marked by a ©.)*

1933: "Opening Night" (© Feb. 10); "The Last Mail" (© Mar. 24); "Runaway Blackie" (© Apr. 7); "Bubbles and Troubles" (© Apr. 28); "The Nut Factory" (Davis/Aug. 11); "Cubby's Picnic" (Muffati, Donnelly/Oct. 6/a.k.a. "Picnic Problems"); "The Gay Gaucho" (Hamilton, McKimson/ Nov. 3); "Galloping Fanny" (Muffati, Donnelly/Dec. 1/a.k.a. "Galloping Hooves"); and "Croon Crazy" (Muffati/Dec. 29).

1934: "Sinister Stuff" (Muffati/Jan. 26/a.k.a. "Villain Pursues Her"); "Goode Knight" (Stallings/Feb. 23); "How's Crops?" (Stallings/Mar. 23/a.k.a "Brownie's Victory Garden"); "Cubby's Stratosphere Flight" (Stallings/Apr. 20); "Mild Cargo" (Stallings/May 18/a.k.a. "Brownie Bucks the Jungle"); and "Fiddlin' Fun" (Stallings/June 15).

◎ DAFFY DITTIES

John Sutherland Productions, the same company that produced industrial cartoons for MGM, produced this series. Most were regular animated cartoons, with a few done in stop-motion animation using plastic-and-clay figures à la George Pal's *Puppetoons. Directors and voice credits are unknown. Technicolor. A John Sutherland Production released through United Artists.*

1945: "The Cross-Eyed Bull."

1946: "The Lady Said No" (Apr. 26); "Pepito's Serenade" (July 5); "Choo Choo Amigo" (Aug. 16); and "The Flying Jeep" (Aug. 20).

1947: "The Fatal Kiss" (Nov. 7).

◎ DAFFY DUCK

Daffy was a wisecracking duck whose screen antics originated at Warner Bros. in the late 1930s. The web-footed looney, who first appeared as a costar in Tex Avery's 1937 cartoon "Porky's Duck Hunt," was not officially christened until his second cartoon appearance, "Daffy Duck and Egghead," the following year.

At first, Daffy was nothing like the character audiences grew to love. He was more screwball than the later witty sophisticate who spouted verbal gems in his adversarial sparrings with Bugs Bunny, Porky Pig and Elmer Fudd. Instead, cross-eyed with a squat and round physique, he

Porky Pig orders Daffy Duck to sit on and hatch a mysterious egg in a scene from Bob Clampett's 1946 cartoon "Baby Bottleneck." © *Warner Bros. Inc.* (COURTESY: BOB CLAMPETT ANIMATION ART)

made the quick, jerky movements of a lunatic on the loose, performing handstands, somersaults and other acrobatics that underscored his manic "Woo-hoo! Woo-hoo!" laugh (reportedly inspired by comedian Hugh Herbert's famous "Hoo-hoo! Hoo-hoo!" tag line).

Daffy's unique personality proved infectious, winning support to cast him in additional cartoons of his own. As director Bob Clampett, who animated Daffy's first screen appearance, recalled in an interview: "At the time, audiences weren't accustomed to seeing a cartoon character do these things. And so, when it hit the theaters it was like an explosion. People would leave the theaters talking about this 'daffy duck.'"

Through the 1940s Daffy's character remained "out of control" in the films that followed under the effective direction of Clampett, who streamlined Daffy's design, making him taller, skinnier and thin-limbed. Daffy showed signs of screwballness in his first star-billed effort, "Daffy and the Dinosaur" (1939), directed by Chuck Jones, but Clampett took the character to greater extremes in such notable efforts as "Draftee Daffy" (1945), "The Great Piggy Bank Robbery" (1946), "Book Revue" (1946), and "Baby Bottleneck" (1946).

By the 1950s Daffy became more malevolent in nature and was transformed into a hilarious cartoon foil for Warner cartoon stars Bugs Bunny and Porky Pig in a host of cartoons. It was during this period that Daffy's speech impediment evolved—he was unable to pronounce words having an "s" sound (thus "despicable" became "desthpicable"). In the 1960s, with DePatie-Freleng as his producer, Daffy's character became even more hard-edged when he was cast as a villain of sorts opposite Speedy Gonzales in a series of cartoons.

According to Chuck Jones, the successful formula for Daffy was having him victimized by his own ego: "Daffy was insane. He never settled down. His personality was very self-serving. as if to say 'I may be mean, but at least I'm alive.'"

Perhaps the most memorable cartoons in the series include the Bugs Bunny/Daffy Duck pairings about rabbit/duck season—"Rabbit Fire" (1951), "Rabbit Seasoning" (1952) and "Duck! Rabbit! Duck!" (1953)—as well as the science-fiction favorite, "Duck Dodgers in the 24 1/2 Century" (1953), each directed by Jones. (In 1977 Jones directed a sequel, "The Return of Duck Dodgers in the 24 1/2 Century," intended for theatrical release but instead broadcast as the centerpiece of a TV special, *Daffy Duck's Thank-for-Giving Special* in 1981.)

After a 19-year absence from the silver screen, Daffy starred in an all-new *Looney Tunes* cartoon in 1987, "The Duxorcist," a spoof of the chilling horror flick *The Exorcist*, followed by a new *Merrie Melodies* cartoon a year later: "Night of the Living Duck," this time parodying the cult horror classic *Night of the Living Dead*. Both were directed by Greg Ford and Terry Lennon and were the last Daffy Duck theatrical cartoons to feature the voice of Mel Blanc as Daffy. Blanc died in 1989 at the age of 81.

In the 1990s Daffy appeared in four new cartoon shorts, three of them as costar opposite Bugs Bunny: 1990's "Box Office Bunny," followed by "Invasion of the Bunny Snatchers," which was never released theatrically, and "Carrotblanca" (1995), a cartoon parody of the Warner Bros. classic, *Casablanca* (voiced by Joe Alaskey), directed by Douglas McCarthy. In 1996 Daffy returned to star in the Michael Jordan–Bugs Bunny smash hit feature *Space Jam* and in the first new Daffy Duck cartoon in nine years: "Superior Duck" (voiced by Frank Gorshin), in which Daffy tries to be a superhero. Warner Bros. cartoon legend Chuck Jones produced and directed the film, one of six new *Looney Tunes* he produced and/or directed (under the Chuck Jones Film Productions banner) for the studio after forming a new animation unit on the studio grounds. The cartoon was released jointly to theaters nationwide by Warner Bros. Family Entertainment with the live-action comedy feature *Carpool*, starring Tom Arnold. The cartoon was the last to be directed by the Jones animation unit, which ceased operation in April of 1997. *Directed by Tex Avery, Bob Clampett, Norm McCabe, Charles M. Jones, Frank Tashlin, Friz Freleng, Robert McKimson, Phil Monroe, Art Davis, Rudy Larriva, Alex Lovy, Maurice Noble, Ted Bonnicksen, Greg Ford, Terry Lennon, Darrel Van Citters and Douglas McCarthy. Black-and-white. Technicolor. A Warner Bros. release.*

Voices
Daffy Duck: Mel Blanc, Jeff Bergman, Greg Burson, Frank Gorshin

Looney Tunes

1937: "Porky's Duck Hunt" (with Porky Pig/Avery/Apr. 17).

1938: "What Price Porky" (Clampett/Feb. 26); "Porky and Daffy" (Clampett/Aug. 6); and "The Daffy Doc" (with Porky Pig/Clampett/Nov. 26).

1939: "Scalp Trouble" (with Porky Pig/Clampett/June 24); and "Wise Quacks" (with Porky Pig/Clampett/Aug. 5).

1940: "Porky's Last Stand" (with Porky Pig/Clampett/Jan. 6); and "You Ought to Be in Pictures" (with Porky Pig/Freleng/May 18).

1941: "A Coy Decoy" (with Porky Pig/McCabe/June 7); and "The Henpecked Duck" (with Porky Pig/Clampett/Aug. 30).

1942: "Daffy's Southern Exposure" (McCabe/May 2); "The Impatient Patient" (McCabe/Sept. 5); "The Daffy Duckaroo" (McCabe/Oct. 24); and "My Favorite Duck" (with Porky Pig/Jones/Dec. 5).

1943: "To Duck or Not to Duck" (with Elmer Fudd/Jones/Mar. 6); "The Wise Quacking Duck" (Clampett/May 1); "Yankee Doodle Daffy" (with Porky Pig/Freleng/July 3); "Porky Pig's Feat" (with Porky Pig, Bugs Bunny/Tashlin/July 17); "Scrap Happy Daffy" (Tashlin/Aug. 21); and "Daffy—The Commando" (Freleng/Nov. 28).

1944: "Tom Turk and Daffy" (with Porky Pig/Jones/Feb. 12); "Tick Tock Tuckered" (with Porky Pig/Clampett/Apr. 8/remake of "Porky's Badtime Story"); "Duck Soup to Nuts" (with Porky Pig/Freleng/May 27); "Plane Daffy" (Tashlin/Sept. 16); and "The Stupid Cupid" (with Elmer Fudd/Tashlin/Nov. 25).

1945: "Draftee Daffy" (Clampett/Jan. 27); and "Ain't That Ducky" (Freleng/May 19).

1946: "Book Revue" (Clampett/Jan. 5); "Baby Bottleneck" (with Porky Pig/Clampett/Mar. 16); "Daffy Doodles" (with Porky Pig/McKimson/Apr. 6); and "The Great Piggy Bank Robbery" (Clampett/July 20).

1947: "Birth of a Notion" (with Peter Lorre, Joe Besser–like goose/McKimson/Apr. 12); "Along Came Daffy" (with Yosemite Sam/Freleng/June 4); "The Up-Standing Sitter" (McKimson/July 13); and "Mexican Joy Ride" (Davis/Nov. 29).

1948: "What Makes Daffy Duck?" (with Elmer Fudd/Davis/Feb. 14/Cinecolor); and "The Stupor Salesman" (Davis/Nov. 20).

1949: "Wise Quackers" (with Elmer Fudd/Freleng/Jan. 1); and "Daffy Duck Hunt" (with Porky Pig/McKimson/Mar. 26).

1950: "Boobs in Woods" (with Porky Pig/McKimson/Jan. 28); "The Scarlet Pumpernickel" (with Porky Pig, Sylvester the Cat, Elmer Fudd, Momma Bear/Jones/Mar. 4); and "The Ducksters" (with Porky Pig/Jones/Sept. 2).

1951: "Rabbit Fire" (with Bugs Bunny, Elmer Fudd/Jones/May 19).

1952: "Thumb Fun" (with Porky Pig/McKimson/Mar. 1); "The Super Snooper" (McKimson/Nov. 1); and "Fool Coverage" (with Porky Pig/McKimson/Dec. 13).

1954: "Design for Leaving" (with Elmer Fudd/McKimson/Mar. 27).

1955: "Dime to Retire" (with Porky Pig/McKimson/Sept. 3).

1956: "The High and the Flighty" (with Foghorn Leghorn/McKimson/Feb. 18); "Stupor Duck" (McKimson/July 17); "A Star Is Bored" (with Elmer Fudd, Bugs Bunny/Freleng/Sept. 15); and "Deduce, You Say" (with Porky Pig/Jones/Sept. 29).

1957: "Boston Quackie" (with Porky Pig/McKimson/June 22); and "Show Biz Bugs" (with Bugs Bunny/Freleng/Nov. 2).

1959: "China Jones" (with Porky/McKimson/Feb. 14).

1961: "The Abominable Snow Rabbit" (with Bugs Bunny/Jones, Noble/May 20); and "Daffy's Inn Trouble" (with Porky Pig/McKimson/Sept. 23).

1962: "Good Noose" (McKimson/Nov. 10).

DePatie-Freleng Enterprises releases

1964: "The Iceman Ducketh" (with Bugs Bunny/Monroe, Noble/May 16).

1965: "It's Nice to Have Mouse Around the House" (with Speedy Gonzales, Sylvester/Freleng, Pratt/Jan. 16); "Moby Duck" (with Speedy Gonzales/McKimson/Mar. 27); "Well Worn Daffy" (with Speedy Gonzales/McKimson/May 22); "Tease for Two" (with Goofy Gophers/Aug. 28); and "Chili Corn Corny" (with Speedy Gonzales/Oct. 23).

1966: "The Astroduck" (with Speedy Gonzales/McKimson/Jan. 1); "Daffy Rents" (with Speedy Gonzales/McKimson/Apr. 29); "A-Haunting We Will Go" (with Speedy Gonzales, Witch Hazel/McKimson/Apr. 16); "A Squeak in the Deep" (with Speedy Gonzales/McKimson/July 19); and "Swing Ding Amigo" (with Speedy Gonzales/McKimson/Sept. 17).

Warner Bros. releases

1967: "Quacker Tracker" (with Speedy Gonzales/Larriva/Apr. 29); "The Spy Swatter" (with Speedy Gonzales/Larriva/June 24); "Rodent to Stardom" (with Speedy Gonzales/Lovy/Sept. 23); and "Fiesta Fiasco" (Lovy/Dec. 9/originally "The Rain Maker").

1968: "See Ya Later, Gladiator" (with Speedy Gonzales/Lovy/June 29).

1987: "The Duxorcist" (Ford, Lennon/Nov. 20).

1990: "Box Office Bunny" (with Bugs Bunny, Elmer Fudd/Van Citters/Nov.).

1995: "Carrotblanca" (with Bugs Bunny, Yosemite Sam, Sylvester, Tweety, Foghorn Leghorn, Pepe Le Pew, Penelope/McCarthy/Aug. 25).

Chuck Jones Film Production (released by Warner Bros. Family Entertainment)

1996: "Superior Duck" (Jones/Aug.).

Merrie Melodies

1938: "Daffy Duck and Egghead" (with Egghead/Avery/Jan. 1); and "Daffy Duck in Hollywood" (Avery/Dec. 3).

1939: "Daffy Duck and the Dinosaur" (Jones/Apr. 22).

1942: "Conrad the Sailor" (with Conrad Cat/Jones/Feb. 28).

1944: "Slightly Daffy" (with Porky Pig/Freleng/June 17).

1945: "Nasty Quacks" (Tashlin/Dec. 1).

1946: "Hollywood Daffy" (with Bette Davis, Johnny Weissmuller, Charlie Chaplin, Jimmy Durante, Jack Benny, Bing Crosby, Joe Besser caricatures/Freleng/June 22).

1947: "A Pest in the House" (with Elmer Fudd/Jones/Aug. 3).

1948: "Daffy Duck Slept Here" (with Porky Pig/McKimson/Mar. 6); "You Were Never Duckier" (with Henery Hawk/Jones/Aug. 7); "Daffy Dilly" (Jones/Oct. 21/Cinecolor); and "Riff Raffy Daffy" (with Porky Pig/Davis/Nov. 7/Cinecolor).

1949: "Holiday for Drumsticks" (Davis/Jan. 22/Cinecolor).

1950: "His Bitter Half" (Freleng/May 20); and "Golden Yeggs" (with Porky Pig/Freleng/Aug. 5).

1951: "Dripalong Daffy" (with Porky Pig/Jones/Nov. 17); and "The Prize Pest" (with Porky Pig/McKimson/Dec. 22).

1952: "Cracked Quack" (with Porky Pig/Freleng/July 5); and "Rabbit Seasoning" (with Bugs Bunny, Elmer Fudd/Jones/Sept. 20).

1953: "Duck Amuck" (Jones/Feb. 28/working title: "Daffy Pull"); "Muscle Tussle" (McKimson/Apr. 18); "Duck Dodgers in the 24 1/2 Century" (with Porky Pig, Marvin Martian/Jones/July 25); and "Duck! Rabbit! Duck!" (with Bugs Bunny, Elmer Fudd/Jones/Oct. 3).

1954: "Quack Shot" (with Elmer Fudd/McKimson/Oct. 30); and "My Little Duckaroo" (with Porky Pig/Jones/Nov. 27).

1955: "Beanstalk Bunny" (with Bugs Bunny, Elmer Fudd/Jones/Feb. 12); "Stork Naked" (Freleng/Feb. 26); and "This Is a Life?" (with Elmer Fudd, Bugs Bunny, Yosemite Sam/Freleng/July 9).

1956: "Rocket Squad" (with Porky Pig/Jones/Mar. 10).

1957: "Ali Baba Bunny" (with Bugs Bunny/Jones/Feb. 9); and "Ducking the Devil" (with Tasmanian Devil/McKimson/Aug. 17).

1958: "Don't Axe Me" (with Elmer Fudd/McKimson/Jan. 4); and "Robin Hood Daffy" (with Porky Pig/Jones/Mar. 8).

1959: "People Are Bunny" (McKimson/Dec. 19).

1960: "Person to Bunny" (with Bugs Bunny, Elmer Fudd/Freleng/Apr. 1).

1962: "Quackodile Tears" (Davis/Mar. 31).

1963: "Fast Buck Duck" (McKimson, Bonnicksen/Mar. 9); and "Aqua Duck" (McKimson/Sept. 28).

DePatie-Freleng Enterprises releases

1965: "Assault and Peppered" (with Speedy Gonzales/McKimson/Apr. 24); "Suppressed Duck" (McKimson/June 26); and "Go Go Amigo" (with Speedy Gonzales/McKimson/Nov. 20).

1966: "Muchos Locos" (with Speedy Gonzales/McKimson/Feb. 5); "Mexican Mousepiece" (with Speedy Gonzales/McKimson/Feb. 26); "Snow Excuse" (with Speedy Gonzales/McKimson/May 21); "Feather Finger" (with Speedy Gonzales/McKimson/Aug. 20); and "A Taste of Catnip" (with Speedy Gonzales/McKimson/Dec. 3).

Warner Bros. releases

1967: "Daffy's Diner" (with Speedy Gonzales/McKimson/Jan. 21); "The Music Mice-Tro" (with Speedy Gonzales/Larriva/May 27); "Speedy Ghost to Town" (with Speedy Gonzales, Miguel/Lovy/July 29); and "Go Away Stowaway" (with Speedy Gonzales/Lovy/Sept. 30).

1968: "Skyscraper Caper" (with Speedy Gonzales/Lovy/Mar. 9).

1988: "Night of the Living Duck" (Ford, Lennon/Sept. 23).

⊚ DEPUTY DAWG

Spurred by the success of *The Deputy Dawg Show*, which premiered on television in 1960, 20th Century-Fox released a number of these made-for-TV cartoons, featuring a not-so-bright lawman trying to maintain law and order in Mississippi, to theaters nationwide. The series was one of *Terrytoons'* most successful in the 1960s. *Directed by Bob*

Kuwahara and Dave Tendlar. Technicolor. A Terrytoons Production released through 20th Century-Fox.

Voices
Deputy Dawg: Dayton Allen

1962: "Where There's Smoke" (Kuwahara/Feb.); "Nobody's Ghoul" (Tendlar/Apr.); "Rebel Trouble" (Tendlar/June); and "Big Chief, No Treaty" (Kuwahara/Sept.).

1963: "Astronut" (with Deputy Dawg/Rasinski).

◉ DIMWIT

As the character's name implies, Dimwit was anything but smart in this early 1950s series of *Terrytoon* cartoon adventures. *Directed by Connie Rasinski. Technicolor. A Terrytoons Production released through 20th Century-Fox.*

1953: " How to Keep Cool" (Oct.).

1954: "How To Relax" (Feb.).

1957: "Daddy's Little Darling" (Apr.).

◉ DINGBAT

This nutty cuckoo bird with a wacky laugh and a penchant for causing trouble starred in this short-lived *Terrytoons* cartoon series, following his appearance in the 1949 Gandy Goose cartoon "Dingbat Land" (a sort of *Terrytoons* version of the Warner Bros. classic, "Porky in Wackyland"). *Directed by Connie Rasinki and Mannie Davis. Technicolor. Voice credits unknown. A Terrytoons Production released through 20th Century-Fox.*

1949: "Dingbat Land" (with Gandy Goose, Sourpuss/Feb.)

1950: "All This and Rabbit Stew" (Rasinski/July); and "Sour Grapes" (Davis/Dec.)

◉ DINKY DUCK

A number of studios had a duck star. Walt Disney had Donald Duck and Warner Bros. had Daffy Duck. *Terrytoons* producer Paul Terry developed his own duck character to compete with his cartoon rivals: Dinky Duck. Dinky splashed onto the silver screen to the delight of millions of moviegoers in "The Orphan Duck" (1939). The character managed to endure despite the competition, continuing to entertain audiences in new adventures until 1957. *Directed by Eddie Donnelly, Connie Rasinski, Mannie Davis and Win Hoskins. Black-and-white. Technicolor. A Terrytoons Production released through 20th Century-Fox.*

1939: "The Orphan Duck" (Rasinski/Oct. 6).

1940: "Much Ado About Nothing" (Rasinski/Mar. 22); and "The Lucky Ducky" (Rasinski/Sept. 6/Technicolor).

1941: "Welcome Little Stranger" (Rasinski/Oct. 3).

1942: "Life with Fido" (Rasinski/Aug. 21).

(All cartoons in Technicolor.)

1946: "Dinky Finds a Home" (Donnelly/June 7).

1950: "The Beauty Shop" (Donnelly/Apr. 28).

1952: "Flat Foot Fledgling" (Davis/Jan. 25); "Foolish Duckling" (Davis/May 16); and "Sink or Swim" (Rasinski/Aug. 29).

1953: "Wise Quacks" (Davis/Feb.); "Featherweight Champ" (Donnelly/Feb. 6); "The Orphan Egg" (Donnelly/Apr. 24); and "The Timid Scarecrow" (Donnelly/Aug. 28).

1957: "It's a Living" (Hoskins/Nov. 15).

◉ DOC

Walter Lantz first introduced this highly sophisticated cat, replete with bow tie, top hat and spindly cane, opposite two troublesome mice, Hickory and Dickory, in 1959's "Mouse Trapped," directed by Alex Lovy. The character starred in six additional cartoons through 1962.

Director Alex Lovy left the series in 1960, with Jack Hannah, a former Disney veteran, succeeding him in that role. *Directed by Alex Lovy and Jack Hannah. Technicolor. A Walter Lantz Production released through Universal Pictures.*

Voices
Doc: Paul Frees; **Hickory/Dickory:** Dal McKennon

1959: "Mouse Trapped" (with Hickory and Dickory/Lovy/Dec. 8).

1960: "Witty Kitty" (Lovy/Jan. 5); and "Freeloading Feline" (with Cecil/Hannah/June 15/Walter Lantz Cartune Special).

1961: "Doc's Last Stand" (with Champ/Hannah/Dec. 19).

1962: "Pest of Show" (with Champ/Hannah/Feb. 13); "Punchy Pooch" (with Champ/Hannah/Sept. 4); and "Corny Concerto" (with Champ/Hannah/Oct. 30).

◉ DR. SEUSS

Based on the Dr. Seuss children stories and written by Irving A. Jacoby. Musical score by Phillip Sheib. *Black-and-white. A Warner Bros. release.*

1931: "'Neath the Bababa Tree" (June 1); and "Put on the Spout" (June 1).

◉ THE DOGFATHER

Spoofing Marlon Brando's role in *The Godfather*, Dogfather

The Dogfather gives directions to his henchmen in the cartoon series spoof of Marlon Brando's The Godfather *called* The Dogfather. *© DePatie-Freleng Enterprises*

and canine subordinates, Louie and Pugg, carry out heists and other jobs that run amuck. *Series directors included Bob McKimson, Gerry Chiniquy and Art Leonardi. Technicolor. A DePatie-Freleng/Mirisch Cinema Company Production released through United Artists.*

Voices
Dogfather: Bob Holt; **Louie/Pugg:** Daws Butler

Additional Voices
Frank Welker

1974: "The Dogfather" (June 27); "The Goose That Laid a Golden Egg" (Oct. 4); "Heist and Seek" (McKimson/Oct. 4); "The Big House Ain't a Home" (Oct. 31); "Mother Dogfather" (Oct. 31); "Bows and Errors" (Dec. 29); and "Deviled Yeggs" (Dec. 29).

1975: "Watch the Birdie" (Chiniquy/Mar. 20); "Saltwater Tuffy" (Leonardi/Mar. 20); "M-O-N-E-Y Spells Love" (Apr. 23); "Rock-A-Bye . . . Maybe" (Apr. 23); "Haunting Dog" (Chiniquy/May 2); "Eagle Beagles" (May 5); "From Nags to Riches" (May 5); "Goldilox and the Three Hoods" (Aug. 28); and "Rockhounds" (Nov. 20).

1976: "Medicur" (Apr. 30).

⊚ DONALD DUCK

The ill-tempered Donald Duck made his debut in 1934 in Walt Disney's *Silly Symphony* cartoon, "The Wise Little Hen." Like Warner's Daffy Duck, Donald's features were greatly exaggerated in the beginning: He featured a longer bill, a skinnier neck, a fatter body and overly webbed feet highlighted by a tailor-made navy-blue jacket. (Donald's initial design was by studio animator Dick Lundy.) By the 1940s Donald's physique was modified into the figure known and recognized worldwide today.

Though Donald's first appearance won the unanimous acceptance of moviegoers, it wasn't until his second appearance in "Orphan's Benefit" that his true personality was revealed—that of "a cocky showoff with a boastful attitude that turns into anger as soon as he is crossed," according to animator Fred Spencer, who later animated MGM's *Tom and Jerry* cartoons.

Donald's success onscreen was largely due to his distinctive voice, which broke into nondescriptive jibberish when he became angry. Actor Clarence Nash was the talented individual who created Donald's voice. An Oklahoma native, Nash started at age 13 imitating animal sounds for friends down on the farm, never dreaming that one day he would voice cartoons professionally.

Walt Disney discovered Nash one evening while listening to a Los Angeles radio show. Nash was a local milk company spokesman. "I was talking duck talk on the radio one night when Disney just happened to tune in," Nash once explained. Disney immediately had the studio's personnel director set up a voice audition for Nash and from there everything fell into place.

"When I was 13, I used to recite 'Mary Had a Little Lamb' to my friends, and they'd just cut up," remembered Nash, prior to his death in 1985. "When I got there [the studio], I stuck my tongue into the left side of my mouth and recited the same old 'Mary Had a Little Lamb.' I didn't know it, but the engineer had flipped the switch and my voice was being piped over an intercom into Walt's office."

Midway through Nash's recital, Walt ran out of his office declaring "That's our duck! You're Donald Duck!"

Nash's most difficult voice challenge was presented in dubbing Donald Duck cartoons in foreign languages for theatrical release abroad. "Words were written out for me phonetically," he once recalled. "I learned to quack in French, Spanish, Portuguese, Japanese, Chinese, and German."

Among Nash's favorite cartoons were "The Band Concert," in which Mickey Mouse's attempt to play the "William Tell Overture" is marred by Donald's spiteful insistence at playing "Turkey in the Straw" on a piccolo, and the TV show, *A Day in the Life of Donald Duck*," made in the 1950s, in which he appears with his alter ego.

As the series blossomed, so did Donald's supporting cast. In 1937's "Don Donald," Donald was paired with a young, attractive senorita named Donna, who later became Daisy Duck, Donald's girlfriend. A year later Huey, Dewey and Louie, Donald's hellion nephews, were cast as regulars in the series.

Donald's meteoric rise led to roles in more than 150 cartoon shorts as well as appearances in several memorable feature films, among them: *The Reluctant Dragon* and *The Three Caballeros*. In 1983 he appeared in a featurette cartoon with pals Mickey Mouse and Goofy entitled *Mickey's Christmas Carol*.

Jack King, formerly of Warner Bros., directed the series from 1937 to 1947. King was joined by Jack Hannah and Jack Kinney, who shared assignments with King until his retirement. Kinney is best remembered for directing the 1943 Academy Award–winning Donald Duck wartime short, "Der Fuehrer's Face," winner in the "Best Short Films (Cartoons)" of the year category. *Additional series directors included Clyde Geronimi, Ben Sharpsteen, Dick Lundy, Riley Thomson, Wilfred Jackson, Bob Carlson, Charles Nichols, Hamilton Luske and Bill Roberts. Technicolor. A Walt Disney Production released through United Artists, RKO-Radio Pictures and later Buena Vista.*

Voices
Donald Duck: Clarence Nash

United Artists releases

1934: "The Wise Little Hen" (Jackson/June 9/*Silly Symphony*).

1936: "Donald and Pluto" (Sharpsteen/Sept. 12/Mickey Mouse cartoon).

1937: "Don Donald" (Sharpsteen/Jan. 9/Mickey Mouse cartoon); "Modern Inventions" (King/May 29).

RKO-Radio Pictures releases

1937: "Donald's Ostrich" (King/Dec. 10).

1938: "Self Control" (King/Feb. 11); "Donald's Better Self" (King/Mar. 11); "Donald's Nephews" (King/Apr. 15); "Polar Trappers" (with Goofy/Sharpsteen/June 17); "Good Scouts" (King/July 8/A.A. nominee); "The Fox Hunt" (with Goofy/Sharpsteen/July 29); and "Donald's Golf Game" (King/Nov. 4).

1939: "Donald's Lucky Day" (King/Jan. 13); "Hockey Champ" (King/Apr. 28); "Donald's Cousin Gus" (King/May 19); "Beach Picnic" (with Pluto/Geronimi/June 9); "Sea Scouts" (Lundy/June 30); "Donald's Penguin" (King/Aug. 11); "The Autograph Hound" (King/Sept. 1); and "Officer Duck" (Geronimi/Oct. 10).

1940: "The Riveter" (Lundy/Mar. 15); "Donald's Dog Laundry" (with Pluto/King/Apr. 5); "Billposters" (with Goofy/Geronimi/May 17); "Mr. Duck Steps Out" (King/June 7); "Put-Put Troubles" (with Pluto/Thomson/July 19); "Donald's Vacation" (King/Aug. 9); "Window Cleaners" (with Pluto/King/Sept. 20); and "Fire Chief" (King/Dec. 3).

1941: "Timber" (King/Jan. 10); "Golden Eggs" (Jackson/Mar. 7); "A Good Time for a Dime" (Lundy/May 9); "Early to Bed" (King/July 11); "Truant Officer Donald" (King/Aug. 1/A.A. nominee); "Old MacDonald Duck" (King/Sept. 12); "Donald's Camera" (Lundy/Oct. 24); and "Chef Donald" (King/Dec. 5).

1942: "The Village Smithy" (Lundy/Jan. 16); "The New Spirit" (Jackson, Sharpsteen/Jan. 23); "Donald's Snow Fight" (King/Apr. 10); "Donald Gets Drafted" (King/May 1); "Donald's Garden" (Lundy/June 12); "Donald's Gold Mine" (Lundy/July 24); "The Vanishing Private" (King/Sept. 25); "Sky Trooper" (King/Nov. 6); and "Bellboy Donald" (King/Dec. 18).

1943: "Der Fuehrer's Face" (Kinney/Jan. 1/A.A. winner); "The Spirit of '43" (King/Jan. 7); "Donald's Tire Trouble" (Lundy/Jan. 29); "Flying Jalopy" (Lundy/Mar. 12); "Fall Out, Fall In" (King/Apr. 23); "The Old Army Game" (King/Nov. 5); and "Home Defense" (King/Nov. 26).

1944: "Trombone Trouble" (King/Feb. 18); "Donald Duck and the Gorilla" (King/Mar. 31); "Contrary Condor" (King/Apr. 21); "Commando Duck" (King/June 2); "The Plastics Inventor" (King/Sept. 1); and "Donald's Off Day" (Hannah/Dec. 8).

1945: "The Clock Watcher" (King/Jan. 26); "The Eyes Have It" (with Pluto/Hannah/Mar. 30); "Donald's Crime" (King/June 29/A.A. nominee); "Duck Pimples" (Kinney/Aug. 10); "No Sail" (with Goofy/Hannah/Sept. 7); "Cured Duck" (King/Oct. 26); and "Old Sequoia" (King/Dec. 21).

1946: "Donald's Double Trouble" (King/June 28); "Wet Paint" (King/Aug. 9); "Dumb Bell of the Yukon" (King/Aug. 30); "Lighthouse Keeping" (Hannah/Sept. 20); and "Frank Duck Brings 'em Back Alive" (with Goofy/Hannah/Nov. 1).

1947: "Straight Shooters" (Hannah/Apr. 18); "Sleepy Time Donald" (King/May 9); "Clown of the Jungle" (Hannah/June 20); "Donald's Dilemma" (King/July 11); "Crazy with the Heat" (with Goofy/Carlson/Aug. 1); "Bootle Beetle" (Hannah/Aug. 22); "Wide Open Spaces" (King/Sept. 12); and "Chip an' Dale" (with Chip 'n' Dale/Hannah/Nov. 28/A.A. winner).

1948: "Drip Dippy Donald" (King/Mar. 5); "Daddy Duck" (Hannah/Apr. 16); "Donald's Dream Voice" (King/May 21); "The Trial of Donald Duck" (King/July 30); "Inferior Decorator" (Hannah/Aug. 27); "Soup's On" (Hannah/Oct. 15); "Three for Breakfast" (with Chip 'n' Dale/Hannah/Nov. 5); and "Tea for Two Hundred" (Hannah/Dec. 24/A.A nominee).

1949: "Donald's Happy Birthday" (Hannah/Feb. 11); "Sea Salts" (Hannah/Apr. 8); "Winter Storage" (with Chip 'n'

Dale/Hannah/June 3); "Honey Harvester" (Hannah/Aug. 5); "All in a Nutshell" (with Chip 'n' Dale/Hannah/Sept. 2); "The Greener Yard" (Hannah/Oct. 14); "Slide, Donald, Slide" (Hannah/Nov. 25); and "Toy Tinkers" (with Chip 'n' Dale/Hannah/Dec. 16/A.A. nominee).

1950: "Lion Around" (Hannah/Jan. 20); "Crazy Over Daisy" (with Chip 'n' Dale/Hannah/Mar. 24); "Trailer Horn" (with Chip 'n' Dale/Hannah/Apr. 28); "Hook, Lion and Sinker" (Hannah/Sept. 1); "Bee at the Beach" (Hannah/Oct. 13); and "Out on a Limb" (with Chip 'n' Dale/Hannah/ Dec. 15).

1951: "Dude Duck" (Hannah/Mar. 2); "Corn Chips" (with Chip 'n' Dale/Hannah/Mar. 23); "Test Pilot Donald" (with Chip 'n' Dale/Hannah/June 8); "Lucky Number" (Hannah/July 20); "Out of Scale" (with Chip 'n' Dale/Hannah/Nov. 2); and "Bee on Guard" (Hannah/Dec. 14).

1952: "Donald Applecore" (with Chip 'n' Dale/Hannah/Jan. 18); "Let's Stick Together" (Hannah/Apr. 25); "Uncle Donald's Ants" (Hannah/July 18); and "Trick or Treat" (Hannah/Oct. 10).

1953: "Don's Fountain of Youth" (Hannah/May 30); "The New Neighbor" (Hannah/Aug. 1); "Rugged Bear" (Hannah/Oct. 23/A.A. nominee); "Working for Peanuts" (with Chip 'n' Dale/Hannah/Nov. 11/3-D); and "Canvas Back Duck" (Hannah/Dec. 25).

1954: "Spare the Rod" (Hannah/Jan. 15); "Donald's Diary" (Kinney/Mar. 5); "Dragon Around" (with Chip 'n' Dale/Hannah/July 16); "Grin and Bear It" (Hannah/Aug. 13); "The Flying Squirrel" (Hannah/Nov. 12); and "Grand Canyonscope" (Nichols/Dec. 23/CinemaScope; Buena Vista release).

RKO-Radio releases

1955: "No Hunting" (Hannah/Jan. 14/A.A. nominee/CinemaScope); "Lake Titicaca" (Roberts/Feb. 18/segment from *Saludos Amigos* feature); "Blame It on the Samba" (Geronimi/Apr. 1/from *Melody Time* feature); "Bearly Asleep" (Hannah/Aug. 19/CinemaScope); "Beezy Bear" (Hannah/Sept. 2/CinemaScope); and "Up a Tree" (with Chip 'n' Dale/Hannah/Sept. 23).

1956: "Chips Ahoy" (with Chip 'n' Dale/Kinney/Feb. 24/CinemaScope); and "How to Have an Accident in the Home" (Nichols/July 8/CinemaScope/Buena Vista release).

Buena Vista releases

1959: "Donald in Mathmagic Land" (Luske/June 26); and "How to Have an Accident at Work" (Nichols/Sept. 2).

1961: "Donald and the Wheel" (Luske/June 21); and "The Litterbug" (Luske/June 21).

⊚ DROOPY

Dwarfed, sad-eyed, unflappable bloodhound Droopy had a Buster Keaton physique and comedy style. His creator, Tex Avery, who directed the series until he left MGM in 1954, based the character on Wallace Wimple, a supporting character in radio's *The Fibber McGee and Molly Show*, played by Bill Thompson, who also voiced Droopy. (Thompson was later replaced by veteran voice artists Daws Butler and Don Messick in succession.)

Most adventures followed Avery's trademark survival-of-the-fittest theme, pitting the tiny basset hound against a scene-stealing Wolf, featured between 1949 and 1952, and pesky bulldog, Spike, in situational duels with meek, low-key Droopy always emerging victorious. Situations often were earmarked by imaginative sight gags and hyperboles, complementing Droopy's notorious deadpan, which, like Keaton, convulsed audiences into laughter often without ever uttering a line of dialogue.

Michael Lah was named Avery's successor, directing five cartoons in all, including "One Droopy Knight" (1957), which was nomimated for an Academy Award. (Lah actually codirected several of Avery's last films before he was given full reign.) Dick Lundy, an MGM cartoon veteran, also directed occasional episodes. *Technicolor. CinemaScope. A Metro-Goldwyn-Mayer release.*

Voices

Droopy: Bill Thompson, Daws Butler, Don Messick

1943: "Dumb Hounded" (Avery/Mar. 20).

1945: "Shooting of Dan McGoo" (Avery/Mar. 3/re: Apr. 14, 1951/originally "The Shooting of Dan McScrew," a take-off of MGM's feature *Dan McGrew*) and "Wild And Wolfy" (Avery/Nov. 3/re: Oct. 4, 1952/working title: "Robinson's Screwball").

1946: "Northwest Hounded Police" (Avery/Aug. 13/re: Sept. 19, 1953/working title: "The Man Hunt").

1949: "Senor Droopy" (Avery/Apr. 9/re: Dec. 7, 1956); "Wags to Riches" (with Spike/Avery/Aug. 13/working title: "From Wags to Riches"); and "Out-Foxed" (Avery/Oct. 12).

1950: "The Chump Champ" (with Spike/Avery/Nov. 4).

1951: "Daredevil Droopy" (with Spike/Avery/Mar. 31); "Droopy's Good Deed" (Avery/May 5); and "Droopy's Double Trouble" (Avery/Nov. 17).

1952: "Caballero Droopy" (Lundy/Sept. 27).

1953: "Three Little Pups" (Avery/Dec. 26).

1954: "Drag-Along Droopy" (Avery/Feb. 20); "Homesteader Droopy" (Avery/July 10); and "Dixieland Droopy" (Avery/Dec. 4/first in CinemaScope).

1955: "Deputy Droopy" (Avery/Oct. 28).

1956: (All in CinemaScope); "Millionaire Droopy" (Avery/ Sept. 21).

1957: "Grin and Share It" (Lah/May 17/produced by William Hanna and Joseph Barbera); "Blackboard Jumble" (Lah/Oct. 4/produced by William Hanna and Joseph Barbera); and "One Droopy Knight" (Lah/Dec. 6/produced by William Hanna and Joseph Barbera).

1958: "Sheep Wrecked" (Lah/Feb. 7/produced by William Hanna and Joseph Barbera); "Mutts About Racing" (Lah/Apr. 4/produced by William Hanna and Joseph Barbera); and "Droopy Leprechaun" (Lah/July 4/produced by William Hanna and Joseph Barbera).

⊚ DUCKWOOD

This ordinary-looking duck, who got into all sorts of fixes, was a minor star in this early 1960s Terrytoons cartoon series, starring in only three cartoons for the studio. *Directed by Dave Tendlar. Technicolor. Voice credits unknown. A Terrytoons Production released through 20th Century-Fox.*

1964: "The Red Tractor" (Feb.); "Short Term Sheriff" (with Dokey Otie); and "Oil Thru the Day."

⊚ ELMER FUDD

A "wabbit hunter" by trade, Elmer J. Fudd's comic adventures onscreen often involved his relentless pursuit of his adversarial costar, Bugs Bunny, who successfully outwitted Fudd ("Be vew-wy quiet, I'm hunting wabbits!") in numerous animated film triumphs.

   The plump, chipmunk-cheeked hunter originally debuted in a different body and face as Egghead, a comic-relief character in early Warner Bros. cartoons, replete with brown derby and a nose the color of wine. Patterned after famed radio/film comedian Joe Penner, whose trademark phrase was "Wanna buy a duck?" Cliff Nazzaro has been credited with supplying the character's voice. It is now believed that Dave Weber, who provided the voices of various minor characters in several Warner Bros. cartoons as early as 1938, actually did the voice of Egghead. Among his other voice characterizations were impersonations of Rochester, Jack Benny's sidekick, Fred Allen and Walter Winchell.

   After 11 cartoons, Warner Bros. animators decided to change the character to Elmer Fudd, appearing as such for the first time in "Dangerous Dan McFoo" (1939), supervised by Tex Avery. (Avery also directed Bugs Bunny's first official screen appearance, "A Wild Hare" [1940], in which Fudd also starred.) For this cartoon, Warner Bros. hired a new man to do the voice of Elmer: Arthur Q. Bryan, best known as Doc Gamble on the *Fibber McGee and Molly* radio

" ELMER FUDD "

Elmer Fudd strikes a familiar pose as he prepares for "wabbit season."
© *Warner Bros., Inc.*

program and an actor who did bit parts in movies, including Bela Lugosi's cult classic *The Devil Bat* (1941).

   Even with a new name and face, Elmer went through several additional design changes, beginning with Bob Clampett's "Wabbit Twouble" (1941) and three subsequent cartoons in which he appeared exceedingly portly. According to Clampett, Elmer was redesigned because "we artists were never satisfied with the way he looked—he didn't look funny."

   By now Elmer resembled his alter ego, Arthur Q. Bryan. By Friz Freleng's "The Hare-Brained Hypnotist" (1942), Elmer appeared in the style and form filmgoers would remember, including his most memorable trait—his inability to pronounce the letter *r*.

   In the 1990s Elmer popped up on the screen in two new Bugs Bunny cartoons, "Box Office Bunny" (1990) and "Invasion of the Bunny Snatchers" (not released to theaters), and in the Michael Jordan–Bugs Bunny megahit movie, *Space Jam* (1996). *Directed by Tex Avery, Frank*

Tashlin, Ben Hardaway, Cal Dalton, Bob Clampett, Charles M. Jones, Friz Freleng and Darrel Van Citters. Black-and-white. Technicolor. A Warner Bros. release.

Voices

Egghead: Dave Weber, Cliff Nazzaro; **Elmer J. Fudd:** Arthur Q. Bryan, Mel Blanc, Jeff Bergman

Merrie Melodies

1937: "Egghead Rides Again" (Avery/July 17); and "Little Red Walking Hood" (Avery/Nov. 6).

1938: "Daffy Duck and Egghead" (with Daffy Duck/Avery/Jan. 1); "The Isle of Pingo-Pongo" (Avery/May 28); "Cinderella Meets Fella" (Avery/July 23); "A Feud There Was" (Avery/Sept. 24); "Johnny Smith and Poker-Huntas" (Avery/Oct. 22); and "Count Me Out" (Hardaway, Dalton/Dec. 17).

1939: "Hamateur Nite" (Avery/Jan. 28); A Day at the Zoo (Avery/Mar. 11); "Believe It or Else" (Avery/June 25); and "Dangerous Dan McFoo" (character's named changed to Elmer Fudd/Avery/July 15).

1940: "Elmer's Candid Camera" (with Bugs Bunny/Jones/Mar. 2); "Confederate Honey" (Freleng/May 30); "A Wild Hare" (with Bugs Bunny/Avery/July 27/A.A. nominee); and "Good Night Elmer" (Jones/Oct. 26).

1941: "Elmer's Pet Rabbit" (with Bugs Bunny/Jones/Jan. 4); "All This and Rabbit Stew" (with Bugs Bunny/Avery/Sept. 13); and "Wabbit Twouble" (with Bugs Bunny/Clampett/Dec. 20).

1942: "The Wabbit Who Came to Supper" (with Bugs Bunny/Freleng/Mar. 28); "The Wacky Wabbit" (with Bugs Bunny/Clampett/May 2); "Fresh Hare" (with Bugs Bunny/Freleng/Aug. 22); and "The Hare-Brained Hypnotist" (with Bugs Bunny/Freleng/Oct. 31).

1943: "A Corny Concerto" (with Bugs Bunny, Porky Pig/Clampett/Sept. 18); and "An Itch in Time" (Clampett/Dec. 4).

1944: "The Old Grey Hare" (with Bugs Bunny/Clampett/Oct. 28); and "Stage Door Cartoon" (with Bugs Bunny/Freleng/Dec. 30).

1945: "The Unruly Hare" (with Bugs Bunny/Tashlin/Feb. 10).

1946: "Hare Remover" (with Bugs Bunny/Tashlin/Mar. 23); and "Bacall to Arms" (with Bugs Bunny/Clampett/Aug. 3).

1947: "A Pest in the House" (with Daffy Duck/Jones/Aug. 3).

1948: "Back Alley Oproar" (with Sylvester/Freleng/Mar. 27).

1949: "Hare Do" (with Bugs Bunny/Freleng/Jan. 15); and "Each Dawn I Crow" (Freleng/Sept. 23).

1952: "Rabbit Seasoning" (with Bugs Bunny, Daffy Duck/Jones/Sept. 20).

1953: "Duck! Rabbit! Duck!" (with Bugs Bunny, Daffy Duck/Jones/Oct. 3).

1954: "Quack Shot" (with Daffy Duck/McKimson/Oct. 30).

1955: "Pest for Guests" (with Goofy Gophers/Freleng/Jan. 29); and "Beanstalk Bunny" (with Bugs Bunny, Daffy Duck/Jones/Feb. 12).

1956: "Bugs Bonnets" (with Bugs Bunny/Jones/Jan. 14); "Yankee Dood It" (with Sylvester/Freleng/Oct. 13); and "Wideo Wabbit" (with Bugs Bunny/McKimson/Oct. 27).

1957: "What's Opera, Doc?" (with Bugs Bunny/Jones/July 6); and "Rabbit Romeo" (with Bugs Bunny/McKimson/Dec. 14).

1958: "Don't Axe Me" (with Daffy Duck/McKimson/Jan. 4).

1960: "Person to Bunny" (with Bugs Bunny, Daffy Duck/Freleng/Apr. 1); and "Dog Gone People" (McKimson/Nov. 12).

Looney Tunes

1938: "The Daffy Doc" (with Daffy Duck, Porky Pig/Clampett/Nov. 26).

1944: "The Stupid Cupid" (with Daffy Duck/Tashlin/Nov. 25).

1945: "Hare Tonic" (with Bugs Bunny/Jones/Nov. 10).

1946: "The Big Snooze" (with Bugs Bunny/Clampett/Oct. 5).

1947: "Easter Yeggs" (with Bugs Bunny/McKimson/June 28).

1948: "Kit for Cat" (with Sylvester/Freleng/Nov. 6).

1949: "Wise Quackers" (with Daffy Duck/Freleng/Jan. 1).

1950: "The Scarlet Pumpernickel" (with Daffy Duck, Porky Pig, Sylvester, Momma Bear/Jones/Mar. 4); "What's Up, Doc?" (with Bugs Bunny/McKimson/June 17); and "The Rabbit of Seville" (with Bugs Bunny/Jones/Dec. 16).

1951: "Rabbit Fire" (with Bugs Bunny, Daffy Duck/Jones/May 19).

1953: "Ant Pasted" (Freleng/May 9); and "Robot Rabbit" (with Bugs Bunny/Freleng/Dec. 12).

1954: "Design for Living" (with Daffy Duck/McKimson/Mar. 27).

1955: "Hare Brush" (with Bugs Bunny/Freleng/May 7).

1956: "Heir-Conditioned" (with Sylvester/Freleng/Nov. 26).

1958: "Pre-Hysterical Hare" (with Bugs Bunny/McKimson/Nov. 1).

1959: "A Mutt in a Rut" (McKimson/May 23).

1961: "What's My Lion?" (McKimson/Oct. 21).

1990: "Box Office Bunny" (with Bugs Bunny, Daffy Duck/Van Citters/Nov.).

◉ FABLES

In addition to *Color Rhapsodies*, producer Charles Mintz, who began his career producing silent cartoons, produced another series based on popular children's tales called *Fables*. Directors included Sid Marcus, Ben Harrison, John Hubley, Lou Lilly, Frank Tashlin, Alec Geiss, Bob Wickersham and Art Davis. Technicolor. A Columbia Pictures release.

1939: "The Little Lost Sheep" (with Krazy Kat/Oct. 6); and "Park Your Baby" (with Scrappy/Dec. 22).

1940: "Practice Makes Perfect" (with Scrappy/Apr. 5); "Barnyard Babies" (Marcus/June 14); "Pooch Parade" (with Scrappy/July 19); "A Peep in the Deep" (with Scrappy/Aug. 23); "Farmer Tom Thumb" (Sept. 27); "Mouse Meets Lion" (Oct. 25) and "Paunch 'n' Judy" (Harrison/Dec. 13).

1941: "The Streamlined Donkey" (Marcus/Jan. 17); "It Happened to Crusoe" (Mar. 14); "Kitty Gets the Bird" (June 13); "Dumb Like a Fox" (July 18); "Playing the Pied Piper" (Lilly/Aug. 18); "The Great Cheeze Mystery" (Davis/Oct. 27); and "The Tangled Angler" (Tashlin/Dec. 26).

1942: "Under the Shedding Chestnut Tree" (Wickersham/Feb. 22); "Wolf Chases Pig" (Tashlin, Hubley/Apr. 20); and "The Bulldog and the Baby" (Geiss/July 3).

◉ FANNY ZILCH

Paul Terry produced this *Terrytoons* cartoon series parody of old movie serial melodramas, starting with 1933's "The Banker's Daughter." The serials followed the exploits of beautiful heroine Fanny Zilch and her love interest, Strongheart, who was more concerned about his good looks while the villainous Oil Can Harry snatched Fanny right from under his nose. The series inspired the later *Mighty Mouse* operetta format that became common in that series, and, in 1937, Oil Can Harry was spun off into a short-lived series of his own. *Directed by Paul Terry and Frank Moser. Black and white. Voice credits unknown. A Terrytoons Production released through 20th Century-Fox.*

1933: "The Banker's Daughter" (with Oil Can Harry/June 25); "The Oil Can Mystery" (with Oil Can Harry, Strongheart/July 9); "Fanny in the Lion's Den" (with Oil Can Harry, Strongheart/Aug. 1); and "Hypnotic Eyes" (with Oil Can Harry, Strongheart/Aug. 11)

◉ FARMER AL FALFA

The white-bearded hayseed who first appeared in the silent days returned to star in new sound cartoon adventures under the *Terrytoons* banner for creator Paul Terry. Later adventures costarred two other *Terrytoons* stars, Kiko the Kangaroo and Puddy the Pup. *Directed by Paul Terry, Frank Moser, Mannie Davis, George Gordon and Jack Zander. Black-and-white. Voice credits unknown. A Terrytoons Production released through 20th Century-Fox.*

1931: "Club Sandwich" (Terry, Moser/Jan. 25/known on studio records as "Dancing Mice"); "Razzberries" (Terry, Moser/Feb. 8); "The Explorer" (Terry, Moser/Mar. 22); "The Sultan's Cat" (Terry, Moser/May 17); "Canadian Capers" (Terry, Moser/Aug. 23); and "The Champ" (Terry, Moser/Sept. 20).

1932: "Noah's Outing" (Terry, Moser/Jan. 24); "Ye Olde Songs" (Terry, Moser/Mar. 20); "Woodland" (Terry, Moser/May 1); "Farmer Al Falfa's Bedtime Story" (Terry, Moser/June 12); "Spring Is Here" (Terry, Moser/July 24); "Farmer Al Falfa's Ape Girl" (Terry, Moser/Aug. 7); and "Farmer Al Falfa's Birthday Party" (Terry, Moser/Oct. 2).

1933: "Tropical Fish" (Terry, Moser/May 14); "Pick-Necking" (Terry, Moser/Sept. 22); "The Village Blacksmith" (Terry, Moser/Nov. 3); and "Robinson Crusoe" (Terry, Moser/Nov. 17/copyrighted as "Shipwrecked Brothers").

1934: "The Owl and the Pussycat" (Terry, Moser/Mar. 9); and "Why Mules Leave Home" (Terry, Moser/Sept. 7).

1935: "What a Night" (Terry, Moser/Jan. 25); "Old Dog Tray" (Terry, Moser/Mar. 21); "Moans and Groans" (Terry, Moser/June 28); and "A June Bride" (Terry, Moser/Nov. 1).

1936: "The 19th Hole Club" (Terry, Moser/Jan. 24); "Home Town Olympics" (Terry Moser/Feb. 7); "The Alpine Yodeler" (Terry, Moser/Feb. 21); "Barnyard Amateurs" (Terry, Moser/Mar. 6); "The Western Trail" (Terry, Moser/Apr. 3); "Rolling Stones" (Terry, Moser/May 1); "The Runt" (Terry, Moser/May 15); "The Hot Spell" (with Puddy the Pup/Davis, Gordon/July 10); "Puddy the Pup and the Gypsies" (with Puddy the Pup/July 24); "Farmer Al Falfa's Prize Package" (with Kiko the Kangaroo/July 31); "The Health Farm" (Davis, Gordon/Sept. 4); and "Farmer Al Falfa's Twentieth Anniversary" (Davis, Gordon/Nov. 27).

1937: "The Tin Can Tourist" (Davis, Gordon/Jan. 22); "The Big Game Hunt" (Davis, Gordon/Feb. 19); "Flying South" (Davis, Gordon/Mar. 19); "The Mechanical Cow" (Zander/June 25); "Trailer Life" (Aug. 20); "A Close

Shave" (with Ozzie/Davis/Oct. 1); and "The Dancing Bear" (Oct. 15).

◉ FELIX THE CAT

Clever feline Felix the Cat briefly appeared in a series of sound cartoons, which were accompanied by a musical soundtrack, in which he acted in pantomime in stories that were throwbacks to the silent days of filmmaking. The cartoons were produced as part of Burt Gillett's *Rainbow Parades*. *Directed by Burt Gillett and Tom Palmer. Black-and-white. A Van Beuren Production released through RKO Radio Pictures.*

1936: "Felix the Cat and the Goose That Laid the Golden Eggs" (Feb. 7); "Neptune Nonsense" (Mar. 20); and "Bold King Cole" (May 29).

◉ FIGARO

This series starred the mischief-making cat Figaro, formerly of Walt Disney's *Pinocchio* (1940), in his eternal quest to catch the ever-elusive Cleo the goldfish who likewise debuted in the feature-film classic. Figaro also appeared separately as a supporting player in Pluto cartoons. *Directed by Jack Kinney and Charles Nichols. Technicolor. A Walt Disney Production released through RKO-Radio Pictures.*

Voices
Figaro: Clarence Nash, Kate-Ellen Murtagh

1943: "Figaro and Cleo" (Kinney/Oct. 15).

1946: "Bath Day" (Nichols/Oct. 11).

1947: "Figaro and Frankie" (Nichols/May 30).

◉ FLIPPY

The "chase" formula, so popular in *Terrytoons* and MGM's *Tom and Jerry*, was the basis of this series that revolved around the adventures of a thin yellow canary, Flippy, who is chased by an adversarial cat, Flop. That's until Sam the Dog, the neighborhood watchdog, intervenes. Flippy in some ways resembles Warner Bros.' Tweety bird. The series later inspired its own comic book series. *Directed by Howard Swift and Bob Wickersham. Technicolor. A Columbia Pictures release.*

1945: "Dog, Cat and Canary" (Swift/Jan. 5/*Color Rhapsody*).

1946: "Cagey Bird" (Swift/July 18); and "Silent Treatment" (Wickersham/Sept. 19).

1947: "Big House Blues" (Swift/Mar. 6/*Color Rhapsody*).

◉ FLIP THE FROG

The star of Ub Iwerks's first Celebrity Pictures animated series, this web-footed amphibian was featured in 38 car-

toon adventures released by Metro-Goldwyn-Mayer. Each film had a ragtime musical soundtrack and other vocal effects, as none of the characters in the films ever talked.

Originally to be called Tony the Frog, Flip's debut was in the 1930 cartoon "Fiddlesticks," made in two-strip Cinecolor two years before Walt Disney produced the first Technicolor short, "Flowers and Trees." With the aid of a small staff, Iwerks animated most of the cartoons himself.

After two cartoons, Flip's character was modified at the request of Iwerks's producer Pat Powers, making him "less froglike" with more human qualities. (Taller, he was dressed in plaid pants, white shoes and hand mittens.) The changes to his character were apparent in the 1930 release "The Village Barber," which enabled Powers to sell the series to MGM for distribution.

Most cartoons in the series, except for those filmed in two-strip Cinecolor, cost an average of $7,000 to produce and proved extremely profitable. "The Village Barber," for example, grossed $30,000 in ticket receipts in the United States alone, and the series overall grossed $304,666.61, of which Pat Powers made $110,000 in profit.

The *Flip the Frog* series was MGM's first animated venture and lasted four years. Carl Stalling, who first scored Walt Disney's *Silly Symphony* series and later Warner Bros.' *Merrie Melodies* and *Looney Tunes*, served as the series' musical director. Most cartoons were produced in black-and-white with a few filmed in the then-experimental Cinecolor. *Directed by Ub Iwerks. A Celebrity Pictures Production released through Metro-Goldwyn-Mayer. (Copyright dates are marked by ©.)*

1930: "Fiddlesticks" (Aug. 16/Cinecolor); "Flying Fists" (Sept. 6); "The Village Barber" (Sept. 27); "Little Orphan Willie"; "Cuckoo Murder Case" (Oct. 18); and "Puddle Pranks."

Flip the Frog gets "reeled in" in a scene from UB Iwerks's "Nurse Maid" (1932). (COURTESY: BLACKHAWK FILMS)

1931: "The Village Smithie" (Jan. 31); "The Soup Song" (Jan. 31); "Laughing Gas" (Mar. 14); "Ragtime Romeo" (May 2); "The New Car" (July 25); "Movie Mad" (Aug. 29); "The Village Specialist" (Sept. 12); "Jail Birds" (Sept. 26); "Africa Squeaks" (Oct. 17); and "Spooks" (Dec. 21).

1932: "The Milkman" (Feb. 20); "Fire! Fire!" (Mar. 5); "What a Life" (Mar. 26); "Puppy Love" (Apr. 30); "School Days" (May 14); "Bully" (June 18); "The Office Boy" (July 16); "Room Runners" (Aug. 13); "Stormy Seas" (Aug. 22); "Circus" (Aug. 27); "The Goal Rush" (© Oct. 3); "Phoney Express" (© Oct. 27); "The Music Lesson" (Oct. 29); "Nurse Maid" (Nov. 26), and "Funny Face" (Dec. 24).

1933: "Cuckoo the Magician" (Jan. 21); "Flip's Lunch Room" (Apr. 3); "Techno-Cracked" (May 8/Cinecolor); "Bulloney" (May 30); "Chinaman's Chance" (June 24); "Pale-Face" (Aug. 12); and "Soda Squirt" (Oct. 12).

⊚ FOGHORN LEGHORN

A loudmouthed Southern rooster known for his boisterous babblings on ("Pay attention, boy . . . now listen here!"), Foghorn Leghorn was another popular character in Warner Bros.' stable of cartoon stars. The braggart was first featured in Warner's 1946 release "Walky Talky Hawky," appearing opposite a precocious chicken hawk named Henery Hawk, whose single greatest ambition is to "catch chickens."

Surprisingly, the cartoon won an Academy Award nomination for "Best Short Subject" that year. It also won Foghorn a permanent spot on the Warner's cartoon roster; he was cast in his own starring cartoon series for the next 16 years.

Warner's animator Robert McKimson actually modeled Foghorn, originally considered a parody of the Senator Claghorn character from Fred Allen's radio show, after a sheriff character from an earlier radio program, *Blue Monday Jamboree*. It was from this broadcast that McKimson adapted many of Foghorn's distinctive traits, among them his overstated repartee and other standard lines for which he became famous.

Mel Blanc, the man of 1,000 cartoon voices, was the voice of Foghorn Leghorn. Blanc derived the idea for the character's voice from a 1928 vaudeville show he attended as a teenager. "When I was just a youngster, I had seen a vaudeville act with this hard-of-hearing sheriff. And the fellow would say, 'Say! P-pay attenshun. I'm talkin' to ya, boy. Don't ya know what I'm ah talkin' about.' I thought, 'Gee, this might make a good character if I made a big Southern rooster out of him.' And that's how I happened to get the voice of Foghorn Leghorn," Blanc recalled prior to his death in 1989.

Since pairing Henery Hawk with Foghorn was so successful the first time around, McKimson made the character a regular in the series, alternating him in a supporting role with Br'er Dog, a grumpy backyard dog, as Foghorn's chief nemesis. For romantic interest, Miss Prissy, the husband-seeking hen, was later featured in several films, along with her son, Egghead Jr. (also known as "Junior" in earlier adventures), a bookwormish child prodigy whose intelligence was vastly superior to that of Foghorn's.

In the 1990s Foghorn returned to the screen, first in a minor role in a new Bugs Bunny cartoon: "Carrotblanca" (1995), which pokes fun at the 1942 Warner Bros.' classic *Casablanca* (with Greg Burson as the voice of Foghorn). Then in 1997 Foghorn returned starred in his first new cartoon short in 34 years, entitled "Pullet Surprise," produced by legendary animator Chuck Jones and directed by Darrel Van Citters. Foghorn's nemesis was the slightly impaired Pete Puma (as voiced by Stan Freberg); Frank Gorshin did the voice of Foghorn. The cartoon was the fifth new cartoon short produced by Jones, who had formed a new animation unit on the Warner Bros. lot three years earlier. The short opened with the full-length animated feature *Cats Don't Dance*. Foghorn made his feature-film debut a year earlier in the Michael Jordan–Bugs Bunny hit, *Space Jam*. *Directed by Robert McKimson, Art Davis, Douglas McCarthy and Darrel Van Citters. Technicolor. A Warner Bros. release.*

Voices

Foghorn Leghorn: Mel Blanc, Greg Burson, Frank Gorshin; **Henery Hawk:** Mel Blanc; **Miss Prissy:** Mel Blanc, Bea Benadaret, June Foray, Julie Bennett

Merrie Melodies

1946: "Walky Talky Hawky" (with Henery Hawk/McKimson/Aug. 31/A.A. nominee).

1948: "The Foghorn Leghorn" (with Henery Hawk/McKimson/Oct. 9).

1950: "A Fractured Leghorn" (McKimson/Sept. 16).

1951: "Leghorn Swoggled" (with Henery Hawk/McKimson/July 28).

1952: "The Egg-Cited Rooster" (with Henery Hawk/McKimson/Oct. 4).

1955: "Feather Dusted" (with Prissy, Junior/McKimson/Jan. 15).

1957: "Fox Terror" (McKimson/May 11).

1958: "Feather Bluster" (McKimson/May 10); and "Weasel While You Work" (McKimson/Aug. 6).

1960: "Crockett-Doodle-Doo" (with Egghead Jr./McKimson/June 25); and "The Dixie Fryer" (McKimson/Sept. 24).

1961: "Strangled Eggs" (with Henery Hawk/McKimson/Mar. 18).

1962: "Mother Was a Rooster" (McKimson/Oct. 20).

1963: "Banty Raids" (McKimson/June 29).

Looney Tunes

1947: "Crowing Pains" (with Sylvester, Henery Hawk/McKimson/July 12).

1948: "The Rattled Rooster" (Davis/June 26).

1950: "The Leghorn Blows at Midnight" (with Henery Hawk/McKimson/May 6).

1951: "Lovelorn Leghorn" (with Miss Prissy/McKimson/Sept. 8).

1952: "Sock-a-Doodle Doo" (McKimson/May 10).

1954: "Little Boy Boo" (with Widow Hen, Junior/McKimson/June 5).

1955: "All Fowled Up" (with Henery Hawk/McKimson/Feb. 19).

1956: "The High and the Flighty" (with Daffy Duck/McKimson/Feb. 18).

1959: "A Broken Leghorn" (McKimson/Sept. 26).

1962: "The Slick Chick" (with Widow Hen, Junior/McKimson/July 21).

1995: "Carrotblanca" (with Bugs Bunny, Daffy Duck, Yosemite Sam, Sylvester, Tweety, Pepe Le Pew, Penelope/McCarthy/Aug. 25).

Chuck Jones Film Production (released by Warner Bros. Family Entertainment)

1997: "Pullet Surprise" (with Pete Puma/Van Citters/Mar. 26/produced by Chuck Jones).

◎ FOOFLE

Gene Deitch, the creative director for *Terrytoons* in the late 1950s, created this hapless, voiceless character who pantomimed his way through one failure after another. Deitch derived the concept for Foofle from another one of his sadsack creations, Nudnik, who appeared in 13 cartoons for Paramount. *Directed by Dave Tendlar. Technicolor and CinemaScope. A Terrytoons Production released through 20th Century-Fox.*

1959: "Foofle's Train Ride" (May).

1960: "Foofle's Picnic" (Mar./CinemaScope); and "The Wayward Hat" (July/CinemaScope).

◎ FOOLISH FABLES

Various spoofs of popular children's fables had been done before. That same formula inspired this short-lived series by

Walter Lantz Production, which faltered after only two cartoons. *Directed by Paul J. Smith. Technicolor. Voices credits unknown. A Walter Lantz Production released through Universal Pictures.*

1953: "The Mouse and the Lion" (May 11); and "The Flying Turtle" (June 29).

◎ FOX AND THE CROW

The slick-talking black crow and gluttonous bow-tied fox were the most flamboyant Columbia Pictures cartoon characters to appear on movie screens. The brainchild of director Frank Tashlin, who wrote and directed the first cartoon, "The Fox and the Grapes" (1941), the characters' wild pursuits of each other served as inspiration for Chuck Jones's blackout-style humor (a series of gags joined together by one common theme) in his Road Runner and Coyote series for Warner Bros. From 1941 through most of 1943, they initially starred in seven *Color Rhapsodies* before they were featured in their own series, beginning with 1943's "Room and Bored."

Charles Mintz initially produced the series, with Dave Fleischer and Ray Katz succeeding him as the series producer.

When Columbia Pictures closed its cartoon department, United Productions of America (UPA) picked up the series and continued its production, with Steve Bosustow serving as producer. The characters received two Academy Award nominations: 1948's "Robin Hoodlum," the first *Fox and the Crow* cartoon for UPA, and 1949's "The Magic Fluke." *Series directors were Bob Wickersham, Frank Tashlin, Howard Swift and John Hubley. Technicolor. A Columbia Pictures and UPA Productions release.*

Voices
Fox: Frank Graham; **Crow:** Paul Frees

Columbia Pictures

1941: "The Fox and the Grapes" (Tashlin/Dec. 5/Color Rhapsody).

1942: "Woodman Spare That Tree" (Wickersham/July 2/*Color Rhapsody*); and "Toll Bridge Troubles" (Wickersham/Nov. 27/*Color Rhapsody*).

1943: "Slay It with Flowers" (Wickersham/Jan. 8/*Color Rhapsody*); "Plenty Below Zero" (Wickersham/May 14/Color Rhapsody); "Tree for Two" (Wickersham/June 21); "A Hunting We Won't Go" (Wickersham/Aug. 23/*Color Rhapsody*); "Room and Bored" (Wickersham/Sept. 30/first *Fox and the Crow* cartoon); and "Way Down Yonder in the Corn" (Wickersham/Nov. 25).

1944: "The Dream Kids" (Wickersham/Jan. 5/last cartoon produced by Fleischer); "Mr. Moocher" (Wickersham/Sept. 8); "Be Patient, Patient" (Wickersham/Oct. 27); and "The Egg Yegg" (Wickersham/Dec. 8).

1945: "Ku-Kunuts" (Wickersham/Mar. 30); "Treasure Jest" (Wickersham/Aug. 30); and "Phoney Baloney" (Wickersham/Sept. 13).

1946: "Foxey Flatfoots" (Wickersham/Apr. 11); "Unsure Runts" (Swift/May 16); and "Mysto Fox" (Wickersham/Aug. 29).

1947: "Tooth or Consequences" (Swift/June 5/Phantasy cartoon).

UPA Productions

1948: "Robin Hoodlum" (Hubley/Dec. 23/produced by Steve Bosustow/A.A. nominee).

1949: "The Magic Fluke" (Hubley/Mar. 27/produced by Steve Bosustow/A.A. nominee).

1950: "Punchy De Leon" (Hubley/Jan. 12/Jolly Frolics).

◎ FOXY

Foxy, who resembled Mickey Mouse with pointy ears and a bushy tail, was an early *Merrie Melodies* star who headlined three series entries in 1931. The character was featured in episodes shaped around popular songs of the day. Frank Marsales, who was Warner's first musical director for animation, directed Foxy's screen debut. *Black-and-white. Voice credits unknown. A Warner Bros. release.*

1931: "Lady Play Your Mandolin" (Marsales/Sept.); "Smile, Darn Ya, Smile" (Sept. 5); and "One More Time" (Oct. 3).

◎ FRACTURED FABLES

A series of outlandish tall tales directed by Ralph Bakshi, of *Lord of the Rings* and *Fritz the Cat* fame, and James "Shamus" Culhane. Bakshi also served as executive producer of the series, beginning with 1967's "The Fuz." *Technicolor. A Famous Studios Production released through Paramount Pictures.*

1967: "My Daddy the Astronaut" (Culhane/Apr./released in conjunction with *2001: A Space Odyssey*); "The Stuck-Up Wolf" (Culhane/Sept.); "The Stubborn Cowboy" (Culhane/Oct.); "The Fuz" (Bakshi/Dec.); "The Mini-Squirts" (Bakshi/Dec.); and "Mouse Trek" (Bakshi/Dec. 31).

◎ GABBY

Gabby first appeared as a town crier in the animated feature *Gulliver's Travels* (1939), produced by Max Fleischer. After his film debut, he starred in his own cartoon series. Stories were shaped around Gabby's inability to do anything right. He tried everything, from diapering a baby to cleaning a castle, with predictably disastrous results.

Gabby, a character in the Max Fleischer feature Gulliver's Travels *(1939), starred in his own cartoon series shaped around his incompetence in doing anything right.* (COURTESY: REPUBLIC PICTURES)

Pinto Colvig, the original voice of Walt Disney's Goofy, provided the voice of Gabby. *Directed by Dave Fleischer. Technicolor. A Fleischer Studios Production released through Paramount Pictures.*

Voices
Gabby: Pinto Colvig

1940: "King for a Day" (Oct. 18); and "The Constable" (Nov. 15).

1941: "All's Well" (Jan. 17); "Two for the Zoo" (Feb. 21); "Swing Cleaning" (Apr. 11); "Fire Cheese" (June 20); "Gabby Goes Fishing" (July 18); and "It's a Hap-Hap-Happy Day" (Aug. 15).

◎ GANDY GOOSE

Inspired by comedian Ed Wynn's fluttery voice and mannerisms, sweet-natured Gandy was another *Terrytoons* attempt at copying the success of a noted personality in animated form. Unlike other attempts, this character proved to be a major disappointment after it was first introduced to filmgoers in 1938's "Gandy the Goose." There was no real chemistry or magic to the early films.

Rather than scrap Gandy altogether, the studio resurrected a one-shot cat character, Sourpuss, from an earlier cartoon, "The Owl and the Pussycat," to pair with Gandy in future escapades. The teaming saved the series, with the cat's offbeat personality, which was reminiscent of comedian Jimmy Durante, sparking more interest from theater audiences. The series became so successful that studio animators repeated the Gandy-Sourpuss formula for 10 years until the series ended in 1955.

Several *Terrytoons* veterans were responsible for directing the series. They included John Foster, Eddie Donnelly, Connie Rasinski, Volney White and Mannie Davis. *Black-and-white. Technicolor. A Terrytoons Production released through 20th Century-Fox.*

Voices
Gandy/Sourpuss: Arthur Kay

(The following cartoons were all produced (in black-and-white unless noted otherwise.)

1938: "Gandy the Goose" (Foster/Mar. 4); "Goose Flies High" (Foster/Sept. 9); "Doomsday" (Rasinski/Dec. 16); and "The Frame-Up" (Rasinski/Dec. 30).

1939: "G-Man Jitters" (Donnelly/Mar. 10); "A Bully Romance" (Donnelly/June 16); Barnyard Baseball" (Davis/July 14); "Hook, Line and Sinker" (Donnelly/Sept. 8/first Technicolor); and "The Hitchhiker" (Donnelly/Dec. 1).

1940: "It Must Be Love" (Rasinski/Apr. 5); and "The Magic Pencil" (White/Nov. 15).

1941: "Fishing Made Easy" (Donnelly/Feb. 21); "The Home Guard" (Davis/Mar. 7/Technicolor); "The One Man Navy" (Davis/Sept. 5/Technicolor); "Slap Happy Hunters" (Donnelly/Oct. 31/Technicolor); and "Flying Fever" (Davis/Dec. 26).

1942: "Sham Battle Shenanigans" (Rasinski/Mar. 20/Technicolor); "The Night" (Apr. 17); "Lights Out" (Donnelly/Apr. 17/Technicolor); "Tricky Business" (Donnelly/May 1); "The Outpost" (Davis/July 10); "Tire Trouble" (Donnelly/July 24); and "Night Life in the Army" (Davis/Oct. 12/Technicolor).

(The following cartoons were all produced in Technicolor.)

1943: "Camouflage" (Donnelly/Aug. 27); "Somewhere In Egypt" (Davis/Sept. 17); and "Aladdin's Lamp" (Donnelly/Oct. 22).

1944: "The Frog and the Princess" (Donnelly/Apr. 7); "The Ghost Town" (Davis/Sept. 22); and "Gandy's Dream Girl" (Davis/Dec. 8).

1945: "Post War Inventions" (Rasinski/Mar. 23); "Fisherman's Luck" (Donnelly/Mar. 23); "Mother Goose Nightmare" (Rasinski/May 4); "Aesop Fable: The Mosquito" (Davis/June 29); "Who's Who in the Jungle" (Donnelly/Oct. 19); and "The Exterminator" (Donnelly/Nov. 23).

1946: "Fortune Hunters" (Rasinski/Feb. 8); "It's All in the Stars" (Rasinski/Apr. 12); "The Golden Hen" (Davis/May 24); and "Peace-Time Football" (Davis/July 19).

1947: "Mexican Baseball" (Davis/Mar. 14).

1948: "Gandy Goose and the Chipper Chipmunk" (Davis/Mar. 9).

1949: "Dingbat Land" (with Sourpuss/Feb.); "The Covered Pushcart" (with Sourpuss/Davis/Aug. 26); and "Comic Book Land" (Davis/Dec. 23).

1950: "Dream Walking" (Rasinski/June 9); and "Wide Open Spaces" (Donnelly/Nov. 1).

1951: "Songs of Erin" (Rasinski/Feb. 25); and "Spring Fever" (Davis/Mar. 18).

1955: "Barnyard Actor" (Rasinski/Jan. 25).

◉ GASTON LE CRAYON

Appearing in several new *Terrytoons* series launched in the late 1950s, this talented French artist made his drawings come to life in assorted misadventures. Screen debut: "Gaston Is Here," released in CinemaScope in 1957. *Directed by Connie Rasinksi and Dave Tendlar. Technicolor. CinemaScope. A Terrytoons Production released through 20th Century-Fox.*

1957: "Gaston Is Here" (Rasinski/May).

1958: "Gaston's Baby" (Rasinski/Mar.); "Gaston, Go Home" (Rasinski/May); and "Gaston's Easel Life" (Tendlar/Oct.).

1959: "Gaston's Mama Lisa" (Rasinski/June).

◉ GEORGE AND JUNIOR

Parodying characters George and Lenny from John Steinbeck's novel *Of Mice and Men*, this short-lived series featured stupid, overweight George and his clever straight man bear Junior. They were an uproarious and destructive pair, fashioned by Tex Avery, who also directed the series. *Technicolor. A Metro-Goldwyn-Mayer release.*

Voices
George: Frank Graham; **Junior:** Tex Avery

1946: "Henpecked Hoboes" (Avery/Oct. 26).

1947: "Hound Hunters" (Avery/Apr. 12); and "Red Hot Rangers" (Avery/May 31).

1948: "Half-Pint Pygmy" (Avery/Aug. 7).

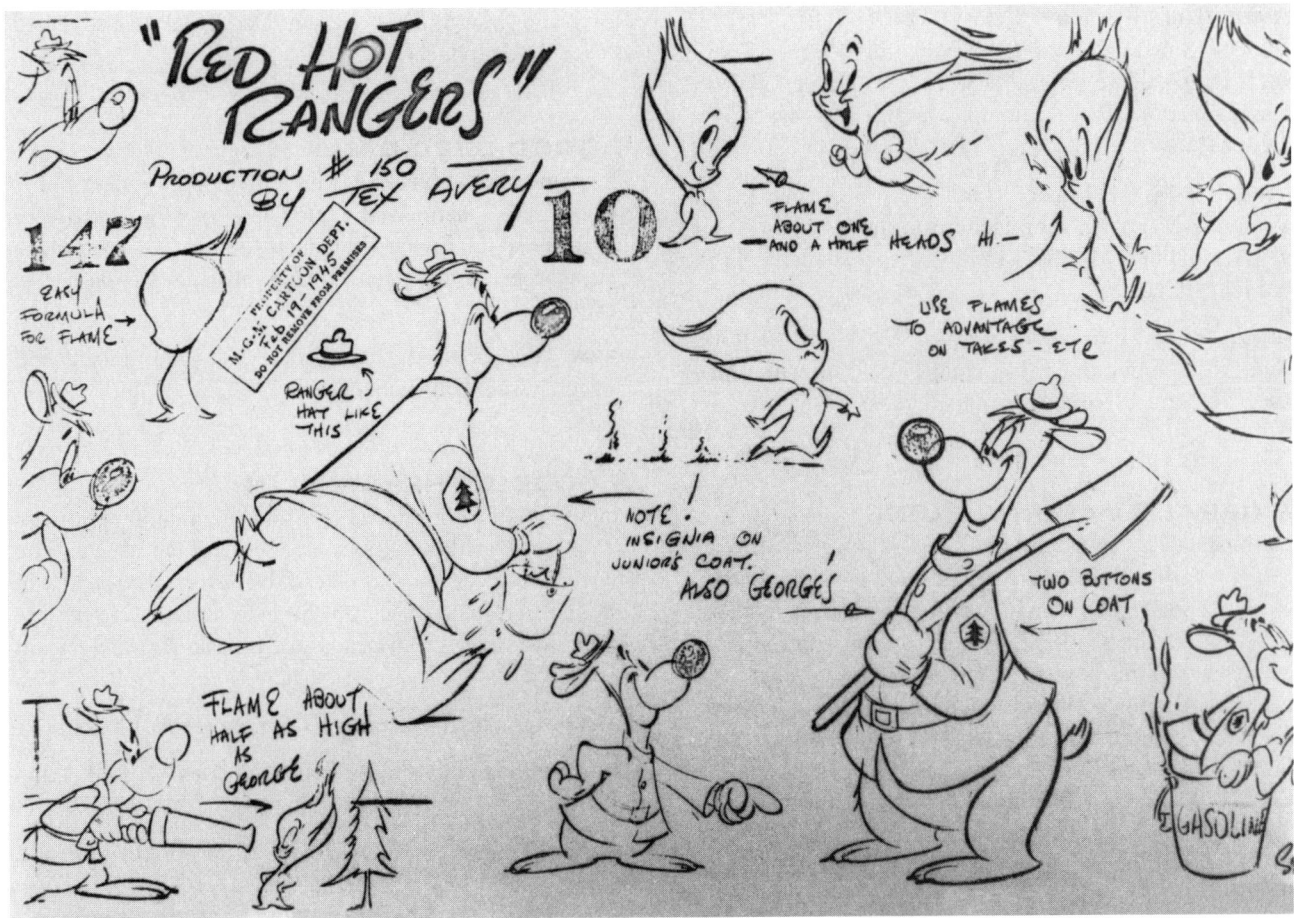

George and Junior, the Abbott and Costello of cartoons, starred in riotous misadventures directed by Tex Avery for MGM. © Turner Entertainment (COURTESY: MARK KAUSLER)

◎ GEORGE PAL PUPPETOONS

Director George Pal, noted for producing such science-fiction classics as *War of the Worlds* and *When Worlds Collide*, created this widely acclaimed stop-action animation series starring the wide-eyed little black boy Jasper and his constant companions, Professor Scarecrow and Black Crow, in Huckleberry Finn–like tales shaped around black folklore.

The characters, which were actually wooden puppets, had flexible limbs that enabled them to move realistically. Pal and his 45 staff members, whom he credits for the series' success, diligently prepared background sets and other movable miniatures before filming each eight-minute one-reel short. A typical production cost $25,000 to create.

According to Pal, "We had all these creative people bouncing ideas around. We were our own masters. We didn't have to get this approval and that approval, the way you do in feature motion pictures. All I had to do was pick up the phone to Paramount and tell them we had an idea, and they said, 'Go ahead.'"

The series won five Academy Award nominations in the Best Short Subject category and critical acclaim from film industry officials, who were amazed by the dexterity of Pal's creations. *Directed by George Pal. Narration by Rex Ingram and Victor Jory. Technicolor. A Paramount Pictures release.*

1941: "Western Daze" (Jan. 7/*Madcap Model* cartoon); "Dipsy Gypsy" (Apr. 4); "Hoola Boola" (June 27); "The Gay Knighties" (Aug. 22); and "Rhythm in the Ranks" (Dec. 26/A.A. nominee).

1942: "Jasper and the Watermelons" (Feb. 26/*Madcap Model* cartoon); "Sky Princess" (Mar. 27); and "Jasper and the Haunted House" (Oct. 23).

1943: "Jasper and the Choo-Choo" (Jan. 1/*Madcap Model* cartoon); "Tulips Shall Grow" (Jan. 26/A.A. nominee); "Bravo Mr. Strauss" (Feb. 26); "The 500 Hats of Bartholomew Cubbins" (Apr. 30/A.A. nominee); "Mr. Strauss Takes a Walk" (May 8); "Jasper's Music Lesson" (May 21); "The Truck Goes Fishing" (Oct. 8); and "Good Night Rusty" (Dec. 3).

1944: "Package for Jasper" (Jan. 28); "Say, Ah Jasper" (Mar. 10); "And to Think I Saw It on Mulberry Street"; "Jasper Goes Hunting" (July 28); "Jasper's Paradise" (Oct. 13); and "Two-Gun Rusty" (Dec. 1).

1945: "Hot Lisp Jasper" (Jan. 5); "Jasper Tell" (Mar. 23); "Jasper's Minstrels" (May 25); "A Hatful of Dreams" (July 6); "Jasper's Close Shave" (Sept. 28); "Jasper and the Beanstalk" (Oct. 9/A.A. nominee); and "My Man Jasper" (Dec. 14).

1946: "Olio for Jasper" (Jan. 25); "Together in the Weather" (Mar. 22); "John Henry and the Inky Poo" (Sept. 6/A.A. nominee); "Jasper's Derby" (Sept. 20); and "Jasper in a Jam" (Oct. 18).

1947: "Shoe Shine Jasper" (Feb. 28); "Wilbur the Lion" (Apr. 18); "Tubby the Tuba" (July 11); "Date with Duke" (Oct. 31); and "Rhapsody in Wood" (Dec. 29).

◎ GERALD McBOING BOING

Based on a Dr. Seuss children's record, Gerald McBoing Boing, a curly-topped, mute boy, uttered only the sound of "Boing Boing" when communicating with his parents and friends. Introduced in 1951, the first cartoon, titled after the character, was released to theaters under the *Jolly Frolics* series produced by United Productions of America (UPA). The film garnered an Academy Award for Best Short Subject of the year.

Three years later the series was distributed under the *Gerald McBoing Boing* name, with the final series release, "Gerald McBoing Boing on the Planet Moo" (1956), winning the series' second Oscar in five years. *Directed by Bob Cannon. Narrated by Hal Peary. Technicolor. A UPA Productions release through Columbia Pictures.*

1951: "Gerald McBoing Boing" (Cannon/Jan. 25/A.A. winner/*Jolly Frolics*).

1953: "Gerald McBoing Boing's Symphony" (Cannon/July 15/*Jolly Frolics*).

1954: "How Now Boing Boing" (Cannon/Sept. 9).

1956: "Gerald McBoing Boing on the Planet Moo" (Cannon/Feb. 9/A.A. winner).

◎ GO-GO TOONS

One of Famous Studios' last cartoon series, *Go-Go Toons* features a wide assortment of outlandish cartoon tales, each starring various characters. *Directed by Ralph Bakshi, James "Shamus" Culhane and Chuck Harriton. Technicolor. A Famous Studios Production released through Paramount Pictures.*

1967: "The Space Squid" (Culhane/Jan.); "The Squaw-Path" (Culhane/May); "The Plumber" (Culhane/May); "A Bridge Grows in Brooklyln" (Harriton/Oct.); "The Opera Caper" (Culhane. Bakshi/Nov. 1/Culhane also served as executive producer); "Keep the Cool, Baby" (Harriton/

Nov.); and "Marvin Digs" (Bakshi/Dec. 1/Bakshi also served as executive producer).

◎ GOOD DEED DAILY

The name of this character, whose lifeblood was performing "good deeds," defined the plot line of this short-lived *Terrytoons* series. *Directed by Connie Rasinski. Technicolor and CinemaScope. A Terrytoons Production released through 20th Century-Fox.*

1956: "Scouts to the Rescue" (Apr.); and "Cloak and Stagger" (Aug./CinemaScope).

◎ GOODIE THE GREMLIN

Famous Studios introduced this lovable gremlin, who tries fitting into Earthly situations, in a series of *Noveltoons*. The character's career was short-lived, however; he appeared in only five cartoons. *Directed by Seymour Kneitel. Technicolor. A Famous Studios Production released through Paramount Pictures.*

1961: "Goodie the Gremlin" (Apr./*Noveltoon*).

1962: "Good and Guilty" (Feb./*Noveltoon*); and "Yule Laff" (Kneitel/Oct./*Noveltoon*).

1963: "Goodie's Good Deed" (Nov./*Modern Madcap*); and "Hiccup Hound" (Nov./*Noveltoon*).

◎ GOOFY

A cross between Mortimer Snerd and Snuffy Smith, Walt Disney's hayseed Goofy lit up the screen with his apologetic laugh, "Uh-hyulk, uh-hyulk . . . yep . . . uh-hyulk," in a series of misadventures that played up his silly but harmless nature.

Affectionately nicknamed the "Goof" by studio animators, Goofy first appeared in the early 1930s as a stringbean character, Dippy Dawg, in a Disney cartoon adventure. Later renamed, his actual personality never came into focus until studio animator Art Babbitt molded Goofy into "a composite of an everlasting optimist, a gullible Good Samaritan, a halfwit and a hick with a philosophy of the barber shop variety," who seldom completes his objectives or what he has started.

Babbitt, who first worked for Paul Terry in New York in 1932, became the studio expert at animating Goofy, with director Jack Kinney, who directed the most memorable cartoons in the series, using the character to good measure. Kinney's "How to Play Football" (1944), one in a series of classic Goofy sports "how-tos," received the series' only Academy Award nomination.

In 1992 Goofy celebrated his 60th birthday by starring in his own daily cartoon series, *Goof Troop*, which premiered in September of that year as part of The Disney Afternoon, a two-hour weekday syndicated cartoon block. The series was the first Disney cartoon series to feature a member of the "Classic 5" characters as its star; Mickey Mouse, Minnie Mouse, Donald Duck and Pluto are the others. The program centered on the slapstick adventures of Goofy and his son, Max. Three years later Goofy starred opposite Max in his first full-length animated feature, *A Goofy Movie. Series directors were Dick Huemer, Jack Kinney, Jack Hannah, Bob Carlson, Clyde Geronimi, Les Clark and Woolie Reitherman. Technicolor. A Walt Disney Production released through RKO-Radio Pictures and later Buena Vista.*

Voices
Goofy: Pinto Colvig (1931–39, 1944–67); George Johnson (1933–44); Bob Jackman (1950–51)

RKO-Radio Pictures releases

1939: "Goofy and Wilbur" (Huemer/Mar. 17).

1940: "Goofy's Glider" (Kinney/Nov. 22).

1941: "Baggage Buster" (Kinney/Apr. 18); "The Art of Skiing" (Kinney/Nov. 14); and "The Art of Self Defense" (Kinney/Dec. 26).

1942: "How to Play Baseball" (Kinney/Sept. 4); "The Olympic Champ" (Kinney/Oct. 9); "How to Swim" (Kinney/Oct. 23); and "How to Fish" (Kinney/Dec. 4).

1943: "Victory Vehicles" (with Pluto/Kinney/July 30).

1944: "How to be a Sailor" (Kinney/Jan. 28); "How to Play Golf" (Kinney/Mar. 10); and "How to Play Football" (Kinney/Sept. 15/A.A. nominee).

1945: "Tiger Trouble" (Kinney/Jan. 5); "African Diary" (Kinney/Apr. 20); "Californy 'er Bust" (Kinney/July 15); and "Hockey Homicide" (Kinney/Sept. 21).

1946: "A Knight for a Day" (Hannah/Mar. 8); and "Double Dribble" (Hannah/Dec. 20).

1947: "Crazy with the Heat" (with Donald Duck/Carlson/Aug. 1); and "Foul Hunting" (Hannah/Oct. 31)

1948: "They're Off" (Hannah/Jan. 23); and "The Big Wash" (Geronimi/Feb. 6).

1949: "Tennis Racquet" (Kinney/Aug. 26); and "Goofy Gymnastics" (Kinney/Sept. 23).

1950: "How to Ride a Horse" (Kinney/Feb. 24/part of *The Reluctant Dragon* feature); "Motor Mania" (Kinney/June 30); and "Hold That Pose" (Kinney/Nov. 3).

1951: "Lion Down" (Kinney/Jan. 5); "Home Made Home" (Kinney/Mar. 23); "Cold War" (Kinney/Apr. 27); "Tomorrow We Diet" (Kinney/June 29); "Get Rich Quick"

(Kinney/Aug. 31); "Fathers Are People" (Kinney/Oct. 21); and "No Smoking" (Kinney/Nov. 23).

1952: "Father's Lion" (Kinney/Jan. 4); "Hello, Aloha" (Kinney/Feb. 29); "Man's Best Friend" (Kinney/Apr. 4); "Two-Gun Goofy" (Kinney/May 16); "Teachers Are People" (Kinney/June 27); "Two Weeks Vacation" (Kinney/Oct. 31); and "How to Be a Detective" (Kinney/Dec. 12).

1953: "Father's Day Off" (Kinney/Mar. 28); "For Whom the Bulls Toil" (Kinney/May 9); "Father's Week End" (Kinney/June 20); "How to Dance" (Kinney/July 11); and "How to Sleep" (Kinney/Dec. 25).

1955: "El Gaucho Goofy" (Kinney/June 10/part of *Saludos Amigos*).

Buena Vista releases

1961: "Aquamania" (Reitherman/Dec. 20).

1965: "Freewayphobia No. 1" (Clark/Feb. 13); and "Goofy's Freeway Trouble" (Clark/Sept. 22).

◎ GOOFY GOPHERS
This pair of polite, swift-talking gophers vaguely resembled Walt Disney's popular Chip 'n' Dale characters, not only in voice but in facial and body features.

Introduced in a 1947 cartoon of the same name, Warner's director Bob Clampett designed the gophers, whose demeanor was modeled after two mild-mannered character actors of the time, Edward Everett Horton and Franklin Pangborn. (The gophers appeared earlier in a 1941 Warner's cartoon, "Gopher Goofy," but were not similar to Clampett's version.) Clampett wrote the story for the first cartoon, which was directed by Art Davis, Clampett's successor. Clampett left Warner's after completing the story to join Columbia Pictures' animation department.

The gophers' inquisitive ways landed them in a half-dozen cartoons. They were often cast in situations that enabled them to display exaggerated politeness towards one another to resolve their differences. The characters acquired the nicknames of "Mac and Tosh" when they later appeared on television's *The Bugs Bunny Show. Directors included Robert McKimson, Friz Freleng and Arthur Davis. Cinecolor. Technicolor. A Warner Bros. release.*

Voices
Mac: Mel Blanc; Tosh: Stan Freberg

Looney Tunes

1947: "Goofy Gophers" (with Bugs Bunny/Davis/Jan. 25).

1949: "A Ham in a Role" (McKimson/Dec. 31).

1951: "A Bone for a Bone" (Freleng/Apr. 7).

1955: "Lumber Jerks" (Freleng/June 25).

1958: "Gopher Broke" (McKimson/Nov. 15).

Merrie Melodies

1948: "Two Gophers from Texas" (Davis/Dec. 27/Cinecolor).

1954: "I Gopher You" (Freleng/Jan. 30).

1955: "Pests for Guests" (with Elmer Fudd/Freleng/Jan. 29).

◎ GOOPY GEER

Considered the first *Merrie Melodies* star, Goopy is a consummate performing dog—he sings, dances and plays the piano—who appeared in a number of music-and-dance shorts for Warner Bros. Unfortunately, Goopy's stardom was short-lived; he appeared in only three *Merrie Melodies* cartoons. *Directors unknown. Black-and-white. Voice credits unknown. A Warner Bros. release.*

1932: "Goopy Geer" (Apr. 16); "Moonlight for Two" (June 11); and "The Queen Was in the Parlor" (July 9).

◎ GRAN' POP MONKEY

This was one of animator Ub Iwerks's last cartoon series, a British-financed production produced by Cartoons Limited, an animation studio headed by Walt Disney veteran Paul Fennell. The short-lived series featured Gran' Pop, an artful and ancient ape created by noted British painter/illustrator Lawson Wood. Wood actually drew many of the key drawings for the series starring this cheerful old chimp in a handful of full-color cartoon shorts. *Produced and directed by Ub Iwerks. Technicolor. A Cartoons Limited Production released through Monogram Pictures.*

1940: "A Busy Day"; "Beauty Shoppe"; and "Baby Checkers."

◎ HALF PINT

This incidental *Terrytoons* star—a tiny Dumboesque elephant who everyone frowned on and yet managed to get into trouble—was unleashed onto the screen in two cartoon shorts, both produced in 1951. Walt Disney later did a similar version of the character in the 1960 Wolfgang Reitherman–directed short, "Goliath II." *Directed by Mannie Davis. Technicolor. Voice credits unknown. A Terrytoons Production released through 20th Century-Fox.*

1951: "Stage Struck" (Feb.); and "The Elephant Mouse" (May).

◎ HAM AND EX

This pair of troublesome pups was first featured as part of an ensemble cast in 1935's "I Haven't Got a Hat," in which Porky Pig made his first official appearance. The characters were later paired with Beans, a mischievous cat, in several *Looney Tunes* cartoons. *Directed by Friz Freleng and Jack King. Black-and-white. Voice credits unknown. A Warner Bros. release.*

Merrie Melodies

1935: "I Haven't Got a Hat" (with Porky Pig, Beans/Freleng/Mar. 9).

Looney Tunes

1936: "The Phantom Ship" (with Beans/King/Feb. 1); and "The Fire Alarm" (with Beans/King/Mar. 9).

◎ HAM AND HATTIE

In the last theatrical series of United Productions of America (UPA), Ham and Hattie made their screen debut

© 1958 UPA PICTURES, INC.

"HAM and HATTIE"

A NEW IDEA IN SHORTS
PRODUCED BY U.P.A. • RELEASED BY COLUMBIA

✻ nominated for Academy Award

UPA's last theatrical cartoon series, Ham and Hattie, *paired two separate cartoons shaped around the adventures of Ham Hamilton (left) and a girl named Hattie (right).* © UPA PRODUCTIONS in the 1948 release, "Trees and Jamaica Daddy," which received the studio's final Academy Award nomination. Each episode paired two three-and-a-half-minute cartoons, the first featuring the adventures of a little girl named Hattie, with the second shaped around the music of Hamilton Ham. *Directed by Lew Keller. Technicolor. A UPA Production released through Columbia Pictures.*

1958: "Trees and Jamaica Daddy" (Jan. 30/A.A. nominee); "Sailing and Village Band" (Feb. 27); and "Spring and Saganaki" (Oct. 16).

1959: "Picnics Are Fun and Dino's Serenade" (Jan. 16).

◎ HAPPY HARMONIES

Another attempt by former Disney animators Hugh Harman and Rudolf Ising to rival Walt Disney's "personality animation," this series of musical cartoons is similar to Disney's celebrated *Silly Symphony* series. This type of cartoon had been mastered before by both animators, who had directed Warner Bros.' *Merrie Melodies* series.

Happy Harmonies resulted after the pair left Warner Bros. in 1933. They formed their own production company in conjunction with MGM to produce cartoons for theatrical release by the studio. Metro developed its own cartoon studio four years later, spurred by Harman's and Ising's inability to keep their films under budget. Animated by MGM's new animation department, the series continued through 1938. *Directed by Rudolf Ising, Hugh Harman and William Hanna. Technicolor. A Metro-Goldwyn-Mayer release.*

1934: "The Discontented Canary" (Ising/Sept. 1); "The Old Pioneer" (Ising/Sept. 29); "A Tale of the Vienna Woods" (Harman/Oct. 27); and "Toyland Broadcast" (Ising/Dec. 22).

1935: "Hey, Hey Fever" (Harman/Jan. 9); "When the Cat's Away" (Ising/Feb. 16); "The Lost Chick" (Harman/Mar. 9); "The Calico Dragon" (Ising/Mar. 30); "The Good Little Monkeys" (Harman/Apr. 13); "The Chinese Nightmare" (Harman/Apr. 27); "Poor Little Me" (Harman/May 11); "Barnyard Babies" (Ising/May 25); "The Old Plantation" (Ising/Sept. 21); "Honeyland" (Ising/Oct. 19); "Alias St. Nick" (Ising/Nov. 16); and "Run, Sheep, Run" (Harman/Dec. 14).

1936: "Bottles" (Harman/Jan. 11); "The Early Bird and the Worm" (Ising/Feb. 8); "The Old Mill Pond" (Harman/Mar. 7); "Two Little Pups" (Ising/Apr. 4); "The Old House" (Harman/May 2); "Pups' Picnic" (Ising/May 30); "To Spring" (Hanna/June 4); "Little Cheezer" (Ising/July 11); and "The Pups' Christmas" (Ising/Dec. 12).

1937: "Swing Wedding" (Harman/Feb. 13); "The Hound and the Rabbit" (Ising/May 29); and "Wayward Pups" (Ising/July 10).

1938: "Pipe Dream" (Harman/Feb. 5); and "Little Bantamweight" (Ising/Mar. 12).

◎ HASHIMOTO

Created by Terrytoons animator Bob Kawahara, Japanese house mouse Hashimoto, a judo expert, was launched in the 1959 Terrytoons "Hashimoto San." The series pilot and subsequent adventures dealt with Hashimoto's reminiscences about the legends of his country, its romantic tradition and numerous other aspects of Japanese lore for American newspaper correspondent G.I. Joe. The cartoon shorts costarred his wife, Hanako, and his children, Yuriko and Saburo. A series of new cartoons were produced as part of NBC's *The Hector Heathcote Show* in the 1960s. *Directors were Bob Kuwahara, Dave Tendlar, Connie Rasinski, Mannie Davis and Art Bartsch. A Terrytoons Production released through 20th Century-Fox.*

Voices
Hashimoto/Hanako/Yuriko/Saburo: John Myhers

1959: "Hashimoto-San" (Kuwahara, Tendlar/Sept. 6).

1960: "House of Hashimoto" (Rasinski/Nov. 30).

1961: "Night Life in Tokyo" (Davis/Feb.); "So Sorry, Pussycat" (Bartsch/Mar.); "Son of Hashimoto" (Rasinski/Apr. 12); "Strange Companion" (Davis/May 12); and "Honorable Cat Story" (Rasinski/Nov.).

1962: "Honorable Family Problem" (Kuwahara/Mar. 30); "Loyal Royalty" (Kuwahara/May 18); and "Honorable Paint in the Neck" (Kuwahara/Aug. 22).

1963: "Tea House Mouse" (Kuwahara/Jan.); "Pearl Crazy" (Kuwahara/May); "Cherry Blossom Festival" (Kuwahara/June 17); and "Spooky-Yaki" (Kuwahara/Nov. 13).

◎ HECKLE AND JECKLE

Conniving, talking magpies Heckle and Jeckle were popular cartoon stars through the mid-1960s. Paul Terry, head of *Terrytoons*, inspired the characters' creation after dreaming of starting a series featuring cartoon twins or look-alikes. Terry's idea came to fruition in "The Talking Magpies," the first Heckle and Jeckle cartoon, released in 1946.

The comical pair were identical in appearance yet featured contrasting accents—Brooklyn and British respectively. The characters became Terry's answer to the bombastic stars of rival Warner Bros. and MGM, becoming his most popular characters next to Mighty Mouse. The cartoons revitalized the "chase" formula characteristic of the Terrytoons cartoons.

Heckle and Jeckle experienced a brief revival when their films were syndicated to television in the 1960s. *Directors were Mannie Davis, Connie Rasinski, Eddie Donnelly, Martin*

Paul Terry's talking magpies Heckle and Jeckle lasted 20 years on screen as mischief makers for Terrytoons. © Viacom International

B. Taras, Dave Tendlar, George Bakes and Al Chiarito. Technicolor. A Terrytoons Production released through 20th Century-Fox.

Voices

Heckle/Jeckle: Dayton Allen, Ned Sparks, Roy Halee

1946: "The Talking Magpies" (Davis/Jan. 4); and "The Uninvited Pest" (Rasinski/Nov. 29).

1947: "McDougal's Rest Farm" (Davis/Jan. 31); "Happy Go Lucky" (Rasinski/Feb. 28); "Cat Trouble" (Rasinski/Apr. 11); "The Intruders" (Donnelly/May 9); "Flying South" (Davis/Aug. 15); "Fishing by the Sea" (Rasinski/Sept. 19); "Super Salesman" (Donnelly/Oct. 24); and "Hitch Hikers" (Rasinski/Dec. 12).

1948: "Taming the Cat" (Rasinski/Jan.); "Sleepless Night" (Rasinski/June); "Magpie Madness" (Donnelly/July); "Out Again, In Again" (Rasinski/Nov. 1); "Free Enterprise" (Davis/Nov. 23); "Gooney Golfers" (Rasinski/Dec. 1); and "Power of Thought" (Donnelly/Dec. 31).

1949: "Lion Hunt" (Donnelly/Mar.); "Stowaways" (Rasinski/Apr.); "Happy Landing" (June); "Hula Lula Land" (Davis/July); and "Dancing Shoes" (Davis/Dec.).

1950: "Fox Hunt" (Rasinski/Feb. 17); "Merry Chase" (Davis/May); and "King Tut's Tomb" (Davis/Aug.).

1951: "Rival Romeos" (Donnelly/Jan.); "Bulldozing the Bull" (Donnelly/Mar. 11); "The Rain Makers" (Rasinski/June); "Steeple Jacks" (Rasinski/Sept.); and "Sno' Fun" (Donnelly/Nov.).

1952: "Movie Madness" (Rasinski/Jan.); "Seaside Adventure" (Davis/Feb.); "Off to the Opera" (Rasinski/May); "House Busters" (Rasinski/Aug.); and "Moose on the Loose" (Davis/Nov.).

1953: "Hair Cut-Ups" (Donnelly/Feb.); "Pill Peddlers" (Rasinski/Apr.); "Ten Pin Terrors" (Rasinski/June); "Bargain Daze" (Davis/Aug.); and "Log Rollers" (Davis/Nov.).

1954: "Blind Date" (Donnelly/Feb.); "Satisfied Customers" (Rasinski/May); and "Blue Plate Symphony" (Rasinski/Oct. 29.).

1956: "Miami Maniacs" (Rasinski/Feb.).

1957: "Pirate's Gold" (Donnelly/Jan.).

1959: "Wild Life" (Taras/Sept.).

1960: "Thousand Smile Checkup" (Taras/Jan.); "Mint Men" (Tendlar/June 23); "Trapeze Please" (Rasinski/June 12); "Deep Sea Doddle" (Tendlar/Sept. 16); and "Stunt Men" (Taras/Nov. 23).

1961: "Sappy New Year" (Nov. 10).

1966: "Messed Up Movie Makers" (Bakes, Chiarito/Mar.).

⊚ HECTOR HEATHCOTE

As with Deputy Dawg, this series was originally produced for television. It focused on the adventures of this good-natured, Revolutionary War–era boy who plays an integral part in the events of this country's history. (George Washington would have never crossed the Delaware River if Hector hadn't built the rowboat.)

Ed Bower, a Terrytoons designer, is credited with creating the character. Cartoons produced for television in the early 1960s also received theatrical distribution. *Directed by Arthur Bartsch, Dave Tendlar, Connie Rasinski, Bill Tytla and Bob Kuwahara. Technicolor. CinemaScope. A Terrytoons Production released through 20th Century-Fox.*

Voices

Hector Heathcote: John Myhers

1959: "The Minute and a Half Man" (Tendlar/July/CinemaScope).

1960: "The Famous Ride" (Rasinski/Apr./CinemaScope); and "Daniel Boone, Jr." (Tendlar/Dec./CinemaScope).

1961: "Railroaded to Fame" (Tendlar/May); "The First Fast Mail" (Tendlar/May); "Crossing the Delaware" (Bartsch/June/CinemaScope); and "Unsung Hero" (July).

1962: Klondike Strikes Out" (Tendlar/Jan.); "He-Man Seaman" (Bartsch/Mar.); "Riverboat Mission" (Tendlar/May); "First Flight Up" (Tytla/Oct.); and "A Flight to the Finish" (Tendlar/Dec.).

1963: "Tea Party" (Tendlar/Apr.); "A Bell for Philadelphia" (Kuwahara/July); and "The Big Clean-Up" (Tendlar/Sept.).

1970: "Land Grab" (Feb.), "Lost and Foundation" (June); and "Belabout Thy Neighbor" (Oct.).

1971: "Train Terrain" (Feb.).

◉ HENERY HAWK

This temperamental diminutive chicken hawk with a fiery attitude was intended to be a "star" in his own right. Known for his supporting roles in mostly Foghorn Leghorn cartoons, Henery was introduced to the screen in 1942 with the intention of featuring him in his own series. Created by legendary Warner Bros. animator Chuck Jones, Henery first splashed onto the screen in "The Squawkin' Hawk," a *Merrie Melodies* cartoon. Four years later he was meant to star in what would be the follow-up cartoon to his first screen appearance, "Walky Talky Hawky," directed by Robert McKimson (which was nominated for an Academy Award). Instead, McKimson turned the cartoon into a starring vehicle for a new character he planned to introduce: a loudmouthed, catankerous rooster named Foghorn Leghorn. Henery also appeared opposite Daffy Duck in one cartoon, "You Were Never Duckier," a 1948 *Merrie Melodies* directed by Chuck Jones.

The voice of Henery was provided by none other than venerable Warner Bros. voice artist Mel Blanc. *Directed by Chuck Jones and Robert McKimson. A Warner Bros. release.*

Voices
Henery Hawk: Mel Blanc

Merrie Melodies

1942: "The Squawkin' Hawk" (Jones/Aug. 8).

1946: Walky Tawky Hawky" (with Foghorn Leghorn/McKimson/Aug. 31/A.A. nominee).

1948: "You Were Never Duckier" (with Daffy Duck/Jones/Aug. 7).

1951: "Leghorn Swoggled" (with Foghorn Leghorn/McKimson/July 18).

1952: "The Egg-Cited Rooster" (with Foghorn Leghorn/McKimson/Oct. 4).

1961: "Strangled Eggs" (with Foghorn Leghorn/McKimson/Mar. 18).

Looney Tunes

1947: "Crowing Pains" (with Foghorn Leghorn, Sylvester/McKimson/July 12).

1950: "The Leghorn Blows at Midnight" (with Foghorn Leghorn/McKimson/May 6).

1955: "All Fowled Up" (with Foghorn Leghorn/McKimson/Feb. 19)

◉ HERMAN AND KATNIP

The idea of a cat-and-mouse team already proved successful for MGM with *Tom and Jerry*. What worked for one studio seemed liked it could work again, so Famous Studios unveiled their own feuding tandem in 1947: Herman, a slick city mouse, and Katnip, a country-bumpkin cat. For 12 years, the pair starred in a series of misadventures with Herman being the target of Katnip's desires to nab him as his personal prize. Like MGM's Jerry, Herman emerged unscathed through his sheer inventiveness and ability to outwit the cat. Initially, the madcap duo starred in cartoons produced under the *Noveltoons* banner before they were given their own series in 1952, the first entry of which was "Mice Capades."

Country-bumpkin cat Katnip and slick-city mouse Herman often feuded onscreen, with, naturally, the cat always on the losing end. © Harvey Cartoons

The pair also appeared independently of each other in individual *Noveltoons. Directors were Isadore Sparber, Seymour Kneitel, Bill Tytla and Dave Tendlar. Technicolor. A Famous Studios Production released through Paramount Pictures.*

Voices

Herman: Arnold Stang; **Katnip:** Syd Raymond

1947: "Naughty But Mice" (Kneitel/Oct. 10/*Noveltoon*).

1950: "Mice Meeting You" (Kneitel/Nov. 10/*Noveltoon*).

1951: "Mice Paradise" (Sparber/Mar. 9/*Noveltoon*); and "Cat Tamale" (Kneitel/Nov. 9/*Noveltoon*).

1952: "Cat Carson Rides Again" (Kneitel/Apr. 4/*Noveltoon*); and "Mice Capades" (Kneitel/Oct. 3/first cartoon in the *Herman and Katnip* series).

1953: "Of Mice and Magic" (Sparber/Feb. 20); "Herman the Cartoonist" (Sparber/May 15); "Drinks on the Mouse" (Tendlar/Aug. 28); and "Northwest Mousie" (Kneitel/Dec. 28).

1954: "Surf and Sound" (Tendlar/Mar. 5); "Of Mice and Menace" (Kneitel/June 25); "Ship A-Hooey" (Sparber/Aug. 20); and "Rail-Rodents" (Tendlar/Nov. 26).

1955: "Robin Rodenthood" (Tendlar/Feb. 25); "A Bicep Built for Two" (Kneitel/Apr. 8); "Mouse Trapeze" (Sparber/Aug. 5); and "Mousieur Herman" (Tendlar/Nov. 25).

1956: "Mouseum" (Kneitel/Feb. 24); "Will Do Mousework" (Kneitel/June 29); "Mousetro Herman" (Sparber/Aug. 10); and "Hide and Peak" (Tendlar/Dec. 7).

1957: "Cat in the Act" (Tendlar/Feb. 22); "Sky Scrappers" (Tendlar/June 14); "From Mad to Worse" (Kneitel/Aug. 16); and "One Funny Knight" (Tendlar/Nov. 22).

1958: "Frighty Cat" (Sparber/Mar. 14); and "You Said a Mouseful" (Kneitel/Aug. 29).

1959: "Owly to Bed" (Kneitel/Jan. 2); "Felineous Assault" (Kneitel/Feb. 20); "Fun on the Furlough" (Kneitel/Apr. 3); and "Katnip's Big Day" (Kneitel/Oct. 30).

Herman by Himself

1944: "The Henpecked Rooster" (with Henry the Rooster/Kneitel/Feb. 18).

1945: "Scrappily Married" (with Henry the Rooster/Kneitel/Mar. 30).

1946: "Cheese Burglar" (Sparber/Feb. 22).

1949: "Campus Capers" (Tytla/July 1).

Katnip by Himself

1952: "City Kitty" (Sparber/July 18).

◎ HIPPETY HOPPER

The high-jumping kangaroo was originally created by Robert McKimson as a running gag in a cartoon with lisping Sylvester. Resembling an overgrown mouse, Hippey became more than a one-shot joke. He lasted for 16 years as a nontalking costar in a dozen cartoons with Sylvester, with his actions speaking louder than words.

In 1950 McKimson added another character to play off Hippety: Sylvester's son, Sylvester Jr., who encounters the kangaroo in situations where he questions his father's knowledge of animals. (Sylvester often mistakens Hippety for a "mouse.") *Directed by Robert McKimson. Technicolor. A Warner Bros. release.*

Looney Tunes

1948: "Hop Look and Listen" (with Sylvester/McKimson/Apr. 17).

1950: "Pop 'em Pop!" (with Sylvester, Sylvester Jr./McKimson/Oct. 28).

1952: "Hoppy Go Lucky" (with Sylvester/McKimson/Aug. 9).

1956: "Too Hop to Handle" (with Sylvester, Sylvester Jr./McKimson/Jan. 28).

1961: "Hoppy Daze" (with Sylvester/McKimson/Feb. 11).

DePatie-Freleng Enterprises release

1964: "Freudy Cat" (McKimson/Mar. 14).

Merrie Melodies

1949: "Hippety Hopper" (with Sylvester/McKimson/Nov. 19).

1953: "Cat's Aweigh" (with Sylvester, Sylvester Jr./McKimson/Nov. 28).

1954: "Bell Hoppy" (with Sylvester/McKimson/Apr. 17).

1955: "Lighthouse Mouse" (with Sylvester/McKimson/Mar. 12).

1956: "The Slap-Hoppy Mouse" (with Sylvester/McKimson/Sept. 1).

1957: "Mouse-Taken Identity" (with Sylvester, Sylvester Jr./McKimson/Nov. 16).

◎ HOMER PIGEON

A 1940s' addition to Walter Lantz's cartoon gallery, this rubelike country bird was based on comedian Red Skelton's famed radio character, Clem Kadiddlehopper. The straw-hatted bird, who was originally cast as comic relief in a number of films, first appeared in the Walter Lantz Cartune Special, "Pigeon Patrol," in 1942. His only other starring appearance came 14 years later before retiring from the screen. *Directed by Alex Lovy. Technicolor. A Walter Lantz Production released through Universal Pictures.*

Voices
Homer Pigeon: Dal McKennon

1942: "Pigeon Patrol" (Aug. 3).

1956: "Pigeon Holed" (Jan. 16).

◉ HONEY HALFWITCH

In an attempt to come up with something different, Famous Studios, producers of *Casper* and *Herman and Katnip*, launched this series featuring Honey Halfwitch, a sweet-natured apprentice who manages to escape trouble through the power of witchcraft. The series' theme song was composed by Winston Sharples, the studio's musical director. *Directors were Howard Post, James "Shamus" Culhane and Chuck Harriton. Technicolor. A Famous Studios Production released through Paramount Pictures.*

1965: "Shoeflies" (Post/Oct.).

1966: "Baggin' the Dragon" (Post/Feb.); "From Nags to Witches" (Post/Feb.); "Trick or Cheat" (Post/Mar.); "The Rocket Racket" (Post/Mar.); "The Defiant Giant" (Culhane/June); "Throne for a Loss" (Culhane/July); and "Potions and Notions" (Culhane/Aug.).

1967: "Alter Egotist" (Harriton/Apr.); "Clean Sweep" (Harriton/June); "High But Not Dry" (Culhane/Aug.); and "Brother Rat" (Harriton/Aug.).

◉ THE HONEY-MOUSERS

What began as a one-shot parody of television's classic comedy series *The Honeymooners* turned into a brief series of hilarious spoofs featuring Ralph (Ralph Crumden), Alice (Alice Crumden), Norton (Ned Morton) and Trixie (Trixie Morton) as mice. Warner Bros. veteran Robert McKimson brought the characters to the screen for the first time in 1956's "The Honey-Mousers." Comedian Jackie Gleason allegedly was unhappy with the idea of a cartoon spoof and threatened to block its release by the studio. McKimson sent Gleason a print of the cartoon and after watching it, Gleason was pleased and dropped his objections. *Directed by Robert McKimson. Technicolor. A Warner Bros. release.*

Voices
Ralph Crumden/Ned Morton: Daws Butler; **Alice Crumden:** June Foray, Julie Bennett; **Trixie Morton:** June Foray

Looney Tunes
1956: "The Honey-Mousers" (Dec. 8).

1957: "Cheese It, The Cat" (May 4).

1960: "Mice Follies" (Aug. 20).

◉ HOOT KLOOT

A redneck, fat-bellied sheriff saddles up to maintain law and order with the help of his silly but faithful horse, Confederate, in cartoon adventures lampooning the Wild West. *Directors were Bob Balser, Durward Bonaye, Gerry Chiniquy, Arthur Leonardi, Sid Marcus, Roy Morita and Hawley Pratt. Technicolor. A DePatie-Freleng/Mirisch Cinema Company Production released through United Artists.*

Voices
Hoot Kloot: Bob Holt; **Confederate:** Larry D. Mann

Additional Voices
Joan Gerber, Allan Melvin, Hazel Shermet

1973: "Kloot's Kounty" (Pratt/Jan. 19); "Apache on the County Seat" (Pratt/June 16); "The Shoe Must Go On" (Chiniquy/June 16); "A Self-Winding Sidewinder" (Morita/Oct. 9); "Pay Your Buffalo Bill" (Chiniquy/Oct. 9);

Fat-bellied Sheriff Hoot Kloot prepares for trouble in a scene from DePatie-Freleng's cartoon series spoofing the Old West. © DePatie-Freleng Enterprises

"Stirrups and Hiccups" (Chiniquy/Oct. 15); and "Ten Miles to the Gallop" (Leonardi/Oct. 15).

1974: "Phony Express" (Chiniquy/Jan. 4); "Giddy-Up Woe" (Marcus/Jan. 9); "Gold Struck" (Morita/Jan. 16); "As the Tumbleweed Turns" (Chiniquy/Apr. 8); "The Badge and the Beautiful" (Balser/Apr. 17); "Big Beef at the O.K. Corral" (Balser/Apr. 17); "By Hoot or by Crook" (Balser/Apr. 17); "Strange on the Range" (Bonaye/Apr. 17); "Mesa Trouble" (Marcus/May 16); and "Saddle Soap Opera" (Chiniquy/May 16).

◉ HUBIE AND BERTIE

Chuck Jones created these two troublesome mice, Hubie and Bertie, who were added to the Warner Bros. cartoon roster in 1943. In subsequent adventures they were paired with a mouse-hungry cat, Claude Cat. The short-lived series produced one Academy Award nomination for the 1949 release "Mouse Wreckers," the pair's second cartoon. *Directed by Chuck Jones. Technicolor. A Warner Bros. release.*

Voices
Hubie: Mel Blanc; **Bertie:** Mel Blanc, Stan Freberg

Merrie Melodies

1943: "The Aristo Cat" (June 12).

1948: "House-Hunting Mice" (Oct. 7).

1949: "Mouse Wreckers" (with Claude Cat/Apr. 23/A.A. nominee).

1950: "The Hypo-Condri-Cat" (with Claude Cat/Apr. 15).

1951: "Cheese Chasers" (with Claude Cat/Aug. 28).

Looney Tunes

1946: "Roughly Squeaking" (Nov. 23).

1952: "Mouse Warming" (with Claude Cat/Sept. 8).

◉ HUGH HARMAN CARTOONS

In the early 1930s Hugh Harman and partner Rudolf Ising moved from Warner Bros. to MGM to produce cartoons independently for their new studio. In 1939, after a brief departure, Harman returned to Metro following overtures from Fred Quimby, head of the studio's new cartoon department. Quimby hired Harman to develop a fresh, new cartoon series that would help establish the studio as a leader in the field of cartoon animation.

Using a familiar formula, Harman produced and directed a series of musical cartoons similar to his former *Merrie Melodies* for Warner Bros., featuring various animated characters as the stars. His finest effort came in 1939 during his

Two determined cherubs of the forest pick blueberries so they can color the nearby waters of the land blue in Hugh Harman's MGM cartoon short "The Blue Danube" (1939). © Turner Entertainment

first year back at the studio, when his "Peach on Earth," a timely war-themed cartoon released that year, won an Academy Award nomination for Best Short Subject and a *Parents Magazine* medal of distinction.

Veteran animator Friz Freleng, who briefly defected to MGM from Warner Bros., directed one cartoon under the series. *Directed by Hugh Harman and Friz Freleng. Technicolor. A Metro-Goldwyn-Mayer release.*

1939: "Art Gallery" (Harman/May 13); "Goldilocks and the 3 Bears" (Harman/July 15/re: Nov. 22, 1947); "Bear Family" (Abandoned); "The Bookworm" (Freleng/Aug. 26); "The Blue Danube" (Harman/Oct. 28); "Peace on Earth" (Harman/Dec. 9/A.A. nominee); and "The Mad Maestro" (Harman/Dec. 30).

1940: "A Rainy Day" (Harman/Apr. 20); "Tom Turkey and His Harmonica Humdingers" (Harman/June 8); "The Bookworm Turns" (Harman/July 20); "Papa Gets the Bird" (Harman/Sept. 7); and "Lonesome Stranger" (Harman/Nov. 23).

1941: "Abdul the Bulbul Ameer" (Harman/Feb. 22); "The Little Mole" (Harman/Apr. 5); "The Alley Cat" (Harman/July 5); and "Field Mouse" (Harman/Dec. 27).

1942: "The Hungry Wolf" (Harman/Feb. 21).

◉ INKI

Paired with a pesty minah bird, Inki, who was a little black jungle boy with a bone in his hair, was used occasionally in a number of Warner Bros. cartoons directed by creator Chuck Jones. Inki first appeared in 1939's "The Little Lion Hunter." *Directed by Chuck Jones. Technicolor. A Warner Bros. release.*

Voices
Mel Blanc

Merrie Melodies

1939: "Little Lion Hunter" (Oct. 7).

1941: "Inki and the Lion" (July 19).

1943: "Inki and the Minah Bird" (Nov. 6).

1947: "Inki at the Circus" (June 21).

Looney Tunes

1950: "Caveman Inki" (Nov. 25).

◎ THE INSPECTOR

The blundering French sleuth of *Pink Panther* fame, Inspector Clouseau starred in a series of cartoon shorts based on Blake Edwards's film character, played by actor-comedian Peter Sellers in several feature films in the 1960s and 1970s.

In 1965 the animated character, who bears more than a fleeting resemblance to Sellers, made his debut along with his equally lamebrained aide, Sergeant Deudeux, when United Artists simultaneously released the James Bond thriller *Thunderball* and the cartoon "The Great de Gaulle Stone" nationwide.

As in the successful feature film series, the animated adventures dealt with Clouseau's inherent ability to solve important cases despite his obvious ineptitude. Blake Edwards actually suggested the idea for the series. *Directors were Gerry Chiniquy, Friz Freleng, Robert McKimson and George Singer. Technicolor. A Mirisch-Geoffrey-DePatie-Freleng Production released through United Artists.*

Voices
The Inspector/Sergeant Deudeux: Pat Harrington Jr.; **The Chief:** Paul Frees, Marvin Miller

Additional Voices
June Foray, Helen Gerald, Joan Gerber, Diana Maddox, Mark Skor, Hal Smith, Larry Storch, Lennie Weinrib

1965: "The Great De Gaulle Stone Operation" (Freleng, Chiniquy/Dec. 21).

1966: "Reaux, Reaux, Reaux Your Boat" (Chiniquy/Feb. 1); "Napoleon Blown-Aparte" (Chiniquy/Feb. 2); "Cirrhosis of the Louvre" (Chiniquy/Mar. 9); "Plastered in Paris" (Chiniquy/Apr. 5); "Cock-a-Doodle Deux Deux" (McKimson/June 15); "Ape Suzette" (Chiniquy/June 24); "The Pique Poquette of Paris" (Singer/Aug. 24); "Sicque! Sicque! Sicque!" (Singer/Sept. 23); "That's No Lady—That's Notre Dame" (Singer/Oct. 26); "Unsafe and Seine" (Singer/Nov. 9); and "Toulouse La Trick" (McKimson/Dec. 30).

1967: "Sacre Bleu Cross" (Chiniquy/Feb. 1); "Le Quiet Squad" (McKimson/May 17); "Bomb Voyage" (McKimson/May 22); "Le Pig-Al Patrol" (Chiniquy/May 24); "Le Bowser Bagger" (Chiniquy/May 30); "Le Escape Goat" (Chiniquy/June 29); "Le Cop on Le Rocks" (Singer/July 3); "Crow De Guerre" (Chiniquy/Aug. 16); "Canadian Can-Can" (Chiniquy/Sept. 20); "Tour De Farce" (Chiniquy/Oct. 25); and "The Shooting of Caribou Lou" (Chiniquy/Dec. 20).

1968: "London Derriere" (Chiniquy/Feb. 7); "Les Mise-robots" (Chiniquy/Mar. 21); "Transylvania Mania" (Chiniquy/Mar. 26); "Bear De Guerre" (Chiniquy/Apr. 26); "Cherche Le Phantom" (Chiniquy/June 13); "Le Great Dane Robbery" (Chiniquy/July 7); "La Feet's De Feat" (Chiniquy/July 24); and "Le Ball and Chain Gang" (Chiniquy/July 24).

1969: "French Freud" (Chiniquy/Jan. 22); "Pierre and Cottage Cheese" (Chiniquy/Feb. 26); and "Carte Blanched" (Chiniquy/May 14).

◎ INSPECTOR WILLOUGHBY

Believing the time was ripe for a new cartoon character to grace the screen, Walter Lantz enlisted former Disney director Jack Hannah to develop story ideas for a new series. Hannah responded with a revised version of a character from his Disney days named Ranger Willoughby. Making a few minor alterations, he gave the character a new identity and new profession as a burly mustachioed secret agent, 6 7/8. Willoughby's low-key demeanor and speaking voice were humanized versions of Tex Avery's popular basset hound, Droopy.

Hannah directed the premiere episode of the series, "Hunger Strife," in 1960, plus a subsequent cartoon, "Eggnapper," the following year. The rest of the series was directed by Lantz veteran Paul J. Smith until 1965. *Directed by Jack Hannah and Paul J. Smith. Technicolor. A Walter Lantz Production released through Universal Pictures.*

Voices
Inspector Willoughby: Dal McKennon

1960: "Hunger Strife" (with Windy/Hannah/Oct. 5).

1961: "Rough and Tumbleweed" (Smith/Jan. 31); "Eggnapper" (Hannah/Feb. 14); "Mississippi Slow Boat" (Smith/July); and "Case of the Red-Eyed Ruby" (Smith/Nov. 28).

1962: "Phoney Express" (Smith/May 15); and "Hyde and Sneak" (Smith/July 24).

1963: "Coming-Out Party" (Smith/Feb.); "Case of the Cold-Storage Yegg" (Smith/Mar.); and "Hi-Seas Hi-Jacker" (Smith/May).

1964: "The Case of the Maltese Chicken" (Smith/Feb. 4).

1965: "The Case of the Elephant's Trunk" (Smith/Jan. 1).

◉ JACKY'S WHACKY WORLD
Based on the comic strip *Jacky's Diary* by cartoonist Jack Mendelsohn that relates a young boy's fractured views of history and fairy tales, Mendelsohn wrote and directed this brief Paramount cartoon series, produced as *Noveltoons* cartoons. *Technicolor. Voice credits unknown. A Famous Studios Production released through Paramount Pictures.*

1965: "The Story of George Washington" (Feb./*Modern Madcap*); and "A Leak in the Dike" (Mar./*Modern Madcap*).

◉ JAMES HOUND
Inspired by Ian Fleming's fictional James Bond character, Terrytoons introduced this canine counterpart of the famed super-sleuth in animated escapades featuring international spies and farfetched gadgets on a smaller scale. Ralph Bakshi, who made his *Terrytoons* directorial debut in 1964, directed the series. *Directed by Ralph Bakshi. Technicolor. A Terrytoons Production released through 20th Century-Fox.*

Voices
James Hound: Dayton Allen

1966: "Dr. Ha Ha Ha" (Feb.), "The Monster Maker" (July), "Rain Drain" (Sept.), "Dream-Napping" (Nov.) and "The Phantom Skyscraper" (Dec. 31).

1967: "A Voodoo Spell" (Jan.); "Mr. Win Lucky" (Feb.); "It's for the Birds" (Mar.); "The Heat's Off" (Apr.); "Traffic Trouble" (May); "Bugged by a Bug" (June); "Fancy Plants" (July); "Give Me Liberty" (Aug.); "Which Is Witch" (Sept.); "Dr. Rhinestone's Theory" (Oct.); "Frozen Sparklers" (Nov.); and "Baron Von Go-Go" (Dec.).

◉ JEEPERS AND CREEPERS
This brief series starred a comic pair of dogs, Jeepers and Creepers, who were the original version of another Paramount cartoon team, Swifty and Shorty, who debuted two years later. *Directed by Seymour Kneitel. Technicolor. A Famous Studios Production released through Paramount Pictures.*

Voices
Jeepers: Jack Mercer; **Creepers:** Syd Raymond, Allen Swift, Jack Mercer

1960: "The Boss Is Always Right" (Jan. 15); "Trouble Date" (Mar. 11/*Modern Madcap*); "Busy Buddies" (June); and "Scouting for Trouble" (Sept.).

◉ JERKY JOURNIES
Two years after Republic Pictures released animator Bob Clampett's experimental TruColor cartoon, "It's a Grand Old Nag," starring Charlie Horse and Hay-dy LaMare, the studio produced this series of animated travelogue spoofs without the guidance of Clampett, who left the studio after producing his single effort. Studio president Herbert Yates proposed making the series to further exploit its new color process in the same manner Disney made Technicolor into a success with his *Silly Symphony* cartoons.

The series became Republic's first and only cartoon series. Technical and voice credits are unknown. *TruColor. A Republic Pictures release.*

1949: "Beyond Civilization" (Mar. 15); "The Three Minnies" (Apr. 15); "Bungle in the Jungle" (May 15); and "Romantic Rumbolia" (June 15).

◉ JOHN DOORMAT
The ups-and-downs of suburban life in the 1950s is comically portrayed in this *Terrytoons* series featuring John Doormat, a poor soul whose encounters deal with a variety of everyday issues. Writer Jules Feiffer later joined the series, changing the direction of the cartoons to a more Thurberish outlook on life. Lionel Wilson, who supplied all the voice characterizations for TV's *Tom Terrific* series, did the voice of John Doormat, who was created by Terrytoons' creative director Gene Deitch. *Directed by Connie Rasinski and Al Kouzel. Technicolor. CinemaScope. A Terrytoons Production released through 20th Century-Fox.*

Voices
John Doormat: Lionel Wilson

1957: "Topsy Turvy" (Rasinski/Jan.); and "Shove Thy Neighbor" (Rasinski/June).

1958: "Dustcap Doormat" (Kouzel/June).

◉ JOLLY FROLICS
When Columbia Pictures' animation department closed down, United Productions of America (UPA) independently produced new cartoons for distribution through the studio to replace the *Phantasy* color classics series. The first cartoon to launch the series was 1949's "Ragtime Bear," starring the myopic Mr. Magoo.

Magoo, Gerald McBoing Boing and other stalwarts from UPA's cartoon gallery appeared in several episodes of this new series. *Directors were John Hubley, Art Babbitt, Steve Bosustow, Bob Cannon, Pete Burness and Ted Parmelee. Technicolor. A UPA Production released through Columbia Pictures.*

1949: "Ragtime Bear" (with Mr. Magoo/Hubley/Sept. 8).

1950: "Spellbound Hound" (Hubley/Mar. 16); "The Miner's Daughter" (Cannon/May 25); "Giddyap" (Babbitt/July 27); and "The Popcorn Story" (Babbitt/Nov. 30).

1951: "Gerald McBoing Boing" (Cannon/Jan. 25); "The Family Circus" (Babbit/Jan. 25); "Georgie the Dragon" (Cannon/Sept. 27); and "Wonder Gloves" (Cannon/Nov. 29).

1952: "The Oompahs" (Cannon/Jan. 24); "Rooty Tooty Toot" (Hubley/Mar. 27/A.A. winner); "Pete Hothead" (Parmelee/Sept. 25); and "Madeline" (Cannon/Nov. 27/ A.A. nominee).

1953: "Little Boy with a Big Horn" (Cannon/Mar. 26); "The Emperor's New Clothes" (Parmelee/Apr. 30); and "Christopher Crumpet" (Cannon/June 25/A.A. nominee).

◉ KARTUNES

In the early 1950s Paramount's Famous Studios resurrected a familiar formula—themed stories with no-named stars— when it introduced *Kartunes*, animated in the same style and manner as its former success, *Noveltoons*.

Kartunes never equaled the success of *Noveltoons* in terms of popularity and longevity. The series only lasted three years. *Directed by Isadore Sparber and Seymour Kneitel. A Famous Studios Production released through Paramount Pictures.*

1951: "Vegetable Vaudeville" (Sparber/Nov. 9); and "Snooze Reel" (Kneitel/Dec. 28).

1952: "Off We Glow" (Sparber/Feb. 29); "Fun at the Fair" (Sparber/May 9/song: "Wait Till the Sun Shines, Nellie"); "Dizzy Dinosaurs" (Kneitel/July 4); "Gag and Baggage" (Sparber/Aug. 8); and "Forest Fantasy" (Kneitel/Nov. 14).

1953: "Hysterical History" (Sparber/Jan. 23/song: "Yankee Doodle Boy"); "Philharmaniacs" (Kneitel/Apr. 3); "Aero-Nutics" (Kneitel/May 8); "Invention Convention" (Sparber/ June 10); and "No Place Like Rome" (Sparber/July 31).

◉ KIKO THE KANGAROO

First appearing in *Farmer Al Falfa* cartoons, Kiko was a playful kangaroo cast in numerous misadventures. The character was created by Paul Terry, who featured the character in his own series of animated shorts beginning in 1936. *Directed by Mannie Davis and George Gordon. Black-and-white. Voice credits unknown. A Terrytoons Production released through 20th Century-Fox.*

1936: "Kiko and the Honey Bears" (Davis, Gordon/Aug. 21); "Kiko Foils a Fox" (Davis, Gordon/Oct. 2); and "Skunked Again" (Davis, Gordon/Dec. 25).

1937: "Red Hot Music" (Davis, Gordon/Mar. 5); "Ozzie Ostrich Comes to Town" (Davis, Gordon/May 28); "Play Ball" (Davis/June 11); and "Kiko's Cleaning Day" (Gordon/ Sept. 17).

◉ KRAZY KAT

The advent of sound revived many silent-film favorites, including George Herriman's popular animated feline, Krazy Kat. Krazy previously had gained fame by starring in more than 80 silent cartoons. He was brought back to life when Columbia Pictures, wanting to become a major force in the cartoon industry, agreed to distribute this proven property in a series of new cartoons produced by Charles Mintz.

The sound cartoons had the same basic stories as the silent adventures, with some dialogue and musical soundtrack accompaniment. Krazy's soft-speaking voice was like Mickey Mouse, who inspired several other sound-alike characters, among them, Warner Bros.' Bosko and Buddy.

As had happened in the silent series, the series suffered several setbacks because of creative differences in bringing Krazy's innate style of humor to the screen. No attempt was made to stay true to creator George Herriman's style or story lines. Consequently, Offisa Pup was rarely used, and the romance between Ignatz and Krazy, ever popular in the comic strip series, was virtually ignored.

At the same time Mintz produced the series for Columbia, Walt Disney supplied cartoons for the studio for release. In 1932, after Disney parted company with Columbia, Mintz became the studio's sole supplier of cartoons, with Krazy leading the pack. (Coincidentally, Mintz was the same producer responsible for taking the *Oswald the Rabbit* series from Disney years earlier.)

Manny Gould and Ben Harrison, who wrote most of the cartoon stories, jointly directed and supervised the animation of each cartoon. Music was supplied by Joe De Nat, a former New York pianist, whose peppy musical scores enlivened each film. *Directed by Manny Gould and Ben Harrison. Black-and-white. Technicolor. A Columbia Pictures release. Voice credits unknown.*

1929: "Ratskin" (Aug. 15); "Canned Music" (Sept. 12); "Port Whines" (Oct. 10); "Sole Mates" (Nov. 7); and "Farm Relief" (Dec. 30).

1930: "The Cat's Meow" (Jan. 2); "Spook Easy" (Jan. 30); "Slow Beau" (Feb. 27); "Desert Sunk" (Mar. 27); "An Old Flame" (Apr. 24); "Alaskan Knights" (May 23); "Jazz Rhythm" (June 19); "Honolulu Wiles" (July 17); "Cinderella" (Aug. 14); "The Band Master" (Sept. 8); "The Apache Kid" (Oct. 9); "Lambs Will Gamble" (Nov. 1); and "The Little Trail" (Dec. 3).

1931: "Take for a Ride" (Jan.); "Rodeo Dough" (Feb. 13); "Swiss Movements" (Apr. 4); "Disarmament Conference" (Apr. 27); "Soda Poppa" (May 29); "Stork Market" (July 11); "Svengarlic" (Aug. 3); "The Weenie Roast" (Sept. 14); "Bars and Stripes" (Oct. 15); "Hash House Blues" (Nov. 2); and "The Restless Sax" (Dec. 1).

1932: "Piano Mover" (Jan. 4); "Love Krazy" (Jan. 25); "Hollywood Goes Krazy" (Feb. 13); "What a Knight" (Mar. 14); "Soldier Old Man" (Apr. 2); "Birth of Jazz" (Apr. 13); "Ritzy Hotel" (May 9); "Hic-Cups the Champ" (May 28); "The Paper Hanger" (June 21); "Lighthouse Keeping" (Aug. 15); "Seeing Stars" (Sept. 12); "Prosperity Blues" (Oct. 8); "The Crystal Gazebo" (Nov. 7); "The Minstrel Show" (Nov. 21); and "Show Time" (Nov. 30).

1933: "Wedding Bells" (Jan. 10); "The Medicine Show" (Feb. 7); "Wooden Shoes" (Feb. 25); "Bunnies and Bonnets" (Mar. 29); "The Broadway Malady" (Apr. 18); "Russian Dressing" (May 1); "House Cleaning" (June 1); "Antique Antics" (June 14); "Out of the Ether" (Sept. 5); "Whacks Museum" (Sept. 29); "Krazy Spooks" (Oct. 13); "Stage Krazy" (Nov. 13); "The Bill Poster" (Nov. 24); and "The Curio Shop" (Dec. 15).

1934: "The Autograph Hunter" (Jan. 5); "Southern Exposure" (Feb. 5); "Tom Thumb" (Feb. 16); "Cinder Alley" (Mar. 9); "Bowery Daze" (Mar. 30); "Busy Bus" (Apr. 20); "Masquerade Party" (May 11); "The Trapeze Artist" (Sept. 1); "Katnips of 1940" (Oct. 12); "Krazy's Waterloo" (Nov. 16); and "Goofy Gondolas" (Dec. 21).

1935: (All the following cartoons were produced in Technicolor.) "The Bird Man" (Feb. 1); "Hotcha Melody" (Mar. 15); "The Peace Conference" (Apr. 26); "The King's Jester" (May 20); "Garden Gaieties" (Aug. 1); "A Happy Family" (Sept. 27); and "Kannibal Kapers" (Dec. 27).

1936: "The Bird Stuffer" (Feb. 1); "Lil' Ainjil" (Mar. 19); "Highway Snobbery" (Aug. 9); "Krazy's Newsreel" (Oct. 24); and "Merry Cafe" (Dec. 26).

1937: "The Lyin' Hunter" (Feb. 12); "Krazy's Race of Time" (May 6); "The Masque Raid" (June 25); and "Railroad Rhythm" (Nov. 20).

1938: "Sad Little Guinea Pigs" (Feb. 22); "The Auto Clinic" (Mar. 4); "Little Buckaroo" (Apr. 11); "Krazy Magic" (May 20); "Krazy's Travel Squawks" (July 4); "Gym Jams" (Sept. 9); "Hot Dogs on Ice" (Oct. 21); and "The Lone Mountie" (Dec. 10).

1939: "Krazy's Bear Tale" (Jan. 27); "Golf Chumps" (Apr. 6); "Krazy's Shoe Shop" (May 12); and "Little Lost Sheep" (Oct. 6/*Fables* cartoon).

1940: "The Mouse Exterminator" (Jan. 26/*Phantasy* cartoon).

Ⓢ LADDY AND HIS LAMP

This brief Paramount cartoon series—following the adventures of a young boy and the genie of the lamp—was brought to the screen in 1964, when studio animators introduced a variety of one-shot characters (including Buck and Wingy, Homer Ranger and King Artie) in the studio's popular *Noveltoons* series. *Directed by Seymour Kneitel. Technicolor. Voice credits unknown. A Famous Studios Production released through Paramount Pictures.*

1964: "Laddy and His Lamp" (Sept./*Noveltoon*); and "A Tiger's Tail" (Dec./*Noveltoon*).

Ⓢ LAND OF THE LOST

The popular children's radio show *The Insgrigs* inspired this series of fantasy cartoons produced as part of Famous Studios' *Noveltoons* series. *Directed by Isadore Sparber and Seymour Kneitel. Technicolor. A Famous Studios Production released through Paramount Pictures.*

1948: "Land of the Lost" (Sparber/June 7).

1950: "Land of the Lost Jewels" (Sparber/Jan. 6).

1951: "Land of Lost Watches" (Kneitel/May 4).

Ⓢ LIL' ABNER

Few comic-strip characters were successful in an animated cartoon environment. Columbia Pictures had learned this before with Krazy Kat and Barney Google, the latter an earlier comic strip–to–film adaptation that failed. Yet the studio tried again, this time with a short-lived series of cartoon shorts based on Al Capp's hillbilly character. The series was dropped after only five films, which pleased creator Capp, who repeatedly expressed his disdain with the studio's simplifications of the characters and situations from his nationally syndicated strip. *Directors were Sid Marcus, Bob Wickersham and Howard Swift. Technicolor. A Columbia Pictures release.*

1944: "Amoozin But Confoozin" (Marcus/Mar. 3); "Sadie Hawkins Day" (Wickersham/May 4); "A Peekoolyar Sitcheeyshun" (Marcus/Aug. 11); "Porkulia Piggy" (Wickersham/Oct. 13); and "Kickapoo Juice" (Swift/Dec. 1).

Ⓢ LIL' EIGHTBALL

Former Disney protégé Burt Gillett was responsible for creating this stereotyped black youngster who, after a brief opportunity at movie stardom, resurfaced in Walter Lantz's comic books of the 1940s. *Directed by Burt Gillett. Black-and-white. Voice credits unknown. A Walter Lantz Production released through Universal Pictures.*

1939: "Stubborn Mule" (July 3); and "Silly Superstition" (Aug. 28).

Ⓢ LITTLE AUDREY

When Paramount lost the rights to Little Lulu in late 1947, the studio produced a series of Little Audrey cartoons as her replacement. This series revolved around the life and loves of a sweet little girl who earlier claimed fame as a Harvey comic-book character. Stories depict her matching wits with a prank-loving boy, Melvin, tracking down hoodlums and lending a helping hand to anyone needing assistance.

Mae Questel, who did most of the female and children's voices for the studio, was Audrey in the series. The first little Audrey comic book was published four months before the series' first cartoon. *Directed by Isadore Sparber, Seymour Kneitel and Bill Tytla. Technicolor. A Famous Studios Production released through Paramount Pictures.*

Voices
Little Audrey: Mae Questel

(All series cartoons were released under the *Noveltoons* banner.)

1948: "Butterscotch and Soda" (Tytla/July 6).

1949: "The Lost Dream" (Tytla/Mar. 18); and "Song of the Birds" (Tytla/Nov. 18).

1950: "Tarts and Flowers" (Tytla/May 26); and "Goofy Goofy Gander" (Tytla/Aug. 18).

1951: "Hold the Lion Please" (Sparber/Apr. 27); and "Audrey the Rainmaker" (Sparber/Oct. 26).

1952: "Law and Audrey" (Sparber/May 23); and "The Case of the Cockeyed Canary" (Kneitel/Dec. 19).

1953: "Surf Bored" (Sparber/July 17).

1954: "The Seapreme Court" (Kneitel/Jan. 29).

1955: "Dizzy Dishes" (Sparber/Feb. 4); and "Little Audrey Riding Hood" (Kneitel/Oct. 14).

1957: "Fishing Tackler" (Sparber/Mar. 29).

1958: "Dawg Gawn" (Kneitel/Dec. 12).

⊚ LITTLE CHEEZER

Rudolph Ising created this cute, cuddly mouse who briefly appeared on the screen in two cartoons of his own. Little Cheezer's first appearance was in a *Happy Harmonies* cartoon bearing his name. *Ising also directed the series. Black-and-white. A Metro-Goldwyn-Mayer release.*

Voice
Little Cheezer: Bernice Hansen

1936: "Little Cheezer" (July 11/*Happy Harmonies*).

1937: "Little Buck Cheezer" (Dec. 15).

⊚ LITTLE KING

Based on the popular comic-strip character penned by cartoonist Oscar E. Soglow, this animated version marked yet another attempt by Van Beuren Studios to find a successful screen character to upgrade its image in the already crowded cartoon marketplace.

Unfortunately, the series never quite lived up to the studio's expectations as a "cartoon savior." The king never talked but acted out his response in pantomime, which may have been part of the reason for the series failure. (Strangely, the king later appeared in several Paramount Betty Boop cartoons and was given a speaking voice for those appearances.) *Directed by Jim Tyer and George Stallings. Black-and-white. A Van Beuren Production released through RKO-Radio Pictures.*

1933: "The Fatal Note" (Sept. 29); "Marching Along" (Tyer/Mar. 27); "On the Pan" (Nov. 24); and "Pals" (Tyer/Dec. 22).

1934: "Jest of Honor" (Stallings/Jan. 19); "Jolly Good Felons" (Stallings/Feb. 16); "Sultan Pepper" (Stallings/Mar. 16); "A Royal Good Time" (Stallings/Apr. 13); "Art for Art's Sake" (Stallings/May 11); and "Cactus King" (Stallings/June 8).

⊚ LITTLE LULU

Animator Max Fleischer adapted the Marjorie H. Bell comic-strip character, Little Lulu, to stories that relate the activities and frustrations of a mischievous little girl trying to show her parents how grown up she can be. Already a favorite in *Saturday Evening Post* cartoon panels, Fleischer added the series to the Paramount/Famous Studios 1943–44 roster.

As he had hoped, Lulu's childish mischief spelled success for his studio, with adventures pitting her against next-door neighbor Tubby, who always harasses her but is vanquished by Lulu's childlike wit.

The series' theme song was written by Fred Wise, Sidney Lippman and Buddy Kaye, becoming as successful a hit as the cartoon series itself.

Paramount dropped the series in 1948 when it was unable to renegotiate the rights to continue with the character. (Thirteen years later Lulu returned to the screen in "Alvin's Solo Flight," a *Noveltoon* coproduced by Lulu's creator Majorie H. Buell.) Lulu ultimately was replaced by a new little girl character, Little Audrey, whose inspiration was clear by her Lulu-like voice and manner.

In 1995 the character experienced a resurgence of interest, starring in an all-new animated television series produced for HBO. *Directors were Isadore Sparber, Seymour Kneitel and Bill Tytla. Technicolor. A Famous Studios Production released through Paramount Pictures.*

Marjorie H. Buell's popular comic-strip character Little Lulu was turned into a theatrical cartoon series by Max Fleischer in 1944.
(COURTESY: NATIONAL TELEFILM ASSOCIATES)

Voices
Little Lulu: Mae Questel, Cecil Roy

1943: "Eggs Don't Bounce" (Sparber/Dec. 24).

1944: "Hullaba-Lulu" (Kneitel/Feb. 25); "Lulu Gets the Birdie" (Sparber/Mar. 31); "Lulu in Hollywood" (Sparber/May 19); "Lucky Lulu" (Kneitel/June 30); "It's Nifty to Be Thrifty" (Kneitel/Aug. 18); "I'm Just Curious" (Kneitel/Sept. 8); "Indoor Outing" (Sparber/Sept. 29); "Lulu at The Zoo" (Sparber/Nov. 17); and "Birthday Party" (Sparber/Dec. 29).

1945: "Magica-Lulu" (Kneitel/Mar. 2); "Beau Ties" (Kneitel/Apr. 20); "Daffydilly Daddy" (Kneitel/May 25); "Snap Happy" (Tytla/June 22); and "Man's Pest Friend" (Kneitel/Nov. 30).

1946: "Bargain Counter Attack" (Sparber/Jan. 11); "Bored of Education" (Tytla/Mar. 1); and "Chick and Double Chick" (Kneitel/Aug. 16).

1947: "Musica-Lulu" (Sparber/Jan. 24); "A Scout with the Gout" (Tytla/Mar. 24); "Loose in a Caboose" (Kneitel/May 23); "Cad and Caddy" (Sparber/July 18); "A Bout with

a Trout" (Sparber/Oct. 30); "Super Lulu" (Tytla/Nov. 21); and "The Baby Sitter" (Kneitel/Nov. 28).

1948: "The Dog Show-Off" (Kneitel/Jan. 30).

1961: "Alvin's Solo Flight" (Kneitel/Apr./*Noveltoon*/ coproduced by Marjorie H. Buell and William C. Erskine).

1962: "Frog's Legs" (Kneitel/Apr./*Comic King*/coproduced by Marjorie H. Buell and William C. Erskine).

Ⓖ LITTLE ROQUEFORT
MGM's Tom and Jerry and Famous Studios' Herman and Katnip preceded this cat-and-mouse tandem—a pesky, pint-size mouse, Little Roquefort, and nemesis cat, Percy—who starred in assorted *Terrytoons* cartoon "chases" reminiscent of the style and humor first popularized in the *Tom and Jerry* series. Unfortunately, most comparisons of the two series end here. The *Terrytoons* version ran five years, while MGM's cat-and-mouse stars remained popular for 26 years, winning seven Academy Awards in the process. *Directed by Connie Rasinski, Mannie Davis and Ed Donnelly. Technicolor. A Terrytoons Production released through 20th Century-Fox.*

Voices
Little Roquefort/Percy the Cat: Tom Morrison

1950: "Cat Happy" (Rasinski/Sept.); and "Mouse Garden" (Davis/Oct.).

1951: "Three Is a Crowd" (Rasinski/Feb.); "Musical Madness" (Donnelly/May); "Seasick Sailors" (Davis/July); "Pastry Panic" (Davis/Oct.); and "The Haunted Cat" (Donnelly/Dec.).

1952: "City Slicker" (Davis/Feb.); "Hypnotized" (Davis/June); "Good Mousekeeping" (Davis/Oct.); and "Flop Secret" (Donnelly/Dec.).

1953: "Mouse Meets Bird" (Rasinski/Mar.); "Playful Puss" (Davis/May); "Friday the 13th" (Davis/July); and "Mouse Menace" (Donnelly/Sept.).

1954: "Runaway Mouse" (Davis/Jan.); "Prescription for Percy" (Davis/Apr.); and "Cat's Revenge" (Davis/Sept.).

1955: "No Sleep for Percy" (Rasinski/Mar. 1).

Ⓖ LOONEY TUNES
Looney Tunes were cartoon specials originally produced and animated in the style of Walt Disney's *Silly Symphony* cartoons, featuring popular music and assorted characters to tell a story. By the late 1930s, following structural changes, the series became a stamping ground for many of Warner Bros.' most renowned characters, including Bugs Bunny, Daffy Duck and Porky Pig.

From 1930 to 1933 the series was directed by Rudolf Ising and Hugh Harman, two ex-Disney animators who later joined MGM to head up its new cartoon department. After Harman and Ising's departure, producer Leon Schlesinger named Friz Freleng head director of the series. Freleng had worked alongside both directors since the inception of Warner's cartoon department. He served as chief animator on Harman and Ising's *Bosko* series. Incidentally, Bosko was the *Looney Tunes* series first regular cartoon star.

Beside Bosko, cartoons featured such studio favorites as Babbit and Catstello, Beaky Buzzard, Beans, Bobo, Buddy, Bugs Bunny, Claude Cat, Conrad Cat, Daffy Duck, Elmer Fudd, Foghorn Leghorn, Goofy Gophers, Hippety Hopper, The Honey-Mousers, Hubie and Bertie, Marc Antony, Pepe Le Pew, Ralph Wolf and Sam Sheepdog, Road Runner, Speedy Gonzales, Sylvester and Tweety. (See individual entries for series episode titles.) *Other series directors included Jack King, Bob Clampett, Norm McCabe, Frank Tashlin, Chuck Jones, Art Davis, Abe Levitow, Maurice Noble, Hawley Pratt, Alex Lovy and Robert McKimson. Black-and-white. Technicolor. A Warner Bros. release.*

Cartoon stars Little Roquefort (pictured) and nemesis cat, Percy, starred in cartoon "chases" reminiscent of MGM's Tom and Jerry for Terrytoons. © Viacom International

Voices

Mel Blanc, June Foray, Stan Freberg, Dick Beals, Daws Butler

(The following filmography is made up of *Looney Tunes* that do not feature a major star.)

1941: "The Haunted Mouse" (Avery/Feb. 15); and "Joe Glow, The Firefly" (Jones/Mar. 8).

1942: "Saps in Chaps" (Freleng/Apr. 11); "Nutty News" (Clampett/May 23); "Hobby Horse-Laffs" (McCabe/June 6); "Gopher Goofy" (McCabe/June 27); "Wacky Blackout" (Clampett/July 11); "The Ducktators" (McCabe/Aug. 1); "Eatin' on the Cuff" (Clampett/Aug. 22); and "The Hep Cat" (Clampett/Oct. 3/first Technicolor *Looney Tunes*).

1943: "Hop and Go" (McCabe/Mar. 27); "Tokio Jokio" (McCabe/May 15); and "Puss N' Booty" (Tashlin/Dec. 11/ last black-and-white *Looney Tunes*).

(All the following cartoons were in Technicolor.)

1944: "I Got Plenty of Mutton" (Tashlin/Mar. 11); "Angel Puss" (Jones/June 3); and "From Hand to Mouse" (Jones/ Aug. 5).

1945: "Behind the Meat Ball" (Tashlin/Apr. 7).

1946: "Of Thee I Sting" (Freleng/Aug. 17).

1948: "The Rattled Rooster" (Davis/June 26); "The Shell Shocked Egg" (McKimson/July 10); and "A Horse Fly Fleas" (McKimson/Dec. 13).

1949: "Swallow the Leader" (McKimson/Oct. 14).

1950: "It's Hummer Time" (McKimson/July 22).

1951: "Chowhound" (Jones/June 16).

1953: "A Peck o' Trouble" (McKimson/Mar. 28); "There Auto Be a Law" (McKimson/Jones/June 6); "Easy Peckins" (McKimson/Oct. 17); and "Punch Trunk" (Jones/Dec. 19).

1954: "From A to Z-Z-Z-Z" (Jones/Oct. 16/A.A. nominee/voice by Dick Beals).

1955: "The Hole Idea" (McKimson/Apr. 16).

1956: "Mixed Master" (McKimson/Apr. 14).

1957: "Three Little Bops" (Freleng/Jan. 5/narrator: Stan Freberg); and "Go Fly a Kit" (Jones/Feb. 23).

1958: "A Waggily Tale" (Freleng/Apr. 26) and "Dog Tales" (McKimson/July 26).

1959: "Mouse-Placed Kitten" (McKimson/Jan. 24).

1960: "High Note" (Jones/Dec. 3/A.A. nominee).

1962: "Martian Through Georgia" (Jones, Levitow/co-director: Noble/Dec. 29).

1963: "Now Hear This" (Jones/codirector: Noble/Apr. 27/ A.A. nominee).

DePatie-Freleng Enterprises releases

1964: "Señorella and the Glass Huarache" (Pratt/Aug. 1).

Warner Bros. releases

1968: "Flying Circus" (Lovy/Sept. 14).

◎ LOOPY DE LOOP

The indomitable French wolf's broken English caused unending communications gaffes that usually resulted in chaos. Loopy was the first theatrical cartoon series produced by William Hanna and Joseph Barbera for their studio, Hanna-Barbera Productions, which they cofounded after leaving MGM in 1957. Loopy later found new life through syndication of the old shorts to television in the 1960s. *Directed by William Hanna and Joseph Barbera. Technicolor. A Hanna-Barbera Production released through Columbia Pictures.*

Voices
Loopy De Loop: Daws Butler

1959: "Wolf Hounded" (Nov. 5); and "Little Bo Bopped" (Dec. 3).

1960: "Tale of a Wolf" (Mar. 3); "Life with Loopy" (Apr. 7); "Creepy Time Pal" (May 19); "Snoopy Loopy" (June 16); "The Do-Good Wolf" (July 14); "Here, Kiddie, Kiddie" (Sept. 1); and "No Biz Like Shoe Biz" (Sept. 8).

1961: "Count Down Clown" (Jan. 5); "Happy Go Lucky" (Mar. 2); "Two Faced Wolf" (Apr. 6); "This My Ducky Day" (May 4); "Fee Fie Foes" (June 9); "Zoo Is Company" (July 6); "Child Sock-Cology" (Aug. 10); "Catch Meow" (Sept. 14); "Kooky Loopy" (Nov. 16); and "Loopy's Hare-Do" (Dec. 14).

1962: "Bungle Uncle" (Jan. 18); "Beef For and After" (Mar. 1); "Swash Buckled" (Apr. 5); "Common Scents" (May 10); "Bearly Able" (June 28); "Slippery Slippers" (Sept. 7); "Chicken Fraca-See" (Oct. 11); "Rancid Ransom" (Nov. 15); and "Bunnies Abundant" (Dec. 13).

1963: "Just a Wolf at Heart" (Feb. 14); "Chicken Hearted Wolf" (Mar. 14); "Whatcha Watchin" (Apr. 18); "A Fallible Fable" (May 16); "Sheep Stealers Anonymous" (June 13); "Wolf in Sheep Dog's Clothing" (July 11); "Not in Nottingham" (Sept. 5); "Drum-Sticked" (Oct. 3); "Bear Up!" (Nov. 7); "Crook Who Cried Wolf" (Dec. 12); and "Habit Rabbit" (Dec. 31).

1964: "Raggedy Rug" (Jan. 2); "Elephantastic" (Feb. 6); "Bear Hug" (Mar. 5); "Trouble Bruin" (Sept. 17); "Bear Knuckles" (Oct. 15); and "Habit Troubles" (Nov. 19).

1965: "Horse Shoo" (Jan. 7); "Pork Chop Phooey" (Mar. 18); "Crow's Fete" (Apr. 14); and "Big Mouse Take" (June 17).

◎ LUNO

The flying horse Luno and his young master Tim relive history and fairy tales through transcendental powers of the great white stallion. *Directed by Connie Rasinski and Arthur Bartsch. Technicolor. A Terrytoons Production released through 20th Century-Fox.*

Voices
Luno, the white stallion/Tim, his companion: Bob McFadden

1963: "The Missing Genie" (Rasinski/Apr. 1); and "Trouble in Baghdad" (Rasinski/Sept. 13).

1964: "Roc-a-Bye Sinbad" (Bartsch/Jan.); "King Rounder" (Rasinski); "Adventure by the Sea" (Bartsch/July 15); and "The Gold Dust Bandit" (Bartsch/Sept.).

◎ MAGGIE AND SAM

Domestic trouble was the basis for comedy misadventures of this husband-and-wife pair who starred briefly in this Walter Lantz series. *Directed by Alex Lovy. Technicolor. A Walter Lantz Production released through Universal Pictures.*

Voices
Maggie: Grace Stafford; **Sam:** Daws Butler

1956: "The Ostrich and I" (Apr. 9) and "Talking Dog" (Aug. 27).

1957: "Fowled-Up Party" (Jan. 14).

◎ MARC ANTONY

A ferocious, bellowing bulldog is reduced to a softie by an adorable tiny pussycat, Pussyfoot, in this Warner Bros. cartoon series. The characters were created by Chuck Jones. *Directed by Chuck Jones. Technicolor. A Warner Bros. release.*

Voices
Marc Antony/Pussyfoot: Mel Blanc

Additional Voices
Bea Benadaret

Merrie Melodies

1952: "Feed the Kitty" (Feb. 2).

Looney Tunes

1953: "Kiss Me Cat" (Feb. 21).

1958: "Cat Feud" (Dec 20).

MARTIAN MOOCHERS

Created under the reign of legendary animator Ralph Bakshi, supervising director of Terrytoons in 1966, these weird little outer space mice wreaked havoc before making their escape in their spaceship in this short-lived series of adventures. *Directed by Bob Kuwahara. Technicolor. Voice credits unknown. A Terrytoons Production released through 20th Century-Fox.*

1966: "Champion Chump" (Apr.); and "The Cowardly Watchdog" (Aug.).

MARVIN MARTIAN

This dwarf, super-intelligent being, whose face was kept hidden under an oversize space helmet, zapped his way into the hearts of filmgoers in the 1948 Bugs Bunny cartoon "Haredevil Hare." Warner's animator Chuck Jones created Marvin for the screen, along with his Commander Flyer Saucer X-2 spacecraft, featuring the character in several command performances. Marvin's most memorable appearance was opposite Daffy Duck and Porky Pig in the 1953 classic, "Duck Dodgers in the 24 1/2 Century."

In 1980, following a 17-year absence, Marvin returned to the screen, at least the small screen, in two cartoons: "Space Out Bunny," produced as part of the *Bugs Bunny's Bustin' Out All Over* TV special for CBS, and "Duck Dodgers and the Return of the 24 1/2 Century," the long-awaited sequel to "Duck Dodgers in the 24 1/2 Century." The latter was originally produced for theaters but never released; it made its television debut on *Daffy Duck's Thank-for-Giving Special* on NBC. *Directed by Chuck Jones and Maurice Noble. Technicolor. A Warner Bros. release.*

Voices
Marvin Martian: Mel Blanc

Looney Tunes

1948: "Haredevil Hare" (with Bugs Bunny/Jones/July 24).

1952: "The Hasty Hare" (with Bugs Bunny/Jones/June 7).

1958: "Hare-Way to the Stars" (with Bugs Bunny/Jones/Mar. 29).

Merrie Melodies

1953: "Duck Dodgers in the 24 1/2 Century" (with Daffy Duck, Porky Pig/Jones/July 25).

1963: "Mad As a Mars Hare" (with Bugs Bunny/Jones, Noble/Oct. 19).

MAW AND PAW

The pug-nosed hillbilly Maw was half the size of her lean, bald husband, Paw. The two characters bore striking resemblances to Marjorie Main and Percy Kilbride, stars of Universal's long-running *Ma and Pa Kettle* film series, on which the cartoon series was based.

Grace Stafford, Walter Lantz's wife and voice of Woody Woodpecker, supplied the voice of Maw. *Directed by Paul J. Smith. Technicolor. A Walter Lantz Production released through Universal Pictures.*

Voices
Maw: Grace Stafford; **Paw:** Dal McKennon

1953: "Maw and Paw" (Smith/Aug. 10); and "Plywood Panic" (Smith/Sept. 28).

1954: "Pig in a Pickle" (Smith/Aug. 30).

1955: "Paw's Night Out" (Smith/Aug. 1).

MEANY, MINY AND MOE

Walter Lantz first introduced these three circus-dressed monkeys as supporting players in an Oswald Rabbit cartoon, "Monkey Wretches," in 1935. The characters were so well received that Lantz starred the trio in their own series, his fourth for Universal. Each episode incorporated the broad comedy gags that had made the Three Stooges popular, here with the monkeys acting out stories in pantomime.

Thirteen cartoons were produced between 1936 and 1937, with the first official Meany, Miny and Moe cartoon being "Turkey Dinner," released in November 1936. Lantz cut the number of Oswald cartoons he usually produced in half so he could start production of this new series, costing

© 1977 Walter Lantz

Universal's successful Ma and Pa Kettle *feature film series inspired this cartoon spinoff,* Maw and Paw, *created by Walter Lantz. © Walter Lantz Productions*

roughly $8,250 for each episode. Lantz discontinued the series in late 1937. "There just wasn't much else we could do with the characters," he said. *Directed by Walter Lantz. Black-and-white. A Walter Lantz Production released through Universal Pictures.*

1936: "Turkey Dinner" (Nov. 30); and "Knights for a day" (Dec. 25).

1937: "The Golfers" (Jan. 11); "House of Magic" (Feb. 8); "The Big Race" (Mar. 3); "Lumber Camp" (Mar. 15); "Steel Workers" (Apr. 26); "The Stevedores" (May 24); "Country Store" (July 5); "Fireman's Picnic" (Aug. 16); "Rest Resort" (Aug. 23); "Ostrich Feathers" (Sept. 6); and "Air Express" (Sept. 20).

☺ MERLIN THE MAGIC MOUSE

Reminiscent of W.C. Fields—even sounding like the great bulbous-nosed comedian—Merlin the Magic Mouse was the second new cartoon creation by Alex Lovy for Warner Bros.' animation department after its reopening in 1967. Stories were based on the globe-trotting adventures of the mouse, who never made a lasting impression on filmgoers and was quickly retired after only five film appearances. Larry Storch (of TV's *F Troop* fame) provided the voice of Merlin in all but one cartoon, that being the first: 1967's "Merlin the Magic Mouse" (voiced by Daws Butler). *Directed by Alex Lovy and Robert McKimson. Technicolor. A Warner Bros. release.*

Voices
Merlin the Magic Mouse: Larry Storch, Daws Butler

Merrie Melodies

1967: "Merlin the Magic Mouse" (Lovy/Nov. 18).

1968: "Feud with a Dude" (Lovy/May 25).

1969: "Shamrock and Roll" (McKimson/June 28).

Looney Tunes

1968: "Hocus Pocus Pow Wow" (Lovy/Jan. 13).

1969: "Fistic Mystic" (McKimson/Mar. 29).

☺ MERRIE MELODIES

Directors Rudolf Ising and Hugh Harman, two former Disney animators, produced independently through Warner Bros. a series based on popular melodies of that era. Leon Schlesinger later served as producer when Harman and Ising left Warner in 1933 to lend their talent to studio rival MGM, which was entering the cartoon field for the first time.

The earliest picture in the series made use of Abe Lyman's Recording Orchestra on soundtracks, playing "whoopee tunes" of the day, like "Smile, Darn Ya Smile" and "Freddie the Freshman." Other initial series entries revolved around "period" subjects—the vaudeville stage, the college football craze, and so on—and spot references to popular culture and current trends.

In the beginning, the series' closest thing to a star was Goopy Geer, a wisecracking entertainer—"part comedian, part musician and part dancer"—inspired by vaudeville showmen of that period. Throughout its history, the series featured a vast array of major and less notable cartoon stars and miscellaneous one-shot characters.

The series' stars were Babbit and Catstello, Beaky Buzzard, Bobo, Bunny and Claude, Bugs Bunny, Charlie Dog, Claude Cat, Conrad Cat, Daffy Duck, Elmer Fudd, Foxy, Goofy Gophers, Goopy Geer, Hippety Hopper, Hubie and Bertie, Inki, Marc Antony, Pepe Le Pew, Piggy, Ralph Phillips, Ralph Wolf and Sam Sheepdog, the Road Runner and Coyote, Speedy Gonzales, Sylvester, The Three Bears, Tweety and Two Curious Dogs. (See individual entries for aforementioned characters for episodic listings.) *Besides Harman and Ising, series directors included Tex Avery, Bernard Brown, Bob Clampett, Cal Dalton, Art Davis, Earl Duvall, Friz Freleng, Ben Hardaway, Chuck Jones, Abe Levitow, Alex Lovy, Frank Marsales, Robert McKimson, Ken Mundie, Tom Palmer, and Frank Tashlin. Black-and-white. Technicolor. A Warner Bros. release.*

Voices
Mel Blanc, Pinto Colvig, Bea Benadaret, June Foray, Daws Butler

Additional Voices
Vivian Dandrige, Tex Avery, Leslie Barrings

(The following filmography is comprised of "Merrie Melodies" that do not feature major Warner cartoon stars.)

1931: "Red-Headed Baby" (Ising/Dec. 26).

1932: "Pagan Moon" (Ising/Jan. 31); "Freddy the Freshman" (Ising/Feb. 20); "Crosby, Columbo and Vallee" (Ising/Mar. 19); "It's Got Me Again" (Ising/May 14/A.A. nominee); "I Love a Parade" (Ising/Aug. 6); "You're Too Careless with Your Kisses" (Ising/Sept. 10); "I Wish I Had Wings" (Ising/Oct. 15); and "A Great Big Bunch of You" (Ising/Nov. 12).

1933: "The Shanty Where Santa Lives" (Ising/Jan. 7); "Three's a Crowd" (Ising/Jan. 17); "One Step Ahead of My Shadow" (Ising/Feb. 4); "Young and Healthy" (Ising/Mar. 4); "The Organ Grinder" (Ising/Apr. 8); "Wake Up the Gypsy in Me" (Ising/May 13); "I Like Mountain Music" (Ising/June 13); "Shuffle Off to Buffalo" (Freleng/July 8); "We're in the Money" (Ising/Aug. 26). (The following

Merrie Melodies were Leon Schlesinger Productions.) "I've Got to Sing a Torch Song" (Palmer/Sept. 23); "The Dish Ran Away with the Spoon" (Ising/Sept. 24); and "Sittin' on a Backyard Fence" (Duvall/Sept. 16).

1934: "Pettin' in the Park" (Brown/Jan. 27); "Honeymoon Hotel" (Duvall/Feb. 17/Cinecolor); "Beauty and the Beast" (Freleng/Apr. 14/Cinecolor); "Those Were Wonderful Days" (Brown/Apr. 26); "Goin' to Heaven on a Mule" (Freleng/May 19); "How Do I Know It's Sunday" (Freleng/June 9); "Why Do I Dream Those Dreams?" (Freleng/June 30); "The Girl at the Ironing Board" (Freleng/Aug. 23); "The Miller's Daughter" (Freleng/Oct. 13); "Shake Your Powder Puff" (Freleng/Oct. 17); "Those Beautiful Dames" (Freleng/Nov. 10/two-strip Technicolor); and "Pop Goes My Heart" (Freleng/Dec. 18/two-strip Technicolor).

1935: "Mr. and Mrs. Is the Name" (Freleng/Jan. 19/two-strip Technicolor); "Rhythm in Bow" (Hardaway/Feb. 1/last *Merrie Melodies* in black-and-white; following were all produced in two-strip Technicolor); "The Country Boy" (with Peter Rabbit/Freleng/Feb. 9/); "Along Flirtation Walk" (Freleng/Apr. 6); "My Green Fedora" (with Peter Rabbit/Freleng/May 4); "Into Your Dance" (Freleng/June 8); "The Country Mouse" (Freleng/July 13); "The Merry Old Soul" (Freleng/Aug. 17); "The Lady in Red" (Freleng/Sept. 7); "Little Dutch Plate" (Freleng/Oct. 19); "Billboard Frolics" (Freleng/Nov. 9); and "Flowers for Madame" (Freleng/Nov. 20).

(All in Technicolor.)

1936: "I Wanna Play House" (Freleng/Jan. 11); "The Cat Came Back" (Freleng/Feb. 8); "Miss Glory" (Avery/Mar. 7); "I'm a Big Shot Now" (Freleng/Apr. 11); "Let It Be Me" (Freleng/May 2); "I Love to Take Orders from You" (Avery/May 18); "Bingo Crosbyana" (Freleng/May 30); "When I Yoo Hoo" (Freleng/June 27); "I Love to Singa" (Avery/July 18); "Sunday Go to Meetin' Time" (Freleng/Aug. 8); "At Your Service Madame" (Freleng/Aug. 29); "Toytown Hall" (Freleng/Sept. 19); "Boulevardier from the Bronx" (Freleng/Oct. 10); "Don't Look Now" (Avery/Nov. 7); and "The Coo Coo Nut Grove" (Freleng/Nov. 28).

1937: "He Was Her Man" (Freleng/Jan. 2); "Pigs Is Pigs" (Freleng/Jan. 30); "I Only Have Eyes for You" (Avery/Mar. 6); "The Fella with the Fiddle" (Freleng/Mar. 27); "She Was an Acrobat's Daughter" (Freleng/Apr. 10); "Ain't We Got Fun" (Avery/Apr. 27); "Clean Pastures" (Freleng/May 22); "Uncle Tom's Bungalow" (Avery/June 5); "Streamlined Greta Green" (Freleng/June 19); "Sweet Sioux" (Freleng/June 26); "Plenty of Money and You" (Freleng/July 31); "A Sunbonnet Blue" (Avery/Aug. 21); "Speaking of the Weather" (Tashlin/Sept. 4); "Dog Daze" (Freleng/Sept. 18); "I Wanna Be a Sailor" (Avery/Sept. 25); "The Lyin' Mouse" (Freleng/Oct. 16); "The Woods Are Full of Cuckoos" (Tashlin/Dec. 4); and "September in the Rain" (Freleng/Dec. 18).

1938: "My Little Buckaroo" (Freleng/Jan. 29); "Jungle Jitters" (Freleng/Feb. 19); "The Sneezing Weasel" (Avery/Mar. 12); "A Star Is Hatched" (Freleng/Apr. 2); "The Penguin Parade" (Avery/Apr. 16); "Now That Summer Is Gone" (Tashlin/May 4); "The Isle of Pingo-Pongo" (Avery/May 28); "Katnip Kollege" (Hardaway, Dalton/June 11); "Have You Got Any Castles?" (Tashlin/June 25); "Love and Curses" (Hardaway, Dalton/July 9); "The Major Lied Till Dawn" (Tashlin/Aug. 13); "Cracked Ice" (Tashlin/Sept. 10); "Little Pancho Vanilla" (Tashlin/Oct. 8); "You're an Education" (Tashlin/Nov. 5); "The Night Watchman" (Jones/Nov. 19); and "The Mice Will Play" (Avery/Dec. 31).

1939: "Robin Hood Makes Good" (Jones/Feb. 11); "Gold Rush Daze" (Hardaway, Dalton/Feb. 25); "Bars and Stripes Forever" (Hardaway, Dalton/Apr. 8); "Thugs with Dirty Mugs" (Avery/May 6); "Hobo Gadget Band" (Hardaway, Dalton/June 17); "Dangerous Dan McFoo" (Avery/July 15); "Snow Man's Land" (Jones/July 29); "Detouring America" (Avery/Aug. 26/A.A. nominee); "Sioux Me" (Hardaway, Dalton/Sept. 9); "Land of the Midnight Fun" (Avery/Sept. 23); "The Good Egg" (Jones/Oct. 21); "Fresh Fish" (Avery/Nov. 4); "Fagin's Freshman" (Hardaway, Dalton/Nov. 18); and "Screwball Football" (Avery/Dec. 16).

1940: "The Early Worm Gets the Bird" (Avery/Jan. 13); "The Mighty Hunters" (Jones/Jan. 27); "Busy Bakers" (Hardaway, Dalton/Feb. 10); "Cross Country Detours" (Avery/Mar. 16); "The Bear's Tale" (Avery/Apr. 13); "A Gander at Mother Goose" (Avery/May 25); "Tom Thumb in Trouble" (Jones/June 8); "Circus Today" (Avery/June 22); "Little Blabbermouse" (Freleng/July 6); "Ghost Wanted" (Jones/Aug. 10); "Ceiling Hero" (Avery/Aug. 24); "Malibu Beach Party" (Freleng/Sept. 14); "Stage Fright" (Jones/Sept. 28); "Holiday Highlights" (Avery/Oct. 12); "Wacky Wildlife" (Avery/Nov. 9); "Of Fox and Hounds" (Avery/Dec. 7); and "Shop, Look and Listen" (Freleng/Dec. 21).

1941: "The Fighting 69th 1/2" (Freleng/Jan. 18); "The Crackpot Quail" (Avery/Feb. 15); "The Cat's Tale" (Freleng/Mar. 1); "Goofy Groceries" (Clampett/Mar. 29); "The Trial of Mister Wolf" (Freleng/Apr. 26); "Farm Frolics" (Clampett/May 10); "Hollywood Steps Out" (with The Three Stooges, Clark Gable, Bing Crosby, Jimmy Stewart, William Powell, Peter Lorre, Groucho Marx, Harpo Marx and Buster Keaton caricatures/Avery/May 24); "The Wacky Worm" (Freleng/June 21); "Aviation Vacation" (Avery/Aug. 2); "Sport Chumpions" (Freleng/Aug. 16); "The Bug Parade" (Avery/Oct. 11); "Rookie Revue" (Freleng/Oct. 25); "Saddle Silly" (Jones/Nov. 8); "The Cagey Canary" (Avery, Clampett/Nov. 22); and "Rhapsody In Rivets" (Freleng/Dec. 6/A.A. nominee).

1942: "Hop, Skip, and Chump" (with Laurel and Hardy–like crows/Freleng/Jan. 3); "Aloha Hooey" (Avery/Jan. 30); "Crazy Cruise" (Avery, Clampett/Mar. 14); "Horton Hatches the Egg" (Clampett/Apr. 11/based on the story by Dr. Seuss); "Dog Tired" (Jones/Apr. 25); "The Draft Horse" (Jones/May 9); "Lights Fantastic" (Freleng/May 23); "Double Chaser" (Freleng/June 27); "Foney Fables" (Freleng/Aug. 1); "Fox Pop" (Jones/Sept. 5/film title was a spoof of a popular radio program); "The Dover Boys" (Jones/Sept. 10); "The Sheepish Wolf" (Freleng/Oct. 17); and "Ding Dog Daddy" (Freleng/Dec. 5).

1943: "Coal Black and de Sebben Dwarfs" (Clampett/Jan. 16/So White voiced by Vivian Dandrige); "Pigs in a Polka" (Freleng/Feb. 2/A.A. nominee); "Fifth Column Mouse" (Freleng/Mar. 6); "Flop Goes the Weasel" (Jones/Mar. 20); "Greetings Bait" (Freleng/May 15/A.A. nominee); "Tin Pan Alley Cats" (Clampett/July 17); "Hiss and Make Up" (Freleng/Sept. 11); and "Fin N' Catty" (Jones/Oct. 23).

1944: "Meatless Flyday" (Freleng/Jan. 29/spider voiced by Tex Avery); "The Weakly Reporter" (Jones/Mar. 25); "Russian Rhapsody" (Clampett/May 20); and "Goldilocks and the Jivin' Bears" (Freleng/Sept. 2).

1945: "Fresh Airedale" (Jones/Aug. 25).

1946: "Holiday for Shoestrings" (with Laurel and Hardy elves/Freleng/Feb. 23); "Quentin Quail" (Jones/Mar. 2); "Hollywood Canine Canteen" (with Edward G. Robinson, Jimmy Durante, Laurel and Hardy, Bing Crosby, Bob Hope, Jerry Colonna, Abbott and Costello, Blondie and Dagwood, Joe Besser and Harry James caricatures in the images of dogs/McKimson/Apr. 20); "The Eager Beaver" (Jones/July 13); and "Fair and Worm-er" (Jones/Sept. 28).

1947: "The Gay Anties" (Freleng/Feb. 15); and "The Foxy Duckling" (Davis/Aug. 23).

1948: "Bone Sweet Bone" (Davis/May 22/Cinecolor); "Dough Ray Me-Ow" (Davis/Aug. 14); "A Horse Fly Fleas" (McKimson/Dec. 13/Cinecolor); and "A Hide, a Slick, and a Chick" (Davis/Dec. 27).

1951: "A Fox in a Fix" (McKimson/Jan. 20); "Corn Plastered" (McKimson/Mar. 3); "Early to Bet" (McKimson/May 12); and "Sleepy Time Possum" (McKimson/Nov. 3).

1952: "Kiddin' the Kitten" (McKimson/Apr. 5); and "The Turn-Tale Wolf" (McKimson/June 28).

1953: "Much Ado About Nutting" (Jones/May 23).

1954: "Wild Wife" (McKimson/Feb. 20); "The Oily American" (McKimson/July 10); and "Goo Goo Goliath" (Freleng/Sept. 18).

1955: "Pizzicato Pussycat" (Freleng/Jan. 1); and "One Froggy Evening" (Jones/Dec. 31).

1956: "Rocket-Bye Baby" (Jones/Aug. 4); and "Two Crows from Tacos" (Freleng/Nov. 24).

1958: "To Itch His Own" (Jones/June 28).

1959: "Mouse-Placed Kitten" (McKimson/Jan. 24); "The Mouse That Jack Built" (with Jack Benny, Rochester, Mary Livingston and Don Wilson as mice/McKimson/Apr. 4/voices performed by Jack Benny, Mary Livingston, Rochester, Don Wilson and Mel Blanc); and "Unnatural History" (Levitow/Nov. 14).

1960: "Wild Wild World" (McKimson/Feb. 27).

1961: "The Mouse on 57th Street" (Jones/Feb. 25); and "Nelly's Folly" (with Nelly the Giraffe/Jones, Noble, Levitow/Dec. 30/A.A. nominee).

1963: "I Was a Teenage Thumb" (with Ralph K. Merlin Jr./Jones, Noble/Jan. 19).

DePatie-Freleng Enterprises releases

1964: "Bartholomew Versus the Wheel" (McKimson/Feb. 29).

Warner Bros. releases

1968: "Chimp and Zee" (Lovy/Oct. 12).

1969: "Rabbit Stews and Rabbits Too" (with Rapid Rabbit/McKimson/June 7).

⊚ MERRY MAKERS

This was the last cartoon series launched by Paramount's Famous Studios. James "Shamus" Culhane produced and directed each cartoon short, shaped around everyday situations and starring various animated characters. Paramount shut down its cartoon department after the 1967 season, the same year *Merry Makers* was created.

Directed by James "Shamus" Culhane. Technicolor. A Famous Studios Production released through Paramount Pictures.

1967: "Think or Sink" (Mar.); "Halt, Who Grows There?" (May); "From Orbit to Obit" (June); and "Forget Me Nuts" (Aug.).

⊚ MGM CARTOONS

The Metro-Goldwyn-Mayer lot was known for more than just producing its share of big-budget musicals and epic films. The studio also produced a number of quality, theatrical sound cartoons. In the early 1930s Hugh Harman and Rudolf Ising produced and directed MGM cartoons, and in the 1940s the studio produced a series of cartoons featuring major stars like Tom and Jerry, Droopy and Barney Bear. During the cartoon divison's halycon days it also produced an assortment of cartoons featuring an all-star cast and no-name characters that, for the most part, were equally entertaining. The following is a listing of the studio's miscellaneous cartoons that were released under the studio's trademark MGM lion logo. (For MGM series entries, see *Barney Bear, Bosko, Droopy, George and Junior, Tom and Jerry, Screwy Squirrel* and Tex Avery, Hugh Harman and Rudolph Ising listings.) *Directed by Milt Gross, George Gordon, Joseph Barbera, William Hanna, Robert Allen and Jerry Brewer. Black-and-white. Technicolor. A Metro-Goldwyn-Mayer release.*

1939: (Sepia-tone) "Jitterbug Follies" (with J.R. the Wonder Dog, Count Screwloose/Gross/Feb. 25); and "Wanted: No Master" (with J.R. the Wonder Dog, Count Screwloose/Gross/Mar. 18).

1940: (All the following cartoons were produced in Technicolor) "Swing Social" (Hanna, Barbera/May 18); and "Gallopin' Gals" (Hanna, Barbera/Oct. 26).

1941: "The Goose That Goes South" (Hanna, Barbera/Apr. 26); "Little Caesario" (Allen/Aug. 30); and "Officer Pooch" (Hanna, Barbera/Sept. 6).

1942: "The First Swallow" (Brewer/Mar. 14); "Bats in the Belfry" (Brewer/July 4); and "Chips Off the Old Block" (Allen/Sept. 12).

1943: "War Dogs" (Hanna, Barbera/Oct. 9); and "Stork's Holiday" (Gordon/Oct. 23).

1944: "Innertube Antics" (Jan. 22/working titles: "Strange Innertube" and "Innertube Interlude"); and "The Tree Surgeon" (Gordon/June 3).

1948: "Make Mine Freedom" (Hanna, Barbera/Feb. 25).

1950: "Why Play Leapfrog?" (produced by John Sutherland for Harding College).

1951: "Meet King Joe" (produced by John Sutherland for Harding College/Sept. 13); "Inside Cackle Corners" (produced by John Sutherland for Harding College/Nov. 13); and "Fresh Laid Plans" (produced by John Sutherland for Harding College/Dec. 11).

1955: "Good Will to Men" (Hanna, Barbera/Dec. 23/ A.A. nominee).

◎ MICHIGAN J. FROG

This high-stepping song-and-dance amphibian, known today to television audiences as the corporate mascot of the WB Network, was the brainchild of legendary animator Chuck Jones. Jones introduced him as a nameless frog in the 1956 *Merrie Melodies* cartoon "One Froggy Evening," considered a cult classic in which the top-hatted frog is exploited for his dancing talent and singing of "Hello, My Ragtime Gal."

In 1995, after forming a new animation studio to produce theatrical cartoon shorts for his former studio, Jones directed a sequel to the original masterpiece, entitled, what else, "Another Froggy Evening." The short continues the story of the mysterious amphibian with a beautiful voice who refuses to sing in public. Jeff McCarthy supplied the crooning in the sequel (following this gig he starred on Broadway as the Beast in the stage rendition of Disney's *Beauty and the Beast*). The film was originally scheduled to be released nationwide with the Batman sequel, *Batman Forever*, but Warner Bros. decided not to release it. The cartoon instead made its premiere at the Telluride Film Festival in September 1995. *Directed by Chuck Jones. Technicolor. A Warner Bros. release.*

Voices
Michigan J. Frog: Jeff McCarthy

1956: "One Froggy Evening (Dec. 31/*Merrie Melodies*).

1995: "Another Froggy Evening" (Sept.).

◎ MICKEY MOUSE

Button-eyed, mischievous Mickey Mouse has been a lovable world-renowned character for more than 60 years. New generations of television viewers continue to rediscover the superstar rodent through reruns of *The Mickey Mouse Club* and Mickey Mouse cartoons.

In the early cartoons, Mickey displayed some of the same physical features as Walt Disney's Oswald the Rabbit character: He wore short, button-down pants and pure-white, four-finger gloves. Disney and veteran animator Ub Iwerks first drew the soft-talking Mickey, and Disney himself supplied the voice through the late 1940s.

In 1928, inspired by the enormous success of *The Jazz Singer*, the first talking picture, which had been released the previous year, Disney cashed in on the opportunity by providing something unique—the first synchronized sound cartoon, "Steamboat Willie," starring Mickey as the captain of his own steamboat.

The cartoon came about following initial tests by Disney and his staff. He first screened a scene using synchronized sound—a process renovated by animator Ub Iwerks—when the film was half finished. The effect of the screening was "nothing less than electric," Disney once said. The reaction was duplicated months later when audiences witnessed this latest innovation for the first time on theater screens across the country.

This landmark film changed the course of cartoon animation, and Disney immediately added soundtracks to two previously produced silent Mickey Mouse cartoons, "Plane Crazy" and "Gallopin' Gaucho," releasing both films with music arranged and composed by Carl Stalling, who later became Warner Bros.' musical director.

Mickey experienced unprecedented worldwide fame in the years ahead, spawning hundreds of thousands of licensed merchandise items, such as games and toys. (The first Mickey Mouse stuffed doll was designed by animator Bob Clampett, then a high school student, and his enterprising aunt Charlotte Clark.) In fact, in 1932 Disney even received a special Academy Award in recognition of Mickey's creation and resulting impact on the cartoon industry.

Supporting characters in the series were Minnie Mouse, Peg Leg Pete, Horace Horsecollar and Clarabelle Cow, each appearing in several episodes during the life of the series.

In 1990 Mickey Mouse starred along with pals Goofy, Donald Duck and Pluto in an all-new 35-minute featurette, *The Prince and the Pauper*, based on the original Mark Twain tale. The film was simultaneously released with the full-length Disney feature *The Rescuers Down Under*. Animator George Scribner, who had worked with legendary animators Chuck Jones and Ralph Bakshi (on the features *American Pop* and *Lord of the Rings* and at Hanna-Barbera (on the feature *Heidi's Song*) and Disney (on the features *The Black Cauldron* and *The Great Mouse Detective*), directed the film.

Following a five-year absence, Mickey returned to the screen in an all-new cartoon adventure, "Runaway Brain," in which he encounters a Frankenstein-like mad scientist who switches his brain with that of his monster creation. It was Mickey's 119th cartoon short and his first in 42 years. The seven-minute cartoon opened with the live-action feature, *A Kid in King Arthur's Court*. Mickey was redesigned for the occasion by supervising animator Andreas Deja and his fellow animators (so was costar Minnie Mouse, who had a retro makeover; the film also featured Pluto). They reviewed Mickey's other short films and archival "model sheets," 67 years' worth of drawings, before settling on the personality and look Mickey had around 1941 in films such as "The Nifty Nineties." Wayne Allwine, who took over as the voice of Mickey in 1983, provided Mickey's voice characterization, with wife Russi Taylor as Minnie and Kelsey Grammer as the mad scientist. The short was produced by Ron Tippe and directed by Chris Bailey. *Directors were Walt Disney, Wilfred Jackson, Bert Gillett, David Hand, Ben Sharpsteen, Hamilton Luske, Pinto Colvig, Walt Pfeiffer, Ed Penner, Jack King, Dick Huemer, Bill Roberts, Clyde Geronimi, Riley Thomson, Charles Nichols, Jack Hannah, Milt Schaffer, Burny Mattinson, George Scribner and Chris Bailey. Black-and-white. Technicolor. A Walt Disney Production released through Celebrity Pictures, Columbia Pictures, United Artists, RKO-Radio Pictures and later Buena Vista.*

Voices

Mickey Mouse: Walt Disney (to 1947), Jim MacDonald (1947–83), Wayne Allwine (1983–); **Minnie Mouse:** Marcellite Garner (to 1940), Thelma Boardman (1940), Ruth Clifford (after 1942), Russi Taylor

Celebrity Pictures

1928: "Plane Crazy" (Disney/never released silent/released in 1929 in sound); "Gallopin' Gaucho" (Disney/released in 1929 in sound); and "Steamboat Willie" (Disney/Nov. 18/ first sound cartoon).

1929: "The Barn Dance" (Disney/Mar. 14); "The Opry House" (Disney/Mar. 28); "When the Cat's Away" (Disney/ Apr. 11); "The Barnyard Battle" (Disney/Apr. 25); "The Plow Boy" (Disney/May 9); "The Karnival Kid" (Disney/ May 23); "Mickey's Follies" (Jackson/June 26); "Mickey's Choo-Choo" (Disney/June 20); "The Jazz Fool" (Disney/ July 5); "The Haunted House" (Disney/Aug. 1); "Wild Waves" (Gillett/Aug. 15); and "Jungle Rhythm" (Disney/ Nov. 15).

Columbia Pictures

(The studio took over distributorship of all previous films as well as new releases.)

1930: "The Barnyard Concert" (Disney/Mar. 3); "Just Mickey" (Disney/Mar. 14/formerly "Fiddlin' Around"); "The Cactus Kid" (Disney/Apr. 11); "The Shindig" (Gillett/July 11); "The Fire Fighters" (Gillett/Aug. 6); "The Chain Gang" (with Pluto/Gillett/Aug. 18); "The Gorilla Mystery" (Gillett/Oct. 1); "The Picnic" (with Pluto/Gillett/ Nov. 14); and "Pioneer Days" (with Pluto/Gillett/Dec. 10).

1931: "The Birthday Party" (Gillett/Jan. 6); "Traffic Troubles" (Gillett/Mar. 20); "The Castaway" (Jackson/Apr. 6); "The Moose Hunt" (with Pluto/Gillett/May 8); "The Delivery Boy" (Gillett/June 15); "Mickey Steps Out" (with Pluto/Gillett/June 22); "Blue Rhythm" (Gillett/Aug. 18); "Fishin' Around" (with Pluto/Gillett/Sept. 14); "The Barnyard Broadcast" (Gillett/Oct. 19); "The Beach Party" (with Pluto/Gillett/Nov. 4); "Mickey Cuts Up" (with Pluto/Gillett/Dec. 2); and "Mickey's Orphans" (with Pluto/Gillett/Dec. 14/A.A. nominee).

1932: "The Duck Hunt" (with Pluto/Gillett/Jan. 28); "The Grocery Boy" (with Pluto/Jackson/Feb. 3); "The Mad Dog" (with Pluto/Gillett/Mar. 5); "Barnyard Olympics" (with Pluto/Jackson/Apr. 18); "Mickey's Revue" (with Pluto, Goofy/Jackson/May 2); "Musical Farmer" (Jackson/ July 11); and "Mickey In Arabia" (Jackson/July 20).

United Artists

1932: "Mickey's Nightmare" (with Pluto/Gillett/Aug. 13); "Trader Mickey" (with Pluto/Hand/Aug. 20); "The Whoopee Party" (with Goofy/Jackson/Sept 17); "Touchdown Mickey" (Jackson/Oct. 5); "The Wayward Canary" (with Pluto/Gillett/Nov. 12); "The Klondike Kid" (with Pluto/Jackson/Nov. 12); and "Mickey's Good Deed" (with Pluto/Gillett/Dec. 17).

1933: "Building a Building" (Hand/Jan. 7/A.A. nominee); "The Mad Doctor" (with Pluto/Hand/Jan. 21); "Mickey's Pal Pluto" (with Pluto/Gillett/Feb. 18); "Mickey's Meller-drammer" (with Goofy/Jackson/Mar. 18); "Ye Olden Days" (with Goofy/Gillett/Apr. 8); "The Mail Pilot" (Hand/May 13); "Mickey's Mechanical Man" (Jackson/June 17); "Mickey's Gala Premiere" (with Pluto, Goofy/Gillett/July 1); "Puppy Love" (with Pluto/Jackson/Sept. 2); "The Steeplechase" (Gillett/Sept. 30); "The Pet Store" (Jackson/Oct. 28); and "Giantland" (Gillett/Nov. 25).

1934: "Shanghaied" (Gillett/Jan. 13); "Camping Out" (Hand/Feb. 17); "Playful Pluto" (with Pluto/Gillett/Mar. 3); "Gulliver Mickey" (Gillett/May 19); "Mickey's Steam Roller" (Hand/June 16); "Orphan's Benefit" (with Donald Duck, Goofy/Gillett/Aug. 11); "Mickey Plays Papa" (with Pluto/Gillett/Sept. 29); "The Dognapper" (with Donald Duck/Hand/Nov. 17); and "Two-Gun Mickey" (Sharpsteen/Dec. 15).

1935: "Mickey's Man Friday" (Hand/Jan. 19); "The Band Concert" (with Donald Duck, Goofy/Jackson/Feb. 23/first color); "Mickey's Service Station" (with Donald Duck, Goofy/Sharpsteen/Mar. 16); "Mickey's Kangaroo" (with Pluto/Hand/Apr. 13/last black-and-white Mickey Mouse cartoon); "Mickey's Garden" (with Pluto/Jackson/July 13); "Mickey's Fire Brigade" (with Donald Duck, Goofy/Sharpsteen/Aug. 3); "Pluto's Judgement Day" (with Pluto/Hand/Aug. 31); and "On Ice" (with Donald Duck, Goofy, Pluto/Sharpsteen/Sept. 28).

1936: "Mickey's Polo Team" (with Donald Duck, Goofy/Hand/Jan. 4); "Orphan's Picnic" (with Donald Duck/Sharpsteen/Feb. 15); "Mickey's Grand Opera" (with Donald Duck, Pluto/Jackson/Mar. 7); "Thru the Mirror" (Hand/May 30); "Moving Day" (with Donald Duck, Goofy/Sharpsteen/June 20); "Mickey's Rival" (Jackson/June 20); "Alpine Climbers" (with Donald Duck, Pluto/Hand/July 25); "Mickey's Circus" (with Donald Duck/Sharpsteen/Aug. 1); and "Mickey's Elephant" (with Pluto/Luske/Oct. 10).

1937: "The Worm Turns" (with Pluto/Sharpsteen/Jan. 2); "Magician Mickey" (with Donald Duck/Hand/Feb. 6); "Moose Hunters" (with Donald Duck, Goofy/Sharpsteen/Feb. 20); and "Mickey's Amateurs" (with Donald Duck/Colvig, Pfeiffer, Penner/Apr. 17).

RKO-Radio Pictures

1937: "Hawaiian Holiday" (with Donald Duck, Goofy Pluto/Sharpsteen/Sept. 24); "Clock Cleaners" (with Donald Duck, Goofy/Sharpsteen/Oct. 15); and "Lonesome Ghosts" (with Donald Duck, Goofy/Gillett/Dec. 24).

1938: "Boat Builders" (with Donald Duck, Goofy/Sharpsteen/Feb. 25); "Mickey's Trailer" (with Donald Duck, Goofy/Sharpsteen/May 6); "The Whalers" (with Donald Duck, Goofy/Huemer/Aug. 19); "Mickey's Parrot" (with Pluto/Roberts/Sept. 9); and "Brave Little Tailor" (Gillett/Sept. 23/A.A. nominee).

1939: "Society Dog Show" (with Pluto/Roberts/Feb. 3); and "The Pointer" (with Pluto/Geronimi/July 21/A.A. nominee).

1940: "Tugboat Mickey" (with Donald Duck, Goofy/Geronimi/Apr. 26); "Pluto's Dream House" (with Pluto/Geronimi/Aug. 30); and "Mr. Mouse Takes a Trip" (with Pluto/Geronimi/Oct. 1).

1941: "The Little Whirlwind" (Thomson/Feb. 14); "The Nifty Nineties" (with Donald Duck, Goofy/Thomson/June 20); and "Orphan's Benefit" (with Donald Duck, Goofy/Thomson/Aug. 12).

1942: "Mickey's Birthday Party" (with Donald Duck, Goofy/Thomson/Feb. 7); and "Symphony Hour" (with Donald Duck, Goofy/Thomson/Mar. 20).

1947: "Mickey's Delayed Date" (with Pluto/Nichols/Oct. 3).

1948: "Mickey Down Under" (with Pluto/Nichols/Mar. 19); and "Mickey and the Seal" (Nichols/Dec. 3/A.A. nominee).

1951: "Plutopia" (with Pluto/Nichols/May 18); and "R'coon Dawg" (with Pluto/Nichols/Aug. 10).

1952: "Pluto's Party" (Schaffer/Sept. 19); and "Pluto's Christmas Tree" (with Chip 'n' Dale, Donald Duck, Goofy/Hannah/Nov. 21).

1953: "The Simple Things" (with Pluto/Nichols/Apr. 18).

1983: "Mickey's Christmas Carol" (Mattinson/Dec. 16/A.A. nominee).

1990: "The Prince and the Pauper" (with Goofy, Donald Duck, Pluto/Scribner/Nov. 16).

1994: "Runaway Brain" (with Minnie Mouse, Pluto/Bailey/Aug. 11).

Ⓖ THE MIGHTY HEROES

Under the supervision of animator Ralph Bakshi, this series emerged in response to the growing craze for superhero cartoons, only this one poked fun at the idea. Episodes featured five defenders of justice—Diaper Man, Tornado Man, Rope Man, Strong Man and Cuckoo Man—a group of half witted superheros who battle the evil doings of such notorious villains as the Stretcher, the Shrinker and, of course, the Enlarger.

Originally, 26 episodes were made for television, with a scant few actually released to theaters nationwide in the late 1960s and early 1970s. Bakshi was named supervising director of Terrytoons in 1966, the same year the series was first broadcast on television. *Directed by Ralph Bakshi and Bob Taylor. Technicolor. A Terrytoons Production released through 20th Century-Fox.*

Voices:

The Mighty Heroes: Herschel Benardi, Lionel Wilson

1969: "The Stretcher" (Apr.); "The Frog" (Oct.); and "The Toy Man" (Dec.).

1970: "The Ghost Monster" (Apr.); "The Drifter" (Aug.); "The Proton Pulsator" (Sept.); and "The Shocker" (Dec.).

1971: "The Enlarger" (Apr.); "The Duster" (Aug.); and "The Big Freeze" (Dec.).

◎ MIGHTY MOUSE

Combining the power of Superman and the body of Mickey Mouse, Mighty Mouse was animator Paul Terry's most popular cartoon star. For more than 15 years, the character defended the rights of mice in need of his superstrength to stave off trouble and restore order.

I. Klein, a Terrytoons storyman, originated the Mighty Mouse character several years after joining the studio in the spring of 1940. Since most animated characters at that time were humanized animals and insects, Klein initially sketched a "super fly," replete with a red Superman-like cape. The sketches quickly attracted Terry's attention.

"We were putting up ideas for a cartoon at the start of a new cartoon story. It crossed my mind that a 'takeoff' of the new comic-strip sensation, *Superman*, could be a subject for a *Terrytoons* cartoon," Klein once recalled.

Terry changed Klein's superfly to a mouse, dubbing him "Supermouse," as the character was billed in four cartoons

Original character design of Paul Terry's Mighty Mouse (originally called Super Mouse).

beginning in 1942 with "The Mouse of Tomorrow." (He was actually more like a superrat than supermouse in this film.) The cartoon series ultimately saved Terrytoons from losing its distribution contract with 20th Century-Fox, which had considered dropping the studio's cartoons from its roster. With the success of the *Mighty Mouse* series, 20th Century-Fox immediately changed its mind and signed a new deal with Terrytoons to continue releasing its cartoons to theaters.

A year after the cartoon's debut, Terry changed the name of the character, but not because of possible legal action from D.C. Comics, the license holder of Superman, for copyright infringement, as reported elsewhere. A former Terrytoons employee had contributed his own version of the character to a new comic book called *Coo Coo Comics*, with the first issue appearing the same month that "The Mouse of Tomorrow" was officially released. Terry decided he didn't want to compete with a character that was so similar in nature, so he renamed his superrodent "Mighty Mouse."

As a result of the name change, the early Supermouse cartoons were retitled before the films were syndicated to television. The films reappeared on television as part of CBS's *Mighty Mouse Playhouse* in 1955. *Directors were Mannie Davis, Connie Rasinski, Eddie Donnelly, Bill Tytla, and Dave Tendlar. Technicolor. A Terrytoons Production released through 20th Century-Fox.*

Voices

Mighty Mouse: Tom Morrison

1942: "The Mouse of Tomorrow" (Donnelly/Oct. 16); and "Frankenstein's Cat" (Davis/Nov. 27).

1943: "He Dood It Again" (Donnelly/Feb. 5); "Pandora's Box" (Rasinski/June 11); "Super Mouse Rides Again" (Davis/Aug. 6/a.k.a. "Mighty Mouse Rides Again"); "Down with Cats" (Rasinski/Oct. 7); and "Lion and the Mouse" (Davis/Nov. 12).

1944: "Wreck of Hesperus" (Davis/Feb. 11/first cartoon billed as Mighty Mouse); "The Champion of Justice" (Davis/Mar. 17); "Mighty Mouse Meets Jekyll and Hyde Cat" (Davis/Apr. 28); "Eliza on Ice" (Rasinski/June 16); "Wolf! Wolf!" (Davis/June 22); "The Green Line" (Donnelly/July 7); "The Two Barbers" (Donnelly/Sept. 1); "Sultan's Birthday" (Tytla/Oct. 13); and "At the Circus" (Donnelly/Nov. 17).

1945: "Mighty Mouse and the Pirates" (Rasinski/Jan. 12); "Port of Missing Mice" (Donnelly/Feb. 2); "Raiding the Raiders" (Rasinski/Mar. 9); "Mighty Mouse and the Kilkenny Cats" (Davis/Apr. 13); "The Silver Streak" (Donnelly/June 8); "Mighty Mouse and the Wolf" (Donnelly/July 20); "Gypsy Life" (Rasinksi/Aug. 3/A.A. nominee); "Mighty Mouse Meets Bad Bill Bunion" (Davis/Nov. 9); and "Mighty Mouse in Krakatoa" (Rasinski/Dec. 14).

1946: "Svengali's Cat" (Donnelly/Jan. 18); "The Wicked Wolf" (Davis/Mar. 8); "My Old Kentucky Home" (Donnelly/Mar. 29); "Throwing the Bull" (Rasinski/May 3); "The Johnstown Flood" (Rasinksi/June 28); "The Trojan Horse" (Davis/July 26); "Winning the West" (Donnelly/Aug. 16); "The Electronic Mouse Trap" (Davis/Sept. 6); "The Jail Break" (Davis/Sept. 20); "The Crackpot King" (Donnelly/Nov. 15); and "The Hep Cat" (Davis/Dec. 6).

1947: "Crying Wolf" (Rasinski/Jan. 10); "Deadend Cats" (Donnelly/Feb. 14); "Aladdin's Lamp" (Donnelly/Mar. 28); "The Sky Is Falling" (Davis/Apr. 25); "Mighty Mouse Meets Deadeye Dick" (Rasinski/May 30); "A Date for Dinner" (Donnelly/Aug. 29); "The First Show" (Davis/Oct. 10); "A Fight to the Finish" (Rasinski/Nov. 14); "Swiss Cheese Family Robinson" (Davis/Dec. 19); and "Lazy Little Beaver" (Donnelly/Dec. 26).

1948: "Mighty Mouse and the Magician" (Donnelly/Mar.); "The Feuding Hillbillies" (Rasinski/Apr.); "The Witch's Cat" (Davis/July); "Love's Labor Won" (Davis/Sept.); "The Mysterious Stranger" (Davis/Oct.); "Triple Trouble" (Davis/Nov.); and "Magic Slipper" (Davis/Dec.).

1949: "Racket Buster" (Davis/Feb.); "Cold Romance" (Davis/Apr.); "The Catnip Gang" (Donnelly/July); "Perils of Pearl Pureheart" (Donnelly/Oct.); and "Stop, Look and Listen" (Donnelly/Dec.).

1950: "Anti-Cats" (Davis/Mar.); "Law and Order" (Donnelly/June 23); "Beauty on the Beach" (Rasinski/Nov.); and "Mother Goose's Birthday Party" (Rasinski/Dec.).

1951: "Sunny Italy" (Rasinski/Mar.); "Goons from the Moon" (Rasinski/Apr. 1); "Injun Trouble" (Donnelly/June); "A Swiss Miss" (Davis/Aug.); and "A Cat's Tale" (Davis/Nov.).

1952: "Prehistoric Perils" (Rasinski/Mar.); "Hansel and Gretel" (Rasinski/June); and "Happy Holland" (Donnelly/Nov.).

1953: "Soapy Opera" (Rasinski/Jan.); "Hero for a Day" (Davis/Apr.); "Hot Rods" (Donnelly/June); and "When Mousehood Was in Flower" (Rasinski/July).

1954: "Spare the Rod" (Rasinski/Jan.); "Helpless Hippo" (Rasinski/Mar.); and "Reformed Wolf" (Rasinski/Oct.).

1959: "Outer Space Visitor" (Tendlar/Nov.).

1961: "The Mysterious Package" (Davis/Dec. 15); and "Cat Alarm" (Rasinski/Dec. 31).

◉ MR. MAGOO

For a long time United Productions of America (UPA) cartoon producer John Hubley wanted to get away from "funny" cartoon animals and try something different—a human character with a distinct personality of his own. Columbia Pictures, UPA's distributor, reluctantly approved Hubley's new concept: a nearsighted, crotchety old man named Mr. Magoo.

The studio bought the idea when Hubley added an animal character—a bear—to the first cartoon, "Ragtime Bear," released in 1949. Success was immediate, and soon after the studio requisitioned more Magoo cartoon shorts, which became UPA's top moneymaking short-subject series during its long, award-winning run.

Milfred Kaufman, who wrote the story for "Ragtime Bear," was the person most responsible for Magoo's creation. Hubley handled the series from the beginning, producing and directing two more cartoons until he assigned Pete Burness to direct the series. Under Burness, the *Magoo* series received four Academy Award nominations, winning twice for "When Magoo Flew" (1954) and "Magoo's Puddle Jumper" (1956) as Best Short Subjects of the year.

Magoo's character was actually derived from several real-life figures—a bullheaded uncle of Hubley's and bulbous-nosed comedian W.C. Fields, among others. Jim Backus, the voice of Magoo, also drew from remembrances of his businessman father for the character's crinkly voice.

Backus was hired to voice Magoo at the recommendation of Jerry Hausner, who played Magoo's nephew, Waldo, in the series. According to Hausner, Backus "invented a lot of things and brought to the cartoons a fresh, wonderful approach."

By the 1950s Magoo's personality was softened, and he was made into a more sentimental character. Director Pete Burness contends that the character "would have been stronger if he had continued crotchety, even somewhat nasty." Nonetheless, Magoo continued to charm moviegoers with his slapdash humor until 1959, when the series ended. The character later experienced a rebirth in popularity when UPA produced a brand-new series of cartoons for television in the early 1960s.

In 1997 Leslie Nielsen, of *Naked Gun* film fame, reprised the role of Mr. Magoo in a live-action feature film, based on the popular cartoon character. The film fared poorly at the box office and was panned by critics. *Series directors were John Hubley, Pete Burness, Robert Cannon, Rudy Larriva, Tom McDonald, Gil Turner, Chris Ishii and Bill Hurtz. Technicolor. CinemaScope. A UPA Production released through Columbia Pictures.*

Voices
Mr. Magoo: Jim Backus; **Waldo:** Jerry Hausner, Daws Butler

1949: "Ragtime Bear" (Hubley/Sept. 8/Jolly Frolics cartoon).

1950: "Spellbound Hound" (Hubley/Mar. 16/first official Mr. Magoo cartoon in the series); "Trouble Indemnity" (Burness/Sept. 4/A.A. nominee); and "Bungled Bungalow" (Burness/Dec. 28).

1951: "Bare Faced Flatfoot" (Business/Apr. 26); "Fuddy Duddy Buddy" (Hubley/Oct. 18); and "Grizzly Golfer" (Burness/Dec. 20).

1952: "Sloppy Jalopy" (Burness/Feb. 21); "Dog Snatcher" (Burness/May 29); "Pink and Blue Blues" (Burness/Aug. 28/A.A. nominee/working title: "Pink Blue Plums"); "Hotsy Footsy" (Hurtz/Oct. 23); and "Captain's Outrageous" (Burness/Dec. 25).

1953: "Safety Spin" (Burness/May 21); "Magoo's Masterpiece" (Burness/July 30); and "Magoo Slept Here" (Burness/Nov. 19).

1954: "Magoo Goes Skiing" (Burness/Mar. 11); "Kangaroo Courting" (Burness/July 1); and "Destination Magoo" (Burness/Dec. 16).

1955: "When Magoo Flew" (Burness/Jan. 6/A.A. winner); "Magoo's Check-Up" (Burness/Feb. 24); "Madcap Magoo" (Burness/June 23); "Stage Door Magoo" (Burness/Oct. 6); and "Magoo Makes News" (Burness/Dec. 15/CinemaScope).

1956: "Magoo's Caine Mutiny" (Burness/Mar. 8/originally "Canine Mutiny"); "Magoo Goes West" (Burness/Apr. 19/CinemaScope); "Calling Dr. Magoo" (Burness/May 24/CinemaScope); "Magoo Beats the Heat" (Burness/June 21/CinemaScope); "Magoo's Puddle Jumper" (Burness/July 26/A.A. winner/CinemaScope); "Trailblazer Magoo" (Burness/Sept. 13/CinemaScope); "Magoo's Problem Child" (Burness/Oct. 18/CinemaScope); and "Meet Mother Magoo" (Burness/Dec 27/CinemaScope).

1957: "Magoo Goes Overboard" (Burness/Feb. 21/CinemaScope); "Matador Magoo" (Burness/May 30/CinemaScope); "Magoo Breaks Par" (Burness/June 27/CinemaScope); "Magoo's Glorious Fourth" (Burness/July 25/CinemaScope); "Magoo's Masquerade" (Larriva/Aug. 15/CinemaScope); "Magoo Saves the Bank" (Burness/Sept. 26); "Rock Hound Magoo" (Burness/Oct. 24); "Magoo's House Hunt" (Cannon/Nov. 28); and "Magoo's Private War" (Larriva/Dec. 19).

1958: "Magoo's Young Manhood" (Burness/Mar. 13/working title: "The Young Manhood of Mr. Magoo"); "Scoutmaster Magoo" (Cannon/Apr. 10); "The Explosive Mr. Magoo" (Burness/May 8); "Magoo's Three-Point Landing" (Burness/June 5); "Magoo's Cruise" (Larriva/Sept. 11); "Love Comes to Magoo" (McDonald/Oct. 2); and "Gumshoe Magoo" (Turner/Nov.).

1959: "Bwana Magoo" (McDonald/Jan. 9); "Magoo's Homecoming" (Turner/Mar. 5); "Merry Minstrel Magoo" (Larriva/Apr. 9); "Magoo's Lodge Brother" (Larriva/May 7); and "Terror Faces Magoo" (Ishii/July 9).

◎ MODERN MADCAPS

This series was a lame attempt by Paramount's cartoon department to provide a launch for other potential cartoon series. A few notable characters to appear in this series during its nine-year run were Boobie Baboon, The Cat, Goodie the Gremlin, Honey Halfwitch and Sir Blur. (See individual series entries of aforementioned characters for filmographies and more information.) *Directed by Seymour Kneitel, James "Shamus" Culhane, Howard Post and Gene Deitch. Gene Deitch and Allen Swift were series producers. Technicolor. A Famous Studios Production released through Paramount Pictures.*

1958: "Right Off the Bat" (Kneitel/Nov. 7).

1959: "Fit to Be Toyed" (Kneitel/Feb. 6); "La Petite Parade" (Kneitel/Mar. 6); "Spooking of Ghosts" (Kneitel/June 12); "Talking Horse Sense" (Kneitel/Sept. 11); and "T.V. Fuddlehead" (Kneitel/Oct. 16).

1960: "Mike the Masquerader" (Kneitel/Jan. 1); "Fiddle Faddle" (Kneitel/Feb. 26); "Trouble Date" (with Jeepers and Creepers/Kneitel/Mar. 11); "From Dime to Dime" (Kneitel/Mar. 25); "Trigger Treat" (Kneitel/Apr.); "The Shoe Must Go On" (Kneitel/June); "Electronica" (Kneitel/July); "Shootin' Stars" (with The Cat/Kneitel/Aug.); "Disguise the Limit" (Kneitel/Sept.); "Galaxia" (Kneitel/Oct.); "Bouncing Benny" (Kneitel/Nov.); and "Terry the Terror" (Kneitel/Dec.).

1961: "Phantom Moustacher" (Kneitel/Jan.); "The Kid from Mars" (Kneitel/Feb.); "The Mighty Termite" (Kneitel/Apr.); "In the Nicotine" (Kneitel/June); "The Inquisit Visit" (Kneitel/July); "Bopin' Hood" (with The Cat/Kneitel/Aug.); and "The Plot Sickens" (Kneitel/Dec.).

1962: "Crumley Cogwell" (Kneitel/Jan.); "Popcorn and Politics" (Kneitel/Feb.); "Giddy Gadgets" (Kneitel/Mar.); "Hi-Fix Jinx" (Kneitel/Mar.); "Funderful Suburbia" (Kneitel/Mar.); "Samson Scrap" (Deitch/Mar.); "Penny Pals" (Kneitel/Oct.); "The Robot Ringer" (Kneitel/Nov.); and "One of the Family" (Kneitel/Dec.).

1963: "Ringading Kid" (Kneitel/Jan.); "Drump Up a Tenant" (Kneitel/Feb.); "One Weak Vacation" (Kneitel/Mar.); "Trash Program" (Kneitel/Apr.); "Harry Happy" (Kneitel/Sept.); "Tell Me a Badtime Story" (with Goodie the Gremlin/Kneitel/Oct.); "The Pigs' Feat" (Kneitel/Oct.); "Sour Gripes" (Kneitel/Oct.); "Goodie's Good Deed" (with Goodie the Gremlin/Kneitel/Nov.); and "Muggy-Doo, Boycat: Boy Pest with Osh" (with Myron Walman, Boy Animator and Beverly Arnold, Girl Creator/Kneitel/Dec./produced by Hal Seeger of TV's *Batfink* and *Milton The Monster* fame).

1964: "Robot Rival" (with Zippy Zephyr/Kneitel/Sept.); "And So Tibet" (Kneitel/Oct.); "Reading, Writhing and 'Rithmetic" (with Buck and Wingy/Kneitel/Nov.); and "Near Sighted and Far Out" (Kneitel/Nov.).

1965: "Cagey Business" (Post/Feb.); "The Itch" (Post/May).

1966: "Two by Two" (Post/Jan.); "I Want My Mummy" (with José Jimenez/Post/Mar./voiced by Bill Dana).

⊚ MUSICAL MINIATURES

Putting music to animation took new direction with this animated series by Walter Lantz, which used classical music as a backdrop for story elements and character development on screen. Music was performed by a 50-piece orchestra that Universal Pictures, the series' distributor, loaned out to Lantz. Woody Woodpecker's "The Poet and Peasant" inaugurated the series in 1946 and was held over by some theaters for four to six weeks. The films cost more than $30,000 to produce—the most expensive pictures Lantz ever made. *Directed by Dick Lundy. Technicolor. A Walter Lantz Production released through Universal Pictures.*

1946: "The Poet and Peasant" (with Woody Woodpecker, Andy Panda/Lundy/Mar. 18).

1947: "Musical Moments from Chopin" (with Andy Panda, Woody Woodpecker/Lundy/Feb. 24); and "Overture to William Tell" (with Wally Walrus/Lundy/June 16).

1948: "Pixie Picnic" (Lundy/May).

⊚ NANCY AND SLUGGO

Breaking tradition, Paul Terry purchased the rights to an established comic-strip character, in this case Ernie Bushmiller's *Nancy*, which he turned into a short-lived cartoon series. *Technicolor. A Terrytoons Production released through 20th Century-Fox.*

1942: "School Daze" (Sept. 18); and "Doing Their Bit" (Oct. 30).

⊚ NOVELTOONS

A stalwart array of familiar and lesser-known cartoon stars appeared in these full-color productions, created by Paramount's Famous Studios. The series' featured players were Baby Huey, Blackie the Lamb, Buzzy the Crow, Casper the Friendly Ghost, Goodie the Gremlin, Herman and Katnip, Little Audrey, Little Lulu, Tommy Tortoise and Moe Hare, Spunky and Swifty and Shorty, and a few short-lived characters who starred in cartoons of their own: *Jacky's Whacky World, Laddy and His Lamp* and *Raggedy Ann and Raggedy Andy*. (See series entries for aforementioned characters for filmographies and series information.) The studio had used this formula successfully before and found it worth repeating, especially for characters who did not warrant series of their own. *Directors were Seymour Kneitel, Isadore Sparber, Bill Tytla, Dave Tendlar, Howard Post, James "Shamus" Culhane, Jack Mendelsohn and Gene Deitch.*

Cinecolor. Technicolor. A Famous Studios Production released through Paramount Pictures.

Voices

Jackson Beck, Syd Raymond, Arnold Stang

1944: "The Henpecked Rooster" (with Herman and Henry/Kneitel/Feb. 18); "Cilly Goose" (with Goose that laid golden eggs/Kneitel/Mar. 24); and "Gabriel Churchkitten (from the book by Margot Austin/Kneitel/Dec. 15).

1945: "When G.I. Johnny Comes Homes" (Feb. 2/Kneitel); "A Self-Made Mongrel" (with Dog Face/Tendlar/June 29); and "Old MacDonald Had a Farm" (Kneitel/June 7/first to revive "Bouncing Ball" format of Fleischer *Song Car-Tunes*).

1946: "The Goal Rush" (Sparber/Sept. 27); "Sudden Fried Chicken" (Tytla/Oct. 18); and "Spree for All" (with Snuffy Smith/Kneitel/Oct. 18/Cinecolor).

1947: "Madhattan Island" (June 27/narrated by Kenneth Roberts); "The Wee Men" (Tytla/Aug. 8); "The Mild West" (Kneitel/Aug. 22); "Naughty But Mice" (Kneitel/Oct. 10); and "Santa's Surprise" (Kneitel/Dec. 5).

1948: "Cat o' Nine Ails" (Kneitel/Jan. 9); "Flip Flap" (with the Seal/Sparber/Feb. 13); "We're in the Honey" (Kneitel/Mar. 19); "The Bored Cuckoo" (Tytla/Apr. 19); "The Mite Makes Right" (with Tom Thumb/Tytla/Sept. 3); and "Hector's Hectic Life" (with Hector the Dog at Christmas/Tytla/Nov. 19).

1949: "The Little Cutup" (Sparber/Jan. 21); "Hep Cat Symphony" (Kneitel/Feb. 4); "Little Red School Mouse" (Apr. 15); "A Mutt in a Rut" (with Martin Kanine/Sparber/May 27); and "Leprechaun's Gold" (Tytla/Oct 14).

1950: "Quack a Doodle Doo" (Sparber/Mar 3); "Teacher's Pest" (with Junior/Sparber/Mar. 31); "Ups and Downs Derby" (with Lightning/Kneitel/June 9); "Pleased to Eat You" (with The Hungry Lion/Sparber/July 21); "Saved by the Bell" (Kneitel/Sept. 15); and "The Voice of the Turkey" (with turkey voiced by Arnold Stang/Tytla/Oct. 13).

1951: "Slip Us Some Redskin" (with Hep Indians/Kneitel/July 6); and "By Leaps and Hounds" (with Herbert the Dog/Sparber/Dec. 14).

1952: "Feast and Furious" (with Finny the Goldfish/Sparber/Dec. 26).

1954: "Crazytown" (a gag anthology/Sparber/Feb. 26); "Candy Cabaret" (Tendlar/June 11); "The Oily Bird" (with Inchy the Worm/Sparber/July 30); and "Fido Beta Kappa" (with Fido/Sparber/Oct. 29).

1955: "News Hound" (with Snapper the Dog/Sparber/June 10); "Poop Goes the Weasel" (with Wishbone

Duck and Waxy Weasel/Tendlar/July 8); and "Kitty Cornered" (with Kitty Cuddles/Tendlar/Dec. 30).

1956: "Pedro and Lorenzo" (Tendlar/July 13); "Sir Irving and Jeames" (Kneitel/Oct. 19); and "Lion in the Roar" (with Louis the Lion/Kneitel/Dec. 21).

1957: "L'Amour the Merrier" (Kneitel/July 5); "Possum Pearl" (Kneitel/Sept. 20); "Jolly the Clown" (Kneitel/Oct. 25); and "Cock-a-Doodle Dino" (with Danny Dinosaur, Mother Hen/Sparber/Dec. 6).

1958: "Dante Dreamer" (with Little Boy, Dragon/ Sparber/Jan. 3); "Sporticles" (compilation of scenes from earlier cartoons/Kneitel/Feb. 14); "Grateful Gus" (with an obnoxious man/Tendlar/Mar. 7); "Finnegan's Flea" (Sparber/ Apr. 4); "Chew Chew Baby" (Sparber/Aug. 15); "Travelaffs" (compilation of scenes from earlier cartoons/Sparber/Aug. 22); and "Stork Raving Mad" (Kneitel/Oct. 3).

1959: "The Animal Fair" (Kneitel/Jan. 16); "Houndabout" (Kneitel/Apr. 10); and "Out of this Whirl" (Kneitel/ Nov. 13).

1960: "Be Mice to Cats" (with Skit and Skat/Feb. 5); "Monkey Doodles" (Kneitel/Apr.); "Silly Science" (Kneitel/May); "Peck Your Own Home" (Kneitel/May); "The Shoe Must Go On" (Kneitel/June); "Counter Attack" (Kneitel/July); "Turning the Fables" (Kneitel/Aug.); "Fine Feathered Fiend" (Kneitel/Sept.); "Planet Mouseola" (Kneitel/Oct.); "Northern Mites" (Kneitel/Nov.); and "Miceniks" (Kneitel/Dec.).

1961: "The Lion's Busy" (Kneitel/Feb.); "Hound About That" (Kneitel/Apr.); "Trick or Tree" (Kneitel/July); "Cape Kidnaveral" (Kneitel/Aug.); "Munro" (Deitch/Sept.); "Turtle Scoop" (with Hare, Tortoise/Kneitel/Oct.); and "Kozmo Goes to School" (Kneitel/Nov.).

1962: "Perry Popgun" (Kneitel/Jan.); "Without Time or Reason" (Kneitel/Jan.); "T.V. or No T.V." (Kneitel/Mar.); "Anatole" (Deitch/Sept.); "It's for the Birdies" (Kneitel/ Nov.); and "Fiddlin' Around" (Kneitel/Dec.).

1963: "Ollie the Owl" (Kneitel/Jan.); "Good Snooze Tonight" (Kneitel/Feb.); "A Sight for Squaw Eyes" (Kneitel/Mar.); "Gramps to the Rescue" (Kneitel/Sept.); "Hobo's Holiday" (Kneitel/Oct.); "Hound for Hound" (Kneitel/Oct.); and "The Sheepish Wolf" (Kneitel/Nov.).

1964: "Whiz Quiz Kid" (Kneitel/Feb.); and "Homer on the Range" (with Homer Ranger/Post/Dec.).

1965: "Horning In" (with King Artie/Post/Jan.); "A Hair-Raising Tale" (Post/Jan.); "Horning In" (Post/Jan.); "Tally-Hokum" (with Hangdog and Moxie Foxie/Post/Oct.); and "Geronimo and Son" (Culhane/Dec.).

1966: "Sick Transit" (with Roadhog and Rapid Rabbit/ Post/Jan.); "Op Pop Wham and Bop" (Post/Jan.); and "Space Kid" (Kneitel/Feb./this cartoon was released a year and a half after Kneitel's death).

1967: "The Trip" (Culhane/Apr.); and "Robin Hoodwinked" (with Sir Blur/Culhane/June).

◉ NUDNIK

By the early 1960s Paramount began distributing cartoon properties produced overseas, including this Czechoslovakian-made series featuring a galactic alien named Nudnik, animated in the fashion of Terrytoons' *Astronut*.

Nudnik was based on a character named Foofle, who won critical acclaim in a *Terrytoons* cartoon short. Its creator was William Snyder, who produced the Academy Award–winning cartoon "Munro," also released by Paramount.

Story lines centered on Nudnik's problems communicating with Earthlings. Narration and sound effects were used in place of dialogue as the character did not speak. *Directed by Gene Deitch. Technicolor. A Rembrandt Films Production released through Paramount Pictures.*

1965: "Here's Nudnik" (Aug.); and "Drive On, Nudnik" (Dec.).

1966: "Home Sweet Nudnik" (Mar.); "Welcome Nudnik" (May); "Nudnik on the Roof" (July); and "From Nudnik with Love" (Sept.).

1967: "Who Needs Nudnik" (May); "Nudnik on the Beach" (May); "Good Neighbor Nudnik" (June); "Nudnik's Nudnickel" (Aug.); "I Remember Nudnik" (Sept.); and "Nudnik on a Shoestring" (Oct.).

◉ OIL CAN HARRY

Villainous Oil Can Harry, costar of the Terrytoons *Fanny Zilch* cartoon melodrama series of the early 1930s, was cast in his own series of "cartoon serials" four years after his screen debut. The series was short-lived, lasting only two cartoons. *Series directors included Connie Rasinski. Black-and-white. A Terrytoons Production released through 20th Century-Fox.*

1937: "The Villain Still Pursued Her" (Sept. 3); and "The Saw Mill Mystery" (Rasinki/Oct. 29).

◉ OSWALD THE RABBIT

Originally a silent cartoon star, Oswald the Rabbit made the transition to sound, unlike many other characters from that era. Walt Disney originated the series but lost the rights to the character in 1927 after holding out for more money. His partnership with series producer Charles Mintz came to an abrupt end as a result.

Mintz contracted his brother-in-law, George Winkler, to set up a cartoon studio to animate new Oswalds. Universal Pictures, which owned the rights to Oswald, intervened and awarded the series to animator Walter Lantz. Mintz and Winkler were thus put out of business, and Lantz was put in charge of the studio's first cartoon department.

Lantz's first job was to staff his animation department. He hired several former Disney animators, such as Hugh Harman, Rudolf Ising and Friz Freleng. He then added sound to six unreleased Oswald cartoons Winkler had completed, the first called "Ozzie of the Circus."

"It was funny how we did it," Lantz once said, remembering how he stuck sound to the cartoons. "We had a bench with all the props on it—the bells, and so. And we'd project the cartoon on the screen and all of us would stand there in front of the cartoon. As the action progressed, we'd make the sound effects, dialogue, and all. We never prescored these films. We did everything as we watched the picture. It was the only way we knew how to add sound."

Lantz also changed Oswald's character, giving him a cuter look. He shortened the ears and humanized Oswald to resemble a Mickey Mouse–type character. "The Disney stories were great, mind you . . . very funny," he said, "but I didn't like the rabbit. He was just black and white. He wouldn't have any appeal for commercial items like comic books, or that sort of thing. So I redesigned him."

Mickey Rooney, who was nine years old at the time, was the first person to voice Oswald. Lantz hired him because "he had the right squealing voice for Oswald." Rooney had previously starred in a series of Mickey McGuire comedy two-reel shorts. Bernice Hansen, also the voice of Warner Bros.' Sniffles, replaced Rooney when he left the series.

Aside from regular cartoon shorts, Lantz animated the first two-strip Technicolor sequence for Universal's all-talking extravaganza, *The King of Jazz Revue*, featuring an animated Oswald and famed bandleader Paul Whiteman.

Lantz directed most cartoons in the series. William C. Nolan codirected with Lantz from 1931 to 1934, with additional films supervised by Friz Freleng. Alex Lovy, Fred Kopietz, Lester Kline, Rudy Zamora and Elmer Perkins during the series' last years of production. *Black-and-white. A Walter Lantz Production released through Universal Pictures.*

Voices
Oswald the Rabbit: Bernice Hansen, Mickey Rooney

(Copyright dates are marked by ©.)

1929: "Ozzie of the Circus" (Lantz/Jan. 5); "Stage Stunt" (Lantz/May 13); "Stripes and Stars" (Lantz/May 27); "Wicked West" (Freleng/June 10); "Nuts and Bolts" (Lantz/June 24); "Ice Man's Luck" (Luck/July 8); "Jungle Jingles" (Lantz/July 22); "Weary Willies" (Lantz/Aug. 5); "Saucy Sausages" (Lantz/Aug. 19); "Race Riot" (Lantz/Sept. 2); "Oil's Well" (Lantz/Sept. 16); "Permanent Wave" (Lantz/Sept. 30); "Cold Turkey" (Lantz/Oct. 14); "Pussy Willie" (Lantz/Oct. 14); "Amateur Night" (Lantz/Nov. 11); "Hurdy Gurdy" (Lantz/Nov. 24); "Snow Use" (Lantz/Nov. 25); "Nutty Notes" (Lantz/Dec. 9); and "Kounty Fair" (Lantz/© Dec. 17).

1930: "Chile Con Carmen" (Lantz/Jan. 15); "Kisses and Kurses" (Lantz/Feb. 17); "Broadway Folly" (Lantz/Mar. 3); "Bowery Bimbos" (Lantz/Mar. 18/working title: "Bowling Bimboes"); "Hash Shop" (Lantz/Apr. 12/working title: "The Hash House"); "Prison Panic" (Lantz/Apr. 30); "Tramping Tramps" (Lantz/May 6); "Hot for Hollywood"(Lantz/May 19/working title: "Hollywood"); "Hell's Heels" (Lantz/June 2); "My Pal Paul" (Lantz/June 16); "Song of the Caballero" (Lantz/June 29); "Not So Quiet" (Lantz/June 30); "Spooks" (Lantz/July 14); "Sons of the Saddle" (Lantz/July 20); "Cold Feet" (Lantz/© Aug. 13); "Snappy Salesman" (Lantz/© Aug. 18); "Henpecked" (Lantz/© Aug. 20/working title: "Hen Fruit"); "Singing Sap" (Lantz/Sept. 8); "Fanny the Mule" (Lantz/Sept. 15); "Detective" (Lantz/Sept. 22); "The Fowl Ball" (Lantz/Oct. 13); "Strange as it Seems" (Lantz/Oct. 27); "The Navy" (Lantz/Nov. 3); "Mexico" (Lantz/Nov. 17); "Africa" (Lantz/Dec. 1); "Alaska" (Lantz/Dec. 15); and "Mars" (Lantz/Dec. 29).

1931: "China" (Lantz, Nolan/Jan. 12); "College" (Lantz, Nolan/Jan. 27); "Shipwreck" (Lantz, Nolan/Feb. 9); "The Farmer" (Lantz, Nolan/Mar. 23); "Fireman" (Lantz, Nolan/Apr. 6); "Sunny South" (Lantz, Nolan/Apr. 20); "Country School" (Lantz, Nolan/May 5); "The Bandmaster" (Lantz, Nolan/May 18); "North Woods" (Lantz, Nolan/June 1); "Stone Age" (Lantz, Nolan/July 13); "Radio Rhythm" (Lantz, Nolan/July 27); "Kentucky Belle" (Lantz, Nolan/Sept. 2/working title: "Horse Race"); "Hot Feet" (Lantz, Nolan/Sept. 14); "The Hunter" (Lantz, Nolan/Oct. 12); "In Wonderland" (Lantz, Nolan/Oct. 26); "Trolley Troubles" (Lantz, Nolan/Nov. 23); "Hare Mail" (Lantz, Nolan/Nov. 30); "Fisherman" (Lantz, Nolan/Dec. 7); and "The Clown" (Lantz, Nolan/Dec. 21).

1932: "Grandma's Pet" (Lantz, Nolan/Jan. 18); "Oh, Teacher" (Lantz, Nolan/Feb. 1); "Mechanical Man" (Lantz, Nolan/Feb. 15); "Great Guns" (Lantz, Nolan/Feb. 29); "Wins Out" (Lantz, Nolan/Mar. 14); "Beaus and Arrows" (Lantz, Nolan/Mar. 28); "Making Good" (Lantz, Nolan/Apr. 11); "Let's Eat" (Lantz, Nolan/Apr. 21/working title: "Foiled"); "Winged Horse" (Lantz, Nolan/May 9); "To the Rescue" (Lantz, Nolan/May 23); "Catnipped" (Lantz, Nolan/May 23); "A Wet Knight" (Lantz, Nolan/June 20); "A Jungle Jumble" (Lantz, Nolan/July 4); "Day Nurse" (Lantz, Nolan/Aug. 1); "Busy Barber" (Lantz, Nolan/Sept. 12); "Carnival Capers" (Lantz, Nolan/Oct. 10); "Wild and

Woolly" (Lantz, Nolan/Nov. 21); and "Teacher's Pest" (Lantz, Nolan/Dec. 19).

1933: "Oswald the Plumber" (Lantz, Nolan/Jan. 16); "The Shriek" (Lantz, Nolan/Feb. 27); "Going to Blazes" (Lantz, Nolan/Apr. 10); "Beau Best" (Lantz, Nolan/May 22); "Ham and Eggs" (Lantz, Nolan/June 19); "A New Deal" (Lantz, Nolan/July 17); "Confidence" (Lantz, Nolan/July 31); "Five and Dime" (Lantz, Nolan/Sept. 18); "In the Zoo" (Lantz, Nolan/Nov. 6); "Merry Old Soul" (Lantz, Nolan/Nov. 27/A.A. nominee); and "Parking Space" (Lantz, Nolan/Dec. 18).

1934: "Chicken Reel" (Lantz Nolan/Jan. 1); "The Candy House" (Lantz, Nolan/Jan. 15); "County Fair" (Lantz, Nolan/Feb. 5); "The Toy Shoppe" (Lantz, Nolan/Feb. 19); "Kings Up" (Lantz, Nolan/Mar. 12); "Wolf Wolf" (Lantz, Nolan/Apr. 12); "Gingerbread Boy" (Lantz, Nolan/Apr. 16); "Goldilocks and the Three Bears" (Lantz, Nolan/May 14); "Annie Moved Away" (Lantz, Nolan/May 28); "The Wax Works" (Lantz, Nolan/June 25); "William Tell" (Lantz, Nolan/July 9); "Chris Columbus Jr." (Lantz/July 23); "Dizzy Dwarf" (Nolan/Aug. 6); "Happy Pilgrims" (Lantz/Sept. 3/working title: "Ye Happy Pilgrims"); "Sky Larks" (Lantz/Oct. 22); and "Spring in the Park" (Nolan/Nov. 12).

1935: "Robinson Crusoe Isle" (Lantz/Jan. 7); "Hill Billys" (Lantz/Feb. 1); "Two Little Lambs" (Lantz/Mar. 11); "Do a Good Deed" (Lantz/Mar. 25); "Elmer the Great Dane" (Lantz/Apr. 29); "Gold Dust Oswald" (Lantz/May); "Towne Hall Follies" (Lantz/June 3); "At Your Service" (Lantz/July 8); "Bronco Buster" (Lantz/Aug. 5); "Amateur Broadcast" (Lantz/Aug. 26); "Quail Hunt" (Lantz/Sept. 23/Technicolor); "Monkey Wretches" (Lantz/Nov. 11); "Case of the Lost Sheep" (Lantz/Dec. 9); and "Doctor Oswald" (Lantz/Dec. 30).

1936: "Softball Game" (Lantz/Jan. 27); "Alaska Sweepstakes" (Lantz/Feb. 7); "Slumberland Express" (Lantz/Mar. 9); "Beauty Shoppe" (Lantz/Mar. 30); "Barnyard Five" (Lantz/Apr. 20); "The Fun House" (Lantz/May 4); "Farming Fools" (Lantz/May 25); "Battle Royal" (Lantz/June 22); "Music Hath Charms" (Lantz/Sept. 7); "Kiddie Revue" (Lantz/Sept. 21); "Beachcombers" (Lantz/Oct. 5); "Nightlife of the Bugs" (Lantz/Oct. 19); "Puppet Show" (Lantz/Nov. 2); "Unpopular Mechanic" (Lantz/Nov. 6); and "Gopher Trouble" (Lantz/Nov. 30).

1937: "Everybody Sings" (Lantz/Feb. 22); "Duck Hunt" (Lantz/Mar. 8); "The Birthday Party" (Lantz/Mar. 29); "Trailer Thrills" (Lantz/May 3); "The Wily Weasel" (June 7); "The Playful Pup" (July 12); "Love Sick" (Oct. 4); "Keeper of the Lions" (Lantz/Oct. 18); "Mechanical Handyman" (Nov.

8); "Football Fever" (Lantz/Nov. 15); "The Mysterious Jug" (Nov. 29); and "The Dumb Cluck" (Dec. 20).

1938: "The Lamplighter" (Jan. 10); "Man Hunt" (Feb. 7); "Yokel Boy Makes Good" (Lantz/Feb. 21); "Trade Mice" (Feb. 28); "Feed The Kitty" (Lovy/Mar. 14); "Nellie, The Sewing Machine Girl" (Lovy/Apr. 11); "Tail End" (Kline/Apr. 25/*Cartune Special*); "Problem Child" (Zamora/May 16); "Movie Phoney News" (Lovy/May 30); "Nellie, The Indian Chief's Daughter" (June 6/*Cartune Special*); "Happy Scouts" (Kopietz/June 20); "Voodoo in Harlem" (Zamora/July 18/Cartune Special); "Silly Seals" (Kline/July 25); "Queen's Kittens" (Kline/Aug. 8); "Ghost Town Frolics" (Sept. 5); and "Pixieland" (Perkins/Sept. 12/originally "The Busy Body").

ⓖ PARAMOUNT CARTOON SPECIALS

In the 1960s Paramount Pictures distributed a handful of new cartoon shorts labeled as "cartoon specials." Most were produced and directed by outside producers and animators, with one exception: 1961's "Abner the Baseball," which tells the story of Abner Doubleday, the founder of major league baseball. The cartoon was produced by the studio's Famous Studios cartoon division and directed by veteran animator Seymour Kneitel. "Abner" was an animated two-reeler—it was twice as long as the usual seven-minute cartoon normally produced by the studio. Eddie Lawrence, who supplied the voice of Paramount cartoon stars Swifty and Shorty, wrote and narrated the film.

The bulk of the studio's "cartoon specials" were produced by William Snyder and directed by Gene Deitch, a Czechoslovakian director and former artistic director of Terrytoons. (Deitch created the critically acclaimed *Tom Terrific* cartoon series for TV's *Captain Kangaroo* and in the 1960s directed a new series of *Tom and Jerry* cartoons for MGM.) In 1961 the pair produced and directed the studio's Academy Award–winning cartoon, "Munro." Subsequently they teamed up to produce three more cartoons for Paramount— a *Modern Madcap*, entitled "Samson Scrap," followed by the *Noveltoon*, "Anatole" and a Krazy Kat cartoon, "Keeping Up with Krazy," part of the *Comic Kings* series featuring famous King Features comic-stip characters in animated form. Al Brodax, who produced the *Popeye* cartoon series for television in the 1960s, was executive producer of the series. In 1963 Hal Seeger, who produced the 1960s' TV cartoon series *Out of the Inkwell*, *The Milton the Monster Show* and *Batfink*, independently produced under his Hal Seeger Productions (and employing primarily former and moonlighting Paramount animators) the *Modern Madcap* "Muggy-Doo, Boy Cat: Boy Pest with Osh," featuring Myron Waldman, Boy Animator and Beverly Arnold, Girl Creator. It was the only outside cartoon Seeger produced for the studio.

Three years later Oscar-winning producer/director John Hubley, formerly of United Productions of America (UPA), produced and directed another independent release, *Herb Alpert & the Tijuana Brass Double Feature*. The cartoon was nominated for an Academy Award.

It would be 26 years before Paramount released another "cartoon special." In 1992 the studio distributed, '*The Itsy Bitsy Spider*, a cartoon featurette that inspired the television series of the same name for USA Network. The film, produced by Hyperion Studios and directed by Matthew O'Callaghan, was released to theaters with the Paramount animated feature *BeBe's Kids*. *Directed by Gene Deitch, Hal Seeger, John Hubley and Matthew O'Callaghan. Technicolor. A Famous Studios/Rembrendt Films/Hal Seeger/Hubley Studios/Hyperion Studios Production released through Paramount Pictures.*

1961: "Munro" (Deitch/Sept./*Noveltoon*); and "Abner the Baseball" (Kneitel/Nov./two reels/narrated by Eddie Lawrence).

1962: "Samson Scrap" (Deitch/Mar./*Modern Madcap*); "Anatole" (Deitch/Sept./*Noveltoon*); and "Keeping Up with Krazy" (with Krazy Kat/Deitch/*Comic Kings* cartoon).

1963: "Muggy-Doo, Boy Cat: Boy Pest with Osh" (Seeger/Dec.).

1966: *Herb Alpert & the Tijuana Brass Double Feature* (Hubley).

1992: *The Itsy Bitsy Spider* (O'Callaghan/July).

PEPE LE PEW

Warner Bros.' storyman Michael Maltese created and refined Pepe Le Pew, the suave French skunk who charmed moviegoers for more than a decade with his aromatic adventures.

Pepe's unctuous accent and irresistible personality were based on French actor Charles Boyer and others. (His name was derived from Boyer's Pepe Le Moko character in the 1938 film classic *Algiers*.) The character first appeared in Chuck Jones's 1945 *Looney Tunes* cartoon, "The Odor-Able Kitty," but not as Pepe Lew Pew. (On model sheets he was called "Stinky.") Two years later the character was so named and starred in the first "official" Pepe Le Pew film, "Scent-Imental Over You."

In 1949, after just three cartoons, Pepe won an Academy Award for his starring role in "For Scent-Imental Reasons," which Jones also directed. The award marked the second such honor for Jones, who won three Academy Awards during his career.

In an interview, Jones once remarked that he had no problem identifying with Pepe's romantic foibles: "Pepe was everything I wanted to be romantically. Not only was he quite sure of himself but it never occurred to him that anything was wrong with him. I always felt there must be great areas of me that were repugnant to girls, and Pepe was quite the opposite of that."

The series remained a popular Warner Bros. entry through 1962, when "Louvre Come Back to Me," the final Pepe Le Pew cartoon, was released to theaters.

Pepe returned to the screen in the 1990s, first in a new Bugs Bunny cartoon, "Carrotblanca" (1995), a parody of the 1942 Warner Bros. classic, *Casablanca* (with Greg Burson as the voice of Pepe), then in the 1996 hit feature *Space Jam*. *In addition to Jones, series directors were Abe Levitow, Art Davis and Douglas McCarthy. Technicolor. A Warner Bros. release.*

Voices
Pepe Le Pew: Mel Blanc, Greg Burson

Merrie Melodies

1951: "Scent-Imental Romeo" (Jones/Mar. 24).

1952: "Little Beau Pepe" (Jones/Mar. 29).

1953: "Wild Over You" (Jones/July 11).

1955: "Past Perfumance" (Jones/May 21); and "Two Scent's Worth" (Jones/Oct. 15).

1956: "Heaven Scent" (Jones/Mar. 31).

1957: "Touche and Go" (Jones/Oct. 12).

1959: "Really Scent" (Levitow/July 27).

Looney Tunes

1945: "The Odor-Able Kitty" (Jones/Jan. 6).

1947: "Scent-Imental Over You" (Jones/Mar. 8).

1949: "For Scent-Imental Reasons" (Jones/Nov. 12/A.A. winner).

1954: "Cat's Bah" (Jones/Mar. 20).

1960: "Who Scent You?" (Jones/Apr. 23).

1961: "A Scent of the Matterhorn" (Jones/June 24).

1962: "Louvre Come Back to Me" (Jones/Aug. 18).

1995: "Carrotblanca" (with Bugs Bunny, Daffy Duck, Yosemite Sam, Tweety, Sylvester, Foghorn Leghorn, Penelope/McCarthy/Aug. 25).

PHANTASY CARTOONS

In addition to Krazy Kat and Scrappy, its two major cartoon stars, Columbia Pictures' cartoon department produced several catchall series featuring no-name animated characters. The *Phantasy* cartoons were the last of these series, comprised of black-and-white and Technicolor oddities. The series was discontinued in 1948 when Columbia's animation department closed down. United Productions of America (UPA) later replaced the series with *Jolly Frolics*. *Producers were Charles Mintz, Dave Flesicher, Raymond Katz, and Henry Binder. Directors were Frank Tashlin, Alec Geiss, Paul Sommer, Howard Swift, Allen Rose, John Hubley, Sid Marcus, Bob Wickersham and Alex Lovy. Black-and-white. Technicolor. A Columbia Pictures release.*

1939: "The Charm Bracelet" (with Scrappy/Sept. 1); and "Millionaire Hobo" (with Scrappy/Nov. 24).

1940: "The Mouse Exterminator" (with Krazy/Jan. 26); "Man of Tin" (with Scrappy/Feb. 23); "Fish Follies" (May 10); "News Oddities" (July 19); "Schoolboy Dreams" (with Scrappy/Sept. 24); and "Happy Holidays" (Oct. 25).

1941: "The Little Theatre" (with Scrappy/Feb. 7); "There's Music in Your Hair" (Mar. 28); "The Cute Recruit" (May 2); "The Wall Flower" (July 3); "The Merry Mouse Cafe" (Aug. 15); and "The Crystal Gazer" (Sept. 26).

1942: "Dog Meets Dog" (Tashlin/Mar. 6); "The Wild and Woozy West" (Rose/Apr. 30); "A Battle for a Bottle" (Tashlin/May 29); "Old Blackout Joe" (Sommer/Aug. 27); "The Gullible Canary" (Geiss/Sept. 18); "The Dumb Conscious Mind" (Sommer, Hubley/Oct. 23); "Malice in Slumberland" (Geiss/Nov. 20); and "Cholly Polly" (Geiss/Dec. 18).

1943: "The Vitamin G Man" (Sommer, Hubley/Jan. 22); "Kindly Scram" (Geiss/Mar. 5); "Willoughby's Magic Hat" (with Willoughy Wren/Wickersham/Apr. 30); "Duty and the Beast" (Geiss/May 28); "Mass Mouse Meeting" (Geiss/June 25); "The Fly in the Ointment" (Sommer/July 23); "Dizzy Newsreel" (Geiss/Aug. 27); "Nursery Crimes" (Geiss/Oct. 8); "The Cocky Bantam" (Sommer/Nov. 12); and "The Playful Pest" (Sommer/Dec. 3).

1944: "Polly Wants a Doctor" (Swift/Jan. 6); "Magic Strength" (Wickersham/Feb. 4); "Lionel Lion" (Sommer/Mar. 3); "Giddy Yapping" (Swift/Apr. 7); "Tangled Travels" (Geiss/June 9); "Mr. Fore by Fore" (Swift/July 7); "Case of the Screaming Bishop" (Aug. 4); "Mutt 'n' Bones" (Sommer/Aug. 25); and "As the Fly Flies" (Swift/Nov. 17).

1945: "Goofy News Views" (Marcus/Apr. 27); "Booby Socks" (Swift, Wickersham/July 12); and "Simple Siren" (Sommer/Sept. 20).

1946: "Kongo-Roo" (Swift/Apr. 18); "Snap Happy Traps" (Wickersham/June 6); and "The Schooner the Better" (Swift/July 14).

1947: "Fowl Brawl" (Swift/Jan. 9); "Uncultured Vulture" (Wickersham/Feb. 6); "Wacky Quacky" (Lovy/Mar. 20); "Leave Us Chase It" (Swift/May 15); "Tooth or Consequences" (with Fox and the Crow/Swift/June 5); and "Kitty Caddy" (Marcus/Nov. 6).

1948: "Topsy Turkey" (Marcus/Feb. 5); and "Short Snort on Sports" (Lovy/June 3).

1949: "Coo-Coo Bird Dog" (Marcus/Feb. 3).

◉ PHONEY BALONEY

Phoney Baloney, a teller of tall tales who stretched the truth a bit, was a lesser-known character cast in a brief series of one-reel shorts under the *Terrytoons* banner. *Directed by Connie Rasinski. Technicolor. A Terrytoons Production released through 20th Century-Fox.*

1954: "Tall Tale Teller" (May).

1957: "African Jungle Hunt" (Mar.).

◉ PIGGY

Warner Bros. introduced this happy-go-lucky musical pig, called "Patty Pig" on studio model sheets, in a series of musical *Merrie Melodies* cartoon shorts. *Director and voice credits are unknown. Black-and-white. A Warner Bros. release.*

Merrie Melodies

1931: "You Don't Know What You're Doin'" (Oct. 21); and "Hittin' the Trail to Hallelujah Land" (Nov. 28).

◉ THE PINK PANTHER

The egocentric panther was first introduced during the credits of Blake Edwards's popular spy spoof *The Pink Panther*, named after the jewel in the movie. Edwards contracted DePatie-Freleng Enterprises, headed by David H. DePatie and Friz Freleng, to animate titles for the movie using a sly panther being hotly pursued by a cartoon version of Inspector Clouseau.

The film's clever title sequence set the stage for a series of Pink Panther cartoons that followed, produced by DePatie-Freleng for United Artists. The studio unanimously approved the idea after witnessing the widespread attention the character received for its brief appearance in the Blake Edwards feature.

The first "official" Pink Panther cartoon, "The Pink Phink," premiered in 1964 with Billy Wilder's feature *Kiss Me, Stupid* at Grauman's Chinese Theatre in Hollywood. The cartoon was a huge success in more ways than one. It garnered the coveted Oscar statuette for Best Short Subject (it was the only time a cartoon studio won an Oscar with its first cartoon release; only one other Pink Panther cartoon was ever nominated for an Oscar: 1966's "The Pink Blue Print"), and DePatie-Freleng was commissioned to produce one new cartoon per month following the success of their first effort in order to satisfy the public's thirst for more.

The nonspeaking panther did break his silence in two cartoons. In 1965's "Sink Pink," Paul Frees, in a Rex Harrison–type voice, spoke the first lines of dialogue in the character's history ("Why can't man be more like animals?") at the end of film in which he outsmarts a big-game hunter who tries capturing animals of every species by building an ark. He spoke again, this time with more extensive dialogue, in 1965's "Pink Ice" (voiced by Rich Little).

Silent film comedies of the 1920s served as a source of inspiration for creating the series' brand of humor. Many films reenact visual bits first made famous by Charlie Chaplin and Buster Keaton, two of filmdom's greatest slapstick comedians. Even a lively ragtime musical score accompanied the cartoons, similar to the music organists played in theaters to back silent film comedies as they were screened for audiences.

Friz Freleng, who found his niche at Warner Bros., first directed the series before turning it over to his longtime assistant Hawley Pratt. Storyman John Dunn is credited with writing the wildly innovative and clever stories for the series.

In 1993 the Pink Panther returned, this time in a new syndicated television cartoon series, in which he talked (voiced by Matt Frewer of TV's *Max Headroom* fame). The series was produced by MGM/United Artists (UA) in association with Claster Corporation. Creator Friz Freleng and longtime partner David DePatie served as creative consultants on the series, which was produced and directed by Charles Grosvenor and Byron Vaughns. Two years later the Pink Panther was back on the silver screen when MGM/UA released an episode from the television series as a new theatrical cartoon short, "Driving Mr Pink," featuring a new sidekick: Voodoo Man. The short, produced and directed by Grosvenor and Vaughns, opened with Don Bluth's full-length animated feature *The Pebble and the Penguin. Directed by Friz Freleng, Brad Case, Gerry Chiniquy, Art Davis, Dave Detiege, Cullen Houghtaling, Art Leonardi, Sid Marcus, Robert McKimson, Hawley Pratt, Bob Richardson, Charles Grosvenor and Byron Vaughns. Technicolor. A Mirisch-Geoffrey-DePatie-Freleng Production released through United Artists and MGM/United Artists.*

Voices
Pink Panther: Paul Frees, Rich Little, Matt Frewer

Additional voices
Rich Little, Mel Blanc, Paul Frees, Dave Barry, Ralph James

United Artists releases

1964: "The Pink Phink" (Freleng, Pratt/Dec. 18/A.A. winner); and "Pink Pajamas" (Freleng, Pratt/Dec. 25).

1965: "We Give Pink Stamps" (Freleng, Pratt/Feb. 12); "Dial 'P' for Pink" (Freleng, Pratt/Mar. 17); "Sink Pink" (Freleng, Pratt/Apr. 12/Note: Friz Freleng is uncredited as codirector); "Pickled Pink" (Freleng, Pratt/May 12); "Shocking Pink" (Freleng, Pratt/May 13); "Pinkfinger" (Freleng, Pratt/May 13); "Pink Ice" (Freleng, Pratt/June 10); "The Pink Tail Fly" (Freleng, Pratt/Aug. 25); "Pink Panzer" (Pratt/Sept. 15/incorporates live-action footage of tanks in action); "An Ounce of Pink" (Pratt/Oct. 20); "Reel Pink" (Pratt/Nov. 16); and "Bully for Pink" (Pratt/Dec. 14).

1966: "Pink Punch" (Pratt/Feb. 21); "Pink Pistons" (Pratt/Mar. 16); "Vitamin Pink" (Pratt/Apr. 21); "The Pink Blue Print" (Pratt/May 25/A.A. nominee); "Pink, Plunk, Plink" (Pratt/May 25/Note: Contains cameo appearance by Pink Panther theme composer Henry Mancini); "Smile Pretty, Say Pink" (Pratt/May 29); "Pink-a-Boo" (Pratt/June 26); "Genie with the Light Pink Fur" (Pratt/Sept. 14); "Super Pink" (Pratt/Oct. 12); and "Rock-a-Bye Pinky" (Pratt/Dec. 23).

1967: "Pinknic" (Pratt/Jan. 6); "Pink Panic" (Pratt/Jan. 11); "Pink Posies" (Pratt/Apr. 26); "Pink of the Litter" (Pratt/May 17); "In the Pink" (Pratt/May 18); "Jet Pink" (Chiniquy/June 13); "Pink Paradise" (Chiniquy/June 24); "Pinto Pink" (Pratt/July 19); "Congratulations! It's Pink" (Pratt/Oct. 27); "Prefabricated Pink" (Pratt/Nov. 22); "The Hand Is Pinker Than the Eye" (Pratt/Dec. 20); and "Pink Outs" (Chiniquy/Dec. 27).

1968: "Sky Blue Pink" (Pratt/Jan. 3); "Pinkadilly Circus" (Pratt/Feb. 21); "Psychedelic Pink" (Pratt/Mar. 13); "Come on In! The Water's Pink" (Pratt/Apr. 10); "Put-Put Pink" (Chiniquy/Apr. 14); "G.I. Pink" (Pratt/May 1); "Lucky Pink" (Pratt/May 7); "The Pink Quarterback" (Pratt/May 22); "Twinkle, Twinkle Little Pink" (Pratt/June 30); "Pink Valiant" (Pratt/July 10); "The Pink Pill" (Chiniquy/July 31); "Prehistoric Pink" (Pratt/Aug. 7); "Pink in the Clink" (Chiniquy//Sept. 18); "Little Beaux Pink" (Pratt/Oct. 2); "Tickled Pink" (Chiniquy/Oct. 6); "The Pink Sphinx" (Pratt/Oct. 23); "Pink Is a Many Splintered Thing" (Chiniquy/Nov. 20); "The Pink Package Plot" (Davis/Dec. 11); and "Pink-Come Tax" (Davis/Dec. 20).

1969: "Pink-a-Rella" (Pratt/Jan. 8); "Pink Pest Control" (Chiniquy/Feb. 12); "Think Before You Pink" (Chiniquy/Mar. 19); "Slink Pink" (Pratt/Apr. 2); "In the Pink of the Night" (Davis/May 18); "Pink on the Cob" (Pratt/May 29); and "Extinct Pink" (Pratt/June 20).

1971: "A Fly in the Pink" (Pratt/June 23); "Pink Blue Plate" (Chiniquy/July 18); "Pink Tuba-Dore" (Davis/Aug.

4); "Pink Pranks" (Chiniquy/Aug. 18); "Psst Pink" (Davis/Sept. 5); "The Pink Flea" (Pratt/Sept. 15); "Gong with the Pink" (Pratt/Oct. 20); and "Pink-in" (Davis/Oct. 20).

1972: "Pink 8-Ball" (Pratt/Feb. 6).

1974: "Pink Aye" (Chiniquy/May 16); and "Trail of the Lonesome Pink" (Chiniquy/June 27).

1975: "Pink DaVinci" (McKimson/June 23); "Pink Streaker" (Chiniquy/June 27); "Salmon Pink" (Chiniquy/July 25); "Forty Pink Winks" (Chiniquy/Aug. 8); "Pink Plasma" (Leonardi/Aug. 28); "Pink Elephant" (Chiniquy/Oct. 20); "Keep Our Forests Pink" (Chiniquy/Nov. 20); "Bobolink Pink" (Chiniquy/Dec. 30); "It's Pink But Is It Mink?" (McKimson/Dec. 30); "Pink Campaign" (Leonardi/Dec. 30); and "The Scarlet Pinkernel" (Chiniquy/Dec. 30).

1976: "Mystic Pink" (McKimson/Jan. 6); "The Pink Arabee" (Chiniquy/Mar. 13); "The Pink Pro" (McKimson/Apr. 12); "Pink Piper" (Houghtaling/Apr. 30); "Pinky Doodle" (Marcus/May 28); "Sherlock Pink" (McKimson/June 29); and "Rocky Pink" (Leonardi/July 9).

1977: "Therapeutic Pink" (Chiniquy/Apr. 1).

(The following 32 Pink Panther cartoons were originally produced for television's *All New Pink Panther Show*, which aired on ABC from 1978 to 1979, and were released theatrically.)

1978: "Pink Pictures" (Chiniquy/Oct. 21); "Pink Arcade" (Marcus/Oct. 25); "Pink Lemonade" (Chiniquy/Nov. 4); "Pink Trumpet" (Davis/Nov. 4); "Sprinkle Me Pink" (Richardson/Nov. 11); "Dietetic Pink" (Marcus/Nov. 11); "Pink Lightning" (Case/Nov. 17); "Pink S.W.A.T." (Marcus/Nov. 12); "Pink U.F.O." (Detiege/Nov. 16); "Pink Daddy" (Chiniquy/Nov. 18); "Cat and the Pinkstalk" (Detiege/Nov. 18); "Pink and Shovel" (Chiniquy/Nov. 25); "Pinkologist" (Chiniquy/Dec. 2); "Yankee Doodle Pink" (Marcus/Dec. 2/reissue of "Pinky Doodle"); "Pink Press" (Davis/Dec. 9); "Pet Pink Pebbles" (Chiniquy, Leonardi/Dec. 9/reissue of "Rocky Pink"/Note: Art Leonardi is uncredited as codirector); "The Pink of Bagdad" (Davis, Chiniquy/Dec. 9/reissue of "The Pink of Arabee"/Note: Gerry Chiniquy is uncredited as codirector); "Pink in the Drink" (Marcus/Dec. 20); "Pink Bananas" (Davis/Dec. 22); "Pink-Tails for Two" (Davis/Dec. 22); "Pink Z-Z-Z" (Marcus/Dec. 23); and "Star Pink" (Davis/Dec. 23).

1979: "Pink Breakfast" (Case/Feb. 1); "Pink Quackers" (Case/Apr. 4); "Toro Pink" (Marcus/Apr. 4); "String Along in Pink" (Chiniquy/Apr. 12); "Pink in the Woods" (Case/Apr. 27); "Pink Pull" (Marcus/June 15); "Spark Plug Pink" (Case/June 28); "Doctor Pink" (Marcus/Nov. 16); "Pink Suds" (Davis/Dec. 19).

1980: "Supermarket Pink" (Case/Feb. 1).

MGM/United Artists release

1995: "Driving Mr. Pink" (with Voodoo Man/Grosvenor, Vaughns/Apr.).

◎ PLUTO

His lovable, mischievous nature spelled instant stardom for Mickey Mouse's playful pet Pluto in a number of memorable Walt Disney cartoons. By contrast to other cartoon stars of this era, his popularity was somewhat surprising since he displayed few human characteristics and didn't even talk. Nonetheless, film audiences fell in love with this canine creation following his first screen appearance in the 1930 Mickey Mouse cartoon "The Chain Gang."

Norman Ferguson, who animated Pluto in his first cartoon, was mostly responsible for establishing him as a major star. He embellished the dog's personality, adding exaggerated facial expressions and pantomime to his repertoire. Audiences were so taken by Pluto's screen presence that by the 1940s he actually outranked his mentor Mickey Mouse in popularity.

In 1937 Pluto starred in his own series, lasting 15 consecutive years before it was discontinued. *Directors were Ben Sharpsteen, Jack Kinney, Norman Ferguson, Clyde Geronimi, Charles Nichols, Jack Hannah and Milt Schaffer. Technicolor. A Walt Disney Production released through RKO-Radio Pictures.*

1937: "Pluto's Quin-Puplets" (Sharpsteen/Nov. 26).

1940: "Bone Trouble" (Kinney/June 28); and "Pantry Pirate" (Geronimi/Dec. 27).

1941: "Pluto's Playmate" (Ferguson/Jan. 24); "A Gentleman's Gentleman" (Geronimi/Mar. 28); "Canine Caddy" (Geronimi/May 30); and "Lend a Paw" (Geronimi/Oct. 3/A.A. winner).

1942: "Pluto Junior" (Geronimi/Feb. 28); "The Army Mascot" (Geronimi/May 22); "The Sleepwalker" (Geronimi/July 3); "T-Bone for Two" (Geronimi/Aug. 14); and "Pluto at The Zoo" (Geronimi/Nov. 20).

1943: "Pluto and the Armadillo" (with Mickey Mouse/Geronimi/Feb. 19); and "Private Pluto" (with formative Chip 'n' Dale/Geronimi/Apr. 2).

1944: "Springtime for Pluto" (Nichols/June 23); and "First Aiders" (Nichols/Sept. 22).

1945: "Dog Watch" (Nichols/Mar. 16); "Canine Casanova" (Nichols/July 27); "The Legend of Coyote Rock" (Nichols/Aug. 24); and "Canine Patrol" (Nichols/Dec. 7).

1946: "Pluto's Kid Brother" (Nichols/Apr. 12); "In Dutch" (Nichols/May 10); "Squatter's Rights" (with Chip 'n' Dale, Mickey Mouse/Hannah/June 7/A.A. nominee); and "The Purloined Pup" (Nichols/July 19).

1947: "Pluto's Housewarming" (Nichols/Feb. 21); "Rescue Dog" (Nichols/Mar. 21); "Mail Dog" (Nichols/Nov. 14); and "Pluto's Blue Note" (Nichols/Dec. 26/A.A. nominee).

1948: "Bone Bandit" (Nichols/Apr. 30); "Pluto's Purchase" (with Mickey Mouse/Nichols/July 9); "Cat Nap Pluto" (Nichols/Aug. 13); and "Pluto's Fledgling" (Nichols/ Sept. 10).

1949: "Pueblo Pluto" (with Mickey Mouse/Nichols/Jan. 14); "Pluto's Surprise Package" (Nichols/Mar. 4); "Pluto's Sweater" (Nichols/Apr. 29); "Bubble Bee" (Nichols/June 24); and "Sheep Dog" (Nichols/Nov. 4).

1950: "Pluto's Heart Throb" (Nichols/Jan. 6); "Pluto and the Gopher" (Nichols/Feb. 10); "Wonder Dog" (Nichols/ Apr. 7); "Primitive Pluto" (Nichols/May 19); "Puss-Cafe" (Nichols/June 9); "Pests of the West" (Nichols/July 21); "Food for Feudin'" (with Chip 'n' Dale/Nichols/Aug. 11); and "Camp Dog" (Nichols/Sept. 22).

1951: "Cold Storage" (Kinney/Feb. 9); "Plutopia" (with Mickey Mouse/Nichols/May 18); and "Cold Turkey" (Nichols/Sept. 21).

◎ POOCH THE PUP

A cuddly canine, whose happy disposition was typical of other 1930s' cartoon stars, was the central figure in this series launched by creator Walter Lantz. The series was short-lived despite its strong characterizations and story lines based on familiar children's fairy tales and everyday themes with strong morals. *Directed and animated by Walter Lantz and William Nolan. No voice credits. Black-and-white. A Walter Lantz Production released through Universal Pictures.*

1932: "The Athlete" (Aug. 29); "The Butcher Boy" (Sept. 26); "The Crowd Snores" (Oct. 24); "The Underdog" (Nov. 7); and "Cats and Dogs" (Dec. 5).

1933: "Merry Dog" (Jan. 2); "The Terrible Troubador" (Jan. 30); "The Lumber Champ" (Mar. 13); "S.O.S. Icicle" (May 8); "Pin-Feathers" (July 3); "Hot and Cold" (Aug. 14); "King Klunk" (Sept. 4); and "She Done Him Right" (Oct. 9).

◎ POPEYE THE SAILOR

The most loved sailor of all time, Popeye came into the cartoon world in 1919 when Elzie Segar, a world-famous comic-strip artist, first conceived the musclebound sailor, originally known as Ham Gravy, for the classic strip *Thimble Theatre*. Gravy was featured in the strip along with his sticklike girlfriend, Olive Oyl. The strip became enormously popular, and Segar experimented with the Gravy character, changing his name to Popeye on January 17, 1929.

Even then, Popeye displayed many of the same traits that moviegoers became accustomed to in later cartoons: a gruff, straight-talking, hard-hitting sailor whose main source of energy was his can of spinach. The sailor's initial appearance was so well received that Segar made him a regular in the strip. Then, in 1932, Max Fleischer bought the film rights to the character from King Features, which syndicated the strip nationally, to produce a series of Popeye cartoons.

Popeye's first film appearance was in a Betty Boop cartoon, "Popeye the Sailor" (1933). Fleischer chose to feature him opposite a known star like Betty to measure public reaction before starring him in his own series, which began in earnest that same year. Early titles were derived from many of Popeye's popular catch lines, such as "Blow Me Down," "I Eats My Spinach" and others.

Through the years Popeye's voice changed—from gruff to even solemn—due to the switchover in voice artists who played him. William Costello was the first man to do Popeye (he won the job after Fleischer heard a recording of songs from his nightclub act as Red Pepper Sam) but was let go after "success went to his head." Costello was succeeded by another man, whom Dave Fleischer, Max's younger brother, overheard talking while buying a newspaper at a street corner. Fleischer hired the gentleman on the spot. His name was Jack Mercer, who, ironically, was an in-betweener at the Fleischer Studios.

Mercer remained the voice of Popeye for more than 45 years altogether, counting cartoons later produced for television. He gave the character greater dimension through memorable mutterings and other under-his-breath throwaway lines during recording sessions that added to the infectious humor of the series. A singer named Gus Wickie was the original voice of Bluto, who never appeared in the *Thimble Theatre* strip. (He was adapted from a one-shot villain in the strip, Bluto the Terrible.) As for Olive Oyl, Mae Questel, also the voice of Betty Boop, lent her voice for Popeye's lovestruck girlfriend. Questel demonstrated her versatility throughout the series, even doing the voice of Popeye for a handful of cartoons when Mercer was sent overseas during World War II.

Many early cartoons were built around songs by lyricist Sammy Lerner and musician Sammy Timberg, who wrote the original "Popeye the Sailor Man" song for the first Paramount cartoon. In time, various costars were added to the series, among them the hamburger-mooching Wimpy, Swee' Pea and other Segar creations, such as the Jeep, Poopdeck Pappy and the Goon. In the 1940s the series introduced Popeye's nephews: Peep-eye, Pip-eye, Pup-eye and Poop-eye, obviously inspired by Donald Duck's own nephews, Hewey, Dewey and Louie.

Besides starring in hundreds of one-reel shorts, Popeye and his cast of regulars appeared in a series of two-reel Technicolor "featurettes" before Walt Disney's breakthrough *Snow White and the Seven Dwarfs*. Adventures included

Popeye the Sailor Meets Sinbad the Sailor (1936) and *Popeye Meets Ali Baba and His 40 Thieves* (1937).

In all, the Popeye series lasted 24 consecutive years, becoming the longest-running cartoon series in motion picture history. *Produced by Max Fleischer. Directors were Dave Fleischer, Isadore Sparber, Dan Gordon, Seymour Kneitel, Bill Tytla and Dave Tendlar. Black-and-white. Technicolor. A Fleischer Studios and Famous Studios release through Paramount Pictures.*

Voices

Popeye: William Costello (to 1933), Jack Mercer, Mae Questel; **Olive Oyl:** Mae Questel; **Bluto:** Gus Wickie, Pinto Colvig, William Pennell, Jackson Beck; **Swee'pea:** Mae Questel; **Poopdeck Pappy/Peep-eye/Pip-eye/Pup-eye/Poop-eye/Wimpy:** Jack Mercer; **Shorty:** Arnold Stang

(The following cartoons are black-and-white unless indicated otherwise. Copyright dates are marked by a ©.)

1933: "Popeye the Sailor" (Fleischer/July 14); "I Yam What I Yam" (Fleischer/Sept. 29); "Blow Me Down" (Fleischer/Oct. 27); "I Eats My Spinach" (Fleischer/Nov. 17); "Season's Greetniks" (Fleischer/Dec. 17); and "Wild Elephinks" (Fleischer/Dec. 29).

1934: "Sock-a-Bye Baby" (Fleischer/Jan. 19); "Let's You and Him Fight" (Fleischer/Feb. 16); "The Man on the Flying Trapeze" (Fleischer/Mar. 16); "Can You Take It" (Fleischer/Apr. 27); "Shoein' Hosses" (Fleischer/June 1); "Strong to the Finich" (Fleischer/June 29); "Shiver Me Timbers" (Fleischer/July 27); "Axe Me Another" (Fleischer/Aug. 30); "A Dream Walking" (Fleischer/©Sept. 26); "The Two-Alarm Fire" (Fleischer/Oct. 26); "The Dance Contest" (Fleischer/Nov. 23); and "We Aim to Please" (Fleischer/Dec. 28).

1935: "Beware of Barnacle Bill" (Fleischer/Jan. 25); "Be Kind to Animals" (Fleischer/Feb. 22); "Pleased to Meet Cha!" (Fleischer/Mar. 22); "The Hyp-Nut-Tist" (Fleischer/Apr. 26); "Choose Your Weppins" (Fleischer/May 31); "For Better or Worser" (Fleischer/June 28); "Dizzy Divers" (Fleischer/July 26); "You "Gotta Be a Football Hero" (Fleischer/Aug. 30); "King of the Mardi Gras" (Fleischer/Sept. 27); "Adventures of Popeye" (Fleischer/Oct. 25); and "The Spinach Overture" (Fleischer/Dec. 7).

1936: "Vim, Vigor and Vitaliky" (Fleischer/Jan. 3); "A Clean Shaven Man" (Fleischer/Feb. 7); "Brotherly Love" (Fleischer/Mar 6); "I-Ski Love-Ski You-Ski" (Fleischer/Apr. 3); "Bridge Ahoy" (Fleischer/May 1); "What, No Spinach" (Fleischer/May 7); "I Wanna Be a Lifeguard" (Fleischer/June 26); "Let's Get Movin'" (Fleischer/July 24); "Never Kick a Woman" (Fleischer/Aug. 28); "Little Swee' Pea" (Fleischer/Sept. 25); "Hold the Wire" (Fleischer/Oct. 23); "The Spinach Roadster" (Fleischer/Nov. 26); and "I'm in the Army Now" (Fleischer/Dec. 25).

1937: "The Paneless Window Washer" (Fleischer/Jan. 22); "Organ Grinders Swing" (Fleischer/Feb. 19); "My Artistical Temperature" (Fleischer/Mar. 19); "Hospitaliky" (Fleischer/Apr. 16); "The Twisker Pitcher" (Fleischer/May 21); "Morning, Noon and Nightclub" (Fleischer/June 18); "Lost and Foundry" (Fleischer/July 16); "I Never Changes My Altitude" (Fleischer/Aug. 20); "I Like Babies and Infinks" (Fleischer/Sept. 18); "The Football Toucher Downer" (Fleischer/Oct. 15); "Proteck the Weakerist" (Fleischer/Nov. 19); and "Fowl Play" (Fleischer/Dec. 17).

1938: "Let's Celebrake" (Fleischer/Jan. 21); "Learn Polikness" (Fleischer/Feb. 18); "The House Builder Upper" (Fleischer/Mar. 18); "Big Chief Ugh-Amugh-Ugh" (Fleischer/Apr. 25); "I Yam Love Sick" (Fleischer/May 29); "Plumbin' Is a Pipe" (Fleischer/June 17); "The Jeep" (Fleischer/July 15); "Bulldozing the Bull" (Fleischer/Aug. 19); "Mutiny Ain't Nice" (Fleischer/Sept. 23); "Goonland" (Fleischer/Oct. 21); "A Date to Skate" (Fleischer/Nov. 18); and "Cops Is Always Right" (Fleischer/Dec. 29).

1939: "Customers Wanted" (Fleischer/Jan. 27); "Leave Well Enough Alone" (Fleischer/Apr. 28); "Wotta Nightmare" (Fleischer/May 19); "Ghosks Is the Bunk" (Fleischer/June 14); "Hello, How Am I?" (Fleischer/July 14); "It's The Natural Thing to Do" (Fleischer/July 30); and "Never Sock a Baby" (Fleischer/Nov. 3).

1940: "Shakespearian Spinach" (Fleischer/Jan. 19); "Females Is Fickle" (Fleischer/Mar. 8); "Stealin' Ain't Honest" (Fleischer/Mar. 22); "Me Feelin's Is Hurt" (Fleischer/Apr. 12); "Onion Pacific" (Fleischer/May 24); "Wimmen Is a Myskery" (Fleischer/June 7); "Nurse Mates" (Fleischer/June 21); "Fightin' Pals" (Fleischer/July 12); "Doing Impossikible Stunts" (Fleischer/Aug. 2); "Wimmin Hadn't Oughta Drive" (Fleischer/Aug. 16); "Puttin' on the Act" (Fleischer/Aug. 30); "Popeye Meets William Tell" (Fleischer/Sept. 20/Note: Shamus Culhane credits himself as director, even though Fleischer is listed); "My Pop, My Pop" (Fleischer/© Oct. 18); "With Poopdeck Pappy" (Fleischer/Nov. 15); and "Popeye Presents Eugene the Jeep" (Fleischer/Dec. 13).

1941: "Problem Pappy" (Fleischer/Jan. 10); "Quiet! Please" (Fleischer/Feb. 7/uses footage from "Sock-a-Bye Baby"); "Olive's Sweepstakes Ticket" (Fleischer/Mar. 7); "Flies Ain't Human" (Fleischer/Apr. 4); "Popeye Meets Rip Van Wrinkle" (Fleischer/May 9); "Olive's Boithday Presink" (Fleischer/June 13); "Child Psykolojiky" (Fleischer/July 11); "Pest Pilot" (Fleischer/Aug. 8); "I'll Never Grow Again" (Fleischer/Sept. 19); "The Mighty Navy" (Fleischer/Nov. 14); and "Nix on Hypnotricks" (Fleischer/Dec. 19).

1942: "Kickin' the Conga 'Round" (Fleischer/Jan. 16); "Blunder Below" (Fleischer/Feb. 13); "Fleets of Stren'th"

(Fleischer/Mar. 13); "Pip-Eye, Pup-Eye, Poop-Eye and Peep-Eye" (Fleischer/Apr. 10); "Olive Oyl and Water Don't Mix" (Fleischer/May 8); "Many Tanks" (Fleischer/May 15); "Baby Wants a Bottleship" (Fleischer/July 3/last cartoon directed by Fleischer); "You're a Sap, Mr. Jap" (Gordon/Aug. 7); "Alona on the Sarong Seas" (Sparber/Sept. 4); "A Hull of a Mess" (Sparber/Oct. 16); "Scrap the Japs" (Kneitel/Nov. 20); and "Me Musical Nephews" (Kneitel/Dec. 25).

1943: "Spinach fer Britain" (Sparber/Jan. 22); "Seein' Red, White 'n' Blue" (Gordon/Feb. 19); "Too Weak to Work" (Sparber/Mar. 19); "A Jolly Good Furlough" (Gordon/Apr. 23); "Ration fer the Duration" (Kneitel/May 28); "The Hungry Goat" (Gordon/June 25); "Happy Birthdaze" (Gordon/July 16); "Wood-Peckin'" (Sparber/Aug. 6); "Cartoons Ain't Human" (Kneitel/Aug. 27/last Paramount black-and-white cartoon); "Her Honor the Mare" (Sparber/Nov. 26/re: Oct 6, 1950/first Technicolor); and "The Marry-Go-Round" (Kneitel/Dec. 31).

(The following cartoons are in Technicolor unless indicated otherwise.)

1944: "W'ere on Our Way to Rio" (Sparber/Apr. 21/re: Oct. 20, 1950); "The Anvil Chorus Girl" (Sparber/May 26/re: Oct. 5, 1951/remake of "Shoein' Hosses"); "Spinach-Packin' Popeye" (Sparber/July 21/re: Oct. 5, 1951/footage used from *Popeye Meets Ali Baba and His 40 Thieves* and *Popeye the Sailor Meets Sinbad the Sailor*); "Puppet Love" (Kneitel/Aug. 11/re: Oct. 3, 1952); "Pitching Woo at the Zoo" (Sparber/Sept. 1/re: Oct. 3, 1953); "Moving Aweigh" (Sept. 22); and "She-Sick Sailors" (Kneitel/Dec. 8/re: Oct. 5, 1951).

1945: "Pop-Pie a la Mode" (Sparber/Jan. 26/re: Nov. 3, 1950); "Tops in the Big Top" (Sparber/Mar. 16); "Shape Ahoy" (Sparber/Apr. 27/re: Nov. 17, 1950); "For Better or Nurse" (Sparber/June 8/re: Oct. 5, 1951/remake of "Hospitaliky"); and "Mess Production" (Kneitel/Aug. 24/re: Oct. 3, 1952).

1946: "House Tricks?" (Kneitel/Mar. 15/re: Oct. 5, 1952/remake of "House Builder Uppers"); "Service with a Guile" (Tytla/Apr. 19); "Klondike Casanova" (Sparber/May 31); "A Peep in the Deep" (Kneitel/June 7/remake of "Dizzy Divers"); "Rocket to Mars" (Tytla/Aug. 9/Cinecolor); "Rodeo Romeo" (Sparber/Aug 16); "The Fistic Mystic" (Kneitel/Nov. 29); and "The Island Fling" (Tytla/Nov. 29).

1947: "Abusement Park" (Sparber/Apr. 25); "I'll Be Skiing Ya" (Sparber/June 13); "Popeye and the Pirates" (Kneitel/Sept. 12); "The Royal Four-Flusher" (Kneitel/Sept. 12); "Wotta Knight" (Sparber/Oct. 24); "Safari So Good" (Sparber/Nov. 7); and "All's Fair at the Fair" (Sparber/Dec. 19/Cinecolor).

1948: "Olive Oyl for President" (Sparber/Jan. 30); "Wigwam Whoopee" (Sparber/Feb. 27); "Pre-Hysterical Man" (Kneitel/Mar. 26); "Popeye Meets Hercules" (Tytla/June 18/Polacolor); "A Wolf in Sheik's Clothing" (Sparber/July 30); "Spinach Vs. Hamburgers" (Kneitel/Aug. 27/footage used from "Anvil Chorus Girl," "She-Sick Sailors" and "Pop-Pie a La Mode"); "Snow Place Like Home" (Kneitel/Sept. 3); "Robin Hoodwinked" (Kneitel/Nov. 12/Polacolor); and "Symphony in Spinach" (Kneitel/Dec. 31/Polacolor).

1949: "Popeye's Premiere" (Mar. 25/footage used from *Popeye Meets Aladdin and His Wonderful Lamp*); "Lumberjack and Jill" (Kneitel/May 27); "Hot Air Aces" (Sparber/June 24); "A Balmy Swami" (Sparber/July 22); "Tar with a Star" (Tytla/Aug. 12); "Silly Hillbilly" (Sparber/Sept. 9); "Barking Dogs Don't Fite" (Sparber/Oct. 28/remake of "Proteck the Weakerist"); and "The Fly's Last Flight" (Kneitel/Dec. 23).

1950: "How Green Is My Spinach" (Kneitel/Jan. 27); "Gym Jam" (Sparber/Mar. 17/remake of "Vim, Vigor and Vitaliky"); "Beach Peach" (Kneitel/May 12); "Jitterbug Jive" (Tytla/June 23); "Popeye Makes a Movie" (Kneitel/Aug. 11/footage used from *Popeye Meets Ali Baba and His 40 Thieves*); "Baby Wants Spinach" (Kneitel/Sept. 29); "Quick on the Vigor" (Kneitel/Oct. 6); "Riot in Rhythm" (Kneitel/Nov. 10/remake of "Me Musical Nephews"); and "The Farmer and the Belle" (Kneitel/Dec. 1).

1951: "Vacation with Play" (Sparber/Jan. 19); "Thrill of Fair" (Kneitel/Apr. 20/remake of "Li'l Swee Pea"); "Alpine for You" (Sparber/May 18/remake of "I-Ski Love-Ski You-Ski"); "Double Cross Country Race" (Kneitel/June 15); "Pilgrim Popeye" (Sparber/July 13); "Let's Stalk Spinach" (Kneitel/Oct. 19/remake of "Popeye and the Beanstalk"); and "Punch And Judo" (Sparber/Nov. 16).

1952: "Popeye's Pappy" (Kneitel/Jan. 25); "Lunch with a Punch" (Sparber/Mar. 14); "Swimmer Take All" (Kneitel/May 16); "Friend or Phony" (Sparber/June 30/footage used from "Tar with a Star" and "I'll Be Skiing Ya"); "Tots of Fun" (Kneitel/Aug. 15); "Popalong Popeye" (Kneitel/Aug. 29); "Shuteye Popeye" (Sparber/Oct. 3); and "Big Bad Sinbad" (Kneitel/Dec. 12/footage used from *Popeye the Sailor Meets Sinbad the Sailor*).

1953: "Ancient History" (Kneitel/Jan. 30); "Child Sockology" (Sparber/Mar. 27); "Popeye's Mirthday" (Kneitel/May 22); "Toreadorable" (Kneitel/June 12); "Baby Wants a Battle" (Kneitel/July 24); "Firemen's Brawl" (Sparber/Aug. 21); "Popeye, the Ace of Space" (Kneitel/Oct. 2/released in 3-D); and "Shaving Muggs" (Kneitel/Oct. 9/remake of "A Clean Shaven Man").

1954: "Floor Flusher" (Sparber/Jan. 1/remake of "Plumbing Is a Pipe"); "Popeye's 20th Anniversary" (Sparber/Apr. 2);

"Taxi-Turvy" (Kneitel/June 4); "Bride and Gloom" (Sparber/July 2); "Greek Mirthology" (Kneitel/Aug. 13); "Fright to the Finish" (Kneitel/Aug. 27); "Private Eye Popeye" (Kneitel/Nov. 12); and "Gopher Spinach" (Kneitel/Dec. 10).

1955: "Cooking with Gags" (Sparber/Jan. 14); "Nurse to Meet Ya" (Sparber/Feb. 11/remake of "Hospitaliky," "Nurse Mates" and "For Better or Nurse"); "Penny Antics" (Kneitel/Mar. 11/remake of "Customers Wanted"); "Beaus Will Be Beaus" (Sparber/May 20); "Gift of Gag" (Kneitel/May 27); "Car-azy Drivers" (Kneitel/July 22); "Mister and Mistletoe" (Sparber/Sept. 30); "Cops Is Tops" (Sparber/Nov. 4); and "A Job for a Gob" (Kneitel/Dec. 9).

1956: "Hillbilling and Cooling" (Kneitel/Jan. 13); "Popeye for President" (Kneitel/Mar. 30); "Out to Punch" (Kneitel/June 8); "Assault and Flattery" (Sparber/July 6/footage used from "The Farmer and the Belle," "Friend or Phony" and "A Balmy Swami"); "Insect to Injury" (Tendlar/Aug. 10); "Parlez Vous Woo" (Sparber/Sept. 12); "I Don't Scare" (Sparber/Nov. 16); and "A Haul in One" (Sparber/Dec. 14/remake of "Let's Get Movin'").

1957: "Nearlyweds" (Kneitel/Feb. 8); "The Crystal Brawl" (Kneitel/Apr. 5/footage used from "Alpine for You" and "Quick on the Vigor"); "Patriotic Popeye" (Sparber/May 10); "Spree Lunch" (Kneitel/June 21); and "Spooky Swabs" (Sparber/Aug. 9).

Popeye Two-Reel Featurettes

1936: *Popeye the Sailor Meets Sinbad The Sailor* (Fleischer/Nov. 27/A.A nominee).

1937: *Popeye Meets Ali Baba and His 40 Thieves* (Fleischer/Nov. 26/Technicolor).

1939: *Popeye the Sailor Meets Aladdin and His Wonderful Lamp* (Fleischer/Apr. 7/Technicolor).

◎ PORKY PIG

When Warner Bros. began testing several characters as replacements for Hugh Harman's *Buddy* series, director Friz Freleng introduced this timid, simpleminded pig who spoke with a stutter in 1935's "I Haven't Got a Hat," an animal version of Hal Roach's *Our Gang* series. (The idea for the film was suggested by producer Leon Schlesinger, who liked the classic short-subject series.) Created as part of a team called "Pork and Beans" (named after a can of Campbell's Pork & Beans) by animator Bob Clampett, Freleng renamed the pig Porky after a childhood playmate he recalled as being "very fat."

While the other characters had their moments, Porky's recital of "Mary Had a Little Lamb" was the most memorable. Warner Bros. agreed. Afterward they gave the stam-

mering pig his own starring series and, as they say, the rest is history.

Actor Joe Dougherty, a Warner Bros. bit player whose credits included *The Jazz Singer* and *Ziegfield Girl*, was first hired to do the voice of Porky. Dougherty got the job because he actually stammered when he spoke, which turned out to be a problem as the series progressed since it was difficult for him to record his lines of dialogue. Dougherty lasted in the role for only two years; according to Freleng, "When he delivered his lines, he used up excessive amounts of soundtrack film since he couldn't control his stammerings. It just became too expensive to keep him so we finally let him go."

At the advice of Warner story editor Treg Brown, actor Mel Blanc was auditioned as Dougherty's replacement. He was so convincing that Freleng hired him on the spot and Blanc not only became the voice of Porky but practically every Warner Bros. cartoon character until the demise of the animation department in 1963. Blanc created Porky's famous sign-off line of "Th-th-th-th-that's all, folks!" used at the end of most Warner Bros. cartoons.

Porky remained a headliner in his series throughout the 1930s and 1940s. During the 1930s Clampett almost exclusively directed Porky in such early classics as "Porky's Hero Agency" (1937), "Porky in Wackyland" (1938), and "The Lone Stranger and Porky" (1939), a Grand Shorts Award winner, plus two key 1940s films, "Baby Bottleneck" (1946) and "Kitty Kornered" (1946). In the late 1930s Porky was given a sidekick: a short-tempered, irritable goat named Gabby Goat, who appeared in only three cartoons: "Porky's Badtime Story," "Porky and Gabby" and "Get Rich Porky," all produced in 1937. (Gabby was voiced by Warner Bros.

Porky encounters a strange bunch of characters, including a Do-Do bird, in Bob Clampett's "Porky in Wackyland" (1938). © Warner Bros., Inc. (COURTESY: BOB CLAMPETT ANIMATION ART)

animator/director Cal Howard.) Gabby was dropped from the series after movie audiences found his characterization offensive.

Although Porky was a major star, the studio often used him in supporting roles to play off other characters on the studio roster. He was a supporting character for the first appearances of Daffy Duck in "Porky's Duck Hunt" (1937) and of Bugs Bunny in "Porky's Hare Hunt" (1938). At various times he played other comic relief roles. His most notable performances in this realm were under director Chuck Jones, who made Porky more adult-looking and cast him opposite Daffy Duck in a series of misadventures. Their most memorable appearance together is the space-age encounter "Duck Dodgers in the 24 1/2 Century" (1953), which Jones directed. By the 1950s Porky seemed so well suited as a "second banana" that the studio utilized him more often in this capacity for the remainder of his career.

Porky did not remain completely indifferent to members of the opposite sex. In the late 1930s he was given a girlfriend who appeared in a handful of cartoon shorts. Her name: Petunia Pig. Petunia was introduced to moviegoers in 1937's "Porky's Romance."

Porky was reunited with his Bugs Bunny and his *Looney Tunes* pals in two films: "Invasion of the Bunny Snatchers," a 1990s Bugs Bunny cartoon that was never released to theaters, and *Space Jam*, the 1996 feature starring Michael Jordan and Bugs Bunny. Bob Bergen provided the voice of Porky for the latter. *Series directors were Friz Freleng, Tex Avery, Jack King, Frank Tashlin, Ub Iwerks, Bob Clampett, Cal Dalton, Cal Howard, Ben Hardaway, Norm McCabe, Chuck Jones, Art Davis, Robert McKimson and Irv Spector. Black-and-white. Technicolor. A Warner Bros. release.*

Voices
Porky Pig: Joe Dougherty (to 1937), Mel Blanc, Jeff Bergman; **Gabby Goat:** Cal Howard

Looney Tunes

1936: "Gold Diggers of '49" (with Beans/Avery/Jan. 6); "Alpine Antics" (with Beans, Kitty/King/Jan. 18); "Boom Boom" (with Beans/King/Feb. 29); "The Blow Out" (Avery/Apr. 4); "Westward Whoa" (with Beans, Ham, Ex, Kitty/King/Apr. 25); "Plane Dippy" (Avery/Apr. 30); "Fish Tales" (King/May 23); "Shanghaiied Shipmates" (King/June 26); "Porky's Pet" (King/July 11); "Porky the Rainmaker" (Avery/Aug. 1); "Porky's Poultry Plant" (Tashlin/Aug. 22); "Milk and Money" (Avery/Oct. 3); "Porky's Moving Day" (King/Oct. 7); "Little Beau Porky" (Tashlin/Nov. 14); "The Village Smithy" (Avery/Dec. 5); and "Porky of the Northwoods" (Tashlin/Dec. 19).

1937: "Porky the Wrestler" (Avery/Jan. 9); "Porky's Road Race" (Tashlin/Feb. 6); "Picador Porky" (Avery/Feb. 27);

"Porky's Romance" (with Petunia Pig/Tashlin/Apr. 3); "Porky's Duck Hunt" (with Daffy Duck; his first appearance/Avery/Apr. 17); "Porky and Gabby" (with Gabby Goat/Iwerks/May 15); "Porky's Building" (Tashlin/June 19); "Porky's Super Service" (Iwerks/July 3); "Porky's Badtime Story" (with Gabby Goat/Clampett/July 24); "Porky's Railroad" (Tashlin/Aug. 7); "Get Rich Quick Porky" (Clampett/Aug. 28); "Porky's Garden" (Avery/Sept. 11); "Rover's Rival" (Clampett/Oct. 9); "The Case of the Stuttering Pig" (with Petunia Pig/Tashlin/Oct. 30); and "Porky's Hero Agency" (Clampett/Dec. 4).

1938: "Porky's Poppa" (Clampett/Jan. 15); "Porky at the Crocadero" (Tashlin/Feb. 5); "What Price Porky" (Clampett/Feb. 26); "Porky's Phoney Express" (Howard, Dalton/Mar. 19); "Porky's Five and Ten" (Clampett/Apr. 6); "Porky's Hare Hunt" (with formative Bugs Bunny/Hardaway/Apr. 30); "Injun Trouble" (Clampett/May 21); "Porky the Fireman" (Tashlin/June 4); "Porky's Party" (Clampett/June 25); "Porky's Spring Planting" (Tashlin/July 25); "Porky and Daffy" (with Daffy Duck/Clampett/Aug. 6); "Wholly Smoke" (Tashlin/Aug. 27); "Porky in Wackyland" (Clampett/Sept. 24); "Porky's Naughty Nephew" (Clampett/Oct. 15); "Porky in Egypt" (Clampett/Nov. 5); "The Daffy Doc" (with Daffy Duck/Clampett/Nov. 26); and "Porky the Gob" (Hardaway, Dalton/Dec. 17).

1939: "The Lone Stranger and Porky" (with Daffy Duck/Clampett/Jan. 7); "It's an Ill Wind" (Hardaway, Dalton/Jan. 28); "Porky's Tire Trouble" (Clampett/Feb. 18); "Porky's Movie Mystery" (Clampett/Mar. 11); "Chicken Jitters" (Clampett/Apr. 1); "Porky and Teabiscuit" (Hardaway, Dalton/Apr. 22); "Kristopher Kolumbus, Jr." (Clampett/May 13); "Polar Pals" (Clampett/June 3); "Scalp Trouble" (with Daffy Duck/Clampett/June 24); "Porky's Picnic" (with Petunia Pig/Clampett/July 15); "Wise Quacks" (with Daffy Duck/Clampett/Aug. 5); "Porky's Hotel" (Clampett/Sept. 2); "Jeepers Creepers" (Clampett/(Sept. 23); "Naughty Neighbors" (Clampett/Oct. 7); "Pied Piper Porky" (Clampett/Nov. 4); "Porky the Giant Killer" (Hardaway, Dalton/Nov. 18); and "The Film Fan" (Clampett/Dec. 16).

1940: "Porky's Last Stand" (with Daffy Duck/Clampett/Jan. 6); "Africa Squeaks" (Clampett/Jan. 27); "Ali-Baba Bound" (Clampett/Feb. 17); "Pilgrim Porky" (Clampett/Mar. 16); "Slap-Happy Porky" (Clampett/Apr. 13); "Porky's Poor Fish" (Clampett/Apr. 27); "You Ought to Be in Pictures" (with Daffy Duck/Freleng/May 18); "The Chewin' Bruin" (Clampett/June 8); "Porky's Baseball Broadcast" (Freleng/July 6); "Patient Porky" (with Bugs Bunny/Clampett/Aug. 24); "Calling Dr. Porky" (Freleng/Sept. 21); "Prehistoric Porky" (Clampett/Oct. 12); "The Sour Puss" (Clampett/Nov. 2); "Porky's Hired Hand" (Freleng/Nov. 30); and "The Timid Toreador" (Clampett, McCabe/Dec. 21).

1941: "Porky's Snooze Reel" (Clampett, McCabe/Jan. 11); "Porky's Bear Facts" (Freleng/Mar. 29); "Porky's Preview" (Avery/Apr. 19); "Porky's Ant" (Jones/Apr. 10); "A Coy Decoy" (with Daffy Duck/Clampett/June 7); "Porky's Prize Pony" (Jones/June 21); "Meet John Doughboy" (Clampett/July 5); "We, the Animals Squeak" (Clampett/Aug. 9); "The Henpecked Duck" (with Daffy Duck/Clampett/Aug. 30); "Notes to You" (Freleng/Sept. 20); "Robinson Crusoe, Jr." (McCabe/Oct. 25); "Porky's Midnight Matinee" (Jones/Nov. 22); and "Porky's Pooch" (Clampett/Dec. 27).

1942: "Porky's Pastry Pirates" (Freleng/Jan. 17); "Who's Who in the Zoo" (McCabe/Feb. 14); "Porky's Cafe" (with Conrad Cat/Jones/Feb. 21); and "My Favorite Duck" (with Daffy Duck/Jones/Dec. 5).

1943: "Confusions of a Nutzy Spy" (McCabe/Jan. 23); "Yankee Doodle Daffy" (with Daffy Duck/Freleng/July 3); and "Porky Pig's Feat" (with Daffy Duck/Tashlin/July 17).

1944: "Tom Turk and Daffy" (with Daffy Duck/Jones/Feb. 12); "Tick Tock Tuckered" (with Daffy Duck/Clampett/Apr. 8); "The Swooner Crooner" (Tashlin/May 6/A.A. nominee), "Duck Soup Nuts" (with Daffy Duck/Freleng/May 27); and "Brother Brat" (Tashlin/July 15).

1945: "Trap Happy Porky" (Jones/Feb. 24).

1946: "Baby Bottleneck" (with Daffy Duck/Clampett/Mar. 16); "Daffy Doodles" (with Daffy Duck/McKimson/Apr. 16); "Kitty Kornered" (with Sylester/Clampett/June 8); and "Mouse Menace" (Davis/Nov. 2).

1947: "Little Orphan Airedale" (with Charlie Dog/Jones/Oct. 4).

1948: "The Pest That Came to Dinner" (Davis/Sept. 11).

1949: "Porky's Chops" (Davis/Feb. 12); "Paying the Piper" (McKimson/Mar. 12); "Daffy Duck Hunt" (with Daffy Duck/McKimson/Mar. 26); "Curtain Razor" (Freleng/May 21); and "Often an Orphan" (with Charlie Dog/Jones/Aug. 13).

1950: "Boobs in the Woods" (with Daffy Duck/McKimson/Jan. 28); "The Scarlet Pumpernickel" (with Daffy Duck, Sylvester the Cat, Elmer Fudd, Momma Bear/Jones/Mar. 4); and "The Ducksters" (with Daffy Duck/Jones/Sept. 2).

1951: "The Wearing of the Grin" (Jones/July 14).

1952: "Thumb Fun" (with Daffy Duck/McKimson/Mar. 1); and "Fool Coverage" (with Daffy Duck/McKimson/Dec. 13).

1955: "Dime to Retire" (with Daffy Duck/McKimson/Sept. 3).

1956: "Deduce, You Say" (with Daffy Duck/Jones/Sept. 29).

1957: "Boston Quackie" (with Daffy Duck/McKimson/June 22).

1959: "China Jones" (with Daffy Duck/McKimson/Feb. 14).

1961: "Daffy's Inn Trouble" (with Daffy Duck/McKimson/Sept. 23).

DePatie-Freleng Enterprises releases

1965: "Corn on the Cop" (with Daffy Duck/Spector/July 24).

Merrie Melodies

1935: "I Haven't Got a Hat" (first Porky Pig cartoon/Freleng/Mar. 9); and "Into Your Dance" (Freleng/June 8).

(The following cartoons are in Technicolor unless indicated otherwise.)

1939: "Old Glory" (Jones/July 1).

1943: "A Corny Concerto" (with Bugs Bunny, Elmer Fudd/Clampett/Sept. 18).

1944: "Slightly Daffy" (with Daffy Duck/Freleng/June 17).

1945: "Wagon Heels" (Clampett/July 28).

1947: "One Meat Brawl" (McKimson/Jan. 18).

1948: "Daffy Duck Slept Here" (with Daffy Duck/McKimson/Mar. 6); "Nothing But the Tooth" (Davis/May 1); "Riff Raffy Daffy" (with Daffy Duck/Davis/Nov. 7/Cinecolor); and "Scaredy Cat" (with Sylvester/Jones/Dec. 18).

1949: "Awful Orphan" (with Charlie Dog/Jones/Jan. 29); "Dough for the Do-Do" (Freleng/Sept. 3/remake of "Porky in Wackyland"); and "Bye, Bye Bluebeard" (Davis/Oct. 21).

1950: "An Egg Scramble" (with Miss Prissy/McKimson/May 27); and "Golden Yeggs" (with Daffy Duck/Freleng/Aug. 5).

1951: "Dripalong Daffy" (with Daffy Duck/Jones/Nov. 17); "Dog Collared" (McKimson/Dec. 2); and "The Prize Pest" (with Daffy Duck/McKimson/Dec. 22).

1952: "Cracked Quack" (with Daffy Duck/Freleng/July 5).

1953: "Duck Dodgers in the 24 1/2 Century" (with Daffy Duck, Marvin Martian/Jones/July 25).

1954: "Claws Alarm" (with Sylvester/Jones/May 22); and "My Little Duckaroo" (with Daffy Duck/Jones/Nov. 27).

1955: "Jumpin' Jupiter" (with Sylvester/Jones/Aug. 6).

1956: "Rocket Squad" (with Daffy Duck/Jones/Mar. 10).

1958: "Robin Hood Daffy" (with Daffy Duck/Jones/Mar. 8).

⊚ POSSIBLE POSSUM

Set in the tiny town of Happy Hollow, this series spinoff from Terrytoons' *Deputy Dawg* was composed of more

Southern-flavored tales, this time featuring the carefree, guitar-playing Possible Possum and his loyal swamp friends, Billy the Bear, Owlawishus Owl and Macon Mouse. *The cartoons were animated and directed by Terrytoons veterans Connie Rasinski, Art Bartsch, Bob Kuwahara, Cosmo Anzilotti and Dave Tendlar. Technicolor. A Terrytoons Production released through 20th Century-Fox.*

Voices
Possible Possum/Billy Bear/Owlawishus Owl/Macon Mouse: Lionel Wilson

1965: "Freight Fright" (Rasinski/Mar.); "Darn Barn" (Rasinski/June); "Get That Guitar" (Bartsch/Sept.); and "The Toothless Beaver" (Rasinski/Dec.).

1966: "Watch the Butterfly" (Tendlar/Oct.).

1968: "Big Bad Bobcat" (Anzilotti/Apr.); "Surprisin' Exercisin'" (Anzilotti/July); "The Rock Hounds" (Tendlar/Oct.); and "Mount Piney" (Bartsch/Dec.).

1969: "The General's Little Helper" (Feb.); "The Red Swamp Fox" (May); "The Bold Eagle" (May); and "Swamp Snapper" (Nov.).

1970: "Surface Surf Aces" (Mar.); "Swamp Water Taffy" (July); and "Slinky Minky" (Nov.).

1971: "Berry Funny" (Mar.); and "Big Mo" (July).

⊚ PROFESSOR SMALL AND MR. TALL

This capricious pair, who were the complete opposites of their names—the "tall" Professor Small and "small" Mr. Tall—appeared in a short-lived cartoon series for Columbia Pictures. Situations revolved around the twosome's clumsy attempts to refute various superstitions of life. *Directed by John Hubley and Paul Sommer. Technicolor. Voice credits unknown. A Columbia Pictures release.*

1943: "Professor Small and Mr. Tall" (Sommer, Hubley/Mar. 26/*Color Rhapsody*).

1945: "River Ribber" (Sommer/Oct. 4/*Color Rhapsody*).

⊚ PUDDY THE PUP

Paul Terry created this frisky little pup who first appeared opposite Farmer Al Falfa before starring in a theatrical sound series of his own. *Directed by Mannie Davis, George Gordon and Connie Rasinski. Black-and-white. Voice credits unknown. A Terrytoons Production released through 20th Century-Fox.*

1936: "The Hot Spell" (with Farmer Al Falfa/Davis, Gordon/July 10); "Puddy the Pup and the Gypsies" (with Farmer Al Falfa/July 24); "Sunken Treasure" (Davis, Gordon/Oct. 16); and "Cats in the Bag" (Davis, Gordon/Dec. 11).

1937: "The Book Shop" (Davis, Gordon/Feb. 5); "Puddy's Coronation" (Davis, Gordon/May 14); "The Homeless Pup" (Gordon/July 23); and "The Dog and the Bone" (Gordon/Nov. 12).

1938: "His Off Day" (Rasinski/Feb. 4); "Happy and Lucky" (Rasinski/Mar. 18); and "The Big Top" (Davis/May 12).

⊚ RAGGEDY ANN AND RAGGEDY ANDY

Three years after Max Fleischer's two-reel special *Raggedy Ann and Raggedy Andy*, based on the characters and stories created by Johnny Gruelle, Famous Studios produced this short-lived series of one-reel shorts, which premiered with 1944's "Suddenly It's Spring." The cartoons were released as part of the studio's *Noveltoons* series. *Directed by Seymour Kneitel. Technicolor. A Famous Studios Production released through Paramount Pictures.*

1944: "Suddenly It's Spring" (Apr. 28).

1947: "The Enchanted Square" (May 9).

⊚ RAINBOW PARADES

Former Disney director Burt Gillett, who won Academy Awards for his Walt Disney classics "Flowers and Trees" (1932); and "The Three Little Pigs" (1933), created and directed this series of musical children's fables for Van Beuren Studios, whose stars were generally lesser known. Gillett, who had joined the studio in 1933, launched the idea following completion of his first series there, *Toddle Tales*, which combined live-action sequences with animated characters and plot lines.

Rainbow Parades became the first color series for Van Beuren, initially filmed in a two-color process and then in three-strip Technicolor. The cartoons alternated between one-shot stories and episodes with continuing characters, becoming popular installments for the studio.

The series was released to television in the 1950s after Official Films purchased Van Beuren's entire cartoon library to distribute to this thriving medium. *Other series directors were Ted Eshbaugh, Steve Muffati, Tom Palmer, James "Shamus" Culhane and Dan Gordon. Voice credits unknown. Technicolor. An RKO-Radio Pictures release.*

1934: "Pastry Town Wedding" (Gillett, Eshbaugh/July 27); and "The Parrotville Fire Department" (Gillett, Eshbaugh/Sept. 14).

1935: "The Sunshine Makers" (Gillett, Eshbaugh/Jan. 11); "Parrotville Old Folks" (Gillett, Palmer/Jan. 25);

"Japanese Lanterns" (Gillett, Eshbaugh/Mar. 8); "Spinning Mice" (Gillett, Palmer/Apr. 5); "Picnic Panic" (Gillett, Palmer/May 3); "The Merry Kittens" (Gillett, Culhane/May 15); "The Foxy Terrier" (Gillett/May 31); "Parrotville Post Office" (Gillett, Palmer/June 28); "Rag Dog" (Gillett/July 19); "Putting on the Dog" (Gillett/July 19); "The Hunting Season" (Gillett/Aug. 9); "Bird Scouts" (Gillett, Palmer/Sept. 20); "Molly Moo Cow and the Butterflies" (Gillett, Palmer/Nov. 15); "Molly Moo Cow and The Indians" (Gillett, Palmer/Nov. 15); and "Molly Moo Cow and Rip Van Wrinkle" (Gillett, Palmer/Nov. 17).

1936: "Toonerville Trolley" (Gillett, Palmer/Jan. 17); "Felix the Cat and the Goose That Laid the Golden Egg" (Gillett, Palmer/Feb. 7); "Molly Moo Cow and Robinson Crusoe" (Gillett, Palmer/Feb. 28); "Neptune Nonsense" (Gillett, Palmer/Mar. 20); "Bold King Cole" (with Felix the Cat/Gillett/May 29); "A Waif's Welcome" (Palmer/June 19); "Trolley Ahoy" (Gillett/July 3/Toonerville Trolley cartoon); "Cupid Gets His Man" (Palmer/July 24); "It's a Greek Life" (Gordon/Aug. 2); and "Toonerville Picnic" (Gillett/Oct. 2/*Toonerville Trolley* cartoon).

RALPH PHILLIPS

Chuck Jones brought this young boy with an overactive imagination, who daydreams in the fashion of Walter Mitty, to the screen in 1954's "From A to Z-Z-Z-Z," which was nominated for an Academy Award. Ralph appeared in only two cartoons altogether, his second being "Boyhood Daze" (1957); a *Merrie Melodies* cartoon. *Directed by Chuck Jones. Technicolor. A Warner Bros. release.*

Voices
Ralph Phillips: Dick Beals

Looney Tunes

1954: "From A to Z-Z-Z-Z" (Oct. 16/A.A. nominee/voice of teacher by Bea Benaderet).

Merrie Melodies

1957: "Boyhood Daze" (Apr. 20).

RALPH WOLF AND SAM SHEEPDOG

Ralph, a scheming wolf who resembles Wile E. Coyote, tries everything possible to steal sheep under the nose of one clever sheepdog, Sam—only during working hours—in this rib-tickling cartoon series created by Chuck Jones for Warner Bros. The battling pair first starred in 1953's "Don't Give Up the Sheep." *Directed by Chuck Jones, Phil Monroe and Richard Thompson. Technicolor. A Warner Bros. release.*

Voices
Mel Blanc

Looney Tunes

1953: "Don't Give Up the Sheep" (Jan. 3).

1955: "Double or Mutton" (July 13).

1957: "Steal Wool" (June 8).

Merrie Melodies

1954: "Sheep Ahoy" (Dec. 11).

1960: "Ready Woolen and Able" (July 30).

1962: "A Sheep in the Deep" (Feb. 10).

1963: "Woolen Under Where" (Monroe, Thompson/May 11)

ROAD RUNNER AND COYOTE

Director Chuck Jones and storyman Michael Maltese created the incredibly speedy ostrich-necked Road Runner ("Beep! Beep!") and his relentless pursuer Wile E. Coyote in what became known as the "longest chase" in cartoon history.

Jones had always aspired to animate a series using "blackouts" and sound effects in classic fashion. He admits to having been influenced by a series of a similar nature, Columbia Pictures' *Fox and the Crow* cartoons, which was based on the same chase formula but to a different extreme.

As for the Road Runner's voice, Jones recalls he and Maltese got the idea from, of all places, the hallways of Warner Bros.' cartoon studio. "Curiously enough, Mel Blanc didn't come up with the 'Beep! Beep!' That was done by a fellow named Paul Julian. He was walking down the hall carrying a load of backgrounds and couldn't see where he was going," Jones recalled. "He had about 60 drawings in front of him and he kept going 'Beep! Beep!' as he went by to keep people out of his way. Mike and I were laying out the first picture when Paul went by our door making that sound. We looked at each other and thought that must have been the sound the Road Runner makes. Mike looked up and said, 'Okay, God, we'll take it from here.'"

The characters were first introduced in the 1948 Technicolor release, "Fast and Furry-Ous," featuring the type of lunacy that became a staple of the series. Jones imposed certain disciplines when animating the series: The Road Runner always stayed on the road. He was never injured; the Coyote injured himself instead. The same Arizona desert was used in each picture. Sympathy was always on the side of the Coyote. No dialogue was furnished for either character, with the exception of the Road Runner's traditional "Beep! Beep!" sound, which sound-effects man Treg Brown invented while using an electronic horn called a claxon. (Mel Blanc mimed the sound vocally for the second cartoon, "Beep Beep!" [1952], when the instrument got lost. Blanc's sound was used for each and every cartoon there-

The Coyote's never-ending pursuit of the Road Runner is about to end in disaster in the long-running Warner Bros. cartoon series created by Chuck Jones. © Warner Bros., Inc.

after.) The splash technique of the Coyote falling off the cliff was incorporated into almost every film. And, last, the Coyote never catches the Road Runner.

Jones directed the most cartoons in the series, one of which was nominated for an Academy Award for Best Short Subject: 1961's "Beep Prepared." After Warner Bros. shut down its animation department, the series resumed under DePatie-Freleng Enterprises, which produced a new series of Warner cartoons before the studio reopened its animation division in 1967.

In 1994 the Road Runner and Coyote returned to the screen in their first all-new theatrical cartoon in 28 years, "Chariots of Fur," which opened with the live-action feature *Richie Rich*, starring Macaulay Culkin. Series creator Chuck Jones opened a 1990s' version of Termite Terrace, the name of the animation unit in Warner Bros. heyday, to produce new animated cartoon shorts for theaters. The Road Runner cartoon was to be animated by the new unit. *Other series directors were Maurice Noble, Rudy Larriva, Abe Levitow and Robert McKimson. Technicolor. A Warner Bros. release.*

Voices
Road Runner: Mel Blanc

Merrie Melodies

1952: "Beep, Beep" (Jones/May 24); and "Going! Going! Gosh!" (Jones/Aug. 23).

1953: "Zipping Along" (Jones/Sept. 10).

1954: "Stop, Look and Hasten" (Jones/Aug. 14).

1958: "Whoa Be-Gone" (Jones/Apr. 12); and "Hip Hip—Hurry" (Jones/Dec. 6).

1959: "Wild About Hurry" (Jones/Oct. 10).

1960: "Hopalong Casualty" (Jones/Oct. 8)

1961: "Zip 'n' Snort" (Jones/Jan. 21); and "Beep Prepared" (Jones/Nov. 11/A.A. nominee).

1962: "Zoom at the Top" (Jones, Noble/June 30).

1963: "To Beep or Not to Beep" (Jones, Noble/Dec. 28).

DePatie-Freleng Enterprises releases

1965: "Rushing Roulette" (McKimson/July 31); "Run, Run, Sweet Road Runner" (Larriva/Aug. 21); "Tired and Feathered" (Larriva/Sept. 18); "Boulder Wham" (Larriva/Oct. 9); "Just Plane Beep" (Larriva/Oct. 30); "Harried and Hurried" (Larriva/Nov. 13); and "Chaser on the Rocks" (Larriva/Dec. 25).

1966: "Out and Out Rout" (Larriva/Jan. 29).

Looney Tunes

1949: "Fast and Furry-Ous" (Jones/Sept. 16/first Road Runner cartoon).

1955: "Ready, Set, Zoom!" (Jones/Apr. 30); and "Guided Muscle" (Jones/Dec. 10).

1956: "Gee Whiz-z-z" (Jones/May 5); and "There They Go-Go-Go" (Jones/Nov. 10).

1957: "Scramble Aches" (Jones/Jan. 26); and "Zoom and Bored" (Jones/Sept. 14).

1958: "Hook, Line and Stinker" (Jones/Oct. 11).

1959: "Hot Rod and Reel!" (Jones/May 9).

1960: "Fastest with the Mostest" (Jones/Jan. 19).

1961: "Lickety Splat" (Jones, Levitow/June 3).

DePatie-Freleng Enterprises releases

1964: "War and Pieces" (Jones, Noble/June 6).

1965: "Highway Runnery" (Larriva/Dec. 11).

1966: "Shot and Bothered" (Larriva/Jan. 8); "The Solid Tin Coyote" (Larriva/Feb. 29); "Clippety Clobbered" (Larriva/Mar. 12); and "Sugar and Spies" (McKimson/Nov. 5).

Chuck Jones Film Production (released by Warner Bros. Family Entertainment)

1994: "Chariots of Fur" (Jones/Dec.).

⊚ ROCKY AND MUGSY

Longtime supporting players in Warner Bros. cartoons directed by Friz Freleng, this hilarious gangster team—featuring Rocky, the diminutive tough guy with the tall hat and ever-present cigar, and Mugsy, his gullible, dumb sidekick—were used mostly as comic relief in cartoons starring Bugs Bunny. Rocky actually was introduced first on screen in 1950's "Golden Yeggs" starring Daffy Duck and Porky Pig. He appeared next in the 1953 Tweety and Sylvester cartoon, "Catty Cornered," in which he was joined by a sidekick named Nick. In 1954 Rocky and Mugsy made their first joint appearance in "Bugs and Thugs" starring Bugs Bunny, followed by their second appearance three years later in "Bugsy and Mugsy," also a Bugs Bunny cartoon. In 1960 Freleng cast the gangster duo in their only starring vehicle, "The Unmentionables," a clever spoof of TV's *Untouchables*. It was also their final appearance on the screen. *A Warner Bros. release.*

Voices
Rocky/Mugsy/Nick: Mel Blanc

Merrie Melodies

1950: "Golden Yeggs" (with Daffy Duck/Porky Pig/Freleng/Aug. 5/introduced the character Rocky by himself).

1953: "Catty Cornered" (with Tweety and Sylvester/Freleng/Oct. 31).

1963: "The Unmentionables" (with Bugs Bunny/Freleng/Sept. 7/narrator: Ralph James).

Looney Tunes

1954: "Bugs and Thugs" (with Bugs Bunny, Freleng/Mar. 2).

1957: "Bugsy and Mugsy" (with Bugs Bunny/Freleng/Aug. 31).

◎ ROGER RABBIT
Following up on the success of *Who Framed Roger Rabbit*, Walt Disney Studios launched this series of fast-paced, funny tributes to Hollywood cartoons of the 1940s reuniting the film's principal cartoon stars, the zany Roger Rabbit, his voluptuous wife, Jessica Rabbit and the temper-tantrum-throwing Baby Herman.

Under the Maroon Cartoons banner—the fictional studio that employed Roger in the box-office smash cartoon feature—Disney released its first theatrical animated short in 25 years, the 1989 madcap adventure "Tummy Trouble," double-billed with the studio's feature-length *Honey, I Shrunk the Kids*, which grossed more than $87 million at the box office in the first five weeks.

Like the movie, it again paired Roger Rabbit and Baby Herman, who has been left in Roger's less-than-adroit care. When Baby swallows a rattle, Roger rushes the tyke to the hospital—St. Nowhere—and bedlam ensues. Roger's sexy, curvacious wife, Jessica, plays a nurse in the film (again voiced by Kathleen Turner), and MGM's sorrowful blood-

hound Droopy makes a cameo appearance as an elevator operator.

In June 1990 Disney again tied the release of the series' second short, "Rollercoaster Rabbit," with the nationwide premiere of Warren Beatty's long-awaited feature-length comic-strip adaptation *Dick Tracy*. A year later the crazy cottontail character was to return to the screen in another cartoon short, entitled "Hare in My Soup," but the film was never produced.

After a three-year absence from the screen, Roger starred again with Jessica Rabbit in an all-new cartoon, "Trail Mix Up." Directed by Barry Cook, the nine-minute short, produced at Disney-MGM Studios in Florida, opened in theaters with the live-action feature *A Far Off Place. Directed by Rob Minkoff, Barry Cook and Frank Marshall (live action). Technicolor. A Walt Disney/Amblin Entertainment Production released through Touchstone Pictures.*

Voices
Roger Rabbit: Charles Fleischer; **Jessica Rabbit:** Kathleen Turner; **Young Baby Herman:** April Winchell; **Adult Baby Herman:** Lou Hirsch; **Droopy:** Richard Williams

1989: "Tummy Trouble" (Minkoff, Marshall/July 23).

1990: "Rollercoaster Rabbit" (Minkoff, Marshall/June 15).

1993: "Trail Mix-Up" (Cook/March 12).

◎ ROLAND AND RATTFINK
DePatie-Freleng Enterprises seemingly took over where Warner Bros.' animation department left off, producing new cartoon series mirroring the style and humor of the classic Warner cartoons, only with new stars in the leading roles. Produced in the late 1960s, Roland and Rattfink was based on the idea of good versus evil. The series paired Roland, a blond, good-looking upholder of justice, against Rattfink, that all-around sleazy, dastardly, good-for-nothing bad guy who always seems to be on the wrong side of the law. *Series directors were Gerry Chiniquy, Art Davis, Hawley Pratt and Grant Simmons. Technicolor. A DePatie-Freleng/Mirisch Films Production released through United Artists.*

Voices
Roland: Leonard Weinrib, Dave Barry; **Rattfink:** Leonard Weinrib, John Byner

Additional Voices
June Foray, Peter Halton, Athena Lorde

1968: "Hawks and Doves" (Pratt/Dec. 18).

1969: "Hurts and Flowers" (Pratt/Feb. 11); "Flying Feet" (Chiniquy/Apr. 10); "The Deadwood Thunderball" (Pratt/

Good-looking champion of justice Roland makes peace with all-around sleaze Rattfink in the DePatie-Freleng Enterprises theatrical cartoon series Roland and Rattfink. © *DePatie-Freleng Enterprises*

June 6); "Sweet and Sourdough" (Davis/June 25); and "A Pair of Sneakers" (Davis/Sept. 17).

1970: "Say Cheese, Please" (Davis/June 7); "A Taste of Money" (Davis/June 24/Note: Only Rattfink appears in this cartoon); "The Foul Kin" (Simmons/Aug. 5); "Bridgework" (Davis/Aug. 26); "Robin Goodhood" (Chiniquy/Sept. 9); "War and Pieces" (Davis/Sept. 20); and "Gem Dandy" (Chiniquy/Oct. 25).

1971: "Trick or Retreat" (Davis/Mar. 3); "The Great Continental Overland Cross Country Race" (Davis/May 23); "A Fink in the Rink" (Davis/July 4); and "Cattle Battle" (Davis/Aug. 4).

◉ RUDOLF ISING CARTOONS

Producer/animator Rudolf Ising, a former Disney animator, produced and directed this series of musical cartoons, starring miscellaneous characters, on his return visit to MGM in the late 1930s. Ising felt right at home, having worked for the studio previously in 1933 after a brief stint at Warner Bros. Following his arrival, he was responsible for directing MGM's *Barney Bear* series and the studio's first Academy Award–winning cartoon, "Milky Way" (1940).

For additional Rudolf Ising cartoons, see *Barney Bear* series entry. *Directed by Rudolf Ising. Voice credits unknown. Technicolor. A Metro-Goldwyn-Mayer release.*

1939: "The Little Goldfish" (Ising/Apr. 15/re: Nov. 10, 1948); "The Bear That Couldn't Sleep" (Ising/June 10/re: Dec. 5, 1953); and "One Mother's Family" (Ising/Sept. 30).

1940: "Home on the Range" (Ising/Mar. 23); "The Milky Way" (Ising/June 22/re: Feb. 14, 1948/A.A. winner); "Romeo Rhythm" (Ising/Aug. 10); "The Homeless Flea" (Ising/Oct. 12); and "Mrs. Lady Bug" (Ising/Dec. 21/re: Jan. 17, 1958).

1941: "Dance of the Weed" (Ising/June 7).

1942: "The Bear and the Beavers" (Ising/Mar. 28); and "Little Gravel Voice" (Ising/May 16).

1943: "Bah Wilderness" (Ising/Feb. 23); "The Boy and the Wolf" (Ising/Apr. 24); and "The Uninvited Pest" (Ising/July 17).

◉ SAD CAT

Ralph Bakshi, after being elevated to the role of director at Terrytoons, created and directed this series about a scraggly-haired, droopy-eyed cat and his friends, Gadmouse, Impressario, Letimore and Fenimore, in numerous backwoods adventures. Following two seasons, Bakshi turned over the directorial reins to Arthur Bartsch, another Terrytoons veteran. *Directed by Ralph Bakshi and Arthur Bartsch. Technicolor. A Terrytoons Production released through 20th Century-Fox.*

Voices
Sad Cat/Impressario/Letimore/Fenimore: Bob McFadden

1965: "Gadmouse the Apprentice Good Fairy" (Bakshi/Jan.); "Don't Spill the Beans" (Bakshi/Apr.); "Dress Reversal" (Bakshi/July); and "The Third Musketeer" (Bakshi/Oct.).

1966: "Scuba Duba Do" (Bakshi/June).

1968: "Dribble Drabble" (Bartsch/Jan.); "Big Game Fishing" (Bartsch/Feb.); "Grand Prix Winner" (Bartsch); "Commander Great Guy" (Bartsch/May); "All Teed Off" (Bartsch/June); "Judo Kudos" (Bartsch/Aug.); "The Abominable Mountaineers" (Bartsch/Sept.); and "Loops and Swoops" (Bartsch/Nov.).

◉ SAM SMALL

This British-made cartoon series was the only foreign-animated series to be distributed theatrically in the United States, outside of Gene Deitch's Czechoslovakian-produced cartoons for MGM and Paramount in the 1960s. It starred a defiant soldier of the king's army who was also a teller of tall tales. Sam was created by famed British comedian Stanley Holloway and English cartoonist Anson Dyer. Astor Pictures distributed the series in America. *Narrated by Stanley Holloway. Technicolor. An Astor Pictures Corporation release.*

1937: "Halt, Who Goes There" (Apr. 15); "Carmen" (May); "Sam and His Musket" (June); "Sam's Medal" (July); "Beat the Retreat" (Aug.); and "Drummed Out" (Sept.).

◉ SCRAPPY

Produced as a companion to Columbia's *Krazy Kat*, Dick Huemer devised this curly-topped, button-eyed boy and his faithful dog, Yippy, in plots associated with childhood themes and encounters with juvenile nemeses, Vonsey and Oopie. When Huemer left the series in 1933 to join Walt Disney Studios, Art Davis and Sid Marcus, who contributed most of the series' stories, continued with its production. *Directed by Dick Huemer, Ub Iwerks, Sid Marcus, Art Davis and Ben Harrison. Produced by Charles Mintz. Voice credits unknown. Black-and-white. Technicolor. A Columbia Pictures release.*

1931: "Yelp Wanted" (Huemer/July 16); "The Little Pest" (Huemer/Aug. 15); "Sunday Clothes" (Huemer/Sept. 15); "The Dog Snatcher" (Huemer/Oct. 15); "Showing Off" (Huemer/Nov. 11); and "Minding the Baby" (Huemer/Nov. 16).

1932: "Chinatown Mystery" (Huemer/Jan. 4); "Treasure Runt" (Huemer/Feb. 25); "Railroad Wretch" (Huemer/Mar. 23); "The Pet Shop" (Huemer/Apr. 28); "Stepping Stones" (Huemer/May 17); "Battle of the Barn" (Huemer/May 31); "Fare-Play" (Huemer/July 2); "Camping Out" (Huemer/Aug. 10); "The Black Sheep" (Huemer/Sept. 17); "The Great Bird Mystery" (Huemer/Oct. 20/working title: "The Famous Bird Case"); "Flop House" (Huemer/Nov. 9); "The Bad Genius" (Huemer/Dec. 1); and "The Wolf at the Door" (Huemer/Dec. 29).

Scrappy shares a moment with faithful companion, Yippy, in a scene from the popular Columbia Pictures cartoon series. © Columbia Pictures, Inc.

1933: "Sassy Cats" (Huemer/Jan. 25); "Scrappy's Party" (Huemer/Feb. 13); "The Beer Parade" (Huemer/Mar. 4); "The False Alarm" (Huemer/Apr. 22); "The Match Kid" (Huemer/May 9); "Technocracket" (Huemer/May 20); "The World's Affair" (Huemer/June 5); "Movie Struck" (Huemer/Sept. 8); "Sandman Tales" (Huemer/Oct. 6); "Hollywood Babies" (Huemer/Nov. 10); and "Auto Show" (Huemer/Dec. 8).

1934: "Scrappy's Art Gallery" (Jan. 12); "Scrappy's Television" (Jan. 29); "Aw, Nurse" (Mar. 9); "Scrappy's Toy Shop" (Apr. 13); "Scrappy's Dog Show" (May 18); "Scrappy's Theme Song" (June 15); "Scrappy's Relay Race" (July 7); "The Great Experiment" (July 27); "Scrappy's Expedition" (Aug. 27); "Concert Kid" (Nov. 2); "Holiday Land" (Nov. 9/Color Rhapsody/A.A. nominee); and "Happy Butterfly" (Dec. 20).

1935: "The Gloom Chasers" (Jan. 18); "The Gold Getters" (Mar. 1); "Graduation Exercises" (Apr. 12); "Scrappy's Ghost Story" (May 24); "The Puppet Murder Case" (June 21); "Scrappy's Big Moment" (July 28); "Scrappy's Trailer" (Aug. 29); and "Let's Ring Doorbells" (Nov. 7).

1936: "Scrappy's Boy Scouts" (Jan. 2); "Scrappy's Pony" (Mar. 16); "Scrappy's Camera Troubles" (June 5); "Playing Politics" (July 8/Color Rhapsody); "The Novelty Shop" (Aug. 15/Color Rhapsody); "In My Gondola" (Sept. 3/Color Rhapsody); "Looney Balloonists" (Sept. 24); "Merry Mutineers" (Oct. 2/Color Rhapsody); "Birds in Love" (Oct. 28/Color Rhapsody); and "A Boy and His Dog" (Dec. 23/Color Rhapsody).

1937: "Skeleton Frolic" (Iwerks/Jan. 29/Color Rhapsody); "Merry Mannequins" (Iwerks/Mar. 19/Color Rhapsody); "Puttin' Out the Kitten" (Mar. 26); "Let's Go" (Apr. 10/Color Rhapsody); "Scrappy's Band Concert" (Apr. 29); "Mother Hen's Holiday" (May 7/Color Rhapsody); "The Foxy Pup" (Iwerks/May 21/Color Rhapsody); "Scrappy's Music Lesson" (June 4); "I Want to Be an Actress" (July 18); "Spring Festival" (Aug. 6/Color Rhapsody); "Scary Crows" (Aug. 20/Color Rhapsody); "Swing Monkey Swing" (Sept. 10/Color Rhapsody); "The Air Hostess" (Oct. 22); "The Little Match Girl" (Nov. 5/Color Rhapsody); "The Clock Goes Round and Round" (Nov. 6); "Dizzy Ducks" (Nov. 18); and "Scrappy's News Flashes" (Dec. 8).

1938: "Bluebird's Baby" (Jan. 21/Color Rhapsody); "Scrappy's Trip to Mars" (Feb. 4); "The Horses on the Merry-Go-Round" (Iwerks/Feb. 17/Color Rhapsody); "The Foolish Bunny" (Davis/Mar. 26/Color Rhapsody); "Scrappy's Playmates" (Mar. 27); "Showtime" (Iwerks/Apr. 14/Color Rhapsody); "The Big Birdcast" (May 13/Color Rhapsody); "Window Shopping" (Marcus/June 3/Color Rhapsody); "Poor Little Butterfly" (Harrison/ July 4/Color Rhapsody); "The Frog Pond" (Iwerks/Aug. 12/Color Rhapsody);

"Hollywood Graduation" (Davis/Aug. 26/*Color Rhapsody*); "The Early Bird" (Sept. 16); "Animal Cracker Circus" (Harrison/Sept. 23/*Color Rhapsody*); "Happy Birthday" (Oct. 7/*Color Rhapsody*); "Midnight Frolics" (Iwerks/Nov. 24/*Color Rhapsody*); and "Kangaroo Kid" (Harrison/Dec. 23/*Color Rhapsody*).

1939: "Scrappy's Added Attraction" (Jan. 13); "Peaceful Neighbors" (Marcus/Jan. 26/*Color Rhapsody*); "The Gorilla Hunt" (Iwerks/Feb. 24/*Color Rhapsody*); "Scrappy's Side Show" (Mar. 3); "The Happy Tots" (Harrison/Mar. 31/*Color Rhapsody*); "The House That Jack Built" (Marcus/Apr. 14/*Color Rhapsody*); "A Worm's Eye View" (Apr. 28); "Lucky Pigs" (Harrison/May 26/*Color Rhapsody*); "Nell's Yells" (Iwerks/June 30/*Color Rhapsody*); "Scrappy's Rodeo" (June 2); "Hollywood Sweepstakes" (Harrison/July 28/*Color Rhapsody*); "The Charm Bracelet" (Sept. 1 /*Phantasy* cartoon); "Millionaire Hobo" (Nov. 24/*Phantasy* cartoon); and "Park Your Baby" (Dec. 22/*Fable* cartoon).

1940: "Man of Tin" (Feb. 23/*Phantasy* cartoon); "Practice Makes Perfect" (Apr. 5/*Fable* cartoon); "Pooch Parade" (July 19/*Fable* cartoon); "A Peep in the Deep" (Aug. 23/*Fable* cartoon); and "Schoolboy Dreams" (Sept. 24/*Phantasy* cartoon).

1941: "The Little Theatre" (Feb. 7/*Phantasy* cartoon).

⊚ SCREEN SONGS

Animator Seymour Kneitel created the *Follow the Bouncing Ball* series, which was first produced in the late 1920s and was later revived in the late 1940s by Famous Studios. The cartoons worked on the concept popularized in movie theaters of song slides showing lyrics of well-known tunes to invite audiences to sing along with live singers or musicians. Max and Dave Fleischer adapted the idea, committing it to animated drawings with live-action footage featuring the talents of famous musical personalities within the context of the films. The early series installments were actually filmed without sound; the dialogue and sound were synchronized later. In the late 1940s series revival, the animated stars led the sing-a-longs, this time in Technicolor. As before, the bouncing ball was incorporated into the onscreen lyrics. *Isadore Sparber and Seymour Kneitel also directed the series. Black-and-white. Technicolor. A Flesicher Studios and Famous Studios release through Paramount Pictures.*

Voices
Jack Mercer and Mae Questel

(Copyright dates are marked by a ©.)

1929: "The Sidewalks of New York" (Feb. 5); "Yankee Doodle Boy" (Mar. 1); "Old Black Joe" (Apr. 5); "Ye Olde Melodies" (© May 3); "Daisy Bell" (May 31); "Mother Pin a Rose on Me" (© July 6); "Dixie" (Aug. 17); "Chinatown My Chinatown" (Aug. 29); "Goodbye My Lady Love" (© Aug. 31); "My Pony Boy" (© Sept. 13); "Smiles" (Sept. 27); "Oh, You Beautiful Doll" (Oct. 14); "After the Ball" (Nov. 8); "Put on Your Old Gray Bonnet" (Nov. 22); and "I've Got Rings on My Fingers" (Dec. 17).

1930: "Bedilia" (Jan. 3); "In the Shade of the Old Apple Tree" (Jan. 16); "I'm Afraid to Come Home in the Dark" (Jan. 30); "Prisoner's Song" (Mar. 1); "La Paloma" (Mar. 20); "I'm Forever Blowing Bubbles" (Mar. 30); "Yes! We Have No Bananas" (Apr. 25); "Come Take a Trip in My Airship" (May 23); "In the Good Old Summer Time" (June 6); "A Hot Time in the Old Town Tonight" (Aug. 1); "The Glow Worm" (Aug. 18); "The Stein Song" (with Rudy Vallee/Sept. 5); "Strike Up the Band" (Sept. 26); "My Gal Sal" (Oct. 18); "Mariutch" (Nov. 15); "On a Sunday Afternoon" (Nov. 25); and "Row, Row, Row" (Dec. 19).

1931: "Please Go 'Way and Let Me Sleep" (Jan. 9); "By the Beautiful Sea" (Jan. 23); "I Wonder Who's Kissing Her Now" (Feb. 13); "I'd Climb the Highest Mountain" (Mar. 6); "Somebody Stole My Gal" (©Mar. 20); "Any Little Girl That's a Nice Little Girl" (Apr. 16); "Alexander's Ragtime Band" (May 9); "And the Green Grass Grew All Around" (June 1); "My Wife's Gone to the Country" (© June 12); "That Old Gang of Mine" (© July 9); "Betty Go-Ed" (with Rudy Vallee/Aug. 1); "Mr. Gallagher and Mr. Shean" (Aug. 29); "You're Driving Me Crazy" (Sept. 19); "Little Annie Rooney" (Oct. 10); "Kitty from Kansas City" (with Rudy Vallee/Nov. 1); "By the Light of the Silvery Moon" (Nov. 14); "My Baby Cares for Me" (Dec. 5); and "Russian Lullaby" (with Arthur Tracy/Dec. 26).

1932: "Sweet Jenny Lee" (Jan. 9); "Show Me the Way to Go Home" (Jan. 30); "When the Red Red Robin Comes Bob Bob Bobbin' Along" (Feb. 19); "Wait Till the Sun Shines, Nellie" (Mar. 4); "Just One More Chance" (Apr. 1); "Oh! How I Hate to Get Up in the Morning" (Apr. 22); "Shine on Harvest Moon" (with Alice Joy/May 6); "Let Me Call You Sweetheart" (with Ethel Merman/May 20); "It's Ain't Got Nobody" (with The Mills Brothers/June 17); "You Try Somebody Else" (with Ethel Merman/July 29); "Rudy Vallee Melodies" (with Betty Boop/Aug. 5); "Down Along the Sugar Cane" (with Lillian Roth/Aug. 26); "Just a Gigolo" (with Irene Bordini/Sept. 9); "School Days" (with Gus Edwards/Sept. 30); "Romantic Melodies" (with Arthur Tracy/Oct. 21); "When It's Sleepy Time Down South" (with The Boswell Sisters/Nov. 11); "Sing A Song" (with James Melton/Dec. 2); and "Time on My Hands" (with Ethel Merman/Dec. 23).

1933: "Dinah" (with The Mills Brothers/Jan. 13); "Ain't She Sweet" (with Lillian Roth/Feb. 3); "Reaching for the Moon" (with Arthur Tracy/Feb. 24); "Aloha Oe" (with The

Royal Samoans/Mar. 17); "Popular Melodies" (with Arthur Jarrett/Apr. 7); "The Peanut Vendor" (with Armida/Apr. 28); "Song Shopping" (with Ethel Merman, Johnny Green/May 19); "Boilesk" (with The Watson Sisters/June 9); "Sing, Sisters, Sing!" (with The Three X Sisters/June 30); "Down by the Old Mill Stream" (with The Funny Boners/July 21); "Stoopnocracy" (with Stoopnagle and Budd/Aug. 18); "When Yuba Plays the Rumba on the Tuba" (with The Mills Brothers/Sept. 15); "Boo, Boo, Theme Song" (with The Funny Boners/Oct. 3); "I Like Mountain Music" (with The Eton Boys/Nov. 10); and "Sing, Babies, Sing" (with Baby Rose Marie/Dec. 15).

1934: "Keeps Rainin' All the Time" (with Gertrude Niesen/Jan. 12); "Let's All Sing Like the Birdies Sing" (with Reis and Dunn/Feb. 9); "Tune Up and Sing" (with Lanny Ross/Mar. 9); "Lazy Bones" (with Borrah Minevitch and His Harmonica Rascals/Apr. 13); "This Little Piggie Went to the Market" (with Singin' Sam/May 25); "She Reminds Me of You" (with Eton Boys/June 22); and "Love Thy Neighbor" (with Mary Small/July 20).

1935: "I Wished on the Moon" (with Abe Lyman and His Orchestra/Sept. 20); and "It's Easy to Remember" (with Richard Himber and His Orchestra/Nov. 29).

1936: "No Other One" (with Hal Kemp and His Orchestra/Jan. 24); "I Feel Like a Feather in the Breeze" (with Jack Denny and His Orchestra/Mar. 27); "I Don't Want to Make History" (with Vincent Lopez and His Orchestra/May 22); "The Hills of Wyomin'" (with The Westerners/July 31); "I Can't Escape from You" (with Joe Reichman and His Orchestra/Sept. 25); and "Talking Through My Heart" (with Dick Stable and His Orchestra/Nov. 27).

1937: "Never Should Have Told You" (with Nat Bradywine and His Orchestra/Jan. 29); "Twilight on the Trail" (with The Westerners/Mar. 26); "Please Keep Me in Your Dreams" (with Henry King and His Orchestra/May 28); "You Came to My Rescue" (with Shep Fields and His Orchestra/July 30); "Whispers in the Dark" (with Gus Arnheim and His Orchestra/Sept. 24); and "Magic on Broadway" (with Jay Freeman and His Orchestra/Nov. 26).

1938: "You Took the Words Right Out of My Heart" (with Jerry Blaine and His Orchestra/Jan. 28); "Thanks for the Memory" (with Bert Block and His Orchestra/Mar. 25); "You Leave Me Breathless" (with Jimmy Dorsey and His Orchestra/May 27); and "Beside a Moonlit Stream" (with Frank Dailey and His Orchestra/July 29).

Famous Studios

1947: "The Circus Comes to Town" (Sparber/Dec. 26).

1948: "Base Brawl" (Kneitel/Jan. 23); "Little Brown Jug" (Kneitel/Feb. 20); "The Golden State" (Kneitel/Mar. 12);

"Winter Draws On" (Kneitel/Mar. 19); "Sing or Swim" (Kneitel/June 16); "Camptown Races" (Kneitel/July 30); "The Lone Star State" (Sparber/Aug. 20); and "Readin', Writin', and Rhythmetic" (Kneitel/Oct. 22).

1949: "The Funshine State" (Kneitel/Jan. 7/Polacolor/narrator: Charles Irving); "The Emerald Isle" (Kneitel/Feb. 25/song: "McNamara's Band"); "Comin' Round the Mountain" (Sparber/Mar. 11); "The Stork Market" (Kneitel/Apr. 8); "Spring Song" (Sparber/June 3); "Hot Air Aces" (Sparber/June 24); "The Ski's the Limit" (Sparber/June 24); "Toys Will Be Toys" (Kneitel/July 15); "Farm Foolery" (Kneitel/Aug. 5); "Our Funny Finny Friends" (Kneitel/Aug. 26); "Marriage Wows" (Sparber/Sept. 16); "The Big Flame-Up" (Sparber/Sept. 30); "Strolling Through the Park" (Kneitel/Nov. 4); "The Big Drip" (Sparber/Nov. 25/song: "Ain't Gonna Rain No More"); and "Snow Foolin'" (Sparber/Dec. 16/song: "Jingle Bells").

1950: "Blue Hawaii" (Kneitel/Jan. 13); "Detouring Through Maine" (Kneitel/Feb. 17/song: "Maine Stein Song"); "Short'nin Bread" (Sparber/Mar. 24); "Win, Place and Showboat" (Sparber/Apr. 28/song: "Waitin' for the Robert E. Lee"); "Jingle Jangle Jungle" (Kneitel/May 19/song: "Civilization—Bongo Bongo Bongo"); "Heap Hep Injuns" (Sparber/June 30/song: "My Pony Boy"); "Gobs of Fun" (Sparber/July 28/song: "Strike Up the Band"); "Helter Swelter" (Kneitel/Aug. 25/song: "In the Good Old Summertime"); "Boos in the Night" (Sparber/Sept. 22/song: "Pack Up Your Troubles"); "Fiesta Time" (Kneitel/Nov. 17/song: "El Rancho Grande"); and "Fresh Yeggs" (Kneitel/Nov. 17/song: "Give My Regards to Broadway").

1951: "Tweet Music" (Sparber/Feb. 9/song: "Let's All Sing Like the Birdies Sing"); "Drippy Mississippi" (Kneitel/Apr. 13/song: "M-i-s-s-i-s-s-i-p-p-i"); "Miners Forty-Niners" (Sparber/May 18/song: "Clementine"); and "Sing Again of Michigan" (Sparber/June 29/song: "I Wanted to Go Back to Michigan Down on the Farm").

⊚ SCREWY SQUIRREL

The bushy-tailed squirrel was a short-lived MGM character who manifested on screen animator/creator Tex Avery's wild and brash humor. During the planning stages of the first cartoon, MGM animators simply dubbed the character "the squirrel" before he was named. Nonetheless, MGM made quite an effort to sell the new character, releasing three cartoons in the first year. Unfortunately, Screwy was a bit too wild for filmgoers' tastes. Exhibiting the same brashness as Bugs Bunny and Woody Woodpecker, in the eyes of the public, he lacked the endearing qualities that were necessary to make him a "likable" star. *Directed by Tex Avery. Technicolor. Voice credits unknown. A Metro-Goldwyn-Mayer release.*

1944: "Screwball Squirrel" (Apr. 1); "Happy Go Nutty" (June 24); and "Big Heel Watha" (Oct. 21/working title: "Buck of the North").

1945: "Screwy Truant" (Jan. 13).

1946: "Lonesome Lenny" (Mar. 9).

⊚ SIDNEY THE ELEPHANT

The final creation of Gene Deitch's regime as creative director for Terrytoons, this series helped restore the studio's image as a major cartoon producer. Deitch, who joined the studio in 1965, developed a number of starring characters after revamping the animation department. Sidney was by far his most likable character, a neurotic, frustrated elephant who sucks on his trunk for security and feels ill-suited for life in the jungle. Pals Stanley the Lion and Cleo the Giraffe were always on hand to protect him from serious danger.

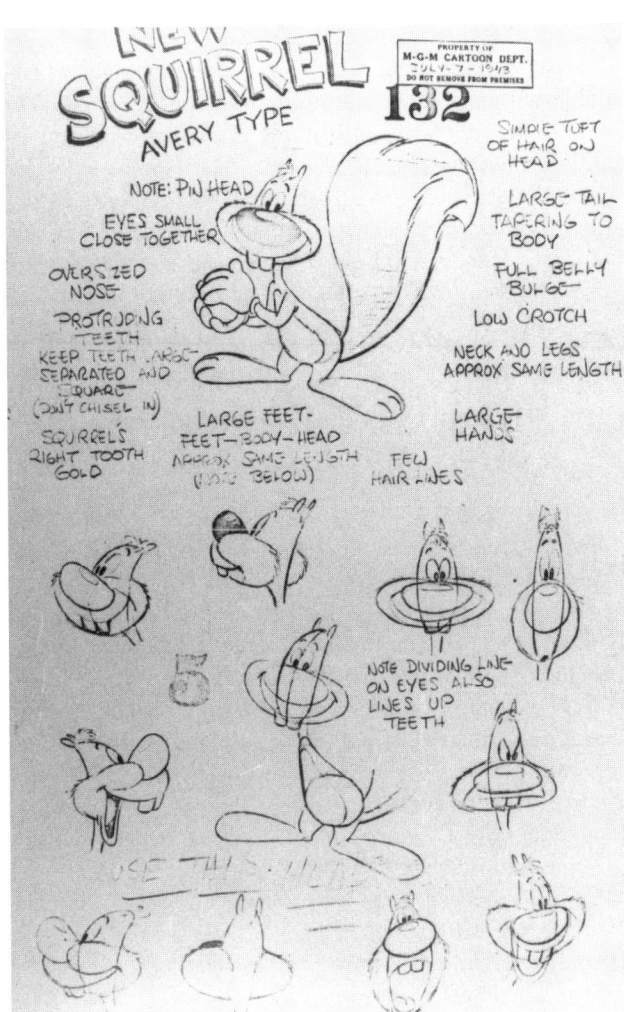

Tex Avery's Screwy Squirrel underwent several changes before appearing in his first cartoon, "Screwball Squirrel." This was the second model sheet for the character who, up to this point, was nameless. © Turner Entertainment

The series' second cartoon, "Sidney's Family Tree," marked another breakthrough for the studio: It won the first Academy Award nomination for Terrytoons. thirteen episodes were later broadcast on television as part of *The Hector Heathcote Show. Directors were Arthur Bartsch, Martin B. Taras, Dave Tendlar and Connie Rasinski. Technicolor. CinemaScope. A Terrytoons Production released through 20th Century-Fox.*

Voices
Sidney the Elephant: Lionel Wilson, Dayton Allen; **Stanley the Lion/Cleo the Giraffe:** Dayton Allen

1958: "Sick, Sick Sidney" (Bartsch/Aug.).

1960: "Hide and Go Sidney" (Bartsch/Jan./CinemaScope); "Tusk Tusk" (Taras/Apr. 3); "The Littlest Bully" (Taras/Aug. 9/CinemaScope); and "Two Ton Baby Sitter" (Tendlar/Sept. 4/CinemaScope).

1962: "Peanut Battle" (Rasinski/Apr. 25/CinemaScope); "Send Your Elephant to Camp" (Bartsch/July 4/CinemaScope); and "Home Life" (Rasinski/CinemaScope).

1963: "To Be or Not to Be" (Rasinski/CinemaScope); "Sidney's White Elephant" (Bartsch/May 1); and "Driven to Extraction" (Bartsch/June 28).

⊚ SILLY SYMPHONIES

Long wanting a series in the form of *Aesop's Fables,* Walt Disney fulfilled his dream by producing this series of nonstandard character cartoons that evoked settings, seasons and events. The series was actually proposed by musical director Carl Stalling, who had composed and arranged music for Mickey Mouse's historic "Steamboat Willie" (1928).

The first cartoon officially to launch the series was entitled "The Skeleton Dance," animated by Disney's longtime associate Ub Iwerks. The series went on to introduce the first three-strip Technicolor cartoon, "Flowers and Trees," perhaps the most imaginatively drawn cartoon from this era. (The film appropriately won an Academy Award for Best Short Film [Cartoon].)

The addition of color ensured the success of the *Silly Symphony* series, which lasted six more years and produced more classic cartoons like "Three Little Pigs." *Directors were Walt Disney, Ub Iwerks, Burt Gillett, Wilfred Jackson, David Hand, Ben Sharpsteen, Dick Lundy, Hugh Harman, Rudolf Ising, Jack Cutting and Graham Heid. Black-and-white. Technicolor. A Walt Disney Production released through Columbia Pictures, United Artists and RKO-Radio Pictures. Columbia Pictures*

1928–29: "The Skeleton Dance" (Disney); "El Terrible Toreador" (Disney); "Springtime" (Iwerks); "Hell's Bell's" (Iwerks); and "The Merry Dwarfs" (Disney).

1930: "Summer" (Iwerks/Jan. 6); "Autumn" (Iwerks/Feb. 13); "Cannibal Capers" (Gillett/Mar. 13); "Frolicking Fish" (Gillett/May 8); "Arctic Antics" (Iwerks/June 5); "In a Toy Shop" (Gillett/July 3/copyrighted as "Midnight in a Toy Shop"); "Night" (Disney/July 31); "Monkey Melodies" (Gillett/Aug. 10); "Winter" (Gillett/Nov. 5); and "Playful Pan" (Gillett/Dec. 28).

1931: "Birds of a Feather" (Gillett/Feb. 10); "Mother Goose Melodies" (Apr. 17); "The China Plate" (Jackson/May 25); "The Busy Beavers" (Jackson/June 22); "The Cat's Out" (Jackson/July 28/originally "The Cat's Nightmare"); "Egyptian Melodies" (Jackson/Aug. 21); "The Clock Store" (Jackson/Sept. 30/originally "In a Clock Store"); "The Spider and the Fly" (Jackson/Oct. 16); "The Fox Hunt" (Jackson/Nov. 18); and "The Ugly Duckling" (Jackson/Dec. 16).

1932: "The Bird Store" (Jackson/Jan. 16).

United Artists Releases

1932: "The Bears and the Bees" (Jackson/July 9); "Just Dogs" (Gillett/July 30); "Flowers and Trees" (Gillett/Sept. 30/first color *Silly Symphony* cartoon); "King Neptune" (Gillett/Sept. 10); "Bugs in Love" (Gillett/Oct. 1); "Babes in the Woods" (Gillett/Nov. 19/all *Silly Symphony* cartoons in color from this point on); and "Santa's Workshop" (Jackson/Dec. 10).

1933: "Birds in the Spring" (Hand/Mar. 11); "Father Noah's Ark" (Jackson/Apr. 8); "Three Little Pigs" (Gillett/May 27/A.A. winner); "Old King Cole" (Hand/July 29); "Lullaby Land" (Jackson/Aug. 19); "The Pied Piper" (Jackson/Sept. 16); and "The Night Before Christmas" (Jackson/Dec. 9).

1934: "The China Shop" (Jackson/Jan. 13); "Grasshopper and the Ants" (Jackson/Feb. 10); "Funny Little Bunnies" (Jackson/Mar. 24); "The Big Bad Wolf" (Gillett/Apr. 14); "The Wise Little Hen" (Jackson/June 9/first appearance of Donald Duck); "The Flying Mouse" (Hand/July 14); "Peculiar Penguins" (Jackson/Sept. 1); and "The Goddess of Spring" (Jackson/Nov. 3).

1935: "The Tortoise and the Hare" (Jackson/Jan. 5/A.A. winner); "The Golden Touch" (Disney/Mar. 22); "The Robber Kitten" (Hand/Apr. 20); "Water Babies" (Jackson/May 11); "The Cookie Carnival" (Sharpsteen/May 25); "Who Killed Cock Robin?" (Hand/June 29/A.A. nominee); "Music Land" (Jackson/Oct. 5); "Three Orphan Kittens" (Hand/Oct. 26/A.A. winner); "Cock o' the Walk" (Sharpsteen/Nov. 30); and "Broken Toys" (Sharpsteen/Dec. 14).

1936: "Elmer Elephant" (Jackson/Mar. 28); "Three Little Wolves" (Hand/Apr. 18); "Toby Tortoise Returns" (Jackson/Aug. 22); "Three Blind Mouseketeers" (Hand/Sept. 26); "The Country Cousin" (Jackson/Oct. 31/A.A. winner); "Mother Pluto" (Nov. 14); and "More Kittens" (Hand/Dec. 19).

1937: "Woodland Cafe" (Jackson/Mar. 13); and "Little Hiawatha" (Hand/May 15).

RKO-Radio Pictures releases

1937: "The Old Mill" (Jackson/Nov. 5/A.A. winner).

1938: "Moth and the Flame" (Gillett/Apr. 1); "Wynken, Blynken, and Nod" (Heid/May 27); "Farmyard Symphony" (Cutting/Oct. 14); "Merbabies" (supervised by Disney, Sharpsteen, Hand, Englander; directed by Rudolf Ising for Harman-Ising Studios/Dec. 9); and "Mother Goose Goes Hollywood" (Jackson/Dec. 23/A.A. nominee).

1939: "The Ugly Duckling" (Cutting/Apr. 7/A.A. winner).

◉ SIR BLUR

A nearsighted knight in King Arthur's time who always has trouble with his glasses, Sir Blur was one of several late 1960s' cartoon creations featured in Paramount/Famous Studios' *Modern Madcap* theatrical cartoon series. The myopic knight made his screen debut in 1966's "A Balmy Knight," directed by James "Shamus" Culhane. *Culhane directed the entire series. Technicolor. Voice credits unknown. A Famous Studios Production released by Paramount Pictures.*

1966: "A Balmy Knight" (June/*Modern Madcap*); and "A Wedding Knight" (Aug./*Modern Madcap*).

1967: "The Blacksheep Blacksmith" (Jan./*Modern Madcap*).

◉ SNIFFLES

Director Chuck Jones created this naive, bewhiskered mouse who spoke with a squealing dialect and constantly found himself in precarious situations. Sniffles personified the "cute" personalities that launched the careers of animators Hugh Harman and Rudolf Ising at Warner Bros. In fact, in some respects, Jones's character bore a striking resemblance to Harman's Little Buck Cheeser.

Introduced in 1939's "Naughty But Mice," even Jones admitted the Sniffles cartoons were "often too long. When I had extra time, I'd tend to make the pans too long and the movement too slow."

Sniffles's squeaky voice was provided by Bernice Hansen, a veteran voice artist best known for her animal characters. Jones derived Sniffles's name from the fact he always had "a code in da nose." *Directed by Chuck Jones. Technicolor. A Warner Bros. release.*

Voices
Sniffles: Bernice Hansen

Merrie Melodies

1939: "Naughty But Mice" (Jones/May 30); "Little Brother Rat" (Jones/Sept. 2); and "Sniffles the Bookworm" (Jones/Dec. 2).

1940: "Sniffles Takes a Trip" (Jones/May 22); "The Egg Collector" (Jones/July 20); and "Bedtime for Sniffles" (Jones/Nov. 23).

1941: "Sniffles Bells the Cat" (Jones/Feb. 1); "Toy Trouble" (Jones/Apr. 12); and "Brave Little Bat" (Jones/Sept. 27).

1943: "The Unbearable Bear" (Jones/Apr. 17).

1944: "Lost and Foundling" (Jones/Aug. 30).

Looney Tunes

1946: "Hush My Mouse" (Jones/May 4).

◎ SPEEDY GONZALES

Possessing the speed of the Road Runner and the quick-wittedness of Tweety bird Speedy Gonzales was the mischievous Mexican mouse, jaunty in his chic sombrero, who boasted a spitfire running speed of 100 miles per hour. He was often paired with Sylvester and Daffy Duck in adventures reminiscent of MGM's *Tom and Jerry* cartoons.

The idea for Speedy's character originated in a Robert McKimson cartoon of 1953 called "Cat-Tails for Two." The story was about an idiotic cat-and-dog team who sneak into a Mexican strip in search of mice but discover that the rodents are too fast to be caught. The head mouse is unnamed in the film and bears little resemblance to the Speedy movie audiences grew up with.

Friz Freleng remembered McKimson's mouse character two years later and redesigned him with animator Hawley Pratt into "the fastest mouse in all of Mexico." Speedy's first cartoon was the 1955 entry "Speedy Gonzales." The film was accorded the film industry's highest honor, an Academy Award, for best cartoon of the year. Three other Speedy cartoons were also nominated for Oscars: "Tabasco Road" (1957), "Mexicali Shmoes" (1959); and "The Pied Piper of Guadalupe" (1961).

In later adventures, Speedy was given a comic sidekick, Slowpoke Rodriguez, whose lethargic personality never caught on. He was limited to occasional guest appearances. *Directors were Robert McKimson, Friz Freleng, Hawley Pratt, Rudy Larriva and Alex Lovy. Technicolor. A Warner Bros. release.*

Voices
Speedy Gonzales: Mel Blanc

Merrie Melodies

1953: "Cat-Tails for Two" (McKimson/Aug. 29).

1955: "Speedy Gonzales" (with Sylvester/Freleng/Sept. 17/ A.A. winner).

1957: "Tabasco Road" (with Sylvester/McKimson/July 20/ A.A. nominee); and "Gonzales' Tamales" (with Sylvester/ Freleng/Nov. 30).

1960: "West of the Pesos" (with Sylvester/McKimson/ Jan. 23).

1963: "Mexican Cat Dance" (Freleng/Apr. 20); and "Chili Weather" (with Sylvester/Freleng/Aug. 17).

DePatie-Freleng Enterprises releases

1964: "Road to Andaly" (with Sylvester/Freleng, Pratt/ Dec. 26).

1965: "Cats and Bruises" (with Sylvester/Freleng, Pratt/ Jan. 30); "The Wild Chase" (Freleng, Pratt/Feb. 27); and "Go Go Amigo" (with Daffy Duck/McKimson/Nov. 20).

1966: "Muchos Locos" (with Daffy Duck/McKimson/Feb. 5); "Mexican Mousepiece" (with Daffy Duck/McKimson/ Feb. 26); "Snow Excuse" (with Daffy Duck/McKimson/May 21); "Feather Finger" (with Daffy Duck/McKimson/Aug. 20); and "A Taste of Catnip" (with Daffy Duck/McKimson/ Dec. 3). Warner Bros. Releases

1967: "Daffy's Diner" (with Daffy Duck/McKimson/Jan. 21); "The Music Mice-Tro" (with Daffy Duck/Larriva/May 27); "Speedy Ghost to Town" (with Daffy Duck/Miguel/ Lovy/July 29); and "Go Away Stowaway" (with Daffy Duck/ Lovy/Sept. 30).

1968: "Skyscraper Caper" (with Daffy Duck/Lovy/Mar. 9).

Looney Tunes

1958: "Tortilla Flaps" (McKimson/Jan. 18).

1959: "Mexicali Shmoes" (with Slowpoke Rodriguez/ Freleng/July 4/A.A. nominee); and "Here Today Gone Tamale" (with Sylvester/Freleng/Aug. 29).

1961: "Cannery Woe" (with Sylvester/McKimson/Jan. 7); and "The Pied Piper of Guadalupe" (with Sylvester, Slowpoke Rodriguez/Freleng, Pratt/Aug. 19/A.A. nominee).

1962: "Mexican Boarders" (with Sylvester, Slowpoke Rodriguez/Freleng, Pratt/May 12).

DePatie-Freleng Enterprises Releases

1964: "A Message to Gracias" (with Sylvester/McKimson/ Feb. 8); "Nuts and Volts" (with Sylvester/Freleng/Apr. 25); and "Pancho's Hideaway" (Freleng, Pratt/Oct. 24).

1965: "It's Nice to Have Mouse Around the House" (with Daffy Duck, Sylvester/Freleng, Pratt/Jan. 16); "Well Worn Daffy" (with Daffy Duck/McKimson/May 22); "Tease for Two" (with Daffy Duck, Goofy Gophers/McKimson/Aug. 28); and "Chili Corn Corny" (with Daffy Duck/McKimson/Oct. 23).

1966: "The Astroduck" (with Daffy Duck/McKimson/Jan. 1); "Daffy Rents" (with Daffy Duck/McKimson/Mar. 26); "A-Haunting We Will Go" (with Daffy Duck, Witch Hazel/McKimson/Apr. 16); "A Squeak in the Deep" (with Daffy Duck/McKimson/July 19); and "Swing Ding Amigo" (with Daffy Duck/McKimson/Sept. 17).

Warner Bros. releases

1967: "Quacker Tracker" (with Daffy Duck/Larriva/Apr. 29); "The Spy Swatter" (with Daffy Duck/Larriva/June 24); "Rodent to Stardom" (with Daffy Duck/Lovy/Sept. 23); and "Fiesta Fiasco" (with Daffy Duck/Lovy/Dec. 9).

1968: "See Ya Later, Gladiator" (with Daffy Duck/Lovy/June 29).

SPIKE

Originally developed as a supporting character in MGM's *Droopy* series, Tex Avery featured this gentle bulldog in traditional chaotic cartoon situations in a starring series of his own. Bill Thompson, also the voice of Droopy, played Spike in the series. *Directed by Tex Avery. Technicolor. A Metro-Goldwyn-Mayer release.*

Voices
Spike: Bill Thompson

1949: "Counterfeit Cat" (Dec. 24).

1950: "Ventriloquist Cat" (May 27); and "Garden Gopher" (Sept. 30/working title: "Sting Time in the Rockies").

1951: "Cock a Doodle Dog" (Feb. 10).

1952: "Rock-a-Bye Bear" (July 12).

SPIKE AND CHESTER

Spike, a tough streetwise dog, and his admiring pal, Chester, were short-lived screen stars, paired with Sylvester (of *Tweety and Sylvester* fame) in two Warner Bros. cartoons. The tandem began their screen careers in 1952's "Tree for Two." *Directed by Friz Freleng. Technicolor. A Warner Bros. release.*

Voices
Spike: Mel Blanc; **Chester:** Stan Freberg

Merrie Melodies

1952: "Tree for Two" (with Sylvester/Oct. 4).

Looney Tunes

1954: "Dr. Jerkyl's Hide" (with Sylvester/May 8).

SPIKE AND TYKE

William Hanna and Joseph Barbera created this father-and-son dog team—Spike, the gruff father, and Tyke, the impish son—as supporting players in MGM's *Tom and Jerry* series. The characters first appeared in *Tom and Jerry* in 1942's "Dog Trouble." Hanna and Barbera later modified and cast the pair in their own series in the late 1950s. Unfortunately, the series had a brief existence.

Spike and Tyke later served as the basis for Hanna and Barbera's popular television characters, Augie Doggy and Doggy Daddy. *Directed by William Hanna and Joseph Barbera. Technicolor. CinemaScope. A Metro-Goldwyn-Mayer release.*

Voices
Spike: Bill Thompson, Daws Butler

1942: "Dog Trouble" (with Tom and Jerry/Apr. 18).

1944: "The Bodyguard" (with Tom and Jerry/July 22); and "Puttin' on the Dog" (with Tom and Jerry/Oct. 28).

1945: "Quiet Please" (with Tom and Jerry/Dec. 22/A.A. winner).

1946: "Cat Fishin'" (with Tom and Jerry/Mar. 15); and "Solid Serenade" (with Tom and Jerry/Aug. 31).

1947: "The Invisible Mouse" (with Tom and Jerry/Sept. 27).

1948: "The Truce Hurts" (with Tom and Jerry/July 17).

1949: "Heavenly Puss" (with Tom and Jerry/July 9); and "Love That Pup" (with Tom and Jerry/Oct. 1).

1950: "The Framed Cat" (with Tom and Jerry/Oct. 21).

1951: "Slicked-Up Pup" (with Tom and Jerry/Sept. 8).

1952: "Fit to Be Tied" (with Tom and Jerry/July 26); and "The Doghouse" (with Tom and Jerry/Nov. 29).

1953: "That's My Pup" (with Tom and Jerry/Apr. 25).

1954: "Hic-Cup Pup" (with Tom and Jerry/Apr. 17); and "Pet Peeve" (with Tom and Jerry/Nov. 20/CinemaScope).

1955: "Pup on a Picnic" (with Tom and Jerry/Apr. 30/CinemaScope).

1956: "Barbecue Brawl" (with Tom and Jerry/Dec. 14).

1957: "Give and Tyke" (Mar. 29/first Spike and Tyke/CinemaScope); "Scat Cats" (July 26/CinemaScope); and "Tom's Photo Finish" (with Tom and Jerry/Nov. 1/CinemaScope).

◎ SPUNKY

Spunky, one of several minor *Noveltoons* characters, appeared on the screen for the first time in 1944's "Yankee Doodle Donkey." The character did not star again in another cartoon until 14 years after his screen debut. *Directed by Isadore Sparber. Technicolor. A Famous Studios Production released through Paramount Pictures.*

1944: "Yankee Doodle Donkey" (Nov. 27).

1958: "Okey Dokey Donkey" (May 16).

◎ STONE AGE CARTOONS

Following the success of *Gulliver's Travels* (1939), Max Fleischer unveiled two cartoon series, the first featuring the comic exploits of Stone Age life. The series predated TV's *The Flintstones* by 20 years, but, unlike the television classic, this novel series died a quick death. No central characters starred in the films, which may have been one reason for the series' failure. *Technicolor. No voice credits. A Fleischer Studios Production released through Paramount Pictures.*

1940: "Granite Hotel" (Apr. 26); "The Foul Ball Player" (May 24); "The Ugly Dino" (June 14); "Wedding Belts" (July 5); "Way Back When a Razberry Was a Fruit" (July 26); "The Fulla Bluff Man" (Aug. 9); "Springtime in the Rock Age" (Aug. 30); "Pedagogical Institution (College to You)" (Sept. 13); and "Way Back When Women Had Their Weigh" (Sept. 26).

◎ SUGARFOOT

Walter Lantz attempted to cast the lame horse Sugarfoot, originally a character in a Woody Woodpecker cartoon, in a cartoon series of his own. The series did not produce much interest, however, as only two films were produced. *Directed by Paul J. Smith. Technicolor. A Walter Lantz Production released through Universal Pictures.*

1954: "A Horse's Tale" (Feb. 15); and "Hay Rube" (June 7).

◎ SUPERMAN

First conceived by Jerry Siegel and Joe Schuster as a newspaper strip and finally published in *Action Comics*, this legendary man of steel was adapted to the screen in 1941.

As in the comics, the city of Metropolis was the newspaper beat for mild-mannered reporter Clark Kent of the *Daily Planet*. Beneath his meek exterior was a Herculean super-hero able to leap tall buildings in a single bound, more powerful than a locomotive and faster than a speeding bullet.

The supporting cast of characters was also intact: pretty newspaper gal Lois Lane, cub reporter Jimmy Olsen and blustering editor-in-chief Perry White.

Both Fleischer Studios and Famous Studios produced the series. "The Japoteurs" was the first Famous cartoon. The original Fleischer cartoons used Rotoscoping to give animation a semirealistic look and attention to detail never to be matched in later television versions of the series. Action and special effects were key elements of the series, which was backed by a tremendous promotional campaign when it was introduced.

Director Dave Fleischer contracted two actors from the radio version, Bud Collyer and Joan Alexander, to voice Clark Kent/Superman and Lois Lane. *Directors were Dave Fleischer, Seymour Kneitel, Isadore Sparber and Dan Gordon. Technicolor. A Fleischer Studios and Famous Studios Production released through Paramount Pictures.*

Voices
Clark Kent/Superman: Clayton "Bud" Collyer; **Lois Lane:** Joan Alexander

Fleischer Studios Releases

1941: "Superman" (Fleischer/Sept. 26/working title: "The Mad Scientist"/A.A. nominee); and "The Mechanical Monsters" (Kneitel/Nov. 21).

1942: "Billion Dollar Limited" (Fleischer/Jan. 9); "The Arctic Giant" (Fleischer/Feb. 27); "The Bulleteers" (Fleischer/Mar. 26); "The Magnetic Telescope" (Fleischer/Apr. 24); "Electric Earthquake" (Fleischer/May 15); "Volcano" (Fleischer/July 10); and "Terror on the Midway" (Fleischer/Aug. 28).

Famous Studios Releases

1942: "Japoteurs" (Kneitel/Sept. 18); "Showdown" (Sparber/Oct. 16); "Eleventh Hour" (Gordon/Nov. 20); and "Destruction, Inc." (Sparber/Dec. 25).

1943: "The Mummy Strikes" (Sparber/Feb. 19); "Jungle Drums" (Gordon/Mar. 26); "Underground World" (Kneitel/June 18); and "Secret Agent" (Kneitel/July 30).

◎ SWIFTY AND SHORTY

A fast-talking con man, Swifty, and his pudgy friend, Shorty, appeared in this series of misadventures patterned after comedy greats Abbott and Costello. Formerly "Jeepers and Creepers," the characters under their new identities were recast in several cartoon shorts—*Noveltoon* and *Modern Madcap* releases—before being given their own star-billed series in 1964. (In the three cartoons released in

1962, they were known as Ralph and Percy.) Comedian Eddie Lawrence supplied the voices for this series. *Directed by Seymour Kneitel and Howard Post. Technicolor. A Famous Studios Production released through Paramount Pictures.*

Voices
Swifty/Shorty: Eddie Lawrence

1962: "Without Time or Reason" (Kneitel/Jan./Noveltoon); "Hi-Fi Jinx" (Kneitel/Mar./Modern Madcap); and "T.V. or No T.V." (Kneitel/Mar./Noveltoon).

1964: "Panhandling on Madison Avenue" (Kneitel/Apr.); "Fizzicle Fizzle" (Kneitel/Apr.); "Sailing Zero" (Kneitel/Apr.); "Fix That Clock" (Kneitel/May); "A Friend in Tweed" (Kneitel/May); "The Once-Over" (Kneitel/June); "Service with a Smile" (Kneitel/June); "Call Me a Taxi" (Kneitel/July); "Highway Slobbery" (Kneitel/July); "Hip Hip Ole" (Kneitel/Sept.); "Accidents Will Happen" (Kneitel/Sept.); and "The Bus Way to Travel" (Kneitel/Oct.).

1965: "Inferior Decorator" (Post/June); "Ocean Bruise" (Post/Sept.); "Getting Ahead" (Post/Dec.); and "Les Boys" (Post/Dec.).

⊚ SWING SYMPHONIES

Popular jazz tunes of the 1940s were the basis of this series produced and created by Walter Lantz. Episodes featured no running characters, and early versions concentrated on boogie-woogie type music evidenced by such series titles as "Yankee Doodle Swing Shift" and "Cow Cow Boogie."

Lantz paid a hefty price to produce these ambitious musical oddities, from $9,500 to $12,000 per one-reeler. As he told biographer Joe Adamson: "I loved to make musicals, but you can't cheat on musicals. You've got to animate to the beat."

In 1944 the series ran its course. Two years later Lantz replaced it with another musical series entitled *Musical Miniatures. Directed by Walter Lantz, Alex Lovy, Ben Hardaway, Emery Hawkins, James "Shamus" Culhane and Dick Lundy. Black-and-white. Technicolor. A Walter Lantz Production released through Universal Pictures.*

1941: "$21,000 a Day Once a Month" (Lantz/Dec. 1).

1942: "The Hams That Couldn't Be Cured" (Lantz/Mar. 4); "Juke Box Jamboree" (Lovy/July 27); "Yankee Doodle Swing Shift" (Lovy/Sept. 21); and "Boogie Woogie Sioux" (Lovy/Nov. 30).

1943: "Cow Cow Boogie" (Lovy/Jan. 5); "Egg Cracker Suite" (with Oswald the Rabbit/Hardaway, Hawkins/Mar. 22); "Swing Your Partner" (with Homer Pigeon/Lovy); "Pass the Biscuits Mirandy" (Culhane/Aug. 23); and "Boogie Woogie Man" (Culhane/Sept. 27).

1944: "Jungle Jive" (Culhane/May 15); and "Abou Ben Boogie" (Culhane/Sept. 18).

1945: "The Pied Piper of Basin Street" (Culhane/Jan. 15); and "The Sliphorn King of Polaroo" (Lundy/Mar. 19).

⊚ SYLVESTER

Sylvester enjoyed an accomplished solo career before teaming up with the slippery yellow canary Tweety. The lisping cat, whose voice was similar to Daffy Duck's, was first used in Friz Freleng's 1945 "Life with Feathers," ironically appearing with a lovelorn lovebird. In this film debut he uttered his now-famous line of "Sufferin' succotash."

Sylvester next appeared in Freleng's "Peck Up Your Troubles" (1945), this time opposite a woodpecker, and as a ringleader of a quartet of cats in Bob Clampett's "Kitty Kornered" (1946), before Freleng paired the exasperated cat with Tweety the bird in 1947's "Tweety Pie." (Clampett did the preliminary story for the film, but Freleng assumed the property after Clampett left the studio that same year.)

While the cartoon became the first starring role for Sylvester (in the film, he is referred to as Thomas, not Sylvester), it also became the first Warner cartoon to win an Oscar for Best Short Subject of the year. It was Sylvester's second of three Oscar-nominated cartoons. His first was 1945's "Life with Feather"; his third and final nominated cartoon was 1961's "The Pied Piper of Guadalupe" starring Speedy Gonzales.

Sylvester was given a series of his own in 1953, appearing in cartoons opposite his ever-energetic son, Sylvester Jr. (simply known as "Junior"), and Hippety Hopper, the hopping kangaroo, whom Sylvester constantly mistakes for an oversize mouse. The sly pussycat made intermittent appearances with Elmer J. Fudd and Porky Pig and was paired with Speedy Gonzales in other cartoon misadventures.

In the 1990s Sylvester resurfaced in minor film roles, first in the new Bugs Bunny cartoon "Carrotblanca" (1995), followed by an appearance in the hit feature *Space Jam* (1996), starring Michael Jordan and the *Looney Tunes* characters. In 1997 Sylvester starred in an all-new cartoon short—his first in 35 years—"Father of the Bird," which opened in theaters with the live-action comedy *The Man Who Knew Too Little*, starring Bill Murray. Produced by legendary animator Chuck Jones (who four years earlier had formed a new animation unit at Warner Bros. to produce new theatrical cartoon shorts for the studio) and directed by Jones's protégé Steve Fossati, the cartoon introduced a new nemesis: Cornbread, a fiesty little bird, voiced by veteran voice artist June Foray. Joe Alaskey provided the voice of Sylvester. *Directed by Friz Freleng, Charles M. Jones, Bob Clampett, Robert McKimson, Hawley Pratt, Gerry Chiniquy, Douglas McCarthy and Steve Fossati. Technicolor. A Warner Bros. release.*

Voices

Sylvester: Mel Blanc, Joe Alaskey; **Sylvester Jr./Tweety:** Mel Blanc; **Cornbread:** June Foray

Merrie Melodies

1945: "Life with Feathers" (Freleng/Mar. 24/A.A. nominee); and "Peck Up Your Troubles" (Freleng/Oct. 20).

1947: "Doggone Cats" (Davis/Oct. 25).

1948: "Back Alley Oproar" (with Elmer Fudd/Freleng/Mar. 27); and "Scaredy Cat" (with Porky Pig/Jones/Dec. 21).

1949: "Mouse Mazurka" (Freleng/June 11); "Swallow the Leader" (McKimson/Oct. 14); and "Hippety Hopper" (with Hippety Hopper/McKimson/Nov. 19).

1952: "Little Red Rodent Hood" (Freleng/May 3); and "Tree for Two" (Freleng/Oct. 4).

1953: "A Mouse Divided" (Freleng/Jan. 31); "A Peck o' Trouble" (McKimson/Mar. 28); and "Cats Aweigh" (with Junior, Hippety Hopper/McKimson/Nov. 28).

1954: "Bell Hoppy" (with Hippety Hopper/McKimson/Apr. 17); and "Claws for Alarm" (with Porky Pig/Jones/May 22).

1955: "Lighthouse Mouse" (with Hippety Hopper/McKimson/Mar. 12); "A Kiddie's Kitty" (Freleng/Aug. 20); "Speedy Gonzales" (with Speedy Gonzales/Freleng/Sept. 17/A.A. winner); and "Pappy's Puppy" (Freleng/Dec. 17).

1956: "The Unexpected Guest" (McKimson/June 2); "The Slap-Hoppy Mouse" (with Hippety Hopper/McKimson/Sept. 1); and "Yankee Dood It" (with Elmer Fudd/Freleng/Oct. 13).

1957: "Tabasco Road" (with Speedy Gonzales/McKimson/July 20); "Mouse-Taken Identity" (with Hippety Hopper, Junior/McKimson/Nov. 16); and "Gonzales' Tamales" (with Speedy Gonzales/Freleng/Nov. 30).

1960: "West of Pesos" (with Speedy Gonzales/Freleng/Jan. 23); and "Trip for Tat" (with Tweety/Freleng/Oct. 19).

1961: "D'Fightin' Ones" (Freleng/Apr. 22).

1963: "Chili Weather" (with Speedy Gonzales/Freleng/Aug. 17); and "Claws in the Lease" (with Junior/McKimson/Nov. 9).

DePatie-Freleng Enterprises Releases

1964: "Road to Adaly" (with Speedy Gonzales/Freleng, Pratt/Dec. 26).

1965: "Cats and Bruises" (with Speedy/Freleng, Pratt/Jan. 30).

Looney Tunes

1946: "Kitty Kornered" (with Porky Pig/Clampett/June 8).

1948: "Hop Look and Listen" (with Hippety Hopper/McKimson/Apr. 17); and "Kit for Cat" (with Elmer/Freleng/Nov. 6).

1950: "The Scarlet Pumpernickel" (with Daffy Duck, Porky Pig, Elmer Fudd and Momma Bear/Jones/Mar. 4); and "Pop 'em Pop!" (with Hippety, Junior/McKimson/Nov. 6).

1951: "Canned Feud" (Freleng/Feb. 3).

1952: "Who's Kitten Who" (with Hippety Hopper, Junior/McKimson/Jan. 5); and "Hoppy Go Lucky" (with Hippety Hopper/McKimson/Aug. 9).

1954: "Dr. Jerkyl's Hide" (with Spike and Chester/Freleng/May 8); and "By Word of Mouse" (Freleng/Oct. 2).

1955: "Jumpin' Jupiter" (with Porky Pig/Jones/Aug. 6).

1956: "Too Hop to Handle" (with Hippety Hopper, Junior/McKimson/Jan. 28); and "Heir-Conditioned" (with Elmer Fudd/Freleng/Nov. 26).

1959: "Cat's Paw" (with Junior/McKimson/Aug. 15); and "Here Today, Gone Tamale" (with Speedy Gonzales/Freleng/Aug. 29).

1960: "Goldimouse and the Three Cats" (with Junior/Freleng/Mar. 16); and "Mouse Garden" (with Junior, Sam/Freleng/July 16).

1961: "Cannery Woe" (with Speedy Gonzales/McKimson/Jan. 7); "Hoppy Daze" (with Hippety Hopper/McKimson/Feb. 11); "Birds of a Father" (with Junior/McKimson/Apr. 1); and "The Pied Piper of Guadalupe" (with Speedy Gonzales, Slowpoke Rodriguez/Freleng, Pratt/A.A. nominee).

1962: "Fish and Slips" (with Junior/McKimson/Mar. 10); and "Mexican Boarders" (with Speedy Gonzales, Slowpoke Rodriguez/Freleng, Pratt/May 12).

DePatie-Freleng Enterprises releases

1964: "A Message to Gracias" (with Speedy Gonzales/McKimson/Feb. 8); "Freudy Cat" (with Hippety Hopper, Junior/McKimson/Mar. 14); and "Nuts and Volts" (with Speedy Gonzales/Freleng/Apr. 25).

1965: "It's Nice to Have Mouse Around the House" (with Speedy Gonzales, Daffy Duck/Freleng, Pratt/Jan. 16).

1995: "Carrotblanca" (with Bugs Bunny, Daffy Duck, Yosemite Sam, Tweety, Pepe Le Pew, Foghorn Leghorn, Penelope/McCarthy/Aug. 25).

Chuck Jones Film Production (released by Warner Bros. Family Entertainment)

1997: "Father of the Bird" (with Cornbread/Fossati/Nov. 14).

⊚ TALKARTOONS

Billed as "actual talking pictures" in theater ads, this series represented the Fleischer Studios' initial entrance into the sound cartoon arena. Films starred a host of subsequently famous characters, including Betty Boop, Bimbo and Koko the Clown.

Early entries featured postsynched dialogue and music added after the productions were complete with dialogue being kept to a minimum and peppy musical scores carrying the films. In the beginning, having no accomplished musical director to create songs, the Fleischers purchased the rights of popular songs to use as soundtracks. The series' first star was Bimbo, resurrected by the Fleischers from the *Out of the Inkwell* series.

While the series celebrated Bimbo's return to the screen, the series' sixth cartoon release of 1930, "Dizzy Dishes," introduced another character in her formative stages—Betty Boop, invented and drawn by animator Grim Natwick. In 1931 Koko the Clown was brought back as a supporting player in the series, after a brief retirement from the screen. *Directed by Dave Fleischer. Black-and-white. A Fleischer Studios Production released through Paramount Pictures.*

(Copyright dates are marked by a ©.)

1929: "Noah's Lark" (© Oct. 25) and "Accordion Joe" (© Dec. 12).

1930: "Marriage Wows" (© Jan. 8); "Radio Riot" (Feb. 13); "Fire Bugs" (May 9); "Wise Flies" (July 18); "Dizzy Dishes" (with Betty Boop/Aug. 9); "Barnacle Bill" (Aug. 31); "Swing, You Sinner" (Sept. 24); "The Grand Uproar" (Oct. 3); "Sky Scraping" (Nov. 1); "Up to Mars" (Nov. 20); and "Mysterious Mouse" (Dec. 26).

1931: "The Ace of Spades" (Jan. 16); "Tree Saps" (Feb. 3); "Teacher's Pest" (Feb. 7); "The Cow's Husband" (Mar. 13); "The Bum Bandit" (Apr. 3); "The Male Man" (Apr. 24); "Silly Scandals" (with Betty Boop/May 23); "The Herring Murder Case" (June 26); "Bimbo's Initiation" (with Betty Boop/July 24); "Bimbo's Express" (with Betty Boop/Aug. 22); "Minding the Baby" (with Betty Boop/Sept. 26); "In the Shade of the Old Apple Sauce" (Oct. 16); "Mask-a-Raid" (with Betty Boop/Nov. 7); "Jack and the Beanstalk" (with Betty Boop/Nov. 21); and "Dizzy Red Riding Hood" (with Betty Boop/Dec. 12).

1932: "Any Rags" (with Betty Boop/Jan. 2); "Boop-Oop-a-Doop" (with Betty Boop/Jan. 16); "The Robot" (Feb. 5); "Minnie the Moocher" (with Betty Boop, Cab Calloway and His Orchestra/Feb. 26); "Swim or Sink" (with Betty Boop/Mar. 11); "Crazy Town" (with Betty Boop/Mar. 25); "The Dancing Fool" (Apr. 8); "A Hunting We Will Go" (with Betty Boop/Apr. 29); "Chess-Nuts" (May 13); "Hide and Seek" (May 26); "Admission Free" (with Betty Boop/June 10); and "The Betty Boop Limited" (with Betty Boop/July 1).

⊚ TASMANIAN DEVIL

One Warner Bros. star who was very popular on screen in a handful of cartoon misadventures was that whirling dervish, the Tasmanian Devil, who buzzsawed his way through everything in his path. Robert McKimson originated the character and Mel Blanc supplied the voice. Blanc, who described his characterization as "growl slobbering, indecipherable gibberish," supposedly told McKimson while voicing the first cartoon, "I defy you or anybody else to tell me he doesn't sound like a Tasmanian Devil."

In all, the Tasmanian Devil appeared in five cartoons, most of them opposite Bugs Bunny.

The character resurfaced again, in a different form, in 1990 on the hit Warner Bros. TV series, *Tiny Toon Adventures.* Known as Dizzy Devil, he made occasional appearances on the show. In 1991 Warner Bros. renamed him "Taz" and awarded him his own series, *Taz-Mania,* which premiered on the Fox Network in 1991. The character later appeared in a supporting role in the critically acclaimed feature *Space Jam* (1996), starring basketball superstar Michael Jordan. *Directed by Robert McKimson. Technicolor. A Warner Bros. release.*

Voices
Tasmanian Devil: Mel Blanc

Looney Tunes

1954: "Devil May Hare" (with Bugs Bunny/McKimson/June 19).

Merrie Melodies

1957: "Bedevilled Rabbit" (with Bugs Bunny/McKimson/Apr. 13); and "Ducking the Devil" (with Daffy Duck/McKimson/Aug. 17).

1962: "Bill of Hare" (with Bugs Bunny/McKimson/June 9).

1964: "Dr. Devil and Mr. Hare" (with Bugs Bunny/McKimson/Mar. 28).

⊚ TERRY BEARS

Originally Terrytoons' mascots, these rascally twin bears starred in their own cartoon series for the studio. *Directors were Connie Rasinski, Ed Donnelly and Mannie Davis. Technicolor. A Terrytoons Production released through 20th Century-Fox.*

Voices

Terry Bears: Roy Halee, Phillip A. Scheib, Doug Moye

1951: "Tall Timber Tale" (Rasinski/July); and "Little Problems" (Donnelly/Sept.).

1952: "Papa's Little Helpers" (Davis/Jan.); "Papa's Day of Rest" (Davis/Mar.); "Little Anglers" (Rasinski/July); "Nice Doggy" (Donnelly/Oct.); and "Picnic with Papa" (Davis/Dec.).

1953: "Thrifty Cubs" (Davis/Jan.); "Snappy Snap Shots" (Donnelly/Mar.); "Plumber's Helpers" (Rasinski/May); "Open House" (Donnelly/Aug.); "The Reluctant Pup" (Davis/ Oct.); and "Growing Pains" (Donnelly/Dec.).

1954: "Pet Problems" (Donnelly/Apr.); and "Howling Success" (Rasinski/July).

1956: "Baffling Business" (Rasinski/Apr.).

⊚ TERRYTOONS

Featuring assembly-line animation and repetitive story formulas, *Terrytoons* was, surprisingly, one of the longest-running continuous series in cartoon history. The series never achieved the critical success or cult status of Disney, Warner and MGM cartoons, yet it endured despite the fact most films starred incidental characters.

Paul Terry created the series after forming his own studio in 1929, with partner Frank Moser. Audio-Cinema Studios agreed to finance the cartoons and provided working space for the animators at the old Edison studio in the Bronx. Under the agreement, Terry and Moser worked without pay until Audio Cinema recouped its costs for these animated adventures.

Educational Pictures distributed the first cartoons, released with a synchronized soundtrack based on popular music of the day. In 1934 Terry broke ground and built his Terrytoons studio in New Rochelle, New York, where the vast majority of these films were produced until the studio closed down in 1968.

Despite the addition of sound, Terry relied mostly on ragtime musical soundtracks and loads of action, featuring little dialogue between characters in these episodes. Except for some films produced in the 1950s, most cartoons had no main character.

Terry was one of the last to change over to color, filming the series in black-and-white. In 1938 he finally gave in to industry pressures and produced his first color *Terrytoons*, "String Bean Jack." However, Terry remained unconvinced about producing more color cartoons because of the great expense; black-and-white animation was considerably less costly. He therefore used color sparingly until 1943, when he completely converted over to the process since black-and-white had faded in popularity altogether.

(For additional *Terrytoons* entries, see *Aesop's Fables, Astronut, Clint Clobber, Deputy Dawg, Dinky Duck, Dimwit, Dingbat, Duckwood, Fanny Zilch, Farmer Al Falfa, Foofle, Gandy Goose, Gaston Le Crayon, Good Deal Daily, Half Pint, Hashimoto, Heckle and Jeckle, Hector Heathcote, James Hound, John Doormat, Kiko the Kangaroo, Little Roquefort, Luno, Martian Moochers, Mighty Mouse, Oil Can Harry, Phoney Baloney, Possible Possum, Puddy the Pup, Sad Cat, Sidney the Elephant, the Terry Bears and Willie Walrus.*) Directors were Paul Terry, Frank Moser, Mannie Davis, George Gordon, Jack Zander, Dan Gordon, John Foster, Connie Rasinski, Volney White, Ed Donnelly, Bob Kuwahara, Dave Tendlar, Al Kouzel and Martin B. Taras. Black-and-white. Technicolor. CinemaScope. A Terrytoons Production released through Educational Pictures and 20th Century-Fox.

Educational Pictures Releases

(Copyright dates are marked by a ©.)

1930: "Caviar" (Terry, Moser/Feb. 23); "Pretzels" (Terry, Moser/Mar. 9); "Spanish Onions" (Terry, Moser/Mar. 23); "Indian Pudding" (Terry, Moser/Apr. 6); "Roman Punch" (Terry, Moser/Apr. 20); "Hot Turkey" (Terry, Moser/May 4); "Hawaiian Pineapple" (Terry, Moser/May 4); "Swiss Cheese" (Terry, Moser/Mat 18); "Codfish Balls" (Terry, Moser/June 1); "Hungarian Goulash" (Terry, Moser/June 15); "Bully Beef" (Terry, Moser/July 13); "Kangaroo Steak" (Terry, Moser/July 27); "Monkey Meat" (Terry, Moser/Aug. 10); "Chop Suey" (Terry, Moser/Aug. 24); "French Fried" (Terry, Moser/Sept. 7); "Dutch Treat" (Terry, Moser/Sept. 21); "Irish Stew" (Terry, Moser/Oct. 5); "Fried Chicken" (Terry, Moser/Oct. 19); "Jumping Beans" (Terry, Moser/Nov. 2); "Scotch Highball" (Terry, Moser/Nov. 16); "Salt Water Taffy" (Terry, Moser/Nov. 30); "Golf Nuts" (Terry, Moser/Dec. 14); and "Pigskin Capers" (Terry, Moser/Dec. 28).

1931: "Popcorn" (Terry, Moser/Jan. 11); "Go West, Big Boy" (Terry, Moser/Feb. 22); "Quack Quack" (Terry, Moser/Mar. 8); "Clowning" (Terry, Moser/Apr. 5); "Sing Sing Prison" (Terry, Moser/Apr. 19); "The Fireman's Bride" (Terry, Moser/May 3); "A Day to Live" (Terry, Moser/May 31); "2000 B.C." (Terry, Moser/June 14); "Blues" (Terry, Moser/June 28); "By the Sea" (Terry, Moser/July 12); "Her First Egg" (Terry, Moser/July 26); "Jazz Mad" (Terry, Moser/Aug. 9); "Canadian Capers" (Terry, Moser/Aug. 23); "Jesse and James" (Terry, Moser/Sept. 6); "Around the World" (Terry, Moser/Oct. 4); "Jingle Bells" (Terry, Moser/Oct. 18); "The Black Spider" (Terry, Moser/Nov. 1); "China" (Terry, Moser/Nov. 15); "The Lorelei" (Terry, Moser/Nov. 29); "Summertime" (Terry, Moser/Dec. 13); and "Aladdin's Lamp" (Terry, Moser/Dec. 27).

1932: "The Villain's Curse" (Terry, Moser/Jan. 10); "The Spider Talks" (Terry, Moser/Feb. 7); "Peg Leg Pete" (Terry, Moser/Feb. 21); "Play Ball" (Terry, Moser/Mar. 6); "Bull-Ero"

(Terry, Moser/Apr. 3); "Radio Girl" (Terry, Moser/Apr. 17); "Romance" (Terry, Moser/May 15); "Bluebeard's Brother" (Terry, Moser/May 29); "The Mad King" (Terry, Moser/June 26); "Cocky Cockroach" (Terry, Moser/July 10); "Sherman Was Right" (Terry, Moser/Aug. 21); "Burlesque" (Terry, Moser/Sept. 4); "Southern Rhythm" (Terry, Moser/Sept. 18); "College Spirit" (Terry, Moser/Oct. 16); "Hook and Ladder Number One" (Terry, Moser/Oct. 30); "The Forty Thieves" (Terry, Moser/Nov. 13); "Toyland" (Terry, Moser/Nov. 27); "Hollywood Diet" (Terry, Moser/Dec. 11); and "Ireland or Bust" (Terry, Moser/Dec. 25)

1933: "Jealous Lover" (Terry, Moser/Jan. 8); "Robin Hood" (Terry, Moser/Jan. 22); "Hansel and Gretel" (Terry, Moser/Feb. 5); "Tale of a Shirt" (Terry, Moser/Feb. 19); "Down on the Levee" (Terry, Moser/Mar. 5); "Who Killed Cock Robin?" (Terry, Moser/Mar. 19); "Oh Susanna" (Terry, Moser/Apr. 2); "Romeo and Juliet" (Terry, Moser/Apr. 16); "Pirate Ship" (Terry, Moser/Apr. 30); "Cinderella" (Terry, Moser/May 28); "Grand Uproar" (Terry, Moser/Aug. 25); "Fanny's Wedding Day" (with Fanny, Strongheart/Terry, Moser/Oct. 6); "A Gypsy Fiddler" (Terry, Moser/Oct. 6); "Beanstalk Jack" (Terry, Moser/Oct. 20); "Little Boy Blue" (Terry, Moser/Nov. 30); "In Venice" (Terry, Moser/Dec. 15); and "The Sunny South" (Terry, Moser/Dec. 29).

1934: "Holland Days" (Terry, Moser/Jan. 12); "The Three Bears" (Davis/Jan. 26); "Rip Van Winkle" (Terry, Moser/Feb. 9); "The Last Straw" (Terry, Moser/Feb. 23); "A Mad House" (Terry, Moser/Mar. 23); "Joe's Lunch Wagon" (Terry, Moser/Apr. 6); "Just a Clown" (Terry, Moser/Apr. 20); "The King's Daughter" (Terry, Moser/May 4); "The Lion's Friend" (Terry, Moser/May 18); "Pandora" (Terry, Moser/June 1); "Slow But Sure" (Terry, Moser/June 15); "See the World" (Terry, Moser/June 29); "My Lady's Garden" (Terry, Moser/July 13); "Irish Sweepstakes" (Terry, Moser/July 27); "Busted Blossoms" (Terry, Moser/Aug. 10); "Mice in Council" (Terry, Moser/Aug. 24); "Jail Birds" (Terry, Moser/Sept. 21); "The Black Sheep" (Terry, Moser/Oct. 5); "The Magic Fish" (Terry, Moser/Oct. 17); "Hot Sands" (Terry, Moser/Nov. 2); "Tom, Tom the Piper's Son" (Terry, Moser/Nov. 16); "Jack's Snack" (Terry, Moser/Nov. 30); "South Pole or Bust" (Terry, Moser/Dec. 14); and "The Dog Show" (Terry, Moser/Dec. 28).

1935: "The First Show" (Terry, Moser/Jan. 11); "The Bullfight" (Terry, Moser/Feb. 8); "Fireman Save My Child" (Terry, Moser/Feb. 22); "The Moth and the Spider" (Terry, Moser/Mar. 8); "Peg Leg Pete, The Pirate" (Terry, Moser/Apr. 19); "A Modern Red Riding Hood" (Terry, Moser/May 3); "Five Puppets" (Terry, Moser/May 17); "Opera" (Terry, Moser/May 31); "King Looney XIV" (Terry, Moser/June 14); "Amateur Night" (Terry, Moser/July 12); "The Foxy-Fox" (Terry, Moser/July 26); "Chain Letters"

(Terry, Moser/Aug. 9); "Birdland" (Terry, Moser/Aug. 23); "Circus Days" (Terry, Moser/Sept. 6); "Hey Diddle Diddle" (Terry, Moser/Sept. 20); "Foiled Again" (with Fanny, Oil Can, Strongheart/Terry, Moser/Oct. 14); "Football" (Terry, Moser/Oct. 18); "Aladdin's Lamp" (Terry, Moser/Nov. 15); "Southern Horse-Pitality" (Terry, Moser/Nov. 29); "Ye Olde Toy Shop" (Terry, Moser/Dec. 13); and "The Mayflower" (Terry, Moser/Dec. 27).

1936: "The Feud" (Terry, Moser/Jan. 10); "Off to China" (Terry, Moser/Mar. 20); "A Wolf in Cheap Clothing" (Terry, Moser/Apr. 17); "The Busy Bee" (May 29); "The Sailor's Home" (June 12); "A Tough Egg" (Terry, Moser/June 26); and "Robin Hood in an Arrow Escape" (Davis, Gordon/Nov. 13).

1937: "Salty McGuire" (Davis, Gordon/Jan. 8); "Bug Carnival" (Davis, Gordon/Apr. 16); "Schoolbirds" (Davis, Gordon/Apr. 30); "The Paper Hangers" (Davis/July 30); "A Bully Frog" (Terry, Davis, Gordon/Sept. 18); "The Timid Rabbit" (Davis/Nov. 26); "The Billy Goat Whiskers" (Foster/Dec. 10); and "The Barnyard Boss" (Rasinski/Dec. 24).

1938: "The Lion Hunt" (Davis/Jan. 7); "Bugs Beetle and His Orchestra" (Foster/Jan. 21); "Just Ask Jupiter" (Davis/Feb. 18); "A Mountain Romance" (Davis/Apr. 1); "Robinson Crusoe's Broadcast" (Foster/Apr. 15); "Maid in China" (Rasinski/Apr. 29); "Here's to Good Old Jail" (Donnelly/June 10); "The Last Indian" (Rasinski/June 24); "Milk for Baby" (Davis/July 8); "Mrs. O'Leary's Cow" (Donnelly/July 22); and "Eliza Runs Again" (Rasinski/July 29/last Educational Pictures release).

20th Century-Fox releases

1938: "Chris Columbo" (Donnelly/Aug. 12); "String Bean Jack" (Foster/Aug. 26/first in Technicolor); "Wolf's Side of the Story" (Rasinski/Sept. 23); "The Glass Slipper" (Davis/Oct. 7); "The Newcomer" (with Panda Bear/Davis/Oct. 21); "The Stranger Rides Again" (Davis/Nov. 4); "Housewife Herman" (Donnelly/Nov. 18); and "Village Blacksmith" (Davis/Dec. 2).

1939: "The Owl and the Pussycat" (Donnelly/Jan. 13/Technicolor); "One Gun Gary in the Nick of Time" (with One Gun Gary/Donnelly/Jan. 27); "The Three Bears" (Davis/Feb. 10/Technicolor); "Frozen Feet" (Rasinski/Feb. 24); "The Nutty Network" (Davis/Mar. 24/Technicolor); "The Cuckoo Bird" (Davis/Apr. 7); "Their Last Bean" (Donnelly/Apr. 21); "Barnyard Eggcitement" (Davis/May 5); "Nick's Coffee Pot" (Rasinski/May 19); "The Prize Guest" (Davis/June 2); "Africa Squawks" (Rasinski/June 30); "Old Fire Horse" (Donnelly/July 28); "Two Headed Giant" (Rasinski/Aug. 11); "The Golden West" (Davis/Aug. 25); "Sheep in the Meadow" (Davis/Sept. 22); "The Watchdog" (Donnelly/Oct. 20); "One Mouse in a Million"

(Rasinski/Nov. 3); "A Wicky-Wacky Romance" (Davis/Nov. 17); "The Ice Pond" (Davis/Dec. 15); and "The First Robin" (Rasinski/Dec. 29/Technicolor).

1940: "A Dog in a Mansion" (Donnelly/Jan. 12); "Edgar Runs Again" (Davis/Jan. 26); "Harvest Time" (Rasinski/Feb. 9/Technicolor); "The Hare and the Hounds" (Donnelly/Feb. 23); "All's Well That Ends Well" (Davis/Mar. 8); "Just a Little Bull" (Donnelly/Apr. 19/Technicolor); "Wot's All th' Shootin' Fer" (White/May 3); "Swiss Ski Yodelers" (Donnelly/May 17); "Catnip Capers" (Davis/May 31); "Professor Offkeyski" (Rasinski/June 14); "Rover's Rescue" (White/June 28); "Rupert the Runt" (Davis/July 12); "Love in a Cottage" (White/July 28); "Billy Mouse's Akwakade" (Donnelly/Aug. 9/Technicolor); "Club Life in Stone Age" (Davis/Aug. 23); "Touchdown Demons" (White/Sept. 20); "How Wet Was My Ocean" (Donnelly/Oct. 4/Technicolor); "Happy Haunting Grounds" (Davis/Oct. 18); "Landing of the Pilgrims" (Rasinski/Nov. 1/Technicolor); "Plane Goofy" (Donnelly/Nov. 29); "Snowman" (Davis/Dec. 13); and "Temperamental Lion" (Rasinski/Dec. 27/Technicolor).

1941: "What a Little Sneeze Will Do" (Donnelly/Jan. 10); "Hairless Hector" (White/Jan. 24); "Mississippi Swing" (Rasinski/Feb. 7/Technicolor); "When Knights Were Bold" (White/Mar. 21); "The Baby Seal" (Rasinski/Apr. 10); "Uncle Joey" (Davis/Apr. 18/Technicolor); "The Dog's Dream" (Donnelly/May 2); "The Magic Shell" (Davis/May 16); "What Happens at Night" (Rasinski/May 30); "Horse Fly Opera" (Donnelly/June 13); "Good Old Irish Tunes" (Rasinski/June 27); "Twelve O'Clock and All Ain't Well" (Donnelly/July 25); "The Old Oaken Bucket" (Rasinski/Aug. 8); "The Ice Carnival" (Donnelly/Aug. 22); "Uncle Joey Comes to Town" (Davis/Sept. 19); "The Frozen North" (Rasinski/Oct. 17); "Back to the Soil" (Donnelly/Nov. 14); "The Bird Tower" (Davis/Nov. 28/Technicolor); and "A Yarn About Yarn" (Rasinski/Dec. 12).

1942: "The Torrid Toreador" (Donnelly/Jan. 9/Technicolor); "Happy Circus Days" (Rasinski/Jan. 23/Technicolor); "Funny Bunny Business" (Donnelly/Feb. 6); "Cat Meets Mouse" (Davis/Feb. 20/Technicolor); "Eat Me Kitty, Eight to a Bar" (Davis/Mar. 6); "Oh Gentle Spring" (Rasinski/Apr. 3); "Neck and Neck" (Davis/May 15/Technicolor); "The Stork's Mistake" (Donnelly/May 29); "All About Dogs" (Rasinski/June 12/Technicolor); "Wilful Willie" (Rasinski/June 26); "All Out for 'V'" (Davis/Aug. 7/Technicolor/A.A. nominee); "School Daze" (with Nancy/Sept. 18/Technicolor); "Doing Their Bit" (with Nancy/Oct. 30/a.k.a. "Nancy's Little Theatre"); "Ickle Meets Pickle" (Rasinski/Nov. 13); "Barnyard Waac" (Donnelly/Dec. 11); and "Somewhere in the Pacific" (Davis/Dec. 25/Technicolor).

(All cartooons below in Technicolor.)

1943: "Barnyard Blackout" (Davis/Mar. 5); "Shipyard Symphony" (Donnelly/Mar. 19); "Patriotic Pooches" (Rasinski/Apr. 9); "The Last Round-Up" (Davis/May 14); "Mopping Up" (Donnelly/June 25); "Keep 'em Growing" (Davis/July 28); "Yokel Duck Makes Good" (Donnelly/Nov. 26); and "The Hopeful Donkey" (Davis/Dec. 17).

1944: "The Butcher of Seville" (Donnelly/Jan. 7); "The Helicopter" (Donnelly/Jan. 21); "A Day in June" (Mar. 3); "My Boy Johnny" (May 12/A.A. nominee); "Carmen Veranda" (Davis/July 28); "The Cat Came Back" (Rasinski/Aug. 18); "A Wolf's Tale" (Rasinski/Oct. 27); and "Dear Old Switzerland" (Donnelly/Dec. 22).

1945: "Ants in Your Pantry" (Davis/Feb. 16); "Smoky Joe" (Rasinski/May 25); "The Fox and the Duck" (Davis/Aug. 24); "Swooning the Swooners" (Rasinski/Sept. 14); and "The Watch Dog" (Donnelly/Sept. 28).

1946: "The Tortoise Wins Again" (Rasinski/Aug. 9); "The Snow Man" (Rasinski/Oct. 11); "The Housing Problem" (Davis/Oct. 25); and "Beanstalk Jack" (Donnelly/Dec. 20).

1947: "One Note Tony" (Rasinski/© Oct. 22); and "The Wolf's Pardon" (Donnelly/Dec. 5).

1948: "Felix the Fox" (Davis/Jan.); "Hounding the Hares" (Donnelly/Apr.); "Mystery in the Moonlight" (Donnelly/May); "Seeing Ghosts" (Davis/June); and "The Hard Boiled Egg" (Rasinski/Oct.).

1949: "The Wooden Indian" (Rasinski/Jan.); "The Lyin' Lion" (Rasinski/Aug.); "Mrs. Jones Rest Farm" (Donnelly/Aug.); "A Truckload of Trouble" (Rasinski/Oct. 25); "Flying Cops and Saucers" (Rasinski/Nov.); and "Paint Pot Symphony" (Rasinski/Dec.).

1950: "Better Late Than Never" (with Victor the Volunteer/Donnelly/Mar. 17); "Aesop's Fable: Foiling the Fox" (Rasinski/Apr.); "The Red Headed Monkey" (Davis/July 7); "The Dog Show" (Donnelly/Aug.); and "If Cats Could Sing" (Donnelly/Oct.).

1951: "Squirrel Crazy" (with Nutsy/Davis/Jan.); "Woodman Spare That Tree" (Donnelly/Feb.); "Aesop's Fable: Golden Egg Goosie" (Donnelly/Aug.); and "The Helpful Genie" (Rasinski/Oct.).

1952: "Mechanical Bird" (Donnelly/Feb.); "Time Gallops On" (Davis/Apr.); "The Happy Cobblers" (Davis/May); "Flipper Frolics" (Rasinski/July); and "Mysterious Cowboy" (Davis/Sept.).

1954: "Nonsense Newsreel" (Davis/Mar.); and "Pride of the Yard" (with Percival Sleuthound/Donnelly/Aug.).

1955: "A Yokohama Yankee" (Rasinski/Jan.); "Bird Symphony" (Rasinski/Apr./CinemaScope); "Phoney News Flashes" (Rasinski/May); "Foxed by a Fox" (Rasinski/May);

"Last Mouse of Hamlin" (Rasinski/June); and "Little Red Hen" (Rasinski/July/CinemaScope).

1956: "Clockmakers Dog" (Rasinski/Jan.); "Park Avenue Pussycat" (Rasinski/Jan./CinemaScope); "Uranium Blues" (Rasinski/Mar./CinemaScope); "Hep Mother Hubbard" (Rasinski/Mar.); "Oceans of Love" (Rasinski/May/Cinema-Scope); "Lucky Dog" (Rasinski/May/CinemaScope); "Police Dogged" (with Clancy the Bull/Rasinski/July/CinemaScope); and "The Brave Little Brave" (Davis/July).

1957: "Gag Buster" (with Spoofy/Rasinski/Feb./Cinema-Scope); "A Hare Breadth Finish" (Rasinski/Feb.); "A Bum Steer" (with Beefy/Davis/Mar./CinemaScope); "The Bone Ranger" (with Sniffer/Rasinski/Apr./CinemaScope); "Love Is Blind" (Davis/May); and "Flebus" (Pintoff/Aug./CinemaScope).

(All cartoons in CinemaScope.)

1958: "The Juggler of Our Lady" (Kouzel/Apr.).

1959: "A Tale of a Dog" (Tendlar/Feb.); "The Fabulous Firework Family" (Kouzel/Aug.); and "The Leaky Faucet" (Taras/Dec.).

1960: "The Misunderstood Giant" (Rasinski/Feb.); "Hearts and Glowers" (Taras/June); and "Tin Pan Alley Cat" (Tendlar/Oct.).

1964: "Search for Misery" (with Pitiful Penelope/Kuwahara).

◉ TEX AVERY CARTOONS

Tex Avery, the former Warner Bros. director who joined MGM in 1942, supervised various spoofs and comedy-musical cartoons with the basic Avery humor of hyperbole and character gyrations intact. His cartoons featured fast-paced, violent, zany moments, punctuated with outrageous takes by his cartoon stars. When a character does a take in an Avery cartoon, his eyes literally pop out, his jaw drops to the floor like porch steps and his tongue gyrates vigorously as he screams. Avery's cartoons were based on the survival-of-the-fittest theme, obviously to some extremes.

Avery produced practically every other major non–Hanna and Barbera MGM cartoon from 1942 to 1955, starting with "Blitz Wolf," which won an Academy Award for Best Short Subject. Like his other MGM series—*Droopy, George and Junior,* and *Screwy Squirrel*—these cartoon specialties delved into the unusual only as Tex Avery could, from lampooning detective mysteries in "Who Killed Who?" (1943) to discovering the formula to create a giant-size canary in "King-Size Canary" (1947).

Avery also took a subject that was taboo—sex—to another level of lunacy, directing his own "updated" versions of nursery tales: "Red Hot Riding Hood" (1943);

"Swing Shift Cinderella" (1945) and "Uncle Tom's Cabana" (1947), all starring a lustful Wolf who at the sight of a curvacious female costar turns into a human pretzel of delirious sexual desire.

In 1954 Avery left MGM to join Walter Lantz Studios, where he directed the *Chilly Willy* series.

See *Droopy, George and Junior, Screwy Squirrel* and *Spike* for additional entries. *Directed by Tex Avery. Technicolor. A Metro-Goldwyn-Mayer release.*

Voices
June Foray

1942: "The Blitz Wolf" (Aug. 22/A.A. winner); and "The Early Bird Dood It" (Aug. 29).

1943: "Red Hot Riding Hood" (May 8); "Who Killed Who?" (June 5); "One Ham's Family" (Aug. 14); and "What's Buzzin' Buzzard" (Nov. 27).

1944: "Batty Baseball" (Apr. 22).

1945: "Jerky Turkey" (Apr. 7); and "Swing Shift Cinderella" (Aug. 25/working titles: "Wolf," "Swingshift Cindy," "Red Hot Cinderella," and "The Glass Slipper").

1946: "The Hick Chick" (June 15).

1947: "Uncle Tom's Cabana" (July 19); "Slap Happy Lion" (Sept. 20/re: May 28, 1955); and "King-Size Canary" (Dec. 6/re: Oct. 21, 1955).

1948: "What Price Fleadom" (Mar. 20/re: Dec. 2, 1955); "Little Tinker" (May 15/re: May 14, 1955); and "The Cat That Hated People" (Nov. 12/re: Jan. 20, 1956).

1949: "Bad Luck Blackie" (Jan. 22/re: Nov. 9, 1956/working title: "Two Black Cats"); "House of Tomorrow" (June 11/re: Mar. 16, 1956); "Doggone Tired" (July 30/re: Apr. 6, 1956); and "Little Rural Red Riding Hood" (Sept. 17/re: Dec. 28, 1956).

1950: "The Cuckoo Clock" (June 10/re: Jan. 19, 1957); and "The Peachy Cobbler" (Dec. 9/re: May 24, 1957).

1951: "Symphony in Slang" (June 6/re: June 13, 1958); and "Car of Tomorrow" (Sept. 22).

1952: "Magical Maestro" (Feb. 9); "One Cab's Family" (May 15); and "Rock-a-Bye Bear" (July 12).

1953: "Little Johnny Jet" (Apr. 18/A.A. nominee); and "T.V. of Tomorrow" (June 6).

1954: "Billy Boy" (May 8); "Farm of Tomorrow" (Sept. 18); and "The Flea Circus" (Nov. 6).

1955: "Field and Scream" (Apr. 30); "The First Bad Man" (Sept. 30); and "Cellbound" (Nov. 25).

1957: "The Cat's Meow" (Jan. 25/remake of "Ventriloquist Cat").

⊚ THE THREE BEARS

Warner animator Chuck Jones originated this series depicting domestic life of an American family, with bears playing the roles of Papa, Mamma and Junior. The trio first appeared in 1944, in "Bugs Bunny and the Three Bears," reenacting the Goldilocks fable with a comical twist. Jones brought the characters back to the screen in four more cartoon adventures, each one offering a humorous view of the trials and tribulations of this abnormal family. *Directed by Chuck Jones. Technicolor. A Warner Bros. release.*

Voices
Papa Bear: Mel Blanc, Billy Bletcher; **Mamma Bear:** Bea Benadaret; **Junior Bear:** Stan Freberg

Merrie Melodies

1944: "Bugs Bunny and the Three Bears" (Feb. 26).

1949: "The Bee-Deviled Bruin" (May 14).

1951: "A Bear for Punishment" (Oct. 20).

Looney Tunes

1948: "What's Brewin', Bruin?" (Feb. 28).

1949: " Bear Feat" (Dec. 10).

⊚ TIJUANA TOADS

This late-1960s series followed the humorous exploits of a bossy Spanish-accented toad, Poncho, who demonstrates for his inexperienced, skinny apprentice, Toro, how to catch flies and cope with basic necessities of life as a toad in inventively funny situations. The toads were later renamed "The Texas Toads" (the characters also changed their names to Fatso and Banjo) when segmented on TV's *The Pink Panther Laff and a Half Hour and a Half Show. Directors were Hawley Pratt, Gerry Chiniquy, Art Davis and Grant Simmons. Technicolor. A DePatie-Freleng/Mirisch Films Production released through United Artists.*

1969: "Tijuana Toads" (Pratt/Aug. 6); "A Pair of Greenbacks" (Davis/Dec. 16); and "Go for Croak" (Pratt/Dec. 25).

1970: "The Froggy Froggy Duo" (Pratt/Mar. 15); "Hop and Chop" (Simmons/June 17); "Never on Thirsty" (Pratt/Aug. 5); and "A Dopey Hacienda" (Pratt/Dec. 6).

1971: "Snake in the Gracias" (Pratt/Jan. 24); "Two Jumps and a Chump" (Mar. 28); "Mud Squad" (Davis/Apr. 28); "The Egg of Ay-Yi-Yi!" (Chiniquy/June 6); "The Fastest Tongue in the West" (Chiniquy/June 20); "A Leap in the Deep" (Chiniquy/June 20); "Croakus Pocus" (Davis/Dec. 26); and "Serape Happy" (Chiniquy/Dec. 26).

1972: "Frog Jog" (Chiniquy/Apr. 23); and "Flight to the Finish" (Davis/Apr. 30).

⊚ TIMON AND PUMBAA

Timon, the wisecracking meerkat, and Pumbaa, his warthog sidekick, from the Disney animated classic *The Lion King* returned to the silver screen in 1995, this time as stars of their first theatrical cartoon short, "Stand by Me." The cartoon, based on the popular song of the same name, opened in theaters nationwide with the live-action feature-length adventure *Tom And Huck*, starring Jonathan Taylor (of TV's *Home Improvement*). Three months before the release of the three-minute cartoon short, the characters starred in their own television series, *The Lion King's Timon and Pumbaa*, which premiered in syndication and on CBS that fall. Nathan Lane, who provided the voice of Timon in *The Lion King*, did not return to reprise the character. The character, in the short and on the television series, was voiced by Kevin Schoen. *Directed by Steve Moore. A Walt Disney Production released by Buena Vista.*

Voices
Timon: Kevin Schoen; **Pumbaa:** Ernie Sabella

1995: "Stand by Me" (Dec. 22).

⊚ TITO

The adventures of a small, portly Mexican boy named Tito and his burro companion, Burrito, comprised this short-lived series for Columbia Pictures. The characters, who were created by Dave Fleischer, later found new life in *Real Screen* and *Fox and the Crow* comics. *Directed by Bob Wickersham and Howard Swift. Produced by Dave Fleischer and later Ray Katz. Technicolor. Voice credits unknown. A Columbia Pictures release.*

1942: "Tito's Guitar" (Wickersham/Oct. 30/Color Rhapsody).

1945: "Fiesta Time" (Wickersham/Apr. 4/Color Rhapsody).

1947: "Loco Lobo" (Swift/Jan. 9/Color Rhapsody).

⊚ TOBY THE PUP

Columbia producer Charles Mintz, who produced several major cartoon series for the studio, hired two of Max Fleischer's best animators, Dick Huemer and Sid Marcus, to head a new animation unit in California to expand his cartoon operations and sell a separate series to RKO-Radio Pictures. It was Marcus who devised the character for that series, Toby the Pup, a malicious, frisky pup who headlined in only 12 films. *Directed by Dick Huemer and Sid Marcus.*

Black-and-white. Voice credits unknown. A RKO-Van Beuren release.

1930: "The Museum" (Aug. 19); "Toby the Fiddler" (Sept. 1); "Toby the Miner" (Oct. 1); "Toby the Showman" (Nov. 22); and "The Bug House" (Dec. 7).

1931: "Circus Time" (Jan. 25); "Toby the Milkman" (Feb. 25); "Brown Derby" (Mar. 22); "Down South" (Apr. 15); "Halloween" (May 1); "Toby The Bull Thrower" (June 7); and "Aces Up."

◉ TODDLE TALES

This series was Burt Gillett's first following his defection from Walt Disney Studios to direct new cartoons for Van Beuren. Only three films were made in the series, which blended live-action sequences of two children with animated animal characters in each adventure. The filmed openings led into each story, which might involve why dogs wag their tails or how ducks evolved, based on discussions with these animals. *Directors were Burt Gillett, Steve Muffati, Jim Tyer and Tom Palmer. Black-and-white. Cinecolor. Voice credits unknown. A RKO-Van Beuren release.*

1934: "Grandfather's Clock" (Gillett, Tyer/June 29); "Along Came a Duck" (Gillett, Muffati/Aug. 10); and "A Little Bird Told Me" (Gillett, Tyer/Sept. 7).

◉ TOM AND JERRY (VAN BEUREN)

This was not MGM's famous cat-and-mouse team but rather an earlier duo of rawboned leader Tom and his dumpy cohort Jerry in primitively animated stories combining action and ragtime music with little onscreen dialogue. The series, produced by Van Beuren, was developed by John Foster and studio newcomers George Stallings and George Rufle, both veteran animators of the New York animation circuit. Following the series' first entry, "Wot a Night" (1931), the studio produced 26 cartoons over the next three years before the characters were retired. *Directors were John Foster, George Stallings, Frank Tashlin, George Rufle, Frank Sherman and Harry Bailey. Black-and-white. Voice credits unknown. An RKO-Van Beuren release.*

1931: "Wot a Night" (Foster, Stallings/Aug. 1); "Polar Pals" (Foster, Rufle/Sept. 5); "Trouble" (Foster, Stallings/Oct. 10); "Jungle Jam" (Foster, Rufle/Nov. 14); and "A Swiss Trick" (Foster, Stallings/Dec. 19).

1932: "Rocketeers" (Foster, Rufle/Jan. 30); "Rabid Hunters" (Foster, Stallings/Feb. 27); "In the Bag" (Foster, Rufle/Mar. 26); "Joint Wipers" (Foster, Stallings/Apr. 23); "Pet and Pans" (May 14); "The Tuba Tooter" (Foster, Stallings/June 4); "Plane Dumb" (Foster, Rufle/June 25); "Redskin Blues" (Foster, Stallings/July 23); "Jolly Fish"

(Foster. Stallings/Aug. 19); "Barnyard Bunk" (Foster, Rufle/Sept. 6); "A Spanish Twist" (Foster, Stallings/Oct. 7); "Piano Tooners" (Foster, Rufle/Nov. 11); and "Pencil Mania" (Foster, Stallings/Dec. 9).

1933: "(Copyright dates are marked by a ©.) "Tight Rope Tricks" (Foster, Rufle/Jan. 6); "The Magic Mummy" (Foster, Stallings/Feb. 7); "Panicky Pup" (Foster, Bailey/Feb. 24/*Aesop's Fable*); "Puzzled Pals" (Stallings, Sherman/© Mar. 31); "Happy Hoboes" (Stallings, Rufle/Mar. 31); "Hook and Ladder Hokum" (Stallings, Tashlin/Apr. 28); "In the Park" (Sherman, Rufle/©May 26); and "The Phantom Rocket" (Sherman, Rufle/July 31).

◉ TOM AND JERRY (MGM)

MGM's madcap adventures of the feuding alley cat, Tom, and his mischief-making nemesis, Jerry the mouse, won seven Academy Awards during their heyday.

The idea for this pairing came from veteran animators William Hanna and Joseph Barbera, who later created the likes of Yogi Bear, Ruffy and Reddy and countless other characters after opening their own studio in the late 1950s. "We asked ourselves what would be a normal conflict between characters provoking comedy while retaining a basic situation from which we could continue to generate plots and stories," Hanna once recalled. "We almost decided on a dog and a fox before we hit on the idea of using a cat and a mouse."

Hanna and Barbera named the characters based on hundreds of suggestions submitted by studio employees in a contest staged at the MGM lot. (In their screen debut Tom was actually called "Jasper.") The first Tom and Jerry cartoon, "Puss Gets the Boot," was produced and released in 1940, despite producer Fred Quimby's reservations about the

Tom and Jerry from their first screen appearance, "Puss Gets the Boot" (1940). The characters were created by William Hanna and Joseph Barbera. © Turner Entertainment

characters. ("What can you do with a cat and a mouse that would be different?")

The first cartoon quickly established the entire tone of the series: Tom, the mischievous house cat, trying to outfox the equally clever mouse, Jerry. The formula remained the same throughout the history of the series, though the characters underwent gradual changes in their appearance.

Besides starring in cartoon shorts, Tom and Jerry also appeared as animated characters in live-action sequences of two clasic MGM musicals: Gene Kelly's *Anchor's Aweigh* (1944) (Jerry only) and Esther Williams' *Dangerous When Wet* (1953), featuring both characters swimming with Williams in complete synchronization.

Quimby produced the series until his retirement in 1955; from then through 1958 Hanna and Barbera performed dual roles as the series' producers and directors.

The popular screen tandem lost some of their comedy flair after Hanna and Barbera left MGM to launch their own production company, Hanna-Barbera Productions. From 1961 to 1962 Gene Deitch, a former artistic director of Terrytoons and a Czechoslovakian cartoon director (whose claim to fame was creating TV's critically acclaimed *Tom Terrific*), tried animating new Tom and Jerry adventures that were unmemorable at best.

In 1963 former Warner Bros. animator/director Chuck Jones and producer Les Golden, who formed Sib-Tower 12 Productions (later renamed MGM Animation/Visual Arts), convinced MGM to allow them to produce a third series of films. But even under the watchful eye of Jones the films failed to generate much excitement. As one anonymous MGM executive remarked after a board of directors screening: "Those are god awful!"

Even Jones has admitted making the cartoons was a mistake: "They were not my characters and I didn't really understand them as well as, let's say, the Road Runner and Coyote. The Tom and Jerrys I did look like the Road Runner and Coyote in cat and mouse drag!"

Other series directors included Ben Washam, Abe Levitow, Tom Ray and Jim Pabian. Veteran voice artist June Foray provided occasional supporting character voices in a number of cartoons for the series. *Technicolor. CinemaScope. A Metro-Goldwyn-Mayer release.*

1940: "Puss Gets the Boot" (with Mammy/Hanna, Barbera/Feb. 10).

1941: "The Midnight Snack" (with Mammy/Hanna, Barbera/July 19/re: Feb. 27, 1948); and "The Night Before Christmas" (Hanna, Barbera/Dec. 6/A.A. nominee).

1942: "Fraidy Cat" (Hanna, Barbera/Jan. 17); "Dog Trouble" (with Spike and Mammy/Hanna, Barbera/Apr. 18); "Puss 'n' Toots" (Hanna, Barbera/May 30); "The Bowling Alley Cat" (Hanna, Barbera/July 18); and "Fine

Feathered Friend" (Hanna, Barbera/Oct. 10/re: Jan. 1, 1949).

1943: "Sufferin' Cats" (with Meathead/Hanna, Barbera/Jan. 16/re: June 4, 1949); "Lonesome Mouse" (with Mammy/Hanna, Barbera/May 22/re: Nov. 26, 1949); "Yankee Doodle Mouse" (Hanna, Barbera/June 26/A.A. winner); and "Baby Puss" (with Meathead/Hanna, Barbera/Dec. 25).

1944: "Zoot Cat" (with Toots/Hanna, Barbera/Feb. 26); "Million Dollar Cat" (Hanna, Barbera/May 6/re: May 6, 1954); "The Bodyguard" (with Spike/Hanna, Barbera/July 22); "Puttin' on the Dog" (with Spike/Hanna, Barbera/Oct. 28/re: Oct. 20, 1951); and "Mouse Trouble" (Hanna, Barbera/Nov. 23/re: Dec. 12, 1951/A.A. winner/working titles: "Cat Nipped" and "Kitty Foiled").

1945: "The Mouse That Comes to Dinner" (with Toots, Mammy/Hanna, Barbera/May 5/re: Jan. 19, 1952/working title: "Mouse to Dinner"); "Mouse in Manhattan" (Hanna, Barbera/July 7/working title: "Manhattan Serenade"); "Tee for Two" (Hanna, Barbera/July 21); "Flirty Birdy" (Hanna, Barbera/Sept. 22/re: July 4, 1953/working title: "Love Boids"); and "Quiet Please" (Hanna, Barbera/Dec. 22/A.A. winner).

1946: "Springtime for Thomas" (with Toots/Hanna, Barbera/Mar. 30); "The Milky Waif" (with Nibbles/Hanna, Barbera/May 18); "Trap Happy" (with Meathead/Hanna, Barbera/June 29/re: Mar. 6, 1954); and "Solid Serenade" (with Spike, Toots, Meathead/Hanna, Barbera/Aug. 31).

1947: "Cat Fishin'" (with Spike/Hanna, Barbera/Feb. 22/re: Oct. 30, 1954); "Part-Time Pal" (with Mammy/Hanna, Barbera/Mar. 15/working title: "Fair Weathered Friend"); "The Cat Concerto" (Hanna, Barbera/Apr. 26/A.A. winner); "Dr. Jekyll and Mr. Mouse" (Hanna, Barbera/June 14/A.A. nominee); "Salt Water Tabby" (with Toots/Hanna, Barbera/July 12); "A Mouse in the House" (with Mammy/Hanna, Barbera/Aug. 30); and "The Invisible Mouse" (Hanna, Barbera/Sept. 27).

1948: "Kitty Foiled" (Hanna, Barbera/May 1); "The Truce Hurts" (with Spike/Hanna, Barbera/July 17); "Old Rockin' Chair Tom" (Hanna, Barbera/Sept. 18); "Professor Tom" (Hanna, Barbera/Oct. 30); and "Mouse Cleaning" (with Mammy/Hanna, Barbera/Dec. 11/A.A. winner).

1949: "Polka Dot Puss" (Hanna, Barbera/Feb. 26/re: Sept. 28, 1956); "The Little Orphan" (with Nibbles/Hanna, Barbera/Apr. 30/A.A. winner); "Hatch Up Your Troubles" (Hanna, Barbera/May 14/A.A. nominee/remade as "The Egg and Jerry"); "Heavenly Puss" (Hanna, Barbera/July 9/re: Oct. 26, 1956); "Cat and Mermouse" (Hanna, Barbera/Sept. 3); "Love That Pup" (with Spike and Tyke/Hanna, Barbera/Oct. 1); "Jerry's Diary" (Hanna, Barbera/Oct. 22); and "Tennis Chumps" (Hanna, Barbera/Dec. 10).

1950: "Little Quacker" (Hanna, Barbera/Jan. 7); "Saturday Evening Puss" (Hanna, Barbera/Jan. 14/working title: "Party Cat"); "Texas Tom" (with Toots/Hanna, Barbera/Mar. 11); "Jerry and the Lion" (Hanna, Barbera/Apr. 8/working title: "Hold That Lion"); "Safety Second" (Hanna, Barbera/July 1/working title: "F'r safety Sake"); "Tom and Jerry in the Hollywood Bowl" (Hanna, Barbera/Sept. 16); "The Framed Cat" (Hanna, Barbera/Oct. 21); and "Cueball Cat" (Hanna, Barbera/Nov. 25).

1951: "Casanova Cat" (Hanna, Barbera/Jan. 6); "Jerry and the Goldfish" (Hanna, Barbera/Mar. 3); "Jerry's Cousin" (Hanna, Barbera/Apr. 7/working title: "City Cousin" and "Muscles Mouse"); "Sleepy Time Tom" (Hanna, Barbera/May 26); "His Mouse Friday" (Hanna, Barbera/July 7); "Slicked Up Pup" (with Spike and Tyke/Hanna, Barbera/Sept. 8); "Nit Witty Kitty" (Hanna, Barbera/Oct. 6); and "Cat Napping" (Hanna, Barbera/Dec. 8).

1952: "Flying Cat" (Hanna, Barbera/Jan. 12); "Duck Doctor" (Hanna, Barbera/Feb. 16); "Two Mouseketeers" (Hanna, Barbera/Mar. 15/A.A. winner); "Smitten Kitten" (Hanna, Barbera/Apr. 12); "Triplet Trouble" (Hanna, Barbera/Apr. 19); "Little Runaway" (Hanna, Barbera/June 14); "Fit to Be Tied" (Hanna, Barbera/July 26); "Push-Button Kitty" (Hanna, Barbera/Sept. 6); "Cruise Cat" (Hanna, Barbera/Oct. 18); and "The Dog House" (Hanna, Barbera/Nov. 29).

1953: "The Missing Mouse" (Hanna, Barbera/Jan. 10); "Jerry and Jumbo" (Hanna, Barbera/Feb. 21); "Johann Mouse" (Hanna, Barbera/Mar. 21/A.A. winner/narration by Hans Conried); "That's My Pup" (with Spike and Tyke/Hanna, Barbera/May 28); "Just Ducky" (Hanna, Barbera/Sept. 5); "Two Little Indians" (Hanna, Barbera/Oct. 17); and "Life with Tom" (Hanna, Barbera/Nov. 21).

1954: "Puppy Tale" (Hanna, Barbera/Jan. 23); "Posse Cat" (Hanna, Barbera/Jan. 30); "Hic-Cup Pup" (with Spike and Tyke/Hanna, Barbera/Apr. 17/working title: "Tyke Takes a Nap"); "Little School Mouse" (Hanna, Barbera/May 29); "Baby Butch" (Hanna, Barbera/Aug. 14); "Mice Follies" (Hanna, Barbera/Sept. 4); "Neopolitan Mouse" (Hanna, Barbera/Oct. 21); "Downhearted Duckling" (Hanna, Barbera/Nov. 13); "Pet Peeve" (Hanna, Barbera/Nov. 20/CinemaScope); and "Touché Pussy Cat" (with Toots/Hanna, Barbera/Dec. 18/re: May 21, 1955/CinemaScope).

1955: "Southbound Duckling" (Hanna, Barbera/Mar. 12/re: June 25, 1955/CinemaScope); "Pup on a Picnic" (with Spike and Tyke/Hanna, Barbera/Apr. 30/CinemaScope); "Mouse for Sale" (Hanna, Barbera/May 21/CinemaScope); "Designs on Jerry" (Hanna, Barbera/Sept. 2/CinemaScope); "Tom and Cherie" (Hanna, Barbera/Sept. 9/CinemaScope); "Smarty Cat" (Hanna, Barbera/Oct. 14/CinemaScope);

"Pecos Pest" (Hanna, Barbera/Nov. 11); and "That's My Mommy" (Hanna, Barbera/Nov. 19/CinemaScope).

(The following were all in CinemaScope.)

1956: "The Flying Sorceress" (Hanna, Barbera/Jan. 27); "The Egg and Jerry" (Hanna, Barbera/Mar. 23/remake of "Hatch Up Your Troubles"); "Busy Buddies" (Hanna, Barbera/May 4); "Muscle Beach Tom" (Hanna, Barbera/Sept. 7); "Down Beat Bear" (Hanna, Barbera/Oct. 21); "Blue Cat Blues" (Hanna, Barbera/Nov. 6); and "Barbecue Brawl" (Hanna, Barbera/Dec. 14).

1957: "Tops with Pops" (Hanna, Barbera/Feb. 22/remake of "Love That Pup"); "Timid Tabby" (Hanna, Barbera/Apr. 19); "Feedin' the Kiddie" (Hanna, Barbera/June 7/remake of "The Little Orphan"); "Mucho Mouse" (Hanna, Barbera/Sept. 6); and "Tom's Photo Finish" (Hanna, Barbera/Nov. 1).

1958: "Happy Go Ducky" (Hanna, Barbera/Jan. 3/working title: "One Quack Mind"); "Royal Cat Nap" (Hanna, Barbera/Mar. 7); "Vanishing Duck" (Hanna, Barbera/May 2); "Robin Hoodwinked" (Hanna, Barbera/June 6); and "Tot Watchers" (Hanna, Barbera/Aug. 1).

Rembrandt Releases

1961: "Switchin' Kitten" (Deitch/Sept. 7); "Down and Outing" (Deitch/Oct. 26); and "It's Greek to Me-Ow" (Deitch/Dec. 7).

1962: "High Steaks" (Deitch/Jan.); "Mouse Into Space" (Deitch/Feb.); "Landing Stripling" (Deitch/Apr.); "Calypso Cat" (Deitch/June); "Dikie Moe" (Deitch/July); "The Tom and Jerry Cartoon Kit" (Deitch/Aug.); "Tall in the Trap" (Deitch/Sept.); "Sorry Safari" (Deitch/Oct.); "Buddies Thicker Than Water" (Deitch/Nov.); and "Carmen Get It" (Deitch/Dec.).

Sib-Tower 12 Productions Releases

1963: "Penthouse Mouse" (Jones).

1964: "The Cat Above, The Mouse Below" (Jones); "Is There a Doctor in the Mouse?" (Jones); and "Unshrinkable Jerry Mouse" (Jones).

1965: "Tom-Ic Energy" (Jones); "Ah—Sweet Mouse Story of Life" (Jones); "The Brothers Carry-Mouse-Off" (Pabian); "Bad Day at Cat Rock" (Jones); "Haunted Mouse" (Jones); "I'm Just Wild About Jerry" (Jones); "Of Feline Bondage" (Jones); "Tom Thumb" (Jones); The Year of the Mouse" (Jones); "The Cat's Me-Ouch" (Jones), and "Jerry-Go-Round" (Levitow).

1966: "Duel Personality" (Jones); "Jerry Jerry Quite Contrary" (Jones); "Love Me, Love My Mouse" (Washam); "Puss 'N' Boats" (Levitow); "Filet Meow" (Levitow);

"Matinee Mouse" (Ray); "A-Tominable Snowman" (Levitow), and "Catty Cornered" (Levitow).

1967: "Cat and Duplicat" (Jones); "O Solar Meow" (Levitow); "Guide Mouse-Ille" (Levitow); "Rock 'n' Rodent" (Levitow); "Cannery Rodent" (Jones); "The Mouse from H.U.N.G.E.R." (Jones); "Surf Bored Cat" (Levitow); "Shutter Bugged Cat" (Ray); "Advance and Be Mechanized" (Washam); and "Purr Chance to Dream" (Washam).

⊚ TOMMY TORTOISE AND MOE HARE

Loosely based on the concept of the timeless children's fable "Tortoise and the Hare," this series concerned the humorous exploits of a smart rabbit, Moe, and a dumb tortoise, Tommy, who somehow manages to outsmart the superintelligent hare in outlandish situations. The films were produced for Paramount's *Noveltoons* series. *Directed by Isadore Sparber and Dave Tendlar. Technicolor. A Famous Studios Production released through Paramount Pictures.*

1953: "Winner by a Hare" (Sparber/Apr. 17).

1955: "Rabbit Punch" (Tendlar/Sept. 30).

1956: "Sleuth But Sure" (Tendlar/Mar. 23).

1957: "Mr. Money Gags" (Sparber/June 7).

⊚ TOONERVILLE TROLLEY

Fontaine Fox's popular comic strip inspired this abbreviated sound cartoon series, featuring the Skipper, the Powerful Katrinka and the Terrible-tempered Mr. Bang, which was released under the RKO-Van Beuren *Rainbow Parade* series. Director Burt Gillett purchased the rights to make the films in hopes of insuring greater box-office success for the fledgling Van Beuren cartoon studio. *Directed by Burt Gillett and Tom Palmer. Black-and-white. An RKO-Van Beuren release.*

1936: "Toonerville Trolley" (Gillett, Palmer/Jan. 17); "Trolley Ahoy" (Gillett/July 3); and "Toonerville Picnic" (Gillett/Oct. 2).

⊚ TWEETY AND SYLVESTER

The bird-hungry cat Sylvester plotted fruitlessly against the clever canary Tweety, whose immortal battle cry for 15 years upon Sylvester's entrance was "I tawt I taw a puddy tat. I did, I did see a puddy tat!"

Both characters made separate film debuts before becoming a team. They shared top billing in 39 cartoons between 1947 and 1964, garnering two Academy Awards—for "Tweetie Pie" (1947) and "Birds Anonymous" (1957)—and three Oscar nominations. The films alternately featured another series regular, sweet, bespectacled Granny, Tweety's

owner, who was far from sweet when Sylvester was around, pounding on him whenever he attempted to lay his lands on her baby-faced, baby-voiced pet bird.

Mel Blanc voiced both characters. His voice for Sylvester was similar to Daffy Duck's, featuring the same sputtering delivery and slurred voice. The only difference was his recorded dialogue was sped up in the sound studio. As for the voice of Tweety, Bob Clampett developed the idea of what the small bird should sound like. Top layout artist Michael Sasanoff and animator/director Robert McKimson both recalled that Clampett used to talk in the "baby-talk voice" later used for Tweety while just kidding around at the studio.

Clampett created Tweety, basing the baby bird's wide-eyed stare on a childhood picture of himself. Tweety's famous catch phrase, "I tawt I taw a putty tat," was actually derived from a phrase Clampett had used years earlier in letters to a friend next to a drawing of a little bird. (The catch phrase became so popular that in 1950 Warner Bros. story man Warren Foster composed a song using the phrase as its title. The record sold more than 2 million copies and became a novelty in England.)

Clampett directed the first three cartoons in the series, beginning with 1942's "A Tale of Two Kitties," which costarred Babbit and Catstello, a pair of cats resembling famed comedians Abbot and Costello. Friz Freleng took over the series after Clampett left the studio in 1946. Freleng directed the bulk of the series, with additional titles produced under the direction of Hawley Pratt and Gerry Chiniquy. (See *Sylvester* entry for other Sylvester cartoon appearances.)

Tweety unknowingly walks into the mouth of a cat who plans on making him his next meal in Bob Clampett's 1944 cartoon "Birdy and the Beast." It was the second Tweety cartoon ever made. © Warner Bros. Inc. (COURTESY: BOB CLAMPETT ANIMATION ART)

Tweety and Sylvester returned to the screen in supporting roles in the 1995 Bugs Bunny cartoon short "Carrotblanca," lampooning the Humphrey Bogart–Lauren Bacall classic *Casablanca* and in the 1996 live-action/animated feature *Space Jam* starring Michael Jordan. Tweety was voiced by Bob Bergen; Sylvester by Joe Alaskey. *Technicolor. A Warner Bros. release.*

Voices
Tweety: Mel Blanc, Bob Bergen; **Sylvester the Cat:** Mel Blanc, Joe Alaskey; **Granny:** Bea Bendaret, June Foray

Merrie Melodies

1942: "A Tale of Two Kitties" (with Babbit and Catstello/Clampett/Nov. 21/first Tweety cartoon).

1944: "Birdy and the Beast" (Clampett/Aug. 19).

1945: "A Grusome Twosome" (Clampett/June 9).

1947: "Tweetie Pie" (Freleng/May 3/A.A. winner).

1948: "I Taw a Putty Tat" (Freleng/Apr. 2).

1949: "Bad Ol' Putty Tat" (Freleng/July 23).

1950: "Home Tweet Home" (Freleng/Jan. 14).

1951: "Room and Bird" (Freleng/June 2); and "Tweety's S.O.S." (with Granny/Freleng/Sept. 22).

1953: "Fowl Weather" (Freleng/Apr. 4); "Tom Tom Tomcat" (Freleng/June 27); and "Catty Cornered" (Freleng/Oct. 31).

1954: "Muzzle Tough" (Freleng/June 26).

1955: "Tweety's Circus" (Freleng/June 4).

1956: "Tree Cornered Tweety" (Freleng/May 19); and "Tugboat Granny" (with Granny/Freleng/June 23).

1957: "Tweet Zoo" (Freleng/Jan. 12); "Tweety and the Beanstalk" (Freleng/May 16); and "Birds Anonymous" (Freleng/Aug. 10/A.A. winner).

1958: "A Bird in a Bonnet" (Freleng/Sept. 27).

1959: "Trick or Tweet" (Freleng/Mar. 21); "Tweet and Lovely" (Freleng/July 18); and "Tweet Dreams" (Freleng/Dec. 5).

1960: "Hyde and Tweet" (Freleng/May 14); and "Trip for Tat" (Freleng/Oct. 29).

1961: "The Last Hungry Cat" (Freleng, Pratt/Dec. 2).

DePatie-Freleng Enterprises releases

1964: "Hawaiian Aye Aye" (Chinquy/June 27).

Looney Tunes

1950: "All A-Bir-r-r-d" (Freleng/June 24); and "Canary Row" (Freleng/Oct. 7).

1951: "Puddy Tat Twouble" (Freleng/Feb. 24); and "Tweet Tweet Tweety" (Freleng/Dec. 15).

1952: "Gift Wrapped" (Freleng/Feb. 16); "Ain't She Tweet" (Freleng/June 21); and "Bird in a Guilty Cage" (Freleng/Aug. 30).

1953: "Snow Business" (Freleng/Jan. 17); and "A Streetcar Named Sylvester" (Freleng/Sept. 5).

1954: "Dog Pounded" (Freleng/Jan. 2).

1955: "Sandy Claws" (Freleng/Apr. 2/A.A. nominee); and "Red Riding Hoodwinked" (Freleng/Oct. 29).

1956: "Tweet and Sour" (Freleng/Mar. 24).

1957: "Greedy for Tweety" (Freleng/Sept. 28).

1958: "A Pizza Tweety Pie" (Freleng/Feb. 22).

1961: "Rebel Without Claws" (Freleng/July 15).

1962: "The Jet Cage" (Freleng/Sept. 22).

1990: "Invasion of the Bunny Snatchers" (with Bugs Bunny/Ford, Lennon).

1995: "Carrotblanca" (with Bugs Bunny, Daffy Duck, Yosemite Sam, Pepe Le Pew, Foghorn Leghorn, Penelope/McCarthy/Aug. 25).

◎ TWO CURIOUS PUPPIES
This nontalking, comical pair—a large brown boxer and a spotted puppy—were introduced by Chuck Jones to moviegoers in 1939, usually cast in everyday situations in which things ran afoul. The entertaining duo starred in two *Merrie Melodies* that first year, "Dog Gone Modern," marking their screen debut, followed by "Curious Puppy." It would be two years before moviegoers were again treated to their unusual antics with the debut of "Snowtime for Comedy," their third and final appearance on the big screen. *The series was directed by Chuck Jones. Technicolor. A Warner Bros. release.*

Merrie Melodies

1939: "Dog Gone Modern" (Jan. 14); and "Curious Puppy" (Dec. 30).

1941: "Snowtime for Comedy" (Aug. 30).

◎ UPA CARTOON SPECIALS
This series featured previous characters such as Gerald McBoing Boing and other cartoon stars in cartoon specials

produced by United Productions of America (UPA), which later produced television strips based on Dick Tracy and Mr. Magoo.

One cartoon in the series, "The Tell-Tale Heart" (1953), was adapted from a story by Edgar Allen Poe. Only one film was nominated for an Academy Award, the series' last entry, "The Jaywalker" (1956). *Directors were Bill Hurtz, Art Babbitt, Theodore Tee Hee, Ted Parmelee, Bob Cannon, Abe Liss, Paul Julian and Osmond Evans. Technicolor. A UPA Production released through Columbia Pictures.*

1953: "A Unicorn in the Garden" (Hurtz/Sept. 24); and "The Tell-Tale Heart" (Parmelee/Dec. 27/narrated by actor James Mason).

1954: "Bringing Up Father" (Hurtz/Jan. 14); "Ballet-Oops" (Cannon/Feb. 11); "The Man on the Flying Trapeze" (Parmelee/Apr. 8); "Fudget's Budget" (Cannon/June 17); "Kangaroo Courting" (Burness/July 22); and "How Now Boing Boing" (with Gerald McBoing Boing/Cannon/Sept. 9).

1955: "Spare the Child" (Liss/Jan. 27); "Four Wheels and No Brake" (with Pete Hothead/Parmelee/Mar. 24); "Baby Boogie" (Julian/May 19); "Christopher Crumpet's Playmate" (Cannon/Sept. 8); and "Rise of Duton Lang" (Evans/Dec. 1).

1956: "The Jaywalker" (Cannon/May 31/A.A. nominee).

ⓦ WALT DISNEY SPECIALS

When *Silly Symphonies* faded into screen history, Walt Disney produced new cartoon specials to replace the old animated favorites. This long-running series proved equally successful for the studio, reaping eight Academy Award nominations and three Oscar statuettes for Best Short Subject of the Year.

Over the years several well-known Disney characters appeared in the series, including Scrooge McDuck, Winnie the Pooh and Roger Rabbit. *Directors were Dick Rickard, Norm Ferguson, Eric Larson, Bob Cormack, Gerry Geronimi, Bill Roberts, Hamilton Luske, Jack Kinney, Charles Nichols, Jack Hannah, Wilfred Jackson, Ward Kimball, Bill Justice, Woolie Reitherman, Les Clark, John Lounsbery, Don Bluth, Tim Burton, Darrell Van Citters, Rick Reinert, Michael Cedeno and Rob Minkoff. Technicolor. A Walt Disney Production released through RKO Radio Pictures and later Buena Vista.*

RKO Radio Pictures Releases

1938: "Ferdinand the Bull" (Rickard/Nov. 25/A.A. winner).

1939: "The Practical Pig" (Rickard/Feb. 24).

1943: "Education for Death" (Geronimi/Jan. 15); "Reason and Emotion" (Roberts/Aug. 27/A.A. nominee); and "Chicken Little" (Geronimi/Dec. 17).

1944: "The Pelican and the Snipe" (Luske/Jan. 7).

1950: "The Brave Engineer" (Kinney/Mar. 3); and "Morris the Midget Moose" (Hannah/Nov. 24).

1952: "Lambert, the Sheepish Lion" (Hannah/Feb. 8/A.A. nominee); "Susie the Little Blue Coupe" (Geronimi/June 6); and "The Little House" (Jackson/Aug. 8).

1953: "Melody" (Nichols, Kimball/May 28/a.k.a.: "Adventures in Music"/Disney's first 3-D cartoon); "Football Now and Then" (Kinney/Oct. 2); "Toot, Whistle, Plunk and Boom" (Nichols, Kimball/Nov. 10/A.A. winner/Disney's first CinemaScope cartoon/a Buena Vista release); and "Ben and Me" (Luske/Nov. 10/A.A. nominee/a Buena Vista release).

1954: "Two for the Record" (Kinney/Apr. 23/from "Make Mine Music"); "Pigs Is Pigs" (Kinney/May 21/A.A. nominee); "Johnny Fedora and Alice Bluebonnet" (Kinney/May 21/from "Make Mine Music"); "Casey Bats Again" (Kinney/June 18); "The Martins and the Coys" (Kinney/June 18/from "Make Mine Music"); "Casey at the Bat" (Geronimi/July 16/from "Make Mine Music"); "Little Toot" (Geronimi/Aug. 13/from "Melody Time"); "Willie the Operatic Whale" (Geronimi, Luske, Cormack/Aug. 17/from "Make Mine Music"/a Buena Vista release); "Once Upon a Wintertime" (Luske/Sept. 17/from "Melody Time"); and "Social Lion" (Kinney/Oct. 15).

1955: "Contrasts in Rhythm" (Kinney, Luske/Mar. 11/from "Melody Time"); "Pedro" (Luske/May 13/from "Saludos Amigos"); "Aquarela Do Brasil" (Jackson/June 24/from "Saludos Amigos"); "The Flying Gauchito" (Ferguson, Larson/July 15/from "The Three Caballeros"); "Peter and the Wolf" (Geronimi/Sept. 14/from "Make Mine Music"/a Buena Vista release); and "Johnny Appleseed" (Jackson/Dec. 25/from "Melody Time"/a Buena Vista release).

Buena Vista Releases

1956: "Hooked Bear" (Hannah/Apr. 27/CinemaScope); "Jack and Old Mac" (Justice/July 18); "Man in Space" (Kimball/July 18); "In the Bag" (Hannah/July 27/CinemaScope); and "A Cowboy Needs a Horse" (Justice/Nov. 6).

1957: "The Story of Anyburg U.S.A." (Geronimi/June 19); "The Truth About Mother Goose" (Reitherman, Justice/Aug. 28/A.A. nominee); and "Mars and Beyond" (Kimball/Dec. 26).

1958: "Paul Bunyan" (Clark/Aug. 1); "Our Friend the Atom" (Luske/Aug.); and "The Legend of Sleepy Hollow" (Kinney, Geronimi/Nov. 26/from "The Adventures of Ichabod and Mr. Toad").

1959: "Noah's Ark" (Justice/Nov. 10/A.A. nominee).

1960: "Goliath II" (Reitherman/Jan. 21/A.A. nominee).

1961: "The Saga of Windwagon Smith" (Nichols/Mar. 16).

1962: "A Symposium on Popular Songs" (Justice/Dec. 19/ A.A. nominee).

1966: "Winnie the Pooh and the Honey Tree" (Reitherman/Feb. 4).

1967: "Scrooge McDuck and Money" (Luske/Mar. 23).

1968: "Winnie the Pooh and the Blustery Day" (Reitherman/Dec. 20/A.A. winner).

1969: "It's Tough to Be a Bird" (Kimball/Dec. 10/A.A. winner).

1970: "Dad, Can I Borrow the Car" (Kimball/Sept. 30).

1971: "Bongo" (Kinney/Jan. 20/from "Fun and Fancy Free").

1974: "Winnie the Pooh and Tigger Too" (Lounsbery/ Dec. 20/A.A. nominee).

1975: "The Madcap Adventures of Mr. Toad" (Kinney/ Dec. 25/from "The Adventures of Ichabod and Mr. Toad").

1978: "The Small One" (Bluth/Dec. 16).

1980: "Mickey Mouse Disco" (June 25/compilation cartoon).

1981: "Once Upon a Mouse" (July 10/compilation cartoon).

1982: "Vincent" (Burton/Oct. 1); and "Fun with Mr. Future" (Van Citters/Oct. 27).

1983: "Winnie the Pooh and a Day for Eeyore" (Reinert/ Mar. 11).

1987: "Oilspot and Lipstick" (Cedeno/July 28).

1989: "Tummy Trouble" (with Roger Rabbit, Baby Herman/animation directed by Rob Minkoff; live action by Frank Marshall/July 23).

⊚ WALTER LANTZ CARTUNE SPECIALS

Walter Lantz, creator of Woody Woodpecker, Andy Panda and others, lived out his love for music by initiating this series of musical cartoon novelties in 1934, produced in the same form as Disney's *Silly Symphonies* and Warner's early *Merrie Melodies*. No main characters were prominent in these animated efforts, which were based on hit songs of the day. Early titles were filmed in two-strip Cinecolor and then later three-strip Technicolor. *Directors were Walter Lantz, Lester Kline, Alex Lovy, Burt Gillett, Ben Hardaway, Emery Hawkins, James "Shamus" Culhane, Dick Lundy, Elmer Perkins, Paul J. Smith, Tex Avery, Pat Lenihan, Don Patterson and Jack Hannah. Cinecolor. Technicolor. A Walter Lantz*

Production released through Universal Pictures and United Artists.

Universal Pictures Releases

1934: "Jolly Little Elves" (Oct. 1/A.A. nominee); and "Toyland Premiere" (Dec. 7).

1935: "Candy Land" (Apr. 12); "Springtime Serenade" (May 27); "Three Lazy Mice" (July 15); and "The Fox and the Rabbit" (Sept. 30).

1938: "Nellie, the Sewing Machine Girl" (Apr. 11); "Tail End" (Apr. 25); "Movie Phoney News" (May 30); "Nellie, the Indian Chief's Daughter" (June 26); "Voodoo in Harlem" (July 18); "Ghost Town Frolics" (Kline/Sept. 5); "Hollywood Bowl" (Perkins/Oct. 5); "Baby Kittens" (Lovy/ Dec. 19); and "Little Blue Blackbirds" (Lenihan/Dec. 26).

1939: "Soup to Mutts" (Kline/Jan. 9); "I'm Just a Jitterbug" (Lovy/Jan. 23); "Magic Beans" (Kline/Feb. 3/ Nertsery Rhyme); "Birth of a Toothpick" (Gillett/Feb. 27); "Little Tough Mice" (Lovy/Mar. 13); "One-Armed Bandit" (Lovy/Mar. 27); "Crackpot Cruise" (Lovy/Apr. 10); "Charlie Cuckoo" (Perkins/Apr. 24); "Nellie of the Circus" (Lovy/May 8); "Bolo Mola Land" (Lovy/May 28); "The Bird on Nellie's Hat" (Lovy/June 19); "Arabs with Dirty Fezzes" (Lovy/July 31); "Snuffy Skunk's Party" (Perkins/Aug. 7); "Slap Happy Valley" (Lovy/Aug. 31/Crackpot Cruise cartoon); "A-Haunting We Will Go" (Gillett/Sept. 4/first cartoon in three-strip Technicolor; previous cartoons filmed in two-strip Cinecolor); "Scrambled Eggs" (Lovy/Nov. 20); and "The Sleeping Princess" (Gillett/Dec. 4/Technicolor/ Nertsery Rhyme cartoon).

1940: "Recruiting Daze" (Lovy/Oct. 28); and "Syncopated Sioux" (Lantz/Dec. 30).

1941: "Fair Today" (Lantz/Feb. 24); "Hysterical High Spots of American History" (Lantz/Mar. 31); "Scrub Me Mama with a Boogie Beat" (Lantz/Mar. 28); "Salt Water Daffy" (Lantz/June 9); "The Boogie Woogie Bugle Boy of Company B" (Lantz/Sept. 1/A.A. nominee); and "Man's Best Friend" (Lantz/Oct. 20).

1942: "Mother Goose on the Loose" (Lantz/Apr. 13); and "Air Radio Warden" (Lovy/Dec. 21).

1943: "Canine Commandos" (Lovy/June 28).

United Artists Releases

1948: "Kiddie Koncert" (Lundy/Apr. 23).

Universal Pictures Releases

1953: "The Dog That Cried Wolf" (Smith/Mar. 23).

1954: "Dig That Dog" (Patterson/Apr. 12); and "Broadway Bow Wows" (Patterson/Aug. 2).

1955: "Crazy Mixed-Up Pup" (Avery/Feb. 14/A.A. nominee); "Sh-h-h-h!!" (Avery/June 6); and "Flea for Two" (Patterson/July 20).

1957: "The Plumber of Seville" (Lovy/Mar. 11); "Goofy Gardener" (Lovy/Aug. 26); and "The Bongo Punch" (with Pepito Chickeeto/Lovy/Dec. 30).

1960: "Freloading Feline" (Hannah/Sept. 7); and "Hunger Strife" (Hannah/Oct. 5).

1961: "Eggnaper" (Hannah/Feb.); "Papoose on the Loose" (Smith/Apr. 11); "Bears and the Bees" (Hannah/May); and "Tin Can Concert" (Hannah/Oct. 31).

◎ WARNER BROS. CARTOON SPECIALS

In 1968, a year after studio head Jack Warner reorganized Warner Bros.' animation department and put William L. Hendricks in place as the studio's newest cartoon producer, Hendricks produced the studio's first and only "Cartoon Special," a non–*Looney Tunes* and *Merrie Melodies* cartoon, entitled "Norman Normal." A contemporary satire on business methods and social behavior as experienced by a young man with a conscience (Norman), the cartoon features the vocal and singing talents of singer/songwriter Noel (Paul) Stockey (Paul of Peter, Paul and Mary fame), who provides all of the character voices but Norman's, and Dave Dixon, the voice of Norman (who is incorrectly identified as Paul Dixon in the opening credits). Stockey and Dixon wrote the story on which the cartoon was based. The theme song, "Norman Normal," sung in the cartoon, was released on Peter, Paul and Mary's 1967 Warner Bros. album *Album*. *Directed by Alex Lovy. Technicolor. A Warner Bros. cartoon release.*

1968: "Norman Normal" (Feb. 3).

◎ WILLIE THE WALRUS

As an experiment, Terrytoons cast a walrus in Arctic misadventures in an effort to develop new cartoon star material. This series, like several other attempts, was short-lived. *Directed by Mannie Davis and Connie Rasinski. Technicolor. A Terrytoons Production released through 20th Century-Fox.*

1954: "Arctic Rivals" (Davis/June).

1955: "An Igloo for Two" (Rasinski/Mar.).

◎ WILLIE WHOPPER

When animator Ub Iwerks ceased production of his *Flip the Frog* series, he created this screen replacement, an imaginative liar named Willie Whopper whose tall tales were the foundation for unusual stories and situations. Adventures opened with Willie standing in front of a *Looney Tunes*–type oval, bragging to viewers "Say, did I ever tell you this one?" The roly-poly, freckle-faced boy never matched the popularity of Iwerks's Flip the Frog, however, and was soon abandoned. Actress Jane Withers, best known as Josephine the Plumber in TV's Comet Cleanser commercials, supplied the voice of Willie when she was seven years old. It was one of her first paying jobs. *Produced and directed by Ub Iwerks. Black-and-white. Cinecolor. A Celebrity Pictures Production released through Metro-Goldwyn-Mayer.*

Voice
Willie Whopper: Jane Withers

1933: "Play Ball" (Sept. 6); "Spite Flight" (Oct. 14); "Stratos-Fear" (Nov. 11); and "Davy Jones" (Dec. 9/Cinecolor).

(Copyright dates are marked by a ©.)

1934: "Hell's Fire" (Jan. 6/Cinecolor); "Robin Hood Jr." (Feb. 3); "Insultin' the Sultan" (Apr. 14); "Reducing Creme" (May 19); "Rasslin' Round" (© June 1); "The Cave Man" (July 6); "Jungle Jitters" (July 24); "Good Scout" (© Sept. 1); and "Viva Willie" (© Sept. 20).

◎ WILLOUGHBY WREN

This abbreviated Columbia Pictures cartoon series starred a canarylike bird who acquires tremendous strength each time he dons a magical cap containing particles of hair from Samson, the legendary strongman. Without the hat, he loses his power and becomes meek and helpless. The cartoons were released under the *Phantasy* and *Color Rhapsody* cartoon banners. Directors were Bob Wickersham and Howard Swift. *Technicolor. Voices credits unknown. A Columbia Pictures release.*

1943: "Willoughby's Magic Hat" (Wickersham/Apr. 20) Phantasy cartoon).

1944: "Magic Strength" (Wickersham/Feb. 4/Phantasy cartoon).

1945: "Carnival Courage" (Swift/Sept. 6/Color Rhapsody).

◎ WINDY

Featured in various misadventures, this dumbfounded country bear starred briefly in his own series for creator Walter Lantz. Veteran voice artist Daws Butler provided the vocal characterization for the bumpkin bear. *Directed by Paul J. Smith. Technicolor. A Walter Lantz Production released through Universal Pictures.*

Voice
Windy: Daws Butler

1958: "Salmon Yeggs" (Smith/Mar. 24); and "Three-Ring Fling" (Lovy/Oct. 6).

1959: "Truant Student" (with Breezy/Smith/Jan. 5); "Bee Bopped" (with Breezy/Smith/June 15).

WINNIE THE POOH

Honey-loving Winnie the Pooh, created by children's author A.A. Milne, was adapted for the screen in a series of delightfully animated cartoon shorts produced by Walt Disney under the studio's *Walt Disney Specials* banner. Joined by Eeyore, Piglet, Rabbit, Tigger and Christopher Robin, Pooh first appeared on movie screens in 1966's "Winnie the Pooh and the Honey Tree," directed by Woolie Reitherman. The series received two Academy Award nominations, winning an Oscar for 1968's "Winnie the Pooh and the Blustery Day." All short subjects in the series were later rebroadcast as prime-time network specials. In 1977 Pooh starred in his first full-length feature, *The Many Adventures of Winnie the Pooh.* He also appeared in his own animated series for ABC, *The New Adventures of Winnie the Pooh,* premiering in the fall of 1988. *Directed by Woolie Reitherman, John Lounsbery and Rick Reinert. Technicolor. A Walt Disney Production released through Buena Vista.*

Voices

Winnie the Pooh: Sterling Holloway, Hal Smith; **Eeyore:** Ralph Wright; **Owl:** Hal Smith; **Piglet:** John Fiedler; **Christopher Robin:** Bruce Reitherman, John Walmsley, Kim Christianson; **Kanga:** Barbara Luddy, Julie McWhirter Dees; **Roo:** Clint Howard, Dori Whitaker, Dick Billingsley; **Rabbit:** Junius Matthews, Will Ryan; **Tigger:** Paul Winchell; **Gopher:** Howard Morris

1966: "Winnie the Pooh and the Honey Tree" (Reitherman/Feb. 4).

1968: "Winnie the Pooh and the Blustery Day" (Reitherman/Dec. 20/A.A. winner).

1974: "Winnie the Pooh and Tigger Too" (Lounsbery/Dec. 20/A.A. nominee).

1983: "Winnie the Pooh and a Day for Eeyore" (Reinert/Mar. 11).

WOODY WOODPECKER

This hammering woodpecker with the "Ha-hah-ha-hah" laugh was Walter Lantz's prized creation. Screwball by nature, the redheaded menace was first introduced as the perfect foil in Andy Panda's 1940 cartoon, "Knock Knock," bearing a strong resemblance to the nutty characterizations of Warner's early Daffy Duck and Bugs Bunny. Legend long had it that Lantz invented Woody after honeymooning with his wife, former Broadway/screen actress Grace Stafford. A pesky woodpecker that pounded the roof of their honeymoon cottage provided inspiration. Unfortunately, the story was a Hollywood press agent's fabrication since Lantz's honeymoon actually occurred one year after Woody's first cartoon appearance.

"My wife suggested that since I had animated animals like mice, rabbits and so forth that maybe I should invent some kind of woodpecker character. I thought it was a good idea so I created Woody," Lantz later recalled.

In 1941 Lantz officially launched Woody in his own series, casting the malicious woodpecker in an eponymous cartoon. Veteran actor Mel Blanc supplied the voice of Woody in the first four or five cartoons. Ben "Bugs" Hardaway, who left Warner to become a story man for Lantz, lent his vocal talents to the character after Blanc's departure and continued to develop new stories for the series.

Hardaway did not handle the dual responsibility for long. In 1948 Lantz decided a change was needed and auditioned

Walter Lantz's Woody Woodpecker experienced many physical changes during his years as a screen star. © Walter Lantz Productions

50 actors for the "new" voice of Woody. Lantz was not present at the auditions, but he was responsible for making the final choice. Of those who auditioned on tape, he picked the talent who sounded the best. His selection: Grace, his wife, who had "tried out" without informing her husband.

Stafford was first employed in the 1948 Woody Woodpecker release "Banquet Busters" and remained the voice of Woody until the series ended 24 years later in 1972. By her request, she did not receive voice credit until 1952; she was afraid children would be "disillusioned if they knew a woman" had voiced the famed woodpecker.

Lantz later packaged the early Woody cartoons in a half-hour television series, *The Woody Woodpecker Show*, which was first broadcast in 1957 on ABC and was sponsored by Kellogg for nine consecutive seasons. The films are still syndicated today throughout most U.S. television markets and abroad. *Directors were Walter Lantz, Don Patterson, Paul J. Smith, Alex Lovy, Jack Hannah, Sid Marcus, Emery Hawkins, Milt Schaffer, James "Shamus" Culhane, Dick Lundy, Ben Hardaway and Cal Dalton. Technicolor. A Walter Lantz Production released through Universal Pictures and United Artists.*

Voices
Woody Woodpecker: Mel Blanc, Ben Hardaway, Grace Stafford

Additional Voices
June Foray

1940: "Knock Knock" (with Andy Panda/Lantz/Nov. 25).

1941: "Woody Woodpecker" (Lantz/July 7/working title: "Cracked Nut"); "The Screwdriver" (Lantz/Aug. 11); and "What's Cookin'?" (Lantz/Nov. 24/working title: "Pantry Panic").

1942: "Hollywood Matador" (Lantz/Feb. 9); "Ace in the Hole" (Lovy/June 22); and "The Loan Stranger" (Lovy/Oct. 19).

1943: "The Screwball" (Lovy/Feb. 25); "The Dizzy Acrobat" (May 31/A.A. nominee); and "Ration Bored" (Hawkins, Schaffer/July 26).

1944: "Barber of Seville" (Culhane/Apr. 10); "The Beach Nut" (Culhane/Oct. 16); and "Ski for Two" (Culhane/Nov. 13).

1945: "Chew-Chew Baby" (Culhane/Feb. 5); "Woody Dines Out" (Culhane/May 4); "Dippy Diplomat" (Culhane/Aug. 27); and "Loose Nut" (Culhane/Dec. 17).

1946: "Who's Cooking Who?" (Culhane/June 24); "Bathing Buddies" (Lundy/July 1); "The Reckless Driver" (Culhane/Aug. 26); and "Fair Weather Friends" (Culhane/Nov. 18).

United Artists Releases

1947: "Musical Moments from Chopin" (with Andy Panda/Lundy/Feb. 24/A.A. nominee/Musical Miniature); "Smoked Hams" (Lundy/Apr. 28); "Coo-Coo Bird" (Lundy/June 9); "Well Oiled" (Lundy/June 30); "Solid Ivory" (Lundy/Aug. 25); and "Woody, the Giant Killer" (Lundy/Dec. 15).

1948: "The Mad Hatter" (Lundy/Feb.); "Banquet Busters" (with Andy Panda/Lundy/Mar. 12); "Wacky-Bye Baby" (Lundy/May); "Wet Blanket Policy" (Lundy/Aug. 27); and "Wild and Woody" (Lundy/Dec. 31).

Universal Pictures Releases

(Copyright dates are marked by a ©.)

1949: "Drooler's Delight" (Lundy/Mar. 25).

1951: "Puny Express" (Lundy/Jan. 22); "Sleep Happy" (Lantz/Mar. 26); "Wicket Wacky" (Lantz/© May 28); "Sling Shot 6 7/8" (Lantz/July 23); "Redwood Sap" (Lantz/Oct. 1); "Woody Woodpecker Polka" (Lantz/Oct. 29); and "Destination Meatball" (Lantz/Dec. 24).

1952: "Born to Peck" (Lantz/Feb. 25); "Stage Hoax" (Lantz/Apr. 21); "Woodpecker in the Rough" (Lantz/June 16); "Scalp Treatment" (Lantz/Sept. 18); "The Great Who Dood It" (Lantz/Oct. 20); and "Termites from Mars" (Patterson/Dec. 8).

1953: "What's Sweepin'?" (Patterson/Jan. 5); "Bucaneer Woodpecker" (Patterson/Apr. 20); "Operation Sawdust" (Patterson/June 15); "Wrestling Wrecks" (Patterson/July 20); "Hypnotic Hick" (Patterson/Sept. 26/in 3-D); "Belle Boys" (Patterson/Sept. 14); and "Hot Noon" (Smith/Oct. 12).

1954: "Socko in Morocco" (Patterson/Jan. 18); "Alley to Bali" (Patterson/Mar. 15); "Under the Counter Spy" (Patterson/May 10); "Hot Rod Huckster" (Patterson/July 5); "Real Gone Woody" (Smith/Sept. 20); "Fine Feathered Frenzy" (Patterson/Oct. 25); and "Convict Concerto" (Patterson/Nov. 20).

1955: "Helter Shelter" (Smith/Jan. 17); "Witch Crafty" (Smith/Mar. 14); "Private Eye Pooch" (Smith/May 19); "Bedtime Bedlam" (Smith/July 4); "Square Shooting Square" (Smith/Sept. 26); "Bunco Busters" (Smith/Nov. 21); and "The Tree Medic" (Lovy/Dec. 19).

1956: "After the Ball" (Smith/Feb. 13); "Get Lost" (Smith/Mar. 12); "Chief Charlie Horse" (Smith/May 7); "Woodpecker from Mars" (Smith/July 2); "Calling all Cuckoos" (Smith/Sept. 24); "Niagra Fools" (Smith/Oct. 22); "Arts and Flowers" (Smith/Nov.19); and "Woody Meets Davy Crewcut" (Lovy/Dec. 17).

1957: "Red Riding Hoodlum" (Smith/Feb. 11); "Box Car Bandit" (Smith/Apr. 8); "The Unbearable Salesman" (Smith/June 3); "International Woodpecker" (Smith/July 1); "To Catch a Woodpecker" (Lovy/July 29); "Round Trip to Mars" (Smith/Sept. 23); "Fodder and Son" (Smith/Nov. 4); and "Dopey Dick and the Pink Whale" (Smith/Nov. 15).

1958: "Misguided Missile" (Smith/Jan. 27); "Watch the Birdie" (Lovy/Feb. 24); "Half-Empty Saddles" (Smith/Apr. 21); "His Better Elf" (Smith/July 14); "Everglade Raid" (Smith/Aug. 11); "Tree's a Crowd" (Smith/Sept. 8); and "Jittery Jester" (Smith/Nov. 3).

1959: "Tom Cat Combat" (Smith/Mar. 2); "Log Jammed" (Smith/Apr. 20); "Panhandle Scandal" (Lovy/May 18); "Woodpecker in the Moon" (Lovy/July 13); "The Tee Bird" (Smith/July 13); "Romp in a Swamp" (Smith/Aug. 7); and "Kiddie League" (Smith/Nov. 3).

1960: "Billion-Dollar Boner" (Lovy/Jan. 5); "Pistol-Packin' Woodpecker" (Smith/Mar. 2); "Heap Big Hepcat" (Smith/Mar. 30); "Ballyhooey" (Lovy/Apr. 20); "How to Stuff a Woodpecker" (Smith/May 18); "Bats in the Belfry" (Smith/June 16); "Ozark Lark" (Smith/July 13); "Southern Fried Hospitality" (with Gabby Gator/Hannah/Nov. 28); and "Fowled-Up Falcon" (Smith/Dec. 20).

1961: "Poop Deck Pirate" (Hannah/Jan. 10); "The Bird Who Came to Dinner" (Smith/Mar. 7); "Gabby's Diner" (with Gabby Gator/Hannah/Apr.); "Sufferin' Cats" (Smith/June); "Frankenstymied" (Hannah/July 4); "Busman's Holiday" (Smith/Aug.); "Phantom of the Horse Opera" (Smith/Oct.); and "Woody's Kook-Out" (Hannah/Nov.).

1962: "Rock-a-Bye Gator" (with Gabby Gator/Hannah/Jan. 9); "Home Sweet Homewrecker" (Smith/Jan. 30); "Room and Bored" (Smith/Mar. 6); "Rocket Racket" (with Gabby Gator/Hannah/Apr. 24); "Careless Caretaker" (Smith/May 29); "Tragic Magic" (Smith/July 3); "Voodoo Boo-Hoo" (Hannah/Aug. 14); "Growin' Pains" (Smith/Sept.); and "Little Woody Riding Hood" (with Gabby Gator/Smith/Oct.).

1963: "Greedy Gabby Gator" (with Gabby Gator/Marcus/Jan.); "Robin Hood Woody" (Smith/Mar.); "Stowaway Woody" (Marcus/May); "Shutter Bug" (Smith/June); "Coy Decoy" (Marcus/July 9); "The Tenants' Racket" (Marcus/Aug. 30); "Short in the Saddle" (Smith/Sept. 30); "Teepee for Two" (Marcus/Oct. 29); "Science Friction" (Marcus/Nov.); and "Calling Dr. Woodpecker" (Smith/Dec. 24).

1964: "Dumb Like a Fox" (Marcus/Jan. 7); "Saddle-Sore Woody" (Smith/Apr. 7); "Woody's Clip Joint" (Marcus/May); "Skinfolks" (Marcus/July 7); "Get Lost! Little Doggy" (Marcus/Sept.); "Freeway Fracus" (Smith/Sept.); and "Roamin' Roman" (Smith/Dec.).

1965: "Three Little Woodpeckers" (Marcus/Jan. 1); "Woodpecker Wanted" (Smith/Feb. 1); "Birds of a Feather" (Marcus/Mar. 1); "Canned Dog Feud" (Smith/Apr. 1); "Janie Get Your Gun" (Smith/May 1); "Sioux Me" (Marcus/June); and "What's Peckin?" (Smith/July 1).

1966: "Rough Riding Hood" (Marcus/Jan. 1); "Lonesome Ranger" (Smith/Feb. 1); "Woody and the Beanstalk" (Smith/Mar. 1); "Hassle in a Castle" (Smith/Apr.); "The Big Bite" (Smith/Apr. 1); "Astronut Woody" (Smith/May); "Monster of Ceremonies" (Smith/May); and "Practical Yolk" (Smith/May 1).

1967: "Sissy Sheriff" (Smith/Jan. 1); "Have Gun—Can't Travel" (Smith/Feb. 1); "The Nautical Nut" (Smith/Mar. 1); "Hot Diggity Dog" (Smith/Mar. 1); "Horse Play" (Smith/Apr. 1); and "Secret Agent Woody" (Smith/May 1).

1968: "Lotsa Luck" (Smith); "Fat in the Saddle" (Smith/June 1); "Feudin', Fightin' 'n' Fussin'" (Smith/June 1); "A Peck of Trouble" (Smith/July 1); "A Lad in Bagdad" (Smith/Aug. 1); "One Horse Town" (Smith/Oct. 1); and "Woody the Freeloader" (Smith).

1969: "Hook Line and Stinker" (Smith); "Little Skeeter" (Smith); "Woody's Knightmare" (Smith/May 1); "Tumbleweed Greed" (Smith/June 1); "Ship Ahoy, Woody" (Smith/Aug. 1); "Prehistoric Super Salesman" (Smith/Sept. 1); and "Phony Pony" (Smith/Nov. 1).

1970: "Seal on the Loose" (Smith/May 1); "Wild Bill Hiccup" (Smith/June 1); "Coo Coo Nuts" (Smith/July 1); "Hi-Rise Wise Guys" (Smith/Aug. 1); "Buster's Last Stand" (Smith/Oct. 1); and "All Hams on Deck" (Smith/Nov. 9).

1971: "Film Flam Fountain" (Smith/Jan. 5); "Sleep Time Chimes" (Smith/Feb. 1); "Reluctant Recruit" (Smith); "How to Trap a Woodpecker" (Smith); "Woody's Magic Touch" (Smith); "Kitty from the City" (Smith); "Snoozin' Bruin Woody" (Smith); and "Shanghai Woody" (Smith).

1972: "Indian Corn" (Smith); "Gold Diggin' Woodpecker" (Smith); "Pecking Holes in Poles" (Smith); "Chili Con Corny" (Smith); "Show Biz Eagle" (Smith); "For the Love of Pizza" (Smith); "The Genie with the Light Touch" (Smith); and "Bye Bye Blackboard" (Smith).

⊚ YOSEMITE SAM

A primary cartoon foil for Bugs Bunny, this pint-size, short-tempered cowboy who called himself "the roughest, toughest hombre" in the West came out guns ablazing in his screen debut opposite the carrot-eating rabbit in 1945's "Hare Trigger."

Friz Freleng, who directed the film, was responsible for creating Yosemite. "I was looking for a character strong enough to work against Bugs Bunny. . . . So I thought to use the smallest guy I could think of along with the biggest voice I could get," Freleng told Warner Bros. historian Steven Schneider.

In his 1944 "Stage Door Cartoon," Freleng used a similar character who looked and sounded like Yosemite and had only a walk-on part. According to writer Michael Maltese, Freleng drew from several personas—himself included—in developing the loud-mouthed Yosemite. His primary influences were Red Skelton's Sheriff Deadeye, a boneheaded cowboy short on smarts, Bob Clampett's gunslinger character based on Deadeye and comic-strip star Red Ryder in his 1944 "Buckaroo Bugs."

Yosemite's appearances were limited to supporting roles throughout his career; he never starred in his own series. Today the character is still seen daily in television reruns of the studio's *Merrie Melodies* and *Looney Tunes* package and in frequent prime-time animated specials.

In 1995 Yosemite returned to movie screens as costar in a brand-new Bugs Bunny cartoon, "Carrotblanca," a spoof of the Humphrey Bogart–Lauren Bacall classic, *Casablanca*, directed by Douglas McCarthy. Voice impressario Maurice LaMarche took over as the voice of Yosemite Sam. Two years later, after returning to Warner Bros. to produce and direct new cartoon shorts, legendary animator Chuck Jones directed Yosemite in a second cartoon opposite Bugs Bunny, "From Hare to Eternity," intended as Jones's tribute to fellow animator, the late Friz Freleng. The film was never released theatrically. Comedian/impressionist Frank Gorshin, best known as The Riddler on the *Batman* TV series, lent his voice as Yosemite. *Directors were Friz Freleng, Ken Harris, Hawley Pratt, Gerry Chiniquy and Douglas McCarthy. Technicolor. A Warner Bros. release.*

Voices
Yosemite Sam: Mel Blanc, Maurice LaMarche, Frank Gorshin

Additional Voices
June Foray, Billy Booth

Looney Tunes

1948: "Bucaneer Bunny" (with Bugs Bunny/Freleng/May 8).

1950: "Mutiny on the Bunny" (with Bugs Bunny/Freleng/Feb. 11); and "Big House Bunny" (with Bugs Bunny/Freleng/Apr. 22).

1951: "Rabbit Every Monday" (with Bugs Bunny/Freleng/Feb. 10); and "The Fair Haired Hare" (with Bugs Bunny/Freleng/Apr. 14).

1952: "14 Carrot Rabbit" (with Bugs Bunny/Freleng/Feb. 16); and "Hare Lift" (with Bugs Bunny/Freleng/Dec. 20).

1954: "Captain Hareblower" (with Bugs Bunny/Freleng/Feb. 16).

1955: "Sahara Hare" (with Bugs Bunny/Freleng/Mar. 26); and "Roman Legion Hare" (with Bugs Bunny/Freleng/Nov. 12).

1956: "Rabbitson Crusoe" (with Bugs Bunny/Freleng/Apr. 28).

1957: "Piker's Peak" (with Bugs Bunny/Freleng/May 25).

1958: "Knighty-Knight Bugs" (with Bugs Bunny/Freleng/Aug. 23/A.A. winner).

1959: "Wind and Wooly Hare" (with Bugs Bunny/Freleng/Aug. 1).

1960: "Horse Hare" (with Bugs Bunny/Freleng/Feb. 13).

1961: "Prince Violent" (with Bugs Bunny/Freleng, Pratt/Sept. 2).

1962: "Shishkabugs" (with Bugs Bunny/Freleng/Dec. 8).

DePatie-Freleng Enterprises Releases

1964: "Dumb Patrol" (with Bugs Bunny, Porky Pig/Chiniquy/Jan. 18).

1995: "Carrotblanca" (with Bugs Bunny, Daffy Duck, Yosemite Sam, Tweety and Sylvester, Foghorn Leghorn, Pepe Le Pew, Penelope/McCarthy).

Merrie Melodies

1945: "Hare Trigger" (with Bugs Bunny/Freleng/May 5)

1948: "Bugs Bunny Rides Again" (with Bugs Bunny/Freleng/June 12).

1950: "Bunker Hill Bunny" (with Bugs Bunny/Freleng/Sept. 23).

1951: "Ballot Box Bunny" (with Bugs Bunny/Freleng/Oct. 6).

1953: "Southern Fried Rabbit" (with Bugs Bunny/Freleng/May 2); and "Hare Trimmed" (with Bugs Bunny/Freleng/June 20).

1959: "Hare-Abian Nights" (with Bugs Bunny/Harris/Feb. 28).

1960: "Lighter than Hare" (with Bugs Bunny/Freleng/Dec. 17).

1962: "Honey's Money" (Freleng/Sept. 1).

1963: "Devil's Feud Cake" (with Bugs Bunny/Freleng/Feb. 9).

⊚ ⊚ ⊚ ⊚ ⊚

FULL-LENGTH ANIMATED FEATURES

⊚ ⊚ ⊚ ⊚ ⊚

The following section is a complete listing of full-length animated features that received limited and wide theatrical distribution in the United States only. The section excludes those features that combine a little animation with live action.

Films that have minor animated sequences that are not mentioned in this section include: *King of Jazz* (1930), which features a four-minute animated opening by Walter Lantz (the first animation to be done in two-color Technicolor); *Hollywood Party* (MGM, 1934), in which an animated Mickey Mouse appears; *She Married a Cop* (1939), featuring Paddy the Pig in a cartoon segment, also seen in the film's remake *Sioux City Sue* (1947), starring Gene Autry; *Victory Through Air Power* (Disney, 1943); *Anchors Aweigh* (MGM, 1944), featuring Gene Kelly and Jerry Mouse in a popular dance sequence; *So Dear to Heart* (Disney, 1945); *My Dream Is Yours* (Warner, 1949), the Doris Day–Jack Carson film highlighted by animated appearances of Bugs Bunny and Tweety bird (Bugs appeared one year earlier in another Jack Carson film, *Two Guys from Texas*); *Destination Moon* (1950), featuring Woody Woodpecker in a brief bit of animated business; *Dangerous When Wet* (MGM, 1953), which teams Tom and Jerry with Esther Williams in an underwater sequence; *Mary Poppins* (1965), in which Julie Andrews and Dick Van Dyke dance in perfect synchronization with several animated penguins; and *Bedknobs and Broomsticks* (1971).

When animated characters play a major part in the story structure of live action/animated films (i.e., *The Incredible Mr. Limpet*, *Pete's Dragon* and *Who Framed Roger Rabbit*), those productions have been included.

Technical credits appear with each listing, limited to the production staff (producer, director, writer, musical director and supervising animators) and voice artists. Production sidelights and other tidbits of interest have been entered under notes about the production (abbreviated as "PN") whenever appropriate.

The following key can be used to translate abbreviations for technical staff listed under each film:

anim dir: animation directors
anim superv: animation supervisor
cart sc: cartoon score
cart st: cartoon story
cpd: coproducer
d: director
dir anim: directing animator
exec prod: executive producer
l/a dir: live-action director
m: music
md: musical direction
ms: musical supervision
m/a: music associates
m/l: music and lyrics
m/s: music and songs
m/sc: musical score
p: producer
prod dir: production director
prod superv: production supervisor
scr: screenplay
scr st: screen story
seq dir: sequence directors
st: story
st dev: story development
superv anim: supervising animators
superv d: supervising directors
w: writer

⊚ THE ADVENTURES OF ICHABOD AND MR. TOAD (1949)

A Walt Disney Production released by RKO Radio Pictures. **p:** Walt Disney; **prod superv:** Ben Sharpsteen; **d:** Jack Kinney, Clyde Geronimi, James Algar; **dir anim:** Frank Thomas, Ollie Johnston, Wolfgang Reitherman, Milt Kahl, John Lounsbery, Ward Kimball; **st:** Erdman Penner, Winston Hibler, Joe Rinaldi, Ted Sears, Homer Brightman, Harry Reeves; **md:** Oliver Wallace. **Songs:** "Ichabod," "Katrina," "The Headless Horseman" and "Merrily on Our Way." **Running time:** 68 minutes.

Voices

Mr. Toad: Eric Blore; **Cyril:** J. Pat O'Malley; **Rat:** Claude Allister; **John Ployard:** John McLeish; **Mole:** Colin Campbell; **Angus MacBadger:** Campbell Grant; **Winky:** Alec Harford. "Ichabod" narrated by Bing Crosby. "Willows" narrated by Basil Rathbone.

This somewhat forgotten Disney feature combines two half-hour adaptations: Washington Irving's *Legend of Sleepy Hollow,* the story of schoolmaster Ichabod Crane's encounter with the famed horseman and his Jack-o'-lantern head, and Kenneth Grahame's *Wind in the Willows,* featuring the misadventures of Mr. Toad Hall, a whimsical toad who is wrongly accused of car thievery and tries proving his innocence. Bing Crosby ("Ichabod") and Basil Rathbone ("Willows") provided narration for the films.

PN: The film's original title was *Two Fabulous Characters* but was changed prior to its release.

⊚ THE ADVENTURES OF THE AMERICAN RABBIT (1986)

A Toei Animation Production released by Clubhouse Pictures. **p:** Masaharu Etoh, Masahisa Saeki, John G. Marshall; **d:** Fred Wolf, Nobutaka Nishizawa; **w:** Norm Lenzer (based on the characters created by Stewart Moskowitz); **m/l:** Mark Volman, Howard Kayland, John Hoier. **Running time:** 85 minutes.

Voices

Theo: Bob Arbogast; **Tini Meeny:** Pat Fraley; **Rob/American Rabbit:** Barry Gordon; **Rodney:** Bob Holt; **Dip/Various Characters:** Lew Horn; **Bruno:** Norm Lenzer; **Vultor/Buzzard:** Ken Mars; **Toos Loose:** John Mayer; **Lady Pig:** Maitzi Morgan; **Ping Pong:** Lorenzo Music; **Bunny O'Hare:** Laurie O'Brien; **Mentor:** Hal Smith; **Mother:** Russi Taylor; **Fred Red:** Fred Wolf

Loosely based on Superman, mild-mannered, bespectacled Rob Rabbit obtains supernatural powers following a bizarre encounter with a mystical rabbit wizard, enabling him to restore peace and order as a superrabbit.

⊚ AKIRA (1988)

An Akira Committee Production released by Streamline Pictures. **p:** Akira Committee; **d:** Mamoru Oshii, Katsuhiro Otomo; **scr:** Isao Hashimoto (based on the comic created by Katsuhiro Otomo); **m:** Shoji Yamashiro. **Songs:** "Kaneda," "Battle Against Clown," "Winds over the Neo-Tokyo," "Tetsuo," "Dolls' Polyphony," "Shohmyoh," "Mutation," "Exodus from the Underground Fortress," "Illusion" and "Requiem." **Running time:** 124 minutes.

Voices

Kaneda: Mitsuo Iwata; **Tetsuo:** Nozomu Sasaki; **Kei:** Mami Koyama; **Kai:** Takeshi Kusao; **The Colonel:** Tara Ishida

Additional Voices

Jimmy Flanders, Barbara Larsen, Lewis Lemay, Drew Thomas

A secret military project endangers Neo-Tokyo when it turns a biker gang member into a rampaging psychopath with telekinetic powers that only a group of teenagers (from the motorcycle gang from which he came) can stop, in this apocalyptic story based on the popular Japanese comicbook novel.

⊚ ALADDIN (1992)

A Walt Disney Picture released by Buena Vista. **p & d:** John Musker, Ron Clements; **scr:** Ron Clements, John Musker, Ted Elliott, Terry Rossio; **m:** Alan Menken (with songs by Howard Ashman, Alan Menken, Tim Rice); **superv anim:** Randy Cartwright, Andreas Deja, Will Finn, Eric Goldberg, Mark Henn, Glen Keane, Duncan Marjoribanks. **Songs:** "Arabian Nights," "Legend of the Lamp," "One Jump Ahead," "Street Urchins," "Friend Like Me," "To Be Free," "Prince Ali," "A Whole New World," "Jafar's Hour," "The Ends of the Earth," "The Kiss," "On a Dark Night," "Jasmine Runs Away," "Marketplace," "Cave of Wonders," "Aladdin's Word," "The Battle" and "Happy End in Agrabah." **Running time:** 87 minutes.

Voices

Aladdin: Scott Weinger; **Genie:** Robin Williams; **Jasmine:** Linda Larkin; **Jafar:** Jonathan Freeman; **Abu:** Frank Welker; **Iago:** Gilbert Gottfried; **Sultan:** Douglas Seale; **Rajah:** Aaron Blaise; **Merchant (singing):** Bruce Adler; **Aladdin (singing):** Brad Kane; **Jasmine (singing):** Lea Salonga; **Gazem/Achmed:** T. Daniel Hofstedt; **Guard:** Chris Wahl; **Beggar/Snake Jafar:** Kathy Zielinski

Additional Voices

Jack Angel, Corey Burton, Philip L. Clarke, Jim Cummings, Jennifer Darling, Debi Derryberry, Bruce Gooch, Jerry Houser, Vera Lockwood, Sherry Lyn, Mickie McGowan, Patrick Pinney, Philip Proctor

Accompanied by his faithful monkey friend Abu, street-urchin Aladdin, with the aid of a mysterious magic lamp with a powerful Genie inside (played for laughs by Robin Williams) who will grant him three wishes, goes up against the evil Jafar, who plots to rule the city of Agrabah. Aladdin falls in love with Princess Jasmine in the process and saves the city from Jafar's ruthless attempt to rule.

PN: *Aladdin* marked a departure from tradition for Disney animated features. Unlike past efforts, this film was an irreverent, high-stakes gamble featuring outrageous one-liners, sight gags and pop references. Comedian Robin Williams, known for his free-form shtick, improvised freely during the recording of dialogue for the film. This was a challenge for the directors: The first scene he recorded for the film he did 25 times, in 25 different ways, to the point that scenes originally meant to last 30 seconds suddenly ended up 10 minutes long.) Williams reportedly mimicked 55 different personalities for the film, with many more ending up on the cutting room floor, including imitations of President Bush and well-known sex therapist Dr. Ruth Westheimer. The work paid off as the film earned a record $217 million in revenue, at one time making it the highest-grossing animated feature film ever. The film was nominated for five Academy Awards, winning the award for Best Original Score and Best Song (for the song: "A Whole New World"). Robin Williams was honored with a special Golden Globe award for his vocal work on the film. Two made-for-video sequels were produced following the success of the animated feature: *The Return of Jafar* (1993) and *Aladdin and the King of Thieves* (1996). Robin Williams reprised his role of the Genie only for the latter.

◉ ALAKAZAM THE GREAT (1961)

A Toei Animation Production released by American International Pictures. **p:** Lou Rusoff (U.S.), Hiroshi Okawa (Japan); **d:** Lee Kresel (U.S.), Teiji Yabushita, Osamu Tezuka, Daisaku Shirakawa (Japan); **scr:** Lou Rusoff, Lee Kresel (U.S.), Keinosuke Uekusa (Japan); **m:** Les Baxter. **Songs:** "Ali the Great," "Bluebird in the Cherry Tree," "Under the Waterfall" and "Aliki-Aliko-Alakazam." **Running time:** 84 minutes.

Voices

Alakazam: Frankie Avalon; **De De:** Dodie Stevens; **Sir Quigley Broken Bottom:** Jonathan Winters; **Lulipop:** Arnold Stang; **Narrator:** Sterling Holloway

Alakazam, a shy and modest monkey, is chosen by his peers to be the monarch of all animals on earth. When the power goes to his head, King Amo, ruler of Majutsoland, the celestial island where all retired magicians reside, imprisons Alakazam in a cave to teach him a lesson. He is later released from confinement with the stipulation that he go about the countryside performing good deeds.

PN: Released in Japan in 1960 in ToeiScope as *Saiyu-ki*, the film was reedited and retitled for American release, running four minutes shorter than the original production.

◉ ALICE IN WONDERLAND (1951)

A Walt Disney Production released by RKO Radio Pictures. **p:** Walt Disney; **prod superv:** Ben Sharpsteen; **d:** Clyde Geronimi, Hamilton Luske, Wilfred Jackson; **anim dir:** Milt Kahl, Ward Kimball, Frank Thomas, Eric Larson, John Lounsbery, Ollie Johnston, Wolfgang Reitherman, Marc Davis, Les Clark, Norman Ferguson; **st:** Winston Hibler, Bill Peet, Joe Rinaldi, Bill Cottrell, Joe Grant, Del Connell, Ted Sears, Erdman Penner, Milt Banta, Dick Kelsey, Dick Huemer, Tom Oreb, John Walbridge; **m/sc:** Oliver Wallace. **Songs:** "Very Good Advice," "In a World of My Own," "All in a Golden Afternoon," "Alice in Wonderland," "The Walrus and the Carpenter," "The Caucus Race," "I'm Late," "Painting the Roses Red," "March of the Cards," "Twas Brillig," "The Unbirthday Song," "We'll Smoke the Blighter Out," "Old Father William" and "A E I O U." **Running time:** 75 minutes.

Voices

Alice: Kathryn Beaumont; **Mad Hatter:** Ed Wynn; **Caterpillar:** Richard Haydn; **Cheshire Cat:** Sterling Holloway; **March Hare:** Jerry Colonna; **Queen of Hearts:** Verna Felton; **Walrus/Carpenter/Tweedledee and Tweedledum:** J. Pat O'Malley; **White Rabbit/Dodo:** Bill Thompson; **Alice's Sister:** Heather Angel; **Door Knob:** Joseph Kearns; **Bill Card Painter:** Larry Grey; **Nesting Mother Bird:** Queenie Leonard; **King of Hearts:** Dink Trout; **The Rose:** Doris Lloyd; **Dormouse:** James Macdonald; **Card Painters:** The Mello Men; **Flamingoes:** Pinto Colvig; **Card Painter:** Ken Beaumont

Based on Lewis Carroll's two books, *Alice in Wonderland* and *Through the Looking Glass*, this classic Disney feature traces young Alice's dream of falling through space and time into a magical land of make-believe where she meets everything from the disappearing Cheshire Cat to the White Rabbit ("I'm late, I'm late for a very important date!").

◉ ALL DOGS GO TO HEAVEN (1989)

A Sullivan Bluth Studios Ireland, Ltd. Production in association with Goldcrest Films released by United Artists. **p:** Don Bluth, Gary Goldman, John Pomeroy; **d:** Don Bluth; **scr:** Davis Weiss; **st:** Don Bluth, Ken Cromar, Gary Goldman, Larry Leker, Linda Miller, Monica Parker, John Pomeroy, Guy Schulman, David Steinberg, David N. Weiss; **m:** Ralph Burns; **anim dir:** John Pomeroy, Linda Miller, Ralph Zondag, Dick Zondag, Lorna Pomeroy-Cook, Jeff Etter, Ken Duncan. **Songs:** "You Can't Keep a Good Dog Down," "Let Me Be Surprised," "What's Mine Is Yours," "Let's Make

Music Together," "Soon You'll Come Home" and "Hallelujah." **Running time:** 84 minutes.

Voices
Charlie B. Barkin: Burt Reynolds; **Itchy:** Dom DeLuise; **Dog Caster:** Daryl Gilley; **Vera:** Candy Devine; **Killer:** Charles Nelson Reilly; **Carface:** Vic Tayback; **Whippet Angel:** Melba Moore; **Anne-Marie:** Judith Barsi; **Harold:** Rob Fuller; **Kate:** Earleen Carey; **Stella Dallas:** Anna Manahan; **Sir Reginald:** Nigel Pegram; **Flo:** Loni Anderson; **King Gator:** Ken Page; **Terrier:** Godfrey Quigley; **Mastiff:** Jay Stevens; **Puppy:** Cyndi Cozzo; **Gambler Dog:** Thomas Durkin; **Puppy:** Kelly Briley; **Fat Pup:** Dana Rifkin; **The Don Bluth Players:** John Carr, John Eddings, Jeff Etter, Dan Hofstedt, Dan Kuenster, Dan Molina, Mark Swan, Taylor Swanson, David Weiss, Dick Zondag

Set in the canine world of New Orleans, c. 1939, this fun-filled, heartwarming story traces the exploit of Charlie B. Barkin, a German shepherd with a con man's charm, who gets a reprieve (he is sent back from heaven to perform some acts of goodness before he will be allowed in) and befriends a little orphan girl, Anne-Marie, kidnapped by his scurvy old gang.

PN: More than 1.5 million individual drawings were needed to produce this animated adventure. The film features a musical score by Academy Award–winning composer Ralph Burns (*Cabaret*, *All That Jazz*) and original songs by Charles Strouse (*Annie*). The film marked the first production for the Sullivan Bluth Studios, relocated from Hollywood to Dublin, Ireland.

ALL DOGS GO TO HEAVEN 2 (1996)
A Metro-Goldwyn-Mayer Production released by Metro-Goldwyn-Mayer. **p:** Jonathan Dern, Paul Sabella; **d:** Larry

Charlie (voiced by Burt Reynolds) leads an all-canine conga line in All Dogs Go to Heaven *(1989), a tale of rascals, puppies and true love. © Goldcrest & Sullivan Bluth, Ltd.*

Leker, Paul Sabella; **scr:** Arnie Olsen, Kelly Ward; **m:** Mark Watters. **Songs:** "It's Too Heavenly Here," "Count Me Out," "My Afghan Hairless," "It Feels So Good to Be Bad," "On Easy Street" and "I Will Always Be with You." **Running time:** 82 minutes.

Voices
Charlie B. Barkin: Charlie Sheen; **Sasha:** Sheena Easton; **Carface:** Ernest Borgnine; **Itchy:** Dom DeLuise; **Red:** George Hearn; **Anabelle:** Bebe Neuwirth; **David:** Adamy Wylie; **Labrador:** Wallace Shawn

Mischievous mutt Charlie B. Barkin is asked to retrieve Gabriel's horn when it is stolen from heaven and returns to earth, joined by sidekick Itchy, only to get sidetracked into trouble in this sequel to 1989's *All Dogs Go to Heaven*.

PN: Don Bluth, who produced and directed the original, was not involved in producing the sequel, which fared poorly at the box office, grossing $8.62 million in ticket sales. Actor Charlie Sheen took over the role of Charlie B. Barkin, which was played by Burt Reynolds in the original movie.

ALLEGRO NON TROPPO (1976)
A Bruno Bozetto Film Production release. **p & d:** Bruno Bozetto; **scr:** Guido Manuli, Maurizio Nichetti, Bruno Bozetto; **m:** Debussy, Dvorak, Ravel, Sibelius, Vivaldi, Stravinsky. **Running time:** 80 minutes.

Cast (live action)
Maurizo Nichetti, Nestor Garay, Maurizio Micheli, Maria Luisa Giovannini

A parody of Walt Disney's famed *Fantasia* featuring six different animated stories fitted to classical music conducted by such noted artists as Herbert von Karajan, Hans Stadlmair and Lorin Maazel. The film intersperses live action between each of the symphonic pieces, which feature English subtitles and animation. Musical selections are: "Prelude of a Faun" by Debussy, "Slavonic Dance No. 7" by Dvorak, "Bolero" by Ravel, "Valse Triste" by Sibelius, "Concerto in C Minor" by Vivaldi and "The Firebird" by Stravinsky.

AMERICAN POP (1981)
A Ralph Bakshi Film released by Columbia Pictures. **p:** Martin Ransohoff; **d:** Ralph Bakshi; **scr:** Ronnie Kern; **m:** Lee Holdridge. **Songs:** "A Hard Rain's a Gonna Fall" (by Bob Dylan), "American Pop Overture" (arranged by Lee Holdridge), "Anything Goes," "As Time Goes By," "Bill," "Blue Suede Shoes," "Body & Soul," "California Dreamin'," "Cantaloupe Island," "Charleston," "Crazy on You," "Devil with the Blue Dress On," "Don't Think Twice It's Allright," "Free Bird" (performed by Lynrd Skynrd), "Give My Regards to Broadway," "Hell Is For Children," "I Don't

Care," "I Got Rhythm," "I'm Waiting for the Man," "Look for the Silver Lining," "Maple Leaf Rag," "Moanin'" (performed by Al Blakey), "Mona Lisa," "Nancy (with the Laughing Face)," "Night Moves," "Onward Christian Soldiers," "Over There," "Palm Leaf Rag," "People Are Strange," "Pretty Vacant," "Purple Haze," "Say Si Si," "Sing, Sing, Sing," "Slaughter on Tenth Avenue," "Smiles," "Somebody Loves Me," "Somebody to Love," "Summertime," "Sweet Georgia Brown," "Take Give" (performed by Dave Brubeck Quartet), "This Train," "Turn Me Loose" (performed by Fabian), "Up, Up and Away," "When the Saints Go Marching In" and "You Send Me." **Running time:** 97 minutes.

Voices

Izzy: Gene Borkan; **Prostitute:** Beatrice Colen; **Crisco:** Frank DeKova; **Nicky Palumbo:** Ben Frommer; **Louie:** Jerry Holland; **Eva Tanguay:** Roz Kelly; **Nancy:** Amy Levitt; **Zalmie:** Jeffrey Lippu; **Poet:** Richard Moll; **Bella:** Lisa Jane Perksy; **Hannele:** Elsa Raven; **Theatre Owner:** Vincent Schiarelli; **Benny:** Richard Singer; **Frankie:** Marya Small; **Leo:** Leonard Stone; **Little Pete:** Eric Taslitz; **Tony:** Ron Thompson; **The Blonde:** Lynda Wiesmeier; **Other:** Hilary Beane

Beginning in 19th-century Russia, this animated musical odyssey follows the adventures of a troubled but talented family and chronicles popular American music from the turn of the century—from the pre-jazz age through soul, '50s rock, drug-laden psychadelia, punk and finally new wave of the early 1980s.

⊚ AN AMERICAN TAIL (1986)

An Amblin Entertainment Production released by Universal Pictures. **p:** Don Bluth, John Pomeroy, Gary Goldman; **d:** Don Bluth; **w:** Judy Freudberg, Tony Geiss (based on the story by David Kirschner, Judy Freudberg, Tony Geiss); **m:** James Horner; **anim dir:** John Pomeroy, Dan Kuenster, Linda Miller. **Songs:** "There Are No Cats in America," "Never Say Never," "Somewhere Out There," "A Duo" and "Stars and Stripes Forever." **Running time:** 80 minutes.

Voices

Mama Mousekewitz: Eric Yohn; **Papa Mousekewitz:** Nehemiah Persoff; **Tanya Mousekewitz:** Amy Green; **Fievel Mousekewitz:** Phillip Glasser; **Henri:** Christopher Plummer; **Warren T. Rat:** John Finnegan; **Digit:** Will Ryan; **Moe:** Hal Smith; **Tony Toponi:** Pat Musick; **Bridget:** Cathianne Blore; **Honest John:** Neil Ross; **Gussie Mausheimer:** Madeline Kahn; **Tiger:** Dom DeLuise.

When a clan of Jewish mice are forced to emigrate, little Fievel Mousekewitz is separated from his family, who is en route to New York. The cherubic mouse makes it to the New Land via a glass bottle and encounters many adventures—including his share of cats—until he is successfully reunited with his family.

PN: This was Steven Spielberg's first animated motion picture. It grossed $47 million and earned the honor of being the highest-grossing animated feature of that time. The song "Somewhere Out There" received a 1986 Oscar nomination for Best Song. A year later the home video edition was released and sold a whopping 1.3 million units.

⊚ AN AMERICAN TAIL: FIEVEL GOES WEST (1991)

A Steven Spielberg and Amblin Entertainment Production released by Universal Pictures. **d:** Phil Nebblink, Simon Wells; **p:** Steven Spielberg, Robert Watts; **exec prod:** Franik Marshall, Kathleen Kennedy, David Kirschner; **st:** Charles Swenson; **scr:** Flint Dille; **m:** James Horner, Will Jennings; **superv anim:** Nancy Beiman, Bibo Begeron, Ulrich W. Meyer, Christoph Serrand, Robert Stevenhagen. **Songs:** "Dreams to Dream," "American Tail Overture," "Cat Rumble," "Headin' Out West," "Way Out West," "Green River/Trek Through the Desert," "Building a New Town," "Sacred Mountain," "Reminiscing," "Girl You Left Behind," "In Training," "Shoot-Out" and "New Land." **Running time:** 75 minutes.

Voices

Fievel Mousekewitz: Phillip Glasser; **Mama:** Erica Yohn, **Papa:** Nehemiah Persoff; **Tanya:** Cath Cavadini; **Cat R. Waul:** John Cleese; **Tiger, Fievel's vegetarian cat friend:** Dom DeLuise; **Wylie Burp, over-the-hill marshall:** James Stewart; **Miss Kitty:** Amy Irving; **T.R. Chula:** Jon Lovitz

Two years after arriving in New York City from Russia, Fievel and his family discover the streets in America are "not paved with cheese" and decide to head West to seek a new promised land in this sequel to the 1986 original.

PN: A follow-up to the 1986 smash hit *An American Tail*, the Universal/Steven Spielberg animated movie premiered on Thanksgiving weekend opposite Disney's *Beauty and the Beast*. Don Bluth, who directed the highly successful *An American Tail*, was replaced by Phil Nibbelink and Simon Wells to direct the sequel, and animation was done by a new group of artists. The song "Dreams to Dream" received a Golden Globe nomination for Best Original Song.

⊚ ANASTASIA (1997)

A Fox Family/20th Century-Fox/Fox Animation Studios Production released by 20th Century-Fox. **p & d:** Don Bluth, Gary Goldman; **exec prod:** Maureen Donley; **scr:** Susan Gauthier, Bruce Graham, Bob Tzudiker, Noni White; **m:** David Newman (with songs by Stephen Flaherty); **dir** anim: Sandro Cleuzo, John Hill, Fernando Moro, Paul Newberry, Troy Saliba, Len Simon. **Songs:** "Once Upon a December," "A Rumor in St. Petersburg," "Journey to the Past," "In the Dark of the Night," "Learn to Do It," "Paris Holds the Key (to Your Heart)" and "At the Beginning." **Running time:** 94 minutes.

Voices

Anastasia: Meg Ryan; **Dimitri:** John Cusack; **Vladimir:** Kelsey Grammer; **Rasputin:** Christopher Lloyd; **Bartok:** Hank Azaria; **Sophie:** Bernadette Peters; **Young Anastasia:** Kirsten Dunst; **Dowager Empress Marie:** Angela Lansbury; **Anastasia (singing):** Liz Calloway; **Young Anastasia (singing):** Lacey Chabert; **Rasputin (singing):** Jim Cummings; **Dimitri (singing):** Jonathan Dokuchitz; **Czar Nicholas/Servant/Revolutionary Soldier/Ticket Agent:** Rick Jones; **Phlegmenkoff/Old Woman:** Andrea Martin; **Young Dimitri:** Glenn Walker Harris Jr.; **Actress:** Debra Mooney; **Travelling Man/Major Domo:** Arthur Malet; **Anastasia Impostor:** Charity James

An orphaned peasant girl who was a Russian princess finds true love in this modern-day romantic fairy tale. This classically animated musical explores what might have happened to the little girl long rumored to have survived the massacre of Russia's royal Romanovs.

PN: The first full-length animated feature ever produced by 20th Century-Fox—and first by the studio's Fox Animation Studios, based in Phoenix, Arizona—*Anastasia* was produced and directed by legendary animator Don Bluth and partner Gary Goldman. (Bluth is Fox Animation's studio head.) Costing an estimated $53 million to produce, the animated musical opened on 2,478 movie screens nationwide, grossing $14.242 million its first weekend and more than $48.36 million (through December 1997).

⊚ ARABIAN KNIGHT (1995)

An Allied Filmmakers/Majestic Film Production released by Miramax Films. **p:** Imogene Sutton, Richard Williams; **d:** Richard Williams; **st:** Margaret French; **scr:** Richard Williams, Margaret French; **m/sc:** Robert Folk. **Songs:** "Am I Feeling Love?" "Tack and Thief," "Polo Game," "She Is More," "The Courtroom," "The Brigands," "Pole Vault," "Club Sahara," "So Incredible," "Bom, Bom, Bom Beem, Bom," "Thief Gets the Ball," "One Eyes Advance," "Witch Riddle" and "Thief After the Balls." **Running time:** 80 minutes.

Voices

Tack, the Cobbler: Matthew Broderick; **Princess Yum Yum:** Jennifer Beals; **The Thief:** Jonathan Winters; **King Nod:** Clive Revill; **Zigzag:** Vincent Price; **Phido:** Eric Bogosian; **Nurse/Good Witch:** Toni Collette; **One-Eye:** Kevin Dorsey; **Princess Yum Yum (singing):** Bobbi Page

Additional Voices
Donald Pleasance

A timid shoemaker (Tack) recovers the three enchanted Golden Balls that protect the ancient city of Baghdad after they were stolen by a wicked wizard, saving the beloved city from destruction.

PN: Originally titled *Thief and the Cobbler*. Oscar-winning animator Richard Williams, of *Who Framed Roger Rabbit* fame, ran into financial trouble trying to get this film finished and released. In May of 1992 the film was over budget, prompting a Los Angeles completion bond firm to take control of the project. That company fired Williams and his London-based crew and hired TV producer Fred Calvert to finish the production. Because of his firing, Williams ceased operation of his London-based Richard Williams Animation and laid off about 30 animators plus other personnel. Warner Bros. originally intended to release the movie at Christmas. (The finished film was released instead by Miramax.) Williams had begun production in 1965. When he lost control of the project, only 70 minutes of the full-length feature had been completed, with 17 minutes of footage left to be animated. Some of the finest American animators came out of retirement to work on the film, including Grim Natwick, the creator of Betty Boop; Art Babbit, who animated the dancing mushroom and thistles in *Fantasia*, and two of the top animators of Warner Bros. cartoons: Ken Harris (who animated many of the Road Runner cartoons) and Emery Hawkins. It was the last animation done by all four, each of whom died before the film was completed. The finished film included animation, dialogue and music added after Williams departed the project. In 1995 Miramax Films released Williams's long-awaited masterpiece to mixed reviews and an even less enthusiastic moviegoing public. Final ticket sales totaled $500,000. The home video release was issued under the film's original title.

⊚ THE ARISTOCATS (1970)

A Walt Disney Production released by Buena Vista. **p:** Wolfgang Reitherman, Winston Hibler; **d:** Wolfgang Reitherman; **st:** Larry Clemmons, Vance Gerry, Frank Thomas, Julius Svendsen, Ken Anderson, Eric Cleworth, Ralph Wright (based on a story by Tom McGowan and Tom Rowe); **m:** George Bruns; **dir anim:** Milt Kahl, Frank Thomas, Ollie Johnston, John Lounsbery. **Songs:** "The Aristocats," "Scales and Arpeggios," "She Never Felt Alone" and "Thomas O'Malley Cat." **Running time:** 78 minutes.

Voices

Thomas O'Malley: Phil Harris; **Duchess:** Eva Gabor; **Roquefort:** Sterling Holloway; **Scat Cat:** Scatman Crothers; **Chinese Cat:** Paul Winchell; **English Cat:** Lord Tim Hudson; **Italian Cat:** Vito Scotti; **Russian Cat:** Thurl Ravenscroft; **Berlioz:** Dean Clark; **Marie:** Liz English; **Toulouse:**

Gary Dubin; **Frou-Frou:** Nancy Kulp; **Georges Hautecourt:** Charles Lane; **Madame Adelaide Bonafamille:** Hermione Baddeley; **Edgar:** Roddy Maude-Roxby; **Uncle Waldo:** Bill Thompson; **Lafayette:** George Lindsey; **Napoleon:** Pat Buttram; **Abigail Gabble:** Monica Evans; **Amelia Gabble:** Carole Shelley; **French Milkman:** Pete Renoudet

Duchess, a cat, and her three well-bred kittens, Berlioz, Toulouse and Marie, try to find their way back to Paris after a jealous butler (Edgar) angrily abandons them in the countryside.

◉ BABAR: THE MOVIE (1989)

A Nelvana Production released by New Line Cinema. **p:** Patrick Loubert, Michael Hirsh, Clive A. Smith; **d:** Alan Bunce; **scr:** Peter Sauder, J.D. Smith, John De Klein, Raymond Jaffelice, Alan Bunce (adapted from a story by Sauder, Loubert and Hirsh based on characters created by Jean and Laurent de Brunhoff); **m/s:** Milan Kymlicka; **anim dir:** John Laurence Collins. Songs: "Elephantland March," "The Best We Both Can Be," "Monkey Business," "Committee Song" and "Rataxes Song." **Running time:** 70 minutes.

Voices

King Babar/the Elder: Gordon Pinsent; **Queen Celeste/ Old Lady:** Elizabeth Hanna; **Isabelle:** Lisa Yamanaka; **Flora:** Marsha Moreau; **Pom:** Bobby Becken; **Alexander:** Amos Crawley: **Boy Babar:** Gavin Magrath; **Young Celeste:** Sarah Polley; **Pompadour:** Stephen Ouimette; **Cornelius:** Chris Wiggins; **Zephir;** John Stocker; **Rataxes:** Charles Kerr; **Old Tusk:** Stuart Stone; **Celeste's Mom:** Angela Fusco

In the form of a bedtime story, King Babar recalls for his children his first day as boy-king of Elephantland and his ensuing battle to save the nearby village—the home of his sweetheart, Celeste—from decimation by a tyrannical cult of elephant-enslavening rhinos.

◉ BALTO (1995)

A Universal Pictures/Amblin Entertainment Production released by Universal Pictures. **p:** Steve Hickner; **d:** Simon Wells; **exec prod:** Steven Spielberg, Kathleen Kennedy, Bonnie Radford; **st:** Clif Ruby, Elana Lesser (based on a true story); **scr:** Cliff Ruby, Elana Lesser, David Steven Cohen, Roger S.H. Schulman; **m:** James Horner (with song "Reach for the Light" written by Barry Mann and James Horner); **superv anim:** David Bowers, Shahin Ersoz, Rodolphe Guenoden, Nicolas Marlet, Patrick Mate, William Salazar, Christoph Serrand, Robert Stevenhagen, Jeffrey James Varab, Dick Zondag. Songs: "Reach for the Light." **Running time:** 78 minutes.

Cast (live action)

Grandma: Miriam Margolyes; **Granddaughter:** Lola Bates-Campbell

Voices

Balto: Kevin Bacon; **Boris:** Bob Hoskins; **Jenna:** Bridget Fonda; **Steele:** Jim Cummings; **Muk/Luk:** Phil Collins; **Nikki:** Jack Angel; **Kaltag:** Danny Mann; **Star:** Robbie Rist; **Rosy:** Juliette Brewer; **Sylvie/Dixie/Rosy's Mother:** Sandra Searles Dickinson; **Doc:** Donald Sinden; **Rosy's Father:** William Roberts; **Telegraph Operator:** Garrick Hagon; **Butcher:** Bill Bailey; **Town Dog:** Big Al; **Grandma Rosy:** Miriam Margolyes; **Granddaughter:** Lola Bates-Campbell

Additional Voices

Michael McShane, Austin Tichenor, Reed Martin, Adam Long, Jennifer Blanc, Jim Carter, Christine Cavanaugh, Brendan Fraser, Michael Shannon

In 1925 a courageous dog named Balto, who is half wolf, half husky, leads a team of sled dogs on a 600-mile trip across the Alaskan wilderness, braving blizzard conditions for five days, to deliver antitoxin to the diphtheria-stricken residents of Nome, Alaska. Based on a true story.

PN: This Steven Spielberg film, with its largely British production team, was headed by Simon Wells and Steve Hickner, who previously supervised animation for Disney's milestone animated feature *Who Framed Roger Rabbit*. The film grossed a disappointing $11.268 million in the United States.

◉ BAMBI (1942)

A Walt Disney Production released by RKO Radio Pictures. **p:** Walt Disney; **superv dir:** David D. Hand; **st (adaptation):** Larry Morey; **st dev:** George Stallings, Melvin Shaw, Carl Fallberg, Chuck Couch, Ralph Wright (based on the book by Felix Salten); **m:** Frank Churchill, Edward H. Plumb; **seq dir:** James Algar, Bill Roberts, Norman Wright, Sam Armstrong, Paul Satterfield, Graham Heid; **superv anim:** Franklin Thomas, Milt Kahl, Eric Larson, Oliver M. Johnston Jr. Songs: "Love Is a Song," "Let's sing a Gay Little Spring Song," "Little April Shower" and "Looking for Romance (I Bring You a Song)." **Running time:** 69 1/2 minutes.

Voices

Bambi: Bobby Stewart; **Bambi:** Donnie Dunagan; **Bambi:** Hardy Albright; **Bambi:** John Sutherland; **Bambi's mother:** Paula Winslowe; **Faline:** Cammie King, Ann Gillis; **Aunt Ena/Mrs. Possum:** Mary Lansing; **Prince of the Forest:** Fred Shields; **Friend Owl:** Bill Wright; **Flower:** Stanley Alexander; **Flower:** Sterling Holloway; **Thumper:** Peter Behn; **Thumper/Flower:** Tim Davis; **Mrs. Quail:** Thelma Boardman; **Mrs. Rabbit:** Marjorie Lee

Additional Voices

Bobette Audrey, Janet Chapman, Jeanne Christy, Dolyn Bramston Cook, Marion Darlington, Otis Harlan, Jack Horner, Thelma Hubbard, Babs Nelson, Sandra Lee Richards, Francesca Santoro, Elouise Woodward

A newborn prince of the forest (Bambi) learns about love, friendship and survival—with the help of fellow forest dwellers including Flower the skunk and Thumper the rabbit—as he conquers both man and nature to take his rightful place as king of the forest.

⊚ BATMAN: MARK OF PHANTASM (1993)

A Warner Bros. Production released by Warner Bros. **p:** Benjamin Melniker, Michael Uslan; **cpd:** Alan Burnett, Erich Radomski, Bruce W. Timm; **exec prod:** Tom Ruegger; **d:** Eric Radomski, Bruce W. Timm; **scr:** Alan Burnett, Paul Dini, Martin Pasko, Michael Reaves (based on the DC Comics character created by Bob Kane); **m:** Shirley Walker; **anim dir:** Se-Won Kim, Young-Hwan Sang, Chung Ho Kim, Sun Hee Lee, Yukio Suzuki, Yutaka Oka, Noburo Takahashi; **superv anim:** Ric Machin. **Songs:** "I Never Even Told You" (performed by Tia Carrere). **Running time:** 77 minutes.

Voices

Batman/Bruce Wayne: Kevin Conroy; **Andrea Beaumont:** Dana Delany; **Councilman Arthur Reeves:** Hart Bochner; **Phantasm/Carl Beaumont:** Stacy Keach Jr.; **Salvatore Valestra:** Abe Vigoda; **Chuckie Sol:** Dick Miller; **Buzz Bronski:** John P. Ryan; **Alfred the Butler:** Efrem Zimbalist Jr.; **Commissioner Gordon:** Bob Hastings; **Detective Bullock:** Robert Coztanzo; **The Joker:** Mark Hamill

Additional Voices

Jeff Bennett, Jane Downs, Ed Gilbert, Mark Hamill, Marilu Henner, Charles Howarton, Vernee Watson-Johnson, Pat Musick, Thom Pinto, Peter Renaday, Neil Ross

Batman tries to save face after being accused of a series of murders he did not commit and attempts to uncover the real killer, known as The Phantasm, in this absorbing, first-ever full-length animated feature based on the popular DC Comics character. A sequel, *Batman: Sub-Zero*, was released direct-to-video in 1998.

PN: Warner Bros. originally planned to produce this animated feature spun off from the popular animated TV series directly to video but, after the project was substantially completed, deemed it strong enough for theatrical release. The feature tallied $5.6 million in ticket sales and was a big hit on home video as well. The film's original working title was *Batman: The Animated Movie*.

⊚ BEAUTY AND THE BEAST (1991)

A Walt Disney Picture released by Buena Vista. **p:** Don Hahn; **d:** Gary Trousdale, Kirk Wise; **exec prod:** Don Hahn; **scr:** Linda Woolverton; **m:** Alan Menken; **superv anim:** Ruben A. Aquino, James Barter, Andreas Deja, Will Winn, Mark Henn, David Pruiksma, Nik Ranieri, Chris Wahl. **Songs:** "Beauty and the Beast," "Be Our Guest," "Belle," "How Long Must This Go On," "If I Can't Love Her," "Something There," "The Mob Song" and "Maison des Lumes." **Running time:** 84 minutes.

Voices

Belle: Paige O'Hara; **Beast:** Robby Benson; **Gaston:** Richard White; **Lumiere:** Jerry Orbach; **Cogsworth/Narrator:** David Ogden Stiers; **Mrs. Potts:** Angele Lansbury; **Chip:** Bradley Michael Pierce; **Maurice:** Rex Everhart; **LeFou:** Jesse Corti; **Philippe:** Hal Smith; **Wardrobe:** Jo Anne Worley; **Bimbette:** Mary Kay Bergman; **Stove:** Brian Cummings; **Bookseller:** Alvin Epstein; **Monsieur D'Arque:** Tony Jay; **Baker:** Alec Murphy; **Featherduster:** Kimmy Robertson; **Footstool:** Frank Welker; **Mimbette:** Kath Soucie

A cruel prince who is turned into a hideous beast must win the love of a beautiful young enchantress to break the spell cast upon him in this animated musical version of the classic children's fairy tale.

PN: In the first eight weeks, *Beauty and the Beast* earned $82.5 million in box-office revenue and broke the previous record set by *The Little Mermaid* (which had earned $84.3 million during its release), becoming the first animated feature to surpass the $100-million mark (final gross: $144.8 million). Originally a dark, straightforward, nonmusical retelling of this classic fairy tale was planned, but it was scuttled after Disney executives saw the first reel. Nominated for six Academy Awards (including an unprecedented three nominations for the film's musical score and songs), it became the first animated feature ever nominated for Best Picture. Joe Grant, who developed the characters and stories for Walt Disney's *Snow White and the Seven Dwarfs*, *Pinocchio*, *Dumbo*, *Fantasia*, among others and had left the studio in 1949, returned for a second stint to work on this film, after a 40-year absence from the film business. He also worked on subsequent Disney animated features, including *Aladdin*, *The Lion King* and *Pocahontas* (the latter at 86 years of age).

⊚ BEAVIS AND BUTT-HEAD DO AMERICA (1996)

A Geffen Pictures/MTV/Paramount Production released by Paramount Pictures. **p:** Abby Terkuhle; **d:** Mike Judge, Yvette Kaplan; **cpd:** John Andrews; **exec prod:** David Gale, Van Toffler; **scr:** Mike Judge, Joe Stillman (based on the television series, *Beavis and Butt-Head*); **m:** John C. Frizzell.

Songs: "Two Cool Guys," "Love Rollercoaster," "Ain't Nobody," "Ratfinks, Suicide Tanks and Cannibal Girls," "I Wanna Riot," "Walk on Water," "Snakes," "Pimp'n Aint Ez," "Lord Is a Monkey," "White Trash," "Gone Shootin'" and "Lesbian Seagull." **Running time:** 80 minutes.

Voices

Beavis/Butt-Head/Tom Anderson/Mr. Van: Mike Judge; **FBI Agent Flemming:** Robert Stack; **Martha:** Cloris Leachman; **Agent Hurly:** Jacqueline Barba; **Flight Attendant/White House Tour Guide:** Pamela Blair; **Ranger:** Eric Bogosian; **Man on Plane/Second Man in Confession Booth/Old Guy/Jim:** Kristofor Brown; **Motley Crue Roadie #2/Tourist Man:** Tony Darling; **Airplane Captain/White House Representative:** John Donman; **Petrified Forest Recording:** Jim Flaherty; **Hoover Guide/ATF Agent:** Tim Guinee; **Motley Crue Roadie #1:** David Letterman; **TV Chief #2/Concierge/Bellboy/Male TV Reporter:** Toby Huss; **Limo Driver/TV Chief #1/Man in Confession Booth #1/Petrified Forest Ranger:** Sam Johnson; **Tour Bus Driver:** Richard Linklater; **Flight Attendant #2:** Rosemary McNamara; **Indian Dignitary:** Harsh Nayyar; **Announcer in Capitol:** Karen Phillips; **President Clinton:** Dale Reeves; **Hoover Technician/General at Strategic Air Command:** Michael Ruschak; **Flight Attendant #3/Female TV Reporter:** Gail Thomas; **FBI Agent Bork:** Greg Kinnear; **Dallas Grimes:** Demi Moore; **Muddy Grimes:** Bruce Willis

Additional Voices
David Spade

MTV junkies Beavis and Butt-Head wake up to find their television stolen. They embark on an epic journey across America to recover it, only to become wanted by the FBI (they're mistaken for two of America's most dangerous men alive) in their first full-length animated feature, based on the popular television series.

PN: Produced at a cost of $12 million, this crudely animated feature opened on 2,190 movie screens and grossed a stunning $20.114 million the weekend it opened. The film's total domestic gross was $63.071 million.

◉ BEBE'S KIDS (1992)
A Hudlin Bros./Hyperion Studio Production released by Paramount Pictures. **p:** William Carroll, Thomas L. Wilhite, David Robert Cobb; **d:** Bruce Smith; **exec prod:** Reginald Hudlin, Warrington Hudlin; **scr:** Reginald Hudlin (based on the album *Bebe's Kids* by Robin Harris); **m:** John Barnes; **superv anim:** Lennie K. Graves. **Songs:** "On Our Worst Behavior," "Standing on the Rock of Love," "Can't Say Goodbye," "I Got the 411," "Your Love Keep Working on Me," "All My Love," "Straight Jackin'," "Freedom Song" and "Oh No." **Running time:** 70 minutes.

Robin Harris (in cartoon form) has his own troubles in this scene from the animated musical based on the late comedian's life, Bebe's Kids. *© Paramount Pictures*

Voices

Robin Harris: Faizon Love; **Jamika:** Vanessa Bell Calloway; **Leon:** Wayne Collins Jr.; **LaShawn:** Jonell Green; **Kahill:** Marques Houston; **Pee Wee:** Tone Loc; **Dorothea:** Myra J.; **Vivian:** Nell Carter; **Card Player #1:** John Witherspoon; **Card Player #2:** Chino "Fats" Williams; **Card Player #3:** Rodney Winfield; **Card Player #4:** George D. Wallace; **Bartender:** Brad Sanders; **Lush:** Reynaldo Rey; **Barfly:** Bebe Drake-Massey; **Richie:** Jack Lynch; **Opie:** Phillip Glasser; **Security Guard #1:** Louie Anderson; **Security Guard #2:** Tom Everett; **Security Guard #2/Fun World Patrolman:** Kerrigan Mahan; **Ticket/Lady/Saleswoman/Nuclear Mother/Rodney Rodent:** Susan Silo; **Announcer/President Lincoln/Impericon/Tommy Toad:** Pete Renaday; **President Nixon:** Rich Little; **Titanic Captain:** David Robert Cobb; **Nuclear Father/Motorcycle Cop:** Barry Diamond

Additional Voices
Stanley B. Clay, Michelle Davison, Judi M. Durand, Greg Finley, Maui France, Jaquita Green, Jamie Gunderson, J.D. Hall, Doris Hess, Barbara Iley, Daamen J. Krall, John Lafayette, Tina Lifford, Josh Lindsay, Arvie Lowe Jr., DeVaughn Nixon, David Randolph, Noreen Reardon, Gary Schwartz, Cheryl Tyre Smith

In this amusing animated musical comedy, based on characters created by the late comedian Robin Harris, Robin's first date with a beautiful woman is foiled when she insists that her well-mannered son and her friend Bebe's three irrepressible kids accompany them, turning their trip to an amusement park into a nightmare.

PN: The first animated featured produced by Hyperion Studios as part of a multifilm deal with Paramount Pictures, *Bebe's Kids* was also the first animated theatrical feature to star all–African American characters. The film was promoted as "Animation with an attitude."

◎ THE BLACK CAULDRON (1985)

A Walt Disney Production in association with Silver Screen Partners II released through Buena Vista. p: Joe Hale; d: Ted Berman, Richard Rich; st: David Jonas, Vance Gerry, Al Wilson, Roy Morita, Ted Berman, Peter Young, Richard Rich, Art Stevens, Joe Hale (based on Lloyd Alexander's five *Chronicles of Prydain* books); m: Elmer Bernstein. **Running time:** 80 minutes.

Voices
Taran: Grant Bardsley; **Eilonwy:** Susan Sheridan; **Dallben:** Freddie Jones; **Fflewddur Fflam:** Nigel Hawthorne; **King Eidilleg:** Arthur Malet; **Gurgi/Doli:** John Byner; **Orddu:** Eda Reiss Merin; **Orwen:** Adele Malia-Morey; **Orgoch:** Billie Hayes; **The Horned King:** John Hurt; **Creeper/Henchman:** Phil Fondacaro; **Narrator:** John Huston; **Fairfolk:** Lindsday Ric, Brandon Call, Gregory Levinson; **Henchmen:** Peter Renaday, James Almanzar, Wayne Allwine, Steve Hale, Phil Nibbelink, Jack Laing

Taran, a young man who dreams of becoming a warrior, is put to the test as he battles the evil Horned King, who is determined to gain possession of the "black cauldron," a source of supernatural power, to use to further his misdeeds. Taran is joined by a cast of characters in his quest, including Princess Elowny, Hen Wen, a psychic pig and Gurgi, a sycophantic creature.

PN: More than 2.5 million drawings were used to create this $25-million feature, which took 10 years to complete. The film was shot in 70 millimeter, only the second to ever be done in that wide-screen format. (The first was *Sleeping Beauty* in 1959.) The movie was also the first Disney cartoon feature to merit a PG rating.

◎ BON VOYAGE, CHARLIE BROWN (AND DON'T COME BACK) (1980)

A Lee Mendelson–Bill Melendez Production released through Paramount Pictures. p & d: Lee Mendelson, Bill Melendez; w: Charles M. Schulz (based on the *Peanuts* characters); m: Ed Bogas, Judy Munsen. **Running time:** 75 minutes.

Voices
Charlie Brown: Arrin Skelley; **Peppermint Patty:** Laura Planting; **Marcie:** Casey Carlson; **Linus:** Daniel Anderson;

Sally Brown: Annalisa Bartolin; **Snoopy:** Bill Melendez; **Waiter/Baron/Driver/Tennis Announcer/English Voice/American Male:** Scott Beach

As exchange students, Charlie Brown and the gang visit both England, where Snoopy competes at Wimbeldon, and France, where they find themselves the guests of a mysterious benefactor in a historic chateau.

◎ A BOY NAMED CHARLIE BROWN (1969)

A Lee Mendelson–Bill Melendez Production released by New General Pictures. p: Lee Mendelson, Bill Melendez; d: Bill Melendez; w: Charles M. Schulz; m: Vince Guaraldi; m/s: Rod McKuen. **Songs:** "Piano Sonata Opus 13 (Pathetique)," "Failure Face," "Champion Charlie Brown," "Cloud Dreams," "Charlie Brown and His All Stars," "We Lost Again," "Blue Charlie Brown," "Time to Go to School," "I Only Dread One Day at a Time," "By Golly I'll Show 'Em," "Class Champion," "School Spelling Bee," "Start Boning Up on Your Spelling, Charlie Brown," "You'll Either Be a Hero . . . or a Goat," "Bus Station," "Do Piano Players Make a Lot of Money?" "I've Got to Get My Blanket Back," "Big City," "Found Blanket," "National Spelling Bee," "B-E-A-G-L-E," "Homecoming," "I'm Never Going to School Again," "Welcome Home, Charlie Brown" and "I Before E." **Running time:** 86 minutes.

Voices
Charlie Brown: Peter Robbins; **Lucy:** Pamelyn Ferdin; **Linus:** Glenn Gilger; **Sally:** Erin Sullivan; **Patty:** Sally Dryer Barker; **Violet:** Ann Altieri, **Pigpen:** Christopher Defaria; **Schroeder:** Andy Pforsich; **Frieda:** Linda Mendelson; **Singers:** Betty Allan; Loulie Norman, Gloria Wood; **Boys:** David Carey, Guy Pforsich; **Snoopy:** Bill Melendez

Charlie Brown, who never seems able to do anything right, surprises himself and his friends by being chosen for the national spelling bee in New York. True to form, he loses, on national television no less, but is nevertheless given a hero's welcome when he returns home.

◎ THE BRAVE LITTLE TOASTER (1987)

A Kushner-Locke/Hyperion Pictures Production released by Walt Disney Pictures. p: Donald Kushner, Thomas L. Wilhite; d: Jerry Rees; coprod: Cleve Reinhard; exec prod: Willard Carroll, Peter Locke; st: Joe Ranft, Jerry Reese, Brian McEntee (based on the novella by Thomas M. Disch); scr: Joe Ranft, Jerry Rees; m: David Newman (with songs by Van Dyke Parks); anim dir: Randy Cartwright, Joe Ranft, Rebecca Rees. **Songs:** "City of Light," "It's a B-Movie," "Cutting Edge," "Worthless," "Hidden Meadow," "Tutti Frutti," "My Mammy" and "April Showers." **Running time:** 90 minutes.

Voices
Radio: Jon Lovitz; **Lampy/Zeke:** Tim Stack; **Blanky/Young Master/Kirby:** Thurl Ravenscroft; **Toaster:** Deanna Oliver; **Air Conditioner/Hanging Lamp:** Phil Hartman; **Elmo St. Peters:** Joe Ranft; **Mish-Mash/Two-Face Sewing Machine:** Judy Toll; **Rob:** Wayne Katz; **Chris:** Colette Savage; **Mother/Two-Face Sewing Machine:** Mindy Stern; **Plugsy:** Jim Jackman; **Entertainment Center:** Randy Cook; **Computer:** Randy Bennett; **Black and White TV:** Jonathan Benair; **Spanish Announcer:** Louis Conti

Based on Thomas M. Disch's charming 1986 novella, five household appliances—Toaster (also known as "Slots" to his pals), Blankey, the electric blanket, Kirby, the grumpy vacuum cleaner, Lampy, the desk lamp, and Radio, the wiseguy chatterbox—abandoned in a rustic family cabin, set out to find their 13-year-old Master, who gave their secret lives meaning.

PN: Following completion of this $1.8-million animated feature, the producers had trouble securing a distributor for the film. In 1988 the film was broadcast on The Disney Channel; in 1989 and 1990 it played in theaters in selected cities.

⊚ BRAVESTARR, THE MOVIE (1988)

A Filmation Production released by Taurus Entertainment. **p:** Lou Scheimer; **d:** Tom Tataranowicz; **scr:** Bob Forward, Steve Hayes; **m:** Frank W. Becker; **superv anim:** Brett Hisey. **Running time:** 91 minutes.

Voices
Charlie Adler, Susan Blu, Pat Fraley, Ed Gilbert, Alan Oppenheimer, Eric Gunden, Erika Scheimer

Bravestarr, who comes from a place steeped in Indian culture to futuristic New Texas, meets his nemesis, Tex-Hex, for the first time.

PN: In movie theater ads, this film was billed as *Bravestarr, The Movie,* even though initially prints of the film reflected the original title, *Bravestarr, The Legend.*

⊚ THE BUGS BUNNY/ROAD RUNNER MOVIE (1979)

A Warner Bros. release. **p & d:** Chuck Jones; **w:** Michael Maltese, Chuck Jones; **m:** Carl Stalling, Milt Franklyn. **Running time:** 92 minutes.

Voices
Mel Blanc

Bugs Bunny looks back on his past triumphs in this entertaining compilation that ties in 20 minutes of new animation with old Warner cartoons, in full or part. (New footage has Bugs giving audiences a tour of his Beverly Hills estate as he fondly recalls the highlights of his 40-year career.) The five complete cartoons featured are "Hareway to Stars," "What's Opera, Doc?", "Duck Amuck," "Bully for Bugs" and "Rabbit Fire," plus excerpts from eight others, along with an 11-minute Road Runner tribute consisting of 31 gags culled from 16 cartoons.

PN: Warner Bros. had a difficult time deciding what to call this feature. The original titles that were bantered about included *The Great Bugs Bunny/Road Runner Chase* and *The Great American Bugs Bunny/Road Runner Chase.*

⊚ BUGS BUNNY'S THIRD MOVIE—1001 RABBIT TALES (1982)

A Warner Bros. release. **p:** Friz Freleng; **seq dir:** Dave Detiege, Friz Freleng; **m:** Rob Walsh, Bill Lava, Milt Franklyn, Carl Stalling. **Running time:** 76 minutes.

Voices
Mel Blanc, Shep Menken, Lennie Weinrib

As rival book salesmen for "Rambling House Publishers," Bugs Bunny and Daffy Duck travel the world to find new areas to market their wares, including the Arabian desert. Other characters featured include Yosemite Sam, Tweety and Sylvester. New animated wraparounds introduce several complete cartoons, previously released to theaters: "Ali Baba Bunny," "Apes of Wrath," "Betwitched Bunny," "Cracked Quack," "Goldimouse and the Three Cats," "Mexican Boarders," "One Froggy Evening," "Pied Piper of Guadalupe" and others.

PN: The sequel to this third Bugs Bunny compilation is 1983's *Daffy Duck's Movie: Fantastic Island.*

⊚ BUGS BUNNY, SUPERSTAR (1975)

A Hair Raising Films Inc. release through Warner Bros. **p & d:** Larry Jackson; **anim dir:** Chuck Jones, Bob Clampett, Tex Avery, Friz Freleng, Robert McKimson. **Running time:** 91 minutes.

Voices
Mel Blanc; **Narrator:** Orson Welles

Famed Warner Warner Bros. animators Friz Freleng, Tex Avery and Bob Clampett appear in this documentary film on Warner Bros. cartoons of the 1940s. Interspersed between interview segments are complete cartoon versions of "What's Cooking Doc?" "A Wild Hare," "I Taw a Putty Tat," "Rhapsody Rabbit," "Corny Concerto," "Walky Talky Hawky," "The Old Grey Hare," "My Favorite Duck" and "Hair Raising Hare."

⊚ THE CARE BEARS ADVENTURE IN WONDERLAND (1987)

A Nelvana Production released by Cineplex Odeon Films. **p:** Michael Hirsh, Patrick Loubert, Clive A. Smith; **d:** Raymond Jafelice; **w:** Susan Snooks, John De Klein (based on a story by Peter Sauder); **m:** Trish Cullen; **m/l:** John Sebastian, Maribeth Solomon; **superv anim:** John Laurence Collins. **Running time:** 75 minutes.

Voices

Grumpy Bear: Bob Dermer; **Swift Heart Rabbit:** Eva Almos; **Brave Heart Lion/Dum:** Dan Hennessey; **Tenderheart Bear:** Jim Henshaw; **Good Luck Bear:** Marla Lukofsky; **Lots-a-Heart Elephant:** Louba Goy; **White Rabbit:** Keith Knight; **Alice:** Tracey Moore; **Wizard:** Colin Fox; **Dim/Cheshire Cat:** John Stocker; **Caterpillar:** Don McManus; **Queen of Wonderland:** Elizabeth Hanna; **Flamingo:** Alan Fawcett; **Mad Hatter/Jabberwocky:** Keith Hampshire; **Princess:** Alyson Court

Combining the flavor of Lewis Carroll's *Alice in Wonderland* and Frank Baum's *Wizard of Oz*, this third Care Bears feature casts the cuddly characters in Wonderland where they search for Alice, who has been abducted by an evildoing wizard who has designs on ruling the great land. Along the way they meet up with all sorts of interesting characters—The Mad Hatter, Tweedledee and Tweedledum, Cheshire Cat and others—who appeared in the Disney classic *Alice in Wonderland*.

PN: Nelvana produced this third and final Care Bears feature, which earned a disappointing $3 million. The first movie in the series made almost three times as much at the box office.

THE CARE BEARS MOVIE (1985)

A Nelvana Production released by Samuel Goldwyn. **p:** Michael Hirsch, Patrick Loubert, Clive Smith; **d:** Arna Selznick; **w:** Peter Sauder; **m:** John Sebastian, Walt Woodward, Trish Cullen; **m/l:** John Sebastian, title song. **Running time:** 75 minutes.

Voices

Mr. Cherrywood: Mickey Rooney; **Love-a-Lot Bear:** Georgia Engel; **Brave Heart Lion:** Harry Dean Stanton

In the land of Care-A-Lot two orphaned siblings, Kim and Jason, develop friendships with the Care Bears and experience the warm, good feelings of these cuddly creatures. Such feelings are temporarily dashed by the Evil Spirit, who casts a third child, Nicholas, under his power. Nicholas is to help the Evil Spirit by creating spells that remove all the care and feeling from the world.

CARE BEARS MOVIE II: A NEW GENERATION (1986)

A Nelvana Production released by Columbia Pictures. **p:** Michael Hirsh, Patrick Loubert, Clive A. Smith; **d:** Dale Schott; **scr:** Peter Sauder; **m:** Patricia Cullen; **anim dir:** Charles Bonifacio. **Songs:** "Our Beginning," "Flying My

Noble Heart Horse (left) and True Heart Bear (second from left), the co-founders of the Care Bear Family, and Care Bears Cubs, Secret Cub (second from right) and Tenderheart (right), look on as Care Cousin Cub Lil' Bright Heart Racoon slides down a rainbow in Care Bears Movie II: A New Generation *(1986).* (COURTESY: NELVANA LIMITED)

Colors," "I Care for You," "Growing Up," "Care Bears Cheer Song" and "Forever Young." **Running time:** 77 minutes.

Voices

True Heart Bear: Maxine Miller; **Noble Heart Horse:** Pam Hyatt; **Dark Heart/The Boy:** Hadley Kay; **Christy:** Cree Summer Francks; **Dawn:** Alyson Court; **John:** Michael Fantini

True Heart Bear and Noble Heart Horse venture from their home base at the Great Wishing Star on a mission to a summer camp to teach a couple of self-centered youngsters the virtues of sharing and caring.

PN: This Nelvana theatrical cartoon feature release grabbed $8 million in ticket sales.

CASPER (1995)

An Amblin Entertainment Production in association with The Harvey Entertainment Company released by Universal Pictures. **p:** Jeff Franklin, Steve Waterman; **d:** Brad Siberling; **exec prod:** Gerald R. Molen, Jeffrey A. Montgomery, Steven Spielberg; **scr:** Sherri Stoner, Deanna Oliver (based on the character of Casper the Friendly Ghost created by Joseph Oriolo in the story by Joseph Oriolo and Seymour Reit); **m:** James Horner; **anim dir:** Armstrong, Phil Nibbelink. **Songs:** "Casper the Friendly Ghost," "That's Life," "Same Song" and "Remember Me This Way." **Running time:** 101 minutes.

Cast/Voices

Kat: Christina Ricci; **Dr. Harvey;** Bill Pullman; **Carrigan:** Cathy Moriarty; **Dibs:** Eric Idle; **Stretch:** Joe Nipote;

Stinkie: Joe Alaskey; **Fatso:** Brad Garrett; **Vic:** Garette Ratliff Henson; **Amber:** Jessica Wesson; **Amelia:** Amy Brenneman; **Casper:** Malachi Pearson; **Nicky:** Chauncey Leopardi; **Andreas:** Spencer Vrooman; **Rugg:** Ben Stein; **Father Guido Sarducci:** Don Novello; **Himself:** Fred Rogers; **Herself:** Terry Murphy; **Woman Being Interviewed:** Ernestine Mercer; **Reporter:** Douglas J.O. Bruckner; **Himself:** Rodney Dangerfield; **The Crypt Keeper:** Jon Kassir; **Mr. Curtis:** Wesley Thompson; **Student #1:** Michael Dubrow; **Student #2:** J.J. Anderson; **Arnold:** Jess Harnell; **Drunk in Bar:** Michael McCarty; **Student:** Micah Winkelspecht; **Phantom:** Mike Simmrin; **Casper on Screen:** Devon Sawa; **Dr. Raymond Stantz:** Dan Aykroyd; **Himself:** Clint Eastwood, Mel Gibson

Determined to get her hands on hidden treasure, the daughter of a late millionaire hires an afterlife therapist, Dr. Harvey, to exorcise ghosts from her father's less-than-livable mansion. The therapist and the daughter take up residence in the mansion until the ghosts are driven away.

PN: Based on the popular theatrical cartoon star and comic-book character, *Casper* featured the first "computer-generated" star of a major motion picture and turned out to be a major performer where it counted: at the box office. Budgeted at $55 million, the film grossed $100 million domestically and $282 million worldwide and even spawned a direct-to-home video sequel.

◎ CAT CITY (1987)

A Pannonia Film/Sefel Pictures release. **d:** Bela Ternovsky; **w:** Jozsef Nepp; **m:** Tamas Deak. **Running time:** 93 minutes.

The entire mouse population may soon be extinct thanks to a secret weapon developed by a group of nasty cats who are slowly taking over the world. Intermaus, an international mouse intelligence agency, enlists the services of its top agent, Grabowski, to find the blueprints to the weapon and restore order.

PN: This film was produced by Budapest's top animation studio, Pannonia. Features English subtitles.

◎ CATS DON'T DANCE (1997)

A Turner Pictures/Turner Feature Animation/David Kirschner Production released by Warner Bros. **p:** Bill Bloom, Paul Gertz, David Kirschner; **d:** Mark Dindal; **cpd:** Jim Katz, Barry Weiss; **exec prod:** David Steinberg, Charles L. Richardson, Sandy Russell Gartin; **st:** Mark Dindal, Robert Lence, Brian McEntee, Rick Schneider, David Womersley, Kelvin Yasuda; "**scr:** Robert Gannaway, Cliff Ruby, Elana Lesser, Theresa Pettengell; **m:** Steve Goldstein (with songs by Randy Newman); **dir anim:** Jill Culton, Lennie K. Graves, Jay Jackson, Kevin Johnson, Bob Scott, Frans Vischer; **superv anim:** Chad Stewart, Steven Wahl. **Songs:** "Our Time Has Come," "I Do Believe," "Danny's Arrival Song," "Little Boat on the Sea," "Animal Jam," "Big

and Loud," "Tell Me Lies," "Nothing's Gonna Stop Us Now," "Once Upon a Time . . ." and "Tea Time for Danny." **Running time:** 75 minutes.

Voices

Danny: Scott Bakula; **Sawyer (speaking):** Jasmine Guy; **Sawyer (singing):** Natalie Cole; **Darla Dimple (speaking):** Ashley Peldon; **Darla Dimple (singing):** Lindsay Rideway; **Tillie Hippo:** Kathy Najimy; **Woolie Mammoth:** John Rhys-Davies; **L.B. Mammoth:** George Kennedy; **Flanigan:** Rene Auberjonois; **Francis:** Betty Lou Gerson; **Cranston:** Hal Holbrook; **T.W. Turtle:** Don Knotts; *Pudge the Penguin:* Matthew Harried, **Francis Betty:** Lou Gerson; **Farley Wink:** Frank Welker; **Bus Driver:** David Johansen; **Max:** Mark Dindal

A young, optimistic cat named Danny heads to Hollywood, with a song in his heart and dance moves in his feet, to become a film star, only to learn that Hollywood is a cruel and unforgiving town.

PN: Songs for *Cats Don't Dance* were written by Randy Newman, of "I Love L.A." fame, who also penned the Oscar-nominated songs for Disney's *Toy Story*. The songs were sung by Natalie Cole. The movie's song-and-dance numbers were choreographed by famed MGM song-and-dance man Gene Kelly, who died that year. A high-speed digital ink and paint system, created by USAnimation, was used to create the film's digitally composited 2-D cel animation look, replacing traditional painting and camera methods. Even though the film was beautifully animated, *Cats Don't Dance* lasted only one week in movie theaters, grossing a mere $3.562 million at the box office.

◎ CHARLOTTE'S WEB (1973)

A Hanna-Barbera Production released by Paramount Pictures. **p:** William Hanna, Joseph Barbera; **d:** Charles A. Nichols, Iwao Takamoto; **w:** Earl Hamner Jr. (based on the book by E.B. White); **m:** Richard M. Sherman, Robert M. Sherman. **Songs:** "Charlotte's Web," "A Veritable Smorgasbord," "There Must Be Something More," "I Can Talk," "Mother Earth and Father Time," "We've Got Lots in Common," "Deep in the Dark" and "Zukerman's Famous Pig." **Running time:** 94 minutes.

Voices

Charlotte: Debbie Reynolds; **Templeton:** Paul Lynde; **Wilbur:** Henry Gibson; **Narrator:** Rex Allen; **Mrs. Arable:** Martha Scott; **Old Sheep:** Dave Madden; **Avery:** Danny Bonaduce; **Geoffrey:** Don Messick; **Lurvy:** Herb Vigran; **The Goose:** Agnes Moorehead; **Fern Arable:** Pam Ferdin; **Mrs. Zuckerman/Mrs. Fussy:** Joan Gerber; **Homer Zuckerman:** Robert Holt; **Arable:** John Stephenson; **Henry Fussy:** William B. White

Wilbur, a runt pig who has been a pet of a New England farmer, is sold to a neighbor where he is told by a sheep that he is ticketed for the slaughterhouse. His life changes upon meeting a spider named Charlotte, who devotes all her energies to saving Wilbur from a pig's fate.

◎ THE CHIPMUNK ADVENTURE (1987)

A Bagdasarian Production released by Samuel Goldwyn. **p:** Ross Bagdasarian Jr.; **d:** Janice Karman; **w:** Janice Karman, Ross Bagdasarian Jr.; **m:** Randy Edelman. **Songs:** "Witch Doctor," "Come on-a My House," "Diamond Dolls," "The Girls of Rock and Roll, "Wooly Bully," "I, Yi, Yi, Yi, Yi/Cuanto Le Gusta," "My Mother" and "Getting Lucky." **Running time:** 76 minutes.

Voices

Alvin/Simon/Dave Seville: Ross Bagdasarian Jr.; **Theodore/Brittany/Jeanette/Eleanor:** Janice Karman; **Miss Miller:** Dodie Goodman; **Claudia Furschtien:** Susan Tyrell; **Klaus Furschtien:** Anthony DeLongis; **Sophie:** Frank Welker

Additional Voices

Charles Adler, Nancy Cartwright, Phillip Clark, Pat Pinney, George Poulos, Ken Samson

Dave Seville goes off to Europe, leaving the unhappy Chipmunks home with their babysitter, Miss Miller. Alvin dreams of world travel and convinces Simon and Theodore to enter a hot-air balloon race around the world against the Chipettes, Brittany, Jeanette and Eleanor. During their globe-trotting the Chipmunks and Chipettes unwittingly assist a pair of international diamond smugglers, hiding illegal gems in toy dolls at shops in Greece, Africa, Egypt, Rio and several other faraway places.

The glass slipper appears to be a perfect fit for poor orphaned Cinderella in a scene from Walt Disney's full-length cartoon release, Cinderella *(1950). © Walt Disney Productions* (COURTESY: THE MUSEUM OF MODERN ART/FILM STILLS ARCHIVE)

◎ CINDERELLA (1950)

A Walt Disney Production released by RKO Radio Pictures. **p:** Walt Disney; **prod superv:** Ben Sharpsteen; **d:** Wilfred Jackson, Hamilton Luske, Clyde Geronimi; **dir anim:** Eric Larson, Ward Kimball, Norman Ferguson, Marc Davis, John Lounsbery, Milt Kahl, Wolfgang Reitherman, Les Clark, Ollie Johnston, Frank Thomas; **st:** Kenneth Anderson, Ted Sears, Homer Brightman, Joe Rinaldi, William Peet, Harry Reeves, Winston Hibler, Erdman Penner (based on the traditional story as told by Charles Perrault); **md:** Oliver Wallace, Paul J. Smith. **Songs:** "Bibbidi-Bobbidi-Boo," "So This Is Love," "A Dream Is a Wish Your Heart Makes," "Cinderella," "The Work Song" and "Oh Sing, Sweet Nightingale." **Running time:** 74 minutes.

Voices

Cinderella: Ilene Woods; **Prince Charming:** William Phipps; **Stepmother:** Eleanor Audley; **Stepsisters:** Rhoda Williams, Lucille Bliss; **Fairy Godmother:** Verna Felton; **King/Grand Duke:** Luis Van Rooten; **Jaq/Gus/Bruno:** James Macdonald

Poor orphaned Cinderella is a slave to her stepmother and two stepsisters in an environment she can endure only through her friendship with animals. Her fairy godmother transforms her rags into a beautiful gown, and she is given only until midnight to attend the king's ball where his son (Prince Charming) yearns to find the girl of his dreams.

Alvin, Theodore and Simon travel the world to several faraway places in their first full-length feature, The Chipmunk Adventure *(1987).* (COURTESY: BAGDASARIAN PRODUCTIONS)

◎ COOL WORLD (1992)

A Frank Mancuso Production released by Paramount Pictures. **p:** Frank Mancuso Jr.; **d:** Ralph Bakshi; **scr:** Michael Grais, Mark Victor, Larry Gross (uncredited); **m:** Mark Isham, John Dickson. **Songs:** "Play with Me," "My Ideal," "Under," "N.W.O.," "Ah-Ah," "The Devil Does Drugs," "The Witch," "Holli's Groove," "Sex on Wheelz," "Do That Thing," "Papua New Guinea, "Next Is the E," "Her Sassy Kiss," "Industry and Seduction," "Mindless," "Sedusa," "Let's Make Love," "Disappointed," "Real Cool World" and "That Old Black Magic." **Running time:** 101 minutes.

Cast/Voices

Holli Would: Kim Basinger; **Jack Deebs:** Gabriel Byrne; **Jennifer Malley:** Michele Abrams; **Isabelle Malley:** Deidre O'Connell; **Mom Harris:** Janni Brenn-Lowen; **Frank Harris:** Brad Pitt; **Cop:** William Frankfather; **Cop:** Greg Collins; **Sparks:** Michael David Lally; **Comic Bookstore Cashier:** Michele Abrams; **Comic Store Patron:** Stephen Worth; **Lonette (performance model):** Jenine Jennings; **Interrogator:** Joey Camen; **Mash:** Maurice LaMarche; **Bash:** Gregory Snegoff; **Bob:** Candi Milo; **Nails:** Charles Adler; **Bouncer:** Patrick Pinney; **Isabelle Malley:** Deidre O'Connell; **Himself:** Frank Sinatra; **Lucky's Bouncer:** Lamont Jackson; **Valet:** Paul Ben-Victor, **Mash (performance model):** Gary Friedkin, **Lonette (performance model):** Clare Hoak; **Dock Whiskers (performance model):** Antonio Hoyos; **Nails (performance model):** Leroy Thompson, **Bob (performance model):** Robert N. Bell

None-too-stable cartoonist Jack Deebs (Gabriel Byrne), who has just finished a jail term for murdering his wife's lover (a returning World War II soldier played by Brad Pitt), is willed into a cartoon world by a character of his own devising: sexy cartoon seductress Holli Would (voiced by Kim Basinger). Trying to return to the real world, Deebs encounters a universe of strange animated "doodles" (cartoon characters) through adventures in Las Vegas, in this live-action/animated fantasy directed by legendary animator Ralph Bakshi of *Fritz the Cat, Heavy Traffic* and *Coonskin* fame and often compared to *Who Framed Roger Rabbit* but taken to extremes.

PN: Animator Ralph Bakshi toned down his trademark outrageousness for this film, which received a PG-13 rating. Screenwriter Larry Gross, of *48 Hours* fame, wrote most of the other screenplay for the film but his work was uncredited. The film cost an estimated $28 million to produce. As with most Bakshi productions, the film was not without controversy; following its release, Jenine Jennings, a 21-year-old actress listed as the film's choreographer and music consultant, went public, claiming that it was she who played the animated Holli Would in the film. Jennings reported that she did the dancing, acting and even the "very hot" love scene with Gabriel Byrne (in the movie Byrne and the animated Holli Would do more than kiss), and dressed in skimpier and skimpier outfits for the animators to get the idea of what the Basinger cartoon character should act like. Frank Sinatra Jr. appeared in the film as himself and also sang the duet, "Let's Make Love," with the film's costar Kim Basinger, who had the dubious distinction of being nominated for a 1993 Razzie Award for Worst Actress for her performance. Rocker David Bowie also sang a song for the film, entitled "Real Cool World."

◎ COONSKIN (1975)

An Albert S. Ruddy Production released by Bryanston Pictures. **p:** Albert S. Ruddy; **d & w:** Ralph Bakshi; **m:** Chico Hamilton; **seq anim:** Irven Spence, Charlie Downs, Ambrozi Palinoda, John E. Walker Sr. **Running time:** 82 minutes.

Voices

Samson/Brother Bear: Barry White; **Preacher/Brother Fox:** Charles Grodone; **Pappy/Old Man Bone:** Scatman Crothers; **Randy/Brother Rabbit:** Phillip Thomas

Three rural black men seek new direction in their lives to escape the ghetto life of crime and other vices.

PN: Paramount Pictures was originally supposed to release this film, which combined live action and animation, but passed due its strong racial content. Upon its release, the film provoked objections to its depictions of blacks from the Congress of Racial Equality (CORE). In 1975, after a brief run, the film was shelved. To calm racial tension, the film was later released on video under a new title: *Streetfight*. The film's working titles were *Bustin' Out, Coon Skin* and *Coonskin No More*.

◎ DAFFY DUCK'S MOVIE: FANTASTIC ISLAND (1983)

A Warner Bros. release. **p & d:** Friz Freleng; **scr:** John Dunn, David Detiege, Friz Freleng; **seq dir:** David Detiege, Friz Freleng, Phil Monroe, **Running time:** 78 minutes.

Voices

Mel Blanc, June Foray, Les Tremayne

In this spoof of TV's *Fantasy Island*, Daffy Duck and Speedy Gonzales become shipwrecked on a desert island. After finding a treasure map belonging to Yosemite Sam, they begin digging for buried treasure and instead discover a wishing well that—after making a wish—magically changes the island into a fantasy paradise. This new footage introduces several complete cartoons: "Bucaneer Bunny," "Stupor Duck," "Greedy Tweety," "Banty Raids," "Louvre Come Back" and others. Other Warner Bros. characters featured are Tweety, Sylvester the Cat, Tasmanian Devil and Pepe Le Pew.

🄯 DAFFY DUCK'S QUACKBUSTERS (1988)

A Warner Bros. release. **p:** Steven S. Greene, Kathleen Helppie-Shipley; **d & w:** Greg Ford, Terry Lennon; **m:** Carl Stalling, Milt Franklyn, Bill Lava. **Running time:** 72 minutes.

Voices

Mel Blanc, Roy Firestone, B.J. Ward

After inheriting $1 million, Daffy starts a ghost-busting business with Bugs Bunny and Porky Pig for the sole purpose of destroying the ghost of J.B. Cubish, his benefactor. Cartoons featured: "Prize Pest," "Water Water Ever Hare," "Hyde and Go Tweet," "Claws for Alarm," "The Abominable Snow Rabbit," "Transylvania 6-500," "Punch Trunk" and "Jumpin' Jupiter." The film also contained the first new cartoon short produced by the studio in several decades, "The Duxorcist."

PN: This compilation featured grossed a dismal $300,000 following its opening.

🄯 THE DAYDREAMER (1966)

A Joseph E. Levine/Arthur Rankin Jr./Videocraft International Production released by Embassy Pictures. **p:** Arthur Rankin Jr.; **d:** Jules Bass; **exec prod:** Joseph E. Levine, **scr:** Arthur Rankin Jr. (based on the stories and characters created by Hans Christian Andersen; with additional dialogue by Romeo Muller); **m/l:** Jules Bass, Maury Laws (with the theme "The Daydreamer" sung by Robert Goulet). **Songs:** "The Daydreamer," "Wishes and Teardrops," "Luck to Sell," "Happy Guy," "Who Can Tell," "Simply Wonderful," "Isn't It Cozy Here," "Tivoli Bells," "Voyage of the Walnut Shell" and "Waltz for a Mermaid." Filmed in Animagic. **Running time:** 105 minutes.

Cast/Voices

The Sandman: Cyril Ritchard; **Chris Andersen:** Paul O'Keefe; **Papa Andersen:** Jack Gilford; **The Pieman:** Ray Bolger; **Mrs. Klopplebobbler:** Margaret Hamilton; **The Little Mermaid:** Hayley Mills; **Father Neptune:** Burl Ives; **The Sea Witch:** Tallulah Bankhead; **The First Tailor:** Terry-Thomas; **The Second Tailor:** Victor Borge; **The Emperor:** Ed Wynn; **Thumbelina:** Patty Duke; **The Rat:** Boris Karloff; **The Mole:** Sessue Hayakawa

Additional Voices

Robert Harter, Larry Mann, Billie Richards, James Daugherty, William Marine

Famous storyteller Hans Christian Andersen, as a young boy, daydreams about his best-loved fairytale adventures—

incorporating the tales of "The Little Mermaid," "The Emperor's New Clothes," "Thumbelina" and "The Garden of Paradise"—in this live-action/"Animagic," full-length feature that includes an all-star cast.

PN: *Daydreamer* was one of three films produced by Arthur Rankin Jr. and Jules Bass in association with famed Hollywood producer Joseph E. Levine. The motion picture was the combined efforts of five countries, the United States, Canada, England, France and Japan. The movie's title song, "The Daydreamer," was sung by Robert Goulet. Other musical numbers were sung by the film's costars, among them: "Wishes and Teardrops" (by Hayley Mills), "Happy Guy" (by Patty Duke), "Who Can Tell" (by Ray Bolger), "Simply Wonderful" (by Ed Wynn).

🄯 DICK DEADEYE—OR DUTY DONE (1975)

A Bill Melendez Production, London released by International Releasing Corporation. **p:** Steven C. Melendez; **d:** Bill Melendez; **st:** Robin Miller and Leo Rost; **m:** Jimmy Horowitz (with additional lyrics by Robin Miller); **anim dir:** Dick Horn. **Running time:** 80 minutes.

Voices

Dick Deadeye: Victor Spinetti; **Yum Yum:** Linda Lewis; **Sorcerer, Captain of the Pinafore:** Peter Reeves; **Pirate King:** George A. Cooper; **Little Buttercup:** Miriam Karlin; **Nanki/Poo:** John Newton; **Rose Maybud:** Julia McKenzie; **Monarch of the Sea/Major General:** Francis Ghent; **Judge:** Barry Cryer; **Princess Zara/Queen Elizabeth:** Beth Porter; **Singing voice of Monarch of the Sea/Major General:** John Baldry; **Singing voice of Nanki/Poo:** Casey Kelley; **Singing voice of Rose Maybud:** Lisa Strike; **Singing voice of Pirate King:** Ian Samwell

Dick Deadeye, that scurrilous villian of Gilbert and Sullivan's most popular operetta, *H.M.S. Pinafore*, is transformed into the most unlikely hero in this cartoon parody, featuring rock versions of 26 classic Gilbert and Sullivan tunes from five operettas: *H.M.S. Pinafore, The Mikado, The Pirates of Penzance, The Sorcerer* and *Trial by Jury.* The plot line involves Deadeye's attempts to rescue the Ultimate Secret from the Sorcerer and the Pirate King; he is commissioned to do so by no other than the Queen herself.

PN: Bill Melendez, best known as the creator of countless *Peanuts* television specials, directed this cartoon feature, which was produced in England and released theatrically in the United Kingdom and America.

🄯 DIRTY DUCK (1977)

A Murakami-Wolf Production released by New World Pictures. **p:** Jerry Good; **d, w & anim:** Charles Swenson; **m:** Mark Volman, Howard Kaylan-Flo and Eddie. **Running time:** 75 minutes.

Voices

Mark Volman, Robery Ridgeley, Walker Emiston, Cynthia Adler, Janet Lee, Lurene Tuttle, Jerry Good, Howard Kaylan

Willard Eisenbaum, a shy, lonely, inept, sexually frustrated insurance company employee, is thrown by fate into the company of a large, sailor-suited duck who is convinced that some good sex will straighten Willard out.

PN: Like Ralph Bakshi's *Fritz the Cat*, this film was X-rated.

DUCKTALES: THE MOVIE, TREASURE OF THE LOST LAMP (1990)

A Walt Disney Animation (France) S.A. Production released by Buena Vista. **p & d:** Bob Hathcock; **scr:** Alan Burnett; **m:** David Newman; **seq dir:** Paul Brizzi, Gaetan Brizzi, Clive Pallant, Mattias Marcos Rodric, Vincent Woodcock; **anim:** Gary Andrews, James Baker, Javier Gutierrez Blas, Eric Bouillette, Moran Caouissin, Caron Creed, Caroline Cruikshank, Roberto Curilli, Sylvain DeBoissy, Joe Ekers, Mark Eoche-Duval, Pierre Fassal, Al Gaivoto, Manolo Galiana, Bruno Gaumetou, Dina Gellert-Nielsen, Arnold Gransac, Teddy Hall, Peter Hausner, Francisco Alaminos Hodar, Daniel Jeannette, Nicholas Marlet, Bob McKnight, Ramon Modiano, Sean Newton, Brent Odell, Catherine Poulain, Jean-Christopher Roger, Pascal Ropars, Stephane Sainte-Foi, Alberto Conejo Sanz, Anna Saunders, Ventura R. Vallejo, Jan Van Buyten, Duncan Varley, Simon Ward-Horner and Johnny Zeuten. **Songs:** "Duck Tales Theme." **Running time:** 74 minutes.

Voices

Scrooge McDuck: Alan Young; **Launchpad:** Terence McGovern; **Huey/Duey/Louie/Webby:** Russi Taylor; **Dijon:** Richard Libertini; **Merlock:** Christopher Lloyd; **Mrs. Featherby:** June Foray; **Duckworth:** Chuck McCann; **Mrs. Beakley:** Joan Gerber; **Genie:** Rip Taylor

Additional Voices

Charlie Adler, Jack Angel, Steve Bulen, Sherry Lynn, Mickie T. McGowan, Patrick Pinney, Frank Welker

Scrooge McDuck travels to the far ends of the earth in search of the elusive buried treasure of legendary thief Collie Baba. With his companions Huey, Dewey and Louie, Webby and Launchpad McQuack, Scrooge discovers not only the treasure but also that there's a mysterious madman named Merlock who's out to stop him.

PN: The success of the *DuckTales* syndicated TV series inspired this feature-length release. Box-office receipts totaled $18 million.

DUMBO (1941)

A Walt Disney Production released by RKO Radio Pictures. **p:** Walt Disney; **super dir:** Ben Sharpsteen; **scr st:** Joe Grant, Dick Huemer (based on a story by Helen Aberson and Harold Pearl); **st dev:** Bill Peet, Aurie Battaglia, Joe Rinaldi, George Stallings, Webb Smith; **m:** Oliver Wallace, Frank Churchill, Ned Washington; **seq dir:** Norman Ferguson, Wilfred Jackson; Bill Roberts, Jack Kinney, Sam Armstrong; **anim dir:** Vladimir Tytla, Fred Moore, Ward Kimball, John Lounsbery, Arthur Babbitt, Wolfgang Reitherman. **Songs:** "Look Out for Mr. Stork," "Baby Mine," "Pink Elephants on Parade," "Casey Junior," "Song of the Roustabouts," "When I See an Elephant Fly." **Running time:** 63 1/2 minutes.

Voices

Narrator: John McLeish; **Timothy Mouse:** Ed Brophy; **Ringmaster:** Herman Bing; **Casey Jr.:** Margaret Wright; **Messenger Stork:** Sterling Holloway; **Elephant:** Verna Felton; **Elephant:** Sarah Selby; **Elephant:** Dorothy Scott; **Elephant:** Noreen Gamill; **Joe/Clown:** Billy Sheets; **Clown:** Billy Bletcher; **Skinny:** Malcolm Hutton; **Crows:** Cliff Edwards; **Crows:** Jim Carmichael; **Crows:** Hall Johnson Choir; **Clown:** Eddie Holden; **Roustabouts:** The King's Men; **Boy:** Harold Manley; **Boy:** Tony Neil; **Boy:** Charles Stubbs

Mrs. Jumbo, a circus elephant, patiently awaits the stork's delivery of her own baby elephant. The young elephant is like no other—with ears as large as sails, he is affectionately dubbed "Dumbo." Dumbo's imperfection becomes an asset when he discovers he can use his ears to fly. He is billed as a top circus attraction, experiencing triumphs and failures of circus life.

FANTASIA (1940)

A Walt Disney Production released by RKO Radio Pictures. **p:** Walt Disney; **prod superv:** Ben Sharpsteen; "Toccata and

Baby elephant Dumbo takes his first flight in a scene from the classic Walt Disney feature Dumbo (1941). © Walt Disney Productions
(COURTESY: THE MUSEUM OF MODERN ART/FILM STILLS ARCHIVE)

Mickey Mouse hypnotizes the brooms to do his water chores in "The Sorcerer's Apprentice" scene from Walt Disney's Fantasia *(1940).* © *Walt Disney Productions* (COURTESY: THE MUSEUM OF MODERN ART/FILM STILLS ARCHIVE)

Fugue in D Minor" by Johann Sebastian Bach: **d:** Samuel Armstrong; **st:** Lee Blair, Elmer Plummer, Phil Dike; "The Nutcracker Suite" by Peter Ilich Tchaikovsky: **d:** Samuel Armstrong; **st:** Sylvia Moberly-Holland, Norman Wright, Albert Heath, Bianca Majolie, Graham Heid; "The Sorcerer's Apprentice" by Paul Dukas: **d:** James Algar; **st:** Perce Pearce, Carl Fallberg; **superv anim:** Fred Moore, Vladimir Tytla; "The Rite of Spring" by Igor Stravinsky: **d:** Bill Roberts, Paul Satterfield; **st:** William Martin, Leo Thiele, Robert Sterner, John Fraser McLeish; **superv anim:** Wolfgang Reitherman, Joshua Meador; "Pastoral Symphony" by Ludwig van Beethoven: **d:** Hamilton Luske, Jim Handley, Ford Beebe; **st:** Otto Englander, Webb Smith, Erdman Penner, Joseph Sabo, Bill Peet, George Stallings: **superv anim:** Fred Moore, Ward Kimball, Eric Larson, Arthur Babbitt, Oliver M. Johnston Jr., Don Towsley; "Dance of the Hours" by Amilcare Ponchielli: **d:** T. Hee, Norman Ferguson; **superv anim:** Norman Ferguson; "Night on Bald Mountain" by Modest Mussorgsky and "Ave Maria" by Franz Schubert: **d:** Wilfred Jackson; **st:** Campbell Grant, Arthur Heinemann, Phil Dike; **superv anim:** Vladimir Tytla. **Running time:** 120 minutes.

Cast

Himself: Deems Taylor; **Themselves:** Leopold Stokowski and the Philadelphia Symphony Orchestra; **Sorcerer's Apprentice:** Mickey Mouse

Walt Disney set new standards for animation with this film, featuring eight different pieces of classical music—Tchaikovsky's "The Nutcracker Suite," Bach's "Toccata and Fugue in D Minor" and others—visually interpreted by the Disney artists. The most memorable moment of the film is

Mickey Mouse's performance in "The Sorcerer's Apprentice," where he tries to cast his master's spells.

PN: Among Walt Disney's plans for this animated, symphony-laden classic was to shoot the film in wide screen and stereophonic sound, film some scenes in 3-D and perfume theaters with floral scent during the "Nutcracker Suite" flower ballet. Although tight money stymied Disney's plans, he did embellish the film with an innovative fully directional sound system he called "Fantasound."

◉ FANTASTIC PLANET (1973)

A Les Films Armorial/Service De Recherche Ortif Production released by New World Pictures. **p:** Simon Damiani, Andre Valio-Cavaglione; **d:** Rene Laloux; **w:** Rene Laloux, Roland Topor (based on the novel *Ems en Serie* by Stefen Wul); **m:** Alain Gorogeur. **Running time:** 71 minutes.

Voices

Barry Bostwick, Marvin Miller, Olan Soule, Cynthia Adler, Nora Heflin, Hal Smith, Mark Gruner, Monika Ramirez, Janet Waldo.

This avant-garde-styled film is a tale of social injustice, relating the story of the Draggs, 39-foot-tall inhabitants of the planet Yagam, who keep the Oms—who have evolved from humans—as pets. Terr, one of the Oms, is accidentally educated by the Draggs and, after uniting with his people, helps them achieve equality with the Draggs once and for all.

PN: This French Czech full-length animated fantasy was winner of a Grand Prix award at the 1973 Cannes Film Festival.

◉ FERNGULLY . . . THE LAST RAINFOREST (1992)

An FAI Films Production in association with Youngheart Productions released by 20th Century-Fox. **p:** Peter Faiman, Wayne Young, Jim Cox, Brian Rosen, Richard Harper; **d:** Bill Kroyer; **exec prod:** Ted Field, Robert W. Cort, Jeff Dowd, William F. Willett; **scr:** Jim Cox (based on the stories of *Ferngully* by Diana Young); **m:** Alan Silvestri: **m/sc:** Tim Sexton, Becky Mancuso; **anim dir:** Tony Fucile. **Songs:** "Life Is a Magic Thing," "Batty Rap," "If I'm Gonna Eat (It Might as Well Be You)," "Toxic Love," "Raining Like Magic," "Land of a Thousand Dances," "A Dream Worth Keeping," "Lithuanian Lullaby," "Spis, Li Milke Le," "Bamnqobile," "Tri Jetrve," "Some Other World." **Running time:** 76 minutes

Voices

Hexxus: Tim Curry; **Crysta, a fairy wise-woman-in-training:** Samantha Mathis; **Pips, Crysta's boyfriend:** Christian Slater; **Zak, a young human logger:** Jonathan

Ward; **Batty Koda:** Robin Williams; **Magi Lune, the wise forest mother:** Grace Zabriski; **Ralph:** Geoffrey Blake; **Tony:** Robert Pastorelli; **Stump:** Cheech Marin; **Root:** Tommy Chong; **The Goanna, a ravenous blue goanna lizard: Tone Loc; Knotty:** Townsend Coleman; **Ock:** Brian Cummings; **Elder #1:** Kathleen Freeman; **Fairy #1:** Janet Gilmore: **Elder #2:** Naomi Lewis; **Ash/Voice Dispatch:** Danny Mann; **Elder #3:** Neil Ross; **Fairy #2:** Pamela Segall; **Rock:** Anderson Wong

Additional Voices
Lauri Hendler, Rosanna Huffman, Harvey Jason, Dave Mallow, Paige Nan Pollack, Holly Ryan, Gary Schwartz

In this animated ecological fantasy, the lives of rain forest inhabitants nestled in a secret world known as Fern-Gully, home to an unusual girl named Crysta and her friend Pips, the rowdy Beetle Boys, a singing lizard and a bat named Batty, are threatened by the forces of destruction. The only human who has ever been there fights to save them and their magical place.

PN: Adapted from stories by Australian author Diana Young and written for the screen by Jim Cox, who penned Disney's *The Rescuers Down Under*, the film marked the feature-film directorial debut of Bill Kroyer and was the first feature for Kroyer's Kroyer Films. Released in the spring of 1992, the film grossed $25 million. Music for the film was performed by Sheena Easton, Elton John, Johnny Clegg, Tone Loc, and Raffi among others.

◉ FIRE AND ICE (1984)

A Ralph Bakshi/Frank Frazetta Production released by 20th Century-Fox/Producers Sales Organization. **p:** Ralph Bakshi, Frank Frazetta; **d:** Ralph Bakshi; **w:** Roy Thomas, Gerry Conway (based on a story and characters by Ralph Bakshi); **m:** William Kraft. **Running time:** 81 minutes.

Voices
Larn: Randy Norton; **Teegra:** Cynthia Leake; **Darkwolf:** Steve Sandor; **Nekron:** Sean Hannon; **Jarol:** Leo Gordon; **Taro:** William Ostrander; **Juliana:** Eileen O'Neill; **Roleil:** Elizabeth Lloyd Shaw; **Otwa:** Micky Morton; **Tutor:** Tamara Park; **Monga:** Big Yank; **Pako:** Greg Elam; **Subhuman Priestess:** Holly Frazetta; **Envoy:** Alan Koss; **Defender Captain:** Hans Howes; **Subhumans:** James Bridges, Shane Callan, Archie Hamilton, Michael Kellogg, Dale Park, Douglas Payton.

Teegra, the beautiful young daughter of the evil Ice Lord, is taken hostage by the Subhumans, which were considered extinct after the glacial destruction of the city Fire Keep. The Subhumans prove to be no match for the Ice Lord and his powerful Dragonhawks, but a mysterious hero, Darkwolf, prevails in destroying the sorcerer once and for all.

PN: Working title: *Sword and the Sorcery*.

◉ THE FOX AND THE HOUND (1981)

A Walt Disney Production released through Buena Vista. **p:** Wolfgang Reitherman, Art Stevens; **d:** Art Stevens, Ted Berman, Richard Rich; **st:** Larry Clemmons, Ted Berman, Peter Young, Steve Hulett, David Michener, Burny Mattinson, Earl Kress, Vance Gerry (based on the book by Daniel P. Mannix); **superv anim:** Randy Cartwright, Cliff Nordberg, Frank Thomas, Glen Keane, Ron Clements, Ollie Johnston. **Running time:** 83 minutes.

Voices
Tod: Mickey Rooney; **Cooper:** Kurl Russell; **Big Mama:** Pearl Bailey; **Amos Slade:** Jack Albertson; **Vixey:** Sandy Duncan; **Widow Tweed:** Jeanette Nolan; **Chief:** Pat Buttram; **Porcupine:** John Fiedler; **Badger:** John McIntire; **Dinky:** Dick Bakalyan; **Boomer:** Paul Winchell; **Young Tod:** Keith Mitchell; **Young Copper:** Corey Feldman

A young fox and a puppy become the best of friends one summer but are separated when the dog's owner, a hunter, takes the dog away for the winter. Returning the following spring, the dog (now a fully trained hunting dog) and the fox learn what it is like to be enemies.

PN: The first Disney feature to display the talents of a new crop of artists developed during a 10-year program at the studio under the supervision of veteran Disney animators Wolfgang Reitherman, Eric Larson and Art Stevens. Working title: *The Fox and the Hounds.*

◉ FRANK AND OLLIE (1995)

A Walt Disney/Theodore Thomas Production released by Buena Vista Pictures. **p:** Theodore Thomas, Kuniko Okubo; **d:** Theodore Thomas; **scr:** Theodore Thomas; **m:** John Reynolds. **Songs:** "That's a Plenty," "Speakeasy Charleston," "Lonesome Railroad Blues," "Waltz Marguerite" and "Just a Little While to Stay Here." **Running time:** 90 minutes.

Cast
Frank Thomas, Oliver M. Johnston Jr., Sylvia Roemer, John Canemaker, John Culhane, Marie E. Johnston, Jeanette A. Thomas, Glen Keane, Andy Gaskill

Featuring clips from such Disney animated classics as *Snow White and the Seven Dwarfs, Pinocchio, Alice in Wonderland, Peter Pan, Lady and the Tramp, Sword and the Stone, The Jungle Book* and *Robin Hood*, this well-produced documentary chronicles the lives and careers of legendary Disney animators Frank Thomas and Ollie Johnston.

PN: Premiering at the Cleveland Film Festival in April 1995, this feature-length documentary was first released theatrically in Los Angeles in October of that year for Oscar consideration. The film's producer, Theodore Thomas, happens to be Frank Thomas's son. A previous 21-minute documentary honoring the two veteran Disney animators was produced in 1978, *Frank and Ollie: Four Decades of Disney Animation.*

⊙ FREDDIE AS F.R.O.7 (1992)

A Shapiro Glickenhaus/Hollywood Motion Pictures (of London) Ltd. Production. **p:** Norman Priggen, Jon Acevski; **d:** Jon Acevski; **scr:** Jon Acevski, David Ashton; **m:** David Dundas, Rick Wentworth; **anim dir:** Ton Guy. **Songs:** "The Narrator," "I'll Keep Your Dreams Alive," "Evilmainya," "Shy Girl," "Lay Down Your Arms," "Fear Not the Sword My Son," "F.R.O.7," and "Suite from Freddie." **Running time:** 72 minutes.

Voices

Freddie: Ben Kingsley; **El Supremo:** Brian Blessed; **Trilby:** Jonathan Pryce; **Nessie:** Phyllis Logan: **Brigadier G:** Nigel Hawthorne; **King:** Michael Hordern; **Queen/Various Voices:** Prunella Scales; **Daffers:** Jenny Agutter; **Messina:** Billie Whitelaw; **Scott/Various Voices:** John Sessions

An extraordinary young frog prince–turned–secret agent with superpowers and a leaping green fighting machine battles the forces of evil to stop the wicked Aunt Messina from conquering the earth in this animated fantasy adventure.

PN: Of the non-Disney features released in 1992, this one fared the worst, grossing only $1 million in revenue. Songs featured in the production were sung by such well-known recording artists as George Benson, Grace Jones and Boy George. The film is also known as *Freddie the Frog.*

⊙ FRITZ THE CAT (1972)

A Steve Krantz Production released by Cinemation Industries. **p:** Steve Krantz; **d & w:** Ralph Bakshi (based on characters created by Robert Crumb); **m:** Ed Bogas, Ray Shanklin; **superv anim:** Virgil Ross, Manuel Perez, John Sparey. **Running time:** 78 minutes.

Voices

Fritz the Cat: Skip Hinnant: Rosetta LeNoire; John McCurry; Judy Engles

Re-creating the pop culture and social agonies of the 1960s, this political, racial and sexual satire traces the sexual and political exploits of Fritz the Cat, a college-age cat who dabbles in drugs, radical politics and hedonism. By film's end, following his many encounters, he rejects violence and cruelty but still embraces sex.

PN: The first animated film ever to receive an X rating. The feature was to become the first of three projects planned by producer Steve Krantz. The others: *Arrivederci, Rudy!* based on the life of Valentino, and *Dick Tracy, Frozen, Fried and Buried Alive,* tracing the career of Chester Gould's detective through the 1930s and 1940s. These two films were never produced.

⊙ FRIZ FRELENG'S LOONEY LOONEY BUGS BUNNY MOVIE (1981)

A Warner Bros. release. **p & d:** Friz Freleng; **scr:** John Dunn, David Detiege, Friz Freleng, Phil Monroe, Gerry Chinquy; **m:** Rob Walsh, Don McGinnis, Milt Franklyn, Bill Lava, Shorty Rogers, Carl Stalling. **Running time:** 80 minutes.

Voices

Mel Blanc, June Foray, Frank Nelson, Frank Welker, Stan Freberg, Ralph James

Veteran Warner Bros. director Friz Freleng was given a shot at producing and directing this compilation feature following the success of Chuck Jones's *The Bugs Bunny/Road Runner Movie.* Freleng combined new animation with previously presented cartoons, broken into three acts: Yosemite Sam, playing the devil (shaped around 1963's "Devil's Feud Cake"); Bugs outsmarting a dopey gangster duo, Rocky and Mugsy, who are holding Tweety hostage; and Bugs serving as master of ceremonies for a humorous spoof of Hollywood awards programs. Cartoons featured during the film are: "Knighty Knight Bugs," "Sahara Hare," "Roman Legion Hare," "High Diving Hare," "Hare Trimmed," "Wild and Wooly Hare," "Catty Cornered," "Golden Yeggs," "The Unmentionables," "Three Little Bops" and "Show Biz Bugs," the latter an Academy Award winner.

⊙ FUN AND FANCY FREE (1947)

A Walt Disney Production released by RKO Radio Pictures. **p:** Walt Disney; **prod superv:** Ben Sharpsteen; **l/a dir:** William Morgan; **anim dir:** Jack Kinney, Bill Roberts, Hamilton Luske; **st:** Homer Brightman, Harry Reeves, Ted Sears, Lance Nolley, Eldon Dedini, Tom Oreb, with "Bongo" based on an original story by Sinclair Lewis; **md:** Charles Wolcott; **m/sc:** Paul J. Smith, Oliver Wallace, Eliot Daniel; **anim dir:** Ward Kimball, Les Clark, John Lounsbery, Fred Moore, Wolfgang Reitherman. **Songs:** "Fun and Fancy Free, "Lazy Countryside," "Too Good to Be True," "Say It with a Slap," "Fee Fi Fo Fum," "My Favorite Dream," "I'm a Happy Go-Lucky Fellow," "Beanero" and "My, What a Happy Day." **Running time:** 73 minutes.

Cast

Edgar Bergen, Luana Patten, Charlie McCarthy, Mortimer Snerd

Voices

Narrator/Bongo: Dinah Shore; **The Singing Harp:** Anita Gordon; **Jiminy Cricket:** Cliff Edwards; **Willie the Giant:** Billy Gilbert; **Donald Duck:** Clarence Nash; The King's Men, The Dinning Sisters, and The Starlighters

Radio stars Edgar Bergen and Charlie McCarthy and cartoon star Jiminy Cricket appear in this Walt Disney feature composed of two animated stories threaded together by live action and animated wraparounds. Cartoon sequences include: "Bongo, the Wonder Bear," about a circus bear who escapes from the circus and finds the companionship of Lulubelle, a cute female bear, and "Mickey and the Beanstalk," a clever retelling of the famed "Jack and the Beanstalk" tale featuring Mickey, Donald, Goofy and, of course, the Giant (Willie).

◎ GAY PURR-EE (1962)

A UPA (United Pictures of America) Production released by Warner Bros. **p:** Henry G. Saperstein; **d:** Abe Levitow; **w:** Dorothy and Chuck Jones, Ralph Wright. **Songs:** "Mewsette," "Roses Red-Violets Blue," "Take My Hand, Paree," "The Money Cat," "Little Drops of Rain," "Rubbles," "Paris Is a Lonely Town" and "The Horses Won't Talk." **Running time:** 85 minutes.

Voices

Mewsette: Judy Garland, **Jaune-Tom:** Robert Goulet; **Robespierre:** Red Buttons; **Mme. Rubens-Chatte:** Hermione Gingold; **Meowrice:** Paul Frees;

Additional Voices

Morey Amsterdam: Mel Blanc; Julie Bennett; and Joan Gardiner

Mewsette, a naive country girl cat, becomes tired of peasant-type cats and leaves the farm on the next train to Paris to explore new adventures. She is followed on foot by her boyfriend, Jaune Tom, and his tiny companion, Robespierre, who set out to rescue her from Meowrice, a suave city cat who plans to marry her.

Mewsette, a naive country girl cat (voiced by Judy Garland), is the object of boyfriend Jaune-Tom's love in Gay Purr-ee (1962). © Warner Bros. Inc.

◎ GOBOTS: BATTLE OF THE ROCKLORDS (1986)

A Hanna-Barbera/Tonka Toys Production released by Clubhouse Pictures/Atlantic Releasing. **p:** Kay Wright; **d:** Ray Patterson; **w:** Jay Segal; **md:** Hoyt Curtin; **anim dir:** Paul Seballa; **superv anim:** Janine Dawson. **Running time:** 75 minutes.

Voices

Solitaire: Margot Kidder; **Nuggit:** Roddy McDowall; **Boulder:** Michael Nouri; **Magmar:** Telly Savalas; **Turbo/ Cop-Tur/Talc:** Arthur Burghardt; **Nick:** Ike Eisenmann; **Cy-Kill:** Bernard Erhard; **Crasher:** Marilyn Lightstone; **Matt:** Morgan Paull; **Leader-1** Lou Richards; **A.J.:** Leslie Speights; **Scooter/Zeemon/Rest-Q/Pulver Eye/Sticks/ Narliphant:** Frank Welker; **Slime/Stone/Granite/Narligator:** Michael Bell; **Stone Heart/Fossil Lord:** Foster Brooks; **Vanguard:** Ken Campbell; **Herr Friend/Crack-Pot/Tork:** Philip Lewis Clarke; **Pincher/Tombstone/Stone:** Peter Cullen; **Brimstone/Klaws/Rock Narlie:** Dick Gautier; **Marbles/Hornet:** Darryl Hickman; **Small Foot:** B.J. Ward; **Fitor:** Kelly Ward; **Heat Seeker:** Kirby Ward

The evil Rock Lord Magmar is bent on seizing control of the entire planet of Quartex, which is peopled by various species of living rock. This spurs the noble Guardian Go-Bots into action, using a variety of devices to thwart the enemy Renegade GoBots to prevent the Rock Lords from taking control.

◎ A GOOFY MOVIE (1995)

A Walt Disney Pictures Production released by Buena Vista Pictures. **p:** Dan Rounds; **d:** Kevin Lima; **st:** Jymm Magon; **scr:** Jymn Magon, Chris Matheson, Brian Pimenthal; **m/sc:** Carter Burwell (with songs by Tom Snow, Jack Feldman, Patrick DeRener and Roy Freeland); **anim superv:** Nancy Beiman, Matias Marcos, Dominique Monfery, Stephane Sainte-Foi. **Songs:** "After Today," "Stand Out," "Leslie's Possum Pork," "On the Open Road," "121" and "Nobody Else But You." **Running time:** 78 minutes.

Voices

Goofy: Bill Farmer; **Max:** Jason Marsden; **Pete:** Jim Cummings; **Roxanne:** Kellie Martin, **PJ:** Rob Paulsen; **Principal Mazur:** Wallace Shawn; **Stacey:** Jenna von Oy; **Bigfoot:** Frank Welker; **Lester:** Kevin Lima; **Waitress:** Florence Stanley; **Miss Maples:** Jo Anne Worley; **Photo Studio Girl:** Brittany Alyse Smith; **Lester's Grinning Girl:** Robyn Richards; **Lisa:** Julie Brown; **Tourist Kid:** Klee Bragger; **Chad:** Joey Lawrence; **Possum Park Emcee:** Pat Buttram (listed as Butrum in credits); **Mickey Mouse:** Wayne Allwine; **Security Guard:** Herschel Sparber; **Powerline:** Tevin Campbell; **Max (singing):** Aaron Lohr; **Robert Zimmeruski (Bobby):** Pauly Shore

Additional Voices

Dante Basco, Sheryl Bernstein, Corey Burton, Pat Carroll, Elizabeth Daily, Carol Holiday, Steve Moore, Brian Pimental, Jason Willinger

Lovable canine klutz Goofy is a suburban dad who tries to bond and regain the closeness he once had with his teenage son, Max, during a cross-country trip.

PN: A spinoff of the Disney animated series *Goof Troop*, Disney struck gold with this new animated feature (and the first full-length animated feature to star the 63-year-old canine), grossing $35 million at the box office. Principal animation was produced overseas at studio facilities in France and Sydney, Australia, as well as the Burbank studios.

◎ THE GREAT MOUSE DETECTIVE (1986)

A Walt Disney/Silver Screen Partners II Production released by Buena Vista. **p:** Burny Mattinson; **d:** John Musker, Ron Clements, Dave Michener, Burny Mattinson; **st dev:** Pete Young, Vance Gerry, Steve Hulett, Ron Clements, John Musker, Bruce M. Morris, Matthew O'Callaghan, Burny Mattinson, Dave Michener, Melvin Shaw (based on the book *Basil of Baker Street* by Eve Titus); **m:** Henry Mancini; **superv anim:** Mark Henn, Glen Keane, Robert Minkoff, Hendel Butoy. **Songs:** "The World's Greatest Criminal Mind," "Goodbye, So Soon" and "Let Me Be Good to You." **Running time:** 74 minutes.

Voices

Professor Ratigan: Vincent Price; **Basil/Bartholomew:** Barrie Ingham; **Dawson:** Val Bettin; **Olivia:** Susanne Pollatschek; **Fidget:** Candy Candido; **Mrs. Judson:** Diana Chesney; **The Mouse Queen:** Eve Brenner; **Flaversham:** Alan Young; **Sherlock Holmes:** Basil Rathbone; **Watson:** Laurie Main; **Lady Mouse:** Shani Wallis; **Bar Maid:** Ellen Fitzhugh; **Citizen/Thug Guard:** Walker Edmiston; **Thug Guards:** Wayne Allwine, Val Bettin, Tony Anselmo

Ratigan, an evil rat, wants to control the mouse world and kidnaps a brilliant mouse toymaker to build a mechanical rodent robot to begin his quest. His initial plans are to dethrone the mouse queen, but he never counted on two factors getting in his way: Basil and Dr. Dawson, two Holmesian mice hired by the toymaker's daughter to track down her father. The pair not only find the toymaker but successfully thwart Ratigan's plans.

PN: This Disney mouse-tale/adventure grossed $25 million at the box office and used digital animation for the first time in an animated movie.

◎ GULLIVER'S TRAVELS (1939)

A Fleischer Studios Production released by Paramount Pictures. **p:** Max Fleischer; **d:** Dave Fleischer; **w:** Dan Gordon, Ted Pierce, Izzy Sparber, Edmond Seward (based on a story by Seward from the novel by Jonathan Swift); **m:** Victor Young; **anim dir:** Seymour Kneitel, Willard Bowsky, Tom Palmer, Grim Natwick, William Hanning, Rolland Crandall, Tom Johnson, Robert Leffingwell, Frank Kelling, Winfield Hoskins, Orestes Calpini: **Songs:** "It's a Hap-Hap-Happy Day," "Bluebirds in the Moonlight," "All's Well," "We're All Together Again," "Forever," "Faithful" and "Faithful Forever." **Running time:** 75 minutes.

Voices

Singing voice of the Prince: Lanny Ross; **Singing voice of the Princess:** Jessica Dragnotte

With the success of Walt Disney's *Snow White and the Seven Dwarfs*, animators Max and Dave Fleischer tried their own hand at a full-length animated feature shaped around the popular romance of Jonathan Swift. The film centers on the adventures of shipwrecked Lemuel Gulliver on an island inhabited by tiny people in the kingdom of Lilliput and his attempts to escape the island and return to his homeland.

◎ GULLIVER'S TRAVELS BEYOND THE MOON (1966)

A Toei Films Production released through Continental Distributing. **p:** Hiroshi Okawa; **d:** Yoshio Kuroda; **w:** Shinichi Sekizawa (based on the character in the novel by Jonathan Swift); **m/s:** Milton and Anne Delugg; **anim dir:** Hideo Furusawa. **Songs:** "The Earth Songs," "I Wanna Be Like Gulliver," "That's the Way It Goes" and "Keep Your Hopes High." **Running time:** 85 minutes.

Voice credits unknown.

In an effort to rival Disney's feature-length cartoons, Max Fleischer countered with his own full-length film, Gulliver's Travels *(1939).*
(COURTESY: REPUBLIC PICTURES)

Hit by a car and knocked unconscious, a young boy dreams he is with Dr. Gulliver, a toy-soldier colonel, a crow and a dog on a trip to the planet Hope. There they discover a princess who tells them the planet is being run by robots who have gone out of control. The boy and Dr. Gulliver destroy the robots—who melt when hit by water—and free the planet.

PN: Produced in Japan, this full-length animated feature was retitled for American release. It was formerly titled *Gulliver No Uchu Ryoko.*

☺ GUMBY: THE MOVIE (1995)

An Arrow/Premavision Production released by Arrow Releasing. **p:** Art Clokey, Gloria Clokey; **d:** Art Clokey; **scr:** Art Clokey, Gloria Clokey; **m/sc:** Jerry Gerber (with songs by David Ozzie Ahlers). **Songs:** "Take Me Away," "Rockin' Arc Park," "This Way 'n That" and "He Was Once." **Running time:** 88 minutes.

Voices

Gumby/Claybery/Fatbuckle/Kapp: Charles Farrington; **Pokey/Prickle/Gumbo:** Art Clokey; **Goo:** Gloria Clokey; **Thinbuckle:** Manny LaCarruba; **Ginger:** Alice Young; **Gumba:** Janet MacDuff; **Lowbelly/Farm Lady:** Bonnie Rudolph; **Tara:** Patti Morse; **Radio Announcer:** Ozzie Ahlers

In this spinoff of the 1950's "claymation" cartoon series, the spunky green clay hero and his orange sidekick Pokey experience thrills and spills as they travel to Camelot, Toyland and beyond in their first feature-length adventure.

☺ HAPPILY EVER AFTER (1990)

A Filmation/First National Production released by Kel-Air Entertainment. **p:** Lou Scheimer; **d:** John Howley; **scr:** Robby London, Martha Moran; **m:** Frank W. Becker; **seq dir:** Gian Celestri, Ka Moon Song, Lawrence White. **Running time:** 74 minutes.

Voices

Snow White: Irene Cara; **Scowl:** Edward Asner; **Muddy:** Carol Channing; **Looking Glass:** Dom DeLuise; **Mother Nature:** Phyllis Diller; **Blossom:** Zsa Zsa Gabor; **Critterina/Marina:** Linda Gary; **Sunflower:** Jonathan Harris; **"Prince:** Michael Horton; **Sunburn:** Sally Kellerman; **Lord Maliss:** Malcolm McDowell; **Moonbeam/Thunderella:** Tracey Ullman; **Batso:** Frank Welker

The evil queen's brother, Lord Maliss, seeks to avenge his sister's death by evening the score with Snow White, who is rescued by the Prince.

PN: This unauthorized sequel to the Walt Disney classic *Snow White and the Seven Dwarfs* began production in 1986 simultaneously with another unauthorized sequel to a Dis-

ney masterpiece, *Pinocchio and the Emperor of the Night,* which was released in 1987. Unlike the Disney original, the film produced a small return, grossing only $3.2 million. Originally released in 1990 and doing only marginal business, the film was re-released in 1993 hoping to attract a wider audience but didn't.

☺ HEATHCLIFF: THE MOVIE (1986)

A DIC-Audiovisual-LBS Communications-McNaught Syndicate Production released by Atlantic Releasing and Clubhouse Pictures. **p:** Jean Chalopin; **d:** Bruno Bianchi; **w:** Alan Swayze (based on the comic strip *Heathcliff* by George Gately). **Running time:** 73 minutes.

Voices

Heathcliff: Mel Blanc

Featuring new introductory footage, the film incorporates numerous adventures from the television series with the famed comic-strip feline becoming involved in all kinds of escapades.

☺ HEAVY METAL (1981)

An Ivan Reitman/Leonard Mogel Production released by Columbia Pictures. **p:** Ivan Reitman; **d:** Gerald Potterton; **w:** Dan Goldberg and Len Blum (based on work and stories by Richard Corben, Angus McKie, Dan O'Bannon, Thomas Warkentin, Berni Wrightson); **m:** Elmer Bernstein. **Running time:** 91 minutes.

Voices

Roger Bumpass, Jackie Burroughs, John Candy, Joe Flaherty, Don Francks, Martin Lavut, Eugene Levy, Marlyn Lightstone, Alice Playten, Harold Ramis, Susan Roman, Richard Romanos, August Schellenberg, John Vernon, Zal Yanovsky

Seven segments backed by original rock music comprise this adult cartoon fantasy based on stories from *Heavy Metal* magazine.

☺ HEAVY TRAFFIC (1973)

A Steve Krantz Production released by American International Pictures. **p:** Steve Krantz; **d & scr:** Ralph Bakshi, **m:** Ray Shanklin, Ed Bogas. **Running time:** 78 minutes.

Voices

Joseph Kaufmann, Beverly Hope Atkinson, Frank DeKova, Terri Haven, Mary Dean Lauria, Jacqueline Mills, Lillian Adams, Jim Bates, Jamie Farr, Robert Easton, Charles Gordone, Michael Brandon, Morton Lewis, Bill Striglos, Jay Lawrence, Lee Weaver

Young cartoonist Michael, the virginal offspring of a Mafia member, leaves home after quarreling violently with his Jewish mother and takes a black girl, Rosa, as his mistress.

PN: Like *Fritz the Cat*, the film received an X rating, even though the content was not as visually and aurally explicit as Bakshi's first effort. It was originally to be based on Hubert Selby's *Last Exit to Brooklyn*, but a deal between Selby and Bakshi fell through. In 1974 a scattering of scenes from the film were reanimated for an R rating so the film could be reissued on a double bill with *The Nine Lives of Fritz the Cat*.

⊚ HEIDI'S SONG (1982)

A Hanna-Barbera Production released by Paramount Pictures. **p:** Joseph Barbera, William Hanna; **d:** Robert Taylor; **st:** Joseph Barbera, Jameson Brewer (based on the novel *Heidi* by Johanna Spyri); **scr:** Joseph Barbera, Robert Taylor, Jameson Brewer; **m:** Hoyet S. Curtin; **m/l:** Sammy Cahn, Burton Lane. **Songs:** "Friends," "It's a Christmas Day," "She's a Nothing!," "Can You Imagine," "An Unkind Word" and "You're Not Rat Enough to Be a Rat!" **Running time:** 94 minutes.

Voices

Grandfather: Lorne Greene; **Head Ratte:** Sammy Davis Jr.; **Heidi:** Margery Gray; **Gruffle:** Peter Cullen; **Peter:** Roger DeWitt; **Herr Sessman:** Richard Erdman; **Sebastian:** Fritz Feld; **Klara:** Pamela Ferdin; **Fraulein Rottenmeier:** Joan Gerber; **Willie:** Michael Bell; **Aunt Dete:** Virginia Gregg; **Tinette:** Janet Waldo; **Schnoddle/Hootie:** Frank Welker; **Mountain:** Michael Winslow.

Based on Johanna Spyri's enduring, tear-jerking novel *Heidi*, this animated musical version tells the story of Heidi, who is separated from her beloved grandfather and forced to live with a wealthy crippled girl and a mean-spirited governess who detests her, only to be reunited with her grandfather and her friends in the end.

PN: After years of intensive preparation, *Heidi's Song* was the next major animated feature produced by William Hanna and Joseph Barbera (who also cowrote the story and screenplay), following their last effort, 1973's *Charlotte's Web*.

⊚ HERCULES (1997)

A Walt Disney Production released by Buena Vista Pictures. **p:** Ron Clements, Alice Dewey, John Musker; **d:** Ron Clements, John Musker; **st:** Barry Johnson; **scr:** Ron Clements, Don McEnery, Irene Mecchi, John Musker, Bob Shaw; **m:** Alan Menken; **superv anim:** Chris Bailey, Nancy Beiman, Andreas Deja, Ken Duncan, Eric Goldberg. **Songs:** "Long Ago . . ," "Gospel Truth," "Go the Distance," "Oh Mighty Zeus," "One Last Hope," "Zero to Hero," "I Won't Say (I'm in Love)," "Star Is Born," "Big Olive," "Prophecy,

"Destruction of the Agora," "Phil's Island," "Rodeo," "Speak of the Devil," "Hydra Battle," "Meg's Garden," "Hercules' Villa," "All Time Chump," "Cutting the Thread" and "True Hero." **Running time:** 92 minutes.

Voices

Hercules: Tate Donovan; **Young Hercules (speaking):** Josh Keaton; **Young Hercules (singing):** Roger Bart; **Phil:** Danny DeVito; **Hades:** James Woods; **Meg (Megara):** Susan Egan; **Pain:** Bob Goldthwait; **Panic:** Matt Frewer; **Zeus:** Rip Torn; **Hera:** Samantha Eggar; **Alcmene:** Barbara Barrie; **Hermes:** Paul Shaffer; **The Fates:** Amanda Plummer, Carole Shelley, Paddi Edwards; **Narrator:** Charlton Heston; **Cyclops:** Patrick Pinney; **Calliope:** Lillias White; **Clio:** Vanesse Thomas; **Melpomene:** Cheryl Freeman; **Terpsichore:** La Chanze; **Thalia:** Roz Ryan; **Burnt Man:** Corey Burton; **Nessus:** Jim Cummings; **Apollo:** Keith David; **The Earthquake Lady:** Mary Kay Bergman; **Heavyset Woman:** Kathleen Freeman; **Little Boy:** Bug Hall; **Little Boy:** Kellen Hathaway; **Demetrius:** Wayne Knight; **Ithicles:** Aaron Michael Metchik.

Additional Voices

Tawatha Agee, Jack Angel, Shelton Becton, Bob Bergen, Rodger Bumpass, Jennifer Darling, Debi Derryberry, Bill Farmer, Milt Grayson, Sherry Lynn, Mickie McGowan, Denise Pickering, Philip Protor, Jan Rabson, Riley Steiner, Fronzi Thornton, Erik von Detten, Ken Williams.

Pumped-up Greek muscleman Hercules conquers the villainous Hades' hostile takeover of Mount Olympus in this souped-up, fiendishly funny animated musical-comedy from the producers of *The Little Mermaid* and *Aladdin*.

PN: Much like *The Hunchback of Notre Dame*, *Hercules* was a high-stakes risk for Walt Disney Productions, though the film fared better than expected. Opening the same week as the hit suspense/thriller *Face Off* starring John Travolta, *Hercules* came in a close second, raking in $21.454 million the weekend it premiered and going on to gross more than $99.0446 million nationwide.

⊚ HERE COME THE LITTLES (1983)

A DIC Enterprises Production released by Atlantic Releasing. **p:** Jean Chalopin, Andy Heward, Tetsuo Katayama; **d:** Bernard Deyries; **w:** Woody Kling; **m:** Haim Saban, Shuky Levy; **anim dir:** Tsukasa Tannai, Yoshinobu Michihata. **Running time:** 77 minutes.

Voices

Henry Bigg: Jimmy E. Keegan; **Lucy Little:** Bettina Bush; **Tom Little:** Donovan Freberg; **Uncle Augustus:** Hal Smith; **William Little:** Gregg Berger; **Helen Little:** Patricia Parris; **Grandpa Little:** Alvy Moore; **Dinky Little:** Robert David Hall; **Mrs. Evans:** Mona Marshall

When Henry Bigg's parents are lost in Africa, the boy is sent to live with his mean Uncle Augustus, who wants to be Henry's guardian so he can tear down Henry's house and build a shopping center. The Littles, Tom and Lucy, who accidentally wind up in Henry's suitcase, reveal themselves to Henry, who is astonished to learn of their existence but pledges to help them escape.

HEY, GOOD LOOKIN' (1982)
A Ralph Bakshi Production released through Warner Bros. **p, d & w:** Ralph Bakshi; **m:** John Madara, Ric Sandler. **Running time:** 76 minutes.

Voices
Vinnie: Richard Romanus; **Crazy Shapiro:** David Proval; **Roz:** Tina Bowman; **Eva:** Jesse Welles; **Solly:** Angelo Grisanti; Stompers: Danny Wells, Bennie Massa, Gelsa Palao, Paul Roman, Larry Bishop, Tabi Cooper; **Waitress:** Juno Dawson, **Chaplain:** Shirley Jo Finney; **Yonkel:** Martin Garner; **Alice:** Terry Haven; **Max:** Allen Joseph; **Chaplain:** Philip M. Thomas; **Old Vinnie:** Frank DeKova; **Sal:** Candy Candido; **Italian Man:** Ed Peck; **Italian Women:** Lillian Adams, Mary Dean Lauria; **Gelsa:** Donna Ponterotto; **The Lockers Staging and Choreography:** Toni Basil

Vinnie, a slicked-hair, 1950's type (drawn to look like John Travolta), is the head of a white youth street gang, The Stompers, whose rivals are a black group known as the Chaplains in this 1950's genre spoof.

PN: Ralph Bakshi completed principal work on this animated feature in 1975, but it was shelved by Warner Bros. for seven years before it was released.

HEY THERE, IT'S YOGI BEAR (1964)
A Hanna-Barbera Production released by Columbia Pictures. **p & d:** William Hanna, Joseph Barbera; **w:** William Hanna, Joseph Barbera, Warren Foster; **m:** Marty Paich; **anim dir:** Charles A. Nichols. **Songs:** "Hey There, It's Yogi Bear," "Ven-E, Ven-O, Ven-A," "Like I Like You," "Wet Whistle," "St. Louie" and "Ash Can Parade." **Running time:** 89 minutes.

Voices
Yogi Bear: Daws Butler; **Boo Boo/Ranger Smith:** Don Messick; **Cindy Bear:** Julie Bennett; **Grifter:** Mel Blanc; **Corn Pone:** Hal Smith; **Snively:** J. Pat O'Malley

Additional Voices
James Darren; Jean Vander Pyl

Yogi Bear, the self-proclaimed king of Jellystone Park, and pal Boo Boo travel cross-country in search of Yogi's girlfriend, Cindy, who has been captured by a circus. The

adventure winds up in New York, where Ranger Smith comes to the rescue of all three.

PN: The film was Yogi's first full-length animated feature and the first cartoon feature ever for Hanna-Barbera Productions.

HUGO THE HIPPO (1976)
A Brut/Hungarofilm Pannonia Filmstudio Production released by 20th Century-Fox. **p:** Robert Halmi; **d:** Bill Feigenbaum; **scr:** Thomas Baum; **m:** Bert Keyes; **anim dir:** Joszef Gemes. **Songs:** "It's Really True," "I Always Wanted to Make a Garden," "Somewhere You Can Call Home," "H-I-P-P-O-P-O-T-A-M-U-S," "You Said a Mouthful," "Best Day Ever Made," "Mr. M'Bow-Wow," "Wherever You Go, Hugo," "Harbor Chant" and "Zing Zang." **Running time:** 76 minutes.

Voices
Narrator: Burl Ives; **The Sultan:** Robert Morley; **Aban Khan:** Paul Lynde; **Jorma:** Ronnie Cox; **Jorma's Father:** Percy Rodriguez; **Royal Magician:** Jesse Emmette; **Judge:** Len Maxwell; **Grown Ups and Children:** Tom Scott; Don Marshall, H.B. Barnum III, Marc Copage, Charles Walken, Lee Weaver, Richard Williams, Frank Welker, Ron Pinkard, Michael Rye, Marc Wright. Ellsworth Wright, Vincent Esposito, Court Benson, Peter Benson, Mona Tera, Bobby Eilbacher, Len Maxwell, Peter Fernandez, Allen Swift, Derek Power, Frederick O'Neal, Al Fann, Thomas Anderson, Jerome Ward, Shawn Campbell, Lisa Huggins, John McCoy, Alicia Fleer, Lisa Kohane, Bobby Dorn, Pat Bright, Robert Lawrence; **Special Voice Effects:** Frank Welker, Nancy Wible, Jerry Hausner; **Vocalists:** Marie Osmond, Jimmy Osmond

A forlorn baby hippo struggles to survive against hippo-haters of the world in the Hungarian-produced feature Hugo the Hippo *(1976). © 20th Century-Fox*

A forlorn baby hippo struggles to survive against hippo-haters of the world, led by Aban Khan (voiced by Paul Lynde), and seeks the companionship of others to feel needed and loved.

☺ THE HUNCHBACK OF NOTRE DAME (1996)

A Walt Disney Production released by Buena Vista Pictures. **p:** Roy Conli, Don Hahn; **d:** Gary Trousdale, Kirl Wise; **st:** Tab Murphy (based on the novel *Notre-Dame de Paris*); **scr:** Irene Mecchi, Tab Murphy, Jonathan Roberts, Bob Tzudiker, Noni White; **m:** Alan Menken, Stephen Schwartz; **superv anim:** James Baxter, Dave Burgess, Russ Edmonds, Will Finn, Tony Fucile, Ron Husband, David Pruiksma, Mike Surrey, Kathy Zielinski. **Songs:** "The Bells of Notre Dame," "Out There," "Topsy Turvy," "Humiliation," "God Help the Outcasts," "The Bell Tower," "Heaven's Light/Hellfire," "A Guy Like You," "Paris Burning," "The Court of Miracles," "Sanctuary," "And He Shall Smite the Wicked" and "Someday." **Running time:** 90 minutes.

Voices

Quasimodo: Tom Hulce; **Esmeralda:** Demi Moore; **Frollo:** Tony Jay; **Phoebus:** Kevin Kline; **Clopin:** Paul Kandel; **Hugo:** Jason Alexander; **Victor:** Charles Kimbrough; **Laverne:** Mary Wickes; **The Archdeacon:** David Odgen Stiers; **Esmeralda (singing):** Heidi Mollenhauer; **Quasimodo's Mother:** Mary Kay Bergman; **Brutish Guard:** Corey Burton; **Miscellaneous Guards/Gypsies:** Jim Cummings; **Oafish Guard:** Bill Fagerbakke; **Miscellaneous Guards/Gypsies:** Patrick Pinney; **The Old Heretic:** Gary Trousdale; **Baby Bird:** Frank Welker; **Laverne (additional dialogue:** Jane Withers

Quasimodo, the 15th-century misshapen, gentle-souled bell ringer who lives in the belltower of the Notre Dame cathedral, defends the beautiful gypsy girl Esmeralda and the very cathedral he calls home from the evil Minister of Justice in this animated retelling of the classic Victor Hugo story.

PN: Costing $70 million to produce, *The Hunchback of Notre Dame* was not as successsful as some of Disney's other animated features in the 1990s. The film grossed $100.117 million in this country and $184.7 million worldwide. Talented songwriter/lyricist Alan Menken, who penned the award-winning musical scores for *Beauty and the Beast, Aladdin* and others, wrote the original music for the film along with Stephen Schwartz. Menken and Schwartz were honored with an Academy Award nomination for Best Original Score for their work.

☺ THE INCREDIBLE MR. LIMPET (1962)

A Warner Bros. release. **p:** John C. Rose; **d:** Arthur Lubin; **scr:** James Brewer and John C. Rose; **m:** Frank Perkins;

anim dir: Vladimir Tytla, Gerry Chiniquy, Hawley Pratt; **seq dir:** Robert McKimson. **Running time:** 99 minutes.

Cast

Henry Limpet: Don Knotts; **Bessie Limpet:** Carole Cook; **George Stickle:** Jack Weston; **Commander Harlock:** Andrew Duggan; **Admiral Spewter:** Larry Keating; **Admiral Fivestar:** Charles Meredith; **Admiral Doemitz:** Oscar Beregi

Voices

Limpet: Don Knotts; **Ladyfish:** Elizabeth MacRae; **Crusty:** Paul Frees

In this live-action/animated feature, Don Knotts plays a retiring Walter Mitty–type bookkeeper who, depressed by his inability to join the navy (he's classified as 4-F because of his eyesight), accidentally falls into the ocean and is suddenly transformed into a fish. In his new role, he makes friends, finds a sweetheart and aides the U.S. war effort by helping convoys cross the ocean to knock off enemy U-boats.

PN: Working titles were *Henry Limpet, Mister Limpet* and *Be Careful How You Wish.*

☺ JAMES AND THE GIANT PEACH (1996)

A Walt Disney/Skellington Production released by Buena Vista Pictures. **p:** Tim Burton; **d:** Henry Selick; **cpd:** John Engel, Henry Selick; **exec prod:** Jake Eberts; **scr:** Steven Bloom, Karey Kirkpatrick, Jonathan Roberts (based on the novel by Roald Dahl); **m:** Randy Newman; **anim superv:** Paul Berry. **Songs:** "My Name Is James," "That's Life," "Eating the Peach," "Family," "Heroes Return" and "Sail Away." **Running time:** 79 minutes.

Cast/Voices

Grasshopper: Simon Callow; **Centipede:** Richard Dreyfuss, **Ladybug:** Jane Leeves; **Aunt Spiker:** Joanna Lumley; **The Glowworm/Aunt Sponge:** Miriam Margolyes; **Old Man:** Pete Postlethwaite; **Spider:** Susan Sarandon; **James:** Paul Terry; **Earthworm:** David Thewlis; **Reporter #2:** J. Stephen Coyle; **James's Father:** Steven Culp; **Girl with Telescope:** Cirocco Dunlap, **Reporter #1:** Michael Girardin; **Reporter #3:** Tony Haney; **Woman in Bathrobe:** Katherine Howell; **Newsboy:** Chae Kirby; **Hard Hat Man:** Jeff Mosely; **Cabby:** Al Nalbandian; **Beat Cop:** Mike Starr; **James's Mother:** Susan Turner-Cray; **Street Kid:** Mario Yedidia

Additional Voices

Emily Rosen

After saving the life of a spider, a wildly imaginative young boy (James) embarks on a fantastic adventure after boarding a magical giant peach, only to become friends with a ladybug and a centipede who help him with his plan to get to New York, in this live-action/stop-motion animated featured based on Roald Dahl's popular children's story.

PN: Randy Newman, who scored the music for the Disney blockbuster feature *Toy Story,* wrote the music for this feature and received an Oscar nomination for Best Original Score.

◉ JETSONS: THE MOVIE (1990)
A Hanna-Barbera Production released by Universal Pictures. **p & d:** William Hanna and Joseph Barbera; **w:** Dennis Marks; **m:** John Debney (with original songs by Tiffany); **anim dir:** David Michener; **anim:** Frank Adriana, Oliver "Lefty" Callahan, David Feiss, Don MacKinnon, and Irv Spence. **Songs:** "Jetsons Main Title," "Gotcha," "Maybe Love, Maybe Not," "Staying Together," "I Always Thought I'd See You Again," "First Time in Love," "You and Me," "Home," "We're the Jetsons" (Jetsons' RAP) and "With You All the Way." **Running time:** 82 minutes.

Voices
George Jetson: George O'Hanlon; **Cosmo C. Spacely:** Mel Blanc; **Jane Jetson:** Penny Singleton; **Judy Jetson:** Tiffany; **Elroy Jetson:** Patric Zimmerman; **Astro:** Don Messick; **Rosie the Robot:** Jean Vander Pyl; **Rudy 2:** Ronnie Schell; **Lucy 2:** Patti Deutsch; **Teddy 2:** Dana Hill; **Fergie Furbelow:** Russi Taylor; **Apollo Blue:** Paul Kreppel; **Rocket Rick:** Rick Dees

Additional Voices
Michael Bell, Jeff Bergman, Brian Cummings, Brad Garrett, Rob Paulsen, Susan Silo, Janet Waldo, B.J. Ward, Jim Ward, Frank Welker

This film version of the classic cartoon show finds the fun-loving foursome, accompanied by their faithful companion/dog, Astro, moving to outer space when George receives a promotion. While their family adjusts to their new home in the Intergalactical Garden estates, George heads for his new job as vice president of the Spacely Sprocket factory. Trouble looms, however, with the discovery that someone is sabotaging the factory and its machinery.

PN: Based on the popular 1960s' TV show, this full-length feature grossed $5 million during the first weekend of its release and $20 million overall. One unpopular move was the ousting of actress Janet Waldo, the original voice of Judy Jetson, who recorded all her dialogue and was then dumped for the youthful pop singer Tiffany. The film's settings and vehicles were designed using advanced computer-animated techniques created by deGraf/Wahrman and Kroyer Films.

◉ JOURNEY BACK TO OZ (1974)
a Filmation Associates Production released by EBA. **p:** Norm Prescott, Lou Scheimer; **w:** Fred Ladd, Norm Prescott

d: Hal Sutherland; **m/l:** Sammy Cahn, James Van Heusen; **anim superv:** Amby Paliwoda. **Running time:** 90 minutes.

Voices
Dorothy: Liza Minelli; **Scarecrow:** Mickey Rooney; **Tin-Man:** Danny Thomas; **Cowardly Lion:** Milton Berle; **Aunt Em:** Margaret Hamilton; **Mombi, the Bad Witch;** Ethel Merman; **Glinda, the Good Witch:** Rose Stevens; **Pumpkinhead:** Paul Lynde; **Woodenhead:** Herschel Bernardi; **The Signpost:** Jack E. Leonard

Additional Voices
Mel Blanc; Paul Ford; Dallas McKennon; Larry Storch

Ever since the classic 1939 MGM/Judy Garland film filmmakers have wanted to return to the land of Oz, which is the focal point of this animated sequel featuring the same well-known characters—Dorothy, Tin Man, Scarecrow and the Cowardly Lion—in all-new adventures in the "land over the rainbow."

PN: This animated feature was originally produced in 1964 but was not released until nearly 10 years later.

◉ THE JUNGLE BOOK (1967)
A Walt Disney Production released by Buena Vista. **p:** Walt Disney; **d:** Wolfgang Reitherman; **dir anim:** Milt Kahl, Frank Thomas, Ollie Johnston Jr., John Lounsbery; **st:** Larry Clemmons, Ralph Wright, Ken Anderson, Vance Gerry (based on Rudyard Kipling's *The Jungle Book* stories); **m:** George Bruns. **Songs:** "I Wanna Be Like You," "Trust in Me," "My Own Home," "That's What Friends Are For," "Colonel Hathi's March" and "The Bare Necessities." **Running time:** 78 minutes.

Voices
Baloo the Bear: Phil Harris; **Bagheera the Panther:** Sebastian Cabot; **King Louise of the Apes:** Louis Prima; **Shere Kahn, the tiger:** George Sanders; **Kaa, the snake:** Sterling Holloway; **Colonel Hathi, the elephant:** J. Pat O'Malley; **Mowgli, the man-cub:** Bruce Reitherman; **Elephants:** Verna Felton, Clint Howard; **Vultures:** Chad Stuart, Lord Tim Hudson, J. Pat O'Malley, Digby Wolfe **Wolves:** John Abbott, Ben Wright; **Girl:** Darleen Carr

This animated adaptation of Rudyard Kipling's classic stories deals with Mowgli, an Indian boy abandoned at birth who is raised as a wolf cub and 10 years later is returned to his people by Bagheera, the panther who protected him as a child. In his jungle setting, Mowgli makes friends with Baloo, a happy-go-lucky bear, and lives life anew in the jungle, but not without a few close encounters with King Louie, Colonel Hathi and Shere Khan.

PN: The last animated film to bear the creative stamp of Walt Disney, who died in 1966.

Dorothy, Tin Man, Scarecrow and the Cowardly Lion return to Oz in the full-length animated feature Journey Back to Oz. © *Filmation*

☺ LADY AND THE TRAMP (1955)

A Walt Disney Production released by Buena Vista. **p:** Walt Disney; **d:** Hamilton Luske, Clyde Geronimi, Wilfred Jackson; **dir anim:** Milt Kahl, Frank Thomas, Ollie Johnston, John Lounsbery, Wolfgang Reitherman, Eric Larson, Hal King, Les Clark; **st:** Erdman Penner, Joe Rinaldi, Ralph Wright, Donald Da Gradi (based on an original story by Ward Greene); **m/sc:** Oliver Wallace. **Songs:** "He's a Tramp," "La La Lu," "Siamese Cat Song," "Peace on Earth" and "Bella Notte." **Running time:** 76 minutes.

Voices

Darling/Si/Am/Peg: Peggy Lee; **Lady:** Barbara Luddy; **Tramp:** Larry Roberts; **Trusty:** Bill Baucom; **Aunt Sarah:** Verna Felton; **Tony:** George Givot; **Jim Dear/Dog Catcher:** Lee Millar; **Bull/Dachsie/Jock/Joe:** Bill Thompson; **Beaver/Pet-Store Clerk:** Stan Freberg; **Boris:** Alan

Reed; **Toughby/Professor/Pedro:** Dallas McKennon; **Dogs in Pound:** The Mello Men

Lady, a pretty female cocker spaniel, falls in love with Tramp, a stray who values his liberty above all else. The heart of the story deals with the unusual bonding of the two characters—the more refined Lady and the outcast Tramp, who battles with two neighborhood mutts, Jock and Caesar, who yearn for Lady's love.

☺ THE LAND BEFORE TIME (1988)

A Sullivan Bluth Studios Production released by MGM/United Artists. **p:** Don Bluth, Gary Goldman, John Pomeroy; **d:** Don Bluth; **scr:** Stu Krieger; **st:** Judy Freudberg; Tony Geiss; **m:** James Horner; **anim dir:** John Pomeroy, Linda Miller, Ralph Zondag, Dan Kuenster, Lorna Pomeroy, Dick Zondag. **Running time:** 69 minutes.

Voices

Narrator/Rooter: Pat Hingle; **Littlefoot's Mother:** Helen Shaver; **Littlefoot:** Gabriel Damon; **Grandfather:** Bill Erwin; **Cera:** Candy Hutson; **Daddy Topps:** Burke Barnes; **Ducky:** Judith Barsi; **Petrie:** Will Ryan

A young brontosaurus named Littlefoot is orphaned when a tyrannosaurus attacks and separates his herd. He sets off in search of the Great Valley, a legendary land of lush vegetation where dinosaurs can live and thrive in peace. Along the way he meets four other youngsters, each a member of a different dinosaur family. Together they encounter incredible obstacles while learning unforgettable lessons about life.

PN: Three direct-to-video sequels were produced following the original feature: *The Land Before Time II: The Great Valley Adventure* (1994), *The Land Before Time III: The Time of the Great Giving* (1995) and *The Land Before Time IV: Journey Through the Mists* (1996).

THE LAST UNICORN (1982)

A Rankin-Bass Production released by ITC. **p & d:** Arthur Rankin Jr., Jules Bass; **w:** Peter S. Beagle (based on the novel by Peter S. Beagle); **m:** Jimmy Webb. **Running time:** 88 minutes.

Voices

Schmendrick the Magician: Alan Arkin; **Prince Lir:** Jeff Bridges; **The Last Unicorn/Lady Amalthea:** Mia Farrow; **Molly Grue:** Tammy Grimes; **The Butterfly:** Robert Klein; **Mommy Fortuna:** Angela Lansbury; **King Haggard:** Christopher Lee; **Capt. Cully:** Keenan Wynn; **The Talking Cat:** Paul Frees; **The Speaking Skull:** Rene Auberjonois

A young unicorn accompanied by a magician journeys to release the rest of her species from the tyranny of an evil king.

THE LION KING (1994)

A Walt Disney Production released by Walt Disney Pictures. **p:** Don Hahn; **d:** Roger Allers, Rob Minkoff; **exec prod:** Sarah McArthur, Thomas Schumacher; **scr:** Irene Mecchi, Jonathan Roberts, Linda Woolverton; **m:** Elton John, Hans Zimmer; **superv anim:** Tony Fucile, Mark Henn, Ellen Woodbury, Anthony de Rosa. **Songs:** "Circle of Life," "I Just Can't Wait to Be King," "Be Prepared," "Hakuna Matata," "Can You Feel the Love Tonight," "The Lion Sleeps Tonight," "I've Got a Lovely Bunch of Coconuts," "It's a Small World," "Hawaiian War Chant" and "Rhythm of the Pride Lands." **Running time:** 88 minutes.

Voices

Adult Simba: Matthew Broderick; **Young Simba:** Jonathan Taylor Thomas; **Mafasa:** James Earl Jones; **Adult Nala:** Moira Kelly; **Young Nala:** Niketa Calame; **Shenzi:** Whoopi Goldberg; **Banzai:** Cheech Marin; **Timon:** Nathan Lane; **Pumbaa:** Ernie Sabella; **Scar:** Jeremy Irons; **Rafiki:** Robert Guillaume; **Sarabi:** Madge Sinclair; **Sarafina:** Zoe Leader; **Zazu:** Rowan Atkinson; **Ed, the Laughing Hyena:** Jim Cummings; **Adult Simba (singing):** Joseph Williams; **Young Simba (singing):** Jason Weaver; **Adult Nala (singing):** Sally Dworsky; **Young Nala (singing):** Laura Williams

Additional Voices

Cathy Cavadini, Judi M. Durand, Daamen J. Krall, David McCharen, Linda Phillips, Philip Proctor, David J. Randolph, Frank Welker

Set amid the majestic beauty of the Serengeti, this coming-of-age saga tells of the love between a proud lion ruler, Mufasa, and his son, Simba, and follows Simba's heroic journey when he is forced into exile by his evil uncle after the death of his father, the King.

PN: This Disney animated feature was the most successful in the studio's history, earning $312.8 million in ticket sales and winning two Oscars for Best Original Score and Best Song. The home video release did even better than the movie, grossing more in its first two weeks than its entire theatrical run. A mild controversy followed the release of the film. Cult "Japanimation" fans raised questions over similarities between the hit Disney film and the 1960s' Japanese-created TV cartoon series *Kimba the White Lion*, which was based on a comic-book series from the 1950s called *The Jungle Emperor* by animator Osamu Tezuka, crowned "the Walt Disney of Japan." Disney cited *Hamlet* as one of the film's main influences. Disney pulled the movie from theaters in late September 1994, after grossing more than $270 million through the summer and falling out of the Top 10 for the first time since opening. The studio re-released the film at Thanksgiving, breeding new life at the box office and sending it on its way to the biggest-grossing animated feature in motion picture history.

THE LITTLE MERMAID (1989)

A Walt Disney Pictures presentation in association with Silver Screen Partners IV released by Buena Vista. **p:** Howard Ashman, John Musker; **d:** Ron Clements, John Musker; **scr:** Ron Clements, John Musker; **m:** Alan Menken; **anim dir:** Mark Henn, Glen Keane, Duncan Marjoribanks, Ruben Aquino, Andreas Deja, Matthew O'Callaghan. **Songs:** "Under the Sea," "Part of Your World," "Poor Souls," "Les Poissons," "Fathoms Below" and "Daughters of Triton." **Running time:** 82 minutes.

Voices

Louis: Rene Auberjonois; **Eric:** Christopher Daniel Barnes; **Ariel:** Jodi Benson: **Ursula:** Pat Carroll; **Scuttle:** Buddy

Hackett; **Flounder:** Jason Marin; **Triton:** Kenneth Mars; **Grimsby:** Ben Wright; **Sebastian:** Samuel E. Wright

Against her father's wishes, young mermaid princess Ariel travels beyond her world to the one above the sea, where she falls in love with a human prince in this cartoon adaptation of the Hans Christian Andersen tale.

PN: *Little Mermaid* set a box-office record for a modern-day fully animated feature, grossing $84.4 million. The record was soon surpassed by *Beauty and the Beast,* which grossed more than $141 million. Prior to *Little Mermaid*'s record-setting performance, Disney's *Oliver & Company* (1988) was the studio's top animated performer with $53.1 million.

⊚ LITTLE NEMO: ADVENTURES IN SLUMBERLAND (1991)

A Tokyo Movie Sinsha Company Production released by Hemdale Pictures Corporation. **p:** Yutaka Fujioka; **d:** Masami Hata, William T. Hurtz; **scr:** Chris Columbus, Richard Outten (based on the comic strip by Winsor McCay and on a concept for the screen by Ray Bradbury); **st:** Jean Mobius Giraud, Yutaka Fujioka; **m:** Thomas Chase, Steve Rucker (with songs by Richard M. Sherman and Robert B. Sherman); **superv anim:** Kazuhide Tomonaga, Nobuo Tomizawa. **Running time:** 85 minutes.

Voices

Little Nemo: Gabriel Damon; **Flip:** Mickey Rooney; **Professor Genius:** Rene Auberjonois; **Icarus:** Danny Mann; **Princess Camille:** Laura Mooney; **King Morpheus:** Bernard Erhard; **Nightmare King:** William E. Martin; **Oomp:** Alan Oppenheimer; **Oompy:** Michael Bell; **Oompe:** Sidney Miller; **Oompa:** Neil Ross; **Oompo:** John Stephenson; **Nemo's Mother:** Jennifer Darling; **Nemo's Father/Flap:** Greg Burson; **Bon Bon:** Sherry Lynn; **Dirigible Captain:** John Stephenson; **Courtier/Cop:** Guy Christopher; **Page:** Nancy Cartwright; **Page:** Ellen Gerstell; **Elevator Creature:** Tress MacNeille; **Etiquette Master:** Michael McConnohie; **Teacher #1/Cop:** Beau Weaver; **Teacher #2:** Michael Gough; **Dance Teacher:** Kathleen Freeman; **Fencing Teacher:** Michael Sheehan; **Librarian:** June Foray; **Equestrian Master:** Gregg Barger; **Goblin General:** Ben Kramer; **Woman:** Bever-Leigh Banfield

A young boy (Little Nemo) falls asleep and is carried off by a blimp to Slumberland, where he helps Princess Camille and her father, King Morpheus, defeat the armies of the evil Nightmare King in this feature-length adaptation of Winsor McCay's stylistic newspaper strip and animated cartoon of the same name.

PN: This feature was in production for 15 years before it was finally released. The film was big flop, grossing only $1.1 million in ticket sales. Famed fantasy novelist Ray Bradbury conceived the story of this feature-length treatment, and *Home Alone* director Chris Columbus was one of

the film's screenwriters. Former Disney and UPA animator William T. Hurtz codirected the movie, and veteran Disney animators Frank Thomas and Oliver Johnston served as story consultants. Original songs for the movie were written by Richard M. Sherman and Robert B. Sherman, the famed songwriting brothers who wrote the music for the Disney classic *Mary Poppins.* The title songs for the movie were sung by famed singer/songwriter Melissa Manchester.

⊚ LORD OF THE RINGS (1978)

A Fantasy Films/Saul Zaentz Production released by United Artists. **p:** Saul Zaentz; **d:** Ralph Bakshi; **w:** Chris Conkling, Peter S. Beagle (based on the stories by J.R.R. Tolkien); **m:** Leonard Roseman. **Running time:** 131 minutes.

Voices

Frodo: Christopher Guard; **Gandalf:** William Squire; **Sam:** Michael Scholes; **Aragon:** John Hurt; **Merry:** Simon Chandler; **Pippin:** Dominic Guard; **Bilbo:** Norman Bird; **Boromir:** Michael Graham-Fox; **Legolas:** Anthony Daniels; **Gimli:** David Buck; **Gollum:** Wood Thorpe; **Saruman:** Fraser Kerr; **Theoden:** Phillip Stone; **Wormtongue:** Michael Deacon; **Elrond:** Andre Murell; **Innkeeper:** Alan Tilvern; **Galadriel:** Annette Crosbie; **Treebeard:** John Westbrook

The Dark Lord Sauron possesses rings of great evil with which he can control Middle Earth, but that all changes when one of the rings falls into the hands of Hobbit Bilbo Baggins, who passes the ring and its inherent power on to his nephew, Frodo, to take up the battle.

PN: The film employs Bakshi's Rotoscope technique of animating live-action characters to create a lifelike effect.

⊚ MAD MONSTER PARTY (1967)

A Videocraft International Production released by Embassy Pictures. **p:** Arthur Rankin Jr.; **d:** Jules Bass; **exec prod:** Joseph E. Levine; **scr:** Len Korobkin, Harvey Kurtzman, Forrest J. Ackerman (based on a story by Rankin); **m/l:** Maury Laws, Jules Bass. **Songs:** "Mad Monster Party," "Waltz for a Witch," "Never Was a Love," "Cocktails," "The Mummy," "Drac," "The Baron," "You're Different," "Our Time to Shine" and "One Step Ahead." Filmed in Animagic. **Running time:** 94 minutes.

Voices

Baron Boris von Frankenstein/Uncle Boris: Boris Karloff; **Monster's Mate:** Phyllis Diller

Additional Voices

Ethel Ennis; Gale Garnett; Allen Swift

Using 3-D figures in a process called Animagic, this stop-action animated film lampoons the horror-film genre. This musical comedy features all the monsters—The Werewolf, Dracula, the Creature from the Black Lagoon, King Kong, Dr. Jekyll and Mr. Hyde, The Mummy and others—as attendees at a convention for the Worldwide Organization of Monsters. Their purpose: to select a new leader for the soon-to-be retired Baron Boris von Frankenstein.

PN: This was third and final full-length theatrical release produced by Arthur Rankin and Jules Bass in association with Joseph E. Levine for Embassy Pictures and was the most popular of the three. Veteran character designer Jack Davis did the character designs for the film. He was later responsible for the character designs for such popular Rankin/Bass television series as *The King Kong Show* and *The Jackson 5*. The character Yetch was modeled after well-known horror film star Peter Lorre, who died in 1964. Newspaper advertisements used to promote the film featured the headline, "At long last a Motion Picture with absolutely no cultural value!!"

THE MAGICAL WORLD OF CHUCK JONES (1992)

A Magical World/IF/X Production of a George Daughtery Film released by Warner Bros. **p:** George Daughtery, David Ka Lik Wong; **d:** George Daughtery: **exec prod:** Valerie Kausen; **m:** Cameron Patrick. **Running time:** 100 minutes.

Cast

Steven Spielberg, Whoopi Goldberg, Ron Howard, Matt Groenig, Leonard Maltin, Joe Dante, George Lucas, Steve Guttenberg, Chris Connelly, Danny Elfman, Gary Rydstrom, Friz Freleng, Roddy McDowall, June Foray, Maurice Noble, Roger Mayer, Linda Jones Clough, Marian Jones, Valerie Kausen, Chuck Jones

This "What's Up Doc-umentary" pays tribute to three-time Oscar winner and legendary Warner Bros. animator Chuck Jones, featuring excerpts from his greatest cartoon masterpieces—with Bugs Bunny, Daffy Duck, Elmer Fudd, Porky Pig, the Road Runner and Coyote et al. and clips from "One Froggy Evening," "What's Opera, Doc?" "Long-Hair Hare," "A Bear for Punishment," among others—plus interviews with former colleagues and friends.

PN: The documentary was released shortly after Jones's 80th birthday.

THE MAGIC PONY (1979)

A Soyuzmultifilm Studios Production released by Action Entertainment. **p:** C.B. Wismar; **d:** Ivan Ivanov-Vano; **scr:** George Malko (based on the Russian folktale by Peter Yershow); **m:** Tom Ed Williams; **superv anim:** Lev Milchin. **Songs:** "Ride a Magic Pony," "Lonely Child," "A Whale of a Day" and "On This Beautiful Day." **Running time:** 80 minutes.

Voices

King: Jim Backus; **Red Haired Groom:** Hans Conried; **Zip the Pony:** Erin Moran; **Ivan:** Johnny Whitaker

Additional Voices

Diane Alton; Robb Cigne; John Craig; Wayne Heffley; Jason Wingreen; Sandra Wirth

Ivan and his three brothers are sent to watch over the fields, in hope of catching the culprit responsible for the destruction of the wheat crop. Ivan catches the person—a Magic Pony, who leads him on a fascinating adventure where he encounters a range of characters, from an emperor to a terrifying whale.

MAKE MINE MUSIC (1946)

A Walt Disney Production released by RKO Radio Pictures. **p:** Walt Disney; **prod superv:** Joe Grant; **d:** Jack Kinney, Clyde Geronimi, Hamilton Luske, Robert Cormack, Joshua Meador; **st:** Homer Brightman, Dick Huemer, Dick Kinney, John Walbridge, Tom Oreb, Dick Shaw, Eric Gurney, Sylvia Holland, T. Hee, Dick Kelsey, Jesse Marsh, Roy Williams, Ed Penner, James Bodero, Cap Palmer, Erwin Graham; **md:** Charles Wolcott; **m/a:** Ken Darby, Oliver Wallace, Edward H. Plumb. **Songs:** "Johnny Fedora and Alice Bluebonnet," "All the Cats Join In," "Without You," "Two Silhouettes," "Casey, the Pride of Them All," "The Martins and the Coys," "Blue Bayou," "After You've Gone" and "Make Mine Music." **Running time:** 75 minutes.

Voices

Nelson Eddy, Dinah Shore, Benny Goodman and Orchestra, The Andrew Sisters, Jerry Colonna, Andy Russell, Sterling Holloway, The Pied Pipers, The King's Men, The Ken Darby Chorus, and featuring Tania Riabouchinska and David Lichine

Like *Fantasia*, this Disney production adapted popular music to the screen, featuring a collection of melodies in animated sequences, including "The Martins and the Coys," a cartoon version of an age-old hillbilly feud; "A Tone Poem," a mood piece based on Ken Darby's chorus of "Blue Bayou"; "A Jazz Interlude," with Benny Goodman and his orchestra leading a vignette drawn version of "All the Cats Join In."

THE MAN CALLED FLINTSTONE (1966)

A Hanna-Barbera Production released by Columbia Pictures. **p & d:** William Hanna, Joseph Barbera; **w:** Harvey Bullock, R.S. Allen (based on a story by Harvy Bullock and R.S. Allen and story material by Joseph Barbera, William Hanna, Warren Foster, Alex Lovy); **m:** Marty Paich, Ted Nichols; **anim dir:** Charles A. Nichols. **Songs:** "Pensate Amore," "Team Mates," "Spy Type Guy," "The Happy Sounds of

Paree," "The Man Called Flintstone," "When I'm Grown Up" and "Tickle Toddle." **Running time:** 90 minutes.

Voices
Fred Flintstone: Alan Reed Sr.; **Barney Rubble:** Mel Blanc; **Wilma Flintstone:** Jean Vander Pyl; **Betty Rubble:** Gerry Johnson

Additional Voices
Paul Frees; June Foray; Harvey Korman; Don Messick; John Stephenson; Janet Waldo

Resembling American spy Rock Slag, who was wounded while chasing international spy Green Goose and his girlfriend, Tanya, Fred Flintstone is asked to take Rock's place and fly to Rome (with his family, of course) to help corral Green Goose once and for all. The whole thing turns out to be a trap and the real Slag, now fully recovered, comes to Fred's rescue.

PN: The film's working title was *That Man Flintstone*.

THE MAN FROM BUTTON WILLOW (1965)

An Eagle Film Production released by United Screen Artists. **p:** Phyllis Bounds Detiege; **d & w:** Dave Detiege; **m:** George Stoll, Robert Van Eps. **Running time:** 81 minutes.

Voices
Justin Eagle: Dale Robertson; **Sorry:** Edgar Buchanan; **Stormy:** Barbara Jean Wong

Additional Voices
Herschel Bernardi; Buck Buchanan; Pinto Colvig; Cliff Edwards; Verna Felton; John Hiestand; Howard Keel; Ross Martin; Shep Menken; Clarence Nash; Edward Platt; Thurl Ravenscroft

Intrigue and espionage are key elements of this action-packed adventure about the first U.S. government undercover agent, Justin Eagle, who recovers a kidnapped government official and thwarts plans to sabotage a state railroad.

THE MANY ADVENTURES OF WINNIE THE POOH (1977)

A Walt Disney Production released through Buena Vista. **p:** Wolfgang Reitherman; **d:** Wolfgang Reitherman, John Lounsbery; **st:** Larry Clemmons, Vance Gerry, Ken Anderson, Ted Berman, Ralph Wright, Xavier Atencio, Julius Svendsen, Eric Cleworth; **m/l:** Richard Sherman, Robert B. Sherman. **Running time:** 74 minutes

Voices
Narrator: Sebastian Cabot; **Winnie the Pooh:** Sterling Holloway; **Tigger:** Paul Winchell; **Roo:** Clint Howard; **Roo:** Dori Whitaker; **Christopher Robin:** Timothy

Turner; **Christopher Robin:** Bruce Reitherman; **Christopher Robin:** Jon Walmsley; **Kanga:** Barbara Luddy; **Eeyore:** Ralph Wright; **Rabbit:** Junius Matthews; **Gopher:** Howard Morris; **Piglet:** John Fiedler; **Owl:** Hal Smith

A.A. Milne's beloved children's stories come alive in this collection of Winnie the Pooh cartoon shorts ("Winnie the Pooh and the Honey Tree," "Winnie the Pooh and the Blustery Day" and "Winnie the Pooh and Tigger Too") combined with new animation and released as a full-length feature.

MELODY TIME (1948)

A Walt Disney Production released by RKO Radio Pictures. **p:** Walt Disney; **prod superv:** Ben Sharpsteen; **anim dir:** Clyde Geronimi, Wilfred Jackson, Hamilton Luske, Jack Kinney; **st:** Winston Hibler, Harry Reeves, Ken Anderson, Erdman Penner, Homer Brightman, Ted Sears, Joe Rinaldi, Art Scott, Bob Moore, Bill Cottrell, Jesse Marsh, John Walbridge. "Little Toot" by Hardie Gramatky; **md:** Eliot Daniel, Ken Darby; **dir anim:** Eric Larson, Ward Kimball, Milt Kahl, Oliver M. Johnston Jr., John Lounsbery, Les Clark. **Songs:** "Melody Time," "Little Toot," "The Lord Is Good to Me," "The Pioneer Song," "Once Upon a Wintertime," "Blame It on the Samba," "Blue Shadows on the Trail," "Pecos Bill," "Trees" and "The Flight of the Bumblebee." **Running time:** 75 minutes.

Cast
Roy Rogers, Luana Patten, Bobby Driscoll, Ethel Smith, Bob Nolan, the Sons of the Pioneers

Voices/Musicians
Master of Ceremonies: Buddy Clark; The Andrews Sisters; Fred Waring and his Pennsylvanians: Frances Langford; Dennis Day; **Aracaun Bird:** Pinto Colvig; with Freddy Martin and His Orchestra featuring Jack Fina

The last of Disney's musical fantasies, this musical melange features live action and animated episodes based on popular songs of the day. Several key animated sequences make up the film, among them: "Blame It on the Samba," with Donald Duck and *Saludos Amigos* costar Jose Carioca in this animated samba backed by Ethel Smith and the Dinning Sisters; "Johnny Appleseed," featuring the voice of actor/singer Dennis Day as narrator; and "Little Toot," the story of a young tugboat's determination to be successful, sung by The Andrews Sisters.

METAMORPHOSES (1978)

A Sanrio Films release. **p:** Terry Ogisu, Hiro Tsugawa, Takashi; **d & w:** Takashi (based on Ovid's *Metamorphoses*); **seq dir:** Jerry Eisenberg, Richard Huebner, Sadao Miyamoto, Amby Paliwoda, Ray Patterson, Manny Perez, George Singer, Stan Walsh. **Running time:** 89 minutes.

Six of the most familiar Greek and Roman myths—creation; the hunter Actaeon turned into a stag by the goddess Diana; Orpheus and Eurydice; Mercy and the House of Envy; Perseus and Medusa; and Phaeton and the sun chariot—are integrated into this cartoon adaptation of five tales of classic mythology by Ovid.

PN: Three years in the making, *Metamorphoses* was first screened in the fall of 1977 but pulled back from general release for some additional postproduction work.

⊚ MISTER BUG GOES TO TOWN (1941)

A Fleischer Studios Production released by Paramount Pictures. **p:** Max Fleischer; **d:** Dave Fleischer; **w:** Dave Fleischer, Dan Gordon, Ted Pierce, Isadore Sparber, William Turner, Mike Meyer, Graham Place, Bob Wickersham, Cal Howard; **md:** Leigh Harline; **m/l:** Hoagy Carmichael, Frank Loesser, Herman Timberg, Four Marshals and Royal Guards. **Songs:** "We're the Couple in the Castle," "Boy, Oh Boy," "Katy-Did, Katy-Didn't," "Bee My Little Baby Bumble Bee" and "I'll Dance at Your Wedding." **Running time:** 78 minutes.

Voices

Kenny Gardner, Gwen Williams, Jack Mercer, Ted Pierce, Mike Meyer, Stan Freed, Pauline Loth

Bug life on Broadway sets the stage for this second feature by animators Max and Dave Fleischer chronicling an insect colony's never-ending battle against the human race. The film's central characters are Honey Bee and grasshopper Hoppity, the love interests of the story, and the nasty C. Bagley Beetle and his hoodlum henchmen, Swat the Fly and Smack the Mosquito, who make life miserable in bug town.

⊚ THE MOUSE AND HIS CHILD (1977)

A deFaria-Lockhart-Murakami-Wolf/Sanrio release. **p:** Walt deFaria; **d:** Fred Wolf, Chuck Swenson; **w:** Carol Mon Pere (based on the novel by Russell Hoban); **m:** Roger Kellaway. **Running time:** 83 minutes.

Voices

Manny: Peter Ustinov; **Eutrepe:** Cloris Leachman; **Seal:** Sally Kellerman; **Frog:** Andy Devine; **Mouse:** Alan Barzman; **Mouse Child:** Marcy Swenson; **Iggy:** Neville Brand; **Clock/Hawk:** Regis Cordic; **Elephant:** Joan Gerber; **Muskrat:** Bob Holt; **Startling/Teller:** Maitzi Morgan; **Crow:** Frank Nelson; **Crow:** Cliff Norton; **Serpentina:** Cliff Osmond; **The Paper People:** Iris Rainer; **Jack in the Box:** Bob Ridgely; **Blue Jay/The Paper People:** Charles Woolf; and Mel Leven

Based on Russell Hoban's novel, the film centers around the story of a mechanical mouse and his son who have one wish: to be self-winding.

⊚ MY LITTLE PONY: THE MOVIE (1986)

A Sunbow/Marvel Production in association with Hasbro, Inc. released by DeLaurentis Films. **p:** Joe Bacal, Tom Griffin, Michael Joens; (no director listed); **w;** George Arthur Bloom; **m:** Rob Walsh (theme song "My Little Pony" by Spencer Michilin and Ford Kinder); **superv anim:** Pierre DeCelles, Michael Fallows, Ray Lee. **Running time:** 90 minutes.

Voices

Grundle King: Danny DeVito; **Droggle:** Madeline Kahn; **Hydia:** Cloris Leachman; **Reeka:** Rhea Perlman; **The Moonchick:** Tony Randall; **Megan:** Tammy Amerson; **The Snooze:** Jon Bauman; **Baby Lickety Split/Bushwoolie #1:** Alice Playten; **Spike/Woodland Creature:** Charlie Adler; **Grundle:** Michael Bell; **Buttons/Woodland Creature/Bushwoolie:** Sheryl Bernstein; **Lofty/Grundle/Bushwoolie:** Susan Blu; **North Star:** Cathy Cavadini; **Gutsy/Bushwoolie #4:** Nancy Cartwright; **Grundle/Ahgg:** Peter Cullen; **Sundance/Bushwoolie #2:** Laura Dean; **Magic Star:** Ellen Gerstell; **Molly:** Keri Houlihan; **Fizzy/Baby Sunshine:** Katie Leigh; **Danny:** Scott Menville; **Sweet Stuff:** Laurel Page; **Wind Whistler:** Sarah Partridge; **Morning Glory/Rosedust/Bushwoolie/Shunk:** Russi Taylor; **Shady/Baby Lofty:** Jill Wayne; **Grundle/Bushwoolie #3:** Frank Welker

In Ponyland, the Little Ponies' annual Spring Festival is about to begin. While they are enjoying their festive spring party, the evil witch Hydia is plotting to turn Ponyland into a wasteland. When her attempt fails, she decides to cover Ponyland with a purple ooze called the "Smooze."

⊚ MY NEIGHBOR TOTORO (1993)

A Studio Ghibli Production released by 50th Street Films/Troma, Inc. **p:** Toru Hara (American producer: Carl Macek); **d:** Hayao Miyazaki (American director: Greg Snegoff); **exec prod:** Yasuyoshi Tokuma; **scr:** Hayao Miyazaki; **m:** Jo Hisaishi; **dir anim:** Yoshiharu Sato. **Songs:** "Sanpo" and "Tonarino Totoro." **Running time:** 86 minutes.

Voices

Lisa Michaelson, Cheryl Chase, Greg Snegoff, Kenneth Hartman, Alexandra Kenworthy, Natalie Core, Steve Kramer, Lara Cody, Melanie McQueen

After moving to the country with their professor-father, two young children befriend a giant, lovable supernatural spirit known as Totoro who becomes their magical guardian in a series of high-flying adventures.

PN: Released originally in 1988 in Japan, this English-dubbed version enjoyed modest success in the United States and was directed by accomplished Japanese director Hayao Miyazaki. The movie was a Film Advisory Board award winner.

THE NINE LIVES OF FRITZ THE CAT (1974)

A Steve Krantz Production released by American International Pictures. **p:** Steve Krantz; **d:** Robert Taylor; **scr:** Fred Halliday, Eric Monte, Robert Taylor; **m:** Tom Scott, L.A. Express. **Running time:** 76 minutes.

Voices

Fritz: Skip Hinnant; Reva Rose; Bob Holt

Married and tired of his nagging wife, Fritz gets high on marijuana and reexperiences some of the better times in his life—seducing his kid sister, acting as Hitler's orderly and blasting off to Mars among others—in this sequel to the 1972 original.

NUTCRACKER FANTASY (1979)

A Sanrio Films release. **p:** Walt deFaria, Mark L. Rosen, Arthur Tomioka; **d:** Takeo Nakamura; **w:** Thomas Joachim, Eugene Fornier (based on *The Nutcracker and the Mouse King* by E.T.A. Hoffman, adaptation by Shintaro Tsuji; **m:** Peter Illych Tchaikovsky (adapted and arranged by Akihito Wakatsuki, Kentaro Haneda). **Running time:** 82 minutes.

Voices

Narrator: Michele Lee; **Clara:** Melissa Gilbert; **Aunt Gerda:** Lurene Tuttle; **Uncle Drosselmeyer/Street Singer/ Puppeteer/Watchmaker:** Christopher Lee; **Queen Morphia:** Jo Anne Worley; **Chamberlain/Poet/Wiseman:** Ken Sansom; **King Goodwin:** Dick Van Patten; **Franz Fritz:** Roddy McDowall; **Indian Wiseman/Viking Wiseman:** Mitchel Gardner; **Chinese Wiseman/Executioner:** Jack Angel; **Otto Von Atra/French Wiseman/Clovis:** Gene Moss; **Queen of Time:** Eva Gabor; **Mice Voices:** Joan Gerber, Maxine Fisher; **Princess Mary:** Robin Haffner

A young girl dreams of romance and adventure in a world inhabited by a king whose daughter has been turned into a sleeping mouse and can only be transformed and reawakened by a heroic prince.

PN: This Japanese production, filmed and dubbed in English for American release, featured puppet animation.

THE NUTCRACKER PRINCE (1990)

A Lacewood Production released by Warner Bros. **p:** Kevin Gillis; **d:** Paul Schibli; **scr:** Patricia Watson (based on *The Nutcracker and the Mouseking* by E.T.A. Hoffman); **m:** Peter Ilyich Tchaikovsky (arranged by Victor Davies and performed by the London Symphony Orchestra under the direction of Boris Brott). **Running time:** 72 1/2 minutes.

Voices

Nutcracker Prince: Kiefer Sutherland; **Clara:** Megan Follows; **Mouseking:** Mike MacDonald; **Uncle Drosselmeier:** Peter Boretski; **Mousequeen:** Phyllis Diller; **Pantaloon:** Peter O'Toole

Young Clara Stahlbaum discovers a wooden nutcracker in the shape of a toy soldier under her Christmas tree. Her eccentric Uncle Drosselmeier tells her the story of the nutcracker, a young man named Hans, who was put under a spell by a wicked, vengeful Mousequeen. Clara dismisses the story, but that night everything her uncle told her unfolds before her eyes.

OF STARS AND MEN (1961)

A John and Faith Hubley film. **p:** John and Faith Hubley; **d:** John Hubley; **w:** John and Faith Hubley, Harlow Shapley (based on the book *Of Stars and Men* by Shapley); **anim dir:** William Littlejohn, Gary Mooney. **Running time:** 53 minutes.

Voices

Dr. Harlow Shapley, Mark Hubley, Hamp Hubley

Man's scientific world is interpreted in this film by animation husband-and-wife team John and Faith Hubley. The film's central character, Man, recalls his place in the universe—in space, time, matter and energy—and the meaning of life.

OLIVER & COMPANY (1988)

A Walt Disney/Silver Screen Partners III Production released by Buena Vista. **d:** George Scribner; **st:** Vance Gerry, Mike Gabriel, Joe Ranft, Jim Mitchell, Chris Bailey, Kirk Wise, Dave Michener, Roger Allers, Gary Trousdale, Kevin Lima, Michael Cedeno, Pete Young, Leon Joosen (based on Charles Dickens's *Oliver Twist*); **scr:** Jim Cox, Timothy J. Disney, James Mangold; **m:** Carole Childs (original score by J.A.C. Redford); **superv anim:** Mike Gabriel, Glen Keane, Ruben A. Aquino, Hendel Butoy, Mark Hehn, Doug Krohn. **Running time:** 72 minutes.

Voices

Oliver: Joey Lawrence; **Dodger:** Billy Joel; **Tito:** Cheech Marin; **Einstein:** Richard Mulligan; **Francis:** Roscoe Lee Browne; **Rita:** Sheryl Lee Ralph; **Fagan:** Dom DeLuise; **Roscoe:** Taurean Blacque; **Desoto:** Carl Weintraub; **Sykes:** Robert Loggia; **Jenny:** Natalie Gregory; **Winston:** William Glover; **Georgette:** Bette Midler

A rollicking take-off of Dickens's masterpiece with little orphan Oliver, a homeless kitten, taken in and cared for and taught "street smarts" by a pack of lovable hip dogs led by a human Fagin.

PN: *Oliver & Company* proved to be Disney's most successful fully animated feature in the 1980s, grossing a record $53.1 million.

◉ OLIVER TWIST (1974)

A Filmation Associates Production released by Warner Bros. **p:** Lou Scheimer, Norman Prescott; **d:** Hal Sutherland; **m:** George Blais. **Running time:** 75 minutes.

Voices
Oliver Twist: Josh Albee; **Fagin:** Les Tremayne.

Additional Voices
Phil Clark, Cathleen Cordell, Michael Evans, Lola Fischer, Robert Holt, Davy Jones, Larry D. Mann, Dallas McKennon, Billy Simpson, Larry Storch, Jane Webb, Helen Winston

In mid-19th-century London, an orphan boy finds that he is really the heir to a large fortune in this musical version of Charles Dickens's timeless novel.

PN: Originally released as a full-length feature, the film was reedited and broadcast as a prime-time special on NBC in 1981.

◉ ONCE UPON A FOREST (1993)

A Hanna-Barbera Production released by 20th Century-Fox. **p:** David Kirschner, Jerry Mills; **d:** Charles Grosnevor, David Michener; **scr:** Mark Young, Kelly Ward; **st:** Rae Lambert; **m:** James Horner. **Songs:** "Once Upon a Time With Me," "Forest," "Cornelius's Nature Lesson," "Accident," "Bedside Vigil," "Please Wake Up," "Journey Begins," "He's Back," "Flying," "Escaping from the Yellow Dragons/The Meadow," "Flying Home to Michelle" and "Children/Maybe One Day . . . Maybe One Day." **Running time:** 72 minutes.

Voices
Cornelius: Michael Crawford; **Phineas:** Ben Vereen; **Abigail:** Ellen Blain; **Edgar:** Ben Gregory; **Russell:** Paige Gosney; **Michelle:** Elizabeth Moss; **Abigail's Father:** Paul Eiding; **Edgar's Mother:** Janet Waldo; **Russell's Mother:** Susan Silo; **Willy:** Will Estes; **Waggs:** Charles Adler; **Bosworth:** Rickey Collins; **Bosworth's Mother:** Angel Harper; **Marshbird:** Don Reed; **Truck Driver:** Robert David Hall; **Russell's Brother:** Benjamin Smith; **Russell's Sister:** Haven Hartman

Exploring humans' cavalier encroachment on nature, this politically correct storybook fantasy details the adventures of four young forest animals—a wood mouse named Abigail, a mole named Edgar, a hedgehog named Russell and their little badger friend Michelle—and a wise old badger, Cornelius, who try to stop the deforestation of the forest by man and retrieve an herbal antidote that grows there to save the life of Michelle, who becomes seriously ill after a tanker crashes and releases poison gas in the air.

PN: Box-office gross for this Hanna-Barbera feature only totaled $6.2 million.

◉ ONE HUNDRED AND ONE DALMATIONS (1961)

A Walt Disney Production released by Buena Vista. **p:** Walt Disney; **d:** Wolfgang Reitherman, Hamilton Luske, Clyde Geronimi; **st:** Bill Peet (based on *The Hundred and One Dalmations* by Dodie Smith); **m:** George Bruns; **dir anim:** Milt Kahl, Frank Thomas, Marc Davis, John Lounsbery, Ollie Johnston, Eric Larson. **Songs:** "Cruelle De Vil," "Dalmation Plantation" and "Kanine Krunchie Commercial." **Running time:** 79 minutes.

Voices
Pongo: Rod Taylor; **Perdita:** Lisa Daniels; **Perdita:** Cate Bauer; **Roger Radcliff:** Ben Wright; **Anita Radcliff:** Lisa Davis; **Nanny/Queenie/Lucy:** Martha Wentworth; **The Colonel/Jaspar Badun/etc.:** J. Pat O'Malley, Horace Badun; **Inspector Craven:** Fred Worlock; **Cruella De Vil/Miss Birdwell:** Betty Lou Gerson; **Towser:** Tudor Owen; **Quizmaster/Collie:** Tom Conway; **Danny:** George Pelling; **The Captain:** Thurl Ravenscroft; **Sergeant Tibs:** Dave Frankham; **Television Announcer/Labrador:** Ramsay Hill; **Princess:** Queenie Leonard; **Duchess:** Marjorie Bennett; **Rolly:** Barbara Beaird; **Patch:** Mickey Maga; **Penny:** Sandra Abbott; **Lucky:** Mimi Gibson; **Rover:** Barbara Luddy; **Dirty Dawson:** Paul Frees; **Singer of TV Commercial:** Lucille Bliss

Additional Voices
Sylvia Marriott, Dallas McKennon, Basil Ruysdael, Max Smith, Rickie Sorensen, Bob Stevens

The spotted dogs owned by British couple Roger and Anita grow to multitudes when their prized pets Pongo and Perdita produce 15 beautiful Dalmatian puppies. The newborns fall prey to a rich and cunning woman, Cruella De Vil, a self-professed fur lover. Aided by henchmen Jasper and Horace, she steals the poor pups and makes plans to turn them into fur coats!

PN: Costing approximately $4 million to produce, this Disney classic featured the use of Xerography, whereby Disney animators made multiple copies of drawings, thus eliminating the necessity to draw 101 separate dogs for the mass character scenes.

◉ 1001 ARABIAN NIGHTS (1959)

A UPA (United Productions of America) Production released by Columbia Pictures. **p:** Steve Bosustow; **d:** Jack Kinney; **scr:** Czeni Ormonde; **st:** Dick Kinney, Leo Salakin, Pete Burness, Lew Keller, Ed Notziger, Ted Allan, Margaret Schneider, and Paul Schneider); **m:** George Duning; **dir anim:** Abe Levitow. **Songs:** "You Are My Dream," "Three Little Maids from Damascus" and "Magoo's Blues." **Running time:** 76 minutes.

Voices

Uncle Abdul Azzia Magoo: Jim Backus; **Princess Yasminda:** Kathryn Grant; **Aladdin/Magoo's nephew:** Dwayne Hickman; **The Wicked Wazir:** Hans Conried; **The Jinni of the Lamp:** Herschel Bernardi; **Sultan:** Alan Reed; **Omar the Rug Maker:** Daws Butler; **Three Little Maids from Damascus:** The Clark Sisters

Nearsighted, bumbling Baghdad lamp dealer Azziz Magoo wants his carefree nephew Aladdin to wed and settle down. Aladdin likes his own way of life until he falls in love with the beautiful Princess Yasminda. Yasminda is to wed the Wicked Wazir, who craves absolute power but can't have it until he also gets possession of a magic lamp that lies buried in a treasure cave. Magoo is fooled into giving up the magic lamp to the Wicked Wazir, although Wazir's victory is short-lived as Magoo triumphs in the end by defeating him entirely.

PN: The Technicolor film marked the first full-length feature for UPA and the first animated feature starring the myopic Mr. Magoo.

◎ THE PAGEMASTER (1994)

A 20th Century-Fox/Turner Pictures/David Kirschner Production released by 20th Century-Fox. **p:** David Kirschner, Paul Gertz (animation producers: David J. Steinberg, Barry Weiss; live-action scenes produced by Michael R. Joyce); **d:** Maurice Hunt (animation), Joe Johnston (live action); **st:** David Kirschner, David Casci; **scr:** David Casci, David Kirschner, Ernie Contreras; **m:** James Horner. **Songs:** "Dream Away" and "Whatever You Imagine." **Running time:** 80 minutes.

Cast/Voices

Richard Tyler: Macaulay Culkin; **Mr. Dewey and the Pagemaster:** Christopher Lloyd; **Alan Tyler:** Ed Begley Jr.;

Nearsighted Mr. Magoo takes a flying carpet ride he'll never forget in Columbia Pictures' 1001 Arabian Nights. © Screen Gems

Claire Tyler: Mel Harris; **Adventure:** Patrick Stewart; **Fantasy:** Whoopi Goldberg; **Horror and Dragon:** Frank Welker; **Dr. Jekyll & Mr. Hyde:** Leonard Nimoy; **Captain Ahab:** George Hearn; **Jamaican Pirates:** Dorian Harewood; **George Merry:** Ed Gilbert; **Pirates:** Richard Erdmann, Fernando Escandon, Robert Picardo; **Tom Morgan:** Phil Hartman; **Long John Silver:** Jim Cummings; **Queen of Hearts:** B.J. Ward; **Neighborhood kids:** Canan J. Howell, Alexis Kirschner, Jessica Kirschner, Guy Mansker, Brandon McKay, Stephen Sheehan

Richard Tyler, a bookwormish young boy, is transported to an animated world in which fictional characters from his favorite books come to life—Captain Ahab, Long John Silver, Dr. Jekyll (and Mr. Hyde)—and knowledge is the only key to get him home in this live-action/animated adventure.

◎ THE PEBBLE AND THE PENGUIN (1995)

A Don Bluth Limited Production released by Metro-Goldwyn-Mayer. **p:** Russell Boland; **d:** Don Bluth, Gary Goldman; **exec prod:** James Butterworth; **scr:** Rachel Koretsky, Steve Whitestone; **m/sc:** Mark Watters (with original songs by Barry Manilow and Bruce Sussman); **dir anim:** John Pomeroy, Len Simon, Richard Brazley, Silvia Hoefnagels, Ralf Palmer, John Hill, John Power. **Songs:** "Now and Forever," "Sometimes I Wonder," "The Good Ship Misery," "Don't Make Me Laugh" and "Looks I Got a Friend." **Running time:** 74 minutes.

Voices

Narrator: Shari Wallis; **Chubby/Gentoo:** S. Scott Bullock; **Hubie:** Martin Short; **Marina:** Annie Golden; **Priscilla/Chinstrap:** Louise Vallance; **Pola/Chinstrap:** Pat Music; **Gwynne/Chinstrap:** Angeline Ball; **Timmy:** Kendall Cunningham; **Petra:** Alissa King; **Beany:** Michael Nunes; **Drake:** Tim Curry; **Scrawny:** Neil Ross; **King:** Philip L. Clarke; **Megellenic #1:** B.J. Ward; **Mellegenic #2:** Hamilton Camp; **McCallister:** Stanley Jones; **Royal/Tika:** Will Ryan; **Rocko:** James Belushi

Escaping to Antarctica with his streetwise friend Rocko, Hubie, a lovable but introverted penguin, plans to present his betrothal pebble to the bird of his dreams in this Don Bluth–animated feature, with original songs by award-winning singer/songwriter Barry Manilow.

PN: American filmgoers never warmed up to this film, which was the last feature to originate from Don Bluth's Irish studio. It opened the same weekend as Disney's *A Goofy Movie* and took in only $3.9 million. The original story for the film was based on mating habits observed among Antarctica's Adelie penguins, which engage in an elaborate ritual involving brightly colored stones. A special added attraction, featured with the full-length animated feature, was an all-new Pink Panther cartoon, "Driving Mr. Pink," featuring a new character: Voodoo Man. Five months after its theatrical release, Warner Bros. released the film on home video. During its first two weeks, it ranked number one in sales, according to VideoScan, Inc.

◎ PETER PAN (1953)

A Walt Disney Production released by RKO Radio Pictures. **p:** Walt Disney; **d:** Hamilton Luske, Clyde Geronimi, Wilfred Jackson; **dir anim:** Milt Kahl, Frank Thomas, Wolfgang Reitherman, Ward Kimball, Eric Larson, Ollie Johnston, Marc Davis, John Lounsbery, Les Clark, Norman Ferguson; **st:** Ted Sears, Bill Peet, Joe Rinaldi, Erdman Penner, Winston Hibler, Milt Banta, Ralph Wright, Bill Cottreoll (adapted from the play and books by Sir James M. Barrie); **m/sc:** Oliver Wallace. **Songs:** "The Elegant Captain Hook," "The Second Star to the Right," "What Makes the Red Man Red?" "You Can Fly, You Can Fly, You Can Fly," "Your Mother and Mine," "A Pirate's Life," "March of the Lost Boys (Tee Dum Tee Dee)" and "Never Smile at a Crocodile." **Running time:** 76 1/2 minutes.

Voices

Peter Pan: Bobby Driscoll; **Wendy:** Kathryn Beaumont; **Captain Hook/Mr. Darling:** Hans Conried; **Mr. Smee and other pirates:** Bill Thompson; **Mrs. Darling:** Heather Angel; **John Darling:** Paul Collins; **Michael:** Tommy Luske; **Indian Chief:** Candy Candido; **Narrator:** Tom Conway

Left in the care of a nursemaid, Wendy, Michael and John, the children of Mr. and Mrs. Darling of Bloomsbury, London, are swept away to fascinating adventures with fairy-tale hero Peter Pan, who, along the way, saves the children from his longtime nemesis, Captain Hook.

◎ PETE'S DRAGON (1977)

A Walt Disney Production released by Buena Vista. **p:** Ron Miller, Jerome Courtland; **d:** Don Chaffey; **anim dir:** Don Bluth; **w:** Malcolm Marmorstein (based on a story by Seton I. Miller and S.S. Field); **m:** Irwin Kostal. **Songs:** "Candle on the Water," "I Saw a Dragon," "It's Not Easy," "Every Little Piece," "The Happiest Home in These Hills," "Brazzle Dazzle Day," "Boo Boo Bopbopbop (I Love You Too)," "There's Room for Everyone," "Passamashloddy" and "Bill of Sale." **Running time:** 134 minutes.

Cast

Nora: Helen Reddy; **Dr. Terminus:** Jim Dale; **Lampie:** Mickey Rooney; **Hoagy:** Red Buttons; **Lena Gogan:** Shelley Winters; **Pete:** Sean Marshall; **Miss Taylor:** Jean Kean; **The Mayor:** Jim Backus; **Merle:** Charles Tyner; **Grover:** Gary Morgan; **Willie:** Jeff Conway; **Paul:** Cal Bartlett; **Captain:** Walter Barnes; **Store Proprietor:**

Robert Easton; **Man with Visor:** Roger Price; **Old Sea Captain:** Robert Foulk; **Egg Man:** Ben Wrigley; **Cement Man:** Joe Ross; **Fishermen:** Al Checco, Henry Slate, Jack Collins

Voices

Elliott the Dragon: Charlie Callas

Pete, an orphaned little boy, runs away from his foster family and makes friends with an animated dragon named Elliott, who becomes the child's new companion.

PN: Elliott was the film's only animated star, appearing in live-action scenes with characters throughout the film. The film was cut by 30 minutes for its 1984 rerelease.

◎ THE PHANTOM TOLL BOOTH (1970)

A Chuck Jones Production released by Metro-Goldwyn-Mayer. **p:** Chuck Jones, Abe Levitow, Les Goldman; **d:** Chuck Jones, Abe Levitow, David Monahan; **w:** Chuck Jones, Sam Rosen (based on the book by Norton Juster); **m:** Dean Elliott; **anim dir:** Ben Washam, Hal Ambro, George Nicholas. **Songs:** "Milo's Song," "Time Is a Gift," "Word Market," "Numbers Are the Only Things That Count," "Rhyme and Reason Reign," "Don't Say There's Nothing to Do in the Doldrums" and "Noise, Noise, Beautiful Noise." **Running time:** 90 minutes.

Cast

Milo: Butch Patrick

Voices

Mel Blanc, Daws Butler, Candy Candido, Hans Conried, June Foray, Patti Gilbert, Shep Menken, Cliff Norton, Larry Thos, Les Tremayne

Milo, a young lad bored with life, is taken to the Kingdom of Wisdom where he embarks on a magical journey with new friends, Tock and Humburg, to rescue the Princesses of Rhyme and Reason. He returns home through the toll booth in his room from which he came. The film opens and closes with live-action sequences of Milo, played by *Munsters* star Butch Patrick, who is transformed into an animated character once he is transported into this land of make-believe.

PN: Chuck Jones directed this film, the first full-length feature of his career and the first for MGM.

◎ PINOCCHIO (1940)

A Walt Disney Production released by RKO Radio Pictures. **p:** Walt Disney; **superv dir:** Ben Sharpsteen, Hamilton Luske; **seq dir:** Bill Roberts, Norman Ferguson, Jack Kinney, Wilfred Jackson, T. Hee; **anim dir:** Fred Moore, Franklin Thomas, Milton Kahl, Vladimir Tytla, Ward Kimball, Arthur Babbitt, Eric Larson, Wolfgang Reitherman;

st (adaptation): Ted Sears, Otto Englander, Webb Smith, William Cottrell, Joseph Sabo, Erdman Penner, Aurelius Battaglia (based on the story by Collodi a.k.a. Carlo Lorenzini); **m/l:** Leigh Harline, Ned Washington, Paul J. Smith. **Songs:** "When You Wish Upon a Star," "Little Woodenhead," "Hi Diddle Dee Dee (An Actor's Life for Me)," "I've Got No Strings" and "Give a Little Whistle." **Running time:** 88 minutes.

Voices

Pinocchio: Dickie Jones; **Geppetto:** Christian Rub; **Jiminy Crickett:** Cliff Edwards; **The Blue Fairy:** Evelyn Venable; **J. Worthington Foulfellow:** Walter Catlett; **Gideon:** Mel Blanc; **Lampwick:** Frankie Darro; **Stromboli and the Coachman:** Charles Judels; **Barker:** Don Brodie

The story of toymaker Geppetto and his wooden puppet creation, Pinocchio, became Walt Disney's second feature-length attempt in three years. Given life by the Blue Fairy, Pinocchio is joined by Jiminy Cricket, appointed as "his conscience," to lead him through real-life adventures of boyhood.

⊚ PINOCCHIO AND THE EMPEROR OF THE NIGHT (1987)

A Filmation Associates Production released by New World Pictures. **p:** Lou Scheimer; **d:** Hal Sutherland; **w:** Robby London, Barry O'Brien, Dennis O'Flaherty (based on a story by Dennis O'Flaherty from *The Adventures of Pinocchio* by Collodi a.k.a. Carlo Lorenzini); **m:** Anthony Marinelli, Brian Banks; **m/l:** Will Jennings, Barry Mann, Steve Tyrell, Anthony Marinelli; **superv anim:** John Celestri, Chuck Harvey, Kamoon Song. **Songs:** "Love Is The Light Inside Your Heart," "You're a Star," "Do What Makes You Happy" and "Neon Cabaret." **Running time:** 88 minutes.

Voices

Scalawag: Edward Asner; **Geppetto:** Tom Bosley; **Twinkle:** Lana Beeson; **Emperor of the Night:** James Earl Jones; **Fairy Godmother:** Rickie Lee Jones; **Gee Willikers:** Don Knotts; **Pinocchio:** Scott Grimes; **Bee-Atrice:** Linda Gary; **Lt. Grumblebee:** Jonathan Harris; **Puppetino:** William Windom; **Igor:** Frank Welker

Woodcarver mentor Geppetto assigns former puppet creation Pinocchio to deliver a jewel box to the mayor. Despite a friendly warning from Gee Willikers, a toy glowbug brought to life by the Blue Fairy, Pinocchio becomes sidetracked along the way. He encounters a shifty racoon and monkey assistant who con him out of the jewel box. Ashamed, he joins the traveling circus and continues search for the missing jewel box.

PN: Despite a concerted effort to market the film to fans of the original Disney *Pinocchio*, this Filmation-produced full-length animated feature grossed only $3 million in ticket revenue.

⊚ PINOCCHIO IN OUTER SPACE (1965)

A Swallow/Belvision Production released by Universal Pictures. **p:** Norm Prescott, Fred Ladd; **d:** Ray Goossens; **w:** Fred Laderman (based on an idea by Prescott from the story by Carlo Collodi); **m:** F. Leonard, H. Dobelaere, E. Schurmann; **m/l:** Robert Sharp, Arthur Korb. **Running Time:** 71 minutes.

Voices

Nurtle the Turtle: Arnold Stang; **Pinocchio:** Peter Lazer

Additional Voices

Jess Cain; Conrad Jameson; Kevin Kennedy; Mavis Mims; Cliff Owens; Minerva Pious; Norman Rose

Turned back into a puppet by Gepetto, Pinocchio becomes friends with an outer-space creature, Nurtle the Turtle, whose spaceship has accidentally landed on Earth. Pinocchio helps Nurtle get back on course and joins him on a trip to Mars where they encounter the menacing Astro the Flying Whale, who plans to invade Earth.

PN: Film was titled *Pinocchio Dans Le Space* for its Belgian release. Working title: **Pinocchio's Adventure in Outer Space.**

⊚ PIPPI LONGSTOCKING (1997)

An AB Svensk Filmindustri/Iduna Film/TFC Trickcompany and Nelvana Limited Production released by Legacy Releasing. **p:** Waldemar Bergendahl, Hasmi Giakoumis, Merle-Anne Ridley, Michael Shaack; **d:** Clive Smith; **exec prod:** Michael Hirsh, Patrick Loubert, Clive Smith, Lennart Wilkund (co-exec prod: David Ferguson); **scr:** Catharina Stackelberg (with additional dialogue written by Frank Nissen and Ken Sobol, based on the books by Astrid Lindgren); **m:** Anders Bergund; **anim dir:** Ute V. Minchon-Pohl, Edson Basarin, Robin Budd, Bill Giggle. **Songs:** "What Shall I Do Today," "Hey-Ho I'm Pippi," "Recipe for Life," "A Bowler and a New Gold Tooth," "Pluttifikation" and "The Schottish." **Running time:** 75 minutes.

Voices

Pippi Longstocking: Melissa Altro; **Mrs. Prysselius:** Catherine O'Hara; **Teacher:** Carole Pope; **Thunder-Karlsson:** Dave Thomas; **Captain Longstocking:** Gordon Pinset; **Dunder-Karlsson:** Peter Karlsson; **Constable Kling:** Jan Sigurd; **Constable Klang:** Phillip Williams; **Mrs. Settergren:** Karen Bernstein; **Mr. Settergren:** Martin Zavut; **Mrs. Prysselius:** Wallis Grahn; **Tommy:** Noah Reid; **Blom:** Wayne Robson; **Annika (vocals):** Judy Tate; **Mr. Nillson/Dog:** Richard Binsley; **O'Malley/King:** Rick Jones; **Fridolf:** Chris Wiggins; **Mrs. Klang:** Mari Trainer; **Mrs. Kling:** Elva Mai Hoover; **Ringmaster:** Phillip Williams; **Snake Lady:** Melleny Melody; **Adolp:** Howard

Jerome; **Kids:** Kyle Farley; **Zachary Spider:** Brown Smith; **Group Singers:** Brent Barkman, Emily Barlow, Marleve Herington

A nine-year-old girl lives the way all children wish they could—in charge of their own destiny—in this animated musical adaptation of Astrid Lindgren's popular children's books.

PN: This Canadian-Swedish–produced animated feature was shown in limited release in the United States, opening at only 73 theaters. Consequently, the film did not muster up much in ticket sales, producing a total box-office gross of $478,113.

◎ THE PLAGUE DOGS (1984)
A Nepenthe Productions released by United International Pictures. **p, d & w:** Martin Rosen; **m:** Patrick Gleason; **anim dir:** Tony Guy, Colin White. **Running time:** 103 minutes.

Voices
John Hurt, Christopher Benjamin, James Bolam, Nigel Hawthorne, Warren Mitchell, Bernard Hepton, Brian Stirner, Penelope Lee, Geoffrey Mathews, Barbara Leigh-Hunt, John Bennet, John Franklyn-Robbins, Bill Maynard, Malcolm Terris, Judy Geeson, Phillip Locke, Brian Spink, Tony Church, Anthony Valentine, William Lucas, Dandy Nichols, Rosemary Leach, Patrick Stewart

Two dogs, one of whom already was the victim of experimental brain surgery, escape from a government research establishment in England's Lake District. Their mission is to find a kind master and an island where they may be safe from pursuit and their own dread.

PN: Filmmaker Martin Rosen, of *Watership Down* fame, produced this film, which was originally previewed in London two years before its American release.

◎ POCAHONTAS (1995)
A Walt Disney Production relesed by Walt Disney Pictures. **p:** James Pentescost; **d:** Mike Gabriel, Eric Goldberg; **scr:** Carl Binder, Susannah Grant, Philip LaZebnik; **m:** Alan Menken, Stephen Schwartz; **superv anim:** Renee Holt-Bird, Glen Keane, Duncan Marjoribanks, David Pruiksma. **Songs:** "Virginia Company," "Ship at Sea," "Steady as the Beating Drum," "Just Around the Riverbend," "Grandmother Willow," "Listen with Your Heart," "Mine, Mine, Mine," "Colors of the Wind," "Savages, Part 1," "Savages, Part 2," "I'll Never See Him Again," "Pocahontas," "Council Meeting," "Percy's Bath," "River's Edge," "Skirmish," "Getting Acquainted," "Ratcliffe's Plan," "Picking Corn," "Warriors Arrive," "John Smith Sneaks Out," "Execution," "Farewell" and "If I Never Knew You." **Running time:** 81 minutes.

Voices
John Smith: Mel Gibson; **Pocahontas:** Irene Bedard; **Lon:** Joe Baker; **Thomas:** Christian Bale; **Ben:** Billy Connolly; **Kocoum:** James Apaumut Fall; **Grandmother Willow:** Linda Hunt; **Meeko:** Jon Kassir; **Pocahontas (singing):** Judy Kuhn; **Percy:** Danny Mann; **Powhatan:** Russell Means; **Governor Ratcliffe/Wiggins:** David Odgen Stiers; **Nakoma:** Michelle St. John; **Kekata:** Gordon Tootoosis; **Flit:** Frank Welker

A courageous and free-spirited Indian woman defies her father by falling in love with Captain John Smith, leader of a rag-tag band of English sailors and soldiers to the New World who plunder its riches, even though she has already been pledged to marry a great Indian warrior.

PN: Disney premiered this feature in New York's Central Park, attracting more than 100,000 filmgoers. Overall, the film drummed up less business at the box office than Disney's previous blockbusters *Beauty and the Beast* and *The Lion King*, as it faced stronger-than-usual competition from *Casper*, *Batman Forever* and *Mighty Morphin Power Rangers: The Movie*, released during the summer. Budgeted at $55 million, the film grossed $141.6 million nationally and $342.6 million worldwide.

◎ POGO FOR PRESIDENT— I GO POGO (1984)
A Stowar Enterprises/Possum Productions release. **p, d & w:** Marc Paul Chinoy; **m:** Gary Baker, Thom Flora; **anim dir:** Stephen Chodo. **Running time:** 82 minutes.

Voices
Pogo: Skip Hinnant;

Additional Voices
Jimmy Breslin; Ruth Buzzi; Stan Freberg; Bob Kaliban; Bob McFadden; Len Maxwell; Vincent Price; Marcia Savella; Mike Schultz; Arnold Stang; Jonathan Winters. Special guest appearance by Jimmy Breslin.

Election year fever sweeps the Okenfenokee Swamp as everyone's favorite possum suddenly finds himself recruited for the nation's highest office by all of his friends, including Albert, Howland and Porky Pine. Produced in stop-motion animation, the film is based on Walt Kelly's unforgettable *Pogo* cartoon strip.

◎ PORKY PIG IN HOLLYWOOD (1986)
A Films Incorporated Production released by Warner Bros. **d:** Tex Avery, Friz Freleng, Bob Clampett, Frank Tashlin, Chuck Jones; **w:** Rich Hogan, Tubby Millar, Ben Hardaway, Frank Tashlin, Dave Monahan, Ernest Gee; **m:** Carl Stalling. Compiled by George Feltenstein. **Running time:** 102 minutes.

Voices

Mel Blanc

This limited-release compilation was a tribute to Warner Bros.' famed stuttering pig. It featured Porky in a collection of classic cartoons: "You Oughta Be in Pictures" (1940); "Wholly Smoke" (1938); "Porky's Romance" (1937); "Porky's Preview" (1941); "Daffy Doc" (1938) and "Porky's Movie Mystery" (1938).

POUND PUPPIES AND THE LEGEND OF BIG PAW (1988)

A Family Home Entertainment and Tonka Corp. presentation of an Atlantic/Kushner-Locke Production in association with the Maltese Companies released by Tri-Star. **p:** Donald Kushner, Peter Locke; **d:** Pierre DeCelles; **scr:** Jim Carlson, Terrence McDonnell; **m:** Steve Tyrell. **Running time:** 76 minutes.

Voices

McNasty: George Rose; **Whopper:** B.J. Ward; **Nose Marie:** Ruth Buzzi; **Cooler:** Brennan Howard; **Collette:** Cathy Cadavini; **Bright Eyes:** Nancy Cartwright

The Pound Puppies foil the efforts a nasty old man with an evil laugh (McNasty) whose goal is to take over the world by recovering the Bone of Scone, a mystical relic possessing great magical powers.

THE PRINCESS AND THE GOBLIN (1993)

A Siriol/Pannonia Film/S4C Wales/NHK Enterprises International Production released by Hemdale Pictures Corporation. **p:** Robin Lyons; **d:** Jozsef Grimes; **exec prod:** Steve Walsh, Marietta Dardai; **scr:** Robin Lyons (adapted from the novel by George MacDonald); **m:** Istvah Lerch; **anim dir:** Les Orton. **Song:** "A Spark Inside Us." **Running time:** 82 minutes.

Voices

Joss Ackland, Claire Bloom, Roy Kinnear, Sally Ann Marsh, Rik Mayall, Peggy Mount, Victor Spinetti, Mollie Sugden, Frank Rozelaar Green, William Hootkins, Steve Lyons, Robin Lyons

When a peaceful kingdom is menaced by an army of monstrous goblins, a brave and beautiful princess teams up with a resourceful peasant boy to rescue the noble king and his people in this thrilling adventure based on the timeless fairy tale from master storyteller George MacDonald.

PN: This 1993 British-Hungarian coproduction, known as *A Hercengno es a kobold*, was released in the United States on Memorial Day, 1994. The G-rated feature was winner of the Film Advisory Board's Award of Excellence, The Dove Seal of Approval from the Dove Foundation

Review Board and the Best Children's Film Award from the Fort Lauderdale International Film Festival.

THE PUPPETOON MOVIE (1987)

An Expanded Entertainment release. **p & w:** Arnold Leibovit; **m:** Budy Baker. **Running time:** 80 minutes.

A long-overdue tribute to the work of filmmaker George Pal, whose stop-action technique influenced creators of similar characters from Gumby to the Pillsbury Doughboy. The feature contains ten films from the 1930s and 1940s: "Hoola Boola," "John Henry and the Inky Poo," "Tubby the Tuba," "Tulips Shall Grow," "Jasper in a Jam," "Philips Broadcast of 1938," "Philip's Calvacade," "Sleeping Beauty," "South Sea Sweetheart" and "Together in the Weather."

RACE FOR YOUR LIFE, CHARLIE BROWN (1977)

A Bill Melendez Production released by Paramount Pictures. **p:** Lee Mendelson, Bill Melendez; **d:** Bill Melendez, Phil Roman; **w:** Charles M. Schulz (based on the *Peanuts* characters by Schulz); **m:** Ed Bogas. **Songs:** "Race for Your Life, Charlie Brown," "The Greatest Leader," "Charmine" and "She'll Be Comin' Round the Mountain." **Running time:** 75 minutes.

Voices

Charlie Brown: Duncan Watson; **Schroeder:** Gregory Felton; **Peppermint Patty:** Stuart Brotman; **Sally:** Gail Davis; **Linus:** Liam Martin; **Lucy:** Melanie Kohn; **Marcie:** Jimmie Ahrens; **Bully:** Kirk Jue; **Another Bully:** Jordan Warren; **Another Bully:** Tom Muller; **Singers:** Ed Bogas, Larry Finlayson, Judith Munsen, David Riordan, Roberta Vandervort

Additional Voices

Fred Van Amburg, Bill Melendez

The Peanuts gang is off to camp for a summer of misadventures, including building a raft for the "big race," only to be outdone by the competing team, which "buys" its raft. Aside from the race, Snoopy has an altercation with a nasty feline and Lucy leads the other girls in an antiboy campaign.

RAGGEDY ANN AND ANDY (1977)

A Lester Osterman Production released by 20th Century-Fox. **p:** Richard Horner; **d:** Richard Williams; **scr:** Patricia Thackray and Max Wilk (based on the stories and characters created by Johnny Gruelle); **m:** Joe Raposo; **seq dir:** Gerald Potterton. **Songs:** "I Look and What Do I See!" "No Girl's Toy," "Rag Dolly," "Poor Babette," "A Miracle," "Ho-Yo," "Candy Hearts," "Blue," "The Mirage,"

"I Never Get Enough," "I Love You," "Loony Anthem," "It's Not Easy Being King," "Hooray for Me," "You're My Friend" and "Home." **Running time:** 84 minutes.

Cast
Marcella: Claire Williams

Voices
Raggedy Ann: Didi Conn; **Raggedy Andy:** Mark Baker; **The Camel with the Wrinkled Knees:** Fred Struthman; **Babette:** Niki Flacks; **Captain Contagious:** George S. Irving; **Queasy:** Arnold Stang; **The Greedy:** Joe Silver; **The Loony Knight:** Alan Sues; **King Koo-Koo:** Marty Brill; **Gazooks:** Paul Dooley; **Grandpa:** Mason Adams; **Maxi-Fixit:** Allen Swift; **Susie Pincushion:** Hetty Galen; **Barney Beanbag/Socko:** Sheldon Harnick; **Topsy:** Ardyth Kaiser; **The Twin Pennies:** Margery Gray, Lynne Stuart

A search ensues for Babette, a French doll, who is kidnapped by another doll, Captain Contagious, in the toy-filled playroom of a young girl named Marcella, seen in live action in this animated feature. Doll makes Raggedy Ann and Andy embark on a magical journey to rescue Babette, successfully managing through a forbidding forest, a tossing sea, a looney kingdom and other dangers.

PN: Film was originally designed as a Hallmark Hall of Fame television special; Liza Minelli and Goldie Hawn were considered for Raggedy Ann's role.

RAINBOW BRITE AND THE STAR STEALER (1985)
A DIC Enterprises Production released by Warner Bros. **p:** Jean Chalopin, Andy Heyward, Tetsuo Katayama; **d:** Bernard Deyries, Kimio Yabuki; **w:** Howard R. Cohen (based on a story by Chalopin, Howard R. Cohen, and characters developed by Hallmark Properties); **m:** Haim Saban, Shuki Levy. **Songs:** "Brand New Day" and "Rainbow Brite and Me." **Running time:** 97 minutes.

Voices
Rainbow Brite: Bettina; **Lurky/On-X/Buddy Blue/Dog Guard/Spectran/Slurthie/Glitterbot:** Patrick Fraley; **Murky/Castle Monster/Glitterbot/Guard/Skydancer/Slurthie:** Peter Cullen; **Twin/Shy Violet/Indigo/La La Orange/Spectran/Sprites:** Robbie Lee; **Starlite/Wizard/Spectran:** Andre Stojka; **Krys:** David Mendenhall; **The Princess/The Creature:** Rhonda Aldrich; **Orin/Bombo/TV Announcer:** Les Tremayne; **Red Butler/Witch/Castle Creature/Spectran/Patty O'Green/Canary Yellow:** Mona Marshall; **Count Blogg:** Jonathan Harris; **Stormy:** Marissa Mendenhall; **Brian:** Scott Menville; **Popo:** Charles Adler; **Sergeant Zombo:** David Workman

A spoiled princess steals the planet Spectra for her "jewel collection." Little Rainbow, riding her flying horse Starlites, saves the planet, accompanied by a young boy, Krys, on his mechanical horse, On-X.

THE RELUCTANT DRAGON (1941)
A Walt Disney Production released by RKO Radio Pictures. **p:** Walt Disney; **l/a dir:** Alfred L. Werker; **anim dir:** Hamilton Luske; **scr:** Ted Sears, Al Perkins, Larry Clemmons, Bill Cottrell, Harry Clark. **Songs:** "Oh Fleecy Cloud," "To an Upside Down Cake," "Radish So Red," "'Tis Evening" and "The Reluctant Dragon." **Running time:** 72 minutes.

Cast
Robert Benchley: Himself; **Studio artist:** Frances Gifford; **Mrs. Benchley:** Nana Bryant; **Studio guide:** Buddy Pepper; **Florence Gill and Clarence Nash:** Themselves; Alan Ladd, John Dehner, Truman Woodworth, Hamilton McFadden, Maurice Murphy, Jeff Corey; **Studio cop:** Henry Hall; **Orchestra leader:** Frank Faylen; **Slim:** Lester Dorr; **Guard:** Gerald Mohr; and members of the staff, including Walt Disney, Ward Kimball and Norman Ferguson

Voices
The Dragon: Barnett Parker; **Sir Giles:** Claud Allister; **The Boy:** Billy Lee; **Themselves:** The Rhythmaires; **Donald Duck:** Clarence Nash; **Goofy:** Pinto Colvig; **Baby Weems's narrator:** Gerald Mohr; **Baby Weems:** Leone LeDoux, Raymond Severn; **John Weems:** Ernie Alexander; **Mrs. John Weems:** Linda Marwood; **FDR:** Art Gilmore; **Walter Winchell:** Edward Marr; **How to Ride a Horse narrator:** John McLeish; **Reluctant Dragon narrator:** J. Donald Wilson

Part live action and part animation, this film delves into the behind-the-scenes making of cartoons, with comedian Robert Benchley, in live action, being pursuaded by his onscreen wife (Nana Bryant) to approach Walt Disney about producing a cartoon based on *The Reluctant Dragon*, a delightful children's book by Kenneth Grahame. The film traces Benchley's visit to the Disney studio and the ultimate production of this tale about a dragon who loathes terrorizing people. Goofy appears in the film showing animator Ward Kimball making his latest cartoon, "How to Ride a Horse."

THE RESCUERS (1977)
A Walt Disney Production released by Buena Vista. **p:** Wolfgang Reitherman; **d:** Wolfgang Reitherman, John Lounsbery, Art Stevens; **st:** Larry Clemmons, Ken Anderson, Vance Gerry, David Michener, Burny Mattinson, Frank Thomas, Fred Lucky, Ted Berman, Dick Sebast (from *The Rescuers* and *Miss Bianca* by Margery Sharp); **m:** Artie Butler (songs by Carol Connors, Ayn Robbins, Sammy Fain, and Robert Crawford); **anim dir:** Ollie Johnston, Frank Thomas,

Milt Kahl, Don Bluth. **Songs:** "The Journey," "Rescue Aid Society," "Tomorrow is Another Day," "Someone's Waiting for You" and "The U.S. Air Force Song." **Running time:** 77 minutes.

Voices
Bernard: Bob Newhart; **Miss Bianca:** Eva Gabor; **Mme. Medusa:** Geraldine Page; **Mr. Snoops:** Joe Flynn; **Ellie Mae:** Jeanette Nolan; **Luke:** Pat Buttram; **Orville:** Jim Jordan; **Rufus:** John McIntire; **Penny:** Michelle Stacy; **Chairman:** Bernard Fox; **Gramps:** Larry Clemmons; **Evinrude:** James Macdonald; **Deadeye:** George Lindsey; **TV Announcer:** Bill McMillan; **Digger:** Dub Taylor; **Deacon:** John Fiedler

Two mice, Bernard and Miss Bianca, set out to rescue a girl, Penny, held captive in a swamp by the evil Mme. Medusa.

PN: This beautifully animated feature took four years to make at a cost of nearly $8 million.

◎ THE RESCUERS DOWN UNDER (1990)

A Walt Disney Picture in association with Silver Screen Partners IV released by Buena Vista. **p:** Thomas Schumacher; **d:** Hendel Butoy and Mike Gabriel; **scr:** Jim Cox, Karey Kirkpatrick, Byron Simpson, Joe Ranft; **m:** Bruce Broughton; **superv anim:** Glen Keane, Mark Henn, Russ Edmonds, David Cutler, Ruben A. Aquino, Nik Ranieri, Ed Gombert, Anthony De Rosa, Kathy Zielinski, Duncan Marjoribanks; **anim:** James Baxter, Ron Husband, Will Finn, David Burgess, Alexander S. Kupershmidt, Chris Bailey, Mike Cedeno, Rick Farmiloe, Jacques Muller, Dave Pruiksma, Rejean Bourdages, Roger Chiasson, Ken Duncan, Joe Haidar, Ellen Woodbury, Jorgen Klubien, Gee Fwee Border, Barry Temple, David P. Stephan, Chris Wahl, Larry White, Brigitte Hartley, Doug Krohn, Phil Young, Tom Roth, Leon Joosen. **Songs:** "Black Slacks" and "Waltzing Matilda." **Running time:** 74 minutes.

Voices
Bernard: Bob Newhart; **Miss Bianca:** Eva Gabor; **Wilbur:** John Candy; **Jake:** Tristan Rogers; **Cody:** Adam Ryen; **McLeach:** George C. Scott; **Frank:** Wayne Robson; **Krebbs:** Douglas Seale; **Joanna/Special Vocal Effects:** Frank Welker; **Chairmouse/Doctor:** Bernard Fox; **Red:** Peter Firth; **Baitmouse:** Billy Barty; **François:** Ed Gilbert; **Faloo/Mother:** Carla Meyer; **Nurse Mouse:** Russi Taylor

In Australia, young Cody discovers that evil McLeach has captured the magnificent eagle Marahute. He manages to set her free only to be kidnapped himself and later to see her recaptured.

PN: This sequel to Disney's *The Rescuers* was released simultaneously with a brand-new Mickey Mouse short, *The*

Prince and the Pauper, costarring pals Goofy, Donald Duck and Pluto.

◎ ROBIN HOOD (1973)

A Walt Disney Production released by Buena Vista. **p:** Wolfgang Reitherman; **d:** Wolfgang Reitherman; **st:** Larry Clemmons (based on character and story conceptions by Ken Anderson); **m:** (songs by) Roger Miller, Floyd Huddleston, George Bruns, Johnny Mercer; **dir anim:** Milt Kahl, Frank Thomas, Ollie Johnston, John Lounsbery. **Songs:** "Not in Nottingham," "Whistle Stop," "Love" and "The Phoney King of England." **Running time:** 83 minutes.

Voices
Allan-a-Dale: Roger Miller; **Prince John/King Richard:** Peter Ustinov; **Sir Hiss:** Terry-Thomas; **Robin Hood:** Brian Bedford; **Maid Marian:** Monica Evans; **Little John:** Phil Harris; **Friar Tuck:** Andy Devine; **Lady Kluck:** Carole Shelley; **Sheriff of Nottingham:** Pat Buttram; **Trigger:** George Lindsay; **Nutsy:** Ken Curtis; **Skippy:** Billy Whitaker; **Sis:** Dana Laurita; **Tagalong:** Dora Whitaker; **Toby Turtle:** Richie Sanders; **Otto:** J. Pat O'Malley; **Crocodile:** Candy Candido; **Mother Rabbit:** Barbara Luddy; **Church Mouse:** John Fiedler

All the familiar characters appear in this animated version of the classic story, featuring cartoon animals in the title roles—Robin Hood and Maid Marian are foxes, Little John is a bear and the ever-villainous Prince John is a mangy lion—in this return to Sherwood Forest and Robin's battles with the Sheriff of Nottingham.

◎ ROCK-A-DOODLE (1992)

A Goldcrest Films/Sullivan Bluth Studios Ireland Ltd. Production released by Samuel Goldwyn Company. **p:** Don Bluth, Gary Goldman, John Pomeroy; **d:** Don Bluth; **cd:** Gary Goldman, Dan Kuenster; **exec prod:** John Quested, Morris F. Sullivan; **st:** Don Bluth, John Pomeroy, David Steinberg, David N. Weiss, T.J. Kuenster, Gary Goldman; **scr:** David N. Weiss; **m/sc:** Robert Folk (with original songs by T.J. Kuenster). **Songs:** "Sun Do Shine," "We Hate the Sun," "Come Back to You," "Bouncers' Theme Song," "Tweedle Te Dee," "Treasure Hunting Fever," "Sink or Swim," "Kiss 'n Cod," "Back to the Country," "The Owl's Picnic" and "Tyin' Your Shoes." **Running time:** 74 minutes.

Cast (live action)
Edmond: Toby Scott Ganger; **Mother:** Kathryn Holcomb; **Dad:** Stan Ivar; **Scott:** Christian Hoff; **Mark:** Jason Marin

Voices
Narrator/Patou: Phil Harris; **Chanticleer:** Glen Campbell; **Snipes, the magpie:** Eddie Beezen; **The Grand Duke:**

Christopher Plummer; **Peepers, the mouse:** Sandy Duncan; **Stuey:** Will Ryan; **Hunch, Grand Duke's inept nephew:** Charles Nelson Reilly; **Goldie:** Ellen Greene; **Pinky:** Sorrell Booke

When a young farmboy (Edmond) is turned into an animated kitten by an evil owl, he and his barnyard friends go in search of the singing Elvis-like rooster Chanticleer (who has been banished to a cartoon-world Las Vegas, known as Big City, after he fails to crow one morning), to enlist his help in getting back home in this live-action/animated musical from the creator of *The Secret of NIMH* and *Land Before Time*.

⦿ ROCK AND RULE (1984)

A Nelvana Limited Production released by Metro-Goldwyn-Mayer/United Artists. **p:** Patrick Loubert, Michael Hirsh; **d:** Clive A. Smith; **scr:** Peter Sauder, John Halfpenny; **st:** Patrick Loubert, Peter Sauder; **m:** Patrick Cullen. Songs: "Angel's Song," "Invocation Song," "Send Love Through," "Pain and Suffering," "My Name Is Mok," "Born to Raise Hell," "I'm the Man," "Ohm Sweet Ohm," "Dance, Dance, Dance" and "Hot Dogs and Sushi." **Running time:** 79 minutes.

Voices

Mok: Don Francks; **Omar:** Paul Le Mat; **Angel:** Susan Roman; **Mok's Computer:** Sam Langevin; **Dizzy:** Dan Hennessey; **Stretch/Zip:** Greg Duffell; **Toad:** Chris Wiggins; **Sleazy:** Brent Titcomb; **Quadhole/1st Radio Announcer:** Donny Burns; **Mylar/2nd Radio Announcer:** Martin Lavut; **Cindy:** Catherine Gallant; **Other Computers:** Keith Hampshire; **Carnegie Hall Groupie:** Melleny Brown; **Edna:** Anna Bourque; **Borderguard:** Nick Nichols; **Uncle**

When the only survivors of a war are street animals, a new race of mutants evolve in the fantasy adventure Rock and Rule *(1984). The film was the first feature-length production by Nelvana Limited in Canada.* (COURTESY: NELVANA LIMITED)

Mikey: John Halfpenny; **Sailor:** Maurice LaMarche; **Aunt Edith:** Catherine O'Hara

The war is over. The only survivors are street animals—dogs, cats and rats. From them a new race of mutants evolve. In this new world Mok, an aging superstar, tries to find the last element in a diabolical plan to raise a demon that will give him immense power. The missing element is a voice, and he finds that voice in Angel, a female singer who plays with a local band in the small town of Ohmtown. He steals her away to post-apocalypse Nuke York to launch his plan into action.

PN: The first full-length feature film for Nelvana Limited, a Canadian-based animation company (producers of *The Care Bears*). The film features an original soundtrack by rock artists Cheap Trick, Debbie Harry, Lou Reed, Iggy Pop and a special performance by Earth, Wind and Fire.

⦿ ROVER DANGERFIELD (1991)

A Rodney Dangerfield/Hyperion Pictures Production released by Warner Bros. **p:** Willard Carroll, Thomas L. Wilhite; **d:** Jim George, Bob Seeley; **exec prod:** Rodney Dangerfield; **st:** Roger Dangerfield, Harold Ramis (based on an idea by Rodney Dangerfield) **scr:** Rodney Dangerfield; **m:** David Newman (with songs by Rodney Dangerfield and Billy Tragesser); **seq dir:** Steve Moore, Matthew O'Callaghan, Bruce Smith, Dick Sebast, Frans Vischer, Skip Jones. Songs: "It's a Dog's Life," "Somewhere There's a Party," "I'd Give Up a Bone for You," "I'm in Love with the Dog Next Door," "I'll Never Do It on a Christmas Tree," "I Found a Four-Leaf Clover When I Met Rover," "Respect," "Happy Birthday to You," "Merrily We Roll Along," "I'm Just a Country Boy at Heart," "It's a Big Wide Wonderful World" and "Winter Wonderland." **Running time:** 74 minutes.

Voices

Rover Dangerfield: Rodney Dangerfield; **Daisy:** Susan Boyd; **Eddie:** Ronnie Schell; **Raffles:** Ned Luke; **Connie:** Shawn Southworth; **Danny:** Dana Hill; **Rocky:** Sal Landi; **Coyote/Rooster:** Tom Williams; **Big Boss/Coyote/Sparky/Wolf/Horse:** Chris Collin; **Gangster/Farm Voice:** Robert Bergen; **Count:** Paxton Whitehead; **Mugsy/Bruno:** Ron Taylor; **Max:** Bert Kramer; **Champ:** Eddie Barth; **Truck Driver:** Ralph Monaco; **Queenie/Chorus Girls/Hen/Chickens/Turkey:** Tress MacNeille; **José/Sheep:** Michael Sheehan; **Gigi/Chorus Girl/Sheep:** Lara Cody; **Fisherman #1:** Owen Bush; **Fisherman #2:** Ken White; **Cal:** Gregg Berger; **Katie:** Heidi Banks; **Lem:** Dennis Blair; **Clem:** Don Stuart; **Duke:** Robert Pine; **Wolvies:** Danny Mann, Bernard Erhard

In this canine adventure, Rover Dangerfield, a street-smart dog owned by a Las Vegas showgirl, becomes separated from his owner and winds up living on an idyllic farm where he finds true love and respect.

PN: Comedian Rodney Dangerfield came up with the idea for this animated feature and served as the film's executive producer, writer and lyricist. The movie had its Los Angeles premiere at the Fourth Los Angeles International Animation Celebration.

SALUDOS AMIGOS (1943)

A Walt Disney Production released by RKO Radio Pictures. **p:** Walt Disney; **st:** Homer Brightman, Ralph Wright, Roy Williams, Harry Reeves, Dick Huemer, Joe Grant; **md:** Charles Wolcott; **m:** Ed Plumb, Paul Smith; **seq dir:** Bill Roberts, Jack Kinney, Hamilton Luske, Wilfred Jackson. **Songs:** "Saludos Amigos," "Brazil" and "Tico Tico." **Running time:** 43 minutes.

Voices
Donald Duck: Charles Nash; **Joe Carioca:** José Oliveira; **Goofy:** Pinto Colvig

This animated production, though far short of feature-film length, was released by Disney as an animated feature. Travelogue footage—filmed on location in South America—is incorporated into the film, which features four cartoon shorts strung together to portray the Latin American influence on the United States.

Sequences include Donald Duck as a naive tourist who runs into trouble while sightseeing; the adventures of Pedro the airplane, who grows up to be an airmail plane just like his dad; "El Gaucho Goofy," the misadventures of Goofy playing out the life of a gaucho—with little success; and, finally, tropical bird José (or Joe) Carioca, who takes Donald on a tour of South America, teaching him the samba along the way.

SANTA AND THE THREE BEARS (1970)

A R and S Film Enterprises Production released by Ellman Enterprises. **p, w & d:** Tony Benedict; **m:** Doug Goodwin, Tony Benedict, Joe Leahy. **Running time:** 63 minutes.

Cast
Grandfather: Hal Smith; **Beth:** Beth Goldfarb; **Brian:** Brian Hobbs

Voices
Ranger/Santa Claus: Hal Smith; **Nana:** Jean Vander Pyl; **Nikomi:** Annette Ferra; **Chinook:** Bobby Riaj

Two cute wide-eyed bear cubs (Nikomi and Chinook) put off hibernating in Yellowstone National Park to wait for the arrival of Santa Claus. So the cubs are not disappointed, the park's cheery, grandfatherly forest ranger agrees to impersonate Santa Claus at the request of their mother. The film opens, in live action, with a kindly old grandfather (played by Hal Smith) relating the tale to his grandchildren.

THE SECRET ADVENTURES OF TOM THUMB (1993)

A bolexbrothers/Lumen Films Production released by Manga Entertainment. **p:** Richard "Hutch" Hutchison; **d:** Dave Borthwick; **exec prod:** Colin Rose, Thierry Garrel; **scr:** Dave Borthwick; **m:** John Paul Jones, Startled Insects. **Running time:** 57 minutes.

Cast
Pa Thumb: Nick Upton; **Ma Thumb:** Deborah Collard; **Man:** Frank Passingham, John Schofield; **Woman in Bar:** Mike Gifford

Voices
Brett Lane, Helen Veysey, Paul Veysey, Peter Townsend, Marie Clifford, Tim Hand, Andrew Bailey, Nick Upton, John Schofield

Additional Voices
John Beedel, George Brandt, Andy Davis, Richard Goleszowski, Robert Heath, Andy Joyce, Andy McCormick, Tim Norfolk, Dave Alex Riddett

In a twisted, much darker version of the classic fairy-tale character, Tom Thumb is kidnapped by a genetic lab for experimentation and meets other small, oppressed creatures who band together to fight against the tyranny of the "giants" in this highly acclaimed, stop-motion, clay-animated feature.

PN: Originally this film was a 10-minute version that caused public outrage when it was shown on BBC2 in the United Kingdom in 1988. Producers Dave Borthwick and Dave Riddett managed to garner enough capital to produce this full-length feature version, which was first released in the United Kingdom in 1993. The film was released in the United States two years later, in January 1995, playing in limited release.

THE SECRET OF NIMH (1982)

A Don Bluth Production released through MGM/UA. **p:** Don Bluth, Gary Goldman, John Pomeroy; **d:** Don Bluth; **anim dir:** John Pomeroy, Gary Goldman; **st:** Don Bluth, John Pomeroy, Gary Goldman, Will Finn (based on the novel *Mrs. Frisby and the Rats of NIMH* by Robert C. O'Brien); **m:** Jerry Goldsmith. **Running time:** 82 minutes.

Voices
Elizabeth Hartman, Dom DeLuise, Hermione Baddeley, Arthur Malet, Peter Strauss, Paul Shenar, Derek Jacobi, John Carradine, Shannen Doherty, Will Wheaton, Jodi Hicks, Ian Fried, Tom Hatten, Lucille Bliss, Aldo Ray

A recently widowed mother mouse (Mrs. Bisby) desperately tries finding a new home for her brood before the old one is destroyed by spring plowing. Her task gets complicated by the severe illness of her son, who is too sick to move.

PN: Co-creators of the film were Don Bluth, Gary Goldman, and John Pomeroy, all three former Disney animators who left the studio in a dispute over standards and struck out on their own. Working title: *Mrs. Frisby and the Rats of NIMH.*

◎ THE SECRET OF THE SWORD (1985)

A Filmation Associates Production released by Atlantic Releasing. **p:** Arthur Nadel; **d:** Ed Friedman, Lou Kachivas, Marsh Lamore, Bill Reed, Gwen Wetzler; **scr:** Larry Ditillo, Robert Forward. **Running time:** 87 minutes.

Voices

He-Man: John Erwin; **She-Ra:** Melendy Britt; **Hordak:** George DiCenzo

Additional Voices

Linda Gary, Eric Gunden, Erika Scheimer, Alan Oppenheimer

He-Man discovers he has a twin sister, She-Ra, who was kidnapped shortly after birth by the evil Hordak. She has been raised by Hordak to combat He-Man. He-Man sets about to reunite her with their family.

PN: Prior to its release the film was called *Princess of Power.*

◎ SHINBONE ALLEY (1971)

A Fine Arts Film released by Allied Artists. **p:** Preston M. Fleet; **d:** John David Wilson; **w:** Joe Darion (based on the

Justin (center) tries to fend off dastardly Jenner, while Mrs. Brisby looks on in a scene from The Secret of NIMH *(1982). © United Artists*

book for the musical play by Darion and Mel Brooks, from the "archy and mehitabel" stories by Don Marquis); **m:** George Kleinsinger. **Songs:** "I Am Only a Poor Humble Cockroach," "Blow Wind Out of the North," "Cheerio My Deario (Toujours Gai)," "Ah, the Theater, the Theater," "What Do We Care If We're Down and Out?" "The Moth Song," "Lullaby for Mehitabel's Kittens," "The Shinbone Alley Song," "The Lightning Bug Song," "Here Pretty Pretty Pussy," "Ladybugs of the Evening," "Archy's Philosophies," "They Don't Have It Here," "Romeo and Juliet" and "Come to Meeoww." **Running time:** 83 minutes.

Voices

mehitabel: Carol Channing; **archy:** Eddie Bracken; **Big Bill Sr.:** Alan Reed; **Tyrone T. Tattersall:** John Carradine

Additional Voices

Sal Delano; Joan Gerber; Ken Sansom; Jackie Ward Singers; Hal Smith

A poet is transmigrated into the body of a cockroach named archy, whose back-alley adventures and love for a sexy street cat (mehitabel) make up the plot line of this surrealistic tale.

PN: Based on the long-running musical of the same name (which was based on Don Marquis's comic strip of the 1920s and 1930s), Carol Channing and Eddie Bracken recreated roles originally played by Eartha Kitt and Bracken on Broadway.

◎ SLEEPING BEAUTY (1959)

A Walt Disney Production released through Buena Vista. **p:** Walt Disney; **d:** Hamilton Luske, Clyde Geronimi, Wilfred Jackson; **st:** Erdmann Penner, Joe Rinaldi, Ralph Wright, Donald Da Gradi (based on an original story by Ward Greene); **m:** Oliver Wallace; **dir anim:** Milt Kahl, Frank Thomas, Marc Davis, Ollie Johnston Jr., John Lounsbery; **seq dir:** Eric Larson, Wolfgang Reitherman, Les Clark. **Songs:** "Once Upon a Dream," "Hail the Princess Aurora," "I Wonder," "The Skumps" and "Sleeping Beauty Song." **Running time:** 75 minutes.

Voices

Princess Aurora/Briar Rose: Mary Costa; **Maleficent:** Eleanor Audley; **Merryweather:** Barbara Luddy; **King Stefan:** Taylor Holmes; **Prince Phillip:** Bill Shirley; **Flora:** Verna Felton; **Fauna:** Barbara Jo Allen; **King Hubert:** Bill Thompson; **Maleficent's Goons:** Candy Candido, Pinto Colvig, Bob Amsberry; **Owl:** Dallas McKennon; **Narrator:** Marvin Miller

Aurora, the daughter of good king Stephen and his wife, is given beauty, goodness and charm by three good fairies only to become victimized by a bad fairy, who casts a spell on her that she will prick her finger on a spindle when she is 16 and die. Fortunately, one of the good fairies intervenes and changes the spell so that Aurora's fate is deep sleep rather than death. She will awaken only with a loving kiss.

◎ THE SMURFS AND THE MAGIC FLUTE (1984)

A First Performance Pictures/Studios Belvision coproduction in association with Stuart R. Ross released by Atlantic Releasing Corporation. **p:** José Dutillieu; **d & w:** John Rust; **m:** Michel Legrand; **superv anim:** Eddie Lateste. **Running time:** 74 minutes.

Voices

Cam Clarke, Grant Gottschall, Patty Foley, Mike Reynolds, Ted Lehman, Bill Capizzi, Ron Gans, X. Phifer, Dudly Knight, John Rust, Richard Miller, David Page, Durga McBroom, Michael Sorich, Robert Axelrod

Somehow a magic flute—which has the power to make people dance uncontrollably when it is played—has gotten out of Smurfland and into the hands of young practical joker Peewit and good knight Johan. But when Peewit loses the flute to the sinister bandit Oilycreep, the Smurfs make plans to retrieve the magical instrument.

PN: Film was called *V'la Les Schtroumpfs* for its Belgian release.

◎ SNOOPY COMES HOME (1972)

A Lee Mendelson–Bill Melendez Production released by National General Pictures. **p:** Lee Mendelson, Bill Melendez; **d:** Bill Melendez; **scr:** Charles Schultz; **m:** Donald Ralke; **m/l:** Richard M. Sherman, Robert B. Sherman. **Songs:** "Snoopy, Come Home," "Lila's Tune," "Fun on the Beach," "Best of Buddies," "Changes," "Partners," "Getting It Together" and "No Dogs Allowed." **Running time:** 80 minutes.

Voices

Charlie Brown: Chad Webber; **Lucy Van Pelt:** Robin Kohn; **Linus Van Pelt:** Stephen Shea; **Schroeder:** David Carey; **Lila:** Johanna Baer; **Sally:** Hilary Momberger; **Peppermint Patty:** Chris DeFaria; **Clara:** Linda Ecroli; **Freida:** Linda Mendelson; **Snoopy:** Bill Melendez

Snoopy learns that his previous owner, Lila, is sick in the hospital and goes to see her. He vows to return to Lila for good, so he drafts a "Last Will and Testament" for the gang, which throws him a farewell party.

◎ THE SNOW QUEEN (1959)

A Soyuzmultfilm Production released by Universal-International. **p:** (American) Robert Faber; **d:** Lev Atamanov (American directors: Bob Fisher, Phil Patton, Alan Lipscott); **scr:** Soyuzmultfilm Productions (based on a story of Hans Christian Andersen; live-action prologue and adaptation written by Alan Lipscott, Bob Fisher); **m:** Frank Skinner. **Songs:** "The Snow Queen," "Do It While You're Young" and "The Jolly Robbers." **Running time:** 70 minutes.

Cast (live action)

Art Linkletter, Tammy Marihugh, Jennie Lynn, Billy Booth, Rickey Busch

Voices

Gerda: Sandra Dee; **Kay:** Tommy Kirk; **Angel:** Patty McCormack; **The Snow Queen:** Louise Arthur; **Ol' Dreamy/The Raven:** Paul Frees; **Court Raven:** June Foray; **The Princess:** Joyce Terry; **The Prince:** Richard Beals; **Granny:** Lillian Buyeff

Two inseparable companions—a boy, Kay, and a girl, Gerda—search for the girl's brother, held captive in the palace of the evil Snow Queen, in this Russian animated color feature, based on the classic Hans Christian Andersen fairy tale, which was rescored and redubbed in English for its American release.

PN: A six-minute live-action prologue, featuring well-known television personality Art Linkletter (host of *House Party* and *Kids Say the Darndest Things*) and a cast of child actors, was produced and added to the film. Dialogue for the animated story was redubbed by American actors, including 1950s' and 1960s' teen stars Sandra Dee and Tommy Kirk (best known for his roles in Disney films, including *The Shaggy Dog, The Absent-Minded Professor* and *Old Yeller*).

◎ SNOW WHITE AND THE SEVEN DWARFS (1937)

A Walt Disney Production released by RKO Radio Pictures. **p:** Walt Disney; **superv d:** David Hand; **seq dir:** Perce Pearce, Larry Morey, William Cottrell, Wilfred Jackson, Ben Sharpsteen; **w:** Ted Sears, Otto Englander, Earl Hurd, Dorothy Ann Blank, Richard Creedon, Dick Richard, Merrill De Maris, Webb Smith (based on the fairy tale "Sneewittchen" in collection of *Kinder-und Hausmarchen* by Jacob Grimm, Wilhelm Grimm); **m:** Frank Churchill, Leigh Harline, Paul Smith, Morey; **superv anim:** Hamilton Luske, Vladimir Tytla, Fred Moore, Norman Ferguson. **Songs:** "I'm Wishing," "One Song," "With a Smile and a Song," "Whistle While You Work," "Heigh Ho," "Bluddle-Uddle-Um-Dum," "The Dwarfs' Yodel Song" and "Some Day My Prince Will Come." **Running time:** 83 minutes.

Voices

Snow White: Adriana Caselotti; **The Prince:** Harry Stockwell; **The Queen:** Lucille LaVerne; **Bashful:** Scotty Mattraw; **Doc:** Roy Atwell; **Grumpy:** Pinto Colvig; **Happy:** Otis Harlan; **Sleepy:** Pinto Colvig; **Sneezy:** Billy

Gilbert; **The Magic Mirror:** Moroni Olsen; **Humbert, the Queen's Huntsman:** Stuart Buchanan

Classic good versus evil tale of ever-sweet orphan princess Snow White, who although she is forced to work as a household servant to the Queen, a vain woman who will have no rival, becomes the most beautiful in the land. In retaliation, the Queen casts a spell on Snow White—brought on by a bite of a poisonous apple—which can be broken only by a kiss from the Prince to bring her back to life.

PN: The first full-length animated feature of any kind, this film is still considered a milestone in animated cartoon history. The picture took four years to complete and went over budget. (Originally set at $250,000, the film cost $1,488,000 to produce.) It grossed $8.5 million during its first release (then the highest-grossing first release film of all time). Subsequent reissues in 1944, 1952, 1967, 1975, 1983 and 1987 have proven even more worthwhile. The 1987 release alone grossed over $50 million.

One sequence involving Snow White's mother dying in childbirth was cut from the story during production, even though stills from the scene were published in *Look* magazine's preview of the film as well as in authorized book versions, comic strips and comic books based on the film.

⊚ SONG OF THE SOUTH (1946)

A Walt Disney Production released by RKO Radio Pictures. **p:** Walt Disney; **anim dir:** Wilfred Jackson; **scr:** Dalton Reymond, Morton Grant, Maurice Rapf; **st:** Dalton Reymond (based on the *Tales of Uncle Remus* by Joel Chandler Harris); **cart st:** William Peet, Ralph Wright, George Stallings; **md:** Charles Wolcott; **cart sc:** Paul J.

Walt Disney's Snow White and the Seven Dwarfs (1937) was the first full-length animated feature in cartoon history. The film remains one of the top-grossing cartoon features of all time. © Walt Disney Productions (COURTESY: THE MUSEUM OF MODERN ART/FILM STILLS ARCHIVE)

Smith; **dir anim:** Milt Kahl, Eric Larson, Oliver M. Johnston Jr., Les Clark, Marc Davis, John Lounsbery. **Songs:** "How Do You Do?" "Song of the South," "That's What Uncle Remus Said," "Sooner or Later," "Everybody's Got a Laughing Place," "Zip-a-Dee-Doo-Dah," "Let the Rain Pour Down" and "Who Wants to Live Like That?" **Running time:** 94 minutes.

Cast

Sally: Ruth Warrick; **Uncle Remus:** James Baskett; **Johnny:** Bobby Driscoll; **Ginny:** Luana Patten; **Grandmother:** Lucile Watson; **Aunt Tempy:** Hattie McDaniel; **Toby:** Glenn Leedy; **The Faver Boys:** George Nokes, Gene Holland; **John:** Erik Rolf; **Mrs. Favers:** Mary Field; **Maid:** Anita Brown

Voices

Brer Fox: James Baskett; **Brer Bear:** Nicodemus Stewart; **Brer Rabbit:** Johnny Lee

In Tom Sawyer–like fashion, Uncle Remus recalls the simple truths of the Old South instilling good morals in the mind of Johnny, a youngster who comes to rely on Remus as his main companion. The two are joined by a friendly little girl, Ginny, and along the way many of Remus's old tales come to life via animated sequences featuring the likes of Brer Rabbit, Brer Fox and Brer Bear.

⊚ SPACE JAM (1996)

A Uli Meyer Features/Warner Brothers/Character Builders/Charles Gammage Animation/Courtside Seats/Northern Lights Entertainment/Rees-Leiva/Spaff Animation/Stardust Pictures Production released by Warner Bros. **p:** Daniel Goldberg, Steven Paul Leiva, Joe Medjuck, Ivan Reitman; **d:** Joe Pytka (live action), Tony Cervone (animation), Bruce W. Smith (animation); **exec prod:** David Falk, Ken Ross; **scr:** Leonardo Benvenuti, Timothy Harris, Steve Rudnick, Herschel Weingrod; **m:** James Newton Howard. **Songs:** "Fly Like an Eagle," "Winner," "Space Jam," "I Believe I Can Fly," "Hit 'em High," "I Found My Smile Again," "For You I Will," "Upside Down ('Round-n-Round)," "Givin' U All That I've Got," "Basketball Jones," "I Turn to You," "All of My Days," "That's the Way (I Like It)" and "Buggin." **Running time:** 81 minutes

Cast (live action)

Himself: Michael Jordan; **Stan Podolak:** Wayne Knight; **Juanita Jordan:** Theresa Randle; **Jeffery Jordan:** Manner Washington; **Marcus Jordan:** Eric Gordon; **Jasmine Jordan:** Penny Bae Bridges; **Michael Jordan, age 10:** Brandon Hammon; **Himself:** Larry Bird; **James Jordan:** Thom Barry; **Themselves:** Charles Barkley, Patrick Ewing, Tyrone Bogues, Larry Johnson, Shawn Bradley, Ahmad Rashad, Del Harris, Vlade Divac, Cedric Ceballos, Jim Rome, Paul Westphal, Danny Ainge; **Jordan Housekeeper:** Bebe Drake; **Woman Fan:** Patricia Heaton; **Male Fan:** Dan Castellaneta; **Female Seer:** Linda Lutz; **Basketball Girl:** Nicky McCrimmon; **Little League Girl:** Kelly Vint; **Golfer:** Willam G. Schilling; **Psychiatrist:** Albert Hague; **Doctor:** Michael Alaimo; **NBA Referee:** James O'Donnell; **Charlotte Coach:** David Ursin; **Commissioner:** Douglas Robert Jackson; **Themselves:** Alonzo Mourning, A.C. Green, Charles Oakley, Derek Harper, Jeff Malone, Anthony Miller, Sharone Wright; **Umpire (as Rosey Brown):** Andre Rosey Brown; **Stars Catcher:** Brad Henke; **Owner's Girlfriend:** Connie Ray; **Baron's Manager:** John Roselius; **Baron's Catcher:** Charles Hoyes; **Players:** Luke Torres, Steven Shenbaum, Bean Miller; **Barons Coach:** Joy Bays; **Himself:** Bill Murray (uncredited)

Voices

Bugs Bunny/Elmer Fudd: Billy West; **Daffy Duck/Tazmanian Devil/Bull:** Dee Bradley Baker; **Swackhammer:** Danny DeVito; **Porky Pig:** Bob Bergen; **Sylvester/ Yosemite Sam/Foghorn Leghorn:** Bill Farmer; **Granny:** June Foray; **Pepe Le Pew:** Maurice LaMarche; **Lola Bunny:** Kath Soucie; **Nerdluck Pound:** Jocelyn Blue; **Nerdluck Blanko:** Charity James; **Nerdluck Bang:** June Melby; **Nerdluck Bupkus:** Catherine Reitman; **Nerdluck Nawt/Sniffles:** Colleen Wainwright; **Monstar Bupkus:** Dorian Harewood; **Monstar Ban:** Joey Camen; **Monstar Nawt:** T.K. Carter; **Monstar Pound:** Darnell Suttles; **Monster Blanko/Announcer:** Steve Kehela

Basketball superstar Michael Jordan is recruited by Bugs Bunny and the Looney Tunes characters to compete in a high-stakes basketball game (their opponent is the Monstars, a team of pumped-up aliens who've stolen the skills of some NBA stars) to win their freedom from an evil amusement park owner who plans to enslave them as his top attractions.

PN: Opening on 2,650 movie screens nationwide, *Space Jam* was an instant hit, grossing $27.528 million during its first weekend and more than $90 million in the United States alone.

STARCHASER: THE LEGEND OF ORIN (1985)

A Steven Hahn Production released by Atlantic Releasing. **p:** Steven Hahn; **d:** Steven Hahn, John Sparey; **w:** Jeffrey Scott; **m:** Andrew Belling; **anim dir:** Mitch Rochon, Jang-Gil Kim. **Running time:** 101 minutes.

Voices

Orin: Joe Colligan; **Dagg:** Carmen Argenziano; **Elan Aviana:** Noelle North; **Zygon:** Anthony Delongis; **Arthur:** Les Tremayne; **Silica:** Tyke Caravelli; **Magreb:** Ken Samson; **Auctioneer/Z. Gork:** John Moschita Jr.; **Mine-**

master: Mickey Morton; **Pung/Hopps:** Herb Vigran; **Shooter:** Dennis Alwood; **Kallie:** Mona Marshall; **Aunt Bella:** Tina Romanus

Additional Voices

Daryl T. Bartley; Phillip Clarke; Joseph Dellasorte; John Garwood; Barbera Harris and Company; Ryan MacDonald; Thomas H. Watkins; Mike Winslow

A young robot/human retrieves a magic sword and overtakes a piratical captain of a spaceship to free other humans in the underground world.

THE SWAN PRINCESS (1994)

A Nest Entertainment/Rich Animation Studios Production released by Columbia Pictures. **p&d:** Richard Rich; **exec prod:** Jared F. Brown, Seldon Young; **st:** Brian Nissen, Richard Rich; **st:** Richard Rich, Brian Nissen; **scr:** Brian Nissen; **m:** Lex de Azevedo (with songs by David Zippel and Lex de Azevedo). **Songs:** "Far Longer Than Forever," "Eternity," "This Is My Idea," "Practice, Practice, Practice," "No Fear," "No More Mr. Nice Guy" and "Princess on Parade." **Running time:** 90 minutes.

Voices

Rothbart: Jack Palance; **Prince Derek:** Howard McGillin; **Princess Odette:** Michelle Nicastro; **Jean-Bob:** John Cleese; **Speed:** Steven Wright; **Puffin:** Steve Vinovich; **Lord Rogers:** Mark Harelik; **Chamberlain:** James Arrington; **Bromley:** Joel McKinnon Miller; **King William:** Dakin Matthews; **Queen Uberta:** Sandy Duncan; **Narrator:** Brian Nissen; **Young Derek:** Adam Wylie; **Young Odette:** Adrian Zahiri; **Musician:** Tom Alan Robbins; **Hag:** Bess Hopper; **Dancers:** Cate Coplin, Tom Slater, Jim Pearce; **Odette (singing voice):** Liz Callaway; **Rothbart (singing voice):** Lex De Azevedo; **Chamberlain (singing voice):** Davis Gaines

A beautiful young princess (Odette) is transformed into a swan by an evil sorcerer's spell, which can be broken only by a vow of everlasting love in this magical musical adventure based on the classic fairy tale *Swan Lake*.

PN: Turner's New Line Cinema lost the battle at the box office with this beautifully animated feature that went head-to-head against Fox's release of Turner's *The Pagemaster*, Disney's *The Lion King* and live-action *The Santa Clause* starring Tim Allen of TV's *Home Improvement*. Final ticket sales totaled only $3 million. At the 1994 Cannes Film Festival in France, 300 guests were given their first peek of the $35-million full-length animated feature at a party held in a medieval castle overlooking the Mediterranean. The film's fairy-tale story was based on the German folk tale, *Swan Lake* (which was also the film's original working title). Eight original songs were written for the movie by Broadway veterans Lex de Azevedo and David Zippel, the same composers who wrote Broadway's *The Goodbye Girl* and *City of Angels*, a Tony Award winner. The song "Far Longer Than Forever" was nominated for a Golden Globe award for Best Original Song. Richard Rich and Matt Mazur, two former Disney employees (Rich is best known for directing the animated feature *Fox and the Hound*) produced the feature as well as the 1997 direct-to-video sequel, *Swan Princess: Escape from Castle Mountain*, which Rich also directed.

⊚ THE SWORD IN THE STONE (1963)

A Walt Disney Production released by Buena Vista. **p:** Walt Disney; **d:** Wolfgang Reitherman; **dir anim:** Frank Thomas, Milt Kahl, Ollie Johnston, John Lounsbery; **st:** Bill Peet (based on the book by T.H. White); **m:** George Bruns. **Songs:** "A Most Befuddling Thing," "Blue Oak Tree," "Mad Madame Mim," "That's What Makes the World Go Round," "Higitus Figitus" and "The Legend of the Sword in the Stone." **Running time:** 79 minutes.

Voices

Wart: Ricky Sorenson; **Sir Ector/Narrator:** Sebastian Cabot; **Merlin:** Karl Swenson; **Archimedes:** Junius Matthews; **Sir Pelinore:** Alan Napier; **Sir Kay:** Norman Alden; **Madame Mim/Granny Squirrel:** Martha Wentworth; **Girl Squirrel:** Ginny Tyler; **Scullery Maid:** Barbara Jo Allen; **Wart:** Richard and Robert Reitherman

As the title implies, the sword embedded in stone is central to this story featuring Wart, a foster son of Sir Ector, who undertakes lessons in life from Merlin the Magician. Setting off for a jousting tournament in London with Ector and his son Sir Kay, Wart returns to retrieve Kay's forgotten sword. To save time, he pulls a sword from the legendary stone, unaware that the man who does so becomes the rightful king of all of England.

⊚ THE THREE CABALLEROS (1945)

A Walt Disney Production released by RKO Radio Pictures. **p:** Walt Disney; **prod superv/dir:** Norman Ferguson; **seq d:** Clyde Geronimi, Jack Kinney, Bill Roberts; **d:** Harold Young (Patzcuaro, Veracruz, Acapulco); **st:** Homer Brightman, Ernest Terrazzas, Ted Sears, Bill Peet, Ralph Wright, Elmer Plummer, Roy Williams, William Cottrell, Del Connell, James Bodrero; **md:** Charles Wolcott, Paul J. Smith, Edward H. Plumb. **Songs:** "The Three Caballeros," "Os Quindins De Yaya," "You Belong to My Heart," "Mexico," "Have You Ever Been to Baia?" "Pandeiro & Flute," "Pregoes Carioca" and "Lilongo." **Running time:** 71 minutes.

Cast

Aurora Miranda, Carmen Molina, Dora Luz, Nestor Amaral, Almirante, Trio Calaveras, Ascencio del Rio Trio and Padua Hill Players

Voices

Donald Duck: Clarence Nash; **José Carioca:** José Oliveira; **Panchito:** Joaquin Garay; **Narrator:** Fred Shields; **Narrator:** Frank Graham; **Narrator:** Sterling Holloway. "Mexico" sung by Carlos Ramirez

The Latin American setting of Brazil serves as a background for this musical combining live-action personalities and cartoon figures on the same screen. Donald Duck is the central cartoon character in the animated story line of his journey to the native lands of Baia, where he falls in love with a beautiful saleslady and sees the city aboard a magic flying serape. Donald is paired in the film with old pal José Carioca, a tropical bird friend who appeared with Donald in 1943's *Saludos Amigos*, and new addition Panchito, a Mexican charro rooster.

⊚ THUMBELINA (1994)

A Don Bluth Film released by Warner Brothers. **p:** Don Bluth, Gary Goldman, John Pomeroy; **d:** Don Bluth, Gary Goldman; **scr:** Don Bluth; **m:** William Ross, Barry Manilow (with original songs by Barry Manilow, Jack Feldman, Bruce Sussman); **superv anim:** John Pomeroy; **dir anim:** John Hill, Richard Bazley, Jean Morel, Len Simon, Piet Derycker, Dave Kupcyk. **Songs:** "Follow Your Heart," "Thumbelina's Theme," "Soon," "Let Me Be Your Wings," "On the Road," "Follow Your Heart," "You're Beautiful Baby," "Marry the Mole." **Running time:** 86 minutes.

Voices

Jacquimo: Gino Conforti; **Mother:** Barbara Cook; **Thumbelina:** Jodi Benson; **Hero:** Will Ryan; **Queen Tabitha:** June Foray; **King Colbert:** Kenneth Mars; **Prince Cornelius:** Gary Imhoff; **Grundel:** Joe Lynch; **Mrs. (Ma) Toad:** Charo; **Mozo:** Danny Mann; **Gringo:** Loren Michaels; **Baby Bug:** Kendall Cunningham; **Gnatty:** Tawny Sunshine Glover; **Li'l Bee:** Michael Nunes; **Mr. Beetle:** Gilbert Gottfried; **Mrs. Rabbit:** Pat Muisick; **Mr. Fox/Mr. Bear:** Neil Ross; **Ms. Fieldmouse:** Carol Channing; **Mr. Mole:** John Hurt; **Reverend Rat:** Will Ryan

This animated adaptation of the timeless Hans Christian Andersen fairy tale tells the enchanting story of a tiny, out-of-place girl ("no bigger than a thumb") who tries to find her place in a giant world, thus setting the stage for a series of romantic adventures that begin with the arrival of a fairy prince and lead to romance by an ugly, wise-cracking beetle who wants to steal her from the handsome prince.

PN: This film marked Don Bluth's last production for his Ireland-based animation studio, producing a disappointing $11 million in ticket sales. Two months following the release of the film, Bluth was hired to head up 20th Century-Fox's theatrical animation studio in Phoenix, Arizona. Opening with the film nationwide was the Steven Spielberg produced short subject, "I'm Mad," the first theatrical short starring TV's Animaniacs.

Thumbelina and Prince Cornelius find true happiness together at last in Don Bluth's animated fantasy Thumbelina. © *Don Bluth Limited*

◎ TIM BURTON'S THE NIGHTMARE BEFORE CHRISTMAS (1993)

A Skellington Production released by Touchstone Pictures. **p:** Tim Burton, Denise Di Novi, Kathleen Gavin; **d:** Henry Selick; **scr:** Caroline Thompson (with adaptation by Michael McDowell based on a poem by Tim Burton); **m:** Danny Elfman. **Songs:** "Overture," "Opening," "This Is Halloween," "Jack's Lament," "Doctor Finklestein/In the Forest," "What's This?" "Town Meeting Song," "Jack & Sally Montage," "Jack's Obsession," "Kidnap the Sandy Claws," "Making Christmas," "Nabbed," "Oogie Boogie's Song," "Sally's Song," "Christmas Eve," "Poor Jack," "To the Rescue," "Finale," "Closing" and "End Titles." **Running time:** 76 minutes.

Voices
Jack Skellington (singing)/Barrel/Clown with the Tear-Away Face: Danny Elfman; **Jack Skellington (speaking):** Chris Sarandon; **Sally/Shock:** Catherine O'Hara; **Dr. Finkelstein:** William Hickey; **Mayor:** Glenn Shadix; **Lock:** Paul Reubens; **Oogie Boogie:** Ken Page; **Santa:** Ed Ivory; **Big Witch:** Susan McBride; **Corpse Kid/Corpse Mom/Small Witch:** Debi Durst; **Harlequin Demon/Devil/Sax Player:** Greg Proops; **Man Under Stairs/Vampire/Corpse Dad:** Kerry Katz; **Mr. Hyde/Behemoth/Vampire:** Randy Crenshaw; **Mummy/Vampire:** Sherwood Ball; **Undersea Gal/Man Under the Stairs:** Carmen Twillie; **Wolfman:** Glenn Walters; **Narrator:** Patrick Stewart

Additional Voices
Mia Brown, L. Peter Callender, Ann Fraser, Jess McClurg, Robert Olague, Jennifer Levey, Elena Praskin, Judi M. Durand, John Morris, Daamen J. Krall, David McCharen, Bobbi Page, David J. Randolph, Trampas Warman, Doris Hess, Christina MacGregor, Gary Raff, Gary Schwartz

Jack Skellington, the Pumpkin King of Halloween Town, discovers the joys of Christmas Town and attempts to fill Santa's shoes in this ghoulish yet wickedly funny dark, stop-motion animated holiday tale, based on a story by Tim Burton.

PN: Unlike the Disney blockbuster animated features, *The Nightmare Before Christmas* was filmed in a laborious process called "stop-motion animation," for which animators move puppets around miniature sets, filming them frame by frame with computerized cameras. Grossing $50 million in box-office revenue, this feature-length treatment was responsible for revitalizing the stop-motion animation industry. Twelve years before making this film, Burton worked as an animator at Disney. Stop-motion expert Henry Selick, the genius behind Pillsbury Doughboy commercials and MTV spots, directed the film.

◎ TOM AND JERRY: THE MOVIE (1993)

A Turner Entertainment/WMG Film/Film Roman Production released by Miramax Films. **p&d:** Phil Roman; **cpd:** Bill Schultz; **exec prod:** Roger Mayer, Jack Petrik, Hans Brockman, Justin Ackerman; **scr:** Dennis Marks; **m/sc:** Henry Mancini (with songs by Henry Mancini and lyrics by Leslie Bricusse); **seq dir:** John Sparey, Monte Young, Bob Nesler, Adam Kuhlman. **Songs:** "Tom And Jerry Theme," "Friends to the End," "What Do We Care? (The Alley Cat Song)," "(Money Is Such) A Beautiful Word," "God's Little Creatures," "I Miss You—Robyn's Song," "I've Done It" and "All in How Much We Give." **Running time:** 84 minutes.

Voices
Tom: Richard Kind; **Jerry:** Dana Hill; **Robyn Starling:** Anndi McAfee; **Lickboot:** Tony Jay; **Captain Kiddie/carnival sea captain:** Rip Taylor; **Doctor Applecheeks, an evil pet snatcher:** Henry Gibson; **Ferdinand/Straycatcher #1:** Michael Bell; **Puggsy/Daddy Starling:** Ed Gilbert; **Frankie Da Flea:** David L. Lander; **Squawk:** Howard Morris; **Straycatcher #2:** Sydney Lassick; **Alleycat/Bulldog:** Raymond McLeod; **Alleycat:** Mitchell D. Moore; **Alleycat:** Scott Wojahn; **Patrolman:** Tino Insana; **Droopy:** Don Messick; **Woman's Voice:** B.J. Ward; **Man:** Greg Burson; **Aunt Pristine Figg, Robyn's aunt:** Charlotte Rae

In their first full-length feature, squabbling cat-and-mouse duo Tom and Jerry are left homeless after Tom's owners accidentally move without him. The lovable duo help a runaway rich girl named Robyn find her missing father.

PN: Tom and Jerry spoke and sang in this movie, which was a joint effort between Turner Entertainment and Film Roman Productions, but not for the first time as the film's promoters made the public believe. Tom spoke many times before in the duo's MGM cartoon shorts, including "Solid Serenade" (1946), in which he used four different voices.

Jerry's most notable talking film appearance was in the MGM feature *Anchors Aweigh,* in which he sang and danced with costar Gene Kelly. Despite the prospects of an all-talking Tom and Jerry feature, the movie proved to be a major disappointment, however, taking in just $3.5 million. Joseph Barbera, who co-created Tom and Jerry with partner Bill Hanna, served as a creative consultant on the film.

◎ TOY STORY (1995)

A Walt Disney/Pixar Animation Studios Production released by Walt Disney Pictures. **p:** Bonnie Arnold, Ralph Guggenheim; **d:** John Lasseter; **st:** John Lasseter, Andrew Stanton, Peter Docter, John Ranft; **scr:** Joss Whedon, Andrew Stanton, Joel Cohen, Alec Sokolow; **m:** Randy Newman; **dir anim:** Ash Brannon. **Songs:** "You've Got a Friend in Me," "Strange Things," "I Will Go Sailing No More," "Andy's Birthday," "Soldier's Mission," "Presents," "Buzz," "Sid," "Woody And Buzz," "Mutants," "Woody's Gone," "Big One," "Hang Together," "Big One," "On the Move" and "Infinity and Beyond." **Running time:** 81 minutes.

Voices

Woody: Tom Hanks; **Buzz Lightyear:** Tim Allen; **Mr. Potato Head:** Don Rickles; **Slinky Dog:** Jim Varney; **Rex:** Wallace Shawn; **Hamm:** John Ratzenberger; **Bo Peep:** Annie Potts; **Andy:** John Morris; **Sid:** Erik von Detten; **Mrs. Davis:** Laurie Metcalf; **Sergeant:** R. Lee Ermey; **Hannah:** Sarah Freeman; **TV Announcer:** Penn Jillette

Additional Voices

Jack Angel, Spencer Aste, Gregg Berger, Lisa Bradley, Kendall Cunningham, Debie Derryberry, Cody Dorkin, Bill Farmer, Craig Good, Gregory Grudt, Danielle Judovits, Sam Lasseter, Brittany Levenbrown, Sherry Lynn, Scott McAfee, Mickie McGowan, Ryan O'Donohue, Jeff Pidgeon, Patrick Pinney, Philip Proctor, Jan Rabson, Joe Ranft, Andrews Stanton, Shane Sweet

A pull-string cowboy toy named Woody ("Reach for the sky") falls out of favor with his six-year-old owner when the young boy receives a flashy space ranger (Buzz Lightyear), sporting laser action and pop-out wings, as a birthday present. The two rival toys become friends in order to defeat the toy-torturing boy next door in this heartwarming, entertaining computer-animated adventure.

PN: A joint venture between Disney and Pixar, this feature was seven years in the making and the first fully computer animated feature made in America. Produced at a cost of $30 million, the film grossed an astounding $191 million in the United States and $354 million worldwide, and was nominated for three Academy Awards: Best Writing (Screenplay Written Directly for the Screen), Best Original Score and Best Song (for the song: "You've Got a Friend,"

written and performed as a solo by Randy Newman and as a duet with Lyle Lovett in the film). Director John Lasseter previously directed five groundbreaking computer-animated shorts for Pixar prior to doing *Toy Story,* including two Oscar-nominated films for Best Short Films: 1988's *Tin Toy* and 1989's *Knicknack.*

◎ THE TRANSFORMERS: THE MOVIE (1986)

A Sunbow-Marvel Entertainment Production released by DEG. **p:** Joe Bacal, Tom Griffin; **d:** Nelson Shin, Kozo Morishita; **w:** Ron Friedman, Flint Dille (based on the Hasbro toy, "The Transformers"); **m:** Vince DiCola. **Running time:** 86 minutes.

Voices

Planet Unicron: Orson Welles; **Ultra Magnus:** Robert Stack; **Galvatron:** Leonard Nimoy; **Wreck Gar:** Eric Idle; **Hot Rod/Rodimus Prime:** Judd Nelson; **Kup:** Lionel Stander; **Blurr:** John Moschitta; **Kranix:** Norm Alden; **Astrotrain:** Jack Angel; **Prowl/Scrapper/Swoop/Junkion:** Michael Bell; **Grimlock:** Gregg Berger; **Arcee:** Susan Blu; **Devastator:** Arthur Burghardt; **Spike/Brown/Shockwave:** Cory Burton; **Cyclonus/Quintession Leader:** Roger C. Carmel; **Quintession Judge:** Rege Cordic; **Prime/Ironhide:** Peter Cullen; **Jazz:** Scatman Crothers; **Dirge:** Bud Davis; **Inferno:** Walker Edmiston; **Perceptor:** Paul Eiding; **Blitzwing:** Ed Gilbert; **Bumblebee:** Dan Gilvean; **Blaster:** Buster Jones; **Scourge:** Stan Jones; **Cliffjumper:** Casey Kasem; **Starscream:** Chris Latta; **Daniel:** David Mendenhall; **Gears:** Don Messick; **Shrapnel:** Hal Rayle; **Kickback:** Clive Revill; **Bonecrusher/Hook/Springer/Slag:** Neil Ross; **Soundwave/Megatron/Rumble/Frenzy/Wheelie/Junkion:** Frank Welker

Set in the year 2005, the Transformers and their archenemies, the Decepticons, are at war with each other when an Earthly group, the Autobots, enter the picture and help send the Decepticons into outer space. The Decepticons return rejuvenated after Unicron, a powerful planetary force, intercedes and refits the group's leader with a new body and new name (he's now called Galvatron) so they can renew the war with Autobots.

PN: *Citizen Kane* director Orson Welles was the voice of Unicron.

◎ TREASURE ISLAND (1972)

A Filmation Associates Production released by Warner Bros. **p:** Lou Scheimer, Norman Prescott; **d:** Hal Sutherland; **m:** George Blais. **Songs:** "Fifteen Men on a Dead Man's Chest," "Find the Boy/Find the Mouse and We Find the Map" and "Proper Punishment." **Running time:** 75 minutes.

Voices
Long John Silver: Richard Dawson; **Captain Flint:** Larry Storch; **Jim Hawkins:** Davy Jones; **Squire Trelawney:** Larry D. Mann; **Mother:** Jane Webb; **Parrot:** Dallas McKennon

Young Jim Hawkins and his newfound friend Hiccup the Mouse take to the high seas in search of buried treasure in this musical version of Robert Louis Stevenson's classic children's tale.

PN: In 1980 NBC aired this feature-length movie as a prime-time special, edited for broadcast.

⊚ A TROLL IN CENTRAL PARK (1993)

A Don Bluth Ireland Ltd. Production released by Warner Bros. Family Entertainment. **p:** Don Bluth, Gary Goldman; **d:** Don Bluth, Gary Goldman; **st:** Don Bluth, Gary Goldman, John Pomeroy, T.J. Kuenster, Stu Krieger; **scr:** Stu Krieger; **m:** Robert Folk (with original songs by Barry Mann, Cynthia Well, Norman Gimbel and Robert Folk); **superv anim:** John Pomeroy. Songs: "Queen of Mean," "Welcome to My World," "Absolutely Green" and "Friends Like Us." **Running time:** 76 minutes.

Voices
Stanley: Dom DeLuise; **Queen Gnorga:** Cloris Leachman; **King Llort:** Charles Nelson Reilly; **Alan:** Jonathon Pryce; **Hilary:** Hayley Mills; **Gus:** Philip Glasser; **Rosie:** Tawny "Sunshine" Glover; **Boss:** Will Ryan; **Snuffy:** Pat Musik

Stanley, a kindly troll with a sweet disposition and a penchant for growing beautiful plants, is exiled by the wicked queen to New York City for growing one too many flowers and to learn how to act like the other trolls (who are mean and like to scare humans) in this classically animated fantasy/adventure from legendary animator Don Bluth.

⊚ THE TUNE (1992)

A Bill Plympton Production released by October Films. **p & d:** Bill Plympton; **scr:** Maureen McElheron, Bill Plympton, P.C. Vey; **m:** Maureen McElheron; **anim:** Bill Plympton. **Running time:** 72 minutes.

Voices
Del: Daniel Nieden; **Didi:** Maureen McElheron; **Mayor/Mr. Mega/Mrs. Mega:** Marty Nelson; **Dot:** Emily Bindiger; **Wiseone/Surfer/Tango Dancer/Note:** Chris Hoffman; **Cabbie:** Jimmy Ceribello; **Houndog:** Ned Reynolds; **Bellhop:** Jeff Knight; **Surfer/Note:** Jennifer Senko

This entertaining series of musical shorts follows the adventures of a songwriter's (Del) quest to write a hit song, leading him to the wacky world of Flooby Nooby, where he learns to write songs from the heart.

PN: This was the first feature film produced almost entirely by an independent animator in a one-room New York loft. Producer-director Bill Plympton worked three years to bring the movie to the big screen. Unlike big-budget animated features which often employ hundreds of people, *The Tune* was made by scarcely a handful of artists. Plympton animated the entire film (using approximately 30,000 drawings) himself while two assistants inked and painted. Financed entirely by Plympton, sections of the feature were released as short films to generate funds to finance the film, including "The Wiseman" and "Push Comes to Shove," which won the 1991 Prix du Jury at the Cannes Film Festival.

⊚ TWICE UPON A TIME (1983)

A Korty Films and Lucasfilm Ltd. Production released by the Ladd Company through Warner Bros. **p:** Bill Couturie; **d:** John Korty, Charles Swenson; **scr:** John Korty, Charles Swenson, Suella Kennedy, Bill Couturie; **m:** Dawn Atkinson, Ken Melville; **seq dir:** Brian Narelle, Carl Willat, Henry Selick. Songs: "Twice Upon a Time," "Life Is But a Dream," "Out on My Own," "Heartbreak Town" and "Champagne Time." **Running time:** 75 minutes.

Voices
Ralph, the All-Purpose Animal: Lorenzo Musi; **The Fairy Godmother:** Judith Kahan Kampmann; **Synonamess Botch:** Marshall Efron; **Rod Rescueman/Scuzzbopper:** James Crana; **Flora Fauna:** Julie Payne; **Greensleeves:** Hamilton Camp; **Narrator/Chief of State/Judges and Bailiff:** Paul Frees

Action-adventure-fantasy-comedy about two oddballs, Ralph, the All-Purpose Animal, and Mum, his prankster sidekick, who are so eager to be heroes that they do something very wrong in trying to do something very right.

PN: This film was the first to utilize a revolutionary new animation process, Lumage animation, developed by Korty Films. The technique enables depth, translucent color and textural effects usually impossible to achieve in standard cel animation.

⊚ VAMPIRES IN HAVANA (1987)

An Insituto del Arte and Industria Cinematográficos-Television Española-Drunoik Production release. **p:** Paco Prats; **d & w:** Juan Padron; **m:** Rembert Egues. **Running time:** 80 minutes.

A group of Chicago-based vampires, who head up a local Mafioso, are after a secret formula developed by a Cuban scientist. The potent serum will enable vampires to survive in the sunlight.

PN: First screened in its native Cuba in 1985 as *Vampiros en la Habana*.

THE WACKY WORLD OF MOTHER GOOSE (1966)

A Videocraft International Production released by Embassy Pictures. **p:** Arthur Rankin Jr.; **d:** Jules Bass; **exec prod:** Joseph E. Levine; **st:** Arthur Rankin Jr.; **scr:** Romeo Muller (based on characters created by Charles Perrault in the book *Mother Goose Tales*); **m/l:** George Wilkins, Jules Bass. Songs: "I Still Believe," "It's Never Too Late," "Half a Chance," "S.S. BBC," "You're Predictable" and "Great Big Wacky World." **Running time:** 77 minutes.

Voices

Mother Goose: Margaret Rutherford

Additional Voices

Robert McFadden, Bradley Bolke, Laura Leslie, James Daugherty, Craig Sechler, Susan Melvin, Kevin Gavin, Bryma Kaeburn, Robert Harter, William Marine

Fabled storybook character Mother Goose gets mixed up with secret agents and well-known storybook characters Sleeping Beauty, Tom Thumb and others in this full-color fantasy adventure.

PN: *The Wacky World of Mother Goose* was the first cel-animated theatrical feature produced by Arthur Rankin Jr. and Jules Bass, who achieved fame with their "Animagic"-produced television specials using stop-motion puppets.

THE WATER BABIES (1979)

A Productions Associates and Adridne Films Production released by Pethurst International. **p:** Peter Shaw; **d:** Lionel Jeffries; **scr:** Michael Robson (based on Charles Kingsley's novel); **st:** Phil Coulter, Bill Martin; **superv anim:** Mirsolaw Kijowiez (Film Polski), J. Stokes (Cuthbert Cartoons). **Running time:** 93 minutes.

Cast

Grimes: James Mason, **Mrs. Doasyouwouldbedoneby:** Billie Whitelaw; **Masterman:** Bernard Cribbins; **Lady Harriet:** Joan Greenwood; **Sir John:** David Tomlinson; **Sladd:** Paul Luty; **Tom:** Tommy Pender; **Ellie:** Samantha Gates

A young chimney sweep's apprentice and his dog accidentally fall into a pond and are transformed into "water babies" who inhabit an eternal underwater playground.

PN: Based on Charles Kingsley's children's novel, the film combines live action and animation. Budget: $2 million.

WATERSHIP DOWN (1978)

A Nepenthe Production released by Avco Embassy Pictures. **p, d & w:** Martin Rosen (based on the novel by Richard Adams); **m:** Angela Morley, Malcolm Williamson; **superv**

anim: Philip Duncan; **anim dir:** Tony Guy; **superv anim:** Philip Duncan. **Running time:** 92 minutes.

Voices

Hazel: John Hurt; **Fiver:** Richard Briers; **Bigwig:** Michael Graham-Cox; **Capt. Holly:** John Bennett; **Blackberry:** Simon Cadell; **Pipkin:** Roy Kinnear; **Dandelion:** Richard O'Callaghan; **Silver:** Terence Rigby; **Chief Rabbit:** Sir Ralph Richardson; **Cowslip:** Denholm Elliott; **Kehaar:** Zero Mostel; **Clover:** Mary Maddox; **Hyzenthlay:** Hannah Gordon; **Cat:** Lyn Farleigh; **Gen. Woundwort:** Harry Andrews; **Campion:** Nigel Hawthorne; **Blackavar:** Clifton Jones; **Black Rabbit:** Joss Ackland; **Narrator:** Michael Hordern

A colony of rabbits, threatened by the destruction of their warren, run off to find a new home safe from the menace of human rule.

PN: First U.S. showing was at the World Science Fiction and Fantasy Convention in Phoenix, Arizona. World premiere: London. Singer/songwriter Art Garfunkel sings two songs in the film.

WE'RE BACK! A DINOSAUR'S STORY (1993)

An Amblin Entertainment Production released by Universal Pictures. **p:** Steve Hickner; **d:** Dick Zondag, Ralph Zondag, Phil Nibbelink, Simon Wells; **cpd:** Thad Weinlein; **exec prod:** Kathleen Kennedy, Frank Marshall, Steven Spielberg; **scr:** John Patrick Stanley (based on the book by Hudson Talbott); **m:** James Horner (with original songs by James Horner and Thomas Dolby); **superv anim:** Jeffrey J. Varab, Bibo Bergeron, Kristof Serrand, Rob Stevenhagen, Thierry Schiel, Sahin Ersoz, Borge Ring. Songs: "Roll Back the Rock (to the Dawn of Time)." **Running time:** 78 minutes.

A scene from Watership Down *(1978), based on Richard Adams's celebrated best-seller about a colony of rabbits who escape the menace of human rule. © Avco Embassy Pictures*

Voices

Rex: John Goodman; **Buster:** Blaze Berdahl; **Mother Bird:** Rhea Perlman; **Vorb:** Jay Leno; **Woog:** Rene LeVant; **Elsa:** Felicity Kendal; **Dweeb:** Charles Fleischer; **Captain NewEyes:** Walter Cronkite; **Louie:** Joe Shea; **Dr. Bleeb:** Julia Child; **Professor ScrewEyes, Captain NewEyes' evil brother:** Kenneth Mars; **Cecilia:** Yeardley Smith; **Stubbs the Clown:** Martin Short

Additional Voices

Eddie Deezen, Larry King, John Malkovich

Four dinosaurs, Elsa, Woog, Rex and Dweeb, are plucked from prehistory by an eccentric captain who raises their IQs with a high-tech breakfast cereal and offers them a chance to grant the wishes of modern-day children.

PN: Based on the popular 32-page children's book by Hudson Talbott, this was the fourth Spielberg-produced animated feature and the second from his London-based Amblimation studio (after *An American Tail: Fievel Goes West*). This film was the least successful of Spielberg's animated films. Adding to its difficulties at the box office was the fact it opened the same weekend as Robin Williams's smash-hit comedy. *Mrs. Doubtfire*. Former CBS newscaster Walter Cronkite lent his voice to the character of Captain NewEyes, making his animated film debut, and Charles Fleischer, the voice of Roger Rabbit, also worked on the film.

◎ WHO FRAMED ROGER RABBIT (1988)

An Amblin Entertainment/Touchstone Pictures Production released by Buena Vista. **d:** Richard Zemeckis; **scr:** Jeffrey Price, Peter Seaman (based on novel *Who Censored Roger Rabbit?* by Gary K. Wolf); **m:** Alan Silvestri; **anim dir:** Richard Williams; **superv anim:** Andreas Beja; Russell Hall, Phil Nibbelink, Simon Wells. **Running time:** 104 minutes

Cast

Eddie Valiant: Bob Hoskins; **Judge Doom:** Christopher Lloyd; **Dolores:** Joanna Cassidy; **Marvin Acme:** Stubby Kaye; **R.K. Maroon:** Alan Tilvern; **Lt. Santino:** Richard Le Parmentier

Voices

Roger Rabbit/Benny the Cab: Charles Fleischer; **Jessica Rabbit:** Kathleen Turner; **Baby Herman:** Lou Hirsch; **Betty Boop:** Mae Questel; **Daffy Duck/Porky Pig/Tweety/ Sylvester the Cat/Bugs Bunny:** Mel Blanc; **Hippo:** Mary T. Radford; **Yosemite Sam:** Joe Alaskey; **Droopy:** Richard Williams; **Lena Hyena:** June Foray; **Mickey Mouse:** Wayne Allwine; **Bullet #1:** Pat Buttram; **Bullet #2:** Jim Cummings; **Bullet #3:** Jim Gallant; **Singing Sword:** Frank Sinatra; **Minnie Mouse:** Russi Taylor; **Goofy/Wolf:** Tony Pope; **Woody Woodpecker:** Cherry Davis

Famed cartoon star Roger Rabbit is sabotaging his screen career by worrying over his wife's carrying on with another "toon." The studio assigns a detective to follow the wife and spy on her in this live-action/animated romp.

PN: This classic live-action/animated feature was rumored to have cost $45 million to produce. It became the most popular film of 1988, grossing an astronomical $154 million in the United States and the same number overseas. In November 1991 the film premiered on CBS, featuring four never-before seen animated minutes cut from the original film. In the added footage, detective Eddie Valiant snoops around Jessica Rabbit's dressing room and gets caught by Judge Doom, who has the Weasels take him to Toontown and give him a "Toonaroo"—they paint a cartoon head on him. The four-minute scene cost $500,000 to produce. Paul Reubens, of "Pee Wee Herman" fame, was originally chosen to do the voice of Roger Rabbit when the film was first in development in 1981. At the time Darrell Van Citters was to be the film's animation director. Mike Giaimo developed the original character design for Roger when Van Citters was handling the project. Some years later, when Robert Zemeckis took over the project, he considered Giaimo's character design "too clownlike" and asked Giaimo to redesign, suggesting that he make Roger "a little more like Michael J. Fox." Fox was then star of TV's *Family Ties* and had recently wrapped up production of the comedy feature *Back to the Future*, which Zemeckis directed.

◎ WILLY McBEAN AND HIS MAGIC MACHINE (1965)

An Arthur Rankin Jr./Videocraft International/Dentsu Motion Picture Production released by Magna Pictures Distribution Corporation. **p, d & scr:** Arthur Rankin Jr.; **assoc prod:** Jules Bass, Larry Roemer; **m/l:** Edward Thomas, Gene Forrell, James Polack; **anim superv:** Tad Mochinaga. Filmed in Animagic. **Running time:** 94 minutes.

Voices

Willie McBean: Billie Richards; **Professor Von Rotten:** Larry Mann

Additional Voices

Alfie Scopp, Paul Kligman, Claude Ray, Corrine Connely, James Doohan, Pegi Loder, Paul Soles

A young boy (Willie McBean) and his sidekick monkey (Pablo) follow a mad professor (Professor Von Rotten) take a mad romp through time on a magic time machine to the days of Christopher Columbus, King Tut, King Arthur, Buffalo Bill and the cavemen—in this "Animagic" color musical comedy-fantasy.

PN: Produced in "Animagic," a lifelike stop-motion process using three-dimensional objects and puppets that move on the screen without strings or hands, this was the first full-length stop-motion animated theatrical feature by the team of Arthur Rankin and Jules Bass, known for such popular television specials as *Rudolph, The Red-Nosed Reindeer, Frosty the Snowman* and others. The movie was produced simultaneously with the *Rudolph, The Red-Nosed Reindeer* special, which premiered first on NBC on December 6, 1964. Actor James Doohan, who later became known as Scotty on TV's *Star Trek*, was one of the voice artists on the film.

The movie had its world premiere in San Francisco on June 23, 1965, in a multiple engagement of 47 theaters.

⊚ WIZARDS (1977)

A Bakshi Production released by 20th Century-Fox. **w, p & d:** Ralph Bakshi; **m:** Andrew Belling; **seq anim:** Irv Spence. **Running time:** 80 minutes.

Voices
Avatar: Bob Holt; **Elinore:** Jesse Wells; **Weehawk:** Richard Romanus; **Peace:** David Proval; **President:** James Connell; **Blackwolf:** Steve Gravers; **Fairy:** Barbara Sloane; **Frog:** Angelo Grisant; **Priest:** Hyman Wien; **Deewhittle:** Christopher Tayback; **Sean:** Mark Hamill; **General:** Peter Hobbs; **Prostitute:** Tina Bowman.

An evil twin brother/wizard named Blackwolf seeks to extend the evil sphere of his domain in the land of Scortch. He battles for supremacy against his brother Avatar, wizard of Montagar, who is totally the opposite of Blackwolf in personality and beliefs.

⊚ YELLOW SUBMARINE (1968)

An Apple Films/King Features Production released by United Artists. **p:** Al Brodax; **d:** George Dunning; **st:** Lee Minoff (based on a song by John Lennon and Paul McCartney); **scr:** Lee Minoff, Al Brodax, Jack Mendelsohn, Erich Segal; **md:** George Martin; **anim dir:** Jack Stokes, Bob Balser. **Running time:** 89 minutes.

The Beatles, in animated form, fight to save the undersea kingdom of Pepperland from a horde of antimusic monsters in Yellow Submarine *(1968).* (COURTESY: KING FEATURES PRODUCTIONS)

Voices
Paul McCartney, Ringo Starr, John Lennon, George Harrison, Dick Emery, Paul Angelus, Lance Percival

Inspired by its title song, this musical fantasy (billed as a "modyssey") finds the legendary lads from Liverpool fighting to save the undersea kingdom of Pepperland from a horde of antimusic monsters, the Blue Meanies. The fearless four meet a multitude of strange and original characters throughout their voyage: the U.S. Calvary, King Kong, Paul's Clean Old Grandad and Lucy in the Sky with Diamonds.

PN: First previewed at the Pavillion in London in July 1968. The film began its exclusive Los Angeles engagement November 13 at the Village Theatre, Westwood. Lance Percival, one of the film's vocal talents, earlier voiced the characters of Paul and Ringo in the 1960's animated television series, which, coincidentally, was produced by Al Brodax, also producer of the Fab Four's animated feature.

◎ ◎ ◎ ◎ ◎

ANIMATED TELEVISION SPECIALS

◎ ◎ ◎ ◎ ◎

◎ ABEL'S ISLAND

Abel, an articulate and sophisticated mouse, is stranded on an island for a full year, separated from his new wife, Amanda, and worried about her, in this award-winning film and Emmy-nominated half-hour special from animator Michael Sporn. Based on a book by William Steig, this intelligent retelling debuted on the long-running PBS anthology series, *Long Ago & Far Away*. *A Michael Sporn Animation Production in association with Italtoons Corporation. Half-hour. Premiered on PBS: February 11, 1989. Rebroadcast on PBS: November 30, 1990; November 1, 1992.*

Voices
Abel: Tim Curry; **Gower the Frog:** Lionel Jeffries; **Amanda:** Heidi Stallings

◎ ACE VENTURA CHRISTMAS SPECIAL

Famous pet detective Ace Ventura (in cartoon form) and his monkey sidekick Spike go after a bunch of reindeer-nappers who've made off with Santa's prized reindeer in this prime-time animated special, based on the popular CBS Saturday morning series. *A Nelvana Enterprises Production. Color. Half-hour. Premiered on CBS: December 13, 1995.*

Voices
Ace: Michael Hall; **Spike:** Richard Binsley; **Shickadance:** Vince Corraza; **Aguado:** Al Waxman; **Emilio:** Bruce Tubbe; **Woodstock:** David Beatty

◎ THE ADVENTURE MACHINE

Buttons, the cub bear, and Rusty, the fox, stars of this fifth in a series of syndicated Chucklewood Critters specials, become stranded in a forest where they meet some unusual characters in this entertaining holiday half-hour program. *An Encore Enterprises Production. Color. Half-hour. Premiered: 1990. Syndicated. Premiered on USA: April 11, 1993.*

Voices
Buttons: Barbara Goodson; **Rusty:** Mona Marshall

◎ ADVENTURES FROM THE BOOK OF VIRTUES: "COMPASSION"

When an immigrant family loses its home in a terrible fire, Plato and Aurora counter Zach's excuses not to get involved with several inspiring stories about the need for compassion in this installment of the popular PBS inspirational series, first broadcast as part of an hour-long block of specials. *A PorchLight Entertainment Production in association with KCET/Hollywoood and Fox Animation Studios. Color. Half-hour. Premiered on PBS: September 3, 1996. Rebroadcast on PBS: September 21, 1996.*

Voices
Plato: Kevin Richardson; **Ari:** Jim Cummings; **Aurora/ Annie:** Kath Soucie; **Zach:** Pam Segall; **Socrates:** Frank Welker

⊚ ADVENTURES FROM THE BOOK OF VIRTUES: "COURAGE"

When Annie Redfeather hits a hurdle and falls flat on her face during a track meet, her friends at Plato's Peak offer several stories to bolster her courage so she can face the next big race in this half-hour episode of the critically acclaimed PBS series, which debuted on PBS as part of an hour-long block of specials. *A PorchLight Entertainment Production in association with KCET/Hollywood and Fox Animation Studios. Color. Half-hour. Premiered on PBS: September 4, 1996. Rebroadcast on PBS: September 21, 1996.*

Voices

Plato: Kevin Richardson; **Ari:** Jim Cummings; **Aurora/Annie:** Kath Soucie; **Zach:** Pam Segall; **Socrates:** Frank Welker

Wraparound

Starter: Jim Cummings; **Bobbi:** Pam Segall

THE MINOTAUR: Theseus: Mark Hamill; **Minotaur/Aegeus:** Frank Welker; **King Minos:** Tim Curry; **Guard #1:** Ed Begley Jr.; **Ariadne:** B.J. Ward; **Father:** Jim Cummings

THE BRAVE MICE: Skinny Male Mouse: Mark Hamill; **Young Lady Mouse:** Kath Soucie; **Old Lady Mouse:** B.J. Ward; **Chubby Mouse:** Kevin Richardson

WILLIAM TELL: William Tell: Ed Begley Jr.; **Gessler:** Tim Curry; **Soldier #1:** Mark Hamill; **Willie:** B.J. Ward; **Soldier #2:** Kevin Richardson

⊚ ADVENTURES FROM THE BOOK OF VIRTUES: "FAITH"

When Annie's elderly friend and neighbor dies suddenly, she questions the use of faith in the telling of three related stories in this half-hour edition of the award-winning PBS cartoon series–and part of a second batch of half-hour specials–aired in an hour-long block. *A PorchLight Entertainment Production in association with KCET/Hollywood and Fox Animation Studios. Color. Half-hour. Premiered on PBS: February 16, 1997.*

Voices

Plato: Kevin Richardson; **Ari:** Jim Cummings; **Aurora/Annie:** Kath Soucie; **Zach:** Pam Segall; **Socrates:** Frank Welker

⊚ ADVENTURES FROM THE BOOK OF VIRTUES: "FRIENDSHIP"

When Annie's "new best friend" breaks her promise and chooses someone else to be her partner on a canoe trip, Annie's feelings are hurt, provoking a discussion about the meaning of true friendship in this animated half-hour–and second grouping of six specials from the critically acclaimed PBS series–which premiered as part of an hour-long block. *A Porchlight Entertainment Production in association with KCET/Hollywood and Fox Animation Studios. Color. Half-hour. Premiered on PBS: February 9, 1997.*

Voices

Plato: Kevin Richardson; **Ari:** Jim Cummings; **Aurora/Annie:** Kath Soucie; **Zach:** Pam Segall; **Socrates:** Frank Welker

"FOR EVERYTHING THERE IS A SEASON" (POEM): Sarah West: Catherine Cavadini; **Betty RedFeather:** Christine Avila

WAUKEWA'S EAGLE: Waukewa: Alex Dent; **Father:** Michael Horse; **Eagle:** Frank Welker

WHY FROG AND SNAKE DON'T PLAY TOGETHER: Frog Child: Christine Cavanaugh; **Snake Child:** Kath Soucie; **Frog Father:** Frank Welker; **Snake Mother:** Catherine Cavanaugh

DAMON & PYTHIAS: Damon: George Newbern; **Pythias/Soldier #1:** Jim Cummings; **King Dionysius:** Peter Strauss

⊚ ADVENTURES FROM THE BOOK OF VIRTUES: "GENEROSITY"

After collecting canned goods for a local shelter, Plato realizes that Zach and Annie are more concerned about getting recognition for their generosity than actually helping people in this animated half-hour–part of a second collection of specials from the popular PBS inspirational series–aired in an hour-long block. *A PorchLight Entertainment Production in association with KCET/Hollywood. Color. Half-hour. Premiered on PBS: February 23, 1997.*

Voices

Plato: Kevin Richardson; **Ari:** Jim Cummings; **Aurora/Annie:** Kath Soucie; **Zach:** Pam Segall; **Socrates:** Frank Welker

ROCKING HORSE LAND: Fredolin: Mike Hughes; **Rocking Horse (Rollande):** Jim Cummings; **Attendant:** Chris Sarandon

OLD MR. RABBIT'S THANKSGIVING DINNER: Old Mr. Rabbit: Lewis Arquette; **Billy Chipmunk:** Frank Welker; **Molly Mouse:** Tippi Hedren; **Tommy Chickadee:** Jim Cummings

THE GIFT OF THE MAGI: Salesman: Lewis Arquette; **Della:** Joanna Gleason; **Madame Sofroni:** Tippi Hedren; **Jim:** Chris Sarandon

ADVENTURES FROM THE BOOK OF VIRTUES: "HONESTY"

When Zach Nichols breaks one of his father's cameras, he concocts a story to escape blame in this half-hour edition of the award-winning PBS series, which debuted as part of an hour-long block of specials. *A PorchLight Entertainment Production in association with KCET/Hollywood and Fox Animation Studios. Color. Half-hour. Premiered on PBS: September 2, 1996. Rebroadcast on PBS: September 21, 1996.*

Voices

Plato: Kevin Richardson; **Ari:** Jim Cummings; **Aurora/ Annie:** Kath Soucie; **Zach:** Pam Segall; **Socrates:** Frank Welker

Wraparound

Mr. Nichols: Jim Cummings

THE FROG PRINCE: Frog/Frog Prince: Jeff Bennett; **Princess** Page O'Hara; **King:** Frank Welker

GEORGE WASHINGTON AND THE CHERRY TREE: George Washington: Kath Soucie; **Mr. Washington:** Frank Welker; **Washington's Siblings:** Page O'Hara, Jeff Bennett

THE INDIAN CINDERELLA: Strong Wind/Chief: Michael Horse; **Sharp Eyes/Morning Light:** Irene Bedard; **Quiet Fire:** Candi Milo; **Mountain Cloud/Maiden:** Jennifer Hale

ADVENTURES FROM THE BOOK OF VIRTUES: "HUMILITY"

When Annie wins the class presidency, the power goes to her head, prompting several stories about the virtue of humility in this animated half-hour, part of second group of six specials aired in hour-long blocks. *A PorchLight Entertainment Production in association with KCET/Hollywood. Color. Half-hour. Premiered on PBS: February 23, 1997.*

Voices

Plato: Kevin Richardson; **Ari:** Jim Cummings; **Aurora/ Annie:** Kath Soucie; **Zach:** Pam Segall; **Socrates:** Frank Welker; **Russ:** Adam Wylie; **Kara:** Pat Musick; **Mrs. Mathers:** Mary Gregory

THE EMPEROR'S NEW CLOTHES: Emperor: Jim Cummings; **Prime Minister:** Frank Welker; **Royal Treasurer** Pat Musick; **Wills/Servant:** Hamilton Camp; **Nils/Child in Crowd:** Charlie Adler; **Herald:** Neilson Ross

KING CANUTE AT THE SEASHORE: King Canute: Neilson Ross; **Courtier #1:** Adam Wylie; **Courtier #2:** Pat Musick; **Courtier #3:** Jim Cummings

PHAETON: Phaeton: John Christian Graas; **Croseus:** Adam Wylie; **Clymene:** Pat Musick; **Phoebus Apollo:** Michael Dorn

ADVENTURES FROM THE BOOK OF VIRTUES: "LOYALTY"

When Zach accidentally breaks a memorial plaque in an "overgrown park, his elderly friend is angered and Zach doesn't understand why until Plato helps by telling several stories about loyalty in this half-hour special from the popular PBS inspirational cartoon series, part of a second batch of specials aired in hour-long blocks. *A PorchLight Entertainment Production in association with KCET/Hollywood and Fox Animation Studios. Color. Half-hour. Premiered on PBS: February 9, 1997.*

Voices

Plato: Kevin Richardson; **Ari/Mr. Cleveland:** Jim Cummings; **Aurora/Annie:** Kath Soucie; **Zach:** Pam Segall; **Socrates:** Frank Welker

YUDISTHIRA AT HEAVEN'S GATE: King Yudisthira: Richard Libertini; **Mongrel Dog:** Frank Welker; **God Indra:** Malcolm McDowell; **God Dharma:** Frank Welker

THE CAP THAT MOTHER MADE: Anders/Anders's Sister/Princess: E.G. Daily; **Lars:** Kath Soucie; **King:** Peter Renaday

QUEEN ESTHER: King Ahasuerus: Brock Peters; **Guest #1:** Peter Renaday; **Queen Vashti:** Kath Soucie; **Haman:** Michael Des Barres; **Queen Esther:** Joan Van Ark; **Mordecai:** Jim Cummings; **Assassin #1:** Kevin Richardson; **Assassin #2:** Frank Welker; **Royal Guards:** Michael Des Barres, Kevin Richardson; **Merchant #1:** Richard Libertini; **Merchant #2:** Brock Peters

ADVENTURES FROM THE BOOK OF VIRTUES: "RESPECT"

When Zach and Annie are rude to a friendly junkyard man who is helping them build a go cart for an upcoming race, Plato decides to tell several stories about the virtue of respect in this uplifting half-hour, part of a second offering of six specials from the PBS animated series. *A PorchLight Entertainment Production in association with KCET/Hollywood and Fox Animation Studios. Color. Half-hour. Premiered on PBS: February 16, 1997.*

Voices

Plato: Kevin Richardson; **Ari:** Jim Cummings; **Aurora/ Annie:** Kath Soucie; **Zach:** Pam Segall; **Socrates:** Frank Welker

PLEASE: Dick: Kath Soucie; **John:** B.J. Ward; **Dick's Please:** Henry Gibson; **John's Please:** Arte Johnson; **Father:** Frank Welker; **Mother:** Joan Gerber

ADVENTURES FROM THE BOOK OF VIRTUES: "RESPONSIBILITY"

Annie vows to safely deliver her mother's cakes on her new bike, but she is tempted by Zach's challenge to a bike race, resulting in an accident that wrecks her new bike and the cakes in this episode about the nature of responsibility from the PBS series, first introduced as part of an hour-long block of specials. *A PorchLight Entertainment Production in association with KCET/Hollywood and Fox Animation Studios. Color. Half-hour. Premiered on PBS: September 3, 1996. Rebroadcast on PBS: September 21, 1996.*

Voices
Plato: Kevin Richardson; **Ari:** Jim Cummings; **Aurora/Annie:** Kath Soucie; **Zach:** Pam Segall; **Socrates:** Frank Welker

Wraparound
Betty Redfeather: Christine Avila

ICARUS AND DAEDALUS: Daedalus: John Forsythe; **Icarus:** Elijah Wood; **King Minos:** Tim Curry; **The Minotaur:** Frank Welker

KING ALFRED AND THE CAKES: King Alfred: Jim Cummings; **Woodcutter's Wife:** Carolyn Seymour; **Woodcuttter:** Tim Curry

THE CHEST OF BROKEN GLASS: Old Woman: Judy Geeson; **Charles:** Charles Shaughnessy; **Emma:** Carolyn Seymour; **Henry:** Julian Sands

ADVENTURES FROM THE BOOK OF VIRTUES: "SELF-DISCIPLINE"

Zach gets into a heated argument with his mother when she refuses to advance him his allowance, prompting several stories from Plato and Aurora about the pitfalls of impatience and losing one's temper. The program premiered on PBS as part of an hour-long block of specials. *A PorchLight Entertainment Production in association with KCET/Hollywood and Fox Animation Studios. Color. Half-hour. Premiered on PBS: September 3, 1996. Rebroadcast on PBS: September 21, 1996.*

Voices
Plato: Kevin Richardson; **Ari:** Jim Cummings; **Aurora/Annie:** Kath Soucie; **Zach:** Pam Segall; **Socrates:** Frank Welker

KING MIDAS: King Midas: Clive Revill; **Marygold:** Sherry Lynn; **Stranger:** Frank Welker

GENGHIS KAHN AND HIS HAWK Khan: Jim Cummings

THE MAGIC THREAD Liese: Pam Dawber; **Peter's Mother/Teacher:** Tress MacNeille; **Old Woman:** Kathy Najimy; **Peter:** Rob Paulsen; **Foreman:** Kevin Richardson; **Priest:** Clive Revill

ADVENTURES FROM THE BOOK OF VIRTUES: "WORK"

When a violent thunderstorm wrecks Plato's Peak, everyone works together to clean up the debris except Sock (short for Socrates), who finds no virtue in "work," in this half-hour episode of the popular PBS animated series. The program premiered as part of an hour-long block of specials. *A PorchLight Entertainment Production in association with KCET/Hollywood and Fox Animation Studios. Color. Half-hour. Premiered on PBS: September 2, 1996. Rebroadcast on PBS: September 21, 1996.*

Voices
Plato: Kevin Richardson; **Ari:** Jim Cummings; **Aurora/Annie:** Kath Soucie; **Zach:** Pam Segall; **Socrates:** Frank Welker

HOW THE CAMEL GOT HIS HUMP: Camel: Jim Cummings; **Horse:** Daniel Davis; **Dog/The Man:** Bronson Pinchot; **Genie: Paula Poundstone**

TOM SAWYER GIVES UP THE BRUSH: Tom Sawyer: Matthew Lawrence; **Joe:** Dana Hill; **School Master:** Daniel Davis; **Aunt Polly:** Kath Soucie; **Ben:** Andrew Lawrence; **Jim:** Pam Segall

THE ADVENTURES OF ENERGY

One in a series of syndicated specials under the title of *LBS Children's Theatre*, this half-hour show chronicled the ways in which man harnessed energy throughout the ages. *A DIC Audiovisual Production. Color. Half-hour. Premiered: 1983—84. Syndicated.*

THE ADVENTURES OF HUCKLEBERRY FINN

Mark Twain's classic adventure is faithfully retold, from rafting down the Mississippi to Huck's friendship with runaway slave Jim, in this animated special sponsored by Kenner Toys. A "Kenner Family Classics" special. *A John Erichsen Production in association with Triple Seven Concepts. Color. Half-hour. Premiered on CBS: November 23, 1984.*

THE ADVENTURES OF MOLE

Mole and his civilized compatriots, Rat, Badger and Toad, discover the joys of fellowship in this hour-long special, based on characters from Kenneth Grahame's *The Wind in the Willows*. The program, preceded by 1995's half-hour holiday special *Mole's Christmas*, debuted on The Disney Channel. *An All Time Entertainment Production. Color. One hour. Premiered on DIS: May 7, 1996.*

THE ADVENTURES OF SINBAD

Sinbad volunteers to recover Baghdad's magic lantern and its genie from the wicked Old Man of the Sea but is met by danger at every turn in this half-hour special produced by Australia's Air Programs International under the series banner *Famous Classic Tales*. *An Air Programs International Production. Color. Half-hour. Premiered on CBS: November 27, 1980.*

Voices
Peter Corbett, Barbara Frawley, Ron Haddrick, Phillip Hinton, Bevan Wilson

THE ADVENTURES OF THE GET ALONG GANG

Six friendly animals—Montgomery, Dotty, Bingo, Zipper, Portia and Woolma—find their values of honesty and friendship tested as they participate in a big scavenger hunt, which is undermined by slimeballs Catchum Crocodile and Leland Lizard. Produced as a TV pilot for the weekly Saturday-morning series, the special aired on CBS the same year the weekly series debuted. *A Scholastic Production in association with Those Characters From Cleveland and Nelvana Limited. Color. Half-hour. Premiered: 1984.*

Voices
Montgomery Moose: Charles Haid; **Dotty Dog:** Mara Hobel; **Zipper Cat:** Jim Henshaw; **Bingo Beaver:** Maria Lufofsky; **Portia Porcupine:** Gloria Figura; **Woolma Lamb:** Julie Cohen; **Catchum Crocodile:** Dan Hennessey; **Leland Lizard:** Dave Thomas; **Officer Growler:** Mark Gordon; **Mr. Hoofnagel:** Wayne Robson; **The Announcer:** Bruce Pirrie

THE ADVENTURES OF THE SCRABBLE PEOPLE IN "A PUMPKIN NONSENSE"

At the site of a magical pumpkin patch, a small boy (Tad) and a girl (Terry), accompanied by Mr. Scrabble, are transported to a town called Nonsense, where they learn of the unhappiness of the Scrabble People and try to help spread goodness among them. *An Arce Production with James Diaz Studios. Color. Half-hour. Premiered: October 31, 1985.*

Voices
Tad/Terry: Brianne Sidall; **Sir Scrabble:** Kevin Slattery; **Rot:** Bob Singer; **Muddler:** George Atkins; **Lexa:** Melissa Freeman; **Rotunda:** Kathy Hart Freeman

THE ADVENTURES OF TOAD

Motor-crazy Mr. Toad ends up on the wrong side of the local constabulary, only to discover upon his return that his mansion has been overrun by rowdies in this second of two one-hour specials to air on The Disney Channel, based on Kenneth Grahame's bestselling novel, *The Wind in the Willows*. *An All Time Entertainment Production. Color. One hour. Premiered on DIS: June 25, 1996.*

AESOP'S FABLES

Comedian Bill Cosby, appearing in live-action wraparounds, hosts two animated *Aesop's Fables* about the tortoise and the hare and the tale of two children (Joey and Marta), in live-action/animation, who are lost in an enchanted forest—in this half-hour special. Cosby's appeal with children was the principal reason for his hosting this special, as his Filmation-produced *Fat Albert and the Cosby Kids* was a popular Saturday-morning installment on CBS, which also aired the special. *A Filmation Associates Production in association with Lorimar Productions. Color. Half-hour. Premiered on CBS: October 31, 1971. Rebroadcast on CBS: December 23, 1974. Rebroadcast on DIS: February 21, 1993.*

Cast
Aesop: Bill Cosby; **Joey:** Keith Hamilton; **Marta:** Jerelyn Fields

Voices
Tortoise: John Byner; **Hare:** Larry Storch; **Eagle:** Roger C. Carmel; **Lady Eagle:** Jane Webb; **Donkey:** John Erwin; **Owl:** Dal McKennon

ALICE IN WONDERLAND (1966)

This musical spoof of the Lewis Carroll classic, follows the adventures of Alice and her dog Fluff in Wonderland where they meet an amusing assortment of characters including several new creations: Hedda Hatter, a female counterpart of the Mad Hatter; Humphrey Dumpty, whose voice was patterned after that of Humphrey Bogart; and the White Knight, voiced by Bill Dana in his José Jimenez character. The full title of the program was *Alice in Wonderland (or*

"What's a Nice Kid Like You Doing in a Place Like This?"). A Hanna-Barbera Production. Color. Half-hour. Premiered on ABC: March 30, 1966. Rebroadcast on ABC: November 19, 1967.

Voices
Alice: Janet Waldo, Doris Drew (singing); **Cheshire Cat:** Sammy Davis Jr.; **White Knight:** Bill Dana; **Queen of Hearts:** Zsa Zsa Gabor; **White Rabbit:** Howard Morris; **Hedda Hatter:** Hedda Hopper; **Mad Hatter:** Harvey Korman; **Alice's Father/Humphrey Dumpty:** Allan Melvin; **King of Hearts/March Hare:** Daws Butler; **Dormouse/Fluff, Alice's dog:** Don Messick; **Caterpillar:** Alan Reed, Mel Blanc

◎ ALICE IN WONDERLAND (1973)

Arthur Rankin Jr. and Jules Bass, who created such classic specials as *Rudolph, the Red-Nosed Reindeer* and *Frosty the Snowman*, produced this second animated version of the children's fairy tale, with Alice making that familiar visit to Wonderland. This wonderfully entertaining syndicated special was broadcast under the umbrella title of *Festival of Family Classics*. A Rankin-Bass Production in association with Mushi Studios. Color. Half-hour. Premiered: February 11, 1973. Syndicated.

Voices
Carl Banas, Len Birman, Bernard Cowan, Peg Dixon, Keith Hampshire, Peggi Loder, Donna Miller, Frank Perry, Henry Ramer, Billie Mae Richards, Alfie Scopp, Paul Soles

◎ ALICE'S ADVENTURES IN WONDERLAND

Slipping into dreamland, Alice becomes caught up in the whimsical world of Wonderland. Met by the frenetic March Hare, who is late for a very important date, they end up at a tea party with the Mad Hatter, where the rest of her madcap adventure unfolds. A Greatest Tales Production. Color. Half-hour. Premiered: 1983–84. Syndicated.

Voices
Peter Fernandez, Gilbert Mack, Ray Owens, Billie Lou Watt

◎ ALIENS FIRST CHRISTMAS

Christmas comes to the Cosmos when Roger and Fran Peoples and their son Benny try to celebrate the holidays in their new home on the planet Zolognia, marred by unexpected problems in this second in a series of half-hour animated Aliens specials. A Perennial Pictures Film Corporation Production in association with Paragon International. Color.

Half-hour. Premiered on DIS: November 12, 1991. Rebroadcast on DIS: December 21, 1991.

Voices
Roger Peoples: Jerry Reynolds; **Fran Peoples:** Brett Sears; **Mavo Zox:** Rachel Rutledge; **Charlick Zox:** Will Gould

◎ ALIENS NEXT DOOR

Transferred to a new job and feeling insecure, the Peoples family arrives on the planet Zolognia and are as frightened of their new neighbors (Charlick and Mavo Zox) as their neighbors are of them in this first of two charming *Aliens* cartoon specials. A Perennial Pictures Film Corporation Production in association with Paragon International. Color. Half-hour. Premiered on DIS: November 3, 1990. Rebroadcast on DIS: February 8, 1992; February 17, 1992.

Voices
Roger Peoples: Jerry Reynolds; **Fran Peoples:** Peggy Powis; **Mavo Zox:** Rachel Rutledge; **Charlick Zox:** Will Gould; **Boonka Frinx:** Miki Mathioudakis

◎ ALL ABOUT ME

A young boy falls asleep in class and dreams of taking a tour of his own body in this musical fantasy that explores the functions of various organs and other biological wonders. An Animated Cartoon Production. Color. Half-hour. Premiered on NBC: January 13, 1973 (NBC's Children's Theatre).

◎ ALL-AMERICAN SPORTS NUTS

Disney sports cartoons comprise this salute to athletes and Olympic gold medalists, produced for The Disney Channel. A New Wave Production for The Disney Channel. Color. One hour. Premiered on DIS: October 16, 1988.

◎ AN ALL NEW ADVENTURE OF DISNEY'S SPORT GOOFY

Popular Disney canine Goofy is the star of this prime-time special, which included scenes from various cartoon shorts (narrated by Stan Freberg) previously released to theaters (including "Hold That Pose [1950]," "Goofy's Glider" [1940], "Lion Down" [1951], "Mickey's Birthday Party" and "Goofy Gymnastics" [1949]) and combined new footage, narrated by Los Angeles Lakers sports announcer Chick Hearn, who calls the "play by play," leading up to a new 20-minute short, "Sport Goofy in Soccermania." A Happy Feet Production for Walt Disney Television. Color. One hour. Premiered on NBC: May 27, 1987.

Voices
Goofy (old): Pinto Colvig; **Goofy (new):** Jack Angel, Tony Pope; **Scrooge McDuck:** Will Ryan; **Beagle Boys/Gyro Gearloose:** Will Ryan; **Huey/Dewey/Louie:** Russi Taylor; **Museum Curator:** Phil Proctor; **Narrator:** Stan Freberg; **Sportscaster:** Chick Hearn

⦿ ALVIN AND THE CHIPMUNKS TRICK OR TREASON: THE STORY OF PUMPKINHEAD

Alvin tries to pass an initiation to become a member of the exclusive Monster Club in this half-hour, made-for-cable animated special. The Halloween-themed program includes the Chipmunks' rendition of the hit song "Monster Mash." *A Bagdasarian Production in association with The Krislin Company. Color. Half-hour. Premiered on USA: October 28, 1994.*

Voices
Alvin/Simon: Ross Bagdasarian Jr.; **Theodore:** Janice Karman

⦿ THE AMAZING BUNJEE VENTURE

Accidentally sent back to the year 100 million B.C., Karen and Andy Winsborrow encounter prehistoric animals; become friends with an elephantlike creature who can fly (Bunjee); and experience modern-day adventures together in this two-part, one-hour *ABC Weekend Special.* A *Hanna-Barbera Production. Color. One hour. Premiered on ABC: March 24 and March 31, 1984. Rebroadcast on ABC: September 15, 1984 and September 22, 1984; January 18, 1986 and January 25, 1986; September 12, 1987 and September 19, 1987; December 10, 1988 and December 17, 1988.*

Voices
Bunjee: Frank Welker; **Karen Winsborrow:** Nancy Cartwright; **Andy Winsborrow:** Robbie Lee; **Mr. Winsborrow:** Michael Rye; **Mrs. Winsborrow/Baby #1:** Linda Gary; **Baby #2:** Nancy Cartwright; **Waxer/Drasto:** John Stephenson; **Willy/Pterodactyl/Tyrannosaur:** Frank Welker

⦿ THE ANGEL AND THE SOLDIER BOY

A toy soldier and a toy angel try to rescue the contents of their owner's piggy bank from ruthless pirates, who've popped up from a book somebody forgot to put away, in this half-hour special originally produced for Showtime. *A BMG Video Production. Color. Half-hour. Premiered on SHO: May 14, 1991.*

Voices
Marie Brennan (vocals)

⦿ ANIMALYMPICS: WINTER GAMES

Olympic-style sports competition takes on a new meaning as animals compete in events of the first Animalia Winter Games in this cartoon spoof built around songs and vignettes. *A Lisberger Production. Color. Half-hour. Premiered on NBC: February 1, 1980. Rebroadcast on NBC: July 4, 1982. Rebroadcast on DIS: August 20, 1993.*

Voices
Henry Hummel: Michael Fremer; **Rugs Turkel:** Billy Crystal; **Keen Hacksaw:** Harry Shearer; **Barbara Warbles/Brenda Springer:** Gilda Radner

⦿ ANNABELLE'S WISH

A lovable calf named Annabelle, born on Christmas Eve, makes friends with a young boy (Billy) who cannot talk and a friendly bunch of barnyard animals, and has one very special wish—to fly like one of Santa's reindeer—in this tender holiday tale, narrated by and starring country music superstar Randy Travis. *A Ralph Edwards Films/Baer Animation Production. Color. One hour. Premiered on FOX: November 30, 1997.*

Voices
Adult Billy/Narrator: Randy Travis; **Aunt Agnes:** Cloris Leachman; **Grandpa:** Jerry Van Dyke; **Scarlett the Horse:** Rue McClanahan; **Mr. Holder:** Jim Varney; **Annabelle:** Kath Soucie; **Ears:** Jay Johnson; **Emily:** Aria Noelle Curzon; **Young Billy:** Hari Oziol; **Santa:** Kay E. Kuter; **Star the Cow:** Jennifer Darling; **Lawyer/Sheriff:** Clancy Brown; **Buste/Bucky Holder:** James Lafferty, Charlie Cronin; **The Doctor:** Stu Rosen; **Slim the Pig:** Jerry Houser; **Brewster the Rooster:** Brian Cummings; **The Hens:** Mary Kaye Bergman, Tress MacNeille; **Owliver the Owl:** Steven Mackall; **Speaking Animals:** Frank Welker

⦿ THE ARABIAN KNIGHTS

A courageous young teenager Pindar tries to win the hand of his love, Fatha, from her uncle Omar, the Thief of Baghdad, by capturing the treasure guarded by the great and powerful Genie of the lamp and the magic slippers of the Cruel Caliph in this half-hour syndicated *Festival of Family Classics* special. *A Rankin-Bass Production in association with Mushi Studios. Color. Half-hour. Premiered: February 4, 1973. Syndicated.*

Voices
Carl Banas, Len Birman, Bernard Cowan, Peg Dixon, Keith Hampshire, Peggi Loder, Donna Miller, Frank Perry, Henry Ramer, Billie Mae Richards, Alfie Scopp, Paul Soles

ANNABELLE

A little calf's secial Christmas wish becomes legendary in the Fox Television Network special Annabelle's Wish. © Ralph Edwards Productions

ARABIAN NIGHTS

Yogi Bear, Boo Boo, Magilla Gorilla, Scooby-Doo and Shaggy star in this politically correct version of the classic children's tale, broken into three separate acts. The 90-minute special made its debut on Superstation WTBS. A *Hanna-Barbera Production. Color. Ninety minutes. Premiered on TBS: September 3, 1994. Rebroadcast on CAR: December 25, 1997.*

Voices

ACT 1: ALLIYAH-DIN AND THE MAGIC LAMP: Yogi Bear: Greg Burson; **Boo Boo:** Don Messick; **Haman:** John Kassir; **Lord of the Amulet:** Tony Jay; **Sultan:** Brian Cummings; **Prince:** Rob Paulsen; **Scribe:** Paul Eiding; **Alliyah-Din:** Jennifer Hale; **Princess:** Kath Soucie

ACT II: SINBAD: Captain: Charlie Adler; **Magilla Gorilla:** Allan Melvin; **Cyclops:** Maurice LaMarche; **Mrs. Rukh/Baby Rukh:** Frank Welker

ACT III: SCHEHERAZADE: Scooby-Doo: Don Messick; **Shaggy:** Casey Kasem; **Chef:** Greg Burson; **Kitchen Worker/Dress Maker:** Nick Jameson; **Caliph:** Eddie Deezen; **Driver/Guard:** Brian Cummings

ARCHIE AND HIS NEW FRIENDS

Familiar comic-book characters Archie, Jughead, Betty and Veronica are joined by a new character, Sabrina the Teenage Witch, in this prime-time special that tells the story of Sabrina's attempt to fit in with the rest of the Riverdale High School crowd. Sabrina was formally introduced to television audiences one day earlier with the debut of CBS's *The Archie Comedy Hour. A Filmation Associates Production. Color. Half-hour. Premiered on CBS: September 14, 1969.*

Voices

Archie Andrews: Dal McKennon; **Jughead Jones:** Howard Morris; **Veronica Lodge/Betty Cooper/Sabrina:** Jane Webb; **Reggie Mantle/Moose:** John Erwin

THE ARCHIE, SUGAR SUGAR, JINGLE JANGLE SHOW

Selected scenes from the Saturday-morning series *The Archies* were featured in this half-hour special, which presented four popular songs (performed by the rock group The Archies) from the earlier series with comic vignettes. Songs included the Archies' number-one hit record in 1969, "Sugar Sugar." *A Filmation Associates Production. Color. Half-hour. Premiered on CBS: March 22, 1970.*

Voices

Archie Andrews: Dal McKennon; **Jughead Jones:** Howard Morris; **Betty Cooper/Veronica Lodge/Sabrina:** Jane Webb; **Reggie Mantle/Moose:** John Erwin

AROUND THE WORLD IN 80 DAYS

The familiar Jules Verne voyage of Phineas Fogg, who tries to win a wager by making a trip around the globe in 80 days, is the premise of this two-part *Festival of Family Classics* special. *A Rankin-Bass Production in association with Mushi Studios. Color. Half-hour. Premiered: November 12 and 19, 1972. Syndicated. Rebroadcast on NIK: March 28, 1992; July 16, 1993.*

Voices

Carl Banas, Len Birman, Bernard Cowan, Peg Dixon, Keith Hampshire, Peggi Loder, Donna Miller, Frank Perry, Henry Ramer, Billie Mae Richards, Alfie Scopp, Paul Soles

◎ THE ART OF DISNEY ANIMATION

Retrospective look at classic Disney animation, including milestone events in the studio's history, hosted by John Lithgow and produced for The Disney Channel. *A Heath and Associations Production in association with Walt Disney Productions. Color. Half-hour. Premiered on DIS: 1988.*

Cast
John Lithgow, Glen Keane, Roy E. Disney, Burny Mattinson, Cheech Marin, Billy Joel, Richard Mulligan, Bill Berg, Dan Hansen, Barry Cook, Penny Coulter, Donald Towns, Mike Gabriel

◎ AU CLAIR DE LA LUNE

The Prince of Darkness puts the person responsible for changing night into day, into a deep slumber, part of his evil plan to have eternal darkness in this half-hour animated special from Cinar Films' cartoon anthology series, *The Real Story of . . . (a.k.a. Favorite Songs)*, first produced for Canadian television in 1992, then premiering on HBO. *A Cinar Films/France Animation Production. Color. Half-hour. Premiered on HBO: January 15, 1994.*

Voices
Prince of Darkness: Milton Berle

◎ BAA BAA BLACK SHEEP

The toughest sheep in Muttonville Prison break out to set up a wool racket that leaves the whole town fleeced in this cartoon special, featuring the voices of Shelley Long and Robert Stack. The show aired on HBO as part of the Saturday-morning anthology series *The Real Story of . . . (a.k.a. Favorite Stories). A Cinar Films/France Animation Production. Color. Half-hour. Premiered on HBO: January 1, 1994.*

Voices
Lieutenant Littleboy: Robert Stack; **The Dame:** Shelley Long

◎ BABAR AND FATHER CHRISTMAS

King Babar successfully spoils the plans of Retaxes the Rhinoceros, who stops at nothing to foil Father Christmas's goodwill gesture to visit the people of Celesteville in Elephant Land. *An Atkinson Film-Arts/MTR Ottawa Production in association with the CBC. Color. Half-hour. Premiered on HBO: December 5, 1986. Rebroadcast on HBO: December 9–24, 1986; December 22, 1991; December 24, 1991.*

Voices
Babar: Jim Bradford; **Celeste:** Louise Villeneuve; **Arthur:** Kemp Edwards; **Zephir/Lazarro/Podular/Mice:** Rick Jones; **Retaxes/Father Christmas:** Les Lye; **Pom:** Amie Charlebois; **Flora:** Courtney Caroll; **Alexander:** Kai Engstead; **Professor:** Noel Council; **Secretary/Elf #1:** Bridgitte Robinson; **Elderberry/Elf #2/Boatman;** Derek Diorio; **Gendarme:** Roch Lafortune

◎ BABAR COMES TO AMERICA

King Babar and his wife, Queen Celeste, receive a telegram inviting them to America to make a movie in Hollywood in this second animated special based on two of the Babar books—*Travels of Babar* by Jean de Brunhoff and *Babar in America* by his son, Laurent de Brunhoff, who also penned the script. *A Lee Mendelson–Bill Melendez Production in association with Laurent de Brunhoff and with the cooperation of Random House. Color. Half-hour. Premiered on NBC: September 7, 1971. Rebroadcast on NBC: February 27, 1972.*

Voices
Babar, King of Elephant Land/Celeste, his queen/Arthur, Babar's cousin/Cornelius, the elder elephant/Narrator: Peter Ustinov

◎ BABAR, THE LITTLE ELEPHANT

The story of the elephant who would be king is told in this first primetime special based on the first three books from the popular French children's book series. The program was originally entitled *The Story of Babar, the Little Elephant. A Lee Mendelson–Bill Melendez Production in association with Laurent de Brunhoff and the cooperation of Random House. Color. Half-hour. Premiered on NBC: October 21, 1968. Rebroadcast on NBC: April 21, 1969; Rebroadcast on DIS: June 6, 1993.*

Voices
Narrator: Peter Ustinov

◎ BAD CAT

Based on two children's books about one cat's struggle for acceptance, this half-hour adaptation tells the story of Bad Cat, the undisputed "King Cat" of Fulton Street, who, despite his reputation for being a troublemaker, is really a good cat. First, he must overcome the animosity of a new group of cats, led by bully cat Riff, who challenges him to a mouse-catching contest to prove one's superiority over the other. *An ABC Weekend Special. A Ruby-Spears Enterprises Production. Color. Half-hour. Premiered on ABC: April 14, 1984. Rebroadcast on ABC: September 29, 1984; October 28, 1985; November 12, 1988; July 8, 1995; May 18, 1996.*

Voices
Bad Cat: Bart Braverman; **Gordon:** Hal Smith; **Neddy:** Tress MacNeille; **Vernon Turner:** Bobby Ellerbee; **Jim Harrison:** Alan Young; **Steve Harrison:** Steve Spears; **Pam Harrison:** Amy Tunik; **Champ:** Frank Welker; **Diedra:** Judy Strangis; **Dimples:** Didi Conn; **Riff:** Jon Bauman; **Mouser:** Marvin Kaplan

⊚ THE BALLAD OF PAUL BUNYAN

Known for his legendary feats of skill and strength as a respected axeman, a giant lumberjack who wields a magic axe, maintains his title by beating the hated Panhandle Pete, a ruthless lumber boss, in log-rolling, arm-wrestling and hole-digging competitions in this *Festival of Family Classics* special. *A Rankin-Bass Production in association with Mushi Studios. Color. Half-hour. Premiered: January 7, 1973. Syndicated.*

Voices
Carl Banas, Len Birman, Bernard Cowan, Peg Dixon, Keith Hampshire, Peggi Loder, Donna Miller, Frank Perry, Henry Ramer, Billie Mae Richards, Alfie Scopp, Paul Soles

⊚ THE BALLAD OF SMOKEY THE BEAR

Movie tough guy Jimmy Cagney, as Smokey the Bear's big brother Big Bear, narrates this charming, half-hour special that recalls the trials and tribulations of the U.S. Forest Service fire-prevention campaign spokesperson, from his early challenges as a tiny cub to his courageous acts on behalf of those in trouble as a wise adult. The special was filmed using the spectacularly lifelike stop-motion animation process called Animagic. *A Rankin-Bass Production in association with Videocraft International. Color. Half-hour. Premiered on NBC: November 24, 1966. Rebroadcast on NBC: May 5, 1968; May 4, 1969.*

Voices
Big Bear: James Cagney; **Smokey:** Barry Pearl

Smokey's friends:
Turtle: William Marine; **Beaver:** Herbert Duncan; **Mrs. Beaver:** Rose Marie Jun; **Fox:** George Petrie; **Mama:** Bryna Raeburn

⊚ THE BALLOONATIKS®: "CHRISTMAS WITHOUT A CLAUS"

The Balloontiks® (Flator, Squeeker, Airhead, Bouncer and Stretch), five balloon creatures from the planet Balloona whose mission on Earth is to battle dastardly deeds, search for the kidnapped Santa in this animated special, based on the comic-book characters created by Anthony Diloia. The half-hour Saturday-morning special was produced by Jay Poynor, winner of three Emmy Awards for his television work as executive producer of the Film Roman animated *Garfield* prime-time specials for CBS. The Balloonatiks is a registered trademark of Animagic Entertainment Group. *An Animagic Entertainment Group Production. Color. Half-hour. Premiered on FOX: December 14, 1996.*

Voices
Flator/Al Pinhead: James Andrew Pearsons; **Airhead/Boy:** Alexandra Rhodie; **Squeeker/Girl/Mom:** Ashley Albert; **Bouncer:** Brian Mitchell; **L.A. Tee/Santa:** Doug Preis; **Dr. "Pop" Swellhead:** Don Peoples; **Keedler/Tacky Pinhead/Squirt:** Chris Phillips; **Penny Nails/Baloonimal:** Giovanna Godard; **Stinky Pinhead:** Marcia Savella; **Dad/Ned Carpool/Dan Blather:** George Flowers

⊚ BANANA SPLITS IN HOCUS POCUS PARK

Costumed live-action animals Fleegle (the dog), Drooper (the lion), Bingo (the gorilla) and Snorky (the elephant) stars of TV's *The Banana Splits Adventure Hour,* appear in this live-action/animated fantasy in which they meet a magician with special powers. *A Hanna-Barbera Production. Color. One hour. Premiered on ABC: November 25, 1972 (on The ABC Saturday Superstar Movie). Rebroadcast on CAR: October 28, 1994; October 30, 1994; October 31, 1994; October 29, 1995 (Mr. Spim's Cartoon Theatre).*

Voices
Snorky: (no voice); **Drooper:** Allan Melvin; **Bingo/Frog/Octopus:** Daws Butler; **Fleegle/Tree:** Paul Winchell; **Witch:** Joan Gerber; **Hocus/Pocus:** Howard Morris

⊚ BANJO, THE WOODPILE CAT

Banjo, an adventurous young cat, runs away to the big city where he becomes lost. Together with his newfound friend, Crazy Legs, he searches for a truck, from which he came, to take him back home. Program preceded the network premiere of *Stanley, the Ugly Duckling. A Banjo Production in association with Don Bluth Productions. Color. Half-hour. Premiered on ABC: May 1, 1982. Rebroadcast on ABC: August 7, 1983.*

Voices
Banjo, the Woodpile Cat: Sparky Marcus; **Crazy Legs:** Scatman Crothers; **Zazu:** Beah Richards; **Papa Cat/Freeman:** Jerry Harper; **Mama Cat/Cleo:** Georgette Rampone; **Jean:** Ann E. Beesley; **Emily:** Robin Muir; **Farmer/Warehouseman:** Ken Samson; **Announcer:** Mark Elliott; **Vocalists:** Jackie Ward, Sally Stevens, Sue Allen

⊚ BARBIE AND THE ROCKERS

After a successful worldwide concert tour ends, Barbie reveals to the group her greatest tour ever—a concert in outer space. The half-hour syndicated special was based on the popular Mattel Toys doll. *A DIC Enterprises Production in association with Mattel. Color. Half-hour. Premiered: Fall 1987. Syndicated.*

Voices
Barbie: Sharon Lewis

◎ B.C.: A SPECIAL CHRISTMAS

Inspired by John Hart's daily comic strip, Peter and Wiley make plans to cash in on the Christmas season by selling trees and gift rocks that are supposedly from a mythical gift giver they have created named Santa Claus in this half-hour yuletide special. *A Cinera Production in association with Hardlake Animated Pictures and Field Enterprises. Color. Half-hour. Premiered: 1971. Syndicated.*

Voices
Peter: Bob Elliott; **Wiley:** Ray Goulding; **Fat Broad:** Barbara Hamilton; **Cute Chick:** Melleny Brown; **Thor:** Henry Ramer; **Clumsy:** Keith Hampshire; **Curls:** John Stocker

◎ B.C.: THE FIRST THANKSGIVING

Since "there's only one way to flavor rock soup and that's with a dead turkey," Fat Broad sends the cavemen (Peter, Wiley, Thor and Curls) all out on a cross-country chase for the bird, complicated by the fact that nobody knows what a turkey is, in this special based on Johnny Hart's popular strip of the same name. *A Levitow-Hanson Films Production in association with Field Enterprises. Color. Half-hour. Premiered on NBC: November 19, 1972.*

Voices
Peter/Thor/Turkey: Don Messick; **Wiley/Grog:** Bob Holt; **Clumsy:** Daws Butler; **Fat Broad/Cute Chick:** Joanie Sommers

◎ THE BEAR WHO SLEPT THROUGH CHRISTMAS

Ted E. Bear, who has never seen Christmas because he's always snoozing through winter, decides to fight hibernation to witness the glorious event for the first time in his life. *A Sed-bar Production in association with DePatie-Freleng Enterprises. Color. Half-hour. Premiered on NBC: December 17, 1973. Rebroadcast on NBC: December 16, 1974; December 25, 1977; December 19, 1978; December 23, 1980; CBS: December 15, 1979.*

Voices
Ted E. Bear: Tom Smothers; **Patti Bear:** Barbara Feldon; **Professor Werner Von Bear:** Arte Johnson; **Santa Claus:**

Robert Holt; **Weather Bear:** Kelly Lange; **Honey Bear:** Michael Bell

◎ BEAUTY AND THE BEAST (1983)

Of five children who live in a plush mansion, only one is kind and good and full of love. Her name is Beauty. While the others are selfish and greedy, especially sisters Jacqueline and Erwina, Beauty makes the best of everything in life, even when her father falls on hard times and they are forced to move from their mansion to a tiny cottage and lead a meager lifestyle. Based on the Madame Leprince de Beaumont children's story. *A Kenner Family Classics daytime special. A Ruby-Spears Enterprises Production in association with TCG Products. Color. Half-hour. Premiered on CBS: November 25, 1983. Rebroadcast on CBS: November 22, 1984.*

Voices
Beauty/Jacqueline/Queen/Old Crone: Janet Waldo; **Beast/Prince:** Robert Ridgely; **Erwina/Stately Lady/Messenger Boy:** Linda Gary; **Merchant/Sailor/Male Voice:** Stacy Keach Jr.; **Rene/Cockatoo:** Alan Young; **Gerard:** Paul Kirby

◎ BEAUTY AND THE BEAST (1989)

A merchant's daughter volunteers to live in the enchanted palace of the Beast to save her father's life in this half-hour animated film, originally produced by Joshua Greene for Lightyear Entertainment as part of his "Stories to Remember" series, a collection of international children's stories told in picture books, recordings and animated films. Narrated by actress Mia Farrow (who also portrays the voice of every character), the award-winning production debuted as an installment of the long-running PBS live-action/animated anthology series, *Long Ago & Far Away*. *A Lightyear Entertainment Production. Color. Half-hour. Premiered on PBS: September 8, 1990. Rebroadcast on PBS: December 20, 1992.*

Voices
Narrator/All Others: Mia Farrow

◎ BEAVIS AND BUTT-HEAD CHRISTMAS SPECIAL (1993)

The moronic twosome starred in what was billed as their "first" Christmas special for music cable network, MTV, featuring back-to-back cartoon episodes. *An MTV Production. Color. Half-hour. Premiered on MTV: December 1993.*

Voices
Beavis/Butt-Head: Mike Judge

BEAVIS AND BUTT-HEAD CHRISTMAS SPECIAL (1995)

In comic twists, Beavis and Butt-Head star in a pair of holiday parodies—"It's a Miserable Life," in which the boys receive a visit from their guardian angel Charlie, and "Huh Huh Humbug," wherein Beavis nods off at Burger World and dreams he's the Scrooge-like manager—in this second prime-time Christmas special for MTV. *An MTV Production. Color. Half-hour. Premiered on MTV: December 19, 1995.*

Voices
Beavis/Butt-Head: Mike Judge

BEAVIS AND BUTT-HEAD DO AMERICA: AN MTV MOVIE SPECIAL

In a rare, up-close and personal interview with that moronic twosome, MTV news reporter Chris Connelly reveals a side of Beavis and Butt-Head never before seen on television, including clips from their 1997 world-premiere movie, *Beavis and Butt-Head Do America. An MTV Production. Color. Half-hour. Premiered on MTV: December 1996.*

Voices
Beavis/Butt-Head: Mike Judge

BEAVIS AND BUTT-HEAD DO THANKSGIVING WITH KURT LODER

MTV's popular suburban misfits hosted this "live" Thanksgiving Day special, along with MTV news anchor Kurt Loder, from MTV's Times Square studios during which they talked about Thanksgiving Day traditions around the country. Features interview bites from musicians talking about what Thanksgiving means to them. Also included is Loder's interview with the boys about their series finale, "Beavis and Butt-Head Are Dead," the final original episode from the long-running cartoon series, which aired the following day. *An MTV Production. Color. Half-hour. Premiered on MTV: November 27, 1997.*

Voices
Beavis/Butt-Head: Mike Judge

BEAVIS AND BUTT-HEAD HALLOWEEN SPECIAL

The B&B boys get into the Halloween spirit in this half-hour spooky spectacular featuring the animated episode "Buttonween," in which an evening of trick-or-treating takes a strange turn when Beavis becomes the Great Cornholio (Beavis's alter ego, who first appeared in four episodes a year earlier). *An MTV Production. Color. Half-hour. Premiered on MTV: October 31, 1995.*

Voices
Beavis/Butt-Head: Mike Judge

BE MY VALENTINE, CHARLIE BROWN

It's Valentine's Day and Cupid is already busy at work, especially at Birchwood School, where Linus displays his affection for his homeroom teacher by buying her a huge box of candy and Sally thinks the candy is for her. Meanwhile, Lucy continues her quest to win Schroeder's affection, while poor hopeless heart Charlie Brown continues to wait for his cards to arrive in the mail. *A Lee Mendelson–Bill Melendez Production in cooperation with United Feature Syndicate. Color. Half-hour. Premiered on CBS: January 28, 1975. Rebroadcast on CBS: February 10, 1976; February 14, 1977; February 9, 1979; February 11, 1983; February 11, 1984; February 14, 1987.*

Voices
Charlie Brown: Duncan Watson; **Linus Van Pelt:** Stephen Shea; **Lucy Van Pelt:** Melanie Kohn; **Sally Brown:** Lynn Mortensen; **Schroeder:** Greg Felton; **Violet/Frieda:** Linda Ercoli

BE OUR GUEST: THE MAKING OF DISNEY'S BEAUTY AND THE BEAST

Combining clips and interviews with original cast members, this half-hour Disney Channel original special looks behind the scenes at the making of the studio's classic full-length feature, hosted by David Ogden Stiers. *A Blue Streak Production in association with Walt Disney Productions. Color. Half-hour. Premiered on DIS: 1991.*

Cast
Roger Allers, James Baxter, Robby Benson, Andreas Deja, Angela Lansbury, Nik Ranieri, Jerry Orbach, Brian McEntee, Will Finn, Don Hahn, Glen Keane, Alan Menken, Paige O'Hara, Bradley Michael Pearce, David Pruiksma, David Ogden Stiers, Gary Trousdale, Kirk Wise, Lindan Woolverton

THE BERENSTAIN BEARS' CHRISTMAS TREE

Papa Bear goes against the advice of Mama Bear not to get a Christmas tree by deciding to find the perfect tree himself in the woods of Bear Valley. During his journey, he encounters the animals of the forest and realizes that by taking a tree he could jeopardize the homes of other creatures less fortunate. *A Cates Brothers Company Production in association with Perpetual Motion Pictures. Color. Half-hour. Premiered on NBC: December 3, 1979. Rebroadcast on NBC: December 15, 1980.*

Voices

Papa Bear: Ron McLarty; **Mama Bear:** Pat Lysinger; **Brother Bear:** Jonathan Lewis; **Sister Bear:** Gabriela Glatzer; **Narrator:** Ron McLarty

⊚ THE BERENSTAIN BEARS' EASTER SURPRISE

With no sign of spring in sight, Papa Bear takes it upon himself to find the Easter Hare, Boss Bunny, and see why Easter hasn't arrived on time. *A Joseph Cates Production in association with Perpetual Motion Pictures. Color. Half-hour. Premiered on NBC: April 14, 1981. Rebroadcast on NBC: April 6, 1982; April 20, 1984.*

Voices

Papa Bear: Ron McLarty; **Mama Bear:** Pat Lysinger; **Brother Bear:** Knowl Johnson; **Sister Bear:** Gabriela Glatzer; **Boss Bunny:** Bob McFadden; **Narrator:** Ron McLarty

⊚ THE BERENSTAIN BEARS' LITTLEST LEAGUER

The moral of this children's special is that parents should never heap their expectations upon their children. Papa Bear finds that out for himself, in a big way, when he tries making his son—and later his daughter—into successful Little League ballplayers with the dream of them someday turning pro. *A Joseph Cates Production in association with Buzzco Productions. Color. Half-hour. Premiered on NBC: May 6, 1983. Rebroadcast on NBC: May 20, 1984 (as* The Berenstain Bears Play Ball*).*

Voices

Papa Bear: Ron McLarty; **Mama Bear:** Pat Lysinger; **Brother Bear:** Knowl Johnson; **Sister Bear:** Gabriela Glatzer; **Narrator:** Ron McLarty

⊚ THE BERENSTAIN BEARS MEET BIG PAW

The legend of Big Paw—a monster who eats bears at Thanksgiving to punish them because they're "insufficiently grateful" for nature's bounty—is the premise of this holiday prime-time special. *A Joseph Cates Production in association with Perpetual Motion Pictures. Color. Half-hour. Premiered on NBC: November 20, 1980. Rebroadcast on NBC: November 24, 1981.*

Voices

Papa Bear: Ron McLarty; **Mama Bear:** Pat Lysinger; **Brother Bear:** Jonathan Lewis; **Sister Bear:** Gabriela Glatzer; **Big Paw/Announcer:** Bob Kaliban; **Narrator:** Ron McLarty

⊚ THE BERENSTAIN BEARS' VALENTINE SPECIAL

Cupid's arrows get the best of Brother Bear and Sister Bear as both critters become preoccupied with the idea of loving someone. *A Joseph Cates Production in association with Perpetual Motion Pictures. Color. Half-hour. Premiered on NBC: February 13, 1982. Rebroadcast on NBC: February 12, 1983.*

Voices

Papa Bear: Ron McLarty; **Mama Bear:** Pat Lysinger; **Brother Bear:** Knowl Johnson; **Sister Bear:** Gabriela Glatzer; **Bearcaster/Others:** Jerry Sroka; **Narrator:** Ron McLarty

⊚ THE BEST OF DISNEY; 50 YEARS OF MAGIC

This two-hour clipfest paying tribute to Disney's film successes features snippets from the studio's live-action and animated films and a cast of well-known celebrities, including Harry Connick Jr., Annette Funicello, Teri Garr, Daryl Hannah, Sandy Duncan, Shelley Long, Dick Van Dyke and many others. *A Don Mischer Production in association with Walt Disney Productions. Color. Two hours. Premiered on ABC: May 20, 1991.*

⊚ THE BEST OF DISNEY MUSIC: A LEGACY IN SONG, PART I

First of two hour-long specials for CBS, hosted by Angela Lansbury, featuring 50 years of musical numbers and an assortment of clips from *Snow White and the Seven Dwarfs* (1937), *Lady and the Tramp* (1955), *Beauty and the Beast* (1991) and others. *A Don Mischer Production in association with Walt Disney Productions. Color. One hour. Premiered on CBS: February 3, 1993.*

⊚ THE BEST OF DISNEY MUSIC II: A LEGACY IN SONG

Second hour-long prime-time special combining memorable musical scores and clips from Disney animated features and cartoon shorts, including *Fantasia* (1940), *Pinocchio* (1940), *Dumbo* (1941), *Cinderella* (1950) and *The Little Mermaid* (1989), hosted by Oscar-winning actress Glenn Close, with a special appearance by Placido Domingo. *A Don Mischer Production in association with Walt Disney Productions. Color. One hour. Premiered on CBS: May 21, 1993.*

☺ BILL AND BUNNY

Tells the story of a young boy (Bill) who can't wait for his baby sister (Bunny) to grow up and become a true playmate, based on the book by Gunilla Bergstroms. The Swedish-produced program premiered on the PBS anthology series *Long Ago & Far Away*. A *Svenska Filminstitutet, Sweden Production. Color. Half-hour. Premiered on PBS: April 29, 1989. Rebroadcast on PBS: December 14, 1990.*

☺ BILL THE MINDER

A clever inventor (Bill) who solves problems for his family and friends by constructing absurd and elaborate machines. Based on a classic picture-book series by W. Heath Robinson, the award-winning film was televised as a special on the PBS anthology series *Long Ago & Far Away*. A *Bevanfield Film, Britain Production in association with Link Licensing Ltd. Color. Half-hour. Premiered on PBS: November 3, 1990. Rebroadcast on PBS: January 17, 1993.*

Voices
Narrator: Peter Chelsom

☺ THE BIRTHDAY DRAGON

Young Emily invites her age-old dragon friend to her birthday party, while taking time to stop two dragon hunters and make the world safe for dragons once again, in this sequel to 1991's *The Railway Dragon*. A *Lacewood Production. Color. Half-hour. Premiered on DIS: September 15, 1992.*

☺ THE BLACK ARROW

Adapted from the Robert Louis Stevenson story, this half-hour special re-creates the adventures of a young heir, orphaned at birth, who joins the band of forest outlaws known as the Brotherhood of the Black Arrow. A *Famous Classic Tales* special. An *Air Programs International Production. Color. Half-hour. Premiered on CBS: December 2, 1973. Rebroadcast on CBS: September 22, 1974.*

Voices
Alistair Duncan, Jeannie Drynan, Tim Elliott, Barbara Frawley, Ron Haddrick, John Llewellyn, Owen Weingott

☺ BLACK BEAUTY

Born and raised in the lush English countryside, a sweet-tempered horse named Black Beauty is taught by his mother to be a friend to man. In true testimony to his mother, Beauty's faith in the goodness of man is put to the test again and again in this touching and heartwarming story based on Anna Sewell's children's novel, first published in 1877. A *Famous Classic Tales* special. A *Hanna-Barbera Production. Color. Half-hour. Premiered on CBS: October 28, 1978. Rebroadcast on CBS: November 11, 1979; November 6, 1983 (as Kenner Family Classics).*

Voices
Alan Young (Narrator), Robert Comfort, Cathleen Cordell, Alan Dinehart, Mike Evans, David Gregory, Colin Hamilton, Laurie Main, Patricia Sigris, Barbara Stevens, Cam Young

☺ THE BLINKINS

Blink, Sparkle, Flicker, Flashy and Shady are selected to perform in the annual Flower of Spring Ceremony to bring the first ray of spring sunshine to Blinkin Land but Slime, a swamp monster, has different plans. An *MCA Television Production in association with TMS Entertainment. Color. Half-hour. Premiered: Spring 1986. Syndicated.*

Voices
Mr. Benjamin the Owl: Burgess Meredith; **Grog the Frog:** Paul Williams; **Blink:** Missy Gold; **Shady:** Tracey Gold; **Baby Twinkle:** Brandy Gold; **Flashy:** Sagan Lewis; **Sparkle:** Carrie Swenson; **Flicker/Pettiford:** Louise Chamis; **Slime:** Chris Latta; **Announcer:** Henry Gibson

☺ THE BLINKINS AND THE BEAR

New challenges await the spunky Blinkins as they follow Mr. Benjamin Owl's advice by gathering food for the winter—but their precious supply is endangered by bad guys, Grog the Frog and Sneed the Bear, who disrupt the proceedings. An *MCA Television Production in association with TMS Entertainment. Color. Half-hour. Premiered: September, 1986. Syndicated.*

Voices
Blink: Noelle North; **Flash:** Daryl Wood; **Sparkle:** Carrie Swenson; **Flicker/Baby Twinkle:** Louise Chamis; **Shady:** Jennifer Darling; **Mr. Benjamin the Owl:** Burgess Meredith; **Sneed the Bear:** Chris Latta; **Grog the Frog:** Hamilton Camp; **Announcer:** Alan Young

☺ THE BLINKINS AND THE BLIZZARD

The Blinkins come to the aid of a poor little girl who is lost in the woods after she loses her precious doll. Villainous Grog the Frog and Sneed the Bear make life miserable for them until the Blinkins lead the girl home safely. An *MCA Television Production in association with TMS. Color. Half-hour. Premiered: December, 1986. Syndicated.*

Voices

Blink: Noelle North; **Flashy:** Daryl Wood; **Sparkle:** Carrie Swenson; **Flicker/Baby Twinkle:** Louis Chamis; **Shady:** Jennifer Darling; **Mr. Benjamin, the Owl:** Burgess Meredith; **Sneed the Bear:** Chris Latta; **Grog the Frog:** Hamilton Camp; **Announcer:** Alan Young

⊚ BLONDIE AND DAGWOOD

The world's favorite comic-strip couple trade places when Blondie gets a job after Dagwood Bumstead gets fired. Loni Anderson provides the voice of Blondie. Based on the comic strip *Blondie* by Dean Young and Stan Drake. *A Marvel Animation Production with King Features Entertainment in association with Toei Animation. Color. Half-hour. Premiered on CBS: May 15, 1987. Rebroadcast on CBS: October 12, 1988.*

Voices

Blondie Bumstead: Loni Anderson; **Dagwood Bumstead:** Frank Welker; **Alexander Bumstead:** Ike Eisenmann; **Cookie Bumstead:** Ellen Gerstell; **Daisy, the Bumsteads' dog:** Pat Fraley; **Julius Dithers:** Alan Oppenheimer; **Cora Dithers/Mrs. Hannon:** Russi Taylor; **Tootsie Woodley:** Laurel Page; **Mr. Beasley/Herb Woodley:** Jack Angel

⊚ BLONDIE AND DAGWOOD: "SECOND WEDDING WORKOUT"

In their second prime-time special, the Bumsteads' 20th wedding anniversary falls on the same day as the deadline for a building project Dagwood must complete in order to receive a bonus to pay for Blondie's new ring—which he loses. *A King Features Entertainment Production in association with King Services Inc. Color. Half-hour. Premiered on CBS: November 1, 1989.*

Voices

Blondie Bumstead: Loni Anderson; **Dagwood Bumstead:** Frank Welker; **Alexander Bumstead:** Ike Eisenmann; **Cookie Bumstead:** Ellen Gerstell; **Daisy, the Bumsteads' dog:** Pat Fraley; **Julius Dithers:** Alan Oppenheimer; **Cora Dithers:** Russi Taylor

⊚ BLUETOES, THE CHRISTMAS ELF

One pint-size, clumsy elf, appropriately named Small One can't seem to do anything right, until his misadventures land him on Santa's toy-filled sleigh to deliver toys to all the children of the world (earning him the name, Bluetoes) in this adorable half-hour animated special, originally produced in 1988 for Canadian television by Lacewood Productions. *A Lacewood Production. Color. Half-hour. Premiered on DIS: December 8, 1991. Rebroadcast on DIS: December 20, 1992; December 7, 1993.*

Voices

Small One (Bluetoes): Polly Jones; **Santa Claus:** Dave Broadfoot; **Woody:** James Bradford; **The Girl:** Jennifer Finestone; **Lonesome/Whitey:** Rick Jones; **Hattie/Elf:** Anna MacCormack; **Elf/Gummy:** Michael O'Reilly; **Boy/Elf:** Ben Mulroney

⊚ THE BOLLO CAPER

On the verge of extinction, two leopards—Bollo and Nefertiti—try to save their species from a band of trappers who are capturing and killing the animals to sell the skins to their boss, a famed New York furrier. *An ABC Weekend Special. A Rick Reinert Pictures Production. Color. Half-hour. Premiered on ABC: February 2, 1985. Rebroadcast on ABC: November 16, 1985; August 16, 1986; November 29, 1986; July 11, 1987; October 5, 1991; January 9, 1993; April 26, 1997.*

Voices

Bollo: Michael Bell; **Nefertiti/Lulu La Looche:** Ilene Latter; **Clamper Carstair:** Hal Smith; **Snag Carstair:** Will Ryan; **Lion/Iceberg/Emperor:** Hal Smith; **Chestnut/Monkey #1:** Will Ryan; **Felix the Furrier:** Pete Renaday; **President/Monkey #2:** Pete Renaday

⊚ BOOP OOP A DOOP

Steve Allen hosts and narrates this 90-minute, clip-filled biography of the evolution of Max Fleischer's famed cartoon sex symbol, Betty Boop, featuring scenes from many of the femme fatale's classic cartoons. *A Nobul/Crystal Pictures Production. Color. Ninety minutes. Premiered on ABC: 1986.*

⊚ BOO! TO YOU TOO, WINNIE THE POOH

Winnie the Pooh and friends, Tigger and Piglet, prepare to celebrate the Bestest Halloween ever and find themselves caught up in an adventure on Halloween night, during which Piglet finds his courage and learns the benefits of sticking together. *A Walt Disney Television Animation Production. Color. Half-hour. Premiered on CBS: October 25, 1996.*

Voices

Winnie the Pooh/Tigger: Jim Cummings; **Piglet:** John Fiedler; **Eeyore:** Peter Cullen; **Rabbit:** Ken Samson; **Gopher:** Michael Gough; **Owl:** Andre Stojka; **Narrator:** John Rhys-Davies

⊚ THE BOY WHO DREAMED CHRISTMAS

A greedy boy learns about giving when Nilus the Snowman transports him to the North Pole on Christmas Eve in this holiday special, first aired on The Disney Channel. *A Cambium Film & Video/Delaney and Friends Production. Color. Half-hour. Premiered on DIS: December 10, 1991. Rebroadcast on DIS: December 22, 1991.*

⊚ THE BRADY KIDS ON MYSTERIOUS ISLAND

Teenagers Greg, Peter, Bobby, Marcia, Janice and Cindy of television's *The Brady Bunch* perform as rock musicians and encounter a few spooks on a strange island in this one-hour animated adventure, which officially launched the first season for *The ABC Saturday Superstar Movie. A Filmation Associates Production for Paramount Television. Color. One hour. Premiered on ABC: September 9, 1972.*

Voices
Greg Brady: Barry Williams; **Peter Brady:** Christopher Knight; **Bobby Brady:** Michael Lookinland; **Marcia Brady:** Maureen McCormick; **Janice Brady:** Eve Plumb; **Cindy Brady:** Susan Olsen; **Marlon:** Larry Storch

⊚ "BUBSY" WHAT COULD POSSIBLY GO WRONG?

In his first celluloid adventure, Bubsy, an unpredictable bobcat with an attitude and a heart of gold, and his reluctant sidekick Arnold, the Armadillo, set out to test mad scientist Virgil Reality's new invention, the Virtual Reality helmet. The villainous Allycassandra and her henchmen scheme to steal in this half-hour syndicated special, broadcast Thanksgiving weekend 1993 as part of Bohbot Entertainment's "Kid's Day Off" block. *A Calico Entertainment/Imagination Factory Inc. Production in association with Accolade Inc. Color. Half-hour. Premiered: November 27–28, 1993.*

Voices
Bubsy: Rob Paulsen; **Arnold, the Armadillo/Virgil Reality:** Pat Fraley; **Sid, the Vicious Shrew:** Jim Cummings; **Oblivia/Bubsy Twin:** Tress MacNeille; **Bozwell, the Gourmet Buzzard/Bubsy Twin:** Neil Ross; **Allycassandra:** B.J. Ward

⊚ BUGS BUNNY: ALL-AMERICAN HERO

The carrot-eating rabbit recalls past events in America's glorious history in this half-hour special, which combines full versions and clips from several old Warner's cartoons reedited to tell a complete story. The program was primarily shaped around the 1954 Bugs Bunny cartoon "Yankee Doodle Bugs." Other cartoons, in whole or in part, included:

Bubsy, a bobcat who's a loose cannon with heart of gold, stars in his first cartoon adventure, "Bubsy" What Could Possibly Go Wrong? produced by Calico Creations. © Accolade Inc. All rights reserved. Property of Calico Entertainment/Imagination Factory, Inc.

"Bunker Hill Bunny," "Dumb Patrol," "Rebel Without Claws" and "Ballot Box Bunny." *A Warner Bros. Television Production. Color. Half-hour. Premiered on CBS: May 4, 1981. Rebroadcast on CBS: March 10, 1982; April 16, 1983; May 26, 1984; May 10, 1985; January 7, 1986; June 18, 1987; September 20, 1988; September 5, 1990; July 1, 1993.*

Voices
Mel Blanc, June Foray

⊚ BUGS BUNNY CREATURE FEATURES

Animated sci-fi parodies starring Bugs Bunny and Daffy Duck, with new introductions by that carrot-chomping rabbit, make up this animated trilogy, including a new cartoon short, "Invasion of the Bunny Snatchers," and two theatrical cartoon shorts, "The Duxorcist" (1987) and "Night of the Living Duck (1988)." *A Warner Bros. Television Animation Production. Color. Half-hour. Premiered on CBS: February 1, 1992. Rebroadcast on CAR: October 31, 1997.*

Voices
Jeff Bergman

◉ THE BUGS BUNNY EASTER SPECIAL

When the Easter Bunny becomes ill, Granny turns to Bugs to help her find the right recruit who can deliver baskets of eggs to children throughout the world. Offered the job himself, Bugs demurs but stages an audition for others to apply for the position. (One persistent applicant is Daffy Duck, who doesn't understand why he isn't taken seriously for the job.) Program includes complete versions of theatrical cartoon favorites, such as "For Scenti-mental Reasons," "Knighty Knight Bugs," "Robin Hood Daffy," "Sahara Hare" and "Birds Anonymous," plus clips from five other cartoons. A *DePatie-Freleng Production for Warner Bros. Television. Color. Half-hour. Premiered on CBS: April 7, 1987. Rebroadcast on CBS: March 18, 1978; April 13, 1979; April 2, 1980; April 14, 1984; March 30, 1985; March 25, 1989.*

Voices
Mel Blanc, June Foray

◉ BUGS BUNNY IN SPACE

Following the box-office sensation of *Star Wars*, CBS aired this half-hour collection of the best moments from science-fiction–oriented Warner Bros. cartoons put together to represent a common theme. The special contained several cartoons featuring Bugs Bunny as well as the classic "Duck Dodgers in the 24 1/2 Century." A *Warner Bros. Television Production. Color. Half-hour. Premiered on CBS: September 6, 1977. Rebroadcast on CBS: April 18, 1978.*

Voices
Mel Blanc

◉ BUGS BUNNY/LOONEY TUNES ALL-STAR 50TH ANNIVERSARY SPECIAL

In honor of Warner Bros.' golden cartoon anniversary, several well-known stars—David Bowie, Steve Martin, Bill Murray, Kirk Douglas, Cher, George Burns and others—are featured in this tribute in the form of interviews recalling their favorite memories of Bugs Bunny and the other Warner cartoon characters. Cartoon footage and rare pencil tests round out the program, plus interviews with Mel Blanc, Friz Freleng and Chuck Jones. Other guest stars: Eve Arden, Candice Bergen, Jeff Goldblum, Jeremy Irons, Quincy Jones, Penny Marshall, Mike Nichols, Geraldine Page, Molly Ringwald, Danny Thomas, Billy Dee Williams and Chuck Yeager. A *Broadway Video Production in association with Warner Bros. Television. Color. One hour. Premiered on CBS: January 14, 1986. Rebroadcast on CBS: July 24, 1987 (as* The Bugs Bunny/Looney Tunes Jubilee).

Voices
Mel Blanc

◉ THE BUGS BUNNY MOTHER'S DAY SPECIAL

When Bugs and Granny encounter a blundering stork, their discussion turns to Mother's Day, which acts as a bridge to various sequences culled from Warner Bros. cartoons, including "Stork Naked," "Apes of Wrath" and "Goo Goo Goliath." A *Warner Bros. Television Production. Color. Half-hour. Premiered on CBS: May 12, 1979. Rebroadcast on CBS: May 12, 1984; May 10, 1985; May 8, 1987; May 8, 1991.*

Voices
Mel Blanc, June Foray

◉ THE BUGS BUNNY MYSTERY SPECIAL

In the role of Alfred Hitchcock, Porky Pig hosts this compilation of crime cartoons, both complete cartoons and excerpts, which entail a string of "whodunit" plots starring a melange of Warner characters. A *Warner Bros. Television Production. Color. Half-hour. Premiered on CBS: October 15, 1980. Rebroadcast on CBS: December 5, 1981; March 8, 1983; March 10, 1984; September 14, 1984; June 5, 1987.*

Voices
Mel Blanc

◉ BUGS BUNNY'S BUSTIN' OUT ALL OVER

Three new cartoons created by Chuck Jones are presented in this half-hour special: Bugs recalling his childhood and first encounter with an infant Elmer Fudd; his capture by Marvin Martian; and Wile E. Coyote's near completion of a 30-year chase to catch the Road Runner. A *Chuck Jones Enterprises Production in association with Warner Bros. Television. Color. Half-hour. Premiered on CBS: May 21, 1980. Rebroadcast on CBS: March 20, 1981; May 5, 1984; April 6, 1985; June 5, 1987; April 19, 1988; April 19, 1989; April 22, 1993.*

Voices
Mel Blanc

◉ BUGS BUNNY'S HOWL-OWEEN SPECIAL

Monstrous events occur in this compendium of old Warner Bros. cartoons as Tweety, Daffy Duck, Porky Pig, Sylvester the Cat and, of course, Bugs Bunny experience strange encounters of the Halloween kind. Cartoons featured are "Bedeviled Rabbit," "Rabbit Every Monday" and clips from eight additional one-reelers, including "Beep Beep," "Canned Feud" and "Trip for Tat." A *Warner Bros. Television Production. Color. Half-hour. Premiered on CBS: October 26,*

1977. *Rebroadcast on CBS: October 25, 1978; October 31, 1979; October 29, 1980; October 27, 1981; October 25, 1989; Rebroadcast on CAR: October 31, 1997.*

Voices
Mel Blanc, June Foray

◎ BUGS BUNNY'S LOONEY CHRISTMAS TALES

Warner cartoon directors Friz Freleng and Chuck Jones animated three all-new cartoons, each with a Christmas theme, for this half-hour special that spotlights the traditional values of the yuletide season in using an assortment of Warner characters. Included are "Bugs Bunny's Christmas Carol" (directed by Freleng), a spoof of Charles Dickens's classic with Porky Pig as Bob Cratchit, Yosemite Sam as Scrooge and Tweety as Tiny Tim; "Freeze Frame" (directed by Jones), starring Wile E. Coyote and the Road Runner chasing each other through the ice and snow; and "Fright Before Christmas" (by Freleng), featuring the Tasmanian Devil, who visits Bugs's house dressed as Santa. *A DePatie-Freleng Enterprises Production with Chuck Jones Enterprises and Warner Bros. Television. Color. Half-hour. Premiered on CBS: November 27, 1979. Rebroadcast on CBS: December 13, 1980; November 27, 1981; December 6, 1982; December 4, 1984; December 24, 1987; December 17, 1988; December 8, 1990; December 4, 1991; Rebroadcast on FAM: December 11, 1996; December 25, 1996.*

Voices
Mel Blanc, June Foray

◎ BUGS BUNNY'S MAD WORLD OF TELEVISION

In new footage, Bugs Bunny is the new head of entertainment for the QTTV Network. His first task is to bolster the station's sagging ratings with new, original programming. He explores a number of options, most of which are represented in footage from previously exhibited cartoons made for theaters. *A Warner Bros. Television Production. Color. Half-hour. Premiered on CBS: January 11, 1982. Rebroadcast on CBS: April 2, 1983; September 14, 1983; July 28, 1984; September 6, 1985.*

Voices
Mel Blanc

◎ BUGS BUNNY'S OVERTURES TO DISASTER

Bugs Bunny stars in this half-hour animated tribute to classical music, featuring the rabbit's own classic cartoon shorts,

"What's Opera, Doc?" (1957), "Rabbit of Seville" (1950) and "Baton Bunny" (1959), and including new sequences of Daffy and Porky (in a cartoon version of "The William Tell Overture" directed by Daniel Haskett), with appearances by Mr. Meek, The Three Bears, Yosemite Sam and Granny. Debuting in 1991, the prime-time special kicked off CBS's "Toon Night," a weekly Wednesday-night attraction featuring animated specials and animated series. *A Warner Bros. Television Production. Color. Half-hour. Premiered on CBS: April 17, 1991.*

Voices
Jeff Bergman, Mel Blanc, June Foray, Stan Freberg, Ronnie Scheib

◎ BUGS BUNNY'S THANKSGIVING DIET

Bugs Bunny, playing a diet doctor, counsels his patients—Porky Pig, Sylvester the Cat and others—against holiday overeating, presenting his favorite cure: a series of cartoons to reduce the urge. Features full versions of "Bedeviled Rabbit" and "Rabbit Every Monday" and clips from eight others. *A Warner Bros. Television Production. Color. Half-hour. Premiered on CBS: November 15, 1979. Rebroadcast on CBS: November 10, 1981; November 12, 1983; November 20, 1984; November 26, 1985; November 26, 1987; November 23, 1988; November 22, 1989.*

Voices
Mel Blanc, June Foray

◎ BUGS BUNNY'S VALENTINE

In the unusual role of "Cupid," Elmer Fudd strikes love into the heart of Bugs Bunny, who experiences the fresh bloom of romance through a series of classic Warner cartoons, complete and edited, strung together in one common theme. *A Warner Bros. Television Production. Color. Half-hour. Premiered on CBS: February 14, 1979. Rebroadcast on CBS: February 13, 1980; February 4, 1981; February 2, 1982; February 11, 1984; February 11, 1986; February 4, 1988.*

Voices
Mel Blanc

◎ BUGS BUNNY'S WILD WORLD OF SPORTS

The "Sportsman of the Year Award" is announced in ceremonies at the Arthur Q. Bryan Pavillion, utilizing many clips of sporting activities from previous Warner Bros. cartoons, including "Raw Raw Rooster," "Sports Chumpions," "To Duck or Not to Duck" and others. Oh, yes, the winner is Foghorn Leghorn, of all characters. A *Warner Bros. Television Production. Color. Half-hour. Premiered on CBS: February 15, 1989.*

Voices
Mel Blanc, Roy Firestone, Paul Kuhn

◉ BUGS VS. DAFFY: BATTLE OF THE MUSIC VIDEO STARS

As cross-town rival disc jockeys, Bugs Bunny, of music channel W.A.B.B.I.T., and Daffy Duck, of radio station K.P.U.T., try topping each other as they introduce various song sequences from old Warner cartoons. Naturally, Bugs gets the higher ratings. *A Warner Bros. Television Production. Color. Half-hour. Premiered on CBS: October 21, 1988.*

Voices
Mel Blanc

◉ A BUNCH OF MUNSCH: "BLACKBERRY SUBWAY JAM" AND "MOIRA'S BIRTHDAY"

Robert Munsch's beloved stories come to life in this half-hour edition of Showtime's *A Bunch of Munsch* series, featuring two episodes: "Blackberry Subway Jam," about a little boy who accepts a man's help to stop a train showing up in his house in exchange for blackberry jam, and "Moira's Birthday," about a young girl whose parents insist she can only invite six of her friends to her birthday party but 200 show up instead. *A Cinar/TMP IX Limited Partnership Production in association with CTV Television Network/ Showtime Networks Inc./The Maclean Hunter Television Fund/Telefilm Canada. Color. Half-hour. Premiered on SHO: December 2, 1992.*

Voices
Andrew Bauer-Gabor, Holly Frankel-Gauthier, A.J. Henderson, Gary Jewell, Rick Jones, Tamar Kozlov, Shayne Olszynko-Gryn, Patricia Rodriguez, Terence Scammell, Jory Steinberg, Jacob D. Tierney, Jane Woods

◉ A BUNCH OF MUNSCH: "THE FIRE STATION" AND "ANGELA'S AIRPLANE

Part of Showtime's original *A Bunch of Munsch* children's series, this sixth half-hour special spotlights two adventures: "The Fire Station," about a boy (Michael) and a girl (Sheila) who get into "fun" kind of trouble after exploring a real fire station; and "Angela's Airplane," which follows the adventures of a young girl (Angela) and her stuffed rabbit (Ralph). *A Cinar/TMP IX Limited Partnership Production in association with CTV Television Network/Showtime Networks Inc./The Maclean Hunter Television Fund/Telefilm*

Canada. Color. Half-hour. Premiered on SHO: November 11, 1992. Rebroadcast on SHO: December 23, 1992.

Voices
Sonja Ball, Tia Caroleo, Richard Dumont, Norman Groulx, Arthur Holden, Liz MacRae, Carlyle Miller, George Morris, Haley Reynolds, Jacob D. Tierney, June Wallack

◉ A BUNCH OF MUNSCH: "MURMEL, MURMEL, MURMEL" AND "THE BOY IN THE DRAWER"

Combined in this half-hour adaptation of the work of famous children's author Robert Munsch are two separate animated stories presented in one broadcast: "Murmel, Murmel, Murmel," about a young girl's (Robin) quest to find a home for a very small baby she uncovers in a sandbox; and "The Boy in the Drawer," which follows the exploits of an impish gnome messing up the life a schoolgirl (Shelley). *A Cinar/TMP IX Limited Partnership Production in association with CTV Television Networks/Showtime Networks Inc./The Maclean Hunter Television Fund/Telefilm Canada. Color. Half-hour. Premiered on SHO: November 4, 1992. Rebroadcast on SHO: December 16, 1992.*

Voices
Amy Fulco, Eramelinda Boquer, Harry Standjofsky, Tamar Kozlov, Sonja Ball, Liz MacRae, Kathleen Fee, Michael Rudder, Rick Jones

◉ A BUNCH OF MUNSCH: "THE PAPER BAG PRINCESS"

Princess Elizabeth, an itty-bitty tyke, has a vivid picture of the man she likes and that man is Ronald, the "perfect prince next door," in this faithful half-hour rendition of a book by Robert Munsch (also narrated by him), broadcast as part of this Showtime anthology series. The episode was the only installment of the series to feature one complete 30-minute story. Subsequent episodes combined two stories per half-hour. *A Cinar/TMP IX Limited Partnership in association with CTV Television Network/Showtime Networks Inc./The Maclean Hunter Television Fund/Telefilm Canada. Color. Half-hour. Premiered on SHO: October 14, 1992.*

Voices
Robert Munsch (Narrator), Mark Hellman, Rick Jones, Jory Steinberg, Christian Tessier

◉ A BUNCH OF MUNSCH: "PIGS" AND "DAVID'S FATHER"

Another entertaining half-hour from this 1992 Showtime series, produced by Canada's Cinar Films, highlighting two animated adaptations of author Robert Munsch's children's stories: "Pigs," in which a young girl named Megan thinks pigs are "stupid" until she finds out otherwise; and "David's Father," about a boy who claims his father is really a "giant," much to the disbelief of his next-door neighbor (Julie). *A Cinar/TMP IX Limited Partnership Production in association with CTV Television Networks/Showtime Networks Inc./The Maclean Hunter Television Fund/Telefilm Canada. Color. Half-hour. Premiered on SHO: October 21, 1992. Rebroadcast on SHO: November 25, 1992.*

Voices

Sonja Ball, Rick Jones, Gordon Masten, Michael O'Reilly, Mark Hellman, Lianne Picard-Poiriero, Matthew Barrot, Tia Caroleo, Jess Gryn, Lisa Hull, Kaya Scott, Vlasta Vrana, Carlysle Miller

◉ A BUNCH OF MUNSCH: "SOMETHING GOOD" AND "MORTIMER"

Robert Munsch's best selling children's books, "Something Good," about a grocery store expedition with three kids (Julie, Andrew and Tyya) run amok and an exasperated father who is forced to buy something good for his daughter (Julie); and "Mortimer," about a rambunctious child who creates pandemonium in his quiet suburban town by making "tumultous noise," comprise this half-hour special and third installment of the critically acclaimed Showtime series *A Bunch of Munsch. A Cinar/TMP IX Limited Partnership Production in association with CTV Television Network/Showtime Networks Inc./The Maclean Hunter Television Fund/Telefilm Canada. Color. Half-hour. Premiered on SHO: October 28, 1992. Rebroadcast on SHO: December 9, 1992.*

Voices

Sonja Ball, Liz MacRae, Haley Reynolds, Gabriel Taraboulsy, Michael Rudder, Lisa Hull, Mark Hellman, Bronwen Mantel, Carlyle Miller, Rick Jones, Terrence Scammel, Kathleen Fee, Harry Standjofsky, Thor Bishopric, Patricia Rodriguez, Norman Groulx

◉ A BUNCH OF MUNSCH: "THOMAS' SNOWSUIT" AND "FIFTY BELOW ZERO"

Two cartoon adaptations of stories by world-renowned author Robert Munsch appear in this half-hour special (part of the *A Bunch of Munsch* series), which aired on Showtime in 1992. Included are: "Thomas's Snowsuit," about a young boy whose mother forces him to wear his new ugly brown snowsuit; and "Fifty Below Zero," the companion episode about the freezing cold and a boy named Jason who deals with his father's sleepwalking problem. *A Cinar/TMP IX Limited Partnership Production in association with CTV Televi-*

sion Network/Showtime Networks, Inc./The Maclean Hunter Television Fund/Telefilm Canada. Color. Half-hour. Premiered on SHO: November 18, 1992.

Voices

Julian Bailey, Sonja Ball, Rick Jones, Gordon Masten, Michael O'Reilly, Anik Matern, Liz MacRae

◉ BUNNICULA, THE VAMPIRE RABBIT

This spooky but comical tale tells the story of a supernatural rabbit and his loving friendship with a small-town family and its pets as told by the family's dog, Harold, an easygoing, intelligent mutt, in this adaptation of Deborah and James Howe's popular children's book, *Bunnicula, A Rabbit-Tale of Mystery. An ABC Weekend Special. A Ruby-Spears Enterprises Production. Color. Half-hour. Premiered on ABC: January 9, 1982. Rebroadcast on ABC: April 17, 1982; October 9, 1982; October 29, 1983.*

Voices

Harold/Roy: Jack Carter; **Chester/Stockboy/Hank:** Howard Morris; **Toby Monroe:** Pat Peterson; **Mr. Monroe/Storekeeper:** Alan Young; **Mrs. Monroe/Gertie/Alice:** Janet Waldo; **Boss/Andy:** Alan Dinehart

◉ BUTT-BOWL (1994)

MTV offered this alternative to traditional Super Bowl halftime fare with the network's first "Butt-Bowl" special, featuring two brand-new Beavis and Butt-Head cartoons. *An MTV Production. Color. Half-hour. Premiered on MTV: January 1994.*

Voices
Beavis/Butt-Head: Mike Judge

◉ BUTT-BOWL (1995)

Two cartoon adventures highlight this second annual "Butt-Bowl" special broadcast during 1995's Super Bowl halftime on MTV: "The Party," in which the world's biggest losers get thrown out of their "own" party; and "Wet Behind the Rears," in which the boys are forced to take a shower during gym class. *An MTV Production. Color. Half-hour. Premiered on MTV: January 29, 1995.*

Voices
Beavis/Butt-Head: Mike Judge

◉ BUTT-BOWL (1996)

Beavis and Butt-Head return for more halftime Super Bowl antics in this MTV special, highlighted by two cartoon shorts: "Prank Call," in which the boys engage in prank calls with disastrous results with a person they pick out of the phone book; and "No Service," wherein Beavis gets a call to work at Burger World and Butt-Head shows up to harass him. *An MTV Production. Color. Half-hour. Premiered on MTV: January 26, 1996.*

Voices
Beavis/Butt-Head: Mike Judge

◎ BUTT-BOWL (1997)

MTV continued the Super Bowl halftime tradition with the airing of this half-hour special, starring Beavis and Butt-Head, which included the animated episode "Vaya Con Cornholio," in which Beavis is mistaken for an illegal alien when federal agents conduct a spot check at Burger World. *An MTV Production. Color. Half-hour. Premiered on MTV: January 26, 1997.*

Voices
Beavis/Butt-Head: Mike Judge

◎ THE CABBAGE PATCH KIDS' FIRST CHRISTMAS

When the Cabbage Patch Kids help a disabled girl and one of their own get adopted, they discover the true meaning of Christmas spirit in this Ruby-Spears animated holiday special. *A Ruby-Spears Enterprises Production in association with Heywood Kling Productions. Color. Half-hour. Premiered on ABC: December 7, 1984. Rebroadcast on ABC: December 13, 1985. Rebroadcast on TBS: December 19, 1993.*

Voices
Otis Lee: Scott Menville; Dawson Glenn: Josh Rodine; Cannon Lee: David Mendenhall; Sybil Sadie: Phenina Segal; Rachel "Ramie" Marie: Ebony Smith; Tyler Bo: Vaughn Jelks; Paula Louise: Ann Marie McEvoy; Jenny: Gini Holtzman; Colonel Casey: Hal Smith; Xavier Roberts: Sparky Marcus; Lavender Bertha: Tress MacNeille; Cabbage Jack/Gus: Arthur Burghardt; Beau Weasel/Fingers: Neil Ross

◎ THE CANTERVILLE GHOST

When the Otis family moves into their new house in Canterville, they get more than they bargained for when a 300-year-old ghost attempts to scare them from the house in this delightful adaptation of the Oscar Wilde story. *A CBS Television Production in association with Orkin-Flaum Productions and Calabash Productions. Color. Half-hour. Premiered: Fall 1988. Syndicated. Rebroadcast on DIS: October 26, 1991. Rebroadcast on USA: October 28, 1994.*

Voices
The Ghost: Dick Orkin; General: Brian Cummings; Father: Louis Arquette; Mother: Janet Waldo; Virginia Otis, their daughter: Susan Blu; Washington: Michael Sheehan; Ned and Ted, the twins: Nancy Cartwright, Mona Marshall; Mrs. Umney, the maid: Kathleen Freeman

◎ CAP'N O.G. READMORE MEETS CHICKEN LITTLE

A true child of the TV age, Chicken Little now believes the sky is falling when his hero, Rocket Rooster, experiences danger in an episode, and it's up to the traveling librarian Cap'n O.G. to save him from a broadcast-manipulating Foxy Loxy. *An ABC Entertainment Production in association with Rick Reinert Productions. Color. Half-hour. Premiered on ABC: April 18, 1992. Rebroadcast on ABC: October 24, 1992; June 10, 1995; April 27, 1996.*

Voices
Cap'n O.G. Readmore/Rocket Rooster: Neil Ross; Foxy Loxy/Ol' Tome: Stanley Jones; Goosey Loosy/Kitty Literature: Ilene Latter; Turkey Lurkey/Ducky Lucky: Hal Smith; Chicken Little: Susan Blu; Kitty Literature: Lucille Bliss

◎ CAP'N O.G. READMORE MEETS DR. JEKYLL AND MR. HYDE

While holding their Friday Night Book Club meeting, Cap'n O.G. and his friends, Kitty Literature, Ol' Tome Cat, Wordsy and Lickety Page, turn to reading the Robert Louis Stevenson classic, *The Strange Case of Dr. Jekyll and Mr. Hyde.* The story becomes so enthralling that Wordsy is sucked into it—literally—and Cap'n O.G. follows to save him in this ABC Weekend Special. *An ABC Entertainment Production in association with Rick Reinert Pictures. Color. Half-hour. Premiered on ABC: September 13, 1986. Rebroadcast on ABC: August 8, 1987; May 3, 1989; November 4, 1989; January 18, 1992; January 23, 1993; October 28, 1995.*

Voices
Cap'n O.G. Readmore: Neil Ross; Wordsy/Ol' Tome Cat/Poole: Stanley Jones; Vendor/Master of Ceremonies: Neil Ross; Robert Louis Stevenson: Stanley Jones; Kitty Literature/Olivia/Heathpote: Ilene Latter; Lickety Page/Calypso LaRose: Lucille Bliss; Edward Hyde/Newcommon: Hal Smith

◎ CAP'N O.G. READMORE MEETS LITTLE RED RIDING HOOD

To teach him a lesson for hating villains, Cap'n O.G. is turned into the Big Bad Wolf from the classic children's tale "Little Red Riding Hood," so he can understand what being a villain is really like. *An ABC Entertainment Production in association with Rick Reinert Pictures. Color. One hour. Premiered on ABC: October 1, 1988. Rebroadcast on ABC: January 13, 1990; April 14, 1990; November 13, 1993; April 15, 1995; February 17, 1996; August 17, 1996; April 19, 1997.*

Voices

Cap'n O.G. Readmore: Neil Ross; **Lickety Page:** Lucille Bliss; **Ol' Tome:** Stanley Ross; **Wordsy:** Will Ryan; **Kitty Literature:** Ilene Latter

◎ CAP'N O.G. READMORE'S JACK AND THE BEANSTALK

In an effort to promote reading, this Saturday-afternoon special takes a unique approach, featuring a bright, articulate cat, Cap'n O.G. Readmore and his friends, Kitty Literature, Ol' Tome Cat, Wordsy, Lickety Page and Dog-Eared, as vehicles to encourage a love of literature among young people. As members of the Friday Night Book Club, they meet to discuss classic literature. Their discussion of the favorite fairy tale, *Jack and the Beanstalk* transports them to this land of make-believe. *An ABC Weekend Special. An ABC Entertainment Production in association with Rick Reinert Pictures. Color. Half-hour. Premiered on ABC: October 12, 1985. Rebroadcast on ABC: October 4, 1986; January 7, 1989; July 15, 1995; June 8, 1996.*

Voices

Cap'n O.G. Readmore: Neil Ross; **Kitty Literature:** Ilene Latter; **Ol' Tome Cat:** Stanley Jones; **Wordsy:** Will Ryan; **Lickety Page:** Lucille Bliss; **Jack:** Stanley Jones; **Jack's Mother:** Lucille Bliss; **Giant:** Hal Smith; **Giant's Wife:** Ilene Latter; **Harp:** Ilene Latter; **Humpty Dumpty:** Will Ryan; **Little Old Man:** Hal Smith; **Hen:** Lucille Bliss

◎ CAP'N O.G. READMORE'S PUSS IN BOOTS

It turns out the original "Puss in Boots" is an ancestor of literate feline, Cap'n O.G., who stars, along with his friends Lickety Page, Ol' Tome and Kitty Literature, in this faithful retelling of the well-known fairy tale, broadcast as an *ABC Weekend Special. An ABC Entertainment Production in association with Rick Reinert Pictures. Color. One hour. Premiered on ABC: September 10, 1988. Rebroadcast on ABC: January 13, 1990; May 22, 1993.*

Voices

Cap'n O.G. Readmore/Puss: Neil Ross; **Lickety Page:** Lucille Bliss; **Ol' Tome/King:** Stanley Jones; **Kitty Literature/Princess:** Ilene Latter; **Wordsy/Francois:** Will Ryan; **The Giant:** Hal Smith

◎ THE CARE BEARS BATTLE THE FREEZE MACHINE

Diabolical Professor Coldheart plans to use his Freeze Machine to no good by freezing all the children in town. The Care Bears (with new characters, Hugs and Tugs) prevent this fiendish plot from being carried out. *A MAD Production in association with Those Characters from Cleveland and Atkinson Film-Arts. Color. Half-hour. Premiered: April, 1984. Syndicated.*

Voices

Dominic Bradford, Bob Dermer, Abby Hagyard, Rick Jones, Les Lye, Anna MacCormack, Brodie Osome, Noreen Young

◎ THE CARE BEARS IN THE LAND WITHOUT FEELINGS

The Care Bears, popular greeting card characters, bring friendship, love and caring to a young boy named Kevin, a runaway, who becomes ensared by the evil Professor Coldheart. The program was the first special based on this wholesome gang. *A MAD Production in association with Those Characters from Cleveland and Atkinson Film-Arts. Color. Half-hour. Premiered: April, 1983.*

Voices

Andrea Blake, Justin Cammy, Abby Hagyard, Rick Jones, Les Lye, Anna MacCormack, Kathy MacLennan

◎ THE CARE BEARS NUTCRACKER SUITE

A tyrant takes over Toyland in this feature-length story produced in 1986 by Canadian animation giant Nelvana around the same time as the studio's popular ABC Saturday-morning series *The Care Bears Family*. The animated production, which ultimately was released on home video, received airplay in the United States on The Disney Channel. *A Nelvana Limited Production in association with Global Television Network/Telefilm Canada. Color. Sixty-five minutes. Premiered on DIS: December 1988.*

Voices

Grumpy Bear: Bob Dermie; **Braveheart Lion/Loyal Heart Dog/Good Luck Bear:** Dan Hennessey; **Mr. Beastley:** John Stocker; **Birthday Bear:** Melleny Brown; **Lotsa Heart Elephant/Gentle Heart Lamb:** Luba Goy; **Tenderheart Bear:** Billie Mae Richards

◎ CARLTON YOUR DOORMAN

This misfit of society who was heard but not seen on the television sitcom *Rhoda*, was transformed into a full-figure character whose adventures were unusual at best in this prime-time special based on the character created by James L. Brooks, Allan Burns, David Davis and Lorenzo Music (the voice of the Carlton in the sitcom and the special). *An MTM Production in association with Murakami-Wolf-Swenson. Color. Half-hour. Premiered on CBS: May 21, 1980.*

Voices
Carlton: Lorenzo Music; **Charles Shaftman:** Jack Somack; **Mrs. Shaftman:** Lucille Meredith; **Carlton's Mother:** Lurene Tuttle; **Darlene:** Kay Cole; **Mr. Gleanson/Fat Man:** Paul Lichtman; **Dog Catcher:** Alan Barzman; **Parrot:** Bob Arbogast; **Pop:** Charles Woolf; **D.J.:** Roy West

◉ CARNIVAL OF ANIMALS

Chuck Jones wrote, produced and animated this half-hour special based on the music of Camille Saint-Saens and the poetry of Ogden Nash, starring a variety of animals—lions, roosters, elephants and others—and Warner cartoon stars Bugs Bunny, Daffy Duck and Porky Pig. One major highlight: Bugs and Daffy, resplendent in black tie and tails, playing twin concert pianos along with a live orchestra conducted by Michael Tilson Thomas. *A Chuck Jones Enterprises Production in association with Warner Bros. Television. Color. Half-hour. Premiered on CBS: November 22, 1976. Rebroadcast on CBS: July 12, 1979.*

Voices
Bugs Bunny/Daffy Duck/Porky Pig: Mel Blanc

◉ CARTOON ALL-STARS TO THE RESCUE

More than 20 animated characters from Saturday-morning cartoon shows band together to help a 14-year-old (Michael) lick his addiction to drugs in this half-hour special shown on all three networks, some 200 independent stations and numerous cable services. The antidrug program produced a record-high 22.0 rating (more than 30 million viewers), the highest rating ever for a Saturday-morning children's program. The program's theme song: "Wonderful Ways to Say 'No.'" *An Academy of Television Arts and Sciences Foundation Production in cooperation with Alien Productions, Bagdasarian Productions, Columbia Pictures Television, DIC Enterprises, Film Roman, Hanna-Barbera Productions, Henson Associates, Marvel Productions, Murakami-Wolf-Swenson Films, Southern Star Productions, The Walt Disney Company and Warner Brothers. Color. Half-hour. Premiered: April 21, 1990.*

Voices
Michael: Jason Marsden; **Corey:** Lindsey Parker; **Mom:** Laurie O'Brien; **Dad:** Townsend Coleman; **Alf:** Paul Fusco; **Bugs Bunny/Daffy Duck:** Jeff Bergman; **The Chip-**munks: **Alvin/Simon:** Ross Bagdasarian; **Theodore:** Janice Karman; **Papa Smurf:** Don Messick; **Brainy Smurf:** Danny Goldman; **Smurfette:** Julie Dees; **Garfield:** Lorenzo Music; **Huey/Duey/Louie:** Russi Taylor; **Winnie the Pooh/Tigger:** Jim Cummings; **Slimer/Baby Kermit:** Frank Welker; **Michaelangelo:** Townsend Coleman; **Baby Piggy:** Laurie O'Brien; **Baby Gonzo:** Russi Taylor; **Smoke:** George C. Scott

◉ CARTOON MADNESS—THE FANTASTIC MAX FLEISCHER CARTOONS

Film critic Leonard Maltin hosts and narrates this tribute to legendary animators Max and Dave Fleischer in this hour-long clip fest, including the likes of Ko-Ko the Clown, Popeye, Betty Boop and others. *A Republic Pictures Corporation Production in association with the Arts & Entertainment Network. Color. Black-and-white. One hour. Premiered on A&E: October 27, 1992.*

◉ CASPER'S FIRST CHRISTMAS

A joyful group of characters—Yogi Bear, Boo Boo, Snagglepuss and others—get lost and decide to make Christmas Eve merry by visiting Casper. Hairy Scary tries to scare their Christmas spirits away until a touching gesture changes his heart. *A Hanna-Barbera Production. Color. Half-hour. Premiered on NBC: December 18, 1979. Rebroadcast on NBC: December 5, 1980; December 14, 1981. Rebroadcast on DIS: December 12, 1990; December 13, 1991; December 15, 1992; December 7, 1993; December 20, 1994. Rebroadcast on CAR: November 25, 1995.*

Voices
Casper: Julie McWhirter; **Hairy Scary:** John Stephenson; **Augie Doggie/Doggie Daddy:** John Stephenson; **Huckleberry Hound:** John Stephenson; **Quick Draw McGraw:** John Stephenson; **Snagglepuss/Quick Draw McGraw:** John Stephenson; **Yogi Bear:** John Stephenson; **Boo Boo:** Don Messick; **Santa Claus:** Hal Smith

◉ CASPER'S HALLOWEEN SPECIAL

It's Halloween night and Casper, the friendly ghost, decides to dress up and go out trick or treating like the rest of the children. Hairy Scary tries to spoil the fun by playing a few pranks and goes beyond the limits of good fun when he disappoints a group of orphan children. The special's story title was "He Ain't Scary, He's Our Brother." *A Hanna-Barbera Production. Color. Half-hour. Premiered on NBC: October 30, 1979. Rebroadcast on NBC: November 1, 1981. Rebroadcast on DIS: October 16, 1991; October 25, 1992; October 18, 1993; October 30, 1994.*

Voices

Casper: Julie McWhirter; **Hairy Scary:** John Stephenson; **Mr. Duncan/Skull:** Hal Smith; **J.R.:** Diane McCannon; **Winifred the Witch:** Marilyn Schreffler; **Black Cat:** Frank Welker; **Butler/Rural Man:** John Stephenson; **Nice Man/Dog:** Frank Welker; **Lovella:** Ginny Tyler; **Bejewelled Dowager/Rural Lady:** Ginny Tyler; **Gervais/Carmelita/Nice Lady:** Lucille Bliss; **Screech:** Michael Sheehan; **Dirk:** Greg Alter

☺ CASTLE

This public television special, based on the book by David Macaulay (also one of the principal voice artists), follows the construction of a 13th-century Welsh castle while examining life in medieval England, combining live action and animation. *A Unicorn Projects Production. Color. One hour. Premiered on PBS: October 5, 1983.*

Voices

Sarah Bullen, David Macaulay

☺ CATHY

Comic-strip heroine Cathy Andrews searches for happiness in this half-hour animated special based on creator Cathy Guisewite's nationally syndicated strip. The story comically plays the upswing in Cathy's career (a nomination for her company's "Employee of the Year") against the downswing in her personal life (her longtime boyfriend is seeing another woman). Seeing red, Cathy reluctantly renews her quest for Mr. Right, prodded by her chum Andrea. *A Lee Mendelson–Bill Melendez Production in association with Universal Press Syndicate and Bill Melendez Productions. Color. Half-hour. Premiered on CBS: May 15, 1987. Rebroadcast on CBS: January 5, 1988.*

Voices

Cathy: Kathleen Wilhoite; **Irving:** Robert F. Paulsen; **Andrea:** Allison Argo; **Anne, Cathy's mother:** Shirley Mitchell; **Bill, Cathy's father:** William L. Guisewite; **Charlene:** Emily Levine; **Mr. Pinkley:** Gregg Berger; **Brenda:** Desiree Goyette; **M.C.:** Robert Towers

☺ CATHY'S LAST RESORT

While on a romantic island vacation with Charlene, the receptionist, career woman Cathy manages to meet a nice single guy and must contend with the sudden appearance of her ever-undependable, workaholic boyfriend, Irving, who, at the last minute, had backed out on the trip. Program was written and illustrated by *Cathy* creator/cartoonist Cathy Guisewite. *A Lee Mendelson–Bill Melendez Production in association with Universal Press Syndicate. Color. Half-hour. Premiered on CBS: November 11, 1988.*

Voices

Cathy: Kathleen Wilhoite; **Irving, her boyfriend:** Robert F. Paulsen; **Anne, Cathy's mother:** Shirley Mitchell; **Bill, Cathy's father:** William L. Guisewite; **Andrea:** Allison Argo; **Mr. Pinkley:** Gregg Berger; **Charlene:** Emily Levine

Additional Voices

Heather Kerr, Jamie Neal, Frank Welker

☺ CATHY'S VALENTINE

Cathy and boyfriend, Irving, try rekindling their romance before Valentine's Day, with Cathy going all out to impress her beau by getting a makeover and buying a new dress even though her mother believes "romance has nothing to do with what you wear, it's what you have in your cupboard." *A Lee Mendelson–Bill Melendez Production in association with Universal Press Syndicate. Color. Half-hour. Premiered on CBS: February 10, 1989.*

Voices

Cathy: Kathleen Wilhoite; **Irving:** Robert F. Paulsen; **Anne, Cathy's mother:** Shirley Mitchell; **Bill, Cathy's father:** William L. Guisewite; **Andrea:** Allison Argo; **Mr. Pinkley:** Gregg Berger; **Charlene:** Emily Levine

☺ CELEBRITY DEATHMATCH DEATHBOWL '98

Clay rendering of today's hottest celebrities from the worlds of music and television appeared as commentators and competitors in three no-holds-barred fights (Howard Stern vs. Kathie Lee Gifford, Pamela Anderson vs. RuPaul and Hanson vs. The Spice Girls) in this MTV Super Bowl half-time special that premiered in 1988. Sports commentator Marv Albert made a special "clay animated" guest appearance. *An MTV Animation Production. Color. Half-hour. Premiered on MTV: January 25, 1998.*

☺ CHARLES DICKENS' DAVID COPPERFIELD

Young quixotic feline David Copperfield is forced into the employ of his villainous stepfather at a moldy London cheese factory in this two-hour musical spectacular, loosely based on Charles Dickens's classic 1849 novel. *A Cinemotion Inc/PMMP National Production. Color. Two hours. Premiered on CBS: December 10, 1993.*

Voices

David Copperfield: Julian Lennon; **Agnes:** Sheena Easton; **Murdstone:** Michael York; **Mealy:** Howie Mandel; **Micawber:** Joseph Marcell; **Clara:** Kelly LeBrock

◉ A CHARLIE BROWN CELEBRATION

This one-hour animated special consists of several different stories of various lengths derived from the best comic strips ever done by *Peanuts* creator/cartoonist Charles Schulz. Segments include Charlie Brown's ill-fated attempt at kite flying, Peppermint Patty going to Dog Obedience School and Lucy and Schroeder at the piano discussing marriage. Schulz hosts the program, which was originally to be called *The Best of Charlie Brown. A Lee Mendelson–Bill Melendez Production in association with Charles M. Schulz Creative Associates and United Feature Syndicate. Color. Half-hour. Premiered on CBS: May 24, 1982. Rebroadcast on CBS: February 18, 1984.*

Voices

Charlie Brown: Michael Mandy; **Lucy Van Pelt:** Kristen Fullerton; **Linus Van Pelt:** Earl "Rocky" Reilly; **Sally Brown:** Cindi Reilly; **Schroeder:** Christopher Donohoe; **Peppermint Patty:** Brent Hauer; **Polly/Truffles:** Casey Carlson; **Marcie:** Shannon Cohn; **Snoopy:** Bill Melendez; **Announcer:** John Hiestand

◉ A CHARLIE BROWN CHRISTMAS

It may be Christmas but Charlie Brown is depressed. Acting as his psychiatrist, Lucy suggests that he get involved with the holiday festivities by directing their Christmas play. To set the proper mood, he is sent out to find the "perfect" Christmas tree to decorate the stage. The first *Peanuts* special ever produced (prompted by some Coca-Cola advertising executives who asked producer Lee Mendelson and creator Charles Schulz if they had ever considered doing a Christmas special for TV), the program was the first half-hour prime-time cartoon without a laugh track and the first to have kids—not adults—do the voices. The special won Emmy and Peabody awards for program excellence. For its 1997 encore showing, CBS restored the 1965 special to its original format, including a 45-second scene, since cut from network rerairings, focusing on Linus's use of his blanket in a snowball fight. *A Lee Mendelson–Bill Melendez Production in association with Charles M. Schulz Creative Associates and United Feature Syndicate. Color. Half-hour. Premiered on CBS: December 9, 1965. Rebroadcast on CBS: December 11, 1966; December 10, 1967; December 8, 1968; December 7, 1969; December 5, 1970; December 7, 1971; December 12, 1972; December 6, 1973; December 17, 1974; December 15, 1975; December 18, 1976; December 12, 1977; December 18, 1978; December 10, 1979; December 9, 1980; December 10, 1981; December 16, 1982; December 12, 1983; December 5, 1984; December 4, 1985; December 12, 1986; December 11, 1987; December 14, 1988; December 22, 1989; December 19, 1990; December 20, 1991; December 2, 1992; December 22, 1993; December 7, 1994; December 9, 1995; December 19, 1996; December 3, 1997.*

Voices

Charlie Brown: Peter Robbins; **Lucy Van Pelt:** Tracy Stratford; **Linus Van Pelt:** Christopher Shea; **Schroeder:** Chris Doran; **Peppermint Patty:** Karen Mendelson; **Sally Brown:** Cathy Steinberg; **Freida:** Ann Altieri; **Pigpen/Shermy:** Chris Doran; **Violet:** Sally Dryer-Barker

◉ CHARLIE BROWN'S ALL STARS

His team having just lost their 99th game in row, Charlie Brown reaches new depths of depression until his team is sponsored—to be in a real league with real uniforms. Unfortunately, he later learns that his sandlot crew can't play in the real league because his players include a dog and several girls. *A Lee Mendelson–Bill Melendez Production in association with Charles M. Schulz Creative Associates and United Feature Syndicate. Color. Half-hour. Premiered on CBS: June 6, 1966. Rebroadcast on CBS: April 10, 1967; April 6, 1968; April 13, 1969; April 12, 1970; April 3, 1982.*

Voices

Charlie Brown: Peter Robbins; **Linus Van Pelt:** Christopher Shea; **Lucy Van Pelt:** Sally Dryer-Barker; **Schroeder:** Glenn Mendelson; **Sally Brown:** Cathy Steinberg; **Peppermint Patty:** Lynn Vanderlip; **Freida:** Ann Altieri; **Pigpen:** Jeff Ornstein; **Violet:** Karen Mendelson; **Shermy/Umpire:** Kip DeFaria

◉ A CHARLIE BROWN THANKSGIVING

Charlie Brown celebrates America's oldest holiday in a rather unorthodox fashion. With his little stand-by, Linus, and the slightly questionable help of Snoopy and Woodstock, Charlie devises the most unusual Thanksgiving menu (potato chips, popcorn, jelly beans, buttered toast and ice cream) since 1621, served, traditionally enough, around a Ping Pong table in Charlie's backyard. *A Lee Mendelson–Bill Melendez Production in association with Charles M. Schulz Creative Associates and United Feature Syndicate. Color. Half-hour. Premiered on CBS: November 20, 1973. Rebroadcast on CBS: November 21, 1974; November 22, 1975; November 22, 1976; November 21, 1977; November 15, 1978; November 19, 1979; November 25, 1980; November 23, 1981; November 20, 1984; November 26, 1985; November 25, 1986; November 24, 1987; November 23, 1989.*

Voices

Charlie Brown: Todd Barbee; **Linus Van Pelt:** Stephen Shea; **Lucy Van Pelt:** Robin Kohn; **Peppermint Patty:** Kip DeFaria; **Sally Brown:** Hilary Momberger; **Marcie:** Jimmy Ahrens; **Franklin:** Robin Reed; **Snoopy:** Bill Melendez

◎ THE CHARMKINS
The Charmkins find themselves in the throes of danger when their friend Lady Slipper, a talented dancer, is abducted by Dragonweed and his band of henchmen. His scheme to keep her is foiled by the Charmkins, who rescue Lady Slipper and return her to Charm World unharmed. *A Sunbow Production in association with Marvel Productions. Color. Half-hour. Premiered: June 1983. Syndicated.*

Voices
Dragonweed: Ben Vereen; **Brown-Eyed Susan:** Aileen Quinn; **Poison Ivy:** Sally Struthers; **Skunkweed:** Ivy Austin; **Willie Winkle:** Martin Biersbach; **Lady Slipper:** Lynne Lambert; **Bramble Brother #1:** Chris Murney; **Bramble Brother #2:** Bob Kaliban; **Briarpatch/Crocus:** Chris Murney; **Thorny:** Gary Yudman; **Popcorn:** Peter Waldren; **Blossom:** Freddi Webber; **Announcer:** Patience Jarvis, Tina Capland; **Vocalists:** Helen Leonhart; Jamie Murphy; Helen Miles

◎ A CHILD'S GARDEN OF VERSES
Nursed by his parents, a young Robert Louis Stevenson fights a childhood illness and is allowed to let his imagination run wild in this half-hour animated special featuring songs and poems from the book by Robert Louis Stevenson. The program was part of the popular cartoon anthology series *HBO Storybook Musicals. A Michael Sporn Animation Production in association with Italtoons Corporation. Color. Half-hour. Premiered on HBO: April 13, 1992. Rebroadcast on HBO: August 8, 1993.*

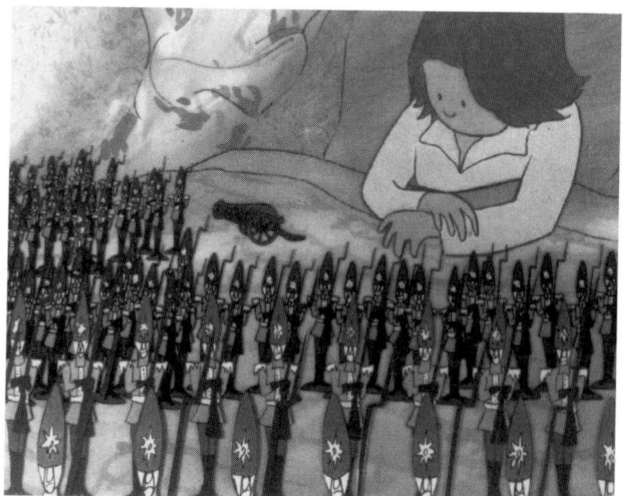

A sick child lets his imagination run wild in a scene from animator Michael Sporn's A Child's Garden of Verses *for HBO. © Michael Sporn Animation*

Voices
Narrator (grown Robert Louis Stevenson): Jonathan Pryce; **The Mother:** Heidi Stallings

◎ A CHIPMUNK CHRISTMAS
The Chipmunks (Alvin, Theodore and Simon) show their Christmas spirit when helping a gravely ill boy (Tommy Waterford) by giving him Alvin's prized harmonica to perform at Carnegie Hall on Christmas Eve. *A Bagdasarian Production. Color. Half-hour. Premiered on NBC: December 14, 1981. Rebroadcast on NBC: December 13, 1982; December 9, 1983; December 5, 1986; December 16, 1988. Rebroadcast on USA: December 11, 1991; December 17, 1992; December 8, 1993; December 1, 1994; December 16, 1995.*

Voices
Alvin/Simon/David Seville: Ross Bagdasarian Jr.; **Theodore:** Janice Karman

◎ A CHIPMUNK REUNION
Alvin, Theodore and Simon embark on a personal journey to uncover their real mother, while David Seville and the Chipettes—Brittany, Jeanette and Elenore—form a search party to find them. *A Bagdasarian Production in association with Ruby-Spears Productions. Color. Half-hour. Premiered on NBC: April 13, 1985. Rebroadcast on NBC: December 22, 1985.*

Voices
Alvin/Simon/David: Ross Bagdasarian Jr.; **Theodore/Brittany/Jeanette/Elenore:** Janice Karman; **Vinnie:** June Foray

◎ THE CHIPMUNKS ROCKIN' THROUGH THE DECADES
Alvin, Theodore and Simon headline this pop-music retrospective, hosted by Will Smith (star of TV's *Fresh Prince*) and featuring guest appearances by Little Richard, Kenny Loggins, Ben Vereen, Shelly Duvall, Raven Symone, Richard Moll and Markie Post. Also included is a special music video by Michael Jackson. *A Bagdasarian Production. Color. Half-hour. Premiered on NBC: December 9, 1990. Rebroadcast on USA: December 17, 1992; December 19, 1992; December 8, 1993; December 19, 1993.*

Voices
Alvin/Simon: Ross Bagdasarian Jr.; **Theodore:** Janice Karman

◎ CHIP 'N DALE RESCUE RANGERS TO THE RESCUE
Chip and Dale try solving a big ruby heist when they help

Detective Don Drake and Plato, a police dog, who suspect the notorious Clawdane is somehow behind the crime in this two-hour special based on the hit syndicated series. *A Walt Disney Television Animation Production. Color. Two hours. Premiered: September 30, 1989. Syndicated.*

Voices
Chip/Gadget: Tress MacNeille; **Dale/Zipper/Snout/Mole:** Corey Burton; **Kirby/Muldoon:** Peter Cullen; **Monterey Jack/Fat Cat/Professor Nimnul:** Jim Cummings

☺ A CHRISTMAS CAROL (1970)

In this hour-long adaptation of Charles Dickens's classic tale money-grubbing businessman Ebenezer Scrooge is visited by several ghostly beings that make him understand the importance of giving. *A Famous Classic Tales special. An Air Programs International Production. Color. One hour. Premiered on CBS: December 13, 1970. Rebroadcast on CBS: December 12, 1971; December 10, 1972; December 8, 1973; December 14, 1974; December 13, 1975; December 18, 1976; December 10, 1977; November 26, 1978; November 25, 1979; November 28, 1980; December 6, 1981; November 28, 1982; December 4, 1983.*

Voices
C. Duncan, Ron Haddrick, John Llewellyn, T. Mangan, Bruce Montague, Brenda Senders, T. Kaff (vocalist), C. Bowden (vocalist)

☺ A CHRISTMAS CAROL (1971)

Actor Alistair Sim, who portrayed the character of Scrooge in a 1951 live-action feature, re-creates the role in this half-hour special that tells the story of one man's greed versus the true meaning of Christmas. *A Richard Williams Production. Color. Half-hour. Premiered on ABC: December 21, 1971. Rebroadcast on ABC: December 15, 1972; December 14, 1973; December 7, 1974.*

Voices
Ebenezer Scrooge: Alistair Sim; **Bob Cratchit:** Melvin Hayes; **Mrs. Cratchit:** Joan Sims; **Tiny Tim:** Alexander Williams; **Marley's Ghost:** Sir Michael Hordern; **Ragpicker/Fezziwig:** Paul Whitsun-Jones; **Scrooge's nephew/Charity Man:** David Tate; **Ghost of Christmas Past:** Diana Quick; **Ghost of Christmas Present:** Felix Felton; **Ghost of Christmas Yet to Come:** Annie West; **Mrs. Dilber:** Mary Ellen Ray; **Narrator:** Sir Michael Redgrave

☺ A CHRISTMAS CAROL (1984)

Unlike previous versions, this syndicated special based on the Charles Dickens story was 90 minutes in length, faithfully re-creating the famed children's classic for another generation of television viewers. *A Burbank Films Production. Color. Ninety minutes. Premiered: November 1984. Syndicated.*

Voices
Bill Conn, Barbara Frawley, Ron Haddrick, Philip Hinton, Anne Hardy, Sean Hinton, Liz Horne, Derani Scarr, Robin Stewart

☺ CHRISTMAS CARTOON CLASSICS

A selection of public-domain, holiday-themed cartoons from the 1930s and 1940s, including Ub Iwerks's "Jack Frost," the Max Fleischer Color Classic "Christmas Comes But Once a Year" and several Paramount theatrical cartoons, such as "Santa's Surprise" and "Hector's Hectic Life," highlight this one-hour syndicated extravaganza. *A Starcross Entertainment/Cable Films/Originamics Production. Color. One hour. Premiered: December 21, 1991. Syndicated.*

☺ CHRISTMAS COMES TO PAC-LAND

When Santa Claus develops sleigh trouble and crash lands in Pac-Land, the Pac family, along with policemen Morris and O'Pac, pool their resources to repair the sleigh and get Santa and his reindeer back on course. *A Hanna-Barbera Production. Color. Half-hour. Premiered on ABC: December 16, 1982. Rebroadcast on ABC: December 8, 1983. Rebroadcast on CAR: December 24, 1992; November 28, 1993; December 17, 1993; December 24, 1993. Rebroadcast on TNT: November 29, 1993 (as Pac-Man's Christmas). Rebroadcast on CAR: November 26, 1994.*

Voices
Pac-Man: Marty Ingels; **Mrs. Pac:** Barbara Minkus; **Pac-Baby:** Russi Taylor; **Chomp Chomp/Morris/Reindeer:** Frank Welker; **Sour Puss/Santa:** Peter Cullen; **O'Pac/Blinky/Pinky Monsters:** Chuck McCann; **Sue Monster:** Susan Silo; **Clyde Monster:** Neilson Ross; **Inky Monster:** Barry Gordon

☺ CHRISTMAS EVERY DAY

Based on a short story by William Dean Howells, this first-run special tells the story of a young girl (Lucy) who wishes that Christmas lasted forever. Her father relates a story, told in flashback, of another girl who made the same wish but lived to regret it. *A CBS Television Production in association with Orkin-Flaum Productions and Calabash Productions. Color. Half-hour. Premiered: December 20, 1986. Syndicated.*

Rebroadcast on USA: December 15, 1993; December 7, 1994; December 16, 1995.

Voices
Tilly/Cissy: Stacy Q. Michaels; **Ned/Butcher/Policemen:** Brian Cummings; **Helen/Franny/Will:** Miriam Flynn; **Christmas Fairy:** Edie McClurg; **Grace/Lucy:** Marla Frumkin; **George/Pete:** Dick Orkin

◎ CHRISTMAS IS
The religious meaning of Christmas is witnessed through the eyes of a young boy (Benji) and his shaggy dog (Waldo) who are sent back to the scene of the Nativity, where Christ is born. The characters appeared in three additional specials, each underwritten by the International Lutheran Layman's League. *A Screen Images Production for Lutheran Television. Color. Half-hour. Premiered: November 7, 1970. Syndicated.*

Voices
Benji: Richard Susceno; **Innkeeper:** Hans Conried; **Waldo/Joseph:** Don Messick; **Mary:** Colleen Collins

◎ CHRISTMAS LOST AND FOUND
Young Davey Hanson, star of the stop-motion animation series *Davey and Goliath*, conveys the Christian meaning of the yuletide season in this holiday special—one of six specials sponsored by the Lutheran Church of America—as he helps a discouraged young boy find happiness by letting him play the part of a king in an upcoming Christmas pageant, a role originally intended for Davey. Gumby creator Art Clokey produced the special. *A Clokey Production for the Lutheran Church of America. Color. Half-hour. Premiered: 1965. Syndicated.*

Voices
Davey Hanson/Sally Hanson/Mary Hanson: Norma McMillan, Nancy Wible; **Goliath/John Hanson:** Hal Smith

◎ THE CHRISTMAS MESSENGER
Encouraged by a friendly stranger whose real identity is later revealed, a young boy joins a group of Christmas carolers, which enhances his appreciation of the holiday season. Richard Chamberlain narrated the special. *A Shostak and Schwartz/Gerald Potterton Production in association with Narrator's Digest. Color. Half-hour. Premiered: 1975. Syndicated.*

Voices
Narrator: Richard Chamberlain

◎ THE CHRISTMAS RACCOONS
Cyril Sneer, in his desire to harvest all the trees in the Evergreen Forest, cuts down the "Raccoondominium" of Ralph,

Melissa and Bert. The Raccoons set out to thwart Cryil's plans and save the forest. Based on the characters of the Canadian-produced series *The Raccoons*. *A Gills-Wiseman Production in association with Atkinson Film-Arts. Color. Half-hour. Premiered: December 1980. Syndicated.*

Voices
Dan: Rupert Holmes; **Julie:** Tammy Bourne; Tommy: Hadley Kay; **Schaeffer:** Carl Banas; **Ralph:** Bobby Dermer; **Melissa:** Rita Coolidge; **Bert:** Len Carlson; **Cyril Sneer:** Michael Magee; **Cedric Sneer:** Fred Little; **Narrator:** Rich Little; **Vocalists:** Rita Coolidge, Rupert Holmes

◎ A CHRISTMAS STORY
With Christmas not too far away, Timmy, a bright little boy, makes a special request of Santa in the form of a letter he believes has been mailed but instead has been misplaced. Pals Goober the dog and Gumdrop the mouse discover the letter and set out to deliver it to Santa so Timmy's wish comes true at Christmas. *A Hanna-Barbera Production. Color. Half-hour. Premiered: December, 1972. Syndicated. Rebroadcast on CAR: November 28, 1992. Rebroadcast on TNT: December 20, 1992. Rebroadcast on CAR: December 15, 1993; November 26, 1994; December 14, 1994; November 25, 1995.*

Voices
Mother/Girl: Janet Waldo; **Timmy/Boy:** Walter Tetley; **Dad/Squirrel:** Don Messick; **Goober/Sleezer/Runto:** Paul Winchell; **Gumdrop/Second Dog:** Daws Butler; **Santa/Fatcat:** Hal Smith; **Polecat/Postman/First Dog:** John Stephenson; **Vocalists:** Paul DeKorte, Randy Kemner, Stephen McAndrew, Susie McCune, Judi Richards

◎ A CHRISTMAS TREE
Charles Dickens himself, in animated form, takes two children, Peter and Mary, on the adventure of their lives as they relive tales of the Christmases of his youth, including the story of a magical Christmas tree that grows as high as the sky, in this *Festival of Family Classics* special. *A Rankin-Bass Production in association with Mushi Studios. Color. Half-hour. Premiered: December 17, 1972. Syndicated. Rebroadcast on USA: December 17, 1991; December 17, 1992; December 5, 1993.*

Voices
Carl Banas, Len Birman, Bernard Cowan, Peg Dixon, Keith Hampshire, Peggi Loder, Donna Miller, Frank Perry, Henry Ramer, Billie Mae Richards, Alfie Scopp, Paul Soles

◎ THE CHRISTMAS TREE TRAIN
Buttons, a young bear, and Rusty, a young fox, are accidentally transported, along with evergreens cut by lumberjacks,

to the big city on a train known as "The Christmas Tree Train." Rusty's and Buttons's parents, Rosey and George Fox and Bridget and Abner Bear, seek help in finding them from Jonesy, the Ranger of the forest. The first in a series of Chucklewood Critters specials. *An Encore Enterprises Production. Color. Half-hour. Premiered: December, 1983. Syndicated. Rebroadcast on USA: December 11, 1991; December 12, 1992; December 4, 1993.*

Voices
Rusty/Rosie: Kathy Ritter; **Buttons:** Barbara Goodson; **Ranger Jones:** Bill Boyett; **Abner/Santa Claus:** Alvy Moore; **George:** Bill Ratner; **Bridgett:** Morgan Lofting

⊚ THE CHRISTMAS WITCH

Angela Lansbury tells the story of a neophyte witch named Gloria who doesn't cut it at the wicked-witch academy and decides to become a good witch instead in this special holiday edition of *Shelley Duvall's Bedtime Stories*, airing on Showtime. *A Think Entertainment/MCA Family Entertainment/Universal Cartoon Studios Production. Color. Half-hour. Premiered on SHO: December 11, 1994.*

Voices
Narrator: Angela Lansbury

⊚ CHRISTOPHER THE CHRISTMAS TREE

A pint-size pine tree gets his heartfelt wish of being cut down so he can be displayed with all the trimmings in the home of a loving family in this half-hour musical cartoon special, which showed on Fox Network's Saturday-morning schedule. *A Chuck Glaser/Delaney and Friends Production. Color. Half-hour. Premiered on FOX: December 24, 1994.*

Voices
Bill Reiter, Lelani Marrell, Kyle Lebine, Tony Dakota, Chuck Glaser, George Bowers, Babs Shula, Kathleen Barr, Kevin Hayes, Hugh Delaney, Jim Glaser, Scott McNeil, Paul Dobson, John Payne, Mikal Grant

⊚ A CHUCKLEWOOD EASTER

Rusty and Buttons are put on trial for stealing eggs after invading the secret home of the Easter Bunny in this entertaining half-hour and fourth in a series of Chucklewood Critters specials. *An Encore Enterprise Production. Color. Half-hour. Premiered: April, 1987. Syndicated. Rebroadcast on USA: April 11, 1993.*

Voices
Rusty/Bluebell: Mona Marshall; **Buttons:** Barbara Goodson; **Abner:** Alvy Moore; **George/Easter Bunny:** Robert

Axelrod; **Bridgett:** Oceana Mars; **Skipper:** Dan Roth; **Ranger Jones:** Bill Boyett

⊚ CINDERELLA

Clever spoof of the classic children's tale in which the misfit Cinderella is transformed into a radiant beauty by her fairy godmother. The other characters are not as perfect as they seem, however; Cinderella's fairy godmother is absent-minded; Prince Charming is a bumbling fool. Yet somehow everything comes out right as Cinderella and Prince Charming get married in this first-run special for television. *A Festival of Family Classics special. A Rankin-Bass Production. Color. Half-hour. Premiered: September 17, 1972. Syndicated.*

Voices
Carl Banas, Len Birman, Bernard Cowan, Peg Dixon, Keith Hampshire, Peggi Loder, Donna Miller, Frank Perry, Henry Ramer, Billie Mae Richards, Alfie Scopp, Paul Soles

⊚ CIRCUS DREAMS

Enchanced by sophisticated animation, this program takes viewers inside the magical world of a traveling circus in this imaginative program (and sequel to the French clay-animated "The Happy Circus") which premiered on the PBS series *Long Ago & Far Away. A La Maison du Cinema de Grenoble/Antenne 2/Folimage-Valence Production. Color. Half-hour. Premiered on PBS: September 29, 1990. Rebroadcast on PBS: February 7, 1993.*

Voices
Narrator: Tammy Grimes

⊚ A CITY THAT FORGOT ABOUT CHRISTMAS

When Benji is impatient with the long wait for Christmas, his grandfather relates to him, his friend Martin and Benji's dog, Waldo, the story of a visitor (Matthew) who changed the lives of the townspeople in preparation for the coming of Jesus on Christmas Eve. *A Screen Images Production for Lutheran Television. Color. Half-hour. Premiered: December, 1974. Syndicated.*

Voices
Benji's grandfather: Sebastian Cabot; **Benji:** David Kelly; **Matthew, the wood carver:** Sebastian Cabot; **Wicked Mayor:** Charles Nelson Reilly; **Henchman:** Louis Nye; **Waldo, Benji's dog:** Don Messick

⊚ A CLAYMATION CHRISTMAS CELEBRATION

The California Raisins join a host of other animated clay figures in song-and-dance renditions of traditional Christmas carols. In 1992 the special was rebroadcast on The Disney Channel under the title of *Will Vinton's Claymation Christmas Special*. *A Will Vinton Production. Color. Half-hour. Premiered on CBS: December 21, 1987. Rebroadcast on CBS: December 23, 1988; December 21, 1989; December 7, 1990; December 6, 1991. Rebroadcast on DIS: December 11, 1992 (as Will Vinton's Claymation Christmas); December 4, 1993; December 22, 1994; December 17, 1995; December 21, 1996.*

◉ CLAYMATION COMEDY OF HORRORS SHOW

The ever-scheming Wilshire Pig talks Sheldon Snail into visiting the castle of Dr. Frankenswine to seek scientific secrets that could be worth a fortune in this prime-time comedy/adventure Halloween special, produced by claymation-master Will Vinton (of *California Raisins* fame). *A Will Vinton Production. Color. Half-hour. Premiered on CBS: May 29, 1991.*

◉ CLAYMATION EASTER

Porkster Wilshire Pig kidnaps the Easter Bunny, then dresses up as a cottontail to enter a competition to become the rabbit's successor in this third in a series of prime-time "claymation" specials. *A Will Vinton Production. Color. Half-hour. Premiered on CBS: April 18, 1992.*

◉ CLEROW WILSON AND THE MIRACLE OF P.S. 14

Re-creating characters introduced on his NBC series, *The Flip Wilson Show*, comedian Flip Wilson, as the voice of his nine-year-old self Clerow Wilson (his rightful name), recalls the struggle of his early childhood at the New Jersey school he attended in this prime-time network special, one of two based on Wilson's childhood adventures. *A DePatie-Freleng Enterprises Production in association with Clerow Productions and NBC. Color. Half-hour. Premiered on NBC: November 12, 1972. Rebroadcast on NBC: November 19, 1973.*

Voices
Clerow/Geraldine Jones/Herbie/Reverend LeRoy/The Devil: Flip Wilson; **Freddie:** Richard Wyatt Jr.; **Miss Davis:** Vivian Bonnett; **Li'l David:** Kenney Ball; **Robert Jackson:** Phillip Brown; **Dicke Porter:** Larry Oliver

◉ CLEROW WILSON'S GREAT ESCAPE

Comedian Flip Wilson plays many of his favorite characters—Geraldine Jones, Freddie the playboy, Ralph the invisible dog, Li'l David, Reverend Leroy and others—in this animated story as a small boy who is adopted into a mean family and attempts to escape. *A DePatie-Freleng Enterprises Production in association with Clerow Productions and NBC. Color. Half-hour. Premiered on NBC: April 3, 1974. Rebroadcast on NBC: December 16, 1974.*

Voices
Clerow Wilson/Geraldine Jones/Ralph/Reverend LeRoy/Herbie/The Devil: Flip Wilson

◉ COMPUTERS ARE PEOPLE, TOO!

The technology of computer animation is demonstrated through a variety of film clips showing the marvels of computer-generated images. The tale is told by talking computers and hosted by Elaine Joyce, who takes viewers through this world of visual entertainment. *A Walt Disney Production. Color. One-hour. Premiered: May 22, 1982. Syndicated.*

Voices
Billy Bowles, Joe Campanella, Nancy Kulp

◉ COMPUTER WARRIORS

In this half-hour fantasy adventure, based on the popular Mattel toy line, four computer warriors (Rod, Grid, Micron and Scanner) are developed to neutralize malfunctioning A1 programs, which have transformed into dangerous computer viruses (named Megahert, Indexx, Hull and Minus) and have the potential to cause irreparable damage to a computer network they've entered unless they are stopped. The program was produced by Carl Macek and directed by Bill Kroyer, who also cowrote the script. *A Kroyer Films Production in association with Mattel Toys/Island Animation and American Film Technologies. Color. Half-hour. Premiered: September 23, 1990. Syndicated.*

◉ THE CONEHEADS

That unusual alien family from the planet Remulak, first seen in a series of comedy sketches on NBC's *Saturday Night Live*, continue their mission to rebuild their space fleet, using humans as their slaves. Based on characters created by Dan Aykroyd, Tom Davis and Lorne Michaels. *A Rankin-Bass Production in association with Broadway Video Color. Half-hour. Premiered on NBC: October 14, 1983.*

Voices
Beldar: Dan Aykroyd; **Prymaat:** Jane Curtin; **Connie:** Laraine Newman

◉ A CONNECTICUT RABBIT IN KING ARTHUR'S COURT

Bugs Bunny plays a wise-guy Connecticut "rabbit" as Daffy Duck (King Arthur), Porky Pig (a varlat), Elmer Fudd (Sir

Elmer Fudd) and Yosemite Sam join the fun in this loosely based adaptation of the Mark Twain classic "plagiarized" by Chuck Jones, who produced this all-new special for CBS. The program was later retitled *Bugs Bunny in King Arthur's Court*. *A Chuck Jones Enterprises Production for Warner Brothers Television. Color. Half-hour. Premiered on CBS: February 23, 1978. Rebroadcast on CBS: November 22, 1978; (as Bugs Bunny in King Arthur's Court) November 17, 1979; August 19, 1981; March 10, 1982.*

Voices
Mel Blanc

A CONNECTICUT YANKEE IN KING ARTHUR'S COURT

Through clever thinking and the use of modern inventions, the inventive Connecticut Yankee encounters the likes of Merlin the Magician and King Arthur's knights in a series of medieval battles in this made-for-television daytime special under the *Famous Classic Tales* banner. *An Air Programs International Production. Color. Half-hour. Premiered on CBS: November 26, 1970. Rebroadcast on CBS: November 25, 1971; November 23, 1972 (in New York on WPIX).*

Voices
Connecticut Yankee: Orson Bean

COOL LIKE THAT: THE CHRISTMAS SPECIAL

Urban depiction of holidays in the 'hood following the exploits of a 15-year-old inner-city teen named Orlando (voiced by Tommy Davison of *In Living Color* fame) and his band of homeboys who experience Christmas in an underprivileged neighborhood. *A Warner Bros. Television Animation/Quincy Jones Production. Color. Half-hour. Premiered on FOX: December 23, 1993.*

Voices
Orlando: Tommy Davison; **Orlando's Mom/Drug Dealer:** Whoopi Goldberg

A COSMIC CHRISTMAS

Three creatures from outer space and their pet mascot journey to Earth on their mission to discover the bright star, the Star of Bethlehem, and find the true meaning of Christmas. *A Nelvana Limited Production in association with the CBC. Color. Half-hour. Premiered: December 6, 1977. Syndicated.*

Voices
Peter: Joey Davidson; **Dad/Plutox/Santa Joe:** Martin Lavut; **Lexicon:** Richard Davidson; **Amalthor:** Duncan

Regehr; **Mom:** Patricia Moffat; **Grandma:** Jane Mallett; **Police Chief Snerk:** Marvin Goldhar; **Marvin:** Greg Rogers; **The Mayor:** Chris Wiggins; **Townies:** Nick Nichols, Marion Waldman

THE COUNT OF MONTE CRISTO

Escaping from prison 15 years after his imprisonment Edmond Dantes, a young sailor, assumes the identify of his dead companion and sets sail to the Isle of Monte Cristo, where he uncovers fabulous treasure and acquires a new persona, the Count of Monte Cristo, with which to wage war on his enemies. *A Hanna-Barbera Production. Color. One hour. Premiered on CBS: September 23, 1973. Rebroadcast on CBS: December 7, 1974. Rebroadcast on CAR: October 22, 1995 (Mr. Spim's Cartoon Theatre).*

Voices
Elizabeth Crosby, Tim Elliott, Barbara Frawley, Ron Haddrick, Richard Meike

THE COUNTRY MOUSE AND THE CITY MOUSE: A CHRISTMAS TALE

Emily, a humble mouse living underneath the floor of a quaint country home, is invited by her cousin Alexander to spend Christmas with him in New York. They encounter trouble when the owner of the restaurant where Alexander lives purchases a "Christmas Cat" to help get rid of pests, and the two barely escape with their lives in this half-hour animated special, produced as part of the *HBO Storybook Musicals* series. *A Michael Sporn Animation Production in association with Italtoons Corporation. Color. Half-hour. Premiered on HBO: December 8, 1993. Rebroadcast on HBO: December 11, 1993.*

Voices
Emily, the Country Mouse: Crystal Gayle; **Alexander, the City Mouse:** John Lithgow

THE CRICKET IN TIMES SQUARE

Adapted from the 1960 book by George Selden, a liverwurst-loving cricket named Chester C. Cricket is transported in a picnic basket from a field in Connecticut to the Times Square subway. There the genteel Chester is befriended by Tucker Mouse, Harry the Cat and Mario the Newsboy, whose parents' newsstand is suffering from a severe lack of sales. When Tucker and Harry discover that Chester has the uncanny gift of being able to reproduce any music he hears, they convince him to perform during rush hour to attract business to the newsstand. The special was the recipient of the Parents' Choice Award for excellence in television programming. *A Chuck Jones Enterprises Production.*

Color. Half-hour. Premiered on ABC: April 24, 1973. Rebroadcast on ABC: January 30, 1974; November 9, 1974. Rebroadcast on NIK: March 14, 1992.

Voices
Chester C. Cricket/Harry the Cat: Les Tremayne; **Tucker the Mouse:** Mel Blanc; **Mario Bellini:** Kerry MacLane; **Mario's Father:** Les Tremayne; **Mario's Mother:** June Foray; **Music Teacher:** Les Tremayne

⊚ THE CRICKET ON THE HEARTH

Cricket Crockett is no ordinary cricket. He has a heart and soul and becomes the saving grace of poor toymaker Caleb Plummer and his troubled daughter, Bertha, who make him a permanent member of their family at Christmas, in this musical adaptation of the Charles Dickens fantasy. The one-hour special starred Danny Thomas and was broadcast during his weekly network series, *The Danny Thomas Hour*. Daughter Marlo Thomas costarred and joined Thomas in several musical numbers, their first such feat on film together. *A Rankin-Bass Production in association with Videocraft International. Color. One hour. Premiered on NBC: December 18, 1967 (on The Danny Thomas Hour). Rebroadcast on NBC: November 25, 1971.*

Voices
Cricket Crockett: Roddy McDowell; **Caleb Plummer:** Danny Thomas; **Bertha:** Marlo Thomas; **Edward:** Ed Ames; **Tackleton:** Hans Conried; **Moll:** Abbe Lane; **Uriah/Sea Captain:** Paul Frees

⊚ CURIOUS GEORGE

Named for his natural inquisitiveness, this little monkey and his big-city friend, the Man in the Yellow Hat, encounter numerous misadventures in this half-hour special comprised of several four-minute cartoons from the *Curious George* cartoon series broadcast on Canadian television. *A Lafferty, Harwood and Partners Production in association with Milktrain Productions. Color. Half-hour. Premiered: 1983. Syndicated.*

Voices
Narrator: Jack Duffy

⊚ CYRANO

French folk hero Cyrano de Bergerac conquers injustice in his quest to help his beautiful friend, Roxanne, in this adaptation of Edmond de Rostand's romantic play. The special was first broadcast as an *ABC Afterschool Special. A Hanna-Barbera Production. Color. Half-hour. Premiered on ABC: March 6, 1974. Rebroadcast on ABC: April 9, 1975. Rebroad-*

cast on DIS: April 22, 1992. Rebroadcast on CAR: October 22, 1995 (Mr. Spim's Cartoon Theatre).

Voices
Cyrano de Bergerac: José Ferrer; **Roxanne:** Joan Van Ark; **Ragueneau:** Kurt Kasznar; **Comte de Guiche:** Martyn Green; **Christian de Neuvillette:** Victor Garber; **Duenna:** Jane Connell; **First Cadet/de Brigny:** Alan Oppenheimer; **Richelieu:** John Stephenson

⊚ DAFFY DUCK AND PORKY PIG MEET THE GROOVIE GOOLIES

Warner Bros.' cartoon stars Daffy Duck and Porky Pig join forces with Horrible Hall's the Groovie Goolies in this comic tale of Phantom's efforts to sabotage the movie studio. The made-for-television cartoon premiered on *The ABC Saturday Superstar Movie. A Filmation Associates Production in cooperation with Warner Bros. Color. One hour. Premiered on ABC: December 16, 1972 (on ABC Saturday Superstar Movie). Rebroadcast on ABC: December 29, 1973.*

Voices
Daffy Duck/Porky Pig: Mel Blanc; **The Groovie Goolies: Count Dracula/Hagatha/Frankie/Bella La Ghostly/Sabrina/Wolfie/Bonapart/Mummy/Dr. Jekyll-Hyde/Ghouliland/Hauntleroy/Ratso and Batso:** Jane Webb, Howard Morris, Larry Storch, Larry D. Mann

⊚ DAFFY DUCK'S EASTER SHOW

The malevolent mallard stars in three new cartoon adventures related to the Easter season—"Yolks on You," "The Chocolate Chase" and "Daffy Goes North"—in his first-ever prime-time special, which preceded NBC's Saturday-morning series *The Daffy and Speedy Show*, introduced in the fall of 1981. In 1992 CBS rebroadcast the show under a new title: "Daffy Duck's Easter Egg-citement." *A DePatie-Freleng Enterprises Production for Warner Bros. Television. Color. Half-hour. Premiered on NBC: April 1, 1980. Rebroadcast on NBC: April 14, 1981; April 6, 1982. Rebroadcast on CBS: April 16, 1984; April 6, 1985; April 18, 1992 (as Daffy Duck's Easter Egg-citement).*

Voices
Mel Blanc

⊚ DAFFY DUCK'S THANK-FOR-GIVING SPECIAL

In trying to convince the studio to buy his idea for a sequel to his classic film, "Duck Dodgers in the 24 1/2 Century," Daffy Duck shows the producer all of his great films of the past, interspersed with clips from his earlier theatrical film accomplishments. After the producer finally relents, the show concludes with a screening of "The Return of Duck Dodgers in the 24 1/2 Century," a 1977 cartoon Chuck Jones produced as a companion piece for the science-fiction thriller, *Star Wars*. In 1991, the special was rebroadcast on CBS and retitled, *Daffy Duck Goes Hollywood*, ranking second in the ratings behind ABC's powerhouse sitcom, *Growing Pains*. A *Chuck Jones Enterprises Production for Warner Bros. Television. Color. Half-hour. Premiered on NBC: November 20, 1980. Rebroadcast on NBC: November 24, 1981. CBS: November 12, 1983; November 26, 1987; May 1, 1991 (as* Daffy Duck Goes Hollywood*).*

Voices
Mel Blanc

◎ DAISY-HEAD MAYZIE
A little girl (Mayzie) becomes an instant celebrity—and the target of exploitation—when a daisy grows out of her head one morning in this Emmy-nominated half-hour animated special, based on a 20-year-old unpublished manuscript written by the late Dr. Seuss (alias Ted Geisel). A *Hanna-Barbera/Tony Collingwood Production. Color. Half-hour. Premiered on TNT: February 5, 1995. Rebroadcast on TNT: February 11, 1995.*

Voices
Mayzie: Fran Smith; **Cat in the Hat:** Henry Gibson; **Finagle:** Tim Curry; **Mayor:** George Hearn; **Principal:** Lewis Arquette; **Dr. Eisenbart:** Jonathan Winters; **Miss Sneetcher:** Susan Silo; **Mrs. McGrew:** B.J. Ward; **Mr. McGrew:** Paul Eiding; **Finch:** Robert Ridgely

◎ DANIEL BOONE
Daniel Boone tells his true life story, separating fact from fable, as he reflects upon his life and accomplishments for the benefit of a writer eager to portray the real story in this daytime children's special produced for CBS's *Famous Classic Tales* series. A *Hanna-Barbera Production. Color. Half-hour. Premiered on CBS: November 27, 1981. Rebroadcast on CBS: November 25, 1982.*

Voices
Daniel Boone: Richard Crenna; **Rebecca:** Janet Waldo; **Daniel Boone, age 14:** Bill Callaway; **Henry Miller:** Mike Bell; **Running Fox:** Bill Callaway; **First Settler/Mr. Harding:** Mike Bell; **Stearns/Assemblyman/Squire Boone:** John Stephenson; **Sarah/James/Quiet Dove:** Joan Gerber; **Washington/Col. Morgan/Second Settler:** Joe Baker; **White Top/Painter/Floor Leader:** Vic Perrin; **Blackfish/Business Man/Indian Dragging Canoe:** Barney Phillips; **Girty/Oconostata/Finley:** Michael Rye

◎ DARKWING DUCK: IT'S A WONDERFUL LEAF
Bushroot plots to ruin Christmas by making Christmas trees in order to steal the presents in this half-hour holiday special, based on the popular *Disney Afternoon* syndicated series. A *Walt Disney Television Animation Production. Color. Half-hour. Premiered: December 23, 1991. Syndicated.*

Voices
Darkwing Duck: Jim Cummings; **Gosalyn Mallard:** Christine Cavanaugh; **Launchpad McQuack:** Terry McGovern; **Bushroot:** Tino Insana

◎ THE DARKWING DUCK PREMIERE/BACK TO SCHOOL WITH THE MICKEY MOUSE CLUB
The debut of Disney's newest cartoon series, *Darkwing Duck*, and the return of The Disney Channel's *The Mickey Mouse Club* are celebrated in this two-hour, first-run syndicated special featuring the episode "Darkly Dawns the Duck," which tells the origin of Darkwing Duck, and several segments from a new season of *The Mickey Mouse Club*. A *Walt Disney Television Animation Production. Color. Two hours. Premiered: September 8, 1991. Syndicated.*

Cast (live action)
Fred Newman, Terri Misner, Josh Ackerman, Lindsey Alley, Rhona Bennett, Nita Booth, Mylin Brooks, Blaine Carson, JC Chasez, Tasha Danner, Dale Godboldo, Tony Lucca, Ricky Lunda, Jennifer McGill, Terra McNair, Ilana Miller, Jason Minor, Matt Morris, Kevin Osgood, Keri Russell, Marc Worden. **The Party:** Albert Fields, Tiffini Hale, Chase Hampton, Deedee Magno, Damon Pampolina

Voices
Darkwing Duck: Jim Cummings; **Gosalyn Mallard:** Christine Cavanaugh; **Launchpad McQuack:** Terry McGovern; **Taurus Bulba:** Tim Curry; **Hammerhead Hannigan:** Laurie Faso; **Huge Jerk:** Hal Rayle; **Clovis/Mrs. Cavanaugh:** Marcia Wallace

◎ DAVID COPPERFIELD
The story of David Copperfield, one of Charles Dickens's most beloved creations, is revealed in this 90-minute cable-television special that takes viewers through every stage of his life and the many struggles he encounters along the way. A *Burbank Films Production. Color. Ninety minutes. Premiered on HBO: October 2, 1984.*

Voices
Ross Higgins, Phillip Hinton, Robyn Moore, Judy Nunn, Moya O'Sullivan, Robin Steward, John Stone

⊚ DAVY CROCKETT
ON THE MISSISSIPPI

American frontiersman Davy Crockett and his talking pet bear, Honeysuckle, are joined by an orphaned boy, Matt Henry, as they journey to meet the Indians on behalf of the U.S. president as part of a peacekeeping mission. *A Hanna-Barbera Production. Color. One hour. Premiered on CBS: November 20, 1976. Rebroadcast on CBS: October 22, 1977; November 2, 1980; November 26, 1982. Rebroadcast on CAR: October 8, 1995 (Mr. Spim's Cartoon Theatre).*

Voices
Davy Crockett: Ned Wilson; **Matt Henry:** Randy Gray; **Honeysuckle/Pete/The Settler:** Mike Bell; **Mike Fink/Flatboat Sailor:** Ron Feinberg; **Running Wolf/Jake:** Kip Niven; **Settler's Wife/Amanda/Susie:** Pat Parris; **Sloan/Andrew Jackson/Blacksmith:** John Stephenson

⊚ DECK THE HALLS

It is nearly Christmas when two recently orphaned children have to choose with which of their relatives they will live—eccentric, stingy Aunt Edwina or kindly Uncle Robert—

Edwina Benson puts the crowning touch on her Christmas tree, as her nephew, niece and butler look on, in Deck the Halls, *a half-hour animated special from Perennial Pictures. © Perennial Pictures*

only to have surprises in store for them when they make their choices in this half-hour holiday special, produced for first-run syndication. *A Perennial Pictures Film Corporation Production. Color. Half-hour. Premiered: November 24, 1994. Syndicated.*

Voices
Aunt Edwina: Rachel Rutledge; **Uncle Robert/Baxter:** Jerry Reynolds; **Wadsworth:** Chris Cawthorne; **Andrew:** Peter Schmutte; **Allison:** Kimberly Ann Harris

⊚ DECK THE HALLS
WITH WACKY WALLS

Six Wallwalkers (Wacky, Big Blue, Springette, Stickum, Crayzlegs and Bouncing Baby Boo) are sent to Earth from their distant planet to find what Christmas is all about in this half-hour animated special based on the Wacky Wall-walker toys. *An NBC Entertainment Production in association with Buzzco Productions. Color. Half-hour. Premiered on NBC: December 11, 1983.*

Voices
Wacky: Daws Butler; **Big Blue:** Peter Cullen; **Springette:** Tress MacNeille; **Stickum:** Marvin Kaplan; **Crazylegs:** Howard Morris; **Bouncing Baby Boo:** Frank Welker; **Darryl:** Scott Menville

⊚ DENNIS THE MENACE:
MAYDAY FOR MOTHER

In his first prime-time special, neighborhood terror Dennis the Menace encounters a variety of problems in attempting to create a special Mother's Day gift for his mother, Alice Mitchell. The special was based on an original story by creator Hank Ketcham. *A DePatie-Freleng Enterprises Production in association with Mirisch Films. Color. Half-hour. Premiered on NBC: May 8, 1981. Rebroadcast on NBC: May 6, 1983.*

Voices
Dennis Mitchell: Joey Nagy; **Alice Mitchell:** Kathy Garver; **Henry Mitchell:** Bob Holt; **George Wilson:** Larry D. Mann; **Martha Wilson:** Elizabeth Kerr; **Margaret:** Nicole Eggert

⊚ THE DEVIL AND DANIEL MOUSE

Jan and Daniel Mouse, recently unemployed folk singers, try making a fresh start with their careers, only for Jan to sign a contract with B.L. Zebub, the devil in disguise, to sell her soul to become a rock star legend. *A Nelvana Limited Production in association with the CBC. Color. Half-hour. Premiered: October 22, 1978. Syndicated.*

Voices
Daniel Mouse: Jim Henshaw, John Sebastian (singing); **Jan:** Annabelle Kershaw, Laurel Runn (singing); **B.L. Zebub, the devil:** Chris Wiggins; **Weez Weasel/Pawnbroker:** Martin Lavut; **Rock Emcee:** John Sebastian; **Interviewer:** Dianne Lawrence

◎ DIG

Explaining the wonders of Earth, Adam and his dog, Bones, explore the geological structure of the planet during a fascinating journey in which they meet strange characters and encounter various phenomena. The special aired in place of CBS's *The Monkees*, which was in reruns on Saturday mornings. *A Hubley Studio Production. Color. Half-hour. Premiered on CBS April 8, 1972. Rebroadcast on CBS: May 5, 1973.*

Voices
Adam: Ray Hubley; **Mother:** Maureen Stapleton; **Rocco:** Jack Warden; **Fossil Pillar:** Morris Carnovsky; **First Rock:** Phil Leeds; **Vocalists:** Harry "Sweets" Edison, Don Elliott, Ruth Price

◎ A DISNEY CHANNEL CHRISTMAS

Jiminy Cricket hosts (and also sings a special version of "When You Wish Upon a Star") this holiday look at the Christmas season featuring a medley of clips from numerous Christmas-themed cartoons, including "A Night Before Christmas," "Santa's Workshop" and "Pluto's Christmas Tree," plus a look at "Mickey's Christmas Carol" in this Disney Channel original production. *A Film Landa Inc. Production for The Disney Channel. Color. Ninety minutes. Premiered on DIS: December 3, 1983.*

◎ A DISNEY CHRISTMAS GIFT

Favorite scenes from Walt Disney Studios' classic animated features, including *Bambi*, *Peter Pan*, *The Three Caballeros* and *Cinderella* and a few memorable cartoon shorts, namely "The Clock Watcher" starring Donald Duck, are tied together in this prime-time holiday special celebrating Christmases past. *A Walt Disney Television Production. Color. One hour. Premiered on CBS: December 20, 1983.*

Voices
Peter Pan: Bobby Driscoll; **Fairy Godmother:** Verna Felton; **Cinderella:** Ilene Woods

◎ A DISNEY HALLOWEEN

Disney's treatment of witches, ghosts and goblins from the studio's classic films and cartoons make up this Disney Channel original production. It includes Mickey, Donald and Goofy as ghost hunters, the frenzied dance demons from the classic animated feature *Fantasia* (1940) and Donald Duck in the 1952 cartoon short, "Trick Or Treat." *A Film Landa Inc. Production for The Disney Channel. Color. Ninety minutes. Premiered on DIS: October 1, 1983.*

◎ DISNEY'S ALL-STAR MOTHER'S DAY ALBUM

The subject of motherhood is celebrated in this compilation special featuring clips from assorted Disney cartoons including the memorable feature film *Peter Pan* (1953), and many classic cartoon shorts, among them "Mickey and the Seal" (1948), "Pluto's Fledgling" (1948) and "Donald's Nephews" (1938). The special closes with a segment featuring the fairy godmother from *Cinderella* (1950) transforming a depressed girl into a fairy princess. *A Walt Disney Television Production. Color. One hour. Premiered on CBS: May 11, 1984.*

◎ DISNEY'S ALL-STAR VALENTINE PARTY

Popular Los Angeles radio disc jockey Rick Dees narrates this collection of scenes from classic Disney cartoons that depict love and friendship. Scenes were culled from "Mickey's Rival" (1936), "The Brave Tin Soldier" (1938), "Pluto's Heart Throb" (1949) and others. *A Walt Disney Television Production. Color. One hour. Premiered on CBS: February 14, 1984.*

Voices
Narrator: Rick Dees

◎ DISNEY'S DTV DOGGONE HITS

(See DISNEY'S DTV DOGGONE VALENTINE.)

◎ DISNEY'S DTV DOGGONE VALENTINE

Hosted by Mickey Mouse, Minnie Mouse, Professor Ludwig von Drake and others, this one-hour special salutes man's best friend with a series of entertaining clips of favorite dog scenes and characters, culled from Disney full-length features and cartoon shorts, set to a rock beat and featuring the music of Kenny Rogers, Huey Lewis and Deniece Williams. *An Andrew Solt Production in association Walt Disney Television. Color. One hour. Premiered on NBC: February 13, 1987. Rebroadcast on NBC: February 19, 1988 (as Disney's DTV Doggone Hits). Rebroadcast on DIS: February 4, 1992; February 2, 1994.*

Voices
Mickey Mouse: Wayne Allwine; **Minnie Mouse/Dalamation Puppy:** Russi Taylor; **Professor Ludwig von Drake:**

Albert Ash; **Jiminy Cricket:** Eddie Carroll; **Goofy:** Bill Farmer; **Pongo:** Will Ryan; **Dalamation Puppies:** Lisa St. James; **Radio Announcer:** Maurice LaMarche; **Announcer:** J.J. Jackson

◉ DISNEY'S DTV MONSTER HITS

In the style of past "DTV" specials, Disney salutes Halloween in this slightly scary collection of cartoon clips featuring scenes from classic Disney cartoons set to music. Includes "Lonesome Ghosts" (1937), starring Mickey Mouse, Donald Duck and Goofy, with Ray Parker's "Ghostbusters" theme, "Bad Moon Rising" by Creedence Clearwater Revival and Bobby "Boris" Pickett's classic Halloween romp, "Monster Mash." Also included is a special montage salute to Disney's villains set to the Eurythmics' hit song "Sweet Dreams." *A Walt Disney Television Production. Color. Half-hour. Premiered on NBC: October 30, 1987. Rebroadcast on DIS.*

◉ DISNEY'S DTV ROMANCIN'

(See DISNEY'S DTV VALENTINE.)

◉ DISNEY'S DTV VALENTINE

Clips from Disney cartoons timed to rock-and-roll music highlight this Valentine's Day special hosted by Mickey Mouse, Donald Duck, Jiminy Cricket and Professor Ludwig von Drake. *An Andrew Solt Production in association with Walt Disney Television. Color. One hour. Premiered on NBC: February 14, 1986. Rebroadcast on NBC: September 7, 1986 (as Disney's DTV Romancin').*

Voices
Mickey Mouse: Les Perkins; **Donald Duck:** Tony Anselmo; **Jiminy Cricket:** Eddie Carroll; **Professor Ludwig von Drake:** Paul Frees; **Gruffi Gummi:** Corey Burton; **Goofy/Pongo:** Will Ryan; **Chip/Dale/Female Voice:** Judith Searle; **Dalamatian Puppies:** Lisa St. James; **Sleeping Beauty:** Mary Costa; **Princess Aura:** Mary Costa; **Prince Phillip:** Bill Shirley; **Announcer:** Paul Frees

◉ DISNEY'S FLUPPY DOGS

Off course from their real destination, several out-of-this-universe dogs (Stanley, Ozzie, Tippi, Bink and Dink), who possess magical powers, arrive on Earth, where they are forced to act like normal dogs when their real presence sends panic into local citizens. Their teenage friends, Jaimie and Claire, aid their escape in order for them to return home through the interdimensional doorway from which they came. *A Walt Disney Television Production in association with TMS Entertainment. Color. One hour. Premiered on ABC:* *November 27, 1986. Rebroadcast on ABC: August 30, 1987 (as* The Sunday Disney Movie*).*

Voices
Jaimie Bingham: Carl Stevens; **Bink/Tippi:** Susan Blu; **Stanley:** Marshall Efron; **Mrs. Bingham:** Cloyce Morrow; **Ozzie:** Lorenzo Music; **Claire:** Jessica Pennington; **Wagstaff:** Michael Rye; **Haimish/Attendant/Dink:** Hal Smith

◉ DISNEY'S GOOF TROOP

Disney's syndicated series *Goof Troop* premiered as this two-hour special season opener in which Goofy returns to his hometown of Spoonerville with his teenage son Max to experience a whole new series of adventures as a 1990s-style dad. Also featured: a new music video, "Gotta Be Gettin' Goofy" by rap artist The CEO and "The Goofy Success Story," a cartoon short chronicling Goofy's remarkable career. *A Walt Disney Television Animation Production. Color. Two hours. Premiered: September 5, 1992.*

◉ DISNEY'S HALLOWEEN TREAT

Halloween is the theme of this Disney prime-time special, featuring witches, goblins and ghouls and classic Disney characters in a collection of excerpts from favorite screen moments of the past. *A Walt Disney Television Production. Color. One hour. Premiered on CBS: October 30, 1982. Rebroadcast on NBC: October 29, 1983. Rebroadcast on DIS: October 18, 1992.*

Voices
Peter Pan: Bobby Driscoll; **Si/Am (Lady and the Tramp):** Peggy Lee

◉ DISNEY'S POCAHONTAS . . . THE MUSICAL TRADITION CONTINUES

The music of Oscar-winning composer Alan Menken is celebrated in this starstudded half-hour animated musical special weaving clips from *Aladdin, Beauty and the Beast* and the studio's 33rd full-length animated feature, *Pocahontas* with video-style recorded performances of songs from the films' soundtracks by popular recording artists Regina Belle, Peabo Bryson, Celine Dion, Jon Secada, Vanessa Williams and Shanice Wilson. *A Walt Disney Production. Color. Half-hour. Premiered on ABC: June 20, 1995.*

◉ DISNEY'S ROOTIN' TOOTIN' ROUNDUP

Animated host Saddlesore Sam introduces this showcase of classic Disney cartoons about the Wild West including

"The Legend of Coyote Rock," "Donald's Gold Mine," "Little Hiawatha" and "The Lone Chipmunks," which are presented in this Disney Channel original production. A *Robert Heath Inc. Production for The Disney Channel. Color. Ninety minutes. Premiered on DIS: 1990.*

◎ DISNEY'S SALUTE TO MOM

Memorable clips from Disney full-length features and cartoon shorts—including *Bambi, Lady and the Tramp, Dumbo* and *One Hundred and One Dalmatians*—are featured in this hour-long clip fest, originally shown on The Disney Channel in 1994 under the title *A Tribute to Mom* (a 90-minute version), which celebrated mothers of all ages. A *Film Landa Inc. Production for The Disney Channel. Color. One hour. Premiered on DIS: May 14, 1955.*

◎ DISNEY'S TALE SPIN PLUNDER & LIGHTNING

Cargo pilot Baloo is aided by a young thief named Kit Cloudkicker (who hides in Baloo's plane) in foiling the evil Don Karnage, who plots to steal a precious jewel in this two-hour pilot for the Disney weekday syndicated series *Tale Spin. A Walt Disney Television Animation Production. Color. Two hours. Premiered: September 7, 1990. Syndicated.*

Voices
Baloo: Ed Gilbert; **Don Karnage/Louie:** Jim Cummings; **Kit Cloudkicker:** R.J. Williams; **Rebecca Cunningham:** Sally Struthers; **Molly Cunningham:** Janna Michaels; **Shere Khan:** Tony Jay; **Dumptruck:** Chuck McCann; **Mad Dog:** Charlie Adler; **Wildcat:** Pat Fraley

◎ DISNEY'S THE LITTLE MERMAID: "A WHALE OF A TALE"

Beautiful young mermaid Ariel tries to prevent King Triton from finding about her pet killer whale, whom he feels would be better off in the wild, in this half-hour "preview" special to the Saturday-morning series that aired on CBS. A *Walt Disney Television Animation Production. Color. Half-hour. Premiered on CBS: September 11, 1992. Rebroadcast on CBS: September 10, 1993.*

Voices
Ariel: Jodi Benson; **Sebastian:** Samuel E. Wright; **Flounder:** Edan Gross; **King Triton:** Kenneth Mars

◎ DR. SEUSS' HALLOWEEN IS GRINCH NIGHT

The people of Whoville are plagued by a "sour-sweet wind," suggesting only one thing—the nasty Grinch, who dwells atop dreadful Mt. Crumpit, cannot be far away. A young lad, Ukariah, bravely faces the evil Grinch in order to save his people. Joining the Grinch in his acts of evil-doing: his dog, Max. Hans Conreid, effective in earlier specials, returns as the program's narrator. A *Dr. Seuss and A.S. Giesel Production in association with DePatie-Freleng Enterprises. Color. Premiered on ABC: October 29, 1977. Rebroadcast on ABC: October 26, 1978; October 28, 1979; October 30, 1980. Rebroadcast on DIS: October 13, 1991; October 17, 1992. Rebroadcast on CAR: November 1, 1997.*

Voices
Grinch: Hans Conried; **Grandpa Joseph:** Hal Smith; **Grandma Mariah:** Irene Tedrow; **Ukariah:** Gary Shapiro

◎ DR. SEUSS' HORTON HEARS A WHO!

Hearing a small voice—"as if some tiny person were calling for help"—Horton the Elephant discovers microscopic creatures floating aboard a speck of dust, headed by the minuscule Dr. Whoovy, who is trying to convince his followers there is another world outside theirs. For "pretending" to talk to his unseen dust friends, Horton is finally seized by his jungle companions, but all comes to a happy ending as Whoovy in turn hears a voice from an even smaller fleck of dust. Based on the Dr. Seuss children's fable of the same name, the program played up the theme: "A person's a person no matter how small." A *Chuck Jones Enterprises Production in association with The Cat in the Hat Productions and MGM-TV. Color. Half-hour. Premiered on CBS: March 19, 1970. Rebroadcast on CBS: September 19, 1971; July 31, 1972; April 20, 1973; February 4, 1974; March 24, 1975; March 19, 1976; May 13, 1977; August 4, 1978. Rebroadcast on CAR: June 3, 1994 (Turner Family Showcase); August 14, 1995.*

Voices
Narrator: Hans Conried

◎ DR. SEUSS' HOW THE GRINCH STOLE CHRISTMAS

Perennial favorite based on the popular Dr. Seuss fable about old meanie Grinch almost ruining Christmas for the townspeople of the little village of Whoville because either "his heart was two sizes small or he wore tight shoes." CBS reportedly spent $350,000 for this animated special, originally sponsored by the Foundation for Commercial Banks. The program preempted the network's *Lassie* series, airing in its time slot. A *Chuck Jones Enterprises Production in association with The Cat in the Hat Productions and MGM-TV. Color. Half-hour. Premiered on CBS: December 18, 1966. Rebroacast on CBS: December*

17, 1967; December 22, 1968; December 21, 1969; December 2, 1970; December 7, 1971; December 4, 1972; December 10, 1973; December 13, 1974; December 12, 1975; December 18, 1976; December 10, 1977; December 16, 1978; December 19, 1979; November 28, 1980; December 16, 1981; December 18, 1982; December 12, 1983; December 5, 1984; December 7, 1985; December 17, 1986; December 11, 1987. Rebroadcast on TNT: December 6, 1990; December 5, 1991 (opposite Dr. Seuss' The Butter Battle Book); December 1, 1992. Rebroadcast on TBS: December 13, 1992; November 28, 1993. Rebroadcast on TNT: November 29, 1993. Rebroadcast on TBS: December 5, 1993. Rebroadcast on CAR: November 25, 1995; December 4, 1996. Rebroadcast on TNT: December 14, 1996. Rebroadcast on TBS: December 17, 1995; December 6, 1996.

Voices
Grinch: Thurl Ravenscroft (singing); **Cindy Lou:** June Foray; **Narrator:** Boris Karloff

DR. SEUSS' HOW THE GRINCH STOLE CHRISTMAS SPECIAL EDITION

Phil Hartman hosts this hour-long show that includes, in addition to the original half-hour special, never-before seen footage and an interview with the show's animator, director and coproducer, the legendary Chuck Jones. *A Turner Network Television Production. Color. One hour. Premiered on TNT: December 3, 1994. Rebroadcast on TNT: December 1, 1996.*

DR. SEUSS ON THE LOOSE

Dr. Seuss returns in this animated trilogy based on three of his classic fables—*The Sneetches*, featuring ostrichlike creatures who learn to treat each other as equals; *Green Eggs and Ham*, showing the silliness of prejudging; and *The Zax*, dealing with the subject of stubborness—which Seuss (Ted Geisel) coproduced. *A DePatie-Freleng Enterprises Production in association with CBS. Color. Half-hour. Premiered on CBS: October 15, 1973. Rebroadcast on CBS: October 28, 1974; November 21, 1975; March 9, 1976; July 12, 1979.*

Voices
The Cat in the Hat (host): Allan Sherman; **Zax (narrator):** Hans Conried; **Joey/Sam-I-Am:** Paul Winchell; **Zax/Sylvester McMonkey McBeam:** Bob Holt

DR. SEUSS' PONTOFFEL POCK, WHERE ARE YOU?

Misfit Pontoffel Pock has blown his opportunity at the pickle factory and gets a second chance when some good fairies provide him with a push-button piano that has the power to transport him anywhere. *A Dr. Seuss and A.S. Gelsel Production in association with DePatie-Freleng Enterprises. Color. Half-hour. Premiered on ABC: May 2, 1980. Rebroadcast on ABC: July 31, 1981. Rebroadcast on DIS: February 23, 1992. Rebroadcast on CAR: August 17, 1995.*

Voices
Pontoffel Pock: Wayne Morton; **Neepha Pheepha:** Sue Allen; **McGillicuddy:** Hal Smith

DR. SEUSS' THE BUTTER BATTLE BOOK

In the first new Dr. Seuss special in seven years, a musical adaptation of Dr. Seuss's parable about the arms race, the Yooks square off against the Zooks, separated by a Great Wall and by a philosophical disagreement over which side to butter their bread on. *A Bakshi Production in association with Ted S. Geisel. Color. Half-hour. Premiered on TNT: November 13, 1989. Rebroadcast on TNT: September 29, 1991. Rebroadcast on CAR: June 3, 1994: (Turner Family Showcase); March 5, 1995 (Mr. Spim's Cartoon Theatre); May 26, 1996 (Mr. Spim's Cartoon Theatre).*

Voices
Narrator: Charles Durning

DR. SEUSS' THE CAT IN THE HAT

Two children who are bored by the prospects of staying home all day because of the rain are greeted by a surprise visitor, the Cat in the Hat, who turns the house upside

Which side of the bread to butter becomes a source of disagreement for the Yooks and the Zooks in the Dr. Seuss animated parable, Dr. Seuss' The Butter Battle Book. © Bakshi Productions

down looking for his moss-covered three-handled gradunza. He virtually destroys the home in the process, but magically restores the structure to its former state before the kids' mother returns. *A DePatie-Freleng Enterprises Production. Color. Half-hour. Premiered on CBS: March 10, 1971. Rebroadcast on CBS: April 11, 1972; February 20, 1973; January 4, 1974; January 31, 1975; March 30, 1976; August 20, 1979; September 20, 1980; May 15, 1987; January 5, 1988. Rebroadcast on CAR: August 15, 1995.*

Voices
Cat in the Hat: Allan Sherman; **Karlos K. Krinklebein:** Daws Butler; **Boy:** Tony Frazier; **Girl:** Pamelyn Ferdin; **Mother:** Gloria Camacho; **Thing 1:** Thurl Ravenscroft; **Thing 2:** Lewis Morford

⊚ DR. SEUSS' THE GRINCH GRINCHES THE CAT IN THE HAT

Grouchy Grinch employs a variety of self-made contraptions to get even with the Cat in the Hat but instead is taught manners by the amiable cat. *A Dr. Seuss and A.S. Geisel Production in association with Marvel Productions. Color. Half-hour. Premiered on ABC: May 20, 1982. Rebroadcast on ABC: August 7, 1983. Rebroadcast on DIS: November 2, 1991; May 5, 1992.*

Voices
Mason Adams, Joe Eich, Bob Holt, Marilyn Jackson, Melissa Mackay, Frank Welker, Richard B. Williams

⊚ DR. SEUSS' THE HOOBER-BLOOB HIGHWAY

Young humans are sent down an imaginary ribbon of light—known as the Hoober-Bloob Highway—to Earth by the chief dispatcher, Hoober-Bloob, who briefs them on the pros and cons of Earthbound living. Dr. Seuss (Ted Geisel) wrote the special. *A De-Patie Freleng Enterprises Production. Color. Half-hour. Premiered on CBS: February 19, 1975. Rebroadcast on CBS: March 23, 1976; November 15, 1977; September 9, 1981. Rebroadcast on DIS: October 31, 1993. Rebroadcast on CAR: May 26, 1996 (Mr. Spim's Cartoon Theatre).*

Voices
Bob Holt, Hal Smith

⊚ DR. SEUSS' THE LORAX

The Lorax, a spokesman for saving trees from the woodsman's axe, sets out to stop the evil Once-ler from destroying all the trees in the forest to help local industrialists prosper.

Program originally aired in the time slot usually reserved for CBS's *Gunsmoke. A DePatie-Freleng Enterprises Production. Color. Half-hour. Premiered on CBS: February 14, 1972. Rebroadcast on CBS: March 28, 1973; March 25, 1974; July 19, 1977; August 4, 1978. Rebroadcast on DIS: October 26, 1993. Rebroadcast on CAR: August 16, 1995; May 26, 1996 (Mr. Spim's Cartoon Theatre).*

Voices
Lorax/Once-ler: Bob Holt; **Boy:** Harlen Carraher; **Other Voices:** Athena Lorde; **Narrator:** Eddie Albert

⊚ DONALD DUCK'S 50TH BIRTHDAY

Comedian Dick Van Dyke hosts this hour-long golden anniversary retrospective of Hollywood's favorite duck utilizing clips from films spanning his career and introduced by special guests including Ed Asner, Bruce Jenner, Cloris Leachman, John Ritter, Kenny Rogers, Donna Summer, Andy Warhol, Henry Winkler and *Star Wars* characters C-3P0 and R2D2. *An Andrew Solt Production in association with Walt Disney Television. Color. One hour. Premiered on CBS: November 13, 1984. Rebroadcast on CBS: October 29, 1985.*

Voices
Donald Duck: Clarence Nash; **C-3P0:** Anthony Daniels; **R2D2:** (electronic)

⊚ DONALD'S 50TH BIRTHDAY

Donald Duck's illustrious career is recounted through clips from many of his cartoon and film appearances in this 90-minute special for The Disney Channel. *A Film Landa Inc. Production for The Disney Channel. Color. Ninety minutes. Premiered on DIS: 1984.*

⊚ A DOONESBURY SPECIAL

Zonker Harris, the lead character in Garry Trudeau's popular *Doonesbury* strip, reflects on social and political issues of the past—flower children, college campus bombings and other cynical observations—in this nostalgic half-hour special, which was released to theaters as well as television and received an Academy Award nomination for Best Animated Film. *A John and Faith Hubley Films Production in association with Universal Press Syndicate. Color. Half-hour. Premiered on NBC: November 27, 1977.*

Voices
Zonker Harris: Richard Cox; **Joanie Caucus:** Barbara Harris; **Mike:** David Grant; **Mark Slackmeyer/Ralphie:** Charles Levin; **B.D.:** Richard Bruno; **Boopsie:** Rebecca Nelson; **Rev. Scott Sloan:** Rev. William Sloane Coffin Jr.; **Referee:**

Jack Gilford; **Kirby:** Mark Baker; **Frank:** Eric Elice; **Calvin:** Ben Haley, Jr.; **Sportscaster:** Will Jordan; **Ellie:** Linda Baer; **Howie:** Eric Jaffe; **Jeannie:** Michelle Browne; **Rufus:** Thomas Baxton; **Magus:** Lenny Jackson; **Virgin Mary:** Patrice Leftwich; **Jimmy Thudpacker:** Jimmy Thudpacker

◎ DOUG AND RUGRATS CHRISTMAS

Two half-hour holiday episodes from Nickelodeon's popular animated series, *Doug* and *Rugrats*, were repackaged in this hour-long syndicated special. *A Jumbo Pictures/Klasky Csupo Production. Color. One hour. Premiered: December 1, 1996. Syndicated.*

◎ DOUG'S HALLOWEEN ADVENTURE

Bristle-haired Doug and his best friend Skeeter go to an amusement park for the grand opening of "the scariest ride ever made" in his first prime-time cable network special, spun off from the popular Nickelodeon cartoon series. *A Jumbo Pictures Production. Color. Half-hour. Premiered on NIK: October 30, 1993.*

Voices
Doug Funnie: Billy West; **Skeeter Valentine:** Fred Newman

◎ DOUG'S SECRET CHRISTMAS

Doug experiences a major crisis (at least major to him) in his life: He doesn't understand why his family fails to celebrate Christmas in the traditional way in this prime-time holiday special, based on the ABC animated series *Brand Spanking New Doug*. The program premiered opposite *Edith Ann's Christmas* on ABC. *A Jumbo Pictures Production in association with Walt Disney Television. Color. Half-hour. Premiered on ABC: December 14, 1996.*

Voices
Doug Funnie: Billy West; **Judy Funnie:** Becca Lish; **Skeeter Valentine:** Fred Newman; **Patti Mayonnaise:** Constance Shulman

◎ DOWN AND OUT WITH DONALD DUCK

The up-and-down life of Donald Duck is chronicled in this *60 Minutes*–style "duckumentary" that combines clips from more than 30 hours of previously exhibited Donald Duck cartoons. *A Garen-Albrecht Production in association with Walt Disney Television. Color. One hour. Premiered on NBC: March 25, 1987. Rebroadcast on NBC: April 29, 1988.*

Voices
Donald Duck/Daisy Duck: Tony Anselmo; **Huey/Dewey/Louie:** Tony Anselmo; **Professor Ludwig von Drake:**

Albert Ash; **Mickey Mouse:** Les Perkins; **Goofy/Peg-Leg Pete:** Will Ryan; **Narrator:** Stan Freberg; **Announcer:** Harry Shearer

◎ DTV²: THE SPECIAL

Classic Disney animation, set to the music of Huey Lewis, Elton John and other performers and featuring such hit songs as "1, 2, 3," "Come On, Let's Go" and "Heart and Soul," fill out this music video-styled (dubbed "DTV") live-action/animated special hosted by Nina Peoples for The Disney Channel. *A Brighton Group Production for The Disney Channel. Color. Half-hour. Premiered on DIS: 1989.*

◎ DUCKTALES: THE MOVIE SPECIAL

Tracey Golden and Kadeem Hardison are hosts of this half-hour preview special produced to hype the release of Disney's full-length animated feature *DuckTales The Movie: The Treasure of the Lost Lamp*. Featured are clips from the movie as well as various adventures from the popular syndicated series. *A Walt Disney Television Animation Production. Color. Half-hour. Premiered: August 1, 1990.*

◎ DUCKTALES: "TIME IS MONEY"

When Scrooge McDuck buys an island that ends up being full of diamonds, his heartless rival, the notorious Flintheart Glomgold, blows the island in two so he'll have all the diamonds while McDuck has only the other worthless half in this two-hour special based on the syndicated series. The special was later rebroadcast in five parts. *A Walt Disney Television Animation Production. Color. Two hours. Premiered: November 25, 1988.*

Voices
Uncle Scrooge McDuck: Alan Young; **Launchpad McQuack:** Terence McGovern; **Huey/Dewey/Louie/Webbigail Vanderduck:** Russi Taylor; **Duckworth:** Don Hills, Chuck McCann; **Gyro Gearloose/Flintheart Glomgold:** Hal Smith; **Mrs. Beakley/Webra Walters:** Joan Gerber; **Sen-Sen:** Haunani Minn; **Bubba Duck/Big Time Beagle:** Frank Welker; **Myng-Ho:** Keone Young

◎ DUCKTALES: "TREASURE OF THE GOLDEN SUNS"

Donald Duck's cantankerous canard uncle, Scrooge McDuck, the world's richest tightwad, is joined by Donald's nephews, Huey, Dewey and Louie, in daring exploits and risky undertakings in this two-hour preview special of the popular syndicated series, which debuted three days later.

The special was then shown in five parts during the series' regular syndicated run. *A Walt Disney Television Animation Production. Color. Two hours. Premiered: September 18, 1987.*

Voices
Uncle Scrooge McDuck: Alan Young; **Donald Duck:** Tony Anselmo; **Huey/Dewey/Louie:** Russi Taylor; **Duckworth:** Joan Gerber, Chuck McCann; **El Capitan:** Peter Cullen, Jim Cummings; **Skittles:** Terence McGovern, Patty Parris

THE EASTER BUNNY IS COMIN' TO TOWN

Through the wonders of Animagic, Fred Astaire, as old friend/mailman S.D. Kluger from *Santa Claus Is Comin' to Town*, relates how the traditions of Easter and the excitement brought by the holiday—the Easter bunny, decorating eggs and chocolate bunnies—first came about in the town of Kidville, a city reserved for children. Astaire sings the title song and "Can Do," one of six original songs written for the program. *A Rankin-Bass Production. Color. One hour. Premiered on ABC: April 6, 1977. Rebroadcast on ABC: March 20, 1978; April 14, 1978; April 5, 1980. Rebroadcast on DIS: March 23, 1994; March 29, 1997.*

Voices
S.D. Kluger (narrator): Fred Astaire; **Sunny, the Easter Bunny:** Skip Hinnant; **Chugs:** Robert McFadden; **Hallelujah Jones:** Ron Marshall; **King Bruce:** James Spies; **Lilly Longtooth:** Meg Sargent

EASTER EGG MORNIN'

The voice and songs of pop music superstar Bobby Goldsboro highlight this animated Easter tale following the adventures of Picasso "Speedy" Cottontail. Known to boast of his fame as the "egg-painting Easter bunny," Cottontail finds himself in a fix when, with Easter fast approaching, the chickens go on strike and won't lay eggs. This half-hour holiday special was produced by Goldsboro. *A Bobby Goldsboro Production in association with Peeler-Rose Productions. Color. Half-hour. Premiered on DIS: 1990.*

Voices
Picasso "Speedy" Cottontail: Bobby Goldsboro; **Henrietta/Snake:** Pat Childs; **Owlbert:** Tim Tappan

EASTER FEVER

The Easter Bunny, alias Jack the Rabbit, is the subject of a celebrity-type roast in honor of his retirement from the Easter egg business. Don Rattles and Steed Martin (animal characterizations of comedians Don Rickles and Steve Martin) head the all-star salute. Just when he thinks his career is over, however, Jack is convinced by a pleading aardvark to change his mind. *A Nelvana Limited Production in association with the CBC. Color. Half-hour. Premiered: March 30, 1980. Syndicated.*

Voices
Jack, the Easter Bunny: Garrett Morris; **Don Rattles/Steed Martin:** Maurice LaMarche; **Santa Claus/Baker:** Chris Wiggins; **Madame Malegg:** Jeri Craden; **Aardvark:** Jim Henshaw; **Scarlett O'Hare:** Catherine O'Hara; **Scrawny Chicken:** Melleny Brown; **Ratso Rat:** Larry Mollin; **Announcer:** Don Ferguson

EASTER IS

Benji is confronted with the prospect of losing his pet dog, Waldo, if he doesn't pay the dog's captor ransom: $5. Waldo manages to escape, making his return home even more dramatic by coming back to his master on Easter morning. *A Screen Images Production for Lutheran Television. Color. Half-hour. Premiered: March, 1974. Syndicated.*

Voices
Benji: David Kelly; **Schoolteacher:** Leslie Uggams; **Martin:** Phillip Morris

EDITH ANN: A FEW PIECES OF THE PUZZLE

Upset that nobody in her family remembered her birthday, Edith Ann plays hooky and lands in the school counselor's office. Her meeting with the counselor and subsequent situations provide a waif's-eye view of her imperfect life in the first of three half-hour animated adaptations of Lily Tomlin's classic comedy character, written by Tomlin's longtime collaborator Jane Wagner. Two more specials followed this effort: *Edith Ann: Homeless Go Home* (1994) and *Edith Ann Christmas* (1996), also on ABC. *A Klasky-Csupo/Anivision/Tomlin/Wagner Production. Color. Half-hour. Premiered on ABC: January 18, 1994.*

Voices
Edith Ann: Lily Tomlin

EDITH ANN: HOMELESS GO HOME

Edith Ann opposes a petition that would ban a proposed shelter for the homeless, which one petitioner claims would leave Edgetown jammed with "bums and bag ladies bumper to bumper," in this second in a series of Edith Ann specials. *A Klasky-Csupo/Tomlin/Wagner Production. Color. Half-hour. Premiered on ABC: May 27, 1994.*

Voices
Edith Ann: Lily Tomlin

◎ EDITH ANN'S CHRISTMAS
When Edith's older sister Irene gets her bottom tattooed, Edith tattles to her parents, causing Irene to run away and leaving Edith trying to patch things up in time for Christmas in this third half-hour outing based on Lily Tomlin's popular character. *A Kurtz & Friends/Tomlin and Wagner Theatricalz Production. Color. Half-hour. Premiered on ABC: December 14, 1996.*

Voices
Edith Ann: Lily Tomlin

◎ EEK! THE CAT CHRISTMAS
Eek! gets into the holiday spirit by helping his mortal enemy Sharkey the Sharkdog search for his missing relatives and aiding Santa in settling a dispute with his reindeer in this prime-time animated special based on the popular Saturday-morning cartoon series. *A Nelvana/Savage Studios Production in association with Fox Children's Network. Color. Half-hour. Premiered on FOX: December 5, 1993.*

Voices
Eek! the Cat: Bill Kopp

◎ THE ELEPHANT'S CHILD
Rudyard Kipling's most beloved "Just So" story about how the elephant got his trunk is told in this half-hour animated special, produced as part of Rabbit Ears Video's *Storybook Classics* series. *A Rabbit Ears Video Production. Color. Half-hour. Premiered on SHO: 1989.*

Voices
Narrator: Jack Nicholson

◎ THE ELF AND THE MAGIC KEY
Santa Claus is kidnapped on Christmas Eve and it's up to Toby the elf to free him in time for Christmas in this holiday half-hour. *A RIM/World Production. Color. Half-hour. Premiered on USA: December 4, 1993. Rebroadcast on USA: December 5, 1993; December 14, 1994; December 24, 1995.*

◎ THE ELF WHO SAVED CHRISTMAS
Disappointed Santa tries to retire when no children's letters arrive, so a determined elf sets out in this half-hour holiday special to find the messages in order to change Santa's mind. *A RIM/World Production. Color. Half-hour. Premiered on USA: December 12, 1992. Rebroadcast on USA: December 4, 1993; December 24, 1995.*

Voices
Santa Claus: Harry Frazier; **Elf:** Wendy Cooke

Additional Voices
Jo Anne Worley

◎ THE EMPEROR AND THE NIGHTINGALE
Actress Glenn Close tells this story of the Emperor and his court in ancient China who discover a little gray bird with an enchanting song, part of Rabbit Ears Video's award-winning *Storybook Classics* series. *A Rabbit Ears Video Production. Color. Half-hour. Premiered on SHO: 1989.*

Voices
Narrator: Glenn Close

◎ THE EMPEROR'S NEW CLOTHES (1972)
Danny Kaye lends his voice to this animated version of the Hans Christian Andersen classic about the vain Emperor Klockenlocher, who is duped into paying $1 million for a suit made from "invisible cloth" in this live-action/animation special featuring the stop-motion process of Animagic, which utilizes the lifelike qualities of three-dimensional figures and the magical fantasy of animation. Portions of the special were shot on location in Andersen's native Denmark. Kaye was most familiar with the famed storyteller, as he played the title role in a 1952 movie about Andersen's life. *A Rankin-Bass Production. Color. One hour. Premiered on ABC: February 21, 1972 (as The Enchanted World of Danny Kaye: The Emperor's New Clothes).*

Voices
Marmaduke (narrator): Danny Kaye; **Emperor Klockenlocher:** Cyril Ritchard; **Princess Klockenlocher:** Imogene Coca; **Mufti:** Allen Swift; **Jasper:** Robert McFadden

◎ THE EMPEROR'S NEW CLOTHES (1989)
Two clever swindlers claiming to be the creators of the richest and most beautiful cloth in the world take advantage of the emperor's passion for new clothes in this animated retelling of the popular Hans Christian Andersen tale, part of Rabbit Ears Video's *Storybook Classics* series. *A Rabbit Ears Video Production. Color. Half-hour. Premiered on SHO: 1989.*

Voices
Narrator: Sir John Gielgud

THE EMPEROR'S NEW CLOTHES (1991)

The tale of a little weaver who convinces a vain emperor that he is wearing the finest garments in the land—until a young child dares to point out that he is wearing nothing at all—in this PBS animated special based on Hans Christian Andersen's timeless tale. Produced by Emmy-award winning animator Michael Sporn (whose affinity for the stories of Hans Christian Andersen is seen in his animated versions of "The Little Match Girl" and "The Red Shoes") and narrated by Regis Philbin, the half-hour adventure aired as part of PBS's award-winning series, *Long Ago & Far Away*. *A Michael Sporn Animation/WGBH Boston Production in association with Italtoons Corporation. Color. Half-hour. Premiered on PBS: October 19, 1991. Rebroadcast on PBS: September 20, 1992.*

Voices

Emperor/Narrator: Regis Philbin; **Scribe:** Courtney Vance; **Mancy:** Peggy Cass; **Treasurer:** Barnard Hughes; **Dresser:** Heidi Stallings; **Weaver:** Phillip Schopper

EVERYBODY RIDES THE CAROUSEL

Based on the works of psychiatrist Erik H. Erikson, this unusual 90-minute prime-time special deals with the eight stages of human life—from infancy to old age—presented in fablelike form and skillfully animated by John and Faith Hubley. Cicely Tyson hosted the special and actress Meryl Streep contributed her voice to the production. *A Hubley Studio Production. Color. Ninety minutes. Premiered on CBS: September 10, 1976.*

Voices

Mother: Judith Coburn; **Baby #1/Maura #2/Adolescent:** Georgia Hubley; **Baby #2:** Ray Hubley; **Baby (cries)/Emily/Adolescent #5:** Emily Hubley; **Babies' Relative #1/Cafeteria Woman:** Jane Hoffman; **Babies' Relative #2:** Lou Jacobi; **Babies' Relative #3:** Lane Smith; **Babies' Relative #4:** Eleanor Wilson; **Maura #1:** Maura Washburn; **Maura's Mother:** Linda Washburn; **Maura's Father:** Mike Washburn; **Bruce/Student #2:** Bruce E. Smith; **Bruce's Mother:** Jane E. Smith; **Bruce's Father:** Mortimer Shapiro; **Student #1:** John Infantanza; **Boy:** Leeds Atkinson; **Girl:** Jenny Lumet; **Oracle:** Jo Carrol Stoneham; **Adolescent #1:** Alvin Mack; **Adolescent #2:** Michael Hirst; **Adolescent #3:** Barbara Gittleman; **Lovers:** Charles Levin, Meryl Streep; **Dinah:** Dinah Manoff; **Dinah's Father:** John Randolph; **Dinah's Mother:** Sarah Cunningham; **Tulane:** Tulane Bridgewater; **Tulane's Mother:** DeeDee Bridgewater; **Librarian:** William Watts; **Couple in Bed:** Lawrence (David) Pressman, Lanna Saunders; **Cafeteria Man:** Jack Gilford; **Halloween Woman:** Juanita Moore; **Halloween Man:** Harry Edison

Scene from John and Faith Hubley's cartoon special about the eight stages of life, Everybody Rides the Carousel. *© Hubley Studios*

THE FABULOUS SHORTS

Lee Mendelson, coproducer of television's *Peanuts* specials, produced this collection of Academy Award–winning cartoons, which included domestic and foreign winners. Clips were featured from nearly 20 films, including Mickey Mouse's "Steamboat Willie" (1928), Bugs Bunny's "Knighty Knight Bugs" (1958) and two Mr. Magoo shorts, "When Magoo Flew" (1954) and "Mr. Magoo's Puddle Jumper" (1956). The special was hosted by actor Jim Backus, also the voice of Mr. Magoo. *A Lee Mendelson Production. Color. Half-hour. Premiered on NBC: October 17, 1968.*

FAERIES

Oisin, a middle-age hunter who is magically transformed into a 15-year-old, offers his help to the Trows to save the faerie world from the evil shadow of the Faerie King, who is threatening their very existence. *An MHV and Friends Production in association with Tomorrow Entertainment. Color. Half-hour. Premiered on CBS: February 25, 1981. Rebroadcast on CBS: July 31, 1982; August 13, 1983.*

Voices

Faerie King/Shadow: Hans Conried; **Oisin:** Craig Schaefer; **Princess Niamh:** Morgan Brittany; **Puck/Fir Darrig:** Frank Welker; **Kobold:** Bob Arbogast; **Hags:** June Foray, Linda Gary; **Trows/Hunters:** Mel Wells, Frank Welker, Bob Arbogast

A FAMILY CIRCUS CHRISTMAS

Daddy, Mommy, Billy, P.J., Dolly and Jeffy are preparing for Christmas when Jeffy gives Santa a near-impossible request: bring his deceased grandfather back to visit the family for the holidays. *A Cullen-Kasden Production in association with the Register and Tribune Syndicate. Color. Half-hour. Premiered* on NBC: December 18, 1979. Rebroadcast on NBC: December 5, 1980; December 20, 1981. Rebroadcast on DIS: December 21, 1992; December 21, 1993; December 13, 1994.

Voices
Mommy: Anne Costello; **Daddy:** Bob Kaliban; **Billy:** Mark McDermott; **Dolly:** Missy Hope; **Jeffy/P.J.:** Nathan Berg; **Santa Claus:** Allen Swift; **Vocalist:** Sarah Vaughan

◎ A FAMILY CIRCUS EASTER

Billy, Dolly and Jeffy succeed in trapping the Easter Bunny to find out why it hides the eggs in this prime-time holiday special that premiered on NBC. *A Cullen-Kasden Productions in association with the Register and Tribune Syndicate. Color. Half-hour. Premiered on NBC: April 8, 1982. Rebroadcast on NBC: April 1, 1983. Rebroadcast on DIS: March 20, 1992; April 16, 1995; April 7, 1996.*

Voices
Mommy: Anne Costello; **Daddy:** Bob Kaliban; **Billy:** Mark McDermott; **Dolly:** Missy Hope; **Jeffy/D.J.:** Nathan Berg; **Easter Bunny:** Dizzy Gillespie

◎ THE FAMILY DOG

The story of a suburban middle-class family and their pet pooch is told from the dog's perspective in three related stories that showcase the animal's true feelings about its owners in humorous fashion. The program was billed as "A Special Animated Adventure" of Steven Spielberg's short-lived NBC series, *Amazing Stories. A Hyperion-Kushner-Locke Production in association with Amblin Entertainment and Universal Television. Color. Half-hour. Premiered on NBC: February 16, 1987 (on Amazing Stories). Rebroadcast on NBC: September 11, 1987.*

Voices
Father: Stan Freberg; **Mother:** Mercedes McCambridge; **Billy:** Scott Menville; **Baby Sister:** Annie Potts

◎ FANTASIA: THE CREATION OF A DISNEY CLASSIC

Celebrates the making of this Disney masterpiece, featuring clips from the film and interviews with some of its original animators. Produced in conjunction with the film's 50th anniversary for The Disney Channel. *A Robert Heath/ Wrightwood Group Production for The Disney Channel. Color. Forty minutes. Premiered on DIS: 1990.*

Cast
Ken Anderson, Pete Comandini, John Culhane, Marc Davis, Roy E. Disney, Carl Fallberg, Joe Grant, Ron Haver, Ollie Johnston, Ward Kimball, Leonard Maltin, Terry Porter, Frank Thomas, Michael Tucker

◎ THE FAT ALBERT CHRISTMAS SPECIAL

The true meaning of Christmas—to love one another—is portrayed in this third Fat Albert special. Tyrone, the owner of the junkyard where Fat Albert's clubhouse sits, threatens to demolish the shack as an act of nastiness while the Cosby Kids, busily working up a Christmas pageant, help a little boy (voiced by Marshall Franklin) whose father and pregnant mother are stranded outside in their car. *A Filmation Associates Production in association with Bill Cosby Productions. Color. Half-hour. Premiered on CBS: December 18, 1977. Rebroadcast on CBS: November 27, 1978; November 27, 1979; December 24, 1980.*

Voices
Fat Albert/Mushmouth/Bill: Bill Cosby; **Russell:** Jan Crawford; **Weird Harold:** Gerald Edwards; **Rudy:** Eric Suter; **Little Boy:** Marshall Franklin

◎ THE FAT ALBERT EASTER SPECIAL

The spirit of Easter is conveyed as Fat Albert and the gang observe the joy of the holiday season by spreading good cheer to others. *A Filmation Associates Production in association with Bill Cosby Productions. Color. Half-hour. Premiered on CBS: April 3, 1982. Rebroadcast on CBS: March 10, 1983.*

Voices
Fat Albert/Mushmouth/Mudfoot/Bill: Bill Cosby; **Russell:** Jan Crawford; **Weird Harold:** Gerald Edwards; **Rudy:** Eric Suter

◎ THE FAT ALBERT HALLOWEEN SPECIAL

Fat Albert and the Cosby Kids are treated to an old-fashioned Halloween, with a trip to the cemetery where a witch jumps out, a visit to that ol' bum Mudfoot who teaches them how to get tricked out of their treats and an encounter with a frightening widow who lives in a house on the hill. *A Filmation Associates Production in association with Bill Cosby Productions. Color. Half-hour. Premiered on CBS: October 24, 1977. Rebroadcast on CBS: October 24, 1978; October 22, 1979; October 22, 1980; October 27, 1981.*

Voices
Fat Albert/Mushmouth/Bill: Bill Cosby; **Russell:** Jan Crawford; **Weird Harold:** Gerald Edwards; **Rudy:** Eric Suter; **Other Voices:** Erika Carroll

FATHER CHRISTMAS

After delivering presents one Christmas season, a weary Santa Claus decides to spend "the other 364 days" tending his garden, doing housework and basking in the sunny climes on a holiday adventure. He returns home in time to prepare Christmas stockings for another yuletide season in this British-produced hour-long animated special that aired on PBS. *An Iain Harvey/Blooming Production in association with Channel 4 International. Color. One hour. Premiered on PBS: December 21, 1994.*

Voices
Santa Claus: Mel Smith

THE FIRST CHRISTMAS: "THE STORY OF FIRST CHRISTMAS SNOW"

In this heartwarming holiday special set in a small abbey in the south of France, a nun cares for a young boy (Lukas) who is blinded by a lightning bolt. *A Rankin-Bass Production. Color. Half-hour. Premiered on NBC: December 19, 1975. Rebroadcast on NBC: December 18, 1976; December 15, 1979. Rebroadcast on FAM: December 3, 1992; November 28, 1993; December 4, 1997.*

Voices
Sister Theresa (narrator): Angela Lansbury; **Father Thomas:** Cyril Ritchard; **Lukas:** David Kelly; **Sister Catherine:** Iris Rainer; **Sister Jean:** Joan Gardner; **Louisa:** Diana Lynn

THE FIRST EASTER RABBIT

Folksy Burl Ives sings and tells the story of the first Easter rabbit, whose special assignment from the good fairy is to deliver painted Easter eggs to children. His mission is not without its obstacles, however, as three comedic con bunnies try to stop him. Adapted from the bestselling book *The Velveteen Rabbit.* Ives sings four songs, including Irving Berlin's famous melody, "Easter Parade." *A Rankin-Bass Production. Color. Half-hour. Premiered on NBC: April 9, 1976. Rebroadcast on NBC: March 19, 1978; April 7, 1979; April 9, 1981. Rebroadcast on DIS: March 24, 1993; March 19, 1994.*

Voices
Great Easter Bunny (narrator): Burl Ives; **Stuffy:** Robert Morse; **Flops:** Stan Freberg; **Zero/Spats:** Paul Frees; **Mother:** Joan Gardner; **Whiskers:** Don Messick; **Glinda:** Dina Lynn; **Vocalists:** Burl Ives, Robert Morse, Christine Winter

THE FISHERMAN AND HIS WIFE

Academy Award–winning actress Jodie Foster narrates this animated half-hour adaptation of the Brothers Grimm tale about a poor fisherman who catches and then frees an enchanted flounder who is able to grant him any wish. Produced for Rabbit Ears Video's *Storybook Classics* series. *A Rabbit Ears Video Production. Color. Half-hour. Premiered on SHO: 1989.*

Voices
Narrator: Jodie Foster

FIVE WEEKS IN A BALLOON

Inspired by the Jules Verne story, three adventurers travel across the wilds of Africa via a hot-air balloon, led by famed explorer Dr. Samuel Ferguson, to reclaim for Queen Victoria a priceless diamond thought to be located on Devil's Peak. *A Hanna-Barbera Production. Color. One hour. Premiered on CBS: November 24, 1977. Rebroadcast on CBS: September 30, 1978; November 23, 1981.*

Voices
Narrator: John Stephenson; **Dr. Samuel Ferguson/Duke of Salisbury:** Laurie Main; **Oliver:** Loren Lester; **Queen Victoria:** Cathleen Cordell; **Irumu/King Umtali:** Brooker Bradshaw; **Le Griffe/1st & 2nd Poacher:** Johnny Hayner; **Native:** Gene Whittington

THE FLAGSTONES SPECIAL

Part of a two-month celebration of all things stone age, the Cartoon Network aired this two-hour special featuring the never-before seen, full-color pilot of *The Flintstones* cartoon series. Known as "The Flagstones," the existence of this 1-minute 45-second clip was rumored for over 30 years before it was finally discovered in a warehouse. Featured during the broadcast were original black-and-white prints of the first three episodes of *The Flintstones* with vintage commercials. *A Hanna-Barbera Production. Black-and-white. Color. Two hours. Premiered on CAR: May 7, 1994. Rebroadcast on CAR: May 14, 1994.*

FLASH GORDON: THE GREATEST ADVENTURE OF ALL

This full-length, made-for-television fantasy tells the complete story of space-age hero, Flash Gordon, who, as a State Department employee in Warsaw, takes it upon himself to prevent the powerful Ming the Merciless from bringing his wave of destruction to the planet Earth. *A Filmation Associates Production in association with King Features. Color. Two hours. Premiered on NBC: August 21, 1982. Rebroadcast on NBC: September 5, 1982; September 26, 1982.*

Voices
Flash Gordon: Robert Ridgely; **Dale Arden:** Diane Pershing; **Dr. Zarkov:** David Opatoshu; **Ming the Merciless:**

Bob Holt; **Vultan:** Vic Perrin; **Princess Aura:** Melendy Britt; **Prince Barin:** Robert Douglas; **Thun:** Ted Cassidy

◉ THE FLIGHT OF DRAGONS

The good wizards select a young Boston writer, Peter Dickenson, to stop the menacing Red Wizards and reclaim a magic crown belonging to their race in this two-hour stop-motion (Animagic) special, produced by Arthur Rankin Jr. and Jules Bass of *Rudolph*, *The Red-Nosed Reindeer* and *Frosty the Snowman* television fame. A *Rankin-Bass Production. Color. Two hours. Premiered on ABC: August 3, 1986. Rebroadcast on DIS: December 1, 1992. Rebroadcast on CAR: July 30, 1995 (Mr. Spim's Cartoon Theatre).*

Voices

Peter Dickenson: John Ritter; **Carolinus:** Harry Morgan; **Ommadon:** James Earl Jones; **Smrgol:** James Gregory; **Gorbash:** Cosie Costa; **Arak:** Victor Buono; **Danielle:** Nellie Bellflower; **Princess Melisande:** Alexandra Stoddart; **Pawnbroker:** Larry Storch; **Vocalist:** Don McLean

◉ A FLINTSTONE CHRISTMAS

Fred's holiday job as a part-time Santa at a Bedrock department store lands him in the real Santa's shoes on Christmas Eve in this half-hour holiday special, which was subtitled "How the Flintstones Saved Christmas." A *Hanna-Barbera Production. Color. Half-hour. Premiered on NBC: December 7, 1977. Rebroadcast on NBC: December 11, 1978. Rebroadcast on CAR: December 13, 1992, November 28, 1993. Rebroadcast on TNT: November 29, 1993. Rebroadcast on CAR: December 18, 1993, November 26, 1994. Rebroadcast on TBS: December 17, 1995. Rebroadcast on TNT: December 13, 1995; December 12, 1996; December 7, 1997.*

Voices

Fred Flintstone: Henry Corden; **Barney Rubble:** Mel Blanc; **Betty Rubble:** Gay Hartwig; **Wilma Flintstone:** Jean VanderPyl; **Pebbles Flintstone:** Gay Hartwig; **Bamm-Bamm Rubble:** Lucille Bliss; **Mrs. Santa:** Virginia Gregg; **Real Santa:** Hal Smith; **Ed the Foreman/Otis:** Don Messick; **George Slate, Fred's boss:** John Stephenson

◉ A FLINTSTONE FAMILY CHRISTMAS

In the spirit of the holiday season, Fred and Wilma invite a caveless street urchin named Stony from "the wrong side of the tarpits" into their home and face a world of trouble while trying to teach the boy the difference between naughty and nice. A *Hanna-Barbera Production. Color. Half-hour. Premiered on ABC: December 18, 1993.*

Voices

Fred Flintstone: Henry Corden; **Wilma Flintstone:** Jean VanderPyl; **Barney Rubble:** Frank Welker; **Betty Rubble/Dino:** B.J. Ward

◉ THE FLINTSTONE KIDS' "JUST SAY NO" SPECIAL

While Freddy, Betty, Barney and Philo are vacationing in exotic locales, Wilma's stuck in Bedrock. Lonely, she makes some new friends, one of whom (Stoney) tries turning Wilma on to drugs. This half-hour prime-time special tied in with former First Lady Nancy Reagan's national campaign to fight drug addiction. A cartoon take-off of rock singer Michael Jackson (called "Michael Jackstone") appears on the program. Featured songs: LaToya Jackson's "Just Say No" and Michael Jackson's "Beat It," with new lyrics added. The program was first broadcast in primetime and then rebroadcast as an *ABC Weekend Special.* A *Hanna-Barbera Production. Color. Half-hour. Premiered on ABC: September 15, 1988. Rebroadcast on ABC: September 24, 1988 (on ABC Weekend Special).*

Voices

Wilma: Elizabeth Lyn Fraser; **Freddy:** Scott Menville; **Barney:** Hamilton Camp; **Betty:** B.J. Ward; **Philo:** Bumper Robinson; **Stoney:** Dana Hill; **Dottie:** Shuko Akune; **Joey:** David Markus; **Clyde:** Scott Menville; **Mr. Slaghoople:** Michael Rye; **Mrs. Slaghoople/Fluffy Woman:** Jean VanderPyl; **Dino/Fang/Crusher:** Frank Welker; **Officer Quartz:** Rene Levant; **Edna Flintstone:** Henry Corden; **Irate Man:** Michael Rye; **Angry Adult:** Jean VanderPyl; **Mrs. Gravelson/Female Announcer:** B.J. Ward; **Michael Jackstone:** Kip Lennon

◉ A FLINTSTONES CHRISTMAS CAROL

Christmas is nearly ruined when Fred, who plays Ebenezer Scrooge in the Bedrock Community Players Christmas production, becomes a scrooge himself in this 1994 Christmas special produced for first-run syndication. A *Hanna-Barbera Production. Color. Half-hour. Premiered: December 1994. Syndicated. Rebroadcast on TBS: December 15, 1995; December 6, 1996. Rebroadcast on TNT: December 7, 1997.*

Voices

Fred Flintstone: Henry Corden; **Wilma Flintstone:** Jean VanderPyl; **Barney Rubble/Spirit of Christmas Past/Belle:** Frank Welker; **Betty Rubble/Dino/Bronto/Cragit/Fezzing:** B.J. Ward; **Urchin #1/Kid/Joe Rockhead:** Don Messick; **Bamm-Bamm/Pin Bird/Slate:** John Stephenson; **Marbly/Banner Hanger #1/Whistle Bird/Santa Claus:** Brian Cummings; **Pebbles/Spirit of Christmas Present/Passerby/Wrapper/Constable:** Russi Taylor; **Martha/Garnet Shale/**

Saleswoman/Ned: Will Ryan; **Miss Feldspar:** Marsha Clark; **Fanny/Maggie/Urchin #2/Chip:** Maurice LaMarche; **Mother Pterodactyl/Banner Hanger #1/Philo Quartz/Customer #1:** Rene Levant

Pebbles shows Bamm-Bamm her "stuff" as Fred and Barney look on in a scene from the Hanna-Barbera special The Flintstones: Little Big League. © *Hanna-Barbera Productions*

☉ THE FLINTSTONES: FRED'S FINAL FLING

With just 24 hours to live (or so he believes), Fred takes a final fling until his eyes close . . . with exhaustion. He awakens to discover the predictions of his demise were premature, but the lesson he learned will last a lifetime. *A Hanna-Barbera Production. Color. Half-hour. Premiered on NBC: October 18, 1981. Rebroadcast on NBC: August 1, 1982. Rebroadcast on DIS: February 30, 1992. Rebroadcast on CAR: November 5, 1995 (Mr. Spim's Cartoon Theatre).*

Voices

Fred Flintstone: Henry Corden; **Barney Rubble:** Mel Blanc; **Betty Rubble:** Gay Autterson; **Wilma Flintstone/Pebbles Flintstone:** Jean VanderPyl; **Dino:** Mel Blanc; **Frank Frankenstone:** John Stephenson; **Monkey #2/Turtle #2:** Henry Corden; **Elephant:** Jean VanderPyl; **Monkey #3:** Mel Blanc; **Nurse/Turtle #1:** Gay Autterson; **Dinosaur/Monkey #1:** John Stephenson; **Doctor/Fish #1 & 2/Parrot/Pigasaurus:** Don Messick

☉ THE FLINTSTONES: JOGGING FEVER

Fred gets it from all sides about his bulging waistline. Even his boss, Mr. Slate, tells him to shape up. Fred decides to take up jogging and finds out how badly out of shape he is. *A Hanna-Barbera Production. Color. Half-hour. Premiered on NBC: October 11, 1981. Rebroadcast on NBC: July 25, 1982. Rebroadcast on DIS: December 31, 1991; January 26, 1992; June 6, 1993.*

Voices

Fred Flintstone: Henry Corden; **Barney Rubble:** Mel Blanc; **Wilma Flintstone:** Jean VanderPyl; **Betty Rubble:** Gay Autterson; **Pebbles Flintstone:** Jean VanderPyl; **Dino:** Mel Blanc; **Frank Frankenstone/George Slate, Fred's boss:** John Stephenson; **Nurse #1:** Jean VanderPyl; **Nurse #2:** Gay Autterson; **Workman #2:** Henry Corden; **Turtle:** Mel Blanc; **Dinosaur/Pterodactyl/Bird/Snake:** John Stephenson; **Creeply/Announcer:** Frank Welker; **Control Tower Operator/Workman #1/Hipposaurus:** Wayne Norton

☉ THE FLINTSTONES: LITTLE BIG LEAGUE

Fred and Barney go to bat as coaches of opposing Little League teams and find their friendship crumbles as the big playoff game approaches in this hour-long, primetime special. *A Hanna-Barbera Production. Color. One hour. Premiered on NBC: April 6, 1976. Rebroadcast on NBC: October 10, 1980. Rebroadcast on CAR: June 4, 1994; November 5, 1995 (Mr. Spim's Cartoon Theatre).*

Voices

Fred Flintstone: Henry Corden; **Barney Rubble:** Mel Blanc; **Wilma Flintstone:** Jean VanderPyl; **Betty Rubble:** Gay Hartwig; **Pebbles Flintstone:** Pamela Anderson; **Bamm-Bamm Rubble:** Frank Welker; **Dino:** Mel Blanc; **Officer:** Ted Cassidy; **Judge:** Herb Vigran; **Dusty:** Lucille Bliss; **Lefty:** Randy Gray

☉ THE FLINTSTONES MEET ROCKULA AND FRANKENSTONE

The Flintstones and the Rubbles don crazy costumes to compete on the "Make a Deal or Don't" game show and to win a romantic trip to Count Rockula's castle in Rocksylvania. *A Hanna-Barbera Production. Color. One hour. Premiered: on NBC: October 3, 1980. Rebroadcast on CAR: June 4, 1994: October 29, 1995 (Mr Spim's Cartoon Theatre).*

Voices

Fred Flintstone: Henry Corden; **Barney Rubble:** Mel Blanc; **Wilma Flintstone:** Jean VanderPyl; **Betty Rubble:** Gay Autterson; **Count Rockula:** John Stephenson; **Frankenstone:** Ted Cassidy; **Frau G.:** Jean VanderPly; **Monty Marble:** Casey Kasem; **Igor/Wolf:** Don Messick; **Silica/Bat:** Lennie Weinrib

THE FLINTSTONES' NEW NEIGHBORS

Fred and Wilma are reluctant to greet their new neighbors, the Frankenstones, whose house is furnished with the weirdest creature comforts. *A Hanna-Barbera Productions. Color. Half-hour. Premiered on NBC: September 26, 1980. Rebroadcast on DIS: September 26, 1991. Rebroadcast on CAR: November 5, 1995 (Mr. Spim's Cartoon Theatre).*

Voices
Fred Flintstone: Henry Corden; **Barney Rubble:** Mel Blanc; **Wilma Flintstone:** Jean VanderPyl; **Betty Rubble:** Gay Autterson; **Pebbles Flintstone:** Jean VanderPyl; **Bamm-Bamm Rubble:** Don Messick; **Dino:** Mel Blanc; **Frank Frankenstone:** John Stephenson; **Oblivia Frankenstone:** Pat Parris; **Stubby Frankenstone:** Jim MacGeorge; **Hidea Frankenstone:** Julie McWhirter; **Creeply/Mother Pterodactyl:** Frank Welker; **Scorpion:** Henry Corden; **Vulture:** Don Messick; **Pterodactyl Chicks:** Don Messick, Mel Blanc, Frank Welker

THE FLINTSTONES' 25TH ANNIVERSARY CELEBRATION

Using clips from past *Flintstones* episodes, along with all-new animation created especially for this program, Tim Conway, Harvey Korman and Vanna White, seen in live-action segments, host this nostalgic special tracing the unique history of television's first prime-time animated program. *A Hanna-Barbera Production. Color One hour. Premiered on CBS: May 20, 1986.*

Voices
Fred Flintstone: Alan Reed, Henry Corden; **Wilma Flintstone:** Jean VanderPyl; **Barney Rubble:** Mel Blanc; **Betty Rubble:** Bea Benadaret; **Yogi Bear/Huckleberry Hound/Quick Draw McGraw:** Daws Butler; **Scooby-Doo/Scrappy-Doo:** Don Messick

THE FLINTSTONES: WIND-UP WILMA

Wilma's mean wind-up in the supermarket, where she throws a melon and knocks two thieves unconscious for trying to steal her grocery money, turns her into an instant local celebrity. She is offered a baseball contract to pitch for the local Bedrock Dodger team, who since their attendance is lagging, could use her talent to boost interest in the team. *A Hanna-Barbera Production. Color. Half-hour. Premiered on NBC: October 4, 1981. Rebroadcast on NBC: March 7, 1982. Rebroadcast on DIS: September 3, 1991.*

Voices
Fred Flintstone: Henry Corden; **Barney Rubble:** Mel Blanc; **Wilma Flintstone:** Jean VanderPyl; **Betty Rubble:**
Gay Autterson; **Pebbles Flintstone:** Jean VanderPyl; **Dino:** Mel Blanc; **Frank Frankenstone:** Julie McWhirter; **Turtle #2/Elephant:** Henry Corden; **Clothespin Bird:** Jean VanderPyl; **Female Cop/Cuckoo Bird:** Gay Autterson; **Animal/La Shale/Rocky:** Julie McWhirter; **Announcer/Bird #1/Turtle #1:** Don Messick; **Mean/Checker/Chick #1:** Joe Baker; **Stub/Cop:** Jim MacGeorge; **Sheep/Rooster/Umpire/Reporter #1/Thief/1st Man/Voice:** Paul Winchell; **Creeply/Bird #2/Finrock:** Frank Welker

THE FOOL OF THE WORLD AND THE FLYING SHIP

Nearly two years went into producing this endearing two-part, stop motion puppet animated production derived from a classic Russian folktale (presented in two half-hour installments on PBS's *Long Ago and Far Away* anthology series) which tells the story a kind-hearted peasant boy (Pyotr) who tries to win an evil czar's daughter's hand in marriage by bringing him a "flying ship." David Suchet, best known as Agatha Christie's Poirot on the PBS series *Mystery!* narrates both segments. *A Cosgrove Hall/WGBH Boston Production. Color. Half-hour. Premiered on PBS: October 5, 1991 (Part 1) and October 12, 1991 (Part 2). Rebroadcast on PBS September 6, 1992 (Part 1) and September 13, 1992 (Part 2).*

Voices
Narrator: David Suchet

FOR BETTER OR FOR WORSE: "A STORM IN APRIL"

Elly is discouraged when the whole Patterson family seems to be constantly self-absorbed: Michael is playing video games nonstop, Elizabeth is working madly on a school project on the electric typewriter, John is busy puttering about his electric train set and April is glued to the television set. So when Elly is asked to work more hours at the library, she jumps at the chance, only to find life isn't so easy when their regular babysitter is unavailable and she tries to take baby April to work with her in this sixth and final half-hour special in the *For Better or for Worse* series, which premiered on The Disney Channel. *A Lacewood Production. Color. Half-hour. Premiered on DIS: October, 1992.*

FOR BETTER OR FOR WORSE: "THE BABE MAGNET"

Michael complains that though he now has a driver's license, he never gets to use the Patterson family car. He and a friend decide to buy their own car—the perfect "Babe Magnet"—and hope that it will attract girls in this half-hour *For Better or for Worse* special. The program was the fifth of six specials, originally produced for Canadian television, to air on The Disney Channel. *A Lacewood Production. Color. Half-hour. Premiered on DIS: September, 1992.*

FOR BETTER OR FOR WORSE: THE BESTEST PRESENT

Originally made for Canadian television audiences, this special—the first based on cartoonist Lynn Johnston's syndicated comic strip, *For Better or for Worse*—deals with the nightmarish adventures of the Patterson family during Christmas when daughter Lizzie loses her precious stuffed bunny while Christmas shopping. *An Atkinson Film-Arts Production in association with Telefilm, Canada. Color. Half-hour. Premiere (U.S.) on HBO: December 1986. Rebroadcast on DIS: December 11, 1991; December 12, 1993; December 6, 1994; December 2, 1996.*

Voices

Michael Patterson: Aaron Johnston; **Elizabeth "Lizzy" Patterson:** Katherine Johnston; **Elly Patterson:** Abby Hagyard; **John Patterson:** William H. Stevens, Jr.; **Walter Lederhaus:** Billy Van; **Connie:** Anna MacCormick; **Lawrence:** Dominic Bradford; **Vocalist:** Scott Binkley

FOR BETTER OR FOR WORSE: "THE CHRISTMAS ANGEL"

"Too little to be big and too big to be little," Lizzie is suffering from the middle-child syndrome. When the rest of the Patterson family seems to have no time for her or for decorating their Christmas tree, Lizzie undertakes the task herself, aided and abetted by the family dog, Farley, which leads to disaster in this half-hour holiday special, part of the *For Better or for Worse* series specials. *A Lacewood Production. Color. Half-hour. Premiered on DIS: September, 1992. Rebroadcast on DIS: December 7, 1992; December 19, 1993; December 6, 1994; December 2, 1996.*

FOR BETTER OR FOR WORSE: "THE GOOD FOR NOTHING"

The Patterson family is busily preparing for the fall fair—Elizabeth is grooming Farley for the dog show and Elly is planning to enter the squash from her garden—only for things to go from bad to worse when Farley makes a mess of Elly's garden and his performance in the dog show is a fiasco. The half-hour special, originally produced for Canadian television, premiered in the United States as part of a series of *For Better or for Worse* cartoon specials on The Disney Channel. *A Lacewood Production. Color. Half-hour. Premiered on DIS: September, 1992. Rebroadcast on DIS: December 20, 1992; November 1, 1994.*

FOR BETTER OR FOR WORSE: "THE LAST CAMPING TRIP"

In this half-hour animated special based on cartoonist Lynn Johnston's popular comic strip, Michael is looking forward to the last day of school and to going up to his friend's cottage but is horrified to discover that his parents have planned a camping trip to the East Coast and insist that he go with them. The Canadian-produced special was the first of six *For Better or for Worse* specials to air on The Disney Channel. *A Lacewood Production. Color. Half-hour. Premiered on DIS: August 28, 1992.*

FOR BETTER OR FOR WORSE: "VALENTINE FROM THE HEART"

Difficulties abound when Michael cons his parents into letting him throw a Valentine's Day party, only to have bully Brad Luggsworth crash the event and wreak unintentional havoc when the rest of the kids turn against him. Michael and his friends later try to make amends when Brad decides to leave town in this half-hour *For Better or for Worse* special, one of six animated specials broadcast on The Disney Channel. *A Lacewood Production. Color. Half-hour. Premiered on DIS: September, 1992. Rebroadcast on DIS: February 6, 1993.*

THE FOURTH KING

Spotting a "strange new light in the sky"—the star of Bethlehem—the animals of the land decide to send emissaries of their own—a lion, sparrow, rabbit, beaver and turtle—so they also will be represented along with the three traveling kings at the manger where the Christ child is to be born. *A RAI Television Production in association with NBC. Color. Half-hour. Premiered on NBC: December 23, 1977.*

Voices

Lion: Ted Ross; **Sparrow:** Laurie Beechman; **Turtle:** Arnold Stang; **Beaver:** Bob McFadden; **Rabbit:** Ed Klein

FREEDOM IS

In his dreams, Benji and his pet dog, Waldo, are transported back in time to the Revolutionary War, where they learn all about freedom with the help of new friend, Jeremiah Goodheart. *A Screen Images Production for Lutheran Television. Color. Half-hour. Premiered: Summer 1976. Syndicated.*

Voices

Benji: David Kelly; **Jeremiah Goodheart:** Jonathan Winters; **Samuel:** Richard Roundtree; **Ben Franklin:** Joseph Cotton; **John Adams:** Edward Asner; **Thomas Jefferson:** Dan Dailey; **Jason:** Philip Morris

◎ FRERE JACQUES

Frere Jacques is in trouble until, with the help of his friend, the Wizard Owl, he breaks an evil spell of eternal sleep cast upon the king in this half-hour animated interpretation of the classic children's song, which aired as part of HBO's Storybook Musicals "The Real Story Of . . ." series. Best-selling recording star Stevie Nicks (of Fleetwood Mac fame) provides the voice of the owl. A Cinar Films/France Animation Production. Color. Half-hour. Premiered on HBO: January 3, 1994.

Voices
The Wizard Owl: Stevie Nicks

◎ FROG AND TOAD

Nine of Arthur Lobel's best-loved "Frog and Toad" stories—from Frog and Toad Together and Frog and Toad Are Friends—come to life in this two-part stop-motion puppet-animated special, following the adventures of the blustery Toad and patient Frog, produced for PBS's award-winning series Long Ago & Far Away. A Churchill Films Production. Color. Half-hour. Premiered on PBS: May 6, 1989 (Part 1) and May 13, 1989 (Part 2). Rebroadcast on PBS: November 24, 1990 (Part 1) and December 1, 1990 (Part 2); February 21, 1992 (Part 1) and February 28, 1992 (Part 2).

◎ FROM DISNEY, WITH LOVE

This 90-minute animated salute to Disney's female characters, produced by The Disney Channel to tie in with Valentine's Day, features clips from many of the studio's classic films, including Lady and the Tramp, Bambi, Snow White, Cinderella and Sleeping Beauty, among others. A Film Landa Inc. Production for The Disney Channel. Color. Ninety minutes. Premiered on DIS: 1984.

◎ FROM THE EARTH TO THE MOON

The early triumphs of an adventurous group, the Gun Club, that attempts to reach the moon by launching a manned vessel is related in this half-hour syndicated special produced overseas. An Air Programs International Production. Color. Half-hour. Premiered: 1976. Syndicated.

Voices
Alistair Duncan, Ron Haddrick, Phillip Hinton, Shane Porteous

◎ FROSTY RETURNS

The lovable snowman with the "corncob pipe and a button nose and two eyes made out of coal" (voiced by John Goodman) battles a nasty old inventor, Mr. Twitchell, who wows the town of Beansborough with his Summer Wheeze de-

icing spray. The spray threatens to alter weather cycles dramatically and put an end to Frosty's existence, when the jolly old snowman comes up with a plan that saves the day (thanks to his new pal, a little girl named Holly), in this second sequel to the 1969 holiday classic Frosty the Snowman. A Bill Melendez Production in association with Broadway Video and CBS Entertainment Productions. Color. Half-hour. Premiered on CBS: December 1, 1995. Rebroadcast on CBS: December 6, 1996; December 12, 1997.

Voices
Frosty the Snowman: John Goodman; Narrator: Jonathan Winters

◎ FROSTY'S WINTER WONDERLAND

In this first sequel to 1969's Frosty the Snowman, Frosty's moppet friends create a wife for the usually joyful snowman whom they find is really lonely. Jack Frost, jealous of the snowman's newfound happiness, makes every effort to make life miserable for him once again. Andy Griffith narrates and sings in this imaginatively wrought special. Songs featured include "Frosty" and "Winter Wonderland." A Rankin-Bass Production. Color. Half-hour. Premiered on ABC: December 2, 1976. Rebroadcast on ABC: December 3, 1977; December 13, 1978; November 25, 1979; December 23, 1981; December 1, 1982: Rebroadcast on DIS: December 4, 1993. Rebroadcast on FAM: December 10, 1995. Rebroadcast on DIS: December 25, 1996.

Voices
Frosty the Snowman: Jackie Vernon; Crystal the Snowgirl: Shelley Winters; Parson: Dennis Day; Jack Frost: Paul Frees; Children: Shelley Hines, Eric Stern; Others: Manfred Olea, Barbara Jo Ewing; Narrator: Andy Griffith; Vocalists: The Wee Winter Singers

◎ FROSTY THE SNOWMAN

Based on a song of the same name by Jack Rollins and Steve Nelson, this perennial favorite traces the origin of America's best-known snowman—brought to life by a magic hat on Christmas Eve—and his struggle to get to the North Pole before spring arrives. A Rankin-Bass Production. Color. Half-hour. Premiered on CBS: December 7, 1969. Rebroadcast on CBS: December 5, 1970; December 5, 1971; December 4, 1972; December 10, 1973; December 8, 1974; December 12, 1975; December 17, 1976; December 10, 1977; November 30, 1978; December 8, 1979; November 28, 1980; November 27, 1981; December 21, 1982 December 14, 1983; December 11, 1984; December 7, 1985; December 12, 1986; December 9, 1987; November 28, 1988; December 22, 1989; December 19, 1990; December 18, 1991; December 16, 1992; December 6, 1993; November 30, 1994; December 1, 1995; December 6, 1996; December 12, 1997.

Voices

Frosty the Snowman: Jackie Vernon; **Professor Hinkle:** Billy DeWolfe; **Karen, Frosty's friend:** June Foray; **Santa Claus:** Paul Frees; **Narrator:** Jimmy Durante

◎ A GARFIELD CHRISTMAS SPECIAL

Jon goes home to the farm for the holidays. While Odie works on a mystery gift, Garfield plans to surprise Grandma. An Emmy Award nominee. *A Film Roman Production in association with United Media and Paws. Color. Half-hour. Premiered on CBS: December 21, 1987. Rebroadcast on CBS: December 23, 1988; December 21, 1989; December 7, 1990: December 6, 1991; December 2, 1992; December 19, 1996.*

Voices

Garfield: Lorenzo Music; **Jon Arbuckle:** Thom Huge; **Odie:** Gregg Berger; **Mom:** Julie Payne; **Dad:** Pat Harrington; **Doc Boy:** David Lander; **Grandma:** Pat Carroll

◎ GARFIELD GETS A LIFE

Follows the hapless social antics of Garfield's dweeb owner, Jon, as Garfield tries to help him "get a life" and a girlfriend. This prime-time half-hour special features music by Lou Rawls, B.B. King and The Temptations. *A Film Roman Production in association with United Media/Mendelson and Paws Inc. Color. Half-hour. Premiered on CBS: May 8, 1991.*

Voices

Garfield: Lorenzo Music; **Jon:** Thom Huge; **Odie:** Gregg Berger; **Lorenzo:** Frank Welker; **Mona:** June Foray

Additional Voices

Julie Payne

◎ GARFIELD GOES HOLLYWOOD

When the TV show *Pet Search* announces a pet talent, contest Jon devises an act for himself, Garfield and Odie: Jonny Bop and the Two Steps. They win the local event and head to Hollywood for the finals, where Garfield and Odie cut Jon out of the act and become The Dancing Armandos. An Emmy Award nominee. *A Film Roman Production in association with United Media and Paws. Color. Half-hour. Premiered on CBS: May 8, 1987. Rebroadcast on CBS: March 16, 1988.*

Voices

Garfield: Lorenzo Music; **Jon Arbuckle:** Thom Huge; **Odie/Bob/Grandma Fogerty/Announcer:** Gregg Berger; **Herbie:** Nino Tempo; **National TV Host:** Frank Welker

◎ GARFIELD: HIS NINE LIVES

Garfield hosts a look at his nine lives. At the end, he is luckily given an additional nine. Ten segments actually make up the special: "In the Beginning," with the "creator" deciding to design a cat; "Cave Cat," showing the prehistoric origins of cats; "King Cat," revealing Garfield's royal heritage; "In the Garden," the story of Garfield's sharing joy in a whimsical world of fantasy with a young girl (Cloey); "Court Musician," with Garfield as the inventor of jazz; "Stunt Rat," featuring Garfield working in silent films; "Diana's Piano," a touching tale about the cycle of life and death; "Lab Animal," offering a strange tale of an experiment that goes awry; "Garfield," the origin of the famed comic-strip character; and "Space Cat," his travels in the distant future and a distant galaxy. *A Film Roman Productions in association with United Media and Paws. Color. One hour. Premiered on CBS: November 22, 1988.*

Voices

Garfield: Lorenzo Music; **Odie:** Gregg Berger, **The Creator:** Lindsay Workman; **Narrator ("Cave Cat"):** Gregg Berger; **Junior:** Thom Huge; **Black Bart:** Nino Tempo; **Announcer ("In the Garden"):** Desiree Goyette; **Jester ("Court Musician"):** Gregg Berger; **Director ("Stunt Kat"):** Jim Davis; **Sara ("Diana's Piano"):** Desiree Goyette; **Jon Arbuckle ("Garfield"):** Thom Huge; **Garfield's Mom ("Garfield"):** Desiree Goyette; **Captain Mendelson ("Space Cat"):** Frank Welker

◎ GARFIELD IN PARADISE

Garfield, Odie and Jon vacation in the tropics at a cheap resort. When they go exploring, they meet a lost tribe that worships 1950's automobiles and is preparing a human and cat sacrifice for the volcano god. An Emmy Award nominee. *A Film Roman Production in association with United Media and Paws. Color. Half-hour. Premiered on CBS: May 27, 1986. Rebroadcast on CBS: January 16, 1987; November 23, 1988; April 24, 1989.*

Voices

Garfield: Lorenzo Music; **Jon Arbuckle:** Thom Huge; **High Rama Lama:** Wolfman Jack; **Hotel Clerk/Salesman:** Frank Nelson; **Odie Pigeon:** Gregg Berger; **Owooda:** Desiree Goyette; **Mai Tai/Stewardess:** Julie Payne; **Monkey:** Nino Tempo; **Woman/Cat:** Carolyn Davis; **B.G. Voices:** Hal Smith; **Vocalists:** Desiree Goyette, Thom Huge, Lorenzo Music, Lou Rawls

◎ GARFIELD IN THE ROUGH

Garfield's enthusiasm for a vacation wanes when he discovers Jon plans a camping trip. Life in the wild gets dangerous when an escaped panther enters the campgrounds. An

Garfield's enthusiastic arrival at a flea-bitten resort is further punctuated by the discovery of Odie, who has stowed away in a suitcase, in the prime-time special Garfield in Paradise. *© United Feature Syndicate Inc.* (COURTESY: CBS)

Emmy Award winner. *A Film Roman Production in association with United Media and Paws. Color. Half-hour. Premiered on CBS: October 26, 1984. Rebroadcast on CBS: March 23, 1985; August 21, 1987.*

Voices
Garfield: Lorenzo Music; **Jon Arbuckle:** Thom Huge; **Odie/Ranger #1/Announcer:** Gregg Berger; **Ranger #2:** George Wendt; **Dicky Beaver:** Hal Smith; **Billy Rabbit:** Orson Bean; **Girl Cats/Arlene:** Desiree Goyette; **Vocalists:** Desiree Goyette, Thom Huge, Lou Rawls

◉ GARFIELD ON THE TOWN

On the way to the vet's, Garfield slips out of the car and attempts to make it as a street cat. While in the inner city, he discovers his birthplace and family. An Emmy Award winner. *A Lee Mendelson–Bill Melendez Production in association with United Media Productions. Color. Half-hour. Premiered on CBS: October 28, 1983. Rebroadcast on CBS: March 10, 1984; December 28, 1985; September 5, 1990.*

Voices
Garfield: Lorenzo Music; **Jon Arbuckle:** Thom Huge; **Raoul:** George Wendt; **Ali Cat:** Gregg Berger; **Mom, Garfield's mother:** Sandi Huge; **Liz:** Julie Payne; **Grandfather:** Lindsay Workman; **Girl Cat #2 & #3:** Allyce Beasley; **Girl Cat #1:** Desiree Goyette; **Vocalists:** Desiree Goyette, Lou Rawls

◉ GARFIELD'S BABES AND BULLETS

In this satire of detective films of the 1940s, Garfield fantasizes (in black-and-white) on a rainy day about being Sam

Spayed, a private investigator handling a case involving a mysterious woman. An Emmy Award winner. *A Film Roman Production in association with United Media and Paws. Color. Half-hour. Premiered on CBS: May 23, 1989.*

Voices
Garfield: Lorenzo Music; **Jon Arbuckle:** Thom Huge; **Odie/Burt Fleebish:** Gregg Berger; **Thug:** Thom Huge; **Kitty:** Julie Payne; **Tanya:** Desiree Goyette; **Professor O'Felix:** Lindsay Workman; **Lt. Washington:** Nino Tempo

◉ GARFIELD'S HALLOWEEN ADVENTURE

Garfield and Odie get dressed up as pirates to go trick or treating. They accidentally end up at a haunted house where ghostly pirates are expected any minute. An Emmy Award winner. *A Film Roman Production in association with United Media Productions. Color. Half-hour. Premiered on CBS: October 30, 1985. Rebroadcast on CBS: October 24, 1986; October 23, 1987; October 28, 1988; October 30, 1989.*

Voices
Garfield: Lorenzo Music; **Jon Arbuckle:** Thom Huge; **Odie:** Gregg Berger; **Old Man:** Lindsay Workman; **TV Announcer:** Gregg Berger; **Woman:** Desiree Goyette; **Vocalists:** Lorenzo Music, Lou Rawls

◉ GARFIELD'S THANKSGIVING SPECIAL

The day before Thanksgiving, Garfield is put on a diet and Liz, the veterinarian, agrees to have Thanksgiving dinner with Jon. However, when Jon's manages to destroy the meal, Grandma arrives in time to save the day and Garfield is given a reprieve from fasting. An Emmy Award winner. *A Film Roman Production in association with United Media and Paws. Color. Half-hour. Premiered on CBS: November 22, 1989.*

Voices
Garfield: Lorenzo Music; **Jon Arbuckle:** Thom Huge; **Odie:** Gregg Berger; **Liz/Scale:** Julie Payne; **Grandma:** Pat Carroll; **Vocalists:** Lou Rawls, Desiree Goyette

◉ GARY LARSON'S TALES FROM THE FAR SIDE

Syndicated cartoonist Gary Larson's sadistic comic strip *The Far Side* comes to life in this humorous Halloween-themed special showcasing his trademark bugs, monsters, redneck hunters and zombies as they meet their comical fates in parodies of familiar spooky tales. *An International Rocketship Production for FarWorks Inc. Color. Half-hour. Premiered on CBS: October 26, 1994.*

Voices
Kathleen Barr, Doug Parker, Lee Tokar, Dale Wilson

⊚ GIDGET MAKES THE WRONG CONNECTION

In this animated spinoff of the *Gidget* television series, Frances "Gidget" Lawrence and her surfer friends expose a ring of gold smugglers in this one-hour movie originally broadcast on the *The ABC Saturday Superstar Movie* series. *A Hanna-Barbera Production. Color. One hour. Premiered on ABC: November 18, 1972 (on The ABC Saturday Superstar Movie). Rebroadcast on ABC: October 6, 1973; March 16, 1974. Syndicated.*

Voices
Gidget: Kathy Gori; **Rink/Steve:** Denny Evans; **Killer/Gorgeous Cat/Capt. Parker:** Don Messick; **Ralph Hightower/R.C. Man:** Mike Road; **Radio (Voice):** Don Messick; **Bull/Capt. Shad:** Bob Hastings; **Barbara Hightower:** Virginia Gregg; **Jud:** David Lander

⊚ G.I. JOE: THE GREATEST EVIL

The G.I. Joe team and COBRA organization unite in the war against drugs, forming the Drug Elimination Force (DEF), and make the Head Man's local drug factory their primary target in this hour-long special, which premiered in daytime syndication in 1991. The program was rebroadcast in syndication in 1992 as a two-part special in most markets. *A DIC Enterprises Production. Color. One hour. Premiered: December 1, 1991. Rebroadcast: October 24, 1992–November 7, 1992. Syndicated.*

⊚ THE GINGHAM DOG AND THE CALICO CAT

Popular singer Amy Grant tells this story of two bickering stuffed animals—a dog and a cat—who fall out of Santa's sleigh, and work together to find their way to their new home in this half-hour animated special. First broadcast on Showtime, it featured a music soundtrack by country music guitar legend Chet Atkins. Part of Rabbit Ears *Holiday Classics* video series. *A Rabbit Ears Video Production. Color. Premiered on SHO: December 3, 1991. Rebroadcast on SHO: December 23, 1991.*

Voices
Narrator: Amy Grant

⊚ THE GLO FRIENDS SAVE CHRISTMAS

When the Wicked Witch of the North Pole unveils her fiendish plans to prevent Santa Claus from delivering toys to the creatures of Gloland, the Glo Friends unleash their own counterattack on the mean witch so Santa can spread his good cheer to everyone. *A Sunbow Production in association with Marvel Productions. Color. Half-hour. Premiered: November 1985. Syndicated.*

Voices
Santa Claus: Carroll O'Connor; **Blanche, Wicked Witch of the North Pole:** Sally Struthers

⊚ GNOMES

Revenge is the order of the day when Tor, a young gnome, is set to marry Lisa from the city, but the archrival trolls, angry because the gnomes keep releasing their prey before they can eat it, decide to grab the unsuspecting gnomes when they're assembled for the nuptial ceremony. *A Zanders Animation Parlor Production in association with Tomorrow Entertainment. Color. One hour. Premiered on CBS: November 11, 1980. Rebroadcast on CBS: August 28, 1982; August 27, 1983.*

Voices
Arthur Anderson, Rex Everhart, Anne Francine, Hetty Galen, Gordon Halliday, Bob McFadden, Corrinne Orr, Joe Silver

⊚ GOING BONKERS

A group of once-famous cartoon characters are replaced by muscle-bound movie stars in this one-hour preview special to the syndicated series *Disney's Bonkers. A Walt Disney Production. Color. One hour. Premiered: September 4, 1993. Syndicated.*

Voices
Bonkers D. Bobcat/Lucky Piquel: Jesse Corti, Jim Cummings; **W.W. Wacky:** David Doyle; **Grumbles Grizzly:** Rodger Bumpass; **Jitters D. Dog:** Jeff Bennett; **Police Chief Leonard Kanifky:** Earl Boen; **Donald Duck:** Tony Anselmo; **Fawn Deer:** Nancy Cartwright; **Marilyn Piquel:** Sherry Lynn; **Dylandra "Dyl" Piquel:** April Winchell; **Fall Apart Rabbit/Toots/Toon Radio:** Frank Welker; **Toon Siren:** Charlie Adler

⊚ GOLDILOCKS

The familiar children's tale of "Goldilocks and the Three Bears" is re-created in this live-action/animation version, which features the voices of the Crosby family (Bing,

Kathryn, Mary Frances and Nathaniel). A *DePatie-Freleng Enterprises Production in association with NBC. Color. Half-hour. Premiered on NBC: March 31, 1970. Rebroadcast on NBC: October 24, 1970.*

Voices
Goldilocks: Mary Frances Crosby; **Papa Bear:** Bing Crosby; **Mama Bear:** Kathryn Crosby; **Baby Bear:** Nathaniel Crosby; **Bobcat:** Paul Winchell

Other Voices
Avery Schreiber

THE GOOD, THE BAD AND HUCKLEBERRY HOUND

Huckleberry Hound cleans up the Old West town of Two Bit, after the notorious Dalton gang (Dinky, Pinky and Frinky) steal his gold nugget, so he becomes the new sheriff. First in a series of feature-length cartoons made for first-run syndication for "Hanna-Barbera's Superstars 10" package. *A Hanna-Barbera Production. Color. Two hours. Premiered: 1988, Syndicated. Rebroadcast on CAR: March 19, 1995 (Mr. Spim's Cartoon Theatre). Rebroadcast on DIS: December 5, 1996.*

Voices
Huckleberry Hound: Daws Butler; **Baba Looey/Peter Potamus/Yogi Bear/Hokey Wolf/Snagglepuss/Quick Draw McGraw:** Daws Butler; **Boo Boo/Narrator:** Don Messick; **Finky/Fat Boy Kid/Rooster/Baby/Little Boy:** Pat Fraley; **Magilla Gorilla/Dinky/Announcer:** Alan Melvin; **Pinky/News Anchorman/Pig:** Charlie Adler; Stinky/Steer/Station Announcer/Bailiff/Laughing Donkey: Michael Bell; **Dentist/Governor/Mr. Peebles/Photographer/Chuckling Chipmunk:** Howie Morris; **Judge Flopner/Horse/Chef/Race Track Announcer/Mission Control:** Frank Welker; **Rusty/Desert Flower/Wife/Little Old Lady/Fat Girl:** B.J. Ward; **Red Eye:** Pat Buttram

A GOOF TROOP CHRISTMAS

Pete and his family take off on a ski vacation to Aspirin, Colorado, only to have Goofy and son Max follow (in the episode entitled "Have Yourself a Goofy Little Christmas") in this half-hour holiday special spun off from the popular series *Goof Troop*. The special, which first aired in syndication in 1992, was comprised of two holiday-themed episodes, including "Have Yourself a Goofy Little Christmas, "Up a Tree, The Art of Skiing" and a behind-the-scenes look at some of Disney's animated classics. The program returned in 1993, still featuring the "Have Yourself a Goofy Little Christmas" episode, plus two new animated additions: "On Ice, the Hockey Champ" and "Toy

Tinkers." *A Walt Disney Television Animation Production. Color. Half hour. Premiered: December 5, 1992; December 11, 1993. Syndicated.*

Voices
Goofy: Bill Farmer; **Max:** Dana Hill; **Pete:** Jim Cummings; **Pistol:** Nancy Cartwright; **P.J.:** Rob Paulsen; **Peg:** April Winchell; **Grizz/Waffles/Chainsaw:** Frank Welker

GOOFY'S GUIDE TO SUCCESS

Featuring clips from classic cartoons, this Disney Channel original production takes a look at Goofy's success in the workforce, with the help of the show's animated host, Paddy O'Riley. *A Robert Heath Production for The Disney Channel. Color. Ninety minutes. Premiered on DIS: November 18, 1990.*

GOOFY'S SALUTE TO FATHER

Goofy's life from his devil-may-care bachelor days to the joys and frustration of parenthood is chronicled in this collection of snippets from past Goofy cartoons. *A Walt Disney Production. Color. Half-hour. Premiered on DIS: June 19, 1994.*

GRANDPA

A kindly old grandfather (voiced by Peter Ustinov) lovingly introduces his granddaughter Emily to the worlds of books and imagination in this half-hour animated adaptation of John Burningham's book of the same name, first aired on Showtime. *A TVC Grandpa Ltd. Production for TVS Television and Channel 4. Premiered on SHO: November 5, 1991. Rebroadcast on SHO: November 20, 1991; November 29, 1991.*

Voices
Grandpa: Peter Ustinov; **Emily:** Emily Osborne

THE GREAT BEAR SCARE

In the small forest community of Bearbank, the resident bear population is menaced by a group of monsters. Ted E. Bear (voiced by Tommy Smothers) is selected to quell the dastardly bunch and becomes hero to the populace and to his special friend, Patti Bear, anchorbear for the local TV station's "Bear Witness News." *A DimenMark Films Production. Color. Half-hour. Premiered: October 1982. Syndicated.*

Voices
Ted E. Bear: Tom Smothers; **Patti Bear:** Sue Raney; **Professor Werner Von Bear:** Hans Conried; **Dracula:** Louis Nye; **C. Emory Bear:** Hal Smith; **Miss Witch:** Lucille Bliss

THE GREAT CHRISTMAS RACE

The Lollipop Dragon and his friends must defeat Baron Bad Blood to save the children from having to eat liver lollipops on Christmas morning. *A Blair Entertainment Production in association with Pannonia Film. Color. Half-hour. Premiered: November 1986. Syndicated.*

Voices

Lollipop Dragon: Gary Wilmot; **Princess Gwendolyn:** Jill Lidstone; **Prince Hubert:** Pat Starr; **Blue Eyes:** Karen Fernald; **Glider/Queen:** Eva Hadden; **Baron Bad Blood:** Stephen Thorne; **Cosmo the Cunning/King:** Dennis Greashan

THE GREAT EXPECTATIONS

Overcoming early misfortunes as a child, Phillip Pirrip—called "Pip"—inherits a sizable fortune and learns many valuable lessons in a series of adventures that follow. *A Burbank Films Production. Color. Half-hour. Premiered: Fall, 1984. Syndicated.*

Voices

Barbara Frawley, Marcus Hale, Philip Hinton, Simon Hinton, Liz Horne, Bill Kerr, Moya O'Sullivan, Robin Stewart

THE GREAT HEEP

In this hour-long fantasy/adventure, *Star Wars* droids R2-D2 and C-3PO arrive on the planet Biitu to meet their new master. They are shocked to find that a gigantic evil droid, the Great Heep, has turned the planet into a wasteland and captured their master, Mungo Baobab, a merchant/explorer. *A Nelvana Limited Production in association with Hanho Heung-Up and Mi-Hahn Productions for Lucasfilm. Color. One hour. Premiered on ABC: June 7, 1986.*

Voices

C3-PO: Anthony Daniels; **R2-D2:** (electronic); **Mungo Baobab:** Winston Rekert; **Admiral Screed:** Graeme Campbell; **Fridge:** Noam Zylberman; **Captain Cag/Announcer/Gulper:** Dan Hennessey; **KT-10/Darva:** Melleny Brown; **The Great Heep:** Long John Baldry

GROWING AND CHANGING

Produced for UNICEF in conjunction with the International Day of the Child in 1995. First Lady Hillary Clinton introduces this half-hour animated special, narrated by Dr. T. Berry Brazelton and produced by Emmy Award–winning animator Michael Sporn for the Disney Channel. *A Michael Sporn Animation Production in association with Italtoons Corporation. Color. Half-hour. Premiered on DIS: December 8, 1995.*

GULLIVER'S TRAVELS

The adventure-seeking Gulliver learns the true meaning of friendship as he assists the Lilliputians in this colorful adaptation of the Jonathan Swift classic. *A CBS Famous Classic Tales special. A Hanna-Barbera Production. Color. One hour. Premiered on CBS: November 18, 1979. Rebroadcast on CBS: November 9, 1980.*

Voices

Gulliver: Ross Martin; **Filmnap/Jester Pirate:** Hal Smith; **Bolgolam/Lilliputian King/Brobdingnag King:** John Stephenson; **Lilliputian/Mob Member #1:** Ross Martin; **Reldresal/Old Fisherman/Blefuscu King:** Don Messick; **Farmer/Brobdingnag Minister/Mob Member #2:** Regis Cordic; **Lilliputian Queen/Brogdingnag Queen:** Julie Bennett; **Farmer's Wife/Glumdalclitch:** Janet Waldo

HAGAR THE HORRIBLE: "HAGAR KNOWS BEST"

Hagar the Horrible, the most famous Viking of all, is on his way home from a two-year business trip ravaging foreign lands. As his ship nears the port, visions of a *Father Knows*

The most famous Viking of all heads home from a two-year business trip, but home doesn't quite meet his expectations in the CBS prime-time special Hagar the Horrible: Hagar Knows Best. *© King Features Entertainment*

Best family life dance in his helmeted head. But once he is home, reality doesn't match up. *A Hanna-Barbera Production in association with King Entertainment. Color. Half-hour. Premiered on CBS: November 1, 1989.*

Voices
Hagar: Peter Cullen; **Honi:** Lydia Cornell; **Helga:** Lainie Kazan; **Hamlet:** Josh Rodine; **Lucky Eddie:** Jeff Doucett; **Olaf:** Hank Saroyan; **Lute/Instructor:** Donny Most; **Doorman:** Hank Saroyan; **Kid:** Josh Rodine; **Principal:** Frank Welker; **Joe:** Jeff Doucette; **Al/Snert/Kvaak:** Frank Welker; **Teacher:** Jack Tice; **Narrator:** Frank Welker

☺ THE HALLOWEEN TREE
Well-known novelist Ray Bradbury is author and narrator of this 90-minute animated tale about five young children who take a frightful journey 4,000 years into the past to rescue the spirit of their friend Pip from the malevolent Mr. Moundshroud (voiced by Leonard Nimoy, alias Mr. Spock from TV's original *Star Trek*), who introduces them to the holiday's customs in various ages and countries. *A Hanna-Barbera Production. Color. Ninety minutes. Premiered on TBS and syndication: October 30, 1993.*

Voices
Narrator: Ray Bradbury; **Mr. Moundshroud:** Leonard Nimoy; **Pip:** Alex Greenwald; **Jenny:** Annie Barker

☺ HALLOWEEN WHO-DUN-IT?
Davey Hanson and his dog, Goliath, stars of the popular religious stop-motion animation series *Davey and Goliath*, return in this first-run special providing a new lesson on Christian living tied in with Halloween. *A Clokey Production for the Lutheran Church of America. Color. Half-hour. Premiered: 1977 Syndicated.*

Voices
Davey Hanson/Sally Hanson/Mary Hanson: Norma McMillan, Nancy Wible; **Goliath/John Hanson:** Hal Smith

☺ HANNA-BARBERA'S 50TH: A YABBA DABBA DOO CELEBRATION
Hosts Tony Danza and Annie Potts lead a madcap cast of live and animated guests in this festive two-hour special celebrating 50 years of animated magic by Oscar-winning animators William Hanna and Joseph Barbera. Interspersed throughout the special are clips from assorted Hanna-Barbera cartoons, plus new animated segments. *A Hanna-Barbera Production. Color. Two hours. Premiered on TNT: July 17, 1989. Rebroadcast on CAR: June 4, 1994.*

Voices
Greg Berg, Mel Blanc, Henry Corden, Casey Kasem, Don Messick, Penny Singleton, John Stephenson, Jean VanderPyl

☺ HAPPILY EVER AFTER
Troubled by the news of her parents' divorce, Molly Conway, who like most children dreams of living happily ever after, forms a group with her offbeat friends ("The Skywalkers") to try to prevent her parents from breaking up. *A JZM–Bill Melendez Production in association with Wonderworks and Bill Melendez Productions, London, England. Color. One hour. Premiered on PBS: October 21, 1985 (on PBS's Wonderworks anthology series).*

Voices
Narrator: Carol Burnett; **Molly Conway:** Cassandra Coblentz; **Alice Conway:** Carrie Fisher; **Carl Conway:** Henry Winkler; **Tommy Johnson:** Danny Colby; **George Johnson:** Danny DeVito; **Rose Johnson:** Rhea Perlman; **Joey Fabrizio:** Jeremy Schoenberg; **Dom Fabrizio:** Dana Ferguson; **Mary O'Connell:** Gini Holtzman; **Darlene Kashitani:** Karrie Ullman; **Woody Coleman:** Carl Stevens; **Molly's Daughter:** Keri Houlihan; **What's His Name:** Brett Johnson

☺ HAPPY ANNIVERSARY, CHARLIE BROWN
Twenty-five years of the *Peanuts* comic strip is celebrated in this retrospective special, containing clips from 14 Charlie Brown television specials. The special is hosted by Carl Reiner and features wraparound interview segments with *Peanuts* creator Charles Schulz. *A Lee Mendelson Production in association with Charles M. Schulz Creative Associates and United Feature Syndicate. Color. One hour. Premiered on CBS: January 9, 1976.*

Voices
Charlie Brown: Duncan Winston; **Schroeder:** Greg Felton; **Sally Brown:** Gail M. Davis; **Lucy Van Pelt:** Lynn Mortensen; **Linus Van Pelt:** Liam Martin; **Peppermint Patty:** Stuart Brotman

☺ HAPPY BIRTHDAY BUGS: 50 LOONEY YEARS
Bugs Bunny, the Oscar-winning rabbit of Warner Bros. fame, turns 50, and his golden anniversary is celebrated in grand style in this freewheeling one-hour special. The program includes a musical salute by Little Richard; an *Entertainment Tonight* portrait by Mary Hart; *A Current Affair* spoof with Maury Povich and Milton Berle, who plays an actor claiming to be the real Bugs; a tribute by Bill Cosby

and Whoopie Goldberg to the late Mel Blanc, who created the voice of Bugs Bunny; and recurrent reports by Joe Garagiola on anti-Bugs protests being mounted by Daffy Duck, who's upset because he wasn't feted two years earlier for his own 50th anniversary in show business. Clips from various Warner cartoons are interspersed throughout the program, starring Elmer Fudd, Porky Pig, Road Runner and Wile E. Coyote. *A Warner Bros. Television Production. Color. One hour. Premiered on CBS: May 9, 1990.*

⊚ HAPPY BIRTHDAY BUNNYKINS

Mr. and Mrs. Bunnykin overlook making plans for a birthday for their son William, who hopes to get his very own marching drum, like the one used in his father's band. This half-hour animated special, originally produced for Canada's CTV network in 1995, was based on the Bunnykins China by Royal Doulton. The program debuted in the United States on The Disney Channel. *A Rabbits Unlimited/Lacewood Production in association with CTV Television Network/Cat's Pyjamas/MTR Entertainment. Color. Half-hour. Premiered on DIS: April 7, 1996.*

Voices
Mr. Bunnykins: James Bradford; **Mrs. Bunnykins:** Denis Killock; **Susan:** Rebecca Overall; **William:** Tia Carello; **Harry:** Amy Fulco; **Lady Rattley:** Leonie Gardner; **Stoatworth:** Terrence Scammel; **Reginald:** Dylan Shaw Lane; **Queen Sophie:** Natalie Stern; **Mr. Shortbread:** Dean Hagopian; **Adrian:** Catherine Lewis

Other Voices
Rick Jones

⊚ HAPPY BIRTHDAY, CHARLIE BROWN

In honor of Charlie Brown's 30th year as a comic-strip character and 15th year on television, CBS's Phyllis George hosts this hour-long salute combining clips from past specials and a special guest appearance by creator Charles Schulz. *A Lee Mendelson Production in association with Charles M. Schulz Creative Associates and Bill Melendez Productions. Color. One hour. Premiered on CBS: January 5, 1979.*

Voices
Charlie Brown: Arrin Skelley, Peter Robbins; **Linus Van Pelt:** Daniel Anderson; **Sally Brown:** Annalisa Bortolin; **Marcie:** Casey Carlson; **Lucy Van Pelt:** Sally Dryer-Barker, Michelle Muller; **Dolores:** Leticia Ortiz; **Peppermint Patty:** Laura Planting; **Franklin:** Ronald Hendrix; **Vocalists:** Don Potter, Becky Reardon, Larry Finlayson

⊚ HAPPY BIRTHDAY, DONALD DUCK

Expanding on the story of the 1949 cartoon "Donald's Happy Birthday," Huey, Dewey and Louie, Donald's mischievous nephews, make plans for a special birthday party for their famed but temperamental uncle. Donald surprises his nephews with his own plans for his birthday—watching footage of his old cartoons. The special was retitled and rebroadcast in two other versions on NBC after its initial premiere on rival network ABC. *A Walt Disney Television Production. Color. One hour. Premiered on ABC: November 21, 1956 (as "At Home with Donald Duck" on the program* Disneyland*). Rebroadcast on ABC: May 8, 1957. Rebroadcast on NBC: November 7, 1976 (on* The Wonderful World of Disney*); April 4, 1979 (as* Happy Birthday, Donald Duck*).*

Voices
Donald Duck: Clarence Nash

⊚ HAPPY BIRTHDAY MICKEY

Mickey Mouse's illustrious career is highlighted in this birthday special loaded with clips from his first screen appearances and his roles in *Fantasia* and *The Mickey Mouse Club*, originally produced for The Disney Channel. *A Film Landa Inc. Production for The Disney Channel. Color. Ninety minutes. Premiered on DIS: 1983.*

⊚ HAPPY BIRTHDAY TO YOU

It's Olivia Orderly's birthday and her only friend at Orderly Mansion is Charley the Horse . . . until Barnaby the stable hand shows up. This story of one girl's search for the perfect birthday song was part of Canadian television's *The Real Story of . . .* series (a.k.a. *Favorite Songs*) produced in 1991 by Cinar Films. It premiered in the U.S. a year later on HBO's popular anthology series *HBO Storybook Musicals*. *A Cinar/France Animation Production in association with Western Publishing Company Inc/The Family Channel/Telefilm Canada/Cofimage 3. Color. Half-hour. Premiered on HBO: January 4, 1992.*

Voices
Barnaby: Roger Daltrey; **Charley the Horse:** Ed Asner

⊚ THE HAPPY CIRCUS

Three magical episodes from the French claymation series *Le Cirque Bonheur*, which takes viewers into a world of dreams, fantasy and childhood with unusual stories, all set in a traveling circus, are featured in this half-hour special based on original stories by Jacques-Remy Girerd, Renaud Terrier and Toni Bauza. It was first introduced to American television audiences on the award-winning PBS series *Long Ago & Far Away*. *A La Maison du Cinema de Grenoble/Antenne 2/Folimage-Valence, France Production. Color. Half-hour. Premiered on PBS: February 18, 1989.*

HAPPY EASTER

The lesson of Easter is delivered as Davey attends the Easter pageant and is overtaken by emotion after watching a rehearsal of the Passion Play. *A Clokey Production for the Lutheran Church of America. Color. Half-hour. Premiered: 1967. Syndicated.*

Voices

Davey Hanson/Sally Hanson/Mary Hanson: Norma McMillan, Nancy Wible; Goliath/John Hanson: Hal Smith

HAPPY NEW YEAR, CHARLIE BROWN

The *Peanuts* gang rings in 1986 with Marcie and Peppermint Patty throwing a big New Year's Eve bash that Charlie Brown at first decides not to attend. *A Lee Mendelson–Bill Melendez Production in association with Charles M. Schulz Creative Associates and United Feature Syndicate. Color. Half-hour. Premiered on CBS: January 1, 1986. Rebroadcast on CBS: January 1, 1987; December 28, 1988.*

Voices

Charlie Brown: Chad Allen; **Charlie Brown (singing):** Sean Collins; **Peppermint Patty:** Kristi Baker; **Lucy Van Pelt:** Melissa Guzzi; **Lucy Van Pelt (singing):** Tiffany Billings; **Linus Van Pelt:** Jeremy Miller; **Sally Brown:** Elizabeth Lyn Fraser; **Schroeder:** Aron Mandelbaum; **Marcie:** Jason Muller; **Off-Camera Singer:** Desiree Goyette

THE HAPPY PRINCE

The story of a royal statue that makes friends with a small swallow is told in this bittersweet tale based on the Oscar Wilde story. *A Gerald Potterton Production in association with Narrator's Digest. Color. Half-hour. Premiered: 1975. Syndicated.*

Voices

Statue: Christopher Plummer; **Swallow:** Glynis Johns

THE HARLEM GLOBETROTTERS MEET SNOW WHITE

The wizards of the basketball court play gargoyles working for a wicked witch—really a vain queen—who has cast a spell on Snow White. *A Hanna-Barbera Production. Color. Ninety minutes. Premiered on NBC: September 27, October 4, October 11 and October 18, 1980 (as a four-part serial on* Fred and Barney Meet the Shmoo*). Syndicated.*

Voices

Curly Neal: Stu Gilliam; **Geese:** John Williams; **Marques:** Robert DoQui; **Li'l John:** Buster Jones; **Dunbar:** Adam Wade; **Nate:** Scatman Crothers; **Baby Face Paige:**

Mork Davitt; **Snow White:** Russi Taylor; **Prince:** Michael Bell; **Marva:** Diane McCannon; **Queen of Grimmania:** Gay Autterson; **Count Revolta:** John Stephenson

HE-MAN AND SHE-RA— A CHRISTMAS SPECIAL

The villainous Skeletor, archrival of He-Man and She-Ra, tries to stop the spread of Christmas joy on Earth, but his diabolical plan is squelched when Prince Adam (He-Man) and Princess Adora (She-Ra) launch their own counterattack. *A Filmation Associates Production. Color. One hour. Premiered: November 1985. Syndicated.*

Voices

Adam/He-Man: John Erwin; **Adora/She-Ra:** Melendy Britt; **Skeletor:** Alan Oppenheimer; **Madam Razz/Shadow Weaver:** Linda Gary; **Hordak/Bow:** George DiCenzo; **Orko:** Eric Gunden

HENRY'S CAT: "THE MYSTERY OF THE MISSING SANTA" AND "WHEN TIME WENT WRONG"

The bedraggled orange feline, star of the British imported animated series *Henry's Cat*, appears in two madcap holiday adventures, which were combined into this half-hour special that premiered on Showtime. (It also aired the *Henry's Cat* cartoon series.) In the opener, Henry plays the "world-famous master detective" when Santa is found missing; then, in the second adventure, he finds himself in a time-tripping predicament. *A Bob Godfrey Films Ltd. Production. Color. Half-hour. Premiered on SHO: December 24, 1991. Rebroadcast on SHO: December 4, 1994; December 20, 1994; December 23, 1994.*

Voices

Bob Godfrey

HERE COMES GARFIELD

In his first prime-time animated special, Garfield the cat lives up to his reputation as being "both thorny and funny" when he and his pint-size playmate, Odie the mutt, play havoc with a nasty neighbor. Unfortunately, their friskiness lands Odie in the city pound and it is up to rueful Garfield to get him out. An Emmy Award nominee. *A Lee Mendelson–Bill Melendez Production in association with United Feature Syndicate. Color. Half-hour. Premiered on CBS: October 25, 1982. Rebroadcast on CBS: November 26, 1983; May 17, 1985; October 12, 1988.*

Voices

Garfield: Lorenzo Music; **Jon Arbuckle:** Sandy Kenyon; **Odie:** Gregg Berger; **Hubert:** Henry Corden; **Reba/**

Skinny: Hal Smith; **Fast Eddie/Fluffy:** Hank Garrett; **Salesman:** Gregg Berger; **Little Girl:** Angela Lee; **Vocalists:** Lou Rawls, Desiree Goyette

HERE COMES PETER COTTONTAIL

Danny Kaye hosts and narrates this whimsical hour-long Animagic special—using stop-motion puppet animation—recounting the delightful tale of Peter Cottontail and his efforts to deliver more eggs than Irontail, an evil rabbit, who is interested in dethroning him as "the Easter Rabbit." Based on the popular children's book *The Easter That Overslept*, the program was conceived by the same team that produced earlier seasonal favorites, including *Rudolph, The Red-Nosed Reindeer* and *Little Drummer Boy*. *A Rankin-Bass Production in association with Videocraft International. Color. One hour. Premiered on ABC: April 4, 1971. Rebroadcast on ABC: March 30, 1972. Rebroadcast on CBS: April 13, 1976; April 8, 1977; March 24, 1978; April 10, 1979; March 28, 1980; April 10, 1981.*

Voices
Seymour S. Sassafrass: Danny Kaye; **Peter Cottontail:** Casey Kasem; **Irontail:** Vincent Price; **Donna:** Iris Rainer; **Antoine/Wellington B. Bunny:** Danny Kaye; **Bonnie:** Joan Gardner

HERE COMES THE BRIDE

Actress/comedienne Carol Kane lends her voice to this imaginative adaptation of the well-known song in which klutzy Maximillian Mole meets acrobat Margaret Mouse when the circus comes to town and it's love at first sight. From Cinar Films *The Real Story of . . .* series. *A Cinar Films/France Animation Production. Color. Half-hour. Premiered on HBO: January 24, 1994.*

Voices
Margaret Mouse: Carol Kane

HERE'S TO YOU, MICKEY MOUSE

Mark Linn-Baker and Soleil Moon-Frye host this 90-minute birthday salute honoring Mickey Mouse's 60th birthday in 1988, complete with clips from many memorable Mickey Mouse cartoons, produced for The Disney Channel. *A George Paige Associates Production for The Disney Channel. Color. Ninety minutes. Premiered on DIS: 1988.*

HE'S YOUR DOG, CHARLIE BROWN

Snoopy's sudden attack of bad manners makes him so unpopular with the *Peanuts* clan that Charlie Brown decides to send him back to the Daisy Hill Puppy Farm for a refresher course in obedience training. The program marked Snoopy's first starring role in primetime. *A Lee Mendelson–Bill Melendez Production in association with Charles M. Schulz Creative Associates and United Feature Syndicate. Color. Half-hour. Premiered on CBS: February 14, 1968. Rebroadcast on CBS: February 20, 1969; February 15, 1970; February 13, 1971; February 14, 1972; June 5, 1973.*

Voices
Charlie Brown: Peter Robbins; **Linus Van Pelt:** Chris Shea; **Lucy Van Pelt:** Sally Dryer-Barker; **Peppermint Patty:** Gail DeFaria; **Frieda/Patty:** Anne Altieri; **Violet:** Linda Mendelson

HEY ARNOLD! THE CHRISTMAS SHOW

Entitled "Arnold's Christmas," this half-hour holiday special follows the adventures of street-smart fourth-grader Arnold as he arranges an elaborate gift for lonely Mr. Hyunh by reuniting him with his long-lost daughter. *A Games Animation Production in association with Snee-Osh, Inc. Color. Half-hour. Premiered on NIK: December 14, 1996. Rebroadcast on NIK: December 20, 1996; December 25, 1996.*

Voices
Arnold: Toran Caudell (Lane T. Caudell); **Gerald:** Jamil W. Smith; **Helga:** Francesca Marie Smith; **Grandma:** Tress MacNeille; **Grandpa:** Dan Castellaneta; **Oskar:** Steve Viksten; **Harold:** Justin Shenkarow; **Phoebe:** Anndi McAfee; **Stinky:** Christopher P. Walberg; **Brainy:** Craig M. Bartlett; **Rhonda:** Olivia Hack; **Mr. Hyunh:** Baoan Coleman; **Big Bob Pataki/Shoe Salesman:** Maurice LaMarche; **Mrs. Pataki:** Kath Soucie; **Ernie:** Dom Irrera; **Mai Hyunh:** Hiep Thi Le; **Mr. Bailey #2:** Vincent Schiavelli

HEY, HEY, HEY, IT'S FAT ALBERT

The first cartoon adaptation of comedian Bill Cosby's fictional childhood characters, this half-hour special combined sketchy-style animated drawings superimposed over live-action footage to tell the story of Cosby's boyhood chums from North Philadelphia who are preparing for a big football match against rival street-gang members the Green Street Terrors. *A Filmation Associates Production in association with Bill Cosby Productions. Color. Half-hour. Premiered on NBC: November 12, 1969. Rebroadcast on NBC: April 17, 1970; September 12, 1971.*

Voices
Fat Albert/Mushmouth/Mudfoot/Dumb Donald: Bill Cosby; **Russell:** Stephen Cheatham; **Weird Harold:** Gerald Edwards; **Bucky:** Jan Crawford; **Rudy:** Eric Suter

HIAWATHA

Legendary brave Hiawatha encounters his greatest test of courage when his tribe is put under the spell of Pearl Feather, an evil medicine man, who seeks revenge by starving the tribe. Based on the Henry Wadsworth Longfellow poem, this program was broadcast in syndication as part of the *Festival of Family Classics*. *A Rankin-Bass Production in association with Mushi Studios. Color. Half-hour. Premiered: September 24, 1972. Syndicated.*

Voices

Carl Banas, Len Birman, Bernard Cowan, Peg Dixon, Keith Hampshire, Peggi Loder, Donna Miller, Frank Perry, Henry Ramer, Billie Mae Richards, Alfie Scopp, Paul Soles

THE HOBBIT

Self-doubting hobbit Bilbo Baggins leads a quest through Middle Earth to recover stolen treasure from the terrifying dragon, Smaug, and finds a magical ring in this 90-minute special based on the J.R.R. Tolkein literary classic. Glen Yarborough sings the special's theme song, "The Greatest Adventure." *A Rankin-Bass Production. Color. Ninety minutes. Premiered on NBC: November 27, 1977. Rebroadcast on CBS: May 19, 1979. Rebroadcast on DIS: December 4, 1992. Rebroadcast on CAR: June 18, 1995 (Mr. Spim's Cartoon Theatre).*

Voices

Bilbo Baggins: Orson Bean; **Gandalf the wizard:** John Huston; **Thorin Oakenshield, king dwarf:** Hans Conreid; **Dragon Smaug:** Richard Boone; **Gollum:** Theodore; **Elvenking:** Otto Preminger; **Elrond:** Cyril Ritchard

HOLLYROCK-A-BYE BABY

When Pebbles and Bamm-Bamm, now married, move to Hollyrock, the first thing they produce is a "double" feature: twins. Meanwhile, Fred tangles with jewel thieves and a glamorous starlet while helping his son-in-law sell a screenplay in this two-hour made-for-TV animated special. *A Hanna-Barbera Production. Color. Two hours. Premiered on ABC: December 5, 1993.*

Voices

Fred Flintstone: Henry Corden; **Wilma Flintstone:** Jean VanderPyl; **Barney Rubble/Dino/J. Rocko:** Frank Welker; **Betty Rubble:** B.J Ward; **Pebbles Flintstone Rubble:** Kath Soucie; **Bamm-Bamm Rubble:** Jerry House; **Mr. Slate:** John Stephenson; **Mrs. Slaghoople:** June Foray; **Rocky:** Charlie Adler; **Mr. Pyrite:** Michael Bell; **Big Rock:** Brad Garrett; **Slick:** Mark Hamill; **Mary Hartstone:** Mary Hart; **John Teshadactyl:** John Tesh; **Shelly Millstone:** Raquel Welch

A HOLLYWOOD HOUNDS CHRISTMAS

A Caucasian country guitar-playing dog learns cultural tolerance and understanding when he teams up with an African American sax-playing canine and a timbale-playing Latina cat to form the first multiethnic pet singing group and discover the true meaning of Christmas. *A DIC Enterprises Production in association with Bohbot Entertainment. Color. Half-hour. Premiered: November 25, 1994. Syndicated.*

Voices

Rosie: Candi Milo; **Dude:** Jeff Bennett; **Cuz:** Chris Broughton; **Michael:** Theodore Borders; **Holly:** Jania Foxworth

HOORAY FOR THE THREE WISEMEN

In the year 2000, three wise men are sent to Earth in a spacecraft to deliver gifts to the newborn Christ child in this Italian-produced special made in six episodes. *A Cineteam Realizzazioni Production in association with Radiotelevisione Italiana. Color. One hour. Premiered: 1987. Syndicated.*

Voices

Gaspar: Albert Eddy; **Balthasar:** Leroy Villanueva; **Melchor:** Tony McShear; **Kid:** Dennis Khalili-Borna; **Joseph:** Michael Connor; **Mary:** Eric Rose; **Herod:** Ken Dana, Michael McComohle; (singing); **Shepherd:** Simon Prescott

THE HORSE THAT PLAYED CENTERFIELD

The New York Goats, a professional baseball team, are perennial losers. Their luck turns when a baseball-playing horse, Oscar, joins the team. The *ABC Weekend Special* was aired in two parts. *A Ruby-Spears Enterprises Production for ABC. Color. Half-hour. Premiered on ABC: February 24, 1979 and March 3, 1979. Rebroadcast on ABC: September 29, 1969 and October 6, 1969; July 5, 1980 and July 12, 1980; June 13, 1981 and 20, 1981; June 5, 1982 and June 12, 1982; May 28, 1983 and June 4, 1983; June 15, 1985 and June 22, 1985; March 4, 1989 and March 11, 1989; September 16, 1989 and September 23, 1989.*

Voices

John Erwin, Joan Gardner, Allan Melvin, Don Messick, Howard Morris, Alan Oppenheimer, Brad Sanders

HOW BUGS BUNNY WON THE WEST

Actor Denver Pyle, well-known for various roles in movie westerns, tells how Bugs Bunny and Daffy Duck were true pioneers of the West in this half-hour special featuring excerpts from previously released Warner cartoons. A

Warner Bros. Television Production. Color. Half-hour. Premiered on CBS: November 15, 1978. Rebroadcast on CBS: September 10, 1979; September 18, 1980; March 8, 1983; January 13, 1984; May 30, 1984; January 18, 1985; September 20, 1985; August 21, 1987.

Voices
Mel Blanc

◎ HOW DO YOU SPELL GOD?

Children from diverse religious and cultural backgrounds answer candid and touching questions emphasizing the importance of unity and understanding among people of all faiths in this HBO special, featuring cartoon renditions of the Hindu parable "The Blind Men and the Elephant" as well as works by Maya Angelou, Isaac Bashevis Singer and A.A. Milne. Opening the half-hour program is a live-action introduction by the Dalai Lama. *A Debra Solomon/HBO Production. Color. Half-hour. Premiered on HBO: December 22, 1996.*

◎ HOW THE LEOPARD GOT HIS SPOTS

Actor Danny Glover narrates this beloved children's tale of a light-coated African leopard whose only chance of survival is to acquire spots for himself in this inspired half-hour animated adaptation of the Rudyard Kipling classic, produced as part of Rabbit Ears Video's *Storybook Classics* series. *A Rabbit Ears Video Production. Color. Half-hour. Premiered on SHO: 1989.*

Voices
Narrator: Danny Glover

◎ HOW THE RHINOCEROS GOT HIS SKIN/HOW THE CAMEL GOT HIS HUMP

Two of Rudyard Kipling's best-known "Just So" stories—the first about a man who seeks revenge on a nasty piggish rhino, the second about how arrogance becomes the downfall of a lazy camel—are presented in this half-hour animated adaptation, told by award-winning actor Jack Nicholson. Produced for Rabbit Ears Video's *Storybook Classics* series, it made its debut on Showtime. *A Rabbit Ears Video Production. Color. Half-hour. Premiered on SHO: 1989.*

Voices
Narrator: Jack Nicholson

◎ HUNGARIAN FOLK TALES

Produced by MTV Enterprises in Hungary, these three delightful animated folktales—"John Raven," about a young man's journey to find his fortune, and two others, "The Hedehog" and "Pinko," classic stories of unlikely heroes rewarded for their kindness and remarkable feats—debuted in the United States on PBS's long-running *Long Ago & Far Away* series. *A MTV Enterprises, Hungary Production. Color. Half-hour. Premiered on PBS: February 25, 1989. Rebroadcast on PBS: November 23, 1990.*

◎ THE ICE QUEEN'S MITTENS

With no kitten fur for mittens to warm her hands during the upcoming winter, Freezelda, the evil Ice Queen bribes her henchman, Hoodwink the Rat, to fetch three little kittens to make fur, only to have Old Man Winter summon a blizzard and thwart her in this half-hour animated musical, originally produced for Canadian television as part of Cinar Films' *The Real Story of . . .* series (retitled from *Three Little Kittens*). The special aired on HBO under the pay-cable network's *HBO Storybook Musicals* series. *A Cinar Films/Crayon Animation Production in association with Western Publishing Company/CTV Television Network/Telefilm Canada. Color. Half-hour. Premiered on HBO: October 2, 1991. Rebroadcast on HBO: October 7, 1991; October 18, 1991; October 31, 1991.*

Voices
Freezelda, the Ice Queen: Lauren Bacall; **Hoodwink:** Bryan Adams

◎ I LOVE CHIPMUNKS, VALENTINE SPECIAL

Valentine's Day to the Chipmunks marks the long-awaited social event of the year—the Valentine's Day dance and a chance to win the prestigious Valentine's couple award. Alvin and Chipette Brittany learn a lesson in honesty and love as they become the model Valentine's couple. *A Ruby-Spears Enterprises Production in association with Ross Bagdasarian Productions. Color. Half-hour. Premiered on NBC: February 12, 1984. Rebroadcast on NBC: February 13, 1985.*

Voices
Alvin/Simon/David Seville: Ross Bagdasarian Jr.; **Theodore:** Janice Karman; **The Chipettes: Brittany/Jeanette/Elenore:** Janice Karman

◎ THE INCREDIBLE BOOK ESCAPE

Actress Quinn Cummings, as a young boy named P.J. (in live action), accidentally gets locked in the children's reading room of the local public library and becomes acquainted with the characters from several picture books who come to life in a blend of live action and animation. *A CBS Library Special. A Bosustow Entertainment Production. Color. One hour. Premiered on CBS: June 3, 1980. Rebroadcast on CBS: November 28, 1980.*

Voices
Mrs. Page: Ruth Buzzi; **Myra:** Penelope Sundrow; **Ghost-in-the-Shed:** George Gobel; **Princess:** Tammy Grimes; **Lord Garp/Prince:** Arte Johnson; **Professor Mickimecki:** Hans Conried; **Melvin Spitznagle:** Sparky Marcus; **Mrs. Spitznagle:** June Foray; **Mr. Spitznagle:** Jack Angel

⊚ THE INCREDIBLE DETECTIVES

On a visit to a local museum, Davey Morrison is kidnapped by two guards with few clues left behind for the police to track his whereabouts. Davey's three talented pets—Madame Cheng, a slightly vain Siamese cat; Hennesy, a gabby black crow; and Reggie, a sophisticated but stuffy bulldog—investigate Davey's whereabouts. *A Ruby-Spears Enterprises Production. Color. Half-hour. Premiered on ABC: November 17, 1979. Rebroadcast on ABC: March 20, 1980; September 27, 1980.*

Voices
Madame Chen: Mariene Aragon; **Reggie:** Laurie Main; **Hennesey:** Frank Welker; **Davey Morrison:** Albert Eisenmann

⊚ THE INCREDIBLE, INDELIBLE, MAGICAL, PHYSICAL MYSTERY TRIP

This educational and entertaining fantasy entails the journey of two young children, Joey and Missy, through the mistreated body of their Uncle Carl, who has done little in his life to maintain his health. The kids make their trip after being miniaturized by their cartoon companion, Timer, in this *ABC Afterschool Special* that combines live action and animation. *A DePatie-Freleng Enterprises Production in association with ABC. Color. Half-hour. Premiered on ABC: Feb-*

Reggie the bulldog, Madame Cheng the cat and Hennesy the crow become detectives to right the wrong and save the day in the Ruby-Spears cartoon special The Incredible Detectives. *© Ruby-Spears Enterprises*

ruary 7, 1973. Rebroadcast on ABC: October 24, 1973; March 4, 1978 (on ABC Weekend Specials).

Voices
Timer: Len Maxwell; **Joey:** Peter Broderick; **Missy:** Kathy Buch

⊚ IN SEARCH OF DR. SEUSS

This two-hour live-action/animated special celebrated the life and work of bestselling children's author Dr. Seuss (a pen name of Theodor Geisel), featuring such celebrity performers as Robin Williams, Christopher Lloyd and Eileen Brennan impersonating famous Seuss characters, and includes clips from popular animated specials. *A Point Blank Production. Color. Two hours. Premiered on TNT: November 6, 1994. Rebroadcast on TNT: December 8, 1994.*

Cast (live action)
Brady Bluhm, Eileen Brennan, Andrae Crouch, Billy Crystal, Matt Frewer, Graham Jarvis, Terry Lindholm, Christopher Lloyd, Howie Mandel, Andrea Martin, Kathy Najimy, David Paymer, Patrick Stewart, Robin Williams

⊚ INSPECTOR GADGET SAVES CHRISTMAS

There's trouble at the North Pole: Dr. Claw has changed the elves into drones and jailed the real Santa. His plot to ruin Christmas is thwarted by Inspector Gadget's tag-along friends Brain and Penny, as well as some fast bumbling on the part of the great inspector himself in this Emmy-nominated holiday special. *A DIC Enterprises Production. Color. Half-hour. Premiered on NBC: December 4, 1992. Rebroadcast on ABC: December 14, 1996.*

Voices
Inspector Gadget: Don Adams

⊚ INTERGALACTIC THANKSGIVING

Two families who are dissimilar in nature (one is hardworking and dedicated, the other is self-centered) travel in space to parts unknown in search of a new planet where they can settle in this Canadian produced holiday special. *A Nelvana Limited Production in association with the CBC. Color. Half-hour. Premiered: October 1979. Syndicated.*

Voices
King Goochie: Sid Caesar; **Ma Spademinder:** Catherine O'Hara; **Pa Spademinder:** Chris Wiggins; **Victoria Spademinder:** Jean Walker; **Magic Mirror:** Martin Lavut; **Notfunnyenuf:** Derek McGrath; **The Bug:** Al Waxman; **Bug Kid:** Toby Waxman

⊚ IRA SLEEPS OVER

Based on the book by Bernard Waber, a young boy (Ira) spends his first night away from home at his playmate Reggie's house. Even though he's afraid that his friend will tease him, he brings along his beloved teddy bear in this half-hour animated musical special, part of the *HBO Storybook Musicals* series. *A Michael Sporn Animation Production in association with Italtoons Corporation. Color. Half-hour. Premiered on HBO: November 6, 1991. Rebroadcast on HBO: November 15, 1991.*

Voices
Ira: Danny Gerard; **Sister:** Grace Johnston

⊚ IS THIS GOODBYE, CHARLIE BROWN?

In this funny yet poignant treatment of the trauma friends suffer when they must separate, Lucy and Linus's father is transferred to a new job in another city and the children must move away from their pint-size community. Charlie Brown finds the situation so appalling that he's left speechless . . . well, almost. *A Lee Mendelson–Bill Melendez Production in association with Charles M. Schulz Creative Associates and United Media Syndicate. Color. Half-hour. Premiered on CBS: February 21, 1983. Rebroadcast on CBS: February 13, 1984.*

Voices
Charlie Brown: Brad Kesten; **Linus Van Pelt:** Jeremy Schoenberg; **Lucy Van Pelt:** Angela Lee; **Marcie:** Michael Dockery; **Sally Brown:** Stacy Heather Tolkin; **Peppermint Patty:** Victoria Vargas; **Schroeder/Franklin:** Kevin Brando; **Snoopy:** José C. Melendez

⊚ IT'S A BRAND NEW WORLD

Four children experience the wonders of the Bible in stories about Noah and Samson told in music and song. The pro-

gram was one of six specials that aired on NBC under the heading "NBC Special Treat." *An Elias Production in association with D & R Productions. Color. One hour. Premiered on NBC: March 8, 1977. Rebroadcast on NBC: April 9, 1977; December 5, 1977.*

Voices
Teacher/Noah: Joe Silver; **Elijah/Samson:** Malcolm Dodd; **Aaron:** Dennis Cooley; **Jezebel:** Boni Enten; **Barnabas:** George Hirsch; **Samson's Brother:** Charmaine Harma; **Vocalists:** Sylvester Fields, Hilda Harris, Maeretha Stewart

⊚ IT'S A MYSTERY, CHARLIE BROWN

Sally needs something to bring to show and tell at school and takes Woodstock's nest as an example of a prehistoric bird nest. Meanwhile, Snoopy, thinking he's Sherlock Holmes, tries to find the thief of his little friend's nest. *A Lee Mendelson–Bill Melendez Production in association with Charles M. Schulz Creative Associates and United Feature Syndicate. Color. Half-hour. Premiered on CBS: February 1, 1974. Rebroadcast on CBS: February 17, 1975.*

Voices
Charlie Brown: Todd Barbee; **Lucy Van Pelt:** Melanie Kohn; **Linus Van Pelt:** Stephen Shea; **Peppermint Patty:** Donna Forman; **Marcie:** Jimmie Ahrens; **Sally Brown:** Lynn Mortensen; **Pigpen:** Thomas A. Muller

⊚ IT'S AN ADVENTURE, CHARLIE BROWN

This one-hour animated special was one of a series of programs featuring different stories based on the best comic strips by *Peanuts* cartoonist Charles M. Schulz. Segments include Lucy's plot to get rid of Linus's security blanket and Peppermint Patty's and Marcie's stint as "caddies" at a golf course. Host: Charles M. Schulz. *A Lee Mendelson–Bill Melendez Production in association with Charles M. Schulz Creative Associates and United Feature Syndicate. Color. Half-hour. Premiered on CBS: May 16, 1983. Rebroadcast on CBS: November 5, 1983; September 19, 1987.*

Voices
Charlie Brown: Michael Catalano; **Lucy Van Pelt:** Angela Lee; **Linus Van Pelt:** Earl "Rocky" Reilly; **Sally Brown:** Cindi Reilly; **Peppermint Patty:** Brent Hauer; **Schroeder:** Brad Schachter; **Marcie:** Michael Dockery; **Ruby:** Jenny Lewis; **Austin:** Johnny Graves; **Leland:** Joel Graves; **Milo:** Jason Muller; **Caddymaster:** Gerard Goyette Jr.; **Camp Kids:** Brandon Crane, Brian Jackson, Kevin Brando; **Snoopy:** José Melendez; **Announcer:** John Hiestand

Ira is excited at the invitation to sleep over at his best friend Reggie's house in Ira Sleeps Over. © Michael Sporn Animation

IT'S ARBOR DAY, CHARLIE BROWN

Sally's lack of knowledge of the significance of Arbor Day inspires some members of the *Peanuts* gang to set things right by embarking on a seed-planting spree using the baseball field as their garden plot. Meanwhile, unsuspecting Charlie Brown is busy preparing strategy for the opening game of the baseball season, unaware that the baseball diamond has been turned into a jungle without his consent. *A Lee Mendelson–Bill Melendez Production in association with Charles M. Schulz Creative Associates and United Feature Syndicate. Color. Half-hour. Premiered on CBS: March 16, 1976. Rebroadcast on CBS: March 14, 1977; April 10, 1978; March 24, 1980.*

Voices

Charlie Brown: Dylan Beach; **Lucy Van Pelt:** Sarah Beach; **Linus Van Pelt:** Liam Martin; **Schroeder:** Greg Felton; **Frieda:** Michelle Muller; **Sally Brown:** Gail Davis; **Peppermint Patty:** Stuart Brotman; **Rerun/Pigpen:** Vinny Dow

IT'S A WONDERFUL TINY TOONS CHRISTMAS

In this parody of the Jimmy Stewart classic *It's a Wonderful Life*, Buster Bunny is fired as director of the Christmas pageant and wishes he had never been on Tiny Toons. He gets his wish and an angel shows him what life would have been like in Acme Acres without him in the first prime-time animated special starring the characters of the popular animated series. *A Warner Bros./Amblin Entertainment Production. Color. Half-hour. Premiered on FOX: December 6, 1992. Rebroadcast on FOX: December 5, 1993; December 25, 1994. Rebroadcast on NIK: December 25, 1996.*

Voices

Buster Bunny: Charlie Adler; **Babs Bunny:** Tress MacNeille; **Hamton J. Pig:** Don Messick; **Plucky Duck:** Joe Alaskey; **Elmyra Duff:** Cree Summer; **Dizzy Devil:** Maurice LaMarche; **Shirley Loon:** Gail Matthius

IT'S CHRISTMAS TIME AGAIN, CHARLIE BROWN

After airing the first *Peanuts* holiday special, *A Charlie Brown Christmas*, for 26 consecutive seasons, CBS ordered this new holiday-themed half-hour—a series of vignettes that focus on the normal *Peanuts* characters and themes. Features music by the late Vince Guaraldi (as performed by jazz pianist David Benoit), who wrote and performed the classic music from the Christmas and Halloween Charlie Brown specials. The 1992 special was the first for creator Charles M. Schulz since the 40th anniversary Charlie Brown retrospective airing in 1990. *A Lee Mendelson–Bill Melendez Production in association with Charles M. Schulz Creative Associates and United Media. Color. Half-hour. Premiered on CBS: November 27, 1992.*

Voices

Lindsay Bennish, John Graas, Philip Lucier, Minday Martin, Sean Mendelson, Marne Patterson, Matthew Slowik, Jamie Smith, Denna Tello, Brittany Thornton

IT'S FLASHBEAGLE, CHARLIE BROWN

Snoopy plays a John Travolta-type character in this animated musical parody of such films as *Flashdance* and *Staying Alive*, featuring various musical vignettes that center around a hoedown, aerobic exercise, a game of "Lucy Says" and, of course, Snoopy on the disco dance floor. *A Lee Mendelson–Bill Melendez Production in association with Charles M. Schulz Creative Associates and United Feature Syndicate. Color. Half-hour. Premiered on CBS: April 16, 1984. Rebroadcast on CBS: January 1, 1985; May 27, 1986; April 19, 1988.*

Voices

Charlie Brown: Brett Johnson, Brad Kesten; **Charlie Brown (singing):** Kevin Brando; **Sally Brown:** Stacy Ferguson; **Peppermint Patty:** Gini Holtzman; **Marcie:** Keri Houlihan; **Schroeder/Tommy, the kid:** Gary Goren, Kevin Brando; **Linus Van Pelt:** Jeremy Schoenberg; **Linus (singing):** David Wagner; **Lucy Van Pelt:** Heather Stoneman; **Lucy (singing):** Jessie Lee Smith; **Snoopy:** José Melendez; **Vocalists:** Joseph Chemay, Joey Harrison Scarbury, Desiree Goyette

IT'S MAGIC, CHARLIE BROWN

While practicing magic tricks, Snoopy succeeds at making Charlie Brown invisible, but he encounters trouble in making him reappear. *A Lee Mendelson–Bill Melendez Production in association with Charles M. Schulz Creative Associates and United Feature Syndicate. Color. Half-hour. Premiered on CBS: April 28, 1981. Rebroadcast on CBS: March 22, 1982; March 23, 1985; May 24, 1988.*

Voices

Charlie Brown: Michael Mandy; **Snoopy:** José Melendez; **Linus:** Earl "Rocky" Reilly; **Sally:** Cindi Reilly; **Marcie:** Shannon Cohn; **Peppermint Patty:** Brent Hauer; **Lucy:** Sydney Penny; **Schroeder/Kid/Franklin:** Christopher Donohoe

IT'S THE EASTER BEAGLE, CHARLIE BROWN

Linus insists that an Easter beagle will magically appear to hand out candy on Easter morning. But, with fresh memories of their futile vigil for the Great Pumpkin, the *Peanuts* gang make their own novel preparations, including boiling eggs without the shells. *A Lee Mendelson–Bill Melendez Production in association with Charles M. Schulz and United Feature Syndicate. Color. Half-hour. Premiered on CBS: April 9, 1974. Rebroadcast on CBS: March 26, 1975; April 12, 1976; April 4, 1977; March 19, 1978; April 9, 1979; March 26, 1986. Rebroadcast on DIS: April 7, 1996.*

Voices
Charlie Brown/Schroeder: Todd Barbee; **Lucy Van Pelt:** Melanie Kohn; **Linus Van Pelt:** Stephen Shea; **Peppermint Patty:** Linda Ercoli; **Sally Brown/Violet/Frieda:** Lynn Mortensen; **Marcie:** James Ahrens

◎ IT'S THE GIRL IN THE RED TRUCK, CHARLIE BROWN

Live action and animation combine in this tale of puppy love in the desert as Snoopy's brother Spike relates in a letter to Charlie Brown and Snoopy that he has found a special someone who brings new meaning to his quiet, carefree days of cooking flapjacks and listening to French-language tapes. She is Jenny (played by Jill Schulz, the daughter of *Peanuts* creator Charles M. Schulz), a perky aerobics instructor who drives a clunky red pickup truck. But Spike's happiness does not last: Jenny has a boyfriend, Jeff, who lures her from the idyllic desert life she has come to love. *A Lee Mendelson–Bill Melendez Production in association with Charles M. Schulz Creative Asscociates and United Feature Syndicate. Color. One hour. Premiered on CBS: September 27, 1988.*

Voices
Charlie Brown: Jason Riffle; **The French Instructor:** Steve Stoliar

Cast (live action)
Jenny: Jill Schulz; **Jeff:** Greg Deason; **Mollie:** Mollie Boice

◎ IT'S THE GREAT PUMPKIN, CHARLIE BROWN

The Halloween season is here and Linus convinces Charlie and his pals from the Charles Schulz *Peanuts* comic strip that the arrival of the Great Pumpkin "with his bag of toys for all the good children" is near. The show featured the first appearance of Snoopy's Red Baron character. Because of Charlie Brown's complaint that all he got for Halloween was a "rock," gifts poured in to CBS and Charles Schulz's office after the special first aired. *A Lee Mendelson–Bill Melendez Production in association with Charles M. Schulz Creative Associates and United Feature Syndicate. Color. Half-hour. Pre-*

miered on CBS: October 27, 1966. Rebroadcast on CBS: October 26, 1967; October 24, 1968; October 26, 1969; October 24, 1970; October 23, 1971; October 28, 1974; October 23, 1976; October 30, 1978; October 22, 1979; October 24, 1980; October 30, 1981; October 25, 1982; October 28, 1983; October 26, 1984; October 30, 1985; October 24, 1986; October 23, 1987; October 25, 1989; October 30, 1991; October 25, 1996; October 31, 1997.*

Voices
Charlie Brown: Peter Robbins; **Linus Van Pelt:** Chris Shea; **Lucy Van Pelt:** Sally Dryer-Barker; **Sally Brown:** Cathy Steinberg; **Frieda/Violet:** Anne Altieri; **Peppermint Patty:** Kip DeFaria; **Pigpen:** Gail DeFaria; **Patty:** Lisa DeFaria; **Schroeder** (*off camera*)**/Shermy:** Glenn Mendelson

◎ IT'S YOUR FIRST KISS, CHARLIE BROWN

Unlikely hero Charlie Brown is faced with two horrendous challenges in this half-hour animated special: He is the kicker for the local football team at the annual homecoming football game and he has been chosen to escort Heather, the homecoming queen, to the celebration dance and give her the "traditional kiss." *A Lee Mendelson–Bill Melendez Production in association with Charles M. Schulz Creative Associates and United Feature Syndicate. Color. Half-hour. Premiered on CBS: October 24, 1977. Rebroadcast on CBS: January 8, 1979; January 14, 1980; January 30, 1981; November 24, 1987.*

Voices
Charlie Brown/Roy/Kid: Arrin Skelley; **Peppermint Patty:** Laura Planting; **Linus/Schroeder:** Daniel Anderson; **Lucy/Heather:** Michelle Muller; **Franklin/Shermy/Pigpen:** Ronald Hendrix

◎ IT'S YOUR 20TH TELEVISION ANNIVERSARY, CHARLIE BROWN

Peanuts creator Charles M. Schulz hosts a toast to his characters' 20th television anniversary, with most of the hour dedicated to clips from 26 *Peanuts* specials which have aired in prime time since 1965. *A Lee Mendelson–Bill Melendez Production in association with Charles M. Schulz Creative Associates and United Feature Syndicate. Color. One hour. Premiered on CBS: May 14, 1985. Rebroadcast on CBS: February 10, 1987.*

◎ IT WAS A SHORT SUMMER, CHARLIE BROWN

Assigned to write a 500-word theme on his summer vacation, Charlie Brown agonizes over the remembrance of things past, including summer camp and his tent-mates' competing against the girls in baseball, swimming and canoeing, all ending in defeat and disaster. His last hope of beating the girls is the Masked Marvel (Snoopy), who enters a wrist-wrestling match against Lucy. *A Lee Mendelson–Bill Melendez Production in association with Charles M. Shulz Creative Associates and United Feature Syndicate. Color. Half-hour. Premiered on CBS: September 27, 1969. Rebroadcast on CBS: September 16, 1970; September 29, 1971; September 7, 1972; June 27, 1983.*

Voices
Charlie Brown: Peter Robbins; **Lucy Van Pelt:** Pamelyn Ferdin; **Linus Van Pelt:** Glenn Gilger; **Sally Brown:** Hilary Momberger; **Peppermint Patty:** Kip DeFaria; **Frieda:** Ann Altieri; **Sophie/Shirley/Clara:** Sally Dryer-Barker; **Shermy:** David Carey; **Pigpen:** Gail DeFaria; **Violet:** Linda Mendelson; **Schroeder:** John Daschback; **Roy/Kid/Boy:** Matthew Liftin; **Snoopy:** Bill Melendez

◎ IT ZWIBBLE: EARTHDAY BIRTHDAY
Two star-touched baby dinosaurs join forces and recruit other creatures to save the planet. Led by the magical dinosaur fairy, It Zwibble, and the Zwibble Dibbles, a group of adorable, socially responsible baby dinosaurs who pledge to care for the Earth and give it a birthday party, this half-hour tied in with the international celebration of Earth Day, April 22, 1990. Featuring a voice cast that included actors Christopher Reeve (as It Zwibble), Fred Gwynne (of TV's *The Munsters* fame) and acclaimed songstress/actress Lainie Kazan, the program was produced and directed by Emmy-nominated animator Michael Sporn (*Lyle, Lyle Crocodile*). *A Michael Sporn Animation Production. Color. Half-hour. Premiered on HBO: April 22, 1990. Rebroadcast on HBO: April 22, 1991; April 22, 1992; April 22, 1993; April 22, 1994; April 22, 1995; April 22, 1996; April 22, 1997.*

Voices
Christopher Reeve, Lainie Kazan, Fred Gwynne, Gregory Perler, Jonathan Goch, Jonathan Gold, Meghan Andrews, Gina Marle Huaman, Larry White, John Cannemaker

◎ IVANHOE
Twelfth-century knight Ivanhoe, aided by Robin Hood and his Merry Men, rescues Lady Rebecca, held captive by Prince John in this loosely based adaptation of Sir Walter Scott's romantic fantasy adventure. *An Air Programs International Production. Color. Half-hour. Premiered on CBS: November 27, 1975. Syndicated.*

Voices
Alistair Duncan, Barbara Frawley, Chris Haywood, Mark Kelly, John Llewellyn, Helen Morse, Bevan Wilson

◎ I YABBA-DABBA DO!
Longtime sweethearts Pebbles Flintstone and Bamm-Bamm Rubble tie the knot (get married, in other words), making Fred and Barney proud parents in this two-hour made-for-TV movie extravaganza directed by cartoon legend William Hanna (who also coproduced with longtime partner Joseph Barbera). The ABC special was the first of two new animated specials by the Oscar-winning cartoon team, followed by the sequel, *Hollyrock-a-Bye Baby* (1993), also for ABC. *A Hanna-Barbera Production. Color. Two hours. Premiered on ABC: February 7, 1993. Rebroadcast on ABC: December 31, 1994.*

Voices
Fred Flintstone: Henry Corden; **Wilma Flintstone:** Jean VanderPyl; **Barney Rubble/Dino:** Frank Welker; **Betty Rubble:** B.J. Ward; **Pebbles Flinstone:** Megan Mullaly; **Bamm-Bamm Rubble:** Jerry Houser

◎ IZZY'S QUEST FOR GOLD
Young Izzy asks the Tribunal Elders if he can compete in the Olympic Games and they agree if he first obtains the Five Olympic Rings given for perseverance, integrity, sportmanship, excellence and brotherhood before taking his giant leap into Olympic-hood. This half-hour animated special featured the mascot of the 1996 Summer Olympics Games, produced less than a year before the games were held in Atlanta. The special was the first of a planned two-part series of cartoon specials to be produced by Emmy Award–winning animation giant Film Roman (producers of such hits as *The Simpsons* and *Garfield and Friends*) for Turner Network Television, but only the first special was ever produced. *A Film Roman Production in association with Atlanta Centennial Olympic Properties. Color. Half-hour. Premiered on TNT: August 12, 1995. Rebroadcast on CAR: August 3, 1996; August 4, 1996.*

Voices
Izzy: Justin Shenkarow; **Coriba:** Alice Ghostly; **Fortius:** Victoria Carroll; **Citius:** Kay E. Kuter; **Altius:** Jeff Bennett; **Mom:** Tress MacNeille; **Dad:** Rob Paulsen; **Martin:** Scott Menville; **Spartin:** Mike Simmrin; **Narrator:** Jim Cummings

◎ JACK AND THE BEANSTALK
Gene Kelly heads the cast of live actors and animated characters who appear in this live-action/animation musical based on the popular children's fable. The original story remains intact as Jack (played by Bobby Riha) is conned by street peddler Jeremy Keen (Gene Kelly) into exchanging the family cow for a handful of magic beans that will sprout a giant beanstalk and take him to the giant's skyward castle,

where treasures of every kind abound. The special reunited Kelly with producers Joe Barbera and William Hanna, who animated Kelly's spectacular dance sequence with Jerry Mouse (of *Tom and Jerry* fame) in the 1945 MGM musical *Anchors Aweigh*. A Hanna-Barbera Production. Color. One hour. Premiered on NBC: February 26, 1967. Rebroadcast on NBC: January 16, 1968. Rebroadcast on CBS: January 15, 1971. Syndicated.

Cast
Jeremy Keen: Gene Kelly; **Jack:** Bobby Riha; **Mother:** Marian McKnight

Voices
Around the Mouse: Chris Allen; **Monster Cat:** Dick Beals; **Princess Serena:** Janet Waldo, Marni Nixon (singing); **Giant:** Ted Cassidy; **Woggle Bird:** Cliff Norton; **Announcer:** Art Gilmore

Other Voices
Jack DeLeon

JACK FROST

After falling in love with beautiful blond Elisa of January Junction—a village terrorized by Kubla Kraus, an ogre who lives in a castle—Jack Frost is granted his wish to become human but is foiled in his pursuit of the girl when she falls for a handsome knight instead. A Rankin-Bass Production. Color. One hour. Premiered on NBC: December 13, 1979. Rebroadcast on NBC: December 5, 1980. Rebroadcast on DIS: December 15, 1992; December 4, 1993. Syndicated.

Voices
Pardon-Me-Pete, the groundhog: Buddy Hackett; **Jack Frost:** Robert Morse; **Elisa:** Debra Clinger; **Elisa's Father/ Danny, the ventriloquist's dummy:** Larry Storch; **Elisa's Mother:** Dee Stratton; **Kubla Kraus/Father Winter:** Paul Frees; **Snip, the Snowflake Maker:** Don Messick; **Holly:** Diana Lynn; **TV Announcer:** Dave Garroway

Other Voices
Sonny Melendrez

THE JACKIE BISON SHOW

Animation and live action were blended in this unsold comedy pilot that aired as a prime-time special about a buffalo (billed as "America's beast of buffoonery") who is the host of his own TV show. The program was inspired by *The Jack Benny Show*. A Stein & Illes Production in association with Brillstein/Grey Productions, Akom Productions and Broadcast TV Arts. Color. Half-hour. Premiered on NBC: July 2, 1990.

Voices
Jackie Bison: Stan Freberg; **Larry J. Lizard, his announcer:** Richard Karron; **Jill St. Fawn, his girlfriend:** Jane Singer; **Mrs. St. Fawn, Jill's mother:** Jayne Meadows

JACK O'LANTERN

In an unusual plot line, Jack O'Lantern, a staple of Halloween, encounters trouble in the form of an evil witch, Zelda, who is fervent in her attempt to snatch Jack's magic pot of gold, and her doting warlock husband, Sir Archibald. The tale is recalled by the grandfather of two children, Michael and Colleen, whose interest in the story serves as a subplot. A *Festival of Family Classics* special. A *Rankin-Bass Production in association with Mushi Studios*. Color. Half-hour. Premiered: October 29, 1972. Syndicated.

Voices
Carl Banas, Len Birman, Bernard Cowan, Peg Dixon, Keith Hampshire, Peggi Loder, Donna Miller, Frank Perry, Henry Ramer, Billie Mae Richards, Alfie Scopp, Paul Soles

JAZZTIME TALE

In New York City circa 1919 a young city girl (Lucinda) befriends a lonely girl (Rose) from the other side of town, who feels left out of her father's busy schedule. They experience Jazztime history while forming a lifelong friendship in this half-hour animated special from animator Michael Sporn, broadcast in 1991 on PBS's award-winning anthol-

The spooky spirit of Halloween is captured in the Rankin-Bass animated fantasy Jack O'Lantern. © Rankin-Bass Productions

ogy series *Long Ago & Far Away*. A Michael Sporn Animation/WGBH Boston Production in association with Italtoons Corporation. Color. Half-hour. Premiered on PBS: November 2, 1991. Rebroadcast on PBS: October 4, 1992.

Voices
Old Lucinda/Narrator: Ruby Dee

◎ THE JEAN MARSH CARTOON SPECIAL
Jean Marsh and Grover Monster, one of the original Muppets, host this collection of animated cartoons for children, including films by animators Chuck Jones, John Hubley and others. Program is also known as *The Grover Monster Cartoon Special*. A KQED-TV Production for PBS. Color. One hour. Premiered on PBS: March 10, 1975.

◎ THE JETSONS MEET THE FLINTSTONES
A time machine catapults the Jetsons (George, Jane, Judy and Elroy) back in time to come face to face with Stone Age citizens Fred and Wilma Flintstone and their best friends, Betty and Barney Rubble, in this two-hour special, the third in a series of original animated movies for first-run syndication distributed as part of *Hanna-Barbera's Superstars 10* package. A Hanna-Barbera Production. Color. Two hours. Premiered: 1987. Syndicated. Rebroadcast on TBS: September 5, 1993. Rebroadcast on CAR: May 28-30, 1994.

Voices
Fred Flintstone/Knight: Henry Corden; **Wilma Flintstone/Rosie/Mrs. Spacely:** Jean VanderPyl; **Barney Rubble/Cosmo C. Spacely/Dino:** Mel Blanc; **Betty Rubble/Jet Rivers/Investor/Panelist/Harem Girl:** Julie Dees; **George Jetson:** George O'Hanlon; **Jane Jetson:** Penny Singleton; **Judy Jetson/Female computer:** Janet Waldo; **Elroy Jetson/Cogswell/Henry:** Daws Butler; **Astro/Rudi/Mac/Announcer/Store Manager/Robot:** Don Messick; **Didi:** Brenda Vaccaro; **George Slate/Moderator/Investor/Poker Player:** John Stephenson; **Turk Tarpit:** Hamilton Camp; **Iggy:** Jon Bauman; **Dan Rathmoon/Johnny/Mr. Goldbrick:** Frank Welker

◎ JIM HENSON'S MUPPET BABIES
Stars of their own successful Saturday-morning cartoon show, the Muppet Babies made their first appearance in cartoon form in this prime-time special for CBS. The premise has the characters acting like show-biz stars in situations taped before a video camera, including a movie take-off (*Star Wars*) and a rock music video. The story title for the program was "Gonzo's Video Show." A Henson Associates Production in association with Marvel Productions. Color. Half-hour. Premiered on CBS: December 18, 1984.

Voices
Kermit/Beaker: Frank Welker; **Piggie:** Laurie O'Brien; **Fozzie/Scooter:** Greg Berg; **Rowlf:** Katie Lee; **Skeeter/Animal:** Howie Mandel; **Gonzo:** Russi Taylor; **Nanny:** Barbara Billingsley

◎ JIMINY CRICKET: STORYTELLER
Famous fables and fairy tales make up this 90-minute special, hosted by Jiminy Cricket, and later released overseas on home video as *Jiminy Cricket's Fabulous Fables, Fairy Tales and Other Wonderful Stuff*. The program premiered on The Disney Channel. A Disney Channel Production. Color. Ninety minutes. Premiered on DIS: 1986.

Voices
Jiminy Cricket: Eddie Carroll

◎ JINGLE BELL RAP
The K9-4 (Fetch, Licks, Rollover and Bones) is a merry group of musical dogs that rap and rock their way back to their hometown for a special Christmas concert and a very special reunion for Rollover in this colorful half-hour Christmas special, first broadcast in first-run syndication in 1991. A Perennial Pictures Film Corporation Production. Color. Half-hour. Premiered: November 1991. Syndicated.

Voices
Rollover: Scott Tyring; **Fetch/Licks:** Jerry Reynolds; **Roxie:** Rachel Rutledge; **Dad:** Russ Harris; **Collie Flower:** Lisa Roe Ward

◎ JINGLE BELL ROCK
Santa is forced to lay off some of his elves as a result of "budget cuts." And three of them decide to hoof it to Hollywood to raise money by competing for the big cash prize on a *Star Search*–type variety show (hosted and voiced by an animated Milton Berle). But the show's host has rigged the contest so his niece will win in this prime-time holiday special for ABC. A DIC Enterprises Production. Color. Half-hour. Premiered on ABC: December 22, 1995.

Voices
Milton Berle, Jay Brazeau, Terry King

◎ JIRIMPIMBIRA: AN AFRICAN FOLKTALE
Temba, a lionhearted young boy whose kindness is as great as "the generosity of his heart," sets off with a trio of ill-intentioned peers to search for food and water to save his

starving North African village. He gets off track after meeting a mysterious old man who gives him some magic bones that will grant him his every wish (after saying the magic word: "jirimpimbira") in this half-hour *ABC Weekend Special*, produced in celebration of Black History Month, based on the classic African folktale of the same name. *A Ruby-Spears/Huff-Douglas Production in association with Greengrass Productions. Premiered on ABC: February 25, 1995. Rebroadcast on ABC: March 15, 1997.*

Voices
Temba: Jamil Smith; **Old Man:** Paul Winfield; **Featherbrain:** Dave Fennoy; **Greedy:** Rembrandt Sabel; **Rat:** Meshach Taylor; **Mother:** Bianca Fergusso; **Storyteller:** Diahann Carroll; **Sly:** Greg Eagles; **Headman:** James Avery; **She Hawk:** Gwen Shepard; **Sister:** Dawn Lewis; **Villager:** Kelly Huff

JOHANN'S GIFT TO CHRISTMAS

In a small mountain village in the early 19th century, a mouse named Johann takes shelter in a church on Christmas Eve and, with the help of a guiding angel, writes a song (with an elderly church mouse, Viktor). In this live-action/clay-animated holiday special produced in 1991, the song provides the inspiration for the church's pastor and his organist to create the classic yuletide carol "Silent Night." The U.S. premiere date is unknown, but the program aired on Nickelodeon in 1993. Clay-animation sequences were directed by Anthony LaMolinera and Jeff Mulcaster (of California Raisins commercials fame). *An O'B & D Films Production. Color. Half-hour. Broadcast on NIK: December 9, 1993.*

JOHNNY APPLESEED

Folk hero Johnny Appleseed goes up against a quack doctor who claims his bottled medicine cures more ills than Johnny's own bottle of apple medicine. A *Family Festival of Classics* special. *A Rankin-Bass Production in association with Mushi Studios. Color. Half-hour. Premiered: November 5, 1972. Syndicated.*

Voices
Carl Banas, Len Birman, Bernard Cowan, Peg Dixon, Keith Hampshire, Peggi Loder, Donna Miller, Frank Perry, Henry Ramer, Billie Mae Richards, Alfie, Scopp, Paul Soles

JOLLY OLD ST. NICHOLAS

Scuddle Mutt and Clawdia dress up as elves and sing "Jolly Old St. Nicholas" to win the $50 first prize at a talent show. During the Christmas Eve performance, two of Santa's elves are mistaken for the impostors and are pushed on stage to sing while the real Scuddle Mutt and Clawdia go on an unexpected sleigh ride with Santa they'll never forget in this heartwarming, half-hour syndicated special. *A Perennial Pictures Film Corporation Production. Color. Half-hour. Premiered: November 24, 1994. Syndicated.*

Voices
Scuddle Mutt/O'Toole the Mule: Jerry Reynolds; **Clawdia/Miss Posey:** Rachel Rutledge; **Santa Claus:** Andy Kuhn; **Poinsetta Pig:** Lisa Buetow

JONNY QUEST VS. THE CYBER INSECTS

The Quest Team again matches wits with the evil Dr. Zin (he's baaaack!) and his army of genetically engineered insects as Zin wreaks havoc on Earth's climate through the use of high-tech satellites in this second feature-length adventure starring the characters from the popular 1960s cartoon series, animated in their original form. Originally titled *Jonny's Global Impact*, the two-hour cartoon spectacular marked the last appearance of Jonny Quest and the gang in their original animated form before the arrival of a new animated series, *The Real Adventures of Jonny Quest*, in the fall of 1996, featuring 1990s' makeovers. *A Hanna-Barbera Production. Color. Two hours. Premiered on TNT: November 19, 1995.*

Voices
Jonny Quest: Kevin Michaels; **Dr. Benton Quest:** Don Messick; **Race Bannon:** Granville Van Dusen; **Hadji:** Rob Paulsen; **Jessie:** Anndi McAfee; **Dr. Zin:** Jeffrey Tambor; **Dr. Belage:** Teresa Saldana; **4-DAC:** Tim Matheson; **Atacama:** Hector Elizondo

JONNY'S GOLDEN QUEST

Jonny, Dr. Quest, Race Bannon, Hadji and company battle the evil Dr. Zin and his ecosystem-threatening genetic mutants in a global chase that takes them to such international locales as Peru, Tokyo, Rome and Australia in this full-length—and first—ever-animated feature produced exclusively for USA Network. Produced 28 years after the original 1964–65 television series, *The Adventures of Jonny Quest*, the film introduced two new female characters: Mrs. Quest, the wife of Dr. Quest (said to have been "lost" all this time), and Jessie Bannon, daughter of Race Bannon (also now married). *A Hanna-Barbera Production in association with USA Network and Fil-Cartoons Inc., Phillipines. Color. Two hours. Premiered on USA: April 4, 1993. Rebroadcast on USA: August 20, 1995.*

Voices
Jonny Quest: Will Nipper; **Race Bannon/Stilt Walker/Cook:** Granville Van Dusen; **Dr. Benton Quest/Bandit/Man:** Don Messick; **Hadji/Announcer:** Rob Paulsen;

Rachel Quest: Meredith MacRae; **Jade Kenyon:** JoBeth Williams; **Dr. Zin/Guard:** Jeffrey Tambor; **3-Dac/Ms. Moo Moo:** B.J. Ward; **Jessie:** Anndi McAfee; **Dr. Devlon/Scientist #1/Stilt Walker:** Peter Renaday; **Commander/College President/Robot:** Ed Gilbert; **Chief/Policeman/Local Boy:** Marcelo Tubert; **Snipe/Replicant/Dolphins:** Frank Welker; **President/Scientist #2/Chikara:** George Hearn; **Agent Melendez/Local Boy/Stilt Walker:** Pepe Serna; **Young Jonny Quest:** Whitby Hertford

◎ JOURNEY BACK TO OZ

Dorothy and her friends, the Scarecrow, the Tin-Man and the Cowardly Lion, return to save Oz from Mombi, the Bad Witch, in this sequel to the 1939 MGM classic that was released originally to theaters and later repackaged as a holiday special with additional live-action sequences of Bill Cosby as the program's Host Wizard. Margaret Hamilton, an original *Wizard of Oz* cast member, played the role of Aunt Em. *A Filmation Associates Production. Color. Two hours. Premiered on ABC: December 5, 1976. Syndicated. Rebroadcast: December 1978 (SFM Holiday Network).*

Voices

Dorothy: Liza Minelli; **Scarecrow:** Mickey Rooney; **Tin-Man:** Danny Thomas; **Cowardly Lion:** Milton Berle; **Aunt Em:** Margaret Hamilton; **Mombi, the Bad Witch:** Ethel Merman; **Glinda, the Good Witch:** Rise Stevens; **Pumpkinhead:** Paul Lynde; **Woodenhead:** Herschel Bernardi; **The Signpost:** Jack E. Leonard

◎ JOURNEY TO THE CENTER OF THE EARTH

Professor Linderbrook, his friend Alex and their guide Hans take the journey of their lifetimes as they head out on a mission to explore Earth's core in this animated adaptation of the Jules Verne science-fiction novel. *A Famous Classic Tales special. An Air Programs International Production. Color. One hour. Premiered on CBS: November 13, 1977. Rebroadcast on CBS: November 23, 1978. Syndicated.*

Voices

Lynette Curran, Alistair Duncan, Barbara Frawley, Ron Haddrick, Bevan Wilson

◎ KIDNAPPED

David Balfour, the rightful heir of the Master of the House of Shaws, gets kidnapped so that his uncle can control his inheritance and remove him from the picture altogether. Program was adapted from the Robert Louis Stevenson novel. *A Famous Classic Tales special. An Air Programs International Production. Color. One hour. Premiered on CBS: October 22, 1973. Syndicated.*

◎ THE KINGDOM CHUMS: LITTLE DAVID'S ADVENTURE

Based on the biblical story of David and Goliath, this holiday special, which opens with live-action footage, details the adventures of Little David, Christopher and Magical Mose who welcome three children—transformed into cartoon form—to the world of the Kingdom Chums where the world's greatest stories unfold, all leading up to David's man-to-man challenge of Goliath. *An ABC Production in association with DIC Enterprises and Diana Kerew Productions. Color. One hour. Premiered on ABC: November 28, 1986. Rebroadcast on ABC: August 15, 1992 (Part 1) and August 22, 1992 (Part 2).*

Cast

Mary Ann: Jenna Van Oy; **Peter:** Christopher Fitzgerald; **Sauli:** Andrew Cassese

Voices

Little David: Scott Menville, Sandi Patti (singing); **Magical Mose:** John Franklin; **Christopher/Cat Soldier:** Billy Bowles; **Goliath/Fox Soldier #3:** Jim Cummings; **Eliab/Fox Soldier #2:** Townsend Coleman; **King Saul:** Paul Winchell; **Frog Servant/Fox Soldier #1/Rat Soldier #1:** Phil Proctor; **Vocalists:** John Franklin, Sandi Patti, Mitchell Winfield

◎ THE KINGDOM CHUMS: ORIGINAL TOP TEN

Debby Boone, Tony Orlando, Marilyn McCoo, Billy Preston and Frankie Valli lend their voices to this tuneful, inspirational tale of three kids who discover the original Top 10 Songs were the Ten Commandments in this two-part, hour-long animated special for Saturday-morning's *ABC Weekend Specials* series. Originally produced in 1989, the program was shelved when ABC's children's programming head left the network. Briefly offered on home video via point-of-purchase television commercials with an 800-number (the idea was dropped when sales were less than expected), it premiered three years after its making. *A Rick Reinert Pictures Production. Color. One hour. Premiered on ABC: August 15, 1992 and August 22, 1992. Rebroadcast on ABC: April 10, 1993 and April 17, 1993.*

Voices

Essie: Debby Boone; **Miriam:** Marilyn McCoo; **Christopher:** Tony Orlando; **Mose:** Billy Preston; **Little David:** Frankie Valli; **Petey:** Mayim Bialik; **Osborn:** Scott Menville; **Annie:** Marine Patterson

◎ THE KING KONG SHOW

The great ape, whose colossal strength and great size enable him to conquer others, was featured in two episodes shown

The world's greatest biblical story, David and Goliath, is transformed into cartoon form in the ABC Weekend Special The Kingdom Chums: Little David's Adventure. © *American Broadcasting Companies, Inc. All rights reserved.* (COURTESY: DIC ENTERPRISES)

back to back in this one-hour preview of the Saturday-morning series that premiered on ABC. *A Rankin-Bass Production. Color. One-hour. Premiered on ABC: September 6, 1966.*

⊚ KING OF THE BEASTS

The animal cast from TV's *Noah's Ark* returns in this half-hour sequel about a lion who assumes the role of "king of the beasts," only to drive one of his rivals, Croc the crocodile, into setting up his own solitary kingdom atop a mount. Songs and story were written by executive producer Charles G. Mortimer Jr., director Shamus Culhane and John Culhane. *A Shamus Culhane Production in association with Westfall Productions. Color. Half-hour. Premiered on NBC: April 9, 1977. Rebroadcast on NBC: April 19, 1978: Rebroadcast on DIS: July 29, 1993; August 6, 1993. Syndicated.*

Voices
Noah: Henry Ramer; **Crocodile:** Paul Soles; **Lion:** Carl Banas; **Male Elephant:** Murray Westgale; **Female Elephant:** Bonnie Brooks; **Male Giraffe/Camel:** Jay Nelson; **Polar Bear:** Don Mason; **Ostrich/Female Penguin:** Ruth Springford; **Walrus:** Jack Mather; **Female Baby Croc:** Judy Sinclair; **Male Baby Croc/Mouse:** Cardie Mortimer

⊚ KISSYFUR: BEAR ROOTS

Gus and Kissyfur, a father-and-son team of performing circus bears, escape from the big top to join the community of Paddlecab County, but are not welcomed by the other resident animals until they rescue the community from the jaws of two hungry alligators, Jolene and Floyd. The program was based on characters created by Phil Melendez and also

inspired their own Saturday-morning series. *An NBC Production in association with DIC Enterprises. Color. Half-hour. Premiered on NBC: December 22, 1985.*

Voices
Kissyfur: R.J. Williams; **Gus:** Edmund Gilbert; **Jolene:** Terence McGovern; **Floyd/Stuckey:** Stu Rosen; **Duane:** Neil Ross; **Beehonie/Miss Emmy/Toot:** Russi Taylor; **Lennie:** Lennie Weinrib; **Uncle Shelby:** Frank Welker

⊚ KISSYFUR: THE BIRDS AND THE BEARS

In their attempt to impress Miss Emmy Lou's smarter-than-average niece, Donna, Kissyfur and his swamp friends build a raft and recklessly travel upstream, only to get caught in a strong undertow and become the target of swamp 'gators, Jolene and Floyd, returning characters from the first Kissyfur special, *Bear Roots. An NBC Production in association with DIC Enterprises. Color. Half-hour. Premiered on NBC: March 30, 1986.*

Voices
Kissyfur: R.J. Williams; **Gus:** Edmund Gilbert; **Jolene:** Terence McGovern; **Floyd/Stuckey:** Stu Rosen; **Duane:** Neil Ross; **Beehonie/Miss Emmy/Toot:** Russi Taylor; **Lennie:** Lennie Weinrib; **Uncle Shelby:** Frank Welker

⊚ KISSYFUR: THE LADY IS A CHUMP

When the search begins for a new babysitter for Kissyfur, Gus hires a sweet nanny who turns out to be Floyd the alligator—bent on a good meal—in disguise. *An NBC Production in association with DIC Enterprises. Color. Half-hour. Premiered on NBC: June 1, 1986.*

Voices
Kissyfur: R.J. Williams; **Gus:** Edmund Gilbert; **Jolene:** Terence McGovern; **Floyd/Stuckey:** Stu Rosen; **Duane:** Neil Ross; **Beehonie/Miss Emmy/Toot:** Russi Taylor; **Lennie:** Lennie Weinrib; **Uncle Shelby:** Frank Welker

⊚ KISSYFUR: WE ARE THE SWAMP

Old buzzard Floyd and his snake Reggie lure Kissyfur and his swamp buddies up to a magical place high in a tree where anything is possible—even swimming in a water-filled hole—as part of a plan to make the critters their main dish for dinner. *An NBC Production in association with DIC Enterprises. Color. Half-hour. Premiered on NBC: July 6, 1986.*

Voices
Kissyfur: R.J. Williams; **Gus:** Edmund Gilbert; **Jolene:**

Terence McGovern; **Floyd/Stuckey:** Stu Rosen; **Duane:** Neil Ross; **Beehonie/Miss Emmy/Toot:** Russi Taylor; **Lennie:** Lennie Weinrib; **Uncle Shelby:** Frank Welker; **Flo:** Marilyn Lightstone

◎ LASSIE AND THE SPIRIT OF THUNDER MOUNTAIN

Television's most famous collie appeared in cartoon form for the first time in this one-hour feature-length story, later rebroadcast as two episodes on Saturday-morning's *Lassie Rescue Rangers* series. *A Filmation Associates Production with Lassie Television. Color. One hour. Premiered on ABC: November 11, 1972 (on* The ABC Saturday Superstar Movie*).*

Voices
Ben Turner: Ted Knight; **Laura Turner, his wife:** Jane Webb; **Susan Turner:** Lane Scheimer; **Jackie Turner:** Keith Sutherland; **Ben Turner/Gene Fox:** Hal Harvey; **Lassie:** Lassie; **Narrator:** Ted Knight

◎ THE LAST HALLOWEEN

Blending live action and computer-generated animation, four bumbling Martians—Gleep, Romtu, Scoota and Bing—crash-land on Earth in search of candy (called "koobie" on their planet) to replenish their planet's supply. They hook up with two small-town kids who help the aliens with their mission and take them trick-or-treating, only to discover an evil scientist (played by Rhea Perlman) who has been stealing the lake water for her experiments in this half-hour Halloween special originally broadcast on CBS. The special's animated stars, Gleep, Romtu, Scoota and Bing, were originally created at Industrial Light & Magic for a series of television commercials. *A Hanna-Barbera/Pacific Data Images Production. Color. Half-hour. Premiered on CBS: October 28, 1991.*

Cast (live action)
Michael: Will Nipper; **Jeanie:** Sarah Martineck; **Mrs. Gizborne, evil scientist:** Rhea Perlman; **Hans, her sinister henchman:** Richard Moll; **Grandpa:** Eugene Roche; **Hubble:** Stan Ivar; **Accountant:** Michael D. Roberts; **Others:** Grant Gelt, Tim Anderson, Sean Roche, Darwyn Carson, Bill Hanna

Voices
Gleep: Paul Williams; **Romtu:** Don Messick; **Scoota/Bing:** Frank Welker

◎ THE LAST OF THE CURLEWS

Native to the arctic shoreland, the curlews, tall striped birds, are on the verge of extinction. As the two survivors search for mates to keep their species alive, they encounter hunters who are unconcerned with their survival. This *ABC Afterschool Special* was an Emmy Award winner. *A Hanna-Barbera Production. Color. One hour Premiered on ABC: October 4, 1972. Rebroadcast on ABC: March 7, 1973. Rebroadcast on CAR: September 10–12, 1993, April 1, 1994 (Turner Family Showcase).*

Voices
Stan: Ross Martin; **Mark:** Vinnie Van Patten; **Bird Calls:** Ginny Tyler; **Narrator:** Lee Vines

◎ THE LAST OF THE MOHICANS

During the French and Indian War, Cora, the daughter of French Commander Allan Munro, is abducted by the traitorous Magua Indians. Scout Hawkeye and the last two Mohicans, Chingachook and his son, Unca, work to free the girl from her captors and aid the French in the capture of the Magua tribe. Based on a novel by James Fenimore Cooper. *A Famous Classic Tales special. A Hanna-Barbera Production. Color. One hour. Premiered on CBS: November 27, 1975. Rebroadcast on CBS: November 25, 1981. Syndicated.*

Voices
Hawkeye: Mike Road; Uncas: Casey Kasem; **Chingachook:** John Doucette; **Cora Munro:** Joan Van Ark; **Alice Munro:** Kristina Holland; **Duncan Heyward:** Paul Hecht; **Magua/Soldier:** Frank Welker; **Colonel Allen Munro/Delaware Chief:** John Stephenson

◎ THE LAST OF THE RED-HOT DRAGONS

A once-powerful old flying dragon who has lost his fire-breathing ability regains it in time to save Noah's ark-bound animals, who are left stranded at the North Pole by melting a block of ice that traps them in a dark cave. *A Shamus Culhane Production in association with Erredia Productions and Westfall Productions. Color. Ninety minutes. Premiered on NBC: April 1, 1980. Syndicated. Rebroadcast on DIS: August 14, 1993.*

Voices
Dragon: John Culhane; **King Lion:** Carl Banas; **Crocodile:** Paul Soles; **Elephant:** Murray Westgate; **Penguin:** Ruth Springford; **Polar Bear:** Don Mason; **Baby Girl Crocodile:** Judy Sinclair; **Baby Boy Crocodile:** Cardie Mortimer

◎ THE LEGEND OF HIAWATHA

Great Indian legend Hiawatha, who is half man and half god, teaches his people how to meet the challenges of everyday life in this adaptation of the famed Henry Wadsworth Longfellow poem. A *Kenner Family Classics* special. *An Atkinson Film-Arts Production in association with Triple Seven Concepts. Color. One hour. Premiered on CBS: November 24, 1983. Rebroadcast on NBC: December 4, 1984 (as NBC Special Treat). Syndicated.*

Voices
Tim Atkinson, Barry Edward Blake, Gary Chalk, Arline Van Dine, Les Lye, Anna MacCormick, Michael Voss

◎ THE LEGEND OF LOCHNAGAR

A reclusive Scotsman's quest for peace and quiet and a warm bath bring him to a cave carved into Lochnagar Mountain, where, boasting an "encyclopedic knowledge of indoor plumbing," he outfits his new home with all the modern conveniences. The plumbing ultimately causes ecological problems that threaten elfin creatures who live beneath Earth's surface in this *ABC Weekend Special*, written and narrated by England's Prince Charles (who appears in a live-action introduction). The prince wrote the story when he was 21 and first told it to his his younger brothers, Andrew and Edward. *A Mike Young Production in association with Dave Edwards Ltd. Color. Half-hour. Premiered on ABC: April 24, 1993. Rebroadcast on ABC: April 1, 1995; November 4, 1995.*

Voices
Scotsman: Robbie Coltrane

◎ THE LEGEND OF ROBIN HOOD

The classic tale of Robin Hood and his Merry Men, who rob from the rich to give to the poor, is colorfully retold in this hour-long adaptation that traces Robin's crusade to rid England of the underhanded Prince John. A *Famous Classic Tales* special. *An Air Programs International Production. Color. One hour. Premiered on CBS: November 14, 1971. Rebroadcast on CBS: November 11, 1972; September 30, 1973. Syndicated.*

Voices
Tim Elliott, Peter Guest, Ron Haddrick, John Kingley, John Llewellyn, Helen Morse, Brenda Senders

◎ THE LEGEND OF SLEEPY HOLLOW

Washington Irving's eerie tale of romantic rivalry along the Hudson River, pitting the new schoolmaster, Ichabod Crane, against the local hero and bully, Brom Bones, is told by Oscar-winning actress Glenn Close in this spirited 1988-produced, half-hour adaptation, part of Rabbit Ears Video's *Holiday Classics* video series, which aired on Showtime. *A Rabbit Ears Video Production. Color. Half-hour. Premiered on SHO: 1989. Rebroadcast on DIS: December 20, 1991.*

Voices
Narrator: Glenn Close

◎ THE LEPRECHAUN'S CHRISTMAS GOLD

Art Carney, as the oldest of the Killakilarney clan, narrates and sings this story of a young cabin boy lost on an uncharted island who unwittingly frees a caterwauling Banshee who tries to steal the leprechauns' pot of gold. *A Rankin-Bass Production. Color. Half-hour. Premiered on ABC: December 23, 1981. Syndicated. Rebroadcast on ABC: December 20, 1983. Rebroadcast on DIS: December 22, 1992.*

Voices
Barney Killakilarney (narrator): Art Carney; **Faye Killakilarney:** Peggy Cass; **Dinty Doyle:** Ken Jennings; **Old Mag:** Christine Mitchell; **Child/Others:** Glynnis Bieg; Michael Moronosk

◎ LIBERTY AND THE LITTLES

On their way to New York City for the Fourth of July, a storm forces the Littles (Dinky, Grandpa, William, Helen, Tom and Lucy) to crash near the Statue of Liberty. There they make friends with two children, Michelle and Pierre, and help them escape from a tiny 19th-century community contained inside the statue. Michelle and Pierre learn the meaning of liberty in a free land. Based on John Peterson's popular children's book series, the special aired in three parts as an *ABC Weekend Special*. The characters appeared in their own successful Saturday-morning series, *The Littles*, also broadcast on ABC. *An ABC Entertainment Production in association with DIC Enterprises. Color. Half-hour. Premiered on ABC: October 18, October 25 and November 1, 1986. Rebroadcast on ABC: August 18, August 25 and September 1, 1989; June 20, June 27 and July 4, 1992.*

Voices
Tom Little: David Wagner; **Lucy Little:** Bettina Rush; **Grandpa Little:** Alvy Moore; **Dinky Little:** Robert David Hall; **Helen Little:** Patti Parris; **William Little:** Gregg Berger; **Michelle/Pierre:** Katie Lee; **Pere Egalitaire:** Jim Morgan; **General/Massey:** Earl Boen

◎ THE LIFE AND ADVENTURES OF SANTA CLAUS

The origin of jolly old St. Nick, alias Santa Claus, is recounted in this Animagic stop-motion animation special that traces the life of this merry old soul, from his early childhood to his rise as the world's foremost agent of goodwill in this hour-long holiday special adaptation of the 1902 story by *Wizard of Oz* author L. Frank Baum. *A Rankin-Bass Production. Color. One hour. Premiered on CBS: December 17, 1985. Rebroadcast on CBS: December 2, 1986; December 3, 1987; December 24, 1988. Rebroadcast on DIS: December 11, 1992; December 14, 1993; December 12, 1995.*

Voices

Great Ak: Alfred Drake; **Old Santa:** Earl Hammond; **Young Santa:** J.D. Roth; **Tingler:** Robert McFadden; **Necile:** Lesley Miller; **King Awgwa:** Earle Hyman; **Wind Demon:** Larry Kenney; **Weekum:** Joey Grasso; **Children:** Amy Anzelowitz, Josh Blake, Ari Gold, Jamie Lisa Murphy; **Others:** Lynne Liptor, Peter Newman; **Vocalists:** Al Dana, Margaret Dorn, Arlene Mitchell, Marty Nelson, David Ragaini, Robert Ragaini; Annette Sanders

⊚ LIFE IS A CIRCUS, CHARLIE BROWN

Snoopy leaves home, becomes a big-top star ("Hugo the Great") in a traveling circus and falls in love with a fancily preened French poodle named Fifi, a circus performer. Charlie Brown is understandably distraught over his lost pet, receiving little comfort from Linus, who philosophizes, "It's difficult not to be enticed by romance and excitement, Charlie Brown. There's more to life than a plastic supper dish." *A Lee Mendelson–Bill Melendez Production in association with Charles M. Schulz Creative Associates and United Feature Syndicate. Color. Half-hour. Premiered on CBS: October 24, 1980. Rebroadcast on CBS: January 11, 1982; January 17, 1983.*

Voices

Charlie Brown: Michael Mandy; **Snoopy:** Bill Melendez; **Schroeder/Kids:** Christopher Donohoe; **Linus Van Pelt:** Earl "Rocky" Reilly; **Lucy Van Pelt:** Kristen Fullerton; **Peppermint Patty:** Brent Hauer; **Marcie:** Shannon Cohn; **Polly:** Casey Carlson

⊚ LIFE WITH LOUIE: A CHRISTMAS SURPRISE FOR MRS. STILLMAN

Stand-up comedian Louie Anderson, as his eight-year-old alter ego, helps his father decorate his lonely neighbor's house in this half-hour holiday misadventure that preceded the popular Fox Saturday-morning series. *A Hyperion Animation Production. Color. Half-hour. Premiered on FOX: December 18, 1994.*

Voices

Little Louie/Dad (Andy Anderson)/Narrator: Louie Anderson; **Mom (Ora Anderson):** Edie McClurg; **Tommy:** Miko Hughes; **Mike Grunewald/Glen Glenn:** Justin Shenkarow; **Jeannie Harper:** Debi Derryberry; **Mrs. Stillman:** Liz Sheridan

⊚ "THE LION KING": A MUSICAL JOURNEY WITH ELTON JOHN

Flamboyant pop star Elton John provides the melodies from the big-screen cartoon in this half-hour clip fest, offering an impressive sampling of scenes from the blockbuster movie and songs from the film's music score, including the chart-climbing ballad "Can You Feel the Love Tonight?" *A Walt Disney Production. Color. Half-hour. Premiered on DIS: June 15, 1994.*

Cast

Elton John, Tim Rice, Roy E. Disney, Jeffrey Katzenberg, Don Hahn, Ron Minkoff, Hans Zimmer, James Earl Jones, Jeremy Irons, Andreas Deja

⊚ THE LION, THE WITCH AND THE WARDROBE

Based on the children's book of the same name, four children are magically transported, via a giant wardrobe, into the wonderful land of Narnia, where they help a kingly lion vanquish a wicked queen who holds the land in the grip of winter. The program was broadcast in two parts. *A Children's Television Workshop Production in association with Bill Melendez Productions, the Episcopal Radio-TV Foundation, T.V. Cartoons and Pegbar Productions. Color. Two hours. Premiered on CBS: April 1 and April 2, 1979. Rebroadcast on CBS: April 22 and April 23, 1980. Rebroadcast on DIS: May 9, 1992; September 4, 1993; October 6, 1995.*

Voices

Lucy: Rachel Warren; **Susan:** Susan Sokol; **Peter:** Reg Williams; **Edmund:** Simon Adams; **Mr. Tumnus:** Victor Spinetti; **Professor:** Dick Vosburgh; **Mr. Beaver:** Don Parker; **Mrs. Beaver;** Liz Proud; **Asian:** Stephen Thorne; **White Witch:** Beth Porter

⊚ THE LITTLE BROWN BURRO

A dejected little burro, who finds he has no place in society, is reassured when he is bought by Joseph and travels to Bethlehem, carrying Mary to the site of baby Jesus' birth. *A Titlecraft/Atkinson Film-Arts Production in association with D.W. Reid Films. Color. Half-hour. Premiered (U.S.): December, 1978. Syndicated.*

Voices:

Little Brown Burro: Bonnie Brooks; **Omar:** Paul Soles; **Narrator:** Lorne Greene

A menagerie of Hanna-Barbera's most famous cartoon stars—Scooby-Doo, Captain Caveman, Barney Rubble, Fred Flintstone, Yogi Bear and Huckleberry Hound—celebrated the studio's golden anniversary in the 1989 TNT special Hanna-Barbera's 50th: A Yabba Dabba Doo Celebration. © Hanna-Barbera Productions. (COURTESY: TURNER NETWORK TELEVISION)

Famous western star hero the Lone Ranger galloped off to brand-new animated adventures in the CBS Saturday morning series The Lone Ranger. © Lone Ranger Productions.

The B.C. gang, from John Hart's beloved syndicated comic strip, make plans to cash in on the Christmas season by selling trees and gift rocks that are supposedly from a mythical gift-giver they create named "Santa Claus" in a scene from the yuletide special B.C.: A Special Christmas. © 1971 Cinera Productions/Hardlake Animated Pictures and Field Enterprises. (COURTESY: MG/PERIN INC.)

Myopic Mr. Magoo joins up with Davy Crockett in a scene from the NBC animated special Uncle Sam Magoo. © 1969 UPA Pictures, Inc. (COURTESY: UPA)

The lovable bears of Care-A-Lot come down to earth in their cloud mobiles to help children with their problems in the first-run, syndicated series The Care Bears. *The program was based on the popular children's book characters of the same name.* © 1985 American Greetings Corp. All program material © 1985 Kenner Parker Toys, Inc. (COURTESY: DIC ENTERPRISES INC.)

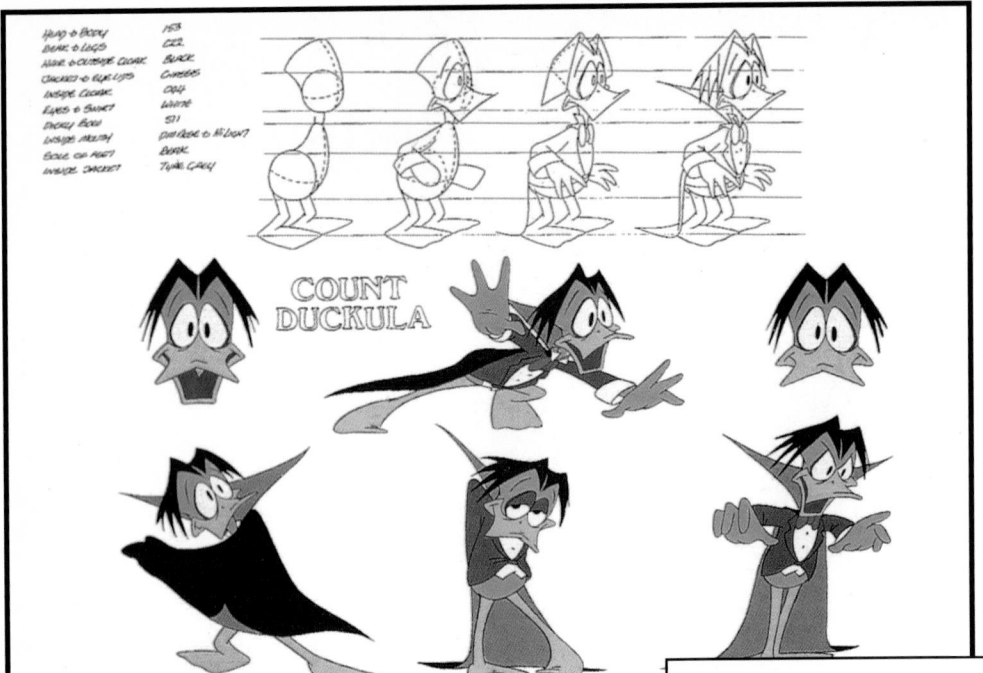

Model sheet for Count Duckula, a reluctant vampire with an aversion for blood who tries to find fame and fortune in show business. The British-produced series was a hit in the United States on Nickelodeon. © 1988 Cosgrove Hall Productions, Inc. (COURTESY: COSGROVE HALL PRODUCTIONS)

Mike reflects on social and political issues of the past in A Doonesbury Special, based on Gary Trudeau's popular syndicated strip. © Universal Press Syndicate. (COURTESY: THE HUBLEY STUDIO)

Charlie Brown decides to send Snoopy back to obedience school after suffering from a sudden attack of bad manners in the prime-time CBS television special He's Your Dog, Charlie Brown. © United Feature Syndicate. (COURTESY: BILL MELENDEZ PRODUCTIONS)

Bert Raccoon (center), Ralph (left) and Melissa (right) plot their strategy in a scene from the Canadian-produced series The Raccoons. © 1989 Evergreen Productions. (COURTESY: EVERGREEN PRODUCTIONS)

Hermy the Elf sings joyfully as friend Rudolph looks on in the perennial prime-time Christmas special Rudolph, The Red-Nosed Reindeer. *© Rankin-Bass Productions.* (COURTESY: FAMILY HOME ENTERTAINMENT)

Miyagi (center) demonstrates the fine art of self-defense for students Taki and Daniel in the animated adaptation of the famed motion picture The Karate Kid. © 1989 Columbia Pictures Television, Inc. All rights reserved. (COURTESY: DIC ENTERPRISES INC.)

Madeline, the smallest and bravest of 12 girls, experiences many new adventures shaped around the importance of love, sharing and friendship in the HBO special Madeline. © 1988 DIC Enterprises, Inc. (COURTESY: DIC ENTERPRISES INC.)

Opening title sequence from the popular HBO animated series
The Little Lulu Show. © *1997 Cinar Productions, Inc.*
"Little Lulu" is a trademark of Western Publishing Company,
Inc. (COURTESY: CINAR PRODUCTIONS)

A young girl is forced to sell matches on the streets of New
York on New Year's Eve in order to survive in the Michael
Sporn–animated special The Little Match Girl, *produced for*
HBO. © *Michael Sporn Animation.* (COURTESY: MICHAEL
SPORN ANIMATION)

Europe's leading animated film studio, Halas and Batchelor, produced this television series adaptation of Alexander Dumas's classic novel The Count of Monte Cristo. © Halas & Batchelor Productions.

THE *NEW* ADVENTURES OF BAT MAN

Actors Adam West and Burt Ward reprised the roles of their famed caped-crusading characters in The New Adventures of Batman, *originally produced for CBS. Joining the cast: Bat-Mite (far left).* © Filmation Associates–DC Comics Inc.
(COURTESY: FILMATION)

Television tough guy Mr. T fights crime with a team of teenage gymnasts in Saturday morning's Mr. T. *© 1983 Ruby-Spears Enterprises.* (COURTESY: RUBY-SPEARS ENTERPRISES)

Uncle Martin and his magazine friend Tim O'Hara, of TV's My Favorite Martian, *joined by two new cast members, Andromeda, Martin's nephew (far left), and Katy O'Hara, Tim's niece (second from left), experienced all-new animated adventures in the Saturday morning spin-off* My Favorite Martians. *© Filmation.* (COURTESY: FILMATION)

Felix the Cat with his magic bag of tricks has the last laugh in this original cel from Joe Oriolo's Felix the Cat *cartoon series. © Joe Oriolo Productions.* (COURTESY: JOE ORIOLO PRODUCTIONS)

The universe-zapping exploits of Flash Gordon, originally brought to the screen by Buster Crabbe as a favorite movie matinee serial in the 1930s, was revived by Filmation Studios in the form of the Saturday morning cartoon series The New Adventures of Flash Gordon. *© Filmation/King Features Syndicate.* (COURTESY: KING FEATURES SYNDICATE)

Homer Simpson shows his smart-mouthed son Bart that he means business in a scene from the critically acclaimed, long-running Fox Network animated series The Simpsons. © 1990 20th Century-Fox Film Corp. (COURTESY: KLASKY/CSUPO PRODUCTIONS)

A team of newly trained cadets, members of Robotech Defense Force, defend Earth from being destroyed by a fleet of giant alien spaceships in the Japanese television series cult favorite Robotech. © 1984 Tatsunoko Productions, Co., Ltd. *"Robotech" is a trademark owned and licensed by Revell, Inc.* (COURTESY: HARMONY GOLD)

Captain Harlock (pointing), head of an interstellar space galleon, protects and defends his home planet in the Japanese-imported series Captain Harlock and the Queen of a Thousand Years. © 1981 ZIV International, Inc. All rights reserved. (COURTESY: HARMONY GOLD)

The robotic droids R2D2 and C3PO from the Star Wars film series returned in animated form in the ABC Saturday morning series Droids: The Adventures of R2D2 and C3PO. The series was produced in association with Star Wars creator George Lucas's company, Lucasfilm. © and ™ 1985 Lucasfilm Ltd. All rights reserved. (COURTESY: LUCASFILM LTD.)

Popular recording stars Alvin and the Chipmunks in a scene from their 1960s animated series The Alvin Show. *© 1961 Bagdasarian Productions.* (COURTESY: BAGDASARIAN PRODUCTIONS)

An eight-year-old boy with the head of an aardvark confronts and solves problems in the half-hour PBS cartoon series Arthur. *© 1997 WGBH Educational Foundation and Cinar Productions. All rights reserved.* (COURTESY: CINAR FILMS)

book characters. A DIC Enterprises Production in association with Western Publishing Company. Color. Half-hour. Premiered: 1989.

Voices
Tootle the Train: Dillan Bouey; **Pokey Little Puppy:** Chiara Zanni; **Shy Little Kitten:** Tony Balshaw; **Katy Caboose:** Emily Perkins; **Scuffy the Tugboat:** Tony Ail; **Tawny Scrawny Lion:** Graham Andrews; **Saggy Raggy Elephant:** Lelani Marrell; **Baby Brown Bear:** Tony Dakota; **Beamer:** Imbert Orchard

THE LITTLE MATCH GIRL
Young Angela is selling matches on the streets of New York on New Year's Eve 1999. In order to survive the freezing weather, she lights three of her matches and has visions of warmth, great feats, loved ones and powerful people who can help her and the homeless in this modern-day adaptation of the Hans Christian Andersen fairy tale. Produced by New York animator Michael Sporn, the special aired on HBO's Storybook Musicals series. A Michael Sporn Animation Production in association with Italtoons Corporation. Color. Half-hour. Premiered on HBO: December 10, 1990.

Voices
Narrator: F. Murray Abraham; **Angela, the Match Girl:** Theresa Smythe

THE LITTLE MERMAID
Once comfortable with her lifestyle under the sea, a beautiful mermaid princess experiences a change of heart when she is saved by a young prince in this philosophical adaptation of the popular Han Christian Andersen tale. The program preceded a rebroadcast of Dr. Seuss's Horton Hears a Who in its original broadcast on CBS. A Gerald Potterton Production in association with Narrator's Digest. Color. Half-hour. Premiered on CBS: February 4, 1974. Rebroadcast on CBS: January 31, 1975. Syndicated.

Voices
Narrator: Richard Chamberlain

THE LITTLE RASCALS CHRISTMAS SPECIAL
Filmdom's The Little Rascals, who cavorted in more than 100 live-action comedy shorts for Hal Roach in the 1920s and 1930s, return in a prime-time animated special revolving around Spanky and his younger brother, Porky, who mistakenly think they're getting an electric train for Christmas. Former "Rascals" Darla Hood Granson (playing Spanky's mother) and Matthew "Stymie" Beard (the town

butcher), both since deceased, lend their voices to the program. A King World Presentation in association with Muller-Rosen Productions and Murakami-Wolf-Swenson Films. Color. Half-hour. Premiered on NBC: December 3, 1979. Rebroadcast on NBC: December 15, 1980; December 20, 1981.

Voices
Alfalfa: Jimmy Gatherum; **Spanky:** Phillip Tanzini; **Darla:** Randi Kiger; **Stymie:** Al Jocko Fann; **Porky:** Robby Kiger; **Mom:** Darla Hood Granson; **Sidewalk Santa:** Jack Somack; **Butcher:** Matthew "Stymie" Beard; **Man:** Cliff Norton; **Sales Clerk:** Frank Nelson; **Delivery Man:** Melville A. Levin; **Uncle Hominy:** Hal Smith; **Sales Lady:** Naomi Lewis; **Tough Kid:** Ike Eisenmann

LITTLE SPARROW: A PRECIOUS MOMENTS THANKSGIVING SPECIAL
A settler boy and a young Indian brave overcome their differences to work together to find the special berry that will cure the sickness affecting both their families in this half-hour Thanksgiving special, aired in first-run syndication on the Bohbot Kids Network. The program was one of five Precious Moments specials. Only two ever aired on U.S. television, the first being 1991's Timmy's Gift—produced by Westlake Village, California–based Rick Reinert Pictures, producers of the popular Cap'n O.G. Readmore/ABC Weekend Specials. A Rick Reinert Pictures Production. Color. Half-hour. Premiered: November 24, 1995. Syndication.

Voices
Little Sparrow: Alex McKenna; **Jon:** E.G. Daily; **Timmy:** Justin Garms; **Angie:** Debi Derryberry; **Indian Father/Settler Father:** Neil Ross

THE LITTLE TROLL PRINCE
Set among the rustic fjords and snow-covered villages of scenic Norway, this delightful parable tells the story of Bu, the crown prince of the trolls, who learns the true meaning of Christmas. This first-run syndicated special was produced in conjunction with the International Lutheran Laymen's League. A Hanna-Barbera Production in association with Wang Film Productions, Inc. and Cuckoo Nest Studios. Color. Half-hour. Premiered: 1987. Syndicated.

Voices
Bu: Danny Cooksey; **Borch, his two-headed brother:** Rob Paulsen; Laurie Faso; **Prag, his two-headed brother:** Neilson Ross; Frank Welker; **King Ulvik Head #1:** Vincent Price; **King Ulvik Head #2:** Jonathan Price; **Queen Sirena:** Cloris Leachman; **Professor Nidaros:** Don Knotts; **Stav:** Charlie Adler; **Ribo/Krill/Father:** Michael Bell; **Kristi:** Ami Foster; **Sonja:** Christina Lange; **Bjorn:**

The hit movie Ghostbusters was animated for Saturday morning television, featuring the same cast of wacko characters. Added for comic relief: Slimer (center). © 1986 Columbia Pictures Television, a division of CPT Holdings Inc. All rights reserved. (COURTESY: DIC ENTERPRISES INC.)

Black-hooded interplanetary space hero Space Ghost interviews health and fitness guru Susan Powter in the 1994 premiere episode of the hour-long late-night talk show from outer space Space Ghost Coast to Coast, produced for the Cartoon Network. "Space Ghost Coast to Coast" © 1994 Cartoon Network, Inc. Animated characters ™ & © 1966 Hanna-Barbera Productions, Inc. All rights reserved.
(COURTESY: CARTOON NETWORK)

🌀 THE LITTLE CROOKED CHRISTMAS TREE

Christopher Plummer narrates this timeless story of a Christmas tree that is spared from being chopped down to protect a nest of dove's eggs. The 1993 special originally produced for Canadian television, aired in the United States on The Disney Channel. *A Lacewood Production. Color. Half-hour. Premiered on DIS: 1993.*

🌀 LITTLE DRUMMER BOY

An exceptional tale set in ancient times about Aaron, a six-year-old orphaned drummer boy, who, along with his drum and three animal friends—a lamb, a camel and a donkey—learns the lesson of love and the true meaning of the holy season by journeying with the Three Wise Men to Bethlehem to witness the birth of the Christ child. The Teachers Guide to Television listed the special as "a specially selected program of educational value" prior to its network premiere. Animation for the program was by Animagic, a stop-motion process using puppets and making their movements appear life-like. The program was backed by the Vienna Boys Choir. *A Videocraft International Production in association with NBC. Color. Half-hour. Premiered on NBC: December 19, 1968. Rebroadcast on NBC: December 18, 1969; December 16, 1970; December 14, 1971; December 10, 1972; December 9, 1973; December 14, 1974; December 14, 1975; December 23, 1977; December 23, 1980. Rebroadcast on FAM: December 11, 1996.*

Voices

Aaron: Teddy Eccles; **Haramed:** José Ferrer; **Ali/Other voices:** Paul Frees; **Narrator:** Greer Garson

🌀 LITTLE DRUMMER BOY, BOOK II

In this sequel to 1968's *The Little Drummer Boy*, Aaron returns to undertake an incredible journey with one of the wise men, Melchoir—to find a man named Simeon who has constructed a set of Silver Bells to be rung to herald the birth of Christ. This Animagic special was produced by Arthur Rankin Jr. and Jules Bass, who created such perennial holiday special favorites as *Santa Claus Is Comin' to Town* and *Frosty the Snowman*. Greer Garson, who narrated the first special, served as the program's story teller. *A Rankin-Bass Production. Color. Half-hour. Premiered on NBC: December 13, 1976. Rebroadcast on NBC: December 23, 1977; December 21, 1978; December 23, 1980. Rebroadcast on FAM: December 9, 1995; December 13, 1996.*

Voices

Aaron: David Jay; **Melchoir:** Allen Swift; **Brutus:** Zero Mostel; **Simeon:** Ray Owens; **Plato:** Robert McFadden; **Narrator:** Greer Garson

🌀 THE LITTLE ENGINE THAT COULD

The plucky little locomotive of children's storybook fame who pulls a trainload of toys over a treacherous, snow-packed mountain, chugging "I think I can" learns the power of positive thinking to overcome difficult odds in this half-hour, made-for-video adaptation of the age-old children's classic by Watty Piper. First released on home video, the program also aired as an Easter special for two weeks—the end of March through early April of 1993—on 56 independent stations around the country. *A Dave Edwards Studio Production in association with MCA/Universal. Color. Half-hour. Premiered: March–April 1993.*

Voices

Bever-Leigh Banfield, Peter Cullen, Scott Menville, Billy O'Sullivan

🌀 LITTLE GOLDEN BOOKLAND

Little Golden Bookland is in danger. Storms have created a hole in the breakwater, and Harbortown and Beamer, the venerable old lighthouse, could be washed away. Scuffy the Tugboat saves the day, along with his friends Tootle the Train, Katy Caboose, Pokey Little Puppy and Shy Little Kitten in this animated version of the well-known children's

Aaron, a six-year-old orphan, conveys his happiness by beating his drum in a scene from the perennial Christmas favorite, Little Drummer Boy. © Rankin-Bass Productions (COURTESY: FAMILY HOME ENTERTAINMENT)

William Christopher; **Witch/Mrs. Bjorn:** B.J. Ward; **Spectator #1:** Rob Paulsen; **Spectator #2:** Laurie Faso; **Spectator #3:** Neilson Ross; **Troll:** Frank Welker

LOST IN SPACE

Hopping aboard their space shuttle *Jupiter II*, Craig Robinson and his crew embark on a peace-saving mission to help the peaceful Throgs ward off the Tyranos, metallic creatures who have declared war on the Throg planet, in this animated version of television's popular science-fiction series, *Lost in Space*. The hour-long movie, which featured several new characters, premiered on *The ABC Saturday Superstar Movie* series. A *Hanna-Barbera Production. Color. One hour. Premiered on ABC: September 8, 1973 (on* The ABC Saturday Superstar Movie). *Rebroadcast on ABC: January 5, 1974. Syndicated.*

Voices
Craig Robinson: Mike Bell; **Deana Carmichael:** Sherry Alberoni; **Linc Robinson:** Vince Van Patten; **Dr. Smith:** Jonathan Harris; **Robot:** Don Messick

Throgs:
Lar/Tyrano Twin One: Sidney Miller; **Kal/Tyrano Twin Two:** Ralph James; **Brack (child)/Announcer/Narrator:** Don Messick; **Tyrano Guard:** Mike Bell

LOVE AMERICAN STYLE: "LOVE AND THE OLD-FASHIONED FATHER"

Tom Bosley, of TV's *Happy Days* fame, plays the father of teenage daughter (Alice), who creates consternation in her middle-class American home when she asks her parents' permission to go away on a water-skiing weekend with her hippie boyfriend in this *All in the Family*–style cartoon scripted by R.S. Allen and Harvey Bullock, executive producers of the live-action *Love American Style* series. The all-animated show was one of two half-hour pilots produced and directed by William Hanna and Joseph Barbera. (Its predecessor was entitled, *Love and the Private Eye*.) A *Hanna-Barbera Production for Paramount Television. Color. Half-hour. Premiered on ABC: February 11, 1972.*

Voices
Father: Tom Bosley; **Mother:** Joan Gerber; **Alice:** Tina Holland

LOVE AMERICAN STYLE: "LOVE AND THE PRIVATE EYE"

Private eye Melvin Danger, a master of disguises who believes he is irresistible to women, delivers a large payroll to an industrial tycoon but loses both payroll and tycoon in

the process in this half-hour pilot produced and directed by William Hanna and Joseph Barbera. Originally entitled *Melvin Danger Plus Two*, the story was written by R.S. Allen and Harvey Bullock. Voice artist Lennie Weinrib is credited with having done six character voices for the show. A *Hanna-Barbera Production for Paramount Television. Color. Half-hour. Premiered on ABC: January 28, 1972.*

Voices
Melvin Danger: Richard Dawson; **Others:** Lennie Weinrib

LUCKY LUKE

This made-for-television movie returns viewers to the wild and woolly days of the Old West, with all the ingredients of a classic sagebrush saga: the strong, silent hero (Lucky Luke), his gallant horse (Jolly), the loyal dog (Bushwhack) and the gang of hardened desperadoes (the Dalton Boys) in an affectionate spoof of the western. A *Hanna-Barbera Production in association with Gaumont Productions and Dargaud Editeur. Color. Two hours. Premiered: 1985. Syndicated.*

Voices
Lucky Luke: Bill Callaway; **Jolly Jumper:** Bob Ridgely; **Averell:** Bob Holt; **Ma Dalton:** Mitzi McCall; **Jack:** Rick Dees; **Bushwhack:** Paul Reubens; **William:** Fred Travalena; **Joe:** Frank Welker

LYLE, LYLE CROCODILE: THE MUSICAL: "THE HOUSE ON EAST 88TH ST."

This music-filled family special tells the enchanting tale about a family who moves into a new home to find it's already inhabited by a talented reptile named Lyle the Crocodile. The charming green character wins their hearts, until Lyle's rightful owner returns to claim him in this animated version of Bernard Waber's popular tale, "The House on East 88th St." Animator Michael Sporn produced and directed this program, which was first released as a theatrical cartoon short in 1985, then given its world television premiere on the *HBO Storybook Musicals* series showcase. A *Michael Sporn Animation Production in association with Italtoons Corporation. Color. Half-hour. Premiered on HBO: November 18, 1987. Rebroadcast on HBO: November 23, 1987.*

Voices
Hector P. Valenti/Narrator: Tony Randall; **Mrs. Primm:** Liz Callaway; **Joshua:** Devon Michaels

MADELINE

Twelve little girls live in an old vine-covered house in Paris. The smallest and bravest of them all is Madeline. She experiences many adventures with her housemates and their loving guardian, Miss Clavel, in this musical tale based on the classic 1930s' children's book. The Emmy-nominated special premiered as part of the *HBO Storybook Musicals* series. *A DIC Enterprises Production. Color. Ninety minutes. Premiered on HBO: November 7, 1988. Rebroadcast on FAM: October 7, 1990.*

Voices
Madeline: Marsha Moreau; **Miss Clavel:** Judith Orban; **Vendor:** John Stocker; **Madeline's friends:** Loretta Jafelice, Linda Kash, Wendy Lands, Daccia Bloomfield, Tara Charendoff; **Narrator:** Christopher Plummer

⊚ MADELINE AND THE BAD HAT

Madeline and crew try to tame Pepito, the son of a Spanish ambassador ("The Bad Hat," as Madeline calls him withwith a capital "B"), who pulls all sorts of dastardly deeds on them. One day the young boy goes too far and must learn his lesson in the second of four half-hour specials produced for The Family Channel. *A DIC Enterprises Production. Color. Half-hour. Premiered on FAM: March 3, 1991. Rebroadcast on FAM: October 18, 1991; February 7, 1992.*

Voices
Madeline: Marsha Moreau; **Narrator:** Christopher Plummer

⊚ MADELINE AND THE GYPSIES

Pepito invites Madeline and the girls to a Gypsy carnival and, after getting separated, Pepito and Madeline meet the Gypsy mama who dresses them in a lion's costume. They roam the countryside, inadvertently frightening people and animals alike and discovering, like many children before them, that there's "no place like home," in this half-hour special produced for The Family Channel. *A DIC Enterprises Production. Color. Half-hour. Premiered on FAM: October 14, 1991. Rebroadcast on FAM: August 21, 1992.*

Voices
Madeline: Marsha Moreau; **Narrator:** Christopher Plummer

⊚ MADELINE IN LONDON

Pixieish Parisian Madeline, Miss Clavel and her friends surprise Pepito, who's moved to London with his father, the Spanish ambassador, by giving him a horse. Madcap mishaps ensue and Madeline ends up with a medal from the queen in this Family Channel special whose debut coincided with the repeat performance of 1990's *Madeline's Christmas*. *A DIC Enterprises Production. Color. Half-hour. Premiered on FAM: November 28, 1991. Rebroadcast on FAM: December 20, 1991; April 12, 1992.*

Voices
Madeline: Marsha Moreau; **Narrator:** Christopher Plummer

⊚ MADELINE'S CHRISTMAS

One year at Christmastime, Madeline, her friends and Miss Clavel get ready by making presents for family and friends, but the holiday is nearly ruined when the whole group (except for Madeline) come down with bad colds in this original half-hour special produced for The Family Channel. *A DIC Enterprises Production. Color. Half-hour. Premiered on FAM: November 11, 1990. Rebroadcast on FAM : December 20, 1991; December 3, 1992.*

Voices
Madeline: Marsha Moreau; **Narrator:** Christopher Plummer

⊚ MADELINE'S RESCUE

Madeline's teacher Miss Clavel almost dies, after nearly being scared to death during Madeline's clowning around. She survives thanks to the intercession of a charming dog who becomes the "hero of the day" in this Family Channel original production. *A DIC Enterprises Production. Color. Half-hour. Premiered on FAM: June 6, 1991. Rebroadcast on FAM: June 9, 1991; March 12, 1992; February 5, 1993.*

Voices
Madeline: Marsha Moreau; **Narrator:** Christopher Plummer

⊚ THE MAD, MAD, MAD COMEDIANS

The comedy routines of several well-known comedians, culled from excerpts of radio programs and television sketches, are brought to life in this simplistic animated special. *A Bruce Stark Production in association with ABC. Color. Half-hour. Premiered on ABC: April 7, 1970.*

Voices
Jack Benny: himself; **George Burns:** himself; **The Marx Brothers:** Groucho Marx, Chico Marx, Harpo Marx; **Smothers Brothers:** Tom Smothers, Dick Smothers; **Christopher Columbus:** Flip Wilson; **George Jessel:** himself; **Phyllis Diller:** herself; **Jack E. Leonard:** himself; **Henny Youngman:** himself; **W.C. Fields:** Paul Frees

⊚ MAD, MAD, MAD MONSTERS

Baron von Frankenstein invites his old friends—Count Dracula, the Wolfman, the Mummy, the Invisible Man and his wife, and his own assistant, Igor—to the ballroom of the Transylvania-Astoria to witness his monster's wedding to the "perfect bride" he has created for him in this hour-long program that was first broadcast as part of the *ABC Satur-*

day *Superstar Movie* series. The production was later broadcast on its own as a children's special in reruns on the network and then in syndication. *A Rankin-Bass Production. Color. One hour. Premiered on ABC: September 23, 1972 (on ABC Saturday Superstar Movie). Syndicated.*

Voices
Bradley Bolke, Rhoda Mann, Bob McFadden, Allen Swift

◉ THE MAGIC FLUTE
Prince Tamino (voiced by Mark Hamill) embarks on an adventurous quest and, with help from the magic flute, subdues dragons, mercenaries and a duplicitious queen in order to rescue a kidnapped princess in this two-part, hour-long animated adaptation of the famous Mozart opera, broadcast as an *ABC Weekend Special. A Ruby-Spears Production in association with Greengrass Productions. Color. One hour. Premiered on ABC: April 30, 1994 (Part 1) and May 7, 1994 (Part 2). Rebroadcast on ABC: March 18, 1995 (Part 1) and March 25, 1995 (Part 2); February 3, 1996 (Part 1) and February 10, 1996 (Part 2); June 29, 1996 (Part 1) and July 6, 1996 (Part 2); March 1, 1997 (Part 1) and March 8, 1997 (Part 2).*

Voices
Prince Tamino: Mark Hamill; **Sarastro:** Michael York

◉ THE MAGIC LOLLIPOP ADVENTURE
In his animated debut, Lollipop Dragon, named for his love of lollipops, appears doomed when Baron Bad Blood, bent on undermining the success of the lollipop industry in the land of Tumtum, steals the magic wand that gives the lollipops their flavor. *A Blair Entertainment Production in association with Pannonia Film. Color. Half-hour. Syndicated. Premiere: 1986.*

Voices
Lollipop Dragon/Hairy Troll: Gary Wilmot; **Cosmo the Cunning/King/Herald:** Dennis Greashan; **Baron Bad Blood:** Stephen Thorne; **Blue Eyes:** Karen Fernald; **Magic Mirror/Prince Hubert:** Pat Starr; **Princess Gwendolyn:** Jill Lidstone; **Glider/Queen/Lady of the Forest:** Eva Hadden

◉ THE MAGIC OF DR. SNUGGLES
Kindly Dr. Snuggles enters the great balloon race in hopes of winning prize money to help Granny Toots build a new cat hospital. However, a couple of treacherous hoodlums have their own plan to win the race—at any cost. This hour-long special was based on the popular television series *Dr. Snuggles. An American Way Production in association with DePatie-Freleng Enterprises. Color. One hour. Premiered: 1985. Syndicated.*

Voices
Cindy Kozacik, Lacoya Newsome, Danielle Romeo, Tony Rosscia, David Scott, Pearl Terry

◉ THE MAGIC PAINTBRUSH
Nib, a young boy, acquires a magic paintbrush with which he grants life to objects he chooses to illustrate. The mystical gift brings him more heartache than fulfillment in this prime-time animated special, based on Robin Muller's book of the same name. Sponsored by McDonald's (dubbed *McDonald's Family Theater*), the half-hour program premiered in prime time on CBS. In 1995 ABC reaired the special on its Saturday-evening schedule. *A Marvel Films Production in association with American Film Technologies. Color. Half-hour. Premiered on CBS: April 22, 1993. Rebroadcast on ABC (ABC Weekend Special): June 25, 1995; July 1, 1995.*

Voices
Greedy King: Michael York; **Nib:** Aaron Metchik; **Sara:** Christa Larson

◉ THE MAGIC PEARL
Follows the story of a Chinese American brother and sister, Peter and Jamie Leung, and their grandfather, Popo, who are magically transported to mythical ancient China where they encounter an evil sorceress protected by a white pearl that possesses extraordinary powers in this 90-minute animated special first aired as part of ABC's *Kids Movie Matinee* series. *A Film Roman Production in association with Greengrass Productions. Color. One hour and a half. Premiered on ABC: August 4, 1996. Rebroadcast on ABC: (as an ABC Weekend Special) February 8, 1997 (Part 1) and February 15, 1997 (Part II).*

Voices
Tsai Chin, Amy Hill, France Nuyen, George Takei

◉ THE MAGIC SCHOOL BUS FAMILY HOLIDAY SPECIAL
Award-winning country singer Dolly Parton provides the voice of Ms. Frizzle's cousin, teaching her students all about "the gift that keeps on giving-recycling," in this hour-long, song-filled yuletide animated special, based on the long-running PBS animated series. *A Nelvana/Scholastic Production. Color. One hour. Premiered on PBS: December 25, 1996.*

Voices
Ms. Frizzle: Lily Tomlin; **Frizzle's cousin:** Dolly Parton; **Producer:** Malcolm-Jamal Warner; **Arnold:** Daniel Tamberelli; **Dorothy Ann:** Tara Meyer; **Wanda:** Lisa

Yamanaka; **Carlos:** Daniel DeSanto; **Keesha:** Erica Luttrell; **Phoebe:** Maia Filar; **Ralphie:** Stuart Stone; **Tim:** Andre Ottley-Lorant

◎ A MAGIC SCHOOL BUS HALLOWEEN
Ms. Frizzle (voiced by Lily Tomlin) and her gang visit a museum where three classmates get separated from the pack and overcome their fears of unusual creatures in this hour-long live-action/animated adventure based on the popular PBS cartoon series. *A Nelvana/Scholastic Production. Color. One hour. Premiered on PBS: (week of) October 28, 1995.*

Voices
Ms. Frizzle/Institute Inhabitant: Lily Tomlin; **Producer:** Malcolm-Jamal Warner; **Arnold:** Daniel Tamberelli; **Dorothy Ann:** Tara Meyer; **Wanda:** Lisa Yakanaka; **Carlos:** Daniel DeSanto; **Keesha:** Erica Luttrell; **Phoebe:** Maia Filar; **Ralphie:** Stuart Stone; **Tim:** Andre Ottley-Lorant

◎ THE MAGICAL MYSTERY TRIP THROUGH LITTLE RED'S HEAD
Live action and animation are combined in this story of Little Red, a young girl, who is used in an experiment by two youngsters (Carol and Larry) who, reduced in size, explore the girl's mind and learn how people express and deal with their feelings from the inside. *An ABC Afterschool Special. A DePatie-Freleng Enterprises Production. Color. One hour. Premiered on ABC: May 15, 1974. Rebroadcast on ABC: December 11, 1974; April 29, 1978 (as ABC Weekend Specials).*

Voices
Timer: Lennie Weinrib; **Carol:** Diane Murphy; **Larry:** Ike Eisenmann; **Little Red:** Sarah Kennedy; **Mother/Adeline/Diane:** Joan Gerber

◎ THE MAKING OF A GOOFY MOVIE
Jenna von Oy hosts this behind-the-scenes look at the feature-length film *A Goofy Movie*, based on the hit series *Goof Troop*. Included is a clip-filled look at Goofy's film career and a visit to Disney's animation studio in France, where most of the film was animated. *A Wrightwood Group Production for The Disney Channel. Color. Half-hour. Premiered on DIS: 1995.*

◎ THE MAKING OF THE HUNCHBACK OF NOTRE DAME
Half-hour special, hosted by Jason Alexander, chronicling the making of Disney's 34th full-length animated feature, featuring clips from the movie and interviews with the film's creators. *A Wrightwood Entertainment Production for The Disney Channel. Color. Half-hour. Premiered on DIS: 1996.*

◎ THE MAKING OF THE LION KING
Robert Guillaume, who lends his voice to this Disney classic, hosts this behind-the-scenes look at the making of the studio's 32nd full-length animated extravaganza. *A Walt Disney Production. Color. Half-hour. Premiered on DIS: June 16, 1994.*

◎ THE MAKING OF POCAHONTAS: A LEGEND COMES TO LIFE
Irene Badard, the speaking voice of Pocahontas in the feature-length cartoon, hosts this special chronicling the making of the first Disney animated feature to be based on a real person. Produced for the Disney Channel. *A Wrightwood Group Production for The Disney Channel. Color. Half-hour. Premiered on DIS: 1995.*

◎ THE MAKING OF TOY STORY
Annie Potts narrates this half-hour special examining the making of this hit computer-animated feature starring the voices of Tom Hanks and Tim Allen. *A Bonifer/Bogner Production for The Disney Channel. Color. Half-hour. Premiered on DIS: 1995.*

◎ THE MAN WHO PLANTED TREES
Winner of 1988 Oscar for Best Animated Short Subject, this inspiring story of how one man, shepherd Elzear Bouffler, selflessly dedicates his life to growing a forest in a barren, desolate region of the French Alps premiered as a half-hour special on the PBS anthology series *Long Ago & Far Away*. Based on an original story by Jean Giono, Christopher Plummer narrates the film, originally produced by animator Frederic Back in 1987. *A Societe Radio-Canada Production. Color. Half-hour. Premiered on PBS: April 15, 1989. Rebroadcast on PBS: December 7, 1990; November 8, 1992.*

Voices
Narrator: Christopher Plummer

◎ MARCO POLO
Famed adventurer Marco Polo is thrust in the middle of a war between the forces of Kublai Khan and the city of Siangyan Fu in China in the year A.D. 1260. Aided by his servant Ton-Ton, Polo wins the respect of the Khan as he saves the province of Yunnan from destruction and returns the Khan's captured daughter to safety. *An Air Programs International Production. Color. One hour. Premiered: 1972. Syndicated.*

Voices
Alistair Duncan, Tim Elliott, Ron Haddrick, Mark Kelly, John Llewellyn, Helen Morse

◎ MARVIN: BABY OF THE YEAR

Tom Armstrong's witty, precocious, diapered comic-strip character is entered into a "baby of the year" contest by his grandparents in the first prime-time special based on Armstrong's beloved creation. A *Southern Star Production. Color. Half-hour. Premiered on CBS: March 10, 1989. Rebroadcast on DIS: August 1, 1992; September 11, 1993.*

Voices
Marvin: Dana Hill; **Chrissy's Mother:** Ruth Buzzi; **Grandma:** Erin Donica; **Meagan:** Patti Dworkin; **Mom:** Kathy Garver; **Dad:** Dave Madden; **Vince:** Jerry Sroka; **Grandpa:** John Stephenson; **Announcer:** Frank Welker

◎ MARVIN—FIRST FLIGHT

Marvin, a man of average looks who builds robots in his underground laboratory, creates a robot (Maxwell) that can change shape, from robot to rocket to automobile, to accommodate Marvin with whatever form of transportation he requires. This program aired on *Special Delivery* on Nickelodeon several years after its United Kingdom television debut. All character voices were performed by voice artist Chris Harris. A *Link Licensing Limited Production. Color. Half-hour. Premiered on NIK: August 1, 1987.*

Voices
Chris Harris

◎ MARVIN—LONDON CALLING

Sid and Stan are a couple of naughty but likable villains who have invented a "Blitzer"—a gun that stuns people briefly, enabling the bad guys to steal lots of money from shops and banks. With help from his robots Buffer, Maxwell and Micron, Marvin puts the culprits behind bars where they belong. A *Link Licensing Limited Production. Color. Half-hour. Premiered on NIK: 1989.*

Voices
Chris Harris

◎ THE MARZIPAN PIG

The tale of the marzipan pig, whose sweetness would enchant a lonely mouse, a lovesick owl, a curious bee and a weary hibiscus flower, inspires a dance of love under the light of the moon in this half-hour animated special produced by Emmy Award–winning animator Michael Sporn

for HBO. A *Michael Sporn Animation Production in association with Italtoons Corporation. Color. Half-hour. Premiered on HBO: November 5, 1990.*

Voices
Narrator: Tim Curry

◎ MASTER OF THE WORLD

Captain Robur, the mad inventor of a fantastic flying machine who bills himself as "Master of the World," sets out to destroy Washington, D.C., with Inspector Strock of the Federal Police fresh on his heels. A *Famous Classic Tales* special. *An Air Programs International Production. Color. One hour. Premiered on CBS: October 23, 1976. Syndicated.*

Voices
Tim Elliott, John Ewart, Ron Haddrick, Judy Morris, Matthew O'Sullivan

◎ MEET JULIE

David McAlister, owner of a small security company, takes his nine-year-old daughter along on a trip to Paris, where he has been assigned to guard a jeweled collar to be worn by a rare snow leopard at an exhibit. As an added surprise, he gives his daughter a special computerized doll, Julie, to take with her on the trip. A *DIC Enterprises Production. Color. Half-hour. Premiered: Fall 1987. Syndicated.*

Voices
Julie: Nicole Lyn; **Carol:** Karen Burthwright

◎ MEET THE RAISINS: THE STORY OF THE CALIFORNIA RAISINS

The California Raisins return in their second prime-time special, this time given recognizable personalities and names (A.C., Red, Stretch, and Beebop), in a clever rock documentary parody, tracing the Raisins' rise to stardom from their early days in a band called the Vine-yls. A *Will Vinton Production. Color. Half-hour. Premiered on CBS: November 4, 1988. Rebroadcast on CBS: August 22, 1990. Rebroadcast on DIS: November 7, 1992.*

◎ MERLIN AND THE DRAGONS

Kevin Kline narrates this animated chronicle highlighted by dark magic, flying serpents, valorious knights, and wicked and bold adventure. In the days of the wise magical warlord Merlin, young King Arthur doubts his ability to rule. Arthur's prophetic dream leads to Merlin's downfall and reveals to Arthur that he is the true heir to the throne in this animated half-hour based on the characters from the King Arthur legends. Originally produced by Lightyear Entertain-

◉ PAC-MAN HALLOWEEN SPECIAL

Pac-Baby experiences Halloween for the first time, but Mez-maron and his chomping Ghost Monsters threaten to disrupt the seasonal fun in this half-hour prime-time special based on the popular Atari video game characters. Entitled "Trick or Chomp," the program was originally broadcast on the characters' popular Saturday-morning series. *A Hanna-Barbera Production. Color. Half-hour. Premiered on ABC: October 30, 1982.*

Voices
Pac-Man: Marty Ingels; **Ms. Pac:** Barbara Minkus; **Baby Pac:** Russi Taylor; **Chomp Chomp:** Frank Welker; **Sour Puss:** Peter Cullen; **Mezmaron:** Alan Lurie; **Sue Monster;** Susan Silo; **Inky Monster;** Barry Gordon; **Blinky Monster/Pinky Monster:** Chuck McCann; **Clyde Monster:** Neilson Ross

◉ PADDINGTON GOES TO SCHOOL

Disaster strikes the Brown household when Paddington is told he must attend school in this 1986 special—the third in a series of puppet-animated specials from producer George Clutterback of FilmFair Animation-directed by Martin Pullen. The program, along with the other two, made its American television debut on the Disney Channel. *A FilmFair Animation/Paddington & Company, Ltd. Production. Color. Half-hour. Premiered on DIS. Rebroadcast on DIS: September 17, 1990; September 11, 1991.*

Voices
Narrator: Sir Michael Hordern

◉ PADDINGTON GOES TO THE MOVIES

The incorrigible Paddington, inspired by the magic of the "silver screen" and a sudden rainstorm, follows the famous footsteps of Gene Kelly and in his own way "dances in the rain" with hilarious consequences in this half-hour special produced by FilmFair Animation (producers of the 1981 PBS stop-motion animated series *Paddington Bear. A FilmFair Animation/Paddington & Company, Ltd. Production. Color. Half-hour. Premiered on DIS. Rebroadcast on DIS: June 2, 1992.*

Voices
Narrator: Sir Michael Hordern

◉ PADDINGTON'S BIRTHDAY BONANZA

Mr. Brown's birthday is drawing near and Paddington is worried because he can't afford to buy him a present in this half-hour puppet-animated special—the first in a series produced by London's FilmFair Animation in 1986. *A FilmFair Animation/Paddington & Company, Ltd. Production. Color. Half-hour. Premiered on DIS. Rebroadcast on DIS: August 11, 1991; February 21, 1993.*

Voices
Narrator: Sir Michael Hordern

◉ PEGASUS

Narrated by Mia Farrow, this contemporary animated half-hour captures the glorious adventures of the mythic winged horse who helps slay a three-headed monster and survives a falling out with Zeus, only to be made immortal. The program aired on PBS's long-running *Long Ago & Far Away* series. *A Lightyear Entertainment Production. Color. Half-hour. Premiered on PBS: November 16, 1991. Rebroadcast on PBS: October 18, 1992.*

Voices
Narrator: Mia Farrow

◉ PETER AND THE MAGIC EGG

Peter Paas the rabbit helps Mama and Papa Doppler, who raised him, save their farm from greedy Tobias Tinwhiskers in this Easter tale told by Uncle Amos Egg, an egg farmer, whose mortgage is about to be foreclosed on by the same evil Tinwhiskers. *An RLR Associates in association with Murakami-Wolf-Swenson Films. Color. Half-hour. Premiered: March, 1983. Syndicated. Rebroadcast on DIS: March 20, 1992; March 7, 1993; March 22, 1994.*

Voices
Uncle Amos Egg: Ray Bolger; **Tobias Tinwhiskers/Cotton:** Bob Ridgely; **Peter Paas:** Al Eisenmann; **Terrence:** Charles Woolf; **Feathers:** Joan Gerber; **Lollychops:** Russi Taylor; **Papa Doppler/Kookybird:** Bob Holt

◉ PETER AND THE WOLF

Kirstie Alley narrates this warm-hearted story of a family reunion, based on Sergei Prokofiev's classic musical tale, told in live action and animation (the latter by cartoon legend Chuck Jones). The hour-long spectacular premiered in prime time on ABC, with versions of the program also offered on home video, audiocassette and CD-ROM. *An IF/X Production/Chuck Jones Enterprises Production for BMG Entertainment International. Color. One hour. Premiered on ABC: December 8, 1995.*

Cast/Voices
Mother: Kirstie Alley; **Peter:** Ross Malinger; **Grandfather:** Lloyd Bridges

◉ THE PICKWICK PAPERS

The humorous escapades of Samuel Pickwick and the members of his literary group, the Pickwick Club, are the premise for this 90-minute adaptation of the Charles Dickens novel. *A Burbank Films Production. Color. Ninety minutes. Premiered: 1985.*

⊚ THE PIED PIPER OF HAMELIN

A mysterious stranger saves the town of Hamelin from a plague of rats by luring them away with his magic pipe in this half-hour stop-motion puppet-animated special produced by England's Cosgrove Hall Productions for the award-winning PBS anthology series *Long Ago & Far Away.* *A Cosgrove Hall Production. Color. Half-hour. Premiered on PBS: January 28, 1989. Rebroadcast on PBS: November 10, 1990; February 28, 1992.*

Voices
Narrator: Robert Hardy

⊚ PINK PANTHER IN "A PINK CHRISTMAS"

In this heartwarming animated holiday special, the Pink Panther, appearing in his first prime-time animated special, is alone, cold and hungry in New York's Central Park in the 1890s, trying desperately to get himself a Christmas dinner even if it entails getting arrested. *A DePatie-Freleng Enterprises Production in association with Mirisch-Geoffrey Productions. Color. Half-hour. Premiered on ABC: December 7, 1978. Rebroadcast on ABC: December 16, 1979. Syndicated.*

⊚ PINK PANTHER IN "OLYMPINKS"

Timed to coincide with the 1980 Winter Olympics, the Pink Panther finds the odds stacked against him in this cartoon version of the Olympics—called "Olympinks"—in which he tries to win at any cost but often pays the price for his effort. The special aired during the Lake Placid Winter Olympics and was also broadcast on ABC. *A DePatie-Freleng Enterprises Production in association with Mirisch-Geoffrey Productions. Color. Half-hour. Premiered on ABC: February 22, 1980. Syndicated.*

⊚ PINK PANTHER IN "PINK AT FIRST SIGHT"

In this Valentine's Day special, the Pink Panther longs for a lady panther and fantasizes about every female he meets. He is ready to give up until a pretty panther comes along and wins not only his attention but his love. *A Marvel Production in association with Mirisch-Geoffrey Productions and DePatie-Freleng Enterprises. Color. Half-hour. Premiered on ABC: May 10, 1981. Rebroadcast on ABC: May 29, 1982. Syndicated.*

Voices
Weaver Copeland, Brian Cummings, Marilyn Schreffler, Hal Smith, Frank Welker

⊚ A PINKY AND THE BRAIN CHRISTMAS

Traveling to the North Pole, Brain sets up in Santa's workshop to mass produce a "fantastically powerful doll" that he will use to broadcast hypnotic suggestions to unsuspecting viewers in this Emmy Award–winning half-hour special based on the popular WB Network series. *A Warner Bros. Television Animation/Amblin Entertainment Production. Color. Half-hour. Premiered on WB: December 17, 1995. Rebroadcast on WB: December 22, 1996.*

Voices
Pinky: Rob Paulsen; **The Brain:** Maurice LaMarche

⊚ PINOCCHIO'S CHRISTMAS

Back in an all-new Christmas adventure, Pinocchio falls in love with a little girl marionette, Julietta. Along the way he meets up with a sly old fox and money-hungry cat and, of course, Papa Geppetto in this Animagic adventure. *A Rankin-Bass Production. Color. One hour. Premiered on ABC: December 3, 1980. Rebroadcast on ABC: December 24, 1982. Syndicated. Rebroadcast on FAM: December 10, 1996; December 11, 1997.*

Voices
Pinocchio: Todd Porter; **Geppetto:** George S. Irving; **Maestro Fire-Eater:** Alan King; **The Cat:** Pat Bright; **Julietta/Lady Azura:** Diane Leslie; **Dr. Cricket:** Robert McFadden; **Children:** Tiffany Blake, Carl Tramon, Alice Gayle

⊚ PINOCCHIO: THE MAKING OF A MASTERPIECE

Robbie Benson, the voice of the Beast in Disney's *Beauty and the Beast*, hosts this behind-the-scenes look at the history of the classic 1940 Disney animated feature. *A Walt Disney Home Video Production. Color. Half-hour. Premiered on DIS: June 11, 1993.*

⊚ PLAY IT AGAIN, CHARLIE BROWN

For years Lucy has tried to get Schroeder's attention. She makes yet another attempt after Peppermint Patty tells her that she has an opening in the PTA program at school for Schroeder to play the piano. Lucy thus offers Schroeder his first "big break," for which he is most appreciative, but her only reward is a "thank you" in return. *A Lee Mendelson–Bill Melendez Production in association with Charles M. Schulz Creative Associates and United Feature Syndicate. Color. Half-hour. Premiered on CBS: March 28, 1971. Rebroadcast on CBS: April 11, 1972; February 11, 1973.*

Voices

Charlie Brown: Chris Inglis; **Lucy Van Pelt;** Pamelyn Ferdin; **Linus Van Pelt:** Stephen Shea; **Sally Brown:** Hilary Momberger; **Schroeder:** Danny Hjeim; **Frieda:** Linda Mendelson; **Peppermint Patty:** Kip DeFaria

⊚ POCAHONTAS: THE LEGEND COMES TO LIFE

Documentary-style special combining interviews with the film's composers and animators and animated clips from the movie—Disney's first to feature a heroine based on a historical figure. *A Walt Disney Production. Color. Half-hour. Premiered on DIS: June 11, 1995.*

⊚ THE POGO SPECIAL BIRTHDAY SPECIAL

Walt Kelly's charming comic-strip character, known for his wit and pointed satire, comes to life in this television special based on classic Pogo stories. Kelly, who coproduced the special with animator Chuck Jones, is credited with writing the program and providing voices for three of the characters. *A Chuck Jones Enterprises Production in association with MGM-TV. Color. Half-hour. Premiered on NBC: May 18, 1969. Rebroadcast on NBC: February 22, 1970; February 20, 1971.*

Voices

Pogo Possum/Mam'selle Hepzibah: June Foray; **Porky Pine/Bunny Rabbit/Basil the Butterfly:** Chuck Jones; **P.T. Bridgeport the Bear/Albert the Alligator/Dr. Howland Owl:** Walt Kelly; **Churchy-la-Femme/Beauregard Bugleboy:** Les Tremayne

⊚ THE POINT

Oblio, a young lad, searches for acceptance after he is banished from his homeland to the Pointless Forest because his head is not pointed like the rest of the locals and because not having a "point" is against the law. Academy Award–winning actor Dustin Hoffman originally narrated this 90-minute special produced for ABC's *Movie of the Week*. (In rebroadcasts of the program, Hoffman was replaced by Alan Barzman [1974] as the father/narrator; Ringo Starr [1976] performed the same task for the videocassette version.) Harry Nilsson, who wrote the original story, also composed seven songs for the program. In August of 1993, the Dustin Hoffman version was rebroadcast in nationwide syndication and on PBS stations. *A Nilsson House Music Production in association with Murakami-Wolf-Swenson Films. Color. Ninety minutes. Premiered on ABC: February 2, 1971. Rebroadcast on ABC: December 7, 1974. Rebroadcast on PBS: December 25, 1993. Syndicated: (week of) August 14, 1993.*

Oblio, a young lad, searches for acceptance in The Point. *© Nilsson House Music, Inc./Murakami-Wolf Productions* (COURTESY: MURAKAMI-WOLF-SWENSON)

Voices

Father (narrator): Dustin Hoffman, Alan Barzman, Ringo Starr; **Son/Oblio:** Michael Lookinland; **Oblio's Father:** Alan Thicke; **The King/Leaf Man:** Paul Frees; **The Count:** Lennie Weinrib; **Rockman:** Bill Martin; **Oblio's Mother:** Joan Gerber; **Count's Son:** Buddy Foster

⊚ THE POKY LITTLE PUPPY'S FIRST CHRISTMAS

A playful little puppy wanders off while the family searches for the perfect Christmas tree, only to fall into a deep hole through the fresh snow. He's rescued later, but that's not the last of the family's misfortunes in this half-hour animated special based on the popular children's storybooks. *A Michael Sporn Animation Production for Italtoons Corporation and Western Publishing Co. Inc. Color. Half-hour. Premiered on SHO: December 13, 1992. Rebroadcast on SHO: December 10, 1993.*

Voices

Narrator: Donald Sutherland

⊚ POOCHIE

Poochie, a lovable pink pup, goes on an exciting journey to Egypt with her computer robot, Hermes, to help a young boy, Danny Evans, find his father, who has disappeared inside a pyramid. *A DIC Enterprises Production in association with Mattel. Color. Half-hour. Premiered: June 1984. Syndicated.*

Voices

Poochie: Ellen Gerstell; **Hermes:** Neil Ross; **Zipcode:** Fred Travalena; **Koom:** Jennifer Darling; **Danny Evans:** Katie Leigh

⊚ POPEYE MEETS THE MAN WHO HATED LAUGHTER

Seafaring sailor Popeye and a bumper crop of comic-strip favorites (Blondie and Dagwood, the Katzenjammer Kids, the Little King, Steve Canyon, Flash Gordon, the Phantom, Tim Tyler, Beetle Bailey, and Jiggs and Maggie) who appear in animation for the first time meet their match when an evil man tries to prevent the spread of laughter in the world in this *ABC Saturday Superstar Movie*. The made-for-television feature was directed by cartoon veterans Jack Zander and Hal Seeger and written by Lou Silverton. Original music was scored by Elliott Schiprut. *A King Features Production. Color. One hour. Premiered on ABC: October 7, 1972 (on The ABC Saturday Superstar Movie). Rebroadcast on ABC: February 9, 1974. Syndicated.*

Voices
Popeye: Jack Mercer

⊚ THE POPEYE SHOW

Aired in prime time, this half-hour special was comprised of four excerpts from the Saturday-morning series *The All-New Popeye Hour*, in which the spinach-gulping sailor; string-bean girlfriend, Olive, and world-class bully, Bluto, are subjected to a series of misadventures. *A Hanna-Barbera Production in association with King Features Entertainment. Color. Half-hour. Premiered on CBS: September 13, 1978.*

Voices
Popeye: Jack Mercer; **Olive Oyl:** Marilyn Schreffler; **Bluto:** Allan Melvin; **Wimpy:** Daws Butler

⊚ THE POPEYE VALENTINE SPECIAL

Olive Oyl sets sail on a Valentine's Day Sweetheart Cruise, captained by hamburger-eating Wimpy, in search of "Mr. Right." She discovers in the end that the best man for her is Popeye. The story title of the program was "Sweethearts at Sea." *A Hanna-Barbera Production in association with King Features Entertainment. Color. Half-hour. Premiered on CBS: February 14, 1979. Rebroadcast on CBS: February 13, 1980; January 30, 1981; February 2, 1982.*

Voices
Popeye: Jack Mercer; **Olive Oyl/Sea Hag/Bathing Beauty #1:** Marilyn Schreffler; **Bluto:** Allan Melvin; **Wimpy:** Daws Butler; **King Neptune/Man-In-The-Moon:** Barney Phillips; **Jeep/Princess/Bathing Beauty #2:** Ginny McSwain

⊚ POUND PUPPIES

The Pound Puppies operate the Pound Puppy Mission Control Center. Their mission is to find homes for hapless pup-

pies that get caught in the net of Dabney Nabbit, the diligent if sloppy dogcatcher in this first-run movie inspired by the Saturday-morning series *Pound Puppies*, which was broadcast on ABC. *A Hanna-Barbera Production. Color. Two hours. Premiered: October, 1985. Syndicated.*

Voices
Cooler: Dan Gilvezan; **Violet/TV Newscaster:** Gail Matthius; **Scounger:** Ron Palillo; **Bright Eyes/Mom:** Adrienne Alexander; **Howler/Fat Cat:** Frank Welker; **Barkerville/Dad:** Alan Oppenheimer; **Mayor Fisk:** Sorrell Brooke; **Chief Williams:** Garrett Morris; **Bigelow:** Jonathan Winters; **Tubbs/Pound Puppy #4:** Avery Schreiber; **Nabbit/Pound Puppy #3:** Henry Gibson; **The Nose:** Jo Anne Worley; **Flack/Nathan/Pound Puppy #1:** Charles Adler; **Itchy/Snitchy/Louie:** Don Messick; **Fist/Pound Puppy #2:** Ed Begley Jr.; **Mother Superior/Old Lady:** June Foray; **Doc West/Chelsea:** Victoria Carroll; **Sarah:** Laura Duff

⊚ THE PRINCE AND THE PAUPER

This 1990, 35-minute theatrical featurette starring Mickey Mouse, Pluto, Donald Duck and Goofy, first premiered by itself on The Disney Channel in 1992 and a year later was broadcast on ABC as an hour-long prime-time "world premiere event"—in which Mickey, in a comic variation of the Mark Twain classic, plays a royal heirhead and a look-alike urchin who trade places. The ABC presentation included the broadcast of "Mickey and the Beanstalk" (narrated by Corey Burton as Ludwig Von Drake), an animated sequence from the 1947 Disney full-length classic *Fun and Fancy Free*. *A Walt Disney Production. Color. Thirty-five minutes. One hour. Premiered on DIS: January 12, 1992. Rebroadcast on ABC: March 26, 1993.*

Voices
Mickey Mouse/The Prince: Wayne Allwine; **Pluto/Goofy-Horace/Weasel #1:** Bill Farmer; **Donald Duck:** Tony Anselmo; **Clarabelle:** Elvia Allman; **Pete:** Arthur Burghardt; **Archbishop/Dying King:** Frank Welker; **Weasels #2 and #3/Pig:** Charles Adler; **Kid #1:** Tim Eyster; **Kid #2:** Rocky Krakoff; **Narrator (The Prince and the Pauper):** Roy Dotrice; **Ludwig Von Drake:** Corey Burton

⊚ THE PRINCE'S RAIN

Inspired by the popular children's nursery rhyme "Rain, Rain, Go Away," this half-hour adaptation tells the tale of cool Prince Vince who angers Mother Nature by asking the palace magician to stop the skies from raining on his tanning season in this animated musical special, broadcast as part of the *HBO Musical Storybook* series in 1991. Canadian animation giant Cinar Films produced the special, which was part of the 13-part *The Real Story of . . .* anthology series. *A Cinar Films/Crayon Animation in association with Western Publishing Company/Global Television Network/Telefilm Canada. Color. Half-hour. Premiered on HBO: November 13, 1991. Rebroadcast on HBO: November 21, 1991, November 26, 1991, November 29, 1991.*

Voices
Prince Vince: Joe Piscopo; **Narrator:** Robin Leach

◎ PRINCE VALIANT: KNIGHT OF THE ROUND TABLE

In this intriguing saga, Prince Valiant struggles with his own sense of pride and must choose his path—to remain true to his father's throne or to continue his journey to become a knight of the Round Table in this feature-length compilation of episodes of the Family Channel's original series *The Legend of Prince Valiant*. *A Hearst/IDDH Groupe Bruno Rene Huchez/Polyphonfilm und Fernschgesellschaft mbH/Sei Young Studios/King Features/Family Channel Production. Premiered on FAM: September 4, 1992.*

Voices
Prince Valiant: Robby Benson; **Arn:** Michael Horton; **King Arthur:** Efrem Zimbalist, Jr; **Guinevere:** Samantha Eggar; **Sir Gawain:** Tim Curry

◎ PRINCE VALIANT: THE VOYAGE OF CAMELOT

This feature-length companion-the first of two reedited from The Family Channel's *The Legend of Prince Valiant* series—tells the story of how the young Valiant comes to serve King Arthur. It features the voices of Robby Benson (Prince Valiant) and Efrem Zimbalist Jr. (King Arthur). *A Hearst/IDDH Groupe Bruno Rene Huchez/Polyphonfilm und Fernschgesellerschaft mbH/Sei Young Studios/King Features/ Family Channel Production. Premiered on FAM: January 3, 1992. Rebroadcast on FAM: July 24, 1992.*

Voices
Prince Valiant: Robby Benson; **King Arthur:** Efrem Zimbalist Jr.

◎ PUFF AND THE INCREDIBLE MR. NOBODY

An insecure young boy (Terry) creates his own imaginary friend, Mr. Nobody. He soon believes his ability to make up songs, jokes and games and to paint pictures originates from the mythical character. Puff the Magic Dragon teaches the young lad that his creativity comes from within and not from his friend. *A Yarrow-Muller/Murakami-Wolf-Swenson Films Production for the My Company. Color. Half-hour. Premiered on CBS: May 17, 1982. Rebroadcast on CBS: August 30, 1985. Syndicated. Rebroadcast on DIS: May 19, 1992; May 30, 1992.*

Voices
Puff: Burgess Meredith; **Terry:** David Mendenhall; **Mr. Nobody:** Robert Ridgely; **Girl:** Diana Dumpis; **Boy:** Billy Jacoby; **Mom:** Joan Gerber; **Dad:** Bob Holt; **Professor K:** Hal Smith

◎ PUFF THE MAGIC DRAGON

Puff comes to the aid of a small boy who is afraid to face life and helps solve the boy's problems by taking him on a trip to his homeland, teaching him to be brave and to see things as they really are. Based on the Peter, Paul and Mary song of the same name, writer Peter Yarrow added new lyrics to go with the story. *A Yarrow-Muller/Murakami-Wolf-Swenson Films Production for the My Company. Color. Half-hour. Premiered on CBS: October 30, 1978. Rebroadcast on CBS: September 10, 1979; April 28, 1981. Syndicated. Rebroadcast on DIS: April 25, 1992.*

Voices
Puff: Burgess Meredith; **Jackie Draper:** Phillip Tanzini; **Pirate/Pieman/Sneeze:** Bob Ridgely; **Mother/Star:** Maitzi Morgan; **Father:** Peter Yarrow; **Bald Doctor:** Regis Cordic; **Tall Doctor:** Frank Nelson; **Short Doctor:** Charles Woolf

◎ PUFF THE MAGIC DRAGON IN THE LAND OF THE LIVING LIES

The irresistible Puff deals with a young girl who lies to make herself feel better after her parents' divorce by taking her to the Land of Living Lies so she can recognize that her lying fools nobody and only hurts herself. *A Yarrow-Muller/Murakami-Wolf-Swenson Films Production for the My Company. Color. Half-hour. Premiered on CBS: November 17, 1979. Rebroadcast on CBS: October 22, 1980. Syndicated.*

Voices
Puff: Burgess Meredith; **Sandy:** Mischa Lenore Bond; **Talking Tree:** Alan Barzman; **Kid Umpire/Boy Who Cried Wolf/Boy with Huge Ears:** Ike Eisenmann; **Mother/Talking Pumpkin/Little Girl:** Joan Gerber; **Judge/Bailiff/Zealot:** Gene Moss; **Baron Munchausen/Snake/Attorney/Basketball Player:** Robert Ridgely; **Father:** Peter Yarrow

THE PUPPY'S AMAZING RESCUE

While celebrating Tommy's birthday in his parents' mountaintop cabin, Petey the puppy and Dolly, Tommy's sister, get separated from Tommy and his father during a massive snowslide. Petey and Dolly head up a search party to find them. An ABC Weekend Special. A Ruby-Spears Enterprises Production. Color. Half-hour. Premiered on ABC: January 26, 1980. Rebroadcast on ABC: May 3, 1980; September 6, 1980; March 26, 1983.

Voices

Petey: Bryan Scott; **Tommy:** John Joseph Thomas; **Dolly:** Nancy McKeon

THE PUPPY SAVES THE CIRCUS

In his fourth afternoon children's special, Petey, the frisky pup, suffers a serious bout of amnesia after he is accidentally struck by a car and, with no memory of his past, he winds up performing in the circus (as Rags II, the Funny Wonder Puppy), where his life is put in great danger. The program marked the fifth-season debut of the ABC Weekend Specials. A Ruby-Spears Enterprises Production. Color. Half-hour. Premiered on ABC: September 12, 1981. Rebroadcast on ABC: March 6, 1982; October 23, 1982; March 3, 1984.

Voices

Petey: Sparky Marcus; **Dolly:** Nancy McKeon; **Tommy:** Tony O'Dell; **George Goodbee/Sligh:** Alan Young; **Gloria Goodbee:** Janet Waldo; **Emily:** Linda Gary; **Dad/Abdullah:** John Stephenson; **Kiki/Vet:** Alan Dinehart; **Tiger/Lead Pony/Clown:** Frank Welker

THE PUPPY'S GREAT ADVENTURE

Petey the puppy's happiness turns to bitter sorrow when his master, Tommy, is adopted out of the Public Home for Boys by a wealthy jeweler and his wife who refuse to take Petey in this sequel to The Puppy Who Wanted a Boy. An ABC Weekend Special. A Ruby-Spears Enterprises Production. Color. Half-hour. Premiered on ABC: February 3, 1979. Rebroadcast on ABC: May 12, 1979; September 2, 1979.

Voices

Petey: Bryan Scott; **Tommy:** John Joseph Thomas; **Dolly:** Nancy McKeon

THE PUPPY WHO WANTED A BOY

The natural bond between a dog and a boy is the core of this half-hour special, adapted from Catherine Woolley's sentimental children's story in which Sonny, a lonely puppy, seeks the companionship of a 12-year-old orphan (Tommy) to fulfill his search for an owner to call his own. An ABC Weekend Special. A Ruby-Spears Enterprises Production. Color. Half-hour. Premiered on ABC: May 6, 1978. Rebroadcast on ABC: September 23, 1978; January 21, 1979; October 27, 1979.

Voices

Sonny/Petey: Todd Turquand; **Tommy:** John Joseph Thomas

PUSS-IN-BOOTS

Wearing boots that possess magical powers, Orlando the cat is given the ability to speak and uses his newfound talent to elevate his master (Jacques) in the community, thus enabling him to pursue his first and only love—the king's daughter. A Rankin-Bass Production in association with Mushi Studios. Color. Half-hour. Premiered: December 9, 1972. Syndicated. Rebroadcast on NIK: May 6, 1993.

Voices

Carl Banas, Len Birman, Bernard Cowan, Peg Dixon, Keith Hampshire, Peggi Loder, Donna Miller, Frank Perry, Henry Ramer, Billie Mae Richards, Alfie Scopp, Paul Soles

THE RACCOONS AND THE LOST STAR

Bert Raccoon and his friends foil the evil Cyril Sneer's plan to recover a special "gold star," and to conquer Earth in this third special based on the popular Canadian cartoon series Raccoons. A Gillis-Wiseman Production in association with Atkinson Film-Arts Productions. Color. Half-hour. Premiered (U.S.): December, 1983. Syndicated.

Voices

Bert Raccoon/Pig General: Len Carlson; **Ralph Raccoon:** Bobby Dermer; **Melissa Raccoon:** Dottie West; **Julie:** Tammy Bourne; **Tommy:** Hadley Kay; **Dan the Ranger:** John Schneider; **Schaeffer, Julie and Tommy's dog:** Carl Banas; **Cyril Sneer/Snag:** Michael Magee; **Cedric Sneer/Pig General:** Fred Little; **Sophia Tu Tu/Broo:** Sharon Lewis; **Narrator:** Rich Little

RACCOONS ON ICE

The Raccoons and their friends wage a courageous effort to save Evergreen Lake, climaxing with an exciting game of ice hockey against sinister Cyril Sneer's ferocious team of "Bears" in this half-hour syndicated cartoon that coincided with the beginning of the 1982 National Hockey League Stanley Cup playoffs. A Gillis-Wiseman Production in association with Atkinson Film-Arts Productions. *Color. Half-hour. Premiered: December 20, 1981. Syndicated.*

Voices
Bert Raccoon: Len Carlson; **Ralph Raccoon:** Bobby Dermer; **Melissa Raccoon:** Rita Coolidge; **Schaeffer:** Carl Banas; **Cyril Sneer/Snag:** Michael Magee; **Cedric Sneer:** Fred Little; **Sophia Tu Tu:** Sharon Lewis; **Julie:** Tammy Bourne; **Tommy:** Hadley Kay; **Ferlin:** Danny Gallivan; **Narrator:** Rich Little; **Vocalist:** Leo Sayer

◎ RAGGEDY ANN AND ANDY IN THE GREAT SANTA CLAUS CAPER

Alexander Graham Wolf, the inventor of "Gloopstick," plans to use the breakable plastic cube to sabotage Christmas, but not before Raggedy Ann and Raggedy Andy ruin his sinister scheme. *A Chuck Jones Enterprises Production in association with Bobbs-Merrill Company. Color. Half-hour. Premiered on CBS: November 30, 1978. Rebroadcast on CBS: December 10, 1979; December 9, 1980. Syndicated. Rebroadcast on DIS: December 23, 1991; December 25, 1993.*

Voices
Raggedy Ann/Comet: June Foray; **Raggedy Andy:** Daws Butler; **Alexander Graham Wolf/Santa:** Les Tremayne

◎ RAGGEDY ANN AND ANDY IN THE PUMPKIN WHO COULDN'T SMILE

Raggedy Ann and Raggedy Andy bring together a lonely boy and lonely pumpkin—to make Halloween special in this touching tale based on the famous ragdoll characters created by Johnny Gruelle. *A Chuck Jones Enterprises Production in association with Bobbs-Merrill Company. Color. Half-hour. Premiered on CBS: October 31, 1979. Rebroadcast on CBS: October 29, 1980. Syndicated. Rebroadcast on DIS: October 27, 1991; October 18, 1992; October 26, 1993; October 30, 1994; October 21, 1995.*

Voices
Raggedy Ann/Aunt Agatha: June Foray; **Raggedy Andy:** Daws Butler; **The Pumpkin:** Les Tremayne; **Ralph:** Steven Rosenberg

◎ THE RAILWAY DRAGON

Keenly aware of the magic that lurks beneath the old railway tunnel, young Emily's ultimate wish comes true in the form of a centuries-old dragon who takes her on an exciting, fun-filled adventure. This Canadian-animated half-hour special was the first of two *Railway Dragon* produced by

Canada's Lacewood Productions. *A Lacewood Production. Color. Half-hour. Premiered on DIS: 1991.*

Voices
Narrator: Leslie Nielsen; **The Dragon:** Barry Morse; **Emily:** Tracey Moore; **Father/Conductor:** Noel Counsil; **Mother:** Beverly Wolfe; **A Dragon/Hunter:** Chuck Collins; **Hunter's Son/Chef:** Rick Jones

◎ RAINBOW BRITE: PERIL IN THE PITS

Archenemy Murky Dismal and his henchman, Lurky, try to drain Earth of its color and remove all the happiness from the world but are foiled by Rainbow Brite and her special friends of Rainbowland in this animated special based on the popular greeting card characters. *A Hallmark Properties Production in association with DIC Enterprises Productions. Color. Half-hour. Premiered: June 1984. Syndicated.*

Voices
Rainbow Brite: Bettina Rush; **Starlite/Spectran:** Andre Stojka; **Brian:** Scott Menville; **Murky Dismal:** Peter Cullen; **Lurky/Buddy Blue/Puppy Brite:** Patrick Fraley; **Twink/Shy Violet/Indigo/La La Orange:** Robbie Lee; **Krys:** David Mendenhall; **Count Blogg:** Jonathan Harris; **Stormy:** Marissa Mendenhall; **Princess/Moonglow/Tickled Pink:** Ronda Aldrich; **Patty O'Green/Red Butler/Canary Yellow/Castle Creature:** Mona Marshall

◎ RAINBOW BRITE: THE BEGINNING OF RAINBOWLAND

In this two-part special based on the Hallmark greeting card characters, Rainbow Brite relates the history of Rainbowland,

Emily shares an adventure with a dragon during which they learn more about themselves and their world in the half-hour animated special The Railway Dragon. *© Lacewood Productions (now Paragon Entertainment)*

including the beginning of her own magical power. Broadcast in half-hour time slots over two consecutive days. *A Hallmark Properties Production in association with DIC Enterprises Productions. Color. One hour. Premiered: April 1985. Syndicated.*

Voices

Rainbow Brite: Bettina Rush; **Starlite/Spectran:** Andre Stojka; **Brian:** Scott Menville; **Murky Dismal:** Peter Cullen; **Lurky/Buddy Blue/Puppy Brite:** Patrick Fraley; **Twink/Shy Violet/Indigo/La La Orange:** Robbie Lee; **Krys:** David Mendenhall; **Count Blogg:** Jonathan Harris; **Stormy:** Marissa Mendenhall; **Princess/Moonglow/Tickled Pink:** Ronda Aldrich; **Patty O'Green/Red Butler/Canary Yellow/Castle Creature:** Mona Marshall

◉ RAINBOW BRITE: THE MIGHTY MONSTROMURK MENACE

Terror strikes Rainbowland when Monstromurk, a powerful monster held captive in a bottle for 700 years, is let loose by that good-for-nothing aardvark Murky Dismal, who wants to make the people of this happy-go-lucky world as miserable as he is. *A Hallmark Properties Production in association with DIC Enterprises Productions. Color. One hour. Premiered: December 1984. Syndicated.*

Voices

Rainbow Brite: Bettina Rush; **Starlite/Spectran:** Andre Stojka; **Brian:** Scott Menville; **Murky Dismal:** Peter Cullen; **Lurky/Buddy Blue/Puppy Brite:** Patrick Fraley; **Twink/Shy Violet/Indigo/La La Orange:** Robbie Lee; **Krys:** David Mendenhall; **Count Blogg:** Jonathan Harris; **Stormy:** Marissa Mendenhall; **Princess/Moonglow/Tickled Pink:** Ronda Aldrich; **Patty O'Green/Red Butler/Canary Yellow/Castle Creature:** Mona Marshall

◉ THE RAISINS: SOLD OUT!

In this fanciful claymation rockumentary, slick manager Leonard Limabean pressures the California Raisins to accept a new member into the group, hotshot performer Lick Broccoli, in this stop-motion animated special. *A Will Vinton Production. Color. Half-hour. Premiered on CBS: May 2, 1990. Rebroadcast on DIS: February 18, 1993; November 26, 1994.*

Voices

Brian Cummings, Jim Cummings, Dorian Harewood, Brian Mitchell, David Scully, Todd Tolces

◉ RARG

British animator Tony Collingwood created this award-winning animated film, based on his original short story

(written in 1982) about a place called Rarg in which the sun never rises and things are blissful until the citizens discover that they exist in the dream of a man who is about to wake up. Premiered on PBS anthology series *Long Ago & Far Away. A Hit Communications Production. Color. Half-hour. Premiered on PBS: September 22, 1990. Rebroadcast on PBS: December 13, 1992.*

Voices

Nigel Hawthorne, Michael Gough, Ronnie Stevens

◉ THE REAL GHOSTBUSTERS CHRISTMAS

Those ghostbusting fools—Peter, Egon, Ray and Winston—unwittingly aid Ebenezer Scrooge when they trap the ghosts of Christmas Past, Present and Future in this regular episode from the popular Saturday-morning series, rebroadcast as a holiday special on USA Network in 1993. (For voice credits, see series entry in *Animated Television Series* section.) *A DIC Enterprises Production in association with Columbia Pictures Television. Color. Half-hour. Premiered on USA: December 19, 1993.*

◉ REALLY ROSIE

Singer-composer Carole King takes on the role of Rosie, who, dressed up like a film star, persuades her friends, the Nutshell Kids, into making musical screen tests for a picture she wants to make. Based on characters from Maurice Sendak's *Nutshell Library. A Sherriss Production in association with D & R Productions. Color. Half-hour. Premiered on CBS: February 19, 1975. Rebroadcast on CBS: June 8, 1976 (as "Maurice Sendak's Really Rosie"). Rebroadcast on DIS: September 2, 1993.*

Voices

Rosie: Carole King

◉ THE RED BARON

When the princess of Pretzelheim is kidnapped by the evil cat, Putzi, legendary flying ace the Red Baron (played by a schnauzer) leads a new squadron of flyers to reclaim the princess and defeat Catahari, the mastermind behind the sinister plan. Program originally aired as an episode of *The ABC Saturday Superstar Movie. A Rankin-Bass Production. Color. Half-hour. Premiered on ABC: December 9, 1972 (on The ABC Saturday Superstar Movie). Rebroadcast on ABC: January 26, 1974. Syndicated.*

Voices

Bradley Bolke, Rhoda Mann, Robert McFadden, Allen Swift

◉ RED RIDING HOOD AND GOLDILOCKS

Actress Meg Ryan narrates this half-hour animated retelling of two of the most cherished stories in children's literature. Part of Rabbit Ear Video's *Storybook Classics* series. *A Rabbit Ears Video Production. Color. Half-hour. Premiered on SHO: 1989.*

Voices
Narrator: Meg Ryan

◉ THE RED SHOES

Based on a story by Hans Christian Andersen, this animated rendition weaves a timeless tale about the importance of friendship. Two girls, Lisa and Jennie, are best friends until Lisa's parents win the lottery. Thereafter Lisa ignores Jennie, until a pair of magic dancing shoes appears and teaches her that money cannot buy happiness. Part of the award-winning anthology series *HBO Storybook Musicals. A Michael Sporn Animation Production in association with Italtoons Corporation. Color. Half-hour. Premiered on HBO: February 7, 1990.*

Voices
The Shoemaker/Narrator: Ossie Davis

◉ THE RELUCTANT DRAGON

In this stop-motion, puppet-animated half-hour special based on the book by Kenneth Grahame, a simple shepherd's son discovers lurking in a cave a dragon who is more inclined to compose poetry than attack frightened villagers. Produced by England's Cosgrove Hall Productions, the special, winner of the British Academy of Film and Television Arts' "Best Animation" award, premiered on PBS's critically acclaimed anthology series *Long Ago & Far Away. A Cosgrove Hall Production. Color. Half-hour. Premiered on PBS: February 4, 1989. Rebroadcast on PBS: November 17, 1990; November 15, 1992.*

Voices
Boy/Narrator: Martin Jarvis; **Dragon:** Simon Callow

◉ THE REMARKABLE ROCKET

An incredible fireworks rocket (Remarkable Rocket) that displays the attitudes and emotions of humans is the subject of this charming adaptation of the Oscar Wilde story about the experiences of a group of fireworks that prepare to be set off during a royal wedding celebration. *A Potterton Production in association with Narrator's Digest. Color. Half-hour. Premiered: 1974. Syndicated.*

Voices
Narrator: David Niven; **Other Voices:** Graham Stark

◉ THE RETURN OF THE BUNJEE

Bunjee, the elephantlike prehistoric creature, and his two young friends, Karen and Andy, wind up in the Middle Ages when the children's father's time-traveling machine is accidentally switched on in this sequel to *The Amazing Bunjee Venture*, adapted from the popular children's book *The Bunjee Venture* by Stan McMurty. *A Hanna-Barbera Production. Color. Half-hour. Premiered on ABC: April 6 and 12, 1985. Rebroadcast on ABC: September 21 and 28, 1985; April 21 and 28, 1990.*

Voices
Bunjee: Frank Welker; **Karen Winsborrow:** Nancy Cartwright; **Andy Winsborrow:** Robbie Lee; **Mr. Winsborrow:** Michael Rye; **Mrs. Winsborrow:** Linda Gary; **Others:** Peter Cullen, Pat Musick; **Narrator:** Michael Rye

◉ THE RETURN OF THE KING

Continuing J.R.R. Tolkien's saga of the Hobbits, Frodo—kin to the aged Bilbo—sets off to destroy the now-evil Ring in the fires of Mount Doom, thereby making it possible for the noble Aragon to return to his kingdom victorious over the hideous realm of Sauron. *A Rankin-Bass Production in association with Toei Animation. Color. Two hours. Premiered on ABC: May 11, 1980. Rebroadcast on ABC: July 21, 1983. Syndicated. Rebroadcast on CAR: June 25, 1995 (Mr. Spim's Cartoon Theatre).*

Voices
Frodo: Orson Bean; **Samwise:** Roddy McDowall; **Gandalf:** John Huston; **Aragorn:** Theodore Bikel; **Denethor:** William Conrad; **Gollum:** Theodore; **Minstrel:** Glenn Yarborough

◉ RETURN TO OZ

In this *General Electric Fantasy Hour* production, Dorothy returns to the Land of Oz to help her former cronies—Socrates (Strawman), Rusty (Tinman) and Dandy Lion (Cowardly Lion)—who have lost their brain, heart and courage, respectively. The program marked the first special produced by filmmakers Arthur Rankin Jr. and Jules Bass. *A Rankin-Bass Production in association with Videocraft International and Crawley Films. Color. One hour. Premiered on NBC: February 9, 1964. Rebroadcast on NBC: February 21, 1965. Syndicated. Rebroadcast on DIS: November 25, 1995.*

Voices
Dorothy: Susan Conway; **Dandy Lion/Wizard:** Carl Banas; **Socrates (Strawman):** Alfie Scopp; **Rusty (Tinman):**

Larry D. Mann; **Munchkins:** Susan Morse; **Glinda/Wicked Witch:** Peggi Loder

⊚ RING RAIDERS

A group of heroic aviators from all eras of flight, led by Ring Commander Victor Vector defend the world from the evil pilots of the Skull Squadron and Skull Commander Scorch in this two-hour special (entitled "Ring Fire"), partially inspired by the box-office success of the Tom Cruise movie *Top Gun*. The special preceded a five-part daily animated series that aired in syndication. *A DIC Enterprises Production in association with Those Characters from Cleveland and Bohbot Entertainment. Color. Half-hour. Premiered: 1989. Syndicated.*

Voices

Victor Vector: Dan Gilvezan; **Joe Thundercloud:** Efrain Figueroa; **Hubbub:** Stuart Goetz; **Cub Jones:** Ike Eisenmann; **Kirchov:** Gregory Martin; **Mako:** Jack Angel; **Jenny Gail:** Chris Anthony; **Max Miles:** Roscoe Lee Browne; **Scorch:** Rodger Bumpass; **Yasu Yakamura:** Townsend Coleman; **Baron Von Clawdeitz:** Chuck McCann; **Siren:** Susan Silo

⊚ RIKKI-TIKKI-TAVI

Adopted by a British family in India, Rikki-Tikki-Tavi, a brave mongoose, fights to protect the people who've been so kind to him, saving them from two dreaded cobras in this wonderful cartoon adaptation of Rudyard Kipling's *The Jungle Book. A Chuck Jones Enterprises Production. Color. Half-hour. Premiered on CBS: January 9, 1975. Rebroadcast on CBS: April 12, 1976; April 4, 1977; January 23, 1978; February 9, 1979. Syndicated. Rebroadcast on NIK: October 12, 1991; February 29, 1992.*

Voices

Rikki-Tikki-Tavi: Orson Welles; **Nag/Chuchundra:** Shepard Menken; **Teddy:** Michael LeClaire; **Nagaina/Dazee's Wife/Mother:** June Foray; **Father:** Les Tremayne; **Darzee:** Lennie Weinrib; **Narrator:** Orson Welles

⊚ THE RISE AND FALL OF HUMPTY DUMPTY

The walking, talking egg of children's nursery rhyme fame saves a beautiful princess from the curses of an evil witch in this half-hour animated special originally produced in 1991 for Cinar Films' *The Real Story of . . .* (retitled from its former name, simply *Humpty Dumpty*). HBO premiered the special as part of its musical cartoon anthology series *HBO Storybook Musicals. A Cinar Production in association with Crayon Animation. Color. Half-hour. Premiered on HBO: December 18, 1991. Rebroadcast on HBO: December 20, 1991.*

Voices

Glenda Jackson, Huey Lewis

⊚ ROBIN HOOD

The Sheriff of Nottingham finally captures Robin Hood and his Merry Men with a plan involving a woodcutter, his son and the boy's sheepdog in this new version of the popular tale. *A Festival of Family Classics special. A Rankin-Bass Production. Color. Half-hour. Premiered: November 26, 1973. Syndicated.*

Voices

Carl Banas, Len Birman, Bernard Cowan, Peg Dixon, Keith Hampshire, Peggi Locker, Donna Miller, Frank Perry, Henry Ramer, Billie Mae Richards, Alfie Scopp, Paul Soles

⊚ ROBIN HOODNIK

Animals are cast in human roles in this colorful rendition of the classic fantasy tale. This time, Robin and his pack of happy critters are prime targets of the Sheriff of Nottingham (aided by his faithful deputy, Oxx) who tries to stop Robin from marrying the lovely Maid Marian by using a secret potion. The hour-long program first aired on *The ABC Saturday Superstar Movie* series (the working title of the production was *Cartoon Adventures of Robin Hound*). *A Hanna-Barbera Production. Color. One hour. Premiered on ABC: November 4, 1972 (on The ABC Saturday Superstar Movie). Syndicated.*

Voices

Robin Hood/Alan Airedale/Whirlin' Merlin/Lord Scurvy/Friar Pork/Little John: Lennie Weinrib; **Sheriff of Nottingham/Carbuncle:** John Stephenson; **Oxx:** Joe E. Ross; **Donkey/Town Crier/Buzzard:** Hal Smith; **Scrounger/Richard the Iron-Hearted:** Daws Butler; **Maid Marian/Widow Weed:** Cynthia Adler

⊚ ROBINSON CRUSOE (1972)

The resourceful Robinson Crusoe is shipwrecked on a tropical island and must find new means of survival until the day he will be rescued in this animated retelling of Daniel Defoe's beloved adventure novel. *A Famous Classic Tales special. An Air Programs International. Color. One hour. Premiered on CBS: November 23, 1972. Rebroadcast on CBS: October 8, 1973. Syndicated.*

Voices

Alistair Duncan, Ron Haddrick, Mark Kelly, John Llewellyn, Owen Weingott

⊚ ROBINSON CRUSOE (1973)

Robinson Crusoe and his talking parrot, Poll, save the captain of a ship from his mutinous crew and find their ticket to freedom from the island on which they have been stranded in this *Festival of Family Classics* special for first-run syndication. *A Rankin-Bass Production in association with Mushi Studios. Color. Half-hour. Premiered: February 18, 1973. Syndicated.*

Voices
Carl Banas, Len Birman, Bernard Cowan, Peg Dixon, Keith Hampshire, Peggi Loder, Donna Miller, Frank Perry, Henry Ramer, Billie Mae Richards, Alfie Scopp, Paul Soles

◎ ROBOTMAN AND FRIENDS
An evil robot (Roberon) tries to convert three friendly robots (Robotman, Stellar and Oops) into hating people instead of loving them, but fails on all counts thanks to the robot's Earthbound friends. Based on the Kenner toy product, which was also turned into a daily comic strip for United Features Syndicate in 1985. *A DIC Enterprises Production in association with United Media. Color. Ninety minutes. Premiered: October, 1985. Syndicated.*

Voices
Robotman: Greg Berg; **Roberon/Sound-Off:** Frank Welker; **Stellar:** Katie Leigh; **Uncle Thomas Cooper:** Phil Proctor; **Michael/Oops:** Adam Carl

◎ ROCKIN' WITH JUDY JETSON
News of intergalactic rock star Sky Rocker's surprise concert sends George and Jane Jetson's teenage daughter, Judy, into orbit, inspiring her to write a song for her music idol in this two-hour movie based on the *Jetsons* cartoon series. *A Hanna-Barbera Production. Color. Two hours. Premiered: 1988. Syndicated. Rebroadcast on CAR: March 5, 1995 (Mr. Spim's Cartoon Theatre).*

Voices
Judy Jetson: Janet Waldo; **Jane Jetson, her mother:** Penny Singleton; **George Jetson, her father:** George O'Hanlon; **Elroy Jetson, her brother:** Daws Butler; **Rosie, the Jetson's maid:** Jean VanderPyl; **Astro, the Jetson's dog:** Don Messick; **Mr. Microchips/Manny:** Hamilton Camp; **Nicky:** Eric Suter; **Ramm/Dee-Jay:** Beau Weaver; **Iona:** Cindy McGee; **Starr/Fan Club President/Zowie:** Pat Musick; **Felonia:** Ruth Buzzi; **Quark/Zappy:** Charlie Adler; **Gruff/Commander Comsat/Bouncer:** Peter Cullen; **Sky Rocker/Zany:** Rob Paulsen; **Rhoda Starlet:** Selette Cole; **High Loopy Zoomy:** P.L. Brown; **Zippy:** B.J. Ward; **Zilchy:** Pat Fraley; **Cosmo C. Spacely:** Mel Blanc

◎ ROCKO'S MODERN LIFE CHRISTMAS AND TATTERTOWN
This hour-long syndicated special features two half-hour Christmas episodes from Nickelodeon's *Rocko's Modern Life*,

in which Rocko's Christmas party guestlist includes his new neighbors-the elves-and Ralph Bashki's 1988 Nickelodeon special, *Tattertown*, about a stranger who visits visits a world populated by unwanted objects. *A Games Animation/Bashki Animation Production. Color. One hour. Premiered: December 10, 1995. Syndicated.*

◎ THE ROMANCE OF BETTY BOOP
It's 1939 and Betty's working two jobs to keep body and soul together: selling shoes by day and headlining at her Uncle Mischa's club at night. While dreaming of millionaire Waldo, she is pursued by humble iceman Freddie and gangster Johnny Throat, Uncle Mischa's ruthless creditor. Desiree Goyette, who displayed her singing prowess in several Charlie Brown television specials, is the voice of Betty. *A King Features Entertainment Production in association with Lee Mendelson–Bill Melendez Productions. Color. Half-hour. Premiered on CBS: March 20, 1985. Rebroadcast on CBS: December 31, 1987.*

Voices
Betty Boop: Desiree Goyette; **Freddie:** Sean Allen; **Waldo Van Lavish:** Derek McGrath; **Johnny Throat/Punchie:** George R. Wendt; **Mischa Bubbles:** Sandy Kenyon; **Parrot:** Frank W. Buxton; **Chuckles:** Robert Towers; **Ethnic Voices:** Ron Friedman; **Announcer:** John Stephenson; **Vocalists:** Desiree Goyette, Sean Allen

◎ ROMAN CITY
This hour-long live-action/animated special, winner of a nighttime Emmy Award for Outstanding Animated Program, tells the story of life in a fictional but historically accurate Roman city, Verbonia. Based on the book by acclaimed author-illustrator David Macaulay, the PBS special examines the social significance of Roman cities and the age-old conflict between the generations. *A Unicorn Films Production. Color. One hour. Premiered on PBS: May 7, 1994.*

◎ ROMIE-O AND JULIE-8
Two robots fall in love with each other and are kept apart by the two companies that manufactured them in this innovative rendition of the classic love story. *A Nelvana Limited Production in association with CBC. Color. Half-hour. Premiered (U.S.): April 1979. Syndicated.*

Voices
Romie-O: Greg Swanson; **Julie-8:** Donann Cavin; **Mr. Thunderbottom:** Max Ferguson; **Ms. Passbinder:** Marie Aloma; **Gizmo:** Nick Nichols; **Junk Monster:** Bill Osler; **Vocalists:** John Sebastian, Rory Block, Richard Manuel

Two robots, kept apart by the companies that manufactured them, hopelessly fall in love in the Romeo and Juliet–*inspired* Romie-O and Julie-8. © *Nelvana Limited*

⊚ THE ROOTS OF GOOFY

In this Disney Channel original production, Gary Owens hosts and narrates this retrospective special telling the story of Goofy's ancestors, featuring a variety of cartoon clips. *A Left Coast Television Production for The Disney Channel. Color. Ninety minutes. Premiered on DIS: 1984.*

⊚ ROSE-PETAL PLACE

A magical flower's beauty and kindness triumphs over evil in an enchanting garden world known as Rose-Petal Place in this live-action/animation special. *A Ruby-Spears Enterprises Production. Color. Half-hour. Premiered: May, 1984. Syndicated.*

Cast
Little Girl in the Garden: Nicole Eggert

Voices
Rose-Petal: Marie Osmond; **Nastina:** Marilyn Schreffler; **Sunny Sunflower/Daffodil:** Susan Blu; **Orchid/Little Girl/Lily Fair:** Renae Jacobs; **Iris:** Candy Ann Brown; **P.D. Centipede/Seymour J. Snailsworth/Tumbles/Elmer/Horace Fly:** Frank Welker

⊚ ROSE-PETAL PLACE II: REAL FRIENDS

In this sequel to *Rose-Petal Place*, Rose Petal returns to help her garden friends learn an important lesson about friendship and trust. *A Ruby-Spears Enterprises Production in association with David Kirschner Productions and Hallmark Properties. Color. Half-hour. Premiered: April, 1985. Syndicated.*

Cast
Little Girl in the Garden: Nicole Eggert

Voices
Rose-Petal: Marie Osmond; **Sunny Sunflower/Canterbury Belle/Fuschia:** Susan Blu; **Elmer/Horace Fly/Seymour J. Snailsworth/P.D. Centipede/Tumbles:** Frank Welker; **Nastina/Lily Fair/Marigold:** Marilyn Schreffler; **Sweet Violet/Cherry Blossom:** Renae Jacobs; **Ladybug:** Stacy McLaughlin

⊚ THE ROSEY AND BUDDY SHOW

Pulling their motorhome into Cartoonland, Rosey and Buddy (played by then real husband and wife Roseanne and Tom Arnold) star in their own television show and find out that the network Powers (as in "the powers that be") care only about profits. *A Little Rosey Production in association with Wapello County Productions/Nelvana Limited. Color. Half-hour. Premiered on ABC: May 15, 1992.*

Voices
Rosey: Roseanne Arnold; **Buddy:** Tom Arnold

⊚ ROTTEN RALPH: "NOT SO ROTTEN RALPH"

Inspired by many weeks of being grounded, Rotten Ralph tries his best to be good and behave himself, but his good deeds have unpredicted results. Second in a series of *Rotten Ralph* specials for The Disney Channel. *An Italtoons Corporation/Matthews Production. Color. Half-hour. Premiered on DIS: August 26, 1996.*

Voices
Rotten Ralph: Hal Rayle; **Mae Whitman/Maggie Roswell:** Corey Burton

⊚ ROTTEN RALPH: "THE TAMING OF THE RALPH"

The Disney Channel originally commissioned four episodes for this stop-motion animated series of specials, but stopped production after only two programs. In this first installment, Ralph watches silly TV shows all day and annoys everyone in the family. As punishment for his rotten deeds, Ralph has to stay home while the rest of the family goes to the circus. The specials were based on the popular children's books written by Jack Gantos and illustrated by Nicole Rubel, published by Houghton-Mifflin. *An Italtoons Corporation/Matthews Production. Color. Half-hour. Premiered on DIS: May 18, 1996.*

Voices
Rotten Ralph: Hal Rayle; **Mae Whitman/Maggie Roswell:** Corey Burton

⊚ RUDOLPH AND FROSTY'S CHRISTMAS IN JULY

Frosty the Snowman and Rudolph the Red-Nosed Reindeer leave the cozy confines of the North Pole to help an ailing circus but find trouble in the form of the villainous Winterbolt. A Rankin-Bass Production. Color. Half-hour. Premiered on ABC: November 25, 1979. Rebroadcast on ABC: December 20, 1981. Rebroadcast on CBS: December 22, 1991. Rebroadcast on DIS: December 18, 1996.

Voices
Santa Claus (narrator): Mickey Rooney; **Rudolph:** Billie Richards; **Frosty:** Jackie Vernon; **Crystal, Frosty's wife:** Shelley Winters; **Mrs. Santa Claus:** Darlene Conley; **Winterbolt:** Paul Frees; **Milton, the ice cream salesman:** Red Buttons; **Scratcher, the jealous reindeer:** Alan Sues; **Lilly, the circus owner:** Ethel Merman; **Lanie, Lilly's daughter:** Shelby Flint; **Big Ben:** Harold Peary

⊚ RUDOLPH'S SHINY NEW YEAR

Happy, the Baby New Year, has run away from Father Time and unless he's found there will be no new year and the calendar will remain locked on December 31st forever. Rudolph the Red-Nosed Reindeer saves the day with Santa's help. Program features an original score by Johnny Marks, including his original hit song, "Rudolph the Red-Nosed Reindeer." A Rankin-Bass Production. Color. One hour. Premiered on ABC: December 10, 1976. Rebroadcast on ABC: December 11, 1977; December 9, 1978; December 16, 1979; December 14, 1980; December 10, 1981; December 6, 1982. Rebroadcast on DIS: December 22, 1992; December 1, 1993; December 6, 1993; December 18, 1993; December 23, 1993; December 20, 1995; December 25, 1996. Syndicated.

Voices
Father Time (narrator): Red Skelton; **Rudolph:** Billie Richards; **Sir Tentworthree/Camel:** Frank Gorshin; **One Million B.C.:** Morey Amsterdam; **Santa Claus/Aeon:** Paul Frees; **Big Ben:** Hal Peary

⊚ RUDOLPH, THE RED-NOSED REINDEER

Inspired by Johnny Marks's bestselling song (recorded in 1949 and selling more than 8 million copies), this gaily colored Animagic special tells the story of Rudolph, the reindeer with the illuminating red nose, who saves Christmas by safely guiding Santa through a terrible storm on Christmas Eve. Burl Ives, appearing as Sam the Snowman, narrates the program, which was first broadcast on NBC in 1964 under the title of *General Electric's Fantasy Hour*. A Videocraft International Production. Color. Half-hour. Premiered on NBC: December 6, 1964 (*on General Electric Fantasy Hour*).

Rebroadcast on NBC: December 5, 1975; December 4, 1966; December 8, 1967; December 6, 1968; December 5, 1969; December 4, 1970; December 6, 1971. Rebroadcast on CBS: December 8, 1972; December 7, 1973; December 13, 1974; December 3, 1975; December 1, 1976; November 30, 1977; December 6, 1978; December 6, 1979; December 3, 1980; December 14, 1981; December 1, 1982; December 3, 1983; December 1, 1984; December 3, 1985; December 9, 1986; December 15, 1987; December 5, 1988; December 15, 1989; December 14, 1990; November 29, 1991; December 11, 1992; December 2, 1993; November 29, 1994; November 28, 1995; November 29, 1996; December 1, 1997.

Voices
Sam the Snowman (narrator): Burl Ives; **Rudolph:** Billie Richards; Hermy the Elf: Paul Soles; **Yukon Cornelius:** Larry D. Mann; **Santa Claus:** Stan Francis; **Clarice:** Janet Orenstein

⊚ RUGRATS CHANUKAH

It's Chanukah and everyone's off to the synagogue to watch Grandpa Boris perform at the holiday fair, while the Rugrats track down a mysterious "villain" of their own in this 1997 holiday special based on the popular Nickelodeon cartoon series. (For voice credits, see series entry in Television Cartoon Series section.) A Klasky-Csupo Production. Color. Half-hour. Premiered on NIK: December 20, 1997.

⊚ RUGRATS: "HOLLYWEEN"

Tommy Pickles and the rest of his preschool age friends get a lesson in trick-or-treating and suspect there's a monster in the garage in their first prime-time animated special based on the popular Nickelodeon cartoon series. (For voice credits, see series entry in "Television Cartoon Series" section.) A Klasky Csupo Production. Color. Half-hour. Premiered on NIK: October 30, 1993.

⊚ RUGRATS MOTHER'S DAY SPECIAL

While the precocious kids scurry around to find the right Mother's Day gifts for their moms, first they lend a hand to Chuckie, who doesn't have a mother, to find an appropriate surrogate in this half-hour special featuring the cast of characters from the Nickelodeon cartoon series. (For voice credits, see series entry in Television Cartoon Series section.) A Klasky-Csupo Production. Color. Half-hour. Premiered on NIK: May 6, 1997.

⊚ A RUGRATS PASSOVER

On Seder night, after locking the kids in the attic, Grandpa Boris entertains them with the story of Passover ("the greatest holiday of the year") in this prime-time animated special. (For voice credits, see entry in Television Cartoon Series section.) *A Klasky-Csupo Production. Color. Half-hour. Premiered on NIK: April 13, 1995. Rebroadcast on NIK: March 30, 1996.*

RUGRATS THE SANTA EXPERIENCE

The families spend Christmas together in the mountains where Tommy and Chuckie set traps for Santa Claus in this fun-filled, prime-time holiday special. (For voice credits, see entry in *Television Cartoon Series* section.) *A Klasky Csupo Production. Color. Half-hour. Premiered on NIK: December 21, 1996. Rebroadcast on NIK: December 25, 1996.*

RUGRATS VACATION

Taking their RV on the road, the Pickles family travels to the entertainment capital of the world—Las Vegas—in this springtime half-hour special. (For voice credits, see series entry in Television Cartoon Series section.) *A Klasky-Csupo Production. Color. Half-hour. Premiered on NIK: March 3, 1998.*

RUMPELSTILTSKIN

A maiden is forced to spin straw into gold to save her father or face death in this animated rendition of the Grimm Brothers' fairy tale which debuted on Canadian television and was syndicated in the United States. *An Atkinson Film-Arts Production in association with Telefilm Canada and CTV. Color. Half-hour. Premiered (U.S.): December 1985. Syndicated. Rebroadcast on NIK: February 8, 1992; April 4, 1992.*

Voices
Rumplestiltskin: Robert Bockstael; **Miller:** Les Lye; **Miller's Daughter/Queen:** Charity Brown; **King:** Al Baldwin; **Narrator:** Christopher Plummer

THE RUNAWAY TEAPOT

Toby the Teapot and Jenny the Milk Jug escape from the clutches of the Mad Hatter and find true love in New York City in this half-hour animated musical, part of the *HBO Storybook Musicals* series, inspired by Lewis Carroll's children's classic *Alice in Wonderland.* Originally called *I'm a Little Teapot,* the special was originally produced as part of Cinar Films' 13-part *The Real Story of . . .* series. *A Cinar Films/Crayon Animation Production in association with Western Publishing Company Inc./Global Television Network. Color. Half-hour. Premiered on HBO: December 4, 1991. Rebroadcast on HBO: December 11, 1991.*

Voices
Julian Lennon

RUPERT AND THE FROG SONG

Music legend Paul McCartney, in live-action wraparounds, hosts (he also produced) this half-hour program featuring two animated stories of popular British cartoon characters Seaside Woman and Oriental Nightfish (for which McCartney and wife, Linda, provided some of the voices), which premiered in the United States on The Disney Channel. *An MPL Communications Production. Color. Half-hour. Premiered on DIS: September 20, 1986.*

Voices
Linda McCartney, Paul McCartney

SANTA AND THE THREE BEARS

Two bear cubs, Nikomi and Chinook, experience the joy and magic of Christmas for the very first time in this hour-long musical originally released theatrically in 1970 and rebroadcast via syndication as a holiday special. Live-action sequences of a kindly old grandfather relating the tale to his grandchildren introduce the animated story. *A Tony Benedict Production in association with Key Industries. Color. One hour. Premiered: 1970. Syndicated. Rebroadcast on USA Network: December 5, 1991; December 12, 1992; December 1, 1993; December 25, 1994; December 24, 1995. Rebroadcast on FAM: December 24, 1995; December 6, 1996; December 10, 1997.*

Cast
Grandfather: Hal Smith; **Beth:** Beth Goldfarb; **Brian:** Brian Hobbs

Voices
Ranger: Hal Smith; **Nana:** Jean VanderPyl; **Nikomi:** Annette Ferra; **Chinook:** Bobby Riha

SANTABEAR'S FIRST CHRISTMAS

Santa Claus recognizes a young bear's giving nature and appoints him as his helper to deliver toys to the animals of the forest. Thus he becomes known as Santabear. *A Rabbit Ears Video Production. Color. Half-hour. Premiered on ABC: November 22, 1986. Rebroadcast on SHO: December 17, 1991; December 22, 1991.*

Voices
Narrator: Kelly McGillis

SANTABEAR'S HIGH-FLYING ADVENTURE

Santa Claus asks Santabear to deliver his toys to the South Pole, but when the naughty Bullybear steals Santabear's bag of toys and his identity, all chances for a merry Christmas seem lost. Second in a series of Santabear Christmas specials. *A Michael Sporn Animation Production. Color. Half-hour. Premiered on CBS: December 24, 1987.*

Voices
Santabear/Bullybear: Bobby McFerrin; **Missy Bear:** Kelly McGillis; **Santa Claus:** John Malkovich

◎ SANTA CLAUS IS COMING TO TOWN

The life and times of Santa Claus—his abandonment as a child, his christening as Kris Kringle, and his eventual marriage to Jessica, the schoolmarm—are the essence of this holiday favorite produced in Animagic and narrated by actor/singer Fred Astaire, who likewise appears, in puppet form, as the town's mailman, S.D. Kluger. *A Rankin-Bass Production. Color. Half-hour. Premiered on ABC: December 14, 1970. Rebroadcast on ABC: December 3, 1971; December 1, 1972; November 30, 1973; December 5, 1974; December 9, 1975; December 12, 1976; December 1, 1977; December 10, 1978; December 2, 1979; December 8, 1980; December 19, 1981. Syndicated. Rebroadcast on FAM: December 4, 1996.*

Voices
S.D. Kluger (narrator): Fred Astaire; **Kris Kringle:** Mickey Rooney; **Jessica:** Robie Lester; **Winter Warlock:** Keenan Wynn; **Tanta Kringle:** Joan Gardner; **Burgermeister:** Paul Frees; **Children:** Diana Lyn, Greg Thomas

◎ SANTA VS. THE SNOWMAN

A lonely snowman (in a nonspeaking role) grows jealous of all the attention Santa Claus always receives and creates an army of snow-minions out of ice cubes, waging an all-out battle against Santa and his elves in this computer-generated holiday special. Created by Steve Oedekerk (of *Ace Ventura: When Nature Calls* fame) and writer-animator John

Santa and the Snowman square off in a scene from the ABC holiday special Santa Vs. The Snowman. *© O Entertainment*

Davis. *An O Entertainment Production. Color. Half-hour. Premiered on ABC: December 13, 1997.*

Voices
Santa Claus: Jonathan Winters; **Security Elf:** Mark Decarlo; **Tour Guide Elf:** Ben Stein; **Communications Elf:** Victoria Jackson; **Narrator:** Don LeFontaine

◎ THE SAVIOR IS BORN

Morgan Freeman reads this poignant retelling of Mary and Joseph's journey to Bethlehem culminating in the birth of Jesus. Part of Rabbit Ears Video's *Holiday Classics* video series, the program debuted on The Family Channel. *A Rabbit Ears Video Production. Color. Half-hour. Premiered on FAM: December 24, 1992.*

Voices
Narrator: Morgan Freeman

◎ SCOOBY AND THE GHOUL SCHOOL

Scooby-Doo, Shaggy and Scrappy-Doo get mixed up with monsters when they accept jobs as gym teachers at a girls' finishing school in this two-hour made-for-television movie. Part of *Hanna-Barbera's Superstars 10* movie package for first-run syndication. *A Hanna-Barbera Production. Color. Two hours. Premiered: 1988. Syndicated.*

Voices
Scooby-Doo/Scrappy-Doo: Don Messick; **Shaggy:** Casey Kasem; **Miss Grimwood:** Glynis Johns; **Elsa Frankensteen:** Pat Musick; **Winnie Werewolf:** Marilyn Schreffler; **Sibella Dracula:** Susan Blu; **Tannis the Mummy:** Patty Maloney; **Phantasma the Phantom:** Russi Taylor; **Matches/Papa Werewolf:** Frank Welker; **Colonel Calloway:** Ronnie Schell; **Daddy Dracula/Frankenstein Senior:** Zale Kessler; **Phantom Father:** Hamilton Camp; **Mummy Daddy/The Grim Creeper:** Andre Stojka; **Revolta:** Ruta Lee; **Baxter:** Rene Auberjonois; **Tug:** Scott Menville; **Miguel:** Aaron Lohr; **Jamaal:** Bumper Robinson; **Grunt:** Jeff B. Cohen

◎ SCOOBY AND THE RELUCTANT WEREWOLF

Scooby-Doo and Shaggy are funny-car drivers, who get into monstrous trouble involving a new werewolf. Produced for *Hanna-Barbera's Superstar 10* movie package for first-run syndication. *A Hanna-Barbera Production. Color. Two hours. Premiered: 1988. Syndicated. Rebroadcast on TBS: December 13, 1992. Rebroadcast on CAR: March 12, 1995 (Mr. Spim's Cartoon Theatre). Rebroadcast on DIS: October 31, 1996; October 31, 1997.*

Voices

Scooby-Doo/Scrappy-Doo: Don Messick; **Shaggy:** Casey Kasem; **Googie:** B.J. Ward; **Vana Pira:** Pat Musick; **Dracula:** Hamilton Camp; **Dreadonia:** Joan Gerber; **Repulsa:** B.J. Ward; **Bonejangles:** Brian Mitchell; **Frankenstein/Skull Head:** Jim Cummings; **Mummy:** Alan Oppenheimer; **Brunch:** Rob Paulsen; **Crunch:** Frank Welker; **Screamer:** Mimi Seton; **Dr. Jeckyll/Mr. Hyde:** Ed Gilbert

◎ SCOOBY-DOO MEETS THE BOO BROTHERS

A search for lost treasure turn the visit of Scooby-Doo, Scrappy-Doo and Shaggy to a Southern plantation into spine-tingling adventure. Part of *Hanna-Barbera's Superstar 10* syndicated movie package. A Hanna-Barbera Production. Color. Two hours. Premiered: 1987. Syndicated.

Voices

Scooby-Doo/Scrappy-Doo/Hound: Don Messick; **Shaggy:** Casey Kasem; **Sheriff:** Sorrell Booke; **Farquard/Skull Ghost/Skeleton:** Arte Johnson; **Freako/Demonstrator Ghost:** Ronnie Schell; **Shreako:** Rob Paulsen; **Meako:** Jerry Houser; **Sadie Mae:** Victoria Carroll; **Billy Bob/Confederate Ghost/Uncle Beauregard/Ape:** Bill Callaway; **Mayor:** Michael Rye

◎ SCOOBY GOES HOLLYWOOD

Scooby-Doo, the clumsy but lovable canine, romps through delightful capers in order to hit the big time in Hollywood by landing his own prime-time television show. A Hanna-Barbera Production. Color. One hour. Premiered on ABC: December 23, 1979. Rebroadcast on ABC: January 25, 1981.

Voices

Scooby-Doo/Bulldog/Second Man: Don Messick; **Shaggy/First Man/Pilot's Voice:** Casey Kasem; **Fred/Afghan/The Groove:** Frank Welker; **Velma/First Woman/Lucy Lane:** Pat Stevens; **Daphne/Treena/Mail girl:** Heather North Kenney; **Baby Scooby-Doo:** Frank Welker; **C.J.:** Rip Taylor; **Director/First V.P./Terrier:** Stan Jones; **Jesse Rotten/V.P./Jackie Carlson:** Michael Bell; **Cherie/Sis/Receptionist:** Marilyn Schreffler; **Lavonne/Second Woman/Waitress:** Joan Gerber; **Kerry/Girl Fan/Executive Secretary:** Ginny McSwain; **Brother/Guard/Announcer's Voice:** Patrick Fraley

◎ SCHOOL . . . WHO NEEDS IT?

Davey (of TV's *Davey and Goliath*) and his friends protest going back to school but come around when their teacher extends an understanding hand and initiates the beginning of a special friendship. A *Clokey* Production for the Lutheran Church of America. Color. Half-hour. Premiered: August-September 1971. Syndicated.

Voices

Davey Hanson/Sally Hanson/Teacher: Norma McMillan, Nancy Wible; **Goliath:** Hal Smith

◎ SCRUFFY

In this three-part adventure, Scruffy, an orphaned puppy, searches for a new home and seeks to find true love in her life for the first time, becoming friends with a Shakespearean street actor, Joe Tibbles, and another stray dog, Butch, in this ABC Weekend Special. A Ruby-Spears Enterprises Production. Color. Half-hour. Premiered on ABC: October 4, October 11 and October 18, 1980. Rebroadcast on ABC: February 7, February 14 and February 21, 1981; February 13, February 20 and February 27, 1982; February 26, March 5 and March 12, 1983.

Voices

Scruffy: Nancy McKeon; **Tibbles:** Hans Conried; **Butch:** Michael Bell; **Dutchess:** June Foray; **Narrator:** Alan Young

◎ SEBASTIAN'S CARIBBEAN JAMBOREE

Sebastian, the musical crab from *The Little Mermaid*, and his partner, Sam Wright, perform a concert taped at Walt Disney World in this live-action/animated special—the second of two—that aired on The Disney Channel. A One Heart Production. Color. Half-hour. Premiered on DIS: 1991.

Cast (live action)

Autumn Hoff, Sam Wright

Voices

Sebastian: Sam Wright

◎ SEBASTIAN'S PARTY GRAS

The Little Mermaid's Sebastian the crab prepares to sing a concert with his friend (and alter ego) Sam Wright in this live-action/animated special taped at Walt Disney World. A Blue Streak Production. Color. Half-hour. Premiered on DIS: 1991.

Cast (live action)

Sam Wright

Voices

Sebastian: Sam Wright; **King Triton:** Kenneth Mars; **Seahorse:** Will Ryan

THE SECRET GARDEN

Sent to live in Yorkshire, England, at the manor house of her aloof, hunchbacked uncle, 11-year-old orphan Mary Lennox finds refuge in her magical hideaway in this animated musical adaptation—and first offering of ABC's quarterly *Kids Movie Matinees* series—of Frances Hodgson Burnett's book. *A Mike Young Production in association with Greengrass Productions. Color. Ninety minutes. Premiered on ABC: November 5, 1994.*

Voices
Mary: Anndi McAfee; **Mrs. Medlock:** Honor Blackman

THE SECRET WORLD OF OG

Five brothers and sisters—Penny, Pamela, Patsy, Peter and their baby brother, Pollywog—are taken to a world of games and make-believe in a strange underground world called OG, inhabited by small green creatures who live in mushroom-shape buildings and play games. *A Hanna-Barbera Production. Color. Ninety minutes (three parts). Premiered on ABC: April 30, 1983, May 7, 1983 and May 14, 1983. Rebroadcast on ABC: December 3, 1983, December 10, 1983 and December 17, 1983; October 27, 1984, November 10, 1984 and November 17, 1984: March 15, 1986, March 22, 1986 and March 29, 1986; February 21, 1987, February 28, 1987 and March 7, 1987; March 7, 1992, March 14, 1992 and March 21, 1992.*

Voices
OG: Fred Travalena; **Penny:** Noelle North; **Pamela:** Marissa Mendenhall; **Patsy:** Brittany Wilson; **Peter:** Josh Rodine; **Pollywod/Green Lady/Woman's Voice:** Julie McWhirter Dees; **Mother/Old Lady:** Janet Waldo; **Old Man/Glub Villager:** Fred Travalena; **Yukon "Yukie" Pete, family dog/Earless, Pollywog's cat/Long John Silver:** Peter Cullen; **Flub/Blib/Little Green Man #2/; Sheriff/Little Green Man #1/; Butcher/Villager/Mushroom Harvester:** Hamilton Camp; **Teacher:** Beth Clopton; **Pirate #1/Mayor/Man's Voice:** Dick Erdman; **Worker/Cowboy #1/Green Deputy/Narrator:** Michael Rye; **Victim #2/Green Man:** Joe Medalis; **Victim #1/Elder OG/OG Father:** Andre Stojka

THE SELFISH GIANT

A giant, who sees his selfish ways, makes an effort to reform himself, opening up his heart to a stray child in this faithful retelling of Oscar Wilde's short story of the same name. Originally produced for theaters, the film was nominated for an Academy Award as Best Animated Short Subject in 1972. The program had first been broadcast in Canada. David Niven narrated the original version of the production and was later replaced by Paul Hecht. *A Gerald Potterton Production in association with Narrator's Digest. Color. Half-hour. Premiered on CBS: March 28, 1973. Rebroadcast on CBS: March 25, 1974; April 6, 1976. Syndicated. Rebroadcast on DIS: September 12, 1991.*

Voices
Narrator: David Niven, Paul Hecht

SHE'S A GOOD SKATE, CHARLIE BROWN

Peppermint Patty enters her first major ice skating competition. With her coach, Snoopy, and faithful companion Marcie at her side, she runs into the usual Charlie Brown–like problems en route to the competition, where a real disaster strikes. Woodstock saves the day. *A Lee Mendelson–Bill Melendez Production in association with Charles M. Schulz Creative Associates and United Feature Syndicate. Color. Half-hour. Premiered on CBS: February 25, 1980. Rebroadcast on CBS: February 25, 1981; February 10, 1982; February 23, 1988.*

Voices
Charlie Brown: Arrin Skelley; **Marcie:** Casey Carlson; **Peppermint Patty:** Patricia Patts; **Coach/Announcer:** Scott Beach; **Teacher:** Debbie Muller; **Bully:** Tim Hall; **Snoopy:** José Melendez; **Woodstock (singing):** Jason Serinus; **Singer:** Rebecca Reardon

SILENT NIGHT

The heartwarming tale of Austrian pastor Joseph Mohr, who wrote the famed Christmas carol, is the premise of this animated production, which tells the origin of the popular yuletide song and its author, including the first time it was performed on Christmas Eve in 1818. *A National Telefilm Associates Presentation. Color. Half-hour. Premiered: December 1977. Syndicated.*

SILVERHAWKS

In the year 2839 a volunteer android team—part metal and part human—is sent by Earth to keep law and order in the galaxy in this hour-long special marking the debut of the first-run syndicated series. *A Rankin-Bass Production in association with Pacific Animation. Color. One hour. Premiered: January 1986. Syndicated.*

Voices
Quicksilver: Peter Newman; **Melodia/Steelheart:** Maggie Jackson; **Windhammer:** Doug Preis; **Mon*Star/Stargazer:** Earl Hammond; **Poker-Face/BlueGrass/Time-Stopper:** Larry Kenney; **HardWare/Steelwill/Yes-Man/Mo-Lec-U-Lar:** Robert McFadden; **Hotwing:** Adolph Caesar, Doug Preis

◎ SIMPLE GIFTS

The spirit of holiday gift-giving in its simplest form is the running theme of this one-hour collection of cartoon segments—each adapted from well-known stories and produced by some of America's most noted animators and artists. *An R.O. Blechman Production for PBS. Color. One hour. Premiered on PBS: December 16, 1978.*

Voices

Narrators: José Ferrer ("A Memory of Christmas"); Hermione Gingold ("The Great Frost")

◎ SIMPLY MAD ABOUT THE MOUSE

Songs performed by contemporary artists, including Billy Joel, Harry Connick Jr., LL Cool J, Ric Ocasek and Michael Bolton, accompany clips from classic Disney cartoons in this half-hour compilation first released on home video, then broadcast on The Disney Channel. *A Walt Disney Production. Color. Half-hour. Premiered on DIS: 1992.*

◎ THE SIMPSONS CHRISTMAS SPECIAL

It's rough sledding for husband and father Homer, who is forced to resort to desperate measures when his Christmas bonus is canceled and Marge's family money goes to erase the tattoo son Bart thought would be the perfect gift. Entitled "Simpsons Roasting Over an Open Fire," the show was originally produced as part of the first season of *The Simpsons* television show. *A Gracie Films/Klasky-Csupo Production in association with 20th Century-Fox Television. Color. Half-hour. Premiered on FOX: December 17, 1989. Rebroadcast on FOX: December 23, 1989; July 1, 1990; December 19, 1991.*

Voices

Homer J. Simpson/Krusty: Dan Castellaneta; **Marge Simpson:** Julie Kavner; **Bart Simpson:** Nancy Cartwright; **Lisa Simpson:** Yeardley Smith; **Maggie Simpson:** (no voice); **Other Voices:** Harry Shearer

◎ THE SIMPSONS HALLOWEEN MARATHON: "TREE HOUSE OF HORROR V"

This two-hour spooky spectacular sandwiches a brand-new half-hour trilogy featuring tributes to more favorite horror and sci-fi movies between reruns of past Halloween specials from 1991 to 1993. In "The Shinning," Mr. Burns cuts off beer and cable TV to caretaker Homer who then becomes an axe-wielding maniac. "Time and Punishment" casts Homer as a time traveler who returns to the present under the totalitarian rule of Ned Flanders. "Nightmare Cafeteria"

tells the tale of students at Springfield Elementary who go to detention only to return as "lunch." *A Gracie Films/Film Roman Production in association with 20th Century-Fox Television. Color. Two hours. Premiered on FOX: October 30, 1994.*

Voices

Homer J. Simpson: Dan Castellaneta; **Marge Simpson:** Julie Kavner; **Bart Simpson:** Nancy Cartwright; **Lisa Simpson:** Yeardley Smith; **Maggie Simpson:** (no voice); **Charles Montgomery Burns/Ned Flanders:** Harry Shearer

◎ THE SIMPSONS HALLOWEEN SPECIAL: "TREE HOUSE OF HORROR"

Bart and Lisa swap scary stories about moving into a haunted house ("Bad Dream House"), their family's abduction by one-eyed extraterrestials ("Hungry Are the Damned") and their own rendition of Edgar Allan Poe's "The Raven" in their first prime-time Halloween special. *A Gracie Films/Klasky-Csupo Production in association with 20th Century-Fox Television. Color. Half-hour. Premiered on FOX: October 25, 1990. Rebroadcast on FOX: December 27, 1990; October 31, 1993; October 30, 1994.*

Voices

Homer J. Simpson/Kodos: Dan Castellaneta; **Marge Simpson:** Julie Kavner; **Bart Simpson/Raven:** Nancy Cartwright; **Lisa Simpson:** Yeardley Smith; **Maggie Simpson:** (no voice); **Moving Man/Serak The Preparer/Narrator:** James Earl Jones; **House:** Harry Shearer

◎ THE SIMPSONS HALLOWEEN SPECIAL: "TREEHOUSE OF HORROR VIII"

More bizarre Halloween tales are told in this eighth annual prime-time trilogy. Homer is the last man left in Springfield after a neutron missile explodes; Bart mixes up his DNA with that of a fly; and Marge and her sisters go trick-or-treating during witch-hunting season. (For voice credits, see entry in Television Cartoon Series section.) *A Gracie Films/Film Roman Production in association with 20th Century-Fox Television. Color. Half-hour. Premiered on FOX: October 26, 1997. Rebroadcast on FOX: October 25, 1998; October 29, 1998.*

◎ THE SIMPSONS HALLOWEEN: "TREEHOUSE OF HORROR III"

Homer Simpson is stalked by a murderous Krusty the Clown doll who threatens to kill him; Mr. Burns and Smithers put Homer's giant, shackled form on stage as a monstrous ape; and son Bart unleashes brain-eating zombies into the world in this third annual half-hour Halloween cartoon trilogy. A *Gracie Films/Film Roman Production in association with 20th Century-Fox Television. Color. Half-hour. Premiered on FOX: October 29, 1992. Rebroadcast on FOX: October 30, 1994.*

Voices
Homer J. Simpson/Krusty: Dan Castellaneta; **Marge Simpson:** Julie Kavner; **Bart Simpson:** Nancy Cartwright; **Lisa Simpson:** Yeardley Smith; **Maggie Simpson:** (no voice); **House of Evil Owner:** James Hong

⊚ THE SIMPSONS NEW HALLOWEEN SPECIAL: "TREE HOUSE OF HORROR II"

Following the success of their first Halloween special produced in 1990, the Simpsons starred in this hilarious trilogy of terrifying tales in which Lisa buys a magic monkey's paw that grants four wishes; Mr. Burns fires Homer then cuts out his brain; and everyone in Springfield fears Bart for his mind-reading abilities. A *Gracie Films/Klasky-Csupo Production in association with 20th Century-Fox Television. Color. Half-hour. Premiered on FOX: October 31, 1991. Rebroadcast on FOX: October 31, 1993; October 30, 1994.*

Voices
Homer Simpson: Dan Castellaneta; **Marge Simpson:** Julie Kavner; **Bart Simpson:** Nancy Cartwright; **Lisa Simpson:** Yeardley Smith

⊚ THE SIMPSONS THANKSGIVING SPECIAL: "BART VS. THANKSGIVING"

It's Thanksgiving Day and Bart leaves rather than apologize to Lisa after accidentally destroying her historical centerpiece in this prime-time Thanksgiving special. A *Gracie Films/Klasky Csupo Production in association with 20th Century-Fox Television. Color. Half-hour. Premiered on FOX: October 25, 1990. Rebroadcast on FOX: March 21, 1991; November 28, 1991.*

Voices
Homer Simpson: Dan Castellaneta; **Marge Simpson:** Julie Kavner; **Bart Simpson:** Nancy Cartwright; **Lisa Simpson:** Yeardley Smith; **Rory:** Gregg Berger

⊚ THE SIMPSONS: "TREE HOUSE OF HORROR IV"

In this spook-tacular Halloween trilogy Homer and the gang parody "The Twlight Zone" episode "Nightmare at 20,000 Feet" called "Nightmare at 5 1/2 Feet"; Homer sells his soul to Ned Flanders as the devil; Mr. Burns is suspected of being a vampire. A *Gracie Films/Film Roman Production in*

association *with 20th Century-Fox Television. Color. Half-hour. Premiered on FOX: October 30, 1993.*

Voices
Homer Simpson: Dan Castellaneta; **Marge Simpson:** Julie Kavner; **Lisa Simpson:** Nancy Cartwright; **Bart Simpson:** Yeardley Smith

⊚ THE SIMPSONS: "TREE HOUSE OF HORROR VI"

In the sixth annual Simpsons Halloween trilogy, a two-dimensional Homer Simpson gets trapped in a weird 3-D universe; an animated Paul Anka croons to help Springfield combat giant advertising characters; and Groundskeeper Willie menaces children (á la Freddy Krueger). A *Gracie Films/Film Roman Production in association with 20th Century-Fox Television. Color. Half-hour. Premiered on FOX: October 29, 1995.*

Voices
Homer J. Simpson/Groundskeeper Willie: Dan Castellaneta; **Marge Simpson:** Julie Kavner; **Bart Simpson:** Nancy Cartwright; **Lisa Simpson:** Yeardley Smith; **Paul Anka:** Himself

⊚ THE SIMPSONS: "TREEHOUSE OF HORROR VII"

Three unrelated stories make up this seventh annual "Treehouse of Horror" trilogy special. Aliens Kang and Kudos interrogate Homer about the identity of Earth's leaders; the Simpsons search for a missing Siamese twin; and Lisa's lost baby tooth is turned into a miniature city. (For voice credits, see entry in Television Cartoon Series section.) A *Gracie Films/Film Roman Production in association with 20th Century-Fox Television. Color. Half-hour. Premiered on FOX: October 27, 1996.*

⊚ SLEEPING BEAUTY

This show retells the story of the beautiful young princess who is cast under a spell by the wicked old witch, but with a new twist. During her curse, the princess and all the subjects in the kingdom remain in perpetual sleep. None of them, including the princess, can be awakened until the handsome, bravehearted Prince Daring puckers up and kisses the sleeping beauty. A *Festival of Family Classics special. A Rankin-Bass Production in association with Mushi Studios. Color. Half-hour. Premiered: January 21, 1973. Syndicated.*

Voices
Carl Banas, Len Birman, Bernard Cowan, Peg Dixon, Keith Hampshire, Peggi Loder, Donna Miller, Frank Perry, Henry Ramer, Billie Mae Richards, Alfie Scopp, Paul Soles

◎ SLIMER! AND THE REAL GHOSTBUSTERS: "THE HALLOWEEN DOOR"

In their first prime-time special, the Ghostbusters are hired by the chairman of the Citizens United Against Halloween assist him in his crusade to abolish the holiday and its traditions. Originally produced as an episode of the popular Saturday-morning series on ABC. *A DIC Enterprises Production in association with Columbia Pictures Television. Color. Half-hour. Premiered on ABC: October 29, 1989.*

Voices

Slimer/Ray Stantz: Frank Welker; **Peter Venkman:** Dave Coulier; **Winston Zeddmore:** Edward L. Jones; **Egon Spengler:** Maurice LaMarche; **Janine Melintz:** Kath Soucie

◎ THE SMURFIC GAMES

The Smurfs discover the spirit of friendly competition when they hold their first Olympic-style "Smurfic Games," and Gargamel tries to activate a special medallion with deadly powers to use against them. Nominated for an Emmy. *A Hanna-Barbera Production in association with SEPP International. Color. Half-hour. Premiered on NBC: May 20, 1984. Rebroadcast on NBC: May 11, 1985.*

Voices

Papa Smurf/Azrael: Don Messick; **Baby Smurf:** Julie McWhirter Dees; **Smurfette:** Lucille Bliss; **Clumsy/Painter/Dragon:** Bill Callaway; **Grouchy/Handy/Lazy/Argus:** Michael Bell; **Greedy/Harmony:** Hamilton Camp; **Jokey:** June Foray; **Hefty/Frog/Bird/Poet:** Frank Welker; **Tailor:** Kip King; **Gargamel:** Paul Winchell; **Bigmouth:** Lennie Weinrib; **Vanity:** Alan Oppenheimer

◎ SMURFILY EVER AFTER

As the Smurfs celebrate the wedding of their beloved Laconia, the mute wood elf, Smurfette hopes to find her own "Mr. Right." The special was closed-captioned for the hearing impaired. *A Hanna-Barbera Production in association with SEPP International. Color. Half-hour. Premiered on NBC: February 13, 1985. Rebroadcast on NBC: March 30, 1986.*

Voices

Papa Smurf/Azrael: Don Messick; **Smurfette:** Lucille Bliss; **Hefty/Monster:** Frank Welker; **Handy/Lazy/Grouchy:** Michael Bell; **Jokey:** June Foray; **Gargamel:** Paul Winchell; **Clumsy:** Bill Callaway; **Vanity:** Alan Oppenheimer; **Brainy:** Danny Goldman; **Greedy/Woody:** Hamilton Camp; **Tailor:** Kip King; **Farmer:** Alan Young; **Elderberry:** Peggy Webber; **Bramble:** Robbie Lee; **Pansy:** Susan Blu; **Lilac:** Janet Waldo; **Holly:** Alexandria Stoddart; **Acorn:** Patti Parris

◎ THE SMURFS

Two months after its successful debut on Saturday morning, this colony of little blue people was featured in their first prime-time special, featuring three episodes from their weekly series: "Supersmurf," "The Smurfette" and "The Baby Smurf." *A Hanna-Barbera Production in association with SEPP International. Color. One hour. Premiered on NBC: November 29, 1981.*

Voices

Papa Smurf/Azrael: Don Messick; **Gargamel:** Paul Winchell; **Brainy:** Danny Goldman; **Clumsy:** Bill Callaway; **Hefty:** Frank Welker; **Jokey:** June Foray; **Smurfette:** Lucille Bliss; **Vanity:** Alan Oppenheimer; **Greedy/Harmony:** Hamilton Camp; **Lazy/Handy/Grouchy:** Michael Bell

◎ THE SMURFS' CHRISTMAS SPECIAL

The Smurfs must use every little ounce of goodness they can muster to battle an even greater evil than Gargamel in this half-hour holiday special. *A Hanna-Barbera Production in association with SEPP International. Color. Half-hour. Premiered on NBC: December 13, 1982. Rebroadcast on NBC: December 9, 1983; December 22, 1984; December 5, 1986. Rebroadcast on CAR: December 24, 1992; November 28, 1992. Rebroadcast on TNT: November 29, 1993. Rebroadcast on CAR: December 13, 1993; December 12, 1994; November 25, 1995.*

Voices

Papa Smurf/Azrael/Horse: Don Messick; **Harmony/Greedy/Bailiff:** Hamilton Camp; **Jokey/Squirrel:** June Foray; **Gargamel:** Paul Winchell; **Smurfette:** Lucille Bliss; **Grouchy/Lazy/Handy:** Michael Bell; **Grandfather/Vanity/Servant:** Alan Oppenheimer; **Stranger:** Rene Auberjonois; **William:** David Mendenhall; **Gwenevere:** Alexandra Stoddart; **Brainy:** Danny Goldman; **Clumsy/Painter/Wolf #1:** Henry Polic; **Hefty:** Frank Welker

◎ THE SMURFS SPRINGTIME SPECIAL

The Smurfs prepare for their big Easter festival, while Gargamel, the Smurfs' archenemy, conspires with his wizardly godfather, Balthazar, to ruin the festivities. An Emmy Award winner. *A Hanna-Barbera Production in association with SEPP International. Color. Half-hour. Premiered on NBC: April 8, 1982. Rebroadcast on NBC: April 1, 1983; April 20, 1984.*

Voices

Gargamel: Paul Winchell; **Papa Smurf/Azrael:** Don Messick; **Smurfette:** Lucille Bliss; **Mother Nature/Jokey:** June Foray; **Handy/Grouchy/Lazy:** Michael Bell; **Clumsy:** Bill Callaway; **Harmony:** Hamilton Camp; **Balthazar:** Keene Curtis; **Brainy/Tailor:** Danny Goldman; **Vanity:** Alan Oppenheimer; **Hefty/Poet/Duckling:** Frank Welker

◎ SNOOPY'S GETTING MARRIED, CHARLIE BROWN

Snoopy's plans to marry a worldly French poodle who runs off with a golden retriever. A *Lee Mendelson–Bill Melendez Production in association with Charles M. Schulz Creative Associates and United Feature Syndicate. Color. Half-hour. Premiered on CBS: March 20, 1985. Rebroadcast on CBS: January 16, 1987; March 16, 1988.*

Voices

Charlie Brown: Bett Johnson; **Lucy Van Pelt:** Heather Stoneman; **Linus Van Pelt:** Jeremy Schoenberg; **Schroeder:** Danny Colby; **Peppermint Patty:** Gini Holtzman; **Sally Brown:** Stacy Ferguson; **Sally (singing):** Dawnn S. Leary; **Marcie:** Keri Houlihan; **Pigpen/Franklin:** Carl Steven; **Snoopy:** José Melendez

◎ SNOOPY'S REUNION

Glancing into the *Peanuts* past, the story of Snoopy's life is told in this nostalgic and entertaining prime-time animated special, written by *Peanuts* creator Charles M. Schulz. The half-hour program was highlighted by a vignette involving Snoopy's first owner, an apparent reference to the 1972 animated feature *Snoopy Come Home. A Bill Melendez Production in association with Charles M. Schulz Creative Association and United Media. Color. Half-hour. Premiered on CBS: May 1, 1991.*

Voices

Charlie Brown: Philip Shafran; **Sally:** Kaitlyn Walker; **Farmer/Bus Driver:** Steve Stoliar; **Linus:** Josh Weiner; **Mother:** Laurel Page; **Little Girl:** Megan Parlen; **Other Voices:** Bill Melendez

◎ SNOOPY: THE MUSICAL

Based on the popular 1974 play, this one-hour animated special is comprised of a series of tuneful vignettes, with Snoopy headlining. Musical interludes include "Edgar Allen Poe," a clever melody about the jitters experienced when being called on in school; "Poor Sweet Baby," a lighthearted ballad pairing hapless Charlie Brown and lovelorn Peppermint Patty; and "The Vigil," a song about Linus's woeful watch for the Great Pumpkin. Music and lyrics were written by Larry Grossman and Hal Hackady. A *Lee Mendelson–Bill Melendez Production in association with Charles M. Schulz Creative Associates and United Feature Syndicate. Color. One hour. Premiered on CBS: January 29, 1988.*

Voices

Snoopy: Cameron Clarke; **Charlie Brown:** Sean Collins; **Lucy:** Tiffany Billings; **Peppermint Patty:** Kristi Baker; **Linus:** Jeremy Miller; **Sally:** Ami Foster

◎ THE SNOWMAN

Tells the story of a young boy who builds a snowman that comes to life during a dream on Christmas Eve in this Oscar-winning animated film based on the book by Raymond Briggs (who also wrote the screenplay). Film premiered as a half-hour special on HBO in 1983 and was subsequently rebroadcast on PBS with rocker David Bowie serving as host. A *Snowman Enterprises Production for Channel 4 in association with TVC London. Color. Half-hour. Premiered on HBO: December 26, 1983. Rebroadcast on PBS: December 2, 1985; December 25, 1986. Rebroadcast on SHO: October 22, 1991; Rebroadcast on DIS: December 20, 1991; November 21, 1992; December 22, 1993.*

◎ THE SNOW QUEEN

Two small children, Gerta and Kay, embark on a dangerous journey to rescue Gerta's brother, who has been kidnapped by the evil Snow Queen in this charming adaptation of the Hans Christian Andersen classic. Originally produced overseas, the program was reedited and redubbed for American broadcast. A *Greatest Tales Production. Color. Half-hour. Premiered: 1977. Syndicated.*

Voices

Gerta: Donna Ellio; **Kay:** Peter Nissen

◎ SNOW WHITE

Ruled by her cruel stepmother, the Queen, the enslaved Snow White escapes to the forest where she receives shelter and protection from the Seven Dwarfs, only to be hunted down by the Queen disguised as a wicked old witch, who sells her a poisoned apple. A *Festival of Family Classics* special. A *Rankin-Bass Production in association with Mushi Studios. Color. Half-hour. Premiered: March 4, 1973. Syndicated. Rebroadcast on NIK: February 22, 1992.*

Voices

Carl Banas, Len Birman, Bernard Cowan, Peg Dixon, Keith Hampshire, Peggi Loder, Donna Miller, Frank Perry, Henry Ramer, Alfie Scopp, Paul Soles

◉ A SNOW WHITE CHRISTMAS

Adapted from the Grimm Brothers' fairy tale, the story of Snow White is given a new twist and new characters as she teams up with seven giants (not dwarfs)—Thinker, Finicky, Corney, Brawny, Tiny, Hicker and Weeper—to stop the evil Queen from ruining Christmas. *A Filmation Studios Production. Color. One hour. Premiered on CBS: November 19, 1980. Rebroadcast on CBS: December 7, 1983.*

Voices

Snow White: Erika Scheimer; **Finnicky/Corney/Tiny/Brawny/Hicker/Weeper/Villager:** Arte Johnson; **Wicked Queen/Hag:** Melendy Britt; **Queen:** Diane Pershing; **Grunyon:** Charlie Bell; **Mirror:** Larry D. Mann; **Thinker:** Clinton Sundberg

◉ THE SOLDIER'S TALE

In this post–World War I story, a young soldier sells his soul—represented by his violin—to the Devil, only to have second thoughts about the idea in this animated version of the classic Russian children's fable written by Igor Stravinsky. *An R.O. Blechman Production for PBS. Color. One hour. Premiered on PBS: March 19, 1981. Rebroadcast on PBS: October 30, 1981.*

Voices

Devil: Max Von Sydow; **Princess:** Galina Panova; **Narrator:** André Gregory

◉ SOMEDAY YOU'LL FIND HER, CHARLIE BROWN

Charlie Brown falls in love with a little girl (Mary Jo) he sees on television during the telecast of a local football game and sets out to find her with the help of codetective Linus. *A Lee Mendelson–Bill Melendez Production in association with Charles M. Schulz Creative Associates and United Features Syndicate. Color. Half-hour. Premiered on CBS: October 30, 1981. Rebroadcast on CBS: March 21, 1983.*

Voices

Charlie Brown: Grant Wehr; **Linus Van Pelt:** Earl Reilly; **Little Girl (Mary Jo):** Jennifer Gaffin; **Snoopy:** José Melendez; **Loretta:** Nicole Eggert; **Teenager:** Melissa Strawmeyer; **Singer:** Rebecca Reardon

◉ THE SORCERER'S APPRENTICE

A poor young boy (Hans) accepts a job as the Sorcerer's apprentice, only to learn that the Sorcerer uses his magical powers for the purposes of evil in this adaptation of the Jacob Grimm fairy-tale classic. *A Gary Moscowitz Production*

in association with Astral Bellevue Pathé. Color. Half-hour. Premiered: October, 1984. Syndicated.

Voices

Narrator: Vincent Price

◉ SPACE GHOST COAST TO COAST HOLIDAY SPECIAL

Interplanetary superhero Space Ghost and his less-than-merry archenemies Moltar and Zorak are featured in three encore presentations of the Cartoon Network's critically acclaimed talk show *Space Ghost Coast to Coast*, plus a brand-new 15-minute Christmas episode in this holiday-filled hour special. *A Hanna-Barbera/Cartoon Network Production. Color. One hour. Premiered on CAR: December 21, 1994. Syndicated: December 1995.*

Voices

Space Ghost: George Lowe; **Moltar/Zorak:** C. Martin Croker

◉ THE SPECIAL MAGIC OF HERSELF THE ELF

Nasty King Thorn and his daughter, Creeping Ivy, steal Herself the Elf's magical wand in order to take nature into their own evil hands in this half-hour syndicated special featuring music composed and performed by Judy Collins. *A Scholastic Production in association with Those Characters From Cleveland and Nelvana Limited. Color. Half-hour. Premiered: April 1983. Syndicated.*

Voices

Herself the Elf: Priscilla Lopez; **Creeping Ivy:** Ellen Greene; **King Thorn:** Jerry Orbach; **Willow Song:** Georgia Engel; **Meadow Morn:** Denny Dillon; **Snow Drop:** Terri Hawkes; **Wilfie:** Jim Henshaw; **Wood Pink:** Susan Roman; **Vocalist:** Judy Collins

◉ A SPECIAL VALENTINE WITH THE FAMILY CIRCUS

In this television debut of Bill Keane's *Family Circus* characters, P.J., Dolly, Billy and Jeffy do everything possible to outdo each other in impressing their parents with "love" for Valentine's Day. *A Cullen-Kasden Production in association with the Register and Tribune Syndicate. Color. Half-hour. Premiered on NBC: February 10, 1978. Rebroadcast on NBC: February 8, 1980; February 13, 1983; Rebroadcast on DIS: February 6, 1993; February 1, 1994; February 12, 1994.*

Voices
Mommy: Anne Costello; **Daddy:** Bob Kaliban; **Billy:** Mark McDermott; **Dolly:** Missy Hope; **Jeffy:** Nathan Berg; **P.J./Teacher:** Suzanne Airey; **Bus Driver:** Sammy Fain

◎ SPIDER JUNIOR HIGH
Itsby Bitsy ("I.B." for short) Spider yearns to play in the Three Bad Bugs. He tags along with an ultra-cool school rock band from Spider Junior High, having to rescue them after they get sealed in a jar in this update of the popular children's nursery rhyme. Premiering in 1991 on HBO's popular anthology series *HBO Storybook Musicals*, the half-hour special was originally produced under the title *Itsy Bitsy Spider* for Cinar Films' *The Real Story of . . .* series. A *Cinar Films/Crayon Animation Production in association with Western Publishing Company/CTV Television Network/Telefilm Canada. Color. Half-hour. Premiered on HBO: October 16, 1991. Rebroadcast on HBO: October 21, 1991.*

Voices
Miss Widow: Patti LaBelle; **Spinner:** Malcolm-Jamal Warner

◎ SPIDER-MAN
The web-slinging comic-book superhero springs into action in this half-hour Saturday-morning special that premiered before the popular Fox Network animated series. *A Marvel Films/New World Entertainment/Saban Entertainment/Graz Entertainment Production. Color. Half-hour. Premiered on FOX: November 19, 1994.*

Voices
Peter Parker/Spider-Man: Christopher Daniel Barres

◎ THE SPIRIT OF '76
Historical events relating to the birth of the United States are presented through live action, animation and song in this overture of five-minute stories. *An MG Films Productions. Color. Half-hour. Premiered: July, 1984. Syndicated.*

Voices
Narrator: Oscar Brand

◎ SPOT'S MAGICAL CHRISTMAS
Based on Eric Hill's lift-the-flap books, Spot and his friends come to the aid of Santa's reindeer to help them find his lost sleigh. This direct-to-video special premiered on The Disney Channel. *A King Rollo Films Ltd./Walt Disney Home Video Production. Color. Half-hour. Premiered on* DIS: December 25, 1995. Rebroadcast on DIS: December 4, 1997.

◎ STANLEY, THE UGLY DUCKLING
A klutzy young duck tries to be anything but a duck and becomes friends with a loner fox who tries to help him become somebody. *An ABC Weekend Special. A Fine Arts Production in association with I Like Myself Productions. Color. Half-hour. Premiered on ABC: May 1, 1982. Rebroadcast on ABC: February 4, 1984. Rebroadcast on NIK: July 20, 1986.*

Voices
Stanley: Susan Blu; **Nathan the Fox:** Jack DeLeon; **Eagle One:** Wolfman Jack

◎ STAR FAIRIES
A tiny band of star creatures (Spice, Nightsong, Jazz, True Love and Whisper) embarks on a very special mission—to grant the wishes of every child in the world—in this half-hour special broadcast as part of a two-hour package that included *Pound Puppies* and *The Harlem Globetrotters Meet Snow White. A Hanna-Barbera Production. Color. Two hours. Premiered: October, 1985. Syndicated.*

Voices
Spice: Didi Conn; **True Love:** Jean Kasem; **Jazz:** Susan Blu; **Nightsong:** Ta Tanisha; **Whisper:** Marianne Chinn; **Sparkle/Michelle/Mother:** B.J. Ward; **Troll:** Billy Barty; **Giant:** Michael Nouri; **Dragon Head #1:** Howard Morris; **Dragon Head #2:** Arte Johnson; **Harvey:** Shavar Ross; **Benjamin:** Matthew Gotlieb; **Jennifer:** Holly Berger; **Puppy/Lavandar/Vanity:** Frank Welker; **Freddie/Frump/Spectre:** Michael Bell; **Giggleby:** Jerry Houser; **Blunderpuff/Elf:** Don Messick; **Wishing Well:** Herschel Bernardi; **Winthrop the Wizard:** Jonathan Winters; **Hillary:** Drew Barrymore

◎ A STAR FOR JEREMY
On Christmas Eve, young Jeremy learns in a dream the meaning of the Christmas star that transports him to the place where God assigns stars to their place in the universe. *A TPC Communications Production. Color. Half-hour. Premiered: December 1984. Syndicated.*

Voices
Leif Ancker, James Gleason, Charlotte Jarvis, Larry Kenny, Stacy Melodia, Christopher Potter, Tia Relbling

◎ THE STEADFAST TIN SOLDIER
Actor Jeremy Irons tells this story of the tin soldier and the hardships he endures for the love of a beautiful ballerina in

a delightful half-hour animated adaptation of Hans Christian Andersen's classic tale. Part of Rabbit Ears Video's *Storybook Classics* series. *A Rabbit Ears Video Production. Color. Half-hour. Premiered on SHO: 1989.*

Voices
Narrator: Jeremy Irons

⊚ THE STINGIEST MAN IN TOWN

Charles Dickens's classic *A Christmas Carol* is revisited, set in 1840s London with the phantoms, known as Christmas Past and Christmas Present, paying the penny-pinching Scrooge a visit to change his self-centered ways. *A Rankin-Bass Production. Color. One hour. Premiered on NBC: December 23, 1978. Rebroadcast on NBC: December 22, 1979. Syndicated. Rebroadcast on DIS: December 14, 1992; December 7, 1993; December 19, 1995; December 17, 1996.*

Voices
B.A.H. Humbug (narrator): Tom Bosley; **Ebenezer Scrooge:** Walter Matthau; **Young Scrooge:** Robert Morse; **Ghost of Marley:** Theodore Bikel; **Fred:** Dennis Day; **Tiny Tim:** Robert Rolofson; **Mrs. Cratchit:** Darlene Conley; **Ghost of Christmas Past:** Paul Frees; **Martha:** Debra Clinger; **Belinda:** Steffanie Calli; **Peter:** Eric Hines; **Boy:** Charles Matthau; **Scrooge's fiancee:** Diana Lee

⊚ THE STORY OF SANTA CLAUS

A kindly old toymaker named Nicholas Claus starts the tradition of delivering a toy on Christmas to every child around the world in this prime-time one-hour animated musical. *An Arnold Shapiro/Film Roman Production in association with CBS Productions. Color. One hour. Premiered on CBS: December 4, 1996. Rebroadcast on CBS: December 12, 1997.*

Voices
Nicholas Claus: Ed Asner; **Gretchen Claus:** Betty White; **Nostros:** Tim Curry; **Clement:** Miko Hughes; **Aurora:** Kathryn Zaremba

⊚ THE STORY OF THE DANCING FROG

George is a multifaceted frog whose leaps and bounds in this parody of a Hollywood musical bring him fame and fortune as he and his devoted friend, Gertrude, set out on a dance adventure around the world. *An HBO Storybook Musicals* series special. *A Michael Sporn Animation Production in association with Italtoons Corporation. Color. Half-hour. Premiered on HBO: October 3, 1989.*

Voices
Narrator: Amanda Plummer

⊚ STRAWBERRY SHORTCAKE AND THE BABY WITHOUT A NAME

Strawberry Shortcake and her friends, Plum Puddin' and Peach Blush, set out to rescue Baby Without a Name, only to be kidnapped themselves by the evil Peculiar Purple Pieman and Sour Grapes. The special was one of six programs based on the American Greetings card characters. *A MAD Production in association with Those Characters From Cleveland and Nelvana Limited. Color. Half-hour. Premiered: March 1984. Syndicated.*

Voices
Sun (narrator): Chris Wiggins; **Strawberry Shortcake:** Russi Taylor; **Peculiar Purple Pieman:** Bob Ridgely; **Sour Grapes/Fig-Boot:** Jeri Craden; **Plum Puddin':** Laurie Waller; **Lemon Meringue/Lime Chiffon:** Melleny Brown; **Peach Blush/Orange Blossom:** Susan Roman; **Lullaberry Pie:** Monica Parker; **Orange Blossom:** Cree Summer Francks

⊚ STRAWBERRY SHORTCAKE IN BIG APPLE CITY

Strawberry Shortcake ventures to Big Apple City to compete in a bake-off against the nasty Peculiar Purple Pieman, who does everything possible to prevent her from winning. *An RLR Associates Production in association with Those Characters From Cleveland and Perpetual Motion Pictures. Color. Half-hour. Premiered: April 1981. Syndicated. Rebroadcast on DIS: September 25, 1993.*

Voices
Sun (narrator): Romeo Muller; **Strawberry Shortcake:** Russi Taylor; **Peculiar Purple Pieman:** Bob Ridgely; **Coco Nutwork:** Bob Holt; **Orange Blossom:** Diane McCan-

Strawberry Shortcake displays her homemade strawberry shortcake in a scene from the half-hour syndicated special Strawberry Shortcake in Big Apple City. *© RLR Associates/Those Characters From Cleveland*

non; **Blueberry Muffin/Apple Dumplin'/Apricot:** Joan Gerber; **Vocalists:** Flo and Eddie

◎ STRAWBERRY SHORTCAKE MEETS THE BERRYKIDS

Thanks to Strawberry Shortcake and her friends, the Peculiar Purple Pieman and Sour Grapes are foiled in their plan to make exotic perfume out of the little Berrykins, tiny fairies who give scent and flavor to fruit. *A MAD Production in association with Those Characters From Cleveland and Nelvana Limited. Color. Half-hour. Premiered: Spring 1985. Syndicated.*

Voices
Sun (narrator): Chris Wiggins; **Strawberry Shortcake:** Russi Taylor; **Peculiar Purple Pieman:** Bob Ridgely; **Sour Grapes:** Jeri Craden; **Banana Twirl/Banana Berrykin:** Melleny Brown; **Berry Princess/Peach Blush/Peach Berrykin:** Susan Roman; **Plum Puddin'/Plum Berrykin/Orange Blossom:** Laurie Waller; **Raspberry Tart/Blueberry Muffin:** Susan Snooks; **VO:** Patrick Black; **Vocalists:** Nadia Medusa, Ben Sebastian, John Sebastian, Russi Taylor, Nicole Wills

◎ STRAWBERRY SHORTCAKE: PETS ON PARADE

Strawberry Shortcake is entrusted with guarding a new tricycle that will be given to the winner of the annual pet show and parade from the villainous Peculiar Purple Pieman and his cohort Sour Grapes who try to ruin all of the fun. *A Muller-Rosen Production in associaton with Those Characters From Cleveland and Murakami-Wolf-Swenson Films and Toei Doga Productions. Color. Half-hour. Premiered: April 1982. Syndicated.*

Voices
Sun (narrator): Romeo Muller; **Strawberry Shortcake:** Russi Taylor; **Pecular Purple Pieman:** Bob Ridgely; **Blueberry Muffin/Apple Dumplin':** Joan Gerber; **Huckleberry Pie:** Julie McWhirter; **Vocalists:** Flo and Eddie

◎ STRAWBERRY SHORTCAKE'S HOUSEWARMING SURPRISE

After Strawberry Shortcake moves into a big new house, her friends give her a surprise housewarming party, but two uninvited guests—Peculiar Purple Pieman and Sour Grapes—try to eat everything in sight and steal Strawberry Shortcake's famous recipes. *A MAD Production in association with Those Characters From Cleveland and Nelvana Limited. Color. Half-hour. Premiered: April 1983. Syndicated.*

Voices
Sun (narrator): Chris Wiggins; **Strawberry Shortcake:** Russi Taylor; **Peculiar Purple Pieman:** Bob Ridgely; **Sour Grapes:** Jeri Craden; **Captain Cackle/VO:** Jack Blum; **Lime Chiffon:** Melleny Brown; **Huckleberry/Parfait/Lem:** Jeanine Elias; **Blueberry/Crepe Suzette/Ada:** Susan Roman; **Vocalists:** Phil Glaston, Bill Keith, Sharon McQueen, Ben Sebastian, John Sebastian

◎ SUPER DUCKTALES

Scrooge McDuck, Huey, Dewey and Louie fight the Beagle Boys' attempts to steal the McDuck fortune in this prime-time special based on the popular weekday series *DuckTales*. *A Walt Disney Television Production. Color. One hour. Premiered on NBC: March 26, 1989 (on The Magical World of Disney).*

Voices
Scrooge McDuck: Alan Young; **Huey/Dewey/Louie:** Russi Taylor

◎ SUPERMAN

The infant Kal-El is sent to Earth before his home planet, Krypton, explodes. Raised by adoptive parents, he develops great powers, which he uses to combat crime in Metropolis in this 90-minute prime-time movie detailing the origins of the "Man of Steel." Also the series opener for 1996's *Superman* animated series, based on the popular DC Comics character. *A Warner Bros. Television Animation Production in association with DC Comics. Color. Ninety minutes. Premiered on WB: September 8, 1996.*

Voices
Clark Kent/Superman: Tim Daly; **Lois Lane:** Dana Delany; **Perry White:** George Dzundza; **Martha Kent:** Shelley Fabares; **Jonathan Kent:** Mike Farrell; **Jor-El:** Christopher McDonald; **Lara-El:** Finola Hughes; **Lex Luthor:** Clancy Brown

◎ SUR LE PONT D'AVIGNON

A ghost appears before a clock shop's owner (Amedee Carillon) and his grandson (Jerome), who have been threatened with eviction from their clock shop. They embark on an exciting adventure to find gold, save the ghost's reputation and keep their shop in this half-hour animated musical that premiered on HBO's cartoon anthology series *The Real Story of. . . . A Cinar Films/France Animation Production in association with Western Publishing Company/The Family Channel/Telefilm Canada/Cofimage 3. Color. Half-hour. Premiered on HBO: January 10, 1994.*

Voices
Amedee Carillon: Robert Guillaume

◎ SVATOHOR (SAINT MOUNTAIN)
A young Russian hunter must complete a seemingly impossible task to save the czar from his enemies and win the hand of the czar's daughter in this stop-motion puppet-animated film based on a popular Russian folktale. From PBS's award-winning series *Long Ago & Far Away*. A *Czechoslovak Television Production. Color. Half-hour. Premiered on PBS: March 25, 1989.*

◎ THE SWISS FAMILY ROBINSON (1973)
Fritz and Franz, the shipwrecked sons of the Robinson family, return to civilization with a young girl they discover on the island. A *Family of Festival Classics* special. A *Rankin-Bass Production in association with Mushi Studios. Color. Half-hour. Premiered: January 13, 1973. Syndicated.*

Voices
Carl Banas, Len Birman, Bernard Cowan, Peg Dixon, Keith Hampshire, Peggi Loder, Donna Miller, Frank Perry, Henry Ramer, Billie Mae Richards, Alfie Scopp, Paul Soles

◎ THE SWISS FAMILY ROBINSON (1973)
Survival is the name of the game for a family of travelers who become shipwrecked on a deserted island in this one-hour special based on Johann Wyss's popular adventure story. *An Air Programs International Production. Color. One hour. Premiered on CBS: October 28, 1973. Rebroadcast on CBS: November 28, 1974. Syndicated.*

Voices
Jeannie Drynan, Alistair Duncan, Barbara Frawley, Ron Haddrick, Brender Senders

◎ TABITHA AND ADAM AND THE CLOWN FAMILY
Tabitha and Adam Stephens, the offspring from television's *Bewitched*, are a teenage witch and warlock in a circus setting in this hour-long animated spinoff of the popular weekly sitcom. A *Hanna-Barbera Production. Color. One hour. Premiered on ABC: December 2, 1972 (on* The ABC Saturday Superstar Movie*). Syndicated.*

Voices
Tabitha Stephens: Cindy Eilbacher; **Adam Stephens/ Scooter:** Michael Morgan; **Max/Glenn/Yancy:** John Stephenson; **Julie:** Shawn Shepps; **Ernie:** Gene Andrusco; **Mike:** Frank Welker; **Ronk/Mr. McGurk/Haji/ Ducks/Railroad Conductor:** Paul Winchell; **Muscles/ Boris/Third Cyclone:** Hal Smith; **Big Louie/Count Krumley/Mr. McGuffin:** Lennie Weinrib; **Second Cyclone/ Trumpet/Voice:** Don Messick; **Marybell/Georgia:** Janet Waldo; **Hi-Rise/First Cyclone:** Pat Harrington

◎ THE TAILOR OF GLOUCESTER
Sensitive retelling of Beatrix Potter's wry tale of a tailor who, thanks to his naughty cat Simpkin, has no more silk thread to finish the coat he has promised the mayor for his wedding on Christmas day. Part of Rabbit Ears Video's *Holiday Classics* video series, produced in 1988. A *Rabbit Ears Video Production. Color. Half-hour. Premiered on SHO: 1989.*

Voices
Narrator: Meryl Streep

◎ TAKE ME UP TO THE BALLGAME
A sandlot baseball team consisting of animals is pitted against the Outer-Space All-Stars, a team that has never lost a game, in an intergalactic playoff to determine the best team in the universe. The half-hour fantasy special aired in Canada and in the United States. A *Nelvana Limited Production in association with CBC. Color. Half-hour. Premiered (U.S.): September 1980. Syndicated.*

Voices
Irwin: Phil Silvers; **Beaver:** Bobby Dermer; **Eagle:** Derek McGrath; **Commissioner:** Don Ferguson; **Announcer:** Paul Soles; **Edna:** Anna Bourque; **Jake:** Maurice LaMarche; **Mole:** Melleny Brown; **Vocalist:** Rick Danko

◎ THE TALE OF PETER RABBIT
Mrs. Rabbit tells her children—Flopsy, Mopsy, Cottontail and Peter—to stay out of Mr. McGregor's garden, but naughty Peter disobeys. This leads to a high-speed chase with an angry Mr. McGregor in pursuit. An *HBO Storybook Musicals* series special. A *Hare Bear Production. Color. Half-hour. Premiered on HBO: June 11, 1991. Rebroadcast on HBO: June 17, 1991; April 5, 1993.*

Voices
Narrator/Mrs. Rabbit/Mr. McGregor's cat: Carol Burnett

◎ THE TALE OF PETER RABBIT AND THE TALE OF MR. JEREMY FISHER
Two enchanting stories by Beatrix Potter—the first about a curious and disobedient rabbit, the second about a gentle-

man frog's minnow-fishing trip that turns into a surprising adventure—are featured in this delightful half-hour adaptation, narrated by actress Meryl Streep. Part of Rabbit Ears Video's *Storybook Classics* series. *A Rabbit Ears Video Production. Color. Half-hour. Premiered: 1989.*

Voices
Narrator: Meryl Streep

⊚ A TALE OF TWO CITIES

During the French Revolution, Sidney Carton, a dispirited English barrister, saves French aristocat Charles Darnay from execution at the guillotine in this vivid adaptation of Charles Dickens's well-known story. *A Burbank Films Production. Color. Ninety minutes. Premiered: 1984. Syndicated.*

Voices
John Benton, John Everson, Phillip Hinton, Liz Horne, Moya O'Sullivan, Robin Stewart, John Stone, Henri Szeps, Ken Wayne

⊚ A TALE OF TWO WISHES

In this live-action/animated special about wish-making, Jane, a girl whose wishes never seem to come true, becomes friends with Skeeter (voiced by rock-'n'-roll legend Rick Nelson), a wise but gentle storyteller. As hosts they introduce a series of animated tales that help Jane understand how to turn her dreams into reality. *A Bosustow Entertainment Production. Color. One hour. Premiered on CBS: November 8, 1981. Rebroadcast on CBS: July 6, 1982. Syndicated.*

Cast
Jane: Tracey Gold; **Skeeter:** Rick Nelson; **Grandmother:** Bibi Osterwald; **Mother:** Judy Farrell; **Father:** Bob Ross; **Margaret:** Seeley Ann Thumann; **Daniel:** Chad Krentzman

⊚ TALES OF WASHINGTON IRVING

Author Washington Irving's two most popular folktales, "The Legend of Sleepy Hollow" and "Rip Van Winkle," are featured in this one-hour special produced as part of CBS's *Famous Classic Tales* package of animated children's specials. *An Air Programs International Production. Color. One hour. Premiered on CBS: November 1, 1970. Rebroadcast on CBS: October 24, 1971. Syndicated.*

Voices
Mel Blanc, George Firth, Joan Gerber, Byron Kane, Julie McWhirter, Don Messick, Ken Samson, Lennie Weinrib, Brian Zax, Larraine Zax

⊚ THE TALKING EGGS

When a young girl named Selina befriends a mystical elderly woman, magical things happen. This half-hour animated production—one of three new half-hours produced for the fourth season of the PBS series *Long Ago & Far Away. A Michael Sporn Animation Production. Color. Half-hour. Premiered on PBS: December 6, 1992.*

Voices
Narrator: Danny Glover

⊚ THE TALKING PARCEL

A 12-year-old girl and talking parrot set out on a remarkable journey to return the land of Mythologia to its rightful leader in this two-part special, based on the book by Gerald Durrell (and adapted by Rosemary Anne Sisson). Originally debuting in syndication in 1983, the special was rebroadcast in 1989 on the award-winning PBS anthology series *Long Ago & Far Away. A Cosgrove-Hall Production. Color. Half-hour. Premiered: 1983–84. Syndicated. Rebroadcast on PBS: March 4, 1989 (Part 1) and March 11, 1989 (Part II).*

Voices
Penelope: Lisa Norris; **Parrot:** Freddie Jones; **Hortense, the Flying Train:** Mollie Sugden; **Ethelred:** Roy Kinnear; **H.H. Junketbury:** Edward Kelsey; **Chief Cockatrice:** Windsor Davies; **Oswald, the Sea Serpent:** Sir Michael Hordern; **Werewolf:** Peter Woodthorpe; **Duke Wensleydale:** Harvey Ashby; **Others:** Raymond Mason, Daphne Oxenford

⊚ TATTERTOWN

In a mystical town where everything comes to life—misfit toys, broken machines and discarded musical instruments—Debbie, a young girl, tries to prevent her stuffed doll, Muffett, from joining forces with the evil Sidney Spider to take over the town. The half-hour Christmas special was the pilot for what was announced as the first prime-time animated series for the all-kids network, Nickelodeon. Ralph Bakshi based the idea on a concept he originated 30 years earlier called "Junk Town." *A Bakshi Animation Production. Color. Half-hour. Premiered on NIK: December 1988. Rebroadcast: December 10, 1995 (as "Rocko's Modern Life Christmas and Tattertown"); December 1, 1996 (syndication).*

⊚ THE TEDDY BEARS CHRISTMAS

Ben, an adorable teddy bear, wants to buy his boy owner's little sister, Sally, a teddy bear for Christmas in this sequel to 1989's *The Teddy Bears' Picnic. A Lacewood Production. Color. Half-hour. Premiered on DIS: December 19, 1992. Rebroadcast on DIS: December 24, 1995; December 19, 1996.*

THE TEDDY BEARS' PICNIC

Two warmhearted teddys, Wally and Benjamin Bear, come to the aid of a sad and lost little girl named Amanda in this first of two Teddy Bears specials, produced by Canada's Lacewood Productions. Originally produced for Canadian television, the half-hour special debuted in the United States on The Disney Channel. *A Lacewood Productions/ Hinton Animation Studios Production in association with C.T.V. and Telefilm Canada. Color. Half-hour. Premiered on DIS: 1989.*

Voices

Benjamin Bear: Jonathan Crombie; **Amanda:** Marsha Moreau; **Wally:** Stuart Stone; **Doc:** Tracey Moore: Sally: Elissa Marcus

TEENAGE MUTANT NINJA TURTLES: "PLANET OF THE TURTLETOIDS"

The animated reptiles go out of this world to save a peaceful planet from a monster in their second half-hour prime-time special. *A Murakami-Wolf-Swenson Production in association with Mirage Studios. Color. Half-hour. Premiered on CBS: August 31, 1991.*

Voices

Michaelangelo: Townsend Coleman; **Leonardo:** Cam Clarke; **Donatello:** Barry Gordon; **Raphael:** Rob Paulsen

TEENAGE MUTANT NINJA TURTLES: "THE CUFFLINK CAPER"

Following its decision to pick up the hit syndicated series based on the early 1980s' comic books about the Turtles, CBS premiered this episode as a prime-time special the night before the show's Saturday morning bow. In the special the Turtles join the mob of a notorious gangster (Big Louie) to find out why the big-time crook is robbing all the best places and taking only cuff links. *A Murakami-Wolf-Swenson Production in association with Mirage Studios. Color. Half-hour. Premiered on CBS: September 14, 1990.*

Voices

Michaelangelo: Townsend Coleman; **Leonardo:** Cam Clarke; **Donatello:** Barry Gordon; **Raphael:** Rob Paulsen

THANKSGIVING IN THE LAND OF OZ

Dorothy returns to Oz and joins forces with her friends Jack Pumpkinhead (the Scarecrow), the Hungry Tiger (the Cowardly Lion) and Tic-Toc (the Tin Man) to stop Tyrone the Terrible Toy Maker, from gaining control of Winkle Country. Later retitled and rebroadcast as *Dorothy*

in the Land of Oz. *A Muller-Rosen Production in association with Murakami-Wolf-Swenson Films. Color. Half-hour. Premiered on CBS: November 25, 1980. Rebroadcast on CBS: December 10, 1981 (as Dorothy in the Land of Oz). Rebroadcast on SHO: November 1985; November 1986. Syndicated.*

Voices

Wizard of Oz (narrator): Sid Caesar; **Dorothy:** Mischa Bond; **Jack Pumpkinhead/Tyrone, the Terrible/Toy Tinker:** Robert Ridgely; **Tic Toc/Ozma, Queen of Oz:** Joan Gerber; **Hungry Tiger:** Frank Nelson; **Aunt Em:** Lurene Tuttle; **Uncle Henry:** Charles Woolf

THE THANKSGIVING THAT ALMOST WASN'T

Johnny Cooke, a young Pilgrim boy, and Little Bear, an Indian boy, are discovered to be missing. Jeremy Squirrel hears of his friends' plight and goes to find them in the woods, putting himself at risk. The story ends happily as the Pilgrims and Indians invite Jeremy to be their guest of honor for Thanksgiving. *A Hanna-Barbera Production. Color. Half-hour. Premiered: November, 1972. Syndicated. Rebroadcast on CAR: November 21, 1993; November 23, 1994; November 19, 1995.*

Voices

Johnny Cooke: Bobby Riha; **Little Bear:** Kevin Cooper; **Janie/Mom/Mary Cooke:** Marilyn Mayne; **Jimmy/Son Squirrel/Mom Squirrel:** June Foray; **Jeremy Squirrel/Dad:** Hal Smith; **Dad Squirrel/Francis Cooke/Indian (Massasoit):** Vic Perrin; **Wolf/Rabbit/Sparrow #1:** Don Messick; **Sparrow #2:** John Stephenson

THAT GIRL IN WONDERLAND

Marlo Thomas, in the role of Ann Marie from her popular prime-time series *That Girl*, portrays a children's book editor who daydreams and imagines herself as the heroine of various fairy tales. Originally broadcast as part of *The ABC Saturday Superstar Movie*. *A Rankin-Bass Production. Color. One hour. Premiered on ABC: January 13, 1973 (on The ABC Saturday Superstar Movie). Rebroadcast on ABC: March 2, 1974. Syndicated.*

Voices
Ann Marie: Marlo Thomas

THERE'S NO TIME FOR LOVE, CHARLIE BROWN

Charlie Brown and his gang go on a school field trip to the local supermarket (they mistake it for a museum) and do their report on that instead. Discovering their mistake, they all fear that they'll get failing grades. *A Lee Mendelson–Bill Melendez Production in association with Charles M. Schulz Creative Associates and United Feature Syndicate. Color. Half-hour. Premiered on CBS: March 11, 1973. Rebroadcast on CBS: March 17, 1974.*

Voices
Charlie Brown: Chad Webber; **Linus Van Pelt:** Stephen Shea; **Lucy Van Pelt:** Robin Kohn; **Sally Brown:** Hillary Momberger; **Peppermint Patty:** Kip DeFaria; **Schroeder:** Jeffrey Bailly; **Franklin:** Todd Barbee; **Marcie:** Jimmie Ahrens

⊚ THIS IS YOUR LIFE, DONALD DUCK
Spoofing Ralph Edwards's *This Is Your Life* television series, host Jiminy Cricket recounts the life of honored guest Donald Duck, in a series of cartoon flashbacks derived from several classic Disney cartoons—"Donald's Better Self" (1938), "Donald's Lucky Day" (1938), "Donald Gets Drafted" (1942), "Sky Trooper" (1942), "Working for Peanuts" (1953), "Mickey's Amateurs" (1937), "Bee at the Beach" (1950) and "Donald's Diary" (1954)—in this hour-long special that first aired on ABC in 1960. The program was later rebroadcast in primetime on NBC as an episode of *The Wonderful World of Disney* and then in 1980 as an NBC special. *A Walt Disney Television Production. Color. One hour. Premiered on ABC: March 11, 1960 (as Walt Disney Presents). Rebroadcast on NBC: February 13, 1977 (on The Wonderful World of Disney); February 22, 1980 (as NBC Special).*

Voices
Jiminy Cricket: Cliff Edwards; **Donald Duck:** Clarence Nash

⊚ THE THREE BILLY GOATS GRUFF AND THE THREE LITTLE PIGS
Two popular nursery rhymes—the first about a greedy troll who is no match for the biggest of the Billy Goats Gruff, the second based on one of the most beloved children's classics, about a wolf who threatens to blow the three little pigs' house down—are featured in this colorful half-hour special, part of Rabbit Ears Video's *Storybook Classics* series. *A Rabbit Ears Video Production. Color. Half-hour. Premiered on SHO: 1989.*

Voices
Narrator: Holly Hunter

⊚ THE THREE FISHKETEERS
A trio of adventuresome fish—(Toby, Finner and Gillis) comically help a "damsel" (Tika) recover a large pearl, then

learn what heroism really is in this half-hour animated special produced for first-run syndication. *A Perennial Pictures Film Corporation Production. Color. Half-hour. Premiered: November 21, 1987. Syndicated.*

Voices
Finner: Jerry Reynolds; **Gillis:** Russ Harris; **Toby:** Adam Dykstra; **Tika:** Rachel Rutledge

⊚ THE THREE MUSKETEERS
Swashbuckling heroes Athos, Porthos and Aramis foil the plan of the ruthless Cardinal de Richelieu who conspires against the honorable King Louis XIII in this colorful rendition of Alexandre Dumas's famed historical novel. *A Hanna-Barbera Production. Color. One hour. Premiered on CBS: November 23, 1973. Rebroadcast on CBS: November 28, 1974; November 22, 1979. Syndicated. Rebroadcast on CAR: October 8, 1995 (Mr. Spim's Cartoon Theatre.)*

Voices
James Condon, Neil Fitzpatrick, Barbara Frawley, Ron Haddrick, Jane Harders, John Martin, Richard Meikle

⊚ THUMBELINA
A beautiful baby girl, no bigger than a thumb, is snatched from her family by an ugly toad who wants to marry her in this colorful half-hour animated adaptation of the classic Hans Christian Andersen story. From Rabbit Ears Video's *Storybook Classics* series. *A Rabbit Ears Video Production. Color. Half-hour. Premiered on SHO: 1989.*

Voices
Narrator: Kelly McGillis

⊚ THUNDERCATS
Years into the future a group of noble, moralistic humanoids from a distant planet thwart the evil efforts of an ageless devil-priest. Based on characters created by Ted Wolf, this one-hour special preceded the popular syndicated series. *A Rankin-Bass Production in association with Pacific Animation. Color. One hour. Premiered: January–February 1985. Syndicated.*

Voices
Lion-O/Jackalman: Larry Kenney; **Snarft/S-S-Slithe:** Robert McFadden; **Cheetara/Wilykit:** Lynne Lipton; **Panthro:** Earle Hyman; **Wilykat/Monkian/Tygra:** Peter Newman; **Mumm-Ra/Vultureman/Jaga:** Earl Hammond

⊚ THUNDERCATS HO!
The Thundercats square off again with their archenemy Mumm-Ra, who assigns the evil Ma-Mut to search out and

destroy the heroic gladiators of outer space. The feature-length special was later edited into five half-hour segments to be broadcast as a miniseries. *A Rankin-Bass Production in association with Pacific Animation. Color. Two hours. Premiered: October 1986. Syndicated.*

Voices
Lion-O/Jackalman: Larry Kenney; **Lynx-O/Snarf/S-S-Slithe:** Robert McFadden; **Cheetara/Wilykit:** Lynne Lipton; **Panthro:** Earle Hyman; **Wilykat/Monkian/Ben-Gali/Tygra:** Peter Newman; **Mumm-Ra/Vultureman/Jaga:** Earl Hammond; **Pumyra:** Gerrianne Raphael

⊚ TIMMY'S GIFT: A PRECIOUS MOMENTS CHRISTMAS SPECIAL
One of heaven's smallest and most inexperienced angels helps deliver a priceless crown to a special giant, in the first of two Precious Moments holiday specials. The special was one of five Precious Moments specials that were produced but only two ever aired on U.S. television. *A Rick Reinert Pictures Production. Color. Half-hour. Premiered on NBC: December 25, 1991.*

Voices
Timmy: Zachary Bostrom; **Baruch:** Billy O'Sullivan; **Simon:** Jaclyn Bernstein; **Simon:** Ziad LeFlore; **Harold:** Giant Gelt; **Nicodemus:** Dom DeLuise; **Titus:** Don Knotts; **Snowflake:** Julie DiMattia

⊚ THE TIN SOLDIER
The one-legged Tin Soldier of the famed Hans Christian Andersen tale comes to life in this colorful adaptation, featuring two new characters, a pair of mice named Fred and Sam, who befriend the Tin Soldier. *An Atkinson Film-Arts Production in association with Telefilm Canada and CTV. Half-hour. Premiered (U.S.): December 1986. Syndicated. Rebroadcast on NIK: August 10, 1991.*

Voices
Fred: Terrence Scammell; **Sam:** Pier Kohl; **Boy:** Adam Hodgins; **Lefty/Rat #1/Rat #3:** Rick Jones; **King Rat/Rat #2/Rat #4:** Robert Bockstael; **Narrator:** Christopher Plummer

⊚ TINY TOON ADVENTURES: HOW I SPENT MY VACATION
Plucky Duck joins Hamton on a nightmarish car trip to the ultimate amusement park—Happy World Land. Elmyra terrorizes Wild Safari Zoo; Fifi sets her sights on movie star Johnny Pew; and Buster harasses Babs, only to have her retaliate in this hour-long, prime-time "summer vacation" special featuring the characters from the popular series *Tiny Toon Adventures*. *A Warner Bros./Amblin Entertainment Production. Color. One hour. Premiered on FOX: September 5, 1993.*

Voices
Buster Bunny: Charlie Adler; **Babs Bunny:** Tress MacNeille; **Plucky Ducky:** Joe Alaskey; **Hamton J. Pig:** Don Messick; **Elmyra Duff:** Cree Summer; **Dizzy Devil:** Maurice LaMarche; **Shirley Loon:** Gail Matthius; **Wade Pig:** Jonathan Winters; **Winnie Pig:** Edie McClurg; **Uncle Stinky:** Frank Welker; **Big Daddy Boo:** Sorrell Booke; **Foulmouth:** Rob Paulsen; **Fifi:** Kath Soucie; **Sweetie:** Candi Milo

⊚ TINY TOON ADVENTURES SPRING BREAK SPECIAL
It's Spring Break at the ACME Looniversity and the gang heads to sunny Fort Lauderdale, where Plucky Duck finally meets his "dream girl" and Elmyra mistakes Buster for the Easter Bunny. *A Warner Bros./Amblin Entertainment Production. Color. Half-hour. Premiered on FOX: March 27, 1994.*

Voices
Buster Bunny: Charles Adler; **Babs Bunny:** Tress MacNeille; **Plucky Duck:** Joe Alaskey; **Hamton J. Pig:** Don Messick; **Montana Max:** Danny Cooksey; **Dizzy Devil:** Maurice LaMarche; **Elmyra Duff:** Cree Summer

⊚ TINY TOON ADVENTURES: THE LOONEY BEGINNING
Warner Bros.' adolescent versions of the studio's popular Looney Tunes characters—Buster and Babs Bunny (as in Bugs), Plucky Duck (as in Daffy), Hamton Pig (as in Porky) and others—were introduced to television audiences in this "sneak preview" prime-time special prior to the premiere of their hit syndicated series *Tiny Toon Adventures*. The Friday night half-hour special premiered on CBS opposite the Teenage Mutant Ninja Turtles special, "The Cufflink Caper," in 1990. *A Warner Bros./Amblin Entertainment Production. Color. Half-hour. Premiered on CBS: September 14, 1990.*

Voices
Buster Bunny: Charles Adler; **Babs Bunny:** Tress MacNeille; **Plucky Duck:** Joe Alaskey; **Hamton J. Pig:** Don Messick; **Montana Max:** Danny Cooksey; **Dizzy Devil:** Maurice LaMarche

⊚ TINY TOONS' NIGHT GHOULERY
Emmy-nominated prime-time scarefest in which the Tiny Toons Gang poke fun at popular TV horror anthology series

such as *Night Gallery* and *The Twilight Zone* and cult creature features from *Frankenstein* to *Night of the Living Dead* (even executive producer Steven Spielberg's TV-suspenser *Duel*, is played for laughs). Hosted by Babs Bunny. *A Warner Bros./Amblin Entertainment Production. Premiered on FOX: May 28, 1995. Rebroadcast on CAR: October 31, 1997.*

Voices
Plucky Duck: Joe Alaskey; **Babs Bunny:** Tress MacNeille; **Buster Bunny:** John Kassir; **Hamton J. Pig:** Don Messick; **Elmyra Duff:** Cree Summer; **Dizzy Devil:** Maurice LaMarche; **Shirley Loon:** Gail Matthius; **Sneezer (the Sneezin' Ghost):** Kath Soucie; **Montana Max:** Danny Cooksey; **Furrball:** Frank Welker; **Mr. Scratch:** Ron Perlman; **Paddy:** Jim Cummings; **Shamus:** Jeff Bennett; **Witch Hazel:** June Foray

◎ THE TINY TREE
A lonely young crippled girl and several small meadow animals transform a tiny whispering tree into a glowing Christmas tree. Johnny Marks provides music and lyrics for the songs, with narrator Buddy Ebsen singing one of the melodies in this half-hour Christmas special produced under the *Bell System Family Theatre* banner. *A DePatie-Freleng Enterprises Production. Color. Half-hour. Premiered on NBC: December 14, 1975 (on Bell System Family Theatre). Rebroadcast on NBC: December 12, 1976. Rebroadcast on ABC: December 18, 1977. Rebroadcast on CBS: December 16, 1978; December 19, 1979. Syndicated.*

Voices
Squire Badger (narrator): Buddy Ebsen; **Hawk:** Allan Melvin; **Turtle:** Paul Winchell; **Lady Bird/Little Girl:** Janet Waldo; **Boy Bunny/Girl Raccoon:** Stephen Manley; **Groundhog/Father/Beaver/Mole:** Frank Welker; **Vocalist:** Roberta Flack

◎ 'TIS THE SEASON TO BE SMURFY
The other Smurfs learn a lesson about the true meaning of Christmas when they help bring some holiday cheer to the lives of an old toy seller and his gravely ill wife. *A Hanna-Barbera Production in association with SEPP International. Color. Half-hour. Premiered on NBC: December 13, 1987. Rebroadcast on CAR: December 14, 1993; December 13, 1994; November 25, 1995.*

Voices
Papa Smurf/Azrael/Chitter: Don Messick; **Smurfette:** Lucille Bliss; **Hefty/Monster/Poet/Puppy:** Frank Welker; **Handy/Lazy/Grouchy:** Michael Bell; **Jokey:** June Foray; **Gargamel:** Paul Winchell; **Clumsy/Rich Man:** Bill Callaway; **Vanity/Doctor:** Alan Oppenheimer; **Brainy:** Danny

Goldman; **Greedy/Woody:** Hamilton Camp; **Tailor:** Kip King; **Farmer:** Alan Young; **Timber:** Bernard Erhard; **Snappy/Anna:** Pat Musick; **Slouchy:** Noelle North; **Nat/Thief:** Charlie Adler; **Baby Smurf/Sassette:** Julie Dees; **Grandpa:** Jonathan Winters; **Gustav:** Les Tremayne; **Hans:** Justin Gocke; **Willem:** William Schallert; **Elise:** Peggy Weber; **Sheriff:** Jess Douchette

◎ TOM SAWYER
An animated Mark Twain narrates this popular story that follows the adventures of Tom Sawyer and Becky Sharpe who get lost during a cave exploration and are thought to be dead by the townspeople. *A Festival of Family Classics special. A Rankin-Bass Production in association with Mushi Studios. Color. Half-hour. Premiered: February 25, 1973. Syndicated. Rebroadcast on NIK: April 13, 1993.*

Voices
Carl Banas, Len Birman, Bernard Cowan, Peg Dixon, Keith Hampshire, Peggi Loder, Donna Miller, Frank Perry, Henry Ramer, Billie Mae Richards, Alfie Scopp, Paul Soles

◎ TOP CAT AND THE BEVERLY HILLS CATS
The fortunes for Top Cat and his pals (Benny the Ball, Brain, Spook, Fancy and Choo Choo) suddenly change when Benny inherits the Beverly Hills estate of an eccentric old lady. Part of *Hanna-Barbera's Superstars 10* movie package. *A Hanna-Barbera Production. Color. Two hours. Premiered: 1988. Syndicated.*

Voices
Top Cat: Arnold Stang; **Benny the Ball:** Avery Schreiber; **Choo Choo:** Marvin Kaplan; **Spook/Brain:** Leo de Lyon; **Fancy-Fancy/Officer Dibble:** John Stephenson; **Mrs. Vandergelt:** Linda Gary; **Snerdly:** Henry Polic II; **Rasputin:** Frank Welker; **Kitty Glitter:** Teresa Ganzel; **Sid Buckman/Manager:** Dick Erdman; **Lester Pester:** Rob Paulson; **Warden:** Kenneth Mars

◎ TO THE RESCUE
During summer camp, Davey, his dog Goliath and a group of youngsters form an emergency rescue squad to help a man and his daughter trapped in the wreckage of their light airplane. *A Clokey Production for the Lutheran Church of America. Color. Half-hour. Premiered: 1975. Syndicated.*

Voices
Davey Hanson/Sally Hanson/Mary Hanson: Norma McMillan, Nancy Wible; **Goliath/John Hanson:** Hal Smith

☺ THE TOWN THAT SANTA FORGOT

In this Emmy-nominated, prime-time holiday special, Dick Van Dyke is the voice of a kindly grandfather who tells his grandchildren the story of Jeremy Creek, a spoiled brat of a boy who learns that it is better to give than receive. *A Hanna-Barbera Production. Color. Half-hour. Premiered on NBC: December 3, 1993.*

Voices

Narrator: Dick Van Dyke; **Other Voices:** Miko Hughes; Troy Davidson

☺ TREASURE ISLAND (1971)

In this high-seas journey, young Jim Hawkins joins Long John Silver and his crew of buccaneers in search of the buried treasure. This hour-long special is based on Robert Louis Stevenson's illustrious pirate story. *A Famous Classic Tales special. An Air Programs International Production. Color. One hour. Premiered: November 28, 1971. Syndicated.*

Voices

Ron Haddrick, John Kingley, John Llewellyn, Bruce Montague, Brenda Senders, Colin Tilley

☺ TREASURE ISLAND (1980)

Young Jim Hawkins's quest to uncover buried treasure and save his life at the same time is recounted in this musical version based on Robert Louis Stevenson's popular adventure story. This time several new faces are added to the standard cast of characters, among them Hiccup the Mouse, Jim's special friend, who keeps him safe although trouble lurks around every corner. The program was originally released in 1972 as a full-length feature and reedited for television broadcast. Melissa Sue Anderson hosted the program. *A Filmation Studios Production in association with Warner Bros. Television. Color. One hour. Premiered on NBC: April 29, 1980. Rebroadcast on NBC: January 31, 1981. Syndicated. Rebroadcast on CAR: August 8, 1995 (Mr. Spim's Cartoon Theatre).*

Voices

Long John Silver: Richard Dawson; **Captain Flint:** Larry Storch; **Jim Hawkins:** Davy Jones; **Squire Trelawney:** Larry D. Mann; **Mother:** Jane Webb; **Parrot:** Dal McKennon

☺ TREASURE ISLAND REVISITED

Long John Silver, Jim Hawkins and the rest of the cast are depicted as animals in this rendition of the familiar children's tale. Made for Japanese television, the program was later dubbed into English and released in the United States.

An American International Television Production in association with Toei Animation and Titan Productions. Color. One hour. Premiered: February 1972. Syndicated.

☺ A TRIBUTE TO MOM

The Disney Channel's look at the importance of mothers through an assemblage of clips culled from memorable Disney cartoons and featuring such popular songs as "Your Mother and Mine," by Sammy Fain and Sammy Cahn, and "The Bare Necessities," sung by Phil Harris. The original 90-minute special (1984) was shortened to an hour and rebroadcast in 1995 with the title *Disney's Salute to Mom. A Film Landa Inc. Production for The Disney Channel. Color. Ninety minutes. Premiered on DIS: May 13, 1984.*

Voices

Narrator: Charles Aidman

☺ THE TROLLS AND THE CHRISTMAS EXPRESS

Christmas is almost ruined when six dastardly trolls dress up as elves to prevent the delivery of toys on Christmas Eve. *A Titlecraft Production in association with Atkinson Film-Arts. Color. Half-hour. Premiered on HBO: December 9, 1981.*

Voices

Trogio: Hans Conried; **Narrator:** Roger Miller

☺ THE TROUBLE WITH MISS SWITCH

A good witch disguised as a schoolteacher enlists two students to help her carry out a special plan to foil the bad witch Saturna and become a witch of good standing again in this two-part fantasy/adventure. An ABC Weekend Special. *A Ruby-Spears Enterprises Production. Color. Half-hour. Premiered on ABC: February 16 and 23, 1980. Rebroadcast on ABC: May 31 and June 7, 1980; September 13 and 20, 1980; April 18 and 25, 1981; July 3 and 10, 1982; January 22 and 29, 1983; May 25 and June 1, 1985; October 14 and 21, 1989.*

Voices

Miss Switch: Janet Waldo; **Rupert P. Brown III ("Rupe"):** Eric Taslitz; **Amelia Matilda Daley:** Nancy McKeon; **Bathsheba/Saturna:** June Foray

☺ TUKIKI AND HIS SEARCH FOR A MERRY CHRISTMAS

A young Eskimo boy travels around the world and experiences the meaning of Christmas through a variety of celebrations. *A Titlecraft Production in association with Atkinson*

Film-Arts. Color. Half-hour. Premiered (U.S.): December 1979. Syndicated.

Voices
Tukiki: Adam Rich; **Northwind:** Sterling Holloway; **Vocalist:** Stephanie Taylor

◉ THE TURKEY CAPER

In this third Chucklewood Critters special, bear cub Buttons and his young fox friend Rusty encounter two young turkeys, who ask for their help in rescuing the wild turkeys of the forest that have been captured. *An Encore Enterprises Production. Color. Half-hour. Premiered: November 1985. Syndicated. Rebroadcast on USA: November 23, 1991; November 21, 1992; November 21, 1993.*

Voices
Rusty/Rosie: Kathy Ritter; **Buttons:** Barbara Goodson; **Ranger Jones:** Bill Boyett; **Abner:** Alvy Moore; **George:** Bill Ratner; **Bridgett:** Morgan Lofting

◉ 'TWAS THE NIGHT BEFORE BUMPY

Mr. Bumpy and his pal Squishington take a trip to the North Pole to snag some of Santa's presents. En route, they become sidetracked and held captive in the jungles of Peru by an earthworm soldier (voiced by Cheech Marin), in this 90-minute Saturday-morning special spunoff from the popular television series, *Bump in the Night. A Danger/Greengrass Production. Color. Ninety minutes. Premiered on ABC: December 19, 1995. Rebroadcast on ABC: December 14, 1996.*

◉ 'TWAS THE NIGHT BEFORE CHRISTMAS

The hearts of every child in Junctionville are broken when their letters to Santa Claus are returned marked "Not Accepted by Addressee!" Father Mouse sets out to find the culprit responsible so his children and others are not disappointed in this holiday special loosely based on Clement Moore's Christmas poem. *A Rankin-Bass Production. Color. Half-hour. Premiered on CBS: December 8, 1974. Rebroadcast on CBS: December 9, 1975; December 17, 1976; December 12, 1977; December 18, 1978; December 8, 1979; December 13, 1980; December 16, 1981; December 18, 1982; December 14, 1983; December 11, 1984; December 4, 1985; December 17, 1986; December 9, 1987; December 8, 1990; December 11, 1991; December 24, 1992; December 23, 1993. Rebroadcast on FAM: December 9, 1995; December 11, 1996.*

Voices
Joshua Trundel, the Clockmaker (narrator): Joel Grey; **Albert Mouse:** Tammy Grimes; **Mayor of Junctionville:** John McGiver; **Father Mouse:** George Gobel; **Vocalists:** The Wee Winter Singers

◉ TWELVE DAYS OF CHRISTMAS

Based on that age-old Christmas carol ("12 lords-a-leaping, 11 ladies dancing, 10 pipers piping" . . . not to mention "a partridge in a pear tree") a blowhard boss, Sir Carolbloomer, wants to use the abovementioned gifts to woo the gloomy Princess Silverbelle. The program was premiered on NBC opposite another new Hanna-Barbera Christmas special, *The Town That Santa Forgot. A Hanna-Barbera Production. Color. Half-hour. Premiered on NBC: December 3, 1993.*

Voices
Carter Cathcart, John Crenshaw, Donna Divino, Merwin Goldsmith, Earl Hammond, Phil Hartman, Larry Kenny, Frank Sims, Marcia Savella

◉ 20,000 LEAGUES UNDER THE SEA (1972)

Scientific journalist Pierre Aronnax, his 16-year-old assistant Conrad, and famed harpooner Ned Land join Captain Nemo for a fantastic undersea journey to the fabled lost continent of Atlantis in this two-part special based on Jules Verne's famous novel. *A Festival of Family Classics special. A Rankin-Bass Production in association with Mushi Studios. Color. One hour. Premiered: October 1972. Syndicated.*

Voices
Carl Banas, Len Birman, Bernard Cowan, Peg Dixon, Keith Hampshire, Peggi Loder, Donna Miller, Frank Perry, Henry Ramer, Billie Mae Richards, Alfie Scopp, Paul Soles

◉ 20,000 LEAGUES UNDER THE SEA (1973)

Captain Nemo dispels the rumor about a giant sea monster by bringing his ship *Nautilus* to the surface and making believers out of marine research scientist Pierre Aronnax and famed harpooner Ned Land. *A Famous Classic Tales special. A Hanna-Barbera Production. Color. Half-hour. Premiered on CBS: November 22, 1973. Rebroadcast on CBS: November 16, 1974. Syndicated.*

Voices
Tim Elliott, Ron Haddrick, Don Pascoe, John Stephenson

◉ THE 2000 YEAR OLD MAN

Carl Reiner and Mel Brooks wrote and created this half-hour animated special, geared more toward adults than children, featuring an interviewer (Reiner) talking about life with a 2,000-year-old man who has lived a full life. ("When I say 'the old days' I don't mean the George M. Cohan days!") Dialogue for the special was recorded before a live studio audience. *A Crossbow/Acre Enterprises Production in association with Leo Salkin Films. Color. Half-hour. Premiered on CBS: January 11, 1975. Rebroadcast on CBS: April 11, 1975. Syndicated.*

Voices
Interviewer: Carl Reiner; **Old Man:** Mel Brooks

◎ TWINKLE TWINKLE LITTLE STAR

A young girl (Lea), who should be practicing her violin, fiddles with her dad's super telescope and, with her dog Paggy and a very young rematerialized Mozart, float through space and come upon a tap-dancing star named Twinkle. From Cinar Films' *The Real Story of . . .* series. *A Cinar Films/France Animation Production in association with Western Publishing Company/The Family Channel/Telefilm Canada/Cofimage 3. Color. Half-hour. Premiered on HBO: January 22, 1994.*

Voices
Twinkle: Vanna White; **Mozart:** Martin Short

◎ THE UGLY DUCKLING

Award-winning singer/actress Cher narrates this adaptation of the beloved Hans Christian Andersen fairy tale about a lonely outcast duckling who is transformed into a beautiful swan. Produced in 1987, it was shown two years later on Showtime as part of Rabbit Ears Video's *Storybook Classics* series. *A Rabbit Ears Video Production. Color. Half-hour. Premiered on SHO: 1989.*

◎ UNCLE ELEPHANT

Based on the award-winning book by author-illustrator Arnold Lobel, this animated musical relates a sensitive story about the special bond between a wistful young elephant who mourns the disappearance of his parents at sea and his older Uncle Elephant, who introduces his nephew to a world full of hope and wonder. This beautifully animated half-hour premiered on PBS's *Long Ago & Far Away* series. *A Churchill Films/WGBH Boston Production. Color. Half-hour. Premiered on PBS: October 26, 1991. Rebroadcast on PBS: September 27, 1992.*

◎ UNCLE SAM MAGOO

Myopic Mr. Magoo wanders through the full spectrum of American history and encounters the likes of George Washington, Ben Franklin, Davy Crockett, Mark Twain and Paul Bunyan in this well-written animated special with a lively

Mr Magoo retraces moments in America history in a scene from the NBC network special Uncle Sam Magoo. © UPA Productions

musical score by award-winning composer Walter Scharf. *A UPA Production. Color. One hour. Premiered on NBC: February 15, 1970. Syndicated. Rebroadcast on DIS: June 23, 1992; June 29, 1992; June 15, 1993; July 9, 1993.*

Voices
Mr. Magoo: Jim Backus; **Uncle Sam/John Alden/Miles/Standish/Paul Revere/Davy Crockett/James Marshall/Johnny Appleseed/Captain John Parker/Robert E. Lee/Daniel Webster/John F. Kennedy:** Lennie Weinrib; **Mark Twain/John Sutter/President/Daniel Boone/Patrick Henry/U.S. Grant/Martin Luther King/Abraham Lincoln:** Barney Phillips; **Indian Chief (American)/Indian Chief (Tropical)/John Smith/Powhattan/Massasoit/Francis Scott Key/Kit Carson/Paul Bunyan/Franklin D. Roosevelt/Harry Truman/Wendell Willkie:** Bob Holt; **Leif Ericson/Columbus/Elder Brewster/Tom Paine/Thomas Jefferson/Woodrow Wilson:** Dave Shelley; **Priscilla/Betsy Ross/Tom Sawyer/Amelia Earhart/Eleanor Roosevelt/Susan B. Anthony:** Patti Gilbert; **George Washington/Walt Whitman/Oliver Wendell Holmes:** John Himes; **Dwight D. Eisenhower/Herbert Hoover/Carl Sandburg:** Bill Clayton; **Benjamin Franklin/Thomas Wolfe/George Washington Carver:** Sid Grossfield; **Others:** Sam Rosen

◎ UP ON THE HOUSETOP

In this half-hour syndicated Christmas special Curtis Calhoun just isn't in the mood for Christmas and wishes it would all go away. It appears he has gotten his wish, at least until he finds a strange little man in a red suit stuck in his chimney on Christmas Eve. *A Perennial Pictures Film Corporation Production. Color. Half-hour. Premiered: November 1993. Syndicated.*

Voices
Curtis Calhoun/Dad/David/Santa: Jerry Reynolds; **Gash:** Russ Harris; **Mrs. Wimbley:** Rachel Rutledge; **Reporter:**

Natalie Bridgegroom Harris; **Mr. Peterson:** Michael N. Ruggiero

⊚ VACATIONING WITH MICKEY AND FRIENDS

Gary Owens, the owner of a travel agency, suggests a series of trips designed to alleviate the stress of everyday life for his customers Donald Duck, Goofy, Mickey Mouse, Minnie Mouse and Pluto in this 90-minute live-action/animated special featuring a collection of classic Disney cartoons. *A Left Coast Television Production for The Disney Channel. Color. Ninety minutes. Premiered on DIS: 1988.*

⊚ THE VELVETEEN RABBIT (1985)

Academy Award–winning actress Meryl Streep narrates the story of a velveteen toy rabbit given to a small boy at Christmas. The rabbit is made real by the child's love in this award-winning half-hour, part of Rabbit Ear Video's *Storybook Classics* series. *A Rabbit Ears Production in association with Random House Home Video. Color. Half-hour. Premiered on PBS: March 9–24, 1985. Rebroadcast on SHO: December 10, 1991. Rebroadcast on ABC (ABC Weekend Special): April 11, 1992. Rebroadcast on SHO: April 29, 1992; May 7, 1992; May 18, 1992. Rebroadcast on ABC (ABC Weekend Special): March 13, 1993; December 23, 1995.*

Voices
Narrator: Meryl Streep; **Others:** Chub Bailey, Josh Rodine

⊚ THE VELVETEEN RABBIT (1985)

Margery Williams's classic tale of a stuffed toy rabbit who comes to life in this special narrated by actor Christopher Plummer. *An Atkinson Film-Arts Production in association with Telefilm Canada and CTV. Color. Half-hour. Premiered (U.S.): April, 1985. Syndicated.*

Voices
Jones: Don Westwood; **Tin Soldier:** Jim Bradford; **Rabbit #1/Rabbit #2:** Rick Jones; **Skin Horse:** Bernard McManus; **Doctor:** Eddie Nunn; **Fairy Queen:** Charity Brown; **Narrator:** Christopher Plummer

⊚ THE VELVETEEN RABBIT (1985)

Young Robert's favorite Christmas gift is a velveteen toy rabbit named Velvee. The special friendship they share is threatened when Robert turns seriously ill and Velvee is on the verge of being destroyed. *A Hanna-Barbera Production. Color. Half-hour. Premiered on ABC: April 20, 1985. Rebroadcast on ABC: October 19, 1985; December 20, 1986.*

Voices
Velvee: Chub Bailey; **Robert:** Josh Rodine; **Skin Horse/Nana:** Marilyn Lightstone; **Father:** Peter Cullen; **Tug:** Bill Scott; **Scungilli:** Barry Dennen; **Spinner:** Hal Smith; **Mouse:** Frank Welker; **Brenda:** Jodi Carlisle; **Harry:** Brian Cummings; **Mother/Nursery Fairy:** Beth Clopton

⊚ A VERY MERRY CRICKET

Chester C. Cricket returns in this sequel to 1973's *The Cricket in Times Square*, this time with pals Tucker R. Mouse and Harry the Cat. Tired of the cacophony and commercialism of Manhattan yuletide, they set off from Connecticut to return Chester to the Big Apple and use his musical attributes to bring the real meaning back to Christmas. *A Chuck Jones Enterprises Production. Color. Half-hour. Premiered on ABC: December 14, 1973. Rebroadcast on ABC: November 28, 1974; December 5, 1978. Syndicated. Rebroadcast on NIK: December 22, 1991; December 9, 1993.*

Voices
Chester C. Cricket/Harry the Cat: Les Tremayne; **Tucker the Mouse/Alley Cat:** Mel Blanc

⊚ A VERY SPECIAL ACTION LEAGUE NOW! SPECIAL

Four hapless crimefighting action-figure heroes, known as the Action League (from Nickelodeon's *Kablam!* series), take on two missions—first, to save the pop star Blandi (voiced by Swedish singer Robyn) from a marauding robot, then to rescue Stinky Diver from the clutches of the dreaded canine Spotzilla, in their first prime-time special. *A Nickelodeon Production. Color. Half-hour. Premiered on NIK: March 28, 1998.*

⊚ VIRTUAL BILL

When President Bill Clinton made his State of the Union Address to the nation in January of 1998, MTV countered with this computer-animated special featuring America's first artificially intelligent bio-digital President who engaged in his own one-hour "fireside chat." The special was written and voiced by Scott Dikkers. *An MTV Animation Production. Color. One hour. Premiered on MTV: January 27, 1998.*

Voice
Virtual Bill: Scott Dikkers

⊚ VOLTRON: DEFENDER OF THE UNIVERSE

In the 25th century, Voltron, a giant flying samurai robot, battles the evil reptile alien King Zorkon of Planet Doom and his army in this 90-minute feature-length cartoon, first syndicated in 1983. The special, shown in 76 markets, was the "pilot" for the weekly half-hour series of the same name, which premiered a year later. *A World Events Production. Color. Ninety minutes. Premiered: 1983.*

Voices
Jack Angel, Michael Bell, Peter Cullen, Tress MacNeille, Neil Ross, B.J. Ward, Lennie Weinrib

⦿ WALT DISNEY PRESENTS SPORT GOOFY'S OLYMPIC GAMES SPECIAL

Like the previously syndicated "Sports Goofy" specials, this version features a selection of memorable Goofy sports cartoons, among them, "Olympic Champ" (1942), "Goofy Gymnastics" (1949), "How To Swim" (1942) and "The Art of Self-Defense" (1941). *A Walt Disney Television Production. Color. Half-hour. Premiered: June 8, 1984. Syndicated.*

Voices
Goofy: Pinto Colvig, George Johnson

⦿ WALT DISNEY'S MICKEY AND DONALD PRESENTS SPORT GOOFY

Athletic competition and sporting events comprise this half-hour compilation special starring lovable dope Goofy in a collection of theatrical shorts from the 1940s, including "How to Play Baseball" (1942), "How To Swim" (1942) and "Tennis Racquet" (1949). *A Walt Disney Television Production. Color. Half-hour. Premiered: May 21–June 12, 1983. Syndicated.*

Voices
Goofy: Pinto Colvig, George Johnson

⦿ WALT DISNEY'S MICKEY AND DONALD PRESENTS SPORT GOOFY #2

Goofy returns in this second in a series of half-hour compilation specials of sports-oriented cartoons: "How to Play Football" (1944), "Goofy's Glider" (1940) and "Get Rich Quick" (1951). *A Walt Disney Television Production. Color. Half-hour. Premiered: August 21, 1983–September 24, 1983. Syndicated.*

Voices
Goofy: Pinto Colvig, George Johnson

⦿ WALT DISNEY'S MICKEY AND DONALD PRESENTS SPORT GOOFY #3

In his third sports spoof special, Goofy is featured in four memorable cartoons originally released to theaters: "Hockey Homicide" (1945), "Double Dribble" (1946), "The Art of

Skiing" (1941) and "Aquamania" (1961). *A Walt Disney Television Production. Color. Half-hour. Premiered: November 6–December 19, 1983. Syndicated.*

Voices
Goofy: Pinto Colvig, George Johnson

⦿ WALT DISNEY'S MICKEY, DONALD AND SPORT GOOFY: GETTING WET

Goofy, Mickey Mouse, Pluto, Donald Duck and Chip and Dale are all featured in this half-hour special—part of a continuing series of Goofy sports specials—originally produced for syndication. Among the cartoons featured are: "The Simple Things" (1953), starring Mickey Mouse and Pluto; "Chips Ahoy" (1956), featuring that pesky pair Chip and Dale; and "Aquamania" (1961), with Goofy. *A Walt Disney Production. Half-hour. Color. Premiered: September 14, 1984. Syndicated.*

Voices
Goofy: Pinto Colvig; **Mickey Mouse:** Jim MacDonald; **Donald Duck:** Clarence Nash

⦿ WALT DISNEY'S MICKEY, DONALD AND SPORT GOOFY: HAPPY HOLIDAYS

Mickey Mouse, Donald Duck and Goofy star in a collection of old cartoon shorts in this holiday season compilation entitled *Happy Holidays*. The show features "Pluto's Christmas Tree" (1952), "The Clock Watcher" (1945) and "How to Ride a Horse" from *The Reluctant Dragon* (1941) full-length feature. *A Walt Disney Television Production. Color. Half-hour. Premiered: December 14, 1984. Syndicated.*

Voices
Mickey Mouse: Jim MacDonald; **Donald Duck:** Clarence Nash; **Goofy:** Pinto Colvig

⦿ WALT DISNEY'S MICKEY, DONALD AND SPORT GOOFY SHOW: SNOWTIME

Subtitled *Snowtime*, various Disney characters appear in this first-run special presenting a collection of previously released cartoons, including "Lend a Paw" (1941), "Chip 'n' Dale" (1947) and "How to Fish" (1942). *A Walt Disney Television Production. Color. Half-hour. Premiered: November 30, 1984.*

Voices
Mickey Mouse: Jim MacDonald; **Donald Duck:** Clarence Nash; **Goofy:** Pinto Colvig

WHICH WITCH IS WITCH?

WEEP NO MORE, MY LADY

In the Mississippi backwoods, Skeeter, a 13-year-old boy, adopts a stray dog, (he names My Lady) and accepts a challenge from Alligator Ike to see whose dog is the best. An *ABC Weekend Special. A Ruby-Spears Enterprises Production. Color. Half-hour. Premiered on ABC: February 10, 1979. Rebroadcast on ABC: May 19, 1979; September 8, 1979; July 19, 1980; May 30, 1981; September 5, 1981; April 9, 1983; June 2, 1984; May 30, 1981; September 5, 1981; April 9, 1983; June 2, 1984.*

Voices
Skeeter: Jeremy Lawrence; **Uncle Jess:** Alan Oppenheimer; **Alligator Ike:** Larry D. Mann; **Mr. Rackman:** Michael Rye

WEIRD HAROLD

Fat Albert relies on Weird Harold to participate with the group in the Great Go-Cart Race. Unfortunately, the race turns into disaster when Weird Harold and Young Bill crash their soap-box derbies and are arrested. This program was the second Fat Albert special following 1969's *Hey, Hey, Hey, It's Fat Albert. A Filmation Associates Production in association with Bill Cosby Productions. Color. Half-hour. Premiered on NBC: May 4, 1973. Rebroadcast on NBC: September 7, 1973.*

Voices
Fat Albert/Mushmouth/Young Bill/Father: Bill Cosby; **Weird Harold:** Gerald Edwards; **Judge:** Henry Silva

WE WISH YOU A MERRY CHRISTMAS

A shellless turtle named Harold, who uses an army helmet as a substitute, suddenly becomes popular (under the name of Bob)—that is, until he is called upon to save the life of a drowning baby turtle. *A Perennial Pictures Film Corporation Production. Color. Half-hour. Premiered on FAM: December 5, 1996.*

Voices
Harold (Bob): Scott Tyring; **Monsieur Volture:** Jerry Reynolds; **Celeste:** Rachel Rutledge; **Mother Turtle:** Lisa Buetow; **Butch:** Russ Harris

WHAT A NIGHTMARE, CHARLIE BROWN

After devouring too much pizza, Snoopy has a nightmare that he is at the North Pole as part of a husky dog sled team and, in the adventures that follow, attempts to adapt to being a "real dog." *A Lee Mendelson–Bill Melendez Production in association with Charles M. Schulz Creative Associates and United Feature Syndicate. Color. Half-hour. Premiered on CBS: February 23, 1978. Rebroadcast on CBS: April 13, 1987.*

Voices
Charlie Brown: Liam Martin; **Snoopy:** Bill Melendez

WHAT HAVE WE LEARNED, CHARLIE BROWN?

In this mostly serious and reflective Memorial Day salute, Charlie Brown reminisces about the *Peanuts* group's adventures while taking part in a student-exchange program in France. Their visit to Omaha Beach triggers a retelling of the D-day attack in animation and newsreel footage. A later visit to the World War I battlefield of Ypres in Belgium sparks historical views on the "war to end all wars," with Linus movingly reciting John McCrae's famous poem, "In Flanders Field." *Peanuts* creator Charles Schulz hosted the program. *A Lee Mendelson–Bill Melendez Production in association with Charles M. Schulz Creative Associates and United Feature Syndicate. Color. Half-hour. Premiered on CBS: May 30, 1983. Rebroadcast on CBS: May 26, 1984; May 29, 1989.*

Voices
Charlie Brown: Brad Kesten; **Sally Brown:** Stacey Heather Tolkin; **Linus Van Pelt:** Jeremy Schoenberg; **Marcie/Shermy:** Michael Dockery; **Peppermint Patty:** Victoria Vargas; **French Madam:** Monica Parker; **Snoopy:** Bill Melendez

WHAT'S UP DOC?: A SALUTE TO BUGS BUNNY

In celebration of Bugs Bunny's 50th birthday, this two-hour retrospective spectacular features a tapestry of cartoon clips, behind-the-scenes footage of the Warner Bros. studio and interviews with directors Tex Avery, Chuck Jones, Friz Freleng, Bob Clampett and the "man of a thousand voices," Mel Blanc. *A Communicreations Production in association with Turner Network Television. Color. Two hours. Premiered on TNT: November 12, 1990. Rebroadcast on TNT: November 17, 1990; January 24, 1993.*

Voices
Narrator: Harlan Rector

WHICH WITCH IS WITCH?

Buttons and Rusty, stars of the Chucklewood Critters specials, experience their first Halloween together, dressed up in costumes, and overcome trouble at a Halloween party

Ranger Jones shows Buttons the bear and Rusty the fox the right way to carve a pumpkin in the Halloween special Which Witch Is Witch? *© Encore Enterprises*

thrown by Ranger Jones. *An Encore Enterprises Production. Color. Half-hour. Premiered: October 1984. Syndicated. Rebroadcast on USA: October 26, 1991; October 27, 1991; October 31, 1992.*

Voices
Rusty/Rosie: Kathy Ritter; **Buttons/Christie:** Barbara Goodson; **Abner:** Alvy Moore; **George:** Bill Ratner; **Bridgett:** Morgan Lofting; **Ranger Jones:** Bill Boyett

◎ WHITE BEAR'S SECRET
Bumbling bachelor Brown Bear (in this sequel to the United Kingdom television hit *Brown Bear's Wedding*) finds that adapting to married life isn't easy in this half-hour special from London's FilmFair Animation that premiered on The Disney Channel. *A FilmFair Animation Production. Color. Half-hour. Premiered on DIS: August 1, 1992. Rebroadcast on DIS: August 4, 1992.*

Voices
Brown Bear: Joss Ackland; **White Bear:** Helena Bonham-Carter; **Owl:** Hugh Laurie

◎ THE WHITE SEAL
In the second of two *Jungle Book* animated specials ordered for the 1974–75 season by CBS, Roddy McDowall narrates the story of Kotick the white seal, who grows up from playful sprout to become leader of his group, taking them to a spectacular island safe from the savage seal hunters. *A Chuck Jones Enterprises Production. Color. Half-hour. Premiered on CBS: March 24, 1975. Rebroadcast on CBS: October 17, 1975; May 13, 1977; September 9, 1981. Syndicated.*

Voices
Kotick/Sea Catch/Sea Cow/Killer Whale/Walrus: Roddy McDowall; **Matkah:** June Foray; **Narrator:** Roddy McDowall

◎ WHITEWASH
Attacked and sprayed white by a gang of white young men, a young black girl comes to terms with what has happened and goes on with her life thanks to her loving grandmother, in this half-hour animated special, written by Ntozake Shange and produced by award-winning animator Michael Sporn for HBO. *A Michael Sporn Animation Production. Color. Half-hour. Premiered on HBO: August 16, 1994.*

Voices
Grandmother: Ruby Dee; **Teacher:** Linda Lavin; **Helene Angel:** Serena Henry; **Mauricio:** Ndehru Roberts

◎ WHY, CHARLIE BROWN, WHY?
Janice, a new *Peanuts* character, is a school friend of Linus and Charlie Brown's who develops leukemia. The story traces her treatment—and eventual recovery—and how the gang deals with it. *A Lee Mendelson–Bill Melendez Production in association with Charles M. Schulz Creative Associates and United Feature Syndicate. Color. Half-hour. Premiered on CBS: March 16, 1990.*

Voices
Charlie Brown: Kaleb Henley; **Janice Emmons:** Olivia Burnette; **Linus Van Pelt:** Brandon Stewart; **Sally Brown:** Andrienne Stiefel; **Little Sister:** Brittany Thorton; **Big Sister:** Lindsay Sloane; **The Bully:** Dion Zamora

◎ WILLIE MAYS AND THE SAY-HEY KID
Baseball great Willie Mays, playing himself, recounts the tale of the near-impossible catch he made to clinch the National League pennant, thanks to a special wish he is granted by an eccentric angel, and a poor orphan girl (Veronica) who turns out to be his godchild in this one-hour special, which originally aired as part of *The ABC Saturday Superstar Movie* series. *A Rankin-Bass Production. Color. One hour. Premiered on ABC: October 14, 1972 (on The ABC Saturday Superstar Movie). Rebroadcast on ABC: September 22, 1973; February 16, 1974. Syndicated.*

Voices
Willie Mays: himself; **Veronica:** Tina Andrews; **Iguana:** Paul Frees; **Veronica's aunt:** Ernestine Wade

THE WILLOWS IN WINTER

Michael Palin and Vanessa Redgrave lent their voices to this 90-minute sequel to a British animated production of Kenneth Grahame's *The Wind in the Willows*, one of two feature-length coproductions produced by Carlton UK Television, HIT Entertainment and Animation House, TVC London. The Emmy-nominated sequel premiered in the United States on The Family Channel. *A TVC London/HIT Entertainment/Carlton UK Television Production. Color. Ninety minutes. Premiered on FAM: September 8, 1996.*

Voices
Michael Palin, Vanessa Redgrave

THE WIND IN THE WILLOWS (1987)

Ratty, Badger and Mole struggle to keep boastful Mr. Toad from danger and try to save Toad Hall from destruction by evil weasels in this two-hour made-for-television movie based on Kenneth Grahame's popular children's classic. *A Rankin-Bass Production in association with Cuckoos Nest Animation. Color. Two hours. Premiered on ABC: July 5, 1987. Rebroadcast on ABC: September 12, 1987. Rebroadcast on NIK: March 28, 1992.*

Voices
Mr. Toad: Charles Nelson Reilly; **Ratty:** Roddy McDowall; **Badger:** José Ferrer; **Moley:** Eddie Bracken; **Wayfarer:** Paul Frees; **Magistrate:** Robert McFadden; **Vocalist:** Judy Collins

THE WIND IN THE WILLOWS (1989)

England's Cosgrove Hall Productions produced this two-hour, stop-motion, puppet-animated film following an unusual group of friends (wise old Badger, kind and innocent Mole, brave and generous Rat and reckless and impetuous Toad)—and their misadventures in 1908 Edwardian England, based on the book by Kenneth Grahame. Part of the award-winning series *Long Ago & Far Away* on PBS, it was the only film from the series longer than a half hour. *A Cosgrove Hall Production. Color. Two hours. Premiered on PBS: March 18, 1989. Rebroadcast on PBS: December 25, 1992 (as a 90-minute special).*

Voices
Badger: Sir Michael Hordern; **Rat:** Ian Carmichael; **Toad:** David Jason; **Mole:** Richard Pearson

WINNIE THE POOH AND A DAY FOR EEYORE

Winnie the Pooh and his friends—Rabbit, Piglet and Roo—happen to forget Eeyore's birthday and with Christopher Robin's help, they throw a surprise party for the sorrowful-looking donkey. The special was the first production starring the characters since *Winnie the Pooh and Tigger Too* produced 12 years earlier. *A Walt Disney Television Production. Color. Half-hour. Premiered on DIS: May 6, 1986.*

Voices
Winnie the Pooh: Hal Smith; **Eeyore:** Ralph Wright; **Piglet:** John Fiedler; **Rabbit:** Will Ryan; **Christopher Robin:** Kim Christianson; **Roo:** Dick Billingsley; **Kanga:** Julie McWhirter Dees; **Tigger:** Paul Winchell

WINNIE THE POOH AND CHRISTMAS, TOO

Winnie the Pooh and the gang write a letter to Santa Claus and take it upon themselves to make sure all their friends in the woods get they want in this prime-time half-hour special that marked the return of TV legend Paul Winchell as the voice of Tigger. *A Walt Disney Television Animation Production. Color. Half-hour. Premiered on ABC: December 14, 1991. Rebroadcast on ABC: December 11, 1992; December 8, 1993; Rebroadcast on CBS: December 21, 1995; December 5, 1996.*

Voices
Winnie the Pooh: Jim Cummings; **Tigger:** Paul Winchell

WINNIE THE POOH AND THE BLUSTERY DAY

Broadcast as a prime-time special, this Academy Award–winning short subject relates Pooh and Piglet's frightening encounter with a giant windstorm that blows them skyward, crashing into and destroying the Owl's treehouse. *A Walt Disney Television Production. Color. Half-hour. Premiered on NBC: November 30, 1970. Rebroadcast on NBC: December 1, 1971; November 29, 1972; November 28, 1973; November 26, 1974; December 1, 1978.*

Voices
Winnie the Pooh: Sterling Holloway; **Eeyore:** Ralph Wright; **Owl:** Hal Smith; **Christopher Robbin:** Jon Walmsley; **Kanga:** Barbara Luddy; **Roo:** Clint Howard; **Rabbit:** Junius Matthews; **Gopher:** Howard Morris; **Tigger:** Paul Winchell; **Piglet:** John Fiedler; **Narrator:** Sebastian Cabot

WINNIE THE POOH AND THE HONEY TREE

Winnie the Pooh's love for honey gets the better of him as he becomes overweight from overconsumption of the sweet stuff in this theatrical short subject broadcast as a prime-time special. *A Walt Disney Television Production. Color.*

Half-hour. Premiered on NBC: March 10, 1970. Rebroadcast on NBC: March 22, 1971; March 14, 1972; April 4, 1973: March 26, 1974; November 25, 1977; January 21, 1990 (on Magical World of Disney).

Voices

Winnie the Pooh: Sterling Holloway; **Eeyore:** Ralph Wright; **Owl:** Hal Smith; **Christopher Robin:** Bruce Reitherman; **Kanga:** Barbara Luddy; **Roo:** Clint Howard; **Rabbit:** Junius Matthews; **Gopher:** Howard Morris; **Narrator:** Sebastian Cabot

⊚ WINNIE THE POOH AND TIGGER TOO

Tigger is so joyfully bouncy that his friends Pooh, Rabbit and Piglet look for ways to "unbounce" him in this animated special originally produced as a theatrical cartoon short. *A Walt Disney Television Production. Color. Half-hour. Premiered on NBC: November 28, 1975 (as NBC Holiday Special). Rebroadcast on ABC: November 25, 1976; CBS: December 11, 1982; August 30, 1983.*

Voices

Winnie the Pooh: Sterling Holloway; **Tigger:** Paul Winchell; **Rabbit:** Junius Matthews; **Piglet:** John Fiedler; **Kanga:** Barbara Luddy; **Roo:** Dori Whitaker; **Christopher Robin:** Timothy Turner; **Narrator:** Sebastian Cabot

⊚ A WISH FOR WINGS THAT WORK: OPUS & BILL'S FIRST CHRISTMAS SPECIAL

Characters from Berkeley Breathed's *Bloom County* and *Outland* comic strips star in this half-hour Christmas special in which Opus the Penguin writes to Santa to ask for wings that work—since he can't handle being a bird that can't fly. *A Universal Cartoon Studios/Amblin Entertainment Production. Color. Half-hour. Premiered on CBS: December 18, 1991. Rebroadcast on CBS: December 24, 1992.*

Voices

Opus the Penguin: Michael Bell; **Bill the Cat:** John Byner; **Cockroach:** Sudy Nim

⊚ THE WISH THAT CHANGED CHRISTMAS

A lonely orphan, a lonely Christmas doll and a lonely childless couple each wish to change their lives at Christmas in this animated adaptation of Rumer Godden's heartwarming story "The Story of Holly and Ivy." *A Children's Television Workshop Production. Color. Half-hour. Premiered on CBS: December 20, 1991. Rebroadcast on CBS: December*

16, 1992. Rebroadcast on ABC: December 23, 1994.

Voices

The Owl: Jonathan Winters; **Mr. Smith:** Paul Winfield; **Ivy:** Brittany Thornton; **Holly:** Lea Floden; **Officer Jones:** Bill Boyett; **Mrs. Jones:** Tress MacNeille; **Mrs. Sheperd:** Beverly Garland; **Mr. Blossom:** Lindsey Workman; **Peter:** Marc Robinson

⊚ WITCH'S NIGHT OUT

Gilda Radner provides the voice of a washed-up witch who turns two small children into the monsters of their choice only to fulfill the fantasies of the town's entire adult population as well in this prime-time Halloween special. *A Leach-Rankin Production in association with Rankin-Bass Productions. Color. Half-hour. Premiered on NBC: October 27, 1978. Rebroadcast on NBC: October 30, 1979. Syndicated. Rebroadcast on DIS: October 25, 1992; October 31, 1992; October 30, 1993.*

Voices

Witch ("The Godmother"): Gilda Radner; **Rotten:** Bob Church; **Goody:** John Leach; **Tender:** Naomi Leach; **Small:** Tony Molesworth; **Malicious:** Catherine O'Hara; **Mincely:** Fiona Reid; **Bazooey:** Gerry Salsberg

⊚ WOLVES, WITCHES AND GIANTS

British comic Spike Milligan narrates and provides character voices for three classic children's fairy tales—"Red Riding Hood," "The Witch and the Comb" and "The Little Tailor"—featured in this half-hour special, which premiered on The Disney Channel. The program was culled from a series of 10-minute episodes originally produced for United Kingdom's ITV Network. *A Honeycomb Animation Production. Color. Half-hour. Premiered on DIS: January 29, 1997.*

Voices

Narrator/Other Voices: Spike Milligan

⊚ THE WOMAN WHO RAISED A BEAR AS HER SON

Set in the high Arctic, an old Inuit woman, who lives alone becomes an unlikely mother when an orphaned polar cub tumbles into her life—in this heartwearming adventure adapted from Arctic legend. *A Lacewood Production. Color. Half-hour. Premiered on DIS: 1990.*

⊚ THE WORLD OF PETER RABBIT AND FRIENDS

Originally airing on The Family Channel, CBS broadcast this hour-long re-creation of books by Beatrix Potter, culled from two previously broadcast half-hours: "The Tale of Peter Rabbit and Benjamin Bunny" and "The Tale of Flopsy Bunnies and Mrs. Tittlemouse." (For full voice credit information, see the series entry in the Television Cartoon Series section.) A *TVC London Production for Frederick Warne and Co./BBC in association with Pony Canyon, Inc. Color. One hour. Premiered on CBS: March 27, 1997.*

Cast *(live action)*
Beatrix Potter: Niamh Cusack

THE WORLD OF PETER RABBIT AND FRIENDS: "THE TAILOR OF GLOUCESTER"

This timeless yuletide tale, featuring an ailing tailor and an altruistic group of mice, weaves a story about the joy of giving in this fourth animated installment of the Emmy-nominated Family Channel series, adapted from work of well-known children's author Beatrix Potter. (For full voice credit information, see the series entry in the Television Cartoon Series section.) A *TVC London Production for Frederick Warne and Co./BBC in association with Pony Canyon, Inc. Color. Half-hour. Premiered on FAM: November 26, 1993. Rebroadcast on FAM: November 29, 1993; December 5, 1993; December 12, 1993; December 4, 1994; December 23, 1994; December 25, 1994; January 8, 1995; May 7, 1995; December 2, 1995; December 17, 1995; December 22, 1995; December 7, 1996; December 8, 1997; December 19, 1997.*

Cast *(live action)*
Beatrix Potter: Niamh Cusack

THE WORLD OF PETER RABBIT AND FRIENDS: "THE TALE OF FLOPSY BUNNIES AND MRS. TITTLEMOUSE"

Two more timeless tales—the first dealing with a group of bunnies who naughtily get into Mr. McGregor's lettuce patch, the second following the exploits of a tidy little wood mouse who lives under a hedge—by renowned children's author Beatrix Potter are featured in this colorfully animated installment of the popular Family Channel series. (For full voice credit information, see the series entry in the Television Cartoon Series section.) A *TVC London Production for Frederick Warne and Co./BBC in association with Pony Canyon, Inc. Color. Half-hour. Premiered on FAM: November 13, 1995. Rebroadcast on FAM: November 16, 1995; November 24, 1995.*

Cast *(live action)*
Beatrix Potter: Niamh Cusack

THE WORLD OF PETER RABBIT AND FRIENDS: "THE TALE OF MRS. TIGGY-WINKLE AND MR. JEREMY FISHER"

The sixth of the Family Channel's Emmy-nominated live-action/animated series, this half-hour special combines two of Beatrix Potter's favorite stories in this seven-part series of specials, following the adventures of a young farm girl, Lucie Carr, a talkative pet hedgehog, Mrs. Tiggy-Winkle and a gentleman frog, Mr. Jeremy Fisher, who have a frightful story of their own. (For full voice credit information, see the series entry in the Television Cartoon Series section.) A *TVC London Production for Frederick Warne and Co./BBC in association with Pony Canyon, Inc. Color. Half-hour. Premiered on FAM: April 3, 1994. Rebroadcast on FAM: April 4, 1994; April 11, 1994; April 17, 1994; October 9, 1994; November 18, 1994; March 27, 1995.*

Cast *(live action)*
Beatrix Potter: Niamh Cusack

THE WORLD OF PETER RABBIT AND FRIENDS: "THE TALE OF PETER RABBIT AND BENJAMIN BUNNY"

Cousins Peter and Benjamin experience some hair-raising escapades in Mr. McGregor's vegetable patch in this first installment in a series of half-hour live-action/animated specials, based on two of Beatrix Potter's popular children's stories. The series of specials were produced for The Family Channel. (For full voice credit information, see the series entry in the Television Cartoon Series section.) A *TVC London Production for Frederick Warne and Co./BBC in association with Pony Canyon, Inc. Color. Half-hour. Premiered on FAM: March 29, 1993. Rebroadcast on FAM: April 4, 1993; April 11, 1993; May 10, 1993; May 16, 1993; September 13, 1993; November 16, 1993; March 13, 1994; March 21, 1994; March 27, 1994; April 3, 1994; April 29, 1994; October 3, 1994; November 11, 1994; April 3, 1995; April 9, 1995; November 16, 1995.*

Cast *(live action)*
Beatrix Potter: Niamh Cusack

THE WORLD OF PETER RABBIT AND FRIENDS: "THE TALE OF PIGLING BLAND"

In this fifth of six animated specials based on Beatrix Potter's lovable and laughable creations, Pigling and his addle-brained brother Alexander head to the market, ignoring the sage advice of Aunt Pettitoes, and find themselves in a stew. (For full voice credit information, see the series entry in the Television Cartoon Series section.) A *TVC London*

Production for Frederick Warne and Co./BBC in association with Pony Canyon, Inc. Color. Half-hour. Premiered on FAM: March 13, 1994. Rebroadcast on FAM: March 21, 1994; March 27, 1994; October 3, 1994; March 27, 1995; May 8, 1995.

Cast (live action)
Beatrix Potter: Niamh Cusack

◎ THE WORLD OF PETER RABBIT AND FRIENDS: "THE TALE OF SAMUEL WHISKERS AND THE ROLY-POLY PUDDING"

When Mrs. Kitten misplaces her rebellious son Tom, Kitten Dumpling Roly-Poly Pudding becomes the dinner item of choice for a rotund cat named Samuel Whiskers, in this delightful animated half-hour, part of *The World of Peter Rabbit and Friends* series, produced by Oscar-winning British producer John Coates for The Family Channel. (For full voice credit information, see the series entry in the Television Cartoon Series section.) *A TVC London Production for Frederick Warne and Co./BBC in association with Pony Canyon, Inc. Color. Half-hour. Premiered on FAM: May 10, 1993. Rebroadcast on FAM: May 16, 1993; May 23, 1993; September 19, 1993; November 17, 1993; December 5, 1993; November 17, 1994; May 8, 1995.*

Cast (live action)
Beatrix Potter: Niamh Cusack

◎ THE WORLD OF PETER RABBIT AND FRIENDS: "THE TALE OF TOM KITTEN AND JEMINA PUDDLE-DUCK"

This richly animated half-hour special combines two fine adaptations of Beatrix Potter's classic children's stories. The opener follows the adventures of three little mischievous kittens named Tom Kitten, Mittens and Moppet. Next is a farmyard tale of a duck who becomes annoyed when the farmer's wife won't let her hatch her own eggs. Both premiered on this Emmy-nominated series, produced for The Family Channel. (For full voice credit information, see the series entry in the Television Cartoon Series section.) *A TVC London Production for Frederick Warne and Co./BBC in association with Pony Canyon, Inc. Color. Half-hour. Premiered on FAM: September 13, 1993. Rebroadcast on FAM: September 19, 1993; September 26, 1993; November 19, 1993; November 29, 1993; April 3, 1994; April 4, 1994; April 11, 1994; October 9, 1994; November 15, 1994; January 8, 1995; May 7, 1995; November 13, 1995.*

Cast (live action):
Beatrix Potter: Niamh Cusack

◎ THE WORLD OF SECRET SQUIRREL AND ATOM ANT

The first cartoon preview aired in prime time, this hour-long special gave viewers a glimpse of the characters from the Saturday-morning series, *The Atom Ant/Secret Squirrel Show* in two back-to-back episodes. The series officially debuted on October 2, 1965. *A Hanna-Barbera Production. Color. One hour. Premiered on NBC: September 12, 1965.*

Voices
Secret Squirrel: Mel Blanc; **Morocco Mole:** Paul Frees; **Atom Ant:** Howard Morris; **Mr. Moto/Others:** Don Messick

◎ THE WORLD OF STRAWBERRY SHORTCAKE

In this Easter special based on the popular greeting card characters, the happiness of Strawberry Shortcake and her friends of the fantasy world, Strawberry Land, is intruded upon by the diabolical Peculiar Purple Pieman, who is always out to spoil their fun. The first of six Strawberry Shortcake specials produced for first-run syndication. *An RLR Associates Production in association with Those Characters From Cleveland and Murakami-Wolf-Swenson Films. Color. Half-hour. Premiered: March–April, 1980. Syndicated. Rebroadcast on DIS: August 11, 1992.*

Voices
Sun (narrator): Romeo Muller; **Strawberry Shortcake:** Russi Taylor; **Peculiar Purple Pieman:** Bob Ridgely; **Huckleberry Pie:** Julie McWhirter; **Blueberry Muffin/Apple Dumplin:** Joan Gerber; **Raspberry Tart:** Pamela Anderson; **Ben Bean/Escargot:** Bob Holt; **Vocalists:** Flo and Eddy

◎ YABBA DABBA 2

Host Bill Bixby salutes the prolific careers of animators William Hanna and Joseph Barbera in this compilation special of clips from their cartoon successes, from their MGM days and their days as the head of their own studio, Hanna-Barbera Productions. The show featured clips of Tom and Jerry, Scooby-Doo, Ruff and Reddy, the Flintstones, and others. *A Hanna-Barbera Production in association with Robert Guenette Productions. Color. One hour. Premiered on CBS: October 12, 1979. Rebroadcast on CBS: June 1, 1982. Rebroadcast on CAR: June 4, 1994.*

◎ YANKEE DOODLE

The spirit of the Revolutionary War, including Paul Revere's historic midnight ride to warn the colonials, is witnessed by Danny, a 12-year-old boy, and his Midnight Militia friends, Freddy and Timmy, in this special about freedom and independence. A *Festival of Family Classics* special. A *Rankin-Bass Production in association with Mushi Studios.* Color. Half-hour. Premiered: 1972–1973. Syndicated,

Voices
Carl Banas, Len Birman, Bernard Cowan, Peg Dixon, Keith Hampshire, Peggi Loder, Donna Miller, Frank Perry, Henry Ramer, Billie Mae Richards, Alfie Scopp, Paul Soles

⊚ YANKEE DOODLE CRICKET

Chester C. Cricket, star of *The Cricket in Times Square* and *A Very Merry Cricket*, stars in this fanciful view of American history re-created by the ancestors of Chester, Harry the Cat and Tucker R. Mouse. A *Chuck Jones Enterprises Production.* Color. Half-hour. Premiered on ABC: January 16, 1975. Rebroadcast on ABC: June 28, 1976. Syndicated.

Voices
Chester C. Cricket/Harry the Cat: Les Tremayne; **Tucker R. Mouse:** Mel Blanc; **Other Voices:** June Foray

⊚ YEAR WITHOUT A SANTA CLAUS

This stop-motion "Animagic" special features the voice of Mickey Rooney, again picking up Santa's reins—as he did in the 1970 *Santa Claus Is Coming to Town*—only this time feeling the world has lost the Christmas spirit. Santa recovers from his disenchantment in time to make his traditional sleigh ride on Christmas Eve to distribute toys to the children of the world. Features the hit songs "Blue Christmas" and "Here Comes Santa Claus." A *Rankin-Bass Production.* Color. One hour. Premiered on ABC: December 10, 1974. Rebroadcast on ABC: December 10, 1975; December 14, 1976; December 9, 1977; December 10, 1978; December 9, 1979; December 21, 1980; Rebroadcast on DIS: December 18, 1992; December 14, 1993; December 13, 1995; December 14, 1996; December 10, 1997. Syndicated.

Voices
Mrs. Santa Claus (narrator): Shirley Booth; **Santa Claus:** Mickey Rooney; **Snowmiser:** Dick Shawn; **Heatmiser:** George S. Irving; **Jingle Bells:** Robert McFadden; **Jangle Bells:** Bradley Bolke; **Mother Nature:** Rhoda Mann; **Mr. Thistlewhite:** Ron Marshall; **Ignatius Thistlewhite:** Colin Duffy; **Blue Christmas Girl/Vocalists:** Christine Winter

⊚ YES, VIRGINIA, THERE
IS A SANTA CLAUS

Animated retelling of eight-year-old Virginia O'Hanlon's letter to a *New York Sun* editor in 1897 asking if Santa Claus

really exists. Program was coproduced by Bill Melendez, who was also associated with Charles M. Schulz's *Peanuts* specials—cornerstones of prime-time animation. A *Burt Rosen Company Production in association with Wolper Productions and Bill Melendez Production.* Color. Half-hour. Premiered on ABC: December 6, 1974. Rebroadcast on ABC: December 5, 1975. Syndicated. Rebroadcast on CBS: December 22, 1991. Rebroadcast on USA: December 17, 1993; December 7, 1994; December 24, 1995. Rebroadcast on FAM: December 11, 1996; December 4, 1997.

Voices
Virginia O'Hanlon: Courtney Lemmon; **Miss Taylor:** Susan Silo; **Billie:** Billie Green; **Specs:** Sean Manning; **Mary Lou:** Tracy Belland; **Arthur:** Christopher Wong; **Amy:** Vickey Ricketts; **Peewee:** Jennifer Green; **Officer Riley:** Herb Armstrong; **Sergeant Muldoon:** Arnold Ross; **Vocalist:** Jimmy Osmond; **Narrator:** Jim Backus

⊚ YOGI AND THE INVASION
OF THE SPACE BEARS

Yogi Bear is on a rampage—and no picnic basket is safe in Jellystone Park. He swears to turn over a new leaf but before he does so, he and Boo-Boo are kidnapped by aliens who plan to clone them. Part of *Hanna-Barbera's Superstar 10* movie package. A *Hanna-Barbera Production.* Color. Two hours. Premiered: 1988. Syndicated.

Voices
Yogi Bear: Daws Butler; **Boo-Boo/Ranger Smith:** Don Messick; **Cindy Bear:** Julie Bennett; **Ranger Jones/Guy:** Michael Rye; **Ranger Brown/Ranger Two:** Patric Zimmerman; **Ranger Roubidoux/Owner:** Peter Cullen; **Boy/Zor Two/Wife:** Rob Paulson; **Little Girl:** Maggie Roswell; **Man/Zor One/Boy:** Townsend Coleman; **Dax Nova/Worker Kid:** Frank Welker; **Mountain Bear/Ranger One:** Sorrell Booke; **Girl:** Victoria Carroll

⊚ YOGI AND THE MAGICAL
FLIGHT OF THE SPRUCE GOOSE

Everyone's favorite bear leads a gang of his friends on a tour of the Spruce Goose, the largest cargo plane ever built. To their amazement, the plane suddenly takes off, taking them on the voyage of a lifetime. Syndicated as part of *Hanna-Barbera's Superstar 10* movie package. A *Hanna-Barbera Production.* Color. Two hours. Premiered: 1988. Syndicated. Rebroadcast on DIS: December 3, 1996.

Voices
Yogi Bear/Quick Draw McGraw/Snagglepuss/Huckleberry Hound/Augie Doggie: Daws Butler; **Boo-Boo/Mumbley:** Don Messick; **Doggie Daddy/Pelican:** John Stephenson;

Dread Baron: Paul Winchell; **Merkin:** Frank Welker; **Firkin:** Dave Coulier; **Bernice:** Marilyn Schreffler

◉ YOGI BEAR'S ALL-STAR COMEDY CHRISTMAS CAPER

Yogi Bear and Boo-Boo sneak off into the city and make Christmas merry for a lonely little rich girl, Judy Jones, with some help from their old friends in this all-star Hanna-Barbera holiday special. *A Hanna-Barbera Production. Color. Half-hour. Premiered on CBS: December 21, 1982. Rebroadcast on CBS: December 18, 1984. Rebroadcast on DIS: December 12, 1990; December 13, 1991; December 19, 1992; December 7, 1993.*

Voices

Yogi Bear/Quick Draw McGraw/Huckleberry Hound/Snagglepuss/Hokey Wolf/Snooper/Blabber/Augie Doggie/Mr. Jinks/Dixie/Wally Gator: Daws Butler; **Boo-Boo/Ranger Smith/Pixie:** Don Messick; **Judy Jones:** Georgi Irene; **Doggie Daddy/Butler/Announcer:** John Stephenson; **Mr. Jones/Zookeeper #1/Sergeant:** Hal Smith; **Mrs. Jones/P.A. Voice/Lady in the Street:** Janet Waldo; **Yakky Doodle/Zookeeper #2:** Jimmy Weldon; **Magilla Gorilla/Chief Blake/Murray:** Allan Melvin; **Fred Flintstone/Policeman/Security Guard #1:** Henry Corden; **Barney Rubble/Bulldog/Security Guard #2:** Mel Blanc

◉ YOGI'S ARK LARK

The biblical tale of Noah's Ark is given a different twist in this animated rendering featuring Yogi Bear, Boo Boo and a host of Hanna-Barbera cartoon favorites. The feature-length story, which originally aired on *The ABC Saturday Superstar Movie,* served as the successful pilot for the Saturday-morning series *Yogi's Gang,* in which the program was rebroadcast in two parts. *A Hanna-Barbera Production. Color. One hour. Premiered on ABC: September 16, 1972 (on The ABC Saturday Superstar Movie). Syndicated.*

Voices

Yogi Bear/Baba Looey/Wally Gator/Huckleberry Hound/Lambsy/Quick Draw McGraw/Snagglepuss/Top Cat: Daws Butler; **Boo Boo/Atom Ant/So So/Moby Dick/Touche' Turtle:** Don Messick; **Paw Rugg/1st Truck Driver/Paw Rugg:** Henry Corden; **Magilla Gorilla/2nd Truck Driver:** Allan Melvin; **Maw Rugg/Floral Rugg/Woman:** Jean VanderPyl; **Squiddly/Hokey Wolf/Yakky Doodle:** Walker Edmiston; **Cap'n Noah:** Lennie Weinrib; **Benny/Doggie Daddy/Hardy:** John Stephenson

◉ YOGI'S FIRST CHRISTMAS

Huckleberry Hound, Snagglepuss, Augie Doggie and Doggie Daddy all arrive at Jellystone Lodge for their annual Christmas celebration with cartoon pals Yogi Bear and Boo-Boo. Their festivities gain added meaning when they discover that the owner, Mrs. Throckmorton, plans to sell the lodge to make way for a freeway in this two-hour made-for-television movie. *A Hanna-Barbera Production. Color. Half-hour. Premiered: November 22, 1980. Syndicated. Rebroadcast: December 22, 1991 (syndication). Rebroadcast on DIS: December 12, 1992; December 7, 1993. Rebroadcast on CAR: November 26, 1994; July 23, 1995 (Mr. Spim's Cartoon Theatre). Rebroadcast on TNT: December 17, 1995; December 1, 1996.*

Voices

Yogi Bear/Huckleberry Hound/Augie Doggie/Snagglepuss: Daws Butler; **Boo-Boo/Ranger Smith/Herman the Hermit:** Don Messick; **Doggie Daddy/Mr. Dingwell:** John Stephenson; **Cindy Bear/Mrs. Throckmorton:** Janet Waldo; **Otto the Chef/Santa Claus:** Hal Smith; **Snively:** Marilyn Schreffler

◉ YOGI'S GREAT ESCAPE

Because of a financial crisis, Jellystone Park will be closed and Yogi Bear and all the other bears must move to a zoo. To avoid incarceration, Yogi and his diminutive sidekick, Boo-Boo, lead Ranger Smith on a cross-country chase in this two-hour made-for-television movie, broadcast as part of *Hanna-Barbera's Superstar 10* series of first-run animated films for television. *A Hanna-Barbera Production. Color. Two hours. Premiered: 1987. Syndicated.*

Yogi Bear heads a cast of characters in some yuletide fun in the two-hour, made-for-television movie Yogi's First Christmas. *© Hanna-Barbera Productions.*

Voices

Yogi Bear/Quick Draw McGraw/Wally Gator/Snagglepuss: Daws Butler; **Boo-Boo/Ranger Smith:** Don Messick; **Buzzy/Little Cowgirl/Swamp Fox Girl/Girl/Swamp Fox Kid #2:** Susan Blu; **Bopper/Yapper/Real Ghost:** Frank Welker; **Bitsy:** Edan Gross; **Skinny Kid:** Josh Rodine; **Chubby Kid:** Dustin Diamond; **Leader Kid:** Scott Menville; **Trapper/Dad:** Bill Callaway; **Bandit Bear:** Allan Melvin; **Li'l Brother Bear:** Hamilton Camp; **Reporter/Cowboy Kid #1/Swamp Fox Kid:** Patrick Fraley; **Swamp Fox Boy/Cowboy Kid #2/Mom/Boy:** Tress MacNeille

🔘 YOGI, THE EASTER BEAR

In this first-run syndicated special, after swiping the sweets marked for the Jellystone Easter Jamboree, Yogi hatches a plan to pacify the enraged Ranger Smith and find the Easter Bunny in time for the big event. *A Hanna-Barbera Production. Color. Half-hour. Premiered: April 3, 1994. Syndicated. Rebroadcast on CAR: April 16, 1995 (Mr. Spim's Cartoon Theatre).*

Voices

Yogi Bear: Greg Burson; **Boo Boo/Ranger Smith:** Don Messick; **Paulie:** Charlie Adler; **Clarence:** Gregg Berger; **Easter Chicken:** Marsha Clark; **Ernest:** Jeff Doucette; **Commissioner:** Ed Gilbert; **Easter Bunny:** Rob Paulsen; **Mortimer/Grand Grizzly:** Jonathan Winters

🔘 YOU DON'T LOOK 40, CHARLIE BROWN

Television star Michele Lee hosts this hour-long retrospective covering 40 years in the life of cartoonist Charles Schulz and his blockheaded alter ago, Charlie Brown. The tribute features highlights from, appropriately, 40 television specials, including the first, *A Charlie Brown Christmas.* Special guests were B.B. King, David Benoit, Joe Williams, Desiree Goyette, Joey Scarbury, Bill Melendez and Cathy Guisewite. *A Lee Mendelson–Bill Melendez Production in association with Charles M. Schulz Creative Associates and United Feature Syndicate. Color. One hour. Premiered on CBS: February 2, 1990.*

🔘 YOU'RE A GOOD MAN, CHARLIE BROWN

This hour-long cartoon adaptation of the 1967 off-Broadway musical featuring the *Peanuts* characters charts the ups and downs of hapless Charlie Brown, for whom life is a constant source of frustration. The program marked Snoopy's speaking debut, with his voice supplied by Robert Tower, a member of the 1967 Los Angeles stage cast. *A Lee Mendelson–Bill Melendez Production in association with Charles M. Schulz Creative Associates and United Feature Syndicate. Color. Half-hour. Premiered on CBS: November 6, 1985.*

Voices

Charlie Brown: Brad Keston; **Charlie Brown (singing):** Kevin Brando; **Linus Van Pelt:** David Wagner; **Lucy Van Pelt:** Jessie Lee Smith; **Schroeder:** Jeremy Reinbolt; **Marcie:** Michael Dockery; **Sally Brown:** Tiffany Reinbolt; **Snoopy:** Robert Tower

🔘 YOU'RE A GOOD SPORT, CHARLIE BROWN

Charlie Brown enters a motocross race, but not until Lucy pulls the ol' place-kick trick on him. To win the race, Charlie finds himself up against some pretty stiff competition: Peppermint Patty and the Masked Marvel (Snoopy). In a separate subplot, Snoopy gets a "tennis lesson" from his pal Woodstock. *A Lee Mendelson–Bill Melendez Production in association with Charles M. Schulz Creative Associates and United Feature Syndicate. Color. Half-hour. Premiered on CBS: October 28, 1975. Rebroadcast on CBS: January 23, 1978.*

Voices

Charlie Brown: Duncan Watson; **Linus Van Pelt:** Liam Martin; **Lucy Van Pelt:** Melanie Kohn; **Peppermint Patty:** Stuart Brotman; **Marcie:** Jimmie Ahrens; **Sally Brown:** Gail M. Davis; **Schroeder:** Liam Martin; **Loretta:** Melanie Kohn; **Franklin/Kid:** Duncan Winston

🔘 YOU'RE IN LOVE, CHARLIE BROWN

For the first time, Charlie Brown is in love! The object of his affection is a little girl in his class. Gravel-voiced, tomboy Peppermint Patty makes her debut in the program, first trying to solve "Chuck's" baseball problems and what she thinks is "an affair d'amour" between Charlie and Lucy. *A Lee Mendelson–Bill Melendez Production in association with Charles M. Schulz Creative Associates and United Feature Syndicate. Color. Half-hour. Premiered on CBS: June 12, 1967. Rebroadcast on CBS: June 10, 1968; June 11, 1969; June 10, 1970; June 7, 1971; June 3, 1972.*

Voices

Charlie Brown: Peter Robbins; **Linus Van Pelt:** Christopher Shea; **Sally Brown:** Cathy Steinberg; **Lucy Van Pelt:** Sally Dryer-Barker; **Peppermint Patty:** Gail DeFaria; **Violet:** Anne Altieri

🔘 YOU'RE IN THE SUPER BOWL, CHARLIE BROWN

Coached by that ever-feisty Snoopy ("the Bear Bryant of the beagle and birdie world") who uses all the motivation he can muster to overcome their brawnier opponents,

Woodstock and his fine-feathered team of Grid Iron birds take on the Bison in a football free-for-all in this 1993 prime-time special, which bowed on NBC (the station that also carried the year's Super Bowl in Atlanta). *A Lee Mendelson–Bill Melendez Production in association with Charles Schulz Creative Associates and United Media. Color. Half-hour. Premiered on NBC: January 18, 1993.*

Voices

Charlie Brown: Jimmy Guardino; **Linus:** John Graas; **Lucy:** Molly Dunham; **Peppermint Patty:** Haley Peel; **Marcie:** Nicole Fisher; **Melody:** Crystal Kuns; **Announcer:** Steve Stoliar; **Snoopy/Woodstock:** Bill Melendez

ⓖ YOU'RE NOT ELECTED, CHARLIE BROWN

After taking a private poll, Lucy determines that Charlie Brown is not suited to run for student body president at school but finds that her insecure brother, Linus, is the perfect candidate. Linus has the election in the bag, but throws it all away during a debate with his opponent by mentioning "the Great Pumpkin," whereupon he is laughed out of the election. *A Lee Mendelson–Bill Melendez Production in association with Charles M. Schulz Creative Associates and United Feature Syndicate. Color. Half-hour. Premiered on CBS: October 29, 1972. Rebroadcast on CBS: October 15, 1973; September 23, 1976.*

Voices

Charlie Brown: Chad Webber; **Lucy Van Pelt:** Robin Kohn; **Linus Van Pelt:** Stephen Shea; **Sally Brown:** Hilary Momberger; **Russell:** Todd Barbee; **Violet:** Linda Ercoli; **Schroeder:** Brian Kazanjian; **Loud Child in Audience:** Brent McKay

Additional Voices

Danny Lettner, Joshua McGowan, Jay Robertson, David Zuckerman

ⓖ YOU'RE THE GREATEST, CHARLIE BROWN

With his school hosting the local Junior Olympics, Charlie Brown enters the decathalon event in hopes of helping his school win. Everyone has faith in him except the *Peanuts* gang. *A Lee Mendelson–Bill Melendez Production in association with Charles M. Schulz Creative Associates and United Feature Syndicate. Color. Half-hour. Premiered on CBS: March 19, 1979. Rebroadcast on CBS: March 5, 1980; March 20, 1981.*

Voices

Charlie Brown: Arrin Skelley; **Lucy Van Pelt/Girl:** Michelle Muller; **Marcie/Crowd:** Casey Carlson; **Linus Van Pelt/Crowd:** Daniel Anderson; **Fred Fabulous:** Tim Hall; **Peppermint Patty:** Patricia Patts; **Announcer:** Scott Beach; **Snoopy:** Bill Melendez

TELEVISION CARTOON SERIES

◉ AAAHH!!! REAL MONSTERS

From the producers of *The Simpsons* and *Rugrats* comes this half-hour series (whose working title was simply *Real Monsters*) about three funny-looking teenage monsters—Ickis, Krumm and Oblina—who learn to scare people at the subterranean Monster Academy (where their teacher is the charming, high-pitched voiced Gromble). Produced in 11-minute half episodes per half-hour, with occasional full half-hour episodes, the series began airing Saturday nights on Nickelodeon in 1994.

A Klasky-Csupo Production. Color. Half-hour. Premiered on NIK: October 29, 1994.

Voices
Ickis: Charlie Adler; **Krumm:** David Eccles; **Oblina:** Christine Cavanaugh; **The Gromble:** Gregg Berger; **Bradley:** Brett Alexander; **The Library Monster:** Beverly Archer; **Simon the Monster Hunter:** James Belushi; **Zimbo:** Tim Curry; **Dizzle:** Cynthia Mann; **Exposia:** Lisa Raggio; **Hairyette:** Marcia Strassman; **Slickis:** Billy Vera; **Dr. Buzz Kutt:** Edward Winter

◉ ABBOTT AND COSTELLO

The antics of one of Hollywood's most memorable comedy teams, Bud Abbott and Lou Costello, inspired this series of 156 five-minute animated misadventures. Bud Abbott, the fast-talking straightman in dire financial straits at the time of the filming, actually voiced his own character. Abbott passed away in 1974. His gullible partner, roly-poly Lou

Costello, who succumbed to a heart attack in 1959, was played by actor Stan Irwin.

A Hanna-Barbera Production for RKO-Jomar Productions. Color. Half-hour. Premiered: Fall 1967. Syndicated.

Voices
Bud Abbott: Himself; **Lou Costello:** Stan Irwin

◉ THE ABC SATURDAY SUPERSTAR MOVIE

This popular Saturday-morning series marked the birth of feature-length cartoons for television. Famous television and cartoon figures were adapted into hour-long stories, along with new concepts especially made for television. In all, 16 films were made during the first season, each costing approximately $300,000 to produce.

A number of popular television sitcoms of the 1960s and 1970s were spun off into feature-length cartoons during the series' first season. *The Brady Bunch*, which enjoyed a five-season run on ABC (1970–74), starred in *The Brady Kids on Mysterious Island* (Filmation), with cast members supplying their own voices. The movie, originally titled *Jungle Bungle*, was the "pilot" for the Saturday-morning cartoon series *The Brady Kids*, broadcast on ABC from 1972 to 1974. Other animated adaptations included: *Nanny and the Professor* (Fred Calvert Productions), based on the television comedy series starring Juliet Mills and Richard Long; *That Girl in Wonderland* (Rankin-Bass), featuring Marlo Thomas as the character Ann Marie (from the ABC sitcom *That Girl*) in this loosely based version of the classic children's story *Alice in Wonderland*; *Gidget Makes a Wrong Connection* (Hanna-Barbera Productions), an animated spin-off of the mid-1960s' teen comedy sensation starring Sally Field (with voice artist Kathy Gori assuming the role); and *Tabitha and Adam and the Clown Family* (Hanna-Barbera), featuring the teenage offspring from television's *Bewitched*.

Other live-action characters turned animated that first season were: *Lassie and the Spirit of Thunder Mountain* (Fred Calvert Productions), featuring television's most famous collie in her first animated adventure (Lassie later starred in the ABC Saturday-morning animated series *Lassie's Rescue Rangers*, from 1973 to 1975); *Mad, Mad, Mad Monsters* (Rankin-Bass), reuniting Count Dracula, the Wolfman, the Mummy and the Invisible Man in stop-motion animated form; and even baseball great Willie Mays in an animated retelling of the 1951 feature film *Angels in the Outfield*, entitled *Willie Mays and the Say-Hey Kid* (Rankin-Bass), in which Mays did his own voice.

Popular animated film and television stars were also cast in feature-length cartoons. Hanna-Barbera produced *Yogi's Ark Lark*, starring "everyone's favorite bear" Yogi Bear, in an animated rendition of the biblical tale of Noah's Ark. King Features brought back the spinach-eating Popeye the Sailor in *Popeye Meets the Man Who Hated Laughter*, while Warner Bros. and Filmation merged some of their most popular characters in *Daffy Duck and Porky Pig Meet the Groovie Goolies*. (The latter were introduced on 1970's *Sabrina and the Groovie Goolies* series on CBS.)

Other original made-for-television feature-length stories were presented during that first season: the two-part *Oliver Twist; and the Artful Dodger*, an animated re-creation of the classic Charles Dickens novel *Oliver Twist*; *Robin Hoodnik* (originally to be called *Cartoon Adventures of Robin Hood*), a colorful rendition of the classic character Robin Hood in animal form; *The Banana Splits in Hocus Pocus Park*, featuring the popular costumed live-action animals from TV's *The Banana Splits Adventure Hour*. (The last three shows were all produced by Hanna-Barbera.) Two other feature-length stories were *The Red Baron* (Rankin-Bass), the story of the legendary flying ace; and *Luvcast U.S.A.*

In 1973–74 the series returned for a second season (retitled *The New Saturday Superstar Movie*), featuring mostly reruns of shows from the first season and only three new cartoons: *Lost in Space*, based on the space-traveling Robinson family ("Danger! Danger!") from the 1960s' cult classic television show; *Nanny and the Professor and the Phantom Circus* and *The Mini-Munsters*, spotlighting Herman and the gang (from the cult television comedy classic *The Munsters*) in their first and only animated adventure.

Most series entries were produced by Hanna-Barbera Productions, then considered the leading producer of animated cartoons for television. Additional series entries were produced by Rankin-Bass Productions, Fred Calvert Pro-

ductions and King Features Productions. (Details for each production, except for *Luvcast U.S.A.*, are available in the Animated Television Specials section.)

A *Hanna-Barbera/Rankin-Bass/Fred Calvert/Filmation/Warner Brothers/King Features Production. Color. One hour. Premiered on ABC: September 9, 1972–August 31, 1974.*

⊚ ABC WEEKEND SPECIALS

Mostly a weekly offering of live-action dramas, this Saturday anthology series occasionally featured hour-long animated specials produced by several major studios. Some stories were one-shot productions, while others were told over the course of two or more broadcasts.

Series installments included the critically acclaimed *The Trouble with Miss Switch* (1980) and *Miss Switch to the Rescue* (1982), about a witch who tries to do good with her witchcraft, each two-part specials, and *Scruffy* (1980), the adventures of an orphaned puppy; all were produced by Ruby-Spears Productions.

Other popular specials included the three-part *Liberty and the Littles* (1986), in which the tiny, near-human Littles learn about liberty, based on John Peterson's popular children's book series and spun off from the ABC animated series *The Littles*, produced by DIC Enterprises. The *Cap'n O.G. Readmore* (Rick Reinert Pictures) series of specials about a literature-loving, articulate cat who discusses classic literature with members of his "Friday Night Book Club" also was popular and included *Cap'n O.G. Readmore's Jack and the Beanstalk* (1985), *Cap'n O.G. Readmore Meets Dr. Jekyll and Mr. Hyde* (1986), *Cap'n O.G. Readmore Meets Little Riding Hood* (1988) and *Cap'n O.G. Readmore's Puss in Boots* (1988). Additional half-hours were comprised of Marvel Productions' *The Monster Bed* (1989), about a young boy trapped in a world of monsters, and *P.J. Funnybunny: Lifestyles of the Funny and Famous* (1989), the first of three such specials produced by independent animator Marija Diletic Dail's Animation Cottage.

More half-hour specials followed between 1992 and 1997, including *The Kingdom Chums: Original Top Ten* (1992), an inspirational tale of three young kids who discover the original top 10 were the 10 Commandments; *The Legend of Lochnagar* (1993), a Scottish story written and narrated by Prince Charles of Wales; *The Magic Flute* (1994), adapted from the famous Mozart opera; *The Magic Paintbrush* (1993), a prime-time animated special originally broadcast on CBS, based on Robin Muller's book; *Jirimpimbira: An African Folktale* (1995), produced in celebration of Black History Month; and *The Magic Pearl* (1996), the story of a Chinese American brother and sister that originally premiered on ABC's quarterly *Kids Movie Matinee* series. (For each title, see the entries in Animated Television Specials section for further details.)

A *Hanna-Barbera/Ruby-Spears/Dave Edwards Ltd./DIC Entertainment/Film Roman/Greengrass/Huff-Douglas/Marvel*

Films/Rick Reinert Pictures/Mike Young Production. Color. One hour. Premiered on ABC: September 10, 1977.

ACE VENTURA: THE ANIMATED SERIES

Wacky pet detective Ace Ventura and his sidekick, Spike the monkey, tackle new capers in this half-hour cartoon series spinoff based on the box-office comedy hit movie starring comedian Jim Carrey. Carrey did not supply his voice for this Saturday-morning cartoon version, which began as a midseason replacement on CBS.

A Nelvana Entertainment Production in association with Morgan Creek Productions. Color. Half-hour. Premiered on CBS: January 20, 1996–August 30, 1997.

Voices
Ace Ventura: Michael Hall; **Spike:** Richard Binsley; **Shickadance:** Vince Corraza; **Aguado:** Al Waxman; **Emilio:** Bruce Tubbe; **Woodstock:** David Beatty

ACME RADIO HOUR

Described as "a radio show from another dimension," this weekly showcase, airing Sundays on the Cartoon Network, features the "hottest toons of the week," from old favorites to brand new *World Premiere Toons*, hosted by its decidedly dizzy deejay, longtime radio personality Don Kennedy and his lovely assistant.

A Cartoon Network Production. Color. One hour. Premiered on CAR: July 9, 1995.

THE ADDAMS FAMILY (1973)

Popular TV ghouls Gomez Addams, wife Morticia, bald Uncle Fester and zombie butler Lurch travel across the country with the rest of the family, telling hair-raising stories in a haunted wagon, complete with moat. The 16-episode series enjoyed a two-season run on NBC.

A Hanna-Barbera Production. Characters' copyrights owned by Charles Addams. Color. Half-hour. Premiered on NBC: September 8, 1973–August 30, 1975. Rebroadcast on CAR: June 1, 1996– (Saturdays).

Voices
Gomez Addams: Lennie Weinrib; **Morticia/Grandmamma:** Janet Waldo; **Uncle Fester:** Jackie Coogan; **Lurch:** Ted Cassidy; **Wednesday:** Cindy Henderson; **Pugsley:** Pat Harrington Jr.

THE ADDAMS FAMILY (1992)

Cartoonist Charles Addams's macabre characters live in the suburb of Happydale Heights, where their normal neighbors seem weird, in brand-new half-hour animated adventures

Time-honored stories including Greek mythology, European fairy tales, African folklore and many others illustrate different virtues for young Zach and Annie in the award-winning PBS cartoon series Adventures from the Book of Virtues. *© PorchLight Entertainment.*

inspired by the success of the 1991 live-action feature. John Astin, who portrayed Gomez in the original hit television series, reprised the character for the new series.

A Hanna-Barbera Production. Color. Half-hour. Premiered on ABC: September 12, 1992–January 7, 1995.

Voices
Gomez Addams: John Astin

ADVENTURES FROM THE BOOK OF VIRTUES

Positive topics using classic American stories, European fairy tales, African fables, biblical adventures, Greek mythology, Asian folktales and Native American legends were brought to life in this first-ever, half-hour prime-time animated series for PBS, based on William J. Bennett's bestseller, *The Book of Virtues*. The series was originally presented as a series of 10 prime-time specials and aired in hour-long blocks, first in September of 1996, then in February of 1997 (two half-hour episodes, back to back). (See Animated Television Specials section for details.) This was before the series entered its regular weekly run.

A Porchlight Entertainment/Fox Animation Studios Production in association with KCET/Hollywood. Color. Half-hour. Premiered on PBS: September 2, 1996 (as a series of specials).

Voices (main cast)
Plato: Kevin Richardson; **Ari:** Jim Cummings; **Aurora/Annie:** Kath Soucie; **Zach:** Pam Segall; **Socrates:** Frank Welker

◎ THE ADVENTURES OF BATMAN

In Gotham City, millionaire playboy Bruce Wayne and his youthful ward, Dick Grayson, battle the nefarious schemes of the Joker, the Penguin, the Riddler, the Catwoman, Mr. Freeze, Mad Hatter and Simon the Pieman in this half-hour action series spun off from 1968's *The Batman/Superman Hour* (see entry for information), which was broadcast on CBS.

A Filmation Associates Production in association with Ducovny Productions. Color. Half-hour. Premiered on CBS: September 13, 1969–September 6, 1970. Syndicated.

Voices
Bruce Wayne/Batman: Olan Soule; **Dick Grayson/Robin:** Casey Kasem; **Barbara Gordon/Batgirl:** Jane Webb; **Alfred Pennyworth, Wayne's butler:** Olan Soule

◎ THE ADVENTURES OF BATMAN AND ROBIN

The caped crusader and his loyal crimefighting partner battle their famous archenemies—the Riddler, the Joker, Two-Face, Catwoman and many others—in this relabeled Saturday morning (and later weekday afternoon) version of *Batman: The Animated Series*, which aired on the Fox Network beginning in 1994. (Complete voice credits are under *Batman: The Animated Series*.)

A Warner Bros. Television Animation Production. Color. Half-hour. Premiered on FOX: September 10, 1994–September 5, 1997.

◎ THE ADVENTURES OF BLINKY BILL

Based on a series of books written by Dorothy Wall, this half-hour series from famed Australian animator Yoram Gross follows the far-reaching adventures of a mischievous koala bear who relies on his imagination to help his furry friends Down Under rebuild their Australian Bush community after it's ruined by construction.

A Yoram Gross Film Studio Production. Color. Half-hour. Premiered: September 24, 1994. Syndicated.

Voices
Robyn Moore, Keith Scott

◎ THE ADVENTURES OF DON COYOTE AND SANCHO PANDA

Hanna-Barbera coproduced this first-run, half-hour animated series of calamitous 17th- and 18th-century adventures about a gangly coyote knight-errant and his paunchy panda sidekick who fight on the side of truth, justice and innocence (aided by Coyote's noble steed, Rosinante, and Sancho's dyed-in-in-the-horsehair cynic donkey, Dapple).

The series was first broadcast in Europe in 1989, based on Miguel Cervantes's original literary classic *Don Quixote*.

A Hanna-Barbera Production in association with RAI (Radiotelevisione Italiana Raiuno). Color. Half-Hour. Premiered: September 23, 1990 (The Fantastic World of the Hanna-Barbera). Rebroadcast on CAR: September 5, 1994. Syndicated.

Voices
Don Coyote/Dapple: Frank Welker; **Sancho Panda:** Don Messick; **Rosinante:** Brad Gilbert

◎ THE ADVENTURES OF GULLIVER

The tiny folks of Lilliput hold captive the giant, Gulliver, who saves the city and people from destruction. In return they help him find his missing father and buried treasure, and overcome the foul deeds of the evil Captain Leech in this animated adaptation of the Jonathan Swift tale.

A Hanna-Barbera Production. Color. Half-hour. Premiered on ABC: September 14, 1968–September 5, 1970.

Voices
Gary Gulliver: Jerry Dexter; **Thomas Gulliver/Captain Leech/King Pomp:** John Stephenson; **Flirtacia:** Jenny Tyler; **Eger/Glum:** Don Messick; **Tagg:** Herb Vigran; **Bunko:** Allan Melvin

◎ THE ADVENTURES OF HOPPITY HOOPER

Naive, lovable frog Hoppity Hooper (originally slated to be called Hippity Hooper, but that was deemed too similar to the name of Warner Bros.' own hopping kangaroo, Hippity Hopper) and associates, Professor Waldo Wigglesworth, a fast-thinking fox, and Fillmore, a dim witted but good-natured bear—travel across the country to explore get-rich schemes in this cartoon series created by Jay Ward, the father of such cartoon favorites as Rocky and Bullwinkle, Dudley Do-Right and Crusader Rabbit.

The comical trio was featured in two episodes of four-part cliffhanging adventures each week, along with episodes of three other components: "Fractured Fairytales" (repeated from *Rocky and His Friends*), which spoofed beloved fairy tales; "Mr. Know-It-All," with Bullwinkle Moose offering solutions to common everyday problems (first seen on *The Bullwinkle Show*); and "Commander McBragg," a boastful, bushy-browed retired naval commander who tells tall tales about his career, which premiered on *Tennessee Tuxedo and His Tales*. The program later contained reruns of "Peabody's Improbable History," hosted by intelligent beagle Peabody and his brainy adopted son, Sherman, who transport themselves back in time to visit historical events through the power of their WABAC machine.

In the fall of 1965, after the first 26 episodes aired on ABC, they were reedited and repackaged for syndication under the title of *Uncle Waldo*. With the network series still on the air, the syndicated version featured only two other recurring segments besides the Hoppity Hooper reruns: "Fractured Fairytales" and "Peabody's Improbable History," the latter repeated from *Rocky and His Friends*. (See series entry for further information.)

A *Hooper Production in association with Jay Ward Productions/Leonardo Television. Color. Half-hour. Premiered on ABC: September 12, 1964–September 2, 1967. Syndicated.*

Voices

Hoppity Hooper: Chris Allen; **Professor Waldo Wigglesworth:** Hans Conried; **Fillmore, the bear:** Bill Scott; **Narrator:** Paul Frees; **Narrator, "Fractured Fairytales":** Edward Everett Horton; **Commander McBragg:** Kenny Delmar; **Bullwinkle Moose:** Bill Scott

⊚ THE ADVENTURES OF HYPERMAN

Befriended by teenage genius Emma C. Squared, who helps him out in his weekly battles while teaching various science lessons along the way, Hyperman, an intergalactic secret agent superhero, along with his faithful dog, Studd Puppy, are assigned to stop bad-guy Entrobe (and his sidekick Kidd Chaos) from destroying Earth in this comedy/educational series that aired on CBS during the 1994–95 season.

A *Hyperion Animation/Illumina Studios/IBM Production. Premiered on CBS: October 14, 1995–August 10, 1996.*

Voices

Hyperman: Steve Mackall; **Entrobe:** Frank Welker; **Emma C. Squared:** Tamera Mowry; **Studd Puppy:** Kevin McDonald; **Kidd Chaos/Comptroller:** Maurice LaMarche

⊚ THE ADVENTURES OF JONNY QUEST

One of the most nostalgically popular animated television series of the 1960s, *The Adventures of Jonny Quest* was developed by artist Doug Wildey for Hanna-Barbera Productions. The 26-episode series—the first cartoon series ever to depict realistic human characters in an action adventure format—recounted the adventures of 11-year-old Jonny and his brilliant scientist father, Dr. Benton Quest (voiced by Don Messick in 20 of the series' original episodes). Accompanied by bodyguard-tutor Roger "Race" Bannon, a mysterious Indian boy named Hadji and fearless bulldog Bandit, they embark on a global expedition that becomes more fantastic with each stop. The series premiered on ABC in September of 1964 (the opening episode was "The Mystery of the Lizard Men") and, surprisingly, lasted only one full season. In 1967 the series was dusted off and rebroadcast on CBS for three full seasons, then again on NBC in 1972 and 1979 (the latter as part of *Godzilla and the Super 90*).

In 1986 Hanna-Barbera revived this animated classic and produced 13 all-new half-hour episodes, packaged for weekend syndication as part of *The Funtastic World of Hanna-Barbera* series. Of the original main cast, only Don Messick returned to voice Dr. Benton Quest and Bandit.

Both series were rebroadcast on The Cartoon Network beginning in October of 1992. The characters were again revived in all-new animated adventures in 1996 under the title of *The Real Adventures of Jonny Quest*. (See entry for details.) Preceding the series were two made-for-TV movies reintroducing the character to viewers: *Jonny's Golden Quest* (1993), produced exclusively for USA Network, and *Jonny Quest Vs. The Cyber Insects* (1995), which premiered on TNT.

A *Hanna-Barbera Production. Color. Half-hour. Premiered on ABC: September 18, 1964–September 9, 1965 (switched nights December 31, 1964). Rebroadcast on CBS: September 6, 1967–September 5, 1970. Rebroadcast on ABC: September 13, 1970–September 2, 1972; NBC: November 4, 1978– September 1, 1979 (as part of* Godzilla and the Super 90*): September 7, 1979–November 3, 1979; April 12, 1980– September 6, 1981. Rebroadcast on CAR: October 1, 1992– October 30, 1992 (weekdays); November 10, 1992–December 5, 1992 (weekdays); January 4, 1993–September 17, 1993 (weekdays); January 3, 1994–June 2, 1995; September 4, 1995–(weekdays, Saturdays). Premiere (new series): September 1986 (as part of* The Funtastic World of Hanna-Barbera*). Syndicated. Rebroadcast on CAR: November 2, 1992–November 9, 1992; December 6, 1992–January 3, 1993; January 3, 1994–June 2, 1995.*

Voices

Dr. Benton Quest: Don Messick, John Stephenson; **Jonny Quest:** Tim Matthieson, Scott Menville (1986); **Roger "Race" Bannon:** Mike Road, Sonny Granville Van Dusen (1986); **Hadji, Indian companion:** Danny Bravo, Rob Paulsen (1986); **Bandit, their dog:** Don Messick; **Dr. Zin/Others:** Vic Perrin; **Jezebel Jade:** Cathy Lewis

⊚ THE ADVENTURES OF LARIAT SAM

Written especially for *The Captain Kangaroo Show*, this preschooler series cast honest but friendly cowboy Lariat Sam and his poetry-reading horse, Tippytoes (known as the "Wonder Horse"), in 13 offbeat stories—presented in three parts— about the Old West. Sam's recurring nemesis: Badlands Meeney. The series was created by Robert Keeshan's company, Robert Keeshan Associates. (Keeshan is best known to viewers as Captain Kangaroo). The cartoons were later packaged for syndication.

A *CBS Terrytoons Productions. Black-and-white. Color. Five minutes. Half-hour. Premiered on CBS: September 10, 1962– August 27, 1965. Syndicated.*

Voices
Lariat Sam/Tippytoes, his horse: Dayton Allen

⊚ THE ADVENTURES OF POW POW

The stories of a young Indian boy (based on Indian folklore and related fables) were recounted in this limited-animated, 26-episode series first telecast on *Captain Kangaroo* in 1957. In 1958 the program was syndicated to local stations nationwide.

A Sam Singer Production. Black-and-white. Five minutes. Half-hour. Premiered on CBS: 1957. Syndicated: 1958.

⊚ THE ADVENTURES OF RAGGEDY ANN AND ANDY

Secretly coming to life in Marcella's playroom, Raggedy Ann and brother Andy and their friends—Raggedy Cat, Raggedy Dog, Grouchy Bear, the Camel with the Wrinkled Knees and others—are hurled into a world where anything is possible: dragons, perriwonks, fairies and even the presence of evil. Based on Johnny Gruelle's famed children's story, *Raggedy Ann and Andy.*

A CBS Animation Production. Color. Half-hour. Premiered on CBS: September 17, 1988–September 1, 1990.

Voices
Raggedy Ann: Christina Lange; **Raggedy Andy:** Josh Rodine; **Marcella:** Tracy Rowe; **Grouchy Bear:** Charlie Adler; **Raggedy Cat:** Kath Soucie; **Raggedy Dog:** Dana Hill; **Camel:** Ken Mars; **Sunny Bunny:** Katie Leigh

⊚ THE ADVENTURES OF SONIC THE HEDGEHOG

Programmed for daily syndication, this 65-episode companion series to the ABC network series, *Sonic the Hedgehog* followed the trials and tribulations of the popular video-game star as he tries to save the planet Mobrius from his favorite enemy, Dr. Robotnik. The series debuted five days before the premiere of the ABC series.

A DIC Enterprises Production in association with Sega of America, Inc. and Bohbot Entertainment. Color. Half-hour. Premiered: September 13, 1993. Syndicated.

Voices
Sonic the Hedgehog: Jaleel White; **Tails:** Christopher Welch; **Dr. Robotnik:** Long John Baldry; **Scratch:** Phil Hayes; **Grounder:** Gary Chalk

⊚ THE ADVENTURES OF TEDDY RUXPIN

Flying in a wonderous airship, Teddy Ruxpin, Newton Gimmick (an eccentric genius inventor) and Grubby (a valiant octopede) try to uncover the true purpose of a series of long-lost ancient crystals in half-hour adventures that bring them face to face with the evil overlords, M.A.V.O. (Monsters and Villains Organization), whose sole purpose is to rule the Land of Grundo. The series, based on the popular interactive toy of the mid-1980s, originally premiered as a five-part syndicated series in 1986. Sixty-five episodes were produced for daily syndication in 1987.

A DIC Enterprises Production. Color. Half-hour. Premiered: 1986 (five-part series); September 1987 (syndicated series). Syndicated.

Voices
Teddy Ruxpin: Phil Barron; **Gimmick:** John Stocker; **Grubby:** Wili Ryan; **Tweeg:** John Koensgen; **L. B. Prince Arin:** Robert Bauxthall; **Leota:** Holly Larocque; **Aruzia:** Abby Hagyard; **Wooly What's It:** Pierre Paquette

⊚ THE ADVENTURES OF THE GALAXY RANGERS

In 2086, to keep peace in the universe, the World Federation forms an organization called BETA (Bureau of Extra-Terrestrial Affairs), led by Commander Joseph Walsh, who heads a special team of crimefighters—Zachary Fox, Doc Hartford, Niko and Goose—to protect mankind from alien enemies in outer space.

A Gaylord Production in association with Transcom Media and ITF Enterprises. Color. Half-hour. Premiered: September 15, 1986. Syndicated.

Voices
THE GALAXY RANGERS: Zachary Fox: Jerry Orbach; **Doc Hartford:** Hubert Kelly; **Niko:** Laura Dean; **Goose:** Doug Preis

OTHERS: Commander Joseph Walsh/Lazarus Slade/Captain Kidd/Wildfire Cody/King Spartos: Earl Hammond; **Buzzwang:** Sandy Marshall; **Mogel the Space Sorcerer/The General/Nimrod/Jackie Subtract/Bubblehead the Memory Bird:** Doug Preis; **Queen of the Crown/The Kiwi Kids:** Corinne Orr; **Zozo/Squeegie/GV/Little Zach Foxx/Brappo:** Bob Bottone; **Waldo/Geezi the Pedulont/Q-Ball/Larry/Scarecrow/Kilbane/Crown Agent:** Henry Mandell; **Maya/Annie Oh/Mistwalker:** Maia Danzinger; **Macross:** Ray Owen; **Aliza Foxx/Jessica Foxx:** Laura Dean

⊚ THE ADVENTURES OF THE LITTLE KOALA

Roobear, a koala bear, experiences various adventures through which he learns the importance of life, parents and friends and the world around him. The 26-episode series made its American television debut on Nickelodeon in 1987, airing weekdays.

A *Cinar Films/Tohokushinsha Film Production. Color. Half-hour. Premiered on NIK: June 1, 1987–April 2, 1993.*

Voices
Roobear: Steven Bednarski; **Laura, his sister:** Morgan Hallett; **Papa, Roobear's father:** Walter Massey; **Mama, Roobear's mother:** Jane Woods; **Miss Lewis:** Bronwen Mantel; **Floppy:** Tim Webber; **Mimi:** Barbara Poggemiller; **Betty:** Cleo Paskal

⊚ THE ADVENTURES OF THE LITTLE PRINCE

Based on the tiny planet of B-612, the Little Prince, an extraordinarily small boy, travels to Earth and other planets, where he makes new friends and helps solve their problems in this series originally produced for French television in 1979, then syndicated in the United States in 1981 over ABC-owned and operated stations. Jameson Brewer, who scripted the Walt Disney classic *Fantasia,* wrote and produced the series.

A *Jambre/Gallerie International Films Production. Color. Half-hour. Premiered: September 1982. Syndicated. Rebroadcast on NIK: 1985.*

Voices
The Little Prince: Julie McWhirter Dees; **Swifty, the space bird:** Hal Smith

⊚ THE ADVENTURES OF T-REX

Five stand-up comic Tyrannosaurus brothers (Buck, Bubba, Bugsy, Bruno and Bernie) transform into the crimefighting superhero group "T-REX" and become heroes when they save Rep City from a sophisticated underground mob, headed by the sinister "Big Boss" Graves." This 52-episode series premiered in syndication in 1992.

A *Gunther-Wahl/Kitty Film Production. Color. Half hour. Premiered: September 1992. Syndicated.*

Voices
Kathleen Barr, Michael Beattie, Gary Chalk, Jennifer Chopping, Ian Corlett, Michael Dobson, Kevin Hayes, Phil Hayes, Janyce Jaud, Allesandro Juliani, Annabel Kershaw, Scott McNeil, Robert O. Smith, Venus Terzo, Dale Wilson

⊚ AEON FLUX

MTV premiered this cartoon spinoff of the network's cutting-edge anthology series *Liquid Television* four years after

An extraordinary small boy travels to Earth and other planets where he makes friends and helps solve their problems in the syndicated favorite The Adventures of the Little Prince. © *Jambre/Gallerie International Films*

its original network debut. The weekly half-hour series continued the exploits of the dangerously sexy, futuristic female "terror agent" (from Colossal Pictures' creator Peter Chung). Due to the unique graphic design and adult subject matter, a viewer disclaimer was required after the series was expanded to a regular half-hour format.

A *Colossal Pictures/MTV Production. Color. Half-hour. Premiered on MTV: August 1995.*

Voices
Aeon Flux: Denis Poirier; **Trevor Goodchild:** John Rafter Lee

⊚ ALF

That wonderful, wise-cracking alien Alf relives his pre-Earth days on the planet Melmac—in this 26-episode half-hour animated series, based on the hit NBC comedy series of the same name. Premiering on NBC in 1987, the series was so successful that it was expanded to 60 minutes in length during its second season run. Added to the show was a new weekly feature: "Alf Tales," offbeat retellings of classic fairy tales, which was spun off into its own series.

An Alien Production in association with DIC Enterprises and Saban Productions. Color. Half-hour. Premiered on NBC: September 26, 1987–September 21, 1989. Rebroadcast on FAM: 1990.

Voices

Alf: Paul Fusco; **Sgt. Staff/Cantfayl:** Len Carlson; **Flo:** Peggy Mahon; **Augie/Rhoda:** Pauline Gillis; **Stella:** Ellen-Ray Hennessey; **Skip:** Rob Cowan; **Larson Petty/Bob:** Thick Wilson; **Curtis:** Michael Fantini; **Harry:** Stephen McMulkin; **Sloop:** Dan Hennessey

◎ ALF TALES

Alf and friends star in irreverent versions of classic children's fairy tales—Robin Hood, Sleeping Beauty, Cinderella, Jack and the Beanstalk, among others—in 21 original adaptations originally broadcast on NBC's animated *Alf* series.

An Alien Production in association with DIC Enterprises. Color. Half-hour. Premiered on NBC: September 10, 1988–September 1990. Rebroadcast on FAM: 1990.

Voices

Alf: Paul Fusco; **Flo:** Peggy Mahon; **Augie/Rhoda:** Paulina Gillis; **Stella:** Ellen-Ray Hennessey; **Skip:** Rob Cowan; **Larson Petty/Bob:** Thick Wilson; **Sloop:** Dan Hennessey

◎ ALL DOGS GO TO HEAVEN

Lovable German shepherd Charlie B. Barkin and pal dachsund Itchy Itchiford are sent back to Earth as guardian angels to perform acts of goodness in this 20-episode half-hour syndicated series based on the animated feature film series, originally created by animator Don Bluth. Dom DeLuise, a cast member in both movies (as the voice of Itchy), and Charles Nelson Reilly (as Killer), who starred in the first *All Dogs Go to Heaven* (1989) movie, reprised their roles for the television series, as did Ernest Borgnine (Carface), Sheena Easton (Sasha) and Bebe Neuwirth (Annabelle), each of whom starred in the 1996 sequel.

An MGM Animation Production in association with Claster Television. Color. Half-hour. Premiered: September 21, 1996. Syndicated.

Voices

Charlie B. Barkin: Steven Weber; **Itchy:** Dom DeLuise; **Carface:** Ernest Borgnine; **Killer:** Charles Nelson Reilly; **Sasha:** Sheena Easton; **Annabelle/Belladonna:** Bebe Neuwirth

◎ ALL-NEW DENNIS THE MENACE

Six years after the successful debut of the first-run syndicated series *Dennis The Menace*, CBS commissioned this all-new, half-hour animated series starring the mischievous hellraiser from artist Hank Ketcham's long-running syndicated comic-strip. The character more closely mirrors the 1960s live-action sitcom role of child star Jay North.

A DIC Enterprises Production in association with General Mills. Color. Half-hour. Premiered on CBS: September 11, 1993–August 10, 1994.

Voices

Dennis Mitchell: Adam Wylie; **Mr. Wilson:** Greg Burson; **Henry Mitchell, Dennis's father/Ruff:** Dan Gilvezan; **Alice Mitchell, Dennis's mother:** Ana Mathias; **Mrs. Wilson:** June Foray; **Margaret/Peebee:** Jeannie Elias; **Joey:** Katie Leigh

◎ THE ALL-NEW EWOKS

The fuzzy little creatures of *Star Wars* fame appear in all-new adventures on the distant forest moon of Endor, led by young scout Wicket, in this new package of 21 episodes broadcast on ABC in 1986. The series ran for only one season.

A Lucasfilm Production in association with Nelvana Limited, Hanho Heung-Up and Mi-Hahn Productions. Color. Half-hour. Premiered on ABC: November 8, 1986–September 5, 1987.

Voices

Wicket: Denny Delk; **Teebo:** Jim Cranna; **Princess Kneesa:** Jeanne Reynolds; **Latara:** Sue Murphy; **Shodu:** Esther Scott; **Logray:** Rick Cimino

◎ THE ALL-NEW GUMBY

The famous "green man" returned in these all-new, first-run syndicated episodes produced by the character's creator, Art Clokey. The program intermixed episodes from the original cult series with new original stories.

Dal McKennon, the original voice of Gumby, trained several actors through his company, Dalmac Productions, to alternate as the character's voice in this series revival. Creator Art Clokey reprised the role of Pokey (he also voiced Prickle), while wife Gloria lent her vocal talent to the character, Goo.

Initially, the series premiered in 80 television markets nationwide and received airplay on stations in Australia and Europe.

A Clokey Production in association with Premavision. Color. Half-hour. Premiered: September 1988. Syndicated.

*Famous green man Gumby and pal Pokey from a promotional still for
The All-New Gumby series. © Premavision*

Voices
Gumby/Professor Cap: Dalmac Productions; **Pokey/
Prickle:** Art Clokey; **Goo:** Gloria Clokey

◎ THE ALL-NEW PINK PANTHER SHOW

The never-discouraged feline starred in this series of new
cartoons made for television, including cartoons of a new
character: Crazylegs Crane, a mixture of Red Skeleton's
Klem Kadiddlehopper and Edgar Bergen's Mortimer Snerd,
joined by his smarter son Crane Jr. and Dragonfly. The 1978
series lasted one season on ABC.

*A DePatie-Freleng Enterprises Production. Color. Half-
hour. Premiered on ABC: September 9, 1978–September 1,
1979.*

Voices
Crazylegs Crane: Larry D. Mann; **Crane Jr./Dragonfly:**
Frank Welker

◎ THE ALL-NEW POPEYE HOUR

In this third television series featuring the famed spinach-
gulping sailor, Popeye picks up where he left off, defending
his love for his girlfriend, Olive Oyl, by battling the bully-
ing, girl-stealing Bluto, in adventures that were less violent
than the theatrical cartoon shorts originally produced by
Max Fleischer.

Jack Mercer, the veteran salty voice of Popeye, wrote
many of the cartoon scripts for the show, which featured
several other familiar characters: hamburger-munching
Wimpy; Pappy, Popeye's father; and Popeye's four nephews.

The program contained three segments in the 1978–79
season: "The Adventures of Popeye," following the continuing exploits of Popeye and Bluto; "Dinky Dog," the misadventures of the world's largest dog; and "Popeye's Treasure
Hunt," tracing Popeye and Olive Oyl's search for buried

treasure, foiled by the ever-scheming Bluto. For the
1979–80 season, a fourth segment was added to the show:
"Popeye's Sports Parade," featuring Popeye in various sports
competitions. Thirty-second spots, known as "Popeye
Health and Safety Tips," were featured on the show during
each season.

*A Hanna-Barbera Production in association with King Fea-
tures Syndicate. Color. One hour. Premiered on CBS: September 9, 1978–September 5, 1981.*

Voices

POPEYE: Popeye: Jack Mercer; **Olive Oyl, his girl-
friend/Sea Hag:** Marilyn Schreffler; **Bluto, Popeye's
nemesis:** Allan Melvin; **Wimpy, Popeye's friend:** Daws
Butler

DINKY DOG: Dinky: Frank Welker; **Uncle Dudley,
Dinky's owner:** Frank Nelson; **Sandy, his niece:** Jackie
Joseph; **Monica, his niece:** Julie Bennett

◎ THE ALL-NEW POUND PUPPIES

In the fall of 1987, following the success of 1986's *Pound
Puppies*, ABC returned with 20 new episodes of this Saturday-morning favorite about adorable puppies who live in a
pound waiting to be adopted.

*A Hanna-Barbera Production. Color. Half-hour. Premiered
on ABC: September 26, 1987–September 3, 1988.*

Voices
Nose Marie: Ruth Buzzi; **Cooler:** Dan Gilvezan; **Holly:**
Ami Foster; **Katrina Stoneheart:** Pat Carroll; **Brattina
Stoneheart:** Adrienne Alexander; **Cat Gut/Nabbit:** Frank
Welker; **Bright Eyes:** Nancy Cartwright; **Millie Trueblood:**
June Lockhart; **Whopper:** B.J. Ward; **Howler:** Bobby
Morse

◎ THE ALL-NEW SCOOBY
AND SCRAPPY-DOO SHOW

Cowardly great Dane Scooby-Doo and his feisty pint-size
nephew Scrappy-Doo brave ghosts, goblins and ghouls to
crack a series of mysteries in all-new comedy adventures.
Daphne, who starred in the original Scooby-Doo cartoons,
rejoined the cast as a reporter for a teen magazine investigating mysteries. The series was broadcast in combination with
The Puppy's Further Adventures. (See entry for information.)

*A Hanna-Barbera Production. Color. Half-hour. Premiered
on ABC: September 10, 1983–September 1, 1984 (Puppy's
Further Adventures/The All-New Scooby and Scrappy-Doo
Show). Rebroadcast on CAR: November 22, 1994–December
9, 1994 (weekdays); December 19, 1994–December 20,
1994; August 16, 1997– (Saturdays, Sundays).*

Voices

Scooby-Doo/Scrappy-Doo: Don Messick; **Shaggy Rogers:** Casey Kasem; **Daphne Blake:** Heather North

☺ THE ALL-NEW SUPER FRIENDS HOUR

Even though Hanna-Barbera's first superheroes cartoon series failed, the amazing popularity of TV's *Wonder Woman* and *The Six Million Dollar Man* spurred network interest in reviving the old *Super Friends* program. This 1977 version was a huge ratings success for ABC. Four additional comic-book characters joined the Justice League in these adventures.

A Hanna-Barbera Production. Color. One hour. Premiered on ABC: September 10, 1977–September 2, 1978.

Voices

Narrators: Bill Woodson, Bob Lloyd; **Wonder Woman:** Shannon Farnon; **Superman:** Danny Dark; **Aquaman:** Norman Alden; **Batman:** Olan Soule; **Robin:** Casey Kasem; **Zan:** Mike Bell; **Jayna:** Liberty Williams

☺ ALVIN AND THE CHIPMUNKS

Alvin, Theodore, Simon and manager David Seville returned in this series of all-new adventures produced by Ross Bagdasarian's son, Ross Jr., who took over the family business in 1977. Adventures dealt with more contemporary and modern issues and introduced the Chipmunks' female companions, the Chipettes (Jeanette, Brittany and Eleanor). In 1988 the series was retitled *The Chipmunks*, and episodes from the series' first four seasons, including several new half-hour shows, were offered for syndication. The series was later rebroadcast on the Fox Network and Nickelodeon.

A Bagdasarian Production in association with DIC Enterprises. Color. Half-hour. Premiered on NBC: September 17, 1983–September 1, 1990. Rebroadcast on FOX: September 14, 1992–September 1993. Rebroadcast on NIK: October 3, 1994–June 30, 1995. Syndicated: 1988 (under the title The Chipmunks).

Voices

Alvin/Simon/David Seville: Ross Bagdasarian Jr.; **Theodore/ Jeanette/Brittany/Eleanor:** Janice Karman; **Miss Miller:** Dodie Goodman

☺ THE ALVIN SHOW

Popular recording stars the Chipmunks (Alvin, Theodore and Simon) and their writer-manager, David Seville, starred in this weekly half-hour cartoon series that premiered in prime-time opposite TV's *Wagon Train.* (In 1960 ABC had introduced two prime-time cartoon programs, *Bugs Bunny* and *The Flintstones*; CBS followed suit in 1961 with the Chipmunks.)

The series combined three Chipmunk episodes every week, two of which were sing-along segments built around their songs, and another sequence featuring "The Adventures of Clyde Crashcup," a wacky inventor who took credit for inventing everything, accompanied by his whispering, bald-domed assistant Leonardo.

Songwriter Ross Bagdasarian, who adopted the pseudonym David Seville in real life, created and supplied the voice of all four characters: Alvin, the egotistical, girl-loving leader; Theodore, the faithful, giggling follower; Simon, the intelligent, bespectacled bookworm always dragged into trouble by his brothers; and David Seville, the Chipmunks' peacemaking manager whose temper was known to explode following Alvin's excessive mischief ("Aaaalllviiinn!").

In 1958, after Bagdasarian first employed a recording technique of speeding up the voices (voices recorded at a slow speed then played back twice as fast) to record his first hit record, "Witch Doctor," the Chipmunks were born. Using this technique, he introduced the squirrely foursome that same year with their first record, "The Chipmunk Song," which sold more than 5 million copies within seven weeks of its release.

Bagdasarian deserves no credit for giving the group its name, however. His children, Carol, Ross Jr. and Adam, are the ones responsible for doing so. After hearing sound recordings, they told their father the voices sounded like chipmunks to them. (Until then he had planned to make the characters rabbits or butterflies.)

As for the characters' individual names, Bagdasarian reportedly named them after Liberty Records executives Al (Alvin) Bennett and Si (Simon) Warnoker and recording engineer Ted (Theodore) Keep. Liberty was the exclusive recording label for the Chipmunks songs.

The following season, CBS moved the 26-episode series to Saturday morning. It lasted in reruns before the network canceled the show in 1965. The series remained on television in syndication through the end of the summer of 1966, even though only one season of cartoons was made. NBC brought back the series in 1979 when the characters experienced a resurgence in popularity, appealing to a whole new generation of children. In the spring of 1994 the series resurfaced again, this time weekdays on Nickelodeon.

A Format Films/Bagdasarian Film Corp. Production. Color. Half-hour. Premiered on CBS: October 14, 1961–September 5, 1962. Rebroadcast on CBS: September 12, 1962–September 18, 1966. Rebroadcast on NBC: February 17, 1979–September 1, 1979 (broadcast under the title Alvin and the Chipmunks). Rebroadcast on NIK: March 7, 1994–December 31, 1995.

Voices

Alvin/Theordore/Simon/David Seville: Ross Bagdasarian; **Clyde Crashcup:** Shepard Menken

⊚ AMAZIN' ADVENTURES

Seven individual animated series initially made up this two-hour syndicated weekend cartoon block, first offered to independent television stations by television syndicator Bohbot Entertainment in 1992. The first block, known as "Amazin' Adventures I," featured animated series from producers DIC Entertainment and Saban Entertainment, namely *Double Dragon, King Arthur and the Knights of Justice, The Hurricanes, Mighty Max, Saban's Around the World in Eighty Dreams, Saban's Gulliver's Travels* and *The Wizard of Oz*, broadcast on more than 143 stations. Bohbot introduced a second block of weekend programming in 1994, dubbed "Amazin' Adventures II," which included DIC Entertainment's *Gadget Boy and Heather, Street Sharks* and *Ultraforce*, Ruby-Spears Productions' *Mega Man* and SKY-SURFER *Strike Force* and New Frontier Entertainment's *Princess Gwenevere and the Jewel Riders*.

A *DIC Enterprises/Saban Entertainment Production in association with Bohbot Entertainment. Color. Two hours. Syndicated: September 7, 1992.*

⊚ THE AMAZING CHAN AND THE CHAN CLAN

Fictional Chinese detective Charlie Chan, aided by his 10 children, combine comedy and adventure in crime investigations in 16 half-hour episodes that aired for two seasons on CBS. Chan was voiced by actor Keye Luke, who portrayed Charlie Chan's number-one son in several Charlie Chan films of the 1930s and later the wise monk Master Po on TV's *Kung Fu.*

A *Hanna-Barbera Production in association with Leisure Concepts, Incorporated. Color. Half-hour. Premiered on CBS: September 9, 1972–September 22, 1974. Rebroadcast on CAR: December 6, 1992; March 14, 1993 (part of Boomerang, 1972); April 10, 1994– (Sundays).*

Voices
Charlie Chan: Keye Luke; **Henry:** Bob Ito; **Stanley:** Stephen Wong, Lennie Weinrib; **Suzie:** Virginia Ann Lee, Cherylene Lee; **Alan:** Brian Tochi; **Anne:** Leslie Kumamota, Jodie Foster; **Tom:** Michael Takamoto, John Gunn; **Flip:** Jay Jay Jue, Gene Andrusco; **Nancy:** Beverly Kushida; **Mimi:** Leslie Juwai, Cherylene Lee; **Scooter:** Robin Toma, Michael Morgan; **Chu-Chu, the dog:** Don Messick

⊚ THE AMAZING THREE

First released in Japan as "W 3"—meaning "Wonder Three"—this Japanese-made series was edited and dubbed by Joe Oriolo Productions for syndication in America. It involved three outer-space aliens sent to Earth by the Galactic Congress to determine whether the "warlike planet" should be destroyed in order to preserve universal peace. In disguise, the trio—Bonnie (a rabbit), Ronnie (a horse) and Zero (a duck with a Beatle haircut)—are aided in their fight against evil by a young Earthling, Kenny Carter. Japanese cartoon legend Osamu Tezuka, the father of *Astro Boy*, created and produced the series.

A *Mushi/Erika Production. Color. Half-hour. Syndicated: September 1967.*

Voices
Jack Curtis, Jack Grimes, Corinne Orr

⊚ AMERICAN HEROES & LEGENDS

From the producer of *Storybook Classics* and *We All Have Tales,* never-before-told true folktale legends—from Annie Oakley to Moby Dick, celebrating the ethnic and regional diversity of the United States—were re-created in this 15-episode half-hour series that originally debuted on Showtime in October 1992. Stories were narrated by such big-name celebrities as Keith Carradine, Danny Glover, John Candy, Sissy Spacek, Nicholas Cage and others. A *Rabbit Ears Video Production. Color. Half-hour. Premiered on SHO: October 14, 1992.*

⊚ AMIGO AND FRIENDS

A friend from across the border, Spanish-speaking Amigo (actually a cartoon version of popular Mexican film comedian Cantiflas) takes children on educational and entertaining adventures, from pyramids, to Shakespeare, to electricity, to life on the moon in this half-hour syndicated series produced between 1980 and 1982. Hanna-Barbera Productions and Diamex S.A. coproduced the 52 episodes of this series, redubbed in English and syndicated in the United States under the title of *Amigo and Friends.* Later the original package was resyndicated under its original title, *Cantiflas,* in a bilingual format dubbed in both English and Spanish.

A *Televisa, S.A. Production in association with Hanna-Barbera Productions. Color. Half-hour. Premiered: 1980–82. Syndicated.*

Voices
Amigo: Don Messick; **Narrator:** John Stephenson

⊚ ANGRY BEAVERS

Riled and accident-prone Daggett and devil-may-care Norbert, a pair of dam-building brother beavers, try to make it in the big world in this half-hour series, from the producers of the *Edith Ann* specials, for Nickelodeon.

A Gunther-Wahl Production. Color. Half-hour. Premiered on NIK: October 7, 1996.

Voices
Norbert: Nick Bakay; **Daggett;** Richard Horwitz; **Barry the Bear:** John Garry; **Truckee:** Mark Klastorin; **Tree-flower:** Cynthia Mann; **Bing:** Victor Wilson; **Scientist #1:** Ed Winter

◎ ANIMANIA

In the tradition of MTV's "Liquid Television," this short-lived half-hour anthology series, also on MTV, mixed live-action and stop-motion animated films. The series opener featured "Slow Bob in the Lower Dimensions."

An MTV Production. Color. Half-hour. Premiered on MTV: December 21, 1991–December 28, 1991.

◎ ANIMANIACS

(SEE STEVEN SPIELBERG PRESENTS ANIMANIACS.)

◎ ANIMATED HERO CLASSICS

The stories of historical figures who made significant contributions to society—including Christopher Columbus, George Washington, Abraham Lincoln, Thomas Edison, Benjamin Franklin and Florence Nightingale—are told in this weekly half-hour HBO series, created by former Disney director Richard Rich, whose credits include *The Swan Princess* and *The Fox and the Hound.*

A Nest Entertainment/Rich Animation Studios Production. Color. Half-hour. Premiered on HBO: March 1, 1997.

◎ ANIMATION STATION

This two-hour cartoon program block was the successor to the Sci-Fi Channel's original program block, *Cartoon Quest.* Premiering in March of 1995, the newly titled assemblage featured many popular fantasy and science-fiction cartoon series as well as a few live-action shows, on a rotating basis, aired Mondays through Fridays and Sundays. Carryovers from the network's former program block included *The Bionic Six, Defenders of Earth, The Ewoks, Droids: The Adventures of R2D2 and C3PO, Fantastic Voyage, Flash Gordon, Galaxy High School, Journey to the Centre of the Earth, Lazer Patrol* (actually *Lazer Tag Academy*), *Little Shop, The New Adventures of Gigantor* and *Transformers.* New to this series, also in reruns, were the animated *Back to the Future* and *The Bionic Six.* Three live-action puppet shows were included in the mix: *Captain Scarlett and the Mysterons* (created by Gerry Anderson of *Thunderbirds* fame), *The Terrahawks* and an original 1960s' British fave, *Stingray,* plus Sid and Marty Krofft's prehistoric 1970's live-action series.

"Land of the Lost." In 1996 a Japanese cartoon series import, *Ronin Warriors,* also aired, albeit briefly.

Color. Two hours. Premiered on SCI: March 27, 1995–August 29, 1997.

◎ ANIMATOONS

Thirty-one well-known fairy tales and original children's stories made up this educational and entertaining half-hour series aimed at encouraging development of verbal skills, vocabulary and creative expression in children. Stories included "Peter and the Wolf," "Goldilocks and the Three Bears" and "Ali Baba and the Forty Thieves."

An Animatoons Production in association with Language Arts Films/Radio and Television Packagers. Color. Half-hour. Syndicated: 1967.

Voices
Narrator: Nancy Berg

◎ AQUAMAN

Born in Atlantis, Aquaman, who rules the Seven Seas and water creatures through telepathic brain waves, protects his kingdom from intruders and possible destruction in this half-hour series, which repeated episodes from the CBS Saturday-morning series *The Superman/Aquaman Hour.*" (See entry for details.) The series featured 36 seven-minute Aquaman adventures—one each week—and 18 "Guest Superheroes" adventures featuring such comic-book stars as the Teen Titans, Flash, Hawkman, Green Lantern and Atom.

A Filmation Associates Production. Color. Half-hour. Premiered on CBS: September 14, 1968–September 7, 1969.

Voices
Aquaman: Ted Knight; **Aqualad:** Jerry Dexter; **Mera:** Diana Maddox

◎ THE ARCHIE COMEDY HOUR

In response to first-season ratings success of *The Archie Show,* CBS brought back creator Bob Montana's *Archie* comic-book characters in this expanded hour-long version of *The Archie Show,* (see the latter for voice credits) featuring musical numbers and further adventures of the gang. Included was "Sabrina, the Teenage Witch," whose popularity later spawned a spin-off series of her own. The show lasted one season in this new format. In the fall of 1970, the show returned as the half-hour, *Archie's Funhouse.* (See entry for further details.)

A Filmation Associates Production. Color. One hour. Premiered on CBS: September 13, 1969–September 5, 1970.

◎ ARCHIE'S BANG-SHANG LALAPALOOZA SHOW

Archie and his regular cohorts, Jughead, Betty, Veronica, and Reggie, share the blame as they encounter new situations in the city of Riverdale in this shortened and retitled version of *The New Archie/Sabrina Hour*. The program also featured Sabrina, the Teenage Witch. Two new characters were added to the series: an Hispanic student named Carlos (voiced by José Flores) and Ophelia (voiced by Treva Frazce.) (See *The New Archie/Sabrina Hour* for voice credits.)

A *Fils-Cartoons/Filmation Associates Production. Color. Half-hour. Premiered on NBC: November 26, 1977–January 28, 1978.*

◎ ARCHIE'S FUNHOUSE FEATURING THE GIANT JUKE BOX

Assisted by a Giant Juke Box, Archie and the gang play favorite dance numbers and perform sketches in a music-comedy-variety show format that mixed live footage of a studio audience composed of children responding to the skits, jokes and other blackout comedy sketches (some written by former *Rowan and Martin's Laugh-In* writers Jack Mendelsohn and Jim Mulligan) in this half-hour retitled version of CBS's *The Archie Comedy Hour*. (See voice credits for *The Archie Show*.)

A *Filmation Associates Production. Color. Half-hour. Premiered on CBS: September 12, 1970–September 4, 1971.*

◎ THE ARCHIE SHOW

Perennial students Archie, Jughead, Betty, Reggie, Veronica and Sabrina cause scholastic havoc in the classrooms of Riverdale High School. Based on the *Archie* comic book by Bob Montana, the show comprised two 10-minute skits and a dance-of-the-week selection.

A *Filmation Associates Production. Color. Half-hour. Premiered on CBS: September 14, 1968–September 6, 1969.*

Voices
Archie Andrews: Dallas McKennon; **Jughead Jones:** Howard Morris; **Betty Cooper/Veronica Lodge:** Jane Webb; **Reggie Mantle:** John Erwin; **Sabrina, the Teenage Witch:** Jane Webb; **Big Moose/Pops/Dilton Doily/Hot Dog Jr.:** Howard Morris; **Big Ethel/Miss Grundy/Aunt Hilda/Aunt Zelda/Hagatha:** Jane Webb; **Hexter/Irwin/Dad:** John Erwin; **Hot Dog Jr./Chili Dog/Harvey/Spencer:** Don Messick; **Mr. Weatherbee/Salem/Mr. Andrews/Mr. Lodge/Coach Cleats/Chuck Clayton:** Dallas McKennon

◎ ARCHIE'S TV FUNNIES

Following *Archie's Funhouse*, CBS added this half-hour series to its 1971 fall Saturday-morning cartoon show lineup. This time Archie and his gang produce their own weekly television show featuring their favorite comic-strip stars, in addition to appearing in 16 new madcap adventures of their own.

Nine popular comic strips were adapted for the "TV Funnies" portion of the program: "Dick Tracy," "Broom Hilda," "Moon Mullins," "Emmy Lou," "The Gumps," "The Dropouts," "Smokey Stover," "Nancy and Sluggo" and the "Captain and the Kids." The Archie episodes were later repeated in 1973's *Everything's Archie* series. Meanwhile, "The Captain and the Kids," "Alley Oop," "Nancy and Sluggo" and "Broom Hilda" were resurrected on NBC's *Fabulous Funnies*.

A *Filmation Associates Production. Color. Half-hour. Premiered on CBS: September 11, 1971–September 1, 1973.*

Voices
Archie Andrews: Dallas McKennon; **Jughead Jones:** Howard Morris; **Betty Cooper:** Jane Webb; **Veronica Lodge:** Jane Webb; **Reggie Mantle:** John Erwin; **Big Moose:** Howard Morris; **Big Ethel:** Jane Webb; **Carlos:** Jose Flores; **Mr. Weatherbee:** Dallas McKennon; **Miss Grundy:** Jane Webb

TV FUNNIES: Captain Katzenjammer: Dallas McKennon; **Hans Katzenjammer:** Dallas McKennon; **Fritz Katzenjammer:** Howard Morris; **Kayo/Chief/Sam Ketchum/Pat Patton/B.O. Plenty:** Dallas McKennon; **Inspector/Sluggo/Sandy/Moon Mullins:** Howard Morris; **Mama/Miss Della/Fritzi Ritz/Grave Gertie:** Jane Webb; **Dick Tracey/Alvin/Smokey Stover:** John Erwin; **Nancy:** Jayne Hamil; **Broom Hilda/Sluggo/Oola:** June Foray; **King Guzzle:** Alan Oppenheimer; **Alley Oop:** Bob Holt

◎ AROUND THE WORLD IN 80 DAYS

Based on Jules Vernes's novel of the same name, millionaire Phileas Fogg embarks on a voyage around the world to prove himself worthy of marrying Lord Maze's niece, Belinda, and to win a wager made by Maze against his chances of fulfilling the trip. The 16-episode half-hour series lasted only one season NBC.

An *Air Programs International Production. Color. Half-hour. Premiered on NBC: September 9, 1972–September 1, 1973. Rebroadcast on CAR: December 6, 1992 (part of Boomerang, 1972). Syndicated.*

Voices
Phileas Fogg: Alistair Duncan; **Jean Passepartout:** Ross Higgins; **Mister Fix:** Max Obinstein

◎ ARTHUR

An eight-year-old boy with the head of an aardvark confronts and solves a series of big problems—from training a puppy to encountering a mean bully—in this half-hour series for PBS, based on a bedtime story by author Marc Brown. Premiering in October of 1996, the half-hour series became an instant hit with children, attracting more than 9 million viewers by March of 1997.

A Cinar Production in association with WGBH Educational Foundation. Color. Half-hour. Premiered on PBS: October 7, 1996.

Voices
Arthur: Michael Yarmush; **D.W.:** Michael Caloz; **Binky/ Dad:** Bruce Dinsmore; **Mom:** Sonja Ball; **Buster:** Danny Brochu; **Francine:** Jodie Resther; **Muffy:** Melissa Altro; **Brain:** Luke Reid

◎ ARTHUR AND THE SQUARE KNIGHTS OF THE ROUND TABLE

In Camelot King Arthur's legendary square knights "protect" the royal crown of England in this British-made half-hour cartoon sendup produced for syndication.

An Air Programs International Production. Color. Half-hour. Premiered: 1968. Syndicated.

◎ ASTRO BOY

Based on one of Japan's most popular comic-strip and cartoon characters—known as Tetsuan-Atoma (the Mighty Atom)—this pint-size android was brought to America by NBC Films, which syndicated the English-dubbed series in 1963. Like the original series, Astro Boy—his Americanized name—was a modern-looking crime fighter created by Dr. Boynton (Dr. Tenma in the Japanese version) of the Institute of Science, who sells the mechanical boy to a circus as a side-show attraction. Rescued by kindly Dr. Elefun (formerly Dr. Ochanomizu), Astro Boy uses his remarkable powers to defend justice and fight the galaxy's most fiendish villains: Phoenix Bird, Sphinx, Long Joan Floater, Crooked Fink, the Mist Men and Zero, the invisible. In all, 104 action-packed episodes were broadcast in the United States.

A Mushi Production. Black-and-white. Color. Half-hour. Premiered: September 7, 1963. Syndicated.

Voices
Astro Boy/Astro Girl: Billie Lou Watt; **Dr. Elefun:** Ray Owens

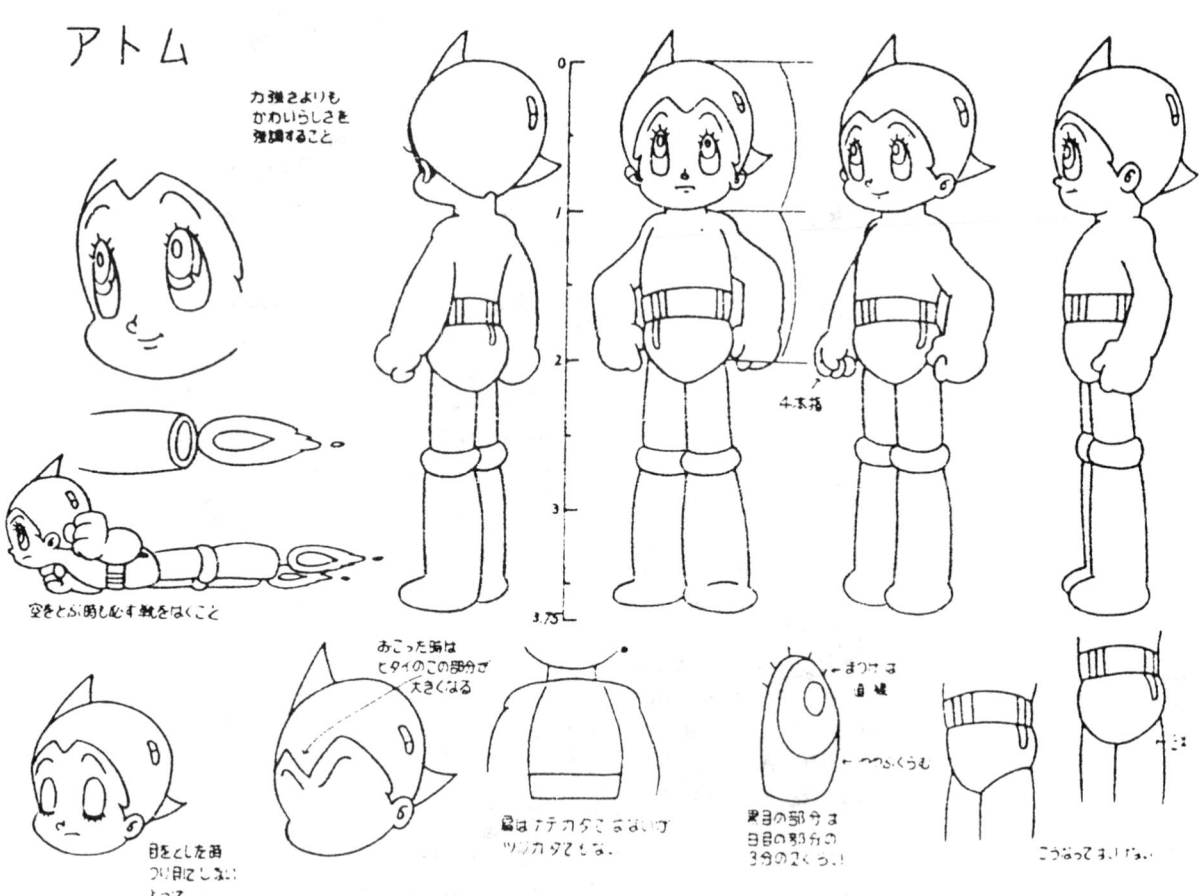

Model sheet for the popular Japanese cartoon series Astro Boy.

THE ASTRONUT SHOW

First seen in an episode of *Deputy Dawg* and in several theatrical cartoons from 1964 to 1965, Astronut, a friendly alien, was featured in his own half-hour series, combining theatrical cartoon shorts and new six-minute episodes, for syndication. In the late 1960s the program contained the following components: "Hashimoto," "Sidney" and "Luno, the Flying Horse," each stars of their own theatrical film series. In the 1970s Viacom, the program's distributor, reprogrammed the series with supporting episodes from other Terrytoons' favorites: "Sad Cat," "Possible Possum" and "James Hound."

A *Terrytoons Production. Color. Half-hour. Premiered: August 23, 1965. Syndicated.*

Voices

Astronut: Dayton Allen, Lionel Wilson, Bob McFadden; **Oscar Mild, his friend/Sad Cat/Gadmouse/Impressario/Letimore/Fenimore:** Bob McFadden; **Hashimoto/Hanako, his wife/Yuriko/Saburo:** John Myhers; **Sidney, the Elephant:** Lionel Wilson, Dayton Allen; **Stanley the Lion/Cleo the Giraffe/James Hound:** Dayton Allen; **Possible Possum/Billy Bear/Owlawishua Owl/Macon Mouse:** Lionel Wilson

THE ATOM ANT/SECRET SQUIRREL SHOW

Essentially two half-hour programs combined, "The Atom Ant/Secret Squirrel Show" was a one-hour block of cartoons comprised of two main stars and their supporting regulars. Each show featured Atom Ant, a superhero ant whose power was derived from a pair of atomized eyeglasses, in two six-minute action adventures, followed by one episode each of "The Hillbilly Bears," the rustic adventures of an idiotic backwoods family, and "Precious Pupp," a troublesome, snickering hound who fools his kindly millionaire owner (Granny Sweet) into thinking he's faithful, obedient and "precious."

Trench-coated Secret Squirrel, a parody of Ian Fleming's James Bond, was the series' other main star, featured in six-minute adventures. Along with his partner Morocco Mole (who sounded like Peter Lorre), the ever-clever squirrel encountered danger in assignments throughout the world. The cartoon components for this half of the show were "Squiddly Diddly," a star-struck squid who hoped to break into show business, and "Winsome Witch," a good-natured witch who used her evil sorcery to perform good deeds. Each appeared in one six-minute cartoon, sandwiched between the adventures of Secret Squirrel.

To promote the new Saturday-morning series, NBC broadcast a special hour-long preview on September 12, 1965, entitled *The World of Secret Squirrel and Atom Ant.*

A *Hanna-Barbera Production. Color. One hour. Premiered on NBC: October 2, 1965–December 31, 1966. Rebroadcast on NBC: September 9, 1967–September 7, 1968.*

Voices

Atom Ant: Howard Morris, Don Messick; **Secret Squirrel:** Mel Blanc; **Morocco Mole:** Paul Frees

THE HILLBILLY BEARS: Paw Rugg: Henry Corden; **Maw Rugg/Floral Rugg:** Jean VanderPyl; **Shag Rugg:** Don Messick

PRECIOUS PUPP: Precious Pupp: Don Messick; **Granny Sweet:** Janet Waldo

SQUIDDLY DIDDLY: Squiddly Diddly: Paul Frees; **Chief Winchley:** John Stephenson

WINSOME WITCH: Winsome Witch: Jean VanderPyl

THE ATOM ANT SHOW

Atomized glasses transform a peek-eyed ant into the world's mightiest insect superhero in this Hanna-Barbera favorite. Other cartoons featured were "Precious Pupp" and "Hillbilly Bears." The series was first broadcast in combination with the adventures of Secret Squirrel as *The Atom Ant/Secret Squirrel Show.* In January 1967 the two were separated and given their own shows, only to be rejoined again in the original format in September of that year. (See *The Atom Ant/Secret Squirrel Show* for details.)

A *Hanna-Barbera Production. Color. Half-hour. Premiered on NBC: January 7, 1967–September 2, 1967. Rebroadcast on CAR: September 20, 1993–December 31, 1993 (weekdays); March 5, 1994–September 3, 1994 (Saturdays); September 11, 1994–September 3, 1995 (Sundays, Wednesdays).*

ATTACK OF THE KILLER TOMATOES

Nefarious, angry (not mad) scientist Dr. Putrid T. Gangreen and his crazed, beach-hunk assistant Igor, armed with every variation on the common garden tomato that perverted science can produce, try to conquer the little town of San Zucchini and make the world safe for plant life. Opposing their evil designs are Chad Finletter, a dynamic teenage pizza-delivery boy; his uncle Wilbur; the lovely Tara (part girl/part tomato) and their "dog," F.T., in this weekly half-hour animated series based on the 1979 cult horror classic. John Astin, who played the character of Dr. Putrid T. Gangreen in the original full-length feature (and the sequel), reprised his character. The series was the first fully computer-generated cartoon series for the Fox Network.

A *Marvel/Four Square Production in association with Akom Productions/Fox Children's Productions. Color. Half-hour. Premiered on FOX: September 8, 1990–September 12, 1992. Rebroadcast on FOX: September 19, 1992–October 26, 1996.*

Voices

Dr. Putrid T. Gangreen: John Astin; **Chad:** Chris Guzek; **Tara:** Kath Soucie; **Whitley White:** Neil Ross; **Wilbur**

Finletter: Thom Bray; **Igor:** Cam Clarke; **F.T.:** S. Scott Bullock; **Zoltan:** Maurice LaMarche

◎ BABAR

That playful pachyderm who has delighted generations of young readers stars in this 65-episode half-hour series broadcast on HBO following its original debut on Canada's CBC-TV. Flashbacks depict the mythical world of Babar, recounting personal conflicts that arise when, as a little boy, he tries to juggle growing up along with handling grown-up responsibilities. Laurent de Brunoff, the son of Babar's creator, Jean de Brunoff, authorized the series, which won an Ace Award (1989) for outstanding programming achievement.

A Nelvana Production in association with The Clifford Ross Company and the CBC. Color. Half-hour. Premiered on HBO: April 9, 1989–September 1993. Rebroadcast on FAM: September 12, 1993–December 23, 1994.

Voices
Adult Babar: Gordon Pinsent; **Young Babar:** Gavin Magrath; **Queen Celeste:** Dawn Greehaigh; **Young Celeste:** Tara Charendoff; **Pompadour:** Stephen Ouimette; **Cornelius:** Chris Wiggins; **Basil:** John Stocker; **The Old Lady:** Elizabeth Hanna; **Rataxes:** Alan Stewart-Coates; **Lady Rataxes:** Corinne Koslo; **Lisa Yamanaka:** Flora; **Pom:** Bobby Becker; **Alexander:** Amos Crawford

◎ THE BABY HUEY SHOW

The daffy, diapered, 250-pound baby duckling with the strength of Superman made famous in a string of 1950s Paramount theatrical cartoons (again voiced by Syd Raymond), returns in 13 all-new syndicated adventures, packaged with classic Harvey cartoons, including Casper the Friendly Ghost, Buzzy the Crow, Herman and Katnip and Little Audrey.

A Harvey Entertainment Production in association with Claster Television. Color. Half-hour. Premiered: September 17, 1994. Syndicated.

Voice
Baby Huey: Syd Raymond

◎ BACK TO THE FUTURE

Marty McFly, the time-traveling teenager from the highly successful *Back to the Future* movie trilogy series (played by Michael J. Fox), embarks on all-new adventures in this animated spinoff. Only three stars from the *Back to the Future* films reprised their roles for the series: Christopher Lloyd as Doc, the eccentric inventor (who appeared in live-action educational wraparounds); Thomas F. Wilson as Biff, the peabrained bully who gives Marty trouble; and Mary Steenburgen, back as Clara, Doc's wife. The series was later rebroadcast on the Sci-Fi Channel.

An Amblin/Wang Film Production. Color. Half-hour. Premiered on CBS: September 4, 1991–August 14, 1993. Rebroadcast on SCI: October 1, 1994–June 28, 1996.

Cast (live action)
Doc: Christopher Lloyd; **The Science Guy:** Bill Nye

Voices
Doc: Dan Castellaneta; **Marty:** David Kaufman; **Biff:** Thomas F. Wilson; **Jules:** Josh Weiner; **Verne:** Troy Davidson; **Einstein:** Danny Mann; **Clara:** Mary Steenburgen

◎ B.A.D. (BUREAU OF ALIEN DECTECTORS)

When aliens invade Earth, a special resistance task force of seasoned military professionals and townspeople— including two determined teenagers, Zach Trainer and Amanda Burke—seek to protect the world from supernatural encounters in this 13-episode action/adventure series, for UPN.

A Saban Entertainment Production. Color. Half-hour. Premiered on UPN: September 8, 1996.

◎ BAGGY PANTS AND NITWITS

Friz Freleng, who created the pantominic Pink Panther, co-produced this half-hour Saturday-morning series with partner David H. DePatie, which premiered on NBC and lasted one season. Featured were: "Baggy Pants," the adventures of a Chaplinesque cat in silent comedy routines, and "The Nitwits," the misadventures of Tyrone and Gladys (characters created by comedians Arte Johnson and Ruth Buzzi on TV's *Rowan and Martin's Laugh-In* and reprised by them for this series), a comic pair of crimefighting superheroes.

A DePatie-Freleng Enterprises Production. Color. Half-hour. Premiered on NBC: September 10, 1977–October 28, 1978.

Voices
Tyrone: Arte Johnson; **Gladys, his wife:** Ruth Buzzi

◎ BAILEY'S COMETS

Comet members Barnaby, Bunny, Wheelie, Sarge and Pudge skate against 17 roller-derby teams in a continuing race around the world in search of $1 million in buried treasure, told in two 10-minute adventures each week. Created by Joe Ruby and Ken Spears, the series lasted four months into the first Saturday-morning season. It was shifted to Sunday mornings, then canceled.

A DePatie-Freleng Enterprises Production. Color. Half-hour. Premiered on CBS: September 9, 1973–August 31, 1975.

Voices
Barnaby Bailey: Carl Esser; **Pudge:** Frank Welker; **Wheelie:** Jim Begg; **Candy:** Karen Smith; **Bunny:** Sarah Kennedy; **Sarge:** Kathi Gori; **Dude:** Robert Holt; **Dooter Roo:** Daws Butler; **Gabby/Henry Jekyll-Hyde:** Don Messick

BANANAMAN
After consuming his daily ration of bananas, unassuming, mild-mannered Eric Wimp becomes the unstoppable crime-fighting superhero Bananaman in this British-produced half-hour animated series based on a character created for Britain's *Nutty Comics* in 1980. The series debuted in the United States on Nickelodeon.

A 101 Production. Color. Half-hour. Premiered on NIK: October 7, 1985–August 31, 1987.

Voices
Tim Brooke-Taylor, Graeme Garden, Bill Oddie

THE BANANA SPLITS ADVENTURE HOUR
Live actors in animal suits—known as the Banana Splits (Fleegle, Drooper, Bingo and Snorky)—hosted this hour-long format composed of their own misadventures, a live-action adventure series "Danger Island," and four cartoon segments: "The Three Musketeers," "The Arabian Knights," "Hillbilly Bears" and "The Micro Venture." The program marked Hanna-Barbera's first live-action/animation show for television. (For voice credits to the "Hillbilly Bears," see *The Atom Ant/Secret Squirrel Show*.)

A Hanna-Barbera Production. Color. One hour. Premiered on NBC: September 7, 1968–September 5, 1970. Rebroadcast on CAR: September 20, 1993–April 29, 1994 (weekdays); December 5, 1994–June 2, 1995 (weekdays); June 5, 1995–September 1, 1995 (part of hour-long block with The Cattanooga Cats).

Voices
Fleegle, the dog: Paul Winchell; **Drooper, the lion:** Allan Melvin; **Bingo, the gorilla:** Daws Butler; **Snorky, the elephant:** Don Messick

THE THREE MUSKETEERS: D'Artagnan: Bruce Watson; **Porthos:** Barney Phillips; **Aramis:** Don Messick; **Athos:** Jonathan Harris; **Toulie*:** Teddy Eccles; The Queen/Lady Constance: Julie Bennett

THE ARABIAN KNIGHTS: Bez: Henry Corden; **Evil Vangore:** Paul Frees; **Raseem:** Frank Gerstle; **Princess Nida:**

*The character Toulie was misspelled as "Tooly" in episode titles of this series.

Shari Lewis; **Prince Turhan:** Jay North; **Fariik:** John Stephenson

THE MICRO VENTURE: Professor Carter: Don Messick; **Jill Carter:** Patsy Garrett; **Mike Carter:** Tommy Cook

DANGER ISLAND: Professor Irwin Hayden: Frank Aletter; **Leslie Hayden:** Ronnie Troup; **Link Simmons:** Michael Vincent; **Morgan, the castaway:** Rockne Tarkington; **Chongo:** Kahana; **Mu-Tan:** Victor Eberg; **Chu:** Rodrigo Arrendondo

BARBAPAPA
Reminiscent of *The Smurfs*, this Netherlands-produced, half-hour series, following the adventures of a family of troll-like creatures known as the Barbapapas, was offered in syndication in 1977 but was not broadcast in the United States until 1981, when the series was picked up by LBS Communications, a U.S. television syndicator that earlier had syndicated another Dutch import, *Dr. Snuggles*.

A Polyscope (Netherlands)/LBS Communications Production. Color. Half-hour. Premiere: 1981. Syndicated.

Voices
Storyteller: Allen Swift

BARKER BILL'S CARTOON SHOW
This first network weekday cartoon series served as a daily showcase for the vintage black-and-white films from the Terrytoons library. Sponsored by Post Sugar Jets, the 15-minute cartoon show was seen twice a week, with only the picture of the program's host seen on camera. An off-camera announcer provided the introductions of the animated films. Terrytoons characters featured on the show included Farmer Al Falfa, Kiko the Kangaroo, Puddy the Pup and others. In 1956 *Barker Bill's Cartoon Show* ended and was replaced by the syndicated *Terry Toons Club* (later retitled *Terry Toons Circus*), hosted by Claude Kirchner on WOR-TV, New York.

A Terrytoons Production. Black-and-white. Fifteen minutes. Premiered on CBS: November 18, 1953–November 25, 1956.

THE BARKLEYS
An outspoken, opinionated canine bus driver, Arnie Barkley (copied after TV's Archie Bunker) clashes with his progressive family over timeworn socially related topics in this half-hour Saturday-morning series inspired by the success of the CBS sitcom, *All in the Family*. The series debuted on rival network NBC, with 13 original episodes. It lasted two seasons.

A DePatie-Freleng Enterprises Production. Color. Half-hour. Premiered on NBC: September 9, 1972–September 1, 1973.

Voices
Arnie Barkley: Henry Corden; **Agnes, his wife:** Joan Gerber; **Terri, Barkley's daughter:** Julie McWhirter; **Chester, the eldest son:** Steve Lewis; **Roger, the youngest son:** Gene Andrusco

◉ BARNYARD COMMANDOS
Planned as a regular series, this short-lived, four-episode cartoon miniseries featured the ongoing battle between two fiercely competitive animal armies: the pigs (whose code name was P.O.R.K.S.: Platoon of Rebel Killers) versus the sheep (known as the R.A.M.S.: Rebel Army of Military Sheep) in this *Teenage Mutant Ninja Turtles* knock-off from the same producers. The series premiered in first-run syndication on Labor Day weekend of 1990.

A Murikami-Wolf-Swenson Production in association with those Characters From Cleveland and Sachs-Finley. Color. Half-hour. Syndicated: September 4, 1990–September 7, 1990.

Voices
Scott Bullock, Thom Bray, Pat Fraley, Paul Kreppel, John Mariano, Bob Ridgely, Lennie Weinrib, Danny Wells

◉ BATFINK
Called into action on a private hotline by the Chief of Police, this pointy-eared crimefighter with wings of steel and his Super Sonic Sonar foils ruthless criminals, mobsters and all-around bad guys with the help of his Japanese assistant Karate in this animated parody of comic-book superhero Batman. The 100-episode series, consisting of 5 five-minute cartoons per each half-hour program, was created by former Fleischer animator Hal Seeger, who originated TV's *Milton the Monster*.

A Hal Seeger Production. Color. Half-hour. Premiered: Fall 1967. Syndicated.

Voices
Batfink: Frank Buxton; **Karate:** Len Maxwell

◉ BATMAN AND THE SUPER SEVEN
NBC broadcast this hour-long compendium of previous episodes of Filmation's *The New Adventures of Batman*, originally aired on CBS in 1977, and four components ("Isis and the Freedom Force," "Microwoman and Super Stretch," "Web Woman" and "Manta and Moray") first broadcast on the 1978 CBS series *Tarzan and the Super Seven*. (See *The New Adventures of Batman* and *Tarzan and the Super Seven* for details and voice credits.)

A Filmation Associates Production. Color. One hour. Premiered on NBC: September 27, 1980–September 5, 1981.

◉ THE BATMAN/SUPERMAN HOUR
Well-known comic-book heroes Superman and Batman appear in separate segments of this Saturday-morning series. Three action-filled Superman episodes, repeated from *The New Adventures of Superman* (1966–1967), were packaged with one new 12-minute adventure of Batman and Robin (17 brand-new cartoons were produced exclusively for the program) on each half-hour broadcast. (Episodes of the latter were rebroadcast as part of *The Adventures of Batman.*)

A Filmation Associates Production. Color. One hour. Premiered on CBS: September 14, 1968–September 6, 1969.

Voices
Clark Kent/Superman: Bud Collyer; **Lois Lane:** Joan Alexander; **Narrator:** Jackson Beck; **Bruce Wayne/Batman:** Olan Soule; **Dick Grayson/Robin:** Casey Kasem; **Alfred Pennyworth:** Olan Soule

◉ THE BATMAN/TARZAN ADVENTURE HOUR
This hour-long fantasy/action series combined new adventures of famed caped crusaders Batman and Robin from 1977's *The New Adventures of Batman and Robin* and eight new episodes of Tarzan, mixed with reruns from his half-hour series, *Tarzan, Lord of the Jungle*.

A Filmation Associates Production. Color. One hour. Premiered on CBS: September 10, 1977–September 2, 1978.

Voices
Tarzan: Robert Ridgely; **Batman:** Adam West; **Robin:** Burt Ward; **Bat-Mite:** Lennie Weinrib

◉ BATMAN: THE ANIMATED SERIES
DC Comics caped-crusader Batman, whose alter ego is millionaire playboy Bruce Wayne, continues his mission to squelch evildoers of Gotham City, joined by his crimebusting counterparts Robin (alias Dick Grayson) and Batgirl (alias Barbara Gordon), in this dark and often humorous version of the classic comic-book superhero. The 85-episode half-hour series debuted on the Fox Network with a special Sunday-night premiere in September 1992, before airing the following day in its Monday-through-Friday weekday afternoon slot. The series was the number-one-rated afternoon show in its time slot.

In an effort to boost ratings of its Saturday-morning lineup, Fox simultaneously aired episodes of the series on Saturdays and, in December of 1992, for five months on Sunday nights, opposite CBS's *60 Minutes*. The series itself earned two Emmy nominations for Outstanding Animated Program, winning the award in 1993.

During the 1994–95 season on Fox, the show was retitled *The Adventures of Batman and Robin*, featuring new episodes, plus previously aired ones from *Batman: The Ani-*

mated *Series.* In 1997 the characters jumped to the WB Network to costar in *The New Batman/Superman Adventures.*

Inspired by the success of the television show, Warner Bros. produced a feature-length movie, *Batman: Mask of the Phantasm,* which was released to movie theaters in 1993. The film originally was produced as a direct-to-video production. A sequel, *Batman: Sub-Zero,* was released direct to video in 1998.

A Warner Bros. Television Production. Color. Half-hour. Premiered on FOX September 6, 1992 (Sunday-night premiere); September 7, 1992–September 10, 1993; September 13, 1993–September 2, 1994.

Voices
Batman/Bruce Wayne: Kevin Conroy; **Batgirl/Barbara Gordon:** Melissa Gilbert; **Alfred Pennyworth:** Clive Revill, Efrem Zimbalist Jr.; **Robin/Dick Grayson:** Loren Lester; **Mayor Hamilton:** Lloyd Bochner; **Commissioner Jim Gordon:** Bob Hastings; **Detective Harvey Bullock/Harry Fox:** Bobby Costanzo; **Dr. Leslie Thompkins:** Diana Muldaur; **Summer Gleason:** Mari Devon; **Lucius Fox:** Brock Peters; **The Joker/Other Villains:** Mark Hamill; **Catwoman/Selena Kyle:** Adrienne Barbeau; **The Penguin/Oswald Cobblepot:** Paul Williams; **The Mad Hatter:** Roddy McDowall; **Mr. Freeze:** Michael Ansara; **The Riddler:** John Glover; **District Attorney Dent/Two Face:** Richard Moll; **Poison Ivy/Pamela Isley:** Diane Pershing

BATTLE OF THE PLANETS

G-Force, a superhuman watchdog squad—Jason, Tiny, Princess and Keyop—commanded by their daring leader, Mark Venture, defend Earth's galaxy from the ever-villainous Zoltar, the ruler of the dying planet Spectra, who aims to conquer the galaxy in this futuristic space-age adventure series. The first major Japanese import hit since 1967's *Speed Racer,* the program was produced by Tatsunko Productions, which also produced the latter. First televised in Japan from 1972 to 1974 under the title *Gatchamans,* the program was retitled and dubbed by producer Sandy Frank, who acquired the property for syndication in the United States. Eighty-five episodes (out of 100 episodes originally produced) were syndicated to independent television stations in 1978. Following its American premiere, the series was rebroadcast on WTBS as G-Force.

A Tasunko Production. Color. Half-hour. Syndicated: October 1978.

Voices
7-Zark-7/Keyop: Alan Young; **Zoltar:** Keye Luke; **Mark Venture:** Casey Kasem; **Princess:** Janet Waldo; **Jason:** Ronnie Schell; **Tiny/Dr. Anderson:** Alan Dinehart

BATTLETECH

Far into the future, Major Adam Steiner and his team of his high-tech, freedom-fighting warriors battle genetically engineered soldiers (led by the ruthless Star Colonel, Nikolai Malthius), who have invaded Earth for no good purpose in this computer-generated half-hour cartoon series adaptation of the popular virtual reality and role-playing game.

A Saban Entertainment Production. Color. Half-hour. Premiered: September 12, 1994. Syndicated.

THE BEAGLES

Canine rock-and-roll duo, Stringer and Tubby (called "The Beagles") croon their way in and out of trouble in this timely cartoon parody of Liverpool's Fab Four, The Beatles. Featuring five-minute serialized adventures, the program was produced by the creators of TV's *Underdog* and *Tennessee Tuxedo.*

A Total Television Production. Color. Half-hour. Premiered on CBS: September 10, 1966–September 2, 1967. Rebroadcast on ABC: September 9, 1967–September 7, 1968. Voices unknown.

Major Adam Steiner and his freedom fighters battle genetically engineered soldiers to save their families, who live on a distant planet, in the state-of-the-art, computer-animated series Battletech. *© Saban Entertainment*

BEANY AND CECIL (1962)

Created by Bob Clampett, formerly an animator for Warner Bros. the high-seas adventures of Cecil (the seasick serpent) and his friends Beany Boy and Captain Huffenpuff (Beany's uncle) began as a daily 15-minute puppet show first broadcast in 1949 on Los Angeles television station KTLA Channel 5. The show became so popular locally that Paramount Television picked up the series and offered it nationwide in 1950. It won three Emmy Awards during its run.

The puppet series inspired a short-lived cartoon series produced in 1959 by Elliot Hyman of Associated Artists Productions (the films were distributed to foreign countries only, including Australia, Canada and Europe, by Associated Artists' parent company, United Artists) and ultimately a weekly animated series that debuted on ABC in 1962. Sponsored by Mattel Toy Company, the show was first billed as *Matty's Funnies with Beany and Cecil.* (After three months the program's title was appropriately shortened to *Beany and Cecil.*) Each week, sailing on the *Leakin' Lena,* Beany and company encountered a host of unusual characters, such as Homer the Baseball Playing Octupuss, Careless the Mexican Hareless, Tear-a-Long the Dotted Lion, the Terrible Three-Headed Threep and the most dastardly Dishonest John ("Nya-hah-hah!"), a series regular, in 78 high-sea adventures (including the five theatrically produced cartoon shorts, such as "Beany and Cecil Meet Billy the Squid").

The cartoons became a particular favorite of many adults during its long run, including such surprising notables as Lionel Barrymore, Jimmy Stewart, Albert Einstein and Joan Crawford. (Groucho Marx, who was a fan of the puppet version, once told Clampett that "Time for Beany" is the only kid's show adult enough for my daughter Melinda to watch.")

Clampett admittedly drew from various influences to create each character. Captain Huffenpuff was based on a Baron Munchausen–type teller of tall tales. (Originally Clampett considered naming him Captain Hornblower.) Cecil was inspired out of a 1920s' silent feature Clampett remembered as a child called *Lost World,* featuring prehistoric dinosaurs. Beany was reminiscent of the precocious Charlie McCarthy, one of Clampett's personal favorites. And Dishonest John was patterned, in part, after one of Clampett's previous bosses at Warner Bros. whom he and his fellow animators affectionately called "Dirty Dalton."

Jim MacGeorge lent his voice for Beany and Captain Huffenpuff, while Irv Shoemaker spoke for Cecil and Dishonest John. (Stan Freberg and Daws Butler did the voices during the first few years of the puppet show.)

Like many cartoons from this era, Beany and Cecil ran into censorship problems with the network. "It was rather ridiculous what the network would censor," Clampett once recalled. "In one cartoon, I had Dishonest John packaging the moon as cheese and bringing it back to Earth to sell it. On the package, I had the word 'Krafty' and ABC was afraid the Kraft Cheese Company would sue them."

One element of the series Clampett and his peers initially underestimated was the popularity of the trademark propellor cap worn by Beany. Prior to his death in 1984, Clampett recalled: "The funny thing about that is, when I first put the propellor on Beany's cap nearly everyone I showed the sketches to said, 'That would be funny for a one time use, but it will never wear well.' Their feelings were so unanimous that, for a short time, I switched to another type of cap before using my own intuition and going back to the propellor cap."

Following its prime-time run on ABC, the series remained on the network until 1968. The cartoons were then syndicated the following year by ABC Films. In the fall of 1989, the series was resyndicated in the United States, where it had been absent from the airwaves for more than a decade. (The series continued to be shown overseas, where it still plays in many markets.) In markets where the show premiered—Baltimore, Chicago, Houston, Dallas, Tampa, San Francisco and Boston—the program scored high ratings and refueled interest in the series nationwide.

A Bob Clampett Production. Color. Half-hour. Premiered on ABC: January 1962–December 1968. Syndicated: 1968–76; 1989.

Voices

Captain Huffenpuff/Beany Boy: Jim MacGeorge; **Cecil, the sea-sick serpent/Dishonest John:** Irv Shoemaker

BEANY AND CECIL (1988)

In the fall of 1988, Bob Clampett's Beany and Cecil characters were featured in this short-lived series revival, this time poking fun at 1980s' culture and themes. ABC canceled the Saturday-morning series after only five episodes. The series was produced and directed by animator John Kricfalusi, who went on to create the Nickelodeon megahit, *The Ren and Stimpy Show.* Actor Billy West, who provided the voice of Cecil the Sea-Sick Serpent, also served as the voice of Stimpy.

A Bob Clampett Production in association with DIC Enterprises. Color. Half-hour. Premiered on ABC: September 10, 1988–October 8, 1988.

Voices

Beany Boy: Mark Laurence Hildreth; **Cecil the Sea-Sick Serpent:** Billy West; **Captain Huffenpuff:** Jim MacGeorge; **Dishonest John:** Maurice LaMarche

BEAST WARS: TRANSFORMERS

The heroic Maximals, animals transformed into robots, hope to stop the evil Predacons from controlling a powerful energy source and conquering the galaxy in this 3-D, computer-animated series, based on the popular action figures.

A Mainframe Entertainment/BLT/Alliance Communications/YTV/Transformer Production. Color. Half-hour. Premiered: September 16, 1996. Syndicated.

Voices
Scorponok: Donald Brown; **Inferno:** Jim Byrnes; **Optimus Primael:** Gary Chalk; **Cheetor/Sentinel:** Ian Corlett; **Megatron:** David Kaye; **Tigatron:** Blue Mankuma; **Dinobot/Rattrap/Silverbolt/Waspinator:** Scott McNeil; **Rhinox:** Richard Newman; **Airazor:** Pauline Newstone; **Terrorsaur:** Doug Parker; **Predacon Ship Computer:** Elizabeth Carol Savenkoff; **Blackarachnia:** Venus Terzo; **Tarantulas:** Alec Willows

⊚ THE BEATLES
Throughout the 1960s, these mop-headed musicians (better known as John, Paul, George and Ringo) dominated the musical scene like no other group. Their music landed them atop national record charts and on several major television shows, including *The Ed Sullivan Show*, wowing teenagers throughout America in the process. The group's success also inspired a weekly animated cartoon series.

Produced in 1965, the series came about through the efforts of producer Al Brodax at King Features after he was approached by an ABC executive with the idea of producing "a Beatles cartoon." Famous toymaker A.C. Gilmer, who envisioned a merchandising goldmine, financed the series.

Premiering on ABC on Saturday, September 25, 1965 at 10:30 A.M., the show was an instant ratings hit. It racked up a 13 score (or 52 share), then unheard of in daytime television. Each half-hour show consisted of two sing alongs, emceed by the Beatles. (Lyrics were flashed on the screen so viewers could join in.) The first episodes that aired were "I Want to Hold Your Hand" and "A Hard Day's Night."

Besides two weekly cartoons, the Beatles show was famous for its clever bridges between episodes and commercials. These included dry, comic vignettes, such as Ringo buying a newspaper from a street vendor and getting hit by a car, only to complain afterward "There's not a word in here [in the paper] about me accident!"

The voices of the Beatles' cartoon look-alikes were supplied by two voice actors, Paul Frees (John and George) and Lance Percival (Paul and Ringo). Animation was sent overseas (TVC of London, which produced the Beatles cult feature, *The Yellow Submarine*, and Astransa, an Australian company, did the bulk of the animation), and scripts were turned out rather easily since episodes were based on popular Beatles songs.

"It took about four weeks to animate each film and I enjoyed it immensely," recalled Chris Cuddington, a series animator. "The characters were easy to draw, and the stories were simple and uncomplicated."

Paul, George and John enjoy Ringo's appearance on television in The Beatles *cartoon series, featuring actual recordings of the famed Liverpool musicians. © King Features Entertainment*

Following the first season's success, Brodax considered producing four Beatles prime-time animated specials. But plans to produce them and several other musical-based cartoon series—animated versions of Herman's Hermits and Freddie and the Dreamers—never materialized.

The Beatles remained on ABC for three more years, the last season consisting of repeats from the previous three seasons. The series lost ground during its second season after it was slated opposite CBS's *Space Ghost*, part of a powerful Saturday-morning lineup that included *Frankenstein Jr. and the Impossibles*, *Mighty Mouse* and *The Mighty Heroes*. (*Space Ghost* won the time slot with a 9.6, a 44 share, while the Beatles slid into second with 7.6, a 36 share.)

In the fall of 1968, the series was moved to Sunday mornings, where it remained until its final broadcast in 1969.

A King Features Production. Color. Half-hour. Premiered on ABC: September 25, 1965–April 20, 1969. Syndicated.

Voices
John Lennon/George Harrison: Paul Frees; **Paul McCartney/Ringo Starr:** Lance Percival

⊚ BEAVIS AND BUTT-HEAD
Originally featured as stars of the cartoon short "Frog Baseball (in which they were called Bobby and Billy), part of MTV's *Liquid Television* series in 1992, this idiotic, repulsive pair of hard-rock music fans—blond Beavis, the one in a Metallica T-shirt, and dark-haired Butt-Head, traditionally dressed in an AC/DC T-shirt—starred in this long-running half-hour series, which quickly became MTV's highest rated show. Each half-hour program consisted of two cartoon adventures with these suburban misfits amusing themselves by watching bad TV shows, working at the local "Burger

World" (and creating chaos at the drive-up window) or attending enriching events such as the "All-Star Monster Tractor Trashathon."

Originally slated to premiere in March 1993, production problems delayed the series, so only two complete programs were aired that month. In May of 1993 MTV "officially" premiered the series in prime time, airing the program Monday through Thursday night. Fierce criticism of the show erupted five months later after an episode prompted an Ohio mother to charge that a "Beavis" episode caused her five-year-old son to start a fire that killed his two-year-old sister. The network subsequently moved the series out of prime time to a late-night slot. Soon producers developed *Beavis & Butt-Head* episodes "more suitable for prime time."

Daria Morgendorffer, the only female friend of Beavis and Butt-Head, debuted that first season. (In March of 1997 she was given her own animated series.) Other series regulars added were: Mr. Buzzcut, the boys' ex-marine gym and hygiene teacher; Tom Anderson, B&B's tormented neighbor; Principal McKicker, the boys' high school principal; and Stewart and Mr. Stevenson, Stewart's dad.

During the series' original run, the characters were spun off into a series of annual "Butt-Bowl" specials that aired during Super Bowl halftimes, beginning in January of 1994. They also appeared on two Christmas specials, in 1994 and 1995 respectively.

In December of 1996 the boys took on Hollywood in their feature film debut, *Beavis and Butt-Head Do America*.

The movie was launched with a pre-release MTV special, *Beavis and Butt-Head Do America: An MTV Movie Special*. After producing more than 200 episodes, the series concluded its original network run on November 28, 1997 with the finale, "Beavis and Butt-Head Are Dead," only to return on the network in reruns with the promise of future specials. The show's final original broadcast was followed by a "live" special, *Beavis and Butt-Head Do Thanksgiving with Kurt Loder* (an MTV news anchor).

An MTV Networks Production. Color. Half-hour. Premiered on MTV: March 1993; (official "premiere"): May 17, 1993–November 28, 1997. Rebroadcast on MTV: November 29, 1997– .

Voices
Beavis/Butt-Head/Tom Anderson/David van Dreesen/Bradley Buzzcut/Principal McVicker: Mike Judge; **Cassandra/Daria/Lolitta/Tanqueray/Heather/Jennifer:** Tracy Grandstaff; **Mr. Graham:** Guy; **Todd:** Rottilio Michieli; **Stewart:** Adam Welch

⊚ BEETHOVEN

The blubbery St. Bernard, immortalized in two comedy films, returns with the family in tow in weekly half-hour misadventures based on the popular movie series.

A Universal Cartoon Studios Production. Color. Half-hour. Premiered on CBS: September 17, 1994–September 2, 1995.

⊚ BEETLEJUICE

Based on the characters from director Tim Burton's hit movie of the same name, this weekly animated series tells the story of an eccentric con artist and his relationship with a 12-year-old Earth girl (Lydia Deetz) that centers around the surrealistic adventures in the Neitherworld, the place where Beetlejuice resides. The series was an instant hit with young viewers on ABC following its debut in the fall of 1989. Series regulars included Doomie the Cat, a reckless auto with a penchant for chasing cars. In 1991, the series jumped to The Fox Network's weekday lineup, featuring 65 new episodes that included spoofs of popular motion pictures and fairy tales. (The original series continued in reruns on ABC.) Beginning in 1994, the series was repeated on Nickelodeon.

A Warner Bros./Nelvana Production in association with The Geffen Film Company and Tim Burton, Inc. Color. Half-hour. Premiered on ABC: September 9, 1989–September 5, 1992. Rebroadcast on FOX: November 1991–September 1993. Rebroadcast on NIK: April 4, 1994–March 31, 1998.

Voices
Beetlejuice: Stephen Ouimette; **Lydia Deetz:** Alyson Court; **Charles Deetz, Lydia's father:** Roger Dunn; **Delia Deetz, Lydia's mother:** Elizabeth Hanna

⊚ BELLE AND SEBASTIAN

Produced in Japan, this 30-minute series tells the story of a abandoned young boy (Sebastian), who makes friends with a lonely big white dog, Belle. The two experience high adventure and the special bonds of friendship in this touching adaptation of the successful children's book series by author Cecile Aubrey.

An MK Company and Visual 80 Production in association with Toho Company, Ltd. Color. Half-hour. Premiered on NIK: June 1984–1990.

⊚ THE BERENSTAIN BEARS

Beartown, a tiny hamlet whose economy is based solely on honey, is home to the Bear Family: Papa Q. Bear; Mama; Brother and Sister Bear; Grizzly and Gran, grandparents; and the hilarious incompetent group of ne'er-do-wells, chief among them Raffish Ralph and Weasel McGreed, whose antics always seem to throw a monkey wrench into the Bear Family's best-laid plans. This CBS Saturday-morning series adapted the beloved children's book characters created by Stan and Jan Berenstain. Previously the characters starred in five half-hour animated specials for NBC.

A *Southern Star Production. Color. Half-hour. Premiered on CBS: September 14, 1985–September 5, 1987.*

Voices
Mama: Ruth Buzzi; **Papa Q. Bear:** Brian Cummings; **Sister:** Christine Lange; **Brother:** David Mendenhall; **Raffish Ralph:** Frank Welker

◎ THE BEST OF SCOOBY-DOO

Classic episodes of the cowardly canine detective Scooby-Doo and his companions, Fred, Shaggy, Daphne and Velma, were rebroadcast in this best-of format for Saturday-morning television. The show combined 49 previously broadcast episodes from past Scooby-Doo programs—25 from 1969's *Scooby-Doo, Where Are You?* and 24 from 1976's *The Scooby-Doo/Dynomutt Hour.* (See programs for complete voice credits.) The series lasted one full season on ABC.

A *Hanna-Barbera Production. Color. Half-hour. Premiered on ABC: September 10, 1983–September 1, 1984.*

◎ THE BETTY BOOP SHOW

National Television Associates (NTA), which earlier had acquired the rights to Betty Boop, tried to rekindle interest in the "Boop-Boop-a-Doop" girl by distributing color-painted prints of Max Fleischer's original theatrical cartoons in half-hour packages. (The master negatives were sent overseas to Korea where they were meticulously hand-colored.)

A *Max Fleischer Production distributed by NTA. Color. Half-hour. Premiered: Fall 1971. Syndicated.*

Voices
Betty Boop: Mae Questel

◎ BEVERLY HILLS TEENS

This series centers around the lives, loves and longings of a group of typical, fun-loving American teenagers, who just happen to be fabulously wealthy.

A *DIC Enterprises Production. Color. Half-hour. Premiered: September 1987. Syndicated.*

Voices
Buck/Wilshire: Michael Beattie; **Pierce Thorndyke:** Stephen McMulkin; **Shanelle Spencer:** Michelle St. John; **Tara/Jett:** Karen Bernstein; **Jillian/Bianca/Blaise:** Tracy Moore; **Switchboard:** Joanna Schellenberg; **Fifi:** Linda Sorensen; **Nikki Darling:** Corrine Koslo; **Gig/Dad:** Mark Saunders; **Larke/Dog:** Mary Long; **Troy:** Jonathan Potts; **Radley/Guitar:** Hadley Kay

A look into the fantastic future of space adventure is told vividly through the eyes of two boys in the action-packed series The Big World of Little Adam. © *Little Adam Productions Inc.*
(COURTESY: FRED LADD)

◎ BIG BAG

Six animated "shorties" ("Samuel and Nina," "Koki," "Slim Pig," "Tobias Totz and His Lion," "Troubles the Cat" and "William's Wish Wellingtons"), plus short music videos make up this hour-long live-action/animated preschool series, hosted by several new Muppet characters (Chelli, Bag and their sock-puppet friends Lyle and Argyle) from Children's Television Workshop (producers of *Cro*), produced for the Cartoon Network.

A *Children's Television Workshop Production. Color. One hour. Premiered on CAR: June 2, 1996.*

◎ THE BIG WORLD OF LITTLE ADAM

The fantastic future of space exploration is seen through the eyes of Little Adam and his big brother Wilbur in this half-hour series consisting of 110 action-packed five-minute episodes. Fred Ladd, the American producer of TV's *Speed Racer* and others, produced the series. John Megna, the voice of Little Adam, is actress Connie Stevens's brother.

A *Little Adam Production Inc. Color. Half-hour. Premiered: 1965. Syndicated.*

Voices
Little Adam: John Megna; **Wilbur, his brother:** Craig Seckler

◎ BIKER MICE FROM MARS

Trying to mirror the success of CBS's *Teenage Mutant Ninja Turtles,* this half-hour, syndicated fantasy series follows the adventures of three space-cycling Martian mice (Modo,

Throttle and Vinnie), each victims of a terrible lab experiment, who wage an interplanetary revolt against a team of revolutionaries who plan to own the galaxy, and the evil scientist (Dr. Karbunkle) who made them into the mutants they are.

A Marvel Production in association with Brentwood TV Funnies and New World Family Filmworks. Color. Half-hour. Premiered: September 1993. Syndicated.

Voices
Modo: Dorian Harewood; **Throttle:** Rob Paulsen; **Vinnie:** Ian Ziering; **Charlie:** Leeza Miller-McGee; **Lawrence Limburger:** Morgan Sheppard; **Dr. Karbunkle:** Susan Silo; **Sweet Georgie Brown:** Jess Harnell; **Grease Pit:** Brad Garrett

BILL & TED'S EXCELLENT ADVENTURES
Rockin', southern California teens Bill and Ted of the two-man rock band "Wyld Stalyns" zoom through the annals of history—from ancient Rome to Mozart's Vienna—with the help of their phone-booth time machine and extremely "cool" guide Rufus in this half-hour, animated spin-off of the 1989 hit movie, featuring Alex Winter (Bill), Keanu Reeves (Ted) and George Carlin (Rufus) reprising their movie roles. The series premiered on CBS in 1990 with 13 original episodes. It joined the Fox Network's Saturday-morning lineup in 1991, where it completed its run with a season of new episodes, minus the original cast.

A Hanna-Barbera Production in association with Nelson Entertainment and Orion Television. Color. Half-hour. Premiered on CBS: September 1990–August 31, 1991; premiered on FOX: September 14, 1991–September 5, 1992.

Voices
Bill: Alex Winter (1990–91); **Ted:** Keanu Reeves (1990–91); **Rufus:** George Carlin (1990–91); **Mr. Preston, Bill's father:** Dave Madden; **Missy, Bill's stepmom:** Vicki Juditz; **Mr. Logan, Ted's father:** Peter Renaday; **Deacon, Ted's younger brother:** Danny Cooksey

BIONIC SIX
The Bennett family employ their bionic talents to combat the evil Dr. Scarab and his minions whose goal is to use science for their own selfish motives. This half-hour fantasy/adventure series was originally produced for first-run syndication in 1987. The series resurfaced on the Sci-Fi Channel (in reruns).

A TMS Production in association with MCA/Universal. Color. Half-hour. Premiered: April 19, 1987–November 16, 1987. Rebroadcast on SCI: January 2, 1995–August 29, 1997. Syndicated.

Voices
J.D. Bennett: Norman Bernard; **Helen Bennett:** Carol Bilger; **Meg Bennett:** Bobbi Block; **Jack Bennett:** John Stephenson; **Eric Bennett:** Hal Rayle; **Bunji Bennett:** Brian Tochi; **Madam O:** Jennifer Darling; **Dr. Scarab:** Jim MacGeorge; **F.L.U.F.F.I.:** Neil Ross; **Klunk:** John Stephenson; **Glove/Mechanic/Chopper:** Frank Welker

BIRDMAN AND THE GALAXY TRIO
Three winged superheroes—Birdman, assistant Birdboy and eagle companion Avenger—encounter world forces under the command of Falcon 7. The other half of the superhero talent, billed on the same show, was the Galaxy Trio. Stories depict the adventures of the spaceship *Condor 1* and its principal pilots, Vapor Man, Galaxy Girl and Meteor Man, who all possess superhuman strength. In wake of programming changes from hard-action fantasy cartoons to tamer comedy programs, NBC canceled the series midway into its second season, along two others: *Samson and Goliath* and *Super President And Spy Shadow*, resulting in a loss of $750,000 by the network. *Birdman and the Galaxy Trio* was one of NBC's higher-rated cartoon shows.

A Hanna-Barbera Production. Color. Half-hour. Premiered on NBC: September 9, 1967–September 14, 1968. Rebroadcast on NBC: September 1968–December 28, 1968. Rebroadcast on CAR: October 1, 1992–April 2, 1993 (weekdays); April 3, 1993–January 1, 1994 (Saturdays); January 9, 1994–April 3, 1994 (Sundays); March 4, 1994 (Super Adventure Saturdays); July 29, 1995 (Power Zone).

Voices

THE BIRDMAN: Ray Randall/Birdman: Keith Andes; **Birdboy:** Dick Beals; **Falcon 7:** Don Messick

THE GALAXY TRIO: Vapor Man: Don Messick; **Galaxy Girl:** Virginia Eiler; **Meteor Man:** Ted Gassidy

THE BISKITTS
A group of pint-size pups—only a doggie-biscuit tall—named caretakers of the royal treasure following the death of Biskitt Island's good wise king thwart the ongoing efforts of King Max, despot of the rundown kingdom of Lower Suburbia, to steal the treasure along with mangy dogs, Fang and Snarl, and his inept jester, Shecky, in 14 half-hour shows produced for CBS. The series was later rebroadcast on USA Network's *Cartoon Express.*

A Hanna-Barbera Production. Color. Half-hour. Premiered on CBS: September 17, 1983–September 1, 1984. Rebroadcast on CBS: May 30, 1985–September 7, 1985. Rebroadcast on USA: March 3, 1989–March 29, 1991.

Voices

Waggs: Darryl Hickman; **Lady:** B.J. Ward; **Scat:** Dick Beals; **Sweets:** Kathleen Helppie; **Spinner/Bump/Flip:** Bob Holt; **Shecky:** Kip King; **Shiner:** Jerry Houser; **Scatch/Fang/Dog Foot:** Peter Cullen; **King Max/Fetch/Snarl:** Kenneth Mars; **Wiggle:** Jennifer Darling; **Downer:** Henry Gibson; **Mooch:** Marshall Efron

◎ BLACKSTAR

Astronaut John Blackstar, an intergalactic soldier of fortune, is drawn through a black hole into an alternate universe. There he uses a mystical Power Star to undertake fantastic adventures to the planet Sagar and battle the Overlord of the Underworld, aided by the beautiful sorceress Mara.

A Filmation Associates Production. Half-hour. Color. Premiered on CBS: September 12, 1981–August 20, 1983.

Voices

John Blackstar: George DiCenzo; **Balkar/Terra/Klone:** Pat Pinney; **Gossamear/Burble/Rif:** Frank Welker; **Carpo/Overlord:** Alan Oppenheimer; **Mara:** Linda Gary

◎ BLAZING DRAGONS

Set in Camelhot, gallant and generous dragons King Allfire and his members of the Square Table—Sir Galahot, Queen Griddle and Sir Burnevere—battle greedy humans for gemstones, rescue damsels in distress and generally make the world a better place in which to live in this cartoon-series spoof of King Arthur and the Knights of the Round Table, based on characters created by *Monty Python's* Terry Jones.

A Nelvana Enterprises/Ellipse Animation Production. Color. Half-hour. Premiered: September 9, 1996. Syndicated.

Voices

King Allfire: Aron Tager; **Queen Griddle:** Steve Sutcliffe; **Sir Blaze/Minstrel:** Richard Binsley; **Sir Loungealot/Count Geoffrey:** Juan Chioran; **Evil Knight #1:** Cedric Smith; **Evil Knight #2/Sir Burnevere:** John Stocker; **Evil Knight #3:** Dan Hennessey; **Flicker:** Edward Glen; **Flame:** Stephanie Morgenstern; **Cinder/Clinker:** Richard Waugh

◎ BLUE'S CLUES

A live-action host (Steve) and his animated blue puppy (Blue) help kids follow visual clues to solve a puzzle in this play-a-long, educational live-action/animated daytime series for preschoolers.

A Nickelodeon Production. Color. Half-hour. Premiered on NIK: September 9, 1996.

Cast (live action)

Steve: Steven Burns

◎ BOBBY'S WORLD

Comedian Howie Mandel created the character of this half-hour animated series, debuting on The Fox Network, in which his highly imaginative preschool alter ego, four-year-old Bobby, presents his point of view of the world and family life through a series of daydreams. Each episode opens and closes with live-action wraparounds of the comedian talking about the show and at times talking to his animated self. Situations usually revolve around Bobby's home life—with his stubborn father, his sympathetic mother, his taunting older brother Derek and his whiny sister Kelly, and next-door neighbors, including his best friend, Jackie, and his sheepdog, Roger—often confronting some sort of dilemma. One series milestone included was the season-long pregnancy of Bobby's mother, resulting in a guest-appearance by Paul Anka, in a blend of live-action and animation, serenading the cartoon mother-to-be in the episode in which she gave birth with his composition "(You're) Having My Baby."

Airing Saturday mornings and weekday afternoons, the series' last original episode was broadcast in February of 1998. The show continues to air in reruns.

A Film Roman Production in association with Alevy Productions and Fox Children's Television Network. Color. Half-hour. Premiered on FOX: September 8, 1990–February 23, 1998.

Voices

Bobby Generic/Howie: Howie Mandel; **Martha:** Gayle Matthius; **Uncle Ted:** Tino Insana; **Kelly:** Charity James; **Derek:** Benny Grant, Pam Segall; **Roger:** Danny Mann, Frank Welker; **Aunt Ruth:** Susan Tolsky; **Jackie:** Debi Derryberry; **Captain Squash:** Gary Owens

◎ BONKERS!

Bonkers D. Bobcat, formerly of the Disney CBS Saturday-morning series *Raw Toonage*, starred in this 65-episode half-hour animated series that captured his manic missions to protect Tinseltown as a member of the Tinseltown Police Force. His well-meaning efforts end in disaster, thwarting the attempts of his mismatched human partner (Sergeant Lucky Piquel) to get promoted. Debuting on the Disney Channel in 1993, the series was also syndicated that September as part of The Disney Afternoon two-hour block, replacing *Chip 'n' Dale's Rescue Rangers*.

A Walt Disney Television Animation Production. Color. Half-hour. Premiered on DIS: February 1993–September 1993. Syndicated: September 6, 1993–September 10, 1995.

Voices

Bonkers/Sergeant Lucky Piquel: Jim Cummings

◎ BOTS MASTER

Set in the year 2015, a child prodigy, Zig Zulaner, develops futuristic 3A manual-labor robots—known as "bots"—for the Robot Megafact Corporation, but the corporation's evil Lewis Paradim plans to build his own version in order to take over the world in this half-hour syndicated series.

A *Nuoptix/Avid Arad/Creativite et Developpement Production in association with All American Television. Color. Half-hour. Premiered: 1993. Syndicated.*

Voices
Ian James Corlett, Richard Cox, Mike Donovan, Steve Guilinetti, Mark Hildreth, Janyce Jaud, Surya Keller, Terry Klassen, Sam Kouth, Rob Lehane, Gusse Mankuma, Pamela Martin, Crystaleen Obray, Kim Restell, Chelan Simmons, Dale Wilson

⊚ BOZO THE CLOWN

Frizzy redhaired clown Bozo, former comic-strip favorite and Capitol Records star, found new avenues via syndicated television when Larry Harmon produced this series of 156 five-minute color cartoons featuring Bozo and his circus pal Butchy Boy. The series has remained in continuous syndication since its premiere in 1959.

A *Larry Harmon/Ticktin/Jayark Films Production. Color. Half-hour. Syndicated: 1959.*

Voices
Bozo the Clown/Butchy Boy: Larry Harmon

Additional Voices
Paul Frees

⊚ THE BRADY KIDS

Re-creating their roles from TV's *The Brady Bunch*, Greg, Peter, Bobby, Marcia, Janice and Cindy were featured in this animated spinoff focusing on the kids' problems as independent-minded young adults. Joining the wholesome youngsters were Ping and Pong. Chinese-speaking twin pandas, and Marlon, a magical black mynah bird. The Brady characters were voiced by members of the original television series cast.

The series pilot, *Jungle Bungle* (retitled *The Brady Kids on Mysterious Island* and broadcast as a feature-length cartoon on *The ABC Saturday Superstar Movie* series), was broadcast as the series opener in 1972. The half-hour cartoon series ran for two seasons on ABC, producing 22 episodes (including the two-part pilot). Original cast members Maureen McCormick, Barry Williams and Christopher Knight did not reprise their characters for the second season. Their voices were supplied by voice actors Erika Scheimer, Lane Scheimer and Keith Allen.

A *Filmation Associates Production. Color. Half-hour. Premiered on ABC: September 16, 1972–August 31, 1974.*

Voices
Marcia Brady: Maureen McCormick, Erika Scheimer; **Greg Brady:** Barry Williams, Lane Scheimer; **Janice Brady:** Eve Plumb; **Peter Brady:** Christopher Knight, Keith Allen; **Cindy Brady:** Susan Olsen; **Bobby Brady:** Michael Lookinland; **Marlon the Magic Bird/Ping/Pong:** Larry Storch; **Babs:** Jane Webb; **Moptop:** "Lassie"

⊚ BRAND NEW SPANKING DOUG

Bristle-topped Doug Funnie, the heartwarming, parent-pleasing, likable 12-year-old with his trademark green sweater vest and brown shorts (from Nickelodeon's hit series *Doug*), enters seventh grade at a newly built middle school in Bluffington and deals with a whole new set of trials and tribulations, including his mom's pregnancy and the arrival of a new addition to the Funnie family, in this all-new weekly half-hour animated series. Cast in new situations are regulars from the old series: Doug's best friend, Skeeter Valentine; Tony; the elusive girl of his dreams, Patti Mayonnaise; big, bad bully Roger Klotz and Porkchop, the dog. ABC initially ordered 13 episodes, including a prime-time holiday special, *Doug's Secret Christmas* for the series first season in 1996. The program was so successful that the network expanded the show to one hour.

A *Jumbo Pictures Production. Color. Half-hour. One hour. Premiered on ABC: September 7, 1996–October 26, 1996 (half-hour version); November 2, 1996 (one-hour version)– .*

Voices
Doug Funnie: Thomas McHugh; **Judy Funnie/Theda Funnie/Connie Benge:** Becca Lish; **Misquito Valentine/Ned Valentine/Mr. Dink:** Fred Newman; **Roger Klotz:** Chris Phillips; **Bebe Bluff:** Alice Playten; **Patti Mayonnaise:** Constance Shulman

⊚ BRAVESTARR

Combining the best of the Old West and of the space-age future, this western fantasy/adventure takes place on the distant planet of New Texas in the 24th century. Horse-riding lawman Marshal Bravestarr draws on his super powers to fight for the cause of justice where evil lurks, aided by his Equestroid talking horse, Thirty-Thirty, in this daily series of 65 half-hour programs produced for syndication. Other characters featured in this high-energy action/adventure included Judge B.J., the female magistrate of New Texas, and pint-size alien lawman, Deputy Fuss.

A *Filmation Production. Color. Half-hour. Syndicated: September 1987.*

Voices
Scuzz/Deputy Fuss: Charlie Adler; **Judge B.J.:** Susan Blu; **Marshal Bravestarr:** Pat Fraley; **Thirty-Thirty/Shaman:** Ed Gilbert

◎ THE BROTHERS GRUNT

Originally developed as characters for MTV network I.D.'s by creator Danny Antonucci (of "Lupo the Butcher" fame), six gross-looking, bug-eyed brothers (Perry, Frank, Tony, Bing, Dean and Sammy), who love cheese, wear bermuda shorts, knee-high black socks and wingtips and communicate only by grunting and twitching, escape from a local monastery and set out on a series of slapstick adventures in this 65-episode half-hour animated series, which premiered on MTV in August of 1994. Each animated half-hour featured three seven-minute cartoons per broadcast.

An a.k.a. Cartoon, Inc. Production in association with MTV. Color. Half-hour. Premiered on MTV: August 15, 1994.

◎ BRUNO

Bruce Willis (known in some circles as "Bruno") co-created and lent his voice to this bespectacled, 11-year-old computer whiz kid with the bulbous head, whose computer-generated superspy alter ego gets him recruited by Globe, an international law-enforcement agency (who assigns Globe operative Jarlsburg to work with him) into the high-stakes world of international espionage. This 36-episode half-hour syndicated adventure series was produced in association with Willis's company, Flying Heart Inc.

A Film Roman Production in association with Flying Heart, Inc. Color. Half-hour. Premiered: September 23, 1996. Syndicated.

Voices
Bruno the Kid: Bruce Willis; **Jarlsburg:** Tony Jay; **Leecy Davidson:** Jennifer Hale; **Grace:** Kath Soucie; **Howard:** John Bower; **Lazlo Gigahertz:** Tim Curry; **Booby Vicious:** Matt Frewer; **Harris:** Mark Hamill; **Globe Member 1:** Earl Boen; **Globe Member 2:** Mark Hamill; **Globe Member 3:** Kath Soucie; **Von Trapp:** Kenneth Mars; **Koos Koos:** Frank Welker; **General Armando Castrato:** Bronson Pinchot; **Mr. X:** Paul Edig; **Professor Wisenstein:** Ben Stein; **Di Archer:** Dawnn Lewis

◎ BUCKY AND PEPITO

This early animated series dealt with the adventures of Bucky, a young boy with a wild imagination and the spirit of an explorer, and his best friend, Pepito, the inventor.

A Sam Singer Production. Half-hour. Black-and-white. Premiered: 1959. Syndicated.

Voices
Bucky: Dallas McKennon

◎ BUCKY O'HARE AND THE TOAD WARS

Based on the graphic novel *Echo of Futurepast*, illustrated by Michael Golden, this series followed the misadventures of fearless S.P.A.C.E. (Sentient Protoplasm Against Colonial Encroachment) Captain Bucky O'Hare and his animal cohorts—Deadeye Duck, Bruiser, the gorilla, and Blinky, the adolescent android—who battle evil outer-space amphibians from the planet Genus.

A Sunbow Entertainment Production in association with Continuity Comics and IDDH. Color. Half-hour. Premiered: September 1991. Syndicated.

Voices
Long John Baldry, Jay Brazeau, Gary Chalk, Doc Harris, Simon Kendall, Sam Kouth, Terry Klassen, Scott McNeil, Shane Meier, Jason Michas, Richard Newman, Doug Parker, Margot Pindvic, David Steele, Dale Wilson

◎ BUDGIE—THE LITTLE HELICOPTER

The series chronicles the adventures of a high-flying friendly copter and his friends who constantly get into mischief, based on four children's books by Sarah Ferguson, the Duchess of York. Debuting first in overseas syndication in 1994 (becoming a hit in England), one year later the series premiered in the United States on The Fox Network's revamped weekday preschool series, *Fox Cubhouse*. Episodes were shown in combination with the serialized adventures of a new animated series, *Magic Adventures of Mumfie*. The duchess got the idea for Budgie in 1987 while practicing for her helicopter pilot's license.

A Fred Wolf Studios/Dublin Production in association with Westinghouse Broadcasting. Color. Half-hour. Premiered on FOX: October 19, 1995–August 15, 1996.

◎ BUFORD AND THE GALLOPING GHOST

This half-hour mystery series was composed of two weekly cartoon segments—"The Buford Files," following the exploits of Buford the bloodhound and two teenagers solving crimes; and "The Galloping Ghost," the misadventures of Nugget Nose, a ghost of an Old West prospector who haunts a dude ranch—which originally aired as part of ABC's 90-minute series *Yogi's Space Race* in 1978. (See *Yogi's Space Race* for voice credits.)

A Hanna-Barbera Production. Color. Half-hour. Premiered on NBC: February 3, 1979–September 1, 1979. Rebroadcast on CAR: September 11, 1994 (Sundays).

◎ THE BUGS BUNNY AND TWEETY SHOW

Bugs Bunny, Tweety and Sylvester star in this program containing classic Warner Bros. cartoons. Added to ABC's

Saturday morning schedule in 1986, the half-hour series continues to air weekly.

A *Warner Bros. Production. Color. Half-hour. Premiered on ABC: September 13, 1986.*

Voices
Mel Blanc

⊚ THE BUGS BUNNY/LOONEY TUNES COMEDY HOUR

Hour-long anthology of cartoon adventures featuring Bugs Bunny, the Road Runner, Daffy Duck, Foghorn Leghorn, Sylvester the Cat and Pepe Le Pew. The series' debut on ABC marked the end of the rascally rabbit's long association with CBS, where *The Bugs Bunny/Road Runner Hour* has remained a staple of Saturday-morning television since its premiere in 1968.

A *Warner Bros. Production. Color. One hour. Premiered on ABC: September 7, 1985–September 6, 1986.*

Voices
Mel Blanc

⊚ THE BUGS BUNNY/ROAD RUNNER HOUR

Bugs Bunny and the Road Runner and Coyote combined to become one of the most popular Saturday-morning vehicles when reruns of their old cartoons were broadcast for the first time on CBS in September 1968. The pairing of these Warner Bros. superstars resulted in consistently high ratings for its time period throughout its 17-year run on CBS. The format was changed only once: In April 1976 the program was aired simultaneously on Tuesday nights in primetime under the title of *The Bugs Bunny/Road Runner Show.* By November 1977 the series was expanded to 90 minutes, remaining in this mode through the beginning of the 1981–82 season, when it returned to one hour, the length it stayed and continued in this until ending its reign on CBS in September 1985.

A *Warner Bros. Production. Color. One hour. Ninety minutes. Premiered on CBS: September 14, 1968–September 4, 1971. Rebroadcast on CBS: September 6, 1975–November 1977 (as The Bugs Bunny/Road Runner Hour); April 1972–June 1976 (as The Bugs Bunny/Road Runner Show); November 1977–September 1981 (as The Bugs Bunny/Road Runner Show); September 12, 1981–September 7, 1985.*

⊚ THE BUGS BUNNY SHOW

Like its rival CBS, which brought *The Flintstones* to prime time, ABC premiered this package of Warner Bros. cartoons starring "the screwy rabbit" and his friends (Elmer Fudd, Yosemite Sam, Tweety and Sylvester the Cat, and the Road Runner), which contained significant amounts of new animated material specially made for television. The program remained in prime time for two seasons before it was moved to Saturday mornings, where it dominated kiddie-show ratings in its time slot for more than 20 years.

A *Warner Bros. Production. Color. Half-hour. Premiered on ABC: October 11, 1960–September 25, 1962. Rebroadcast on ABC: April 1962–September 1968. Rebroadcast on CBS: September 11, 1971–September 1, 1973. Rebroadcast on ABC: September 8, 1973–August 30, 1975.*

Voices
Mel Blanc, Arthur Q. Bryan, Daws Butler, June Foray, Julie Bennett, Stan Freberg, Billy Bletcher, Bea Benadaret

⊚ BUGS N' DAFFY

Continuing to program classic animated shorts from Warner Bros. past, the WB Network aired this package of *Looney Tunes* and *Merrie Melodies* shorts (formerly titled *That's Warner Bros.!*), retitling the series and featuring legendary Warner Bros. toonsters Bugs Bunny and Daffy Duck as the stars of the show. This half-hour series debuted on the kids' WB lineup in 1996.

A *Warner Bros. Production. Color. Half-hour. Premiered on WB: August 26, 1996*

Voices
Mel Blanc (primary voice)

⊚ THE BULLWINKLE SHOW

With new components added, this program was basically a retitled version of the *Rocky and His Friends* series, previously broadcast on ABC from 1959 to 1961. Again, Rocky, the flying squirrel, and Bullwinkle, the moose, tangle with the nefarious Mr. Big, a midget with grandiose ideas, and his two Russian agents, Boris Badenov and Natasha Fatale, in two cliffhanging episodes.

Other holdovers from the former series were "Aesop and Son," "Fractured Fairy Tales" (which alternated each week with "Aesop and Son"), "Peabody's Improbable History" and "Mr. Know-It-All." (For episode titles of each see *Rocky and His Friends.*) Two new segments were added to the show: "Dudley Do-Right of the Mounties" (which rotated every week with "Aesop and Son"), repackaged later as *The Dudley Do-Right Show,* and "Bullwinkle's Corner," short, nonsensical poetry readings by the famed cartoon moose.

In 1981, after eight years off network television, the series returned for a brief run on NBC, then 10 years later for a short run in prime time on CBS as part of the network's Wednesday-night anthology series "Toon Night." Nickelodeon then picked up the series, repeating it on weeknights (under the title of *Bullwinkle's Moose-A-Rama*) from 1992 to 1996. After its final year on Nick, the program returned in reruns on the Cartoon Network.

A *Jay Ward Production in association with Producers Associates for Television. Color. Half-hour. Premiered on NBC: September 24, 1961–September 15, 1963. Rebroadcast on NBC: September 21, 1963–September 5, 1964. Rebroadcast on ABC: September 20, 1964–September 2, 1973. Rebroadcast on NBC: September 12, 1981–July 24, 1982. Rebroadcast on CBS: May 29, 1991–June 12, 1991. Rebroadcast on NIK: August 3, 1992–May 31, 1996 (as Bullwinkle's Moose-A-Rama). Rebroadcast on CAR: June 3, 1996–October 5, 1996 (weekdays).*

Voices
Bullwinkle: Bill Scott; **Rocky/Natasha Fatale/Nell, Dudley's girlfriend:** June Foray; **Boris Badenov/Inspector Fenwick:** Paul Frees; **Aesop:** Charles Ruggles; **Peabody/Dudley Do-Right:** Bill Scott; **Sherman:** Walter Tetley; **Snidely Whiplash:** Hans Conried; **Narrators:** William Conrad ("Bullwinkle"), Edward Everett Horton; ("Fractured Fairy Tales"), Charles Ruggles ("Aesop and Son")

◎ BUMP IN THE NIGHT

Friendly, 10-inch creature Mr. Bumpy—who lives under the bed of a 10-year-old boy and has a penchant for eating socks and car keys—and his playmates wreak all sorts of havoc when they come to life at night in this weekly Saturday-morning series that combined stop-motion animation, live action and computer-animated inserts. ABC, which premiered the series in the fall of 1994 and had ownership interest in the program, took the unusual step of commissioning two years' worth of episodes before the series even debuted. Disney's takeover of Capital Cities/ABC spelled an end for the program. It was canceled in 1996.

A *Danger/Greengrass Production. Color. Half-hour. Premiered on ABC: September 10, 1994–August 31, 1996.*

◎ A BUNCH OF MUNSCH

Canadian humorist Robert Munsch's award-winning, wonderfully wacky children's tales (illustrated by Michael Martchenko) were adapted for this series of Canadian-produced half-hour animated specials, usually featuring two stories about young heroes and imaginary problems in each 30-minute program, often accompanied by original songs. The first Munsch special, "Thomas' Snowsuit and Fifty Below Zero," premiered on Canada's CTV. In the United States, the specials debuted on Showtime on December 17, 1991 and was added to Showtime's fall 1992 lineup, opposite *American Heroes and Legends*, as part of the network's hour-long block of kiddie-oriented programming. The series opener was "The Paper Bag Princess," about a feisty heroine who tilts a rappin', fire-breathing dragon. Additional half-

hours included: "Pigs and David's Father," "Something Good and Mortimer," "Murmel, Murmel, Murmel and the Boy in the Drawer," "The Fire Station and Angela's Surprise" and "Blackberry Subway Jam" and "Moira's Birthday."

A *Cinar Film Production in association with CTV. Color. Half-hour. Premiered on SHO: December 17, 1991.*

Voices
Julian Bailey, Sonja Ball, Rick Jones, Gordon Masten, Michael O'Reilly, Anik Matern, Liz MacRae, Mark Hellman, Lianne Picard-Poirier, Matthew Barrot, Tia Caroleo, Jesse Gryn, Lisa Hull, Kaya Scott, Vlasta Vrana, Carlysle Miller, Haley Reynolds, Gabriel Taraboulsy, Michael Rudder, Bronwen Mantel, Carlyle Miller, Terrence Scammell, Kathleen Fee, Harry Standjofsky, Thor Bishopric, Patricia Rodriguez, Norman Groulx, Jory Steinberg, Christian Tessier, Amy Fulco, Eramelinda Boquer, Tamar Kozlov, Richard Dumont, George Morris, Jacob D. Tierney, June Wallack, Andrew Bauer-Gabor, Holly Frankel-Gauthier, A.J. Henderson, Shayne Olszynko-Gryn, Jane Woods

◎ THE BUSY WORLD OF RICHARD SCARRY

Set in the happy accident-prone burg of Busytown, this weekly half-hour series, based on the popular Scarry storybooks, followed the exploits of funny animal characters Huckle Cat, Lowly Worm and Grouchy Mr. Gronkle. The internationally coproduced series—a cooperative venture between Cinar France Animation in Canada, Paramount Pictures and the British Broadcasting Corporation, Showtime Networks and the Family Channel—aired Wednesday nights on Showtime, beginning in March of 1994.

The series was brought back with all-new episodes in the fall of that year. In the summer of 1995, while episodes continued to air on Showtime, the series began airing weekdays (in reruns) on Nickelodeon.

A *Cinar France Animation/France Co-Production in association with Paramount Pictures/Beta Films/British Broadcasting Corp./Showtime Networks/The Family Channel/Canada's Family Network/Canal J/France 3/Crayon Animation. Color. Half-hour. Premiered on SHO: March 9, 1994. Rebroadcast on NIK: July 3, 1995 (weekdays).*

Voices
Keith Knight, Sonja Ball, Phillip Williams, John Stocker, Peter Wildman, Don Dickinson, Paul Haddad, Len Carlson, Judy Marshak, Cathy Gallant, Tara Meyer, Jeremy Ratchford, Keith Hampshire

◎ BUTCH AND BILLY AND THEIR BANG BANG WESTERN MOVIES

Billy Bang Bang and his brother, Butch, provide commentary for this series of cliffhanging adventures featuring

Bronco Bill, an Old West lawman. The program was composed of back-to-back five-minute episodes.

Color. Half-hour. Premiered: 1961. Syndicated.

Voices
Bronco Bill: Bob Cust; **Billy Bang Bang:** Steve Krieger; **Butch Bang Bang:** Danny Krieger

◎ BUTCH CASSIDY AND THE SUN DANCE KIDS

U.S. government agents work undercover as the rock group Butch Cassidy and the Sun Dance Kids, consisting of teenagers Butch, Merilee, Harvey and Stephanie. Stories depicted the World Wide Talent agency team and its dog, Elvis, engaged in dangerous, global spy adventures represented in 13 half-hour programs.

A Hanna-Barbera Production. Color. Half-hour. Premiered on NBC: September 8, 1973–August 31, 1974.

Voices
Butch: Chip Hand; **Merilee:** Judi Strangis; **Harvey:** Micky Dolenz; **Stephanie (Steffy):** Tina Holland; **Elvis:** Frank Welker; **Mr. Socrates:** John Stephenson

◎ CADILLACS & DINOSAURS

Set in the 26th century, right after a global meltdown of epic proportions, dinosaurs roam Earth and classic cars race a group of underground woolly mammoths (known as The Mechanics), while two survivors, Jack Tenrac and Hannah Dundee, search for ways to make it in the "Xenozoic" era in this Saturday-morning cartoon adaptation of the popular comic book by writer/artist Mark Schultz. Developed by Steven E. de Souza, writer of such big-screen action hits as *Die Hard* and *Commando*, the action/adventures series premiered on CBS.

A Nelvana Entertainment/Galaxy Films/deSouza Production. Color. Half-hour. Premiered on CBS: September 18, 1993–March 11, 1994.

Voices
Jack: David Keeley; **Hannah:** Susan Roman; **Mustapha:** Bruce Tubbe; **Scharnhorst:** Dawn Greenhaigh; **Hammer:** Tedd Dillon; **Wrench:** Colin O'Meara; **Vice:** Frank Pellegrino; **Kirgo:** David Fox; **Grith/Hobbs:** Don Francks; **Dahlgren:** Kristina Nicoll; **Toulouse:** Philip Williams; **Mikla:** Lenora Zann; **Noe:** Don Dickinson

◎ THE CALIFORNIA RAISINS

In this 13 episode Saturday-morning series spinoff that aired on CBS, Will Vinton's "Claymation" stars, noted for their Motown-style singing, take viewers on a "Magical Mystery Tour" from a penthouse above their recording studio, accompanied by their hapless show-biz manager. The Raisins were introduced in 1987, in a series of popular commercials for California raisin growers.

A Murakami-Wolf-Swenson Films Production. Color. Half-hour. Premiered on CBS: September 16, 1989–September 8, 1990.

Voices
Cam Clarke, Dorian Harewood, Jim Cummings, Brian Mitchell, Cree Summer, Rebecca Summers, Gailee Heideman, Michelle Marianna, Todd Tolces, Brian Cummings

◎ CALVIN AND THE COLONEL

Loosely patterned after their long-running radio series *Amos 'n' Andy*, Freeman Gosden and Charles Correll created this animated series featuring the comedy mishaps of two Southern backwoods animals—the shrewd fox, Colonel Montgomery J. Klaxon, and his dimwitted, cigar-smoking bear friend, Calvin Burnside. The series premiered in prime time on ABC on October 3, 1961, opposite the CBS hit comedy series *Dobie Gillis*. The program faltered so ABC yanked the show from its nighttime slot and returned it to the airwaves in January 1962, adding it to the network's Saturday-morning lineup to finish out the season.

A Kayro Production. Color. Half-hour. Premiered on ABC: October 3, 1961–October 31, 1961; January 27, 1962–September 22, 1962. Syndicated.

Voices
Colonel Montgomery J. Klaxon: Freeman Gosden; **Maggie Belle Klaxon, his wife:** Virginia Gregg; **Calvin Burnside:** Charles Correll; **Sister Sue:** Beatrice Kay; **Gladys:** Gloria Blondell; **Oliver Wendell Clutch, lawyer:** Paul Frees

◎ CAMP CANDY

A group of smart-mouthed kids spend summer under the supervision of their camp director, John Candy, the head counselor, head cook and head handyman of Camp Candy, who helps make camp life a special experience for everyone. This half-hour animated series, composed of 39 episodes, ran for two seasons on NBC. The program was honored with the Humanitas Award for the 1991 episode "Wish Upon a Fish." The series entered daily syndication in 1992, after its network run. Providing additional voices on the program were Eugene Levy, Andrea Martin and Dave Thomas, formerly costars with Candy NBC's SCTV series.

A DIC Enterprises Production. Color. Half-hour. Premiered on NBC: September 2, 1989–September 7, 1991. Syndicated: 1992.

Voices
John: John Candy; **Binky:** Tony Ail; **Rex de Forest:** Lewis Arquette; **Nurse Molly:** Valri Bromfield; **Iggy:** Tom Davidson; **Robin:** Danielle Fernandes, Cree Summer Francks; **Vanessa:** Willow Johnson; **Botch:** Brian George;

Chester: Danny Mann; **Duncan:** Gary MacPherson; **Rick:** Andrew Seebaran; **Alex:** Chiara Zanni

◉ CANTIFLAS

This series of 52 six-minute cartoons, produced in Mexico by Hanna-Barbera and Diamex S.A., featured the popular Mexican film comedian in entertaining and educational adventures. (See *Amigo and Friends* for details.) First syndicated in America in 1980 under the umbrella title *Amigo and Friends*, the half-hour series featured four cartoon episodes each half-hour, redubbed in English. The package was later resyndicated under the *Cantiflas* title in a bilingual format.

A Hanna-Barbera/Diamex S.A./Televisa S.A. Production. Color. Half-hour. Premiered: 1980–1982. Syndicated.

Voices
Cantiflas (a.k.a. Amigo): Don Messick; **Narrator:** John Stephenson

◉ CAPITOL CRITTERS

Max, a young field mouse from Nebraska (voiced by Neil Patrick of TV's *Doogie Howser*), moves into the critter-cluttered basement of the White House with his new family of friends—Berkley, a hippie mouse; Trixie, a wise cockroach; Jammet, a combat veteran squirrel; and Mugger, a lab rat survivor—in this short-lived half-hour animated series that poked fun at politics and life in the nation's capital. ABC premiered the series on Tuesday night, January 25, 1992, with a "sneak preview." (The series normally aired on Saturday nights.) Producer Steven Bocho (of *Hill Street Blues* and *St. Elsewhere* fame) and Nat Mauldin, son of Pulitzer Prize–winning cartoonist Bill Mauldin, co-created the series, which never caught on with viewers.

A Steven Bocho Production in association with Hanna-Barbera Productions. Color. Half-hour. Premiered on ABC: January 28, 1992 (sneak preview); January 31, 1992–March 14, 1992. Rebroadcast on CAR: November 11, 1995–December 29, 1996 (Saturdays, Sundays).

Voices
Max: Neil Patrick Harris; **Muggle:** Bob "Bobcat" Goldthwait

◉ CAPTAIN CAVEMAN
AND THE TEEN ANGELS

The idea of three luscious nubile sleuths named "Charlie's Angels" in teasing one-hour TV dramas uncorked several parodies and late-night variety-show spoofs. This animated knock off featured a primitive supersleuth caveman and his three Teen Angels (Dee Dee, Brenda and Taffy) in tame but clever half-hour mysteries. Episodes originally aired as part of *Scooby's All-Star Laff-A-Lympics* and *Scooby's All-Stars* and

were repeated in this half-hour series. (It replaced ABC's *Spider-Woman*.) During the 1980–81 season, Captain Caveman returned in new adventures on *The Flintstones Comedy Show*, which was broadcast on NBC. In 1989 the series was shown in reruns on USA Network's *Cartoon Express*. (See *Scooby's All-Star Laff-A-Lympics* for voice credits.)

A Hanna-Barbera Production. Color. Half-hour. Premiered on ABC: March 8, 1980–June 21, 1980. Rebroadcast on USA: February 20, 1989–March 19, 1991.

◉ CAPTAIN FATHOM

Filmed in "Superanivision," this 1966 animated series, whose pilot was filmed four years earlier, follows the adventures of a submarine captain and his battle against evil in this underwater counterpart of Cambria Studios' *Clutch Cargo* and *Space Angel* series. The series was produced in the same limited illustrative art style and also using the famed "Syncro-Vox" process in which live-action footage of the actors' mouths were superimposed on the cartoon characters' faces. The series consisted of 195 five-minute serialized color adventures that had no story titles but were numbered in order of production. First offered for local syndication in 1966, episodes from the series were shown along with various other cartoons and short subjects as part of the syndicated afternoon kiddie show *Capt. 'n Sailor Bird*, hosted in cartoon wraparounds by a talking parrot, distributed by Sterling Films.

A Cambria Studios Production. Black-and-white. Color. Half-hour. Syndicated: 1966.

Voices
Captain Fathom: Warren Tufts

◉ CAPTAIN HARLOCK AND
THE QUEEN OF 1,000 YEARS

The aging queen and members of a nomadic planet, Millenia, plan to invade Earth and claim it as their new homeland. Earth's only hope against this alien threat is Captain Harlock, head of an interstellar space galleon, who protects and defends his home planet.

A Harmony Gold Production. Color. Half-hour. Premiered: September 1985. Syndicated.

◉ CAPTAIN INVENTORY

Various network-run series from Hanna-Barbera's cartoon library were redistributed to television via syndication for local programming. The program rotated adventures from the following: *Birdman and the Galaxy Trio, The Fantastic Four, Frankenstein Jr. and the Impossibles, Herculoids, Moby Dick and the Mighty Mightor, Shazzan!* and *The Space Ghost and Dino Boy.* (See individual series for details.)

A Hanna-Barbera Production. Color. Half-hour. Premiered: 1973. Syndicated.

◎ CAPTAIN N: THE GAME MASTER

Keven Keene, a young Nintendo gamestar, is "sucked" into his TV set and becomes Captain N, the ultimate hero who saves Videoland from the evil machinations of Mother Brain and her host of video villains, including King Hippo and the Eggplant Wizard. Along with his loyal dog, Duke, Kevin pulls together the disorganized heroes of Videoland—Simon Belmont, Mega Man and Kid Icarus—to become The N-Team, charged with keeping Princess Lana in power and holding the forces of evil at bay. The 1989 series, broadcast on NBC, was based on the phenomenally successful Nintendo game Captain N: The Game Master. The series returned for a second season in 1990 and was made part of a 60-minute block known as *Captain N: The Adventures of the Super Mario Brothers 3*. Captain N and the Super Mario Brothers were featured in half-hour shows back to back, with three other Nintendo properties—Zelda, Gameboy and Link—in animated adventures. In 1991 the program block returned for a third and final season on NBC, retitled *Captain N and the New Super Mario World*. The series was canceled a year later after NBC stopped producing cartoons for Saturday morning. The series was syndicated to television nationwide in 1991 under the name of *Captain N and the Video Game Masters*.

A DIC Enterprises Production in association with Nintendo Of America, Inc. Color. Half-hour. Premiered on NBC: September 9, 1989–September 1, 1990. Premiered on NBC (as Captain N: The Adventures of the Super Mario Brothers 3*): September 8, 1990–September 7, 1991.*

Premiered on NBC (as Captain N and the New Super Mario World*): September 14, 1991–July 25, 1992. Syndicated: 1992.*

Voices

CAPTAIN N: Kevin Keene/Captain N: Matt Hill; **King Hippo:** Gary Chalk; **Dr. Wiley:** Ian James Corlett; **Eggplant Wizard:** Mike Donovan; **Kid Icarus:** Alessandro Juliani; **Simon Belmont:** Andrew Kavadas; **Megaman:** Doug Parker; **Princess Lana:** Venus Terzo; **Duke:** Tomm Wright; **Mother Brain:** Levi Stubbs Jr.; **Narrator:** Matt Hill

SUPER MARIO BROTHERS 3: Mario: Walker Boone; **Luigi:** Tony Rosato; **Princess:** Tracey Moore; **Toad:** John Stocker; **Koopa:** Harvey Atkin; **Cheatsy:** James Rankin; **Kooky:** Michael Stark; **Kootie Pie:** Paulina Gillis; **Big Mouth:** Gordon Masten; **Bully:** Dan Hennessey; **Hip:** Stuart Stone; **Hop:** Tara Charendof

◎ CAPTAIN PLANET AND THE PLANETEERS

The world's first environmental superhero (originally to be voiced by actor Tom Cruise) and his heroic quintet— Kwame (Earth), Linka (Wind), Ma-Ti (Heart), Gi (Water) and Wheeler (Fire)—each bestowed with special powers, team up to rid the world of eco-villains (Hoggish Greedly, Verminous Skumm, Duke Nukem, Sly Sludge, Dr. Blight and others) who are polluting and plundering Earth's resources in this long-running weekly animated series, based on an original idea by media mogul Ted Turner, founder of superstation WTBS and the Turner networks.

Simultaneously premiering on TBS and 223 independent stations in the fall of 1990, the series (which opened with the episode "A Hero for Earth") was developed in close collaboration with Burbank, California–based cartoon studio DIC Enterprises, which produced the series for the first three seasons until 1993. Production was taken over by Hanna-Barbera beginning with the 1994–95 season, the show's fourth and final season of original episodes (retitled *The New Adventures of Captain Planet*). Following the show's 1990 debut, the series became a showcase for Hollywood's environmental activism. Many major Hollywood stars lent their voices to the series (including Elizabeth Taylor, who played Donna, the mother of a young boy—voiced by *Doogie Howser's* Neil Patrick Harris—who tested positive for HIV, a switch from the series' usually eco-conscious story lines), all working for scale, and each episode focused on different environmental concerns. In 1995 the series was rebroadcast on the Cartoon Network.

A DIC Entertainment/Hanna-Barbera Cartoons/TBS Production. Color. Half-hour. Premiered on TBS and Syndication: September 10, 1990. Rebroadcast on CAR: March 25, 1995 (episode "Tears in the Hood," part of "Stop the Violence Week"); September 5, 1995–(weekdays).

Voices

Captain Planet: David Coburn; **Kwame:** Levar Burton; **Wheeler:** Joey Dedio; **Gi:** Janice Kawaye; **Ma-Ti:** Scott Menville; **Linka:** Kath Soucie; **Sushi the Monkey/Lead Suit:** Frank Welker; **Gaia:** Whoopi Goldberg, Margot Kidder

POLLUTING PERPETRATORS: Hoggish Greedly: Ed Asner; **Hoggish Greedly Jr.:** Charlie Schlater; **Dr. Blight:** Meg Ryan, Mary Kay Bergman; **Argos Bleak:** S. Scott Bullock; **Looten Plunder:** James Coburn; **Jane Goodair:** Phyllis Diller; **Commander Clash:** Louis Gossett Jr.; **MAL:** Tim Curry, David Rappaport; **Verminous Skumm:** Jeff Goldblum, Maurice LaMarche; **Rigger:** John Ratzenberger; **Sly Sludge:** Martin Sheen; **Zarm:** Sting, David Warner; **Duke Nukem:** Dean Stockwell, Maurice LaMarche; **Ooze:** Cam Clarke

CAPTAIN SIMIAN AND THE SPACE MONKEYS

A lost-in-space NASA astro-chimp named Charlie (supposedly one of the original chimpanzee astronauts back in the *Sputnik* era) is captured by a group of fed-up superintelligent aliens who turn him into the new defender of the universe. Joined by an intelligent all-primate space crew, he sets out to conquer the once-powerful Lord Nebula and his minions who want to take over the universe in this 26-episode half-hour science-fiction cartoon series, made for first-run syndication. Voice regulars included *Babylon 5*'s Jerry Doyle as Captain Simian and *Star Trek*'s Michael Dorn as the archvillian Nebula.

A Monkeyshine/Hallmark Entertainment Production in association with Epoc Ink/Toon Us In. Color. Half-hour. Premiered: September 2, 1996. Syndicated.

A lost-in-space astro chimp heads a team of outer-space primates who protect the universe in Captain Simian and the Space Monkeys. *© Hallmark Entertainment/Monkeyshine Productions*

Voices
Captain Simian: Jerry Doyle; **Gor:** James Avery; **Spider:** Dom Irrera; **Splittzy:** Maurice LaMarche; **Shao Lin:** Karen Maruyama; **Rhesus 2:** Malcolm McDowell; **Apax:** Frank Welker; **Orbitron:** Jeff Bennett; **Nebula:** Michael Dorn; **The " " :** Oliver Muirhead

THE CARE BEARS (1985)

The lovable bears of Care-A-Lot come down to Earth in their cloud mobiles to help children with their problems. Along with the Care Bear Cousins, who live in the Forest of Feelings, the Care Bears make the world a happier place with their motto of caring and sharing. First series to be based on the popular children's book characters.

A DIC Enterprises Production. Color. Half-hour. Premiered: September 1985. Syndicated.

Voices
Tenderheart Bear: Billie Mae Richards; **Friend Bear:** Eva Almos; **Grumpy Bear:** Bobby Dermie; **Birthday Bear:** Melleny Brown; **Bedtime Bear:** Laurie Waller Benson; **Love A Lot Bear:** Linda Sorenson; **Wish Bear:** Janet Lane Green; **Good Luck Bear:** Dan Hennessy; **Share Bear:** Patrice Black; **Champ Bear:** Terry Sears

Care Bear Cousins
Brave Heart Lion/Loyal Heart Dog: Dan Hennessy; **Gentle Heart Lamb:** Luba Goy; **Swift Heart Rabbit:** Eva Almos; **Bright Heart Raccoon:** Jim Henshaw; **Lotsa Heart Elephant:** Luba Goy; **Playful Heart Monkey:** Marla Lukovsky; **Proud Heart Cat:** Louise Vallance; **Cozy Heart Penguin/Treat Heart Pig:** Pauline Penny

CARE BEARS (1988)

Tenderheart, Grumpy, Cheer, Champ, Grams Bear, Hugs and Tugs are but a few of the cuddly characters of Care-A-Lot, a place where feelings of "caring" are expressed by symbols on the tummies of the bears in this syndication version of the hit ABC Saturday-morning series, *The Care Bears Family*. The series combined old episodes from the former plus additional new episodes. (See *The Care Bears Family* for voice credits.)

A Nelvana Limited Production. Half-hour. Color. Premiered: September 1988. Syndicated.

THE CARE BEARS FAMILY

Based on the hit motion picture, each of the bears, from the founding fathers to the little cubs, represent an individual human emotion in brand-new adventures of this Canadian-produced Saturday-morning series that aired on ABC beginning in 1986. A total of 27 episodes were produced for the first season. The program was so well received that ABC renewed it for a second season, which combined 10 new episodes with old ones. The series went straight into syndication following the end of its network run under the title *Care Bears*. Canadian animation house Nelvana Enterprises, which produced the series, also produced three feature-length films starring the cuddly characters.

A Nelvana Production. Color. Half-hour. Premiered on ABC: September 13, 1986–September 5, 1987; September 26, 1987–January 23, 1988.

Voices

Grumpy Bear: Bob Dermie; **Brave Heart Lion/Loyal Heart Dog/Good Luck Bear:** Dan Hennessey; **Mr. Beastley:** John Stocker; **Birthday Bear:** Melleny Brown; **Lotsa Heart Elephant/Gentle Heart Lamb;** Luba Goy; **Tenderheart Bear:** Billie Mae Richards

◎ CARROT TOP'S A.M. MAYHEM

Popular stand-up comedian Carrot Top and a cast of alter-ego characters, including Granny Top, Aunt Zelda and Cousin Chet, star in this weekday morning, two-hour showcase of classic cartoons produced for the Cartoon Network.

A Cartoon Network Production. Color. Two hours. Premiered on CAR: October 9, 1995.

◎ CARTOON CAPERS

Adapted from popular children's stories and children's fables, this series, first syndicated in 1966, features 170 seven-minute cartoons, complete with dialogue, music and effects, which were offered to independent television stations for flexible daytime programming. Series titles included "Boots and Saddles," "Robin Hood," "Jack and the Beanstalk," "Santa's Caper," "Roscoe the Rabbit," "Goldilocks," "Three Blind Mice," "Don Quixote," "Sleeping Beauty" and "Night in Toyland."

A Thea/Telewide Production. Color. Half-hour. Premiered: 1966. Syndicated.

◎ CARTOON CLASSICS

A collection of serialized animated features grouped and sold to more than 100 worldwide television markets in the 1960s. The package included science-fiction thrillers and fairy-tale classics segmented into cliffhanging episodes. The first package of cartoons went on the air in 1958, with additional fully animated stories syndicated in 1960 and 1965. Boxing promoter Bill Cayton, who entered television with his *Greatest Fights of the Century* series, produced the *Cartoon Classics* series. (Cayton later served as boxing manager for heavyweight champion Mike Tyson.)

A Radio and Television Packagers Production. Color. Half-hour. Syndicated: 1958.

◎ CARTOON EXPRESS

Initially begun as a weekday cartoon block featuring off-network cartoon series in reruns, mostly from Hanna-Barbera's library and other independent studios including DIC Entertainment, Ruby-Spears Productions and UPA Productions. USA Network offered this program alternative for young viewers on its schedule beginning in February of 1989. The first shows to debut that month included *Huckleberry Hound and Friends, Help! It's the Hair Bear Bunch, The Flintstones, Gobots, Huckleberry Hound and Friends, Jana of the Jungle, Mr. T, The Pac-Man Show, She-Ra* and *Young Samson* (featuring "The Space Kidettes").

That year, the program block, airing weekday mornings and afternoons and four-and-a-half hours on weekends, featured other popular television favorites, including *Captain Caveman and the Teen Angels, Dragon's Lair, Dynomutt, Dog Wonder, The New Fred and Barney Show, Goober and the Ghost Chasers, He-Man, Hong Kong Phooey, JEM, Monchichis, Mr. Magoo and Friends, Paw Paws, Pebbles and Bamm-Bamm, Popeye and Son, Scooby's All-Star Laff-A-Lympics, Shirt Tales, Smurfs, Snorks, Teen Force* (from Hanna-Barbera's "Space Stars" series), *Turbo Teen, Where's Huddles? Wheelie and the Chopper Bunch* and *Yogi's Treasure Hunt.*

She-Ra and *Where's Huddles?* were the first programs to be yanked in 1989. Other casualties dropped from the schedule the following year included *He-Man, Mr. Magoo and Friends* and *Popeye and Son.* For the 1991–92 season, the programming was dramatically overhauled. *Captain Caveman and the Teen Angels, Dynomutt, Dog Wonder, Help! It's the Hair Bear Bunch, Gobots, Goober and the Ghost Chasers, Monchhichis, Snorks, Wheelie and the Chopper Bunch* and *Young Samson* were all taken off the air. Only one show was added that year: the syndicated *Voltron: Defender of the Universe.* As a result of Ted Turner's acquisition of Hanna-Barbera and ultimate launching of his 24-hour Cartoon Network in October 1992, USA was unable to continue airing those Hanna-Barbera shows that had been a key component of "Cartoon Express" for several years. Thus the network dropped a number of Hanna-Barbera shows from the schedule, including *Hong Kong Phooey, Huckleberry Hound and Friends, The Flintstones, Magilla Gorilla and Friends, The New Fred and Barney Show, The Pac-Man Show, Paw Paws, Pebbles and Bamm-Bamm, Scooby's All-Star Laff-A-Lympics, Shirt Tales, Teen Force,* and *Yogi's Treasure Hunt.* Other shows terminated were three Ruby-Spears series, *Dragon's Lair, Mr. T* and *Turbo Teen.* Making the jump to "Cartoon Express" from syndication was 1985's *G.I. Joe* series.

With the start of the 1993–94 season, USA, for the time in history, added original first-run cartoon series to its weekend schedule, weaning itself from old programming, by featuring two new shows, *Itsy Bitsy Spider* and *Problem Child*. That season only one previously syndicated series was added, *Dinosaucers*, while two shows, *The Smurfs* and *Voltron: Defender of the Universe*, were canceled.

The following season *Itsy Bitsy Spider* and *Problem Child* returned with new episodes on the weekend "Cartoon Express," while four previously broadcast shows joined the weekend schedule (now six hours long): *Cadillacs & Dinosaurs*, *Hulk Hogan's Rock n' Wrestling*, *Jayce and the Wheeled Warriors* (which lasted only five months on the air) and *Super Mario Bros. 3*. USA dropped two series, *The Real Ghosbusters* and *Scooby-Doo, Where Are You?*

In 1995 USA axed a number of shows from the weekend lineup: *Denver, the Last Dinosaur*, *Dinosaucers*, *Hulk Hogan's Rock n' Wrestling* and *Super Mario Bros. 3*, adding the off-network *Woody Woodpecker and Friends* and two new action adventure series instead: *Savage Dragon* and *Street Fighter*. Also joining the weekend block, reduced to five hours of programming from the previous season, were two other animated series, *Exosquad* and *Wild C.A.T.S.*

In the fall of the following year, the weekend block featured two new first-run series, *Wing Commander Academy*, featuring Mark Hamill as one of the voices, and *Mortal Kombat: Defenders of the Realm*. Also rebroadcast that season on weekends was *Dennis the Menace*, while *G.I. Joe* completed its network run.

A USA Network Production. Color. Three and a half hours. Four and a half hours. Five hours. Six hours. Premiered on USA: February 17, 1989.

◎ CARTOON FUN
In the fall of 1965, ABC added this short-lived series to its Saturday-morning lineup. The half-hour program featured a collection of Jay Ward and Total Television characters seen in repeat episodes, among them Hoppity Hooper, Dudley Do-Right, Commander McBragg and Aesop and Son. (See original series entries for voice credits.)

A Producers Associates for Television Production. Color. Half-hour. Premiered on ABC: September 26, 1965–December 19, 1965.

◎ CARTOONIES
Ventriloquist Paul Winchell and his famed wooden sidekicks, Jerry Mahoney and Knucklehead Smith, hosted this half-hour program of theatrical cartoon shorts, featuring films originally produced for Paramount's *Modern Madcaps* and *Noveltoons* series. Characters featured were Goodie the Gremlin, the Cat and Jeepers and Creepers. Initially the program was titled *Cartoonsville*.

A Paramount Cartoon Studios Production. Color. Half-hour. Premiered on ABC: April 6, 1963–September 28, 1963.

◎ CARTOON JUNCTION
Animation classics from the 1930s, 1940s and 1950s, mostly public domain cartoons, highlight this syndicated package produced in the early 1990s.

A Pacific Family Entertainment Production. Black-and-white. Color. Half-hour. Premiered: September 3, 1993. Syndicated.

◎ CARTOON PLANET
Familiar yellow-caped, black-hooded interplanetary crusader Space Ghost is the host of this Monday-through-Friday night, hour-long anthology series, presenting "the brightest stars" in the cartoon solar system, from Bugs Bunny to Yogi Bear, in cartoon reruns, broadcast on the Cartoon Network.

A Cartoon Network Production. Color. One hour. Premiered on CAR: September 4, 1995.

◎ CARTOON QUEST
The Sci-Fi Channel developed this popular two-hour cartoon program block in 1992. Airing Mondays through Fridays and Sundays, the package featured mostly off-network and out-of-syndication science-fiction and fantasy cartoon series favorites mixed with a few live-action puppet shows and broadcast on a rotating basis. The original two-hour block (rotated) included the animated *Defenders of Earth*, *Fantastic Voyage*, *The New Adventures of Flash Gordon*, *Return of the Planet of the Apes*, *Star Trek* and *Transformers*, each of which debuted in September of 1992. Added to the mix were the popular live-action marionette puppet series, *Captain Scarlett and the Mysterons* (created by Gerry Anderson of *Thunderbirds* fame), which joined the rotation three months later, and 1960s' favorite *Stingray*, debuting in June of that year.

Other animated series were added to the rotation in 1993: *Droids: The Adventures of R2D2 and C3PO*, *The Ewoks*, *Galaxy High School*, *Here Comes The Grump*, *Journey to the Centre of the Earth*, *Lazer Patrol* (actually *Lazer Tag Academy*), *Little Shop*, *The New Adventures of Gigantor* and *Robotech*, as well as two more live-action shows: the marionette-puppet–led *The Terrahawks* and Sid and Marty Krofft's formerly popular 1970s Saturday-morning prehistoric series, *Land of the Lost*.

Rounding out the program block were additional components, added between 1994 and 1996: the animated *Back to the Future*, *The Bionic Six* and a Japanese imported series, *Ronin Warriors*.

Many animated series featured on this program also aired in time slots of their own. In March of 1995, the Sci-Fi Channel changed the name to *Animation Station*. Many of the original components from *Cartoon Quest* remained until that series was canceled in August of 1997.

A Sci-Fi Channel Production. Color. Two hours. Premiered on SCI: September 25, 1992–March 25, 1995.

CARTOON SUSHI

Similar in format to MTV's successful anthology series *Liquid Television*, the network unveiled this fresh and funny collection of four or five animated short films from around the world from its own New York studio as a weekly series in July of 1997. The premiere episode featured John Dilworth's "Dirty Bird."

An MTV Animation Production. Color. Half-hour. Premiered on MTV: July 1997.

CASPER

The lovable, friendly ghost, who still hates to scare people, has a whole new attitude (except for his revolting uncles) in this contemporary version of the famed theatrical cartoon star, based on the hit 1995 live-action/animated feature produced by Steven Spielberg. The 52-episode half-hour series, produced for Saturday-mornings, debuted on the Fox Network as a midseason show in February 1996. The series won its time period every week that it aired and an Emmy during its first season. In the fall of 1997, the show was added to Fox's weekday afternoon schedule. The series ended its run in January 1998.

A Universal Cartoon Studios Production in association with Harvey Comics Entertainment. Color. Half-hour. Premiered on FOX: February 24, 1996–August 30, 1997; September 6, 1997–December 28, 1997. Rebroadcast on FOX: September 9, 1997–January 30, 1998 (weekdays).

CASPER AND THE ANGELS

The year is 2179, and Casper the friendly ghost is assigned to help a pair of Space Patrol Officers, Minnie and Maxi, maintain law and order in Space City, tangling with cosmic criminals and solving space emergencies in the process. A new character featured in the series of 26 half-hour adventures (composed of two 11-minute cartoons per show) was the ghostly Hairy Scary, who provided comic relief.

A Hanna-Barbera Production. Color. Half-hour. Premiered on NBC: September 22, 1979–May 3, 1980. Rebroadcast on CAR: March 18, 1995–March 19, 1995 (Look What We Found!); December 1995 (70s Super Explosion).

Voices
Casper: Julie McWhirter; **Hairy Scary, his assistant/ Harry Scary/Commander:** John Stephenson; **Officer Minni:** Laurel Page; **Officer Maxie:** Diane McCannon

CASPER THE FRIENDLY GHOST AND COMPANY

Repackaged version of previously exhibited Paramount Pictures cartoons—retitled "Harveytoons" in the early 1960s—starring Casper the Friendly Ghost, Baby Huey, Little Audrey and Herman and Katnip. The package was resyndicated in 1991 as *Casper and Friends* by Harvey Comics Entertainment.

A Paramount Cartoon Studios Production for Harvey Films. Color. Half-hour. Premiered: 1974, 1991. Syndicated.

THE CATTANOOGA CATS

This all-animated series featured a feline rock group (Cheesie, Kitty Jo, Scoots, Groove and Country), who not only starred in segments of their own but also hosted the cartoon-filled show.

Cartoon segments were: "It's the Wolf," the madcap adventures of an overzealous wolf (Mildew) whose meal plans are based on snatching one elusive lamb named Lambsy; "Around the World in 79 Days," the globe-trotting adventures of Phineas Fogg Jr., who travels around the world with two teenage friends (Jenny and Happy) in 79 days instead of 80; and "Autocat and Motormouse," a cat and mouse who beat each other at a different game: race car competitions.

Following the first season, the program was reduced to a half-hour.

A Hanna-Barbera Production. Color. One hour. Half-hour. Premiered on ABC: September 6, 1969–September 5, 1970. Rebroadcast on ABC: September 12, 1970–September 5, 1971 (half hour). Rebroadcast on CAR: December 5, 1994–September 1, 1995 (weekdays).

Voices
Cheesie/Kitty Jo: Julie Bennett; **Scoots:** Jim Begg; **Groove:** Casey Kasem; **Country:** Bill Callaway; **Mildew, the wolf:** Paul Lynde; **Lambsy/Crumdon:** Daws Butler; **Bristle Hound, Lamby's protector/Bumbler:** Allan Melvin; **Phineas Fogg, Jr.:** Bruce Watson; **Jenny Trent:** Janet Waldo; **Happy/Smerky:** Don Messick; **Autocat:** Marty Ingels; **Motormouse:** Dick Curtis

CAVE KIDS ADVENTURES

The Flintstones characters Pebbles and Bamm-Bamm appear as prehistoric preschoolers, along with babysitter Dino, in imaginative, lesson-teaching adventures in this half-hour animated series, produced for first-run syndication.

A Hanna-Barbera Production. Color. Half-hour. Premiered: 1996. Syndicated.

Voices
Pebbles: Aria Noelle Curzon; **Bamm-Bamm:** Christine Cavanaugh; **Baby Pebbles:** Taylor Gunther; **Singing Bamm-Bamm:** E.G. Daily; **Dino:** Frank Welker

C.B. BEARS

Three bruin investigators (Hustle, Bump and Boogie) travel in a rigged-up garbage truck (equipped with C.B. and closed-circuit TV) to solve mysteries and strange encounters. The three clumsy bears were lead-ins to five other cartoon regulars: "Shake, Rattle and Roll," the misadventures of three ghostly innkeepers in need of a rest; "Undercover Elephant," starring a bumbling secret agent in "Mission Impossible"–type situations; "Heyyy, It's the King," an animalized parody of Henry Winkler's "Fonzie" (now a smart-alecky lion) from TV's *Happy Days*; "Blast Off Buzzard," a Road Runner and Coyote re-creation casting a nonspeaking buzzard (Blast-Off) and snake (Crazylegs) in the title roles; and "Posse Impossible," the mishaps of three clumsy cowboys in the Old West.

A *Hanna-Barbera Production. Color. One hour. Premiered on NBC: September 10, 1977–June 17, 1978. Rebroadcast on CAR: July 5, 1995– (Wednesdays).*

Voices

C.B. BEARS: Hustle: Daws Butler; **Bump:** Henry Corden; **Boogie:** Chuck McCann; **Charlie:** Susan Davis

SHAKE, RATTLE & ROLL: Shake: Paul Winchell; **Rattle:** Lennie Weinrib; **Roll:** Joe E. Ross; **Sidney Merciless:** Alan Oppenheimer

UNDERCOVER ELEPHANT: Undercover Elephant: Daws Butler; **Loud Mouse:** Bob Hastings; **Chief:** Michael Bell

HEYYY, IT'S THE KING: The King/Yukayuka: Lennie Weinrib; **Skids:** Marvin Kaplan; **Big H:** Sheldon Allman; **Sheena:** Ginny McSwain; **Clyde the Ape:** Don Messick

POSSE IMPOSSIBLE: Sheriff: Bill Woodson; **Stick/Duke:** Daws Butler; **Blubber:** Chuck McCann

◎ C-BEAR AND JAMAL

Jamal, a 10-year-old boy from south-central Los Angeles, embarks on his journey through adolescence, guided every step of the way by C-Bear, his toy teddy bear (voiced by rapper Tone Loc; also the series' executive producer) who possesses magical powers and teaches Jamal valuable lessons, in this 13-episode half-hour animated series for the Fox Network. Despite its being the highest-rated show in its time slot, Fox canceled the critically acclaimed series prior to its decision to merge with powerhouse cartoon giant Saban Entertainment to supply more of its own programming in house.

A *Film Roman Production. Color. Half-hour. Premiered on FOX: September 7, 1996–April 3, 1998.*

Voices
Jamal: Arthur Reggie III; **C-Bear:** Tone Loc; **Hawthorne:** George Wallace; **Grandma:** Dawnn Lewis; **Grandpa:** Darryl Sivad; **Maya:** Kim Fields Freeman; **Big Chill/Kwame:** Aires Spears; **Chipster:** Jeannie Elias; **Kim:** Margaret Cho; **Javier:** Paul Rodriguez; **Sooner:** Danny Mann

◎ CBS CARTOON THEATER

Comedian Dick Van Dyke hosted this half-hour collection of *Terrytoons* cartoons, which originated from WCBS, New York. Four cartoons were shown on each program, including the madcap adventures of "Heckle and Jeckle," "Little Roquefort" and "Dinky Duck." The program was the first network prime-time series featuring animation.

A *CBS Terrytoons Production. Black-and-white. Half-hour. Premiered on CBS: June 13, 1956–September 5, 1956.*

Voices
Gandy Goose: Arthur Kay; **Heckle/Jeckle:** Dayton Allen, Roy Halee; **Little Roquefort/Percy the Cat:** Tom Morrison

◎ CBS STORYBREAK

Bob Keeshan, of *Captain Kangaroo* fame, hosted this weekly anthology series of half-hour animated films based on popular children's stories. The series, produced by several independent studios, debuted on CBS (the same network on which Keeshan had starred in the long-running children's series) in 1985. CBS broadcast the program—in consecutive years until 1991, when it was replaced by *Inspector Gadget* in the network's fall Saturday-morning lineup. The 26-episode series returned to CBS's Saturday-morning schedule in 1993, combining new half-hour episodes with previously broadcast material. The network dropped the series the following season. In January 1998 the series returned as a midseason replacement in reruns.

A *CBS Television Production. Color. Half-hour. Premiered on CBS: March 30, 1985–January 1, 1986; September 18, 1993–September 3, 1994. Rebroadcast on CBS: January 3, 1987–October 26, 1991; September 17, 1994–August 19, 1995; January 3, 1998.*

◎ THE CENTURIONS

Computer scientist Crystal Kane and her top-secret team of computer-operated warriors, called Centurions, try saving the world from destruction at the hands of Doctor Terror's Doom Drones in this first-run action/adventure series.

A *Ruby-Spears Enterprises Production. Color. Half-hour. Premiered: 1985. Syndicated. Rebroadcast on CAR: October 1, 1992–April 9, 1993 (weekdays); April 10, 1993–October 1, 1994 (Saturdays); October 3, 1994–September 1, 1995 (weekdays, Sundays, Saturdays); August 5, 1996–May 3, 1997 (weekdays).*

Computer-operated warriors try to save the world from destruction in the action/adventure series The Centurions. © *Ruby-Spears Enterprises*

Voices

Ace McCloud: Neil Ross; **Jake Rockwell:** Vince Edwards; **Max Ray/Dr. Wu:** Pat Fraley; **Crystal Kane:** Diane Pershing; **Rex Charger:** Bob Ridgely; **John Thunder:** Michael Bell; **Doc Terror:** Ron Feinberg; **Hacker:** Edmund Gilbert; **Amber:** Jennifer Darling

☺ CHALLENGE OF THE GOBOTS

Earth becomes the battleground in a titanic interplanetary struggle between good and evil when a distant, scientifically advanced world erupts in war. On the high-tech planet GoBotron, the noble Guardian GoBots—a race of robots able to transform into vehicles—pursue the evil Renegade GoBots who scheme to enslave Earth and exploit its resources to conquer GoBotron and the galaxy in this first-run, 65-episode series based on the famed action-figure toys. The series was later rerun on USA Network's *Cartoon Express*.

A Hanna-Barbera Production in association with the Tonka Corporation. Color. Half-hour. Premiered: 1984. Syndicated. Rebroadcast on USA: February 17, 1989–March 28, 1991.

Voices

Leader-1: Lou Richards; **Turbo:** Arthur Burghardt; **Scooter:** Frank Welker; **Cy-Kill:** Bernard Erhard; **Cop-Tur:** Bob Holt; **Crasher:** Marilyn Lightstone; **Matt**

Hunter: Morgan Paull; **A.J. Foster:** Leslie Speights; **Nick Burns:** Sparky Marcus; **Dr. Braxis:** Rene Auberjonois; **General Newcastle:** Brock Peters

☺ CHALLENGE OF THE SUPER FRIENDS

Evil forces unite to annihilate those guardians of humanity—Superman, Batman and Robin, Wonder Woman, Aquaman and other comic-book superheroes of the Hall of Justice—who are forced to use all their superpowers to combat the wicked Legion of Doom, composed of well-known DC comic book villains Lex Luthor, Braniac, Bizarro, Toyman, The Riddler, and others. The 16-episode series was the third collection of DC comic superheroes transformed into a weekly animated series, following 1973's "Super Friends" and 1977's *All-New Super Friends*, on ABC.

A Hanna-Barbera Production. Color. Half-hour. Premiered on ABC: September 8, 1978–September 15, 1979.

Voices

Narrator: Bill Woodson

SUPER FRIENDS: Superman: Danny Dark; **Batman:** Olan Soule; **Robin/Computer:** Casey Kasem; **Wonder Woman:** Shannon Farnon; **Aquaman:** Bill Callaway; **Zan/Gleek:** Mike Bell; **Jayna:** Liberty Williams; **Black Vulcan:** Buster Jones; **Samurai/Flash/Hawkman:** Jack Angel; **Apache Chief/Green Lantern:** Mike Rye

LEGION OF DOOM: Luthor: Stanley Jones; **Brainiac/Black Manta:** Ted Cassidy; **Toyman:** Frank Welker; **Giganta:** Ruth Forman; **Cheeta:** Marlene Aragon; **Riddler:** Mike Bell; **Captain Cold:** Dick Ryal; **Sinestro:** Vic Perrin; **Scarecrow:** Don Messick; **Bizarro:** Bill Callaway; **Solomon Grundy:** Jimmy Weldon; **Grodd the Gorilla:** Stanley Ross

☺ CHANNEL UMPTEE-3

Producer Norman Lear (of *All In The Family* fame) dreamed up the concept of this half-hour Saturday-morning series centering on the exploits of a secret TV station (located in "the white space between channels"), established by a small band of wildly enthusiastic television pirates (a seven-foot hyperactive ostrich named Ogden; his best friend and real-life mole, Holey Moley; and resident genius/introverted sluggish snail, Sheldon S. Cargo), who drive around in an "Umptee-3" news van broadcasting stuff "too cool, too weird and too wonderful" for regular television.

An Act II/Enchante-George/Columbia TriStar TV Animation Production. Color. Half-hour. Premiered on WB: October 25, 1997.

Voices

Stickley Ricketts: Jonathan Harris; **Ed:** Neil Ross; **Bud:** Gregg Berger; **Ogden:** Rob Paulsen; **Sheldon:** David Paymer; **Pandora:** Alice Ghostley; **Professor Relevant:** Greg Burson; **Polly:** Susan Silo

⊚ THE CHARLIE BROWN AND SNOOPY SHOW

Charles Schulz's beloved comic-strip characters come to life in animated vignettes focusing on school, sports and, of course, Snoopy in this half-hour series consisting of three separate stories based on the comic strip. Debuting on CBS in September of 1983, the series aired for three consecutive seasons. (The first two seasons were comprised mostly of original episodes.) The series—as well as practically the entire catalog of *Peanuts* programs—was rebroadcast weekdays on The Disney Channel, beginning in October of 1993. In 1998 the series moved to Nickelodeon.

A Lee Mendelson–Bill Melendez Production in association with Charles M. Schulz Creative Associates and United Feature Syndicate. Color. Half-hour. Premiered on CBS: September 17, 1983–August 16, 1986. Rebroadcast on DIS: October 4, 1993; Rebroadcast on NIK: 1998.

Voices

Charlie Brown: Brad Kesten, Brett Johnson; **Linus:** Jeremy Schoenberg; **Lucy:** Angela Lee, Heather Stoneman; **Schroeder:** Kevin Brando, Danny Colby; **Peppermint Patty:** Victoria Hodges, Gini Holtzman; **Marcie:** Michael Dockery, Keri Holtzman; **Rerun:** Jason Muller (Mendelson); **Frieda:** Mary Tunnell; **Little Girl:** Dana Ferguson; **Franklin:** Carl Steven; **Singer (theme song):** Desiree Goyette; **Singer:** Joseph Chemay; **Singer:** Joey Harrison Scarbury

⊚ CHIP & PEPPER'S CARTOON MADNESS

Zany Canadian comics Chip and Pepper Foster hosted this 30-minute mix of live action and animation featuring special celebrity guests and cartoon favorites, including Casper, Popeye and Captain Caveman.

A Rain Forest Entertainment/DIC Animation City Production. Color. Half-hour. Premiered on NBC: September 14, 1991–July 25, 1992.

⊚ CHIPMUNKS GO TO THE MOVIES

Alvin, Theodore and Simon and the Chipettes (Brittany, Janette and Eleanor), along with record manager David Seville, spoof blockbuster movies of the era—including *Batman* (retitled *Batmunk*) and *Honey, I Shrunk the Kids* (renamed *Funny We Shrunk the Adults*)—in this short-lived,

half-hour animated series for NBC. Interspersed throughout the season were reruns of previous *Alvin* episodes.

A Bagdasarian Production in association with Ruby-Spears Productions. Color. Half-hour. Premiered on NBC: September 8, 1990–September 7, 1991.

Voices

Alvin/Simon/Dave Seville: Ross Bagdasarian Jr.; **Theodore/ Brittany/Janette/Eleanor:** Janice Bagdasarian; **Ms. Miller:** Dody Goodman

⊚ CHIP 'N DALE RESCUE RANGERS

Following the enormous success of its number-one-rated daily animated series *DuckTales*, Walt Disney introduced this first-run, half-hour syndicated animated companion featuring chipmunk favorites Chip 'n Dale in cliffhanger stories filled with mystery and intrigue, Indiana Jones–style. The fast-talking, ever-squabbling pair are heads of a small eccentric group of animal characters who solve cases that lead to bigger crimes with far-reaching consequences. Chip 'n' Dale's team of investigators: Monterey Jack, a raucous, back-slapping musclemouse who is Dale's right hand; Zipper the fly; Gadget, a consummate inventor who doubles as Chip and Dale's romantic interest; and Sewer Al, a six-and-a-half-foot-long cajun alligator who acts as the enforcer. After enjoying a one season run on The Disney Channel in 1988–89, the 65-episode series was syndicated as part of the *Disney Afternoon* two-hour block in September of 1989.

A Walt Disney Television Animation Production. Color. Half-hour. Premiered on DIS: August 27, 1988–September 1989. Syndicated: September 1989.

Voices

Corey Burton, Peter Cullen, Jim Cummings, Tress MacNeille, Rob Paulsen

⊚ CHUCK NORRIS' KARATE KOMMANDOS

Action film star Chuck Norris supplied his own voice in this short-lived, five-part syndicated series in which the former karate champ encounters worldly villains, including Super Ninja and an evil empire known as Vulture.

A Ruby Spears Enterprises Production. Color. Half-hour. Premiered: September 1986. Syndicated. Rebroadcast on CAR: April 23–24, 1994 (under one-hour Look What We Found!).

Voices

Chuck Norris: Himself; **Tabe, Ninja Henchman:** Robert Ito; **Too-Much:** Mona Marshall; **Kimo:** Key Luke; **Reed:** Sam Fontana; **Pepper:** Kathy Garver; **The Claw:** Bill Martin; **Super Ninja:** Keone Young; **The President:** Alan Oppenheimer

⦿ CLUE CLUB

This series followed the adventures of four professional teenage detectives—Pepper, Larry, Dotty and D.D.—who collect clues to unsolvable crimes in the same manner as celebrated London sleuth Sherlock Holmes, with the assistance of two cowardly dogs, Woofer and Wimper. This 16-episode half-hour Saturday-morning series premiered on CBS in 1976 and was briefly retitled *Woofer and Wimper, Dog Detectives* in 1978.

A Hanna-Barbera Production. Color. Half-hour. Premiered on CBS: August 14, 1976–September 3, 1977. Rebroadcast on CBS: September 10, 1978–September 2, 1979. Rebroadcast on CAR: April 10, 1994 (Sundays).

Voices
Larry: David Joliffe; **D.D.:** Bob Hastings; **Pepper:** Patricia Stich; **Dotty:** Tara Talboy; **Woofer:** Paul Winchell; **Wimper:** Jim MacGeorge; **Sheriff Bagley:** John Stephenson

⦿ CLUTCH CARGO

Established author Clutch Cargo travels the globe in search of adventure with his constant companions Swampy, Spinner and dog Paddlefoot. Piloting his plane anywhere a friend needs help, Clutch uses only his wits to defeat the villains. Created by one-time cartoonist Clark Haas, these five-minute, 130-episode serialized adventures combined limited animation and a live-action process called Synchro-Vox, invented by Ed Gillette and first used for "talking animal" commercials in the 1950s. This economical but unsophisticated method superimposed the human lips of voice actors over the mouths of their animated counterparts, the only parts of the characters that moved. Twenty-six half-hour shows, each consisting of five five-minute episodes, were produced for the low-budget series between 1957 and 1960. In 1990 the series was colorized and shown for the first time in nearly three decades on The Comedy Channel.

A Cambria Production. Black-and-white and color. Half-hour. Premiered: March 1959. Syndicated. Rebroadcast on the Comedy Channel: 1990.

Voices
Clutch Cargo: Richard Cotting; **Spinner/Paddlefoot:** Margaret Kerry; **Swampy:** Hal Smith

⦿ COLONEL BLEEP

A universe light-years away is the setting for action and adventure in which Colonel Bleep and his Space Deputies, Scratch the Caveman and Squeek the Puppet, battle Doctor Destructo, master criminal of the universe, in this late 1950s' color series produced by Soundac Studios of Miami, Florida. The series consisted of 104 six-minute episodes, shown in a half-hour block (four episodes per show) in syndication beginning in 1957. Originally the series was packaged as part of a franchised children's series *Uncle Bill's TV Club*, broadcast on independent television stations and hosted by local on-air personalities.

A Robert H. Ullman. Inc/Soundac Color Production. Color. Half-hour. Premiered: 1957. Syndicated.

Voices
Narrator: Noel Taylor

⦿ THE COMIC STRIP

Produced in the manner of "Funtastic World of Hanna-Barbera" and "Super Sunday," this two-hour series was a marathon of first-run cartoons featuring several stars in one episodic adventure each week: "Karate Kat," a klutzy karate expert who heads a detective agency (obviously inspired by the popularity of the *The Karate Kid* feature film series); "The Street Frogs," streetwise frogs who encounter comedy and adventure; "The Mini-Monsters," the antics of two brat youngsters and their summer camp monster pals, Dracky, Franklyn, Mumm-O, Blank-O, and Wolfie; and "Tigersharks," an intrepid group of explorers and their underwater adventures.

A Rankin-Bass Production. Color. Two hours. Syndicated: September 1987.

Voices

KARATE KAT: Earl Hammond, Maggie Jakobson, Larry Kenney, Robert McFadden, Gerrianne Raphael

MINI-MONSTERS: Josh Blake, Jim Brownold, Danielle DuClos, Seth Green, Maggie Jakobson, Robert McFadden, Jim Meskimen, Peter Newman

STREET FROGS: Donald Acree, Gary V. Brown, Carmen De Lavallade, Robert McFadden, Gordy Owens, Ron Taylor, Tanya Willoughby, Daniel Wooten

TIGERSHARKS: Camille Banora, Jim Brownold, Earl Hammond, Larry Kenney, Robert McFadden, Jim Meskimen, Peter Newman

⦿ COMMONWEALTH CARTOON PACKAGE

Cartoon favorites Flip the Frog, Willie Whopper, Paul Terry's *Aesop's Fables* and others composed this series of vintage cartoons offered for local programming. Several early Walt Disney cartoon shorts were also included in this syndicated package.

Black-and-white. Half-hour. Premiered: 1951. Syndicated.

THE COMPLETELY MENTAL MISADVENTURES OF ED GRIMLEY

Comedian Martin Short teamed up with Hanna-Barbera Productions to produce this half-hour Saturday-morning show based on his famed *Saturday Night Live* character, Ed Grimley, a sweetly nerdy guy who lives in a funky Victorian apartment with a goldfish named Moby and a clever rat named Sheldon. Plot lines include his encounters with the ever-cranky Mr. Freebus, Ed's landlord; Miss Malone, his gorgeous down-the-hall neighbor; the Truly Remarkable Gustav Brothers, identical twins who look nothing alike; and Ed's favorite television program, Count Floyd and his "Really Scaaary Stories Show."

A Hanna-Barbera Production. Color. Half-hour. Premiered on NBC: September 10, 1988–September 2, 1989. Rebroadcast on CAR: October 4, 1992–April 4, 1993 (Sundays); February 6, 1994–October 2, 1995 (Sundays, Saturdays); December 18, 1995–December 22, 1995; December 26, 1995–December 29, 1995; January 6, 1996–June 23, 1997.

Voices

Ed Grimley: Martin Short; **Count Floyd:** Joe Flaherty; **Miss Malone:** Catherine O'Hara; **Mr. Freebus:** Jonathan Winters; **Mrs. Freebus:** Andrea Martin; **Sheldon:** Frank Welker

The Gustav Brothers

Roger: Jonathan Winters; **Wendell:** Danny Cooksey

CONAN THE ADVENTURER

Enslaved by the evil warlock who turned his family into stone, young musclebound barbarian warrior Conan (a character created for *Weird Tales* magazine by Robert E. Howard in 1932 and later played by Arnold Schwarzenegger in the *Conan* feature-film series of the early 1980s) manages to escape. He embarks on a fearless mission to save the people of his ancient land and to restore his family to their former selves in this half-hour syndicated series. The program—which tried to live up to adventures of the books and movies—debuted in weekly syndication in September 1992 and ran for 13 weeks. In 1993 the program went into daily syndication, with 52 new and original episodes.

A Sunbow Entertainment/Graz Entertainment Production in association with Conan Properties. Color. Half-hour. Premiered: September 12, 1992. Syndicated: 1993.

Voices

Kathleen Barr, Michael Beattie, Jim Burnes, Gary Chalk, Mike Donovan, John Pyper Ferguson, Janyce Jaud, Scott McNeil, Richard Newman, Doug Parker, Alec Willows

COOL McCOOL

Bumbling detective McCool was created by cartoonist Bob Kane, the co-creator of Batman, in the vein of Maxwell Smart, agent 86, who stumbled his way to the solution of crimes in this popular NBC Saturday morning series. McCool was featured in two short adventures each week, along with one episode in between of Keystone Kops–like adventures of Harry McCool, Cool's father, who chases down thieves and other no-goods with the help of two klutzy policemen, Tom and Dick. Twenty half-hour programs were produced in all, each originally telecast in 1966–67 on NBC. The series lasted two more seasons (in reruns) before it was canceled.

A Cavalier/King Features Production. Color. Half-hour. Premiered on NBC: September 10, 1966–August 31, 1969.

Voices

Cool McCool: Bob McFadden; **Number One, his boss/Riggs, a scientific genius:** Chuck McCann; **Friday, Number One's secretary:** Carol Corbett

C.O.P.S.

Former FBI special agent Baldwin P. Vess tries eradicating organized crime in Empire City with the help of his C.O.P.S. crimefighting force, each member a master of a special skill and dedicated to the cause of justice, in this popular 65-episode half-hour series made for syndication. In the spring of 1993, the series returned as a Saturday-morning network show (retitled *Cyber C.O.P.S.*) on CBS, repeating episodes from the original series.

After CBS canceled the series, it reaired on USA Network's *Cartoon Express.*

A DIC Enterprises Production. Color. Half-hour. Premiered: September 1988. Syndicated. Rebroadcast on CBS: March 27, 1993–September 4, 1993. Rebroadcast on USA: January 2, 1995–March 29, 1995.

Voices

Bulletproof Vess: Ken Ryan; **Longram:** John Stocker; **The Big Boss/Mace:** Len Carlson; **Badvibes:** Ron Rubin; **Buttons McBoomBoom/Bowzer:** Nick Nichols; **Berserko:** Paul De La Rosa; **Rock Krusher:** Brent Titcomb; **Squeeky:** Marvin Goldhar; **Turbo Tu-Tone:** Dan Hennessy; **Nightshade:** Jane Schoettle; **Bullseye:** Peter Keleghan; **Highway/Barricade:** Ray James; **Hardtop:** Darren Baker; **Mainframe:** Mary Long; **Whitney Morgan:** Jeri Craden; **Mirage:** Liz Hanna; **Ms. Demeanor:** Paulina Gillis

COUNT DUCKULA

Unlike most vampires whose thirst for blood knows no earthly limits, Count Duckula is a reluctant vampire with a hankering for show business who, instead of blood, sucks on broccoli sandwiches. His Castle Duckula and its occupants—Igor, Nanny and Dr. Von Goosewing—are transported anywhere in the world on command, where they experience many madcap adventures.

A Cosgrove-Hall Production in association with Thames Television. Color. Half-hour. Premiered on NIK: February 6, 1988–December 26, 1993.

Voices
Count Duckula: David Jason; **Igor:** Jack May; **Nanny:** Brian Trueman; **Von Goosewing:** Jimmy Hibbert; **Narrator:** Barry Clayton

Additional Voice
Ruby Wax

◎ THE COUNT OF MONTE CRISTO

Those who pervert justice for their own ends are the targets of the Count of Monte Cristo and his two friends, Rico and Jacopo. Cristo has one consuming passion—to see injustice of any sort uncovered and denounced. Halas and Batchelor, once the largest animation film production studio in Europe, produced this cartoon import in 1974.

A Halas and Batchelor/R.A.I. Production. Color. Half-hour. Premiered: 1974. Syndicated.

Voices
George Roubicek, Jeremy Wilkin, Bernard Spear, Peter Hawkins, Miriam Margoyles, Jean England, David de Keyser

◎ THE COUNTRY MOUSE AND CITY MOUSE ADVENTURES

Two feisty mice cousins—folksy Emily and dapper urbanite Alexander—travel the globe in this weekly half-hour series, based on characters from Aesop's Fables and presented by *Reader's Digest*. Premiered Sunday mornings on HBO in March of 1998.

A Cinar France Animation/Canada/France Production. Color. Half-hour. Premiered on HBO: March 1, 1998.

Voices
Emily: Julie Burroughs; **Alexander:** Terrence Scammel; **No Tail No Good:** Rick Jones

◎ COURAGEOUS CAT AND MINUTE MOUSE

Comic-book artist Bob Kane, who created TV's *Cool McCool*, parodied his own creation of caped crusaders Batman and Robin in this first-run half-hour series of 100 five-minute cartoons that featured a crimefighting cat and

mouse who fight for truth, justice and self-protection in Empire City (a take-off of Gotham City in the Batman series). Relying on a multipurpose Catgun and Catmobile, Courageous Cat and Minute encounter such villains as the Frog (his real name is "Chauncey" and he is patterned after movie tough guy Edward G. Robinson), his assistant Harry the Gorilla, Rodney Rodent, Black Cat, Professor Noodle Stroodle and Professor Shaggy Dog.

A Sam Singer/Trans-Artist Production. Color. Half-hour. Premiered: September 1960. Syndicated.

Voices
Courageous Cat/Minute Mouse: Bob McFadden

◎ COW AND CHICKEN

Based on the Emmy-nominated cartoon short created by David Feiss for Hanna-Barbera and Cartoon Network's *World Premiere Toons* series. This half-hour series continues the outrageous antics of a surreal pair of siblings, big brother Chicken (all of 460 pounds) and little sister Cow, whose American dream lifestyle—a nice house with a white picket fence and loving human parents—usually turns fowl, thanks to pugnacious Chicken's attitude, which requires his little sister to bail him out. Premiering in July of 1997, the program consists of three seven-minute shorts, two featuring the series stars and a third entitled "I Am Weasel," the fabulous exploits of the internationally famous I.M. Weasel (voiced by Michael Dorn, a.k.a. Commander Worf on TV's *Star Trek: The Next Generation*) and his insanely jealous, mentally challenged archrival, I.R. Baboon.

A Hanna-Barbera Production. Color. Half-hour. Premiered on CAR: July 1997.

Voices
Cow/Chicken/Red Guy: Charles Adler; **Mom:** Candi Milo; **Dad:** Dee Bradley Baker; **Flem:** Howard Morris; **Earl:** Dan Castellaneta; **I.M. Weasel:** Michael Dorn; **I.R. Baboon:** Charles Adler

◎ CREEPY CRAWLERS

In an experiment gone wrong, Chris Carter, a typical teenager, accidentally creates this entourage of kindly crustaceans with special powers (called "The Creepy Crawler Goopmandoes") who end up warring with a bunch of evil goopsters, the Crime Grimes, created by the demented magician Professor Guggengrime, in this weekly half-hour fantasy/adventure series, which debuted in first-run syndication in 1994.

A Saban Entertainment Production. Color. Half-hour. Premiered: September 12, 1994. Syndicated. Voice credits unavailable.

◎ THE CRITIC

Pudgy, bald and unmerciful New York film critic Jay Sherman (described as "balder than Siskel and fatter than Ebert"), who is divorced, hated by his ex-wife and barely tolerated by his adoptive parents, is host of his own weekly cable television show, *Coming Attractions*. He reviews (and parodies) popular movies while constantly struggling to find happiness in his personal life in this half-hour, prime-time animated series from former *Simpsons* producers Mike Reiss and Al Jean and executive producer James L. Brooks, who developed the concept in March 1992 and initially toyed with making the series a live-action sitcom. Premiering on ABC in January of 1994, the series produced respectable ratings but was yanked after only six episodes had aired. (ABC planned to air the remaining seven episodes later that season.) In June 1994 the series slipped back on the air on ABC but was not renewed. The Fox Network picked up the series for the 1994–95 season, ordering new episodes. Comedian Jon Lovitz, of *Saturday Night Live* fame, provided the voice of Jay Sherman. In December of 1995, Comedy Central added the program (in reruns) to its Sunday-night schedule opposite the new hit series *Dr. Katz: Professional Therapist*.

A *Gracie Films/Film Roman Production in association with Columbia Pictures Television. Color. Half-hour. Premiered on ABC: January 26, 1994–March 1994; June 1, 1994–July 20, 1994; Premiered on FOX: March 5, 1995–July 30, 1995. Rebroadcast on COM: December 3, 1995.*

Voices

Jay Sherman/Other Voices: Jon Lovitz; **Margo:** Nancy Cartwright; **Marty Sherman/Other Voices:** Christine Cavanaugh; **Franklin Sherman, Jay's father/Other Voices:** Gerritt Graham; **Eleanor Sherman, Jay's mother:** Judith Ivey, Kath Soucie; **Doris, Makeup Woman:** Doris Grau; **Vlada/Other Voices:** Nick Jameson; **Jeremy Hawke/Other Voices:** Maurice LaMarche; **Duke/Other Voices:** Charles Napier; **Penny Thompkins:** Russi Taylor; **Alice Tompkins:** Park Overall

◎ CRO

When a hip Woolly Mammoth named Phil defrosts in the 20th century, he spins tales about the good ol' days back in the Ice Age, entertaining and informing his modern-day friends Mike and Dr. C about the marvels of science and technology. He switches back and forth between the present and his adventures in the past with Cro, a canny orphaned Cro-Magnon boy, in this 21-episode educational half-hour animated series inspired by the book *The Way Things Work*. The series—aimed to teach children ages six to 11 that science can be fun—was produced by Children's Television Workshop, the people behind PBS's Emmy Award–winning children's series *Sesame Street*. It marked CTW's first animation production for television.

A *Children's Television Workshop/Film Roman Production. Color. Half-hour. Premiered on ABC: September 18, 1993–July 15, 1995.*

Voices

Phil: Jim Cummings; **Dr. C:** April Ortiz; **Mike:** Jussie Smollett; **Cro:** Max Cassella

THE WOOLLY MAMMOTHS: Ivana: Laurie O'Brien; **Esmeralda:** Tress MacNeille; **Earle:** Frank Welker; **Mojo/Steamer:** Charlie Adler; **Pakka:** Candi Milo

THE NEANDERTHALS: Nandy: Ruth Buzzi; **Ogg:** Jim Cummings; **Gogg/Bobb:** Frank Welker

THE CREATURES: Selene: Jane Singer; **Big Red:** Charlie Adler; **Murray:** Jim Cummings

◎ CRUSADER RABBIT

Rocky and Bullwinkle creator Jay Ward and Alexander Anderson, the nephew of cartoon producer Paul Terry, originated the long-eared rabbit, Crusader, and pal Ragland ("Rags") T. Tiger in 1948, one year before the characters were "test-marketed" as what historians call the "first cartoon serial" and "first limited animation series" made for television. Ward and Alexander first placed the characters in a film presentation called *The Comic Strips of Television*, along with two other features, "Hamhock Jones" and "Dudley Do-Right."

For many years it was commonly believed the show was syndicated in 1949. Research proves that the series actually was test-marketed the year before it aired nationally. (Unlike syndication, it was sold on a city-to-city basis, premiering in different cities on different dates due to the method of distribution.) The first Los Angeles air date was found to be Tuesday, August 1, 1950.

Jerry Fairbanks, a contract film supplier, was executive producer of the 1949–51 series, which the network turned down. The program aired during the 1950–51 season on NBC-owned and operated stations in several markets. Initially, 130 five-minute cliff hanging episodes were produced.

In 1957 television producer Shull Bonsall, owner of TV Spots, produced a new color series that was similar in nature to the original program. This time the series was syndicated and appeared on several NBC affiliate stations.

A *Television Arts/Jerry Fairbanks Production/Creston Studios Production. Black-and-white. Color. Premiere: Fall 1949 (original series) and Fall 1957 (new series). Syndicated.*

Voices

Crusader Rabbit: Lucille Bliss, Ge Ge Pearson; **Ragland T. Tiger:** Vern Louden; **Dudley Nightshade:** Russ Coughlan; **Narrator:** Roy Whaley

CURIOUS GEORGE

Enchanting escapades of a precocious monkey and his resourceful master (the Man in the Yellow Hat) based on the popular children's books by H.A. and Margaret Ray. This Canadian-produced series of five-minute cartoon adventures was produced between 1979 and 1982 and was first shown in America on Nickelodeon in 1984. The cartoons were made a regular feature of the Nickelodeon series *Pinwheel* in 1985 and were later broadcast as a daily half-hour series of their own. In 1989 the entertaining series joined the popular Disney Channel series *Lunch Box* and, more recently, the network's weekday morning anthology series *Circle Time*.

A *Lafferty, Harwood and Partners/Milktrain Production. Color. Half-hour. Premiered on NIK: 1984. Rebroadcast on DIS: 1989.*

Voices
Narrator: Jack Duffy

CYBER C.O.P.S.

(See C.O.P.S.)

CYBORG BIG "X"

Akira, a young refugee, is changed into a cyborg by Nazi renegade scientists, who place his brain in the body of a powerful robot. As Cyborg Big "X," he uses a special magnetic pen as his sole weapon to do battle with those who could use science for nefarious ends. Created by Osamu Tezuka, the originator of *Astro Boy*, the half-hour science-fiction series was adapted from Tezuka's comic strip, *Big X*. The series, telecast in Japan in 1964, was broadcast in the United States three years later.

A *Global/Transglobal Production. Color. Half-hour. Premiered: Fall 1967. Syndicated.*

THE DAFFY AND SPEEDY SHOW

Daffy Duck and Speedy Gonzales starred in this half-hour Saturday-morning series for NBC, composed of previously released Warner Bros. theatrical cartoons. Lasting only one season, the comical cartoon pair jumped to rival network CBS the following season to headline the short-lived hour-long series *The Daffy and Speedy/Sylvester and Tweety Show*.

A *Warner Bros. Television Production. Color. Half-hour. Premiered on NBC: September 12, 1981–September 4, 1982.*

Voices
Mel Blanc (primary voice)

THE DAFFY AND SPEEDY/ SYLVESTER AND TWEETY SHOW

CBS aired this hour-long collection of Warner Bros. theatrical cartoons starring Daffy Duck, Speedy Gonzales and Sylvester and Tweety on the 1981–82 Saturday-morning schedule as the lead-in show to the popular *Bugs Bunny/Road Runner Hour*, amounting to a solid two-hour cartoon block of classic Warner Bros. cartoons. The network pulled the show about a month after its debut.

A *Warner Bros. Television Production. Color. One hour. Premiered on CBS: September 18, 1982–October 23, 1982.*

Voices
Mel Blanc (primary voice)

THE DAFFY DUCK SHOW (1978)

For years the wacky, malicious Daffy Duck pleaded with Bugs Bunny for his own TV show. His ardent efforts were finally rewarded when NBC and the Warner Bros. cartoon department packaged a series starring the slurred-talking duck and a host of other Warner characters—Pepe Le Pew, Speedy Gonzales and Foghorn Leghorn—from old theatrical one-reelers. The show consisted of vintage Warner Bros. and DePatie-Freleng cartoons produced during the 1950s and 1960s.

A *Warner Bros. Production. Color. Half-hour. Premiered on NBC: November 4, 1978–September 1981.*

Voices
Daffy Duck/Pepe Le Pew/Speedy Gonzales/Foghorn Leghorn: Mel Blanc

THE DAFFY DUCK SHOW (1996)

The WB Network added this cartoon anthology series to its Saturday-morning Kids' WB lineup in late 1996 to replace the low-rated superhero cartoon series *Freakazoid!* Featuring a new animated opening of Daffy Duck as a "jammin'" duck, the series showcased each half-hour two Daffy Duck cartoons bookended with one cartoon starring other Warner Bros. cartoon luminaries—Elmer Fudd, Tweety and Sylvester or Foghorn Leghorn—and a brief segment called "Hip Clip," featuring excerpts from existing Warner Bros. cartoons.

A *Warner Bros. Production. Color. Half-hour. Premiered on WB: 1996.*

Voices
Mel Blanc (primary voice)

DANGER MOUSE

The British Secret Service's most dashing rodent safeguards the lives of everyone who values justice and liberty, waging war against the forces of evil—usually in the form of Baron Silas Greenback. This British import came from the makers of the hit series *Count Duckula*, and Danger Mouse first appeared in several episodes of that program before he was given his own series. Each program varied, containing either one complete story or two episodes (the latter varied in length) per half-hour broadcast. On September 28, 1981, the 65-episode series premiered on the United Kingdom's ITV Network. It wasn't syndicated in this country until three years later on Nickelodeon.

A Cosgrove Hall Production in association with Thames Television. Color. Half-hour. Premiered on NIK: June 4, 1984–May 31, 1987. Rebroadcast on NIK: September 30, 1991–October 2, 1994. Syndicated: 1984.

Voices
Danger Mouse/Colonel K/Nero/Narrator: David Jason; **Penfold, his faithful assistant:** Terry Scott; **Baron Silas Greenback:** Edward Kelsey; **Stiletto, Greenback's henchman:** Brian Trueman

◉ DARIA

The ultimate "whatever" girl, this dour 16-year-old teen hipster (Daria Morgendorffer), who's almost too smart for her own good, provides observations of the absurdities of life—in high school, with her classmates and as a teenager growing up in the 1990s—in this half-hour weekly spinoff of MTV's immensely popular *Beavis & Butt-Head*. The *My So-Called Life*–styled series—MTV's first full-length animated sitcom—debuted with 13 half-hour episodes, airing regularly on Monday nights on the music cable network in early 1997. In *Beavis & Butt-Head*, Daria was well known to fans as the sardonic "smart kid" who hung around the boys because she found their stupidity entertaining. (In all of her seasons on the show, she was a favorite character of viewers.) For her own series, she moved to a new town, Lawndale, with her stressed-out career-fixated parents, Helen and Jake, and her relentlessly cute and popular younger sister, Quinn. The series was developed by Glenn Eichler and Susie Lewis Lynn, who is also one of the show's producers.

An MTV Animation Production. Color. Half-hour. Premiered on MTV: March 3, 1997–July 21, 1997 (first season).

Voices
Daria Morgendorffer: Tracey Grandstaff; **Quinn/Helen Morgendorffer/Jane Lane:** Wendy Hoopes; **Jake Morgendorffer:** Julian Rebolledo; **Trent Lane:** Alvero J. Gonzalez; **Kevin Thompson/Mr. DeMartino/Mr. O'Neill:** Marc Thompson; **Brittany Taylor:** Lisa Collins

◉ DARKSTALKERS

Originated in video arcades in the summer of 1994 to rave reviews (later released as CD-ROM video game) and following the path of other arcade-inspired cartoon series, this 13-episode half-hour syndicated series from the producers of TV's *X-Men* and *The Tick* featured 10 classic supernatural

characters done with a 1990s' sensibility and touch of humor à la the animated *Ghostbusters*.

A Graz Entertainment/Capcom Production. Color. Half-hour. Premiered: September 1, 1996. Syndicated.

◉ DARKWING DUCK

His true identity known only to his best friend, Launchpad McQuack, Drake Mallard (alias Darkwing Duck), an adoptive father, ace avenger and crimebuster extraordinare, balances parenting his precocious nine-year-old daughter Gosalyn with saving the world. He is the shadowy guardian who protects the city of St. Canard from dangerous and despicable delinquents in this half-hour spinoff of the Disney series *DuckTales*. The popular 91-episode comedy/adventure series (originally titled *Double-O Duck*) premiered on The Disney Channel in April of 1991. It aired through September of that year before being added to ABC's fall lineup, running concurrently on the network (with 13 new episodes produced exclusively for ABC and not seen in syndication) and in syndication as anchor of the two-hour weekday cartoon block the *Disney Afternoon*. Nominated for a daytime Emmy Award in 1993, the program replaced Disney's *Adventures of the Gummi Bears*. The animated opener of the syndicated version debuted on the same day as the ABC series as a two-hour Disney special—combined with a look at the new season of *The Mickey Mouse Club*—before airing in its usual Monday-through-Friday time slot.

A Walt Disney Television Animation Production. Color. Half-hour. Premiered on DIS: April 6, 1991; ABC: September 7, 1991–September 4, 1993. Syndicated: September 7, 1991–September 1, 1995.

Voices
Darkwing Duck (a.k.a. Drake Mallard)/Negaduck/Moliarty/Cousin Globby: Jim Cummings; **Gizmo Duck:** Hamilton Camp; **Gosalyn Mallard:** Cathy Cavadini, Christine Cavanaugh; **J. Gander Hooter:** Danny Mann; **Launchpad McQuack:** Terry McGovern; **Steelbeak:** Rob Paulsen; **Honker Muddlefoot:** Katie Leigh; **Herb Muddlefoot:** Jim Cummings; **Binkie Muddlefoot:** Susan Tolsky; **Tank Muddlefoot:** Dana Hill; **Bushroot:** Tino Insana; **Agent Gryslikoff:** Ron Feinberg; **Megavolt:** Dan Castellaneta; **Morgana Macawber/Aunt Nasty:** Kath Soucie; **Tuskerninni:** Kenneth Mars; **Meraculo Macawber:** Frank Welker

◉ DASTARDLY AND MUTTLEY IN THEIR FLYING MACHINES

Villainous Dick Dastardly, his fumbling henchdog Muttley, and an entourage of World War I flying aces pursue American courier Yankee Doodle Pigeon (who was voiceless) to intercept top-secret information in this offbeat show with bad guys as the series' title characters. Featured each week were two Dastardly and Muttley adventures and four Dick Dastardly Blackouts billed as "Wing Dings." The series theme song, "Stop That Pigeon," was written by Bill Hanna and Hoyt Curtin.

A Hanna-Barbera Production. Color. Half-hour. Premiered on CBS: September 13, 1969–September 3, 1971. Rebroadcast on CAR: April 23, 1995 (Super Chunk).

Voices
Dick Dastardly/The General: Paul Winchell; **Muttley/ Yankee Doodle Pigeon/Klunk/Zilly:** Don Messick

◎ DAVEY AND GOLIATH
Long-running 15-minute religious series conceived by Art Clokey, creator of Gumby and Pokey, tracing the saga of young Davey Hanson and his talking dog, Goliath, who solve everyday problems while relating the word of God in an entertaining and less preachy fashion. Like *Gumby*, the series of 64 adventures was filmed in pixillation, a stop-motion photography process.

Funded by the Lutheran Council of Churches, the series was first syndicated in 1960. (Initial experimental efforts were conducted the year before.) Not only was the series a huge success in the United States, it subsequently was dubbed in Portuguese and Spanish. Six half-hour specials were also produced featuring the same cast of characters ("To the Rescue," "Happy Easter," "School . . . Who Needs It?" "Halloween Who-Dun-It," "Christmas Lost and Found," and "New Year Promise").

Production of the series ended when funding from the church foundation ran out. The program is still seen in many television markets today, without five of the series' original episodes, which were removed from circulation for various reasons ("On the Line," "Polka Dot Tie," "Ten Little Indians," "Man of the House" and "The Gang").

A Clokey Production. Color. Half-hour. Syndicated: 1960–1965.

Voices
Davey: Norma McMillan; **Goliath:** Hal Smith

◎ DEFENDERS OF THE EARTH
The year is A.D. 2015. The human race is about to fall under the control of the evil Ming the Merciless, famous intergalactic villain from the planet Mongo. A team of the universe's most adventurous, powerful, superheroes—Flash Gordon, The Phantom, Mandrake the Magician and Lothar—who join forces to overtake Ming with the help of their descendants: Rick Gordon, Flash's scientific genius son; Jedda Walker, the Phantom's mysterious daughter; L.J.

A daring team of superheroes battle the evil Ming the Merciless in the futuristic fantasy/adventure series Defenders of the Earth. © King Features Entertainment (COURTESY: MARVEL PRODUCTIONS)

Davey Hanson and his talking dog, Goliath, are flanked by Davey's father in a scene from the long-running religious series Davey and Goliath. © Clokey Productions

(Lothar Junior), the streetwise son of Lother; Kshin, a 10-year-old orphaned Oriental boy; and Zuffy, a cute and cuddly ball of alien fur.

Originally produced in 1985, the series aired one year later in first-run syndication. In 1992 the Sci-Fi Channel began rebroadcasting the series as part of its two-hour cartoon program block *Cartoon Quest*.

A Marvel Production in association with King Features Entertainment. Color. Half-hour. Premiered: September 1986. Syndicated. Rebroadcast on SCI: September 25, 1992–September 22, 1995.

Voices
William Callaway, Adam Carl, Ron Feinberg, Buster Jones, Loren Lester, Sarah Partridge, Diane Pershing, Peter Renaday, Lou Richards, Peter Mark Richman, Dion Williams

⊚ DENNIS THE MENACE

Comic-strip artist Hank Ketcham's popular newspaper strip inspired this first-run, 78-episode half-hour animated series starring the All-American handful, Dennis, whose zest for life spells trouble for his neighbor, Mr. Wilson. First syndicated in 1985, the series also aired on CBS in 1988, featuring all-new episodes. The series was later rebroadcast on USA Network's *Cartoon Express*.

A DIC Enterprises Production. Color. Half-hour. Premiered: September 1985. Syndicated. Premiered on CBS: January 2, 1988–September 10, 1988. Rebroadcast on USA: July 7, 1996–March 23, 1997.

Voices
Dennis Mitchell: Brennan Thicke; **Alice Mitchell, his mother:** Louise Vallance, Marilyn Lightstone; **Henry Mitchell, his father:** Brian George, Maurice LaMarche; **Mr. Wilson:** Phil Hartman, Maurice LaMarche; **Martha, his wife:** Marilyn Lightstone; **Joey, Dennis's friend/Margaret, Dennis's friend/Tommy:** Jeanine Elias; **Dick/Jim:** Hark Sound; **Ruff:** Phil Hartman

⊚ DENVER, THE LAST DINOSAUR

The series follows the adventures of fun-loving dinosaur, Denver, and his group of ingenious young friends, Wally, Jeremy, Shades and Mario, who bring him into the mainstream of the 20th century in contemporary situations. Following its debut, the program captured the number-one spot for viewers, aged two to 11, beating all other kids' shows, including *DuckTales*, *Teenage Mutant Ninja Turtles* and *The Jetsons*. In 1991 the series was rebroadcast on USA Network's weekday cartoon block *Cartoon Express*.

A World Events/Calico Productions presentation. Color. Half-hour. Premiered on KTTV-Ch. 11, Los Angeles, April 29, 1988. Syndicated. Rebroadcast on USA: October 18, 1991–September 10, 1995.*

Voices
Wally/Jeremy: Adam Carl; **Mario/Shades:** Cam Clarke; **Morton Fizzback/Professor Funt:** Brian Cummings; **Denver the Last Dinosaur:** Pat Fraley; **Chet/Motley:** Rob Paulsen; **Heather/Casey:** Kath Soucie

⊚ DEPUTY DAWG

A not-so-bright Southern lawman, Deputy Dawg, fumbles his way to maintaining law and order in Mississippi, hounded by a pack of pranksters. His best friends and worst enemies are other animals from the South: Vincent "Vince" Van Gopher, Ty Coon the Racoon, Muskie the Muskrat and Pig Newton. In October 1960 the pot-bellied sheriff debuted in over 47 television markets, sponsored by W.H. Lay Potato Chips. The success of the character inspired Terrytoons to release several of the made-for-television cartoons theatrically in 1962. Seven years later Deputy Dawg premiered on NBC in a new vehicle, *The Deputy Dawg Show*. The series repeated episodes from the original series and featured two additional segments composed of previously released theatrical cartoons: *Gandy Goose* and *Terrytoon Classics*.

A Terrytoons Production. Color. Half hour. Syndicated: October 1960 (Deputy Dawg). Premiered on NBC: September 11, 1971–September 2, 1972 (The Deputy Dawg Show).

Voices
Deputy Dawg/Vincent Van Gopher/Ty Coon/The Sheriff: Dayton Allen

⊚ DEVLIN

Star circus attractions, daredevil stunt motorcyclist Ernie Devlin and his orphaned sister and brother—Sandy and Tod—use their skills to help circus animals and others in this half-hour Saturday-morning series, which also featured a weekly safety tip for young viewers.

A Hanna-Barbera Production. Color. Half-hour. Premiered on ABC: September 11, 1974–February 15, 1976.

Voices
Ernie Devlin: Mike Bell; **Tod Devlin:** Micky Dolenz; **Sandy Devlin:** Michele Robinson; **Hank:** Norman Alden

⊚ DEXTER'S LABORATORY

A squat, bespectacled, neurotic kid genius with a pouf of bright-red hair creates fantastic inventions in his huge bedroom laboratory despite the pesky intolerance of his ditsy big sister Dee Dee in this computer-generated animated half-hour series produced exclusively for the Cartoon Network. The character was the first "breakout" star of

A boy genius who creates fantastic inventions in his bedroom laboratory cooks up all sorts of adventures in the Emmy-nominated series Dexter's Laboratory. © Hanna-Barbera Productions (COURTESY: THE CARTOON NETWORK)

Hanna-Barbera's *World Premiere Toons* series, which had premiered a year earlier on the Cartoon Network featuring the cartoon short "Dexter," produced by then 26-year-old Russian-born filmmaker Genndy Tartakovsky. The film won Tartakovsky both an Emmy nomination in 1995 (and again in 1996 for the series) and a contract from the network to develop "Dexter" into a series. Starring in 39 all-new half-hours, each program includes two *Dexter Laboratory* shorts and a third related segment, either "Dial M for Monkey," about a superpowered, crimefighting primate who sets out to save the world when Dexter isn't looking (1996–97 season), or "Justice Friends," which follows a group of superheroes challenged more by the problems of living together than the evil forces that threaten the world (1997–98 season).

A Cartoon Network Production. Color. Half-hour. Premiered on CAR: April 28, 1996.

Voices

DEXTER: Dexter: Christine Cavanaugh; **Dee Dee:** Allison Moore, Kat Cressida; **Mom:** Kath Soucie; **Dad:** Jeff Bennett

DIAL M FOR MONKEY: Monkey: Frank Welker

JUSTICE FRIENDS: The Infraggable Krunk: Frank Welker; **Major Glory:** Rob Paulsen; **Valhallen/Living Bullet:** Tom Kenny

◎ THE DICK TRACY SHOW

Originally titled *The Adventures of Dick Tracy*, the famed comic-strip hero battles the world's most ruthless criminals (Flattop, B.B. Eyes, Pruneface, Mumbles, the Brow, Oodles, the Mole, Sketch Paree, Cheapskate Gunsmoke, Itchy and Stooge Viller) with the questionable help of his diminutive-brained team of law enforcers—Hemlock Holmes, Jo Jitsu, Heap O'Calory, Go Go Gomez, and The Retouchables—in this series of 130 five-minute episodes first syndicated in 1961. Four episodes were shown on the program, each telling a complete story.

Chester Gould, Dick Tracy's creator, developed the series format and supervised the initial episode. In an interview, he later admitted that he disliked the series. "We were catering to very small fry and I think we would have been smarter to have taken a more serious view of the thing and played it more or less straight," he said.

A UPA Production. Color. Half-hour. Premiered: September 1961. Syndicated.

Voices
Dick Tracy: Everett Sloane

◎ DINK, THE LITTLE DINOSAUR

At a time when Earth was scorched by volcanoes, showered by meteor storms and shaken by giant earthquakes and where survival was an everyday adventure, Dink, a self-assured, sometimes scheming brontosauraus, rallies his group of friends around him in a never-ending quest for fun, adventure and discovery in this original half-hour animated adventure series, which debuted on CBS in 1989. The series lasted two seasons featuring two cartoon episodes each half hour. The second season included a new addition: "Factasaurus," fun facts about dinosaurs.

A Ruby-Spears Enterprises Production. Color. Half-hour. Premiered on CBS: September 2, 1989–August 24, 1991. Rebroadcast on CAR: October 4, 1992–April 10, 1994 (Sundays); September 11, 1994– (Sundays).

Voices
Dink: R.J. Williams; **Amber, the lively corythosaurs:** Andee McAfee; **Shyler, the bashful edaphosaurus:** Ben Granger; **Flapper, the boastful pterodon:** S. Scott Bullock; **Scat, the nervous compsognathus/Crusty, an old sea turtle:** Frank Welker

◉ DINOBABIES

A family of dinosaurs act out famous fairy tales and children's stories presenting a strong pro-literacy message in this wholesome half-hour animated series, created by animator Fred Wolf, whose company (formerly known as Murakami-Wolf-Swenson) produced the hit cartoon series *Teenage Mutant Ninja Turtles*. The series was first sold to foreign television markets in 1994, where it enjoyed great success. Wolf had great difficulty selling the series to American broadcasters. It wasn't until the fall of 1996 that the program was syndicated in this country by Westinghouse Broadcasting International.

A Fred Wolf Films/Shanghai Morning Sun Production in association with Westinghouse Broadcasting International. Color. Half-hour. Premiered: 1996. Syndicated.

◉ DINOSAUCERS

To save the quake-racked planet Reptilon from destruction, the Dinosaucers, the planet's only inhabitants, come to Earth, where they enlist the help of four youngsters, to find the secret that will save their own world and keep them safe from the depredation of their brutal enemies, the Tyrannos. This futuristic half-hour action/adventure series, syndicated in 1987, was reshown on The Family Channel beginning in 1989, then four years later on USA Network's *Cartoon Express*.

A DIC Enterprises Production in association with Michael Maliani Productions. Color. Half-hour. Premiered: September 1987. Syndicated. Rebroadcast on FAM: 1989. Rebroadcast on USA: March 29, 1993–September 3, 1995.

Voices

Bonehead/Bronto-Thunder: Marvin Goldhar; **Genghis 'Rex'/Plesio:** Dan Hennessey; **Quackpot/Allo:** Len Carlson; **Steggy:** Ray Kahnert; **Brachio:** Don McManus; **Tricero:** Rob Cowan; **Ichthyo:** Thick Wilson; **Terrible Dactyl/Ankylo:** John Stocker; **Dimetro:** Chris Wiggins; **Styraco:** Gordon Masten; **Sara:** Barbara Redpath; **Paul:** Richard Yearwood; **Ryan:** Simon Reynolds; **David:** Leslie Toth

◉ DIPSY DOODLE

To tie in with the country's Bicentennial celebration, this hour-long, mostly live-action educational children's show, produced in Cleveland and briefly syndicated in December of 1974 was named after the animated country bumpkin whose supposed heritage linked him to the original Yankee Doodle.

A WJW-TV/SFM/General Foods Production. Color. One hour. Syndicated: 1974.

◉ DISNEY AFTERNOON

Walt Disney Studios launched this two-hour, syndicated weekday afternoon block of programs in the fall of 1990. Offered to independent television stations, it was initially made up of *Disney's Adventures of the Gummi Bears, Duck-Tales, Chip 'n Dale's Rescue Rangers* and *Tale Spin*. In subsequent seasons the programs were changed. In 1991–92, *Darkwing Duck* replaced the *Gummi Bears*. The following season, *Goof Troop* was added, bumping *DuckTales*. With the onset of the 1993–94 season, *Disney's Bonkers* replaced of *Chip 'n Dale's Rescue Rangers*. In the 1994–95 season, Disney added other weekday program blocks: *Monday Mania*, featuring *The Shookums & Meat Funny Cartoon Show*; Tuesday–Thursday: *Disney's Bonkers*; and *Action Friday*, marking the debut of Disney's *Gargoyles* and Disney's *Aladdin*. (For the 1995–96 season, *The Lion King's Timon and Pumbaa* replaced *Disney's Aladdin* on *Action Friday*.) The 1996–97 season included three new additions: *Darkwing Duck, Quack Pack* and *Mighty Ducks: The Animated Series*, joining *Gargoyles*, Disney's *Aladdin* and *The Lion King's Timon and Pumbaa*. For the 1997–98 season, the package was overhauled again. Disney's *Aladdin*, *Gargoyles* and *The Lion King's Timon and Pumbaa* were all dropped, while *Disney's 101 Dalmations: The Series* premiered. (See individual series entries for details.)

A Walt Disney Television Animation Production. Color. Two hours. Premiered: September 1990. Syndicated.

◉ DISNEY'S ADVENTURES IN WONDERLAND

Helping kids improve vocabulary and language skills, the denizens of the fantasy world of Lewis Carroll's *Through the Looking Glass*—Alice (played by Elisabeth Harnois), the Mad Hatter, the Red Queen, Tweedle Dum and Tweedle Dee (in live action)—engage in playful wordplay and introduce stories told through the magic of "Claymation" in this weekday live-action/animated series that premiered on The Disney Channel in 1992. Will Vinton, of California Raisins fame, produced 40 animated clay-on-glass episodes for the series, which was later syndicated.

A Betty Productions in association with The Disney Channel and Will Vinton Productions. Color. Half-hour. Premiered on DIS: March 23, 1992. Syndicated: September 6, 1993–September 10, 1995.

Cast (live action)

Alice: Elisabeth Harnois; **March Hare:** Reece Holland; **Red Queen:** Armelia McQueen; **White Rabbit:** Patrick Richwood; **Mad Hatter:** John Robert Hoffman; **Tweedle Dee:** Harry Waters Jr.; **Tweedle Dum:** Robert Barry Fleming; **Caterpillar:** Wesley Mann; **Cheshire Cat:** Richard Kuhlman; **Dormouse:** John Lovelady

DISNEY'S ADVENTURES OF THE GUMMI BEARS

Zummi, Gruffi, Grammi, Cubbi, Sunni and Tummi Gummi find themselves in enchanting escapades as they face new foes and find new friends in the mythical forests of Gummi Glen. From encounters with menacing giants and ogres, to the excitement of discovering lost treasure, the Gummies join together for a captivating series of intriguing and whimsical adventure in this Saturday-morning series produced by Walt Disney Television Animation. NBC broadcast the first four seasons beginning in September 1985. The show moved to ABC in September 1989, when it merged with *The New Adventures of Winnie the Pooh* for its fifth season. The program combined half-hour and 15-minute episodes. In 1990 the series joined the *Disney Afternoon* two-hour daily cartoon block in syndication (in reruns) opposite *DuckTales, Chip 'n' Dale's Rescue Rangers* and *Tale Spin*.

A *Walt Disney Television Animation Production. Color. Half-hour. Premiered on NBC: September 14, 1985–September 2, 1989. Rebroadcast on ABC: September 9, 1989–September 1, 1990 (as Disney's Gummi Bears/Winnie the Pooh Hour). Rebroadcast on DIS: 1991–1996. Syndicated: 1990 (as part of Disney Afternoon).*

Voices

Cavin: Christian Jacobs, Brett Johnson, David Faustino, R.J. Williams; **Chummi Gummi:** Jim Cummings; **Sunni Gummi:** Katie Leigh; **Tummi Gummi:** Lorenzo Music; **Augustus "Gusto" Gummi:** Rob Paulsen; **Zummi Gummi:** Paul Winchell; Jim Cummings; **Gruffi Gummi:** Bill Scott, Corey Burton; **Cubbi Gummi:** Noelle North; **Grammi Gummi:** June Foray; **Gusto Gummi:** Rob Paulsen; **Toadie:** Bill Scott, Corey Burton, Michael Rye; **Giggalin:** Corey Burton; **Clutch:** Paul Winchell, Corey Burton; **Sir Tuxford:** Bill Scott, Hamilton Camp, Roger C. Carmel, Townsend Coleman, Gino Conforti, Peter Cullen, Brian Cummings, Chuck McCann; **Artie Deco/Chillbeard Sr.:** Townsend Coleman, Gino Conforti, Peter Cullen, Brian Cummings; **Knight of Gumadoon:** Townsend Coleman, Gino Conforti, Peter Cullen, Brian Cummings, David Faustino, Alan Oppenheimer; **Angelo Davini/Ogre:** Bill Scott; **Zorlock:** Lennie Weinrib; **Ditto the Boggle/Mervyns/Mother Griffin:** Frank Welker; **Zummi Gummi/Toadie/Slumber Sprite/Giggalin/Tuck (1987–1989):** Paul Winchell; **King Gregor/Duke Igthorn/Sir Gowan:** Michael Rye; **Sir Paunch:** Allan Melvin, Howard Morris; **Sir Thornberry:** Barry Dennen, Aeryk Egan, Walker Edmiston; **Princess Calla:** Noelle North; **Princess Marie:** Hal Smith, Kath Soucie; **Malsinger/Troll/Horse/Nip:** Michael Rye; **Unwin/Gad/Zook/King Carpie/Knight:** Will Ryan; **Ogre:** Will Ryan, Michael Rye; **Trina/Aquarianne:** Pat Parris; **Mobile Tree:** June Foray, Noelle North, Katie Leigh; **Giant, with the Wishing Stone/Dom:** Linda Gary;

Gordo of Ghent: Ed Gilbert, Dana Hill, Bob Holt; **Tadpole:** Chuck McCann; **Bubble Dragon:** Lorenzo Music; **The Most Peaceful Dragon in the World/Counselor Woodale:** June Foray; **Lady Bane/Great Oak/Marzipan/Mother:** Tress MacNeille; **Zorlock:** Andre Stojka, Les Tremayne, Lennie Weinrib

DISNEY'S ALADDIN

Aladdin, Princess Jasmine and their pals Genie, Iago (no longer a bad parrot) and Abu (the friendly monkey) embark on all-new adventures, set in the ancient land of Agrabah, in this half-hour series based on the popular 1992 animated movie. All of the original characters from the movie and subsequent video sequel, *The Return of Jafar*, returned, with the exception of Jafar, who died (for a second time) in the video. A new group of villains were created for the series, including the bearded bandit Abis Mal (voiced by *Seinfeld's* Jason Alexander), the feline Mirage (whose voice was supplied by Bebe Neuwirth of *Cheers*), barbarian Runter (voiced by Michael Jeter of *Evening Shade*) and his wife, Brawnhilda (brought to life by actress/comedienne Carol Kane).

Premiering weekdays in syndication and Saturdays on CBS in September 1994, CBS commissioned 13 shows for its Saturday-morning lineup (each different from the syndication version), while 65 episodes aired in syndication as part of the *Disney Afternoon* cartoon block. The series finished third in the overall syndication ratings behind the live-action *Mighty Morphin Power Rangers* and Steven Spielberg's *Animaniacs* during its successful first season. (The show was also nominated for an Emmy as Outstanding Animated Children's Program.) CBS picked up the series for a second season in 1995, airing eight first-run episodes, while the program continued to air in syndication. In the fall of 1997, previously aired network episodes began airing on The Disney Channel.

Most of the original actors who provided the voices in the movie reprised their roles in the series: Scott Weinger (of TV's *Full House*) as Aladdin, Linda Larkin as Jasmine, and Gilbert Gottfried as Iago. Dan Castellaneta (the voice of Homer Simpson) replaced Robin Williams as the wise-cracking Genie, his second stint in the role counting the home video sequel *The Return of Jafar*, which Williams also refused to voice.

A *Walt Disney Television Animation Production. Color. Half-hour. Premiered on DIS: February 6, 1994; Premiered on CBS: September 17, 1994–August 24, 1996. Syndicated: September 5, 1994–August 29, 1997 (part of Disney Afternoon). Rebroadcast on DIS: September 1997.*

Voices

Aladdin: Scott Weinger; **Jasmine:** Linda Larkin, Deb LaCusta, Kay Kuter, Janice Kawaye, John Kassir; **Genie:** Dan Castellaneta; **Iago:** Gilbert Gottfried; **Abu/Faisal/Rajah/Xerxes:** Frank Welker; **The Sultan of Agrabah:**

Sheryl Bernstein, Val Bettin; **Abis Mal/al-Bhatros:** Jason Alexander; **Mirage:** Bebe Neuwirth; **Runter:** Michael Jeter; **Brawnhilda:** Carol Kane; **Akbar/Amal al-Kateeb/Dominus Trask/Farouk/Hamar/Mad Sultan/Rasoul/Wazou:** Jim Cummings; **Mozenrath:** Susan Blu, Jonathan Brandis

DISNEY'S GUMMI BEARS/WINNIE THE POOH HOUR

In 1989 Disney's Gummi Bears, which ran for four successful seasons on NBC, moved to rival network ABC and merged with *The New Adventures of Winnie the Pooh* in all-new episodes in this fantasy/adventure hour for Saturday-morning television. (See *Disney's Adventures of the Gummi Bears* and *The New Adventures of Winnie the Pooh* for voice credits.)

A Walt Disney Television Production. Color. One hour. Premiered on ABC: September 9, 1989–September 1, 1990.

DISNEY'S 101 DALMATIONS: THE SERIES

Walt Disney Television Animation produced this half-hour cartoon series based on the successful live-action feature and the classic 1961 Disney animated feature of the same name. Premiering in weekday syndication first, then on ABC and airing concurrently in the fall of 1997, the series featured two nine-minute cartoons each half hour: "101 Dalmations," exploring the lives of Lucky, Rolly, Cadpig and the other polka-dot pups as they grow up on a farm in London, and "The Bark Brigade," following the adventures of the dalmations parents, Pongo and Perdita, as they thwart the plans of the evil Cruella de Vil. Sandwiched between them each week were a series of one- to three-minute comic bits, skits and parodies called "Dalmation Spots."

The syndicated version aired six days a week featuring 52 episodes; the ABC Saturday-morning series exclusively broadcast an additional 13 episodes not seen in syndication. Jim Jinkins and David Campbell of Jumbo Pictures, Inc. (the team who created *Doug* and *Brand Spanking New Doug*) helped develop the concept of the new series along with executive producers Roberts Gannaway and Tony Craig (executive producers of *The Lion King's Timon and Pumbaa*) of Walt Disney Television Animation.

A Walt Disney Television Animation/Jumbo Pictures Inc. Production. Color. Half-hour. Premiered: September 1, 1997 (syndicated); ABC: September 13, 1997.

Voices
Lucky: Pam Segall, Debi Mae West; **Rolly/Cadpig/Anita Dearly:** Kath Soucie; **Spot:** Tara Charendoff; **Cruella de Vil:** April Winchell; **Horace:** David Lander; **Jasper:** Michael McKean; **Scorch:** Frank Welker; **Roger Dearly:** Jeff Bennett; **Nanny:** Charlotte Rae; **Pongo:** Kevin Schon; **Perdy (Perdita):** Pam Dawber

DISNEY'S PEPPER ANN

A spunky, eccentric, opinionated and fiercely independent 12-year-old redhead experiences the trials and tribulations of adolescence—with her reactions to situations seen in vivid fantasies—in this half-hour series based on the childhood memories of the show's creator and executive producer Sue Rose (whose character bears a striking resemblance to her creator). The show debuted in the fall of 1997 as part of ABC's two-hour floating cartoon block *One Saturday Morning*, featuring *Brand Spanking New Doug* and *Disney's Recess*.

A Walt Disney Television Animation Production. Color. Half-hour. Premiered on ABC: September 13, 1997.

Voices
Pepper Ann: Kathleen Wilhoite; **Trinket:** Jenna Von Oy; **Moose:** Pamela Segall; **Nicky:** Clea Lewis; **Nicky's Mum:** Kath Soucie; **Lydia:** April Winchell

DISNEY'S QUACK PACK

Grown-up teens Huey, Dewey and Louie live with their famous uncle Donald, now a cameraman for a popular TV newsmagazine. Along with his longtime love-duck Daisy, a brash and courageous TV reporter with the same show, Donald and his nephews go on assignment and encounter action, adventure and trouble around the globe in this first-run half-hour series/spinoff to *DuckTales*. It premiered in the fall of 1996 as part of the weekday cartoon block "The Disney Afternoon." The series working title was *Duck Daze*.

A Walt Disney Television Animation Production. Color. Half-hour. Premiered: September 3, 1996. Syndicated.

Voices
Donald Duck: Tony Anselmo; **Huey Duck:** Jeannie Elias; **Dewey Duck:** Pamela Segall; **Louie Duck:** Elizabeth Daily; **Gwumpki:** Pat Fraley; **Moltoc:** Tim Curry; **Kent Powers:** Roger Rose

DISNEY'S RAW TOONAGE
(See RAW TOONAGE.)

DISNEY'S RECESS

An enterprising group of fourth-grade kids—four boys (Vince, Mikey, T.J. and Gus) and two girls (Gretchen and Ashley)—run into trouble during breaks at school whenever those domineering sixth graders are around, in this half-hour Saturday-morning cartoon from executive producers and the co-creators of *Rugrats*, Paul Germaine and Joe Ansolabehere. The series premiered on ABC in the fall of 1997 as part of the network's floating two-hour block *One Saturday Morning*.

403

A Walt Disney Television Animation/Beantown Production. Color. Half-hour. Premiered on DIS: August 31, 1997 (preview); ABC: September 13, 1997.

Voices
Vince: Rickey D'Shon Collins; **Mikey:** Jason Davis; **T.J.:** Ross Malinger; **Gus:** Courtland Mead; **Gretchen Grundler:** Ashley Johnson; **Ashley Spinelli:** Pamela Segall; **Miss Grotkey:** Allyce Beasley; **Principal Prickley:** Dabney Coleman

⦿ DISNEY'S SING ME A STORY: WITH BELLE
Lynsey McLeod, who played the beautiful Belle in the animated hit *Beauty and the Beast*, hosts this live-action mix of songs and storytelling, accompanied by a brace of classic Disney animated shorts, that demonstrates to young viewers that taking shortcuts in life "is not always the best solution," in this half-hour syndicated series.

A Patrick Davidson/Buena Vista Television Production. Color. Half-hour. Premiered: September 9, 1995. Syndicated.

⦿ DISNEY'S THE LITTLE MERMAID
Beautiful young "mer-teen" Ariel leaves the sea for life in the human world, enjoying occasional underwater adventures with King Triton and her pals (including Sebastian, the calypso-singing crab), sometimes in the form of spectacular musical numbers, in this half-hour Saturday-morning series, billed as the "prequel" to the blockbuster Disney animated feature on which the series was based. CBS launched the series with a Friday night prime-time special, "A Whale of a Tale," which debuted the night before its Saturday-morning introduction. Jodie Benson, Sam Wright and Kenneth Mars reprised their vocal roles from the movie.

In October of 1995, reruns of the series began airing weekdays on The Disney Channel.

A Walt Disney Television Animation Production. Color. Half-hour. Premiered on ABC: September 12, 1992–September 2, 1995. Rebroadcast on DIS: October 2, 1995 (weekdays).

Voices
Ariel: Jodi Benson; **Sebastian:** Samuel E. Wright; **Ursula:** Pat Carroll; **Urchin:** Danny Cooksey; **Flounder:** Edan Gross; **Scuttle:** Maurice LaMarche; **King Triton:** Kenneth Mars

⦿ DR. KATZ: PROFESSIONAL THERAPIST
Based on the stand-up acts of Jonathan Katz, Dom Irerra and Laura Kightlinger, a droll psychiatrist deals with his 23-year-old unemployed slacker son (Ben), who dreams of wealth and freedom but is too lazy to find a real job, in between counseling his neurotic patients and spending his free time at the local bar ("Jacky's 33") with his friends Stan and Julie. This half-hour animated series airing Sunday nights on Comedy Central premiered in May of 1995.

Unlike traditional cartoon series in which episodes are scripted and voice tracks are then recorded, the stand-up routines of Katz and other artists were recorded prior to animating and scripting each half-hour program, then scripted with the improvisational dialogue set to animation through a computer-animation process dubbed "Squigglevision" (so named because of the constant zigzagging around the edges of the characters to give the impression of movement). Well-known comedians and stand-up comics lent their voices as "patients" in each episode, including: Bob Newhart Al Franken (of *Saturday Night Live* fame), Rodney Dangerfield, Richard Lewis, Ray Romano (of *Everyone Loves Raymond*), Rita Rudner and Garry Shandling.

In 1995 the series won an Emmy for Outstanding Performance in an Animated Program (Jonathan Katz) and was Comedy Central's second-highest rated original series.

A Popular Arts Entertainment/Tom Snyder Production in association with HBO Downtown Productions. Color. Half-hour. Premiered on COM: May 28, 1995.

Voices
Dr. Katz: Jonathan Katz; **Ben:** H. Jon Benjamin; **Laura, the receptionist:** Laura Silverman; **Stanley:** Will Le Bow; **Julie:** Julianne Shapiro

⦿ DR. SNUGGLES
Peter Ustinov is the voice of Dr. Snuggles, a good-natured veterinarian who travels anywhere via his pogo stick to care for animals. Ustinov supplied the voice of several other characters in the series as well.

A KidPix Production. Color. Half-hour. Premiered: September 12, 1981. Syndicated.

Voices
Dr. Snuggles: Peter Ustinov

⦿ DO DO—THE KID FROM OUTER SPACE
This British-made 78-episode color half-hour series, imitated popular Japanese imports, featuring the adventures of Do Do and his pet Company, aliens from the atomic planet Hydro, who come to Earth to help a noted scientist, Professor Fingers, perform research on many scientific mysteries left unresolved. The series was telecast on several NBC-owned and operated stations from 1966 through 1970.

A Halas and Batchelor Production. Color. Half-hour. Premiered: August 23, 1965. Syndicated.

⊚ DOG CITY

Brian Henson, son of the late Muppets creator Jim Henson, was executive producer of this half-hour, film noir–style live-action/animated detective series following the comical exploits of hardboiled dog detective Ace Heart, Ace's artist creator, a muppet dog named Eliot Shag and their canine friends (Eddie, Bugsy, Frisky, Bruiser and Kitty), who solve mysteries—often by resorting to supernatural means—to make the streets of Dog City safe again. The series was based on a live-action sketch that appeared on NBC's *The Jim Henson Hour* in 1989.

A Jim Henson/Nelvana Production. Color. Half-hour. Premiered on FOX: September 19, 1992–January 28, 1995.

Voices
Ace Heart: Ron White; **Chief Rosie O'Gravy:** Elizabeth Hanna; **Bugsy:** John Stocker; **Frisky:** James Rankin; **Bruiser:** Howard Jerome; **Kitty:** Paulina Gillis; **Mad Dog:** Stephen Quimette

Muppet Performers
Eliot Shag: Kevin Clash; **Colleen:** Fran Brill; **Artie:** Joey Mazzarino; **Bruno:** Brian Meehl

⊚ DONALD DUCK PRESENTS

Donald Duck hosts this series of classic cartoons edited into half-hour compilations first aired on The Disney Channel in 1983.

A Left Coast Television/No-g Production for The Disney Channel. Color. Half-hour. Premiered on DIS: 1983.

⊚ DOUBLE DRAGON

Trained from infancy in martial arts and steeped in the non-violent Code of the Dragon, Billy Lee undergoes his greatest challenge when, along with Marian, a dedicated policewoman, he battles to stop the Shadow Warriors and meets his long lost identical twin brother in this half-hour syndicated fantasy/adventure series first broadcast in 1993 as part of the weekend anthology series *Amazin' Adventures*. In 1996, following its run in syndication, the series was rebroadcast on USA Network's *Cartoon Express*.

A DIC Enterprises/Bohbot Production. Color. Half-hour. Premiered: 1993. Syndicated. Rebroadcast on USA: September 22, 1996.

Voices
Billy Lee/Shadow Warrior/Jawbreaker: Mike Donovan; **Jimmy Lee/Shadow Boss/Sickle:** Scott McNeil; **Shadowmaster:** Jim Byrnes; **Trigger Happy:** Terry Klassen; **Vortex:** Ian James Corlett; **Blaster/Countdown:** Alvin Sanders; **Wild Willy/Chopper/Kona:** Gary Chalk; **Oldest Dragon:** French Tichner; **Marian Martin:** Cathy Weseluck; **Michael:** Wezley Morris; **Abobo:** Blu Mankuma

⊚ DOUG

A painfully average 11-year-old kid (Doug Funnie), who spends half his time thinking about popular Patty Mayonnaise and the other half avoiding school bully Roger Klotz, muddles through tough childhood experiences, such as getting a bad haircut or learning to dance for the first time, which he carefully details in a diary each night, in this Emmy-nominated half-hour animated series created by Jim Jinkins. Each episode charted the delightful misadventures of the likable lad, learning another valuable lesson about growing up. A cast of regulars included best friend Skeeter Valentine, vice principal Lamar Bone and teacher Mrs. Wingo. Jinkins got the idea for *Doug* one night in 1985 while sitting in his New York loft. First he tried to sell the idea as a greeting card line, then as a children's book, but he had no takers.

Premiering in August 1991 on Nickelodeon, as part of a 90-minute Sunday-morning cartoon block that included *The Ren & Stimpy Show* and *Rugrats*, the show slowly built a loyal following. It didn't really become a ratings hit until the original 52 episodes ceased production in 1994 and Nickelodeon started airing reruns along with *Rugrats*, Monday through Friday. (*Rugrats* became Nick's highest-rated show; *Doug* ranked a close second.)

During the character's network run, in 1993 Nickelodeon cast Doug in his first prime-time animated special, *Doug's Halloween Adventure*, in which Doug and Skeeter go to an amusement park for the opening of "the scariest ride ever made."

In the fall of 1996 Doug returned, as a seventh grader (and back from summer vacation) in 13 new episodes in *Brand Spanking New Doug* for ABC. (See entry for further details.)

A Jumbo Pictures/Ellipse Animation Production in association with Nickelodeon. Color. Half-hour. Premiered on NIK: August 11, 1991–August 8, 1992; August 15, 1992–September 19, 1993; September 26, 1993–October 1, 1994. Rebroadcast on NIK: October 1994.

Voices
Doug Funnie: Billy West; **Judy Funnie:** Becca Lish; **Patty Mayonnaise:** Constance Shulman; **Bud Dink/Skeeter Valentine:** Fred Newman; **Beebe:** Alice Playten; **Lamar Bone:** Doug Preis; **Mayor White:** Greg Lee

⊚ DRAGON BALL Z

Adapted from the phenomenally successful Japanese cartoon. Goko, a rolypoly boy who came to Earth as an infant with powers far beyond those of mortal men to destroy the planet now is mankind's last, best hope to fend off supervillains from his native planet. Their aim: to find the crystal Dragon Balls that will enable them to conquer the universe. This half-hour mystical adventure series was produced for first-run syndication.

A *Toei Animation/FUNimation/Saban Entertainment Production*. Color. Half-hour. Premiered: September 7, 1996. Syndicated.

Voices
Don Brown, Ted Cole, Paul Dobson, Brian Drummond, Andrew Francis, Paulina Gillis, Jason Gray Stanford, Doc Harris, Saltron Henderson, Mark Hildreth, Terry Klassen, Lalainia Lindjberg, Scott McNeil, Laara Nadiq, Pauline Newstone, Doug Parker, Jane Perry, Ward Perry, Alvin Sanders, Matt Smith, Jerry Todd, Dave "Squatch" Ward, Cathy Weseluck, Alec Willows

ⓖ DRAGON FLYZ
Set in the 41st-century city of Airlandis, three heroic brothers and their valiant sister, allied with their mighty dragons, fight against the evil Dread Wing to keep their beloved city floating free. This futuristic, 26-episode half-hour fantasy series premiered in syndication nationwide in the fall of 1996.

An *Abrams Gentile Entertainment/Gaumont Multimedia Production*. Color. Half-hour. Premiered: September 14, 1996. Syndicated.

Voices
T.J. Benjamin, Saul Bernstein, Thomas Cannizzaro, Donna Daley, Jonathan Kahn, Don Mayo, James Michael, K.C. Noel

ⓖ DRAGON'S LAIR
In King Ethelred's kingdom, one knight outshines them all—Dirk the Daring. He performs great deeds and protects the kingdom and his beautiful Princess Daphne from creepy villains and a fiery dragon in this half-hour ABC Saturday-morning series. After its network run ended, the series was subsequently aired on USA Network's *Cartoon Express* then on the Cartoon Network.

A *Ruby-Spears Enterprise Production*. Color. Half-hour. Premiered on ABC: September 8, 1984–April 27, 1985. Rebroadcast on USA: April 30, 1989–March 19, 1992. Rebroadcast on CAR: September 17, 1994–September 18, 1994 (Look What We Found!).

Voices
Dirk the Daring: Bob Sarlatte; **Princess Daphne:** Ellen Gerstell; **King Ethelred:** Fred Travalena; **Timothy:** Michael Mish; **Cinge:** Arthur Burghardt; **Bertram:** Peter Cullen; **Storyteller:** Clive Revill; **Assorted Voices:** Marilyn Schreffler

ⓖ DRAGON WARRIOR
Prompted by the success of the Nintendo video-game series *Dragon Quest*, this Japanese animated series emulated its sword-and-sorcery format. Thirteen serialized half-hour episodes present the adventures of a dragon-slaying 16-year-old teen (Abel), who must rescue his childhood friend (Tiala) from the evil monster Baramos and save mankind from the deadly fury of the Great Dragon.

A *Saban Entertainment Production*. Color. Half-hour. Premiered: September 22, 1990. Syndicated.

Voices
Long John Baldry, Jay Brazeau, Jim Byrnes, Gary Chalk, Marcy Goldberg, Sam Kouth, Shelley Lefler, Duff McDonald, Richard Newman

ⓖ DRAK PACK
Drak, Frankie and Howler, teenage descendants of the famed monsters Dracula, Frankenstein and the Werewolf, atone for the sins of their ancestors by using their special powers for the good of mankind. Their main adversary: the world's worst villain, Dr. Dred, and his O.G.R.E. group (the Organization Of Generally Rotten Endeavors).

A *Hanna-Barbera Production*. Color. Half-hour. Premiered on CBS: September 6, 1980–September 12, 1982.

Voices
Drak Jr.: Jerry Dexter; **Frankie/Howler:** Bill Callaway; **Big D:** Alan Oppenheimer; **Dr. Dred:** Hans Conried; **Vampira:** Julie McWhirter; **Mummy Man:** Chuck McCann; **Toad/Fly:** Don Messick

ⓖ DRAWING POWER
In this live-action/animated series, Pop, a white-haired chief animator, and his assistants, Lenny and Kari, dream up educational cartoon messages in a small animation studio, leading into one of several cartoon segments featured each week, namely: "The Book Report," "Bus Stop," "Pet Peeves," "Professor Rutabaga," "Superperson U" and "What Do You Do, Dad (Mom)?" The half-hour program was by the producers of the award-winning children's series *Schoolhouse Rock*.

A *Newhall-Yohe Production*. Color. Half-hour. Premiered on NBC: October 11, 1980–May 16, 1981.

Cast
Pop: Bob Kaliban; **Lenny:** Lenny Schultz; **Kari:** Kari Page

ⓖ DROIDS: THE ADVENTURES OF R2D2 AND C3PO
The robotic droids from the *Star Wars* film series return in this series of half-hour animated adventures produced for ABC in 1985. Produced in association with Lucasfilm, the company *Star Wars* creator George Lucas, the series was repackaged with another ABC/Lucas animated series, *The Ewoks*, as the hour-long *The Ewoks and Star Wars Droids*

Adventure Hour, which aired on the network in 1986. (See series entry for voice credits and details.)

A Lucasfilm Production in association with Nelvana Limited, Hanho Heung-Up and Mi-Hahn Productions. Color. Half-hour. Premiered on ABC: September 7, 1985–February 22, 1986. Rebroadcast on SCI: March 29, 1993–June 30, 1997 (part of Cartoon Quest *and* Animation Station*).*

◎ DROOPY, MASTER DETECTIVE

Dour-faced basset hound and MGM cartoon star Droopy and his look-alike son Dripple match wits with the most comical crooks of all time in all-new half-hour animated adventures, spun off from Fox's *Tom and Jerry Kids*, on which the two characters were originally featured. The new series combined 13 previously broadcast cartoons with 13 new seven-minute episodes. Two Droopy cartoons were featured on each show, along with one new episode of new adventures of Tex Avery's nuttier-than-a-fruitcake Screwball Squirrel (better known as Screwy Squirrel), who makes life miserable for a public park attendant named Dweeble. Hanna-Barbera cofounder Joe Barbera, who worked at MGM with Avery, served as one of the series' producers.

A Hanna-Barbera Production in association with Turner Entertainment. Color. Half-hour. Premiered on FOX: October 2, 1993–August 12, 1994.

Voices
Droopy: Don Messick; **Dripple/Lightening Bolt the Super Squirrel:** Charlie Adler; **Miss Vavoom:** Theresa Ganzel; **McWolf:** Frank Welker; **The Yolker:** Pat Fraley

◎ DUCKMAN

A politically incorrect, out-of-step family man and duck detective with an offbeat family and peculiar blend of animal and human friends—his shrewish sister-in-law, Bernice; his Sgt. Friday–like sidekick, Cornfed; his duckdude son, Ajax; his two-headed sons, Charles and Mambo; his perpetually flatulent Grandmama; and his irritatingly sweet assistants, Fluffy and Uranus—experiences the joys and frustrations of life in the 1990s in this adult-oriented cartoon series from creator, illustrator and underground cartoonist Everett Peck (and from the makers of *The Simpsons*). In early 1991 the series pilot was developed. Production began in November of that year, with Howard E. Baker directing and Frank Zappa providing some of the musical compositions for the program. (The late rock artist also contributed his library of music, which was used in many episodes.) The series debuted in April 1992 at the MIP-TV International Television Convention in Cannes, France before USA Network commissioned it as a weekly prime-time series.

Premiering in March of 1994, the series attracted a million viewers each week. *Duckman* went on to become USA's

signature show, nominated twice (in 1996 and 1997) for an Emmy Award for Outstanding Animated Program and named winner of a CableAce Award for Best Animated Program. Jason Alexander (best known as George Costanza on TV's *Seinfield*) supplies the voice of Duckman.

A Klasky-Csupo/Reno and Osborn Production in association with Paramount Television. Color. Half-hour. Premiered on USA: March 5, 1994.

Voices
Duckman: Jason Alexander; **Bernice:** Nancy Travis; **Ajax:** Dweezil Zappa; **Charles:** Dana Hill (1994–96, Pat Musick (1996–); **Mambo:** Elizabeth Daily; **Bernice:** Nancy Travis; **Fluffy/Uranus:** Pat Musick

◎ DUCKTALES

The first daily animated television series from Walt Disney Studios originally intended as a one-hour network series, *DuckTales* was the studio's answer to the highly popular live-action feature films *Raiders of the Lost Ark* and *Romancing the Stone*. It focused on the daring exploits of that cantankerous canard, Scrooge McDuck, Donald Duck's uncle and the world's richest tightwad. Scrooge is joined by a collection of familiar friends and relatives, including Donald's nephews, Huey, Dewey and Louie, in adventures mixed with fowl play and risky undertakings in the far reaches of the world. The 65 episode series premiered in syndication in September of 1987 as a two-hour special (in most markets), entitled *DuckTales: Treasure of the Golden Suns*.

New characters introduced on the show included Launchpad McQuack, a soldier of outrageous fortune; Mrs. Beakley, the governess to Scrooge's grandnephews; Webbigail ("Webby") Vanderduck, Mrs. Beakley's pesky granddaughter; Doofus, Launchpad's greatest fan and biggest hindrance; and a quartet of masked heavies called the Beagle Boys. Other newly created characters included Duckworth, Fenton Crackshell and Bubba Duck.

In 1988 a second two-hour afternoon special was produced, *DuckTales: Time Is Money*, followed by a third in 1989, *Super DuckTales*, which premiered on NBC's *Magical World of Disney*. A year later the characters starred in their only full-length animated feature, *DuckTales the Movie: Treasure of the Lost Lamp*.

That same year, following its initial run in syndication, the series joined Disney studio's two-hour, syndicated *Disney Afternoon* cartoon block.

A Walt Disney Television Animation Production. Color. Half-hour. Premiered: September 21, 1987. Syndicated.

Voices
Uncle Scrooge McDuck: Alan Young; **Launchpad McQuack:** Jim McGeorge, Terence McGovern; **Huey/Dewey/Louie/Webbigail Vanderduck:** Russi Taylor; **Doo-**

fus: Brian Cummings; **Gyro Gearloose/Flintheart Glom-gold:** Hal Smith; **Fenton Crackshell:** Hamilton Camp; **Duckworth:** Chuck McCann; **Magica de Spell/Ma Beagle:** June Foray; **Mrs. Beakley:** Joan Gerber; **Bubba Duck:** Christopher Weeks, Frank Welker; **Ludwig Von Drake:** Steve Bulen, Corey Burton; **Donald Duck:** Tony Anselmo

DUDLEY DO-RIGHT AND HIS FRIENDS

(See THE DUDLEY DO-RIGHT SHOW.)

THE DUDLEY DO-RIGHT SHOW

First introduced on 1961's *Bullwinkle Show*, inept Royal Canadian Mountie Dudley Do-Right returned along with girlfriend Nell, Inspector Fenwick and Snidely Whiplash for more madcap fun in this weekly half-hour series for Saturday-morning television. The program repeated adventures previously seen on *The Bullwinkle Show*, in addition to previous segments that debuted on *Rocky and His Friends*. "Aesop and Son," "Fractured Fairy Tales" and "Peabody's Improbable History." (For voice credits, see *Rocky and His Friends* and *The Bullwinkle Show*.) The series was later retitled and syndicated as *Dudley Do-Right and His Friends*.

A Jay Ward Production with Producers Associates for Television. Color. Half-hour. Premiered on ABC: April 27, 1969–September 6, 1970.

Voices
Dudley Do-Right: Bill Scott; **Nell Fenwick:** June Foray; **Inspector Ray K. Fenwick/Narrator:** Paul Frees; **Snidely Whiplash:** Hans Conried

THE DUKES

The hilarious folks of Hazzard County compete in an around-the-world race in this action adventure series based on the tremendously successful prime-time series *The Dukes of Hazzard*. This time greedy little Boss Hogg and dopey Sheriff Rosco scheme to foreclose the mortgage on the Dukes. This causes Bo, Luke and Daisy to race the trusty General Lee, the hottest supercharged car ever, to raise money for the poor folks in Hazzard County and pay off the mortgage. The animated program features the voices of the stars of the live-action network series.

The animated series debuted as a midseason replacement on CBS in 1982. CBS renewed the program for a second season but cancelled the show after it was on the air for only a month. A Hanna-Barbera Production. Color. Half-hour. Premiered on CBS: February 5, 1983–November 5, 1983.

Voices
Boss Hogg: Sorrell Booke; **Bo Duke:** John Schneider; **Luke Duke:** Tom Wopat; **Daisy Duke:** Catherine Bach; **Vance Duke:** Christopher Mayer; **Uncle Jesse:** Denver Pyle; **Sheriff Rosco Coltrane:** James Best; **Flash/Smokey/General Lee:** Frank Welker

DUMB AND DUMBER: THE ANIMATED SERIES

Capitalizing on the success of the 1994 feature film, classic dumbsters Harry and Lloyd (portrayed by comedian Jim Carrey and actor Jeff Daniels in the film) spend most of their time looking for jobs—and losing them soon after they are hired—in this Saturday-morning half-hour cartoon series.

A Hanna-Barbera Cartoons Production in association with New Line Television. Color. Half-hour. Premiered on ABC: September 1995–July 24, 1996.

Voices
Lloyd: Matt Frewer; **Harry:** Bill Fagerbakke; **Weenie:** Tom Kenny; **Dymbster:** Bronson Pinchot; **Waitress:** Kath Soucie

DUNGEONS AND DRAGONS

Based on the popular fantasy game, this 26 episode half-hour series traces the adventures of six children (Sheila, Hank, Eric, Diana, Presto and Bobby) who pile into an amusement park ride only to find themselves on the most mysterious and terrifying ride of all: a trip through time into the realm of dungeons and dragons.

A Marvel Production in association with Dungeons & Dragons Entertainment Group, a division of TSR Incorporated. Color. Half-hour. Premiered on CBS: September 17, 1983–August 30, 1986. Rebroadcast on CBS: June 20, 1987–September 5, 1987.

Voices
Hank: Willie Aames; **Eric:** Donny Most; **Sheila:** Katie Leigh; **Diana:** Toni Gayle Smith; **Presto:** Adam Rich; **Bobby:** Ted Field III; **Dungeon Master:** Sidney Miller; **Venger:** Peter Cullen

DYNOMUTT, DOG WONDER

In the summer of 1978, ABC repeated the adventures of this caped, crusading bionic dog and his faithful leader, the Blue Falcon, who were introduced in tandem on *The Scooby Doo/Dynomutt Hour* in 1976. Created by Joe Ruby and Ken Spears, who formed their own animation studio, Ruby-Spears Enterprises, Dynomutt's voice and mannerisms were patterned after Ed Norton (Art Carney) of *The Honeymooners*.

Before being given its own half-hour time slot that summer, Dynomutt reappeared that season in four two-part broadcasts as part of *Scooby's All-Star Laff-A-Lympics*. (The cartoons were retitled "The Blue Falcon and Dynomutt.") In the fall of 1980, Dynomutt surfaced again briefly as costar of *The Godzilla/Dynomutt Hour with the Funky Phantom* on NBC.

In the spring of 1989 the series began reairing on USA Network's weekday cartoon block *Cartoon Express*, until the fall of 1991. It has since been rebroadcast on the Cartoon Network. (For *Dynomutt* voice credits, see *The Scooby-Doo/Dynomutt Hour*.)

A Hanna-Barbera Production. Color. Half-hour. Premiered on ABC: June 3, 1978–September 2, 1978. Rebroadcast on USA: April 2, 1989–October 25, 1991. Rebroadcast on CAR: October 3, 1992–January 1, 1994 (weekends); January 8, 1994–April 3, 1994 (Saturdays, Sundays); April 9, 1994–September 4, 1994 (Saturdays, Sundays); September 10, 1994–October 15, 1994 (Saturdays); October 17, 1994–September 1, 1995 (with Mighty Man & Yukk).

EARTHWORM JIM

An extraterrestrial supersuit transforms this slimy, spineless 98-gram weakling into a musclebound defender of Earth, the cosmos and everything in between. Every villain wants to nab the supersuit for himself in this 21 episode half-hour cartoon series, based on the popular video game of the same name.

A Universal Cartoon Studios/Akom Production Company/Flextech PLC/Shiny Entertainment Production. Color. Half-hour. Premiered on WB: September 9, 1995–October 12, 1996.

Voices

Earthworm Jim: Dan Castellaneta; **Queen Slug-for-a-Butt:** Andrea Martin; **Peter Puppy/Narrator:** Jeff Bennett; **Princess What's-Her-Name:** Kath Soucie; **Professor Monkey-for-a-Head:** Charles Adler; **Evil the Cat:** Edward Hibbert; **Snott/Henchrat:** Jon Kassir; **Psy-Crow/Bob, the Killer Goldfish:** Jim Cummings

EEK! AND THE TERRIBLE THUNDERLIZARDS

The ever-neurotic cat returned for two more seasons in this half-hour cartoon combo mixing *Eek! The Cat* cartoons and 15-minute serialized adventures (one segment per week) of "The Terrible Thunderlizards," a trio of New Age dinosaurs—Day Z. Cutter, Doc and Bo "Diddly" Squat—from 135 million years ago. Due to creative disagreements between network executives at Fox (which aired the series) and series creator Savage Steve Holland, the program's scheduled September 1993 premiere date was postponed until November of that year.

A Fox Children's Network Production in association with Savage Studios and Nelvana Entertainment. Color. Half-hour. Premiered on FOX: November 20, 1993–September 2, 1995.

Voices
Eek! The Cat: Bill Kopp

EEK! STRAVAGANZA

Beginning with the fall 1995 season, this new *Eek! The Cat* series became a showcase for new animated series, airing Saturday mornings and weekday afternoons. The season marked the debut of "Klutter," the mischievous adventures of an ambulatory pile of junk from under a bed, produced by Savage Steve Holland (who co-created and produced *Eek! The Cat*), which alternated with new episodes of "The Terrible Thunder Lizards."

A Fox Children's Network Production in association with Savage Studios and Nelvana Entertainment. Color. Half-hour. Premiered on FOX: September 9, 1995–September 5, 1997.

Voices
Bill Kopp, Charlie Adler, Kurtwood Smith, Elinor Donahue, Dan Castellaneta, John Kassir, Cam Clarke, Jason Priestly, Jaid Barrymore, Savage Steve Holland, Curtis Armstrong, E.G. Daily, Gary Owens, Brad Garrett, Corey Feldman, Tawny Kitaen, Karen Haber, Anita Dangler

EEK! THE CAT

The slapstick antics of a fat, nontalking, neurotic cat—whose good deeds always run astray (and whose life with a suburban family that includes two awful kids isn't much better—was the subject of this weekly 13-episode half-hour animated series. Introduced on the Fox Network in September of 1992, it was based on the character created by animator Bill Kopp and director Savage Steve Holland. Featured in two other weekly series on the network—*Eek! And the Terrible Thunderlizards* and *Eek! Stravaganza*—the character also starred in a 1993 prime-time Christmas special, *Eek! The Cat Christmas*.

A Fox Children's Network Production in association with Savage Studios and Nelvana Entertainment. Color. Half-hour. Premiered on FOX: September 11, 1992–November 13, 1993.

Voices
Eek! The Cat: Bill Kopp; **Annabelle:** Tawny Kitaen

THE EIGHTH MAN

Comic-strip adaptation of Japanese bionic crimefighter reborn from the body of a murdered police detective found by Professor Genius, who transforms him into super-robot, Tobor, the Eighth Man. Resuming the chase for his own killers, Tobor's true identity is known only to Chief Fumblethumbs of the Metropolitan International Police, for whom he helps fight crime in the city. Along the way he encounters such notorious villains as the Armored Man, Dr.

Demon, and the Light That Burned, as well as the criminal organization Intercrime. First telecast on Japanese television, the 52 episode half-hour animated series was dubbed in English by Joe Oriolo Productions, producers of TV's *Felix the Cat.*

A TCJ Animation Center/ABC Films Production. Color. Half-hour. Premiered: September 7, 1965. Syndicated.

⊚ EMERGENCY + FOUR

In this cartoon spinoff from the long-running NBC live-action adventure series *Emergency,* four youngsters (Sally, Matt, Jason, and Randy) help Los Angeles County paramedics rescue endangered citizens from burning buildings and other perils in 26 half-hour adventures. The series was first telecast on NBC's Saturday-morning schedule in 1973–74, then rebroadcast in its entirety for two more seasons until it was cancelled in September of 1976, the same year the live-action series ended its network run.

Kevin Tighe and Randolph Mantooth, stars of the original *Emergency,* voiced the animated version of their characters.

A Fred Calvert Production. Color. Half-hour. Premiered on NBC: September 8, 1973–September 4, 1976.

Voices
Roy DeSoto: Kevin Tighe; **John Gage:** Randolph Mantooth; **Sally:** Sarah Kennedy; **Matt:** David Joliffe; **Jason:** Donald Fullilove; **Randy:** Peter Haas

⊚ ENCHANTED TALES

Some of the world's most beloved literary classics ("Snow White," "Peter Rabbit," *Treasure Island,* "Hercules," among others), backed by three original songs and fully orchestrated scores featuring the music of Beethoven, Mozart, Tchaikovsky and others, are brought to life in this award-winning hour-long anthology series produced for first-run syndication.

A Sony Wonder Production. Color. One hour. Premiered: September 20, 1997. Syndicated.

⊚ EVERYTHING'S ARCHIE

The fifth in a series of *Archie* comic-strip series, this entry featured repeat episodes of the previous network shows (*The Archie Show, The Archie Comedy Hour, Archie's Funhouse,* and *Archie's TV Funnies*) combined with new animated wraparounds of the cast. (See *The Archies* for voice credits.)

A Filmation Associates Production. Color. Half-hour. Premiered on CBS: September 8, 1973–January 26, 1974.

⊚ THE EWOKS

The furry, feathered, gnomish clan from George Lucas's *Star Wars* film series star in all-new, animated adventures as fierce defenders of the planet Endor in this ABC Saturday-morning series. The program premiered in September 1985, only to later be combined with its animated counterpart, *Droids: The Adventures of R2D2 and C3PO,* as the hour-long fantasy adventure *The Ewoks and Star Wars Droids Adventure Hour.* (See entry for further details). The series was later reaired on the Sci-Fi Channel's *Cartoon Quest* program block.

A Lucasfilm Production in association with Nelvana Limited, Hanho Heung-Up and Mi-Hahn Productions. Color. Half-hour. Premiered on ABC: September 7, 1985–February 22, 1986. Rebroadcast on SCI: April 16, 1993–May 26, 1997.

⊚ THE EWOKS AND STAR WARS DROIDS ADVENTURE HOUR

The enchantment of George Lucas's box-office sensation *Star Wars* was spun off into this Saturday-morning series, combining two half-hour series of new adventures of those lovable droids, R2-D2 and C3PO, as well as those cuddly creatures, the Ewoks, in this hour-long science-fiction fantasy series.

In *Ewoks,* the furry tribe of peace-loving characters, now the Endorian equivalents of teenagers, enjoy new encounters on the distant forest moon of Endor with friends Princess Kneesa and the mischievous Latara. Young Ewoks scout Wicket leads the pack as they journey through their fantastic world.

The second half, *Droids: The Adventures of R2-D2 and C3PO,* recounts the years between the rise of the Empire and the beginning of the "Star Wars" in animated stories with a liberal comic touch, always told from the droids' point of view.

The series' components each began as separate half-hour shows, debuting on ABC's Saturday-morning schedule in September of 1985. Both shows were combined and broadcast under the new title, *The Ewoks and Star Wars Droids Adventure Hour* beginning in March of 1986.

A Lucasfilm Production in association with Nelvana Limited, Hanho Heung-Up and Mi-Hahn Productions. Color. One hour. Premiered on ABC: March 1, 1986–November 1, 1986.

Voices

THE EWOKS: Wicket: Jim Henshaw; **Widdle, Wicket's brother:** John Stocker; **Weechee, Wicket's oldest brother:** Greg Swanson; **Teebo:** Eric Peterson; **Paploo:** Paul Chato; **Deej:** Richard Donat; **Shodu:** Nonnie Griffin; **Winda/Baby Nippet:** Leanne Coppen; **Princess Kneesaa:** Cree Summer Francks; **Latara:** Taborah Johnson; **Logray, the medicine man:** Doug Chamberlain; **Chief Chirpa/Lumat:** George

Buza; **Aunt Bozzie/Aunt Zephee:** Pam Hyatt; **Malani:** Alyson Court; **Baby Wiley:** Michael Fantini; **Ashma:** Paulina Gillis; **Chukah-Trok:** Don McManus; **Erphram Warrick:** Antony Parr; **Kaink:** Pauline Rennie; **Mring-Mring (Gupin):** Ron James; **Ubel:** Hadley Kay; **Punt:** Rob Cowan; **Morag:** Jackie Burroughs; **Singing Maiden:** Glori Gage; **Bondo:** Don McManus; **Trebla:** Alan Fawcett; **Jinda Boy:** Greg Swanson; **Rock Wizard:** Desmond Ellis; **Mooth/Hoom/Dulok Scout:** John Stocker; **Zut:** Joe Matheson; **Dobah:** Diane Polley; **Nahkee:** George Buza; **Hoona:** Myra Fried; **King Corneesh/Trome #1:** Dan Hennessey; **Urgah:** Melleny Brown; **Dulok Shaman:** Don Francks; **Shaman's Nephew:** Hadley Kay; **Murgoob:** Eric Peterson; **Trome #2:** Marvin Goldhar; **Trome #3:** Peter Blais

DROIDS: R2-D2: (electronic); **C3PO:** Anthony Daniels; **C3PO (guide track):** Graham Haley

THE TRIGON ONE (EPISODES 1–4): Thall Joben: Andrew Sabiston; **Jord Dusat:** Dan Hennessey; **Kea Moll:** Lesleh Donaldson, Terri Hawkes; **Tig Fromm:** Maurice Godin; **Sise Fromm:** Michael Kirby; **Vlix/Clones/Sleazy Guard:** Marvin Goldhar; **Demma Moll:** Toby Tarnow; **Boba Fett:** George Buza, Ken Pogue; **BL-17:** Graham Haley; **Proto 1:** Long John Baldry; **Zebulon Dak:** Donny Burns; **Mercenary Droid:** Dan Hennessey

MON JULPA (EPISODES 5–8, 13): Jann Tosh: Milah Cheylov; **Jessica Meade:** Taborah Johnson; **Uncle Gundy:** Dan Hennessey; **Kleb Zellock:** Donny Burns; **Mon Julpa/Kez-Iban:** Michael Lefebvre; **Kybo Ren:** Don Francks; **Jyn Obah/IG-88/Auctioneer/Miner:** Don McManus; **Sol-lag/Zatec-Cha/Grej/Miner:** John Stocker; **Vinga/Yorpo:** Dan Hennessey; **Doodnik:** George Buza; **Lord Toda:** Graeme Campbell; **Princess Gerin:** Cree Summer Francks; **Coby Toda:** Jamie Dick, Christopher Young; **Captain Stroon:** Chris Wiggins; **Mr. Slarm:** J. Gordon Masten

THE ADVENTURES OF MUNGO BAOBAB (EPISODES 9–12): Mungo Baobab: Winston Reckert, Barry Greene; **Admiral Screed:** Graeme Campbell; **Governor Koong:** Don Francks; **Gaff/Krox:** Rob Cowan; **Auren Yomm:** Jan Austin; **Nilz Yomm/Noop:** Peter MacNeill; **Old Ogger:** Eric Peterson; **Lin-D/Galley Master:** John Stocker; **Bun-Dingo/Announcer at the Games:** Michael Kirby; **Bola Yomm:** Pam Hyatt

◉ EXOSQUAD

In an oppressed, futuristic setting, genetic mutants called Neosapiens and their sinister leader, Phaeton, have taken over Earth (and Venus and Mars), and it's up to the human resistance force (comprised of men and women), Exosquad, to free the solar system from the clutches of Phaeton and his loyalists in the first weekly half-hour animated series from Universal Cartoon Studios. The 52-episode series debuted in first-run syndication in 1993, then returned for a second season in 1994 as part of the *Universal Adventure Hour,* opposite the animated thriller *Monster Force.* Following its syndicated run, USA Network added the series to its Saturday morning action/adventure lineup in 1995, along with the animated *Wild C.A.T.S.*

. *A Universal Cartoon Studios Production in association with MCA Television. Color. Half-hour. Premiered: September 1993. Syndicated. Rebroadcast on USA: September 26, 1995.*

Voices
Lieutenant J.T. Marsh: Robby Benson

◉ EXTREME DINOSAURS

Four of the toughest, smartest and coolest dinos from 65 million years ago reappear on Earth to settle an old score with a gang of marauding raptors bent on turning the planet into a hot, steamy raptor paradise in this half-hour syndicated action/adventure series, produced by DIC Entertainment.

A DIC Entertainment Production. Color. Half-hour. Premiered: September 1, 1997. Syndicated.

Voices
T-Bone: Scott McNeil; **Bad Rap:** Gary Chalk; **Haxx:** Lee Tokar; **Stegz:** Sam Kouth; **Spike:** Cusse Mankuma; **Bullzeye:** Jason Gray Stanford; **Spittor:** Terry Klassen; **Chedra:** Louise Vallance; **Hardrock:** Blu Mankuma; **Dr. Becky Scarwell:** Marcy Goldberg

◉ EXTREME GHOSTBUSTERS

When a new generation of spirits appear on the scene, original ghostbuster Egon Spengler emerges from his reclusive lifestyle to lead a group of four inner-city teens (Roland, Garrett, Eduardo, Kylie) and Slimer! the ghost (now a good ghost) to rid the Big Apple of slime-spewing intruders in this half-hour syndicated cartoon series based on the popular movie series. The 40-episode series premiered Labor Day 1997. The program's working title was *Super Ghostbusters.*

A Columbia TriStar TV Animation/Adelaide Production. Color. Half-hour. Premiered: September 1, 1997. Syndication.

Voices
Egon Spengler: Maurice LaMarche; **Janine Melnitz:** Pat Musick; **Roland Jackson:** Alfonso Ribeiro; **Kylie Griffin:** Tara Charendoff; **Eduardo Rivera:** Rino Romano; **Garrett Miller:** Jason Marsden; **Slimer!/Mayor McShane:** Billy West

⊚ THE FABULOUS FUNNIES

Animated vignettes starring comic-strip characters, such as Nancy and Sluggo, Broom Hilda, Alley Oop and the Katzenjammer Kids. The series featured all-new episodes combined with repeat adventures first shown on *Archie's TV Funnies*.

A Filmation Associates Production. Color. Half-hour. Premiered on NBC: September 9, 1978–September 1, 1979.

Voices
Broom Hilda/Sluggo/Oola/Hans and Fritz Katzenjammer: June Foray; **Nancy:** Jayne Hamil; **Captain Katzenjammer/ King Guzzle:** Alan Oppenheimer; **Alley Oop:** Bob Holt

⊚ FAMILY CLASSICS THEATRE

Thirteen hour-long animated specials, based on popular juvenile novels, comprised this series of literary masterpieces converted to animation. Telecast as holiday specials, the films were produced by two animation studios, Australia's Air Programs International and Hanna-Barbera Productions. Titles included: "Tales of Washington Irving," "The Prince and the Pauper," "Robinson Crusoe," "Gulliver's Travels" and others. (See Animated Television Specials for details on each production.) The final season repeated previously shown specials.

An Air Programs International/Hanna-Barbera Production. Color. One hour. Premiered on CBS: November 14, 1971.

⊚ FAMILY CLASSIC TALES

Following the success of *Family Classics Theatre*, CBS aired this series of 11 new animated features for children, packaged as fall holiday specials (see Animated Television Specials for details on each production).

An Air Programs International/Hanna-Barbera Production. Color. One hour. Premiered on CBS: November 15, 1975.

⊚ FAMILY DOG

Originally produced as a half-hour special for Steven Spielberg's ill-fated NBC anthology series *Amazing Stories*, CBS commissioned this half-hour animated spinoff exploring the life of a family's pet dog, which was unleashed in prime time—with two back-to-back episodes—in June of 1993. The long-awaited series from Spielberg and filmmaker Tim Burton encountered numerous creative delays (including a complete production breakdown during which episodes were sent to a Canadian animation house for "fixes") and rising production costs (originally budgeted at $650,000 per episode, costs soared to more than $1 million), only to generate poor ratings. Although 10 episodes were produced, CBS pulled the plug on the series after airing only five of them.

An Amblin Television Production in association with Warner Bros. Television and Universal Television. Color. Half-hour. Premiered on CBS: June 23, 1993–July 21, 1993.

Voices
Skip Binford, father: Martin Mull; **Bev Binford, mother:** Molly Cheek; **Billy Binford, their son:** Zak Huxtable; **Cassie Cole, their daughter:** Cassie Cole; **Dog:** Danny Mann

⊚ THE FAMOUS ADVENTURES OF MR. MAGOO

The myopic Mr. Magoo portrays various literary and historical characters—William Tell, Long John Silver, Don Quixote and others—in this hour-long series that sometimes combined two half-hour stories in one program. The show marked Magoo's first entry into prime time as a regular weekly series. Installments of the series have since been rebroadcast on The Disney Channel.

A UPA Productions of America Production. Color. One hour. Premiered on NBC: September 19, 1964–August 21, 1965. Rebroadcast on DIS.

Voices
Mr. Magoo: Jim Backus

⊚ FANGFACE

Producers Joe Ruby and Ken Spears, formerly top cartoon show creators for Hanna-Barbera, opened shop and animated for ABC their first Saturday-morning kid series under the production company Ruby-Spears. The program dealt with the misadventures of four teenagers—Biff, Kim, Puggsy and Fangs (the latter two reminiscent of Leo Gorcey and Huntz Hall of *Bowery Boys* fame) who fight the forces of evil with the help of Fangs (actually Sherman Fangsworth), who turns into a werewolf. The ABC Saturday-morning series only lasted one full season, but Fangface returned with a new partner, Fangpuss, in new adventures as part of *The Plastic Man Comedy-Adventure Show* during the 1979–80 season.

A Ruby-Spears Enterprises Production. Color. Half-hour. Premiered on ABC: September 9, 1978–September 8, 1979. Rebroadcast on CAR: July 16, 1994–July 17, 1994 (Look What We Found!); October 3, 1994–December 2, 1994 (weekdays); June 5, 1995–September 1, 1995 (weekdays).

Voices
Fangface: Jerry Dexter; **Biff:** Frank Welker; **Puggsy:** Bart Braverman; **Kim:** Susan Blu

THE FANTASTIC FOUR (1967)

The superhero team of the Fantastic Four is composed of scientist Reed Richards (Mr. Fantastic), who can stretch his body into various contortions; his wife, Sue (The Invisible Girl); Ben Grimm, alias the Thing, who, once transformed, has the power of 1,000 horses; and Johnny Storm, the Human Torch. Twenty-episode half-hour series aired for two seasons on ABC.

A Hanna-Barbera Production in association with Marvel Comics Group. Color. Half-hour. Premiered on ABC: September 9, 1967–August 30, 1969. Rebroadcast on ABC: September 7, 1969–August 30, 1970. Rebroadcast on CAR: October 3, 1992–(Saturdays); February 11, 1995 (Super Adventure Saturdays); July 15, 1995 (Power Zone); March 25, 1996–October 5, 1996 (weekdays, Saturdays).

Voices
Reed Richards, alias Mr. Fantastic: Gerald Mohr; **Sue Richards, alias Invisible Girl:** Jo Ann Pflug; **Ben Grimm, alias The Thing/Dr. Doom:** Paul Frees; **Johhny Storm, alias The Human Torch:** Jack Flounder

THE FANTASTIC FOUR (1994)

Mr. Fantastic (Reed Richards), the Invisible Girl (Sue Richards), the Human Torch (Johnny Storm) and the Thing (Ben Grimm) battle archenemies Hydro-Man, Madam Medusa, The Wizard and others in this updated version of the famed comic-book superheroes (also known as *Marvel Superheroes Fantastic Four*), part of the hour-long syndicated block, "The Marvel Action Hour."

A Marvel Films/New World Entertainment Production. Color. Half-hour. Premiered: September 25, 1994.

Voices
Reed Richards, Mr. Fantastic: Beau Weaver; **Sue Richards, The Invisible Girl:** Lori Alan; **Johnny Storm, The Human Torch;** Quinton Flynn; **Ben Grimm/The Thing:** Chuck McCann; **Alicia Masters:** Pauline Arthur Lomas; **Hydro-Man:** Brad Garrett; **Madam Medusa:** Iona Morris; **The Wizard:** Ron Perlman

FANTASTIC MAX

Part of *The Funtastic World of Hanna-Barbera*, this half-hour syndicated adventure series follows the earthly and outer-space encounters of a precocious 16-month-old toddler who returns from an unscheduled trip aboard a rocket with a few surprises: an alien friend and a robot babysitter, who make life for Max and his family anything but dull.

A Hanna-Barbera Production. Color. Half-hour. Premiered: September 1988. Syndicated. Rebroadcast on CAR: October 2, 1992–June 25, 1993 (weekdays); September 20, 1993–December 31, 1993 (weekdays); September 6, 1994–September 1, 1995; September 4, 1995 (weekdays, Saturdays).

Voices
Fantastic Max: Ben Ryan Ganger; **FX, his pea-green alien friend:** Nancy Cartwright; **A.B. Sitter, his babysitter:** Gregg Berger; **Mom, Max's mother:** Gail Matthius; **Dad, Max's father:** Paul Eiding; **Zoe, his six-year-old sister:** Elisabeth Harnois; **Ben, his five-year-old neighbor:** Benji Gregory

FANTASTIC VOYAGE

Trying to save the life of a famous professor who suffers a serious brain injury, a team of government scientists, by means of a special ruby laser, are reduced to the size of a speck and enter the bloodstream in a miniature submarine, beginning a series of incredible adventures, in this 17-episode weekly cartoon series inspired by the 1966 20th Century-Fox feature film of the same name. Debuting on ABC in 1968, the series ran for two seasons before it was finally canceled. The program enjoyed new life in reruns on the Sci-Fi Channel.

A Filmation Associates Production. Color. Half-hour. Premiered on ABC: September 14, 1968–September 5, 1970. Rebroadcast on the SCI: September 27, 1992–September 20, 1996.

Voices
Scientist Corby Birdwell: Marvin Miller; **Erica Stone:** Jane Webb; **Commander Jonathan Kidd/Professor Carter:** Ted Knight

THE FANTASTIC VOYAGES OF SINBAD THE SAILOR

Guided only by his wits, young seafaring adventurer Sinbad braves the high seas, joined by carefree youth Hakeem and his impressible exotic cat Kulak, as they travel the world in this 26-episode, half-hour cartoon series, which premiered on the Cartoon Network.

A Fred Wolf Films Production. Color. Half-hour. Premiered on CAR: February 2, 1998.

Voices
Bob Bergen, Jim Cummings, Melissa Smith Disney, Eric Jacklin, Bob Ridgely, Kath Soucie

FARMER AL FALFA

The prestigious straw-hatted, overall-clad farmer was the principal star of this film package made up of old Terrytoon cartoons and brand-new segments.

A Terrytoons Production. Black-and-White. Color. Half-hour. Premiered: 1956. Syndicated.

FAT ALBERT AND THE COSBY KIDS

One of the staples of comedian Bill Cosby's stand-up act in the early 1960s was his childhood recollections of Fat Albert and the gang from North Philadelphia. Real-life situations were cleverly adapted to amusing and educational cartoons by Filmation Studios in this long-running half-hour series that earned an Emmy Award nomination in 1974. Topics covered drug addiction, family conflicts and other social problems.

Bill Cosby voiced several characters in the series besides serving as its host in live-action wraparounds that opened and closed the program and introduced the animated segments.

Four years before the original series aired on Saturday mornings, NBC broadcast a prime-time special *Hey, Hey, Hey, It's Fat Albert*, which was well received by critics and viewers alike. Beginning with the 1979–80 season, the series' name was changed to *The New Fat Albert Show*.

In 1984, under the title of *Fat Albert and the Cosby Kids*, Filmation produced a new crop of 50 half-hour shows combined with old episodes of the original series for first-run syndication. The original series was rerun on NBC beginning in February 1989 and the following September on USA Network.

A Filmation Associates Production. Color. Half-hour. Premiered on CBS: September 9, 1972–September 1, 1979 (as Fat Albert and the Cosby Kids); September 8, 1979–August 25, 1984 (as The New Fat Albert Show). Rebroadcast on NBC: February 11, 1989–September 2, 1989. Rebroadcast on USA: September 1989. Syndicated.

Voices

Host: Bill Cosby; **Fat Albert/Mushmouth/LeroyMudfoot/Dumb Donald/Weird Harold/Brown Hornet:** Gerald Edwards; **Russell/Bucky:** Jan Crawford; **Rudy/Devery:** Eric Suter

FELIX THE CAT

Producer Joe Oriolo, who took over production of the *Felix the Cat* comic strip, produced this series of new color episodes in which Felix sported a new sight gag—his magic bag of tricks. Stories depicted the scheming, bald-domed Professor and his bulldog assistant, Rock Bottom, endeavoring to steal Felix's magic bag to make him powerless. Such attempts failed miserably, with Felix always having the last laugh. Other scripts had Felix babysitting the Professor's nephew, Poindexter, an intellectual junior scientist. Other recurring characters included the Master Cylinder and Vavoom. Episodes were produced between 1958 and 1960 for broadcast. Five cliff-hanging episodes comprised a complete story.

A Joe Oriolo/Trans-Lux Production. Color. Half-hour. Premiered: January 4, 1960. Syndicated.

Model sheet for the scheming Professor from TV's original Felix the Cat series. © Felix the Cat Productions (COURTESY: JOE ORIOLO PRODUCTIONS)

Voices

Felix the Cat/The Professor/Poindexter/Rock Bottom/The Master Cylinder/Vavoom: Jack Mercer

FESTIVAL OF FAMILY CLASSICS

Favorite literary classics for children were adapted into fully animated feature-length cartoons for this first-run syndicated series of 18 hour-long specials (see Animated Television Specials for details on each title) produced by Jules Bass and Arthur Rankin in association with Japan's Mushi Studios, producers of the animated *Astro Boy*.

A Rankin-Bass Production in association with the Mushi Studios. Color. One hour. Premiered: 1972. Syndicated.

Voices

Carl Banas, Len Birman, Bernard Cowan, Peg Dixon, Keith Hampshire, Peggi Loder, Donna Miller, Frank Perry, Henry Raymer, Billie Mae Richards, Alfie Scopp, Paul Soles.

FIEVEL'S AMERICAN TAILS

Young Fievel Mousekewitz and his 19th-century family—Papa, Mama, Tanya and baby Yasha—journey west to the American frontier and settle in the rugged town of Green River. There Fievel and his pal Tiger set out to tame the Wild West, in this series of continuing escapades based in part on the 1992 sequel *An American Tail: Fievel Goes West*, produced five years after the original 1986 blockbuster *An American Tail*. The series was well received following its debut on CBS in September of 1992 but declining ratings resulted in its cancellation at the end of the season.

An Amblin Entertainment Production in association with Nelvana Enterprises and Universal Television. Color. Half-hour. Premiered on CBS: September 12, 1992–September 11, 1993.

Voices
Fievel Mousekewitz: Philip Glasser; **Papa Mousekewitz:** Lloyd Battista; **Tanya Mousekewitz:** Cathy Cavadin; **Tiger:** Dom DeLuise; **Chula the Spider:** Dan Castellaneta; **Cat R. Waul:** Gerrit Graham; **Sweet William:** Kenneth Mars; **Hambone:** Arthur Burghardt; **Jorge:** Carlos Carrasco; **Fernando:** Alex Dent; **Miss Kitty:** Cynthia Ferrer; **Stanley:** Paige Gosney; **Dog:** Danny Mann; **Aunt Sophie:** Patty Parris; **Lorna Holcombe:** Lisa Picotte; Clint Mousewood: Hal Rayle; **Jack:** Rolland Thompson

◎ FILM ROMAN PRESENTS . . . ANIMATED CLASSIC SHOWCASE

This classic collection of Russian animated children's stories, from Han Christian Andersen's "The Ugly Duckling" to an Indian folk adventure entitled "The Golden Antelope" (a Cannes Film Festival award winner), were redubbed in English, mixed with stereo music and effects tracks, and syndicated worldwide in the fall of 1993 as part of a coventure between American cartoon producer Film Roman and Russia's Films by Jove, owned by former Russian actor Oleg Vidov, his wife Joan Borsten and their associate Sonja Konbrandt, which had acquired the rights to distribute the 1,200-title cartoon film library of Soyuzmultifilm Studios. Initially a package of 12 one-hour specials were produced for syndication.

A Film Roman/Films by Jove Production. Color. One hour. Premiered: Fall 1993.

◎ FISH POLICE

Fish City's top underwater cop, Inspector Gil (voiced by John Ritter), unravels a series of murders and mysteries— joined by a kooky cast of characters: Chief Abalone, Gil's growly boss; Catfish, master of disguise; Tad, the police gofer; Sandy, Gil's "living" badge; Crabby, the Cabdriver, and Pearl, the waitress—in this half-hour comedy/mysteries series parody of 1940s' detective movies, based on a comic-book series by Steve Moncuse. The brainchild of Hanna-Barbera head David Kirschner, the series was its first prime-time animated series since 1972's *Wait Till Your Father Gets Home* and was the second cartoon series to debut in prime-time in a month, following ABC's *Capitol Critters.* CBS ordered only six episodes of *Fish Police,* and dropped the series after three episodes.

A Hanna-Barbera Production. Color. Half-hour. Premiered on CBS: February 28, 1992–March 13, 1992.

Voices
Inspector Gil: John Ritter; **Chief Abalone:** Edward Asner; **Catfish:** Robert Guillaume; **Tad:** Charlie Schlatter; **Crabby:** Buddy Hackett; **Pearl:** Megan Mullally; **Goldie:** Georgia Brown; **Mayor Cod:** Jonathan Winters; **Sharkster:** Tim Curry; **Calmari:** Hector Elizondo; **Mussels Marinara/Doc Croaker:** Frank Welker; **Angel:** JoBeth Willams

◎ FLASH GORDON

Joined by friends Dale Arden and Dr. Hans Zarkov, a teenage Flash Gordon unites a rebel underground to tumble the dynasty of the evil emperor Ming the Merciless on the planet Mongo in this updated, first-run weekly cartoon version of artist/writer Alex Raymond's famed outer-space comic strip but with a dash of 1990s' technology. The series debuted in 1996 with 26 half-hour episodes.

A Hearst Entertainment/Lacewood Productions/Audiovisuel Dupuis-Carrere Television/France 3 Production. Color. Half-hour. Premiered: September 14, 1996. Syndicated.

◎ THE FLINTSTONE KIDS

The original members of *The Flintstones* cast are seen as 10-year-old children in this 1986-produced Saturday-morning series for ABC in which Fred, Barney, Wilma and Betty, together with their dinosaur "pup" Dino, get in and out of scrapes in the familiar surroundings of Bedrock. Complementing the characters is a rich assortment of supporting cast, including Rocky Ratrock, the neighborhood bully; Dreamchip Gemstone, the classic poor little rich girl; Philo Quartz, a budding private detective; and Nate Slate, who will grow up to be Bedrock's biggest businessman.

Three additional segments appeared on the program: "Captain Caveman and Son," exploits of the world's first superhero and his chip-off-the-old-block offspring, Cavey Jr.; "Dino's Dilemmas," demonstrating perils of prehistoric dogdom; and "Flintstone Funnies," a fantasy-adventure segment in which Fred, Barney, Wilma and Betty let their imaginations lead them into exciting adventures.

The series ran for two full seasons on ABC. The program was rebroadcast on ABC from January to May of 1990 and packaged for syndication as part of Hanna-Barbera's *The Funtastic World of Hanna-Barbera* weekend syndicated series. *A Hanna-Barbera Production. Color. One hour. Premiered on ABC: September 13, 1986–October 22, 1988. Syndicated: 1990 (as part of* The Funtastic World of Hanna-Barbera*). Rebroadcast on ABC: January 6, 1990–May 26, 1990. Rebroadcast on CAR: July 4, 1994–June 2, 1995 (weekdays);*

September 4, 1995–September 29, 1995 (weekdays); December 18, 1995–December 22, 1995; December 26, 1995–December 29, 1995; March 25, 1996 (weekdays).

Voices

Freddy: Lennie Weinrib; Scott Menville; **Barney:** Hamilton Camp; **Wilma:** Julie Dees; Elizabeth Lyn Fraser; **Betty:** B.J. Ward; **Dino:** Mel Blanc; **Ed Flintstone, Fred's father:** Henry Corden; **Edna Flintstone, Fred's mother:** Henry Corden; **Robert Rubble, Barney's dad:** Mel Blanc; **Doris Slaghoople:** Jean VanderPyl; **Rocky Ratrock:** Marilyn Schreffler; **Dreamchip Gemstone:** Susan Blu; **Phil Quartz:** Bumper Robinson; **Nate Slate:** Frank Welker; **Flab Slab:** Hamilton Camp; **Miss Rockbottom:** B.J. Ward; **Officer Quartz:** Rene Levant; **Fang:** Frank Welker; **Micky/Mica:** Julie Dees; **Granite Janet:** Susan Blu; **Tarpit Tommy:** Julie Dees; **Stalagbite:** Frank Welker; **Captain Caveman:** Mel Blanc; **Cavey Jr.:** Charles Adler; **Commissioner:** Lennie Weinrib; **Narrator:** Ken Mars

◎ THE FLINTSTONES

The town of Bedrock spelled bedlam when the Flintstones and their neighbors, the Rubbles, got together, formulating what has been probably the most heralded situation-comedy cartoon series and the first "adult" cartoon show for television.

The familiar phrase "Yabba dabba do!" was made famous by blow-hard caveman and father Fred Flintstone. Whenever he tangled with his next-door pal, halfwitted practical joker Barney Rubble, normal modern Stone Age situations always ran amuck.

The main characters, Fred, Barney and wives, Wilma and Betty, were adapted from *The Honeymooners* TV show personalities. Both Fred and Barney bore more than a vague resemblance to Ralph Kramden (Jackie Gleason) and Ed Norton (Art Carney). In the 1-minute and 45-second full-color pilot that sold the series—called *The Flagstones* (the original name of the series)—venerable voice artist Daws Butler did the voices of both Fred and Barney (later assumed by Alan Reed and Mel Blanc) and June Foray was Betty Rubble. The name of the show was eventually changed to *The Flintstones* because the name sounded too much like the Flagtons, a family in the *Hi and Lois* comic strip.

The show's stars faced their share of physical problems, which almost threatened the future of the series. For a full season after Mel Blanc's near-fatal automobile accident in 1962, the show was taped in his bedroom where he lay in a cast from the neck to his toes. Daws Butler filled in as the voice of Barney for at least two episodes, and research has revealed that Hal Smith, best known as Otis the town drunk on *The Andy Griffith Show*, also filled in for Blanc during his illness. As executive producer Joe Barbera explained, "The easy thing would have been to replace him,

but we kept going and it worked. Sometimes we'd have as many as 16 people crowded into his bedroom and we hung a mike in front of him."

Another season Alan Reed (the voice of Fred Flintstone) had a cataract operation but worked up to 20 minutes before his scheduled surgery. He returned to the job in four weeks.

Before Reed's operation, the studio taped his parts in advance and worked around him until he was healthy enough to work again. While he was suffering from cataracts, the scripts were typed in special one-inch letters so that Reed could read his lines.

When the show entered its fourth season, Barbera's other half, Bill Hanna, was quoted as saying "He [Reed] tours the country in a leopard skin—he is Flintstone!" Reed died in 1977.

The Flintstones, which premiered on ABC (the premiere episode was "The Flintstone Flyer"), was the first made-for-television cartoon series to air in prime time and formerly the longest running prime-time animated series (a record since broken by *The Simpsons*). The program aired on Fridays nights at 7:30. Sponsored by Winston, Alka-Seltzer, One-A-Day Vitamins and Post Cereals, the series ended its 166-episode prime-time run on ABC in the fall of 1966. The following September rival network NBC began rebroadcasting the series. Since the program's original network run, the series has been repeated on TBS, USA Network's *Cartoon Express* and the Cartoon Network (the latter since the first day of its launching in 1992).

A Hanna-Barbera Production. Color. Half-hour. Premiered on ABC: September 30, 1960–September 2, 1966. Rebroadcast: NBC: January 7, 1967–August 1969; September 6, 1969–September 5, 1970. Rebroadcast on TBS; Rebroadcast on USA: February 27, 1989–April 26, 1992; Rebroadcast on CAR: October 1, 1992.

Voices

Fred Flintstone: Alan Reed; **Barney Rubble:** Mel Blanc, Daws Butler, Hal Smith; **Wilma Flintstone:** Jean VanderPyl; **Betty Rubble:** Bea Benadaret; Gerry Johnson; **Pebbles:** Jean VanderPyl; **Dino, the pet dinosaur:** Chips Spam; **Bamm Bamm, the Rubbles' son:** Don Messick; **Hoppy, Barney's pet dinosaur:** Don Messick; **George Slate, Fred's boss:** John Stephenson; **Mrs. Slaghoople:** Janet Waldo; Verna Felton; **Arnold, the newsboy:** Don Messick; **The Great Gazoo:** Harvey Korman

◎ THE FLINTSTONES COMEDY HOUR

Complete episodes of *The Flintstones* that previously had aired on the network in other formats reappeared in this hour-long Saturday-morning series, which featured four new episodes of *Pebbles and Bamm-Bamm*, in combination with 20 episodes originally broadcast on 1971's *Pebbles and Bamm-Bamm*.

Other segments included brief vignettes, comedy gag and dance-of-the-week segments rotated in between the series' main cartoon components. The cartoons were repeated the following season under a new series title, *The Flintstones Show,* then shortened to a half-hour, plus as part of *Pebbles and Bamm-Bamm* and the syndicated *Fred Flintstone and Friends.*

A Hanna-Barbera Production. Color. One hour. Half-hour (as The Flintstones Show). Premiered on CBS: September 9, 1972–September 1, 1973. Rebroadcast on CBS: September 8, 1973–January 26, 1974 (as The Flintstones Show.)

Voices

Fred Flintstone: Alan Reed; **Wilma Flintstone:** Jean VanderPyl; **Pebbles Flintstone:** Mickey Stevens, Sally Struthers; **Barney Rubble:** Mel Blanc; **Betty Rubble:** Gay Hartwig; **Bamm-Bamm Rubble:** Jay North; **Sylvester Slate, Fred's boss:** John Stephenson; **Penny:** Mitzi McCall; **Fabian:** Carl Esser; **Wiggy:** Gay Hartwig; **Moonrock/Bronto:** Lennie Weinrib; **Zonk:** Mel Blanc; **Noodles:** John Stephenson; **Stub:** Mel Blanc

☺ THE FLINTSTONES COMEDY SHOW

The original cast of Fred, Barney, Wilma and Betty were featured in this new format of rollicking, fun-filled comedy set in the Stone Age town of Bedrock, debuting on NBC in the fall of 1980. The program contained six regular cartoon segments of various lengths each week: "The Flintstone Family Adventures," the further comic misadventures of the Flintstones and Rubble families; "Pebbles, Dino and Bamm-Bamm," with Pebbles, Bamm-Bamm, Dino and his friends at work solving various mysteries; and "Captain Caveman," the screw-up prehistoric superhero who is aided by Wilma and Betty in warding off criminals.

Other series components included "The Bedrock Cops," the zany escapades of the Bedrock Police force, joined by part-time deputies Fred and Barney and their supernatural friend, Shmoo, in fighting crime; "Dino and the Cavemouse," in which the Flintstones' pet dinosaur, Dino, squares off with a wild house mouse in this frantic prehistoric version of "watchdog vs. mouse"; and "The Frankenstones," the misadventures of the Flintstones' new and "unusual"-looking neighbors, plus a variety of musical and comedy blackouts featuring the series' prehistoric stars.

Following the series' initial network run, three episodes from the series were rebroadcast on NBC under the title, *The Flintstones Family Adventures Hour* in 1981.

A Hanna-Barbera Production. Color. One hour and a half. Premiered on NBC: November 22, 1980–September 5, 1981. Rebroadcast on NBC: October 4, 1981–October 18, 1981 (as The Flintstones Family Adventure Hour).

Voices

Fred Flintstone: Henry Corden; **Wilma Flintstone, his wife:** Jean VanderPyl; **Barney Rubble, their neighbor:** Mel Blanc; **Betty Rubble, his wife:** Gay Autterson; **Dino:** Mel Blanc; **Pebbles Flintstone:** Russi Taylor; **Bamm-Bamm:** Michael Sheehan; **George Slate, Fred's boss:** John Stephenson; **Lou Granite:** Ken Mars; **Penny:** Mitzi McCall; **Wiggy:** Gay Autterson; **Moonrock:** Lennie Weinrib; **Schleprock:** Don Messick; **Shmoo:** Frank Welker; **Sgt. Boulder:** Lennie Weinrib; **Cave Mouse:** Russi Taylor

THE FRANKENSTONES: **Frank Frankenstone, the hulking father:** Charles Nelson Reilly; **Hidea Frankenstone, his wife:** Ruta Lee; **Atrocia Frankenstone, their kooky daughter:** Zelda Rubinstein; **Freaky Frankenstone, their misfit son:** Paul Reubens; **Rockjaw:** Frank Welker; **Captain Caveman:** Joe Baker

☺ FLYING HOUSE

From the producers of *Speed Racer* and *Robotech,* this 1982 half-hour syndicated religious cartoon series (called *Tondera House* in Japan and redubbed in English) premiered in syndication and simultaneously on the Christian Broadcasting Network in 1982. The series covered events of the New Testament and was telecast at the same time as another companion series, *Superbook.* (See entry for details.)

A CBN/Tatsunoko Production. Color. Half-hour. Premiered: 1982 (in syndication and on CBN). Syndicated.

Voices

Billie Lou Watt, Sonia Owens, Hal Studer, Helen Van Koert, Peter Fernandez, Ray Owens, George Gunneau

☺ FONZ AND THE HAPPY DAYS GANG

Inspired by television's hit prime-time comedy series *Happy Days,* this series has Fonzie and the rest of the gang (Richie, Ralph and Fonzie's cut-up dog, Mr. Cool) spread cool fun as they travel via a time machine to every time and place throughout Earth's history. Showing them the way is Cupcake, a young futuristic girl who pilots the craft, which they repaired for her following her unscheduled landing in Milwaukee in the year 1957.

Three original cast members of the popular television sitcom voiced their characters on the 24-episode animated series, which lasted two seasons on ABC.

A Hanna-Barbera Production. Color. Half-hour. Premiered on ABC: November 8, 1980–September 18, 1982.

Voices

Fonzie: Henry Winkler; **Richie Cunningham:** Ron Howard; **Ralph Malph:** Don Most; **Mr. Cool:** Frank Welker; **Cupcake:** DeeDee Conn

☺ FOO FOO

Somewhat forgotten British-made series of 32 five-minute cartoons about a transparent man in a pencil-sketch world.

Produced by England's most noted animation studio, Halas and Batchelor, the series was animated in the same modernistic style of UPA (United Productions of America), which changed the course of animation through limited animation fare like *Gerald McBoing Boing* and Mr. Magoo.

A Halas Batchelor Production. Color. Half-hour. Syndicated: 1961.

⊚ FOOFUR

A ragtag gang of canines (Fencer, Rocki, Louis, Annabell, Fritz-Carlos and Annabell) try to make it on their own, led by the lanky, good-natured blue hound dog, Foofur, in this half-hour animated series for NBC, based on the world-famous Belgian comic-book character created by cartoonist Freddy Monnickendam.

A Hanna-Barbera Production. Color. Half-hour. Premiered on NBC: September 13, 1986–September 3, 1988.

Voices

Foofur: Frank Welker; **Rocky:** Christina Lange; **Annabell:** Susan Tolsky; **Hazel:** Pat Carroll; **Pepe:** Don Messick; **Chucky:** Allan Melvin; **Dolly:** Susan Blu; **Mel:** David Doyle; **Fencer:** Eugene Williams; **Louis:** Dick Gautier; **Fritz-Carlos:** Jonathan Schmock; **Mrs. Escrow:** Susan Silo; **Sam:** Chick Vennera; **Baby:** Peter Cullen; **Burt:** Bill Callaway; **Harvey:** Michael Bell

⊚ FRAGGLE ROCK

Jim Henson's successful muppet clan, the Fraggles, explore everyday adventures in the fun-loving Fraggle community in this animated spinoff of the popular live-action HBO series. The 24-episode animated half-hour version debuted on NBC in September 1987 and lasted one season. It has since appeared in reruns on The Disney Channel since 1991.

A Jim Henson Production in association with Marvel Productions. Color. Half-hour. Premiered on NBC: September 12, 1987–September 3, 1988. Rebroadcast on DIS: 1991.

Voices

Wembley: Bob Bergen; **Gobo/Architect/Wrench:** Townsend Coleman; **Red/Wingnut:** Barbara Goodson; **Mokey/Cotterpin:** Mona Marshall; **Ma Gorg:** Patti Parris; **Boober/Sprocket/Majory:** Rob Paulsen; **Traveling Matt/Pa Gorg/Flange:** Pat Pinney; **Doc/Philo/Gunge:** John Stephenson; **Storyteller:** Stu Rosen

⊚ FRANKENSTEIN JR.
AND THE IMPOSSIBLES

The awesomely strong, 30-foot-tall Frankenstein Jr. protects the community and his boy owner, Buzz, from danger. Sharing billing with the mechanical monster were "The Impossibles," a trio of crime-fighting agents—Fluid Man, Multi-Man and Coil Man—posing as a rock-and-roll group. NBC later rebroadcast episodes of *Frankenstein Jr.* as part of a midseason replacement series called *The Space Ghost/ Frankenstein Jr. Show.*

A Hanna-Barbera Production. Color. Half-hour. Premiered on CBS: September 10, 1966–September 7, 1968. Rebroadcast on CAR: March 5, 1995 (Super Chunk).

Voices

Frankenstein Jr.: Ted Cassidy; **Buzz Conroy:** Dick Beals; **Dr. Conroy:** John Stephenson;

The Impossibles
Multi-Man/Various Others: Don Messick; **Fluid Man:** Paul Frees; **Coil Man:** Hal Smith

⊚ FRED AND BARNEY
MEET THE SHMOO

This 90-minute program was a collection of previously broadcast episodes of *The New Fred and Barney Show* and *The Thing* (originally combined as *Fred and Barney Meet the Thing*), plus repeat episodes from *The New Shmoo*, only serialized into two parts. (See *Fred and Barney Meet the Thing* and *The New Shmoo* for further details.)

A Hanna-Barbera Production. Color. Ninety minutes. Premiered on NBC: December 8, 1979–November 15, 1980.

⊚ FRED AND BARNEY
MEET THE THING

Hanna-Barbera took prehistoric favorites, Fred Flintstone and Barney Rubble, and paired them with Marvel Comics' The Thing in this hour-long series comprised of new adventures of the Flintstone and Rubble families and separate stories revolving around the exploits of high school student Benjamin Grimm, who changes himself into an orange hulk to fight crime. Episodes of both components were repeated on *Fred and Barney Meet the Shmoo*, a 90-minute trilogy series.

A Hanna-Barbera Production. Color. One hour. Premiered on NBC: September 22, 1979–December 1, 1979.

Voices

FRED AND BARNEY: Fred Flintstone: Henry Corden; **Wilma Flintstone, his wife:** Jean VanderPyl; **Barney Rubble, their friend:** Mel Blanc; **Betty Rubble, his wife:** Gay Autterson; **Pebbles, Fred's daughter:** Jean VanderPyl; **Bamm-Bamm, Barney's son:** Don Messick; **George Slate, Fred's boss:** John Stephenson; **Dino, Fred's pet dinosaur:** Mel Blanc

THE THING: Benjy Grimm: Wayne Norton; **The Thing:** Joe Baker; **Kelly, Benjy's friend:** Noelle North; **Betty, Benjy's friend:** Marilyn Schreffler; **Spike, the bully:** Art

Metrano; **Ronald Redford, the rich kid:** John Erwin; **Miss Twilly, the teacher:** Marilyn Schreffler

⊚ FRED FLINTSTONE AND FRIENDS

In new animated wraparounds, Fred Flintstone (voiced by Henry Corden) hosted this series of Hanna-Barbera cartoons originally broadcast by various networks on Saturday mornings: *The Flintstones Comedy Hour, Goober and the Ghost Chasers, Jeannie, Patridge Family: 2200 A.D., Pebbles and Bamm-Bamm* and *Yogi's Gang.*

A Hanna-Barbera Production. Color. Half-hour. Premiered: September 1977. Syndicated.

⊚ FREE WILLY

Based on the 1993 hit family adventure, youngsters Jesse, Randolph and Marlene and their three-ton orca whale friend Willy (who now talks), joined by sea-lion Lucille and baby dolphin Einstein, engage in environmental and scientific adventures, frequently doing battle with the notorious enviro-villain "The Machine" in this weekly ABC Saturday morning series, which debuted in 1994. One of the movie's producers, Lauren Schuler-Donner, served as the series' executive producer.

A Nelvana Entertainment Production. Color. Half-hour. Premiered on ABC: September 1994–August 31, 1996.

Voices

Jesse: Zachary Bennett; **Willy:** Paul Haddad; **Marlene:** Rachael Crawford; **Randolph:** Michael Fletcher; **The Machine:** Gary Krawford; **Amphonids:** James Kidnie; **Lucille:** Alyson Court; **Ben Shore:** Geordie Johnson; **Einstein:** Kevin Zegers; **Mr. Naugle:** Neil Crone; **P.R. Frickey:** Andrew Sabiston; **Annie:** Sheila McCarthy; **Glenn:** Ron Lea

⊚ THE FUNKY PHANTOM

Three teenagers, Skip, Augie and April, and their dog Elmo, release the ghost of Jonathan Wellington Muddlemore ("Mudsy" for short), a young patriot during the American Revolutionary War who has been trapped for two centuries inside the grandfather's clock at Muddlemore Mansion, where he had taken refuge from the Redcoats. Along with his cat Boo, Mudsy and his new friends travel the countryside to challenge injustice and uphold the ideals of the Declaration of Independence. Produced by Hanna-Barbera, this 17-episode, half-hour animated series premiered on NBC in 1971 and lasted only one season. Episodes were later rebroadcast as part of the syndicated series *The Fun World of Hanna-Barbera* and *The Godzilla/Dynomutt Show.*

A Hanna-Barbera Production. Color. Half-hour. Premiered on ABC: September 11, 1971–September 1, 1972. Syndicated (part of The Fun World of Hanna-Barbera). Rebroadcast on CAR: December 6, 1992; March 14, 1993 (part of Boomerang, 1972); April 10, 1994–MAy 26, 1996 (Sundays).

Voices

Jonathan (Mudsy) Muddlemore: Daws Butler; **April Stewart:** Tina Holland; **Skip:** Micky Dolenz; **Augie:** Tommy Cook

⊚ THE FUNNY COMPANY

As members of the Junior Achievement Club, an enterprising group of neighborhood children take on odd jobs to make money, with mixed results in this educational and entertaining series which included educational wraparounds between each cartoon.

A Funny Company/Ken Snyder Production. Color. Half-hour. Premiered: September 1963. Syndicated.

Voices

Buzzer Bell/Shrinkin' Violette: Dick Beals; **Polly Plum:** Robie Lester; **Merry Twitter/Jasper N. Park:** Nancy Wible; **Terry Dactyl:** Ken Snyder; **Dr. Todd Goodheart/Belly Laguna/Dr. Von Upp:** Hal Smith; **The Wisenheimer:** Bud Hiestand; **Broken Feather:** Tom Thomas

⊚ THE FUNTASTIC WORLD OF HANNA-BARBERA

In 1985 Hanna-Barbera Productions launched this syndicated 90-minute cartoon block broadcast on Saturday and Sunday mornings. It was so successful that it was expanded to two hours of continuous cartoon fare. The package was first comprised of three newly animated half-hour series: *Yogi's Treasure Hunt, The Paw Paws* and *Galtar and the Golden Lance.* In its two-hour form, new weekly adventures of *Jonny Quest* were added to the package.

The series' components changed in the following years. In 1987 the producers added *Sky Commanders* and *The Snorks,* retaining *Yogi's Treasure Hunt* and *Jonny Quest* as the other series regulars. The following season the show consisted of *The Further Adventures of Super Ted, Fantastic Max, The Flintstone Kids* and *Richie Rich,* with *Jonny Quest* and *Galtar and the Golden Lance* being the only returnees. The package was pared down in size for the 1989–90 season. It featured *The Further Adventures of Super Ted, Fantastic Max, Paddington Bear* and *Richie Rich.* Additional series added since 1990 included: *Don Coyote and Sancho Panda, The Midnight Patrol, The Pirates of Dark Water, Swat Kats, Two Stupid Dogs, Yo, Yogi* and *Young Robin Hood* (See individual series entries for further details.)

A Hanna-Barbera Production. Color. Ninety minutes. Two hours. Premiered: September 1985. Syndicated.

◎ FUNTOWN FUNNIES

A weekday morning and afternoon and weekend block of programming created for The Family Channel by DIC Enterprises. With the adventures of *Inspector Gadget* as one of the series anchors, this program block aired at various times of the day on the network, beginning in 1990 for two seasons, then again in June of 1993 through December of that year.

A DIC Enterprises Production. Color. Half-hour. Premiered on FAM: September 1990–December 1992; June 1993–December 1993.

◎ FUN WORLD OF HANNA-BARBERA

Off-network series featuring episodes from past Hanna-Barbera shows: *Wacky Races, Dastardly and Muttley, Perils of Penelope Pitstop, The Funky Phantom* and *Amazing Chan and the Chan Clan*. (See individual series for information.)

A Hanna-Barbera Production. Color. Half-hour. Premiered: 1977. Syndicated.

◎ THE FURTHER ADVENTURES OF DR. DOLITTLE

In classic stories loosely based on Hugh Lofting's nine critically acclaimed novels, veterinarian Dr. Dolittle, who commands the animals of the world with his conversational powers, with the help of his 14-year-old assistant, Tommy Stubbins, and his animal friends, attempts to thwart fiendish Sam Scurvy's efforts at world domination, in this half-hour, Saturday-morning cartoon series that debuted on NBC.

A DePatie-Freleng Enterprises Production in association with TCF-TV. Color. Half-hour. Premiered on NBC: September 12, 1970–September 2, 1971. Syndicated.

Voices
Dr. John Dolittle: Bob Holt; **Sam Scurvy, the pirate:** Lennie Weinrib; **Tommy Stubbins:** Hal Smith; **Mooncat/Various Animals:** Barbara Towers, Don Messick; **The Grasshoppers:** Ronie Fellon, Colin Julian, Annabell

◎ THE FURTHER ADVENTURES OF SUPERTED

A once-discarded teddy bear is brought to life by a spotted alien (Spottyman) who endows the poor teddy with magical powers that turn him into the cuddliest superhero in the universe. Together they battle the evil Texas Pete and his marauding mates, Skeleton and Bulk, in this 13-episode, half-hour fantasy/adventure series, originally broadcast on Sunday mornings on "The Funtastic World of Hanna-Barbera."

A once-discarded teddy bear discovers fun and adventure as the cuddliest superhero in the universe in the Further Adventures of SuperTed. © Hanna-Barbera Productions

A Hanna-Barbera Production. Color. Half-hour. Premiered: September 1988. Syndicated. Rebroadcast on CAR: December 17, 1994–December 18, 1994 (Look What We Found!).

Voices
Superted: Danny Cooksey; **Spottyman:** Patrick Fraley; **Texas Pete:** Victor Spinetti; **Skeleton:** Melvyn Hayes; **Bulk:** Marvin Kaplan

◎ GADGET BOY AND HEATHER

Armed with an arsenal of high-tech crime-fighting accessories, Inspector Gadget, as a juvenile bionic crimefighter, squashes the villainous Spydra, with some help from his coagent Heather, in this first-run, syndicated series that aired as part of the weekend cartoon block "Amazin' Adventures II."

A DIC Enterprises Production. Color. Half-hour. Premiered: September 18, 1995 (part of Amazin' Adventures II). Syndicated.

Voices
Gadget Boy: Don Adams; **Agent Heather:** Tara Charendoff; **Spydra:** Louise Vallance

Other Voices
Maurice LaMarche

◎ GADGET BOY'S ADVENTURES IN HISTORY

Juvenile crimefighter Gadget Boy (a younger version of the bionic Inspector Gadget), coagent Heather and the morphing canine G-9 time-travel through history to undo the evil schemes of nefarious Spydra and at the same time "realign" history in this half-hour series produced for The History Channel. The 26-episode series was produced by DIC Entertainment in consultation with the National Education Association.

A DIC Entertainment Production in association with the National Education Association. Color. Half-hour. Premiered on HIS: January 10, 1998.

Voices
Gadget Boy: Don Adams; **Boris/Dabble/Stromboli/Mulch/ Humus:** Maurice LaMarche; **Agent Heather:** Tara Charendoff; **Spydra:** Louise Vallance

⊚ THE GALAXY GOOF-UPS

When NBC shuffled its Saturday-morning cartoon lineup in November 1978, *The Galaxy Goof-Ups* series, formerly segmented on *Yogi's Space Race*, was given its own half-hour, Saturday-morning time slot in which the series' original 13 episodes were rebroadcast. The cast of characters—Yogi Bear, Huckleberry Hound, Scarebear and Quack-Up—intergalactic army officers under the astute command of Captain Snerdley, find more time for disco dancing than protecting the universe. (For voice credits see *Yogi's Space Race*.)

A Hanna-Barbera Production. Color. Half-hour. Premiered on NBC: November 4, 1978–January 27, 1979. Rebroadcast on CAR: September 20, 1993–December 31, 1993 (weekdays under Yogi's Spin-Offs).

⊚ GALAXY HIGH SCHOOL

These space-age adventures follow the exploits of Doyle Cleverlobe and Aimee Brightower, the first exchange students from Earth to attend an interstellar high school on the asteroid Flutor. Thirteen half-hour shows which aired on CBS. The series' provocative antidrug episode, "Brain Blaster," was nominated for the prestigious Humanitas Award in 1987. In 1993 the program was brought back (in reruns) on the Sci-Fi Channel, its two-hour *Cartoon Quest* program block.

A TMS Entertainment Production. Color. Half-hour. Premiered on CBS: December 13, 1986–September 5, 1987. Rebroadcast on CBS: January 9, 1988–August 27, 1988; Rebroadcast on SCI: September 18, 1993–June 27, 1996.

Voices
Doyle Cleverlobe: Hal Rayle; **Aimee Brightower:** Susan Blu; **Rotten Roland:** Neil Ross; **Beef Bonk:** John Stephenson; **Biddy McBrain/Katrina:** Pat Carroll; **Gilda Gossip/Flat Freddy:** Nancy Cartwright; **Earl Eccchhh:** Guy Christopher; **Ollie Oilslick/Reggie Unicycle:** Gino Conforti; **Booey Bubblehead/Wendy Garbo:** Jennifer Darling; **Coach Frogface/Sludge:** Pat Fraley; **Aimee's Locker/**

Students from Earth attend an interstellar high school on the asteroid Flutor in the animated comedy series Galaxy High School. © TMS Entertainment

Doyle's Locker: Henry Gibson; **Milo DeVenus:** David L. Lander; **The Creep:** Danny Mann; **Professor MacGreed/ Professor Icenstein/Luigi LaBounci:** Howard Morris

⊚ GALTAR AND THE GOLDEN LANCE

Astride his noble steed Thork, the handsome and fearless warrior Galtar uses sword and sorcery to protect the lovely Princess Goleeta and rescue his planet from the scourge of the evil Tormack, whose minions killed Galtar's parents and destroyed his village, in this 20-episode, half-hour fantasy/adventure that was part of the syndicated weekend series *The Funtastic World of Hanna-Barbera*. The series premiered Sunday mornings in 1985 and was rerun on the Cartoon Network.

A Hanna-Barbera Production. Color. Half-hour. Premiered: September 1985. Syndicated. Rebroadcast on CAR: October 3, 1992–December 3, 1993 (weekends, weekdays); December 11, 1993–January 1, 1994 (weekends); January 8, 1994–April 3, 1994 (Saturdays, Sundays); April 9, 1994–September 2, 1995 (Saturdays).

Voices
Galtar: Lou Richards; **Galeeta:** Mary McDonald Lewis; **Tormack:** Brock Peters; **Ither:** Bob Arbogast; **Krimm:** Barry Dennen; **Otar:** George DiCenzo; **Pandat:** Don Messick; **Rak:** Bob Frank; **Zorn:** David Mendenhall; **Tuk/ Thork/Koda:** Frank Welker

GARFIELD AND FRIENDS

Garfield creator Jim Davis oversaw production of this Saturday-morning series featuring the further exploits of Garfield and his comic comrades, Jon, Odie, Nermal and others, in two short weekly animated adventures, which included "blackouts" (usually "teasers" when preceding the credits), almost exclusively adapted from actual comic strips. As in Davis's popular comic strip, Garfield was portrayed as that fat, lazy, lasagna-loving pet of Jon, a cartoonist. Also part of the family was Odie, a very simpleminded dog. Other regulars included Nermal, the world's cutest kitten, and Liz, a veterinarian/love interest of Jon's. Another weekly series component was the series based on Davis's other strip, *U.S. Acres*, which revolved around the misadventures of Orson the pig and his farm friends, Wade the duck, Roy the rooster, Booker the baby chick, Sheldon, a chick still mostly in the egg and the brother-sister sheep pair, Bo and Lanolin. Each episode was backed by its own original music score.

Garfield was first adapted for television in a brace of prime-time, Emmy-winning and Emmy-nominated specials—*Garfield on the Town* (1983), *Garfield in the Rough* (1984), *Garfield's Halloween Special* (1985) and *Garfield in Paradise* (1985), among others—that aired on CBS. The Saturday-morning series debuted five years after the first special, also on CBS, and was so successful that the program was expanded to a full hour beginning with the 1989 season. In 1993 original network episodes were stripped for daily syndication. The series concluded its original network run in 1995 and was subsequently rerun on the Cartoon Network.

A Film Roman Production in association with United Media and Paws, Inc. Color. One-hour. Premiered on CBS: October 15, 1988–October 7, 1995. Syndicated: September 20, 1993. Rebroadcast on CAR: September 4, 1995 (weekdays, Sundays).

Voices

Garfield: Lorenzo Music; **Jon/Blinky/Roy:** Thom Huge; **Odie/Orson:** Greg Berger; **Nermal:** Desiree Goyette; **Sheldon/Booker/Bo:** Frank Welker; **Wade:** Howie Morris; **Liz/Lanolin:** Julie Payne; **Cactus Jake:** Pat Buttram; **Doc Boy:** David L. Lander

GARGOYLES

Frozen in stone since A.D. 994 following a spell cast upon them by the evil dark-age magician Archmage, a band of winged creatures, once perched atop a Viking fortress, are transported to a New York City skyscraper. There they come alive by night, 1,000 years later (headed by good-guy gargoyles Goliath and Hudson), to protect the city from modern-day barbarians in this first-run syndicated, 65-episode fantasy/adventure series—described as "animation's first dramatic series"—produced by Walt Disney Television Animation. The series was used to launch the *Disney Afternoon*'s "Action Friday" two-hour cartoon block in October

of 1994, debuting with a five-part story and airing only once a week. On September 4, 1995, the series expanded from weekly airings to a four-days-a-week schedule. In 1998 USA Network began reairing the series weekday mornings. An 80-minute, direct-to-video feature, *Gargoyles the Movie: The Heroes Awaken*, was produced in 1994, edited from the television series.

A Walt Disney Television Animation Production. Color. Half-hour. Premiered: October 24, 1994–August 29, 1997. Syndicated. Rebroadcast on USA: 1998.

Voices

Goliath: Keith David; **Broadway:** Bill Fagerbakke; **Lexington:** Thom Adcox-Hernandez; **Hudson:** Ed Asner; **Brooklyn/Magus/Owen:** Jeff Bennett; **Hakon:** Clancy Brown; **Tom:** J.D. Daniels; **Xanatos:** Jonathan Frakes; **Demona:** Marina Sirtis; **Brendan:** Patrick Fraley; **Commander:** Peter Renaday; **Captain:** Ed Gilbert; **Elisa Maza, police detective:** Salli Richardson; **Princess Katharine:** Kath Soucie; **Bronx:** Frank Welker

GARGOYLES: THE GOLIATH CHRONICLES

Now with the secret of their existence exposed, Goliath and his small clan of Gargoyle warriors face a growing antigargoyle faction known as the Quarrymen, who will stop at nothing until the Gargoyles are captured, in this weekly Saturday-morning cartoon series based on 1994's *Gargoyles* animated series for ABC.

A Walt Disney Television Animation Production. Color. Half-hour. Premiered on ABC: September 7, 1996–April 12, 1997.

Voices

Goliath: Keith David; **Broadway:** Bill Fagerbakke; **Brooklyn/Owen:** Jeff Bennett; **Lexington:** Thom Adcox-Hernandez; **Hudson:** Edward Asner; **Angela:** Brigitte Bako; **Fox:** Laura San Giacomo; **Bronx:** Frank Welker; **John Castaway:** Scott Cleverdon; **David Xanatos:** Jonathan Frakes; **Margot Yale:** Tress MacNeille; **Elisa Marza:** Salli Richardson; **Matt Bluestone:** Thomas F. Wilson

THE GARY COLEMAN SHOW

Different Strokes star Gary Coleman is the voice of an apprentice guardian angel (Andy LeBeau) who, on probation in heaven, returns to Earth to solve people's problems. His heavenly superior, Angelica, suffers through his mistakes, while the evil character Hornswoggle tries to create problems for the little angel. The 28-episode half-hour series—which featured two cartoons per half-hour show—was based on the character in the NBC-TV movie, *The Kid with the Broken Halo*.

A Hanna-Barbera Production in association with Gary Coleman Productions. Color. Half-hour. Premiered on NBC: September 18, 1982–September 10, 1983. Rebroadcast on CAR: February 19, 1994 (under one-hour Look What We Found!).

Voices
Andy LeBeau: Gary Coleman; **Angelica:** Jennifer Darling; **Hornswoggle:** Sidney Miller; **Spence:** Calvin Mason; **Tina:** La Shana Dendy; **Bartholomew:** Jerry Houser; **Chris:** Lauren Anders; **Lydia:** Julie McWhirter Dees; **Mack:** Steve Schatzberg; **Haggle:** Jeff Gordon; **Announcer:** Casey Kasem

◎ GENTLE BEN

Television's favorite bear, who starred in the popular NBC adventure series, returns as a superhero who embarks on many exciting but dangerous adventures.

A Gentle Ben Animation Production. Color. Half-hour. Premiered: 1981. Syndicated.

◎ GEORGE OF THE JUNGLE

Jay Ward, creator of Rocky and Bullwinkle, produced this animated spoof of Edgar Rice Burrough's famed Tarzan character starring a dimwitted, vine-swinging apeman named George, who protects the jungle and his wife, Ursula (Ward's version of Tarzan's wife, Jane), from the hazardous surroundings of the Imgwee Gwee Valley in Africa. George's main confidant and friend is a purplish gorilla, Ape (whose voice recalls actor Ronald Coleman's), who counsels him whenever he is in trouble. He also calls on his friendly elephant, Shep, whom he thinks is a peanut-loving puppy.

Other cartoon segments featured were: "Super Chicken," the misadventures of simpleminded Henry Cabot Henhouse III, who, after downing his famed Super Sauce, becomes a crimefighting super chicken; and "Tom Slick, Racer," a parody of racecar competition following the exploits of American good ol' boy Tom Slick aided by his girlfriend, Marigold, and his grandmother, Gertie.

The series was the only Jay Ward production ever to lose money (more than $100,000) and went straight into syndication following its network run. In the fall of 1992, the series returned for three-month run on The Fox Network, then again in the fall of 1995 on ABC, preceding the summer 1997 release of the live-action feature of the same name starring Brendan Fraser.

A Jay Ward Production. Color. Half-hour. Premiered on ABC: September 9, 1967–September 5, 1970. Syndicated. Rebroadcast on FOX: September 19, 1992–October 17, 1992. Rebroadcast on ABC: September 9, 1995–October 21, 1995. Rebroadcast on CAR: October 7, 1995–October 5, 1996 (Saturdays, Sundays, weekdays); January 5, 1997–August 29, 1997 (Sundays, weekdays).

Voices
George of the Jungle: Bill Scott; **Ursula, his wife:** June Foray; **Ape/Tom Slick/Gertie Growler:** Bill Scott; **Super Chicken:** Bill Scott; **Fred the lion, his butler:** Paul Frees; **Marigold, Tom Slick's girlfriend/Bella:** June Foray; **Narrator/Dick Two-Lane/Baron Otto Mattic:** Paul Frees; **District Commissioner:** Daws Butler

◎ THE GERALD McBOING BOING SHOW

This festival of UPA cartoons presented regular episodes and one-time features in a swiftly paced half-hour variety show format, hosted by Gerald McBoing Boing, one of UPA's most successful theatrical cartoon stars.

Recurring features on the show included "Meet the Artist," lighthearted stories based on the lives of famous artists; "Meet the Inventor," humorous and instructional stories of the trials and triumphs of the world's greatest inventors; and "The Sleuth's Apprentice," in which the self-confident Sleuth gets all the credit for the mysteries solved by his mild-mannered apprentice.

In addition, the series showcased "The Twirlinger Twins," two energetic little girls with Buster Brown haircuts who sing songs, give recitations and take music lessons; "The Etiquette Series," starring the gentlemanly Mr. Charmley who is so intent on learning proper techniques of etiquette that he frequently overlooks practicing them; and "Dusty of the Circus," the adventures of a young boy who enjoys a special relationship with the animals of his father's circus.

Rounding out the series were such one-time features as "Marvo the Magician," a pompous magician who is outdone by his little bearded assistant; "The Two Magicians," a tiny flutist and a huge tubist whose counterpoint includes outrageous practical jokes; "The Last Doubloon," in which a miserly pirate captain is sunk by one doubloon too many; "The Matador and the Troubador," concerning the little brother of a famous matador who confuses bulls with a heel-tapping, flamenco style of fighting; and many others.

The program first aired on CBS in December 1957 and was repeated in 1958. UPA syndicated the package in the late 1960s. In the late 1980s the series was reshown on USA Network under the title The UPA Cartoon Show.

A UPA Production. Color. Half-hour. Premiered on CBS: December 16, 1956–March 10, 1957. Rebroadcast on CBS: May 30, 1958–October 3, 1958. Syndicated. Rebroadcast on USA: Late 1980s.

Voices
Commentator: Bill Goodwin; **Interpreter of Gerald's sound:** Bill Goodwin

Other Voices
Marvin Miller

THE GET ALONG GANG

Traveling through the countryside in their Clubhouse Caboose, this lovable group of animal friends—Monty, the optimistic, leader moose; Dotty, the superstrong pooch; Woolma, a self-indulgent, cuddly lamb; and Zipper, the supercool cat—lend a helping hand to those in need in this half-hour Saturday-morning series based on a series of popular children's books.

A *DIC Enterprises Production in association with Scholastic/Lorimar Productions. Color. Half-hour. Premiered on CBS: September 15, 1984–September 7, 1985. Rebroadcast on CBS: September 14, 1985–August 30, 1986.*

Voices

Bettina Bush, Donovan S. Freberg, Timothy Gibbs, Eva Marie Hesse, Georgi Irene, Nick Katt, Robbie Lee, Sherry Lynn, Sparky Marcus, Scott Menville, Don Messick, Chuck McCann, Frank Welker

G-FORCE

Short-lived remake of syndicator Sandy Frank's *Battle of the Planets* featuring the same characters as before but with new names and identities. The crew members were now called Ace Goodheart (Mark), Dirk Daring (Jason), Agatha June (Princess), Hootie (Tiny) and Professor Brighthead (Anderson). Even the characters' famous tagline, said when they changed into their battle outfits, was changed from "Transmute!" to "Transform!" Their outer-space archnemesis was renamed Galactor (Zoltar). Only six episodes ever aired on TBS.

A *Turner Entertainment Systems Production. Color. Half-hour. Premiered on TBS. Rebroadcast on CAR: January 2, 1995–June 28, 1995 (weekdays); September 4, 1995–October 5, 1996 (weekdays, Saturdays).*

Voices

Ace Goodheart, the leader: Sam Fontana; **Dirk Daring, second in command:** Cameron Clarke; **Professor Brighthead/Hootie:** Jan Rabson; **Agatha June/Pee Wee:** Barbara Goodson; **Galactor:** Bill Capizzi

GHOSTBUSTERS

In an effort to capitalize on the Ghostbuster fever spawned by the blockbuster movie, this comedy-adventure series was not based on the Bill Murray–Dan Ackroyd comedy feature but rather a live-action comedy series starring former *F Troop* actors Forrest Tucker and Larry Storch entitled *The Ghost Busters*, which ran on CBS's Saturday-morning schedule in 1975. The animated revival has the same theme: three heroes—two human (Kong and Eddie) and a gorilla (Tracy)—track down ghosts, goblins and gremlins, only this time throughout the universe and back and forth in time. The show featured an all-new voice cast.

A *Filmation Studios/Tribune Broadcasting Company Production. Color. Half-hour. Premiered: September 1986. Syndication.*

Voices

Eddie Spencer Jr.: Peter Cullen; **Tracy:** Lou Scheimer; **Jake Kong Jr.:** Patrick Fraley; **Prime Evil:** Alan Oppenheimer; **Futura:** Susan Blu; **Jessica:** Linda Gary; **Jessica's nephew:** Erika Scheimer; **G.B./Haunter:** Erik Gunden

GIGANTOR

Created by Dr. Sparks, this jet-propelled robot, designed for war but reprogrammed as an agent of peace, battles interplanetary evil with the help of 12-year-old Jimmy Sparks, the doctor's son, who takes over control of the robot after his father's death. In keeping the world free from destruction and despair, Gigantor comes face to face with such world-class villains as Dr. Katsmeow, Danger's Dinosaurs, the Evil Robot Brain, invaders from the planet Magnapus and many others.

Shown on Japanese television from 1963 to 1967, the series rocketed to fame in the United States when the property was acquired and edited for American audiences by Trans-Lux, which distributed many other cartoon favorites, including *Felix the Cat* and *Mighty Mr. Titan*. The program was produced by Fred Ladd (who produced *Astroboy* and

A jet-propelled robot reprogrammed as an agent of peace battles interplanetary evil in the Japanese animated cult favorite Gigantor. (COURTESY: SCOTT WHEELER PRODUCTIONS)

Speed Racer) and Al Singer. Theme music was by Lou Singer and Gene Raskin.

In the early 1980s an all-new color series, *The New Adventures of Gigantor*, was produced in Japan, where it aired exclusively before debuting in the United States on the Sci-Fi Channel in the fall of 1993. The network briefly considered rerunning the old black-and-white favorite prior to the debut of the new color series but plans to do so never materialized.

A TCJ Animation Center Production. Black-and-White. Half-hour. Premiered: January 5, 1966. Syndicated. Rebroadcast on SCI: 1993.

Voices
Billie Lou Watt, Peter Fernandez, Gilbert Mack, Cliff Owens

◉ G.I. JOE (1985)
American television viewers first got a glimpse of the heroic escapades of famed comic-book hero G.I. Joe in television's first animated miniseries, *G.I. Joe: A Real American Hero*, broadcast in syndication for the 1983–84 season. A second five-part syndicated miniseries, *G.I. Joe II*, was produced the following season. In the fall of 1985 *G.I. Joe* became a daily, 90-episode animated half-hour series. It featured the further adventures of America's highly trained mission force who outwit the forces of COBRA, a terrorist organization, led by villains Destro and the Baroness.

Because the G.I. Joe characters were so strongly defined as defenders of right against wrong, the series incorporated 30-second messages, with the characters showing young viewers "dos" and "don'ts" in such areas as safety, health and nutrition.

In 1992, at the end of its syndicated run, USA Network began reairing the entire package of first-run episodes through the fall of 1996.

A Marvel Production in association with Sunbow Productions. Color. Half-hour. Premiered: September 23, 1985. Syndicated. Rebroadcast on USA: September 14, 1992–September 15, 1996.

Voices
Charlie Adler, Jack Angel, Liz Aubrey, Jackson Beack, Michael Bell, Arthur Burghardt, Corey Burton, Bill Callaway, Peter Cullen, Brian Cummings, Pat Fraley, Hank Garrett, Dick Gautier, Ed Gilbert, Dan Gilvezan, Dave Hall, Zack Hoffman, Kene Holiday, Jerry Houser, Chris Latta, Loren Lester, Mary McDonald Lewis, Chuck McCann, Michael McConnohie, Rob Paulsen, Pat Pinney, Lisa Raggio, Bill Ratner, Hal Rayle, Bob Remus, Neil Ross, Will Ryan, Ted Schwartz, John Stephenson, B.J. Ward, Lee Weaver, Frank Welker, Stan Wojno, Keone Young

◉ G.I. JOE (1989)
The overall goal of the COBRA special mission force is to master the power of Dragonfire, a natural energy like electricity—only infinitely more powerful—that is found in underground "lakes of fire" in a few locations around the world. Their mission is to tap the most powerful repository of all beneath Sorcerer's Mesa, an American Indian site in New Mexico, in this five-part miniseries based on the adventures of the popular syndicated series of the same name.

A DIC Enterprises Production. Color. Half-hour. Premiered: September 1989. Syndicated.

Voices
Sergeant Slaughter: Bob Remis; **Rock 'N Roll:** Kevin Conway; **Scoop:** Michael Benyaer; **Cobra Commander:** Chris Latta (later Chris Collins); **Destro/Copperhead/Lowlight/Serpentor/Spirit:** Maurice LaMarche; **Alley Viper:** Jim Byrnes; **Gnawga Hyde/Rampart:** Ian Corlett; **Lady J:** Suzanne Emmett-Balcom; **Duke:** Ted Harrison; **Hawk:** Gerry Nairne; **Sub Zero:** Don Brown; **Mutt/Gridiron:** Dale Wilson; **Bullhorn:** David Wills; **Ambush/Night Creeper Leader:** Andrew Koenig; **Stretcher:** Alvin Sanders; **Path Finder/Metal Head:** Gary Chalk; **Salvo:** Brent Chapman; **Stalker:** Lee Jeffrey; **Zarana:** Lisa Corps; **Baroness:** Morgan Lofting

◉ G.I. JOE: EXTREME
A new hand-picked assault team of dedicated, covert operation agents work round-the-clock as peacekeepers, on military maneuvers, to protect the world from the heavily armed forces of SKAR in this third half-hour series based in part on the popular Hasbro toy. The series debuted in syndication in September of 1995.

A Sunbow Production. Color. Half-hour. Premiered: September 16, 1995. Syndicated.

Voices
Mayday: Randall Carpenter; **Stone:** Gary Chalk; **Inferno:** Ian James Corlett; **Sgt. Savage:** Michael Dobson; **Eagle Eye:** Brian Drummon; **Metal Head:** Matt Hill; **Black Dragon:** Terry Klassen; **Mr. Clancy:** Campbell Lane; **Freight/Quick Stryke:** Blu Mankuma; **Rampage:** Colin Murdock; **Iron Klaw:** Richard Newman; **Steel Raven:** Elizabeth Carol Savenkoff; **Harpoon:** Francisco Trujillo; **Wreckage/The President/Red:** Dale Wilson

◉ GILLIGAN'S PLANET
Most of the original cast of television's favorite castaways provided their voices for this updated version of the classic

network sitcom in which the crew board a powerful rocket ship built by the Professor that launches them off their island and maroons them on a remote planet in outer space. One new addition to the cast: a pet alien adopted by Gilligan named Bumper.

A Filmation Associates Production. Color. Half-hour. Premiered on CBS: September 18, 1982–September 10, 1983.

Voices

Gilligan, the first mate: Bob Denver; **Jonas Grumby, the skipper:** Alan Hale, Jr.; **Thurston Howell III:** Jim Backus; **Lovey Howell, his wife:** Natalie Schafer; **Ginger Grant, the movie star:** Dawn Wells; **Mary Ann Summers, the clerk:** Dawn Wells; **Roy Hinkley, the professor:** Russell Johnson

◎ GLO FRIENDS

An influx of soft and cuddly characters entered the mainstream of animated cartoon fare following the success of *The Smurfs* and *Care Bears*. This series was no exception, featuring friendly, fearless creatures whose magical glow makes them extra appealing not only to children but to the mean Moligans.

A Marvel Production in association with Sunbow Productions. Color. Half-hour. Premiered: September 16, 1986. Syndicated.

Voices

Charlie Adler, Michael Bell, Susan Blu, Bettina Bush, Joey Camen, Roger C. Carmel, Nancy Cartwright, Townsend Coleman, Jeanine Elias, Pat Fraley, Ellen Gerstell, Skip Hinnant, Keri Houlihan, Katie Leigh, Sherry Lynn, Mona Marshall, Scott Menville, Sarah Partridge, Hal Rayle, Will Ryan, Susan Silo, Russi Taylor, B.J. Ward, Jill Wayne, Frank Welker

◎ GODZILLA AND THE SUPER 90

Formerly this series was called *The Godzilla Power Hour*, but the half-hour adventures of *Jonny Quest* were added to boost the show's ratings and the title was therefore changed to reflect the program's newly expanded format.

Godzilla, the show's star, appeared in one segment as a friendly dragon joining forces with a scientist, Carl Rogers, to battle evil. Another segment, "Jana of the Jungle," focused on the adventures of a girl searching for her lost father in the rain forest where she lived as a child. The "Jana of the Jungle" cartoons were later bundled in half-hours and rebroadcast on USA Network's *Cartoon Express*.

A Hanna-Barbera Production in association with Toho Co. Ltd. and Benedict Pictures Corporation. Color. Ninety minutes. Premiered on NBC: November 4, 1978–September 1, 1979; September 9, 1978–October 28, 1978 (as The Godzilla Power Hour). Rebroadcast on USA: February 27, 1989–March 22, 1991 (Jana of the Jungle).

Voices

Godzilla: Ted Cassidy; **Capt. Carl Rogers:** Jeff David; **Quinn, Carl's aide:** Brenda Thompson; **Pete, Carl's aide:** Al Eisenmann; **Brock, Pete's friend:** Hilly Hicks; **Godzooky, Godzilla's sidekick:** Don Messick; **Jana of the Jungle:** B.J. Ward; **Montaro:** Ted Cassidy; **Dr. Ben Cooper:** Michael Bell; **Natives:** Ross Martin; **Jonny Quest:** Tim Matthieson; **Dr. Benton Quest, his father:** John Stephenson; **Roger "Race" Bannon:** Mike Road; **Hadji, Indian companion:** Danny Bravo; **Bandit, their dog:** Don Messick

◎ THE GODZILLA POWER HOUR

(See GODZILLA AND THE SUPER 90.)

◎ THE GODZILLA SHOW

The favorite prehistoric monster comes alive again in new tales of adventure and suspense saving the day for all mankind in times of natural or supernatural disaster. This was the third series try for Hanna-Barbera, featuring the 400-foot-tall creature. Previously the character starred in the short-lived *The Godzilla Power Hour*, which was replaced after only two months by *Godzilla and the Super 90*, an expanded version with the addition of classic *Jonny Quest* episodes to its roster.

In November 1979 NBC combined *Godzilla* with reruns of *The Harlem Globetrotters* retitling the series, *The Godzilla/Globetrotters Adventure Hour*. By September 1980 that series had been replaced by *The Godzilla/Dynomutt Hour with Funky Phantom*. Like the former it featured reruns of previously broadcast Godzilla episodes and of network-run episodes of *Dynomutt, Dog Wonder* and *The Funky Phantom*. Two months after its debut, the program was changed again. Dynomutt and the Funky Phantom were shelved in place of Hanna-Barbera's former network hit *Hong Kong Phooey*, which was paired with Godzilla under the title of *The Godzilla/Hong Kong Phooey Hour*. (See *The Godzilla and the Super 90* and individual series for voice credits and further details.)

A Hanna-Barbera Production in association with Toho Co. Ltd. and Benedict Pictures. Color. Half-hour. Premiered on NBC: September 8, 1979–November 3, 1979; November 10, 1979–September 20, 1980 (as The Godzilla/Globetrotters Adventure Hour), September 27, 1980–November 15, 1980 (as The Godzilla/Dynomutt Hour with the Funky Phantom); November 22, 1980–May 16, 1981 (as The Godzilla/Hong Kong Phooey Hour). Rebroadcast on NBC: May 23, 1981–September 5, 1981 (as The Godzilla Show). Rebroadcast on CAR: December 6, 1993–April 29, 1994 (weekdays); September 5, 1994–September 1, 1995 (weekdays); March 25, 1996– (weekdays).

⦿ GO GO GOPHERS

CBS added this half-hour series to its 1968 fall schedule featuring repeat episodes of *Go Go Gophers*, in which renegade Indians Running Board and Ruffled Feathers match wits with the blustering Colonel Kit Coyote of the U.S. calvary, and "Klondike Kat," the exploits of an idiotic mountie and the elusive cheese-stealing mouse Savoir Faire. Each component was originally featured on CBS's *Underdog* cartoon series. (See *Underdog* for voice credits.)

A Total TV Production with Leonardo TV Productions. Color. Half-hour. Premiered on CBS: September 14, 1968–September 6, 1969.

⦿ GOLDIE GOLD AND ACTION JACK

A gorgeous, wealthy 18-year-old, Goldie Gold, publisher of the *Gold Street Journal*, is a female James Bond who embarks on 13 exciting half-hour adventures with her reporter/bodyguard Jack Travis, her editor Sam Gritt and her labrador Nugget to pursue stories and solve madcap capers with the aid of 007-type gadgetry.

A Ruby Spears Enterprises Production. Color. Half-hour. Premiered on ABC: September 12, 1981–September 18, 1982. Rebroadcast on CAR: January 8, 1994 (Saturdays).

Voices
Goldie Gold: Judy Strangis; **Jack Travis, her reporter:** Sonny Melendrez; **Sam Gritt, her editor:** Booker Bradshaw

⦿ GOOBER AND THE GHOST CHASERS

Using a similar format to *Scooby Doo, Where Are You?* Hanna-Barbera animated the adventures of reporters Tina,

A gorgeous gadabout uses limitless wealth to pursue adventure with an exotic array of James Bond–like gadgetry in Goldie Gold and Action Jack. *© Ruby-Spears Enterprises*

Ted, Gillie and Goober, their dog, who investigate haunted houses and ghoulish mysteries for *Ghost Chasers* magazine. Goober is a meek character who actually becomes invisible when frightened by beasties or ghoulies.

The 17-episode half-hour series spotlighted guest stars throughout the season. The most regular were The Partridge Family in cartoon form. The program was later packaged as part of *Fred Flintstone and Friends* for syndication and again rebroadcast on USA Network's *Cartoon Express*.

A Hanna-Barbera Production. Color. Half-hour. Premiered on ABC: September 8, 1973–August 31, 1975. Rebroadcast on USA: February 28, 1989–March 25, 1991.

Voices:
Goober: Paul Winchell; **Gillie:** Ronnie Schell; **Ted:** Jerry Dexter; **Tina:** Jo Anne Harris

THE PARTRIDGE FAMILY: Laurie Partridge: Susan Dey; **Chris Partridge:** Brian Forster; **Tracy Partridge:** Suzanne Crough; **Danny Partridge:** Danny Bonaduce

⦿ GOOD MORNING, MICKEY!

Eighty episodes of this daily series, featuring classic Disney cartoons, were produced. Either edited half-hour compilations or two separate episodes aired daily in this series produced for The Disney Channel.

A Left Coast Television Production for The Disney Channel. Color. Half-hour. Premiered on DIS: 1983.

⦿ GOOF TROOP

Moving to a neighborhood in the small, quiet town of Spoonerville, beloved bumbler Goofy, now a man of the 1990s, is a single father raising a rather obnoxious 11-year-old son, Max, whose outlook on life is far different from his dad's. His neighbor is Mickey Mouse's old nemesis, Pete—alias Pegleg Pet and Black Pete—now a respectable surbubanite, and son Pegleg Pete Jr.—P.J. for short—who hangs out with Max at the local mall. Conflicts between Goofy and Max and Goofy's attempts to fit into his new neighborhood become the basis of weekly story lines in this first-run, 78-episode half-hour series that debuted on The Disney Channel in April of 1992, in celebration of Goofy's 60th birthday. The series was moved to syndication in September of 1992 as part of the *Disney Afternoon* two-hour cartoon block (preceded by a two-hour special, *Disney's Goof Troop*, to launch the syndicated series); it replaced *Duck Tales*. Thirteen additional episodes of the series were broadcast concurrently on ABC's Saturday-morning schedule that September as well. A half-hour holiday special, *A Goof Troop Christmas*, was also produced. In September of

1996, the program began airing weekdays (in reruns) on The Disney Channel.

A Walt Disney Television Animation Production. Color. Half-hour. Premiered on DIS: April 20, 1992; ABC: September 7, 1992–September 11, 1993. Syndicated: September 7, 1992–August 30, 1996. Rebroadcast on DIS: September 2, 1996 (weekdays).

Voices
Goofy: Bill Farmer; **Max:** Dana Hill; **Pete:** Jim Cummings; **P.J.:** Rob Paulsen; **Peg:** April Winchell; **Pistol:** Nancy Cartwright; **Burly Guy/"How-to" Narrator/Melvin/Ring Master/School Dean:** Corey Burton; **Fenton Sludge:** Jay Thomas; **Waffles/Chainsaw:** Frank Welker

⊚ GRIMM'S FAIRY TALES
Recalling those classic children's stories of the past, this beautifully animated half-hour series is a collection of the world-famous Grimm's Fairy Tales, presenting colorful retellings of such favorite tales as "Hansel and Gretel," "Snow White," "Puss N' Boots" and "Little Red Riding Hood." The series premiered on Nickelodeon.

A Nippon Animation/Saban Entertainment Production. Color. Half-hour. Premiered on NIK: September 1989.

⊚ THE GROOVIE GOOLIES
Humble Hall residents Count Dracula; Hagatha, his plump wife; Frankie, their son; Bella La Ghostly, the switchboard operator; Sabrina, the teenage witch; Wolfie, the werewolf; Bonapart, the accident-prone skeleton; Mummy, Bonapart's buddy; and others haunt trespassers with practical jokes and ghoulish mischief in this movie-monster spoof produced for Saturday-morning television. The characters were originally introduced on 1970's *Sabrina and the Groovie Goolies* series on CBS, before they were resurrected by the network in their own weekly series in 1971. The series ran one full season on CBS and was later repeated on ABC during the 1975–76 season, replacing *Uncle Croc's Block.*

A Filmation Associates Production. Color. Half-hour. Premiered on CBS: September 12, 1971–September 3, 1972. Rebroadcast on ABC: October 25, 1975–September 5, 1976.

Voices
Frankie/Wolfie/Mummy/Ghouland: Howard Morris; **Hagatha/Aunt Hilda/Aunt Zelda/Bella La Ghostly/Broomhilda/Sabrina:** Jane Webb, **Count "Drac"/Ratzo:** Larry Storch; **Bonapart/Dr. Jekyll-Hyde/Batzo/Hauntleroy:** Larry Mann

⊚ GROOVIE GOOLIES AND FRIENDS
Like Hanna-Barbera, Filmation Studios packaged for worldwide syndication their own collection of previous cartoon hits: *Groovie Goolies, The Adventures of Waldo Kitty, Lassie's Rescue Rangers, The New Adventures of Gilligan, My Favorite Martian,* and 18 half-hour combinations of *M.U.S.H., Fraidy Cat* and *Wacky and Packy.* (See individual cartoon components for series information.)

A Filmation Associates Production. Color. Half-hour. Premiered: September 1978. Syndicated.

⊚ THE GUMBY SHOW
The adventures of this lovable green clay figure and his pet horse, Pokey, first appeared as a Saturday-morning kids' show on NBC in 1957. Created by Art Clokey (also the creator of TV's *Davey and Goliath*), the stop-action animated series was spun off from *Howdy Doody,* on whose program Gumby was first introduced in 1956. Adventures were filmed via the process of pixillation—filming several frames at a time, moving the characters slightly, and then shooting more frames to achieve continuous motion.

Originally Bob Nicholson, best known for his portrayal of Clarabell and Cornelius Cobb on *Howdy Doody,* hosted the NBC program as the character Scotty McKee, later comedian Pinky Lee was host.

The full-color six-minute, two- and three-part adventures that made up the half-hour series were produced under the direction of superb stop-motion filmmaker Raymond Peck and offered for syndication in late 1959, mostly to NBC affiliates. A new syndicated package was offered to independent television stations in 1966. (In all, 130 *Gumby* episodes were produced.) The original series was rebroadcast on The Disney Channel in 1983, and, in 1988, creator Art Clokey produced a brand-new, daily 65-episode half-hour series of adventures, *All-New Gumby,* for syndication. (See series entry for details.) Nickelodeon reaired the old series weekdays for three seasons beginning in 1994.

An Art Clokey Production. Color. Half-hour. Premiered on NBC: March 16, 1957–November 16, 1957. Syndicated: 1959, 1966. Rebroadcast on DIS: 1983. Rebroadcast on NIK: June 6, 1994–May 31, 1997.

Voices
Gumby: Art Clokey, Dallas McKennon; **Pokey:** Art Clokey

⊚ HAMMERMAN
Rap singer M.C. Hammer, who changed his name simply to Hammer, starred in this weekly half-hour animated series as a mild-mannered children's recreation center employee who, upon donning a pair of "magic dancing shoes," turns into a fleet-footed, urban crime-fighting superhero.

A DIC Enterprises Production in association with Bustin' Productions. Color. Half-hour. Premiered on ABC: September 9, 1991–September 5, 1992

Voices
Hammer/Stanley Kirk Burrell: Hammer

◎ THE HANNA-BARBERA NEW CARTOON SERIES

In the fall of 1962, following the success of its previous syndicated series, Hanna-Barbera introduced this trilogy of original cartoon programming featuring a new stable of stars: "Wally Gator," a "swinging gator from the swamp" who refuses to be confined to his home in the zoo; "Lippy the Lion," a blustering, bragging lion who gets into multiple messes with his buddy, a sorrowful hyena, Hardy Har Har; and "Touché Turtle," a well-meaning but inept swashbuckling turtle who goes on a series of avenging adventures with his dog, Dum Dum, to right the wrongs of the world.

Each series component contained 52 episodes and was produced for flexible programming, allowing stations to use each series together in longer time periods or scheduled separately in their own half-hour time slots. (See *Lippy the Lion, Touche Turtle* and *Wally Gator* for voice credits.)

A *Hanna-Barbera Production. Color. Half-hour. Premiered: September 1962. Syndicated.*

◎ HANNA-BARBERA'S WORLD OF SUPER ADVENTURE

This syndicated package of superhero cartoons was first produced for Saturday morning, including *The Fantastic Four, Frankenstein Jr. and the Impossibles, Space Ghost, Herculoids, Shazzan, Moby Dick and the Mighty Mightor* and *Birdman and the Galaxy Trio.* (See individual series for further details.)

A *Hanna-Barbera Production. Color. Half-hour. Premiered: September 1980. Syndicated. Rebroadcast on CAR: September 20, 1993.*

◎ HAPPILY EVER AFTER: FAIRY TALES FROM EVERY CHILD

This music-filled, once-upon-a-time, half-hour children's series offered new interpretations of classic nursery rhymes and fairy tales, each relating the perspective of different cultural backgrounds. Premiering Sunday nights on HBO in March of 1995, the series opened with a 90-minute episode (normally each show ran a half-hour) featuring three new versions of old favorites, including an African American visualization of "Jack and the Beanstalk," starring Tone Loc as the voice of The Giant (he also sings a rhythm-and-blues song called "Living Large"), a Chinese interpretation of "Little Red Riding Hood" and a Latino variation of "Hansel and Gretel" (featuring Rosie Perez and Cheech Marin).

Other first season episodes included an Asian-styled telling of Hans Christian Andersen's "The Emperor's New Clothes" (including among its cast George Takei of TV's original *Star Trek*), a Jamaican slant on the yarn "Rumplestiltskin" featuring the voices of Robert Townsend, Denzel Washington and Jasmine Guy, among others.

Twenty-six-episodes were produced between 1995 and 1997, including a half-hour prime-time special *Mother Goose: A Rappin' and Rhymin' Special*, featuring a star-studded cast. Robert Guillaume, appearing in live-action wraparounds, served as the series' host.

A *Hyperion Animation Production. Color. Half-hour. Premiered on HBO: March 26, 1995; April 13, 1997.*

◎ HAPPY NESS: THE SECRET OF LOCH

From the depths of Scotland's most famous lake, sea creatures Happy Ness, Lovely Ness, Kind Ness, Bright Ness and Silly Ness to name just a few, do their best to change the world into a wonderful place (not without some resistance from some bad "Nessies") after they are discovered by the McCoy kids, who join them in their musical adventures through Happy Land in this part-fable, part-fantasy series produced for first-run syndication.

An *Abrams Gentile Entertainment/C&D Production. Color. Half-hour. Premiered: September 9, 1995. Syndicated.*

Voices
John Brewster, Dan Conroy, Donna Daley, Eddie Korbich Jr., Connor Matthews, Kathryn Zaremba

◎ THE HARDY BOYS

Teenage sleuths Frank and Joe Hardy double as rock-and-roll musicians on a world tour as they solve crimes and play some popular music (music was performed by a live band called, appropriately enough, The Hardy Boys) in this updated version of Franklin W. Dixon's long-running series of children's detective novels.

A *Filmation Studios Production. Color. Half-hour. Premiered on ABC: September 6, 1969–September 4, 1971.*

Voices
Frank Hardy/Chubby Morton: Dallas McKennon; **Joe Hardy/Pete Jones/Fenton Hardy:** Byron Kane; **Wanda Kay Breckenridge/Gertrude Hardy:** Jane Webb

◎ THE HARLEM GLOBETROTTERS

Famed basketball illusionists Meadowlark Lemon, Curly, Gip, Bobby Joe and Geese perform benefits and defeat evil around the world with the help of their basketball finesse in this popular 21-episode half-hour Saturday-morning entry that was a popular fixture on CBS for three consecutive seasons.

In February 1978, NBC repeated the series as part of the two-hour cartoon extravaganza *Go Go Globetrotters*, which featured several other Hanna-Barbera favorites, including *The C.B. Bears* and *The Herculoids*. All-new adventures of the internationally acclaimed "Wizards of the Court" were produced in 1979 under the new title of *The Super Globetrotters*. (See series entry for details.)

A Hanna-Barbera Production. Color. Half-hour. Premiered on CBS: September 12, 1970–September 2, 1972. Rebroadcast on CBS: September 10, 1972–May 20, 1973. Rebroadcast on NBC: February 4, 1978–September 2, 1978 (as part of Go Go Globetrotters).

Voices

Meadowlark Lemon: Scatman Crothers; **Freddie "Curly" Neal:** Stu Gilliam; **Gip:** Richard Elkins; **Bobby Joe Mason:** Eddie "Rochester" Anderson; **Geese:** Johnny Williams; **Pablo:** Robert Do Qui; **Granny:** Nancy Wible; **Dribbles, the dog:** (no voice)

◎ HBO STORYBOOK MUSICALS

Well-known Hollywood celebrities narrated and provided their voices for this half-hour series of cartoon musical specials, based on popular children's stories, fables and songs and produced for HBO by four independent animation houses. Oscar and Emmy award-winning watercolor-animation specialist Michael Sporn launched the series in 1987 with his Oscar-winning short *Lyle, Lyle Crocodile: The Musical: The House On 88th St.*, which made its world television premiere on HBO as a half-hour special. Sporn's effort was followed a year later by DIC Entertainment's Emmy-nominated special *Madeline*, based on the popular children's book character.

Sporn's New York–based company, Michael Sporn Animation, produced six more half-hours for this anthology showcase. In 1989 he brought to television screens *The Story of the Dancing Frog*, based on Quentin Blake's book, followed by the 1990 adaptation of Hans Christian Anderson's *The Red Shoes*. He also produced *Mike Mulligan and His Steam Shovel* (1990); *Ira Sleeps Over* (1991), adapted from Bernard Weber's book; *A Child's Garden of Verses* (1992), based on the classic Robert Louis Stevenson story; and *The Country Mouse and the City Mouse: A Christmas Tale* (1993).

In 1991 Carol Burnett lent her voice to *The Tale of Peter Rabbit*, the only series entry produced by cartoon studio independent Hare Bear Productions. In the fall of that year, Canadian animation house Cinar Films debuted five half-hours from its *The Real Story of. . .* series, featuring adaptations of popular nursery rhymes and children's tales, beginning with *The Ice Queen Mittens*, starring the voice of Hollywood screen

legend Lauren Bacall. Other half-hour installments from Cinar's *The Real Story of. . .* series to premiere under this showcase included: *Spider Junior High* (1991), featuring pop superstar Patti LaBelle and *Cosby* TV star Malcolm-Jamal Warner; *The Runaway Teapot* (1991), with rock star Julian Lennon as one of the voices; *The Rise and Fall of Humpty Dumpy* (1991), costarring Oscar-winning actress Glenda Jackson and rocker Huey Lewis; and *Happy Birthday to You* (1992).

A Michael Sporn Animation/DIC Entertainment/Cinar Films/Hare Bear Production. Color. Half-hour. Premiered on HBO: November 18, 1987–December 8, 1993.

◎ THE HEATHCLIFF AND DINGBAT SHOW

That tough, orange-striped cat of comic-strip fame costars in this Saturday-morning series in which he typically takes great delight in annoying anyone he encounters in 27 episodic adventures. The program's second segment, "Dingbat and the Creeps," followed the misadventures of a vampire dog (whose vocal characterization is reminiscent of Curly Howard of the Three Stooges), a skeleton and a pumpkin who help people in trouble. The series—the first of three "Heathcliff" cartoon series produced in succession—aired one full season on ABC.

A Ruby-Spears Enterprises Production. Color. Half-hour. Premiered on ABC: October 4, 1980–September 18, 1981. Rebroadcast on CAR: September 6, 1994–December 9, 1994 (weekdays): June 5, 1995–September 1, 1995 (weekdays): December 18, 1995–December 22, 1995; December 26, 1995–December 29, 1995.

Voices

HEATHCLIFF: Heathcliff: Mel Blanc; **Mr. Schultz/Iggy/Spike/Muggsy:** Mel Blanc; **Milkman:** Mel Blanc; **Clem/Digby/Dogsnatcher:** Henry Corden; **Sonja:** Julie McWhirter, Marilyn Schreffler; **Crazy Shirley/Sonja/Grandma/Marcy:** June Foray

DINGBAT AND THE CREEPS: Dingbat: Frank Welker; **Nobody, the pumpkin:** Don Messick; **Sparerib, the skeleton:** Don Messick

◎ THE HEATHCLIFF AND MARMADUKE SHOW

In this series the scruffy tomcat shared the spotlight with that imposing and lovable great Dane, Marmaduke (star of Brad Anderson's popular syndicated comic strip), who was featured in separate six-minute adventures, getting himself into all kinds of mischief without meaning to. Meanwhile, Heathcliff picks up where he left off by triumphing over his adversaries—Spike, the neighborhood bulldog; the garbage collector; the fish store owner; and the chef of the local restaurant. "Dingbat and the Creeps" also returned as an alternating segment in the series, and two 30-second teasers were added: "Marmaduke's Riddles" and "Marmaduke's Doggone Funnies."

A Ruby-Spears Enterprises Production. Color. Half-hour. Premiered on ABC: September 12, 1981–September 18, 1982.

Voices

HEATHCLIFF: Heathcliff: Mel Blanc; **Mr. Schultz/ Iggy/Mugsy:** Mel Blanc; **Spike, the bulldog:** Mel Blanc; **Clem/Digby:** Henry Corden; **Dogcatcher:** Henry Corden; **Crazy Shirley/Sonja/Grandma/Marcy:** June Foray;

DINGBAT AND THE CREEPS: Dingbat: Frank Welker; **Nobody, the pumpkin:** Don Messick; **Sparerib, the skeleton:** Don Messick; **Marmaduke, the Great Dane:** Paul Winchell; **Phil Winslow, his owner:** Paul Winchell; **Dottie Winslow, his wife:** Russi Taylor; **Barbie Winslow, their daughter:** Russi Taylor; **Barbie's sister:** Marilyn Schreffler; **Billy Winslow, their son:** Russi Taylor; **Missy:** Russi Taylor; **Mr. Snyder/Mr. Post:** Don Messick

⊚ HEATHCLIFF AND THE CATILLAC CATS

Crafty cat Heathcliff of comic-strip fame terrorizes the neighborhood with little regard for anyone for himself in this half-hour comedy series, divided into two 15-minute segments. The second half features the lively and imaginative escapades of The Catillac Cats (Hector, Wordsworth and Mungo), led by boss-cat Riff Raff, whose get-rich-quick schemes and search for the ultimate meal keep them embroiled in trouble one episode after another. The latter were billed on screen as "Cats & Company." Heathcliff also appeared in daily 30-second prosocial segments educating young viewers on the dos and don'ts of proper pet care. The 65-episode series—the third and final in a series of *Heathcliff* cartoon series—was produced for first-run syndication in 1984. Previous segments from the television series were combined with new wraparound footage to produce the first and only full-length Heathcliff animated feature, 1986's *Heathcliff: The Movie.*

A DIC Enterprises Production in association with LBS Communications and McNaught Syndicate. Color. Half-hour. Premiered: September 1984. Syndicated. Rebroadcast on FAM: October 2, 1994–February 16, 1996.

Voices
Heathcliff: Mel Blanc; **Cleo/Iggy:** Donna Christle; **Spike/ Muggsy/Knuckles:** Derek McGrath; **Grandma:** Ted Ziegler; **Sonja:** Marilyn Lightstone; **Bush/Raul:** Danny Wells;

Milkman: Stanley Jones; **Fish Market Owner:** Danny Mann;

THE CATILLAC CATS: Riff Raff/Wordsworth: Stanley Jones; **Mungo:** Ted Ziegler; **Hector:** Danny Mann; **Cleo:** Donna Christie; **Leroy, the junkyard dog:** Ted Ziegler

⊚ THE HECKLE AND JECKLE CARTOON SHOW

The two conniving, talking magpies of motion-picture fame host a collection of other theatrically released Terrytoon cartoons (Little Roquefort, Gandy Goose, Dinky Duck, and "Terrytoon Classics," including several starring the Terry Bears) and their own misadventures. In 1977 Heckle and Jeckle were cast in a new CBS series entitled *The New Adventures of Mighty Mouse and Heckle and Jeckle.*

A CBS Terrytoons Production. Color. Half-hour. Premiered on CBS: October 14, 1956–September 1957. Rebroadcast on CBS: September 1965–September 3, 1966. Rebroadcast on NBC: September 6, 1969–September 7, 1971. Syndicated.

Voices
Heckle: Dayton Allen, Roy Halee; **Jeckle:** Dayton Allen, Roy Halee; **Little Roquefort/Percy the Cat:** Tom Morrison; **Gandy Goose/Sourpuss:** Arthur Kay; **Terry Bears:** Roy Halee, Philip A. Scheib, Doug Moye, **Dinky Duck:** (no voice)

⊚ THE HECTOR HEATHCOTE SHOW

A time machine enables a scientist (Hector Heathcote) to rewrite history by transporting him back to famous events in this half-hour Saturday-morning series that featured 39 recycled cartoons originally produced for theaters, plus 32 new cartoon shorts made exclusively for television, including "Hashimoto" and "Sidney the Elephant." (See Animated Theatrical Cartoon Series section entries for details.)

A CBS Terrytoons Production. Color. Half-hour. Premiered on NBC: October 5, 1963–September 25, 1965.

Voices
Hector Heathcote/Hashimoto/Mrs. Hashimoto/Yuriko/ Saburo: John Myhers; **Sidney the Elephant:** Lionel Wilson, Dayton Allen; **Stanley the Lion/Cleo the Giraffe:** Dayton Allen

⊚ HELLO KITTY'S FURRY TALE THEATER

Delightfully entertaining series of two weekly 15-minute fairy tales, loosely adapted and contemporized, staged by this animal theater group—Hello Kitty (the star) and friends Tuxedo Sam, Chip and My Melody—who take different roles from story to story, match wits with series villains Catnip and Grinder. The 26-episode series was based on the popular furry animal doll.

A DIC Enterprises Production in association with MGM/UA Television. Color. Half-hour. Premiered on CBS: September 19, 1987–September 3, 1988.

Voices
Hello Kitty: Tara Charendoff; **Tuxedo Sam:** Sean Roberge; **Chip:** Noam Zylberman; **My Melody:** Maron Bennett; **Grandpa Kitty:** Carl Banas; **Grandma Kitty/Mama Kitty:** Elizabeth Hanna; **Papa Kitty:** Len Carlson; **Catnip:** Cree Summer Francks; **Grinder:** Greg Morton; **Fangora:** Denise Pidgeon

◎ H.E.L.P.!
Lessons on safety and first aid are the premise of this series of educational one-minute fillers (the title is short for Dr. Henry's Emergency Lessons for People), prescreened by a team of respected educators and broadcast through ABC's 1979–80 Saturday-morning schedule. The series was awarded a 1980 Emmy for Outstanding Children's Informational/Instructional Programming—Short Format.

An 8 Films/Dahlia/Phil Kimmelman Production. Color. One minute. Premiered on ABC: 1979–80.

◎ HELP! IT'S THE HAIR BAIR BUNCH!
Wonderland Zoo's three wild bear tenants—Hair, Square and Bubi—campaign for better living conditions in Cave

Hello Kitty and friends Tuxedo Sam, Chip and My Melody in a scene from the CBS Saturday-morning series Hello Kitty's Furry Tale Theater. © MGM/UA Television Productions. Certain Characters © Sanrio Co. Ltd. (COURTESY: DIC ENTERPRISES)

Block #9 in this 1971 CBS series (originally titled, "The Yo Yo Bears. From 1974 to 1979 the series was syndicated; then later it rebroadcast on USA Network's "Cartoon Express" and on The Cartoon Network.

A Hanna-Barbera Production. Color. Half-hour. Premiered on CBS: September 11, 1971–September 2, 1972. Rebroadcast on CBS: September 1973–August 31, 1974. Syndicated: 1974–79. Rebroadcast on USA Network: February 19, 1989–November 7, 1991. Rebroadcast on CAR: January 3, 1994–June 3, 1994 (weekdays); June 5, 1995–September 1, 1995 (weekdays); September 6, 1995– (Wednesdays).

Voices
Hair Bear: Daws Butler; **Bubi Bear:** Paul Winchell; **Square Bear:** Bill Callaway; **Eustace P. Peevly, zoo curator:** John Stephenson; **Botch, Peevly's assistant:** Joe E. Ross

◎ HE-MAN AND MASTERS OF THE UNIVERSE
Residing on the planet Eternia, He-Man (Prince Adam) and She-Ra (Princess Adora) clash with the forces of evil—namely the villainous Skeletor—in this action-adventure series based on the popular Mattel toy line, produced for first-run syndication in 1983. Six years later, the series was rebroadcast on USA Network's "Cartoon Express."

A Filmation Associates Production. Color. Half-hour. Premiered: September 1983. Syndicated. Rebroadcast on USA: September 18, 1989–August 14, 1990.

Voices
Prince Adam/He-Man/Ram-Man: John Erwin; **Princess Adora/She-Ra:** Melendy Britt; **Skeletor/Marman/Beast Man:** Alan Oppenheimer; **Queen/Evil-Lyn/Sorceress/Teela:** Linda Gary; **Orko/King:** Lou Scheimer; **Battlecat/Gringer/Man-At-Arms:** Erik Gunden

◎ HENRY'S CAT
Australian-born animator Bob Godfrey (best known for his 1961 cartoon short, "Do-It-Yourself Cartoon Kit") single-handedly produced this cut-out animated half-hour series of 10-minute cartoons involving a misfit cat named Henry who, along with his many back-alley animal friends, fantasizes about hilarious adventures, spoofing everything from Tarzan to Sherlock Holmes. The series aired on Showtime. Henry's cartoon adventures were repackaged and released on home video, with comedian Dom DeLuise redubbing the narration (supplied by creator Bob Godfrey in the television series).

A Bob Godfrey Films Ltd. Production. Color. Half-hour. Premiered on SHO: 1990

Voices
Bob Godfrey

◎ THE HERCULOIDS

Futuristic animals Zok the laser dragon, Tundro the rhinoceros, Gloop and Gleep the friendly blobs, Igoo the rock-ape and Dorno, a young boy, strive to save Zandor, their benevolent king, and the primitive planet Amzot from alien invaders in this 18-episode, half-hour fantasy/adventure series (two episodes per show), originally produced for CBS in 1967. Nine years after its network run, the series was repackaged as part of NBC's *Go Go Globetrotters*. In 1981 "The Herculoids" returned in new adventures in NBC's *Space Stars*.

A Hanna-Barbera Production. Color. Half-hour. Premiered on CBS: September 9, 1967–September 6, 1969. Rebroadcast on NBC: February 4, 1978–September 2, 1978 (part of Go Go Globetrotters). Rebroadcast on CAR: November 8, 1992 (part of Boomerang, 1968); February 7, 1993 (part of Boomerang, 1967).

Voices
Zandor/Zok: Mike Road; **Tara:** Virginia Gregg; **Dorno:** Ted Eccles; **Gloop/Gleep/Zok:** Don Messick; **Igoo:** Mike Road

◎ HERE COMES THE GRUMP

Young American lad Terry and his dog, Bib, strive to save Princess Dawn from the evil Grump, who has put her under the Curse of Gloom in this half-hour animated fantasy series that debuted on NBC in 1969. The 17-episode series was produced by legendary animator Friz Freleng and partner David H. DePatie for their company, DePatie-Freleng Enterprises. The program later reaired on the Sci-Fi Channel's *Cartoon Quest*.

A DePatie-Freleng Enterprises Production. Color. Half-hour. Premiered on NBC: September 6, 1969–September 4, 1971. Rebroadcast on SCI: September 18, 1993–September 17, 1994.

Voices
Princess Dawn: Stefanianna Christopherson; **Terry, the little boy:** Jay North; **The Grump:** Rip Taylor

◎ HEROES ON HOT WHEELS

Moonlighting as race-car drivers, a well-trained team of space scientists and explorers (known as the Shadow Jets), led by the ever-handsome Michael Valiant, prefer the fast action of the speedway in this half-hour adventure series produced for French television two years before its American television debut on The Family Channel in 1991. The weekday series was the second based on Mattel Toys "Hot Wheels" toy car line. (The first: 1969's, *Hot Wheels*, ABC.) A LaCinq/C & D/Lucky World Productions in association with

Mattel. Color. Half-hour. Premiered on FAM: September 16, 1991–August 28, 1992.

Voices
Ian James Corlett, Mike Donovan, Scott McNeil, Venus Terzo, Dale Wilson

◎ HEY ARNOLD!

Set in the wilds of the big city, this series—described by creator Craig Barlett (the brother-in-law of *Simpsons* creator Matt Groening) as a "kind of Charlie Brown for the '90s—follows the quirky, philosophical nine-year-old Arnold, a boy with two bristly tufts of blond hair. Arnold lives in a boardinghouse run by his grandparents and inhabited by refugees as he braves the trials and tribulations of childhood and city life. In an unusual step, the series used real children to voice the characters.

Produced under Nickelodeon's "Nicktoons" banner and by the network's Games Animation division, the series, featuring two segments per show, premiered midseason in 1996. In December of 1996, the characters were spun off into their prime-time animated special, *Hey Arnold! The Christmas Show*.

A Games Animation Production in association with Snee-Osh, Inc. Color. Half-hour. Premiered on NIK: October 7, 1996.

Voices
Arnold: Phillip Van Dyke, Toran Caudell; **Gerald Johnson:** Jamil W. Smith; **Hegla G. Pataki/Sheena/Gloria:** Francesca Smith; **Grandpa/Various Others:** Dan Castellaneta; **Grandma/Miss Slovak:** Tress MacNeille; **Harold Berman:** Justin Shenkarow; **Sid:** Sam Gifaldi; **Phoebe Heyerdahl:** Anndi McAfee; **Stinky:** Christopher Walberg; **Big Bob Pataki:** Maurice LaMarche; **Miriam Pataki/Mrs. Vitello:** Kath Soucie; **Eugene Horowitz:** Ben Diskin, Christopher Castile; **Olga:** Nika; **Rhonda Wellington Lloyd:** Olivia Hack; **Nadine:** Lauren Robinson; **Kyo Heyerdahl:** George Takei; **Reba Heyerdahl:** Jean Smart; **Ruth P. McDougal:** Lacey Chabert; **Brainy:** Craig Bartlett; **Jamie O. Johanssen:** Ben Aaron Hoag; **Martin Johanssen:** Rick Fitts; **Ernie Potts:** Dom Irrera; **Oskar Kokoshka:** Steve Viksten; **Mr. Hyunh:** Baoan Coleman; **Marty Green:** James Keane; **Mr. Simmons:** Dan Butler; **Mary Scheer:** Suzie Kokoshka; **Brooke Lloyd:** Lori Alan

◎ HIGHLANDER: THE ANIMATED SERIES

The Highlander wages war against immortal enemies as he defends survivors of the Great Catastrophe from Kortan, who claims sovereign power over Earth, in this French-produced 40-episode animated series based on the popular film and television series. The made-for-television series aired concurrently in syndication and on USA Network beginning in September 1994.

A Nelvana Entertainment/Gaumont Multimedia Production. Color. Half-hour. Premiered on USA: September 18, 1994.

⊚ HOLIDAY CLASSICS

Between 1988 and 1991 Rabbit Ears Video produced this enchanting and well-illustrated series of holiday half-hour specials, as told by well-known celebrities, for the home video market and also broadcast on cable networks, such as Showtime and The Family Channel. Productions include *The Gingham Dog and The Calico Cat, The Night Before Christmas, The Tailor of Gloucester, The Savior Is Born* and *The Legend of Sleepy Hollow.* (See individual entries in Animated Television Specials section for further details.)

A Rabbit Ears Video Production. Color. Half-hour. Premiered on SHO: 1989–91; Premiered on FAM: 1992

⊚ HONEYBEE HUTCH

After being separated from his mother, a brave little bee begins a long and arduous search for his real mother and makes countless friends—and a few foes—along the way as he gets into one predicament after another in this heartwarming, 65-episode, half-hour series based on an original story.

A Saban Entertainment Production. Color. Half-hour. Premiered: Fall 1996. Syndicated.

⊚ HONEY HONEY

First telecast in Japan as *The Wonderful Adventures of Honey Honey* from October 1981 through May 1982, this 29-episode half-hour animated series was about a young female moppet who enjoys performing good deeds. The inspirational series was rebroadcast in the United States on CBN.

A Toei Studios/MIC Modern Programs International Production. Color. Half-hour. Premiered on CBN: 1984–1988.

⊚ HONG KONG PHOOEY

The crime-fighting karate expert, Hong Kong Phooey, alias Penrod Pooch, a meek police station janitor, maintains justice through his martial-arts abilities (which he learned in a correspondence course) and kayos his opponents in the process. His means of transportation: the "Phooeymobile." Premiering on ABC in 1974, the 16-episode half-hour series ran for two consecutive seasons. After the series' initial run on ABC, the character was reprised on *The Godzilla/Hong Kong Phooey Hour.* (See entry for details.) In 1989 the series joined USA Network's weekday *Cartoon Express* lineup (in reruns), and was later broadcast on the Cartoon Network.

A Hanna-Barbera Production. Color. Half-hour. Premiered on ABC: September 7, 1974–September 4, 1976. Rebroadcast on NBC: February 4, 1978–September 2, 1978; November 22, 1980–May 15, 1981 (part of The Godzilla/Hong Kong Phooey Hour*); May 1981–September 5, 1981 (as* Hong Kong Phooey*). Rebroadcast on USA: May 1, 1989–March 27, 1992. Rebroadcast on CAR: October 2, 1994–May 26, 1996 (Sundays); February 17, 1997 (Monday–Thursday late night).*

Voices

Penrod Pooch/Hong Kong Phooey: Scatman Crothers **Sergeant Flint:** Joe E. Ross; **Rosemary, the switchboard operator:** Kathy Gori; **Spot, Phooey's surly cat:** Don Messick

⊚ HOT WHEELS

Created and produced by Ken Snyder, of TV's *Roger Ramjet* fame, this was the first series created by Anamorphic computer animation. It starred Jack Wheeler, organizer of a young auto racers' club, who battles antagonists in racing competitions. The series was the first cartoon show to offer safety tips and information tidbits on weather, the physical principles of flight and the hazards of smoking.

Stories depicted club members Janet Martin, Skip Frasier, Bud Stuart, Mickey Barnes, Ardeth Pratt and Kip Chogi explaining to children the dangers of auto racing while engaged in reckless race car competition. The show's theme song was written and performed by Mike Curb and the Curbstones; the characters of Mickey and Kip were voiced by well-known comedian Albert Brooks.

A Pantomime Pictures/Ken Snyder Production in association with Mattel Toys. Color. Half-hour. Premiered on ABC: September 6, 1969–September 4, 1971.

Voices

Jack Wheeler/Doc Warren: Bob Arbogast; **Janice Martin:** Melinda Casey; **Mickey Barnes/Kip Chogi:** Albert Brooks; **Ardeth Pratt:** Susan Davis; **Tank Mallory/Dexter Carter:** Casey Kasem; **Mother O'Hare:** Nora Marlowe; **Mike Wheeler:** Michael Rye

⊚ THE HOUNDCATS

Government intelligence agents Dingdog, Puttypuss, Mussel Mutt, Stutz and Rhubarb undertake impossible missions in the Wild West. The 13-episode comedy/adventure series was a spoof of TV's *Mission Impossible* with cats and dogs as members of the task force. (Unlike the stars of the long-running network series, these characters become hysterical when the recorded voice tells them the message will self-destruct in five seconds.) The series bowed on CBS in 1972 and lasted one season.

A DePatie-Freleng Enterprises Production. Color. Half-hour. Premiered on NBC: September 9, 1972–September 1, 1973.

Voices
Stutz, the group's leader: Daws Butler; **Mussel Mutt, the ex-weightlifter dog:** Aldo Ray; **Rhubarb, the inventor:** Arte Johnson; **Puttypuss, cat of thousand faces:** Joe Besser; **Dingdog, the stuntman:** Stu Gilliam

◎ THE HUCKLEBERRY HOUND SHOW

The noble-hearted, slow-talking, Southern-accented bloodhound, Huckleberry Hound, starred and hosted his own series, sponsored by Kellogg's Cereals and syndicated by Screen Gems, the television arm of Columbia Pictures. The program made its debut in 1958 and, one year later, became the first animated cartoon to be awarded an Emmy by the Television Academy. By the fall of 1960 an estimated 16 million Americans and foreign viewers were watching the droopy-eyed bloodhound who starred in 57 six-minute cartoons (one per show) over the course of four seasons.

The series' two companion cartoons on the show (one episode per show) were "Pixie and Dixie" (in 57 episodes of their own), who are perpetually tormented by Mr. Jinks, a beatnik cat; and "Yogi Bear" (in 35 episodes), who pilfers picnic baskets from vacationers at lovely Jellystone National Park. In 1960 "Hokey Wolf" (in 28 episodes) was substituted for Yogi Bear, who starred in his own series the following season. Later, during the show's syndication run, "Yakky Doodle" was pulled from *The Yogi Bear Show* to replace Pixie and Dixie on the show. Episodes of *Huckleberry Hound* were later recycled as part of 1967's *Yogi and His Friends*.

The off-network version of the series *Huckleberry Hound and Friends* was rebroadcast on USA Network, from 1989 to 1991, and the original series was reshown on the Cartoon Network.

A Hanna-Barbera Production. Color. Half-hour. Premiered: October 2, 1958. Syndicated. Rebroadcast on USA: February 17, 1989–September 10, 1992. Rebroadcast on CAR: January 9, 1993–January 1, 1994 (Saturdays); January 10, 1993 (part of Boomerang, 1963); January 3, 1994–February 25, 1994 (weekdays, Saturdays); February 26, 1994–April 2, 1994 (Saturdays); April 9, 1994 (Saturdays, Sundays); August 11, 1995 (Super Chunk).

Voices
Huckleberry Hound: Daws Butler; **Pixie:** Don Messick; **Dixie/Mr. Jinks, the cat:** Daws Butler; **Yogi Bear:** Daws Butler; **Boo-Boo, his cub companion:** Don Messick; **Ranger John Smith:** Don Messick; **Hokey Wolf:** Daws Butler; **Ding-a-Ling, the fox:** Doug Young

Huckleberry Hound (center) stands as master of ceremonies in The Huckleberry Hound Show, *featuring Jinx the cat, Pixie and Dixie (left), Boo Boo and Yogi Bear (right). © Hanna-Barbera Productions*

⊚ HULK HOGAN'S ROCK N' WRESTLING

One of wrestling's most outrageous stars inspired this animated sendup of the popular spectator sport, lending his name but not his voice to this 39-episode animated series, which premiered on CBS in September of 1985. Backed by a strong rock music soundtrack, the show featured stories about the wild and outrageous personalities of the high-contact sport as well as battles between opponents on the wrestling mats. Interspersed through each hour-long program were live-action comedy sketch wraparounds starring the famous World Wrestling Federation champion and fellow wrestler "Mene" Gene Okerlund. The series was later repackaged in 30-minute versions for syndication and, in 1994, joined USA Network's *Cartoon Express*.

A DIC Enterprise Production in association with Titan Sports. Color. One hour. Premiered CBS: September 14, 1985–September 5, 1987. Syndicated. Rebroadcast on USA: September 18, 1994–March 19, 1995.

Cast (live action)
Hulk Hogan: Himself; Gene Okerlund: Himself;

Voices
Hulk Hogan: Brad Garrett; **Capt. Lou Albano:** George DiCenzo; **Junkyard Dog:** James Avery; **Andre the Giant:** Ronald A. Feinberg; **Moolah/Richter:** Jodi Carlisle; **Volkoff:** Ronald Gans; **Roddy:** Charlie Adler; **The Iron Sheik:** Aron Kincaid; **Big John Studd:** Chuck Licini; **Mr. Fuji:** Ernest Harada; **Tino Santana:** Joey Pento; **Superfly Snuka:** Lewis Arquette; **Mean Gene:** Neil Ross; **Hillbilly Jim:** Pat Fraley

⊚ THE HURRICANES

Inheriting her father's multicutural World Soccer League team, high school–age Amanda Carey turns this team of underachievers into world champions by beating the archrival Gorgons in this globe-trotting half-hour adventure series, which aired in syndication in 1993 as part of the weekend cartoon block *Amazin' Adventures I*. Each episode featured live-action cameos of well-known soccer players delivering prosocial messages. ESPN originally announced plans to rebroadcast the series in the fall of 1994–it was to become the "first" toon series to air on the all-sports network—but the network later abandoned such plans.

A DIC Enterprises/Siriol Productions/Scottish Television Enterprises Production in association with Bohbot Entertainment. Color. Half-hour. Premiered: September 12, 1993 (part of Amazin' Adventures I). Syndicated.

Voices
Andrew Airlie, Carol Alexander, Kathleen Barr, Michael Benyaer, Gary Chalk, Candus Churchill, Ian James Corlett, Roger Crossly, Chris Gaze, Colin Heath, Stuart Hepburn, Carl Hibbert, Mark Hildreth, Chris Humphreys, Christina Lippa, Scott McNeil, Wezley Morris, Alvin Sanders, Louise Vallance, Peter Williams, Jeannie Zahni, Chiara Zanni

⊚ I AM THE GREATEST: THE ADVENTURES OF MUHAMMAD ALI

Former heavyweight boxing champ Muhammad Ali supplied his own voice for this 13-episode animated series for NBC that blended comedy, adventure and mystery in situations shaped around Ali's heroics. Joining him in his encounters are his niece and nephew, Nicky and Damon, and his public relations agent, Frank Bannister. Failing to deliver a knockout blow in the ratings, the series was canceled at mid-season.

A Farmhouse Films Production. Color. Half-hour. Premiered on NBC: September 10, 1977–January 28, 1978. Rebroadcast on NBC: February 11, 1978—September 2, 1978.

Voices:
Muhammad Ali: Himself; **Nicky, his niece:** Patrice Carmichael; **Damon, his nephew:** Casey Carmichael; **Frank Bannister:** Himself

⊚ INCH HIGH PRIVATE EYE

The Finkerton Detective Agency puts its best man on the case: the world's smallest private eye, Inch High, who is fashioned after Maxwell Smart, agent 86, of TV's *Get Smart*. The thumbnail-size detective relies on various weapons and disguises to capture criminals. His best friend in the world is his dog, Braveheart. The 13-episode series aired one full season on NBC.

A Hanna-Barbera Production. Color. Half-hour. Premiered on NBC: September 8, 1973–August 31, 1974. Rebroadcast on CAR: July 9, 1995–May 26, 1996 (Sundays); November 17, 1996– (Sundays).

Voices
Inch High: Lennie Weinrib; **Lorie, his niece:** Kathy Gori; **Gator, his aide:** Bob Luttrell; **Mr. Finkerton, his boss:** John Stephenson; **Mrs. Finkerton:** Jean VanderPyl; **Braveheart, Inch High's dog:** Don Messick

⊚ THE INCREDIBLE HULK (1984)

NBC added this series, featuring the hulking Marvel superhero, to its Saturday-morning cartoon roster late in the 1984–85 season. The program repeated episodes that first aired on *The Incredible Hulk/Amazing Spider-Man Hour*.

A Marvel Production. Color. Half-hour. Premiered on NBC: December 15, 1984–September 7, 1985.

Voices

Michael Bell, Susan Blu, Bill Callaway, Hamilton Camp, Victoria Carroll, Hans Conreid, Robert Cruz, Jerry Dexter, George DiCenzo, Alan Dinehart, Walker Edmiston, Michael Evans, Al Fann, Ron Feinberg, Elliott Field, June Foray, Pat Fraley, Kathy Garver, Dan Gilvezan, John Hayner, Bob Holt, Michael Horton, Stan Jones, Sally Julian, Stan Lee, Anne Lockhart, Keye Luke, Dennis Marks, Allan Melvin, Shepard Menken, Vic Perrin, Bob Ridgely, Neilson Ross, Stanley Ralph Ross, Michael Rye, Marilyn Schreffler, John Stephenson, Janet Waldo, B.J. Ward, Frank Welker, William Woodson, Alan Young

◎ THE INCREDIBLE HULK (1996)

Dr. Bruce Banner, also known as the menacing green-skinned goliath the Incredible Hulk, struggles to conquer the inner beast who comes out whenever his emotions rage in this new half-hour animated version based on the Marvel Comics series. Actor Lou Ferrigno, who played the pea-green gargantuan in the 1970s live-action television series, reprised the character in this cartoon version. (Ferrigno, who suffers from a hearing disability, never spoke in the live-action series but did so in the animated series.) The series bowed Sunday mornings on the UPN Network in the fall of 1996.

A Marvel Films/New World Entertainment Production in association with UPN Kids. Color. Half-hour. Premiered on UPN: September 8, 1996.

Voices

The Incredible Hulk: Lou Ferrigno; **Robert Bruce Banner:** Neal McDonough; **Gabriel Jones:** Thom Barry; **Rick Jones:** Luke Perry; **Betty Ross/Sister Rose Erak:** Genie Francis; **She-Hulk/Jennifer Walters:** Lisa Zane; **General Thaddeus "Thunderbolt" Ross:** John Vernon; **Major Glenn Talbot/Abomination/ZZZAX/Samuel Laroquette/Judge:** Kevin Schon; **Doctor Leonard Samson:** Shadoe Stevens; **Leader:** Matt Frewer; **Gargoyle:** Mark Hamill; **Ogress:** Kathy Ireland

◎ THE INCREDIBLE HULK/ AMAZING SPIDER-MAN HOUR

New episodes of the Incredible Hulk were added to this hour-long fantasy series and combined with previously broadcast episodes of the popular Saturday-morning series *Spider-Man and His Amazing Friends.*

A Marvel Production. Color. One-hour. Premiered on NBC: September 19, 1982–September 8, 1984.

Voices

Jack Angel, Michael Bell, Lee Briley, Bill Boyett, Cory Burton, Susan Blu, Wally Burr, Bill Callaway, Hamilton Camp, Victoria Carroll, Phil Clarke, Hans Conreid, Rege Cordic,

Henry Corden, Brad Crandall, Robert Cruz, Peter Cullen, Brian Cummings, Jeff David, Jack DeLeon, Jerry Dexter, George DiCenzo, Alan Dinehart, Walker Edmiston, Michael Evans, Al Fann, Ron Feinberg, Elliot Field, June Foray, Pat Fraley, Brian Fuld, Kathy Garver, Linda Gary, Dan Gilvezan, John Haymer, Bob Holt, Michael Horton, Ralph James, Lynn Johnson, Stanley Jones, Sally Julian, Lee Lampson, Stan Lee, Anne Lockhart, Morgan Lofting, Keye Luke, Dennis Marks, Mona Marshall, John Mayer, Alan Melvin, Shepard Menken, Don Messick, Vic Perrin, Tony Pope, Richard Ramos, Bob Ridgely, Neilson Ross, Gene Ross, Stanley Ralph Ross, Michael Rye, Marilyn Schreffler, John Stephenson, Ted Schwartz, Gary Seger, Michael Sheehan, Andre Stojka, Janet Waldo, B.J. Ward, Frank Welker, Paul Winchell, William Woodson, Alan Young

◎ THE INHUMANOIDS

A group of ancient subhuman monsters from the center of Earth escape their fiery dwellings to wreak havoc and destruction. Only the Earth Corps, a team of brilliant human scientists, can combat the creatures in this eight-episode series, first aired in a trial run (in two episodes) on Marvel's "Super Sunday" weekend cartoon block in January of 1986. The series went weekly in September of that year.

A Marvel Production in association with Sunbow Productions. Color. Half-hour. Premiered: September 21, 1986. Syndicated.

Voices

Michael Bell, William Callaway, Fred Collins, Brad Crandel, Dick Gautier, Ed Gilbert, Chris Latta, Neil Ross, Stanley Ralph Ross, Richard Sanders, Susan Silo, John Stephenson

◎ INSPECTOR GADGET

Don Adams, formerly TV's Maxwell Smart, agent 86, voiced this bumbling Inspector Clouseau type, originally based in a small provincial town as a local police officer, who becomes the first gadgetized and bionic inspector working for Interpol. With the intelligent help of his young niece, Penny, and faithful, long-suffering dog, Brain, Gadget always manages to vanquish his enemies and come out victorious. The series began as a five-episode preview in syndication in the fall of 1982 and became a regular series in 1983. New episodes were produced in 1985, and, two years later, while still in syndication, the series was rebroadcast on Nickelodeon, beginning in the fall. In 1991 CBS rebroadcast the series Saturday mornings. Episodes of the series also popped up on The Family Channel weekend cartoon block *Fun Town.* The series was the first syndicated property of its producer, DIC Enterprises.

A DIC Enterprises Production in association with Field Communications Corp./LBS/TMS. Color. Half-hour. Pre-

Bumbling Inspector Gadget looks as if he has bumbled his last in the popular syndicated cartoon series Inspector Gadget. © *DIC Animation City, Inc.* (COURTESY: DIC ENTERPRISES)

miered: Fall 1982. Syndicated. Rebroadcast on NIK: October 5, 1987–Fall 1992. November 2, 1991–August 31, 1992. Rebroadcast on FAM (part of Fun Town): 1993.

Voices
Inspector Gadget: Don Adams; **Penny, his niece:** Mona Marshall, Cree Summer Francks, Holly Berger; **Brain, his dog:** Frank Welker; **Chief Quimby:** Maurice LaMarche; **Capeman:** Townsend Coleman; **Dr. Claw/Madcat:** Frank Welker

⊚ INSPECTOR GADGET'S FIELD TRIP

Combining animation with live-action footage, bionic crimebuster Inspector Gadget plays host, tour guide and history teacher as he visits the most colorful, interesting and historical sights throughout the world—places like London, Rome, the NASA Space Center and the Great Wall of China—uncovering colorful facts, quirks and interesting legends and lore, in this half-hour educational series, broadcast on The History Channel in 1996.

A DIC Enterprise Production. Color. Half-hour. Premiered on HIS: November 3, 1996.

Voices
Inspector Gadget: Don Adams

⊚ IRON MAN

After sustaining a severe chest injury from an exploding land mine in Vietnam, millionaire businessman Tony Stark went on to become this flying superhero, wearing an armored suit to keep his damaged heart beating while bat-

tling the war-related archenemy, the Mandarin, in a series of comic books created by Stan Lee (with the assistance of artist Don Heck) in 1963. Stark, as Iron Man, first flew onto television screens in 1966 in the Grantray-Lawrence animated series *The Marvel Superheroes*. In 1994 Marvel Films produced the first series featuring the famed Marvel Superhero in a starring role, aired as part of the hour-long syndicated block, *The Marvel Action Hour*. Joined in some episodes by the ForceWorks Team, Iron Man once again encounters his old foe, the Mandarin, and his evil team of villains in 26 episodes (including four two-parters) broadcast over two seasons beginning in 1994.

A Marvel Films/New World Entertainment Production. Color. Half-hour. Premiered: September 25, 1994.

Voices
Iron Man/Tony Stark: Robert Hays; **Julia Carpenter:** Casey Defranco; **War Machine/Jim Rhodes:** Dorian Harewood; **The Madarin:** Ed Gilbert; **Madam Maque:** Lisa Zane; **Dreadknight:** Neil Dickson; **Blizzard:** Chuck McCann; **Modok:** Jim Cummings; **Justin Hammer:** Tony Steedman; **Hypnotia:** Linda Huldahl; **Fin Fang Foom:** Neil Ross

⊚ IT'S PUNKY BREWSTER

Based on the prime-time live-action comedy hit of 1984 to 1986, NBC commissioned this animated series version. The 42-episode half-hour series experienced even greater success as a Saturday morning vehicle Punky's special friend, Glomer, transports Punky and her friends to the four corners of Earth in the blink of an eye.

A Ruby-Spears Enterprises Production. Color. Half-hour. Premiered on NBC: September 14, 1985–August 22, 1987. Rebroadcast on NBC: November 12, 1988–September 2, 1989.

Voices
Punky Brewster: Soleil-Moon Frye; **Cherie:** Cherie Johnson; **Margaux:** Ami Foster; **Allen Anderson:** Casey Ellison; **Henry Warnimont:** Georges Gaynes; **Glomer:** Frank Welker

⊚ THE ITSY BITSY SPIDER

Originally produced as a 1992 theatrical cartoon short, this wise-guy, four-eyed, spindly-legged troublemaker, whose best friends are a little girl (Leslie) and her young friend (George), tries to keep one step ahead of the Exterminator (a musclebound karate champ who is befriended by the girl's piano teacher/mother) in this half-hour animated spinoff. USA Network commissioned this slapstick-filled Saturday morning series in 1993, the year the network added first-run cartoon series to its regular lineup. (The series aired in tandem with the new animated series *Problem Child*.) In 1995 following its original run, the series was rebroadcast and moved to Sunday-mornings. Frank Welker, who portrayed Itsy in the seven-minute theatrical cartoon short, returned to provide the voice of the title character in the show.

A Hyperion Animation Production in association with Paramount Television. Color. Half-hour. Premiered on USA: October 31, 1993–September 15, 1996.

Voices
Itsy/Langston: Frank Welker; **Adrienne Facts:** Charlotte Rae; **The Exterminator:** Matt Frewer; **Leslie:** Francesca Marie Smith; **George:** Jonathan Taylor Thomas

⊚ JABBERJAW

Capitalizing on the movie *Jaws*, Hanna-Barbera created the lovable but stupid white shark Jabberjaw, who sounds like Curly Howard of The Three Stooges. He serves as mascot for four teenagers (Clam-Head, Bubbles, Shelly and Biff) and their rock group, The Neptunes, living in an underwater civilization in A.D. 2021. Created by cartoon veterans Joe Ruby and Ken Spears, the 16-episode series bowed on ABC in 1976.

A Hanna-Barbera Production. Color. Half-hour. Premiered on ABC: September 11, 1976–September 3, 1977. Rebroadcast on ABC: September 11, 1977–September 3, 1978. Rebroadcast on CAR: (beginning) April 10, 1994 (Sundays); October 19, 1997 (Saturdays).

Voices
Jabberjaw: Frank Welker; **Clam-Head:** Barry Gordon; **Bubbles:** Julie McWhirter; **Shelly:** Pat Paris; **Biff:** Tommy Cook

Other Voices
Don Messick

⊚ THE JACKSON 5IVE

Jackie, Marion, Jermaine, Tito and Michael, as then-members of Motown's popular rock group The Jackson 5ive, star in real-life situations that spotlight their comedic lifestyles, happenings and misadventures in cartoon form. The 23-episode half-hour cartoon series originally aired on ABC from 1971 to 1973. It returned to the airwaves via daily syndication in the mid-1980s and briefly again in 1996 on Saturday mornings on VH1.

A Halas and Batchelor Production for Rankin-Bass Productions and Motown. Color. Half-hour. Premiered on ABC: September 11, 1971–September 1, 1973. Syndicated. Rebroadcast on VH1: September 7, 1996–October 12, 1996.

Voices
Jackie: Sigmund Jackson; **Tito:** Toriano Jackson; **Jermaine:** Jermaine Jackson; **David:** Marion Jackson; **Michael:** Michael Jackson

⊚ JAMES BOND JR.

The 17-year-old nephew of the famed fictional British supersleuth encounters saboteurs, criminals and other bad guys—mostly linked to the enemy organization S.C.U.M. (Saboteurs and Criminals United in Mayhem)—employing high-tech gadgetry and acts of derring-do in this first-run half-hour adventure series spin-off of Ian Fleming's internationally known literary character and popular film series.

A Murikami-Wolf-Swenson Production in association with MGM/United Artists Television. Color. Half-hour. Premiered: September 1991. Syndicated. Rebroadcast on CAR: January 2, 1995–June 2, 1995 (weekdays)

Voices
Jeff Bennett, Corey Burton, Julian Holloway, Mona Marshall, Brian Mitchell, Jean Rabson, Susan Silo, Simon Templeman, Aride Talent, Eddie Barth, Cheryl Bernstein, Susan Blu, Susan Boyd, Hamilton Camp, Jennifer Darling, Mari Devon, Jane Downs, Paul Eiding, Jeannie Elias, Pat Fraley, Linda Gary, Ellen Gerstell, Ed Gilbert, Rebecca Gilchrest, Michael Gough, Gaille Heidemann, Vicki Juditz, Matt N. Miller, Pat Musick, Allan Oppenheimer, Samantha Paris, Tony Pope, Bob Ridgely, Maggie Roswell, Kath Soucie, B.J. Ward, Jill Wayne

⊚ JANA OF THE JUNGLE

(See GODZILLA AND THE SUPER 90.)

⊚ JANOSCH'S DREAM WORLD

Based on the works of award-winning German author/illustrator Horst Eckert (whose pen name was Janosch), this half-hour anthology series, first released on home video in the United States in the early 1990s and produced between 1988 and 1990, featured a series of heartwarming and entertaining cartoon fables animated by Germany's WDR studios. The series made its American television debut on Nickelodeon in 1993.

A Cinar Film/WDG Cologne Production. Color. Half-hour. Premiered on NIK: December 6, 1993–June 10, 1994.

Voices
Dean Hagopian, Terry Haig, Harry Hill, Terrence Labrosse Ross, Elizabeth MacRae, Howard Ryshpan, Sam Stone, Jane Woods

JAYCE AND THE WHEELED WARRIORS

Jayce, the son of a famous scientist, and his space-age crew known as the Lightning League—Herc, a mercenary pilot; Gillian, a wise wizard; Flora, a half-plant/half-human girl; and Oon, a mechanical squire/slave—travel the universe in search of his father to reunite the root of a plant that can prevent Saw Boss and his evil plant followers, the Monster Minds, from taking over the universe. The 65-episode series, based on the popular toy line, was produced for first-run syndication and was later rebroadcast on USA Network's *Cartoon Express*.

A DIC Enterprise Production in association with WWP Productions. Color. Half-hour. Premiered: September 1985. Syndicated. Rebroadcast on USA: June 5, 1994–November 16, 1994.

Voices

Jayce: Darin Baker; **Audric, Jayce's father:** Dan Hennessey; **Flora:** Valerie Politis; **Oon:** Luba Goy; **Gillian:** Charles Joliffe; **Herc Stormsailer:** Len Carlson; **Saw Boss:** Giulio Kukurugya; **Monster Minds:** Dan Hennessey, Len Carlson, John Stocker; **Ko Kruiser/Sawtrooper:** Dan Hennessey; **Terror Tank:** Len Carlson; **Gun Grinner:** John Stocker

JEANNIE

In this cartoon spin-off of TV's *I Dream of Jeannie*, Center City High School teenager Corry Anders discovers a magic lamp containing a lady genie and her bumbling apprentice, Babu. They become his grateful servants and use their magical powers to help him out of trouble in this top-rated 16-episode cartoon series for CBS. Actor Mark Hamill, of *Star Wars*, provided the voice of Corry.

A Hanna-Barbera Production in association with Screen Gems. Color. Half-hour. Premiered on CBS: September 9, 1973–August 30, 1975.

Voices

Jeannie: Julie McWhirter; **Babu:** Joe Besser; **Corry Anders:** Mark Hamill; **Henry Glopp, Corry's friend:** Bob Hastings; **Mrs. Anders, Corry's mother:** Janet Waldo

JEM

Jerrica Benton, a beautiful, ambitious and brilliant music executive and founder of a home for teenage runaways has a double identity: Through a magical transformation, she becomes JEM, a glamorous rock star who wages outrageous battles of the bands. First introduced in 1985 as a separate half-hour series, part of Marvel's *Super Sunday* weekend cartoon block, it was so popular with viewers that producers

offered the series by itself in weekly syndication in 1986. Three years later, the program reaired on USA Network's *Cartoon Express*.

A Marvel Production in association with Sunbow Production. Color. Half-hour. Premiered: August 3, 1986 (originally syndicated in 1985 as component of Super Sunday). Syndicated. Rebroadcast on USA: September 18, 1989–August 8, 1993.

Voices

Charlie Adler, Tammy Amerson, Patricia Albrecht, Marlene Aragon, Allison Argo, Ellen Bernfield, Bobbi Block, Cathianne Blore, Sue Blue, Jan Britain, Anne Bryant, Wally Burr, Angela Cappelli, Kim Carlson, T.K. Carter, Cathy Cavadini, Linda Dangcil, Louise Dorsey, Walker Edmiston, Laurie Faso, Ed Gilbert, Dan Gilvezan, Diva Grey, Desiree Goyette, Lani Groves, Michael Horton, Ford Kinder, Jeff Kinder, Clyde Kusatu, Kathi Marcuccio, Cindy McGee, Ullanda McCulloug, Samantha Newark, Noelle North, Britta Phillips, Neil Ross, Jack Roth, Michael Sheehan, Hazel Shermet, Tony St. James, Terri Textor, Florence Warner, Valerie Wilson, Keone Young

THE JETSONS

Hanna-Barbera's space-age answer to its prehistoric blockbuster *The Flintstones* brought the Jetson family of the 21st century into living rooms in 1963 on ABC. For a one-season show, the program—for which only 24 half-hour episodes were produced—remains immensely popular among viewers today. (Its debut episode was "Rosie the Robot.")

Stories depict the prospects of living in a futuristic society and showcase George Jetson, employee of Spacely Space Age Sprockets; his lovely, practical wife, Jane; his teeny-bopping daughter, Judy; and his inventive son, Elroy. They have the luxury of computer-operated housing facilities, a robot maid named Rosie and compact flying vehicles that fold into the size of a briefcase.

In 1984 Hanna-Barbera produced a new series of half-hour episodes (41 for the first season) for first-run syndication, which were voiced by most of the original cast. One new character was added: a pet alien named Orbity (voiced by Frank Welker). The new series was stripped for daily syndication and combined with episodes from the original 1962 series. In 1987 the syndicated series went back into production, producing 10 more half-hour installments, followed by a two-hour TV movie that same year, *The Jetsons Meet the Flintstones*. A year later the space-age family returned in an animated special, *Rockin' with Judy Jetson*. Members of the original cast were reassembled again to lend their voices to the full-length animated feature *Jetsons: The Movie*, released in 1990.

A Hanna-Barbera Production. Color. Half-hour. Premiered on ABC: September 23, 1962–September 8, 1963. Rebroadcast on ABC: September 21, 1963–April 18, 1964. Rebroadcast on CBS: September 4, 1965–September 5, 1966. Rebroadcast on NBC: October 2, 1965–September 2, 1967; September 10, 1966–September 7, 1967. Rebroadcast on CBS: September 13, 1969–September 4, 1971; Rebroadcast on NBC: September 11, 1971–September 4, 1976; February 3, 1979–September 5, 1981. Rebroadcast on ABC: September 18, 1982–April 2, 1983. Rebroadcast on CAR: October 1, 1992–September 1, 1995; March 4, 1996– (weekdays). Premiere (new series): September 1984. Syndicated.

Voices
George Jetson: George O'Hanlon; **Jane Jetson:** Penny Singleton; **Judy Jetson:** Janet Waldo; **Elroy Jetson:** Daws Butler; **Cosmo C. Spacely, George's boss:** Mel Blanc; **Astro, the family dog:** Don Messick; **Rosie, the robot maid:** Jean VanderPyl; **Henry Orbit, janitor:** Howard Morris; **Cogswell, owner of Cogswell: Cogs:** Daws Butler; **Uniblab:** Don Messick; **Orbity:** Frank Welker (1984)

◎ JIM AND JUDY IN TELELAND

The various adventures of two children are related in this highly imaginative limited-animated adventure show first produced in 1949–50, combining cut-out animation and animation cels to create each story. The two characters, who began and closed each episode framed inside a television, encountered a host of unbelievable characters along the way—spies, pirates, giant insects and others—in this syndicated series, which is believed to have been aired in weekly, five-minute time slots. Fifty-two five-minute, cliffhanging episodes were produced initially. The series was reissued in 1959 under the title of *Bob and Betty in Adventureland*.

A Television Screen/Film Flash, Inc. Production. Black-and-white. Five minutes. Premiered: 1953. Syndicated.

Voices
Jim: Merrill Jolls; **Judy:** Honey McKenzie

◎ JOHNNY BRAVO

This series follows the one-track, never-ending obsession (and perpetual failure) with women of this blond, buff-chested, karate-chopping free spirit who believes he is a gift from God to women of Earth, loves his mother and tolerates his next-door neighbor Suzy all at the same time. Created by 26-year-old independent animator Van Partible (who derived the character's name from the classic television series *The Brady Bunch* in the episode entitled "Adios, Johnny Bravo"), *Johnny Bravo* was the third breakout series from Hanna-Barbera that originated as a cartoon short on the Cartoon Network's *World Premiere Toons* series. In July

This biceps-bulging, karate-chopping free spirit believes he is a gift from God to the women of Earth in the animated comedy series *Johnny Bravo.* (If he only knew!) © Hanna-Barbera Productions (COURTESY THE CARTOON NETWORK)

of 1997 the character debuted in 13 half-hour programs, each including three seven-minute cartoons, some of which featured animated versions of such celebrities as Farrah Fawcett, Adam West, Donny Osmond and Scooby-Doo (each of whom appeared as special "celebrity guests").

A Hanna-Barbera Production. Color. Half-hour. Premiered on CAR: July 1997.

Voices
Johnny: Jeff Bennett; **Little Suzy:** Mae Whitman; **Mama:** Brenda Vaccaro

◎ JOHNNY CYPHER IN DIMENSION ZERO

Brilliant Earth scientist Johnny Cypher finds that he has superhuman powers enabling him to travel through the dimensions of inner space and combat sinister forces. This half-hour series of four six-minute adventures, some of them cliffhangers (adding up to 130 episodes in all), was produced by Joe Oriolo, who also produced television's *Felix the Cat* series.

A Seven Arts Production in association with Joe Oriolo Films. Color. Half-hour. Premiered: February 1967. Syndicated.

Voices
Johnny Cypher: Paul Hecht; **Zena, his female assistant:** Corinne Orr; **Rhom, galactic being/Other voices:** Gene Allen

⊚ JOKEBOOK

Twenty to 25 individually styled animated jokes selected from among a wide assortment of foreign and student films, award-winning cartoon shorts and original concepts highlight this colorful fantasy showcase of entertaining animation from throughout the world. Segments ranged from 20 seconds to three minutes each.

Marty Murphy, a cartoonist for various national magazines, including *Playboy*, was a consultant on the series. Frank Ridgeway, syndicated cartoonist for hundreds of newspapers, and Jack Bonestell, cartoonist for national magazines, also contributed their unique styles to the show.

Some of the films shown included the Oscar-winning animated short subjects, "Crunch Bird" and "The Fly," which took Best Animated Short Film honors at the Academy Awards. The show's theme song was sung by comedian Scatman Crothers.

A Hanna-Barbera Production. Color. Half-hour. Premiered on NBC: April 23, 1982–May 7, 1982.

Voices
Henry Corden, Bob Hastings, Joan Gerber, Joyce Jameson, Don Messick, Sidney Miller, Robert Allen Ogle, Ronnie Schell, Marilyn Schreffler, Hal Smith, John Stephenson, Janet Waldo, Lennie Weinrib, Frank Welker

⊚ JOSIE AND THE PUSSYCATS

Based on characters created by Dan DeCarlo for the *Archie* comic-book series. Music promoter Alexander Cabot manages an all-girl rock group, the Pussycats, led by the ambitious Josie, whose desire to be the center of attention often results in a blow to his ego. The singing on the show was performed by Cathy Douglas, Patricia Holloway and Cherie Moore (short for Cheryl Ann Stopylmore), who is now better known as Cheryl Ladd. The character of Alexandra Cabot was voiced by Sherry Alberoni, a former Mouseketeer. Musical numbers for the series were composed and arranged by Danny Janssen, Bob Ingeman and Art Mogell under the corporate name of LAla Productions. Sixteen songs were derived from the series and were released on the album of the same name for Capitol Records in 1970. The 16-episode series originally debuted on CBS in 1970 and

lasted two full seasons. (It returned in reruns in 1975 as well.) A space-age spinoff was produced in 1972, *Josie and the Pussycats in Outer Space*.

A Hanna-Barbera and Radio Comics, Inc. Production. Color. Half-hour. Premiered on CBS: September 12, 1970–September 2, 1972. Rebroadcast on CBS: September 6, 1975–September 4, 1976. Rebroadcast on CAR: December 6, 1992 (part of Boomerang, 1972); January 9, 1993 (Josie and the Pussycats Marathon); February 1, 1993–October 1, 1993; January 11, 1993–April 29, 1994 (weekdays); June 6, 1994–June 2, 1995 (weekdays); November 6, 1995–November 25, 1996 (weekdays).

Voices
Josie: Janet Waldo; **Melody, the dimwitted blond drummer:** Jackie Joseph; **Valerie, the guitarist:** Barbara Pariot; **Alan:** Jerry Dexter; **Alexandra Cabot III:** Casey Kasem; **Alexandra Cabot, his sister:** Sherry Alberoni; **Alexandra Cabot, his sister:** Sherry Alberoni; **Sebastian, their pet cat:** Don Messick

⊚ JOSIE AND THE PUSSYCATS IN OUTER SPACE

The Pussycats (Josie, Melody and Valerie) and company are accidentally launched into outer space when they become trapped in a NASA space capsule. Joined by their manager, Alexander; his sister, Alexandra; Alan; and a new member, Bleep the space mascot, the three teenage girls explore the vast regions of the universe in this 16-episode series spinoff of 1970's *Josie and the Pussycats*. In 1994 the Cartoon Network began rerunning the series, initially airing four episodes back to back that July on the 25th anniversary of the Apollo 11 moon landing.

A Hanna-Barbera and Radio Comics Inc. Production. Color. Half-hour. Premiered on CBS: September 9, 1972–August 31, 1974. Rebroadcast on CAR: July 20, 1994 (25th Anniversary of the Moon Landing with Josie in Outer Space); November 6, 1995–November 25, 1996 (weekdays).

Voices
Josie: Janet Waldo; **Melody:** Jackie Joseph; **Valerie:** Barbara Pariot; **Alan:** Jerry Dexter; **Alexander Cabot III:** Casey Kasem; **Alexandra Cabot:** Sherry Alberoni; **Sebastian, their cat:** Don Messick; **Bleep, the space mascot:** Don Messick; **Group Vocalists:** Cathy Douglas, Patricia Holloway, Cherie Moore

⊚ JOT

Spiritual and moral lessons are conveyed in this popular syndicated series following the adventures of a happy anthropomorphic white dot, named Little JOT, who encounters problematic situations and learns a valuable lesson. Thirteen four-and-a-half-minute episodes were initially produced by the Southern Baptist Radio-Television Commission and first broadcast on the Dallas-based children's show *Peppermint Place*, which was syndicated to independent television stations in the 1980s and 1990s. A second series of episodes was produced and broadcast in many foreign countries, including Australia, Japan and several western European nations, as well as on a number of independent and religious stations.

A Southern Baptist Radio-Television Commission Production. Color. Half-hour. Syndicated: 1965–1970.

⊚ JOURNEY TO THE CENTRE OF THE EARTH

A Scottish geologist, Professor Oliver Lindenbrook, and his intrepid party of fellow explorers—faithful guide Lars and student Alec McEwen—journey to Earth's core, only to discover an enemy in their midst—the evil Count Saccnusson, who wants to establish his own subterreanean empire—in this 17-episode half-hour cartoon series, inspired by the 1959 20th Century–Fox feature (based on Jules Verne's classic 1864 science-fiction novel, *Voyage au Centre de la Terre*). Certain creative liberties were taken with the characters in this animated version. Among them: Lindenbrook's loyal guide Lars was actually named Hans in the book and in the movie; their bitter enemy Count Saccnusson was formerly known as "Count Sakknussem." Ted Knight, who later played the newsman Ted Baxter on *The Mary Tyler Moore Show*, doubled as the voice of Professor Lindenbrook and the Count. The series was a popular fixture (in reruns) on the Sci-Fi Channel's *Cartoon Quest*.

A Filmation Associates Production. Color. Half-hour. Premiered on ABC: September 9, 1967–August 30, 1969. Rebroadcast on SCI: September 18, 1993–July 31, 1996.

Voices
Professor Lindenbrook/Count Saccnusson: Ted Knight; Cindy Lindenbrook: Jane Webb; **Alec McEwen/Lar/Torg:** Pat Harrington Jr.

⊚ JUMANJI—THE ANIMATED SERIES

Reality and fantasy blend together with frightening results, when young Peter and Judy Sheperd play an accursed board game "Jumanji" in their Aunt Nora's house. The game sucks them into a world bristling with action-packed scrapes and hair-raising experiences, where they are aided by a 26-year Jumanji captive, Alan Parrish, a bearded nature boy in a loincloth (voiced by *Coach's* Bill Fagerbakke), in this weekly, Saturday-morning cartoon series based on the hit 1995 feature starring Robin Williams. The show premiered Sunday mornings on the UPN Network in the fall of 1996.

An Adelaide/Interscope/Titler Films/Columbia-Tristar Children's Television Production. Color. Half-hour. Premiered on UPN: September 8, 1996.

Voices
Peter Sheperd: Ashley Johnson; **Judy Sheperd:** Debi Derryberry; **Alan Parrish:** Bill Fagerbakke; **Aunt Nora:** Melanie Chartoff; **Officer Carl Bentley/Tribal Bob:** Richard Allen; **Van Pelt:** Sherman Howard; **Professor Heinrich Ibsen:** William Sanderson; **Professor J.H. Slick (a.k.a: Trader Slick):** Tim Curry; **Rock:** Pamela Segall; **Brute/Manjis** Billy West; **Dead-Eye/Manjis:** Kevin Schon; **Fang/Manjis** Danny Mann

⊚ JUNGLE CUBS

In this prequel to Walt Disney's 1967 animated feature *The Jungle Book*, the film's beloved characters Bagheera the panther, Baloo the bear, Kaa the snake, Shere Khan the tiger and Prince Louie experience all-new adventures as mischievous youngsters as they learn the laws of life in the jungle and the importance of friendships in this 22-episode half-hour syndicated series, rebroadcast in 1997 on The Disney Channel.

A Walt Disney Television Animation/Wang Film Production. Color. Half-hour. Premiered: October 5, 1996. Rebroadcast on DIS: September 1997. Syndicated.

Voices
Jim Cummings, Jason Marsden, Rob Paulsen, Pamela Segall, Adam Wylie

⊚ KABLAM!

Hosted by the squiggly, unnerving and warped preadolescent computer-animated pair, Henry and June (as in controversial author Henry Miller and his wife), this comic book come-to-life cartoon anthology series, billed as "TV's first animated sketch comedy series," showcased various forms of animation, including paper-cut and clay-animated cartoon shorts and character-based stories on Friday and Saturday nights on Nickelodeon. The off-kilter series premiered on Nick in October of 1996, opening with a pair of segments that served as weekly anchors: "Action League Now!," filmed in "chuck-i-mation" (a combination of stop-motion puppetry and "chucking" of the characters), featuring Barbie-like action figures who tell warped crime-fighting stories and whose archnemesis is the car-crushing Stinky, and "Sniz & Fondue," the cel-animated wiggy adventures of a pair of outrageous cartoon cats and their pals. Other recurring segments, included the paper-cut animation "Life with Loopy," about a young girl with an overactive imagination, and "The Offbeats."

A Nickelodeon Production. Color. Half-hour. Premiered on NIK: October 11, 1996.

Voices
June: Julia McIllvane; **Henry:** Noah Segan

THE KARATE KID

The popular motion picture starring Ralph Macchio and Pat Morita inspired this animated adaptation about the continuing adventures of Daniel and Mr. Miyagi, with stories stressing positive values. The 13-episode Saturday-morning series lasted only one full season on NBC.

A DIC Enterprises Production in association with Jerry Weintraub Productions/Columbia Pictures Television. Color. Half-hour. Premiered on NBC: September 9, 1989–September 1, 1990. Syndicated.

Voices
Daniel: Joe Dedio; **Miyagi Yakuga:** Robert Ito; **Taki:** Janice Kawaye

KATIE AND ORBIE

This fully animated, half-hour syndicated series follows the entertaining adventures of a bright, curious five-year-old girl, Katie, and her best friend, a pint-size, red-speckled, inquisitive reptilian alien, Orbie, who crash-lands in a pumpkin patch and is adopted by Katie's parents. This half-hour Canadian-produced cartoon series aired on PBS stations from 1995 to 1996. Based on a series of popular children's books by internationally syndicated cartoonist Ben Wicks, the series, featuring three seven-minute cartoons per half-hour program, was written by Wicks's daughter Susan and narrated by actor Leslie Nielsen (of *Naked Gun* fame). In the fall of 1997 The Disney Channel began rerunning the series fives days a week.

A Lacewood Television Production in association with Baton Broadcasting Inc./North Texas Public Broadcasting Inc./Worldwide Sports & Entertainment Inc./La Chaine De TV Ontario/Rogers Telefund/The Ontario Film Development Corp./Motion Picture Guarantors Ltd. Color. Half-hour. Premiered on PBS: 1995–1996. Rebroadcast on DIS: September 1997.

Voices
Narrator: Leslie Nielsen

KEWPIES

The Kewpies and their peaceful community of Kewp Valley are threatened by the evil Countess who wants to steal their magical powers in this half-hour fantasy series based on the Kewpie doll characters first drawn by illustrator Rose O'Neill in 1909. The series aired weekends in syndication beginning in the fall of 1997.

A Sachs Family Entertainment Production. Color. Half-hour. Premiered: September 20, 1997.

KIDD VIDEO

Zapped into the fourth dimension, four talented teenage rock musicians (Kidd, Ash, Whiz and Carla) visit the wacky world of the Flip Side, a bright, airy, upbeat, nonthreatening environment except for the diabolical Master Blaster of Bad Vibes. With the dubious help of The Copy Cats (Fat Cat, Cool Kitty and She-Lion), Master Blaster tries to steal the famed musical group's sound. The live-action/animated program was further highlighted by Top 40 hits, each of which was inventively animated. NBC aired the series' original 128 episodes over two consecutive seasons beginning in 1984. The series continued in reruns on NBC through April of 1987 and ended its network run on CBS (in reruns) the following season.

A DIC Enterprise Production in association with Saban Productions. Color. Half-hour. Premiered on NBC: September 15, 1984–April 4, 1987. Rebroadcast on CBS: September 19, 1987–December 26, 1987.

Voices
Kidd Video, the group's leader: Bryan Scott; **Ash:** Steve Alterman; **Whiz:** Robbie Rist; **Carla:** Gabrielle Bennett; **Glitter, Kidd Video's friend:** Cathy Cavadini; **Master Blaster:** Peter Renaday

THE COPY CATS: Fat Cat: Marshall Efron; **She-Lion:** Susan Silo; **Cool Kitty:** Robert Towers

KIDEO TV

This 90-minute spectacle packaged three animated series for first-run syndication, designed for weekend programming on independent television stations. Initially the series was comprised of reruns of the half-hour network series *The Get Along Gang*; new half-hour adventures of *The Popples*, based on the series of dolls and toys created by American Greeting Cards' "Those Characters from Cleveland" division; and *Ulysses 31*, an imported Japanese series following the exploits of the famed Homeric traveler into the 31st century. The latter lasted only 13 weeks and ultimately was replaced in 1987 by *Rainbow Brite*, a half-hour series that was followed by a brace of 1984 and 1985 animated specials, based on characters originally created by Hallmark in 1983. (See individual series entries for further details.)

A DIC Enterprises Production in association with Mattel Toys/Those Characters From Cleveland/Hallmark Cards. Color. Ninety minutes. Premiered: September 1986. Syndicated.

KID KAPERS

One of the first cartoon shows on network weekend television, this 15-minute series consisted of early black-and-white cartoons made for the theaters. Though the content is not known, it is believed the films included Ub Iwerks's *Flip the Frog* and *Willie Whopper* or Paul Terry's silent *Aesop's Fables*.

A worldwide organization of kids struggle to save the environment in the Saturday-morning series Kid Power. © *Rankin-Bass Productions*

An ABC Television Presentation. Black-and-white. Fifteen minutes. Premiered on ABC: October 26, 1952–January 30, 1953.

KID 'N' PLAY

Rappers Christopher "Kid" Reid and Christopher "Play" Martin—best known as the two-man rap music group Kid 'n Play—starred in this short-lived half-hour live-action/animated series in which they played themselves (in live-action wraparounds and rap videos only). The show follows the experiences of two aspiring teen rappers and their neighborhood friends as they get into all sorts of crazy adventures while pursuing their dream of becoming recording stars. The series featured live-action segments in which the famed rappers made fun of themselves, sandwiched between urban animated adventures—involving them, their manager Herbie, Kid's sister Terry and their friends—often conveying prosocial lessons.

A Marvel/Saban Entertainment Production in association with Chriss Cross Inc. and Gordy de Passe Productions. Color. Half-hour. Premiered on NBC: September 8, 1990–September 7, 1991.

Voices
Kid: Christopher Hooks; **Play:** Brian Mitchell; **Lela:** Dawn Lewis; **Marika/Downtown:** Cree Summer Francks; **B.B.:** Rain Pryor; **Pitbull:** J.D. Hall; **Wiz/Hurbie:** Martin Lawrence; **Hairy:** Danny Mann; **Jazzy/Acorn:** Tommy Davidson; **Old Blue:** Dorian Harewood

KID POWER

The Rainbow Club, a worldwide organization of kids from all cultural and ethnic backgrounds, struggles to save the environment and change the world in a positive manner through teamwork, friendship and sharing. Based on cartoonist Morrie Turner's well-known comic strip, *Wee Pals*, the 17-episode series premiered on ABC in 1972, the same year as CBS's *Fat Albert and the Cosby Kids*.

A Rankin-Bass/Videocraft Production. Color. Half-hour. Premiered on ABC: September 16, 1972–September 1, 1974.

Voices
Wellington: Charles Kennedy Jr.; **Oliver:** Jay Silverheels Jr.; **Nipper:** John Gardiner; **Jerry:** Allan Melvin; **Connie:** Carey Wong; **Ralph:** Gary Shapiro; **Sybil:** Michele Johnson; **Diz:** Jeff Thomas; **Albert:** Greg Thomas

THE KID SUPER POWER HOUR WITH SHAZAM

Musical-live action segments of a funky rock group were used to introduce two weekly cartoon adventure series in this hour-long NBC Saturday-morning series: "Hero High," a training school for superheroes, and "Shazam," the exploits of three superheroes—Billy Batson (Shazam), Mary Freeman (Mary Marvel) and Freddy Freeman (Captain Marvel Jr.)—as they battle sinister forces of evil, among them, Sivana and Mr. Mind.

A Filmation Associates Production in association with DC Comics. Color. One hour. Premiered on NBC: September 12, 1981–September 11, 1982.

Voices
HERO HIGH: Captain California: Christopher Hensel; **Gorgeous Gal:** Becky Perle; **Dirty Trixie:** Mayo McCaslin; **Misty Magic:** Jere Fields; **Rex Ruthless:** John Berwick; **Weatherman:** John Greenleaf; **Punk Rock:** John Venocour; **Mr. Sampson:** Alan Oppenheimer; **Miss Grimm:** Erika Scheimer.

SHAZAM!: Billy Batson/Shazam: Burr Middleton; **Mary Freeman/Mary Marvel:** Dawn Jeffery; **Freddie Freeman/Captain Marvel Jr.:** Barry Gordon; **Tawny/Uncle Dudley/Dr. Sivana:** Alan Oppenheimer; **Sterling Morris:** Lou Scheimer; **Narrator:** Norm Prescott

KIMBA, THE WHITE LION

White lion cub Kimba and his friends (Dan'l Baboon, Samson, Pauley Cracker, King Speckle Rex and others) patrol the jungle in order to keep peace in Africa 4,000 years ago in this half-hour syndicated series, originally produced in 1965 by Osamu Tezuka's Mushi Studios in Japan. The Americanized version of the series premiered in the United States in September 1966, distributed by NBC's syndication division, NBC Films. A total of 52 half-hour stories were

Kimba, the lovable white lion cub who patrols the jungle in Africa to keep the peace, fights back in a scene from the popular Japanese action adventure series Kimba the White Lion. (COURTESY: NBC)

produced, followed by a sequel, the 26-episode *Leo the Lion*, which, produced in 1966, did not debut on American television until 1984 on the Christian Broadcasting Network.

A Mushi Studios Production in association with NBC Films. Color. Half-hour. Premiered: September 11, 1966. Syndicated.

Voices
Kimba, the White Lion: Billie Lou Watt

◉ KIMBOO

Set in London, a young African boy, joined by his sidekick parrot, returns to his roots and tells stories about Africa in this British-produced half-hour Saturday-morning series, which aired on Black Entertainment Television. Premiering in 1991, the Parents Choice award-winning program incorporated live-action wraparounds of the show's host introducing that week's animated adventure. Unfortunately, little is known about this production. Network records from the period during which this series was broadcast are skimpy, even as far as the name of company that produced these cartoons.

A Black Entertainment Television Production. Color. Half-hour. Premiered on BET: 1991–1992.

◉ KING ARTHUR AND THE KNIGHTS OF JUSTICE

King Arthur and the Knights of the Round Table are given a new twist in this half-hour animated series, part of the syndicated Sunday-morning cartoon block *Amazin' Adven-*

tures. The real King Arthur has been banished and the powerful Merlin the Magician decides to find a suitable replacement, bringing back a 1990s college quarterback (named Arthur King) and his entire New York Knights football team, to the Middle Ages to save Camelot. The 1992 series debuted on 143 stations in first-run syndication.

A Golden Films/Le Centre Nationale de la Cinematographie Production in association with Bohbot Entertainment. Color. Half-hour. Premiered: September 7, 1992 (part of Amazin' Adventures I). Syndicated.

Voices

Kathleen Barr, Michael Beattie, Jim Byrnes, Gary Chalk, Michael Donovan, Lee Jeffrey, Willow Johnson, Andrew Kabadas, Scott McNeil, Venus Terzo, Mark Wilbreth

◉ KING FEATURES TRILOGY

Designed for flexible programming, this 150-episode half-hour cartoon trilogy featured three comic-strip favorites (in 50 cartoons each) adapted for television: "Beetle Bailey," a numbskull private whose mishaps at Camp Swampy unnerve his less-than-understanding superior, Sgt. Snorkel; "Snuffy Smith," the comic adventures of the moonshining mountain man, his wife, Louisa, and nephew, Jughaid (joined occasionally in guest appearances by hayseed farmer Barney Google), who are constantly at odds with their feuding foe, Clem Cutplug; and "Krazy Kat," the further adventures of the lovable feline and friends Offisa Pup and Ignatz the Mouse.

Al Brodax served as executive producer of the series. The "Beetle Bailey" and "Snuffy Smith" cartoons were directed by Paramount/Famous Studios veteran Seymour Kneitel, while famed Czechoslovakian animator Gene Deitch handled directorial duties for "Krazy Kat."

Although the films were completed in 1962, the series did not make it onto the airwaves until 1963. Prior to the series television run, Paramount released 11 cartoons from the package as theatrical cartoon shorts under the umbrella title of *Comic Kings*. (See Animated Theatrical Cartoon Series entry for details.)

A Paramount Cartoon Studios/King Features Production. Color. Half-hour. Premiered: August 26, 1963, KTLA-TV, Ch. 5., Los Angeles. Syndicated.

Voices

Private Beetle Bailey/General Halftrack: Howard Morris; **Sergeant Snorkel:** Allan Melvin; **Cookie, Beetle's girlfriend:** June Foray; **Krazy Kat:** Penny Phillips; **Ignatz Mouse/Offissa Pup:** Paul Frees; **Snuffy Smith:** Paul Frees; **Barney Google:** Allan Melvin; **Loweezy:** Penny Phillips

◉ THE KING KONG SHOW

American scientist Professor Bond establishes a top research center on the remote island of Mondo in the Java

Sea. His son Bobby becomes friends with the legendary 60-foot jungle beast King Kong, whom the professor feels may be helpful in his research. Instead, the professor, daughter Susan and Bobby battle the diabolical Dr. Who, an evil scientist who plans to capture Kong for sinister designs.

Other cartoons included the adventures of a U.S. government agent, "Tom of T.H.U.M.B." (Tiny Humans Underground Military Bureau), and his Oriental assistant, Swinging Jack. The program originally debuted in prime time with a one-hour preview special featuring two half-hour episodes. (See Animated Television Specials for detail.)

The 24-episode Saturday-morning series—which premiered on ABC in September of 1966—was heralded as the "first" network cartoon series made in Japan expressly for American television.

A *Rankin-Bass Production with Videocraft International. Color. Half-hour. Premiered on ABC: September 10, 1966– August 31, 1969.*

☺ KING LEONARDO AND HIS SHORT SUBJECTS

King Leonardo, the ruler of Bongo Congo, and his loyal skunk companion Odie Cologne (whose principal foes are Itchy Brother and Biggie Rat) headlined this popular Saturday-morning entry. Also featured were the adventures of "Tooter Turtle," a mild-mannered turtle who is transported back in time through feats of legerdemain performed by his friend Mr. Wizard, and "The Hunter," a bumbling bloodhound detective who, under the command of Officer Flim Flanagan, is outwitted by a wily con-artist, the Fox. Sponsored by General Mills, the series also included an additional component: the adventures of Twinkles the Elephant, who wiggles out of difficulties using his magic trunk, produced as tie-ins to General Mills breakfast cereals and narrated by George S. Irving. (The latter was edited from television prints later offered for syndication.) Originally created to fill a Saturday-morning time slot on NBC left vacant by the cancellation of Hanna-Barbera's *Ruffy and Reddy, King Leonardo and His Short Subjects* debuted on NBC in 1960 and lasted three seasons. The series was later syndicated under the title of *King and Odie.*

A *Leonardo TV Production with Total TV Productions. Color. Half-hour. Premiered on NBC: October 15, 1960–September 28, 1963. Syndicated (as King and Odie).*

Voices
King Leonardo/Odie Cologne/Biggie Rat/Itchy Brother: Jackson Beck; **Mr. Tooter:** Allen Swift; **Mr. Wizard:** Frank Milano; **The Hunter:** Kenny Delmar; **The Fox:** Ben Stone

☺ KING OF THE HILL

In the fictitious suburb of Arlen, Texas, a beer-drinking, car-fixing, mind-your-own-business propane salesman, Hank Hill, and his dysfunctional blue-collar, middle-class family (wife Peggy, 12-year-old son Bobby and niece Luanne), neighbors (Dale and Nancy Gribble) and friends (divorced army sergeant Bill Dauterive and ladies' man Boomhauer) poke fun at life in the slow lane and the world of pickups, trailers and supermarket busybodies in this half-hour animated series, created by *Beavis and Butt-Head* creator Mike Judge and former *Simpsons* producer Greg Daniels. (His first-ever prime-time network series, Judge came up with the idea in 1995, thinking up the name Hank Hill at the last minute before heading to the pitch meeting with Fox Network executives.)

Brought in as a midseason replacement, the series premiered on the Fox Network in January of 1997 as a lead-in to *The Simpsons*, winning its time slot 10 of 11 weeks and becoming the second-highest-rated new show of the 1997 season, trailing only NBC's *Suddenly Susan*. The series ended up pumping new life into *The Simpsons*, whose ratings had dropped significantly due to the loss of the hit sit-com *Married . . . With Children* as its lead-in. In 1997 the program earned its first Emmy Award nomination for Outstanding Animated Children's Program.

A *Klasky Csupo Production. Color. Half-hour. Premiered on FOX: January 12, 1997.*

Voices
Hank Hill/Boomhauer/Dooley: Mike Judge; **Peggy Hill:** Kathy Najimy; **Bobby Hill:** Pamela Segall; **Luanne Platter/Joseph Gribble:** Brittany Murphy; **Dale Gribble:** Johnny Hardwick; **Nancy Gribble:** Ashley Gardner; **Bill Dauterive:** Stephen Root

☺ KISSYFUR

Kissyfur, an eight-year-old bear cub, along with his circus father, Gus, escape from civilization to begin life anew deep in a swamp populated by other animals—some good, some bad—living simple lives untouched by human influence in this 26-episode half-hour Saturday-morning series. The series aired for two seasons on NBC, though not consecutively. The show was canceled after the 1986–87 season, then brought back with new episodes for the 1988–89 season. The first season's episodes included four 1985 specials that were simply repeated: *Kissyfur: Bear Roots, Kissyfur: The Birds and the Bears, Kissyfur: The Lady Is a Chump* and *Kissyfur: We Are the Swamp.* (See Animated Television Specials entries for details).

An *NBC Production in association with DIC Enterprises. Color. Half-hour. Premiered on NBC: September 13, 1986–September 5, 1987; September 10, 1988–August 25, 1990.*

Voices

Kissyfur: R.J. Williams, Max Meier; **Gus, Kissyfur's father:** Edmund Gilbert; **Beehonie, a rabbit:** Russi Taylor; **Duane, a persnickety pig:** Neilson Ross; **Stuckey, the porcupine:** Stuart M. Rosen; **Toot, a young beaver:** Devon Feldman, Russi Taylor; **Floyd, the alligator:** Stuart M. Rosen; **Jolene, the alligator:** Terrence McGovern; **Miss Emmy Lou, the schoolmarm:** Russi Taylor; **Cackle Sister/Bessie:** Russi Taylor; **Lenny/Charles:** Lennie Weinrib; **Uncle Shelby/Howie/Claudette:** Frank Welker; **Ralph:** Susan Silo

◉ KLUTTER

Unable to have a real family pet because their newspaper-editor father is allergic to everything from dogs to pet rocks, siblings Ryan and Wade zap a pile of junk under their bunk bed, bringing to life this homemade exuberant creature who wreaks domestic havoc in a series of six half-hour cartoons that aired as a component of Saturday morning's *Eek! Stravaganza* series on the Fox Network in the fall of 1995.

A Film Roman/Savage Studios Ltd. Production in association with Fox Children's Productions. Color. Half-hour. Premiered on FOX: September 9, 1995–September 5, 1997.

Voices

Ryan Heap: Cam Clark; **Wade Heap:** Savage Steven Holland; **Sandee Heap:** Sandy Fox; **Andrea Heap:** Kathy Ireland; **John Heap:** David Silverman; **Klutter:** Kirk Thatcher; **Vanna:** Halle Standford; **Mel, Vann's dad:** Dan Castellaneta; **Nel, Vann's mom:** Amy Heckerling; **Kopp:** Kirk Thatcher

◉ THE KWICKY KOALA SHOW

Cartoon legend Tex Avery developed this series—his last animated production—starring a sweet and superspeedy koala bear, reminiscent of his character Droopy, who becomes entangled in numerous misadventures with the wily but hapless Wilford Wolf. The program featured three additional weekly cartoon segments: "Crazy Claws," a whirlwind wildcat whose snappy one-liners are his only defense against the schemes of Rawhide Clyde; "Dirty Dawg," the con-artist canine of the garbage dump, joined by alley mate Ratso the rodent; and "The Bungle Brothers," two beagles (George and Joey) trying desperately to break into show business, seen in three one-minute segments per show. Avery, whose comedic visual gags created a new dimension in cartoons, worked his last two years of his life at Hanna-Barbera Productions until his death in 1980. The series was later rebroadcast on the Cartoon Network.

A Hanna-Barbera Production. Color. Half-hour. Premiered on CBS: September 12, 1981–September 11, 1982. Rebroadcast on CAR: October 2, 1992–January 1, 1993 (weekdays); January 10, 1993–September 19, 1993 (Sundays).

Voices

Kwicky Koala: Robert Allen Ogle; **Wilfred Wolf:** John Stephenson; **Dirty Dawg:** Frank Welker; **Ratso:** Marshall Efron; **Crazy Claws:** Jim MacGeorge; **Rawhide Clyde:** Robert Allen Ogle; **Bristletooth:** Peter Cullen; **Ranger Rangerfield:** Michael Bell; **George:** Michael Bell; **Joey:** Allen Melvin

◉ LADY LOVELYLOCKS AND THE PIXIETAILS

Set in the mystical Land of Lovelylocks, this action/adventure fairy tale centers on the life of a young ruler who learns the lessons of life and the ways of the world, joined by her worthy aides, The Pixietails (Pixiebeauty, Pixiesparkle and Pixieshine), while struggling against the evil workings of Duchess Ravenwaves, who seeks to take over her realm. The 20-episode first-run syndicated series was developed by American Greetings Cards' "Those Characters from Cleveland" division, the same people who introduced *Care Bears*.

A DIC Enterprises Production in association with Those Characters from Cleveland and Mattel. Color. Half-hour. Premiered: September 1987. Syndicated.

Voices

Lady Lovelylocks: Tony St. Vincent; **Duchess Ravenwaves:** Louise Vallance; **Maiden Fairhair/Snags:** Jeanine Elias; **Lady Curlycrown:** Louise Vallance; **Comb Gnome, the nasty gnome:** Danny Mann; **Strongheart/Prince (as dog):** Danny Mann; **Shining Glory/Hairbell/Tanglet:** Brian George

The Pixietails

Pixiesparkle: Tony St. Vincent; **Pixiebeauty:** Jeanine Elias; **Pixieshine:** Brian George

◉ LASSIE'S RESCUE RANGERS

Jack Wrather's famed TV collie roams the Rocky Mountains under the guidance of the Turner family who, along with Lassie and the forest animals, organize a "Forest Force" rescue team in this half-hour Saturday-morning series, originally broadcast on ABC in 1973.

Production teams from Filmation and Rankin-Bass were behind the weekly series, which borrowed artwork and characters previously seen on the 1972 ABC Saturday Superstar Movie *Lassie and the Spirit of Thunder Mountain*. Stories depicted Lassie and the group's attempts to save the already damaged environment. Actor Ted Knight, (a.k.a. anchorman Ted Baxter on TV's *The Mary Tyler Moore Show*) provided the voice of Ben Turner, the patriarch of the Turner family and head of the Forest Force, and was also the series' narrator. Two other series characters were voiced by three of the offspring of director Hal Sutherland and producer Lou Scheimer.

A Filmation Studios/Rankin-Bass Production in association with Wrather Productions. Color. Half-hour. Premiered on ABC: September 8, 1973–August 31, 1974. Rebroadcast on ABC: September 8, 1974–August 31, 1975.

Voices
Narrator: Ted Knight; **Lassie:** Herself; **Ben Turner:** Ted Knight; **Laura Turner:** Jane Webb; **Jackie Turner:** Lane Scheimer, Keith Sutherland; **Susan Turner:** Erika Scheimer; **Ben Turner Jr./Gene Fox:** Hal Harvey

Ⓢ LAUREL AND HARDY

Temperamental Oliver Hardy (the rotund one) always found himself in "another fine mess" when he and his whining, dimwitted friend, thin Stan Laurel, got together. This basic premise became the recurring theme of a cartoon version of the comic pair, coproduced by Larry Harmon, creator of Bozo the Clown, and Hanna-Barbera Productions, which also produced a series of Abbott and Costello cartoons. With both comedians deceased, the voices of Stan and Ollie were re-created by Harmon and voice-artist Jim MacGeorge. The series, consisting of 130 five-minute color cartoons, debuted in syndication one year after Stan Laurel's death in the fall of 1966.

A Hanna-Barbera Production for Wolper Productions and Larry Harmon Pictures. Color. Half-hour. Premiere: 1966. Syndicated.

Voices
Stan Laurel: Larry Harmon; **Oliver Hardy:** Jim MacGeorge

Ⓢ LAVERNE AND SHIRLEY IN THE ARMY

Prime time's hit characters Laverne DeFazio and Shirley Feeny from the popular sitcom *Laverne and Shirley* become privates in the army, where all efforts to instill some military discipline into these two goof-ups fail.

A Hanna-Barbera Production in association with Paramount Pictures Corporation. Laverne and Shirley © 1981 Paramount Pictures Corporation. All material besides Laverne and Shirley © 1981 Hanna-Barbera Productions Inc. Color. Half-hour. Premiered on ABC: October 10, 1981–September 18, 1982.

Voices
Laverne: Penny Marshall; **Shirley:** Cindy Williams; **Sgt. Turnbuckle:** Ken Mars; **Squealy, his pet pig:** Ron Palillo

Ⓢ LAVERNE AND SHIRLEY WITH THE FONZ

Laverne and Shirley's adventures in the army continue, this time with the ever-cool Fonz (voiced by actor Henry Win-

kler, who played the character in the popular sitcom *Happy Days*), now a chief mechanic for the army's motor pool. Fonzie and his sidekick dog, Mr. Cool, add to the laughs and the messed-up missions in this half-hour comedy/adventure that premiered as part of the hour-long block *The Mork and Mindy/Laverne and Shirley/Fonz Hour* on ABC in 1982. The network programmed the series back to back with Ruby-Spears's half-hour animated *Mork and Mindy* series. Repeated were episodes from 1981's *Laverne and Shirley in the Army*, in addition to all-new episodes with the Fonz (voiced by Henry Winkler). Citing contract problems, Cindy Williams, the original Shirley in the live-action comedy series and the animated spinoff, was replaced by actress Lynn Marie Stewart. (See *The Mork and Mindy/Laverne and Shirley/Fonz Hour* for voice credits.)

A Hanna-Barbera Production in association with Paramount Pictures Corporation. Color. Half-hour. Premiered on ABC: September 25, 1982–September 3, 1983.

Ⓢ LAZER TAG ACADEMY

Thirteen-year-old Jamie Jaren returns to the present from the world of the future and, with the help of two young ancestors and the family's special powers, stops the villainous time-traveler Silas Mayhem from changing the course of history in this short-lived Saturday-morning science-fiction series, originally produced for NBC. Redubbed *Lazer Patrol*, the series was rebroadcast for three seasons on the Sci-Fi Channel's *Cartoon Quest*.

A Ruby-Spears Enterprises Production in association with Alchemy II/Worlds of Wonder Inc. Color. Half-hour. Premiered on NBC: September 13, 1986–August 22, 1987. Rebroadcast on SCI: September 18, 1993–September 10, 1996.

Voices
Jamie Jaren: Noelle Harling; **Draxon Drear:** Booker Bradshaw; **Beth Jaren:** Christina McGregor; **Tom Jaren:** Billy Jacoby; **Nicky Jaren:** R.J. Williams; **Andrew Jaren/Skugg:** Frank Welker; **Genna Jaren:** Tress MacNeille; **Professor Olanga:** Sid McCoy; **Charlie/Skugg:** Pat Fraley; **Other Voices:** Susan Blu

Ⓢ THE LEGEND OF CALAMITY JANE

Wild West's Calamity Jane rides again in search of truth and justice using her wits and her whip to aid the downtrodden, while encountering other shoot-'em-up legends along the way—Wyatt Earp, Doc Holliday, Wild Bill Hickok and Buffalo Bill Cody—in this short-lived animated adventure series produced for the WB Network. Premiering in September of 1997, the series lasted only three weeks before the network dropped it. Film actress Jennifer Jason Leigh was to have provided the voice of Calamity Jane. Barbara Scaff, an American actress living in Paris, instead took her place.

A Contree-Allee/Gangster/Warner Brothers Television Animation Production. Color. Half-hour. Premiered on WB: September 13, 1997–September 27, 1997.

Voices
Calamity Jane: Barbara Scaff; **Wild Bill Hickok:** Clancy Brown; **Joe Presto:** Frank Welker; **Lonely Sue:** Miriam Flynn; **Quanna Parker:** Michael Horse; **Captain John O'Rourke:** Tim Matheson; **Bill Doolin:** Mark Rolston

⊚ THE LEGEND OF PRINCE VALIANT

Called to Camelot by King Arthur, Prince Valiant is joined by a peasant (Arn) and the blacksmith's daughter (Rowanne) in their quest to become Knights of the Round Table, beset by trouble along the way, in this half-hour adventure series and first original cartoon series for The Family Channel. Originally scheduled to debut in January 1992, network executives, after viewing some of the finished episodes and pleased by the results, moved up the series premiere to September 1991. The series aired Tuesday nights in prime time, and 26 episodes were produced for the first season. Entering its second season in the fall of 1992, the series returned on Friday nights. New adventures explored issues of triumph and failure, love and hate, family honor and friendship as the hero, Prince Valiant, comes of age.

In 1993, returning a third season, 39 additional episodes were produced and the series was shifted to a Monday-through-Friday time slot. In 1994 the series aired (in reruns) Saturday mornings. Two feature-length compilations, based on the series, were also produced for the network: 1991's *Prince Valiant: The Voyage of Camelot* and 1992's *Prince Valiant: Knight of the Round Table.*

Actors Mark Hamill (star of the Oscar-winning *Star Wars* trilogy), Noel Harrison (son of legendary actor Sir Rex Harrison), Fred Savage (of TV's *Wonder Years*) and Harry Hamlin (from NBC's Emmy Award–winning series *L.A. Law*) were among celebrity guest voices to be featured in episodes of the series.

A Hearst Entertainment/IDDH Groupe Bruno Rene Huchez/Polyphonfilmund Fernschgesellschaft mbH/Sei Young Studios Production in association with King Features and The Family Channel. Color. Half-hour. Premiered on FAM: September 3, 1991–May 10, 1992; October 10, 1993–May 13, 1994.

Voices
Prince Valiant: Robby Benson; **Arn:** Michael Horton; **King Arthur:** Efrem Zimbalist Jr.; **Guinevere:** Samantha Eggar; **Merlin the Magician:** Alan Oppenheimer; **Sir Gawain:** Tim Curry; **Rowanne:** Noelle North

⊚ THE LEGEND OF WHITE FANG: THE ANIMATED SERIES

HBO kicked off the 1994–95 season with two original animated series, each airing on Saturday mornings. First up was this 26-part action/adventure series, based on the Klondike adventures of author Jack London's part-wolf, part-husky hero who was befriended by a 12-year-old girl (Wendy Scott) during the Gold Rush days of the 1890s. Each episode promoted concerns for the environment and offered lessons in life with morals that young viewers could understand easily. Produced by Canadian animation giant Cinar Films, the half-hour series preceded another Cinar-owned property, *The Real Story of. . .,* a series.

A Cinar Films/Crayon Animation/France Animation Production. Color. Half-hour. Premiered on HBO: January 1, 1994.

Voices
White Fang: Mark Hellman; **Wendy Scott:** Patricia Rodriguez; **Beauty Smith:** Michael Rudder; **Matt Laberge:** Rick Jones; **Sgt. Oakes:** Pierre Lenoir; **Alex de Laslo/Weedon Scott:** Terrence Scammel; **Raven Moon:** Neil Shee

⊚ THE LEGEND OF ZELDA

Based on the celebrated Nintendo video game, this fantasy/adventure series stars a 15-year-old adventurer (Nick) and a princess of the same age (Zelda), who fight monsters, ghosts and icky creatures while trying to save the kingdom of Hyrule from the dark depredations of the evil wizard Ganon. The series debuted in syndication in 1989 as part of the *Super Mario Brothers Super Show.* Episodes were later repeated on another Nintendo-inspired aimated series, 1990's *Captain N and the Super Mario Brothers,* produced for NBC. (See *Super Mario Brothers Show* for voice credits.)

A DIC Enterprises Production in association with Nintendo of America Incorporated. Color. Half-hour. Premiered: September 1989. Syndicated.

⊚ LEO THE LION

This sequel to NBC's *Kimba, the White Lion* was created by Kimba's originator, Osamu Tezuka, and originally produced in 1966. Unlike the first series, however, the character was not called Kimba—he was named Leo instead—and he was cast as an adult and the father of two cubs, who rule the jungle with him and his mate, Kitty. Only 26 episodes were made in the series, which was originally broadcast on Japanese television. In 1984, 18 years after it was originally produced, the series made its American television debut on CBN (Christian Broadcasting Network).

A Mushi/Sonic International Production. Color. Half-hour. Premiered on CBN: 1984.

LIFE WITH LOUIE

Eight-year-old Louie experiences the various trials and joys of growing up with his middle-class family while observing an adult world from a child's perspective in this weekly half-hour series based on the routines of stand-up comic Louie Anderson. Introduced to viewers in the fall of 1995 on the Fox Network, the series was preceded by a fully animated half-hour Christmas special, *Life with Louie: A Christmas Surprise for Mrs. Stillman*, which aired in December of 1994, also on Fox. The special was Fox's highest-rated, non-*Simpsons* animated show of the season.

A Hyperion Animation Production. Color. Half-hour. Premiered on FOX: September 9, 1995.

Voices
Little Louie/Andy Anderson, his father/Narrator: Louie Anderson; **Ora Anderson, Louie's mother:** Edie McClurg; **Tommy:** Miko Hughes; **Mike Grunewald/Glen Glenn:** Justin Shenkarow; **Jeannie Harper:** Debi Derryberry; **Other Voices:** Olivia Hack

LINUS THE LIONHEARTED

Three major stars—Jonathan Winters, Sterling Holloway, Carl Reiner—and Sheldon Leonard lent their voices to characters derived from the boxes of Post cereals (produced by General Mills) and brought to life in this weekly Saturday-morning series. The 26-episode series—which debuted on CBS in 1964—revolved around the adventures of Linus the Lionhearted, the frail, docile ruler of the kingdom of animals in Africa, who first appeared on the boxes of Crispy Critters. His costars, Lovable Truly, the postman, and So-Hi, a small Chinese boy, were used to sell Alphabets and Sugar Crinkles. A third character, Sugar Bear, became famous on boxes of Post Cereals Sugar Crisp.

Not everyone bowed to Linus's command, however. His not-so-loyal subjects–also the custodians of the royal cornfields—were Rory Raccoon, Sascha Grouse, Dinny Kangaroo and Billie Bird. Linus, Sugar Bear, Lovable Truly, Rory Raccoon and So-Hi appeared weekly in their own adventures, with the entire cast spotlighted in episodes termed "The Company."

An Ed Graham/Format Films Production. Color. Half-hour. Premiered on CBS: September 26, 1964–September 3, 1966. Rebroadcast on ABC: September 25, 1966–September 7, 1969. Syndicated.

Voices
Linus: Sheldon Leonard; **Lovable Truly:** Sterling Holloway; **So-Hi:** Jonathan Winters; **Sugar Bear:** Sterling Holloway; **Billie Bird:** Ed Graham; **Sascha Grouse/Dinny Kangaroo/Rory Raccoon:** Carl Reiner; **The Japanese Giant:** Jonathan Winters

THE LION KING'S TIMON AND PUMBAA

The popular meercat-warthog comedy duo, who coined the "hakuna matata" credo (which means "no worries") in the 1994 box-office hit *The Lion King*, experience all-new adventures as they travel the globe—to Antarctica, the Swiss Alps, the Mayan ruins and beyond—in this weekly, half-hour cartoon series adaptation. Joining them were other characters from the movie in their own segments: Rafiki, the sagelike baboon; the hyenas; and the sneaky henchman Scar. Also featured in episodic adventures were several new characters: the Vulture Police; Timon's meerkat cousin, Fred; and an obnoxious, multipurposed foil named Quint. Nathan Lane and Ernie Sabella reprised their roles as Timon and Pumbaa in the series. (Lane shared time with Quinton Flynn, also as the voice of Timon.) In the fall of 1997, previously broadcast episodes began rerunning on The Disney Channel.

A Walt Disney Television Animation Production. Color. Half-hour. Premiered: September 8, 1995–August 25, 1997 (syndicated); CBS: September 16, 1995–March 29, 1997. Rebroadcast on DIS: September 1997.

Voices
Timon: Nathan Lane, Quinton Flynn; **Pumbaa:** Ernie Sabella; **Pumbaa Jr.:** Nancy Cartwright; **Rafiki:** Robert Guillaume; **Quint:** Corey Burtion; **Fred:** S. Scott Bullock; **Vulture Police:** Townsend Coleman, Brian Cummings

LIPPY THE LION

Hanna-Barbera, who created the likes of Huckleberry Hound and Yogi Bear, produced this first-run syndicated series of outlandish jungle misadventures, pairing a con-artist lion (Lippy) with a sorrowful but pessimistic hyena (Hardy Har Har). The series' 52 five-minute cartoons were offered to local stations as part of a trilogy called *The Hanna-Barbera New Cartoon Series*, featuring two other cartoon adventures, *Touché Turtle* and *Wally Gator*. Although the films were sold to television stations as a package, the cartoons often were programmed independently of each other in their own half-hour time slots.

A Hanna-Barbera Production. Color. Half-hour. Premiered: September 3, 1962. Syndicated.

Voices
Lippy: Daws Butler; **Hardy Har Har:** Mel Blanc

LIQUID TELEVISION

First produced as interstitial programming—a brace of animated logos and bumpers inserted between rock videos and other programs—MTV inaugurated this expanded, half-hour showcase and the music cable network's first animated variety series, combining cutting-edge animation, over-the-edge graphics and stories from beyond the fringe. Each episode featured a fluid blend of original and acquired animation, animated versions of underground comics, stories featuring live actors in action settings and short films of any description, packaged in collaboration with Britain's BBC and produced by Prudence Fenton, who produced award-winning station I.D.'s for the popular music cable network. Although animation production values varied on each program, the series became one of the tube's finer animation showcases.

Premiering in June of 1991, the first half-hour included Bardal Animation Coloring House's "Lea Press-on Limbs," directed by Chris Miller; "Art School Girls of Doom" (directed by El Noyes; written by Dan Leo; produced by Mark Reusch); "Ms. Lidia's Makeoever (directed by and written by Gordon Clark); "Invisible Hands" (written and designed by Richard Sala); and Mike McKenna and Bob Sabiston's "Grinning Evil Death."

During the first season, serialized segments included: "Aeon Flux" (later adapted into a series of its own), chronicling the adventures of a female secret agent extraordinare; "Stick Figure Theatre," bringing to life scenes from classic movies and television shows; and "Winter Steele," the story of a tough motorcycle babe in search of action. In September of 1992, for the series' second season, new serialized segments were added, namely: "Dog Boy," the misadventures of a boy with a dog's heart; "The Adventures of Thomas and Nardo," the story of a talking, walking insect-eating tenement building; and "Billy & Bobby," the tale of two normal all-American boys gone haywire.

That September "Frog Baseball," an animated short created by Mike Judge featuring two suburban misfits named Bobby and Billy (Beavis and Butt-Head in their original form), debuted. Shortly thereafter, Judge signed a 65 episode contract with MTV to create a Beavis & Butt-Head series.

In 1993 the series was nominated for a daytime Emmy Award for Outstanding Animated Program.

A Colossal Pictures/BBC/MTV Production. Color. Half-hour. Premiered on MTV: June 1991.

◎ LITTL'BITS

A pack of fun-loving, adventuruous inch-tall elves—Snoozabit, Lillabit, Williebit and Snagglebit—maintain peace, love and harmony in the Foothill Forest while coping in a world designed for humans in this 26-episode half-hour series, first released in Japan, then redubbed in English on Nickelodeon.

A Tatsunoko Productions Co. Ltd./Saban Entertainment Production. Color. Half-hour. Premiered on NIK: May 1, 1991–April 30, 1995.

Voices

Arthur Grosser, Dean Hagopian, A.J. Henderson, Arthur Holden, Rick Jones, Liz MacRae, Walter Massey, Anik Matern, Terrence Scammel, Jane Woods

◎ LITTLE CLOWNS OF HAPPYTOWN

The inhabitants of a small fantasy town (called Itty Bitty City) are all born clowns and their goal in life is to spread the message that "happiness is good for you" in this weekly half-hour series, originally broadcast on ABC.

An ABC Entertainment Production in association with Marvel Productions and Murakami-Wolf-Swenson Films. Color. Half-hour. Premiered on ABC: September 26, 1987–July 16, 1988. Rebroadcast on FAM: 1989–1990.

Voices

Charlie Adler, Sue Blu, Danny Cooksey, Pat Fraley, Ellen Gerstell, Howard Morris, Ron Palillo, Josh Rodine, Frank Welker

◎ LITTLE DRACULA

Unlike his famous Transylvanian father, young Drac prefers to sink his teeth into rock 'n' roll and surfing, with his bizarre family, friends and foes, in this half-hour, five-part miniseries adapted from the popular British children's book character of the same name. In September of 1991 the series aired for one week on the Fox Network.

A Hahn Productions/Island Animation Production. Color. Half-hour. Premiered on FOX: September 3, 1991–September 7, 1991.

Voices

Little Dracula: Edan Gross; **Big Dracula:** Joe Flaherty; **Mrs. Dracula/Millicent:** Kath Soucie; **Werebunny:** Joey Camen; **Garlic Man:** Brian Cummings; **Deadwood:** Melvyn Hayes; **No Eyes/Twin-Beaks:** Danny Mann; **Maggot:** Neil Ross; **Hannah the Barbarian:** Fran Ryan; **Igor/Granny:** Jonathan Winters

◎ THE LITTLE LULU SHOW

Tracey Ullman initially lent her voice as the girl in the signature red dress and corkscrew curls who proves that girls are just as good as boys in all-new, half-hour animated adventures, based on stories from the original 1935 comic strip. Each half-hour program featured three "Lulutoons," reuniting Lulu with characters from the comic strip: sailor-capped Tubby Tompkins; buck-toothed Annie; whiny little Alvin and the rest of the ageless crew. Given a six-week test run on HBO on Sunday nights in October 1995, the series was renewed for a full second season, featuring brand-new episodes and a new actor playing the part of Lulu. Tracey

Ullman left the series after the first six episodes. Voice actress Jane Woods assumed the role thereafter.

A Cinar Production in association with Western Publishing Company, HBO and CTV Television Network. Color. Half-hour. Premiered on HBO: October 22, 1995.

Voices
Little Lulu: Tracey Ullman (episodes 1–6), Jane Woods (episodes 7–26); **Tubby:** Bruce Dinsmore; **Annie:** Michael Caloz; **Alvin:** Ajay Fry; **Iggie:** Jane Woods; **Willie:** Andrew Henry; **Mrs. Moppet:** Pauline Little; **Wilbur:** Jacob B. Tierney; **Gloria:** Angelina Bolvin

⊚ LITTLE MERMAID

(See DISNEY'S THE LITTLE MERMAID; SABAN'S ADVENTURE OF THE LITTLE MERMAID FANTASY.)

⊚ THE LITTLE RASCALS/ RICHIE RICH SHOW

The classic fun and humor of the *Our Gang* short-subject series is recaptured in this animated comedy/mystery series, featuring Spanky, Alfalfa, Darla, Buckwheat and their dog Pete, in new episodes combined with episodes originally broadcast on 1982's *The Pac-Man/Little Rascals/Richie Rich Show.* From their funky treehouse, they plan new schemes and plots that send their adversaries into submission in hilarious fashion. The series was paired with all-new episodes (including reruns from the previous show) of the world's richest youngster, Richie Rich.

A Hanna-Barbera Production in association with King Features Entertainment. Color. Half-hour. Premiered on ABC: September 10, 1983–September 1, 1984.

Voices

THE LITTLE RASCALS: Spanky: Scott Menville; **Alfalfa/Porky/Woim:** Julie McWhirter Dees; **Darla:** Patty Maloney; **Buckwheat:** Shavar Ross; **Butch/Waldo:** B.J. Ward; **Pete, the dog/Police Officer Ed:** Peter Cullen.

RICHIE RICH: Richie Rich: Sparky Marcus; **George Rich, his father:** Stanley Jones; **Mrs. Rich, his mother:** Joan Gerber; **Dollar, Richie's dog:** Frank Welker; **Gloria, Richie's girlfriend:** Nancy Cartwright; **Freckles, Richie's friend:** Christian Hoff; **Irona, the Rich's maid:** Joan Gerber; **Cadbury, the Rich's butler:** Stanley Jones; **Professor Keenbean:** Bill Callaway; **Reggie Van Goh:** Dick Beals

⊚ LITTLE ROSEY

Emmy award–winning comedienne Roseanne Arnold created this half-hour animated series (and served as executive producer with then-husband Tom Arnold) featuring her as a 10-year-old teen who finds adventure in fantasy and real life with her family and friends—her sister Tess, her brother Tater and her best friend, Buddy. Arnold did not supply the voice of her own character in the series (it was provided by actress Kathleen Laskey), which premiered on ABC in 1991, home of her long-running comedy series, *Roseanne.* The comedienne was known to have clashed with network executives over series content—reportedly over their wanting her to "put more boys" into the show, which Arnold adamantly resisted (believing it would result in an increase in violence in each show). Arnold got back at the network for its interference when she financed and produced with Tom Arnold a follow-up half-hour, prime-time animated special, *The Rosey and Buddy Show,* in which network executives were portrayed to look as if they cared only about "money and not children." Strangely, the special aired on ABC.

A Little Rosey Production in association with Nelvana Enterprises. Color. Half-hour. Premiered on ABC: September 8, 1990–August 13, 1991.

Voices
Little Rosey: Kathleen Laskey; **Buddy:** Noam Zylberman; **Tess:** Pauline Gillis; **Nanny/Tater:** Lisa Yamanaka; **Mom:** Judy Marshak; **Dad:** Tony Daniels; **Jeffrey/Matthew:** Stephen Bednarski

⊚ THE LITTLES

These tiny, near-human creatures, who live behind the walls of people's houses, are discovered by a normal-size young boy (Henry Bigg), the son of a globetrotting scientist, who joins them in many of their adventures in this half-hour series, adapted from John Peterson's popular Scholastic children's book series. Produced two years after the success of another cartoon series about tiny people, NBC's *The Smurfs,* the series enjoyed a successful three-season run on ABC.

An ABC Entertainment/DIC Enterprises/Tetsuo Katayama Production. Color. Half-hour. Premiered on ABC: September 10, 1983–September 6, 1986.

Voices
Henry Bigg, the young boy: Jimmy E. Keegan; **George Bigg/Dinky:** Robert David Hall; **Mrs. Bigg:** Laurel Page; **Tom Little:** Donavan Freberg; **Lucy Little:** Bettina Bush; **Grandpa:** Alvy Moore; **Ashley:** B.J. Ward; **Slick:** Patrick Fraley

⊚ LITTLE SHOP

Inspired by the 1986 musical film remake of Roger Corman's classic 1961 black comedy, *Little Shop of Horrors,* this half-hour animated series was a toned-down musical spinoff featuring the comical exploits of the primary characters from both movies: Mushnick, the deviled florist; his nerdy assistant Seymour; Seymour's girlfriend Audrey; and even the talking, people-eating plant Audrey, but differently cast from previous efforts. In the cartoon series of offbeat adventures, Seymour and Audrey are teenagers (with Seymour raising the carnivorous talking plant); Mushnick plays Audrey's father; and Audrey Junior loves to sing rap instead of craving live flesh. Debuting on the Fox Network in 1991, the series was subsequently rebroadcast on the Sci-Fi Channel's "Cartoon Quest."

A Marvel Films/Saban Entertainment Production. Color. Half-hour. Premiered on FOX: September 7, 1991–September 5, 1992. Rebroadcast on SCI: September 18, 1993–September 10, 1996.

Voices

Harvey Atkins, David Huban, Tamar Lee, Roland "Buddy" Lewis, Marlo Vola

Singing Voices

Junior Rap: Terry McGee; **Seymour:** Jana Lexxa; **Audrey:** Jennie Kwan; **Paine:** Mark Ryan Martin; **Mushnick:** Michael Rawls

◉ LITTLEST PET SHOP

A group of cantankerous pets (from Stu the sheepdog to Chloe the cat), mysteriously reduced to teeny-weeny size, experience a series of madcap adventures after they are sold to unwitting pet shop customers by the store's eccentric owner/operator Elwood Funk, only to keep sneaking back to his "Littlest Pet Shop," in this 40-episode half-hour syndicated series, coproduced by U.S.-based Sunbow Entertainment in 1995.

A Sunbow Production in association with Claster Television. Color. Half-hour. Premiered: (week of) September 11, 1995. Syndicated.

Voices

Viv: Lynda Boyd; **Sarge:** Gary Chalk; **Chloe:** Babs Chula; **Squeaks:** Tel Cole; **Elwood:** Ian James Corlett; **Stu:** Mike Donovan; **Delilah:** Shirley Milliner; **Rookie:** Sarah Strange; **Chet:** Lee Tockar

◉ LITTLE WIZARDS

Aided by three tiny helpers, Boo, Winkle and Gump, a young boy-prince, Prince Dexter, seeks to regain his kingdom from his powerful uncle, King Renwick, in this magical half-hour fantasy/adventure series, first telecast on ABC.

A Marvel Production in association with Janson and Menville Productions. Color. Half-hour. Premiered on ABC: September 26, 1987–September 3, 1988.

Voices

Charlie Adler, Joey Camen, Peter Cullen, Katie Leigh, Danny Mann, Scott Menville, Amber Souza, Frank Welker

◉ LONE RANGER

The noted avenger of evil and upholder of justice, also known as the Masked Man, and his faithful Indian companion, Tonto, battle villainous cowboys, cutthroats and ruthless land barons of the Old West in this 26-episode half-hour series that aired weekly on CBS. The series was the first animated version of the popular radio and television series character, originally created for radio in 1933 by George W. Trendle and Frank Striker for Trendle's Detroit radio station WXYZ. The Saturday-morning series, featuring three brief adventures per episode, premiered opposite ABC's *The Beatles* in 1966. The series was canceled three years later. In 1980 Filmation produced a new series of cartoons as part of its *The Tarzan/Lone Ranger Adventure Hour*, also for CBS.

A Lone Ranger Production in association with the Jack Wrather Corporation. Color. Half-hour. Premiered on CBS: September 10, 1966–September 6, 1969.

Voices

Lone Ranger: Michael Rye; **Tonto:** Shepard Menken: **Etcetera:** Marvin Miller, Hans Conried; **Warlock:** Marvin Miller; **Tiny Tom:** Richard Beals; **Black Widow:** Agnes Moorehead

Noted upholder of justice the Lone Ranger and faithful companion Tonto get ready for trouble in a scene from The Lone Ranger *cartoon series. © Lone Ranger Productions*

LONG AGO & FAR AWAY

Hosted by actor James Earl Jones, this weekly dramatic series captured the magic of storytelling for children as well as adults, featuring mostly award-winning animated and some live-action films from around the world, usually as half-hour specials. Many of the programs were based on classic children's books, folktales and fairy tales, with others adapted from original screenplays. Produced by WGBH Boston and presented in partnership with the International Reading Association for Library Service to Children, the series aired Saturday nights on PBS stations beginning in 1989, providing an alternative to traditional commercial cartoon fare shown on the most cable networks.

Opening the first season, which lasted 16 weeks, was *The Pied Piper of Hamelin*, based on the famous poem by Robert Browning and produced by England's preeminent puppet animation studio, Cosgrove Hall Productions. Other first-season specials included *The Reluctant Dragon*, also by Cosgrove Hall; *Abel's Island* by award-winning New York animator Michael Sporn; *The Happy Circus*, an episodic half-hour of French clay animation; *Hungarian Folk Tales*, produced by MTV Enterprises, Hungary; *The Talking Parcel*, a two-part tale based on the book by Gerald Durell; *The Wind in the Willows*, the only two-hour special in the series, based on Kenneth Grahame's book; and *Svatohor*, an animated Russian folktale featuring sophisticated puppet animation of the time.

In 1990 the series returned for a second season, reduced to 13 weeks. The season featured more animated films from England, France, Hungary and the United States and one live-action film from Sweden. Kicking off the season was the haunting animated version of *Beauty and the Beast*, narrated by actress Mia Farrow.

PBS renewed the series for a third season in 1991, increasing the show to 24 weeks of original films. Launching the series' third season was the special two-part premiere of *The Fool of the World and the Flying Ship*, a fanciful adaptation of a classic Russian folktale using groundbreaking animation with "lifelike puppets," made in conjunction with England's Cosgrove Hall Productions. Included among that season's other productions was the Emmy-nominated animator Michael Sporn's adaptation of an old Hans Christian Andersen story, *The Emperor's New Clothes*, narrated by Regis Philbin and Peggy Cass. Sporn also produced the heartwarming musical *Jazztime Tale*, the story of of an interracial friendship between two girls set in Harlem in 1919, which also aired that season. Producer Joshua Greene for Lightyear Entertainment brought to television screens *Merlin and the Dragons*, following two previous memorable installments of the *Long Ago & Far Away* series: *Beauty and the Beast* and *Noah's Ark*.

For the series' fourth and final season in 1992–93, 26 half-hour programs and one 90-minute special were offered, mostly reruns from past seasons with the exception of three new programs: Michael Sporn's *Nightingale*, yet another adaptation of a story by Hans Christian Andersen, veteran animator John Matthews *Mouse Soup*, based on a book by the award-winning children's author/illustrator Arnold Lobel (and featuring the voice of comedian Buddy Hackett); and a second special from Sporn, *The Talking Eggs*, adapted from a Creole folktale and narrated by actor Danny Glover.

Funding for the series was provided by General Cinema Corporation/The Neiman Marcus Group, the National Endowment for the Humanities, The Arthur Vining Davis Foundations and others. WGBH Boston's Sandy Cohen produced the award-winning series, with Carol Greenwald serving as project director and series editor. (For a complete listing of individual shows from each season, see Animated Television Specials section for details.)

A WGBH Boston Production for PBS. Color. Half-hour (mostly). Premiered on PBS: January 28, 1989–May 13, 1990; September 8, 1990–December 1, 1990; October 5, 1991–March 14, 1992; September 6, 1992–February 28, 1993.

LOONEY TUNES

In 1955, in both New York (WABD-TV) and Los Angeles (KTLA-TV), Warner Bros.' library of pre-1948 *Looney Tunes*, a calvacade of the studio's most memorable cartoon stars (Bosko, Buddy, Daffy Duck, Porky Pig and others), made their television premiere. (Initially the films were seen on weekdays with local personalities hosting the show.) At first, the studio released 190 cartoons under the series name to television. Prints of each film were black-and-white. It wasn't until 1969, when television stations across the country demanded color, that Warner Bros. struck color prints of those films that were originally produced in that form. In 1960 Warner added post-1948 color *Looney Tunes* to the package for syndication. Portions of the syndicated package (mostly post-1960 cartoons, black-and-white shorts and "colorized" Porky Pig cartoons from the 1930s) began airing afternoons on Nickelodeon in 1988. The half-hour broadcasts (replete with the opening logo: "Looney Tunes on Nickelodeon") usually featured three to four cartoons, including at least one black-and-white oldie starring Bosko, Buddy and Porky Pig. The *Looney Tunes* show was later added to Nick at Nite's lineup of classic television shows aimed at adults, where it was well received by viewers.

A Warner Bros. Production. Black-and-white. Color. Half-hour. Premiered: April 11, 1955. Rebroadcast on NIK: September 12, 1988.

LUNCH BOX

Aimed at younger viewers, this daily half-hour series broadcast on The Disney Channel beginning in 1989 was comprised of live action and cartoon shorts, including such favorites as "Curious George," "Paddington Bear" and "Rupert," as well as many cartoons never before shown in America.

An Alfred Bestall/Siriol Studios (Cardiff)/Kingroll Films Production (and various others). Color. Half-hour. Premiered on DIS: July 3, 1989.

◉ MACRON I

In the year A.D. 2545, a teleportation experiment goes wrong and test pilot David Jance is rocketed through the center of the galaxy into another universe, where he is caught in a life-and-death struggle against the tyrannical armies of GRIP, led by the villainous Dark Star. The good forces of both universes combine and form Marcon 1 to defeat Dark Star's army in this first-run action-packed adventure series, backed by the latest Top-40 rock tunes. Rock group Duran Duran performed the series' theme song, "Reflex."

A Saban Entertainment Production. Color. Half-hour. Premiered: September 1985. Syndicated.

Voices

Angeria Rigamonti, Bill Laver, Christopher Eric, Octavia Beaumont, Tamara Shawn, Rich Ellis, Susan Ling, Oliver Miller

◉ MADELINE

The first weekly animated series based on a series of popular children's books by critically acclaimed author Ludwig Bemelmans, this series followed the adventures of the precocious and engaging French smallfry and her equally petite friends (Chloe, Nicole and Danielle), set in a boarding school in Paris. The award-winning series, backed by original songs and played against lovely Parisian backgrounds painted in a unique homage to artistic impressionism (and narrated by actor Christopher Plummer), debuted on The Family Channel in 1993, as part of a Sunday-night programming block for kids that featured the animated series *Babar* (in reruns) and a new live-action series, *Baby Races*.

Madeline produced solid enough ratings that the network renewed it for a second season in 1994, featuring new episodes. The weekly series, which won a CableAce Award for Outstanding Children's Series, followed by a brace of prime-time animated specials, the first produced for the *HBO Storybook Musical* series in 1988 (simply entitled *Madeline*), then five new specials (*Madeline's Christmas, Madeline and the Bad Hat, Madeline's Rescue, Madeline and the Gypsies* and *Madeline in London*), each originally broadcast on The Family Channel in 1990 and 1991. Madeline's voice, provided by Marsha Moreau in the animated specials, was performed by Tracey-Lee Smyth in the series.

In 1995 the series moved to ABC, with 13 new episodes, entitled *The New Adventures of Madeline*. (See individual entry for details.) The Family Channel series was rebroadcast on The Disney Channel beginning in the fall of 1997.

A DIC Enterprises Production in association with The Family Channel. Color. Half-hour. Premiered on FAM: September 12, 1993. Rebroadcast on DIS: September 1997.

Voices

Madeline: Tracey-Lee Smyth; **Miss Clavel/Genevieve:** Louise Vallance; **Narrator:** Christopher Plummer

◉ MADISON'S ADVENTURES— GROWING UP WILD

A cartoon cat introduces youngsters to exotic locales and wild animals in their natural habitats through a myriad of real-life video clips in this live-action/animated educational series for children, which aired in first-run syndication and was later rebroadcast on The Learning Channel and Animal Planet.

A BBC/Lionheart Television/Wildvision Entertainment/ Time-Life Video/Kookanooga Toons Production. Color. Half-hour. Premiered: September 10, 1994. Syndicated. Rebroadcast on TLC: 1997; Rebroadcast on AP: 1998.

◉ THE MAD SCIENTIST TOON CLUB

Wacky scientist Doctor Pi performs conducts outrageous experiments and lessons for the benefit of young children in this live-action, hour-long syndicated series (offered as two half-hours to stations as well), which featured two regular cartoon components: "The Wacky World of Tic and Tac," the wild comical adventures of a bird and a hippo done in pantomine, and "Eggzavier the Eggasaurus," a good Samaritan dinosaur whose fluttery voice was like that of comedian Ed Wynn. The 1993 syndicated series followed the success of other live-action educational programs, *Beakman's World* and *Bill Nye the Science Guy*.

A Saban Entertainment Production. Color. One hour. Premiered: 1993. Syndicated.

Cast (live action)
Doctor Pi: Michael Sorich

Voices
Mikey Godzilla, Dave Molen, Steve Norton, Wendy Swan

◉ MAGIC ADVENTURES OF MUMFIE

A little white elephant in a pink rain coat with a big heart, who lives alone, travels to help other creatures overcome life's curious obstacles in this series of serialized, song-filled half-hour adventures (also known as *Britt Alcroft's Magic*

Adventures of Mumfie) broadcast Tuesday mornings on the Fox Network's revamped preschooler series *Fox Cubhouse*, beginning in the fall of 1995. The series, from the co-creator of the hit PBS children's series *Shining Time Station*, made its American television debut on the kiddie-oriented program, which also included the cartoon adventures of "Budgie—The Little Helicopter."

A Britt Alcroft Production. Color. Half-hour. Premiered on FOX: September 12, 1995–January 3, 1997.

Voices
Mumfie/Other Characters: Patric Breen

⊚ THE MAGICAL PRINCESS GIGI

Lighthearted fantasy about the Princess from the Kingdom of Fairyland, who comes to earth as a 12-year-old mortal, but with the powers of a Fairy Princess, to do good deeds. This five-part fantasy/adventure series was reedited from the Japanese animated feature *Magic Princess Miki Momo*. The title of this Japanese import was released as *The Magical World of Gigi* in some countries.

An Ashi/Harmony Gold Production. Color. Half-hour. Premiered: 1985. Syndicated.

Voices
Reva West, Lisa Paulette, Sal Russo, Abe Hurt, Betty Gustavson, Ryan O'Flannigan, Anita Pia, Sam Jones

⊚ THE MAGILLA GORILLA SHOW

The anxious, bewildered owner of Mr. Pebbles Pet Shop in Los Angeles, California, makes futile bids to sell or even give away his permanent animal resident, an amiable and fun-loving gorilla named Magilla, who by nature stumbles into all sorts of fantastic and unbelievable incidents. His best friend is a little neighborhood girl called Ogee.

The gorilla made his entrance into syndicated television in January 1964 (telecast in 151 markets), as the star of this three-segment cartoon series, made up of six-minute cartoons. The two original components of the show were "Punkin Puss and Mush Mouse," a pair of hillbilly cats who engage in a nonstop feud like those of the Hatfields and the McCoys, and "Richochet Rabbit," a fast-paced rabbit sheriff who chases all dirty-deeders out of town with the aide of his deputy, Droop-A-Long Coyote.

In January of 1965 "Richochet Rabbit," which moved over to the syndicated *Peter Potamus and His Magic Flying Baloon* series, was replaced by "Breezly and Sneezly," which had originated on the latter. The series followed the misadventures of a foolish polar bear (Breezly) and clear-minded arctic seal (Sneezly) who spend most of their time trying to infiltrate an Alaskan army base, Camp Frostbite, headed by the commander Colonel Fusby.

In January of 1966, both *The Magilla Gorilla Show* and "Peter Potamus" (now billed as *The Peter Potamus Show*) began airing on ABC's Saturday morning lineup while the original series continued in syndication. New episodes of each component were added during the series' original syndication and network run through September of 1967. Sponsor: Ideal Toys.

USA Network rebroadcast the off-network version of the series, *Magilla Gorilla and Friends*, for three years beginning in 1989. Five years later the original series began airing (in reruns) on the Cartoon Network.

A Hanna-Barbera Production. Color. Half-hour. Premiered: January 14, 1964. Syndicated. Rebroadcast on ABC: January 1, 1966–September 2, 1967. Rebroadcast on USA: April 3, 1989–January 16, 1992. Rebroadcast on CAR: January 10, 1993–May 1, 1993 (Sundays); May 15, 1993–January 2, 1994.

Voices
Magilla Gorilla: Allan Melvin; **Mr. Peebles:** Howard Morris; **Ogee:** Jean VanderPyl; **Punkin Puss:** Allan Melvin; **Mush Mouse:** Howard Morris; **Richochet Rabbit/Various Others:** Don Messick; **Deputy Droopalong:** Mel Blanc; **Breezly:** Howard Morris; **Sneezly:** Mel Blanc; **Colonel Fusby:** John Stephenson

⊚ MAPLE TOWN

Led by Mrs. Raccoon, the cuddy characters of Maple Town (Bobby Bear, Patty Rabbit, Danny Dog, Mayor Lion, Funny Fox, Kevin Cat, Penny Pig, Susie Squirrel and the entire Beaver family: Bernard, Bitty and Bucky) defend their wholesome community from the town's only criminal, Wilde Wolf, in this half-hour live-action/animated series, based on Tonka Toys' bestselling toy line. Lasting only three weeks in syndication following its 1987 debut, the series featured a live-action host, Mrs. Maple (played by Janice Adams) to inform young viewers on the lesson learned that day.

A Saban/Maltese Companies Production in association with Toei Animation. Color. Half-hour. Premiered: Fall 1987. Syndicated.

Cast (live action)
Mrs. Maple: Janice Adams

Voices
Tracey Alexander, Jeff Iwai, Wayne Kerr, Bebe Linet, Heidi Lenhart, Lou Pitt, Alice Smith, Jon Zahler

⊚ MARINE BOY

Campy series imported from Japan ("It's Marine Boy, brave and free, fighting evil beneath the sea. . . .") about a daring aquaboy, the son of aquatic scientist Dr. Mariner, who dedicates himself to preserving the world, most notably beneath the sea, for all mankind. Drawing oxygen from Oxygum, life-sustaining oxygen in gum form, he keeps the world safe as a member of the Ocean Patrol, an international defense organization headed by his father. With shipmates Bulton, Piper and pet dolphin Splasher (named "Whity" in the Japanese version), Marine Boy takes to the watery depths in their P-1 submarine to battle the Patrol's main foes—Captain Kidd, Count Shark and Dr. Slime—using special gear (a bulletproof wet suit, propeller boots and an electric/sonic boomerang) to emerge victorious. Stripped for Monday-through-Friday syndication in 1966, the series was the second Japanese import to be produced in color (NBC's *Kimba the White Lion* was the first), and three of the series' 78 episodes (numbers 42, 55 and 57) never aired in the United States. Japanese series name: *Kaitai Shonen Marine*.

A *Japan Telecartoons//K. Fujita Associates/Seven Arts Production. Color. Half-hour. Premiered: October, 1966. Syndicated.*

Voices
Marine Boy/Neptina/Cli Cli: Corinne Orr; **Dr. Mariner/Various Villains:** Jack Curtis; **Bulton:** Peter Fernandez; **Piper:** Jack Grimes; **Splasher, Marine Boy's dolphin:** Jack Grimes; **Dr. Fumble/Commander:** Jack Grimes

MARSUPILAMI

This former Belgian comic-book sensation—a hyperactive cheetah with the world's largest tail—and his brawny, nontalking gorilla pal Maurice starred in this half-hour Saturday-morning cartoon series for CBS, comprised of weekly adventures originally seen the previous season on Disney's anthology cartoon series *Raw Toonage*, also on CBS. Also repeated from the latter, as weekly components, were: "Shnookums & Meat," the comical exploits of a battling dog and cat; and "Sebastian," adventures of the Calypso-singing crab and costar of the hit Disney animated feature *The Little Mermaid*.

A *Walt Disney Television Animation Production. Color. Half-hour. Premiered on CBS: September 18, 1993–August 27, 1994.*

Voices
Marsupilami: Steve Mackall; **Stuie/Groom:** Charlie Adler, Rene Auberjonois, Sheryl Bernstein, Dan Castellaneta; **Maurice/Norman:** Jim Cummings; **Norman's Aunt:** E.G. Daily, J.D. Daniels, Debi Derryberry, June Foray; **Eduardo:** Brad Garrett, Bill Kopp, Steve Landesberg; **Woman:** Tress MacNeille; **Shnookums:** Danny Mann; Jason Marsden; **Meat:** Andi McAfee, Kathy McAuley, Michael Pace, Malachi Pearson, Hal Rayle, Ronnie Schell, Susan Tolsky, Darryl Tookes, Marcia Wallace, Frank

Welker; **Sebastian:** Ken Williams; April Winchell; Samuel E. Wright

THE MARVEL ACTION HOUR

Marvel Comics creator Stan Lee hosts two superhero-filled half hours, featuring the exploits of *Iron Man* and *The Fantastic Four* in back-to-back adventures (see individual series for details), airing weekends in first-run syndication.

A *Marvel Entertainment Group/New World Entertainment Production. Color. Half-hour. Premiered: September 25, 1994. Syndicated.*

THE MARVEL ACTION UNIVERSE

Spider-Man is among a cast of superhero characters featured in the this 90-minute animated action/adventure series adapted from comic books, for television, which originally aired in syndication in 1988. The series was made up of 24 Spider-Man episodes originally aired on 1981's *Spider-Man and His Amazing Friends* (NBC), plus two other weekly components: "Dino Riders," the adventures of 20th-century robot dinosaurs back in prehistoric times (in 11 episodes), and "RoboCop," about a lawkeeping policeman-turned-indestructible cyborg (Alex Murphy), based on the popular 1985 live-action feature. A cartoon version of the comic-book series *X-Men* was originally planned as a regular segment of the series, but only one episode was produced, "Pryde of the X-Men," which aired during the series' syndicated run.

A *Marvel Production in association with Orion Pictures and New World Entertainment. Color. One hour and a half. Premiered: October 2, 1988. Syndicated.*

Voices
Charlie Adler, Michael Bell, Robert Bockstael, Earl Bowen, Barbara Budd, Wally Burr, Len Carlson, Andi Chapman, Cam Clarkee, Joe Colligen, Peter Cullen, Shawn Donahue, Pat Fraley, Ronald Gans, Dan Gilvezan, Rex Hagon, Dan Hennessy, Ron James, Gordon Matson, Greg Morton, Noelle North, Allen Oppenheimer, Patrick Pinney, Susan Roman, Neil Ross, Susan Silo, Kath Soucie, John Stephenson, Alexander Stoddart, Alan Stewart-Coates, Chris Ward, Frank Welker

MARVEL SUPERHEROES

Five famous Marvel comic-book characters—Incredible Hulk, Iron Man, Sub-Mariner, The Mighty Thor and Captain America—starred in this half-hour children's series, consisting of 195 six-minute cartoons, based on the long-running comic-book adventures. Budgeted at around $6,000 each, the cartoons were animated in the style of comic-book panels, with the characters appearing in a series of still poses. (Only their lips moved.) The series was produced by Steven Krantz of Krantz Films and Bob Lawrence of Grantray-Lawrence Animation, a company created in 1954 in association with longtime studio animators Grant Simmons and Ray Patterson. (The company was founded chiefly to produce advertising cartoons.) The names of the actors who voiced the characters in the series remain unknown.

A *Grantray-Lawrence Animation/ARP/Krantz Films Production. Color. Half-hour. Syndicated: 1966–1968.*

☺ M.A.S.K.

Led by Matt Tracker, the Mobile Armored Strike Kommand (M.A.S.K.) is a secret organization that fights crime in an unusual fashion. By donning specially charged masks, participants gain extraordinary powers to undermine the villainous forces of V.E.N.O.M. (Vicious Evil Network of Mayhem), in their insidious plot for world control. Joining Tracker in *Mission Impossible*–type missions are his team of special agents: master of disguise specialist Buddy Hawkes; kung fu expert Gloria Baker; computer whiz Alex Sector; technical wizards Bruce Sato; weapons specialist Monk McLean; and special vehicle drivers Dusty Hayes (driver of "Gator") and Brad Turner (behind the wheel of "Condor"). Produced for first-run syndication in 1985, the series was close-captioned for the hearing impaired.

A *DIC Enterprises Production in association with Kenner Products, a division of Kenner Parker Toys Incorporated. Color. Half-hour. Premiered: September 1985. Syndicated.*

Voices
Matt Tracker: Doug Stone; **Alex Sector/Floyd Malloy/Miles Mayhem:** Brendon McKane; **Jacques Lafleur/**

Commandeering a secret strike force, Matt Tracke and his team of special agents don specially charged masks that give them special powers in DIC Enterprises' M.A.S.K. © Kenner Products, a division of Kenner Parker Toys, Inc. (COURTESY: DIC ENTERPRISES)

Nevada Rushmore: Brendon McKane; **Brad/Calhoun Burns/T-Bob:** Graem McKenna; **Buddy Hawkes/Ace Riker/Sly Rax:** Mark Halloran; **Gloria Baker/Vanessa Warfield:** Sharon Noble; **Scott, Matt Tracker's son:** Brennan Thicke; **Nash Gorey/Dusty Hayes/Bruno Shepard:** Doug Stone; **Boris Bushkin/Max Mayhem:** Doug Stone; **Lester Sludge/Jimmy Rashad:** Brian George

☺ THE MASK

Wearing an ancient "mask" that possesses special powers, reticent Stanley Ipkiss is converted into a cartoonish master of mayhem who spins, contorts, flattens and twists his way through the crime-infested streets of his own Edge City with the help of Milo the Wonder Dog and a variety of characters in this weekly half-hour cartoon series based on the 1994 blockbuster feature film starring Jim Carrey (who did not lend his voice for this animated spinoff) and featuring many characters from it. Ikpiss's alter ego puts his powers to good use encountering his share of sleazy supervillains: an archetypical madman scientist named Pretorious and a toxic balloonatik named Kablam. The 24-episode series aired for two seasons on CBS beginning in 1995 (a month before the debut of the network's new fall lineup).

A *Sunbow Entertainment Production in association with New Line Television and Film Roman, Inc. Color. Half-hour. Premiered on CBS: August 12, 1995–March 29, 1997.*

Voices
Stanley Ipkiss/The Mask: Rob Paulsen; **Doyle/Lars:** Jim Cummings; **Pretorius:** Tim Curry; **Mrs. Peenan:** Tress MacNeille; **Mrs. Francis Forthwright:** Mary McDonald-Lewis; **Lieutenant Kellaway:** Neil Ross; **Mayor Tilton:** Kevin Richardson; **Peggy Brandt:** Heidi Shannon; **Charlie Schumacher:** Mark Taylor; **Milo/Pepe/Baby Forthwright:** Frank Welker

☺ MATTY'S FUNDAY FUNNIES

Mattel Toys sponsored this repackaged version of former Paramount Famous Studios cartoons—Casper the Friendly Ghost, Herman and Katnip, Little Audrey, Baby Huey and other minor characters from the studio's *Noveltoons* series (Buzzy the Crow, Owly the Owl, Finny the Goldfish, etc.)—which originally premiered on late Sunday afternoons on ABC. The films, renamed *Harveytoons* (after Harvey Publishing Company, which purchased the rights to the old cartoons), were presented in combination with two weekly hosts, a young boy, Matty, and his Sisterbelle, who introduced each cartoon adventure.

Instantly successful with young audiences, the program was moved to prime time in 1960, airing one hour before *The Flintstones*. In 1962 the network overhauled the series by replacing the *Harveytoons'* with the cartoon adventures of

Beany and Cecil, an animated version of Bob Clampett's syndicated puppet show. In April 1962, when ABC decided to drop the series' cartoon hosts, the program was simply named *Beany and Cecil*. The riotious adventures of Beany, Cecil, Captain Huffenpuff and Dishonest John were given their own Saturday-morning time slot in January 1963, after the *Matty's Funday Funnies* series concluded its network run.

A Harvey Films and Bob Clampett Production for ABC. Black-and-white. Color. Premiered on ABC: October 11, 1959– December 29, 1962.

◉ MAURICE SENDAK'S LITTLE BEAR

Based on the popular children's books illustrated by Maurice Sendak and written by Else Holmelund Minarik, this enchanting daily half-hour series revolves around the sweet adventures (imaginary or real) of a bear cub as he learns to take his steps and understand the world and how it works, with the help of his parents and pals, told from a child's point of view. Premiering on Nickelodeon's Nick Jr. preschool daytime block in November 1995, the program was part of the network's $30 million commitment to produce new, original programming for this time period.

Staying true to the book series, the Little Bear was joined in each episode by a cast of supporting animal characters, including a duck and a cat and his beloved Mother Bear, Father Bear and, on occasion, Grand Bears, offering words of wisdom and guidance throughout his many adventures.

For the series, Sendak, who illustrated the book series in the late 1950s, served as story editor and consulted on the look of the characters with the series' producers, Nelvana, a Canadian animation house.

A Nelvana Entertainment Production in association with Nickelodeon. Color. Half-hour. Premiered on NIK: November 6, 1995.

Voices
Little Bear: Kristin Fairlie; **Mother Bear:** Janet-Laine Green; **Father Bear:** Dan Hennessey; **Owl:** Amos Crawley; **Duck:** Tracey Ryan; **Hen:** Elizabeth Hanna; **Cat:** Andrew Sabiston; **Emily:** Jennifer Martini; **Mitzi:** Ashley Taylor; **Grandmother Bear:** Diane D'Aquila; **Grandfather Bear** Sean McCann

◉ MAXIE'S WORLD

One of the most popular students at Surfside High School, Maxie, a tall, pretty young girl and straight-A student, is the center of a series of adventures shaped around her Malibu-bred schoolmates, the loves of her life and her outside interests, including her own local weekly television show, in this 32-episode series that aired in first-run syndication in 1989. Episodes from two other animated series, *Beverly Hills Teens* and *It's Punky Brewster*, rotated on a daily basis with first-run *Maxie* episodes during the series' syndicated run.

A DIC Enterprises Production. Color. Half-hour. Premiered: September, 1989. Syndicated.

Voices
Maxie: Loretta Jafelice; **Rob:** Simon Reynolds; **Carly:** Tara Charendoff; **Ashley:** Susan Roman; **Simone:** Suzanne Coy; **Jeri:** Nadine Rabinovitch; **Ferdie:** Yannick Bisson; **Mushroom:** Geoff Kahnert; **Mr. Garcia:** John Stocker

◉ MAX, THE 2000 YEAR OLD MOUSE

Producer Steve Krantz created Max, a lovable little mouse who takes viewers back through the most exciting world events of the past 2,000 years. The educational cartoon series combined film clips and still pictures to tell each story, hosted at the beginning and the end by the program's mouse historian. Memorable moments include Columbus discovering America, the *Mayflower* voyage and others. For trivia buffs, the theme music for the program was later heard on Siskel and Ebert's movie-review series, *Sneak Previews*, for PBS.

A Krantz Animation/Quality Entertainment/ARP Production. Color. Half-hour. Syndicated 1969.

◉ MAYA THE BEE

Maya, a friendly little female bee, protects her other bug friends—including best friends Willie the bee and Flip, a musical grasshopper—from their natural predators in stories that relate the importance of sharing, loving and friendship in this half-hour series based on Waldemar Bonsals's *The Adventures of Maya the Bee*. Originally produced in Austria in 1982 and 1989, the 55-episode series made its American television debut in 1990 on Nickelodeon.

An Apollo Film Production for Saban International. Color. Half-hour. Premiered on NIK: January 1, 1990–December 31, 1992.

Voices
Maya: Pauline Little; **Willi:** Richard Dumont; **Flip:** R.J. Henderson; **Grimelda:** Anna MacCormack; **Cassandra:** Jane Woods

◉ MEATBALLS AND SPAGHETTI

Rock musicians Meatballs and Spaghetti, his mod singer-wife, turned animated cartoon stars along with Clyde, Meatball's sidekick, and Woofer, Spaghetti's loyal dog, appear in a variety of misadventures featuring original songs performed by the famous rock group in this short-lived Saturday-morning series, originally aired on CBS.

A Marvel Production in association with InterMedia Entertainment. Color. Half-hour. Premiered on CBS: September 18, 1982–September 10, 1983.

Voices

Jack Angel, Wally Burr, Phillip Clarke, Peter Cullen, Ronald Gans, Barry Gordon, David Hall, Sally Julian, Morgan Lofting, Ron Masak, Bill Ratner, Ronnie Schell, Marilyn Schreffler, Hal Smith, Frank Welker, Paul Winchell

◎ MEGA MAN

A 21st-Century superrobot and his robot dog, Rush, match wits with a dialobical scientist's evil robotic creations in this half-tour animated series based on the best-selling Nintendo and Sega video game, produced for first-run syndication as part of Bohbot Entertainment's weekend cartoon block, *Amazin' Adventures II*.

A Ruby-Spears Production. Color. Half-hour. Premiered: September 17, 1994 (part of Amazin' Adventures II*). Syndicated.*

Voices

Megman/Rush: Ian Corlett; **Dr. Wily/Protoman:** Scott McNeil; **Gutsman:** Garry Chalk; **Roll:** Robyn Ross; **Dr. Light:** Jim Byrnes; **Cutman:** Terry Klassen

◎ MEL-O-TOONS

This full-color series of six-minute cartoons were based on popular 45 rpm children's records, some featuring famous legends, fairy tales and literary works as story lines (with narration provided by famous announcers, including Don Wilson of TV's *The Jack Benny Show*). The 104-episode series included adaptations of the works of author Thorton Burgess, of "Peter Cottontail" and "Paddy Beaver" fame.

A New World Productions/United Artists Television Production. Color. Half-hour. Premiered: 1960. Syndicated.

◎ MEN IN BLACK: THE SERIES

A team of sharply dressed, unflappable government agents (Jay and Kay), replete with conservative black suits, skinny ties and sunglasses, who cruise the streets of New York City, are assigned to keep aliens in line in this half-hour animated series closely patterned after the hit live-action feature starring Tommy Lee Jones and Will Smith and produced for the WB Network.

An Amblin Entertainment/Columbia Pictures/Adelaide Production. Color. Half-hour. Premiered on WB: October 11, 1997.

Voices

Jay: Keith Diamond; **Kay:** Ed O'Ross; **Zed:** Charles Napier, Gregg Berger; **Elle:** Jennifer Lien; **Twin/Worm:** Pat Pinney; **Twin/Worm:** Pat Fraley; **Buzzard:** Sherman Howard

◎ METRIC MARVELS

This entertaining and educational series of 150-second bumpers, starring Meter Man, Wonder Gram, Liter Leader and Super Celcius conveying the wonders of the metric system to young viewers, was first broadcast on NBC's Saturday-morning schedule, between the network's animated cartoon programming, in the fall of 1978. Producing the series was Newall-Yohe, which had produced other instructional interstitial series: NBC's *H.E.L.P.* and ABC's *Schoolhouse Rock*.

A Newall-Yohe Production. Color. One second. Premiered on NBC: Fall 1978–Fall 1979.

◎ MGM CARTOONS

First syndicated in 1960, this series offered for the first time Metro-Goldwyn-Mayer's pre-1948 animated films to television stations for local programming. The package included such studio cartoon favorites as *Tom and Jerry, Barney Bear, Screwy Squirrel, George and Junior, Bosko* (not the Warner Bros. version), *Captain and the Kids* and *Happy Harmonies*. (See individual series in Theatrical Sound Cartoon Series for details.)

A Metro-Goldwyn Mayer Production. Black-and-white. Color. Premiered: September 1960. Syndicated.

Voices

Barney Bear/Captain: Billy Bletcher; **Bosko:** Carmen Maxwell; **Little Cheezer:** Bernice Hansen; **George:** Frank Graham; **Junior:** Tex Avery

◎ THE MIDNIGHT PARTROL: ADVENTURES IN THE DREAM ZONE

In a series of dream-making adventures, four young friends (Carter, Nick, Rosie and Keiko), accompanied by the sarcastic springer spaniel Pottsworth and a toy dinosaur named Murphy, meet in their dreams every night—becoming the superpowered "Midnight Patrol"—to protect the peaceful slumber of those in "The Dream Zone" and to conquer the villainous Nightmare Prince and his henchmen, who are constantly trying to turn a pleasant night's sleep into a terrifying nightmare. Lending a hand to the heroic foursome is their mentor, the Grand Dozer, the ever-snoozing sovereign of "The Dream Zone" (the name of the place to which they report), along with his assistant, Sebastian, and the irascible Greystone Giant. The 1990 half-hour fantasy/adventure series aired Sunday mornings as part of *The Funtastic World of Hanna-Barbera*.

A Hanna-Barbera Production in association with the Sleepy Kid Co. Ltd. Color. Half-hour. Premiered: 1990 (as part of The Funtastic World of Hanna-Barbera*) Rebroadcast on CAR: November 19, 1994–November 20, 1994 (Look What We Found!). Syndicated.*

Voices
Carter: George Lemore; **Rosie:** Elisabeth Harnois; **Nick:** Whitby Hertford; **Keiko:** Janice Kamaye; **Pottsworth, Carter's dog:** Clive Revill; **Grand Dozer:** Hamilton Camp; **Sebastian:** Michael Bell; **The Greystone Giant:** Kenneth Mars; **Nightmare Prince:** Rob Paulsen

◎ MIGHTY DUCKS: THE ANIMATED SERIES

Transported to Earth from a parallel universe though a space-time vortex, the Mighty Ducks, now an intergalactic hockey team of superpowered half human, half mallards, get trapped on Earth, turning a defunct hockey rink into their headquarters. They decide to save the planet from their archenemy, the dastardly warlord Draconus, in this half-hour animated series based on the live-action feature-film series. The series premiered simultaneously in syndication and in prime time on ABC on September 6, 1996. Regular episodes aired concurrently as part of ABC's Saturday-morning lineup the following day and in syndication beginning the following Monday as part of the *Disney Afternoon* syndicated two-hour block, which also featured *Darkwing Duck, Gargoyles, Disney's Aladdin, The Lion King's Timon and Pumbaa* and *Disney's Quack Pack.* Voice regulars included actors Jim Belushi, Tim Curry, Dennis Franz and television sports commentator Roy Firestone.

A Walt Disney Television Animation Production. Color. Half-hour. Premiered on ABC/Syndication: September 6, 1996. Premiered on ABC: September 7, 1996–August 30, 1997.

Voices
Charles Adler, James Belushi, Jeff Bennett, Clancy Brown, Corey Burton, Tim Curry, Roy Firestone, Dennis Franz

◎ THE MIGHTY HERCULES

Mythological Greek hero Hercules, beautiful maiden Helena, wholesome satyr Tweet and their half-human horse, Newton, traverse the plush Learien Valley of ancient Greece thwarting the machinations of the villainous, blue-hooded Daedelus in this 1963 syndicated series comprised of 130 five-minute, full-color adventures. Produced by Joe Oriolo (who produced and directed 1960's *Felix the Cat* series). The series' theme song, "The Mighty Hercules," was written by Johnny Nash.

An Oriolo Studios/Adventure Cartoons for Television Production in association with Trans-Lux. Color. Half-hour. Premiered: September 1963. Syndicated.

Voices
Hercules: Jerry Bascombe; **Helena:** Helene Nickerson; **Newton/Tewt/Daedelus:** Jimmy Tapp

◎ THE MIGHTY HEROES

Animator Ralph Bakshi (of *Fritz the Cat* fame), as supervising director of *Terrytoons*, devised this half-hour series for television following the exploits of a strange quintet of crimefighters—Diaper Man, Cuckoo Man, Rope Man, Strong Man and Tornado Man (each with a large "H" emblazoned on his costume)—who use their wit and muscle to champion the likes of such archcriminals as The Ghost Monster, The Enlarger, The Frog, The Scarecrow, The Shrinker, The Shocker and The Toy Man in this half-hour comedy series produced for CBS in 1966. Of the series' twenty-five episodes, 10 were released as theatrical cartoons in 1969–70.

A Terrytoons Production. Color. Half-hour. Premiered on CBS: October 29, 1966–September 2, 1967.

Voices
The Mighty Heroes: Herschel Benardi, Lionel Wilson

◎ MIGHTY MAX

Putting on his skull-shape cap, a precocious 11-year-old teen, left at home by his single working mother, travels through time and space with his talking-bird guide, Virgil, and his giant defender, Norman, doing everything in his power to avoid being captured by the villainous Skullmaster in this half-hour syndicated series, part of the weekend series *Amazin' Adventures*, and based on the popular pocket toy of the same name. One of the top-ranked action/adventure programs for kids ages 6 to 11, the series expanded to five days a week starting in September 1994. In 1996 the series reaired on USA Network.

A Film Roman/Bohbot Production in association with Bluebird Canal and DA. Color. Half-hour. Premiered: 1993 (part of Amazin' Adventures) Syndicated. Rebroadcast on USA: September 22, 1996.

Voices
Max: Rob Paulsen; **Virgil:** Tony Jay; **Norman:** Richard Moll; **Skullmaster:** Tim Curry; **Max's mother:** Tress MacNeille

◎ MIGHTY MR. TITAN

This superrobot who fights crime was featured in a series of three-and-a-half-minute color cartoons, produced by Richard H. Ullman, producer of TV's *Colonel Bleep.* Issued to television by syndicator Trans-Lux, which distributed TV's *Felix the Cat* and *The Mighty Hercules*, the series appeared on television screens in 1965, following the popularity of robotic cartoons such as *Gigantor*, which were captivating moppet-head youngsters in every city in America.

A Mister Titan/Trans-Lux Presentation. Color. Half-hour. Syndicated: 1965.

THE MIGHTY MOUSE PLAYHOUSE

Brawny superhero Mighty Mouse, Terrytoons' most popular character, was the star of this pioneer cartoon show seen regularly on Saturday mornings beginning in 1955. The phenomenal success of the program paved the way for other cartoon studios to follow with their own fully animated series. (In 1957 Hanna-Barbera challenged Mighty Mouse with its long-running *Ruff and Reddy* series.) In addition to impacting the cartoon industry, the series revived the career of the supermouse. The program remained a staple of network television through 1966.

A year later Viacom, which had purchased the Terrytoons library from CBS (the network initially paid a staggering $3.5 million, for Paul Terry's entire library of films), packaged *The Mighty Mouse Show*. In its original format, the series contained one or two Mighty Mouse adventures plus other *Terrytoons* featuring an assortment of Paul Terry's creations. Under the syndicated version, two series joined the package: "Luno," the time-traveling adventures of Tim and his flying white stallion, and "The Mighty Heroes," featuring a group of clumsy crime-fighting superheroes (Diaper Man, Cuckoo Man, Rope Man, Strong Man and Tornado Man). Episodes from both series received theatrical distribution as well.

Mighty Mouse later appeared in two series revivals, *The New Adventures of Mighty Mouse and Heckle and Jeckle*, produced by Filmation, and *Mighty Mouse: The New Adventures*. The latter was produced by animator Ralph Bakshi, who, incidentally, began his career working at Terrytoons.

A CBS Terrytoons Production. Color. Half-hour. Premiered on CBS: December 10, 1955–October 2, 1966. Syndicated: 1967.

Voices

Mighty Mouse: Tom Morrison; **The Mighty Heroes:** Lionel Wilson, Herschel Bernardi; **Luno, the Wonder Horse/Tim:** Bob McFadden

MIGHTY MOUSE: THE NEW ADVENTURES

Tracing back to his origins as ordinary Mike the Mouse, the legendary Terrytoons star forges onward to his status as life-and-limb–saving superhero in new cartoon adventures (three per show) in this half-hour Saturday-morning series cowritten and directed by animator Ralph Bakshi. Bakshi radically overhauled the crime-fighting mouse in this updated version, giving him the new alter ego of Mike Mouse, an assembly-line worker at Pearl Pureheart's factory. Featured in episodes were old *Terrytoons* favorites, including Deputy Dawg, Gandy Goose and Oil Can Harry. While a major hit with adult viewers, the series failed to ignite much interest from the 2-to-11 crowd and was canceled after two seasons.

A Ralph Bakshi Animation Production. Color. Half-hour. Premiered on CBS: September 19, 1987–September 2, 1989.

Voice

Dana Hill, Patrick Pinney, Maggie Roswell, Beau Weaver

MIGHTY ORBOTS

In the 23rd century, robots have reached an advanced stage of sophistication. Five unique but friendly robots (Bo, Boo, Bort, Crunch and Ohno), called "orbots" (and developed by scientist Rob Simmons of Galactic Patrol), come together to form a single, incredible crime-fighting force to thwart the efforts of the villiainous cyborg Umbra, ruler of the Shadow Star, who plans to destroy Earth, in this 13-episode half-hour fantasy/adventure series, produced for ABC.

A TMS Entertainment and MGM/UA Entertainment Company/Intermedia Production. Color. Half-hour. Premiered on ABC: September 8, 1984–August 31, 1985.

Voices

Bo: Sherry Alberoni; **Boo:** Julie Bennett; **Bort:** Bill Martin; **Crunch/Rondu:** Don Messick; **Ohno:** Noelle North; **Robert Simmons:** Barry Gordon; **Dia:** Jennifer Darling; **Umbra/Tor:** Bill Martin; **Returns:** Robert Ridgely; **Narrator:** Gary Owens

MIGRAINE BOY

A young boy whose constant headache gives him a different perspective of life berates his friends and plays with his dog, Tylenol, in this half-hour series that aired briefly on MTV, based on the comic strip created by Greg Fiering. The series sprang from a series of interstitials originally produced for MTV.

An MTV Animation Production. Color. Half-hour. Premiered on MTV: 1997.

MILTON THE MONSTER

By mixing the ingredients of the hillbilly Gomer Pyle and the gothic Frankenstein, the Hal Seeger animators produced one lovable character, Milton the Monster. Milton resides with his goblin companions atop Horrible Hill in the city of Transylvania where they brew trouble for their visitors.

Milton shared the spotlight with five other cartoon characters, each featured in their own episodes, in this ABC Saturday-morning series that premiered in the fall of 1965. They included: "Fearless Fly," a tiny superhero insect who battles sinister bug villains; "Penny Penguin," a precocious child whose good deeds often backfire; "Muggy Doo," a sly, fast-talking fox who cons his way out of predicaments;

"Stuffy Durma," a hobo who inherits a fortune but reverts back to living the simple pleasures of his former lifestyle; and "Flukey Luke," a private-eye cowpoke who, aided by his faithful Irish Indian companion Two Feathers, thwarts the efforts of the evil Spider Webb.

On the day after Thanksgiving in 1966, ABC ran cartoons from its Saturday-morning lineup in place of its regular daytime schedule, and "Fearless Fly" was given a 15-minute slot of its own.

Jack Mercer, the voice of Popeye, cowrote the production with Kin Platt. Cartoon veteran James "Shamus" Culhane was one of the series' directors.

A Hal Seeger Production. Color. Half-hour. Premiered on ABC: October 9, 1965–September 8, 1968. Syndicated.

Voices

MILTON THE MONSTER: Milton the Monster: Bob McFadden; **Professor Weirdo:** Dayton Allen; **Count Kook:** Larry Best;

FEARLESS FLY: Fearless Fly: Dayton Ilen; **Florrie Fly:** Bev Arnold

PENNY PENGUIN: Penny Penguin: Bev Arnold; Chester, Penny's dad: Dayton Allen; **Beulah, Penny's mom:** Hettie Galen

STUFFY DURMA: Stuffy Durma/Bradley Brinkley: Dayton Allen

MUGGY DOO: Muggy Doo: Larry Best;

FLUKEY LUKE: Flukey Luke: Dayton Allen; **Two Feathers:** Larry Best

◎ MISSION MAGIC

By drawing a mystical circle on her blackboard, Miss Tickle, a high-school teacher, magically transports her and her prize pupils Carol, Franklin, Harvey, Kim, Socks and her pet cat Tut-Tut back in time to the lands of fantasy in this half-hour series, originally produced for ABC. Recording star Rick Springfield, who plays a troubleshooter, sang his own songs on each program.

A Filmation Associates Production. Color. Half-hour. Premiered on ABC: September 1973–August 31, 1974.

Voices

Rick Springfield: himself; **Miss Tickle, teacher:** Erika Scheimer; **Carl/Kim:** Lola Fisher; **Vickie/Franklin:** Lane Scheimer; **Harvey/Socks/Mr. Samuels/Tolamy/Tut-Tut:** Howard Morris

◎ MISTER BOGUS

A rambunctions but affable 12-inch gremlin, who resides with a typical American family, decides to change his ways—wearing all sorts of disguises—in a series of harmless escapades presented in this half-hour, syndicated series (also known as "The Mister Bogus Show")—that mixed standard and clay animation—from the same producers as the 1990 syndicated series *Widget, The World Watcher*.

A YC Alligator Films/Zodiac/Calico Entertainment Production. Color. Half-hour. Premiered: Fall 1991. Syndicated.

Voices
Mister Bogus: Cam Clarke

◎ MR. MAGOO

The myopic, often irritable Mr. (Quincy) Magoo, played by actor Jim Backus, was given new life in this first-run series of 130 five-minute misadventures, produced for television between 1960 and 1962, featuring several of his relatives, including his beatnik nephew, Waldo, and his English nephew, Prezley. The Magoo adventures actually began on film as a theatrical cartoon series in 1949. Because of his renewed popularity, he was later featured in several prime-time specials (*Mr. Magoo's Christmas Carol* and *Uncle Sam Magoo*) and his own prime-time show, *The Famous Adventures of Mr. Magoo*, in which he portrayed different historical and literary characters in American history. His nearsighted persona was again revived by DePatie-Freleng's *What's New, Mr. Magoo?*, which debuted on CBS in 1977. Episodes from the latter and the 1960's series were bundled together, along with other UPA cartoons (from *The Gerald McBoing Boing Show*), in 1989 under the title of *Mr. Magoo & Friends*, broadcast on USA Network's *Cartoon Express*.

A UPA Production. Color. Half-hour. Premiered: November 7, 1960. Syndicated. Rebroadcast on USA: September 18, 1989–September 16, 1990.

Voices

Mr. Magoo: Jim Backus; **Prezley:** Daws Butler, Paul Frees, Jerry Hausner; **Waldo:** Jerry Hausner, Daws Butler; **Millie, Waldo's girlfriend:** Julie Bennett; **Mother Magoo:** Jim Backus; **Tycoon Magoo:** Paul Frees; **Hamlet:** Richard Crenna

◎ MR. MEN

Smiling Mr. Happy, clumsy Mr. Bump, dizzy Miss Scatterhorn and a cast of 40 other characters created by Roger Hargraves are featured in this collection of animated shorts designed to educate children about personality traits and emotions. A hit in Europe for more than two decades, the half-hour series, complete with live-action wraparounds starring The Mr. Men Players, premiered in syndication in 1997.

A *Marina/Mr. Film/France 3/Mr. Showbiz Production in association with Breakthrough Films and Television Inc./Telegenic Programs/Lacey Entertainment/The Summit Media Group. Color. Half-hour. Premiered: September 15, 1997.*

Cast (live action)

THE MR. MEN PLAYERS: Catherine Fitch, Peter Keleghan, Marguerite, Pigott, Cliff Saunders, Sean Sullivan

Voices
Len Carlson, Alyson Court, Neil Crone, Catherine Disher, Judy Marshak, Ron Rubin

◉ MR. SPIM'S CARTOON THEATRE

The Cartoon Network's series of *World Premiere Toons* and reruns of full-length animated features were rolled out Sunday evenings as part of this two-and-a-half-hour new showcase. The weekly series premiered on February of 1995 with "Dexter's Laboratory," directed by "2 Stupid Dogs" veteran Genndy Tartakovsky, followed by the feature presentation of *Race for Your Life, Charlie Brown,* starring Charlie Brown and the entire Peanuts gang in their Cartoon Network debut.

Subsequent first-season broadcasts included a mix of previously released theatrical and made-for-TV animated features, including *Rockin' with Judy Jetson, Scooby Doo and the Reluctant Werewolf, The Good, the Bad and the Huckleberry, Charlotte's Web,* Chuck Jones's *The Phantom Tollbooth* and Max Feischer's *Gulliver's Travels.* Also featured that season were the animated specials *Dr. Seuss' The Butter Battle Book, The Hobbit, The Return of the King, Oliver Twist, Twice Upon a Time, Rumpelstiltskin, Yogi's First Christmas, Gay Purr-ee* and *Flight of the Dragon.*

In the fall of 1995, the series returned for a second season, again showcasing theatrical and made-for-TV cartoon features and specials from the past, including *Treasure Island, The Three Musketeers, Davy Crockett on the Mississippi, Race for Your Life, Charlie Brown, Count of Monte Cristo* and *Cyrano.* Other titles featured that season included a series of Flintstones' specials: *The Flintstones Meet Rockula, The Flintstones: Little Big League, The Flintstones: New Neighbors* and *The Flintstones: Fred's Final Fling.*

A *Cartoon Network Production. Color. Two and a half hours. Premiered on CAR: February 26, 1995.*

◉ MR. T

Tough guy Mr. T, of TV's *The A-Team* fame, plays coach to a multiracial team of American teenage gymnasts (Robin, Kim, Spike, Woody and Jeff) who travel the world to competitions and wind up pursuing and capturing criminals in various locales in this weekly half-hour cartoon series that

aired on NBC in 1983. Bracketed around each of the series' 30 episodes were live-action closings of Mr. T delivering a valuable moral lesson to young viewers. The series was rebroadcast on USA Network's *Cartoon Express* and the Cartoon Network.

A *Ruby-Spears Enterprises Production. Color. Half-hour. Premiered on NBC: September 17, 1983–September 6, 1986. Rebroadcast on USA: February 21, 1989–March 26, 1992; Rebroadcast on CAR: March 19, 1994–March 20, 1994 (Look What We Found!); June 17, 1995–June 18, 1995 (Look What We Found!).*

Voices
Mr. T: himself; **Robin:** Amy Linker; **Kim:** Siu Ming Carson; **Spike:** Teddy S. Field III; **Woody:** Phillip LaMarr; **Jeff:** Shawn Lieber; **Miss Bisby:** Takayo Fisher

◉ MOBY DICK AND THE MIGHTY MIGHTOR

Hanna-Barbera produced this half-hour, Saturday-morning action/adventure series for CBS in 1967, which combined two cartoon segments: "Moby Dick," an updated version of Herman Melville's classic literary tale in which the famous Great White Whale protects a pair of marooned youngsters, Tom and Tub, and their seal friend Scooby, in dangerous seafaring adventures, and 18 episodes (one per show) of "The Mighty Mightor," starring a young prehistoric boy, Tor, who draws his strength from his magic club, becoming a masked superhuman guardian of the jungle accompanied by his dinosaur/dragon companion, Tog. Thirty-six "Moby Dick" (two per show) and 18 "The Mighty Mightor" (one per show) cartoons were produced for the weekly series, which concluded its run on CBS in 1969.

A *Hanna-Barbera Production. Color. Half-hour. Premiered on CBS: September 9, 1967–September 6, 1969. Rebroadcast on CAR: February 7, 1993 (part of Boomerang, 1967); February 18, 1995 ("Mighty Mightor," part of Super Adventure Saturdays).*

Voices

MOBY DICK: Tom: Bobby Resnick; **Tub:** Barry Balkin; **Scooby, their pet seal:** Don Messick;

MIGHTY MIGHTOR: Mightor: Paul Stewart; **Tor:** Bobby Diamond; **Sheera:** Patsy Garrett; **Pondo/Ork/Tog/Rollo:** John Stephenson; **Li'l Rok:** Norma McMillan

◉ MONCHHICHIS

A tribe of highly developed monkeylife creatures protect their treetop society in this colorful fantasy tale of good and evil.

Looking out for the loving creatures in the kindly wizard Wizzar, who often conjures up powerful spells to save them from the evil grasp of the Grumplins of Grumplor, led by the horrible Horrg, in this half-hour fantasy series first telecast on ABC in 1983. Rebroadcast on USA Network's *Cartoon Express.*

A Hanna-Barbera Production. Color. Half-hour. Premiered on ABC: September 10, 1983–September 1, 1984. Rebroadcast on USA: March 26, 1989–October 17, 1991.

Voices
Moncho: Bobby Morse; **Kyla:** Laurel Page; **Tootoo:** Ellen Gerstell; **Patchitt:** Frank Welker; **Thumkii:** Hank Saroyan; **Horrg:** Sidney Miller; **Wizzar:** Frank Nelson; **Snogs:** Bob Arbogast; **Shreeker/Snitchitt/Gonker:** Peter Cullen; **Yabbott/Fasit/Scumgor:** Laurie Faso

⊚ MONSTER FORCE

A cadre of supernatural-stalking, college-age bounty hunters battle to save mankind from a marauding band of monsters that include Dracula, Bela the Werewolf, HoTep the Mummy and the Creature from the Black Lagoon in this half-hour syndicated series, based on popular Universal Studio's film monsters and animated by the studio's cartoon division.

A Universal Cartoons Studio Production. Color. Half-hour. Premiered: September 12, 1994. Syndicated.

⊚ MONSTER MANIA

When his aunt mysteriously vanishes after spending the night at her spooky mansion, 10-year-old Brian McKenzie meets his first monster—clumsy, big-hearted Boo Marang—who jumps from a bed post and whisks the young boy off of Monster Mania, a land of crazy monsters (located in dark closets everywhere). He helps the monsters battle the evil Osh and a variety of other monsters, in this weekly, 26-episode half-hour fantasy/adventure series made for first-run syndication.

A Kookanooga Toons Production. Color. Half-hour. Premiered: (week of) September 11, 1995. Syndicated.

Voices
Brian/Jamm/Creature Key: Jeannie Elias; **Olive/Coin #1:** Miriam Flynn; **Stan/Limo:** Mark Taylor; **Boo/Sootybush/Bus:** Jim Cummings; **Gertie/Fudge/Taxi:** Tress MacNeille; **Nougat/Droolblossom/Underwood:** Frank Welker; **Osh/Bellylint/Doorman:** Mark Hamill

⊚ MORK AND MINDY/LAVERNE AND SHIRLEY/FONZ HOUR

Shazbot! the spaced-out spaceman from the planet Ork and friend Mindy, played by Robin Williams and Pam Dawber in the hit prime-time television series that aired on ABC from 1978 to 1982, reprised their roles in these animated

A remarkable young boy discovers there really are monsters living in the world—in his bedroom—in the half-hour syndicated series, Monster Mania. *© Kookanooga Toons Ltd.*

adventures in which Mork enrolls at Mt. Mount High, upon orders from his planet's superior, Orson, to learn more about the experiences of Earthlings during adolescence. Airing on ABC in September of 1982, the half-hour comedy cartoon series was half of the hour-long cartoon block known as the *Mork and Mindy/Laverne and Shirley/Fonz Hour,* sharing the spotlight with another new animated series, "Laverne and Shirley with the Fonz." (See individual entry for details.) Hanna-Barbera and Ruby-Spears Enterprises corproduced the "Mork and Mindy" series, while Hanna-Barbera served as sole producer of the "Laverne and Shirley/Fonz" series, the second such animated adaptation of producer Garry Marshall's popular TV sitcom, following 1981's *Laverne and Shirley in the Army,* also produced by Hanna-Barbera.

A Hanna-Barbera/Ruby Spears Enterprises Production in association with Paramount Television. Color. Half-hour. Premiered on ABC: September 25, 1982–September 3, 1983.

Voices

MORK AND MINDY: Mork: Robin Williams; **Mindy:** Pam Dawber; **Doing, Mork's pet:** Frank Welker; **Fred McConnell, Mindy's father:** Conrad Janis; **Mr. Caruthers,**

the principal: Stanley Jones; **Orson, Mork's superior:** Ralph James; **Eugene, Mork's friend:** Shavar Ross; **Hamilton, Mork's friend:** Mark Taylor

LAVERNE AND SHIRLEY/FONZ: Laverne: Penny Marshall; **Shirley:** Lynn Marie Stewart; **Sgt. Turnbuckle:** Ken Mars; **Squealy:** Ron Palillo; **Fonz:** Henry Winkler; **Mr. Cool:** Frank Welker

⊚ MORTAL KOMBAT: DEFENDERS OF THE REALM

This series was based on the highly successful "Mortal Kombat" franchise, including the popular arcade and video games. A group of "chosen warriors"—a ninja (voiced by Luke Perry), a former riot cop (Ron Perlman) and a special-forces officer (Olivia d'Abo)—band together, forming the Outer World Investigation Agency, to battle the forces of the dreaded Emperor Shao Khan and threats to the Mortal Kombat universe in this half-hour series that premiered in 1996 on USA Network's weekend *Cartoon Express.*

A Film Roman Production in association with Threshold Entertainment. Color. Half-hour. Premiered on USA: September 21, 1996.

Voices
Sub-Zero: Luke Perry; **Stryker:** Ron Perlman; **Sonya Blade:** Olivia d'Abo; **Liu Kang:** Brian Tochi; **Rayden:** Clancy Brown; **Princess Kitana:** Cree Summer; **Jax:** Dorian Harewood; **Nightwolf:** Todd Thawley

⊚ THE MOST IMPORTANT PERSON

Originally seen daily on *Captain Kangaroo,* this educational series aimed at preschoolers starred Mike, a baseball-capped boy, and Nicola, a pigtailed black girl, who present a variety of subjects relating the importance of physical and mental health. The films were subsequently syndicated as a half-hour series.

A Sutherland Learning Associates Production. Color. Half-hour (syndication). Premiered on CBS: April 3, 1972—May 18, 1973 (on Captain Kangaroo).

⊚ MOTHER GOOSE AND GRIMM

Those obnoxious and appealing characters from Pulitzer Prize–winning political cartoonist Mike Peters's comic strip—namely the grannyish Mother Goose and the ever-cynical Grimmy the dog—are paired in a series of offbeat adventures, joined by an equal cast of misfits, in this half-hour Saturday-morning series for CBS. The series, which enjoyed a two-season run, was retitled *Grimmy* for the 1992 season.

A Lee Mendelsohn/Film Roman Production in association with Grimmy, Inc. Tribune Media and MGM/UA Television.

Color. Half-hour. Premiered on CBS: September 14, 1991–March 13, 1993.

Voices
Gregg Berger, Charlie Brill, Greg Burton, Mitzi McCall

⊚ MOTORMOUSE AND AUTOCAT

Sportscar maniac Autocat tries everything possible to beat his speedy archrival, Motormouse, in outlandish contests in this half-hour series for Saturday-morning television. The program, which aired on ABC in 1970, featured repeated episodes of the freewheeling cat and mouse and "It's the Wolf," both originally seen for the first time on 1969's *The Cattanooga Cats.* (See *The Cattanooga Cats* for voice events.)

A Hanna-Barbera Production. Color. Half-hour. Premiered on ABC: September 12, 1970–September 4, 1971.

⊚ THE MOUSE AND THE MONSTER

In the story of the unlikeliest pals, a big-hearted, manic rodent, Chesbro, and his half-brained, good-natured, hulking blue monster companion, Mo, operate on the fringe of utter madness as they stay on the run from Mo's evil creator, the mad Dr. Wackerstein and his haughty highbrow bride, Olga, in this wacky half-hour cartoon series produced for the UPN Network. Created by Jerry Leibowitz, an accomplished graphic artist, painter and print cartoonist who founded the first all-comics newspaper, *L.A. Funnies* in 1983, *The Mouse and the Monster* was born out of Leibowitz's "longing for some of the great non-superhero cartoons of the past, particularly those of Jay Ward ('Rocky and Bullwinkle') and Bob Clampett ('Beany and Cecil')." The series premiered in the fall of 1996 Sunday mornings on UPN.

A Saban Entertainment Production. Color. Half-hour. Premiered on UPN: September 8, 1996.

⊚ MOUSETERPIECE THEATER

George Plimpton, in an Alistair Cooke–type role (Cooke was host of the long-running PBS series *Masterpiece Theater,* on which this was loosely based), served as host and provided his own droll commentary before and after classic Disney cartoons shown on this half-hour series, produced for The Disney Channel. First airing in 1983, 60 episodes were produced for the series, directed by Mitchell Kriegman.

An ESNE Production for The Disney Channel. Color. Half-hour. Premiered on DIS: 1983.

⊚ THE MOXY PIRATE SHOW

Classic cartoons were presented on this hour-long showcase featuring the unpredictable antics of its host, Moxy (played by Bob Goldthwait), airing Sunday nights on the Cartoon Network. In November of 1994 the show was revamped to a half-hour version (simply retitled *The Moxy Show*) in which Moxy, with the addition a new recurring character, Flea (voiced by Penn Jillette, the boisterous half of comic-magician team Penn & Teller), continued to screen his favorite cartoons.

A Cartoon Network Production. Color. Half-hour. Premiered on CAR: December 5, 1993 (one hour); November 6, 1994 (half-hour).

Voices
Bob Goldthwait, Penn Jillette

◎ MTV ODDITIES

In December of 1994, MTV launched this weekly animated series featuring strange characters in unusual worlds and situations. The series kicked off with six episodes of "The Head," the story of an Everyman named Jim and his symbiotic relationship with an alien, created by artist-animator Eric Fogel. In April of 1995, the series returned for a second season, opening with another six-episode commitment of "The Maxx," the adventures of a man who travels between two worlds, based on the Image comic book created by Sam Keith. The series launched its third and final episode in February of the following year with seven new episodes of "The Head" (told in individual half-hour adventures.)

An MTV Production. Color. Half-hour. Premiered on MTV: December 1994.

◎ MUMMIES ALIVE!

After a 3,000-year slumber, a group of Egyptian mummies come back to life in modern-day San Francisco to protect a 12-year-old boy who embodies the spirit of an Egyptian pharaoh and who holds the secret to eternal life in this 52-episode half-hour syndicated series created by film producer Ivan Reitman (of *Ghostbusters* fame).

A DIC Entertainment/Ivan Reitman Production. Color. Half-hour. Premiered: September 15, 1997. Syndicated.

Voices
Rath: Scott McNeil; **Nefertina:** Cree Summer; **Presley:** Bill Switzer; **Ja-Kal:** Dale Wilson; **Armon:** Graeme Kingston; **Scarab:** Gerald Plunkett; **Heka:** Pauline Newstone; **Amanda/Khati:** Louise Vallance

◎ MUPPET BABIES

These "babies" are animated versions of creator Jim Henson's familiar Muppet characters as small children who never actually leave their home yet through their imaginations go anywhere, do anything and be anyone they choose. Henson was executive producer of this long-running series,

which premiered on CBS in 1984 as a half-hour series and during the course of its run was expanded to one hour and later 90 minutes. During the 1985–86 season the series was renamed *Jim Henson's Muppet Babies And Monsters*. In 1989, the series' sixth season on CBS, 65 episodes from previous seasons were packaged for syndication. The same package and later episodes were rebroadcast weekdays on the Fox Children's Network beginning in the fall of 1991. Nickelodeon added the series, in reruns, to its daily schedule in 1992.

A Marvel Production in association with Henson Associates and Akom Productions. Color. Half-hour. One hour. Ninety minutes. Premiered on CBS: September 15, 1984–September 7, 1985 (half hour); September 14, 1985–September 6, 1986 (half-hour); September 13, 1986–September 12, 1987 (one hour); September 19, 1987–September 3, 1988 (90 minutes); September 10, 1988–September 9, 1989 (one hour); September 16, 1989–September 8, 1990 (one hour); September 14, 1991–September 7, 1992. Rebroadcast on FOX: September 2, 1991–September 4, 1992. Rebroadcast on NIK: September 28, 1992. Syndicated: 1989.

Voices
Kermit/Beaker: Frank Welker; **Animal:** Howie Mandel, Dave Coulier; **Skeeter:** Howie Mandel, Frank Welker; **Bean Bunny/Statler/Waldorf/Bunsen:** Dave Coulier; **Fozzie/Scooter:** Greg Berg; **Rowlf:** Katie Leigh; **Piggy:** Laurie O'Brien; **Gonzo:** Russi Taylor; **Nanny:** Barbara Billingsley

◎ MUTANT LEAGUE

Playing like the Mighty Ducks, the Bad News Bears and the New York Mets rolled into one mutated mess, the once-hapless Midway Monsters, after drafting the greatest rookie prospect—the incomparable Bones Justice—finally become a team to reckon with in the anything-goes-style-of-play Mutant League. A cartoon parody of professional sports based on the series of video games from Electronic Arts and produced for first-run syndication.

A Franklin-Watternman Production in association with Claster Television. Color. Half-hour. Premiered: September 17, 1994. Syndicated.

Voices
Bones Justice: Roman Foster; **Zalgor Prigg/Spewter:** Jim Hirbie; **Razor Kidd:** Rich Buchlloyd; **KT Blayer/Kang/Mo:** Mark Fleisher; **Eleanor McWhimple:** Kati Starr; **Bob Babble/George McWhimple/Jukka:** Robert Brousseau

◎ MY FAVORITE MARTIANS

A Martian crash-lands in the vicinity of the Los Angeles freeway and is discovered by writer Tim O'Hara. Convincing O'Hara that revealing his true identity would cause worldwide panic, the alien assumes the identity of Tim's

Uncle Martin and they become roommates. O'Hara (now joined by a teenage niece named Katy) must guard the well-being not only of Uncle Martin but also of his other space friend, Andromeda (or "Andy"), in this cartoon spin-off of the TV hit *My Favorite Martian*, which starred Ray Walston and Bill Bixby. (Neither actor supplied his voice for this animated version.) The animated series featured some of the same supporting characters from the famous science-fiction sitcom, including Tim O'Hara's scatterbrained landlady Lorelei Brown and suspicious police detective Bill Brennan (recast with an equally snoopy son, Brad, and pet chimpanzee, Chump), none voiced by the original actor.

A Filmation Associates/Jack Chertok Production. Color. Half-hour. Premiered on CBS: September 8, 1973–August 30, 1975.

Voices

Martin O'Hara (Uncle Martin): Jonathan Harris; **Tim O'Hara:** Howard Morris; **Andromeda (Andy):** Lane Scheimer; **Katy O'Hara, Tim's niece/Lorelei Brown, Tim's landlady:** Jane Webb; **Bill Brennan, security officer:** Howard Morris; **Brad Brennan, his son:** Lane Scheimer; **Tiny/Crumbs/Chump/Okey:** Howard Morris; **Jan/Coral/Miss Casserole:** Jane Webb

◎ MY LITTLE PONY 'N' FRIENDS

Pastel-colored, talking ponies that possess magical powers help three children—the only people on Earth to know of the existence of the fairy-tale region called Ponyland—overcome the villainy of the evil Stratadons in this first-run fantasy adventure series produced in 1986 and based on Hasbro Toys' "My Little Pony" toy line. Featured on each 30-minute program were two seven-minute "My Little Pony" adventures along with one seven-minute segment of "The Glo Friends," "Potato Head Kids" or "Moondreamers," which alternated as the series' third cartoon segment. Some episodes originated from the 1985 "pilot" TV special, *My Little Pony: Escape from Catrina*. The series spawned the 90-minute theatrical feature, *My Little Pony: The Movie*, also released in 1986.

A Marvel Production in association with Sunbow Productions. Color. Half-hour. Premiered: September 15, 1986. Syndicated.

Voices

Charlie Adler, Michael Bell, Sue Blue, Bettina, Nancy Cartwright, Peter Cullen, Jeanine Elias, Ian Freid, Linda Gary, Susie Garbo, Ellen Gerstell, Melanie Gaffin, Scott Grimes, Skip Hinnant, Keri Houlihan, Christina Lang, Jody Lambert, Katie Leigh, Sherry Lynn, Kellie Martin, Ken Mars, Ann Marie McEvoy, David Mendenhall, Scott Menville, Brecken Meyer, Laura Mooney, Sarah Partridge, Andrew Potter, Russi Taylor, B.J. Ward, Jill Wayne, Frank Welker; Bunny Andrews, William Callaway, Adam Carl, Phillip Clarke, Danny Cooksey, Peter Cullen, Jennifer Dar-

ling, Marshall Efron, Pat Fraley, Elizabeth Lyn Fraser, Liz Georges, Robert Ito, Renae Jacobs, Robin Kaufman, Danny Mann, Tress MacNeille, Terry McGovern, Michael Mish, Clive Revill, Stu Rosen, Neil Ross, Ken Sansom, Rick Segal, Judy Strangis, Lennie Weinrib, Charlie Wolfe, Ted Zeigler

◎ MY LITTLE PONY TALES

The "My Little Pony" characters featured in the popular syndicated series *My Little Pony 'N' Friends* starred in this new half-hour series (minus the The Glo-Friends, Moondreamers and Potato Head Kids characters) in newly filmed adventures, combined with repeated episodes, for The Disney Channel. *A Graz Entertainment/Wildstar/Starwild/Sunbow Production. Color. Half-hour. Premiered on DIS: February 28, 1993.*

Voices

Briggata Dau, Laura Harris, Willow Johnson, Lalainia Lindbherg, Shane Meier, Maggie O'Hara, Kate Robbins, Tony Sampson, Kelly Sheridan, Brad Swaile, Venus Terzo, Chiara Zanni

◎ MY PET MONSTER

Whimsical tale of a young boy (Max) who longs for a best friend and finds one in the form of a furry stuffed animal who is transformed into a lovable six-foot monster in this series from the creators of TV's *Care Bears*, which bowed on ABC.

A Nelvana Limited/Those Characters From Cleveland/Telefilm Canada Production. Color. Half-hour. Premiered on ABC: September 12, 1987–September 3, 1988.

A young boy named Max (left) finds a best friend in the form of a furry stuffed animal transformed into a six-foot monster in My Pet Monster. © Nelvana Limited

Voices
Max: Sunny Bensen Thrasher; **Chuckie:** Stuart Stone; **Monster:** Jeff McGibbon; **Jill:** Alyson Court; **Beastur:** Dan Hennessey; **Mr. Hinkle:** Colin Fox; **Princess:** Tracey Moore; **Ame:** Tara Charandoff

◎ MYSTERIOUS CITIES OF GOLD
Led by young Esteban, the children of the Sun search for the cities of gold, crossing unchartered territory and discovering the unknown in this 39-episode, half-hour adventure series that aired daily on Nickelodeon, beginning in 1986, opposite *Belle and Sebastian* and *Danger Mouse.*

All episodes of the series were untitled, and voices are uncredited.

An MK Company Production. Color. Half-hour. Premiered on NIK: June 30, 1986–June 29, 1990.

◎ NBC COMICS
In 1950 NBC made broadcast history with this series of newspaper-strip adventures that featured strip-art panels filmed sequentially in exciting three-minute adventures comprising this 15-minute program, becoming the first made-for-TV network cartoon program. Actually syndicated in 1949 as *Tele-Comics,* the black-and-white series originally presented serialized adventures of "Brother Goose," "Joey and Jug," "Rick Rack Secret Agent" and "Su Lah."

When NBC picked up the series, four new characters were added appearing in stories of their own. They were: "Danny March," hired by the mayor as his personal detective to stop crime; "Kid Champion," a boxing story about a youth (Eddie Hale) who refuses to talk about his past; "Space Barton," who blasts off to Mars in a rocketship built by Professor Dinehart, an astronomer, and his brother Jackie; and "Johnny and Mr. Do-Right," the exploits of a young boy and his dog.

Once the program finished its network run, it was again syndicated under the title of *Tele-Comics.* The cartoons were never titled.

A Vallee Video Production. Black-and-white. Fifteen minutes. Syndicated: 1949 (as Tele-Comics). Premiered on NBC: September 18, 1950–March 30, 1951 (as NBC Comics).

Voices
Bob Bruce, Pat McGeeham, Howard McNear, Lurene Tuttle

◎ NED'S NEWT
A hyperactive boy's self-made superhero is a 500-pound pet salamander named Newton, created by overfeeding him, who shrinks down to four inches at the most inopportune time, usually when trouble strikes, in this half-hour comedy series airing Saturday mornings on Fox Network.

A Nelvana Entertainment Production. Color. Half-hour. Premiered on FOX: February 7, 1998.

Voices
Ned: Tracey Moore; **Newton:** Harland Williams; **Ned's Mom:** Carolyn Scott; **Ned's Dad:** Peter Keleghan

◎ NELVANAMATION
Totonto-based Nelvana Entertainment, producers of the hit *Care Bears* motion picture and television series, produced this popular anthology series of six half-hour animated specials—*A Cosmic Christmas* (1977), *The Devil and Daniel Mouse* (1978), *Romie-O and Julie-8* (1979), *Intergalactic Thanksgiving* (1979), *Easter Fever* (1980) and *Take Me Up to the Ballgame* (1980)—broadcast in syndication beginning in 1977. (See individual titles under Animated Televsion Specials for further details.)

A Nelvana/CBC Production for Viacom Television. Color. Half-hour. Premiered: 1977–90. Syndicated.

◎ THE NEVERENDING STORY
Bastian Balthazar travels to the magical world of Fantasia to renew fond friendships and confront formidable foes in adventures that take him across curious landscapes, including the Goab Desert of Colors, the floating metropolis of the Silver City, the desolate Swamps of Sadness, the darkest corners of Spook City and the uncharted depths in the Sea of Mist, in this half-hour animated children's series based on Michael Ende's bestselling classic novel, which aired Saturday mornings on HBO.

A Nelvana Limited/CineVox Filmproduktion GmbH & Co. TV KG/Ellipse Animation/The Family Channel, Canada/Pro Sieben, Germany/Canal France/Channel 4 and Nickelodeon, UK Production. Color. Half-hour. Premiered on HBO: December 2, 1995–January 25, 1997.

Voices
Bastian: Christopher Bell; **Barktroll:** Richard Binsley; **Barney:** Geoffrey Barnes; **Laroe Head:** Colin Fox; **Falkor:** Howard Jerome; **Engywook:** Wayne Robson

◎ THE NEW ADVENTURES OF BATMAN
The Caped Crusader and Boy Wonder face new dangers in these half-hour animated segments voiced by TV's original Batman and Robin, actors Adam West and Burt Ward. They are joined in their crime-fighting adventures by Batgirl and their prankish mascot, Bat-Mite, in 16 action-packed episodes broadcast Saturday mornings on CBS in 1977. Episodes from the series were later repeated on *The Batman/Tarzan Adventure Hour, Tarzan and the Super 7,* and *Batman and the Super 7.* (See individual series for details.)

A *Filmation Associates Production. Color. Half-hour. Premiered on CBS: February 10, 1977–September 10, 1977.*

Voices
Bruce Wayne/Batman: Adam West; **Dick Grayson/Robin:** Burt Ward; **Barbara Gordon/Batgirl:** Melendy Britt; **Bat-Mite:** Lennie Weinrib, Lou Scheimer

◎ THE NEW ADVENTURES OF CAPTAIN PLANET
(See CAPTAIN PLANET AND THE PLANETEERS.)

◎ THE NEW ADVENTURES OF FLASH GORDON
Originally brought to the screen by actor Buster Crabbe in a favorite movie matinee serial by Universal Pictures in 1936, this animated re-creation of Alex Raymond's science-fiction epic follows the universe-zapping exploits of pilot Flash Gordon, Dale Arden and Dr. Zarkov as they brave the dangers of the planet Mongo, ruled by the evil dictator Ming the Merciless, now joined by an equally merciless daughter named Aura. The 16-episode series—featuring other regulars such as the kindly Prince Barin and Queen Fria and lionlike Thun—was produced for NBC's Saturday-morning lineup in 1979 by Filmation studios, producers of TV's *The Archies, Fat Albert, Gilligan's Planet* and others. NBC canceled the series in 1980, and episodes were reedited into a two-hour feature film, *Flash Gordon: The Greatest Adventure of All*, released theatrically in Europe and broadcast as a special on NBC in August of 1982. (See entry in Animated Television Specials for details.) In 1992 the series began rebroadcasting on the Sci-Fi Channel's *Cartoon Quest*.

A *Filmation Associates Production in association with King Features. Color. Half-hour. Premiered on NBC: September 22, 1979–September 20, 1980. Rebroadcast on SCI: September 27, 1992–June 24, 1995.*

Voices
Flash Gordon/Prince Barin: Robert Ridgely; **Ming the Merciless/Dr. Zarkov:** Alan Oppenheimer; **Aura/Fria:** Melendy Britt; **Dale:** Diane Pershing; **Thun/Voltan:** Allan Melvin, Ted Cassidy; **Gremlin:** Lou Scheimer

◎ THE NEW ADVENTURES OF GIGANTOR
Young Jimmy Sparks and his jet-propelled robot again keep the world safe from destruction and despair while conquering old foes in this full-color update of the 1960s black-and-white classic. Originally produced for Japanese television in the early 1980s, the series premiered in its own time slot on the Sci-Fi Channel in 1993 and also aired as part of the net-

work's two-hour cartoon program block (on a rotating basis), "Cartoon Quest" (later called "Animation Station").

A *Tokyo Movie Shinsha Company Production. Color. Half-hour. Premiered on SCI: September 9, 1993–June 30, 1997.*

Voices
Barbara Goodson: Jimmy Sparks; **Bob Brilliant/Other Voices:** Doug Stone; **Inspector Blooper/Other Voices:** Tom Wyner

◎ THE NEW ADVENTURES OF GILLIGAN
This series featured tales of the faithful charter ship S.S. *Minnow* and five dissimilar passengers who embark on a pleasure cruise and are shipwrecked on a deserted uncharted isle where they must learn survival techniques. Based on the popular TV series, this animated version starred five of the original cast members: Alan Hale, Bob Denver, Jim Backus, Natalie Schager and Russell Johnson. (Dawn Wells, who played Mary Ann, demurred.) In this animated version, Gilligan was given the first name of Willy and an adopted pet monkey named Snubby. The 24-episode series was broadcast three consecutive seasons.

A *Filmation Associates Production. Color. Half-hour. Premiered on ABC: September 7, 1974–September 4, 1977. Syndicated.*

Voices
Willy Gilligan, bumbling first mate: Bob Denver; **Jonas Grumby, the skipper:** Alan Hale; **Thurston Howell III, millionaire:** Jim Backus; **Lovey Howell, the millionaire's wife:** Natalie Schafer; **Roy Hinkley, the professor:** Russell Johnson; **Ginger Grant, movie actress:** Jane Webb; **Mary Ann Summers, clerk:** Jane Edwards; **Snubby:** Lou Scheimer

◎ THE NEW ADVENTURES OF HE-MAN
Traveling through time from Castle Grayskull to the Triax solar system, He-Man (alias Prince Adam) and his friends defend the planet Primus from the evil deeds of Skeletor in this all-new, 65-episode animated series produced for first-run syndication. The series—the second cartoon series to be based on the He-Man character—debuted as a five-part miniseries in September 1990 before becoming a weekly series.

A *Jetlag Productions/DIC Enterprises Production in association with Mattel Inc. and Parafrance Communication. Color. Half-hour. Premiered: September 17, 1990 (as five-part miniseries). Syndicated.*

Voices
He-Man/President Pell/Alcon/Sgt. Krone/Andros/Gross/Artilla: Gary Chalk; **Skeletor/Sagitar:** Campbell Lane; **Gepple/Optikk/Quake/Kayo/Viser/Hydron/Werban:** Don Brown; **Mara/The Sorceress:** Venus Terzo; **Drissi:** Tracy

Eisner; **Flipshot/Krex/B.H./Captain Zang:** Scott McNeil; **Caz:** Mark Hildreth; **Wall Street/Meldoc/Hoove/Prince Adam:** Doug Parker; **Flogg/Tuskador:** Alvin Sanders; **Gleep/Slushead/Karatti/Staghorn/Spinwit:** Ted Cole; **Sebrian:** Anthony Holland; **General Nifel:** Mike Donovan

⦿ THE NEW ADVENTURES OF HUCK FINN

Mark Twain's immortal characters Huck Finn, Tom Sawyer and Becky Thatcher, fleeing Injun Joe, are engulfed in a whirling sea in this live-action/animated series with superimposed animated backgrounds. The 20-episode series lasted only one season on NBC.

A Hanna-Barbera Production. Color. Half-hour. Premiered on NBC: September 15, 1968–September 7, 1969.

Cast (live action)
Huck Finn: Michael Shea; **Tom Sawyer:** Kevin Schultz; **Becky Thatcher:** Lu Ann Haslam; **Injun Joe:** Ted Cassidy; **Mrs. Thatcher*:** Dorothy Tennant; **Aunt Polly*:** Anne Bellamy

Voices
Daws Butler, Bill Beckly, Julie Bennett, Danny Bravo, Ted Cassidy, Henry corden, Dennis Day, Ted DeCorsia, Bernard Fox, Paul Frees, Jack Kruschen, Charles Lane, Keye Luke, Dayton Lummis, Don Messick, Marvin Miller, John Myhers, Jay Novello, Vic Perrin, Mike Road, Abraham Sofaer, Joe Sirola, Hal Smith, Paul Stewart, Janet Waldo, Peggy Webber, Than Wyenn

⦿ THE NEW ADVENTURES OF MADELINE

In this Saturday-morning series narrated by actor Christopher Plummer), which premiered on ABC in 1995, the French pixie schoolgirl and her boarding school classmates, each dressed in identical yellow uniforms and white gloves, cavort around Paris, experiencing new whimsical adventures (including trading pranks with Madeline's best friend, Pepito, at a nearby boys' school). The "new" half-hour series was the offspring of the highly successful animated series *Madeline*, which aired on The Family Channel beginning in 1993 and was based on the stories by children's author Ludwig Bemelman. The producers moved the series to ABC in 1995, producing 13 new episodes. After it failed to draw young viewers (and landed at the bottom of the Saturday-morning rating heap), ABC dropped the series that October, replacing it with reruns of *The New Adventures of Winnie the Pooh*, which originally aired on ABC from 1988 to 1993. Despite the show's poor ratings, it was nominated for a daytime Emmy in 1996 for Outstanding Animated Children's Program.

---

* This character appeared only in the series' first episode.

A DIC Entertainment Production. Color. Half-hour. Premiered on ABC: September 9, 1995–October 21, 1995.

Voices
Madeline: Tracey-Lee Smyth; **Miss Clavel/Genevieve:** Louise Vallance; **Chloe:** Vanessa King; **Danielle:** Kelly Sheridan; **Nicole:** Kristin Fairlie; **Pepito:** A.J. Bond; **Narrator:** Christopher Plummer

⦿ THE NEW ADVENTURES OF MIGHTY MOUSE AND HECKLE AND JECKLE

Two of Terrytoons' most famous characters from the 1940s and 1950s returned in new animated adventures in this series revival, which was first broadcast on CBS in an hour-long format in 1979, then trimmed to a half-hour for its second and final season. In these updated stories, Heckle and Jeckle still find ways to get into trouble, while Mighty Mouse defends mice everywhere and protects his girlfriend, Pearl Pureheart, from the evil clutches of his archenemy, Oil Can Harry, and his sidekick, Swifty. Two Mighty Mouse cartoons were featured on the show in serialized form, plus one self-contained adventure, along with two short Heckle and Jeckle adventures. Mighty Mouse also appeared in 30-second environmental bulletins cautioning youngsters on wasting resources and littering. Another series component was "Quackula," a vampire mallard who terrorizes his landlord and others.

A Filmation Associates Production. Color. One hour. Half-hour. Premiered on CBS: September 8, 1979–August 30, 1980. Rebroadcast on CBS: September 6, 1980–September 12, 1982.

Voices
Mighty Mouse: Alan Oppenheimer; **Pearl Pureheart, his girlfriend:** Diane Pershing; **Oil Can Harry, the villain:** Alan Oppenheimer; **Heckle/Jeckle/Quackula:** Frank Welker; **Theodore H. Bear:** Norm Prescott

⦿ THE NEW ADVENTURES OF PINOCCHIO

Wooden boy Pinocchio and his creator/mentor Geppetto are featured in 130 modernized five-minute adventures—actually "chapters" that formed a series of five-chapter 25-minute episodes—in this half-hour color series, based on Carlo Collodi's world-renowned characters. The naive puppet is exposed to contemporary subjects, such as beatniks and greedy movie producers. Filmed in the stop-motion animation technique called "Animagic" (a laborious single-frame process using puppetlike figures to animate a complete story), the series was produced by Arthur Rankin Jr. and Jules Bass, heads of Canada's Videocrafts International (later renamed Rankin-Bass Productions), who produced many perennial holiday specials, including *Rudolph, The Red-Nosed Reindeer* and *Jack Frost*. Initially the series aired in syndication from 1960 to 1961 on local TV afternoon kiddie shows, hosted by a local on-air personality, before stations ran the show by itself.

A *Videocraft International Production. Color. Half-hour. Syndicated: 1960–1961.*

Voices
Geppetto: Larry Mann; **Foxy Q. Fibble:** Stan Francis

◉ THE NEW ADVENTURES OF SPEED RACER

Speed Racer, his perky girlfriend, Trixie, best friend Sparky, Speed's brother Spridle, the mischievous monkey Chim Chim and Pops Racer return in this modified, half-hour syndicated version of the 1967 original. Speed Racer travels through time from tropical jungles to futuristic sites in the souped-up Special Formula Mach 5. MTV began airing the 52 episodes of the original *Speed Racer* series prior to the arrival of the new syndicated version.

A *Fred Wolf Films/Speed Racer Entertainment/Murikami-Wolf-Swenson Production. Color. Half-hour. Premiered: 1993. Syndicated.*

◉ THE NEW ADVENTURES OF SUPERMAN

Mild-mannered *Daily Planet* reporter Clark Kent, alias Superman, whose only weakness is kryptonite, frustrates criminal activities in Metropolis and elsewhere in the first Saturday-morning cartoon series ever produced by Filmation studios. Added to CBS's Saturday morning lineup in 1966, the series—brought on by CBS program executive Fred Silverman to compete with ABC's highly successful *The Beatles* cartoon series—scored the highest ratings shares in the history of Saturday-morning network television at that time. The weekly half-hour series was comprised of two six-minute "Superman" cartoons, sandwiched between one six-minute episode of "The Adventures of Superboy," chronicling Superman's youth in the town of Smallville, U.S.A., and featuring Krypto, Superboy's superdog. The series was one of six superhero cartoon programs scheduled back to back on Saturday mornings when it first premiered. Adventures later aired as part of *The Superman/Aquaman Hour* and *The Batman/Superman Hour.* (See individual entries for details.) CBS rebroadcast the series in its entirety during the 1969–70 season before it was canceled.

A *Filmation Associates Production. Color. Half-hour. Premiered on CBS: September 10, 1966–September 2, 1967. Rebroadcast on CBS: September 13, 1969–September 5, 1970.*

Voices
Clark Kent/Superman: Bud Collyer; **Lois Lane:** Joan Alexander; **Superboy:** Bob Hastings; **Narrator:** Jackson Beck

◉ THE NEW ADVENTURES OF TINTIN

The globe-trotting, 16-year-old Belgian journalist, who works for an unnamed newspaper, and his faithful fox terrier, Snowy, invaded U.S. television in this Indiana Jones-styled, fast-moving, 'round-the-world adventure series—with Tintin in hot pursuit of a story—based on 10 of 24 comic books by Tintin creator Herge (pen name of the late Belgian artist Georges Remi), a European favorite among children and young adults since 1929. The Canadian-produced series premiered on HBO in 1991, producing high ratings. An *Nelvana Entertainment/Ellipse Animation Production. Color. Half-hour. Premiered on HBO: November 4, 1991.*

Voices
Tintin: Colin O'Meara; **Haddock:** David Fox; **Calculus:** Wayne Robson; **Thompson:** John Stocker; **Thomson:** Dan Hennessey; **Snowy:** Susan Roman; **Castafiore:** Maureen Forrester; **Nestor:** Vernon Chapman

◉ THE NEW ADVENTURES OF VOLTRON

(See VOLTRON: DEFENDER OF THE UNIVERSE.)

◉ THE NEW ADVENTURES OF WINNIE THE POOH

The unforgettably charming characters of A.A. Milne's "Pooh" stories, who live in the imagination of young Christopher Robin, come to life in these joyful escapades filled with laughter and whimsy. The program marked the first time that a classic Disney character was seen on Saturday-morning television. The series was in production for over a year before its network premiere, producing 25 half-hours for the first season (most Saturday morning shows average between 13 and 17 in a single season), which consisted of either two 11-minute episodes or one 22-minute story. Prior to its network run, the series enjoyed a brief run on the Disney Channel in 1988.

In the fall of 1989, the series was merged with *Disney's Adventures of the Gummi Bears* in all-new episodes in a new one-hour show called *Disney's Gummi Bears/Winnie the Pooh Hour.* (See series entry for details.) The following season *The New Adventures of Winnie Pooh* returned, back as a half-hour series, on ABC, featuring new episodes along with old ones. The well-received series was winner of two Emmy Awards in the Outstanding Animated Program category.

A *Walt Disney Television Animation Production. Color. Half-hour. Premiered on DIS: 1988. Rebroadcast on ABC: September 10, 1988–September 2, 1989; September 7, 1990–September 4, 1993.*

Voices
Winnie the Pooh: Jim Cummings; **Christopher Robin:** Tim Hoskins; **Tigger:** Paul Winchell, Jim Cummings; **Eeyore:** Peter Cullen, Stan Ross; **Piglet:** John Fiedler; **Rabbit:** Ken Samson; **Gopher:** Jackie Gonneau, Michael Gough; **Roo:** Chuck McCann, Nicholas Melody; Kanga: Laura Mooney, Nicholas Omana, Patty Parris **Owl:** Hal Smith

◎ THE NEW ARCHIES

The classic characters of Riverdale High—Archie, Jughead, Reggie, Betty and Veronica—meet new challenges with limitless imagination, dream big dreams and create havoc, this time as a group of nine-year-olds, with friendship always prevailing in spite of their efforts to outdo one another in 26 classic adventures. The series debuted on NBC in 1987 and ran for two seasons.

A DIC Enterprises Production in association with Saban Productions. Color. Half-hour. Premiered on NBC: September 12, 1987–September 3, 1988. Rebroadcast on NBC: November 12, 1988–February 4, 1989.

Voices
Archie: J. Michael Roncetti; **Eugene:** Colin Waterman; **Jughead:** Michael Fantini; **Amani:** Karen Burthwright; **Reggie:** Sunny Bensen Thrasher; **Betty:** Lisa Coristine; **Veronica:** Allyson Court; **Big Ethel:** Jazzman Lausanne; **Coach:** Greg Swanson; **Miss Grundy:** Linda Sorensen; **Mr. Weatherbee:** Marvin Goldhar

◎ THE NEW ARCHIE/SABRINA HOUR

Taking two of its most prized properties, Filmation Studios produced this hour-long comedy series combining 13 previously broadcast episodes of Archie and the Riverdale High School gang from *The Archie Comedy Hour* and of Sabrina, the teenage witch from 1971's *Sabrina, the Teenage Witch* series, plus another animated segment called "Surprise Package."

In November 1977, following poor ratings, NBC yanked the series off the air and put in its place a new, improved version, *Archie's Bang-Shang Lalapalooza Show.* Unfortunately, the show fared no better than the former series since it was opposite CBS's 90-minute version of *The Bugs Bunny/Road Runner Show,* which dominated its time slot. (See *The Archie Comedy Hour* and *Sabrina, the Teenage Witch* for voice credits.)

A Filmation Associatess Production. Color. Half-hour. Premiered on CBS: September 10, 1977–November 5, 1977.

◎ THE NEW BATMAN/ SUPERMAN ADVENTURES

The famed comic-book superheroes shared the spotlight in this hour-long series for the WB Network featuring all-new cartoon adventures. In the new Batman adventures, Bruce Wayne (alias Batman) adopts 13-year-old waif Tim Drake, who becomes the new Robin, joined by Batgirl and occasionally the old Robin (now known as Nightwing) as they fight crime in Gotham City. The Superman adventures followed the Man of Steel's attempt to foil some formidable old adversaries—Lex Luthor, Mr. Mxyzptlk, Braniac, to name a few.

A Warner Bros. Television Animation Production. Color. One hour. Premiered on WB: September 13, 1997.

Voices
Batman/Bruce Wayne: Kevin Conroy; **Robin/Tim Drake:** Mathew Valencia; **Alfred Pennyworth:** Efrem Zimbalist Jr.; **Superman/Clark Kent:** Timothy Daly; **Lois Lane:** Dana Delany; **Lex Luthor:** Clancy Brown; **Mercy Graves:** Lisa Edelstein

◎ THE NEW CASPER CARTOON SHOW

First appearing in his own theatrical cartoon series in the 1940s and 1950s for Paramount's Famous Studios, this friendly ghost, who frightened away those he hoped would be his friends, was the star of this half-hour program for Saturday mornings featuring all-new seven-minute Casper cartoons (including supporting cast members Nightmare the Galloping Ghost, Wendy the Good Little Witch and the Ghostly Trio) as well as several Paramount/Famous theatrical cartoons originally released to theaters between 1959 and 1962. Twenty-six half-hour programs were made, each consisting of three cartoons. Airing six seasons on ABC, the series was briefly retitled *The New Adventures of Casper* before ending its network run and entering syndication. Animator Seymour Kneitel, who directed most of the Paramount Casper theatrical cartoons, directed the series.

A Harvey Films Production in association with Famous Studios. Color. Half-hour. Premiered on ABC: October 5, 1963–January 30, 1970.

Voices
Casper: Ginny Tyler

◎ THE NEW FANTASTIC FOUR

Three transformable humans—the stretchable Mr. Fantastic; his wife, Sue (also known as the Invisible Girl); and the rocklike being The Thing—are joined by a wise-cracking computer, HER-B (Humanoid Electronic Robot "B" model), in 13 half-hour adventures based on the Fantastic Four comic-book series in which they encounter weird machines and villains.

A DePatie-Freleng Production in association with Marvel Comics Group. Color. Half-hour. Premiered on NBC: September 9, 1978–September 1, 1979.

Voices
Mr. Fantastic: Mike Road; **Invisible Girl:** Ginny Tyler; **The Thing:** Ted Cassidy; **HER-B the robot:** Frank Welker; **Dr. Doom:** John Stephenson

◎ THE NEW FRED AND BARNEY SHOW

America's favorite prehistoric families, the Flintstones and the Rubbles, returned in this half-hour program for Saturday mornings that included 13 original *Flintstones* episodes redubbed for broadcast. Pebbles and Bamm-Bamm were back in the fold as well, but as infants. Henry Corden had assumed the voice of Fred Flintstone, replacing Alan Reed, who died in 1977. The series was later rebroadcast on USA Network's *Cartoon Express*.

A Hanna-Barbera Production. Color. Half-hour. Premiered on NBC: February 3, 1979–September 15, 1979. Rebroadcast on USA: March 13, 1989–April 21, 1992.

Voices
Fred Flintstone: Henry Corden; **Wilma Flintstone, his wife:** Jean VanderPyl; **Barney Rubble, their neighbor:** Mel Blanc; **Betty Rubble, his wife:** Gay Autterson; **Pebbles:** Jean VanderPyl; **Bamm-Bamm:** Don Messick; **George Slate, Fred's boss:** John Stephenson

◎ NEW KIDS ON THE BLOCK

The New Kids on the Block (Donnie Wahlberg, Jordan Knight, Joe McIntyre and Danny Wood), the 1990's rhythm 'n' blues teen-singing sensations, starred in this weekly animated series that combined MTV-like, live concert footage segues with animated adventures (voiced by other actors) in which the Kids go on a tour and try to have fun like normal kids and still make it to each concert on time. Each half-hour animated story was punctuated by their popular music.

A DIC Enterprises Production in association with Big Step/Dick Scott Enterprises. Color. Half-hour. Premiered on ABC: September 8, 1990–August 31, 1991. Rebroadcast on DIS: 1992.

Cast (live action)
Donnie Wahlberg: Himself; **Joe McIntyre:** Himself; **Danny Wood:** Himself; **Jordan Knight:** Himself; **Jonathan Knight:** Himself

Voices
Donnie Wahlberg: David Coburn; **Joe McIntyre:** Scott Menville; **Danny Wood:** Brian Mitchell; **Jordan Knight:** Loren Lester; **Jonathan Knight:** Matt Mixer; **Dick Scott, their manager:** Dave Fennoy; **Bizcut, their bodyguard:** J.D. Hall; **Nikko, Jonathan's dog:** David Coburn

◎ THE NEW PINK PANTHER SHOW

The happy-go-lucky cat and his pantomimic ways provided the entertainment in this half-hour children's series for NBC consisting of *Pink Panther*, *The Inspector* and *The Ant and the Aardvark* cartoons, each originally released as theatrical cartoon shorts. (See individual entries in Theatrical Sound Cartoon Series section for details.) Additional network shows followed, among them *The Pink Panther Laugh and a Half Hour and a Half Show*, *Think Pink Panther!* and *The All-New Pink Panther Show*.

A DePatie-Freleng Enterprises Production. Color. Half-hour. Premiered on NBC: September 11, 1971–September 4, 1976.

◎ THE NEW SCOOBY AND SCRAPPY-DOO SHOW

Huge, lumbering great Dane Scooby-Doo acts his way out of scary situations—doing almost any daring act for a Scooby snack—with the help of his pal Shaggy, fiesty nephew Scrappy-Doo and Daphne, whose predicaments as an investigative reporter propel the foursome into trouble in episodes originally broadcast on 1982's *Scooby and Scrappy-Doo/Puppy Hour* on ABC. (See latter for voice credits.)

A Hanna-Barbera Production. Color. Half-hour. Premiered on ABC: January 21, 1984–September 1, 1984.

◎ THE NEW SCOOBY-DOO MOVIES

This one-hour cartoon format starred the bashful canine and his pals who are joined weekly by celebrity guests, such as the Three Stooges, Phyllis Diller, Don Knotts, Jonathan Winters, Laurel and Hardy, the Addams Family and Sonny and Cher, all in animated form. The series premiered on CBS in September of 1972 with the opening episode, "The Ghastly Ghost Town," featuring animated characterizations of the Three Stooges.

Sixteen original shows were produced for the 1972–73 season. Featured were an entertaining collection of movies, including two comedy movies with Don Knotts: "Guess Who's Coming to Dinner?" and "The Spooky Fog"; three Scooby-Doo mystery movies: "The Dynamic Scooby-Doo Affair," "Scooby Doo Meets Laurel and Hardy" and "Scooby-Doo Meets the Addams Family," as well as Phyllis Diller as a guest voice in "A Good Medium Is Rare," Sandy Duncan in "Sandy Duncan's Jekyll and Hydes" and even Sonny and Cher, as themselves, in "The Secret of the Shark Island." Other first season stories included: "The Frickert Fracas" (with Jonathan Winters), "The Phantom of the Country Music Hall" (with country singer/actor Jerry Reed), "The Ghostly Creep from the Deep" (with the Harlem Globetrotters), "Ghost of the Red Baron" (featuring the second appearance of the Three Stooges), "The Loch Ness Mess," "The Haunted Horseman In Hagglethorn

Hall" (starring Davey Jones of The Monkees) and "The Caped Crusader Caper" (with Batman and Robin).

ABC renewed the series for a second season but produced only eight new hour-long installments for the 1973–74 season, combined with repeat episodes from the first season. The stories featured mostly Hanna-Barbera cartoon characters and a few celebrities in their own comedy movies. Comedian Tim Conway, of *McHale's Navy* fame, was the featured voice in "The Spirited Spooked Sports Show." Don Adams, agent 86 from TV's *Get Smart*, starred in "The Exterminator." Singer Cass Elliot of the Momas and the Poppas was an unlikely guest voice in "The Haunted Candy Factory."

The five remaining comedy movies for that season all featured Hanna-Barbera characters in starring roles: "The Haunted Showboat" (with Josie and the Pussycats), "Mystery of Haunted Island" (with the Harlem Globetrotters from *The Harlem Globetrotters* series), "Scooby-Doo Meets Jeannie" (with Jeannie and Babu from Hanna-Barbera's animated *Jeannie* series), "The Weird Winds of Winona" (with Speedy Buggy) and "Scooby-Doo Meets Dick Van Dyke."

ABC canceled the series following the second season.

A Hanna-Barbera Production. Color. One hour. Premiered on CBS: September 9, 1972–August 31, 1974. Rebroadcast on CAR: December 26, 1994–December 30, 1994; February 28, 1995–September 3, 1995 (Tuesdays, Thursdays, Sundays); October 23, 1995–October 27, 1995; October 12, 1996– October 11, 1997 (Saturdays); October 13, 1997 (weekdays).

Voices
Scooby-Doo: Don Messick; **Freddy:** Frank Welker; **Daphne:** Heather North; **Shaggy:** Casey Kasem; **Velma:** Nicole Jaffe

◎ THE NEW SCOOBY-DOO MYSTERIES

Scooby-Doo, Scrappy-Doo, Shaggy and Daphne uncover clues to a series of new mysteries in this half-hour program produced for Saturday-morning television. Former cast members Freddy Jones and Velma Dinkley made guest star appearances in several episodes, though they were not series regulars. The season opener was a two-part celebration of Scooby's 15th birthday and a retrospective of his life. The two-part episode "The Nutcracker Scoob" was rebroadcast on USA Network in 1991 as a Christmas special.

A Hanna-Barbera Production. Color. Half-hour. Premiered on ABC: September 9, 1984–August 31, 1985. Rebroadcast on CAR: December 21, 1994–December 23, 1994; August 16, 1997 (Saturdays, Sundays).

Voices
Scooby-Doo/Scrappy-Doo: Don Messick; **Freddy Jones:** Frank Welker; **Shaggy Rogers:** Casey Kasem; **Daphne Blake:** Heather North; **Velma Dace Dinkley:** Maria Frumkin

◎ THE NEW SHMOO

Al Capp's lovable and trusting comic-strip character uses its ability to change into virtually anything to help three young reporters—Mickey, Nita and Billy Joe—who work for "Mighty Mysteries Comics" and investigate cases of psychic phenomena in this NBC Saturday-morning series. Within three months of its debut in 1979, the series was retooled into the 90-minute extravaganza, *Fred and Barney Meet the Shmoo*, featuring repeat episodes from two previously broadcast Hanna-Barbera cartoon shows: 1979's *The New Fred and Barney Show* and *The Thing*, of Marvel Comics' fame (from 1979's *Fred and Barney Meet the Thing*), both of which originally aired on NBC.

A Hanna-Barbera Production. Color. Half-hour. Premiered on NBC: September 22, 1979–December 1, 1979.

Voices
Shmoo: Frank Welker; **Nita:** Dolores Cantu-Primo; **Billy Joe:** Chuck McCann; **Mickey:** Bill Idelson

◎ THE NEW THREE STOOGES

Moe Howard, Larry Fine and Curly-Joe DeRita (the fourth comedian to play the "third Stooge" in the long-running

Al Capp's lovable comic-strip character shows the comical side of his psychic phenomena in the Saturday-morning series The New Shmoo. © *Hanna-Barbera Productions*

comedy act) starred in this series, which combined live-action wraparounds and animated segments to tell one complete story. The cartoons reflected the Stooges' style and humor yet in a less violent manner. Only 40 live-action openings and endings were filmed for this series. (The live segments were rotated throughout the package's 156 cartoon episodes.) Dick Brown, who produced such animated favorites as *Clutch Cargo* and *Space Angel*, produced the series in association with Normandy III Productions (the Stooges' own company, named after their producer/agent, Norman Maurer).

A Cambria Studios Production in association with Normandy III Productions. Color. Half-hour. Premiered: December 20, 1965. Syndicated.

Cast (live action)
Moe: Moe Howard; **Larry:** Larry Fine; **Curly-Joe:** Joe DeRita

Other Actors
Emil Sitka, Peggy Brown/Margaret Kerry, Emil Sitka, Harold Brauer, Jeffrey Maurer (later Jeffrey Scott), Cary Brown, Tina Brown, Eileen Brown

Voices
The Three Stooges: Themselves

◎ NIGHTMARE NED

A sensitive, solitary eight-year-old boy, who has a rather banal existence—at home, at school and with his family—finds adventure when he drifts off into dreamland, entering a world filled with a host of nutty nocturnal visitors and other nightmarish events, in this half-hour cartoon series, which debuted on ABC.

A Walt Disney Television Animation Production. Color. Half-hour. Premiered on ABC: April 19, 1997–August 30, 1997.

Voices
Ned: Courtland Mead

◎ NOOZLES

Twelve-year-old Sandy discovers that Blinky, her favorite stuffed animal, actually becomes a live koala whenever she rubs noses with him. Together they journey magically throughout the universe in search of fun and excitement in this 26-episode half-hour series that debuted weekday afternoons on Nickelodeon in 1988.

A Saban International Services Production in association with Fuji Eight Company. Color. Half-hour. Premiered on NIK: November 8, 1988–April 2, 1993.

◎ NTA CARTOON CARNIVAL LIBRARY

This late 1950s' syndicated series was comprised of previously released live-action and cartoon short subjects originally produced for Paramount Pictures by the following producers: Fleischer Studios, Famous Studios, Jerry Fairbanks Productions and George Pal Productions.

Cartoons that were telecast as part of the package were such highly acclaimed theatrical series as *Animated Antics, Color Classics, Gabby, Noveltoons, Screen Songs, Stone Age Cartoons, Talkartoons, Inkwell Imps*, plus George Pal's *Puppetoons* and *Speaking of Animals*, the Oscar-winning talking animals short-subject series produced by Jerry Fairbanks, who produced the early television versions of *Crusader Rabbit* with Rocky and Bullwinkle creator Jay Ward.

A National Television Associates (NTA) Presentation. Black-and-white. Color. Premiered: 1956. Syndicated.

◎ THE NUTTY SQUIRRELS

Television's forerunners to Ross Bagdasarian's *Alvin and the Chipmunks*, this animated series boasted the exploits of another recording group, The Nutty Squirrels, who beat Alvin, Theodore, Simon and David Seville to television screens by one full year. Established jazzman Don Elliot and TV composer Alexander "Sascha" Burland made up this musical twosome, which recorded their own speeded-up songs, featuring Chipmunk-like voices for Hanover-Signature records (of which comedian Steve Allen was part owner). The pair's first song, "Uh-Oh!" recorded as a single, ranked number 14 in the "Hit Parade" for the week of December 28, 1959, nearly one year after the Chipmunks' "Chipmunk Song" made the same list. Transfilm-Wilde, which specialized in producing animated television commercials, brought the rights to the Nutty Squirrel characters and produced this half-hour series, consisting of 100 five-minute "Nutty Squirrel" cartoons that premiered in syndication in the fall of 1960.

A Transfilm/Wilde Production. Color. Half-hour. Syndicated: Fall 1960.

◎ O CANADA

One of the world's top producers of innovative animation, the National Film Board of Canada produced this weekly anthology of outstanding Canadian-animated shorts from the 1950s to the present, many of them Oscar winners and nominees and representing all styles of animation. The series opener featured the Oscar-winning cartoon short, "Bob's Birthday," about a dentist who is none too happy about turning 40. The half-hour series premiered on the Cartoon Network.

A National Film Board of Canada Production. Color. Half-hour. Premiered on CAR: January 8, 1997.

THE ODDBALL COUPLE

Adapted from Neil Simon's Broadway and Hollywood film hit and long-running TV series, which mismatched sloppy Oscar Madison and fastidious Felix Unger, this animated spin-off casts the perfectionist cat Spiffy (Unger) and the troublesome dog Fleabag (Madison) in equally funny situations as reporters at large in 16 half-hour episodes, produced for this Saturday-morning series, which originally aired on ABC.

A DePatie-Freleng Enterprises Production. Color. Half-hour. Premiered on ABC: September 6, 1975–September 3, 1977.

Voices
Spiffy: Frank Nelson; **Fleabag:** Paul Winchell; **Goldie, the secretary:** Joan Gerber

OFFICIAL FILMS CARTOONS

In 1950 this program featured a recycled package of old Van Beuren Studio cartoons produced in the 1920s and 1930s, first broadcast on *TV Tot's Time* on ABC stations locally and nationally. Included were several notable cartoon stars, each renamed: "Brownie Bear" ("Cubby Bear"), "Dick and Larry" ("Tom and Jerry"), "Jungle Jinks" ("Aesop's Fables"), "Merry Toons" ("Rainbow Parades") and "The Little King," which remained unchanged. In the early 1950s the cartoons were also used by local stations on programs hosted by station personalities. (See individuals entries in Theatrical Sound Cartoon Series for details.)

An Official Films Presentation. Black-and-white. Half-hour. Premiered: 1950.

OFF TO SEE THE WIZARD

Legendary animators Chuck Jones and Abe Levitow produced and directed animated buffers and wraparounds featuring familiar characters from the 1939 MGM classic *The Wizard of Oz* as "hosts" of this hour-long prime-time series. The series served as an umbrella for 26 live-action properties, including first-run specials and television series pilots. Debuting on ABC in 1967, opposite CBS's *The Wild Wild West* and NBC's *Tarzan*, the Friday-night series lost the ratings battle and was canceled.

An MGM Television Production. Color. One hour. Premiered on ABC: September 8, 1967–September 20, 1968.

ONCE UPON A TIME . . . THE AMERICAS

The fabulous story of the American continent—the first Americans, the pioneer explorers, England and the 13 colonies, Cortez and the Aztec Indians, the Inca Empire and others—is chronicled in this historical half-hour series that debuted on The History Channel. The series was the first of three *Once Upon a Time . . .* anthology series originally produced for French television.

A Procidis Production. Color. Half-hour. Premiered on HIS: January 7, 1995.

ONCE UPON A TIME . . . THE DISCOVERERS

The stories of the great inventions and the illustrious sages who revolutionized the world, from yesterday's famed elders Aristotle, Archimedes, Ptolemy and Hero to modern-day discoverers Leonardo da Vinci, Alexander Graham Bell, Thomas Edison and Albert Einstein, are presented in this well-animated 26 episode half-hour historical series—the second of three—first produced for French television by producer Albert Barille. The series premiered in the United States on The History Channel.

A Procidis Production. Color. Half-hour. Premiered on HIS: April 8, 1995.

ONCE UPON A TIME . . . MAN

The primary focus of this French-produced historical half-hour cartoon series, originally made for French television, is the history of man from his earliest origins. It is on the members of one family (led by Peter, an ordinary man, and his beautiful wife, Pierrette) in different historical settings facing the problems of everyday existence. This third and final edition of French producer Albert Barille's *Once Upon a Time . . .* historical series debuted in the United States on The History Channel in 1996.

A Procidis Production. Color. Half-hour. Premiered on HIS: January 6, 1996.

ONE SATURDAY MORNING

Beginning in the fall of 1997, ABC created this floating two-hour block, from 8:30 to 10:30 A.M., for its Saturday-morning lineup. It consisted of all-new Walt Disney animated series: *Brand Spanking New Doug, Disney's Pepper Ann* and *Disney's Recess*, each of which didn't begin or end in a traditional half-hour but were linked through interstitial programming, including the special weekly segment "Great Minds Think for Themselves." The animated segment featured the voice of Robin Williams as the Genie from Disney's *Aladdin* offering educational snippets. (See individual series for voice credits and further details.)

A Walt Disney Television Animation Production. Color. Two hours. Premiered on ABC: September 13, 1997.

OSCAR'S ORCHESTRA

British animator Tony Collingwood teamed up with actor/comedian Dudley Moore to develop this series about a young music impressario (Oscar) who, with the help of instruments that come to life, presents examples of classical music by the world's legendary composers, including Bach, Mozart, Beethoven, Tchaikovsky, Brahms and many others, interwoven into each week's adventure. Based on an original idea by Jan Younghusband, the series, originally produced in 1996, was first syndicated in the United States in 1997.

A Warner Music Vision and Europe Images/Tony Colling-wood/Rubberneck Television Production in association with Lacey Entertainment and The Summit Media Group. Color. Half-hour. Premiered: September 13, 1997. Syndicated.

Voices

Oscar: Dudley Moore; **Thadius Vent/Tank:** Colin McFarlane; **Rebecca:** Elly Fairman; **Mr. Crotchet:** Michael Kilgarriff; **Lucius:** Murray Melvin; **Narrator:** David DeKyser; **Eric:** Eric Meyers; **Monty:** John Baddeley; **Trevor/Lewis:** Steven Lander; **Goodtooth:** Sean Barrett; **Sylvia:** Eve Karpf

◎ THE OSMONDS

Featuring the voices of the famed brother singing group, the Osmonds and their talking dog, Fugi, embark on a worldwide tour as goodwill ambassadors. This weekly half-hour Saturday-morning series produced for ABC took them to a different country each week. Only 17 half-hour adventures were produced, each originally telecast during the show's first season in 1972–73. The series was canceled in September of 1974.

A Rankin-Bass Production. Color. Half-hour. Premiered on ABC: September 9, 1972–September 1, 1974.

Voices

Allen Osmond: Himself; **Jay Osmond:** Himself; **Jimmy Osmond:** Himself; **Donny Osmond:** Himself; **Merrill Osmond:** Himself; **Wayne Osmond:** Himself; **Fugi, the dog:** Paul Frees

◎ OSWALD THE RABBIT

The floppy-eared rabbit from Walter Lantz's theatrical sound cartoon series headlined this package of formerly released black-and-white cartoons produced by Walter Lantz Studios. Along with Oswald, the package included *Meany, Miny and Moe* and *Pooch the Pup*, both successful theatrical cartoon series. (See individual entries in Theatrical Sound Cartoon Series for complete details.)

A Walter Lantz Production distributed by Revue Productions (MCA-TV). Black-and-white. Half-hour. Premiered: February 28, 1955, KNXT, Los Angeles.

Voices

Oswald the Rabbit: Mickey Rooney, Bernice Hansen

◎ OUT OF THE INKWELL

Max Fleischer's innovative silent cartoon series, which combined live-action and animation and featured the comical exploits of Koko the Clown, was among several other successful cartoon series from the early days of cartoon animation that were issued to television in the early 1950s. Initially shown in some television markets in 1952, this series of films was syndicated nationally in 1956 when Paramount sold the cartoons to a television distributor, UM&M-TV (later renamed NTA).

In 1961 Fleischer's creation was revived in all-new color adventures that featured a new supporting cast of regulars: Kokette, Koko's girlfriend; Koko-nut, Koko's dog; and Mean Moe, Koko's primary adversary. Several published reports in the mid-1960s cited Fleischer's disappointment with the series, especially its animation quality. Larry Storch, of TV's *F Troop*, did most of the characters' voices.

A Max Fleischer Production (old films). A Video House Incorporated Production (new series). Black-and-white. Color. Premiered: 1952 (old series). Premiered: September 10, 1962 (new series).

Voices

Koko/Kokette/Mean Moe: Larry Storch

◎ THE PAC-MAN/LITTLE RASCALS/RICHIE RICH SHOW

The popular video game character starred in this hour-long series that featured more episodes of Pakky, in combination with new premiere episodes of "The Little Rascals" and new episodes of *Richie Rich*. The series aired back to back with the first season run of *The Pac-Man Show* on ABC in 1982 and lasted one full season. In 1983 ABC brought the series back but split its components—*Pac Man* and *The Little Rascals/Richie Rich Show*—into two separate time slots. In 1989 *The Pac-Man Show* was rebroadcast (by itself) on USA Network's *Cartoon Express*.

A Hanna-Barbera Production. Color. One hour. Premiered on ABC: September 25, 1982–September 3, 1983. Rebroadcast on USA: February 26, 1989–March 20, 1992 (The Pac-Man Show).

Voices

PAC-MAN: Pac-Man: Marty Ingels; **Ms. Pepper Pac-Man:** Barbara Minkus; **Baby Pac:** Russi Taylor; **Chomp Chomp:** Frank Welker; **Sour Puss:** Peter Cullen; **Mezmaron:** Alan Lurie; **Clyde Monster:** Neilson Ross; **Blinky/Pinky Monsters:** Chuck McCann; **Inky Monster:** Barry Gordon

THE LITTLE RASCALS: Spanky: Scott Menville; **Alfalfa/Porky/Woim:** Julie McWhirter Dees; **Darla:** Patt

Maloney; **Buckwheat:** Shavar Ross; **Butch/Waldo:** B.J. Ward; **Officer Ed/Pete the Pup:** Peter Cullen

RICHIE RICH: Richie Rich: Sparky Marcus; **Mrs. Rich/Irona:** Joan Gerber; **Reggie Van Goh:** Dick Beals; **Professor Keenbean:** Bill Callaway; **Gloria:** Nancy Cartwright; **Mr. Rich/Cadbury:** Stanley Jones; **Dollar:** Frank Welker

THE PAC-MAN/RUBIK THE AMAZING CUBE HOUR

Pac-Man, Ms. Pac, Baby Pac and the rest of the Pac-Land gang returned in all-new adventures in this hour-long fantasy/adventure series that provided equal time to its costar, Rubik, the Amazing Cube, which made its Saturday-morning television debut. Rubik is discovered by a young boy (Carlos), who brings the colorful cube to life—after he aligns all the cube's sides—and sets out on a magical adventure tour along with his brother and sister, Renaldo and Lisa. (The series was rebroadcast in the spring of 1985 as a mid season replacement.) Hanna-Barbera Productions (Pac-Man) and Ruby-Spears Enterprises (Rubik) coproduced the series.

A Hanna-Barbera and Ruby-Spears Enterprises Production. Color. One hour. Premiered on ABC: September 10, 1983– September 1, 1984.

Voices
Pac-Man: Marty Ingels; **Ms. Pac:** Barbara Minkus; **Baby Pac:** Russi Taylor; **Super-Pac:** Lorenzo Music; **Pac-Junior:** Darryl Hickman; **Chomp Chomp:** Frank Welker; **Sour Puss:** Peter Cullen; **Mezmaron:** Alan Lurie; **Sue Monster:** Susan Silo; **Inky Monster:** Barry Gordon; **Clyde Monster:** Neilson Ross; **Rubik:** Ron Palillo; **Carlos:** Michael Saucedo; **Renaldo, his brother:** Michael Bell; **Lisa, his sister:** Jennifer Fajardo; **Ruby Rodriguez:** Michael Bell; **Marla Rodriguez:** Angela Moya

THE PAC-MAN SHOW

The immensely popular video game character starred in this half-hour series, along with his wife, Ms. Pac, a peppery liberated lady; the energetic Baby Pac; Chomp Chomp, a lovable dog; and Sour Puss, their sly cat, in fantasy adventures that took place in Pac-Land, a pretty pastel world composed of brightly glowing dots. Their perfect world had one enemy, however: the ever-sinister Mezmaron, who tried to rob the Power Pellet Forest of the power pellets Pac-Land thrives on. (His attempts were always bungled by his comical ghost monsters, Inky, Blinky, Pinky, Clyde and Sue.)

In 1983 the series was rebroadcast in combination with Ruby-Spears Enterprises' *Rubik The Amazing Cube* as *The Pac-Man/Rubik/The Amazing Cube Hour.* Several new char-

acters were added during the second season to the Pac-Man cartoons: Pac-Junior, Pac-Man's fast-talking, free-wheeling cousin, and Super-Pac, a vain and powerful superhero.

A Hanna-Barbera Production. Color. Half-hour. Premiered on ABC: September 25, 1982–September 3, 1983. Rebroadcast on ABC: September 10, 1983–September 1, 1984 (as The Pac-Man/Rubik/The Amazing Cube Hour). Rebroadcast on CAR: February 18, 1995–February 19, 1995 (Look What We Found!).

Voices
Pac-Man: Marty Ingels; **Ms. Pac:** Barbara Minkus; **Baby Pac:** Russi Taylor; **Super-Pac:** Lorenzo Music; **Pac-Junior:** Darryl Hickman; **Chomp Chomp:** Frank Welker; **Sour Puss:** Peter Cullen; **Mezmaron:** Alan Lurie; **Sue Monster:** Susan Silo; **Inky Monster:** Barry Gordon; **Blinky/Pinky Monsters:** Chuck McCann; **Clyde Monster:** Neilson Ross

PADDINGTON BEAR (1981)

Author Michael Bond's childlike honeybear who can talk was cast in this short-lived series produced by London's preeminent model animation studio, FilmFair Animation, for public television based on chapters from Bond's popular children's books, including his first, *A Bear Called Paddington.* Oscar-winning entertainer Joel Grey introduced each program, featuring five vignettes that blends stop-action animation of a stuffed bear and flat, cut-out figures to tell each story. Between 1985 and 1986, three additional half-hour specials were also produced: "Paddington's Birthday Bonanza," "Paddington Goes to the Movies" and "Paddington Goes to School." Each aired on The Disney Channel.

A FilmFair Animation/Paddington & Co. Ltd. Production. Color. Half-hour. Premiered on PBS: April 13, 1981–May 18, 1981.

Voices
Narrator/Others: Michael Hordern

PADDINGTON BEAR (1989)

The Brown family discovered a lost little bear at London's Paddington Station, whom they named Paddington and raised as their child in this half-hour animated adaptation of the storybook favorite. The program was broadcast on Sunday mornings as part of *The Funtastic World of Hanna-Barbera.*

A Hanna-Barbera Production. Color. Half-hour. Premiered: September 1989.

Voices
Paddington Bear: Charlie Adler; **Mr. Brown:** John Standing; **Mrs. Brown:** B.J. Ward; **Jonathan Brown, their**

son: Cody Everett; **Judy Brown, their daughter:** Katie Johnson; **Mrs. Bird, their housekeeper:** Georgia Brown; **David Russell, the Browns' cousin:** R.J. Williams; **Mr. Gruber, an antique dealer:** Hamilton Camp; **Mr. Curry, the Browns' neighbor:** Tim Curry

⦿ PANDAMONIUM

Three talking panda bears (Algernon, Chesty and Timothy) and their teenage human friends (Peter Darrow and his sister, Peggy) embarked to find the lost pieces of the magical, mystical Pyramid of Power in this 13-episode half-hour fantasy/adventure series, co-created by Fred Silverman, who also served as one of the series' executive producers. The series originally aired on CBS.

A Marvel Production in association with InterMedia Entertainment. Color. Half-hour. Premiered on CBS: September 18, 1982–September 10, 1985.

Voices

Algernon: Walker Edmiston; **Chesty:** Jesse White; **Timothy:** Cliff Norton; **Peter Darrow:** Neilson Ross; **Peggy, his sister:** Katie Leigh; **Amanda Panda:** Julie McWhirter Dees; **Moondraggor:** William Woodson

⦿ PAPA BEAVER'S STORY TIME

These half-hour weekday series cartoon re-creations of clever fables and wondrous children's stories of French author Pere Castor recounted tales of sacrifice, bravery and redemption. They debuted on Nickelodeon in 1995.

An M5 Production. Color. Half-hour. Premiered on NIK: May 18, 1995–December 31, 1997.

⦿ PARTRIDGE FAMILY: 2200 A.D.

Widow Connie Partridge led an interplanetary rock-and-roll group comprised of family members Keith, Laurie, Danny, Tracy and Chris in futuristic adventures on Earth and in outer space, performing their music to new audiences of every kind—alien and otherwise. A spin-off of the popular TV sitcom *The Partridge Family*, the program featured the voices of the original cast members (except Shirley Jones and David Cassidy) and reprised one of the group's most famous songs in each show. The series' 16 half-hour episodes originally aired on CBS in 1974–75 and were later syndicated as part of 1977's *Fred Flintstone and Friends*.

A Hanna-Barbera Production. Color. Half-hour. Premiered on CBS: September 7, 1974–March 8, 1975. Syndicated: 1977.

Voices

Connie Partridge: Joan Gerber; **Keith Partridge:** Chuck McClendon; **Laurie Partridge:** Susan Dey; **Danny Partridge:** Danny Bonaduce; **Christopher Partridge:** Brian Forster; **Tracy Partridge:** Suzanne Crough; **Reuben Kinkaid:** David Madden; **Marion:** Julie McWhirter; **Veenie:** Frank Welker

⦿ THE PAW PAWS

The muffled patter of small tom-toms was the only clue to the whereabouts of the Paw Paws, a tribe of tiny, tenderhearted bearlets who inhabited the enchanted forest where past, present and future are blended in this half-hour fantasy/adventure series offered as part of weekend syndie package, *The Funtastic World of Hanna-Barbera* in 1985. But all was not rosy for Princess Paw Paw and her tribe, for across the river Dark Paw and his evil tribe, the Meanos, lay waiting for their next chance to conquer the peace-loving Paw Paws. The series was rebroadcast on USA Network's *Cartoon Express* and the Cartoon Network.

A Hanna-Barbera Production. Color. Half-hour. Premiered: September 1985. Syndicated. Rebroadcast on USA: September 18, 1989–March 20, 1992. Rebroadcast on CAR: October 2, 1992–April 2, 1993 (weekdays); July 4, 1993–September 17, 1993 (Sundays); January 5, 1994–June 2, 1995 (weekdays); September 4, 1995– (weekdays).

Voices

Princess Paw Paw: Susan Blu; **Brave Paw:** Thom Pinto; **Mighty Paw:** Bob Ridgely; **Laughing Paw:** Stanley Stoddart; **Wise Paw:** John Ingle; **Trembly Paw:** Howard Morris; **Pupooch:** Don Messick; **Dark Paw:** Stanley Ralph Ross; **Bumble Paw:** Frank Welker; **Aunt Pruney:** Ruth Buzzi

⦿ PB&J OTTER

Three young sibling otters (seven-year-old Peanut, his five-year-old sister Jelly and baby sister Butter) enjoy life on their customized houseboat on Lake Hoohaw, frolicking with their neighbors—families of raccoons, ducks and beavers—in this half-hour animated series created by animator Jim Jinkins (the father of *Doug*) for The Disney Channel.

A Siriol Animation Ltd., Cardiff Production for S4C, Wales. Color. Half-hour. Premiered on DIS: March 15, 1998.

⦿ PEBBLES AND BAMM-BAMM

Barney Rubble's muscular son, Bamm-Bamm, and Fred Flintstone's gorgeous daughter, Pebbles, are young adults experiencing the tribulations of teenagers—dating, finding work and earning money—but in a prehistoric setting in this weekly 16-episode Saturday-morning cartoon series, produced for CBS.

Sally Struthers, of TV's *All in the Family* fame, was the voice of Pebbles. (She was replaced by Mickey Stevens when the character was reprised in new adventures on *The Flintstones Comedy Hour*.) Episodes later appeared on the syndicated *Fred Flintstone and Friends* in the late 1970s and in the late 1980s and 1990s were rebroadcast on USA Network's *Cartoon Express* and the Cartoon Network.

A Hanna-Barbera Production. Color. Half-hour. Premiered on CBS: September 11, 1971–September 2, 1972. Rebroadcast on CBS: May 1973–September 1973; February 1974–September 1974; March 8, 1975–September 4, 1976. Rebroadcast on USA: March 31, 1989–May 25, 1992. Rebroadcast CAR: February 1, 1993–February 7, 1993 (including Pebbles and Bamm-Bamm *Marathon); January 2, 1995–June 2, 1995 (weekdays).*

Voices
Pebbles Flintstone: Sally Struthers; **Bamm-Bamm Rubble:** Jay North; **Moonrock:** Lennie Weinrib; **Penny:** Mitzi McCall; **Wiggy/Cindy:** Gay Hartwig; **Fabian:** Carl Esser

◉ THE PERILS OF PENELOPE PITSTOP
In this spoof of the famed silent movie serial *The Perils of Pauline*, lovely heroine race driver Penelope Pitstop (formerly of Hanna-Barbera's *The Wacky Races*) is imperiled by the Hooded Claw (alias Sylvester Sneekly), who seeks to get rid of her in order to acquire her inheritance. Penelope is protected by her legal guardians, a bevy of buffoons known as the Ant Hill Mob, who also appeared in *The Wacky Races*. (Their car's name was changed from "The Bulletproof Bomb" to "Chug-A-Boom.") The 17-episode half-hour series bowed on CBS in 1969, featuring an entertaining ensemble of voice actors, including veterans Mel Blanc and Don Messick, comedian Paul Lynde (from TV's original *Hollywood Squares*) and former *Rowan and Martin's Laugh-In* announcer Gary Owens. Episodes were later syndicated as part of *The Fun World of Hanna-Barbera* and reshown on the Cartoon Network.

A Hanna-Barbera Production. Color. Half-hour. Premiered on CBS: September 13, 1969–September 5, 1971. Syndicated: 1977. Rebroadcast on CAR: June 28, 1993–October 1993 (weekdays); June 6, 1994–September 2, 1994 (weekdays); June 5, 1995–October 1, 1995 (weekdays, Sundays); March 25, 1996–June 27, 1997 (weekdays).

Voices
Narrator: Gary Owens; **Penelope Pitstop:** Janet Waldo; **Sylvester Sneekly/The Hooded/Claw:** Paul Lynde; **Bully Brothers/Yak Yak:** Mel Blanc; **Clyde/Softly:** Paul Winchell; **Zippy/Dum Dum/Snoozy/Pockets/Narrator:** Don Messick; **Chug-A-Boom:** Mel Blanc

◉ PETER PAN & THE PIRATES
Bad pirates (including the bone-chilling scourge of the seven seas, Captain Hook), magical Indians and mythical beasts and the world of flying urchin Peter Pan and friends, Tinker Bell, Wendy and Tiger Lily, come to life in this daily half-hour cartoon series (also known as *Fox's Peter Pan and the Pirates*), inspired by British author James M. Barrie's novel *Peter and Wendy*. Originally to be called "The Never Told Tales of Peter Pan," this stunning animated series was commissioned by the Fox network prior to the theatrical release of Steven Spielberg's full-length live-action feature *Hook*. It experienced declining ratings in its daily time slot and, in an effort to improve its rating status, was moved to the network's Saturday-morning schedule in January 1991, only to be pulled from the lineup permanently that September.

A Southern Star/TMS Entertainment Production in association with Fox Children's Productions. Color. Half-hour. Premiered on FOX: September 8, 1990–September 11, 1992.

Voices
Peter Pan: Jason Marsden; **Tinker Bell:** Debi Derryberry; **Wendy:** Christina Lange; **John:** Jack Lynch; **Michael:** Whitby Hertford; **Tiger Lily:** Cree Summer; **Captain Hook:** Tim Curry; **Alf Mason:** Tony Jay; **Billy Jukes:** Eugene Williams; **Cookson:** Jack Angel; **Curly:** Josh Wiener; **Great Big Little Panther:** Michael Wise; **Hard-to-Hit:** Aaron Lohr; **Mullins:** Jack Angel; **Nibs:** Adam Carl; **Slightly:** Scott Menville; **Smee:** Ed Gilbert; **Starkey:** David Shaughnessy; **Tootles:** Chris Allport; **Twin #1:** Michael Bacall; **Twin #2:** Aaron Lohr

Additional Voices
Linda Gary

◉ PETER POTAMUS AND HIS MAGIC FLYING BALLOON
Umbrella title for Hanna-Barbera's sixth syndicated series, whose main star was a purple hippo, Peter Potamus (whose voice sounded like comedian Joe E. Brown), and his sidekick, So So the monkey, who travel back in time and make history in the process.

Other series regulars were: "Breezly and Sneezly," the misadventures of a goofy polar bear and smart arctic seal who first debuted on *The Magilla Gorilla Show*; and "Yippee, Yappee and Yahooey," tracing the madcap attempts of three palace guard dogs to serve the king. Two years after its debut, the program was retitled and rebroadcast on ABC as *The Peter Potamus Show* and again in syndication as *The Magilla Gorilla/Peter Potamus Show*.

A Hanna-Barbera Production. Color. Half-hour. Premiered: September 16, 1964. Syndicated.

Voices
Peter Potamus: Hal Smith; **So So:** Don Messick; **Breezly:** Howard Morris; **Sneezly:** Mel Blanc; **Colonel:** John Stephenson; **Yippee:** Doug Young; **Yappee:** Hal Smith; **Yahooey:** Daws Butler; **The King:** Hal Smith

THE PETER POTAMUS SHOW

Network version of the syndicated series that first appeared on television screens nationwide in 1964 under the title *Peter Potamus and His Magic Flying Balloon*. ABC picked up the series and added the program to its Saturday-morning children's lineup in 1966. The cartoon components from the former series remained intact (see entry for voice credits and further details), combining new episodes with cartoons that aired previously in syndication.

A Hanna-Barbera Production. Color. Half-hour. Premiered on ABC: January 2, 1966–December 24, 1967.

PHANTOM 2040

The series is set in a future on the brink of environmental disaster. Kit Walker Jr., a college student who is heir to the 500-year legacy of the Phantom, assumes the famed superhero's identity—known down the ages as "the ghost who walks"—to battle a corrupt corporation that plans to destroy Earth's ecosystem in this 33-episode half-hour series stripped for weekend syndication.

A Hearst Entertainment, MINOS S.S. France 3 Production in association with King Features. Color. Half-hour. Premiered: September 17, 1994. Syndicated.

Voices

Phantom/Kit Walker Jr.: Scott Valentine; **Rebecca Madison:** Margot Kidder; **Guran:** J.D. Hall; **Graft:** Ron Perlman; **Maxwell Madison:** Jeff Bennett; **Vain Gloria:** Deborah Harry; **Dr. Jax:** Mark Hamill

PIGGSBURG PIGS!

In a town entirely populated by pigs, those big-time porkers the Bacon Brothers (Bo, Portley and Pighead) go up against Piggsburg's notorious villain, Rembrandt Proupork, in a series of madcap adventures in this short-lived half-hour series that aired on The Fox Network. Premiering in the fall of 1990, the series went up against stiff competition during its network debut: It was scheduled opposite CBS's hit animated series, *Teenage Mutant Ninja Turtles*. Fox pulled the program from its Saturday-morning lineup in the spring of 1991, replacing it with the live-action series *Swamp Thing*. The program finished its network run, twice returning to replace the latter, albeit briefly, in reruns. Only 13 half-hour episodes were produced. The show's original working title was *Pig Out*.

A Ruby-Spears Production in association with the Fred Silverman Company/Sy Fischer Company/Fox Children's Productions. Color. Half-hour. Premiered on FOX: September 13, 1990–April 13, 1991; May 25, 1991–June 29, 1991; August 10, 1991–August 31, 1991.

Voices

Robert Cait, Tara Charandoff, David Huband, Keith Knight, Jonathan Potts, Susan Roman, Ron Rubin, Norman Spencer, Greg Spottiswood, John Stocker, Peter Wildman, Harvey Atkin, Len Carlson, Don Francks, Catherine Gallant, Rex Hagon, Elizabeth Hanna, Robert Bockstael, Dan Hennessey, Gordon Masten, Allen Stewart-Coates

THE PINK PANTHER

Legendary Warner Bros. animator and Pink Panther creator Friz Freleng served as a creative consultant, along with David H. DePatie, who coproduced with Freleng several previous Pink Panther animated television series on this newly produced half-hour syndicated series in which the suave, shrewd cat talked (voiced by Matt Frewer, of TV's *Max Headroom* and *Doctor, Doctor* fame).

Premiering in the fall of 1993, the series' new adventures combined the same visual humor and slapstick gags as previously made cartoons and featured lesser-known DePatie-Freleng theatrical cartoon characters in supporting roles, including the Ant and the Aardvark (voiced by John Byner) and The Dogfather (voiced by Joe Piscopo) as well as several new characters: Voodoo Man (voiced by Dan Castellaneta), Manly Man (voiced by Jess Harnell), among others.

Fifty-two new and original episodes were filmed for the series, which returned for a second season in 1994, comprised of reruns. One episode, "Driving Mr. Pink," was released as a theatrical short in 1995. It first aired as a syndicated television episode in 1994 combined with two other first-run episodes, "Dazed and Confused" and "Three Pink Porkers." The short opened jointly with Don Bluth's full-length animated feature. *The Pebble and the Penguin*.

An MGM Animation Production in association with Claster Television. Color. Half-hour. Premiered: 1993: Syndicated.

Voices

Pink Panther: Matt Frewer; **The Ant and the Aardvark:** John Byner; **The Dogfather/Puggs:** Joe Piscopo; **Inspector Clouseau:** Brian George; **Voodoo Man:** Dan Castellaneta; **Many Man:** Jess Harnell; **The Parrot:** Charles Nelson Reilly; **The Boss:** Wallace Shawn; **Grandmother/The Witch:** Ruth Buzzi

PINK PANTHER AND SONS

The Pink Panther is the father of three sons, Pinky, Panky, and Punkin, in all-new misadventures that test his skills at fatherhood in managing the terrorsome trio. As in previous films, the witty panther conveys his message via pantomime in this half-hour series comprised of 26 cartoon adventures (two per show) originally broadcast on NBC in 1984.

A DePatie-Freleng Enterprises Production in association with Hanna-Barbera Productions. Color. Half-hour. Premiered on NBC: September 15, 1984–September 7, 1985. Rebroadcast on ABC: March 1, 1986–September 6, 1986.

Voices

Pinky: Billy Bowles; **Panky/Punkin:** B.J. Ward; **Chatta:** Sherry Lynn; **Howl:** Marshall Efron; **Anney/Liona:** Jeanine Elias; **Finko/Rocko:** Frank Welker; **Bowlhead:** Gregg Berger; **Buckethead:** Sonny Melendrez; **Murfel:** Shane McCabe

◎ THE PINK PANTHER LAUGH AND A HALF-HOUR AND A HALF

Following the success of NBC's long-running *The New Pink Panther Show*, DePatie-Freleng Enterprises produced this 90-minute version featuring a myriad of old and new cartoon favorites: *The Pink Panther, The Inspector, The Ant and the Aardvark, The Texas Toads* (formerly *The Tijuana Toads*, Poncho and Toro, who were redubbed by actors Don Diamond and Tom Holland for television) and *Misterjaws.* (See individual entries in Theatrical Sound Cartoon Series for complete details.)

A DePatie-Freleng Enterprises Production. Color. Ninety minutes. Premiered on NBC: September 11, 1976–September 3, 1977.

◎ THE PINK PANTHER MEETS THE ANT AND THE AARDVARK

Following the ratings success of *The Pink Panther Show*, NBC ordered this follow-up half-hour series featuring Pink Panther and *The Ant and the Aardvark* cartoons (see individual entry in Theatrical Animated Cartoon Series section for details), originally produced as cartoon shorts for theaters. The series was as successful as its predecessor, garnering high ratings.

A DePatie-Freleng Enterprises Production. Color. Half-Hour. Premiered on NBC: September 12, 1970–September 11, 1971.

◎ THE PINK PANTHER SHOW

Two madcap adventures of the Academy Award-winning mute feline were presented each week in this half-hour series, hosted by Lenny Schultz and featuring the comical exploits of Paul and Mary Ritts puppets. Backed by Henry Mancini's popular theme song, the series' episodes were comprised of cartoons from the theatrical cartoon series made in the 1960s.

Other segments included *The Inspector*, featuring cartoon shorts originally released to theaters between 1965 and 1969. The program was the first of several Saturday-morning series starring the unflappable feline, followed by 1970's *The Pink Panther Meets the Ant and the Aardvark*, 1971's *The New Pink Panther Show*, 1976's *The Pink Panther Laugh and a Half-Hour and a Half Show*, 1978's *Think Pink Panther!* 1978's *The All-New Pink Panther Show* and 1984's *Pink Panther and Sons*.

A DePatie-Freleng Enterprises Production. Color. Half-hour. Premiered on NBC: September 6, 1969–September 5, 1970.

◎ PINKY & THE BRAIN

(See STEVEN SPIELBERG PRESENTS PINKY & THE BRAIN.)

◎ PIRATES OF DARK WATER

First produced as a 1991 five-part animated miniseries (simply called *Dark Water*), chronicling the noble quest to save a dying alien planet, this weekly half-hour sword-and-sorcery series revolved around the continuing plight of the planet Mer and the Kingdom of Octopon, in danger of becoming ruled by the evil forces of Dark Water, a highly intelligent, dictatorial liquid entity determined to take over the planet. Saving the day are a determined young Prince, a fussy sidekick, a dashing pirate rogue and a highly independent woman who come to the rescue. Premiering as a series in the fall of 1992, the program was part of the weekend syndicated extravaganza *Funtastic World of Hanna-Barbera*.

A Hanna-Barbera Production in association with Fils-Cartoons, Inc. and Tama Production Co. Color. Half-hour. Premiered: February 25, 1991–March 1, 1991 (as the five-part miniseries Dark Water*); 1992 (as a weekly series, part of* Funtastic World of Hanna-Barbera*). Rebroadcast on CAR: January 3, 1994–April 1, 1994 (weekdays); June 6, 1994–September 2, 1994 (weekdays); January 5, 1995–June 2, 1995 (weekdays); March 25, 1996–May 3, 1997 (weekdays, Sundays).*

Voices

Jodi Benson, Regis Cordic, Peter Cullen, Tim Curry, Hector Elizondo, Dick Gautier, Allan Lurie, George Newbern, Dan O'Herlihy, Brock Peters, Les Tremayne, Jessica Walter, Frank Welker

◎ THE PLASTIC MAN/BABY PLAS SUPER COMEDY

As if one superhero in the family wasn't enough, Plastic Man and wife, Penny, give birth to a son, Plastic Baby (Baby Plas for short), who possesses the same fantastic attributes as his famous elastic father, in a series of all-new misadventures for ABC. The series, composed of 13 "Plastic Family" and "Baby Plas" cartoons (one per show) and a series of 30-second consumer tips by Plastic Man himself, was the follow-up series of the two-hour extravaganza *The Plastic Man Comedy-Adventure Show*, which also aired on ABC. In 1993 the series resurfaced in reruns on the Cartoon Network.

A Ruby-Spears Production. Color. Half-hour. Premiered on ABC: October 4, 1980–September 5, 1981. Rebroadcast on CAR: June 28, 1993–September 17, 1993 (weekdays); May 2,

1994–September 2, 1994 (weekdays); January 5, 1995 (weekdays); February 25, 1995 (Super Adventure Saturdays); July 22, 1995 (Power Zone).

Voices
Plastic Man: Michael Bell; **Penny, his wife:** Melendy Britt; **Baby Plas, their son:** Michael Bell; **Chief:** Melendy Britt; **Hula Hula:** Joe Baker

◎ THE PLASTIC MAN COMEDY-ADVENTURE SHOW

Spawned by the success of competing studios' superhero cartoons, Ruby-Spears Enterprises adapted a comic-book super-crimefighter of their own: Plastic Man, whose elasticity enables him to stretch like a rubber band and twist his body into different shapes. Aided by friends Penny and Hula-Hula (whose voice is similar to comedian Lou Costello's), the moldable superhero comes to the rescue wherever evil lurks. The series, which bowed on ABC in 1979 in a two-hour format (three months following its debut the show was shortened to 90 minutes), featured three additional cartoon components on each program: "Mighty Man and Yukk," the adventures of a thimble-size superhero (Mighty) and the ugliest dog in the world (Yukk); "Fangface and Fangpuss," the exploits of a teenage werewolf and his equally wolfy cousin; and "Rickey Rocket," in which four teenagers (Comso, Splashdown, Sunstroke and Venus) with a makeshift rocket head a space detective agency. The series was the first of two programs to star the DC Comics superhero, followed by *The Plastic Man/Baby Plas Super Comedy.*

A Ruby-Spears Enterprises Production. Color. Two hours. One hour and a half. Premiered on ABC: September 22, 1979–September 27, 1980 (two-hour format until December of 1979). Rebroadcast on CBS: November 12, 1983–February 4, 1984.

Voices

PLASTIC MAN: Plastic Man: Michael Bell; **Chief/ Penny:** Melendy Britt; **Hula Hula:** Joe Baker;

MIGHTY MAN AND YUKK: Mighty Man/Brandon Brewster: Peter Cullen; **Yukk:** Frank Welker; **Mayor:** John Stephenson

FANGFACE AND FANGPUSS: Fangface/Fangpuss: Frank Welker; **Kim, their friend:** Susan Blu; **Biff, their friend:** Jerry Dexter; **Puggsy, their friend:** Bart Braverman

RICKETY ROCKET: Rickey Rocket: Al Fann; **Cosmo:** Bobby Ellerbee; **Splashdown:** Johnny Brown; **Sunstroke:** John Anthony Bailey; **Venus:** Dee Timberlake

◎ THE PLUCKY DUCK SHOW

Adolescent Daffy Duck look-alike Plucky Duck, the splentic, frenetic costar of Steven Spielberg's popular *Tiny Toon Adventures* cartoon series, hosted this 1991 Saturday-morning entry, comprised solely of repeat episodes from *Tiny Toon Adventures.* Following a three-month run, the series was changed back to *Tiny Toon Adventures,* offering more repeat adventures.

A Spielberg/Warner Brothers Television Animation Production. Color. Half-hour. Premiered on FOX: September 19, 1992–November 7, 1992.

Voices
Plucky Duck: Joe Alaskey

◎ POLE POSITION

A stunt-racing and daredevil family team puts on thrilling automotive acrobatics at the Pole Position Stunt Show, run by Dan Darret and his two sisters, Tess and Daisy, after their parents disappear in an unexplained explosion during a stunt race. The kids carry on their parents' work, along with pet Kuma and two computerized cars, Roadie and Wheels, using the cutting-edge technology of their high-tech vehicles to fight crime in this 13-episode half-hour Saturday-morning series, based on the popular video arcade game of the same name.

A DIC Enterprise/Namco Ltd. Production. Color. Half-hour. Premiered on CBS: September 15, 1984–August 30, 1985.

Voices
Dan Darret: David Coburn; **Tess, his sister:** Lisa Lindgren; **Daisy, his sister:** Kaleena Kiff; **Dr. Zachary, their uncle:** Jack Angel; **Wheels:** Mel Franklyn; **Roadie:** Daryl Hickman; **Kuma:** Marilyn Schreffler; **Teacher:** Helen Minniear

◎ POLICE ACADEMY: THE SERIES

Those wacky defenders of law and order (Mahoney, Jones, Hightower, Zed, Captain Harris and others), known for their hijinks in a series of live-action feature-length action/comedies, return to the beat in this first-run, daily half-hour series as they attempt to keep the peace while using the most outrageous crime-prevention methods ever seen. Syndicated in 1988, voice work for the series was recorded in Canada.

A Ruby-Spears Enterprise Production. Color. Half-hour. Premiered: September 1988. Syndicated.

Voices
Mahoney: Ron Rubin; **Hightower:** Charles Gray, Greg Morton; **Hooks/Callahan:** Denise Pidgeon; **Jones:** Greg

Morton; **Zed/Tackleberry:** Dan Hennessey; **Sweetchuck/
Professor:** Howard Morris; **Proctor:** Greg Swanson; **Las-
sard:** Gary Krawford; **Harris:** Len Carlson; **House:**
Dorian Joe Clark

◉ POPEYE

The King Features syndicate, which owns the rights to Popeye, produced this new made-for-television series of 210 six-
minute episodic adventures reprising the adversarial
relationship of spinach-gobbling sailor Popeye and seafaring
bully Brutus (whose name was changed to Bluto in the Max
Fleischer cartoons), as they continue to battle over the
affections of fickle Olive Oyl. The rest of the supporting
cast from the original Max Fleischer cartoon shorts were
also featured, including Wimpy, Swee'pea, Sea Hag and
Eugene the Jeep.

The series, sold to local stations based on two "pilot" cartoons, "Hits and Missiles" and "Barbecue for Two," was produced by Al Brodax for King Features within a two-year
period and premiered in syndication in 1960. Five different
independent studios were used to animate the series. Jack
Kinney Studios produced the pilot "Barbecue for Two" and
animated most of the series (101 cartoon shorts in all).

*Seafaring sailor Popeye starred in a new made-for-television series of
episodic adventures in the 1960s. © King Features Entertainment*

Paramount Cartoon Studios produced theatrical "Popeye"
cartoon shorts up until 1957 and handled animation for 63
films, including the pilot "Hits and Missiles." Other studios
engaged to animate the series were producer William L.
Snyder's Rembrandt Films (producers of the Oscar-winning
short "Munro"), which produced 28 new "Popeye" cartoons
in association with Britain's Halas and Batchelor and Czech
cartoon director Gene Deitch's studio in Prague. Larry Harmon Productions, which created and produced TV's *Bozo
the Clown*, handled production of 18 cartoons, while Gerald
Ray's TV Spots, an all-purpose animation factory, produced
10 vehicles for the series.

*A King Features Production in association with Larry Har-
mon Productions/Paramount Cartoon Studios/Jack Kinney Stu-
dios/Gene Deitch Studios/Rembrandt Films, TV Spots/Halas
and Batchelor. Color. Half-hour. Premiered: 1960. Syndicated.*

Voices

Popeye: Jack Mercer; **Brutus:** Jackson Beck; **Olive Oyl:**
Mae Questel; **J. Wellington Wimpy:** Charles Lawrence,
Jack Mercer; **Swee'pea/Sea Hag/Eugene the Jeep:** Mae
Questel; **Rough House:** Jack Mercer

◉ THE POPEYE AND OLIVE SHOW

In this Saturday-morning series of all-new adventures based
on Edgar Segar's popular comic-strip creations, Popeye and
Olive shared top billing. This comedy/adventure show consisted of three weekly segments—one ensemble series, "The
Popeye Show," which starred Popeye, Olive and old
favorites Bluto and Wimpy, in 24 cartoon shorts, plus two
additional series of short cartoons (16 episodes each): "Private Olive Oyl," in which Popeye's stringbean girlfriend
stars as a clumsy army private; and "Prehistoric Popeye,"
with the muscleman sailor trying to contend with caveman
situations before the availability of spinach cans. (The films
were mixed in with other modern-day adventures.) Since
its original network run, the series was rebroadcast on The
Family Channel.

*A Hanna-Barbera Production in association with King Fea-
tures Entertainment. Color. Half-hour. Premiered on CBS:
September 12, 1981–November 27, 1982. Rebroadcast on
FAM: September 15, 1990–September 29, 1996.*

Voices

Popeye: Jack Mercer; **Olive Oyl:** Marilyn Schreffler;
Bluto: Allan Melvin; **Wimpy:** Daws Butler; **Sgt. Bertha
Blast, Olive's sergeant:** Jo Anne Worley; **Alice the Goon:**
Marilyn Schreffler; **Colonel Crumb:** Hal Smith

◉ POPEYE AND SON

Updated adventures of strongman sailor Popeye and spindly
girlfriend Olive Oyl who, now married and living in a ram-

shackle beach house, find they have their hands full with son, Popeye Jr. a feisty, rugged nine-year-old who's a real chip off the old block, except that he hates spinach. Old rival Bluto returns to make trouble, with his own son, Tank, who is more "like father, like son" than Popeye Jr. is to his famous fighting father. The 26-episode Saturday-morning series premiered on CBS in 1987, featured two 11-minute cartoon adventures each week. The series was later run on USA Network's *Cartoon Express* and on The Family Channel.

A Hanna-Barbera Production. Color. Half-hour. Premiered on CBS: September 19, 1987–September 10, 1988. Rebroadcast on USA: September 29, 1989–September 16, 1990. Rebroadcast on FAM: September 4, 1994–December 31, 1995.

Voices
Popeye: Maurice LaMarche; **Olive Oyl:** Marilyn Schreffler; **Popeye Jr.:** Josh Rodine; **Bluto:** Allan Melvin; **Lizzie, Bluto's wife:** Marilyn Schreffler; **Tank, their son:** David Markus; **Woody, Junior's friend:** Nancy Cartwright; **Polly, Junior's friend:** Penina Segall; **Dee Dee, Junior's friend:** Kaleena Kiff; **Rad:** B.J. Ward; **Puggy:** Marilyn Schreffler; **Wimpy:** Allan Melvin; **Eugene the Jeep:** Don Messick

POPEYE THE SAILOR
One of several early series repackaging old films for television, this series was comprised of the six-minute "Popeye the Sailor" cartoons produced between 1933 and 1954 by Paramount Pictures. In many television markets, the cartoons were screened for young viewers in programs hosted by local television celebrities. (See entry in Theatrical Sound Cartoon Series for listing of films.)

A Max Fleischer/Famous Studios Production in association with Paramount Pictures. Black-and-white. Color. Half-hour. Premiered: September 10, 1956. Syndicated.

Voices
Popeye: William Costello, Jack Mercer; **Olive Oyl:** Mae Questel; **Bluto:** Gus Wickie, Pinto Colvig, William Pennell; **J. Wellington Wimpy:** Jack Mercer, Lou Fleischer, Frank Matalone; **Swee'pea:** Mae Questel; **Poodpeck Pappy/Pupeye/Peepeye/Pipeye:** Jack Mercer; **Shorty:** Arnold Stang

POPPLES
Able to produce just about anything they need—from a trampoline to a pair of skates—these furry little creatures live in a world scaled for adults with their human friends, Bonnie and Billy and always come up with creative solutions to any obstacles in their way.

A DIC Enterprises Production. Color. Half-hour. Premiered: 1986–87. Syndicated.

Voices
Bonnie/Billy/Mike: Valerie Bromfield

Furry little creatures bring fun and excitement wherever they go in DIC Enterprises' Popples. © American Greetings Corp.
(COURTESY: DIC ENTERPRISES)

THE POPPLES: Potato Chip: Donna Christie; **Penny:** Jeanine Elias; **Punkster/Putter:** Danny Mann; **Pancake:** Sharon Noble; **Party/Punkity/Prize/Puffball:** Louise Vallance; **Puzzle:** Maurice LaMarche

POP-UPS
Paul Klein produced this series of 12 one-minute education fillers, aimed at encouraging reading among young viewers, that were broadcast sporadically as part of NBC's Saturday-morning schedule in 1971.

An Educational Solutions Production. Color. One minute. Premiered on NBC: January 23, 1971–August 28, 1971.

THE PORKY PIG SHOW
P-P-Porky Pig was the host of his own Saturday-morning series, featuring the cartoons of "Daffy Duck," "Bugs Bunny," "Sylvester and Tweety," "Foghorn Leghorn" and "Pepe Le Pew." In 1971, four years after its network run, the series was syndicated to television under the title *Porky Pig and His Friends*. (See series' entries in Theatrical Sound Cartoon Series for complete details.)

A Warner Bros. Production. Color. Half-hour. Premiered on ABC: September 20, 1964–September 2, 1967.

Voices
Porky Pig: Mel Blanc

POUND PUPPIES
Inspired by the hit toy from Tonka Corporation, this half-hour adventures series centered on the exploits of 11-year-old

Holly and her merry band of canine friends who live in the Wagga Wagga Pound and do everything they can to find happy homes for deserving dogs, despite the efforts of Katrina and Brattina. The series was preceded by a 1985 hour-long animated special, *Pound Puppies*, which aired on ABC. The 13-episode series debuted Saturday mornings on ABC, in September of 1986. In 1987 a second series followed: *All-New Pound Puppies*. The original series was later rebroadcast on The Disney Channel and the Cartoon Network.

A Hanna-Barbera Production. Color. Half-hour. Premiered on ABC: September 13, 1986–September 5, 1987. Rebroadcast on DIS: 1991. Rebroadcast on CAR: April 5, 1993–June 3, 1994 (weekdays); September 4, 1995– (weekdays).

Voices
Cooler, the leader: Dan Gilvezan; **Bright Eyes:** Nancy Cartwright; **Howler:** Bobby Morse; **Whopper:** B.J. Ward; **Nose Marie:** Ruth Buzzi; **Holly, their 11-year-old friend:** Ami Foster; **Katrina Stoneheart:** Pat Carroll; **Brattina Stoneheart, her sister:** Adrienne Alexander; **Nabbit/Cat Gut:** Frank Welker

PRINCE PLANET

Sent to Earth by the Galactic Council to see if the planet is fit to join the Galactic Union of Worlds, Prince Planet, a member of the Universal Peace Corps, takes on a new identity once on Earth (Bobby). Using his awesome powers, whose source is a generator on the planet Radion, he battles criminal conspirators and other sinister beings who plan to take over the world. Corps members Hadji and Dynamo join Prince Planet in the fight. The 52-episode half-hour series was among a handful of many Japanese-made cartoons syndicated in the United States in the 1960s.

A TCJ Animation Center Production in association with American-International. Color. Half-hour. Premiered: September 1966. Syndicated.

PRINCESS GWENEVERE AND THE JEWEL RIDERS

The Princess and two heroic teenage girls, who "ride the wild magic," try to recover Merlin's crown jewels of the kingdom in this half-hour fantasy/adventure series broadcast as part of the syndicated weekend block *Amazin' Adventures II*. Debuting in 1995 with the two-part episode "Jewel Quest," 26 half-hours were produced of the series, which aired for two seasons in first-run syndication.

A New Frontier Entertainment Production. Color. Half-hour. Premiered: September 9, 1995–January 10, 1997 (part of Amazin' Adventures II). Syndicated.

Voices
Princess Gwenevere: Kerri Butler

PROBLEM CHILD

Junior Healy, a "bad boy"–adopted junior high teen, makes big problems for his parents, his teachers (with help from his co-conspirator/classmate, Cyndi) and the world at large, thanks to his insatiable curiosity and hyperactive imagination, in this weekly half-hour series adaptation based on the popular film series. The program was broadcast opposite *The Itsy Bitsy Spider"* cartoon series as part of USA Network's Sunday-morning "Cartoon Express" beginning in 1993.

A D'Ocon Film/Universal Cartoon Studios Production. Color. Half-hour. Premiered on USA: October 31, 1993–September 15, 1996.

Voices
Peabody: Gilbert Gottfried; **Junior Healy:** Nancy Cartwright

PROJECT G.E.E.K.E.R.

The plans of a rich industrialist (Mr. Moloch) to conquer the world with the help of an artificially created "humanoid" (G.e.e.K.e.R.), a skinny, drooling dork in a jumpsuit who possesses unlimited powers but doesn't know how to use them, are foiled when his prized creation is stolen by streetwise thief Lady Macbeth and her highly intelligent 10-foot dinosaur named Noah, who help G.e.e.K.e.R. fight the ruthless corporate conglomerate that would exploit his powers in this half-hour fantasy series created by Douglas TenNapel and Doug Langdale.

A Columbia-Tristar Children's Television Production. Color. Half-hour. Premiered on CBS: September 14, 1996–August 30, 1997.

Voices
G.e.e.K.e.R.: Billy West; **Dr. Maston/Jake Dragonn:** Charles Adler; **Moloch/Will Dragonn:** Jim Cummings; **Lady Macbeth (Becky):** Cree Summer; **Noah:** Brad Garrett

PROSTARS

The world's greatest sports superstars—Wayne Gretzky, Bo Jackson and Michael Jordan—teamed up to save the globe from ecological disasters, armed with an arsenal of high-tech gadgetry, in this action-packed half-hour series of globe-trotting adventures preceded by live-action wrap-arounds of the famous sports figures to introduce each week's cartoon. DIC Enterprises, which produced the series, originally developed the idea in 1990 for ESPN (then under the name of *All-Stars*), but ESPN opted not to produce the series. The series instead premiered on NBC in the fall of 1991 and was later rebroadcast on The Family Channel.

A DIC Enterprises Production in association with Reteitalia, S.P.A. and Telecinco. Color. Half-hour. Premiered on NBC: September 14, 1991–July 25, 1992. Rebroadcast on FAM: September 5, 1992–March 27, 1994.

Cast (live action)
Bo Jackson: Himself; Wayne Gretsky: Himself; Michael Jordan: Himself

Voices
Wayne Gretzky: Townsend Coleman; Bo Jackson: Dave Fennoy; Michael Jordan: Dorian Harewood; Mama: Susan Silo; Denise: Diana Barrows

◎ A PUP NAMED SCOOBY-DOO
Scooby-Doo, the world's favorite chicken-hearted canine, returns as a cute but clumsy puppy along with kid versions of friends Shaggy, Daphne, Velma and Freddy as they solve kid-size mysteries and encounter ghouls, ghosts and goblins in this 21-episode half-hour series for Saturday mornings. The Emmy award–winning series aired from 1988 to 1990 on ABC.

A Hanna-Barbera Production. Color. Half-hour. Premiered on ABC: September 10, 1988–September 1, 1990. Rebroadcast on ABC: August 3, 1991–August 31, 1991; September 12, 1992–September 4, 1993. Rebroadcast on CAR: April 4, 1994 (weekdays, Sundays); February 26, 1995 (Super Chunk); October 13, 1997 (weekdays, Saturdays).

Voices
Scooby Doo: Don Messick; Shaggy Rogers: Casey Kasem; Velma Dace Dinkley: Christina Lange; Daphne Blake: Kellie Martin; Freddy Jones: Carl Stevens; Red Herring: Scott Menville

◎ THE PUPPY'S FURTHER ADVENTURES
Joined by his girlfriend, Dolly, and three delightful canine friends, Petey the Pup embarks on a worldwide search for his lost family in this second Saturday-morning series based on several successful *ABC Weekend Specials*, including 1978's *The Puppy Who Wanted a Boy*, which first introduced the character to television audiences. Ten half-hour episodes were produced for the fall of 1983, airing ahead of Hanna-Barbera's *The All-New Scooby and Scrappy-Doo Show* on ABC.

A Ruby-Spears Enterprises Production. Color. Half-hour. Premiered on ABC: September 10, 1983–January 14, 1984 (Puppy's Further Adventures/The All-New Scooby and Scrappy-Doo Show). Rebroadcast on ABC: January 21, 1984–September 1, 1984.

Voices
Petey the Pup: Billy Jacoby; Dolly: Nancy McKeon; Duke/Dash: Michael Bell; Lucky: Peter Cullen; Tommy: Tony O'Dell; Glyder: Josh Rodine; Mother: Janet Waldo; Father: John Stephenson

◎ THE PUPPY'S GREATEST ADVENTURES
Marking the character's third animated series, Petey the Pup, formerly of 1982's *The Scooby and Scrappy-Doo/Puppy Hour* and 1983's *The Puppy's Further Adventures*, returned in a handful of new episodes in this half-hour weekly series for ABC. The series was the least successful of the three, losing the rating battles against NBC's *Snorks* and CBS's *Shirt Tales*, both produced by Hanna-Barbera.

A Ruby-Spears Enterprises/Hanna-Barbera Production. Color. Half-hour. Premiered on ABC: September 10, 1983–November 10, 1984. Rebroadcast on CBS: September 13, 1986–November 8, 1986.

Voices
Petey the Pup: Billy Jacoby; Dolly: Nancy McKeon; Duke/Dash: Michael Bell; Lucky: Peter Cullen; Tommy: Tony O'Dell; Glyder: Josh Rodine; Mother: Janet Waldo; Father: John Stephenson

◎ Q.T. HUSH
This satirical "who-dun-it?" series spotlighted the adventures of a private eye, Q.T. Hush, and his "private-nose" bloodhound, Shamus, who combine forces to solve baffling crimes and mysteries. Hush succeeded in jailing criminals by transforming himself into a shadow named Quincy, who operated independently in tracking down clues in this half-hour series, comprised of 100 five-minute cliff-hanging adventures (10 segments constituted a complete story), produced for first-run syndication.

An Animation Associates Production. Color. Half-hour. Premiered: September 24, 1960. Syndicated.

Voices
Q.T. Hush: Dallas McKennon

◎ QUACK ATTACK
Daily anthology series, airing since 1992 on The Disney Channel, showcasing classic Disney animated cartoon shorts representing 60 years of work by studio animators.

A Walt Disney Company Production. Color. Half-hour. Premiered on DIS: 1992.

◎ QUICK DRAW McGRAW
Law and order are the name of the game as U.S. Marshall Quick Draw McGraw and his Mexican burro sidekick, Baba Looey, corral cutthroats and other villains in untypical cowboy-hero fashion. (Quick habitually ignores his pal's advice and strides resolutely into catastrophe.) Additional plot lines feature Quick as notorious crime fighter El Kabong, a klutzy takeoff of Disney's popular *Zorro* television series, and his

U.S. Marshall Quick Draw McGraw and sidekick Baba Looey are joined by series stars Blabber, Doggie Daddy, Augie Doggie and Snooper from Hanna-Barbera's Quick Draw McGraw series. © Hanna-Barbera Productions

own romantic entanglements with a frustrated filly named Sagebrush Sal. Snuffles, a "dog-biskit" loving dog, was another recurring character in the series. (Once rewarded, he gently floated in midair, symbolizing his ecstasy.)

McGraw's cartoon adventures were the main ingredient of this popular, 45-episode syndicated series, sponsored by Kellogg's and first syndicated in 1959. The program marked Hanna-Barbera's second syndicated series effort made especially for the children's market. It featured two other series regulars: "Snooper and Blabber," a cat (Super Snooper) and mouse (Blabber Mouse) pair of crime investigators who, operating out of the Super Snooper Detective Agency, flush out the city's most-wanted criminals; and "Augie Doggy and Doggie Daddy," starring the ever-affectionate father dog, Daddy (who sounds like Jimmy Durante) and his canine son, Augie, who get caught up in various misadventures.

The program was later rebroadcast on CBS as part of its Saturday-morning lineup in 1963 before returning to syndication. Ted Turner's Cartoon Network began airing the series in 1994 and packaged episodes from the show as part

of a 1995 weeklong prime-time showcase, "Prime Quick Draw McGraw," hosted by popular hosts Haas and Little Joe, daytime stars of Cartoon Network's "High Noon Toons."

A Hanna-Barbera Production. Color. Half-hour. Premiered: September 29, 1959. Syndicated. Rebroadcast on CBS: September 28, 1963–September 3, 1966. Rebroadcast on CAR: September 11, 1994–June 28, 1995 (Sundays, Wednesdays); February 26, 1995 (Super Chunk); July 24, 1995–June 28, 1995 (Prime Quick Draw McGraw); October 13, 1997– (weekdays).

Voices
Quick Draw McGraw/Baba Looey/Injun Joe/Snuffles: Daws Butler; **Sagebrush Sal:** Julie Bennett; **Snooper/Blabber/Augie Doggie:** Daws Butler; **Doggie Daddy:** Doug Young

Other Voices
Don Messick

⊚ THE RACCOONS

Bert Raccoon is just about the best friend anyone could wish for. He's funny, brave, friendly and slightly crazy. He lives with his good friends Ralph and Melissa in a Raccoondominium. Together they run the forest newspaper, the *Evergreen Standard*. However, Bert is usually more interested in playing detective or flying a hang glider than in writing his news column in this half-hour series, originally created by Kevin Gillis for Canadian television. The series debuted on the Canadian CBC TV network in the late 1970s and premiered in the United States on the Disney Channel in 1985. Previously the characters appeared in several successful animated specials, among them *The Christmas Raccoons* and *The Raccoons on Ice*.

A *Gillis-Wiseman Production in association with Atkinson Film-ARTS. Color. Half-hour. Premiered on DIS: October 1985–1992.*

Voices

Bert Raccoon: Len Carlson; **Ralph Raccoon:** Bob Dermer; **Melissa Raccoon:** Linda Feige, Susan Roman; **Schaeffer:** Carl Banas; **Cyril Sneer/Snag:** Michael Magee; **Cedric Sneer:** Marvin Goldhar; **Dan the Ranger:** Murray Cruchley; **Julie:** Vanessa Lindores; **Tommy:** Noam Zylberman; **Bear:** Bob Dermer; **Sophia/Broo:** Sharon Lewis; **Pig One:** Nick Nichols; **Pig #2/Pig #3:** Len Carlson; **Narrator:** Geoffrey Winter

⊚ RAINBOW BRITE

Rainbow Brite, a courageous young girl with a special rainbow-making belt, travels the world by rainbow roads to spread happiness and hope to those in need and to chase away unhappiness in the form of the miserable and mean Murky and Lurky, who do what they can to take Rainbow's power away. Rainbow is joined in her adventures by her faithful horse, Starlite, and her best friend, Twink. This half-hour series was part of the 90-minute syndicated cartoon block "Kideo TV." (See entry for details.) The characters previously appeared in a brace of half-hour animated specials: *Rainbow Brite: The Peril of the Pits* (1984), *Rainbow Brite: The Mighty Monstermunk Menace* (1984) and *Rainbow Brite: The Beginning of Rainbowland* (1985).

A *DIC Enterprises Production in association with Hallmark Cards. Color. Half-hour. Premiered: 1986. Syndicated.*

Voices

Rainbow Brite: Bettina Nash; **Starlite, her horse:** Andre Stojka; **Twink, her best friend:** Robbie Lee; **Murky/Monstromurk/Narrator:** Peter Cullen; **Lurky/Buddy/Evil Force:** Pat Fraley; **Brian:** Scott Menville; **Indigo/Violet/Lala/Sprites:** Robbie Lee; **Red/Patty/Canary:** Mona Marshall; **Moonglow/Tickled Pink:** Ronda Aldrich

A decorated Vietnam War veteran–turned–freedom fighter leads a team of specially trained agents in Ruby-Spears's Rambo. © Ruby-Spears Enterprises/Anabasis Investments

⊚ RAMBO

Rambo, the leader of the specially trained team, the Force of Freedom, and fellow agents Kat, Turbo, Nomad, Sgt. Havoc and Mad Dog, are unofficially assigned by the U.S. government to accomplish seemingly impossible missions—their target: the diabolical organization, S.A.V.A.G.E., led by the sinister General Warhawk—in this first-run adventure series based on the character played by Sylvester Stallone in the top-grossing action-adventure film series. First syndicated in April of 1986 as a five-part miniseries entitled "The Invasion," in which General Warhawk plans to take over a Third World country for a permanent home base, the program returned as daily series, with 65 original episodes, in the fall of that year.

A *Ruby-Spears Enterprises Production in association with Carolco International. Color. Half-hour. Premiered: April 1986 (five-part miniseries); September 1986 (series). Syndicated.*

Voices

Rambo: Neil Ross; **Colonel Trautman:** Alan Oppenheimer; **Kat:** Mona Marshall; **Turbo:** James Avery; **Nomad:** Edmund Gilbert; **General Warhawk:** Michael Ansara; **Gripper:** Lennie Weinrib; **Sgt. Havoc:** Peter Cullen; **Mad Dog:** Frank Welker; **Black Dragon:** Robert Ito

⊚ RAW TOONAGE

This kiddie-oriented, fully animated half-hour series (a sort of animated *Saturday Night Live* for kids), hosted by a different guest host each week, served as a showcase for a pair of new 'toons featured in their own segments each week: "Bonkers," the madcap adventures of misfit Bonkers T. Bobcat (an unemployed cartoon star) who tries to make it as a delivery boy, and "Marsupilami," based on the Franco-Belgain comic-book character of a quick-witted cheetah who gets out of a series of jams thanks to his tail (which happens to be the world's longest). The series ran for one full season on CBS; thereafter, "Bonkers" and "Marsupilami" were spun off into their own half-hour series.

A Walt Disney Television Animation Production. Color. Half-hour. Premiered on CBS: September 19, 1992–September 4, 1993.

Voices

Jitters A. Dog: Jack Angel, Rene Auberjonois, Jeff Bennett; **Grumbles the Grizzly:** Gregg Berger, Scott Bullock, Rodger Bumpass; **Ludwig Von Drake:** Corey Burton; **Fawn Deer:** Jody Carlisle, Nancy Cartwright; **Gosalyn Mallard:** Christine Cavanaugh; **Bonkers D. Bobcat/Norman/Don Karnage/Roderick Lizzard:** Brian Cummings; **Goofy:** Bill Farmer; **Norman's Aunt:** David Fenoy, June Foray; **Marsupilami:** Pat Fraley, Teresa Ganzel, Maurice LaMarche, Katie Leigh, Steve Mackall; **Launchpad McQuack:** Tress MacNeille, Gail Matthius, Terry McGovern; **Badly Animated Man:** Rita Moreno, Gary Owens; **Maurice:** Rob Paulsen, Joe Piscopo, Hal Rayle, Kath Soucie, Russi Taylor, Dave Thomas, Marcia Wallace, B.J. Ward, Frank Welker; **Sebastian:** Samuel E. Wright; **Scrooge McDuck:** Alan Young

◎ THE REAL ADVENTURES OF JONNY QUEST

Originally called *Jonny Quest: The New Adventures*, this series brought Jonny, Hadji, Bandit, Dr. Benton Quest, Race Bannon and the rest of the crew back from the 1960's cartoon series, this time caught in dangers in the real world and in virtual reality, armed with an array of high-tech gadgets. For this series of 65 new half-hour adventures, the characters were radically revamped and featured an *NYPD Blue*–style theme song and a virtual reality segment called "Questworld." Jonny, now 13, was made more muscular than his punky former self. Race Bannon suddenly went from being a dashing bachelor to a father with a daughter, Jessie, supplying some conflict in the story lines. Johnny's barking dog Bandit was cut form the original cast and was not featured in the new series.

In an attempt to overcome the limited viewership of the Cartoon Network, then beamed into only 12 million homes, Turner Broadcasting System simultaneously premiered the series on TNT and TBS. The series premiered in late August of 1996.

A Hanna-Barbera Production. Color. Half-hour. Premiered on the Cartoon Network/TBS/TNT: August 26, 1996.

Voice

Jonny Quest: J.D. Roth, Quinton Flynn; **Dr. Benton Quest:** George Segal, John de Lancie; **Hadji:** Michael Benyaer, Rob Paulsen; **Bandit:** Frank Welker; **Race Ban-** non: Robert Patrick, Robert Foxworth; **Jessie Bannon:** Jesse Douglas, Jennifer Hale; **Williams Messenger:** Dee Bradley Baker, Michael Benyaer; **Ezekiel Rage:** Michael Bell; **Dr. Forbes:** Earl Boen; **Dr. Karel:** Dean Jones; **Dr. Vedder:** Jim Meskimen; **Iris the Computer:** B.J. Ward

◎ THE REAL GHOSTBUSTERS

To avoid confusion with Filmation's *Ghostbusters* series based on the popular 1975 live-action series, the producers of this series, adapted from the hit motion picture, changed the title of their program to make sure that audiences knew the difference. In this animated update, those three misfits who singlehandedly saved New York from supernatural destruction are up to their same old tricks, keeping the city safe from demons, curses, spooks and every other off-the-wall weirdness known (and unknown) to mortal man. Premiering on ABC in 1986, the series entered daily syndication, with all-new episodes, in 1987.

Comedian Arsenio Hall was the voice of Peter Venkman and Winston Zeddmore for the 1986–87 season. He was replaced the next season by voice artists Lorenzo Music (as Venkman) and Edward L. Jones (as Zeddmore). Ray Parker Jr.'s original hit song is featured as the program's theme. In 1988, after two successful seasons on the network, ABC commissioned a third season of shows under the new title of *Slimer! The Real Ghostbusters*. The concept was reprised in the 1997 syndicated series *Extreme Ghostbusters*, featuring mostly an all-new cast of characters.

USA Network rebroadcast the original series as part of its cartoon program block *Cartoon Express* beginning in 1992.

A DIC Enterprises Production. Color. Half-hour. Premiered on ABC: September 13, 1986–September 3, 1988. Syndicated: 1987. Rebroadcast on USA: September 18, 1992–September 4, 1994.

Voices

Peter Venkman: Arsenio Hall, Lorenzo Music; **Winston Zeddmore:** Arsenio Hall, Edward L. Jones; **Egon Spengler:** Maurice LaMarche; **Janine Melnitz:** Laura Summer, Kath Soucie; **Ray Stantz:** Frank Welker; **Slimer:** Frank Welker

◎ THE REAL STORY OF . . .

Thirteen famous nursery rhymes and classic children's tales, including Humpty Dumpty and others, are brought to life by a cast of well-known motion picture stars and recording artists, many of whom narrate each story and provide other voices, in this series of half-hour specials (repackaged versions of episodes from a 1990 Canadian television cartoon series called *Favorite Songs*) that premiered on HBO on New Year's Day 1994. The series opened with the half-hour adaptation of "Baa Baa Black Sheep," featuring the voices of Robert Stack and Shelley Long. It was preceded each

Saturday morning by another animated series, *The Legend of White Fang* (by the same producer).

Subsequent specials included "Au Clair de la Lune," featuring Milton Berle as the Prince of Darkness; "Frere Jacques," with Stevie Nicks as the Wizard Owl; "Happy Birthday to You," costarring Roger Daltrey and Ed Asner; "Here Comes the Bride," featuring Carol Kane as Margaret Mouse; and "Humpty Dumpty," featuring the voices of Huey Lewis and Oscar-winning actress Glenda Jackson.

Other series titles included: "I'm a Little Teapot," starring Julian Lennon, son of former Beatle John Lennon; "Itsy Bitsy Spider," with voices by Malcolm Jamal-Warner and Patti LaBelle; "O Christmas Tree," costarring John Ritter and Deborah Harry; "Rain, Rain, Go Away," featuring Joe Piscopo and Robin Leach (of TV's *Lifestyles of the Rich and Famous* fame); "Sur le Pont D'Avignon," voiced by Robert Guillaume; "Three Little Kittens," starring Lauren Bacall as the character Freezelda; and "Twinkle Twinkle Little Star," costarring Martin Short and *Wheel of Fortune*'s Vanna White. (See individual entries under Animated Television Specials for further details.)

Some entries in the series—"Rain, Rain Go Away" (retitled, "The Prince's Rain"), "Humpty Dumpty" (instead called, "The Rise and Fall of Humpty Dumpty"), "I'm A Little Teapot" (renamed "The Runaway Teapot"), "Itsy Bitsy Spider" (retitled, "Spider Junior High") and "Three Little Kittens" (renamed, "The Ice Queen's Mittens")—originally debuted in 1991 as part of the HBO cartoon anthology series, *HBO Storybook Musicals*. (See individual entries in Animated Television Specials for further details.)

A Cinar Films Production in association with France Animation. Color. Half-hour. Premiered on HBO: January 1, 1994.

REBOOT

Daring to defy evil, Bob, the heroic digital denizen of a personal computer, battles an evil virus named MegaByte and sister strain Hexadecimal from taking control of the computer metropolis of Mainframe. In so doing he protects his friends Dot Matrix, her brother Enzo and thousands of friendly bionomes from this vicious plague in the first all-computer-generated animated series produced for network television. It took the series' producers three years—and many backers—to bring the innovative 23-episode show, which premiered on ABC in the fall of 1994 (with opening episode "The Tearing"), to the air. In 1996, Disney's takeover of Capital Cities/ABC, resulted in the show's cancellation, despite high ratings. That fall Claster Television, a well-known syndicator, repackaged episodes from both seasons and sold the series to 105 independent stations, airing in daytime syndication through September of 1997. A third season of new *ReBoot* cartoons were produced but have yet to air on U.S. television.

A BLT/Alliance Communications Production in association with Claster Television. Color. Half-hour. Premiered on ABC: September 10, 1994–September 2, 1995; September 9, 1995–July 20, 1996. Syndicated: September 16, 1996–September 12, 1997.

Voices
Bob: Michael Benyaer, Ian James Corlett; **Dot:** Kathleen Barr; **Young Andraia:** Andrea Libman; **Young Enzo:** Jesse Moss, Matthew Sinclair; **Grown Andraia:** Sharon Alexander; **Grown Enzo:** Paul Spencer Dobson; **Megabyte:** Tony Jay; **Hexadecimal:** Shirley Miller; **Slash-2:** Scott McNeil; **Mouse:** Louise Vallance; **Mike the TV/Phong/Cecil:** Michael Donovan; **Hack:** Gary Chalk

THE RED PLANET

Jim and P.J., a brother and sister, are sent to the frightening Lowell Academy, far from home and their parents, on a beautiful but dangerous colony planet where they come of age in this three-part miniseries aired on consecutive Saturday mornings on the Fox Network and based on the novel of the same name. The series was an Environmental Award winner.

A Gunther-Wahl Production. Color. Half-hour. Premiered on FOX: May 14, 1994 (part 1); May 21, 1994 (part 2); May 28, 1994 (part 3). Rebroadcast on FOX: January 7, 1995 (part 1); January 14, 1995 (part 2); January 21, 1995 (part 3); May 4, 1996 (part 1); May 11, 1996 (part 2); May 18, 1996 (part 3).

THE RELUCTANT DRAGON AND MR. TOAD

Based on characters and stories in British author Kenneth Grahame's novel *The Wind in Willows*, the kind-hearted, fire-breathing reluctant dragon of Willowmarsh Village, protected by the bumbling knight Sr. Malcolm, and fun-loving gadabout Mr. Toad, master of Toad Hall, were featured in this 17-episode half-hour series, which premiered on ABC in 1970 opposite CBS's *Bugs Bunny/Road Runner Hour* and NBC's *The Heckle and Jeckle Cartoon Show*.

A Rankin-Bass Production. Color. Half-hour. Premiered on ABC: September 12, 1970–September 17, 1972.

Voices
Paul Soles, Donna Miller, Claude Rae, Carl Banas

THE REN & STIMPY SHOW

Created by John Kricfalusi, this long-running, cynical, wacked-out twist on traditional cartoon teams like Tom and Jerry, featuring a scrawny, asthmatic chihuahua and his obese, dimwitted, tube-sucking feline sidekick in outlandish situations, replete with bad-taste humor, be-bop background music and unhappy endings, was an instant hit with college-age viewers (ages 18–24) following its premiere on

Nickelodeon in 1991. Spawning a brace of licensed toys and other merchandise, the series quickly attained cult status with viewers and went on to become a successful franchise for the network.

Kricfalusi, formerly an animation director for Ralph Bakshi's *Mighty Mouse: The New Adventures,* created the characters years ago as office doodles and had tried to sell CBS, ABC and NBC on making the series, diluting the idea by surrounding the characters with a bunch of kids in a show called *Your Gang.* Neither network jumped at the idea. Animation veteran Vanessa Coffey, whom Nickelodeon hired to develop the network's first animated cartoon lineup, saw the potential in Kricfalusi's characters that the major networks had missed.

The series debuted as part of a 90-minute, Sunday-morning cartoon block on Nickelodeon in August 1991 along with *Doug* and *Rugrats.* Six programs were produced for the 1991 season at costs of up $400,000 per episode (almost twice as much as the average Saturday-morning network cartoon series), each comprised of two 11-minute episodes and occasional commercial "parodies." The series was initially broadcast on Sunday mornings on Nickelodeon and was given an 11-week run on MTV, airing Saturday nights, at the end of that year. It proved to be a such a rating success that Nickelodeon renewed the program for a second season and moved it to Saturday evenings in August 1992.

Kricfalusi was busy at work on 13 new half-hour episodes for the 1992–93 season when creative differences, mostly over story content, erupted between him and network executives and his failure to produce new episodes on time resulted in his ouster that September. (The network was forced to repeat the previous six original episodes because of such delays.) Reportedly, the network rejected at least two episodes because they were "inappropriate and offensive." By the time of his dismissal, Kricfalusi had completed portions of new episodes for the show's third season. Series producer Bob Camp, whom the network had retained, salvaged the shows, bridging them with new animation produced by the network-owned Games Animation division, producers of another Nickelodeon cartoon series, *Rocko's Modern Life.* From 1993 through 1995, the series returned with all-new episodes and was nominated twice for Emmy Awards for Outstanding Animated Program.

A Spumco Company/Games Animation Production. Color. Half-hour. Premiered on NIK: August 11, 1991–August 8, 1992; August 15, 1992–September 9, 1993; September 26, 1993–October 1, 1994; October 8, 1994–September 1995. Rebroadcast on MTV: December 28, 1991–March 7, 1992. Rebroadcast on NIK: September 1995.

Voices

Ren Hoek: John Kricfalusi, Bob Camp, Billy West; **Stimpson J. "Stimpy" Cat:** Billy West; **Powered Toast Man:** Gary Owens; **George Liquor:** Michael Pataki; **Singers:** Randy Creenshaw, Edan Gross, Lesa O'Donovan, Churlie Brissette

⊚ RETURN OF THE PLANET OF THE APES

In the year A.D. 3180, on the futuristic planet Earth, a society of apes rule and humans (a trio of displaced space travelers: Bill Hudson, Judy Franklin and Jeff Carter) are slaves. This 13-episode Saturday-morning series was based on the popular *Planet of the Apes* film series and novel by Pierre Boule and produced for NBC in 1975. Between 1992 and 1994 it was rebroadcast on the Sci-Fi Channel's *Cartoon Quest* (also in its own time slot).

A DePatie-Freleng Enterprises Production in association with 20th Century-Fox. Color. Half-hour. Premiered on NBC: September 6, 1975–September 4, 1976. Rebroadcast on SCI: September 27, 1992–June 25, 1994.

Voices

Bill Hudson/Dr. Zaius: Richard Blackburn; **Jeff Carter:** Austin Stoker; **Judy Franklin/Nova:** Claudette Nevins; **Cornelius:** Edwin Mills; **Zira:** Philipa Harris; **General Urko:** Henry Corden

⊚ RICHIE RICH

Retaining the authenticity of the famed Harvey comic-book character, Richie Rich ("the richest kid in the world") starred in this half-hour syndicated series, made up of 13 *Richie Rich* comedy-mystery cartoon adventures and selected cartoons from the classic Harvey film library. Updated for today's audiences, series regulars included Professor Keenbean, Cadbury, Dollar, Gloria Glad, Reggie Van Dough, Chef Pierre, Bascomb, Mayda Munny, Freckles, Pee Wee and Tiny.

A Film Roman Production in association with Harvey Entertainment. Color. Half-hour. Premiered: September 21, 1996. Syndicated.

Voices

Richie Rich/Irona: Katie Leigh; **Regina Rich:** Susan Silo; **Richard Rich Sr./Professor Keenbean/Chef Pierre:** Rene Auberjonois; **Cadbury/Bascomb:** Martin Jarvis; **Dollar:** Pat Fraley; **Gloria Glad/Reggie Van Dough/Freckles/Tiny:** Jeannie Elias

⊚ THE RICHIE RICH/SCOOBY-DOO SHOW—AND SCRAPPY, TOO!

This hour-long Saturday morning series combined new adventures of Richie Rich, a lucky kid with a $100,000 weekly allowance, who uses his wealth for good causes, and 39 new seven-and-a-half-minute episodes (three per show) of Scooby-Doo and his crazy cousin, who previously appeared in 1979's *Scooby and Scrappy-Doo.* Richie Rich was based on the popular comic-book character owned by Harvey Comics.

In the Scooby and Scrappy-Doo adventures, only Shaggy remained from the original cast. Freddy, Daphne and Velma were dropped as well as the mystery format, which had run its course. The new cartoons marked another cast change: Don Messick took over as the voice of Scrappy-Doo (originally voiced by Lennie Weinrib on 1979's *Scooby and Scrappy-Doo*). In addition, for the first time, rather than build plots about crooks in disguise as ghosts and goblins, the ghosts and monsters in the new episodes were real, and Shaggy, Scooby and Scrappy "splatted" them in the end.

Alternating with the misadventures of Scooby-Doo and Scrappy-Doo were several short comical vignettes starring Richie Rich, each running three minutes, seven minutes and 30 seconds long. (No new 30-second spots were produced for the second season). During its second season, the program was retitled *The Richie Rich/Scooby & Scrappy-Doo Show*.

In the fall of 1982, Richie Rich was paired again with Hanna-Barbera's cartoon version of the Our Gang kids in *The Little Rascals/Richie Rich Show*, in all-new episodes, which ran through the 1983 season. In 1988 the program was repackaged and rebroadcast in syndication as part of *The Funtastic World of Hanna-Barbera*. Five years later it was rebroadcast on the Cartoon Network.

A Hanna-Barbera Production in association with Harvey Comics. Color. Half-hour. Premiered on ABC: November 8, 1980–September 5, 1981; September 12, 1981–September 18, 1982. Rebroadcast on CAR (The Richie Rich Show): January 4, 1993–June 3, 1994; January 2, 1995–June 2, 1995; September 4, 1995– (weekdays).

Voices
Richie Rich: Sparky Marcus; **Freckles, Richie's friend:** Christian Hoff; **Gloria, Richie's girlfriend:** Nancy Cartwright; **Reggie Van Dough, Richie's friend:** Dick Beals; **George Rich, Richie's father:** Stan Jones; **Mrs. Rich, Richie's mother:** Joan Gerber; **Cadbury, the Riches' butler:** Stan Jones; **Irona, the Riches' maid:** Joan Gerber; **Dollar, the Riches' dog:** Frank Welker; **Professor Keenbean:** Bill Callaway; **Scooby-Doo:** Don Messick; **Scrappy-Doo:** Don Messick; **Shaggy:** Casey Kasem; **Velma:** Pat Stevens, Maria Frumkin; **Freddy:** Frank Welker; **Daphne:** Heather North

RICK MORANIS IN GRAVEDALE HIGH
A high school teacher's unorthodox methods land him a job in the scariest school in town, Gravedale High, built in the heart of a creepy cemetery, with coffins for lockers and monsters for students—each a teenage version of popular monsters: Vinnie Stoker, the world's hippest teenage vampire; Reggie Moonshroud, the resident werewolf; Medusa ("Duzer"), a snake-headed Madonna wannabe; Frankentyke, the school prankster; Gill Waterman, a surfing swamp creature; Cleofatra, a rotund teenage mummy; Sid, the invisible kid; Blanche, a Southern belle zombie; and J.P. Ghostly the III—in this half-hour cartoon series for NBC.

The series featured the voices of Rick Moranis, Shari Belafonte, Tim Curry, television talk-show host Ricki Lake and comedian Jonathan Winters.

A Hanna-Barbera Production in association with NBC. Color. Half-hour. Premiered on NBC: September 8, 1990– September 7, 1991.

Voices
Max Schneider: Rick Moranis; **Vinnie Stoker:** Roger Rose; **Reggie Moonshroud:** Barry Gordon; **Medusa ("Duzer"):** Kimmy Robertson; **Frankentyke/J.P. Ghastly:** Frank Welker; **Gill Waterman:** Jackie Earl Haley; **Cleofatra:** Ricki Lake; **Sid:** Maurice LaMarche; **Blanche:** Shari Belafonte; **Miss Dirge:** Eileen Brennan; **Miss Webner:** Sandra Gould; **Boneyard:** Brock Peters; **Mr. Tutner:** Tim Curry; **Coach Cadaver:** Jonathan Winters; **Crone:** Georgia Brown

RING RAIDERS
Led by Ring Commander Victor Vector, a group of heroic aviators from all eras of flight—past, present and future—defend the world. Their enemy: the most sinister airborne threat ever known, the evil pilots of the Skull Squadron. The *Top Gun*–style battles and adventures in this five-part daily miniseries were first introduced as a two-hour special.

A DIC Enterprises Production in association with Those Characters from Cleveland. Color. Half-hour. Premiered: 1989. Syndicated.

Voices
Victor Vector, commander: Dan Gilvezan; **Joe Thundercloud:** Efrain Figueroa; **Hubbub:** Stuart Goetz; **Cub**

A group of heroic aviators from all eras of flight, led by Commander Victor Vector, defend the world from the most sinister airborne threat ever known in Ring Raiders. © Those Characters From Cleveland
(COURTESY: DIC ENTERPRISES)

Jones: Ike Eisenmann; **Kirchov:** Gregory Martin; **Mako:** Jack Angel; **Jenny Gail:** Chris Anthony; **Max Miles:** Roscoe Lee Browne; **Scorch:** Rodger Bumpass; **Yasu Yaka-mura:** Townsend Coleman; **Baron Voin Clawdeitz:** Chuck McCann; **Siren:** Susan Silo

◉ ROAD ROVERS

Following their master's signal, regular run-of-the-mill kennel dogs spring into action as courageous crime-fighting super-hounds to protect and defend all that's good in the galaxy in this 13-episode half-hour action/adventure series, first aired Saturday mornings on the WB Network in 1996.

A Warner Bros. Television Animation Production. Color. Half-hour. Premiered on WB: September 7, 1996–February 23, 1997.

Voices
Hunter: Jess Harnell; **Colleen:** Tress MacNeille; **Exile:** Kevin Richardson; **Blitz:** Jeff Bennett; **Shag:** Frank Welker; **The Master:** Joseph Campanella; **General Parvo:** Jim Cummings; **The Groomer:** Sheena Easton

◉ THE ROAD RUNNER SHOW

The predictable antics of foxy, fleet-footed Road Runner and his constant pursuer Wile E. Coyote were repackaged for television, with theatrical cartoons from the Warner Bros. library produced between 1949 and 1966 added to spice up the proceedings. Warner characters featured in the series were Daffy Duck, Foghorn Leghorn, Porky Pig and others. The Road Runner/Coyote cartoons were subsequently paired with reruns of Bugs Bunny cartoons as *The Bugs Bunny/Road Runner Hour*, which premiered on CBS in 1968.

A Warner Bros. Production. Color. Half-hour. Premiered on CBS: September 10, 1966–September 7, 1968. Rebroadcast on ABC: September 11, 1971–September 2, 1972.

Voices
Mel Blanc

◉ ROBOTECH

When Earth is invaded by a fleet of giant alien spaceships capable of destroying the entire planet in a split second, the only hope for survival lies in Robotech Defense Force, led by Captain Gloval and his troop of newly trained cadets, which protects the planet from destruction in this 85 episode half-hour series produced for first-run syndication in 1985. Eight years after its initial run in syndication, the series was rebroadcast on the Sci-Fi Channel's *Cartoon Quest* (and in its own time slot).

A Tatsunoko Production/Harmony Gold U.S.A. Production. Robotech is a registered trademark owned and licensed by Harmony Gold U.S.A. Color. Half-hour. Syndicated: 1985–1986. Rebroadcast on SCI: September 13, 1993–April 30, 1994.

Voices
Greg Snow, Reba West, Jonathan Alexsander, Drew Thomas, Deanna Morris, Thomas Wyner, Brittany Harlow, Donn Warner, Axel Roberts, Tony Oliver, A. Gregory, Noelle McGraph, Sandra Snow, Guy Garrett, Jimmy Flinders, Anthony Wayne, Eddie Frierson, Leonad Pike, Aline Leslie, Shirley Roberts, Wendee Swan, Larry Abraham, Sam Fontana, Penny Sweet, Mary Cobb, Celena Banas, Chelsea Victoria

◉ ROCKET ROBIN HOOD AND HIS MERRY SPACEMEN

The year is 3000. Headquartered on the floating solar-powered asteroid Sherwood Forest, intergalactic crimefighter Rocket Robin Hood and his Merry Spacemen—Will Scarlet, Little John, Alan A. Dale, Jiles and Friar Tuck—team up to battle the universe's top villain, the wicked Sheriff of N.O.T.T., in this half-hour series comprised of 156 five-minute episodes first syndicated in 1967. Veteran animator James "Shamus" Culhane produced and directed the series in cooperation with Steve Krantz, executive producer of *Marvel Superheroes.*

A Trillium/Steve Krantz Production. Color. Half-hour. Premiere: Fall 1967. Syndicated.

Voices
Carl Banas, Ed McNamara, Chris Wiggins, Bernard Cowan, Len Birman, Paul Kligman, Gillie Fenwick, John Scott

◉ ROCKO'S LIFE

Loosely based on creator Joe Murray's outrageous theatrical cartoon "My Dog Zero," a newly arrived pint-size Australian wallaby, joined by his menagerie of household pets (Heffer the cow and his brain-dead Spunky the dog), finds small-town life difficult. Zero is thrown into situations that incessantly threaten his existence, in the first Nickelodeon-created cartoon series of Games Animation, the network's owned-and-operated cartoon division. Premiering in the fall of 1993 with 13 original episodes, the weekly half-hour series mirrored the same gross-out humor as the network's cult favorite, *The Ren & Stimpy Show*, becoming an instant ratings hit. The show's success prompted Nickelodeon to order 26 new episodes for the 1994–95 season. Beginning in late May 1994, the series was rebroadcast for several weeks on MTV, as part of an experiment to reach a wider audience. The character of Rocko originated in Murray's comic strip *Zak and Travis*, the adventures of Zak, a chubby little man with girls on his mind, and Travis (Rocko).

A Games Animation Production. Color. Half-hour. Premiered on NIK: September 18, 1993. Rebroadcast on MTV: May 1994.

Voices

Rocko: Carlos Alazraqui; **Heffer Wolfe:** Tom Kenny; **Filbert Turtle:** Doug Lawrence; **The Bigheads:** Charlie Adler; **Dr. Hutchinson:** Linda Wallem

⊚ ROCKY AND HIS FRIENDS

The flying squirrel Rocky and simple-minded, bristle-haired Bullwinkle Moose (whose voice was reminiscent of Red Skelton's punch-drunk fighter character, Willie Lump-Lump) battle the evil Mr. Big, a midget underworld gangster who hires sinister Boris Badenov and the fetching agent Natasha Fatale to foil the duo's activities in cliff-hanging, serialized adventures (narrated by actor William Conrad) that first premiered on ABC in 1959.

Other cartoon segments included "Fractured Fairytales," "Aesop and Son," "Peabody's Improbable History," and "Mr. Know It All."

In 1961, following its ABC network run, NBC broadcast a new, expanded edition of the series, retitled *The Bullwinkle Show.* (See entry for information.)

The series was the second all-new cartoon show to air on network television, created by Jay Ward and Alex Anderson (whose uncle was Paul Terry, the man behind *Terrytoons*, and with whom he served as an apprentice at his New York Terrytoons studios). Anderson teamed up with Ward to form Television Arts Productions, based in Berkeley, California, to produce cartoon ideas. Among the characters they created were Crusader Rabbit (and his sidekick, Rags the Tiger) and what became the nucleus of "Rocky and Bullwinkle": Rocket J. Squirrel, Bullwinkle and Dudley Do-Right (of these concepts, only "Crusader" Rabbit was sold to television as a syndicated series in 1949).

Rocky and His Friends, *starring Rocky the flying squirrel, his friend Bullwinkle Moose and villains Natasha and Boris, marked the second all-cartoon show to air on network television. The series was created by Jay Ward, who also created Crusader Rabbit. © Jay Ward Productions*

Several of the series' writers would go on to later glories: Allan Burns to *The Mary Tyler Moore Show,* Lloyd Turner to *All in the Family,* and Chris Hayward to *Barney Miller.*

A Jay Ward Production. Color. Half-hour. Premiered on ABC: September 29, 1959–September 3, 1961.

Voices

Rocky, the flying squirrel: June Foray; **Bullwinkle Moose:** Bill Scott; **Boris Badenov:** Paul Frees; **Natasha Fatale:** June Foray; **Narrator:** William Conrad; **Aesop:** Charles Ruggles; **Aesop's Son:** Daws Butler; **Narrator:** Charles Ruggles; **Mr. Peabody:** Bill Scott; **Sherman, his adopted son:** Walter Tetley; **Narrator ("Fractured Fairytales"):** Edward Everett Horton

⊚ ROD ROCKET

Entertaining and educational space adventures in serial form of Rod Rocket, his sidekick Joey, his sister Casey, and their friend Professor Argus. The half-hour series of five-minute cartoons was the first fully animated series produced by Filmation Studios.

A Filmation Associates Production. Color. Half-hour. Premiered: 1963. Syndicated.

⊚ ROGER RAMJET

The terms "daredevil," "flying fool" and "all-round good guy" fittingly describe American Eagle Squadron antihero scientist Roger Ramjet (voiced by famed radio/television personality Gary Owens). A proton energy pill gives Roger the power of 20 atom bombs for a period of 20 seconds. He battles the evil Noodle Romanoff from N.A.S.T.Y., Jacqueline Hyde, Henry Cabbage Patch, Lance Crossfire, the Solenoid Robots, General G.I. Brassbottom, Clara Finork, Lotta Love, the Height Brothers (Cronk, Horse and Gezundt) and other baddies.

Of course, Roger himself has quite a staff of good-doers on the flying squadron: Yank, Doodle, Dan and Dee.

The show avoided violent confrontations and undue violence by inserting the appropriate title cards "Whack!" "Thunk!" "Hurt!" "Pain!" and "Ouch!" The same technique was later employed on TV's *Batman* series.

In 1996, following a resurgence of interest in the series (which previously was issued on home video), the Cartoon Network began rearing the series.

A Ken Snyder Production. Color. Half-hour. Premiered: September, 1965. Syndicated. Rebroadcast on CAR: June 1, 1996–October 5, 1996 (Saturdays); July 23, 1997– (Saturdays).

Voices

Roger Ramjet: Gary Owens; **Yank/Dan:** Dick Beals; **Doodle/Noodles Romanoff:** Gene Moss; **Dee/Lotta Love:** Joan Gerber; **General G.I. Brassbottom/Ma Ramjet:** Bob Arbogast; **Lance Crossfire/Red Dog:** Paul Shively; **The Announcer:** Dave Ketchum

ⓖ ROMAN HOLIDAYS

Forum Construction Company engineer Gus Holiday, his wife, Laurie, and their children, Precocia and Happius, struggle with 20th-century lifestyles in Rome, A.D. 63 in this 13-episode half-hour series originally produced for NBC.

A Hanna Barbera Production. Color. Half-hour. Premiered on NBC: September 9, 1972–September 1, 1973. Rebroadcast on CAR: January 14, 1994–January 15, 1994 (Look What We Found!); July 9, 1995– Sundays).

Voices

Gus Holiday: Dave Willock; **Laurie, his wife:** Shirley Mitchell; **Precocia, their daughter:** Pamelyn Ferdin; **Happius (Happy), their son:** Stanley Livingston; **Mr. Evictus, the landlord:** Dom DeLuise; **Mr. Tycoonius, Holiday's boss:** Hal Smith; **Brutus, the family lion:** Daws Butler; **Groovia, Happy's girlfriend:** Judy Strangis; **Herman, Gus's friend:** Hal Peary; **Henrietta, his wife:** Janet Waldo

ⓖ RONIN WARRIORS

Five young men (Ryo, Cye, Sage, Rowen and Kento), each gifted with mystical, superpowered samurai armor, fight an otherworldly invasion from the dark dimension known as the "Phantom World," headed by the evil warlord Arago, in this phenomenally popular Japanese series originally produced in 1989 as *Samurai Troopers*. Redubbed in English (with most of the characters renamed as well), the series was imported to the United States by Graz Entertainment under the title *Ronin Warriors*, premiering in first-run syndication in the summer of 1995. The 39-episode series was subsequently reaired on the Sci-Fi Channel's *Animation Station*.

A Sunrise Inc./Graz Entertainment Production. Color. Half-hour. Premiered: 1995. Syndicated. Rebroadcast on SCI: June 30, 1996–December 31, 1996.

Voices

Matt Hill, David Kaye, Paul Dobson, Mira Mina, Ward Perry, Peter Wilds, Christopher Turner, Michael Donovan, Teryl Rothery

ⓖ RUBIK THE AMAZING CUBE

The famous multicolored cube that frustrated consumers in their attempts to figure it out and his human companions, the Rodriguez children—Carlos, Lisa and Renaldo—were featured in this half-hour series of magical adventures, originally produced as part of 1983's *The Pac-Man/Rubik the Amazing Cube Hour*. The original hour-long cartoon block lasted one full season on ABC, with the "Rubik the Amazing Cube" portion repeated as a half-hour show of its own in April of 1985. (See *The Pac-Man/Rubik the Amazing Cube Hour* for voice credits.)

A Ruby-Spears Enterprises Production. Color. Half-hour. Premiered on ABC: September 10, 1983–September 1, 1984

(as part of The Pac-Man/Rubik The Amazing Cube Hour*). Rebroadcast on ABC: April 4, 1985–August 31, 1985 as (Rubik the Amazing Cube).*

ⓖ RUDE DOG AND THE DWEEBS

Rude Dog is a cool, "Fonzie-like" dog who drives a pink 1956 Cadillac. The Dweebs are his equally cool gang of canines. Together they spell problems of every kind in this stylized animated series (in two cartoons per show) featuring a whole new color palette for Saturday-morning animation: "hot pinks and neon." CBS canceled the series in December of 1989, replacing it with *Dungeons and Dragons*. The network brought back the series for a summer run in 1990.

A Marvel Production in association with Akom Productions, Ltd./Sun Sportswear. Color. Half-hour. Premiered on CBS: September 16, 1989–December 9, 1989. Rebroadcast on CBS: June 17, 1990–September 8, 1990.

Voices

Rude Dog: Rob Paulsen; **Barney:** Dave Coulier; **Winston/ Herman:** Peter Cullen; **Satch:** Jim Cummings; **Kibble/ Gloria:** Ellen Gerstell; **Tweek:** Hank Saroyan; **Reggie:** Mendi Segal; **Caboose/Rot/Seymour:** Frank Welker

ⓖ THE RUFF AND REDDY SHOW

Telecast in black-and-white until 1959, Hanna-Barbera created this pioneering made-for-television cartoon series that featured the adventures of a talking dog and cat team, Ruff and Reddy, battling sinister forces of evil (Captain Greedy, Scarey Harry Safari, Killer and Diller and others) in serialized stories that were presented in 10 or more six-minute installments in the fashion of Jay Ward's *Crusader Rabbit*. The original half-hour series, which debuted on NBC, featured *Ruff and Reddy* cartoons as wraparounds bookended with a package of Columbia Pictures theatrical cartoons (*Color Rhapsodies, Fox and the Crow* and *Li'l Abner*) originally released to theaters. Televised live from WNBC, New York, the NBC program was hosted by Jimmy Blaine from 1957 to 1960, when it was canceled and replaced by *King Leonardo and His Short Subjects*. Bob Cottle succeeded Blaine as host from 1962 to 1964, when the series returned to NBC. In all, 156 five-minute *Ruff and Reddy* cartoons were produced, with production ending in 1960. Episodes were rebroadcast on the later NBC series and via syndication in 1964.

A Hanna-Barbera Production. Black-and-white. Color. Half-hour. Premiered on NBC: December 14, 1957–September 24, 1960; September 29, 1962–September 26, 1964. Syndicated: 1964.

Voices

Ruff/Professor Gizmo/Ubble-Ubble/Others: Don Messick; **Reddy/Other Voices:** Daws Butler

RUGRATS

The floor-level antics of a group of young toddlers—one-year-old Tommy Pickles and other diaper-clad tots (his one-toothed friend Chuckie, his bossy cousin Angelica and double-trouble infant twins Phil and Lil)—are seen from their viewpoint in this offbeat and funny half-hour cartoon series (in two 11-minute episodes) from the producers of *The Simpsons*.

Premiering on Nickeleodeon in August 1991 as part of a 90-minute Sunday morning cartoon block that included "Doug," *The Ren & Stimpy Show* and *Rugrats*, the series was a late bloomer and became more successful in reruns than during its original network run. Producers tried to broaden its appeal, introducing some news characters during the 1993–94 season, namely an African American family—a little girl named Susie and her parents, Randy and Lily—but it did little to help the show's ratings. During that season the series' first half-hour prime-time special, *Rugrats: Hollyween*, premiered. In 1995 a second half-hour special, *A Rugrats Passover*, bowed on Nick.

Production ended on the Emmy-nominated series in 1994 after 65 episodes. In 1995 Nickelodeon moved the show from weekends to weekdays (in reruns), where it became the network's top-rated show. Surprised by the series' sudden success, the network ordered 13 new episodes (marking the first time Nickelodeon ever went back to a producer and ordered more than 65 episodes for an animated series), which began airing in May of 1997 with the premiere of *Rugrats Mother's Day Special*. The program was the first new episode since 1996's *Rugrats the Santa Experience* special.) In the spring of 1998, the gang starred in yet another prime-time special, *Rugrats Vacation*.

A Klasky-Csupo, Inc. Production. Color. Half-hour. Premiered on NIK: August 11, 1991–August 8, 1992; August 15, 1992–September 19, 1993; September 26, 1993–October 1, 1994; October 8, 1994–September 30, 1995; May 6, 1997– . Rebroadcast on NIK: 1995–1997.

Voices

Tommy Pickles: E.G. Daily; **Chuckie:** Christine Cavanaugh; **Angelica:** Cheryl Chase; **Phil/Lil/Betty Pickles, Drew's wife:** Kath Soucie; **Charlotte:** Tress MacNeille; **Stu Pickles, Tommy's dad:** Jack Riley; **Didi Pickles, Tommy's mom:** Melanie Chartoff; **Drew Pickles, Stu's brother/Charles Sr., Chuckie's dad:** Michael Bell; **Grandpa Pickles:** David Doyle; **Susie:** Cree Summer; **Randy, Susie's dad:** Ron Glass; **Lily, Susie's mom:** Lisa Dinkins; **Dr. Lucy Carmichael:** Cheryl Carter; **Suzie Carmichael:** Cree Summer; **Lipschitz Hotline:** Tony Jay

RUPERT (1989)

Famed British cartoonist Alfred Bestell produced this limited-animated series of cartoon vignettes featuring the adventures of the bold little bear and his friends from Nut-wood Village from Mary Tourtel's famous comic-strip series of the same name. Bestell, who had taken over drawing the comic strip for Tourtel in 1935 due to her failing eyesight, produced an earlier *Rupert* series consisting of stop-motion puppet shorts in the 1970s. His limited-animated series was broadcast in the United States on the Disney Channel's *Lunch Box* series beginning in 1989.

An Alfred Bestell Production. Color. Half-hour (part of the Disney Channel series Lunch Box*). Premiered on DIS: July 1989.*

RUPERT (1993)

The lovable and well-meaning little bear with a nose for excitement joined by his parents and trusted old friend, The Professor embarks on round-the-world adventures, to Africa, Asia, Europe and elsewhere, in this second series based on Mary Tourtel's long-running British comic-strip character. Produced by Toronto-based Nelvana Enterprises and Ellipse Animation, the half-hour cartoon series originally premiered on the Canadian cable service YTV in 1992. The series made its American television debut on The Family Channel (opposite reruns of *Babar*, another Nelvana-produced series) in 1993. The following fall the series joined Nickelodeon's Nick Jr. daily preschool programming block.

A Nelvana Enterprises/Ellipse Animation Production in association with TVS and YTV. Color. Half-hour. Premiered on FAM: September 6, 1993. Rebroadcast on NIK: September 1994.

Voices

Rupert: Ben Sandford; **Bill Badger:** Torquil Campbell; **Pong Ping:** Oscar Hsu; **Pudgy Pig:** Hadley Kay; **Mr. Bear:** Guy Bannerman; **Mrs. Bear:** Lally Cadeau; **Algy Pig:** Keith White; **The Professor:** Colin Fox; **Tiger Lady:** Stephanie Morgenstern; **Sage of Um:** Wayne Robson

SABAN'S ADVENTURES OF OLIVER TWIST

Set in Victorian London, adorable and adventurous mutt Oliver embarks on numerous adventures as he and streetwise scamp the Artful Dodger explore London Town from top to bottom, only to get into trouble and learn a lesson or two along the way in this weekly, 26-episode syndicated series inspired by Charles Dickens's classic novel.

A Saban Entertainment Production. Color. Half-hour. Premiered: September 9, 1996. Syndicated.

SABAN'S ADVENTURES OF PINOCCHIO

Lovable wooden puppet Pinocchio experiences the trials and joys in his unrelenting quest to become human as he encounters Benny the Mouse, Jack the Fox, Willie the

Weasel and the evil Puppetmaster Sneeroff in adventures that carry strong educational messages. This updated, half-hour cartoon series is an adaptation of the classic children's stories by Italian author Collodi (whose real name was Carlo Lorenzini). The 52-episode series made its American television morning debut on HBO in July of 1992, paired weekday mornings with reruns of the hit cartoon series *Babar*, as part of the "HBO for Kids" program block.

A Tatsunoko/Saban Entertainment Production. Color. Half-hour. Premiered on HBO: July 1, 1992.

SABAN'S ADVENTURES OF THE LITTLE MERMAID FANTASY

No relation to Disney's 1989 classic animated feature and television series spinoff, this half-hour syndicated series tells the story of the Little Mermaid and her earthly friend, the young and noble Prince Justin, as they travel through their wondrous worlds above and below the sea and battle the powers of an evil sea witch, who tries again and again to keep them separated forever. In this syndicated 26-episode series based on the Hans Christian Andersen classic.

A Saban Entertainment Production. Color. Half-hour. Premiered: Fall 1991. Syndicated.

Voices
Marina the Mermaid/Hedwig: Sonja Ball; **Prince Justin:** Thor Bishopric; **Dudhlee:** Ian Finley; **Ridley:** Arthur Holden; **Chauncy:** Gordon Masten; **Winnie:** Annik Matern; **Anselm:** Aaron Tiger; **Narrator:** Jane Woods

SABAN'S AROUND THE WORLD IN EIGHTY DREAMS

Carlos, a seasoned, robust sailor, and his three adopted children, A.J., Koki and Marianne, head out into countless escapades around the world to authenticate Carlos's remarkable stories of his past in this 26-episode half-hour series, part of the syndicated Sunday-morning programming block *Amazin' Adventures*. The series premiered in September 1992, along with three other new cartoon series: *King Arthur and the Knights of Justice*, *Saban's Gulliver's Travels* and *The Wizard of Oz*.

A Saban Entertainment Production in association with Antenna 2/MBC/Silvio Brulsconi Communications/Telecino. Color. Half-hour. Premiered: September 7, 1992. Syndicated.

Voices
Carlos: Mark Camacho; **Oscar/Grandma Tadpole:** Rick Jones; **Koki:** Pauline Little; **A.J.:** Sonja Ball; **Marianne:** Patricia Rodriguez

SABAN'S EAGLE RIDERS

In the not-too-distant future, faced with an alien invasion, an elite team of five teenage freedom fighters—Hunter (code name: "Hawk"), the team leader; Flash ("Falcon"), a cyborg and master strategist; Kelly ("Dove"), skilled at hand-to-hand combat; Ollie ("Owl"), the team's wise-cracking navigator; and Mickey ("Merlin"), the smallest, youngest member—under the direction of brilliant scientist Dr. Thadeaus Keane of the Global Security Council, emerge from their underwater refuge and bravely battle outer space archenemies Galaxor and Cybercon to save the planet from total domination in this half-hour fantasy/adventure series that debuted in first-run syndication in 1996.

A Saban Entertainment/Tatsunoko Production. Color. Half-hour. Premiered: September 9, 1996. Syndicated.

Voices
Auto: Dena Burton; **Hunter Harris:** Richard Cansino; **Dr. Aikens:** Lara Cody; **Joe Thax:** Bryan Cranston; **Mallanox:** R. Martin Klein; **Kelly Jenar:** Heidi Lenhart; **Dr. Keane:** Greg O'Neill; **Ollie Keeawani:** Paul Schrier; **Cyberon:** Peter Spellos

SABAN'S GULLIVER'S TRAVELS

A seafaring cabin boy and his sister venture to distant and wondrous lands in this modified version of Jonathan Swift's famed 17th-century novel. The series aired as a component of the Sunday morning syndicated cartoon block *Amazin' Adventures*.

A Saban Entertainment Production in association with Antenna 2/MBC/Silvio Brulsconi Communications/Telecino. Color. Half-hour. Premiered: September 7, 1992. Syndicated (as part of Amazin' Adventures).

Voices
Gulliver: Terence Scammel; **Rafael:** Danny Brochu; **Folia:** Jessalyn Gilsig; **Fosla:** Sonja Ball; **Film:** A.J. Henderson

SABAN'S THE WHY WHY FAMILY

Centered around the inquisitive Baby Victor, who has an insatiable appetite for information, an eccentric family—a Mr. Fix-it–type father, Max; a nature expert mother, Vanilla; and a "hip" grandma, Eartha—try to answer questions from their ever-curious son and grandson about the scientific origins of everything from genetics to internal combustion in this 26-episode half-hour "edutoonment" series aimed at school-age children produced for first-run syndication.

A Saban Entertainment Production. Color. Half-hour. Premiered: September 9, 1996. Syndicated.

SABER RIDER AND THE STAR SHERIFFS

In this out-of-this-world futuristic fantasy with a western twist, Saber Rider, the dashing leader of the Star Sheriffs

Saber Rider, the dashing leader of the Star Sheriffs, maintains peace and unity for the settlers of a new futuristic frontier in the syndicated series Saber and the Star Sheriffs. © World Events Productions

unit, maintains peace and unity for the settlers of the new frontier by defending against the ghostly "Outrider" foes, mysterious vapor beings who have perfected the technique of "dimension jumping."

The program was the first animated strip to incorporate interactive technology, a revolutionary new concept that enables viewers to participate with the program by using specially designed toys.

A World Events Production. Color. Half-hour. Syndicated: September 1987.

Voices
Townsend Coleman, Peter Cullen, Pat Fraley, Pat Musick, Rob Paulsen

SABRINA AND THE GROOVIE GOOLIES

One year after her debut on *The Archie Comedy Hour*, Sabrina, a teenage sorceress, was coupled with The Groovie

Goolies, a group of strange monsters (see *The Groovie Goolies*), in this hour-long series of new animated misadventures and humorous vignettes. Sabrina was so well received that she was given her own series, *Sabrina, the Teenage Witch*, on CBS.

A Filmation Associates Production. Color. One hour. Premiered on CBS: September 12, 1970–September 4, 1971.

Voices
Sabrina, the Teenage Witch: Jane Webb; **Hot Dog Jr./Chili Dog/Harvey/Spencer:** Don Messick; **The Groovie Goolies:** Jane Web, Howard Morris, **Larry Storch, Larry D. Mann**

SABRINA, SUPERWITCH

In attempt to bolster its sagging ratings, NBC repeated 13 episodes of *Sabrina, the Teenage Witch*, giving the program a new title, as a last-ditch effort to bring some excitement to its Saturday-morning cartoon lineup. (Initially the program was titled *The New Archie/Sabrina Hour*.) Unfortunately, the program failed to cast a spell over its audience and was pulled two months after its debut. The original *Sabrina* was first broadcast on rival network, CBS, in 1971. (See *Sabrina, the Teenage Witch* for voice credits.)

A Filmation Associates Production. Color. Half-hour. Premiered on NBC: November 26, 1977–January 28, 1978.

SABRINA, THE TEENAGE WITCH

A 15-year-old apprentice witch works her sorcery on friends Archie Andrews, Jughead, Veronica Lodge, Reggie Mantle, Riverdale High School principal Mr. Weatherbee and teacher Miss Grundy in this fantasy/comedy series inspired by the success of TV's *Bewitched*. The series ran for three successful seasons on CBS.

Sabrina originally debuted as a recurring character on 1969's *The Archie Comedy Hour*. The fast-thinking witch was later combined with *The Groovie Goolies* in a one-hour time slot under the series of *Sabrina and the Groovie Goolies*, broadcast on CBS in 1970. (The program was later edited into a half-hour for syndication.)

A Filmation Associates Production. Color. Half-hour. Premiered on CBS: September 11, 1971–August 31, 1974.

Voices
Sabrina: Jane Webb

SAILOR MOON

Given awesome powers from mysterious feline Guardians, five ordinary high-schoolers—Sailor Moon (earthly name: Serena), Sailor Mars (Raye), Sailor Mercury (Amy), Sailor Jupiter (Lita) and Sailor Venus (Mina)—are transformed into glamorous and empowered fighters to battle the evil Queen Beryl (ruler of the Negaverse), whose goal is to accummulate enough "life energy" to release an explosive energy force that would destroy the world. This popular first-run action/adventure series was broadcast in syndication in 1995. The series, dubbed in English, was an American version of the runaway hit on Japan's TV Asahi called *Pretty Soldier Sailor Moon*.

A DIC Entertainment Production. Color. Half-hour. Premiered: September 11, 1995. Syndicated.

Voices

Sailor Moon/Serena: Tracey Moore, Terri Hawkes; **Sailor Mercury/Amy:** Karen Bernstein; **Sailor Mars/Raye:** Katie Griffin, Emilie Barlow; **Sailor Jupiter/Lita:** Susan Roman; **Sailor Venus/Mina:** Stephanie Morgenstern; **Sailor Pluto/Luna:** Jill Frappier, Sabrina Grdevich; **Tuxedo Mask/Darien:** Jonathon Potts, Toby Proctor, Rino Romano, Vince Corazza; **Queen Beryl:** Naz Edwards; **Zoycite (a.k.a. Cinnabar)/Emerald:** Kirsten Bishop; **Malachite (a.k.a Kunczite):** Dennis Akiyama; **Jedite (a.k.a. Emery)/Wiseman/Jordan:** Tony Daniels; **Neflite (a.k.a Mica):** Kevin Lund; **Luna:** Jill Frappier; **Artemis:** Ron Rubin; **Melvin (a.k.a. Umino):** Roland Parliament; **Molly (a.k.a. Naru)/Catsy:** Mary Long; **Sammy:** Julie Lemieux; **Andrew:** Colin O'Meara; **Miss Haruna:** Nadine Rabinovitch; **Rini:** Tracey Hoyt; **Alan:** Vince Corazza; **Chad:** Steven Bednarski; **Moonlight Knight:** Toby Proctor; **Metallia/Negaforce:** Maria Vacratsis; **Rubeus:** Robert Tinker; **Tree of Life:** Liz Hannah; **Catsy:** Alice Poon; **Birdie:** Kathleen Laskey; **Avery:** Jennifer Griffiths; **Prisma:** Norma Dell'Agnese; **Grandpa:** David Fraser; **Serena's Dad:** David Huband

⊚ SALTY'S LIGHTHOUSE

Educational preschooler series following the adventures of five-year-old Salty, who plays elaborate make-believe games and dress-up in a lighthouse with his seaside friends (Ocho the octopus, Claude the hermit crab and others), combining traditional cel animated wraparounds of Salty and his pals with model animated and live-action segments to tell each story. The series airs weekdays on The Learning Channel.

A Sunbow Entertainment Production in association with The Learning Channel. Color. Half-hour. Premiered on TLC: March 30, 1998.

Voices

Kathleen Barr, Paul Dobson, Rhys Huber, Janyce Jaud, Andrea Libman, Ian James Corlett, Scott McNeil, French Tickner, Lenore Zann

⊚ SAM AND MAX: FREELANCE POLICE

A pair of crime-solving pets—a gregarious dog and manic rabbit—team up as freelance police officers to solve bizarre mysteries, aided by the Geek, a teenage braniac who invents devices and vehicles to help them out in this half-hour Sat-

urday morning series based on the cult comic book by Steve Purcell for the Fox Network.

A Nelvana Production. Color. Half-hour. Premiered on FOX: October 4, 1997.

Voices

Sam: Harvey Atkin; **Max:** Robert Tinkler; **The Geek:** Tracey Moore

⊚ SAMSON AND GOLIATH

Loosely based on the classic biblical tale, a young boy (Samson) and his pet dog (Goliath) are transformed into superhumans—in a colossal man and golden, ruffled-haired lion—by rubbing two gold bracelets together (and declaring "I need Samson Power!") in order to battle despotic fiends and beastly creatures in this 26-episode half-hour adventure series that originally aired on NBC. Debuting in September of 1967, the show was originally called *Samson and Goliath*. On April 6, 1968 the show was retitled *Young Samson*, perhaps in an effort to differentiate itself from Art Clokey's syndicated Christian stop-motion animated series *Davey and Goliath*.

A Hanna-Barbera Production. Color. Half-hour. Premiered on NBC: September 9, 1967–March 1968 (as Samson and Goliath); April 6, 1968–August 31, 1968 (as Young Samson). Rebroadcast on USA: February 20, 1989–March 26, 1991 (with Space Kidettes). Syndicated.

Voices

Samson: Tim Matthieson

⊚ SAMURAI PIZZA CATS

Using their pizza parlor as headquarters, these young samurai crime-fighters (Speedy Cerviche, Guido Anchovi and Polly Esther) protect the myopic Princess Violet and the city from the force of the evil Big Cheese, head of the Little Tokyo Big Business Association, who plans to force residents into buying anything his slimy vendors have to sell in this action-packed half-hour series made for first-run syndication.

A Saban Entertainment/Tatsunoko Production. Color. Half-hour. Premiered: September 9, 1996. Syndicated.

Voices

Sonja Ball, Mark Camacho, Susan Glover, Dean Hagopian, A.J. Henderson, Rick Jones, Pauline Little, Michael O'Reilly, Terrence Scammell

⊚ SANTO BUGITO

Creator Arlen Klasky, cofounder of Klasky Csupo (original producers of *The Simpsons*), got the idea for this half-hour Saturday-morning cartoon series from her own children who, like most kids, were alternately grossed out and fascinated by bugs. Billed as the "world's first Tex-Mex cartoon," this Latin music–driven cartoon series deals with an all-insect cast who live life to the fullest in a Tex-Mex border town of 64 million insects, led by Paco and Carmen De La Antchez, the free-spirited proprietors of Santo Bugito's Cocina, a popular eatery where all the locals hang out. Premiering on CBS in 1995, the series was the first Saturday-morning effort from independent animation giant Klasky-Csupo and featured music by Mark Mothersbaugh, formerly of DEVO.

A Klasky-Csupo Production. Color. Half-hour. Premiered on CBS: September 16, 1995–August 17, 1996.

Voices
Carmen De La Antchez: Marabina Jaimes; **Paco De La Antchez:** Tony Plana; **Eaton Woode:** Charlie Adler; **Ralph:** George Kennedy; **Clem:** William Sanderson; **Burt:** Michael Stanton; **Amelia:** Joan Van Ark; **Carmen:** Marabina Jaimes; **Lencho:** Cheech Marin; **Rosa:** Candi Milo; **Mr. Mothmeyer:** Henry Gibson; **The Professor:** David Paymer

◎ SATURDAY SUPERCADE

Five segments made up this hour-long series of video game–inspired cartoons that ran for two seasons on CBS. The first season lineup featured: "Donkey Kong," about a gorilla who escapes from the circus and keeps on the run to avoid captivity; "Donkey Kong Jr.," the misadventures of Donkey Kong Jr. and his friend, Bones, in search of Kong's missing father; "Frogger," the story of a frog and his companions (Fanny Frog and Shelly the Turtle) as reporters for the *Swamp Gazette*; "Piffall," the exploits of a treasure hunter, his niece and their cowardly pet who travel the world to unearth lost treasures; and "Q*bert," a teenager who battles the evil Coilee Snake and his accomplices (Viper, Ugh and Wrong Way) with the help of his girlfriend, Q*tee.

"Frogger" and "Pitfall Harry" aired only during the first season. For the second season, they were replaced by two new video game–derived segments: "Space Ace," a handsome, gallant space hero with his lovely partner, Kimberly, who protects the heavens from the evil doings of Commander Borf, who plots to rule the universe; and "Kangaroo," the misadventures of three youngsters, Joey, Katy and Sidney, who run into all sorts of problems at the local zoo.

A Ruby-Spears Enterprises Production. Color. One hour. Premiered on CBS: September 17, 1983–August 24, 1985.

Voices

DONKEY KONG: Donkey Kong: Soupy Sales; **Pauline:** Judy Strangis; **Mario:** Peter Cullen

DONKEY KONG JR.: Donkey Kong Jr.: Frank Welker; **Bones, his friend:** Bart Braverman

FROGGER: Frogger: Bob Sarlatte; **Fanny:** B.J. Ward; **Shellshock:** Marvin Kaplan; **Tex:** Ted Field, Sr.; **Mac:** Alan Dinehart

PITFALL: Pitfall Harry: Bob Ridgely; **Rhonda:** Noelle North; **Quickclaw:** Ken Mars

Q*BERT: Q*bert: Billy Bowles; **Q*tee/Q*val:** Robbie Lee; **Q*bertha/Q*Mom/Viper:** Julie Dees; **Q*bit:** Dick Beals; **Q*mungus/Q*ball/Q*Dad/Coilee Snake/Ugg/Wrongway/Sam Slick:** Frank Welker

SPACE ACE: Space Ace: Jim Piper; **Kimberly:** Nancy Cartwright; **Dexter:** Sparky Marcus; **Space Marshall Vaughn:** Peter Renaday; **Commander Borf:** Arthur Burghardt

KANGAROO: Katy: Mea Martineau; **Joey:** David Mendenhall; **Mr. Friendly:** Arthur Burghardt; **Sidney:** Marvin Kaplan; **Monkey Biz Gang:** Frank Welker, Pat Fraley

◎ SAVAGE DRAGON

In futuristic Chicago, the Chicago Police Department's top cop—the half-reptile, half-human Dragon—helps to overcome a generation of superpowered perversions known as Superfreaks who grip the city in a villainous stranglehold. This 13-episode half-hour cartoon series was based on the bestselling comic book created by Erik Larsen. The series premiered on USA Network's Saturday-morning "Cartoon Express" in the fall of 1995.

A Lacewood Production in association with Studio B Productions/Universal Cartoon Studio/P3 Entertainment. Color. Half-hour. Premiered on USA: October 21, 1995.

Voices

Rene Auberjonois, Jeff Bennett, Jim Cummings, Paul Eiding, Jennifer Hale, Mark Hamill, Dorian Harewood, Tony Jay, Danny Mann, Rob Paulsen, Robert Picardo, Neil Ross, Kath Soucie, Mercelo Tubert, Frank Welker

◎ THE SCARY SCOOBY FUNNIES

Scooby Doo, his feisty dog cousin Scrappy-Doo and their goofy adult companion, Shaggy, undo baffling mysteries in this hour-long mystery/adventure show featuring episodes repeated from *The Richie Rich/Scooby-Doo Show—and Scrappy, Too!* (See the latter for voice credits.) The series was shown opposite *The New Scooby-Doo Mysteries* on ABC.

A Hanna-Barbera Production. Half-hour. Premiered on ABC: October 13, 1984–August 31, 1985.

◎ SCHOLASTIC'S THE MAGIC SCHOOL BUS

Lily Tomlin is the voice of Ms. Frizzle, a schoolteacher who takes a group of elementary school students on unusual field trips that turn into fantastic voyages. With the help of her magic school bus, which can literally go anywhere and be anything, they explore space, the Arctic, the human body and the principles of science in this, and PBS's first fully animated series, based on the bestselling children's books by Joanna Cole and illustrator Bruce Degen.

Various celebrity guest stars, including Carol Channing and Tyne Daly (as Dr. Tonelli), hopped aboard the souped-up yellow bus in episodic adventures. Produced by Scholastic Productions in association with Canadian-based Nelvana Limited, the fun-filled entertainment and educational half-hour series premiered on PBS in September of 1994. The program spawned two prime-time animated specials: *A Magic School Bus Halloween* (1995) and *The Magic School Bus Holiday Family Special* (1996), featuring Dolly Parton as celebrity guest voice. The animated series' hip theme song was written by Peter Lurye and performed by rock 'n' roll legend Little Richard. *Fraggle Rock* cocreator Jocelyn Stevenson was the series head writer. In 1995 Tomlin won a daytime Emmy Award for Outstanding Performer in an Animated Program.

A Scholastic Production in association with Nelvana Limited. Color. Half-hour. Premiered on PBS September 10, 1994 (previewed); September 11, 1994 (premiere).

Voices
Ms. Frizzle: Lily Tomlin; **Producer:** Malcolm-Jamal Warner; **Arnold:** Daniel Tamberelli; **Dorothy Ann:** Tara Meyer; **Wanda:** Lisa Yamanaka; **Carlos:** Daniel Desanto; **Keesha:** Erica Luttrell; **Phoebe:** Maia Filar; **Ralphie:** Stuart Stone; **Tim:** Andre Ottley-Lorant

◉ SCHOOLHOUSE ROCK

The brainchild of advertising executive David McCall, this long-running, award-winning educational series was developed in conjunction with ABC children's television head Michael Eisner (now chairman of the board of the Walt Disney Company) and Warner Bros. cartoon legend Chuck Jones. Beginning as a series of 90- to 180-second musical multiplication films called "Multiplication Rock" shown six times weekly during and between the network's Saturday-morning cartoon shows, 13 problem-solving films were produced for the 1972–73 season, covering such topics as "Zero, My Hero" and "Naughty Number Nine."

Different variations evolved in ensuing seasons to educate young viewers: "Grammar Rock" (1973), info-snippets designed to help children with grammar; "American Rock" (1974), a series of patriotic informational bites; "Bicentennial Rock" (1976), chronicling important historical moments in our nation's 200-year heritage (and begun two years before the bicenntial celebration); "Science Rock" (1978–79), dealing with scentific issues; "Body Rock" (1979), a three-episode series covering the importance of good health; and "Scooter Computer and Mr. Chips"

(1980s), to aid children in understanding computers and related technology.

The four-time Emmy Award–winning series, consisting of 41 episodes, went off the air in September of 1985, only to return with brand-new episodic vignettes (including new episodes of "Grammar Rock") on ABC in October 1993. The new animated films were designed by Tom Yohe Jr., son of *Schoolhouse Rock*'s original executive producer.

A Newall/Yohe-Scholastic Rock, Inc. Production. Color. Half-hour. Premiered on ABC: January 6, 1973–September 1985; October 1993.

◉ SCIENCE COURT

Using a courtroom as the teaching ground, a judge (voiced by stand-up comedienne Paula Poundstone) presides over cases in which attorney Doug Savage and court adversary Alison Kremel present evidence trying to prove basic scientific principles and theories, from evaporation to gravity, in order to win in this educational comedy series. It was created by Bill Braudis (who provides the voice of attorney Doug Savage) and famed radio/television personality Tom Snyder, cocreator and executive producer of Comedy Central's *Dr. Katz*.

A Tom Snyder Production. Color. Half-hour. Premiered on ABC: September 13, 1997.

Voices
Judge Stone: Paula Poundstone; **Doug Savage:** Bill Braudis; **Alison Krempel:** Paula Plum

◉ SCOOBY AND SCRAPPY-DOO

The mystery-solving great Dane, Scooby-Doo, and pals Fred, Shaggy, Daphne and Velma returned to the trail of mystery in this new half-hour series, featuring a new addition: Scooby's overly zealous little nephew, Scrappy-Doo, who instigates all the trouble for the gang.

The series marked the final appearance of Fred, Daphne and Velma, who departed after the series' network run. (In 1983, only Daphne returned in the recurring role of a reporter for a teen magazine investigating mysteries on ABC's *The All-New Scooby and Scrappy-Doo Show*. Former series regulars Freddy Jones and Velma Dinkley reappeared in guest-starring roles on 1984's *The New Scooby-Doo Mysteries*). In 1980–81, 39 new seven-and-a-half-minute episodes were featured in *The Richie Rich/Scooby-Doo Show—and Scrappy, Too!* (see entry for information), also on ABC. In January 1984 Scooby and Scrappy-Doo returned in a newly titled series of cartoon reruns *The New Scooby and Scrappy-Doo Show*.

A Hanna-Barbera Production. Color. Half-hour. Premiered on ABC: September 22, 1979–November 1, 1980. Rebroadcast on ABC: 1984 (as The New Scooby and Scrappy-Doo Show); Rebroadcast on CAR: April 14, 1997 (weekdays).

Voices

Scooby-Doo: Don Messick; **Scrappy-Doo:** Lennie Weinrib; **Freddy Jones:** Frank Welker; **Shaggy Rogers:** Casey Kasem; **Daphne Blake:** Heather Storm; **Velma Dace Dinkley:** Maria Frumkin (replaced Patricia Stevens)

⊚ THE SCOOBY AND SCRAPPY-DOO/PUPPY HOUR

Scooby-Doo, the lovable canine afraid of his own shadow, and his fearless little nephew, Scrappy-Doo, comically extricate themselves from fantastic predicaments in this hour-long series for Saturday morning in 1982 that featured as its second half "The Puppy's New Adventures," the warm-hearted tale of Petey the puppy and his human friend, Dolly, and canine buddies Duke, Dash and Lucky as they search for Petey's lost family. The characters were first introduced in a series of "ABC Weekend Specials" beginning with *The Puppy Who Wanted a Boy*, produced between 1978 and 1981 by Ruby-Spears Productions. Coproduced by Hanna-Barbera Productions ("Scooby and Scrappy-Doo") and Ruby-Spears Enterprises ("The Puppy's New Adventures"), the series, featuring three "Scooby and Scrappy-Doo" cartoons and one half-hour adventure of Petey the Puppy, aired in its full hour format for one season on ABC.

The Scooby and Scrappy-Doo cartoons featured a new addition: Scooby's Wild West cousin, Yabba-Doo, who helped Scrappy maintain law and order in separate show segments. Other weekly segments had Scooby, Scrappy and Shaggy eneountering new mysteries in various locales while vacationing.

In the fall of 1983, a second series of new cartoons was produced, *The Puppy's Further Adventures*, which ran as the lead-in to Hanna-Barbera's *The All-New Scooby and Scrappy-Doo Show*. A third and final Petey the Pup series was produced in 1984, *The Puppy's Great Adventures*.

A Hanna-Barbera/Ruby-Spears Production. Color. One hour. Premiered on ABC: September 25, 1982–January 1, 1983. Rebroadcast on ABC: January 8, 1983–September 3, 1983 (as The Scooby-Doo/Puppy Hour*).*

Voices

Scooby-Doo/Scrappy-Doo/Yabba-Doo: Don Messick; **Freddy Jones:** Frank Welker; **Shaggy Rogers:** Casey Kasem; **Daphne Blake:** Heather North; **Velma Dace Dinkley:** Patricia Stevens; **Deputy Dusty:** Frank Welker; **Petey the Pup:** Billy Jacoby; **Dolly:** Nancy McKeon; **Duke/Dash:** Michael Bell; **Tommy:** Tony O'Dell; **Lucky:** Peter Cullen

⊚ SCOOBY-DOO CLASSICS

Fred, Shaggy, Daphne, Velma, Scooby-Doo and Scooby's courageous nephew Scrappy solve unsolvable mysteries in this half-hour Saturday-morning series featuring 49 repeat episodes from previously broadcast series (25 from 1969's *Scooby-Doo, Where Are You?* and 24 from 1976's *Scooby-Doo/Dynomutt Hour*). (See both entries for voice credits.)

A Hanna-Barbera Production. Color. Half-hour. Premiered on ABC: 1981–1982; 1983–1984.

⊚ THE SCOOBY-DOO/DYNOMUTT HOUR

Canine detective Scooby-Doo and the superhero dog wonder Dynomutt share the spotlight in this one-hour show as each stars in his own half-hour cartoon adventures. The bionic Dynomutt, whose voice recalls Art Carney's, teams up with big-city crime fighter the Blue Falcon to uphold law and order, while Scooby Doo and the gang (Freddy, Daphne, Shaggy and Velma) try cracking unusual mysteries. Joining Scooby and his friends was a new character: Scooby-Dum, Scooby-Doo's country cousin reminiscent of Edgar Bergen's Mortimer Snerd), and the female Scooby-Dee, who appeared in "The Chiller Diller Movie Thriller," a Scooby-Doo segment from the series.

A Hanna-Barbera Production. Color. One hour. Premiered on ABC: September 11, 1976–November 1976; December 1976–September 3, 1977 (as The Scooby-Doo/Dynomutt Show*).*

Voices

Scooby-Doo: Don Messick; **Freddy Jones/Dynomutt, dog wonder:** Frank Welker; **Daphne Blake:** Heather North; **Shaggy Rogers:** Casey Kasem; **Velma Dace Dinkley:** Nichole Jaffe; **Scooby-Dum:** Daws Butler; **Scooby-Dee:** Julie McWhirter; **The Blue Falcon:** Gary Owens

⊚ THE SCOOBY-DOO SHOW

Following the successful three-season run of *Scooby-Doo, Where Are You?* on CBS, the series jumped to ABC in the fall of 1978. Scooby and his courageous teenage mystery solvers picked up where they left off in 16 new episodes, this time under the new title of *The Scooby-Doo Show*.

A Hanna-Barbera Production. Color. Half-hour. Premiered on ABC: September 9, 1979–November 4, 1978.

Voices

Scooby-Doo: Don Messick; **Freddy Jones:** Frank Welker; **Daphne Blake:** Heather North; **Shaggy Rogers:** Casey Kasem; **Velma Dace Dinkley:** Patricia Stevens

⊚ SCOOBY-DOO, WHERE ARE YOU?

A cowardly great Dane, Scooby-Doo, and his four teenage partners–Freddy, Daphne, Velma and Shaggy—tour the country in their "Mystery Machine" van in search of the supernatural. The title of the program was a takeoff on the classic television comedy series *Car 54 Where Are You?*

Following its inital three-season run on CBS, the network rebroadcast the series twice—in 1974–75 and 1975–76—before it switched to ABC in 1978 with 16 brand-new episodes under the title of *The Scooby-Doo Show.* The series was rerun on ABC in 1984 under its former title. During the 1978 repeat season, ABC also aired a new series on the same day, *Scooby's All-Stars,* featuring all-new episodes. In the fall of 1981 ABC rebroadcast 25 episodes from the series under the retitled *Scooby-Doo Classics,* which also featured 24 episodes from 1976's *Scooby-Doo/Dynomutt Hour.* (Episodes also were repeated on two other series: 1977's *Scooby's All-Star Laff-a-Lympics* and 1983's *The Best of Scooby-Doo.*) ABC broadcast the series when Hanna-Barbera's *Laverne and Shirley in the Army* animated series was delayed. The series subsequently aired in reruns on TBS, USA Network's *Cartoon Express* and the Cartoon Network.

A *Hanna-Barbera Production. Color. Half-hour. Premiered on CBS: September 13, 1969–September 2, 1972. Premiered on ABC: September 8, 1978—November 4, 1978 (as The Scooby-Doo Show). Rebroadcast on CBS: September 1974–August 1975; September 1975–August 1976. Rebroadcast on ABC: October 6, 1984–October 13, 1984. Rebroadcast on TBS. Rebroadcast on USA: September 7, 1992–September 11, 1994. Rebroadcast on CAR: November 28, 1994–September 1, 1995; January 1, 1996– .*

Voices
Scooby-Doo: Don Messick; **Freddy Jones:** Frank Welker; **Shaggy Rogers:** Casey Kasem; **Daphne Blake:** Stefanianna Christopherson, Heather North, Velma Dace Dinkley, Nichole Jaffe

◎ SCOOBY'S ALL-STAR LAFF-A-LYMPICS

More than 45 of Hanna-Barbera's favorite cartoon characters participate in track and field competition, spoofing ABC's *Wide World of Sports,* in this two-hour Saturday-morning series, the first in network history. Assigned to different teams—the Really Rottens, the Scooby Doobys and the Yogi Yahooeys—the winner of each event earns the prestigious Laff-a-Lympics gold medallion. Snagglepuss and Mildew Wolf serve as the play-by-play announcers.

Other program segments were: "Captain Caveman and the Teen Angels," "Dynomutt, Dog Wonder" (featured in four new two-part episodes under the title of "The Blue Falcon and Dynomutt," plus reruns of old episodes) and "Scooby Doo" (25 episodes repeated from *Scooby-Doo, Where Are You?*).

Following the 1977–78 season, the program returned for a second season under the title of *Scooby's All-Stars.* The series aired a total of three seasons, concluding its network run as *Scooby's Laff-a-Lympics,* a shortened one-hour version comprised of repeat episodes, later rebroadcast on USA Network's *Cartoon Express* and on The Cartoon Network.

A *Hanna-Barbera Production. Color. Two hours. Premiered on ABC: September 10, 1977–September 2, 1978; September 9, 1978–September 8, 1979 (as Scooby's All-Stars); June 12, 1980–November 1, 1980 (as Scooby's Laff-a-Lympics). Rebroadcast on USA: May 2, 1989–October 17, 1981. Rebroadcast on CAR: October 3, 1994–November 25, 1996 (weekdays).*

Voices

ANNOUNCERS: Snagglepuss: Daws Butler; **Mildew Wolf:** John Stephenson

THE YOGI YAHOOEYS: Yogi Bear/Huckleberry Hound/Hokey Wolf/Snooper/Blabber/Wally Gator/Quick Draw McGraw/Augie Doggie/Dixie/Jinks: Daws Butler; **Doggie Daddy:** John Stephenson; **Boo Boo/Pixie:** Don Messick; **Grape Ape:** Bob Holt; **Yakky Doodle:** Frank Welker; **Cindy Bear:** Julie Bennett

THE SCOOBY-DOOBYS: Scooby-Doo: Don Messick; **Scooby-Dum:** Daws Butler; **Shaggy:** Casey Kasem; **Hong Kong Phooey:** Scatman Crothers; **Jeannie:** Julie McWhirter; **Babu:** Joe Besser; **Dynomutt/Tinker:** Frank Welker; **Blue Falcon:** Gary Owens; **Captain Caveman/Speed Buggy:** Mel Blanc; **Brenda Chance:** Marilyn Schreffler; **Dee Dee Sykes:** Vernee Watson; **Taffy Dare:** Laurel Page

THE REALLY ROTTENS: Mumbly/Dastardly Dalton/Mr. Creepley: Don Messick; **Daisy Mayhem:** Marilyn Schreffler; **Sooey Pig/Magic Rabbit:** Frank Welker; **Dread Baron/The Great Fondoo:** John Stephenson; **Orful Octopus/Dinky Dalton:** Bob Holt; **Dirty Dalton:** Daws Butler; **Mrs. Creepley:** Laurel Page

◎ SCOOBY'S MYSTERY FUNHOUSE

Canine detective Scooby-Doo and pals Shaggy and Scrappy-Doo starred in this half-hour collection of classic ghostbusting tales and mysteries originally broadcast on *The Scooby and Scrappy-Doo/Puppy Hour, The New Scooby and Scrappy-Doo Show, Scary Scooby Funnies* and others. (See programs for voice credits.)

A *Hanna-Barbera Production. Color. Half-hour. Premiered on ABC: September 7, 1985–February 22, 1986.*

◎ SCREEN GEMS CARTOONS

More than 350 black-and-white cartoons produced by Columbia Pictures in the 1930s and 1940s—*Krazy Kat, Scrappy,* and *Phantasy Cartoons*—were offered in this syndicated packaged, which also included three previously exhibited Van Beuren series (*Aesop's Fables, Cubby Bear* and *Tom and Jerry*). Screen Gems, Columbia's television division, purchased the rights to these films in 1956 from

Unity Pictures, which had distributed the cartoons to television since 1947. (See individual cartoon series in Theatrical Sound Cartoon Series for complete details.)

A Screen Gems/Columbia Pictures Television Production. Black-and-white. Half-hour. Premiered: 1956. Syndicated.

◎ SEABERT

Together with human friends Tommy and Aura, Seabert, a lovable seal, travels the globe, by land and by sea, protecting his fellow animals in this 26-episode half-hour animated series produced by Belgian-based Sepp International (coproducers of *The Smurfs*) that debuted on HBO.

A Sepp International Production. Color. Half-hour. Premiered on HBO: April 5, 1987–June 30, 1988.

Voices

Diana Ellington, Melissa Freeman, Ron Knight, Bruce Robertson, Morgan Upton

◎ SEALAB 2020

Earth, A.D. 2020. Dr. Paul Williams leads an underwater expedition to study living conditions while searching for scientific solutions in a domed experimental city operated by 250 inhabitants. Williams is unexpectedly joined on his expedition by Captain Mike Murphy, his niece and nephew, Sallie and Bobby, and radio dispatcher Sparks, who were rescued by three Sealab aquanauts (Hal, Ed and Gail) when their ship ran into trouble. The 13-week half-hour series debuted on NBC in 1972.

A Hanna-Barbera Production. Color. Half-hour. Premiered on NBC: September 9, 1972–September 1, 1973. Rebroadcast on CAR: December 6, 1992; March 14, 1993 (part of Boomerang, 1972).

Voices

Dr. Paul Williams: Ross Martin; **Captain Mike Murphy:** John Stephenson; **Bobby Murphy:** Josh Albee; **Sallie Murphy:** Pamelyn Ferdin; **Sparks:** Bill Callaway; **Hal:** Jerry Dexter; **Gail:** Ann Jillian; **Ed:** Ron Pinckard; **Mrs. Thomas:** Olga James; **Jamie:** Gary Shapiro; **Other Voices:** Don Messick

◎ THE SECRET LIVES OF WALDO KITTY

Based on James Thurber's story, "The Secret Life of Walter Mitty," the series stars cowardly Waldo, a daydreaming cat who imagines himself as the roughriding savior Lone Kitty, the superhero Cat Man and others, fighting swaggering bulldog Tyrone for the honor of his pussycat girlfriend, Felicia, in 13 cartoon adventures. Introduced each week with live-action footage of Waldo, feline friend Felicia and bul-

lying Tyrone, the series was originally produced for NBC in 1975 and lasted only one season.

A Filmation Associates Production. Color. Half-hour. Premiered on NBC: September 6, 1975–September 4, 1976.

Voices

Waldo Kitty/Wetzel/Lone Kitty/Catman/Catzan/Robin Cat/ Captain Herc: Howard Morris; **Felicia/Pronto/Sparrow/ Lt. O-Hoo-Ha:** Jane Webb; **Tyrone/Mr. Crock/Ping/ Brennan Hench Dog/Dr. Moans:** Allan Melvin

◎ THE SECRET SQUIRREL SHOW

Packaged for two seasons as part of the hour-long *The Atom Ant/Secret Squirrel Show*, the buck-toothed squirrel private investigator and the supporting elements—"Squiddly Diddly" and "Winsome Witch"—from his half of the original network series were given their own half-hour show in 1967, repeating episodes from the 1965–66 series, which premiered on the same network. The program concluded its network run the way it began, again paired with Atom Ant and company as *The Atom Ant/Secret Squirrel Show* in September 1967. (See entry for voice credits.)

A Hanna-Barbera Production. Color. Half-hour. Premiered on NBC: January 1967–September 2, 1967. Rebroadcast on CAR: September 20, 1993–December 31, 1993 (weekdays); February 28, 1994–September 3, 1994 (weekdays, Saturdays); September 11, 1994–September 3, 1995 (Sundays, Wednesdays).

◎ SECTAURS

On the distant planet, Symbion, a group of telepathically bonded warriors join with their insect companions in the ultimate battle of survival in this first-run, half-hour miniseries comprised of five episodic adventures.

A Ruby-Spears Enterprises Production. Color. Half-hour. Premiered: September 1985. Syndicated.

Voices

Dargon/Dragonflyer: Dan Gilvezan; **Pinsor/Battle Beetle:** Peter Renaday; **Mantor/Skito/Toxid:** Peter Cullen; **Zak/ Bitaur:** Laurie Faso; **Spidrax/Spiderflyer:** Arthur Burghardt; **Skulk/Trancula/Raplor:** Frank Welker; **Waspax/Wingid:** Neil Ross

◎ SHAKESPEARE: THE ANIMATED TALES

William Shakespeare's literary classics—A *Midsummer Night's Dream*, *Twelfth Night*, *Hamlet*, *Romeo and Juliet*, *Macbeth* and others—are brought to life in this first-ever animated series based on his work. Hosted by Robin Williams, the monthly half-hour condensations—using three different styles: stop-action puppetry, cel animation and painting on glass plates, done at the Soyuzmultifilm

Studios in Moscow, debuted on HBO in 1992. Animated by studio artists in Armenia and Russia as well as in Cardiff, Wales, six half-hour episodes were produced the first year, costing around $850,000 each. Character voices were provided by members of Britain's National Theatre and Royal Shakespeare Company.

A Dave Edwards Studio/Christmas Films/Soyuzmultifilm Studios Production. Color. Half-hour. Premiered on HBO: November 10, 1992.

Voices
Daniel Massey, Menna Tussler

ⓢ SHAZZAN!

Twins Chuck and Nancy find a broken ancient ring inscribed with the word "Shazzan!" that, joined together, transports them back to the age of the Arabian Nights. The leader of the group, Shazzan, a 60-foot genie, guards the children by working his wizardry on evildoers in this 26-episode half-hour fantasy/adventure series that bowed on CBS in 1967.

A Hanna-Barbera Production. Color. Half-hour. Premiered on CBS: September 9, 1967–September 6, 1969. Rebroadcast on CAR: November 8, 1992 (part of Boomerang, 1968); February 7, 1993 (part of Boomerang, 1967); August 5, 1995 (part of Power Zone).

Voices
Shazzan: Barney Phillips; **Nancy:** Janet Waldo; **Chuck:** Jerry Dexter; **Kaboobie, the flying camel:** Don Messick

ⓢ SHELLEY DUVALL'S BEDTIME STORIES

Shelley Duvall, the force behind cable TV's *Faerie Tale Theatre* and *Tall Tales & Legends*, produced and cowrote this live-action/animated series presenting contemporary bedtime stories based on famous children's stories and narrated by big-name stars, including Robin Williams, Jean Stapleton, Tatum O'Neal, Billy Crystal, among others. The series opener featured two tales: "Elbert's Bad Word," about a boy who hears a bad word and uses it (read by Ringo Starr), and "Weird Parents," about a youngster who is totally embarrassed by her mom and dad (voiced by Bette Midler). Two or three segments made up each half-hour show to encourage children to read and write. In Christmas 1994 Duvall produced a holiday special version of "The Christmas Witch" (read by Angela Lansbury). (See Animated Television Specials for details.)

A Think Entertainment/MCA Family Entertainment/Universal Cartoon Studios Production. Color. Half-hour. Premiered on SHO: April 21, 1992.

ⓢ SHE-RA: PRINCESS OF POWER

He-Man's twin sister, Adora, transformed by her magic swords into She-Ra, defender of the Crystal Castle, battles the evil forces of Hordak in this 65-episode companion series to *He-Man and the Masters of the Universe* produced for first-run syndication in 1985 and later rebroadcast on USA Network's *Cartoon Express.*

A Filmation Studios Production in association with Mattel Toys. Color. Half-hour. Premiered: 1985. Syndicated. Rebroadcast on USA: February 28, 1989–July 10, 1989.

Voices
Princess Adora/She-Ra/Madama Raxx/Frosta: Melendy Britt; **Hordak:** George DiCenzo; **Castaspella/Glimmer/ Shadow Weaver/Catra; Linda Gary; Broom/He-Man:** John Erwin; **Skeletor:** Alan Oppenheimer; **Kowl/Mantella/ Leech:** Erik Gundin; **Imp:** Erika Scheimer; **Lightrope/ Sprint/Swiftwind/Horde Soldiers/Loo-Kee:** Lou Scheimer

ⓢ THE SHIRT TALES

Lovable little animals, wearing message-bearing T-shirts, help others in need around the world after receiving holographic messages of distress on their sophisticated wristwatch communicators in this weekly Saturday-morning series based on the Hallmark greeting card character. The series was produced by NBC as Saturday-morning competition to CBS's *Sylvester and Tweety/Daffy and Speedy* and ABC's *The Pac-Man/Little Rascals/Richie Rich Show* in 1982. The series' second season featured a new cast member: Kip Kangaroo, a trusting, loving character with powerful hindquarters. After its two-season run on NBC, the series was rerun on CBS, USA Network's *Cartoon Express* and the Cartoon Network.

A Hanna-Barbera Production. Color. Half-hour. Premiered on NBC: September 18, 1982–September 8, 1984. Rebroadcast on CBS: September 15, 1984–May 23, 1985. Rebroadcast on USA: April 2, 1989–March 23, 1992. Rebroadcast on CAR: October 1, 1992–September 17, 1993 (weekdays); January 3, 1994–September 2, 1994 (weekdays); January 5, 1994–June 2, 1995 (weekdays); September 4, 1995– (weekdays).

Voices
TYG Tiger: Steve Schatzberg; **Pammy Panda:** Pat Parris; **Digger Mole:** Bob Ogle; **Bogey Orangutan:** Fred Travalena; **Rick Raccoon:** Ronnie Schell; **Kip Kangaroo:** Nancy Cartwright; **Mr. Dinkel:** Herb Vigram

ⓢ THE SHNOOKUMS & MEAT FUNNY CARTOON SHOW

Previously featured in two previously unsuccessful series, *Raw Toonage* and *Marsupilami*, this battling off-the-wall cat-and-dog team were cast as the title stars of this series used to launch "Manic Monday," a retooled version of Disney studio's the *Disney Afternoon* two-hour weekday cartoon block in January 1995. The program ran once a week and lasted only one season.

A Walt Disney Television Animation Production. Color. Half-hour. Premiered: January 2, 1995–August 28, 1995. Syndicated.

Voices
Shnookums: Danny Mann, Jason Marsden; **Meat:** Frank Welker; **Chafe:** Charlie Adler; **Pith Possum/Tex Tinstar:** Jeff Bennett; **Ian/Krusty Rustnuckle:** Corey Burton; **Narrator (Tex Tinstar):** Jim Cummings; **Commissioner Stress/Wrongo:** Brad Garrett; **Floyd the Rattler/Lieutenant Tension:** Jess Harnell; **Husband:** Bill Kopp, Steve Mackall; **Wife:** Tress MacNeille; **Doris Deer:** April Winchell; **Obediah/The Wonder Raccoon:** Patric Zimmerman

◎ SILVERHAWKS
Music-driven animated series featuring metallic-looking characters–known as The Silverhawks–led by Commander Stargazer, who fight extraterrestrial gangsters and villains, including Mon Star and his Mob. This series was a follow-up to the Rankin-Bass first-run cartoon series *ThunderCats*.

A Rankin-Bass Production. Color. Half-hour. Syndicated: September 1986.

Voices
Larry Kenney, Robert McFadden, Earl Hammond, Maggie Jakobson, Peter Newman, Adolph Newman, Adolph Caesar, Doug Preis

◎ SILVER SURFER
This flashy-looking Marvel Comics superhero (created by Stan Lee and Jack Kirby) roams the galaxy on his flying board in search of his long-lost home, Zenn-La, and the love of his life, Shalla-Bal, battling evil wherever he finds it in this half-hour series produced for the Fox Network. The 13-episode series debuted in February 1998 with the three-part series opener, "The Origin of Silver Surfer."

A Fox Kids Network/Saban International/Marvel Entertainment Group Production. Color. Half-hour. Premiered on FOX: February 7, 1998.

Voices
James Blendick, Robert Bockstael, Jennifer Dale, Raul Essemere, Colin Fox, Gary Krawford, Tara Rosling, John Neville, Camilla Scott, Alison Sealy-Smith, Elizabeth Sheperd, Cedric Smith, Norm Spencer, Mark Strange, Aron Tager

◎ THE SIMPSONS
Cartoonist Matt Groenig (*Life in Hell*) created this outlandish series based on the adventures of an exuberantly

Cartoonist Matt Groening's outlandish blue-collar family from the longest-running prime-time cartoon series in history, The Simpsons. *© Fox Network*

blue-collar family who are just about everything that most television families are not—crude, loud, obnoxious and sloppily dressed characters, with bizarre hairdos and severe overbites. The characters were originally featured in brief segments on Fox Network's *The Tracy Ullman Show* before the network spotlighted them in their own weekly series. From the series inception in 1989, independent cartoon studio Klasky Csupo animated each episode through the 1991–92 season. Film Roman, producers of TV's *Garfield and Friends*, took over production of the series in March of 1992, in time for the 1992–93 season.

During the series' long and illustrious network run, a long list of notable celebrities have lent their voices in guest appearances, including Tony Bennett, Dustin Hoffman, Michael Jackson, Larry King and Leonard Nimoy. The series also has spawned its share of prime-time specials, including *The Simpsons Christmas Special* (1989) and *The Simpsons Halloween Special: Tree House of Horror*, the first in a series of annual Halloween shows.

With the airing of the series' 167th episode (called "The Itchy & Scratch & Poochie Show") on February 9, 1997, the Emmy-winning series dethroned *The Flintstones* (which aired 166 episodes in prime time from 1960 to 1966) as the longest-running prime-time animation series. In 1993 Dan Casetellaneta (the voice of Homer Simpson) was awarded an Emmy for Oustanding Voice-Over Performance.

A Gracie Films/Klasky-Csupo/Film Roman Production in association with 20th Century-Fox Television. Color. Half-hour. Premiered on FOX: January 14, 1990.

Voices
Homer J. Simpson/Abraham J. Simpson (Grandpa)/Herschel Krustofsky ("Krusty the Clown")/Barney Gumble: Dan Castellaneta; **Marjorie (Marge) Simpson/Patty Bouvier/Selma Bouvier/Jacqueline Bouvier:** Julie Kavner; **Bartholomew (Bart) Jo-Jo Simpson/Nelson Muntz/Rod Flanders/Todd Flanders/Ralph Wiggum:** Nancy Cartwright; **Lisa Maria Simpson:** Yeardley Smith; **Maggie Simpson (pacifier sucking):** Matt Groenig; **Maggie Simpson (speaking, one show only):** Elizabeth Taylor; **Apu Nahasapeemapetilon/Moe Szyslak/Police Chief Clancy Wiggun/Comic Book Guy/Dr. Nick Riviera:** Hank Azaria; **Charles Montgomery Burns/Waylon Smithers/Ned Flanders/Seymour Skinner/Otto Mann:** Harry Shearer; **Charles Montgomery Burns/Moe Szyslak (first two seasons):** Christopher Collins; **Lunchlady Doris:** Doris Grau; **Lionel Hutz/Troy McClure:** Phil Hartman; **Milhouse van Houten/Janey Powell/Jimbo Jones/Dolph:** Pamela Hayden; **Agnes Skinner/Ms. Albright/Mrs. Glick:** Tress MacNeille; **Maude Flanders/Luanne van Houten/Helen Lovejoy/Miss Elizabeth Hoover:** Maggie Roswell; **Bleeding Gums Murphy:** Ron Taylor; **Martin Prince/Uter/Sherri/Terri/Lewis Wendell:** Russi Taylor; **Mrs. Krabappel:** Marcia Wallace

⊚ SINBAD JR., THE SAILOR
Originally called *The Adventures of Sinbad, Jr.*, the cartoons star the son of the famed sea adventurer, Sinbad, who becomes superhuman whenever he draws power from a magic belt. He is assisted in his high-sea adventures by his first mate, Salty, the parrot in this half-hour series, comprised of 100 five-minute cartoon adventures, first syndicated in 1965. The first series of Sinbad cartoons were produced by Sam Singer in 1965. Hanna-Barbera took over production of the series the following season.

A Sam Singer and Hanna-Barbera Production. Sinbad is a trademark of American International Pictures. Color. Half-hour. Premiered: Fall 1965. Syndicated.

Voices
Sinbad: Tim Matthieson; **Salty:** Mel Blanc

⊚ THE SKATEBIRDS
Live-action stars Scooter the Penguin, Satchel the Pelican, Knock Knock the Woodpecker and Scat Cat host

this series comprised of wraparounds, comedy skits and animated cartoons, such as "Woofer and Wimper, Dog Detectives" (formerly of *The Clue Club*); "The Robonic Stooges," featuring Moe, Larry and Curly as bionic crime-fighters; "Wonder Wheels," which pairs two high school journalists and a heroic motorcycle in remarkable adventures; and the film serial "Mystery Island." First broadcast on CBS in 1977, the show was canceled after only four months on the air because of poor ratings. It was replaced by *Speed Buggy* and "The Robonic Stooges" (retitled *The Three Robonic Stooges*). (The cartoon trio received better ratings in *The Skatebirds* than any other segment.) In September 1979 *The Skatebirds* returned to CBS on Sunday mornings, where it completed its network run. *A Hanna-Barbera Production. Color. Half-hour. Premiered on CBS: September 10, 1977–January 21, 1978. Rebroadcast on CBS: September 1979–August 1980; September 1980–January 25, 1981. Rebroadcast on CAR: July 5, 1995– (Wednesdays).*

Voices
Scooter: Don Messick; **Satchel:** Bob Holt; **Knock Knock:** Lennie Weinrib; **Scat Cat:** Scatman Crothers

WOOFER AND WIMPER: Larry: David Joliffe; **D.D.:** Bob Hastings; **Pepper:** Patricia Smith; **Dotty:** Tara Talboy; **Woofer:** Paul Winchell; **Wimper:** Jim MacGeorge; **Sheriff Bagley:** John Stephenson

THE ROBONIC STOOGES: Moe: Paul Winchell; **Larry:** Joe Baker; **Curly:** Frank Welker; **Triple-Zero:** Ross Martin

WONDER WHEELS: Willie Sheeler: Micky Dolenz; **Dooley Lawrence:** Susan Davis

Cast
MYSTERY ISLAND: Chuck Kelly: Stephen Parr; **Sue Corwin:** Lynn Marie Johnston; **Sandy Corwin:** Larry Volk; **Dr. Strange:** Michael Kermoyan; **P.A.U.P.S. (voice):** Frank Welker

⊚ SKELETON WARRIORS
Featuring high-tech, computer-generated effects, the very human Skeleton Hunters, led by Prince Justin Lightstar and his royal family, defend themselves from Baron Dark and his army of Skeleton Warriors to reunite two halves of the Lightstar Stone and rescue the world from eternal night in this futuristic, mythic fantasy/adventure series created by Garry Goddard.

A Landmark/Graz Entertainment Production. Color. Half-hour. Premiered on CBS: September 17, 1994–September 2, 1995.

Voices
Jeff Bennett, Earl Boen, Nathan Carlson, Philip L. Clarke, Michael Corbett, Jim Cummings, Paul Eiding, Jeannie Elias, Linda Gary, Michael Gough, Jennifer Hale, Tony Jay, Danny Mann, Richard Molinare, Valery Pappas, Jan Rabson, Kevin Michael Richardson, Rodney Saulsberry, Kevin Schon

⊚ SKY COMMANDERS

The Sky Commanders, a motley crew of renegade soldiers, battle a world-class villain, the evil General Plague, who is bent on world destruction, in the late 21st century, when technology comes face to face with a perilous new wilderness in this first-run half-hour adventure series based on the popular toy line by Kenner Toys. The program aired on Sunday mornings on *The Funtastic World of Hanna-Barbera*.

A Hanna-Barbera Production in association with Kenner Toys. Color. Half-hour. Premiered: July 1987. Syndicated. Rebroadcast on CAR: January 21, 1995 (Super Adventures); July 8, 1995 (Power Zone).

Voices
General Mike Summit, the Sky Commanders leader: Bob Ridgely; **Cutter Kling, crew member:** William Windom; **R.J. Scott, crew member:** Darryl Hickman; **Books Baxter, crew member:** Richard Doyle; **Jim Stryker, crew member:** Dorian Harewood; **Spider Reilly, crew member:** Triston Rogers; **Kodiak Crane, crew member:** Soon-Teck Oh; **Red McCullough, crew member:** Lauren Tewes; **General Plague:** Bernard Erhard; **Mordax:** Dick Gautier; **Raider Rath:** Paul Eiding; **Kreeg:** Charlie Adler; **Dr. Erica Slade:** B.J. Ward

⊚ SKY DANCERS

Five young dance students are appointed the guardians of the Sky Swirl Stone that safeguards Wingdom from the cyclonic villain Sky Clone in this 26-episode half-hour fantasy/adventure series based on the popular Galoob toy line. The 26 half-hour episode series premiered in syndication in the fall of 1996.

An Abrams Gentile Entertainment/Gaumont Multimedia Production. Color. Half-hour. Premiered: September 9, 1996. Syndicated.

Voices
T.J. Benjamin, Andrea Burns, Thomas Cannizaro, Donna Daley, Jonathan Khan, Ciarrai Ni Mhaiile, James Michael, K.C. Noel

⊚ SKY HAWKS

A former air force colonel, widower Mike Wilson; his children, Steve and Caroline; his World War I flying ace father, Pappy; and Pappy's foster children, Baron Hughes and Little Cindy, head a daredevil air transport rescue service that saves troubled charter planes, helicopter pilots and test pilots. Sponsored by Mattel Toys, the 17-episode series debuted on ABC in 1969, opposite CBS's *The Archies* and NBC's *The Banana Splits*. Despite such stiff competition, the series returned for a second season in 1970, comprised entirely of repeat episodes.

A Pantomime Pictures/Ken Snyder Production. Color. Half-hour. Premiered on ABC: September 6, 1969–September 4, 1971.

Voices
Captain Mike Wilson: Michael Rye; **Steve Wilson, his son/Joe Conway:** Casey Kasem; **Caroline Wilson, his daughter:** Iris Rainer; **Pappy Wilson, Mike's father/Baron Hughes, Pappy's foster child:** Dick Curtis; **Cynthia "Mugs" Hughes:** Melinda Casey; **Maggie McNalley:** Joan Gerber; **Buck Devlin:** Bob Arbogast

⊚ SKYSURFER STRIKE FORCE

A pedestrian-looking bunch are magically transformed into imposing crimefighters who battle evil on antigravity "skyboards" (a cross between Jet Skis and skateboards) in this futuristic sci-fi cartoon series produced for first-run syndication. The series premiered in the fall of 1995 as part of the weekend syndicated block, *Amazin' Adventures II*.

A Ruby-Spears/Ashi Production. Color. Half-hour. Premiered: September 24, 1995 (part of Amazin' Adventures II). Syndicated.

Voices
Skysurfer/Jack, Noxious: Mike Donovan, David Kaye; **Crazy Stunts/Mickey, Chronozoid/Replicon:** Paul Dobson; **Soar Loser/Brad:** Ward Perry; **Lazerette (formerly Darklight), Myko:** Vernus Terzo; **Sliced Ice/Kim, Cerena:** Jansyse Jaud; **Five Eyes/Grenader (formerly X-Ploder)/Garland/Foster:** Richard Newman; **Air Enforcer/Nathan (Nate)/Cybron/Wyland:** Alvin Sanders; **Zachariah Easel (formerly Pablo Palet)/Hagedorn/Adam:** Terry Klassen

⊚ SLIMER! AND THE REAL GHOSTBUSTERS

Those ghostbusting idiots of the 1984 box-office sensation return for more mysteries and mishaps, joined by their tagalong mascot, Slimer! in this half-hour comedy/mystery series that originally aired on ABC (retitled after a two-season run as *The Real Ghostbusters* on the same network). The show was expanded to a full hour for the first season (1988–89), featuring 42 new *Slimer! and the Real Ghostbusters* cartoons, plus several new preteen characters. The character of Peter Venkman, formerly voiced by comedian

Title card from the popular ABC Saturday morning series, Slimer! and the Real Ghostbusters. © Columbia Pictures Television, a division of CPT Holdings Inc. All rights reserved. (COURTESY: DIC ENTERPRISES)

Arsenio Hall and Lorenzo Music (the voice of Garfield the Cat) in the previous Saturday-morning series, was now voiced by Dave Coulier. ABC renewed the series for the 1989–90 season and the program was reduced to a half hour, divided into two 15-minute adventures each week. Among the season's broadcasts was the premiere of the prime-time Halloween special *Slimer! And The Real Ghostbusters: The Halloween Door*. ABC canceled the series after four seasons. It was later rebroadcast on USA Network's *Cartoon Express*.

A DIC Enterprises Production in association with Columbia Pictures Television. Color. One hour. Half-hour. Premiered on ABC: September 10, 1988–September 7, 1992. Rebroadcast on USA: September 18, 1992–September 4, 1994. Syndicated.

Voices

SLIMER: Rafael: Charlie Adler; **Professor Dweeb:** Jeff Altman; **Mrs. Van Huego:** Fay De Witt; **Chilly Cooper:** Cree Summer Francks; **Linguini/Bud:** Danny Mann; **Rudy:** Jeff Marder; **Morris Grout:** Alan Oppenheimer; **Slimer:** Frank Welker

THE REAL GHOSTBUSTERS:: Peter Venkman: Dave Coulier; **Ray Stantz/Slimer:** Frank Welker; **Egon Spengler:** Maurice LaMarche; **Winston Zeddmore:** Edward L. (Buster) Jones; **Janine Melnitz:** Kath Soucie; **Catherine:** April Hong; **Jason:** Katie Leigh; **Donald:** Danny McMurphy

☺ THE SMOKEY BEAR SHOW

The National Forest Fires Commission folk hero and spokesbear, "Only you can prevent forest fires," stars in this animated series, as both a bear and cub, in which he protects the forests and its creatures from fire. The 17-episode series, which debuted on ABC in 1969, fared poorly in the ratings, running third each week behind CBS's *The Bugs Bunny/Road Runner Hour* and NBC's *The Heckle and Jeckle Cartoon Show*. Even though the program was not a ratings blockbuster, ABC reran it for a second season before canceling it.

A Rankin-Bass Production. Color. Half-hour. Premiered on ABC: September 13, 1969–September 5, 1970. Rebroadcast on ABC: September 13, 1970– September 12, 1971.

Voices
Smokey the Bear: Jackson Weaver

☺ THE SMURFS

In a tucked away village populated by little blue people who are only three apples tall and make their homes in mushrooms, Papa Smurf, a wise old magician, guides the rest of his hyperactive crew—Brainy, Vanity, Hefty, Clumsy, Jokey, Greedy, Lazy, Handy, Grouchy, Harmony and Smurfette, the only female Smurf—through their unfriendly encounters with the inept wizard Gargamel and his henchcat Azrael, who want to rid of the world of these happy blue busybodies.

French artist Pierre "Peyo" Culliford created these enchanting characters (called "Schtroumpf" in Flemish) in a Belgian comic strip in 1957, long before they appeared in this Emmy Award-winning series, which following its premiere in 1981—was the highest rated Saturday-morning show in eight years and the highest for an NBC animated series since 1970.

In 1982 NBC expanded the show to an unprecedented 90 minutes. Two new human characters joined the fun that season in cartoon adventures of their own: Johan, a young squire in the swashbuckling Errol Flynn mold, and Peewit, his comical sidekick. That same year *The Smurfs* won its first Emmy as Outstanding Children's Entertainment Series, the first of many awards for the series.

During the 1983–84 season, the series welcomed the arrival of Baby Smurf, and by the 1985–86 season it featured a tiny foursome of Smurf kids: the Smurflings (Nat, Slouchy, Snappy and Sassette, the second female). The following season two new characters, Grandpa Smurf (voiced by comedian Jonathan Winters) and Scruple, were introduced. In 1983 Hanna-Barbera, the series' producers, broke new ground by introducing the first deaf character in an animated series: Laconia, the mute wood elf who used sign language to communicate.

The Smurfs' format returned to one hour in the 1983–84 season. In the 1989–90 season, the Smurfs left Smurf Village and became involved in events and key periods in world history, from the prehistoric days to ancient Egypt.

The series (retitled *The Smurfs' Adventures*) enjoyed long life in syndication as well, beginning in 1986, while the network series continued to win its time slot. In 1989 the program was revived in reruns on USA Network's "Cartoon Express," then again in 1993 on the Cartoon Network.

A Hanna-Barbera Production in association with Sepp International, S.A. Color. One hour. Ninety minutes. Premiered on NBC: September 12, 1981–September 1, 1990. Rebroadcast on USA: April 12, 1989–September 12, 1993. Rebroadcast on CAR: October 1993–September 2, 1994 (weekdays); September 5, 1994–June 2, 1995 (weekdays, Sundays); June 30, 1997– (weekdays). Syndicated: 1986.

Voices
Gargamel: Paul Winchell; **Azrael/Papa Smurf:** Don Messick; **Brainy Smurf:** Danny Goldman; **Clumsy/Painter Smurf:** Bill Callaway; **Hefty/Poet/Peewit Smurf/Clockwork Smurf:** Frank Welker; **Jokey Smurf:** June Foray; **Smurfette:** Lucille Bliss; **Vanity Smurf/Hominbus:** Alan Oppenheimer; **Greedy Smurf/Harmony Smurf:** Hamilton Camp; **Lazy Smurf/Handy Smurf/Grouchy Smurf/Johan:** Michael Bell; **King:** Bob Holt; **Dame Barbara:** Linda Gary; **Tailor:** Kip King; **Sloppy:** Marshall Efron; **Farmer/Scaredy:** Alan Young; **Baby Smurf:** Julie Dees; **Grandpa Smurf:** Jonathan Winters; **Scruple:** Brenda Vaccaro; **Nanny Smurf:** Susan Blu

THE SMURFLINGS: Snappy: Pat Musick; **Nat:** Charlie Adler; **Sassette:** Julie Dees; **Puppy:** Frank Welker; **Slouchy:** Noelle North; **Narrator:** Paul Kirby, Kris Stevens

◎ SNIP SNAP

A stop-motion animated series from English cartoon studio Halas and Batchelor featuring the exploits of a dog (Snap) cut out of paper and a pair of scissors (Snip), presented in 18 episodes. Originally broadcast in Britain under the title *Snip the Magic Scissors* (for which 26-episodes were produced), the series was syndicated in America in 1961 along with another H-B cartoon program, *Foo Foo*.

A Halas and Batchelor Production. Color. Half-hour. Syndicated: 1961.

◎ THE SNORKS

Deep under the sea in the mystical underwater world of Snorkland lives a society: tiny, adorable, snorkel-headed creatures who enjoy remarkable adventures with high school student Allstar and his girlfriend, Casey. Created by Freddy Monnickendam, the Snorks first gained popularity as Belgian comic-book characters. The series premiered on NBC in 1984 with 26 first-run episodes (two per half-hour

program) and lasted four seasons of episodes. An additional 76 episodes were filmed before the series finished its NBC run and entered daily syndication in 1989. The first-run syndicated series combined the 36 new episodes with previously produced ones. A year later *The Snorks* were repackaged for syndication as part of Hanna-Barbera's weekend cartoon block, *The Funtastic World of Hanna-Barbera*. The original series was rebroadcast on USA Network's *Cartoon Express* cartoon, then in 1992 the Cartoon Network.

A Hanna-Barbera/Sepp, S.A. Production. Color. Half-hour. Premiered on NBC: September 15, 1984–September 3, 1988. Syndicated: 1989 (part of "The Funtastic World of Hanna-Barbera" in 1990). Rebroadcast on USA: October 23, 1989–August 28, 1991. Rebroadcast on CAR: October 2, 1992–December 31, 1993 (weekdays); January 3, 1994–September 2, 1994 (weekdays); January 5, 1994–June 2, 1995 (weekdays); September 4, 1995– (weekdays).

Voices
Allstar/Elder #4: Michael Bell; **Tooter/Occy:** Frank Welker; **Dimmy:** Brian Cummings; **Governor Wetworth:** Frank Nelson; **Junior Wetworth:** Barry Gordon; **Casey:** B.J. Ward; **Mrs. Wetworth:** Joan Gardner; **Daffney:** Nancy Cartwright; **Mrs. Seaworthy:** Edie McClurg; **Galeo:** Clive Revill; **Elders 1, 2 & 3:** Peter Cullen; **Baby Smallstar:** Gail Matthius; **Willie:** Fredricka Weber; **Mr. Seaworthy:** Bob Holt; **Auntie Marina:** Mitzi McCall; **Mrs. Kelp:** Joan Gerber; **Mr. Kelp:** Bob Ridgely

◎ SONIC THE HEDGEHOG

Sonic the Hedgehog (voiced by Jaleel White of TV's *Family Matters*) encounters famed archenemy Dr. Robotnik as he attempts to free the people of the planet Morbius in this 26-episode half-hour network series version of the best-selling 1991 Sega Genesis video game. The series premiered on ABC on September 18, 1993, five days after the debut of a second 65-episode syndicated series, *Adventures of Sonic the Hedgehog*. (See entry for details.) Two different versions of the show were produced for ABC and syndication, the latter of which ran six days a week. It marked the first time since the premiere of *Slimer! and the Real Ghostbusters* that a character had debuted in syndication and on a network at same time.

A DIC Enterprises/Bohbot Production in association with Sega of America, Inc. Color. Half-hour. Premiered on ABC: September 18, 1993–June 3, 1995.

Voices
Sonic the Hedgehog: Jaleel White; **Tails:** Bradley Pierce; **Dr. Robotnik:** Jim Cummings; **Antoine:** Rob Paulsen; **Rotor:** Mark Ballou; **Snively:** Charlie Adler; **Princess Sally:** Kath Soucie; **Bunnie:** Christine Cavanaugh

◎ SOUTH PARK

Four foul-mouthed third graders—Kyle, Kenny, Cartman and Stan—in the eerie Colorado town of South Park experience all sorts of strange, unexplainable and weird phenomena, including alien abductions, in this offbeat comedy series done in "paper-cut" animation. The series was based on the animated short "The Spirit of Christmas" by series creators Trey Park and Matt Stone, who also provide most of the character voices. Stone and Park produced the short for Brian Graden, a Hollywood Foxlab executive, who sent it out as a video Christmas card to friends in the industry.

A *Comedy Partners/Celluloid Studios/Braniff Production. Color. Half-hour. Premiered on COM: August 13, 1997.*

Voices
Stan Marsh/Eric Cartman/Mr. Garrision/Officer Barbrady/Various Others: Trey Parker; **Kyle Broslofski/Kenny McCormick/Pip/Jesus/Jimbo Marsh/Various Others:** Matthew Stone; **Chef:** Isaac Hayes; **Sheena:** Jeanie Adler

◎ SPACE ANGEL

This classic animated series follows the intergalactic adventures of Scott McCloud—code name: "Space Angel"—a one-man Marine Corps for the Earth Bureau of Investigation who, working in utmost secrecy, tackles assignments involving the security of the solar system. McCloud's crew aboard the superspaceship *Starduster* includes Taurus, an expert pilot and mechanic; Crystal, a specialist in electronics and astronavigation; and Professor Mace, head of base station Evening Star, who make up the bureau's Interplanetary Space Force. Produced by the creators of *Clutch Cargo* and *Captain Fathom*, these serialized science-fiction stories were strung together in 52 weekly half-hour programs. Former National Comics artist Alexander Toth served as art director for the series, which was created by Dik Darley and Dick Brown. Like *Clutch Cargo*, films featured the Synchro-Vox process, superimposed human lips speaking over the mouths of the characters.

A *Cambria Studios Production. Color. Half-hour. Premiered: February 6, 1962. Syndicated.*

Voices
Scott McCloud/Space Angel: Ned LeFebver

◎ SPACECATS

A highly evolved team of space exploring cats (under the rule of D.O.R.C.: Disembodied Omnipotent Ruler of Cats) from the planet Triglyceride 7, led by Captain Catgut and his assistants, Tom, Scratch and Sniff, battle larger-than-life villains on Earth in this live-action/puppet/animated series from producers Paul Fusco and Bernie Brillstein, who produced the hit live-action sitcom *Alf.*

A *Paul Fusco/Marvel Production. Color. Half-hour. Premiered on NBC: September 14, 1991–July 25, 1992.*

Voices
Charles Nelson Reilly (D.O.R.C.), Jack Angel, Gregg Berger, Sheryl Bernstein, Susan Blu, Hamilton Camp, Cam Clarke, Townsend Coleman, Jennifer Darling, Walker Edmiston, Jeannie Elias, John Erwin, Lea Floden, Pat Fraley, Paul Fusco, Brad Garrett, Barry Gordon, Pat Musick, Rob Paulsen, Jan Rabson, Hal Rayle, Bob Ridgely, Maggie Roswell, Susan Silo, Kath Soucie, John Stephenson, Lennie Weinrib

◎ SPACE GHOST AND DINO BOY

A black-hooded interplanetary crimefighter who draws powers from his magic belt, Space Ghost (voiced by former *Rowan and Martin's Laugh-in* announcer Gary Owens) counters evil forces assisted by two teenage wards, Jan and Jace, and their pet space monkey, Blip. The companion cartoon in this series revolved around the adventures of young boy (Tod) who is left in prehistoric times following a time-warp experiment that kills his father. (He earns the name "Dino Boy" by riding on a brown-spotted brontosaurus named Bronty.) A caveman (Ugh) saves the boy and the pair become inseparable.

First run on CBS in 1966, slated opposite ABC's *The Beatles* and NBC's *Space Kidettes*, *Space Ghost and Dino Boy* featured 42 "Space Ghost" adventures per show and 18 "Dino Boy" cartoons during its two-season run on the network. In 1976 NBC purchased the show and combined repeat episodes with another Hanna-Barbera property, *Frankenstein Jr. and the Impossibles*, packaging them together as *The Space Ghost/Frankenstein Jr. Show* to replace the struggling live-action series *Land of the Lost*.

The character was revived five years later (reprised by Gary Owens) in all-new episodes as part of 1981's *Space Stars* for NBC. In April of 1994 the original series was aired again as a three-hour marathon on the Cartoon Network preceding the debut of the network's first late-night talk show, *Space Ghost Coast to Coast*.

A *Hanna-Barbera Production. Color. Half-hour. Premiered on CBS: September 10, 1966–September 7, 1968. Rebroadcast on NBC: November 27, 1976–September 3, 1977 (as The Space Ghost/Frankenstein Jr. Show). Rebroadcast on CAR: February 7, 1993 (part of Boomerang, 1967); April 15, 1994 (Space Ghost Mini-Marathon); May 2, 1994—July 1, 1994 (weekdays); September 5, 1994–September 30, 1994 (weekdays); March 25, 1996–June 2, 1996 (weekdays); January 1997 (Fridays, Saturdays).*

Voices
Space Ghost: Gary Owens; **Jan:** Ginny Tyler; **Jace:** Tim Matthieson; **Dino Boy (Tod):** Johnny Carson (not the talk-show host); **Ugh:** Mike Road; **Bronty:** Don Messick

● SPACE GHOST COAST TO COAST

The Cartoon Network's first original toon, this surprise cult hit features the black-hooded interplanetary superhero as host of this bizarre, hour-long late-night talk show from outer space (cohosted by archenemies Moltar and Zorak, enslaved as unwilling members of Space Ghost's late-night crew) featuring live-action celebrity interviews. Debuting in April of 1994, the series premiered as a weekly 15-minute talk show airing Friday nights. (Guests on the show's premiere were Susan Powter, Kevin Meaney and the Bee Gees). Celebrities who appeared in series episodes include Catherine Bach, Fran Drescher, Ashley Judd, Donny Osmond, and even the cast of *Gilligan's Island* (Bob Denver, Dawn Wells and Russell Johnson).

Footage from the original 1960s Saturday-morning cartoon series was reedited and composited over a live-action miniature set to create what producers called "the first cartoon talk show." In the beginning, the network hired actors to conduct the off-screen interviews of special guests, with George Lowe (the voice of Space Ghost), rerecording the questions in the studio. Each question-and-answer interview was videotaped, and the video image of that particular celeb was inserted into the finished cartoon—in this case, projected on a suspended TV screen on the miniature set, with the animated Space Ghost appearing to interact like a normal TV talk-show host.

In July of 1997, 24 new episodes began airing on the network. Guests included Billy Mumy, Peter Fonda, and Mark Hamil.

A Hanna-Barbera/Cartoon Network Production. Color. One hour. Premiered on CAR: April 15, 1994–July 11, 1997; July 18, 1997 (new episodes).

Voices

Space Ghost: George Lowe; **Moltar/Zorak:** C. Martin Croker

● THE SPACE GHOST/ FRANKENSTEIN JR. SHOW

As a replacement for the poorly rated *Land of the Lost* live-action series, NBC tried to bolster ratings of that time slot with this half-hour compendium of two Hanna-Barbera favorites who starred in their own successful network series. (See *Space Ghost and Dino Boy* and *Frankenstein Jr. and the Impossibles* for voice credits and details.)

A Hanna-Barbera Production. Color. Half-hour. Premiered on NBC: November 27, 1976–September 3, 1977.

● SPACE GOOFS

In this cutting-edge animated series that premiered on the Fox Network, five alien monsters who crash on Earth find refuge in an abandoned house and do anything they can to keep the house from being rented, including scaring away prospective tenants. Originally the 26-episode series was called *Home to Rent.*

A Gaumont Multimedia Production. Color. Half-hour. Premiered on FOX: September 6, 1997.

● SPACE KIDETTES

Accompanied by their comical pet dog, Pup Star, a group of junior space rangers explore the cosmos from their space-capsule clubhouse and battle with creatures and enemies in outer space. In this 20-episode half-hour fantasy/adventure series originally broadcast on NBC in 1966, the kiddettes' main antagonist was Captain Sky Hook (a parody of Captain Hook in *Peter Pan*), the meanest pirate in the universe. Episodes from the series were rerun as part of *The Go-Go Gophers* on CBS in 1968 and even later in syndication on *Young Samson*. (The latter was rebroadcast in its entirety on USA Network's *Cartoon Express*.) Voice cast regulars included Chris Allen, the voice of Jay Ward's Hoppity Hooper, and Lucille Bliss, best known as the voice of Crusader Rabbit.

A Hanna-Barbera Production. Half-hour. Premiered on NBC: September 10, 1966–September 2, 1967. Rebroadcast on USA: February 20, 1989–March 26, 1991.

Voices

Scooter: Chris Allen; **Snoopy:** Lucille Bliss; **Jennie:** Janet Waldo; **Count Down/Pup Star:** Don Messick; **Captain Sky Hook/Static:** Daws Butler

● SPACE STARS

Average space citizens and superpowered heroes tackle jet-age problems and cosmic evil in five suspenseful and humorous segments. In "Teen Force," three superteenagers (Kid Comet, Moleculad and Elektra) fight for freedom in the tradition of Robin Hood and his merry men. In "Astro and the Space Mutts," a trio of interstellar police officers—the Jetsons' family pet Astro and two clumsy canines, Cosmo and Dipper—fight crime directed by their police boss, Space Ace. In "Space Stars Finale," "Space Stars" are pitted against a collection of galactic rogues and rascals. The remaining two weekly segments were "Herculoids" and "Space Ghost," back in all-new episodes produced for television. The hour-long series debuted on NBC in 1981 as a lead-in for another NBC animated series, *Spider-Man and His Amazing Friends*.

In 1989 the program's "Teen Force" cartoons were rebroadcast on USA Network's *Cartoon Express*.

A Hanna-Barbera Productions. Color. One hour. Premiered on NBC: September 12, 1981–September 11, 1982. Rebroadcast on USA: May 31, 1989–January 2, 1992 (Teen Force).

In the distant future, courageous Captain Nemo and his bold crew battle the evil Phantom Warriors in the three-dimensional animated series Space Strikers. © Saban Entertainment

Voices

TEEN FORCE: Elektra: B.J. Ward; **Moleculad:** David Hubbard; **Kid Comet:** Darryl Hickman; **Plutem/Glax:** Mike Winslow; **Uglor, the terrible:** Allan Lurie; **Narrator:** Keene Curtis

ASTRO AND THE SPACE MUTTS: Astro: Don Messick; **Cosmo:** Frank Welker; **Dipper:** Lennie Weinrib; **Space Ace:** Mike Bell

HERCULOIDS: Zandor/Tundro/Zok/Igoo: Mike Road; **Tara:** Virginia Gregg; **Dorno:** Sparky Marcus; **Gloop/Gleep:** Don Messick; **Narrator:** Keene Curtis

SPACE GHOST: Space Ghost: Gary Owens; **Jan:** Alexandra Stewart; **Jace:** Steve Spears; **Blip:** Frank Welker; **Narrator:** Keene Curtis

◎ SPACE STRIKERS

In this futuristic, 3-D animated version of the Jules Verne classic *20,000 Leagues Under the Sea*, a pumped-up heroic Captain Nemo (now captain of his own starship) and his

bold *Nautilus* crew battle the half-human, half-robot Master Phantom and his evil Phantom Warriors, who have conquered the planet Earth and plan to harvest the Planet's valuable resources. This 26-episode action/adventure series, aired Sunday mornings on the UPN network, featuring state-of-the-art computer-generated 3-D action sequences, beginning in 1995.

A Saban Entertainment Production. Color. Half-hour. Premiered on UPN: September 10, 1995.

◎ SPARTAKUS AND THE SUN BENEATH SEA

Living deep in the center of Earth are the Arcadians, a primitive civilization whose lives depend on the power of their sun, Terra. When this once-reliable source fails, they create a beautiful messenger—Arkanna—to send above for help. The foreign-produced, 52-episode series, with theme song performed by the teen rock group Menudo, made its American television on Nickelodeon in 1986.

A RMC Audio Visual/Monte Carlo Production. Color. Half-hour. Premiered on NIK: October 11, 1986–July 28, 1991.

◎ SPEED BUGGY

Teenagers Debbie, Tinker and Mark and chugging auto partner Speed Buggy travel throughout the country and to foreign locales finding mystery and adventure, with Speedy always saving the day in 16 first-run episodes originally produced for CBS in 1973. Over 10 years, the series aired on two different networks, and Speed Buggy made guest appearances on the popular ABC series *Scooby's All-Star Laff-A-Lympics*.

A Hanna-Barbera Production. Color. Half-hour. Premiered on CBS: September 8, 1973–August 30, 1975. Rebroadcast on ABC: September 6, 1975–September 4, 1976. Rebroadcast on NBC: November 27, 1976–September 3, 1977. Rebroadcast on CBS: January 28, 1978–September 2, 1978. Rebroadcast on CBS: September 18, 1982–September 3, 1983. Rebroadcast on CAR: July 9, 1995–May 26, 1996 (Sundays).

Voices
Speed Buggy: Mel Blanc; **Debbie:** Arlene Golonka; **Tinker:** Phil Luther Jr.; **Mark:** Mike Bell; **Other Voices:** Don Messick

◎ SPEED RACER

Adventure-loving hero, Speed Racer, a young race-car enthusiast, speeds around the world to fight the forces of evil in his super-charged Mach 5 race car. Speed's efforts are supported by his girlfriend, Trixie, kid brother, Spridal, and pet monkey, Chim Chim. The 52-episode series was unquestionably one of the most popular Japanese-made cartoon programs to air on American television. In 1993, the series was rebroadcast on MTV preceding the fall debut of brand-new adventures, entitled *The New Adventures of Speed Racer*, produced for first-run syndication. (See entry for further details.) The Cartoon Network reaired the series beginning in 1996.

A Tatsunoko Production. Color. Half-hour. Premiered: September 23, 1967. Syndicated. Rebroadcast on MTV: 1993. Rebroadcast on CAR: February 18, 1996 (Sundays); March 4, 1996– (weekdays).

Voices
Speed Racer: Jack Grimes; **Trixie, Speed's girlfriend/Spridal, Speed's brother/Mrs. Racer, Speed's mother:** Corinne Orr; **Racer X, Speed's older brother/Pops Racer, Speed's father:** Jack Curtis

SPICY CITY

Veteran animator Ralph Bakshi (*Fritz the Cat, Cool World*) created and produced this late-night, six-part adult animated series—and second HBO Animation adult cartoon series—set in a surreal, retrofuturistic urban landscape. Written in the style of the pulp magazines of the 1930s and 1940s and tied together by the continuing character Raven, the proprietor of a social club (voiced by singer/actress

Adventure-loving Speed Racer (center), kid brother Spridal, pet monkey Chim Chim and girlfriend Trixie stand in front of their Mach 5 race car, ready for action, in the Japanese cartoon favorite Speed Racer. © Tatsunoko Productions

Michelle Phillips), the series is set in a city where nothing is ever what it seems and where everything has a price. Each half-hour episode covered such genres as science fiction, horror and noir. The series debuted in July of 1997 with the opening episode "Love Is a Download" (written by Bakshi's son, Preston).

A Ralph Bakshi/HBO Animation Production. Color. Half-hour. Premiered on HBO: July 11, 1997.

Voices
Raven: Michelle Phillips

SPIDER-MAN (1967)

College student Peter Parker, reporter for the *New York Daily Bugle*, takes on underground syndicates and other criminals as famed superhero Spider-Man. He encounters such formidable foes as the Phantom from Space, The Sorcerer, One-Eyed Idol, Blotto, Scorpion and others in this 52-episode half-hour series based on Stan Lee's *The Amazing Spider-Man* comic-book adventures. Airing on ABC beginning in 1967, the series enjoyed a successful three-season run before entering daily syndication.

Executive producers were Robert L. Lawrence and Ralph Bakshi (uncredited), who also served as story supervisor. Cosmo Anzilotti was assistant director while Martin Taras served as one of the principal animators. Like Bakshi, Anzilotti and Taras were former Terrytoon animators.

A Grantray-Lawrence Animation and Krantz Animation Production in association with Marvel Comics. Color. Half-hour. Premiered on ABC: September 9, 1967–August 30, 1969. Rebroadcast on ABC: March 22, 1970–September 6, 1970. Syndicated.

Voices
Peter Parker/Spider Man: Bernard Cowan, Paul Soles; **Betty Brant, a reporter:** Peg Dixon; **J. Jonah Jameson, the editor:** Paul Kligman

SPIDER-MAN AND HIS AMAZING FRIENDS

A small suburban town is the setting for this comedy-adventure series about the world's most popular superhero, alias Peter Parker, a shy, 18-year-old science major, who teams up with two superhuman teenagers, Angelica Jones (Firestar—the Girl of Fire) and Bobby Drake (Iceman), in the name of peace and justice. Episodes were later repeated on *The Incredible Hulk/Amazing Spider-Man Hour*. (See series entry for information.) In 1984 NBC split the program up and Spider-Man returned for one final bow in his own time slot.

A Marvel Production. Color. Half-hour. Premiered on NBC: September 12, 1981–September 11, 1982. Rebroadcast on NBC: September 15, 1984–September 7, 1985.

Voices

Anne Lockhart, George DiCenzo, Alan Dinehart, Jerry Dexter, Michael Evans, Walker Edmiston, Alan Young, Dennis Marks, William Woodson, John Hammer, Keye Luke, Allan Melvin and Sally Julian.

◉ SPIDER-MAN: THE ANIMATED SERIES

Pop culture's most enduring web-slinging comic-book superhero (alias Peter Parker) battles classic foes the Kingpin, the Scorpion, Mysterio, the Rhino, Dr. Octopus, the Vulture, the Green Goblin and the Lizard, and an array of formidable new supervillains—Hydro-Man, Venom, Morbius the Living Vampire and the Shocker—with his superhuman strength, wall-clinging ability and "spider sense" in and around New York City in this new series of 65 half-hour adventures. Story lines placed greater emphasis on Parker's romances and experiences with friends at college than did previous animated attempts. The first episode debuted in November of 1994 as a half-hour Saturday morning special, with weekly airings beginning in February of 1995. The program's last original Saturday-morning episode was a two-part finale, ending in early February of 1998. It was one of Fox Network's highest-rated animated programs. *A Marvel/New World Entertainment/Saban Entertainment/Graz Entertainment Production. Color. Half-hour. Premiered on FOX: November 19, 1994 (half-hour special); February 4, 1995–February 7, 1998.*

Voices

Peter Parker/Spider-Man: Christopher Daniel Barnes; **Mary Jane Parker:** Sara Ballantine; **Spider-Carnage/Ben Reilly:** Christopher Daniel Barnes; **J. Jonah Jameson:** Ed Asner; **Aunt May:** Linda Gary; **Deborah Whitman:** Liz Georges; **Dr. Curt Connors/The Lizard:** Joseph Campanella; **Eddie Brock/Venom:** Hank Azaria; **Felicia Thompson/Black Cat:** Jennifer Hale; **Flash Thompson:** Patrick Laborteaux; **Harry Osborn/Green Goblin:** Gary Imhoff; **Herman Shultz/Shocker:** Jim Cummings; **Liz Osborn:** Marla Rubinoff; **Mac McGargon/Scorpion:** Martin Landau; **Mariah Crawford/Calypso:** Susan Beaubian; **Norman Osborn/Green Goblin:** Neil Ross; **Otto Octavius/Dr. Octopus:** Efrem Zimbalist Jr.; **Wilson Fisk/The Kingpin:** Roscoe Lee Browne; **Alistair Smythe:** Maxwell Caulfield; **Joe "Robbie" Robertson:** Rodney Saulsberry; **Detective Terri Lee:** Dawnn Lewis

◉ SPIDER-WOMAN

Justice magazine editor-publisher Jessica Drew spins herself into Spider-Woman to fight evil and nab supernatural foes, among them Tomand, ruler of the Realm of Darkness; the Great Magini; and The Fly. This half-hour adventure series was based on a character created by Stan Lee, creator of Marvel Comics' *The Amazing Spider-Man*.

A De Patie-Freleng Enterprises Production in association with Marvel Comics Group. Color. Half-hour. Premiered on ABC: September 22, 1979–March 1, 1980.

Voices

Jessica Drew/Spider-Woman: Joan Van Ark; **Jeff Hunt, Jessica's photographer:** Bruce Miller; **Billy Drew, Jessica's nephew:** Bryan Scott; **Police Chief:** Lou Krugman; **Detective Miller:** Larry Carroll; **Announcer:** Dick Tufield

◉ THE SPIRAL ZONE

An international super force known as the 5 Zone Riders, headed by Commander Dirk Courage and joined by multiracial agents Max, Katarina, Razorback, Tank and Hiro, unite to battle their archrival, Overlord, a renegade scientist and his band of evil villains, the Black Widows, to preserve peace and freedom on Earth. This first-run daily syndicated series featured 65 original half-hour episodes.

An Atlantic-Kushner Locke Production in association with The Maltese Companies. Color. Half-hour. Premiered: September 1987. Syndicated.

Voices

Dirk Courage: Dan Gilvezan; **Max:** Hal Rayle; **McFarland/Reaper:** Denny Delk; **Dr. Lawrence/Razorback:** Frank Welker; **Hiro:** Michael Bell; **Duchess Dire/Katerina/Mommy:** Mona Marshall; **Overlord/Tank/Bandit:** Neil Ross

◉ SPIRIT OF FREEDOM

To celebrate America's Bicentennial, legendary animator Shamus Culhane produced this series of three-minute animated vignettes tracing the nation's heritage.

A Shamus Culhane Production. Color. Three minutes. Syndicated: 1975.

◉ SPORT BILLY

A mascot of major international sports federations is sent to Earth to maintain goodwill and fair play for all those who are involved in sports. Aided by his female companion, Lilly, and pet dog, Willy, Billy crusades to keep the world of sports on the right track.

A Filmation Associates Production. Color. Half-hour. Premiered: June 1982 (syndicated); NBC: July 31, 1982–September 11, 1982.

Voices
Sport Billy: Lane Scheimer; **Sport Lilly/Queen Vanda:** Joyce Bulifant; **Willie/Sporticus XI:** Frank Welker

◉ SPUNKY AND TADPOLE

This series of investigative cliffhangers features the lanky lad Spunky and friend Tadpole, a real-life teddy bear, in 150 exciting five-minute adventures and tall tales first syndicated in 1958. In most markets the cartoons were shown on existing children's programs hosted by television station celebrities as well as independently in half-hour time slots. Ten episodes comprised one complete story. Hanna-Barbera voice legend Don Messick provided the voice of Tadpole and most of the series' supporting characters.

A Beverly Hills Corporation Production. Black-and-white. Color. Premiered: September 6, 1958. Syndicated.

Voices
Spunky: Joan Gardner; **Tadpole:** Don Messick, Ed Janis

◉ STARBLAZERS

Actually Japan's *Space Battleship Yamato* series dubbed into English, this adventure series—set in the year 2199—chronicles the story of a group of patriots, known as Star Force, whose mission is to save Earth from an enemy space fleet. Heading the Star Force fleet is Captain Avatar, whose crew includes Cadet Derek Wildstar, the second-in-command; Nova, Wildstar's girlfriend and the team's radar operator; Cadet Mark Venture, chief of operations; IQ-9, a robot

A bright young lad and his teddy bear experience exciting adventures and tall tales in Spunky and Tadpole. © Beverly Film Corporation

(nicknamed "Tin-Wit" for his good sense of humor); Sandor, the chief mechanic; and Dr. Sane, the team's physician. First offered in U.S. syndication in 1979, the series was comprised of 26 original *Space Battleship Yamato* episodes, previously aired on Japanese television, plus a group of 26 new half-hours produced in 1977. The combined 52 episodes were packaged together and syndicated to selected major markets by Claster Television, which originally considered retitling the series *Star Force*.

An Office Academy/Sunwagon Production in association with Claster Television and Westchester Films Inc. Star Blazers is a registered trademark of Westchester Films Inc. Color. Half-hour. Premiered: September 10, 1979. Syndicated.

◉ STARCOM: THE US SPACE FORCE

A peacekeeping force in a planetary community uses ultra-sophisticated vehicles and state-of-the-art technology to combat the sinister Emperor Dark and his Shadow Force of evil warriors and robot drones in this first-run syndicated series that debuted in 1987. Lasting only 13 weeks in syndication, the series was repeated on The Family Channel beginning in 1993.

A DIC Enterprises Production. Color. Half-hour. Premiered: September 1987. Syndicated. Rebroadcast on FAM: 1993.

Voices
Dash: Rob Cowan; **Crowbar/Torvak:** Robert Cait; **Slim:** Phil Aikin; **Kelsey:** Susan Roman; **Vondar:** Marvin Goldhar; **Malvanna:** Elva May Hoover; **Col. Brickley:** Don Francks; **Klag:** Dan Hennessey; **Romak:** Louis DiBianco

◉ STAR TREK

The indomitable Captain James T. Kirk; his pointy-eared science officer Spock; chief engineer Scotty; Dr. Leonard McCoy; and the crew of the U.S.S. *Enterprise* probe outer space, where they encounter intelligent aliens and new civilizations and battle sophisticated forces of evil in this half-hour animated version that premiered on NBC in 1973. The cartoon spinoff from the cult live-action series earned an Emmy Award in 1975 (for the episode "Yesteryear"), with the stars of the original voicing their own characters. (The character of Ensign Paval Chekov, played by actor Walter Koenig, did not appear on the animated series.) Two new characters were added to this animated version: Arrex, a three-legged alien, and M'Ress, a feline being. Budgeted at $75,000 per episode, the 22-episode series ran for two seasons on NBC. The series was later rebroadcast on Sci-Fi Channel's *Cartoon Quest*.

A Filmation Studios Production in association with Norway/ Paramount Pictures Television. Color. Half-hour. Premiered on NBC: September 8, 1973–August 30, 1975. Rebroadcast on SCI: September 27, 1992–March 26, 1994.

Voices

Capt. James T. Kirk: William Shatner; **Science Officer Spock:** Leonard Nimoy; **Dr. Leonard McCoy:** DeForest Kelley; **Chief Engineer Montgomery Scott:** James Doohan; **Nurse Christine Chapel:** Majel Barrett; **Lieutenant Sulu:** George Takei; **Arrex:** James Doohan; **M'Ress:** Majel Barrett

☺ STEVEN SPIELBERG PRESENTS ANIMANIACS

Created in the 1930s but considered so wild that they were locked in the Warner Bros. studio water tower, three zany offspring—brothers Yakko and Wakko and their sister Dot—are finally set free, running amok at the studio every day and creating havoc in this half-hour comedy/musical series originally produced for The Fox Network. The successor to Steven Spielberg's *Tiny Toon Adventures*, the series featured two to three cartoon shorts a day starring the three Warner siblings, Rita and Runt (a cat and dog who live at the studio), the Goodfeathers (three pigeons), Slappy Squirrel (an old-time sassy female brought out of retirement) and the studio CEO, guard, nurse and psychologist.

Spielberg helped create the characters and added his input between directing the blockbuster hit movie *Jurassic Park*, and the NBC live-action series *seaQuest DSV*, reading every script and approving every cartoon before it aired. Sixty-five episodes were initially ordered for the series, which premiered on The Fox Network in September 1993. The series moved to the WB Network in 1995, where 13 new episodes were ordered to kick off new kids' fall lineup. In January of 1997, the Cartoon Network aired the series in a two-hour time slot for four consecutive Friday night prime-time showings along with *Freakazoid!*, *Pinky & the Brain* and *Superman*. The show was honored with three Emmy Awards for Outstanding Animated Program during its original run.

In the spring of 1994, the crazy nutsos (Yakko, Wakko and Dot) starred in their first and—to date—only theatrical cartoon short, "I'm Mad." (See Theatrical Cartoon Series section for details.) The short, about the travails of taking the bickering siblings on a car trip, made its television debut on November 12, 1994 on Fox's Saturday edition of the series.

A Warner Bros. Television Animation Production. Color. Half-hour. Premiered on FOX: September 13, 1993–September 8, 1995. Rebroadcast on WB: September 9, 1995. Rebroadcast on CAR: January 24, 1997.

Voices

Yakko Warner/Pinky/Dr. Otto Scratchansniff: Rob Paulsen; **Wakko Warner:** Jess Harnell; **Dot Warner/Hello Nurse/Marita Hippo:** Tress MacNeille; **Bobby Pigeon:** John Marino; **Pesto Pigeon:** Chick Vennera; **The Brain/Squit Pigeon:** Maurice LaMarche; **Ralph the Guard/The**

C.E.O./Buttons/Runt/Flavio Hippo/Chicken Boo: Frank Welker; **Slappy Squirrel:** Sherri Stoner; **Skippy:** Nathan Ruegger; **Rita:** Bernadette Peters; **Mindy:** Nancy Cartwright; **Minerva Mink:** Julie Brown; **Newt:** Arte Johnson; **Albert Einstein:** Paul Rugg; **Narrator:** Jim Cummings, Tom Bodett; **Sid the Squid:** Jack Burns; **Katie Kaboom:** Laura Mooney; **Katie's Mom:** Mary Gross; **Beanie the Bison:** Avery Schreiber

☺ STEVEN SPIELBERG PRESENTS FREAKAZOID!

In this comic take on the superhero genre, computer geek Dexter Douglas is an easygoing teenager who, while surfing the Internet, gets sucked into his computer and comes as out as the costumed, uncontrollable, unpredictable high-strung superhero, Freakazoid! in this series of offbeat and witty half-hour action adventures developed and produced by Steven Spielberg in association with Warner Bros. television animation. The series—which the producers treated like a series of half-hour "pilots"—premiered on the WB Network in September 1995 and was the centerpiece of the network's Kids WB Saturday lineup, which included *Steven Spielberg Presents Pinky & the Brain*, *The Sylvester and Tweety Mysteries* and *Earthworm Jim*.

Produced in association with six different animation houses, the series, featuring 24 half-hours, lasted one full season and part of a second season before it was canceled due to low ratings. Originally the series was to be produced as a straight superhero action/adventure series with comedic overtones, as first conceived by animator Bruce Timm, but Spielberg nixed the idea, wanting instead a show that topped *Animaniacs*.

A Warner Bros. Television Animation Production. Color. Half-hour. Premiered on the WB: September 9, 1995–November 29, 1996. Rebroadcast on CAR: January 31, 1997.

Voices

Freakazoid!: Paul Rugg; **Announcer:** Joe Leahy; **Sgt. Mike Cosgrove:** Ed Asner; **Dexter Douglas:** David Kaufman; **Debbie Douglas:** Tress MacNeille; **Douglas Douglas:** John P. McCann; **Duncan Douglas:** Googy Gress; **Steph:** Tracy Rowe; **The Lobe:** David Warner; **Lord Bravery/Cave Guy/Candle Jack/The Huntsman:** Jeff Bennet; **Fan Boy:** Stephen Furst; **Armondo Guittierez:** Ricardo Montalban; **Longhorn:** Maurice LaMarche; **Foamy the Freakadog:** Frank Welker

☺ STEVEN SPIELBERG PRESENTS PINKY & THE BRAIN

Two lab mice—one the genuis (The Brain), the other insane (Pinky)—who live at Acme Labs plan to take over the world in order to prove their mousey worth in this half-hour animated spinoff of Warner Bros. *Animaniacs.* Featuring three seven-minute cartoons each half-hour, the series premiered on the WB Network in September of 1995 and was so successful that it was moved to a prime-time, Sunday-night time slot that same season. Produced that year was the pair's first and only prime-time special, *A Pinky and the Brain Christmas*, which won an Emmy Award for Outstanding Animated Program. In the 1996–97 season, the series began offering full-length stories instead of a brace of cartoon shorts in each half-hour. Sixty-five episodes alone were produced through the 1996–97 season, with 40 new episodes filmed for the 1997–98 season, when the show aired weekdays and Saturday nights.

A *Warner Bros. Television Animation Production. Color. Half-hour. Premiered on the WB: September 9, 1995. Rebroadcast on CAR: February 7, 1997.*

Voices
Pinky: Rob Paulsen; **The Brain:** Maurice LaMarche

⊚ STEVEN SPIELBERG PRESENTS TINY TOON ADVENTURES

Rambunctious adolescent versions of beloved Warner Bros. characters—Buster Bunny (Bugs), Plucky Duck (Daffy), Hampton (Porky), Dizzy Devil (Tazmanian Devil)—run wild as they attend Acme University in this next generation of classic Looney Tunes, which featured recurring characters such as Pinky and the Brain (who were subsequently spun off into their own series), Slappy Squirrel, Mindy and Buttons and Rita and Runt.

Premiering on 135 stations in September of 1990, the syndicated series was a gigantic hit for Warner Bros. Cartoons, which produced the series in association with filmmaker Steven Spielberg, who helped develop characters and stories and critiqued each show before it was finished. (Spielberg himself appeared, in animated form, in the 1991 episode "Buster and Babs Go Hawaiian.") Aiming for a higher quality than its industry competitors, the series used more animation cels (single-frame drawings) than other Saturday-morning or syndicated cartoon series: 25 per frame versus the standard 12.

Initially 65 episodes were produced for the series (which earned two Emmys for Outstanding Animated Program). Thirteen more were produced for the 1991–92 season (as was the CBS prime-time special *Tiny Toon Adventures: The Looney Beginning*), and 22 more for the start of the 1992–93 season, when the series jumped to The Fox Network. In 1995 all 100 *Tiny Toon Adventures* began reairing weekdays on Nickelodeon. The characters starred in a brace of Fox prime-time animated specials as well: *It's a Wonderful Tiny Toons Christmas* (1992), *How I Spent My Vacation* (1993), *Tiny Toons Spring Break Special* (1994) and the Emmy-nom-

inated hour-long, *Tiny Toons' Night Ghoulery* (1995), which pokes fun at horror anthology TV series like *Night Gallery* and *The Twilight Zone.*

A *Warner Bros. Television Animation/Amblin Entertainment Production. Color. Half-hour. Premiered: September 1990 (syndication); FOX: September 19, 1992 (part of* The Plucky Duck Show *until November 24, 1992). Rebroadcast on NIK: September 15, 1995 (weekdays).*

Voices
Buster Bunny: Charlie Adler; **Babs Bunny:** Tress MacNeille; **Plucky Duck:** Joe Alaskey; **Hamton J. Pig:** Don Messick; **Montana Max:** Danny Cooksey; **Elmyra Duff:** Cree Summer; **Dizzy Devil:** Maurice LaMarche; **Shirley the Loon:** Gail Matthius; **Sweetie:** Candi Milo; **Blink/Arnold/Fowlmouth:** Rob Paulsen; **Fifi Le Fume/Sneezer:** Kath Soucie; **Furrball/Calamity Coyote/Gogo/Dodo/Little Beeper:** Frank Welker

⊚ STEPHEN SPIELBERG PRESENTS TOONSYLVANIA

This ghoulishly funny Saturday-morning cartoon parody of the Frankenstein legend focuses on the oddball antics of hunchbacked lab assistant Igor and his lumbering monster sidekick Phil, who answer to Dr. Vic Frankenstein, an overbearing scientist residing in a castle above the TransFernando Valley. Steven Spielberg (overseeing the first animated series for his co-owned company DreamWorks) and Bill Kopp (the voice of *Eek! The Cat*) are executive producers of the half-hour series, which debuted on the Fox Network.

A *DreamWorks Production. Color. Half-hour. Premiered on FOX: February 7, 1998.*

Voices
Charlie Adler, Jocelyn Blue, Nancy Cartwright, Jim Cummings, Brad Garrett, Jess Harnell, Tom Kenny, Wayne Knight, Valery Pappas, David Warner, Billy West

⊚ STICKIN' AROUND

These segments began as a series of one-minute interstitial adventures of imaginary stick figures from the mind of eight-year-old Stacy Stickler and her best friend, Bradley, used to punctuate CBS's 1994–95 Saturday-morning lineup. Created by Robin Steele (of MTV's *Stick Figure Theatre* fame) and Brianne Leary, the segments were expanded to a full half-hour series airing on the Fox Network. Premiering in the fall of 1997, the series, animated to resemble a self-created coloring book, with stick figures drawn against a background of crayon, paste and photocollage, revolved around heartfelt commentaries of growing up in the 1990s, as only kids can tell it.

A *Nelvana Limited/Ellipse Animation/Prima TV, Italy Production. Color. Half-hour. Premiered on CBS: September 1994 (interstitials); FOX: September 26, 1997 (series).*

Voices
Stacy: Ashley Taylor; **Bradley:** Ashley Brown; **Stella:** Catherine Disher; **Stanley:** Phillip Williams; **Lance:** Andrew Craig; **Russell:** Amos Crawley; **Polly:** Marianna Galati; **Mr. Doddler:** Nicholas Rice

◉ THE STONE PROTECTORS

Five teenage rock band musicians (Cornelius, Clifford, Angus, Maxwell and Chester), transformed into superpowered, troll-like creatures by powerful gemstones try to save the planet Mythrandi from the evil warlords Zok and Zinc, in this half-hour series produced for syndication.

A *Graz Entertainment Production in association with Ace Novelty Co. Inc./Fantasy, Ltd./Liu Concept Design and Associates. Color. Half-hour. Premiered: 1993. Syndicated.*

Voices
Don Brown, Ted Cole, Scott McNeil, Cathy Weseluck, Rob Morton, Jim Byrnes, Ian Corlett, John Tench, Terry Klassen, Louise Vallance, Cam Lane

◉ STOP THE SMOGGIES!

A moppet-headed bunch of happy little heroes known as the Suntots find their picturesque coral island is threatened by pollution with the arrival of the garbage-strewing villainous trio—the "Smoggies"—in this groundbreaking 52-episode half-hour series created and directed by Oscar nominee Gerry Potterton. A top-rated show in Canada, both in French- and English-language versions, and in the United Kingdom, the series was sold to more than 40 territories worldwide and earned favorable reviews for its imaginative scripts, environmental content and liquid animation techniques. The first animation production to deal with the environment, the series premiered in the United States via nationwide syndication in 1991 and was subsequently rebroadcast on HBO.

A *Cinar/Initial Groupe Production. An Initial Audiovisual/Cinar Films/Antenne 2 Production. Color. Half-hour. Premiered: September 8, 1991. Syndicated. Rebroadcast on HBO: June 24, 1994.*

Voices
Teddy Lee Dillon, Brian Dooley, Richard Dumont, Karen Marginson, Walter Massey, Stephanie Morgenstern, Joan Orenstein, Harvey Berger, Pier Paquette

◉ STORYBOOK CLASSICS

Well-known motion picture, stage and television personalities narrated this stunning collection of 13 half-hour spe-

cials (not 18 as erroneously reported elsewhere) adapted from classic children's stories, produced for home video, then broadcast on Showtime between 1989 and 1991.

Rabbit Ears Video (producers of *American Heroes & Legends, Holiday Classics* and *We All Have Tales* series) produced this series revisiting the worlds of master storytellers such as Rudyard Kipling, Beatrix Potter and Hans Christian Andersen. Each episode was backed by musical scores and animated by a different illustrator. The series included such award-winning specials as "Red Riding Hood and Goldilocks," "The Ugly Duckling," "The Tale of Peter Rabbit and the Tale of Mr. Jeremy Fisher," "The Three Billy Goats Gruff and The Three Little Pigs." "The Fisherman and His Wife," "The Velveteen Rabbit," "How the Leopard Got His Spots," "The Emperor and the Nightingale," "Thumbelina," "The Emperor's New Clothes," "How the Rhinoceros Got His Skin/How the Camel Got His Hump," "The Elephant's Child" and "The Steadfast Tin Soldier."

Celebrity narrators included Danny Glover, Jodie Foster, Jack Nicholson, Jeremy Irons, Kelly McGillis, Holly Hunter, Meg Ryan, Meryl Streep and John Gielgud. (See individual entries in Animated Television Specials section for more details.)

A *Rabbit Ears Video Production. Color. Half-hour. Premiered on Showtime: 1989–1991.*

◉ STORYTOON EXPRESS

Familiar storybook characters starred in this series of 30 three- to nine-minute black-and-white and color cartoon adventures, packaged for television by Republic Pictures.

Young viewers of the 1960s enjoyed classic fairy tales brought to life in the daytime syndicated series Storytoon Express. (COURTESY: NATIONAL TELEVISION ASSOCIATES)

First syndicated in 1965, the series was offered to independent stations for flexible programming.

A Republic Pictures Production in association with National Television Associates (NTA). Black-and-white. Color. Premiered: 1965. Syndicated.

◎ STREET FIGHTER

Based on the fastest-selling video game in history of the same name. Former UN Forces leader Colonel Guile and his team of martial-arts street fighters (Chun Lii, Dee Jay. T. Hawk, Ken and Ryu) do battle with a secret criminal organization—the big, bad Bison and his no-good gang, Shadowru—in this half-hour action/adventure series that premiered on USA Network's Saturday morning *Cartoon Express*.

A Capcom U.S.A. Production in association with Graz Entertainment/USA Network. Color. Half-hour. Premiered on USA: October 21, 1995.

Voices (main cast)

Kathleen Barr, Lisa Ann Beley, Paul Dobson, Michael Donovan, Tong Lung, Scott McNeil, Richard Newman, John Payne, Donna Yamamoto

◎ STREET SHARKS

Accidentally transformed into monstrous half shark, half humans during an illegal experiment that used an untested DNA genetic formula, four crimefighting brothers join forces to protect the world from the disastrous designs the evil scientist plans to unleash in this 13-episode, half-hour action/adventure series based on top-selling action figures. Introduced as a three-part miniseries in first-run syndication in the spring of 1994, the program went weekly in the fall of 1995 as part of the weekend cartoon block, *Amazin' Adventures II*. In 1996 the series was added to ABC's Saturday morning lineup (in reruns) for a brief run (it was replaced by Disney's *Mighty Ducks: The Animated Series*) while the original syndicated series reaired on USA Network.

A Surge Entertainment/DIC Entertainment Production. Color. Half-hour. Premiered: (week of) September 4, 1995 (part of Amazin' Adventures II). Syndicated. Rebroadcast on ABC: September 14, 1996–October 26, 1996. Rebroadcast on USA: September 22. 1996.

Voices

Dr. Piranoid: J. Michael Lee; **Slammu/Slobster/Killamari:** D. Kevin Williams; **Streex:** Andy Rannells; **Slash:** Terry Berner; **Lena:** Pam Carter; **Bends:** Jim Hoggatt; **Guy in the Sky:** Tony Wike

◎ STUNT DAWGS

The wildest bunch of world-class Hollywood stuntmen and stuntwomen (Crash, Splatter, Sizzle and Lucky), who double as crimefighters, save the world from the wicked Stunt Scabs, a band of villainous Tinseltown athletes, in this 40-episode half-hour syndicated series, inspired by director Hal Needman's 1980 comedy *Hooper* starring Burt Reynolds. The series premiered in first-run syndication.

A Rainforest Entertainment Production for Claster Television. Color. Half-hour. Premiered: September 28, 1992. Syndicated.

Voices

Needham/Whizkid: Neil Crone; **Fungus:** John Stocker; **Splatter/Crash/Velda:** Greg Morton; **Lucky/Skiddd:** Greg Swanson; **Airball/Slyme:** Ron Rubin; **Badyear/Half-a-Mind:** Harvey Atkin; **Sizzle:** Lenore Zann; **Nina Newscaster:** Barbara Budd

◎ SUPER BOOK

This Japanese-produced retelling of stories from the Bible, redubbed in English, was first syndicated in 1982 by the Christian Broadcasting Network (which also broadcast the series simultaneously). Animated by Tatsunoko Studios, the producers of *Speed Racer*, the program, which originally aired on Japanese television, was the first nationally broadcast religious cartoon series since 1960's *Davey and Goliath*, featuring 26 original episodes. *Flying House*, a companion animated series also produced by Tatsunoko Studios, also aired in 1992 in syndication and on the Christian Broadcasting Network. (See entry for details.)

A CBN/Tatsunoko Production. Color. Half-hour. Premiered: 1992 (in syndication and on CBN). Syndicated.

Voices

Bill Mack, Ray Owens, Sonia Owens, Helene Van Koert, Billie Lou Watt

◎ SUPER DAVE

Super Dave Osborne, the world's most inept stuntman (and alter ego of comedian Bob Einstein) is joined by his Asian sidekick, Fuji, as he battles incredible villains, including his semi-bionic archenemy, Slash Hazard, in this live-action/animated series for Fox Network, inspired by Einstein's 1980–85 Showtime live-action series, *Super Dave*. The klutzy stuntman appeared in live-action wraparounds in each program. Preliminary objections from a prominent Asian American psychologist—that the characterization of sidekick Fuji was demeaning to Asian Americans—led to the character's being revised.

A DIC Enterprises/Blye-Einstein/Reteitalia Ltd. Production. Color. Half-hour. Premiered on FOX: September 12, 1992–August 28, 1993. Rebroadcast on FAM: June 11, 1994–September 24, 1994.

Voices

Super Dave: Bob Einstein; **Fuji:** Art Irizawa

SUPER FRIENDS

Justice League superheroes Batman, Robin, Superman, Wonder Woman and Aquaman, along with three new members, Marvin, Wendy and Wonder Dog, are called to fight supernatural creatures and other powerful forces in this second assemblage of famed crimefighters from the pages of DC Comics (the first was *The Superman/Aquaman Hour of Adventure*, in which the "Justice League" superheroes appeared), produced as a weekly Saturday-morning series for ABC in 1975. Sixteen half-hours were produced.

Four spin-off series followed: *The All-New Super Friends Hour* (1977), *Challenge of the Super Friends* (1978), *The World's Greatest Super Friends* (1979) and *The Super Friends Hour* (1980), each with new characters added and each produced for ABC.

A Hanna-Barbera Production. Color. One-hour. Premiered on ABC: September 8, 1973–August 30, 1975. Rebroadcast on ABC: February 1976–September 3, 1977. Rebroadcast on CAR: June 3, 1996–May 3, 1997 (weekdays).

Voices

Narrator: Ted Knight; **Superman:** Danny Dark; **Batman:** Olan Soule; **Robin:** Casey Kasem; **Aquaman:** Norman Alden; **Wonder Woman/Wendy:** Sherry Alberoni; **Marvin/Wonder Dog:** Frank Welker

THE SUPER FRIENDS HOUR

Incorporating newly animated safety tips, this hour-long Saturday-morning series, which aired on ABC in 1980, is a retread of 1977's *All-New Super Friends Hour*, also for ABC, featuring repeat episodes from the latter. (See show entry for voice credits and details.)

A Hanna-Barbera Production in association with DC Comics. Color. One hour. Premiered on ABC: October 4, 1980–September 3, 1983.

SUPER FRIENDS: THE LEGENDARY SUPER POWERS SHOW

Comic-book superheroes Wonder Woman, Batman and Robin take on evil forces with help from several new superhuman characters in this 16-episode half-hour fantasy/adventure series, which originally aired on ABC.

A Hanna-Barbera Production. Color. Half-hour. Premiered on ABC: September 8, 1984–August 31, 1985.

Voices

Superman: Danny Dark; **Wonder Woman:** B.J. Ward; **Batman:** Adam West; **Robin:** Casey Kasem; **Firestorm:** Mark Taylor; **Cyborg:** Ernie Hudson; **Darkseid/Kalibak:** Frank Welker; **Desaad:** Rene Auberjonois

THE SUPER GLOBETROTTERS

The Harlem Globetrotters, America's funniest basketball team, are transformed from terrific basketball players to superheroes (Multi-Man, Sphere Man, Gismo Man, Spaghetti Man and Fluid Man), and use their athletic abilities to fight crime throughout the universe. The series was the third animated version of the internationally known hoopsters. The first was 1971's *The Harlem Globetrotters* for CBS, followed by *Go Go Globetrotters*, comprised of reruns from the latter, for NBC. The superhero format lasted three months before the series was paired with Hanna-Barbera's *Godzilla Power Hour* as *The Godzilla/Globetrotters Adventure Hour*.

A Hanna-Barbera Production. Color. Half-hour. Premiered on NBC: September 22, 1979–December 1, 1979. Rebroadcast on NBC: November 10, 1979–September 20, 1980 (as The Godzilla/Globetrotters Adventure Hour). Rebroadcast on CAR: August 20, 1994–August 21, 1994 (Look What We Found!); July 5, 1995– (Wednesdays).

Voices

Curley Neal (Sphere Man): Stu Gilliams; **Geese Ausbie (Multi-Man):** John Williams; **Sweet Lou Dunbar (Gismo Man):** Adam Wade; **Nate Branch (Fluid Man):** Scatman Crothers; **Twiggy Sander (Spaghetti Man):** Buster Jones; **Crime Globe:** Frank Welker; **Announcer:** Mike Rye

SUPERMAN (1988)

The famed Man of Steel—newspaper reporter Clark Kent of the *Daily Planet* in disguise—keeps the streets of Metropolis safe from the likes of such notorious criminals as Lex Luthor, the Master Shadow and Cybron in this Saturday-morning cartoon series revival of the popular comic-book character, originally broadcast on CBS in 1988. In addition to featuring 13 new adventures of the fabled crimefighter, the series also contained a second segment, "Superman Family Album," tracing Superman's youth in 13 separate episodes.

A Ruby-Spears Enterprises Production in association with DC Comics. Color. Half-hour. Premiered on CBS: September 17, 1988–September 12, 1989

Voices

Superman/Clark Kent: Beau Weaver; **Lois Lane:** Ginny McSwain; **Jimmy Olsen:** Mark Taylor; **Perry White:** Stanley Ralph Ross; **Lex Luthor:** Michael Bell; **Jessica Morganberry:** Lynn Marie Stewart; **Ma Kent:** Tress MacNeille; **Pa Kent:** Alan Oppenheimer

SUPERMAN (1996)

The Man of Steel, alias mild-mannered reporter Clark Kent, defends his native Metropolis from classic comic-book villains Braniac, Lex Luthor, Parasite, the Toyman and a whole new gang of baddies, among them Superman's evil clone, Bizarro, in this new half-hour series of adventures based on the popular DC Comics series. The usual cast of characters from the comic book are featured: *Daily Planet* editor Perry White, reporter Lois Lane and pal Jimmy Olsen, as well as a new character: Angela Chen, star gossip columnist and host of the *Metropolis Today* TV show. Airing Saturday mornings on the WB Network, the series originally premiered in September 1996 as a 90-minute prime-time special.

A Warner Bros. Television Animation Production in association with DC Comics. Color. Half-hour. Premiered on WB: September 6, 1996 (special): September 7, 1996–September 6, 1997 (series). Rebroadcast on CAR: February 14, 1997.

Voices

Superman/Clark Kent: Tim Daly; **Lois Lane:** Dana Delany; **Perry White:** George Dzundza; **Jimmy Olsen:** David Kaufman; **Jonathan Kent:** Mike Farrell; **Martha Kent:** Shelley Fabares; **Jor-El:** Christopher McDonald; **Angela Chen:** Lauren Tom; **Braniac:** Corey Burton; **Corben:** Malcolm McDowell; **Darkseid:** Michael Ironside; **Lana Lang:** Joely Fisher; **Lex Luther:** Clancy Brown; **Live Wire:** Lori Petty; **Mercy Graves:** Lisa Edelstein; **Rudy/ The Parasite:** Jim Belushi

THE SUPERMAN/AQUAMAN HOUR OF ADVENTURE

One year after the debut of his Saturday-morning series, Superman, the Man of Steel, returned in this hour-long fantasy/adventure series that featured the leader of the lost continent of Atlantis, Aquaman, as its costar. Aided by his young sidekick Aqualad, and wife, Mera, Aquaman made the transition to animated cartoon beginning with new episodes produced especially for this series.

Six seven-minute cartoons were rotated during each broadcast. Two episodes each of Superman and Aquaman were shown, along with two episodes of "Superboy" (repeated from *The New Adventures of Superman*), which alternated with "Guest Star" cartoons that marked the cartoon debut of The Atom, Flash, The Green Lantern, Hawkman and Hawkgirl, the Teen Titans and the Justice League of America, each successful comic-book superheroes. (The cartoons were rebroadcast as part of the syndicated *Aquaman* series).

A Filmation Studios Production. Color. One hour. Premiered on CBS: September 9, 1967–September 7, 1968.

Voices

Superman/Clark Kent: Bud Collyer; **Lois Lane:** Joan Alexander; **Superboy:** Bob Hastings; **Aquaman:** Ted Knight; **Aqualad:** Jerry Dexter; **Mera:** Diana Maddox

THE SUPERMAN-BATMAN ADVENTURES

Half-hour syndicated package featuring 130 cartoon episodes of the Caped Crusader and the Man of Steel culled

from several popular Saturday-morning cartoon series, originally produced by Filmation and Hanna-Barbera and broadcast on USA Network.

A Hanna-Barbera/Filmation Production in association with Warner Bros. Television International. Color. Half-hour. Premiered on USA: 1995.

SUPER MARIO BROTHERS SUPER SHOW

World-famous brother act Mario and Luigi play two misfit plumbers from the Italian section of Brooklyn who suddenly find themselves flushed through a Warp Zone to the exciting and ever-changing Mushroom Kingdom. There they set out to rescue the perky Princess Toadstool and her factotum Toad from the dastardly King Koopa and his laughable Nintendo minions. This popular half-hour syndicated series was based on the popular Nintendo video game. Each program included the cartoon adventures of the "Super Mario Brothers" and the fantasy/adventure series "The Legend of Zelda" (see individual entry for details), sandwiched between "Club Mario," a series of live-action wraparound segments featuring Mario and Luigi (played by Captain Lou Albano and Danny Wells, respectively), resident scientist Dr. Know It All and a menagerie of other characters. Except for the latter, the Super Mario Brothers and "The Legend of Zelda" cartoons were repackaged as part of the NBC network series *Captain N and the Super Mario Brothers* (1990–91). New episodes were produced, along with cartoons based on another well-known Nintendo character, "Gameboy," for *Captain N and the New Super Mario World* (1991–92), also on NBC.

In 1994 the original syndicated series joined USA Network's *Cartoon Express* lineup in reruns.

A DIC Enterprises Production in association with Nintendo America Incorporated. Color. Half-hour. Premiered: September 1989 (syndication). NBC: September 8, 1990–September 7, 1991 (part of Captain N and the Super Mario Brothers*). NBC: September 14, 1991–July 25, 1992 (part of* Captain N and the Super Mario World*). Rebroadcast on USA: January 9, 1994–May 28, 1995 (Super Mario Bros. 3). Syndicated.*

Voices

SUPER MARIO BROTHERS: Mario: Lou Albano; **Luigi:** Danny Wells; **King Koopa/Mushroom Mayor/Tryclyde/ Sniffet:** Harvey Atkin; **Toad/Mouser/Troopa/Beezo/ Flurry:** John Stocker; **Princess Toadstool/Shyguy:** Jeanine Elias

THE LEGEND OF ZELDA: Zelda: Cyndy Preston; **Link:** Jonathan Potts; **Harkinian:** Colin Fox; **Triforce of Wisdom:** Elizabeth Hanna; **Moblin:** Len Carlson

CLUB MARIO (LIVE-ACTION CAST): Mario: Captain Lou Albano; **Luigi:** Danny Wells; **Tammy Treehuger:** Victoria Delany; **Tommy Treehugger** Chris Coombs; **Evil**

Eric: Michael Anthony Rawlins; **Dr. Know It All:** Kurt Weldon; **The Big Kid:** James Rose; **The Band:** James Abbott; **Princess Centauri:** Shanta Kahn

◎ SUPER POWERS TEAM: GALACTIC GUARDIANS

An alliance of the world's greatest superheroes (Superman, Wonder Woman, Batman, Robin, Firestorm and Cyborg) work to help mankind resist the incursions of Darkseid, the "Godfather" of intergalactic crime, as they battle injustices on Earth and through the vast reaches of space in this half-hour fantasy/adventure series originally produced for ABC. The series ran a distant second in the ratings to the power-house NBC series *The Smurfs* and was canceled after only one season.

A Hanna-Barbera Production. Color. Half-hour. Premiered on ABC: September 7, 1985–August 30, 1986.

Voices
Superman: Danny Dark; **Wonder Woman:** B.J. Ward; **Batman:** Adam West; **Robin:** Casey Kasem; **Firestorm:** Mark Taylor; **Cyborg:** Ernie Hudson; **Darkseid/Kalibak:** Frank Welker; **Desaad:** Rene Auberjonois

◎ SUPER PRESIDENT AND SPY SHADOW

U.S. President James Norcross inherits supernatural powers, turning into a crimefighter (becoming "Super President"), when a cosmic storm showers him with potent chemical particles. He uses his powers to combat cunning criminals in the nation's capital in the main part of this half-hour animated series, originally broadcast on NBC. The series' second supporting segment was "Spy Shadow," the adventures of private eye Richard Vance and his independently functioning shadow hot on the case.

A DePatie-Freleng Enterprises Production. Color. Half-hour. Premiered on NBC: September 16, 1967–September 14, 1968.

Voices
President James Norcross: Paul Frees; **Richard Vance:** Daws Butler

◎ THE SUPER SIX

Under the organization name of Super Service, Inc., a funky group of superheroes, whose names coincide with their superpowers (Granite Man, Super Scuba, Elevator Man, Magnet Man and Captain Wammy), employ their special powers to fight crime in this weekly half-hour Saturday morning series originally broadcast on NBC in 1966. (A sixth superhero, Super Stretch, was either renamed or dropped from the series and no other information could be found regarding his appearance on the show.) Programmed opposite CBS's rat-

ings champ *The Mighty Mouse Playhouse*, the series offered 21 "Super Six" episodes, bracketed between two supporting segments: "Super Bwoing," a guitar-strumming daredevil, and "The Brothers Matzoriley" (Weft, Wong and Wight), a three-headed brother act occupying one body (who first appeared as the villains in the first "Inspector" cartoon, "The Great DeGaulle Stone Operation").

The series was rerun for two consecutive seasons from 1967 to 1969. This was DePatie-Freleng Enterprises' first production for Saturday-morning television.

A DePatie-Freleng Enterprises/Mirisch-Rich Production. Color. Half-hour. Premiered on NBC: September 10, 1966–September 6, 1969.

Voices
Magnet Man: Daws Butler; **Elevator Man:** Paul Stewart; **Super Scuba:** Arte Johnson; **Granite Man:** Lyn Johnson; **Captain Zammo:** Paul Frees; **Super Bwoing:** Charles Smith

The Brothers Matzoriley:
Weft/Wong: Paul Frees; **Wight:** Daws Butler

◎ SUPER SUNDAY

The short, cliff-hanging serial, once a popular staple of Saturday-morning movie matinees, was revived in this syndicated, animated series comprised of three separate weekly half-hour series—*Robotix*, *Bigfoot and the Muscle Machines* and *JEM*—programmed for weekend syndication in 1985. Produced by Marvel Productions, the series was the studio's first attempt at weekend block programming.

The series' first component, *Robotix*, presented in 15 action-packed episodes, followed the confrontations between two humanoid forces on the planet Skalorr. It acted as a lead-in to another serialized component, *Bigfoot and the Muscle Machines*, told in nine episodes, which dealt with a group of powerful land vehicles that assist a young couple in their attempt to escape the evil Mr. Big. The third component in the mix was the nonserialized *JEM*, the adventures of a beautiful young music executive who doubles as a glamorous rock star. The latter was replaced in January of 1986 by the serialized *Inhumanoids* (only two episodes aired), tracing the exploits of a courageous team of scientists who fight side by side with friendly creatures known as Mutroes against vicious monsters who plan to destroy civilization and the world. The series remained in syndication through the fall of 1986.

A Marvel Production. Color. Ninety minutes. Premiered: October 6, 1985. Syndicated.

Voices
Charlie Adler, Michael Bell, Susan Blu, Bill Callaway, Nancy Cartwright, Fred Collins, Brad Crandel, Peter

Cullen, Linda Gary, Dick Gautier, Ed Gilbert, Chris Latta, Neil Ross, Stanley Ralph Ross, Richard Sanders, Susan Silo, John Stephenson, Frank Welker

⦿ SWAMP THING

This seven-foot-tall, slimy-green, superpowered creature from the Louisiana swamplands, first created in a 1972 DC comic by Len Wein and Berni Wrightston, is given a new twist in this half-hour animated series. Dr. Alec Holland (alias Swamp Thing) discovers a plant-growing formula in his high-tech Tree Lab that could end world hunger and must prevent it from falling into evil hands. The series debuted on the Fox Network as a five-part miniseries in April of 1991, replacing the ill-fated *Piggsburg Pigs*. In July 1991, Fox brought the series back (in reruns) again replacing *Piggsburg Pigs* in its time slot.

A DIC Enterprises/Batfilm Production. Color. Half-hour. Premiered on FOX: April 1991 (as a five-part miniseries). Rebroadcast on FOX: July 6, 1991–August 3, 1991.

Voices

Dr. Alec Holland/Swamp Thing: Len Carlson; **Tomahawk:** Harvey Atkin; **Bayou Jack:** Phil Aikin; **Dr. Arcane:** Don Francks; **Dr. Deemo:** Errol Slue; **Skin Man:** Gordon Masten; **Weed Killer:** Joe Matheson; **Abby, Dr. Arcane's niece:** Paulina Gillis; **J.T.:** Richard Yearwood; **Delbert:** Jonathan Potts

⦿ SWAT KATS: THE RADICAL SQUADRON

Jake Clawson and Chance Furlong, auto mechanics by day, transform into T-Bone and Raxor, crime fighting SWAT Kats by night, to keep the peace in Megakat City (entirely populated by humanized cats), in their high-tech, land-air-sea vehicle. This first-run half-hour series was syndicated as part of the *Funtastic World of Hanna* and also broadcast on superstation WTBS beginning in 1993. In the fall of 1994 the series debuted on The Cartoon Network with all-new episodes.

A Hanna-Barbera Production. Color. Half-hour. Premiered: 1993 (syndication); TBS: September 12, 1993; CAR: September 10, 1994 (new episodes). Rebroadcast on CAR: August 7, 1995–September 1, 1995; September 4, 1995 (weekdays, Saturdays).

Voices

Charlie Adler, Frank Birney, Earl Boen, Keene Curtis, Jim Cummings, Linda Gary, Edmund Gilbert, Barry Gordon, Tress MacNeille, Gary Owens, Frank Welker

⦿ SWISS FAMILY ROBINSON

A shipwrecked family with three children make a new life as castaways on a deserted island in this animated adaptation of Jonathan David Wyss's classic novel. The half-hour series was originally produced for Japanese television in 1989 and debuted in the United States on The Family Channel that same year.

A Nippon Animation/PMT Production. Color. Half-hour. Premiered on FAM: September 8, 1989–August 30, 1992.

Voices

Ernest: Jeremy Platt; **Becca:** Reba West; **Fritz:** R. Dwight; **Jack:** Grace Michaels; **Anna:** Wendee Swann

⦿ THE SYLVANIAN FAMILIES

Young children are transported in time to a warm, wonderful and whimsical forest where they become as tiny as the wee bears, rabbits, raccoons, mice, beavers and foxes, sidestepping trouble by banding together to solve their problems. Based on the popular children's toy line, the 26-episode half-hour series was produced for first-run syndication in 1987.

A DIC Enterprise Production. Color. Half-hour. Premiered: September 1987. Syndicated.

Voices

The Woodkeeper: Frank Proctor; **Packbat/Papa Herb Wildwood:** Len Carlson; **Gatorpossum/Grandpa Smokey Wildwood:** John Stocker; **Mama Honeysuckle Evergreen:** Jeri Craden; **Papa Ernest Evergreen:** Thick Wilson; **Grandma Primrose Evergreen:** Ellen Ray Hennessey; **Ashley Evergreen:** Pauline Gillis; **Preston Evergreen:** Michael Fantini; **Rusty Wildwood:** Noam Zylberman; **Holly Wildwood:** Catherine Gallant; **Papa Slick Slydale:** Brian Belfry; **Mama Velvetter Slydale/Grandma Flora Wildwood/Mama Ginger Wildwood:** Diane Fabian; **Buster Slydale:** Jeremiah McCann; **Scarlette Slydale:** Lisa Coristine

⦿ SYLVESTER & TWEETY

Half-hour anthology series comprised of previously released Warner Bros. theatrical cartoons directed by legendary Warner Bros. animators Friz Freleng, Chuck Jones and Robert McKimson, repackaged as a Saturday-morning network show.

A Warner Bros. Production. Color. Half-hour. Premiered on CBS: September 11, 1976–September 3, 1977.

Voices

Mel Blanc, June Foray

⦿ THE SYLVESTER & TWEETY MYSTERIES

The slurred-voiced pussycat and foxy canary travel the globe with Granny, now a Jessica Fletcher–like detective who investigates strange mysteries and bizarre events, joined by the ever-dutiful Hector the Bulldog (Tweety's guardian, who keeps Sylvester in his place) in this new half-hour series—and the first all-new "puddy-tat" cartoons in 30 years—premiering on the WB Network's Kids' WB Saturday lineup in 1995. Producers tried to recapture the look and feel of legendary Warner Bros. animator Friz Freleng's original Sylvester and Tweety shorts. Supertalented voice artist June Foray reprised her role as Granny for the series.

A *Warner Bros. Television Animation Production. Color. Half-hour. Premiered on WB: September 9, 1995.*

Voices
Sylvester/Tweety: Joe Alaskey; **Granny:** June Foray; **Hector:** Frank Welker

◎ TALES FROM THE CRYPTKEEPER

Spun off from the popular HBO live-action series and full-length features (both based on the *Tales from the Crypt* comic book), this animated horror anthology series served up scary tales hosted by the show's wise-cracking, gruesome host, the Cryptkeeper. Premiering on ABC in the fall of 1993, this Saturday-morning series cost an estimated $400,000 per episode to produce.

A *Nelvana Enterprises Production in association with Tales from The Crypt Holdings, Inc. Color. Half-hour. Premiered on ABC: September 18, 1993–July 15, 1995.*

Voices
Cryptkeeper: John Kassir

◎ TALES OF LITTLE WOMEN

Four young Massachusetts sisters (Meg, Amy, Jo and Beth March), characters from Louisa May Alcott's 19th-century novel, are left temporarily fatherless during the American Civil War in this half-hour, weekly animated adaptation produced for Japanese and North American television markets. The series bowed on HBO.

A *Toei Animation/Harmony Gold Production. Color. Half-hour. Premiered on HBO: July 3, 1988–December 1990.*

◎ TALES OF THE WIZARD OF OZ

L. Frank Baum's "Oz" stories were brought to life in this limited-animated series starring Dorothy, Tin Man, Scarecrow and the Cowardly Lion in all-new animated adventures that patterned the cartoon personalities after the MGM classic stars: Judy Garland, Ray Bolger, Jack Haley and Bert Lahr. The program was produced by Arthur Rankin Jr. and Jules Bass, of *Rudolph, The Red-Nosed Reindeer* and *Frosty the Snowman* fame.

A *Videocrafts International Production. Color. Half-hour. Syndicated: 1961.*

◎ TALE SPIN

Baloo the Bear, now a devil-may-care ace cargo pilot in the tropical seaport of Cape Suzette, and his young feisty cub friend, Kit Cloudkicker, find mystery, intrigue and humor in high-flying adventures as they do battle with a menacing band of pirates in this half-hour animated series produced as part of the weekday syndicated *Disney Afternoon* cartoon block. Reuniting Baloo and characters Louie the Ape (featured as a music-loving nightclub owner) and Shere Khan from the 1967 Disney animated favorite *The Jungle Book*, the program featured several new characters: Baloo's boss, Rebecca Cunningham, who provides the cargo company's down-to-earth business sense; her five-year-old daughter, Molly; and Wildcat, the company's whiz mechanic. Produced as a companion to Disney's *DuckTales* and *Chip 'n' Dale Rescue Rangers*, also parts of the cartoon block, the 65-episode series marked the first time the classic Disney television animation had been combined with state-of-the-art computer animation.

A *Walt Disney Television Animation Production. Color. Half-hour. Premiered: 1990. Syndicated.*

Voices
Baloo the Bear: Ed Gilbert; **Kit Cloudkicker:** R.J. Williams; **Rebecca Cunningham:** Sally Struthers; **Molly Cunningham:** Janna Michaels; **Wildcat:** Patrick Fraley; **King Louie/Don Karnage:** Jim Cummings; **Shere Khan:** Tony Jay; **Dumptruck:** Chuck McCann; **Maddog:** Charlie Adler; **Dunder:** Lorenzo Music; **Spigot:** Michael Gough

◎ TARO, GIANT OF THE JUNGLE

Gifted with a secret power drawn from a radioactive tree, Taro, a jungle-born man, safeguards the jungle in this half-hour action/adventure series from Japan.

A *Global Production. Color. Half-hour. Premiered: 1969. Syndicated.*

◎ TARZAN AND THE SUPER SEVEN

The famous vine-swinging hero Tarzan expanded his horizons in this 90-minute show produced for CBS in 1978, in which he traveled to wherever his interests could best help others. The program mixed eight new episodes with old episodes from *Tarzan, Lord of the Jungle*, originally broadcast on CBS during the 1976–77 season, along with new episodes of seven weekly components: *Batman and Robin, Web Woman, Isis and the Freedom Force, Microwoman and Super Stretch, Web Woman, Manta and Moray* and *Jason of Star Command*, a live-action series that ran only during the

Gifted jungle man Taro maintains peace in the jungle in the Japanese animated action/adventure series Taro, Giant of the Jungle. © Global Productions

first season and was spun off into its own half-hour series. In 1980 the "Super Seven" components reaired as the *Batman and the Super Seven* series.

A *Filmation Associates Production. Color. Ninety minutes. Premiered on CBS: September 9, 1978–August 30, 1980.*

Voices
Tarzan: Robert Ridgely; **Batman:** Adam West; **Robin:** Burt Ward; **Bat Mite:** Lennie Weinrib

THE FREEDOM FORCE: Hercules: Bob Denison; **Isis:** Diane Pershing; **Toshi/Merlin:** Mike Bell; **Microwoman:** Kim Hamilton; **Superstretch:** Ty Henderson; **Web Woman:** Linda Gary; **Manta:** Joan Van Ark; **Moray:** Joe Stern

JASON OF STAR COMMAND (LIVE-ACTION CAST): Jason: Craig Littler; **The Commander:** James Doohan, John Russell; **Professor E. J. Parsafoot:** Charlie Dell; **Samantha:** Tamara Dobson; **Dragos:** Sid Haig; **Voice of Twiki:** Larry Storch; **Peepo the Robot:** Himself

◎ THE TARZAN/LONE RANGER/ ZORRO ADVENTURE HOUR

Zorro, the caped freedom fighter of early California, and famed masked man the Lone Ranger join Tarzan, the jungle lord, in separate adventures full of intrigue and cliff-hanging excitement. The series marked the first appearance of Zorro in animated form. Episodes of Tarzan were repeated from the previously broadcast network series *Tarzan, Lord of the Jungle.*

A *Filmation Associates Production. Color. One hour. Premiered on CBS: September 12, 1981–September 11, 1982.*

Voices
Tarzan: Robert Ridgely; **The Lone Ranger:** William Conrad; **Tonto:** Ivan Naranjo; **Don Diego/Zorro:** Henry Darrow; **Maria:** Christine Avila; **Sergeant Gonzales:** Don Diamond; **Ramon:** Eric Mason; **Migel:** Julio Medina; **Frey Gaspar:** East Carlo

◎ TARZAN, LORD OF THE JUNGLE

Edgar Rice Burroughs's comic-strip and movie character displays his legendary ability to swing by jungle vines and repulse attackers and evil game hunters in this animated version of the famed jungle champion of justice. The 16-episode series premiered on CBS in 1976.

A *Filmation Associates Production. Color. Half-hour. Premiered on CBS: September 11, 1976–September 3, 1977. Rebroadcast on CBS: February 11, 1984–September 8, 1984.*

Voices
Tarzan: Robert Ridgely

◎ TAZ-MANIA

In this toned-down version of the classic Looney Tunes character, Tazmanian Devil (now simply known as Taz) is a whirling dervish from Down Under (Australia, in other words), working as a hotel bellhop and sparking his share of outrageous escapades involving members of his extended family—his dad, Hugh; his mother, Jean; and his "Valley girl-ish" sister, Molly—and many other friends in this half-hour Saturday-morning cartoon series produced for the Fox Network.

A *Warner Bros. Television Animation Production. Color. Half-hour. Premiered on FOX: September 7, 1991–September 6, 1996. Rebroadcast on CAR/TBS/TNT: September 9, 1996.*

Voices
Taz: Jimy Cummings

◎ TEENAGE MUTANT NINJA TURTLES

Crime fighting comes into a new age when a band of feisty, fun-loving, sewer-dwelling, pizza-eating turtles (Michaelangelo, Leonardo, Donatello and Raphael), masters of the fine art of ninja, battle underground criminals and assorted villains using their quick-footed fighting skills to overcome evil in this half-hour syndicated and Saturday-morning favorite. First aired as a miniseries in 1987 and 1988, the series went weekly via syndication in the fall of 1988, then daily in 1989, capturing an astounding 73 percent of the market share. Impressed by the series' syndicated success, CBS commissioned new episodes and expanded the program to one hour, adding the show to its fall 1990 Saturday morning lineup, while the first-run half-hour series still aired in daily syndication. (CBS launched its version with a Friday-night prime-time special, "The Cuff Link Capers." A second special, "Planet of the Turtletoids," aired a year later. CBS's *Teenage Mutant Ninja Turtles* not only won its time slot but became the highest-rated show on Saturday-morning television, amassing 185 episodes during its successful six-season run, which ended in 1996. In the fall of 1993, USA Network began rerunning the series on a daily basis.

A Murakami-Wolf-Swenson/Fred Wolf Films Production in association with Mirage Studios. Color. Half-hour. One hour. Premiered: December 1987 (syndicated); CBS: September 8, 1990–September 1996. Rebroadcast on USA: September 20, 1993.

Voices
Michaelangelo: Townsend Coleman; **Leonardo:** Cam Clarke; **Donatello:** Barry Gordon; **Raphael:** Rob Paulsen; **Shredder:** James Avery; **Krang:** Pat Fraley; **April O'Neil:** Renae Jacobs; **Splinter:** Peter Renaday; **Irma:** Jennifer Darling

⊚ TEEN WOLF

Scott Howard, an average teenager, has a secret known only by his best friends, Styles and Boof: He turns into a werewolf (so does his father Harold, sister Lupe and Grandma) in this weekly Saturday-morning series based on the 1985 hit comedy starring Michael J. Fox. Actor James Hampton (Scott's dad in the original movie) was the only cast member from the film to lend his voice to the series.

A Southern Star/Hanna-Barbera Australia/Kushner-Locke Company/Clubhouse Pictures/Atlantic Entertainment Group Production. Color. Half-hour. Premiered on CBS: September

The Teenage Mutant Ninja Turtles in a scene from their long-running CBS Saturday morning series. Characters © Mirage Studios Inc. Exclusively licensed by Surge Licensing Inc. (COURTESY: MURAKAMI-WOLF SWENSON INC.)

13, 1986–August 27, 1988. Rebroadcast on CBS: October 29, 1988–September 2, 1989.

Voices
Scott Howard/Teen Wolf: Townsend Coleman; **Boof:** Jeannie Elias; **Grandma/Mrs. Sesslick:** June Foray; **Grandpa:** Stacy Keach Sr.; **Harold:** James Hampton; **Stiles:** Donny Most; **Mick:** Craig Schaffer; **Chuck:** Will Ryan

⊚ TEKNOMAN

In the year 2087 an evil intergalactic warlord named Darkon invades Earth. It is up to a young man who possesses a powerful crystal and can transform himself into an unstoppable crime fighting machine and his team of super-agents to save the planet from destruction in this half-hour action/adventure series that originally aired in the United States on the UPN Network's fall 1995 Saturday lineup.

A Saban Entertainment Production. Color. Half-hour. Premiered on UPN: September 10, 1995.

⊚ TELE-COMICS

Regarded as one of the first cartoon series ever produced for television (along with the serialized, cliff-hanging adventures of *Crusader Rabbit*) this half-hour syndicated series, using comic-strip panel illustrations and animation effects, featured four serialized stories: "Brother Goose," "Joey and Jug," "Rick Rack Street Agent" and "Su Lah." Receiving limited television airplay in 1949, NBC optioned the property in 1950 and repackaged (and retitled) the program as *NBC Comics.* The new series, comprised of three-minute vignettes, made broadcast history as the first made-for-TV network cartoon program. Following the conclusion of its run on NBC, the series reverted to its original title and was telecast on live-action children's programs throughout the United States. (See *NBC Comics* entry for further details.)

A Vallee Video Production. Black-and-white. Fifteen minutes. Premiered: 1949. Syndicated.

⊚ TENKO AND THE GUARDIANS OF THE MAGIC

In a mix of live-action and animation, real-life illusionist Princess Tenko uses her special powers as a magician to entertain audiences while scouting the globe with her band of crime-fighting Guardians (Hawk, Bolt, Steel and Ali) to recover lost magical jewels before they fall into the wrong hands in this 26-episode half-hour fantasy/adventure series made for first-run syndication.

A Saban Entertainment Production. Color. Half-hour. Premiered: (week of) September 11, 1995. Syndicated.

TENNESSEE TUXEDO AND HIS TALES

Wisecracking penguin Tennessee Tuxedo (voiced by Don Adams) and walrus Chumley undertake to change the living conditions of the denizens of Megalopolis Zoo. When insoluble situations arise, the pair visit their educator friend, answer man Phineas J. Whoopie, who tackles their problems scientifically and practically. Other recurring characters were Yak, a long-horned steer, and Baldy, a bald American eagle, who portrayed Tennessee's and Chumley's friends.

Also featured were supporting segments of "The King and Odie," "The Hunter" and "Tooter Turtle," each repeated from the NBC series, *King Leonardo and His Short Subjects*. The program later added a new segment, seen first on this program, called "The World of Commander McBragg," the tall-tale adventures of a long-winded ex-naval commander with a fantastic imagination. The segment was later repeated on *The Hoppity Hooper Show* and *Underdog*.

Introduced on CBS in 1963, the series, following its initial three-season run, was rebroadcast on ABC during the 1966–67 and 1967–68 seasons (the latter billed as *The Beagles and Tennessee Tuxedo*).

A Leonardo TV Production with Total TV Productions. Color. Half-hour. Premiered on CBS: September 28, 1963–September 3, 1966. Rebroadcast on ABC: September 10, 1966–December 17, 1966.

Voices

Tennessee Tuxedo: Don Adams; **Chumley:** Bradley Bolke; **Professor Phineas J. Whoopie:** Larry Storch; **Yak/Baldy/The Hunter/Commander McBragg:** Kenny Delmar; **King Leonardo/Biggy Brat:** Jackson Beck; **Odie Cologne/Itchy Brother/Tooter Turtle:** Allan Swift; **Mr. Wizard:** Frank Milano; **The Fox:** Ben Stone

Tennessee Tuxedo tells pal Chumley to hang on in a scene from the 1960s' television favorite Tennessee Tuxedo and His Tales. *© Leonardo-TTV*

TESTAMENT: THE BIBLE IN ANIMATION

The time-tested stories of the Old Testament, scripted and designed based on theological opinions from Jewish, Protestant, Catholic and Muslim experts, are presented in this half-hour series from the producers of *Shakespeare: The Animated Tales*. First premiering overseas in the Welsh language on S4C and in English on BBC 2 in autumn of 1996, the series debuted in the United States on HBO in January 1997, shown every Monday night. That year the series was awarded an Emmy for Outstanding Individual Achievement in Animation.

A BBC Wales/S4C/Cartwyn Cymru (Cardiff)/Christmas Films (Moscow) Production. Half-hour. Color. Premiered on HBO: January 6, 1997.

Voices

Noah: Joss Ackland; **God:** David Burke

THAT'S WARNER BROS.!

One hundred eighty-five classic *Looney Tunes* and *Merrie Melodies* cartoon shorts, culled from the Warner Bros. cartoon library, were repackaged under this weekday offering, telecast on the WB Network's "Kids' WB" lineup in 1995. Each half-hour broadcast included three cartoons and a short recurring segment called "Hip Clip," featuring excerpts reedited from existing cartoons. (Most cartoons were previously broadcast on Nickelodeon's *Looney Tunes* program.) In 1996 the program was overhauled and changed to *The Bugs n' Daffy Show*, featuring a new animated opening of Daffy and Bugs singing the show's theme song.

A Warner Bros. Production. Color. Half-hour. Premiered on WB: September 18, 1995–August 23, 1996.

Voices

Mel Blanc (primary voice)

THESE ARE THE DAYS

In the fashion of TV's dramatic series *The Waltons*, this series chronicled the trials and tribulations of the turn-of-the-century Day family, led by Martha, a widow; her children, Ben, Cathy and Danny; and their grandfather, Jeff Day, owner and proprietor of Day General Store, in their hometown of Elmsville. This weekly Saturday-morning series composed of 16 half-hour episodes, first aired on ABC in 1974.

A Hanna-Barbera Production. Color. Half-hour. Premiered on ABC: September 7, 1974–September 5, 1976. Rebroadcast on CAR: June 28, 1993–September 17, 1993 (weekdays).

Voices

Martha Day: June Lockhart; **Kay Day:** Pamelyn Ferdin; **Danny Day:** Jack E. Haley; **Grandpa Day:** Henry Jones; **Ben Day:** Andrew Parks; **Homer:** Frank Cady

◎ THINK PINK PANTHER!

The Pink Panther returned to NBC's Saturday-morning lineup with this fourth and final series entry for the network. The program repeated episodes of the nonspeaking feline star, "Misterjaws, Supershark" and "The Texas Toads." Each was previously featured in *The Pink Panther Laugh and a Half Hour and a Half Show.*

A De Patie-Freleng Enterprises Production. Color. Premiered on NBC: February 4, 1978–September 2, 1978.

Voices

Misterjaws: Arte Johnson; **Catfish, his friend:** Arnold Stang; **Fatso:** Don Diamond; **Banjo:** Tom Holland

◎ THE THIRTEEN GHOSTS OF SCOOBY-DOO

In his 16th year on television, Scooby-Doo reteams with Shaggy, Daphne, Scrappy-Doo and a new sidekick, Flim Flam, a nine-year-old con man, as they track down the 13 worst ghosts, goblins and monsters in spine-tingling new adventures, narrated by famed movie macabre artist Vincent Price (called Vincent Van Ghoul). In 1986 the ABC Saturday-morning series was replaced by reruns of *Scooby's All-Star Laff-A-Lympics.*

A Hanna-Barbera Production. Color. Half-hour. Premiered on ABC: September 7, 1985–February 22, 1986. Rebroadcast on CAR: December 12, 1994–December 16, 1994.

Voices

Scooby-Doo/Scrappy-Doo: Don Messick; **Shaggy Rogers:** Casey Kasem; **Daphne Blake:** Heather North; **Flim Flam:** Susan Blu; **Vincent Van Ghoul:** Vincent Price; **Weerd:** Artie Johnson; **Bogel:** Howard Morris

◎ THIS IS AMERICA, CHARLIE BROWN

Charlie Brown and the gang (Lucy, Linus, Snoopy, Schroeder, Sally and Peppermint Patty) revisit important events in American history in this weekly CBS cartoon miniseries comprised of eight half-hour stories. Series components included: "The *Mayflower* Voyagers," "The Birth of the Constitution," "The NASA Space Station," "The Wright Brothers at Kitty Hawk," "The Building of the Transcontinental Railroad," "The Great Inventors," "The Smithsonian and the Presidency" and "The Music and Heroes of America." The series was repeated on CBS in its entirety in the summer of 1990.

A Lee Mendelson-Bill Melendez Production in association with Charles M. Schulz Creative Organization and United Features Syndicate. Color. Half-hour. Premiered on CBS: October 21, 1988; November 11, 1988; February 10, 1989; March 10, 1989; April 19, 1989; May 23, 1989; May 30, 1990; July 25, 1990.

Voices

Charlie Brown: Erin Chase, Jason Rifle; **Lucy:** Ami Foster, Eric Gayle; **Linus:** Jeremy Miller, Brandon Stewart; **Sally Brown:** Christina Lange, Brittany Thorton; **Peppermint Patty:** Jason Mendelson; **Schroeder:** Curtis Anderson; **Marcie:** Keri Houlihan, Marie Lynn Wise, Tani Taylor Powers; **Franklin:** Hakeen Abdul Samad, Grant Gelt

◎ THE THREE ROBONIC STOOGES

Originally introduced as a weekly component of CBS's live-action cartoon show *The Skatebirds,* this series of 32 five-minute cartoons was so well received (it drew the best ratings in *The Skateboards*) that CBS decided to give the series (formerly known as "The Robonic Stooges") its own Saturday-morning time slot in 1978 as a midseason replacement. Norman Maurer, a former Three Stooges producer and son-in-law of Moe Howard, wrote the series which cast the boys as bionic-limbed superstooges. Repeated was another supporting cartoon segment, "Woofer and Wimper, Dog Detectives." In 1979, the series was moved to Sunday mornings until concluding its broadcasts two years later. (See *The Skatebirds* for voice credits.)

A Hanna-Barbera Production in association with Norman Maurer Productions. Color. Half-hour. Premiered on CBS: January 28, 1978–September 6, 1981.

◎ THUNDARR THE BARBARIAN

When a new world evolves unlike the one before, savagery, sorcery and evil beings now rule the universe. One man battles these evil elements: Thundarr, a slave who frees himself and tries to bring justice back into the world by taking on the evil elements that prevail in this half-hour Saturday-morning series, first broadcast on ABC. Premiering in 1980, the 21 episode series was a ratings hit on ABC airing two seasons.

A Ruby-Spears Enterprises Production. Color. Half-hour. Premiered on ABC: October 4, 1980–September 12, 1982. Rebroadcast on CAR: October 3, 1992–April 4, 1993 (Sundays); April 5, 1993–September 17, 1993 (weekdays); January 8, 1994–April 3, 1994 (Saturdays, Sundays); April 9, 1994–September 3, 1994 (Saturdays); September 5, 1994–October 5, 1996 (weekdays, Saturdays).

Voices

Thundarr the Barbarian: Bob Ridgely; **Princess Ariel, his aide:** Nellie Bellflower; **Ookla, his aide:** Henry Corden

◉ THUNDERBIRDS: 2086

The heroes of this futuristic series are members of International Rescue, an elite corps of daredevil cadets, who fly fantastic fleets of supersonic vehicles as they protect the world from man-made and natural disasters.

An ITC Entertainment Production. Color. Half-hour. Premiered: September 1988. Syndicated.

Voices

Joan Audiberti, Paollo Audiberti, Earl Hammond, Ira Lewis, Keith Mandell, Alexander Marshall, Terry Van Tell

◉ THUNDERCATS

Originally action-figure toys, this quintet of muscular heroes (Lion-O, Tygra, Panthro, Cheetara, Jaga and Pumrya) battles the sinister Mutants with good always triumphing over evil in these 65 half-hour episodes, produced for first-run syndication. The program was introduced via a one-hour special entitled *ThunderCats*, in January 1985, prior to the distribution of 65 half-hour episodes in the fall. In 1986 a two-hour special was made, *ThunderCats Ho!* which was reedited into a five-part adventure for the weekday strip.

A Rankin-Bass Production. Color. Half-hour. Syndicated: September 1985.

Voices

Lion-O-Jackalman: Larry Kenney; **Snarf/S-S-Slithe:** Robert McFadden; **Cheetara/Wilykit:** Lynne Lipton; **Panthro:** Earle Hyman; **Wilykat/Monkian/Ben-Gali/Tygra:** Peter Newman; **Mumm-Ra/Vultureman/Jaga:** Earl Hammond; **Pumyra:** Gerianne Raphael; **Other Voices:** Doug Preis

◉ THE TICK

Replete with tight-fitting tights, this clumsy, 400-pound blue bug of cult comic-book fame sets out to save The City from villainy with the help of his partner/ex-accountant, Arthur, who dons a moth costume, in this satirical half-hour series based on the hit comic book by cartoonist Ben Edlund (who contributed many of the scripts, storyboards and models for the series). It debuted on the Fox Network in 1994. In September of 1966 Comedy Central picked up the series, airing brand-new episodes, even while Fox Network continued to air the show, through 1997.

An Akom/Graz Entertainment/Sunbow Production. Color. Half-hour. Premiered on FOX: September 10, 1994–September 25, 1997; Premiered on COM: September 22, 1996–March 23, 1997.

Voices

The Tick: Townsend Coleman; **Arthur:** Micky Dolenz (1994–1995); Rob Paulsen (1995–1996); **Speak/Sewer**

Urchin: Jess Harnell; **Die Fledermaus:** Cam Clarke; **Mr. Mental/Multiple Santa:** Jim Cummings; **Taft:** Dorian Harewood; **The Deadly Bulb/Mr. Smartypants/Thrakorzog:** Maurice LaMarche; **American Maid:** Kay Lenz; **Dot:** Kimmy Robertson; **Jungle Janet:** Susan Silo; **Carmelita Vatos:** Jennifer Hale; **Breadmaster:** Martin Jarvis; **Chairface Chippendale:** Tony Jay

◉ TIMELESS TALES FROM HALLMARK

Hanna-Barbera in association with Hallmark Entertainment produced this 1990 series of educational cartoon adaptations, originally made available on home video and laser disc, featuring half-hour editions of eight popular children's stories: "The Elves and the Shoemaker," "The Emperor's New Clothes," "Puss in Boots," "Rapunzel," "Rumpelstiltzkin," "The Steadfast Tin Soldier," "Thumbelina" and "The Ugly Duckling." Hosted by award-winning singer Olivia Newton John (who appears in live action), each episode offered Earth-saving environmental messages for children. In December of 1991 USA Network aired the series for one week. The Cartoon Network rebroadcast the series.

A Hanna-Barbera/Hallmark Entertainment Production. Color. Half-hour. Premiered on USA: December 16, 1991– December 20, 1991. Rebroadcast on CAR: August 14, 1994; April 16, 1995.

Cast (live action)

Host: Olivia Newton-John

◉ TIMON AND PUMBAA

(See THE LION KING'S TIMON AND PUMBAA.)

◉ TIN TIN

A European comic-strip favorite, young teenager reporter Tin Tin and his faithful dog, Snowy, engage in rough adventures and mysterious quests in this animated adaptation of Belgian cartoonist Herge's creation. Produced in France and Belgium from 1961 through 1966, the series was first syndicated in the United States by National Television Associates (NTA) in 1963 and again by Tele-Features in 1971. The company of "Bozo" creator Larry Harmon, Larry Harmon Productions, did the American voice dubbing for the series. (Harmon himself did the voice of Tintin, although he went uncredited, while voice impressario Paul Frees lent his voice to other characters.) In 1991 a new series, *The New Adventures of Tintin*, was produced, airing on HBO.

A Tele-Hatchette/Belvision Production in association with National Television Associates (NTA) and Tele-Features. Black-and-white. Color. Syndicated: 1963, 1971.

Voices (U.S. version)
Tintin: Larry Harmon; **Other Voices:** Paul Frees

☺ TINY TOON ADVENTURES
(See STEVEN SPIELBERG PRESENTS TINY TOON ADVENTURES.)

☺ TODD McFARLANE'S SPAWN
The first project of HBO Animation, a new production division created to develop original animated programming for HBO and explore the largely untapped field of adult-oriented animation, *Todd McFarlane's Spawn* is the story of CIA operative Al Simmons, who cuts a deal with the devil for a second chance on Earth. He returns to the living world five years later as a soldier of evil with incredible powers in this half-hour series adaptation of McFarlane's hit comic book. McFarlane also served as executive producer of the series. The late-night, visually striking, cutting-edge animated series debuted in May of 1997 with the season opener "Burning Visions."

An HBO Animation Production. Color. Half-hour. Premiered: May 23, 1997.

Voices
Spawn: Keith David; **Cogliostro:** Richard Dysart; **Clown:** Michael Nicolosi; **Wanda Blake:** Dominique Jennings; **Terry Fitzgerald:** Victor Love; **Cyan:** Kath Soucie; **Sam Burke/Tony Twist:** James Keane; **Twitch Williams:** Michael McShane; **Jason Wynn:** John Rafter Lee; **Senator Scott McMillan/Billy Kincaid:** Ronny Cox

☺ THE TOM AND JERRY COMEDY SHOW
The popular cartoon cat-and-mouse team, joined by MGM counterparts Barney Bear, Droopy the Dog and his nemesis the Wolf (renamed "Slick"), father-and-son canines Spike and Tyke, and Jerry's nephew Tuffy starred in all-new escapades in this half-hour Saturday-morning series for CBS. As in the Oscar-winning MGM theatrical cartoon series, Tom and Jerry never talked in these new cartoon adventures, which were considerably toned down versions of their slapstick antics. The series marked the first appearance of Droopy since the end of his original MGM theatrical cartoon series in 1957 and the only appearance of Barney Bear since 1954. Other characters were modified. The Spike the bulldog characters from the MGM Tom and Jerry and Droopy cartoon series were combined into one character and sported a Jimmy Durante accent. Droopy opened each program and appeared between each cartoon literally "painting" the entire setting with one stroke of a large brush.

Only 16 half-hour programs, each consisting of two seven-and-a-half minute Tom and Jerry episodes and one seven-and-a-half-minute episode of Droopy and the others, were produced for the series, which premiered on CBS in September 1980. Venerable voice artist Frank Welker provided the voices of the other supporting characters (except during the 1980 industry strike, when producer Lou Scheimer filled in to provide all the voices).

A Filmation Production in association with MGM-TV. Color. Half-hour. Premiered on CBS: September 6, 1980–September 4, 1982.

Voices
Frank Welker, Lou Scheimer

☺ THE TOM AND JERRY/ GRAPE APE SHOW
Bill Hanna and Joe Barbera, the co-creators of this famous cat-and-mouse team, produced this less violent series revival for their studio, Hanna-Barbera Productions, featuring the cautious cat and mischievous mouse in brand-new misadventures, part of this hour-long spectacle first broadcast on ABC in 1975. The show's costar was Grape Ape, a 30-foot purple ape (an oversize version of Magilla Gorilla), and his fast-talking canine associate, Beagle, who engaged in fast-paced comedy capers of their own. In 1976 the series returned as *The Tom and Jerry/Grape Ape/Mumbly Show*. (See entry for details.)

A Hanna-Barbera Production in association with Metro-Goldwyn-Mayer. Color. One hour. Premiered on ABC: September 6, 1975–September 4, 1976.

Voices
Grape Ape: Bob Holt; **Beagle:** Marty Ingels

☺ THE TOM AND JERRY/ GRAPE APE/MUMBLY SHOW
The popular cat-and-mouse team from MGM's cartoon heydays headlined this repackaged hour-long series. It featured their own misadventures plus those of the purple primate, Grape Ape, from 1975–76's *The Tom and Jerry/Grape Ape Show*, combined with new episodes of the investigating dog, Mumbly, who tracks down criminals with the help of his assistant, Schnooker. In December 1976 Grape Ape was removed from the cast and the show was shortened to a half-hour under the title of *The Tom and Jerry/Mumbly Show*.

A Hanna-Barbera Production. Color. One hour. Premiered on ABC: September 11, 1976–November 27, 1976; December 4, 1976–September 3, 1977 (as The Tom and Jerry/Mumbly Show).

Voices
Grape Ape: Bob Holt; **Beagle, his canine associate:** Marty Ingels; **Mumbly:** Don Messick; **Schooker:** John Stephenson

TOM AND JERRY KIDS SHOW

Inspired by the original Tom and Jerry MGM cartoon shorts created by legendary animators William Hanna and Joseph Barbera, the classic nontalking cat-and-mouse team are back for more rousing animated escapades. This time they square off as kids in a half-hour Saturday-morning cartoon series that premiered on the Fox Network in the fall of 1990. Each half-hour program featured two seven-minute Tom and Jerry cartoons, along with one adventure (alternating each week) of MGM cartoon star Droopy the dog (teamed with his look-alike son, Dripple, as they try to outfox the villainous McWolf); father-and-son canines Spike and Tyke: and Tex Avery–style cartoons starring several new characters: Wild Mouse, Slow Poke Antonio, The Mouse Scouts and the Gator Brothers. (Droopy and Dripple were later spun off into their own weekly series, 1993's *Droopy, Master Detective*.) The series debuted as weekly in September 1990 and performed so well in its time slot that Fox expanded it to weekdays in 1992, with 39 new episodes.

A *Hanna-Barbera Production in association with Turner Entertainment. Color. Half-hour. Premiered on FOX: September 8, 1990–October 2, 1993 (weekly); September 14, 1992–August 12, 1994 (daily). Rebroadcast on CAR: September 4, 1995 (weekdays, Sundays): October 13, 1997 (weekdays).*

Voices
Droopy: Don Messick; **Dripple:** Charlie Adler; **McWolf:** Frank Welker; **Spike:** Dick Gautier; **Tyke:** Patric Zimmerman

THE TOM AND JERRY SHOW

MGM's top cartoon stars in the 1940s and 1950s, the nontalking Tom the cat and Jerry the mouse made their way to television in this half-hour program broadcast on CBS between 1965 and 1972. The series repackaged many of the original theatrical films starring the destructive duo plus other MGM cartoon favorites such as Barney Bear and Droopy. MGM later retitled the series *Tom and Jerry and Friends* for syndication.

A *Metro-Goldwyn-Mayer Production. Color. Half-hour. Premiered on CBS: September 25, 1965–September 17, 1972.*

Voices
Barney Bear: Billy Bletcher, Paul Frees; **Droopy:** Bill Thompson, Don Messick, Daws Butler; **Spike, the bulldog:** Bill Thompson, Daws Butler

THE TOMFOOLERYS SHOW

Patterned after NBC's comedy-variety series *Rowan and Martin's Laugh-In* but aimed at children, this half-hour series consisted of riddles, stories, limmericks and jokes based on the characters and events portrayed by Edward Lear in *The Nonsense Books*. Premiering in 1970 on NBC, the purpose of the 17-episode series was to entertain and enlighten young viewers on elements of children's literature.

A *Halas and Batchelor Production for Rankin-Bass Productions. Color. Half-hour. Premiered on NBC: September 12, 1970–September 4, 1971.*

Voices
Peter Hawkins, Bernard Spear, The Maury Laws Singers

TOM TERRIFIC

The world's smallest superhero, this curly-haired boy derived his superpowers from his funnel hat, which enabled him to assume any shape or figure and become anything he wanted—a bird, a rock or a locomotive—to apprehend culprits with the help of his reluctant, droopy-eyed canine, Mighty Manfred the Wonder Dog. His and Manfred's main nemesis was the infamous Crabby Appleton, who was "rotten to the core."

Each story lasted five episodes and was initially presented as a daily cliffhanger on *The Captain Kangaroo Show*, Monday through Friday, beginning in 1957. Foreign cartoon producer Gene Deitch created *Tom Terrific* in late 1956 along with his fellow artists at Terrytoons, one year after the studio was sold to CBS. (It became a division of CBS Films.) Following its serialization on *Captain Kangaroo*, the episodes were edited into 26 half-hour adventures and syndicated nationwide.

A *Terrytoons Production in association with CBS Films. Black-and-white. Half-hour. Premiered on CBS: June 10, 1957–September 21, 1961. Syndicated.*

Voices
Tom Terrific/Mighty Manfred: Lionel Wilson

TOP CAT

Near the outskirts of the 13th Precinct police station in New York City, Top Cat—T.C. for short—is a sly con artist and leader of a pack of Broadway alley cats (Choo-Choo, Benny the Ball, Spook, Fancy-Fancy and The Brain), who do everything possible to outswindle and outsmart the cop on the beat, Officer Dibble, in madcap situations. The series debuted in prime time—becoming Hanna-Barbera's second prime-time cartoon series, following *The Flintstones*—in September of 1961. All 31 episodes originally aired in prime time. Following the series' prime-time run, they were rebroadcast Saturday mornings on ABC in 1962 and on

NBC from 1965 to 1968. In 1992 the series began reairing on the Cartoon Network.

A Hanna-Barbera Production. Color. Half-hour. Premiered on ABC: September 27, 1961–September 26, 1962. Rebroadcast on ABC: October 6, 1962–March 30, 1963; NBC: April 3, 1965–May 10, 1969. Rebroadcast on CAR: October 1, 1992–April 2, 1993 (weekdays); January 10, 1993 (part of Boomerang, 1963); June 28, 1993–September 17, 1993 (weekdays); January 3, 1994 (weekdays); September 4, 1995– (weekdays).

Voices
Top Cat (T.C.): Arnold Stang; **Choo Choo:** Marvin Kaplan; **Benny the Ball:** Maurice Gosfield; **Spook/The Brain:** Leo de Lyon; **Goldie:** Jean VanderPyl; **Fancy Fancy/ Pierre:** John Stephenson; **Office Dibble:** Allen Jenkins

TOUCHÉ TURTLE

Brandishing his trusty sword, knightly Touché Turtle and his simpleminded assistant, Dum Dum, heroically save queens, maidens and other people in distress in a series of 52 five-minute cartoon adventures that were first distributed to television stations in 1962 as part of a trilogy series called *The Hanna-Barbera New Cartoon Series.* Along with the series' two other components—"Wally Gator" and "Lippy the Lion"—stations programmed the cartoons back to back, in separate time slots or as elements of popular daytime children's programs. One of the Touché Turtle cartoons offered in the package was actually produced in 1960, two years before the character appeared in this series. The episode was called "Whale of a Tale." Bill Thompson, who created the voice of MGM's sorrowful basset hound Droopy, supplied the voice of Touché Turtle.

A Hanna-Barbera Production. Color. Half-hour. Premiere: September 3, 1962. Syndicated.

Voices
Touché Turtle: Bill Thompson; **Dum Dum:** Alan Reed

TOXIC CRUSADERS

Hideously deformed creatures of superhuman size fight for the good of their hometown, the only unpolluted town in the country, in this half-hour series based on the popular live-action *Toxic Avenger* films of the mid-1980s and early 1990s. First test marketed as a five-part miniseries in syndication in January of 1991, the program went weekly in the fall of that year. Only 13 episodes were broadcast.

A Murikami-Wolf-Swenson Production in association with Troma Films. Color. Half-hour. Premiered: January 1991 (as five-part miniseries); Fall 1991 (as weekly series). Syndicated.

Voices
Gregg Berger, Susan Blu, Paul Eiding, Chuck McCann, Rodger Bumpass, Rad Rayle, Susan Silo, Kath Soucie, Ed Gilbert, Patric Zimmerman, Michael J. Pollard

TRANSFORMERS

The Autobots, residents of the planet Zobitron, try to stop the Decepticons, deadly robots who want to control the universe in this futuristic battle of good over evil. This half-hour series, first syndicated in 1984, was based on the popular Hasbro toy line. The original series became the longest-running cartoon program (in reruns) on Sci-Fi Channel's *Cartoon Quest* (and its later own time slot).

A Marvel Production in association with Hasbro Inc. Color. Half-hour. Premiered: September 1984. Syndicated. Rebroadcast on SCI: September 25, 1992–August 28, 1997.

Voices
Astro Train: Jack Angel; **Prowler/Scrapper/Swoop/ Junkion:** Michael Bell; **Grimlock:** Gregg Berger; **Arcee:** Susan Blu; **Devastator:** Arthur Burghardt; **Spike/Brawn/ Shockwave:** Corey Burton; **Cyclonus:** Roger C. Carmel; **Optimus Prime/Ironhide:** Peter Cullen; **Jazz:** Scatman Crothers; **Dirge:** Brad Davis; **Inferno:** Walker Edmiston; **Perceptor:** Paul Eiding; **Blitzwing:** Ed Gilbert; **Bumblebee:** Dan Gilvezan; **Blaster:** Buster Jones; **Scourge:** Stan Jones; **Cliffjumper:** Casey Kasem; **Star Scream/Cobra Commander:** Chris Latta; **Daniel:** David Mendenhall; **Gears:** Don Messick; **Blurr:** John Moschitta; **Hot Road/ Rodimus:** Judd Nelson; **Shrapnel:** Hal Rayle; **Kickback:** Clive Revill; **Bone Crusher/Hook/Springer/Slag:** Neil Ross; **Soundwave/Megatron/Galatron/Rumble/Frenzy/ Wheelie:** Frank Welker

TRANSFORMERS: GENERATION II

This second-generation *Transformers* cartoon series was produced for syndication in 1993, featuring episodes from the original 1984 series, modified with computer-enhanced bumpers and segues. The voice cast is the same as in the original series.

A Sunbow Production. Color. Half-hour. Premiered: 1993. Syndicated.

TRANZOR Z

The evil Dr. Demon and his army of powerful robot beasts try to take control of the world but encounter a protector of peace more powerful than all of them combined: Tranzor Z, a superrobot ("the mightiest of machines") created by the great Dr. Wells, in this Japanese-animated series made for first-run syndication.

A 3B Production in association with Toei Animation. Color. Half-hour. Premiered: September, 1985. Syndicated.

Voices
Gregg Berger, Mona Marshall, Paul Ross, Willard Jenkins, Robert A. Gaston, James Hodson, William Lloyd Davis

◎ THE TROLLKINS

A mini-civilization of wee playful folks with purple, blue and green faces find modern living possible by fashioning 20th-century devices out of glow worms, spider threads and other natural wonders in the magical community of Troll-town. This weekly Saturday-morning series was originally broadcast on CBS.

A Hanna-Barbera Production. Color. Half-hour. Premiered on CBS: September 12, 1981–September 4, 1982. Rebroadcast on CAR: June 6, 1993–April 3, 1994 (Sundays); September 11, 1994 (Sundays).

Voices
Sheriff Pudge Trollsom: Allan Oppenheimer; **Pixlee Trollsom/DepuTroll Dolly Durkle:** Jennifer Darling; **Blitz Plumkin:** Steve Spears; **Flooky/Bogg/Top Troll:** Frank Welker; **Grubb Trollmaine:** Michael Bell; **Depu Troll Flake:** Marshall Efron; **Mayor Lumpkin:** Paul Winchell; **Afid:** Hank Saroyan; **Slug:** Bill Callaway

◎ TURBO TEEN

A top-secret government experiment goes awry when a high school journalism student, Bret Matthews, accidentally crashes his sports car through the walls of the test laboratory and is struck by a ray from a machine that causes him to become one with his car. As a result of this freak accident, Matthews is able to transform himself into a car whenever his temperature rises. He then uses his unique ability to solve mysteries and fight crime, assisted by his friends Pattie and Alex, who share his secret. The 12-episode half-hour series premiered on ABC in 1984 and was later rebroadcast on USA Network's *Cartoon Express* and on the Cartoon Network.

A Ruby-Spears Enterprises Production. Color. Half-hour. Premiered on ABC: September 8, 1984–August 31, 1985. Rebroadcast on USA: May 5, 1989–March 4, 1992; Rebroadcast on CAR: October 16, 1994–October 17, 1994 (Look What We Found!)

Voices
Brett Matthews: Michael Mish; **Pattie, his girlfriend:** Pamela Hayden; **Alex, his friend:** T.K. Carter; **Eddie:** Pat Fraley; **Flip/Rusty:** Frank Welker; **Other Voices:** Clive Revill

◎ TURNER FAMILY SHOWCASE

TBS board chairman and president Ted Turner hosted this award-winning, two-hour family literacy series featuring previously released full-length animated features originally produced for theaters. Airing Saturdays and Sundays, first every other month in 1993, then monthly in 1994, the series—which was a 1993 National Educational Association (NEA) award recipient—aired such classic features as Max Fleischer's *Gulliver's Travels* (1939), Chuck Jones's *The Phantom Tollbooth* (1970), and Bill Hanna and Joe Barbera's *Charlotte's Web* (1973).

A Cartoon Network Production. Color. Two hours. Premiered on CAR: March 5, 1993–November 9, 1994.

◎ TV TOTS TIME

One of the first network cartoon shows, this 15-minute program aired on ABC on weekdays and Sundays, presenting a variety of black-and-white films, including animated cartoons originally produced by Van Beuren Studios (retitled under Official Films) and early Paul Terry cartoons (called "Terryland" films) from the 1920s. Before making its network debut, the series was broadcast by local ABC stations (February 4, 1950–April 22, 1950) in several major markets.

Black-and-white. Fifteen minutes. Premiered on ABC: December 30, 1951–March 2, 1952.

◎ TWINKLE, THE DREAM BEING

Set on the planet Possible, this magical, stellar-shaped intergalactic genie helps turn the dreams of his girlfriend, Jedda, and friends the Oogies into reality. Only the wretched sorceress Miss Diva Weed is bent on stopping the twinkling dreamster and making all the denizens of the planet subservient to her needs in this 26-episode half-hour fantasy/adventure series produced for syndication.

A Sei Young/MBC/Calico/Zodiac Entertainment Production. Color. Half-hour. Premiered: 1993. Syndicated.

Voices
Twinkle: Tress MacNeille

◎ THE TWISTED TALES OF FELIX THE CAT

In the fall of 1994 the feisty feline of film and television fame was reintroduced to young viewers in a series of 50 five-second bumpers that aired Saturday mornings on CBS, resulting in production of this half-hour network series (originally to be called *The New Adventures of Felix the Cat*) reported to have been the most expensive cartoon series ever produced by Film Roman studios. Retaining the retro look of creator Otto Messmer's original Felix, the series premiered in the fall of 1995, also on CBS, featuring three cartoon shorts and occasional live-action or computer-animated segments. In all, 58 cartoons were produced during the series' two-season run.

A Film Roman Production in association with Felix the Cat Productions. Color. Half-hour. Premiered on CBS: September 16, 1995–August 23, 1997.

Voices

Felix the Cat: Thom Adcox Hernandez, Charlie Adler; **Poindexter:** Cam Clarke; **Rosco:** Phil Hayes; **Sheba Bepoporeba:** Cree Summer

☺ 2 STUPID DOGS

This breakout Hanna-Barbera cartoon series marked a distinct departure from the studio's past television cartoons, producing a series that was much more in step with 1990s' cartoon fare, such as *The Ren & Stimpy Show*, in which the series' main stars—a pair of dogs, one smart (Little Dog), one dumb (Big Dog)—end up in disastrous situations marked by outrageous gags and toilet humor. Each half-hour program was comprised of two seven-minute "2 Stupid Dogs" cartoons and featured another series component: "Super Secret Squirrel," a retooled version of Hanna-Barbera's mid-1960s cartoon character Secret Squirrel, back with gibbering assistant Morocco Mole, in brand-new adventures (one per show). The series premiered simultaneously in syndication and on TBS in September of 1993.

A Hanna-Barbera Production. Color. Half-hour. Premiered: 1993 (syndication); TBS: September 12, 1993. Rebroadcast on CAR: September 10, 1994–October 2, 1995; August 18, 1995 ("Super Chunk"). Syndicated.

Voices

TWO STUPID DOGS: Big Dog: Brad Garrett; **Little Dog:** Mark Schiff; **Hollywood:** Brian Cummings

SUPER SECRET SQUIRREL: Secret Squirrel: Jess Harnell; **Morocco Mole:** Jim Cummings; **Chief:** Tony Jay

☺ ULTRAFORCE

With the mysterious appearance of hundreds of "Ultras"—ordinary humans suddenly bestowed with extraordinary powers used for pure evil—a team of superhero Ultras (Prime, Prototype, Ghoul, Contrary and Topaz) is born. It is led by reluctant hero Hardcase to combat the evils of notorious archenemies Rune, Lord Pumpkin, Sludge and others and settle mass confusion on Earth in this action-packed, half-hour sci-fi/adventure series based on the popular comic book of the same name. Premiering in September of 1995, the series was originally part of the syndicated *Amazin' Adventures II* two-hour weekend cartoon block. In 1996 USA Network began reairing the series.

A DIC Entertainment Production. Color. Half-hour. Premiered: September 24, 1995 (part of Amazin' Adventures II). Syndicated. Rebroadcast on USA: September 22, 1996.

☺ ULYSSES 31

Originally produced for television in 1981 but unable to find a suitable buyer, this Japanese imported series debuted five years later as a regular component of the 90-minute syndicated spectacular *Kideo TV*, airing only for 13 weeks before it was dropped from the series. The futuristic series, set in the 31st century, followed the exploits of Ulysses. (See *Kideo TV* for details.)

An Osmond International/DIC Enterprises Production. Color. Half-hour. Premiered: September 1986 (part of Kideo TV).

☺ UNCLE CROCK'S BLOCK

Charles Nelson Reilly, in live segments, hosted this 1975 ABC series spoof of local children shows presenting skits and jokes along with his buffoonish assistant, Mr. Rabbit Ears. (He also occasionally engaged in some lighthearted bickering with his program's director, Basil Bitterbottom, played by Jonathan Harris.) Between shticks, Reilly introduced several animated cartoons to round out the program. They were: "Fraidy Cat," a cowardly cat who is haunted by his eight ghostly selves; "M*U*S*H," a satirical takeoff of the television sitcom M*A*S*H; and "Wacky and Packy," a pair of Stone Age characters who become misplaced—in New York, of all places—and learn to deal with modern civilization.

A Filmation Associates Production. Color. One hour. Premiered on ABC: September 6, 1975–February 14, 1976.

Cast

Uncle Croc: Charles Nelson Reilly; **Mr. Rabbit Ears:** Alfie Wise; **Basil Bitterbottom:** Jonathan Harris

Voices

FRAIDY CAT: Fraidy Cat/Tinker/Dog/Mouse/Hokey: Alan Oppenheimer; **Tonka/Wizard/Captain Kitt/Sir Walter Cat/Winston:** Lennie Weinrib

M*U*S*H: Bullseye/Tricky John/Sonar/Hilda: Robert Ridgely; **Sideburns/Coldlips/Colonel Flake/General Upheaval:** Ken Mars

WACKY AND PACKY: Wacky/Packy: Allan Melvin

☺ UNCLE WALDO

In 1965 this syndicated series, a retitled version of *The Adventures of Hoppity Hooper*, first appeared. The show was designed for weekday programming. Two episodes of "Hoppity Hooper" were featured daily, along with one episode each of "Fractured Fairytales" and "Peabody's Improbable History." (See *The Adventures of Hoppity Hooper* for voice information and further details.)

A Jay Ward Production. Color. Half-hour. Premiered: 1965.

UNDERDOG

From his guise of humble, lovable canine Shoeshine Boy, superhero Underdog (voiced by *Mr. Peppers' TV series star Wally Cox*) emerges to overpower criminals in Washington, D.C., in this half-hour comedy series, first introduced on NBC in 1964. His main enemies: mad scientist Simon Bar Sinister and underworld boss Riff Raff.

Two adventures were featured each week, along with repeat episodes of several rotating components: "The Hunter," which was first seen on *King Leonardo and His Short Subjects* and "The World of Commander McBragg," which first appeared on *Tennessee Tuxedo and His Tales*.

In the fall of 1966, after the series' initial run on NBC, the program was restructured and moved to CBS. (It replaced *Tennessee Tuxedo and His Tales*.) The original components were replaced by "Go Go Gophers," the comical exploits of Running Board and Ruffled Feathers, a pair of renegade, buck-toothed gopher Indians, who are rebuffed by Colonel Kit Coyote, a blustering Teddy Roosevelt type, in their continuous scheme to seize the U.S. fort near Gopher Gulch; and "Klondike Kat," the hilarious adventures of a dumb mountie and his hot pursuit of the cheese-stealing mouse, Savior Faire. In 1968 CBS repeated episodes of both components in a half-hour series titled *Go Go Gophers*. That same year NBC began rebroadcasting the *Underdog* series, which lasted three more seasons.

A Total TV Production with Leonardo TV Productions. Color. Half-hour. Premiered on NBC: October 3, 1964–September 3, 1966; CBS: September 10, 1966–September 2, 1967. Rebroadcast on NBC: September 7, 1968–September 1, 1973; Rebroadcast on CAR: July 6, 1996–October 5, 1996 (Saturdays, Sundays).

Voices
Underdog: Wally Cox; **Sweet Polly Purebred, reporter:** Norma McMillan; **The Hunter/Colonel Kit Coyote:** Kenny Delmar; **Ruffled Feathers/Sergeant Okey Homa:** Sandy Becker; **Running Board/Narrator:** George S. Irving; **Commander McBragg:** Kenny Delmar

UNITY PICTURES THEATRICAL CARTOON PACKAGE

In March 1947 this package of Van Beuren-RKO theatrical cartoons—*Aesop's Fables* and *Tom and Jerry* (not the famous cat and mouse)—were broadcast on the first children's television series, *Movies for Small Fry*, hosted by Big Brother Bob Emery of WABD-TV, New York. The program was telecast weekdays on the DuMont Television Network. In 1948 *Cubby the Bear* was added to the package for television viewing.

A Van Beuren-RKO Production for Unity Pictures. Black-and-white. One hour. Premiered: March 11, 1947.

THE UPA CARTOON SHOW

This series is a repackaged version of *The Gerald McBoing Boing Show*, which was first shown on CBS in December 1956. The program was repeated in 1957 and then syndicated in the late 1960s (under the title of *UPA Cartoon Parade*) by United Productions of America (UPA). In 1989 the series was packaged as part of the *Mr. Magoo and Friends* show and broadcast on USA Network.

Hosted by Gerald McBoing Boing, the series features cartoon segments starring The Twirlinger Twins, Dusty of the Circus, among others, as well as 130 five-minute Mr. Magoo cartoons produced in the 1960s and episodes from *What's New Mr. Magoo?* produced in 1977 by DePatie-Freleng Enterprises in association with UPA. (See *The Gerald McBoing Boing Show* for voice credit information.)

A UPA Production. Color. Half-hour. Syndicated. Rebroadcast on USA: September 18, 1989–September 16, 1990 (as part of Mr. Magoo and Friends*).*

U.S. OF ARCHIE

In this half-hour Saturday morning series composed of 16 original episodes, timed to coincide with the country's Bicentennial, Archie, Jughead and Veronica re-create the accomplishments of America's forefathers. It was a major ratings failure for CBS. By mid-season, the program was moved to Sunday mornings, where it completed its network run.

A Filmation Associates Production. Color. Half-hour. Premiered on CBS: September 7, 1974–September 5, 1976.

Voices
John Erwin, Dal McKennon, Howard Morris, Jane Webb

VALLEY OF THE DINOSAURS

A modern-day family gets caught up in a whirlpool while exploring an unchartered river in the Amazon and is transported back in time to the world of prehistoric animals and cave people in this 16-episode half-hour fantasy/adventure series first broadcast on CBS.

A Hanna-Barbera Production. Color. Half-hour. Premiered on CBS: September 7, 1974–September 4, 1976. Rebroadcast on CAR: June 28, 1993–September 17, 1993 (weekdays); May 2, 1994–September 2, 1994 (weekdays); June 5, 1995–September 1, 1995 (weekdays).

Voices
John Butler, the father: Mike Road; **Kim Butler, his wife;** Shannon Farnon; **Katie Butler, their daughter;** Margene Fudenna; **Greg Butler, their son:** Jackie Earle Haley; **Gorak, the prehistoric father:** Alan Oppenheimer; **Gera, his wife:** Joan Gardner; **Tana, their daughter:** Melanie Baker; **Lock:** Stacy Bertheau

Other Voices:
Andrew Parks

◎ VAN-PIRES

Four scrapyard vans and cars (under the leadership of Trac-ula) that acquire human traits following a meteor crash plan to sap Earth of all its natural gases in order to fulfill their gluttonous appetites, unless four teenagers (known as The Motor-Vaters) who know of their plan can stop them in this weekly live-action/computer-animated adventure series made for Saturday-morning television.

An Abrams Gentile Entertainment/MSH Entertainment/ Animation Factory Production. Color. Half-hour. Premiered: September 13, 1997. Syndicated.

Cast (live action)
Snap: Garlikayi Mutambirwa; **Rev:** Melissa Marsala; **Nuke:** Marc Schwarz; **Axle:** Jason Hayes

Voices
James Michael, Jonathan Kahn, Max Grace, Donna Daley, Bruce Jay, Billy Boy, Don Mayo

◎ VIDEO POWER

Established video arcade game stars Kuros, Kwirk, Big Foot and Max Force (properties of the Acclaim and Williams Electronics video companies) appeared in cartoon sequences that made up this live-action/animated series, hosted by video-game junkie Johnny Arcade (played by Stivi Paskoski). The daily half-hour series was a hodge-podge of live-action bits, film clips and animated segments, largely appealing to younger viewers. The series aired for two seasons in syndication, beginning in 1990. (For the final season, the show was all live action.)

A Saban Entertainment/Acclaim/Bohbot Production. Color. Half-hour. Premiered: 1990. Syndicated.

Cast (live action)
Johnny Arcade: Stivi Paskoski

Voices
Mike Donovan, Lee Jeffrey, Terry Klassen, Jason Michas, Richard Newman, John Novak, Dale Wilson

◎ VISIONAIRIES: KNIGHTS OF THE MAGIC LIGHT

On the planet Prysmos, the age of technology has come to an end and a new age of magic has begun under the great wizard, Merklyn, who transforms knights into warriors with spectacular capabilities. Calling themselves The Spectral Knights, they protect the citizens from the evil forces of the Darkling Lords in this first-run half-hour series first syndicated in 1987. Based on the Hasbro action toy figures, the 13-week series was originally planned to be part of a cartoon combo known as *The Air Raiders/Visionaries Shows.* Only the latter was produced.

A TMS Entertainment Production in association with Sunbow Productions. Visionairies are trademarks of Hasbro, all rights reserved. Color. Half-hour. Premiered: Fall 1987. Syndicated.

Voices

SPECTRAL KNIGHTS: Leoric: Neil Ross; **Ectar/Lexor:** Michael McConnohie; **Cyrotek:** Bernard Erhard; **Witterquick/Bearer of Knowledge:** Jim Cummings; **Arzon/Wisdom Owl:** Hal Rayle; **Feryl:** Beau Weaver; **Galadria:** Susan Blu

DARKLING LORDS: Darkstorm/Cravex: Chris Latta; **Mortredd:** Jonathan Harris; **Cindarr:** Peter Cullen; **Reekon:** Roscoe Lee Browne; **Virulina:** Jennifer Darling; **Narrator:** Malachi Throne; **Other Voices:** Ellen Gerstel

◎ VOLTRON: DEFENDER OF THE UNIVERSE

Set in the 25th century, a team of young, dauntless space explorers seek and recover five fierce robot lions who unite to form "Voltron," the most incredible robot warrior ever. Once united, the Voltron force protects the planet Arus and neighboring galaxies and establishes peace in the universe in this daily syndicated series, which originated as a 90-minute special in 1983. The half-hour series was distributed to 76 markets a year later and subsequently was rebroadcast on USA Network's *Cartoon Express.* In 1997 the series was resyndicated under the title, *The New Adventures of Voltron,* while episodes of the original series aired weekdays on the Cartoon Network.

A World Events Production. Color. Half-hour. Syndicated: September 1984; September 13–14, 1997. Rebroadcast on USA: September 16, 1991–June 27, 1993; Rebroadcast on CAR: March 17, 1997.

Voices
Jack Angel, Michael Bell, Peter Cullen, Tress MacNeille, Neil Ross, B.J. Ward, Lennie Weinrib

◎ VOR-TECH

Two antagonistic brothers compete to turn humans into powerful machines as a result of technology in this half-hour science-fiction/fantasy series that premiered in 1996 as part of the weekend cartoon strip "Power Block," featuring

The most incredible robot warrior ever made protects the Planet Arus and neighboring galaxies from intruders in the popular syndicated series Voltron: Defender of the Universe. © World Events Productions

the newly animated *All Dogs Go to Heaven* and first-run animated adventures of *Richie Rich*.

A Universal Cartoon Studios Production. Color. Half-hour. Premiered: September 16, 1996. Syndicated.

THE VOYAGES OF DR. DOLITTLE

With his helpers Tommy and Maggie, the world's most famous doctor sets sail around the world to exotic lands and meets, among others, the Monkey King, the Whiskered Rat and Pushmi-Pullyu, the two-headed creature. In this adaptation of Hugh Lofting's classic tale, the good doctor and his patients converse in animal talk.

A Knack Television Production in association with 20th Century-Fox Television. Color. Half-hour. Premiered: 1984. Syndicated.

Voices
Dr. Dolittle: John Stephenson; **Tommy Stubbins:** B.J. Ward; **Maggie Thompson** Jeanine Elias

VYTOR, THE STARFIRE CHAMPION

This program highlights the adventures of the teenage hero, Vytor, and his female costar, Skyla, who work together to recapture the Starfire Orb, the world's most powerful energy source, and create peace and unity in the world. The program aired via syndication as a one-week miniseries in 1989.

A World Events/Calico Productions presentation. Half-hour. Color. Syndicated: January 1989.

Voices
Vytor: Michael Horton; **Skyla/Lyria:** Liz Georges; **Myzor/ Eldor:** Peter Cullen; **Targil:** Neil Ross, **Baboose:** Allison Argo; **Windchaser/Mutoids:** Patrick Fraley

WACKY RACES

Zany race-car drivers and their equally daffy turbine-driven contraptions enter international competitions, with the single goal of winning the coveted title "the World's Wackiest Racer." Their efforts are endangered by the devious activities of evildoer Dick Dastardly and his snickering dog, Muttley.

Competitors include Pat Pending, Rufus Ruffcut, Sawtooth, Penelope Pitstop, The Slag Brothers (Rock and Gravel), the Ant Hill Mob, the Red Max, the Gruesome Twosome, Luke and Blubber Bear.

Hanna-Barbera produced this weekly Saturday-morning series, first offered on CBS in 1968. Thirteen original half-hour episodes were produced, each airing that first season, then rebroadcast in their entirety the following season, before the series was canceled.

A Hanna-Barbera Production. Color. Half-hour. Premiered on CBS: September 14, 1968–September 5, 1970. Rebroadcast on CAR: October 3, 1992–February 26, 1994 (Saturdays); May 7, 1994–September 3, 1994 (Saturdays); June 5, 1995– October 1, 1995 (weekdays); March 25, 1996–June 27, 1997 (weekdays).

Voices
Dick Dastardly/Private Meekly: Paul Winchell; **Penelope Pitstop:** Janet Waldo; **Red Max/Rufus Ruffcut/Rock and Gravel Slag/Peter Perfect/The Sarge/Big Gruesome:** Daws Butler; **Rock/Muttley Sawtooth/Ring-A-Ding/Little Gruesome/Professor Pat Pending:** Don Messick; **Luke and Blubber Bear/General:** John Stephenson; **The Ant Hill Mob:** Mel Blanc; **Narrator:** Dave Willock

THE WACKY WORLD OF TEX AVERY

The side-splitting, fast-paced, gag-filled style of cartoons, replete with squash-and-stretch animation, pioneered by the late legendary Warner Bros. and MGM animator Tex Avery who died in 1980 is emulated in this daily half-hour syndicated series in which Avery, as a rubber-bodied, in-your-face cartoon cowboy, serves as the host. Produced by DIC Entertainment (which bought the rights to Avery's name from his daughter), the program features seven all-new characters, one-upping their adversaries, in six-minute cartoon shorts, ranging from prehistoric inventor Einstone to pesky Freddy the Fly. Available in 65 half-hours or a package of 197 six-minute shorts for flexible programming. DIC's president Andy Heyward (who worked with Avery at Hanna-Barbera until his death) spearheaded the concept and also served as the series executive producer. The series' working title was *Tex Avery Theater*.

A DIC Entertainment Production. Color. Half-hour. Premiered: September 1997. Syndicated.

Voices
Tex Avery/Freddie The Fly/Sagebrush Kid: Billy West; **Dan The Man:** Alec Willows; **Maurice:** Terry Klassen; **Mooch/Mr. Squab/Narrator:** Maurice LeMarche; **Khannie:** Cree Summer; **Chastity Knott:** Kathleen Barr; **Pompeii Pete/Einstone:** Ian James Corlett; **Amanda Banshee:** Scott McNeil; **Ghengia:** Lee Tockar; **Power Pooch:** Phil Hayes; **Mrs. Squab:** Jane Montifee

⊚ WAIT TILL YOUR FATHER GETS HOME
Cast in the mold of TV's long-running *All in the Family*, this wildly funny first-run syndicated series illustrated the generation gap between an old-fashioned father (Harry Boyle, president of Boyle Restaurant Supply Company) and his modern-day children (Chet, Alice and Jamie), who have difficulty accepting their father's timeworn methods and philosophies of life. Broadcast between 1972 and 1974, the 48-episode series appeared in prime time (Hanna-Barbera's first prime-time cartoon series since 1970's *Where's Huddles?*) in many major markets, including five owned and operated NBC affiliates across the United States.

A Hanna-Barbera Production. Color. Half-hour. Premiered: September 12, 1972. Syndicated. Rebroadcast on CAR: October 4, 1992–May 2, 1993 (Sundays); May 16, 1993–April 3, 1994 (Sundays); April 4, 1994–July 2, 1995 (weekdays, Sundays); July 5, 1995–March 11, 1997 (Wednesdays); March 17, 1997 (Mondays–Thursdays).

Voices
Harry Boyle: Tom Bosley; **Irma Boyle, his wife:** Joan Gerber; **Alice Boyle, the daughter:** Kristina Holland; **Chet Boyle, the son:** David Hayward; **Jamie Boyle, the youngest son:** Jackie Haley; **Ralph, their neighbor:** Jack Burns

⊚ WAKE, RATTLE AND ROLL
In the basement of his family home, a computer-loving teenager (Sam Baxter) enjoys watching cartoons on his talking robot (D.E.C.K.S.), made from old VCR parts. Along with his magician-grandfather (Grandpa Quirk), older sister (Debbie) and young female friend (K.C.), he hosts this live-action/animated series that introduced two all-new weekly cartoon series: "Fender Bender 500," a series of race-car adventures starring Hanna-Barbera favorites Yogi Bear, Huckleberry Hound, Top Cat, Dastardly and Muttley, and "Monster Tails," the offbeat adventures of the pets of Hollywood's most famous movie monsters, left behind in a creepy castle. Created by Hanna-Barbera president and chief executive officer David Kirschner (co-executive producer with Steven Spielberg of *An American Tail*), the daily half-hour series—the first children's program designed specifically for morning weekday time periods since *Captain Kangaroo*—premiered in syndication on 90 stations in September 1990. A year later it was rebroadcast on The Disney Channel under the new title of *Jump, Rattle and Roll*.

A Hanna-Barbera Production in association with Four Point Entertainment. Color. Half-hour. Premiered: September 17, 1990. Syndicated. Rebroadcast on DIS: 1991 (as Jump, Rattle and Roll*).*

Cast (live action)
Sam: R.J. Williams; **K.C.:** Ebonie Smith; **Debbie Detector:** Terri Ivens; **Grandpa Quirk:** Avery Schreiber; **D.E.C.K.S.:** Tim Lawrence; **Voice of D.E.C.K.S.:** Rob Paulsen

Voices
FENDER BENDER 500: Yogi Bear: Greg Burson; **Top Cat:** Arnold Stang; **Choo Choo:** Marvin Kaplan; **Dick Dastardly:** Paul Winchell; **Muttley:** Don Messick; **Announcer:** Shadoe Stevens

MONSTER TAILS: Charlie Adler, Tim Curry, Dick Gautier, Pat Musick, Frank Welker, Jonathan Winters

⊚ WALLY GATOR
Giddy alligator Wally, who speaks like comedian Ed Wynn, yearns for freedom from the confines of his zoo cage in 52 five-minute cartoon adventures first offered to television stations as a component of *The Hanna-Barbera New Cartoon Series*, also featuring *Touché Turtle* and *Lippy the Lion* in their own individual series. Local television programmers broadcast the cartoons in consecutive or individual time slots and as part of daily children's programs hosted by local television personalities.

A Hanna-Barbera Production. Color. Half-hour. Premiered: September 3, 1962. Syndicated.

Voices
Wally Gator: Daws Butler; **Mr. Twiddles, his friend:** Don Messick

⊚ WAYNEHEAD
Comic actor and talk-show host Daymon Wayans (of TV's *Living Color* fame) created this half-hour animated series about the adventures of Damey Walker, a resilient 10-year-old with a physical disability growing up in Manhattan and with his close-knit family and friends, based on real-life experiences.

A Warner Bros. Television Animation Production. Color. Half-hour. Premiered on WB: October 19, 1996.

Voices
Damey Walker: Daymon Wayans

⊚ WE ALL HAVE TALES

This follow-up batch of heartwarming animated children's series from the producers of the award-winning *Storybook Classics* series aired sporadically on Showtime beginning in 1991. Told in a "storybook-animation format," 13 stories were initially adapted for television, including the Japanese tale "The Boy Who Drew Cats"; the classic fable "King Midas and the Golden Touch"; the African folktale "Kai and the Kola Nuts"; and many others. Each program was narrated by famous celebrities, including William Hurt, Michael Caine, Ben Kingsley and Whoopi Goldberg. Comedian Robin Williams narrated the series opener, "Flying Ship." The series' original 13 episodes were broadcast over a two-year period, with new episodes airing in early 1994. Susan Sarandon and Michael Palin were among the new crop of celebrity narrators to lend their voices to the new half-hour editions.

A Rabbit Ears Video Production. Color. Half-hour. Premiered on SHO: April 9, 1991.

⊚ WEINERVILLE

Comedian Marc Weiner and his human-head, puppet-body characters (known as Weinerettes) engage in a manic display of slapstick, games-playing and pun-filled comedy sketches, bracketed by vintage cartoons from the 1940s, 1950s and 1960s (including Popeye, Columbia Pictures' *Mr. Magoo* and *Jolly Frolics* cartoons, *Batfink, Courageous Cat* and cartoons from *The Alvin Show*, including the adventures of Clyde Crashcup) in this CableAce Award–winning, weekly two-hour kiddie show that aired Sunday afternoons on Nickelodeon.

A Weiner Production in association with Nickelodeon. Color. Two hours. Premiered on NIK: July 11, 1993–June 30, 1997.

⊚ WHAT A CARTOON! SHOW

(See WORLD PREMIERE TOONS.)

⊚ WHAT-A-MESS

A royal-born, incredibly grubby puppy, Prince Amir of Kinjan (affectionately dubbed What-A-Mess because of his tousled appearance), tackles everyday mysteries of life, determined to be every bit as brave and heroic as his royal Afghan ancestors, in this 26-episode half-hour Saturday-morning cartoon series based on a character created by British TV personality Frank Muir. The gangly accident-prone puppy was first introduced in a series of interstitials produced for ABC in 1994.

A DIC Entertainment Production. Color. Half-hour. Premiered on ABC: September 1994 (interstitials); ABC: September 16, 1995–August 31, 1996 (series).

Voices
What-A-Mess: Ryan O'Donohue; **Felicia:** Jo Ann Harris Belson; **Trash:** Joe Nipote; **Frank:** Frank Muir; **Duchess:** Charity James; **Mother:** Miriam Flynn; **Father:** Michael Bell; **Daughter:** Debi Derryberry; **Son:** Adam Hendershott

⊚ WHAT'S NEW, MR. MAGOO?

The nearsighted, Academy Award–winning Mr. Magoo is joined by an equally myopic canine companion, McBarker, in further adventures marked by mistaken-identity gags and other improbable situations reminiscent of earlier productions featuring the querulous and sometimes irritable character. The half-hour Saturday-morning series debuted on CBS in 1977 in 13 half-hours, composed of 26 new cartoon adventures (two per show). Episodes from the series were packaged together with the original 1960s' series under the title of *Mr. Magoo & Friends*, rebroadcast on USA Network's *Cartoon Express* from 1989 to 1990.

A DePatie-Freleng Enterprises Production in association with UPA Productions. Color. Half-hour. Premiered on CBS: September 10, 1977–September 9, 1979. Rebroadcast on USA: September 18, 1989–September 16, 1990.

Voices
Mr. Magoo: Jim Backus; **McBarker, his bulldog:** Robert Ogle; **Waldo:** Frank Welker

⊚ WHEELIE AND THE CHOPPER BUNCH

The world's greatest stunt-racing car, Wheelie, a souped-up Volkswagen, takes on the Chopper Bunch motorcyle gang, whose leader tries to win the affections of the "bug" girlfriend, Rota Ree, in situations that involve other rotary-engined characters with distinct personalities in this 1974 Saturday-morning series, first broadcast on NBC. Hanna-Barbera produced 13 half-hour episodes of the series, which lasted only one season. It was later rebroadcast on USA Network's *Cartoon Express* and on the Cartoon Network.

A Hanna-Barbera Production. Color. Half-hour. Premiered on NBC: September 7, 1974–August 30, 1975. Rebroadcast on USA: May 16, 1989–March 28, 1991. Rebroadcast on CAR: July 5, 1995 (Wednesdays).

Voices
Wheelie/Chopper: Frank Welker; **Rota Ree:** Judy Strangis; **Scrambles:** Don Messick; **Revs:** Paul Winchell; **High Riser:** Lennie Weinrib; **Other voices:** Rolinda Wolk

◎ WHEN FUNNIES WERE FUNNY

Series of original black-and-white silent cartoon favorites—the Little King, Mutt and Jeff, Felix the Cat and others—newly colorized with soundtracks (music and sound effects) added and packaged for syndication.

A Radio and Television Packagers Production. Color. Half-hour. Premiered: 1974. Syndicated.

◎ WHERE ON EARTH IS CARMEN SANDIEGO?

The world's greatest thief is on the loose and it's up to two young detectives to find her. The only complication is that they and the thief they are chasing exist inside a computer game and must depend on their human "player" to provide them with essential information in this educational half-hour mystery series, which challenges young viewers to figure out the weekly crimes. Based on the best CD-ROM game (which has sold more than 4 million units since 1985), the series premiered on the Fox Network in 1993.

Burbank-based DIC Entertainment developed and produced the series, which was in the development stage for three years at CBS. Finally, DIC president Andy Heyward sold the series to Fox. The series has earned three daytime Emmy nominations for Outstanding Animated Program, winning the award for the 1994–95 season.

A DIC Entertainment Production. Color. Half-hour. Premiered on FOX: February 5, 1994.

Voices
Carmen: Rita Moreno; **The Chief:** Rodger Bumpass; **Ivy:** Jennifer Hale; **Zack:** Scott Menville; **The Players:** Asi Lang, Joanie Pleasant, Jeffrey Tucker, Justin Shenkarow

◎ WHERE'S HUDDLES?

Originally a prime-time summer replacement for CBS's *The Glen Campbell Goodtime Hour*, the weekly half-hour show revolves around a fumbling football quarterback, Ed Huddles, and his next-door neighbor, team center Bubba McCoy, who are members of the Rhinos, a disorganized pro team that Huddles somehow manages to lead to victory. Given a test run in the summer of 1970, the series was supposed to jump into a permanent nighttime slot in January of 1971, but CBS decided otherwise when the series faltered in the ratings. Instead, the series' original 10 episodes were rebroadcast the following summer. Series regulars include Hanna-Barbera stock players Alan Reed (Mad Dog), Mel Blanc (Bubbs) and Jean VanderPyl (Marge Huddles), best known as Fred, Barney and Wilma on *The Flintstones,* as well as comedian Paul Lynde (a regular on the popular TV game show *Hollywood Squares*), former Duke Ellington orchestra singer/vocalist Herb Jeffries and actress Marie Wilson in her final role before her death in 1972.

In 1989 the series enjoyed a brief run (in reruns) on USA Network's *Cartoon Express* and again returned to the air in 1995 on the Cartoon Network.

A Hanna-Barbera Production. Color. Half-hour. Premiered on CBS: July 1, 1970–September 10, 1970. Rebroadcast on CBS: July 1971–September 5, 1971. Rebroadcast on USA: March 1, 1989–March 21, 1989. Rebroadcast on CAR: December 1995.

Voices
Ed Huddles: Cliff Norton; **Bubba McCoy:** Mel Blanc; **Marge Huddles, Ed's wife:** Marie Wilson, Jean VanderPyl; **Claude Pertwee, perfectionist neighbor:** Paul Lynde; **Mad Dog Mahoney, Rhinos' coach:** Alan Reed; **Freight Train:** Herb Jeffries; **Fumbles/Beverly:** Don Messick; **Sports Announcer:** Dick Enberg

◎ WHERE'S WALDO?

The bespectacled young man with the striped turtleneck sweater and ski cap, featured in the bestselling picture-puzzle book created by British artist Martin Handford, starred in this half-hour network series adaptation. Waldo, his girl-friend, Wilma, and pet dog, Woof, embarked on globetrotting adventures, sometimes to help others, presented in two weekly cartoons (called "Waldo Minutes") in which the action was freeze-framed to give young viewers time to find clues to the mystery.

A DIC Enterprises/Waldo Film Company Production. Color. Half-hour. Premiered on CBS: September 14, 1991–September 7, 1992.

Voices
Townsend Coleman, Jim Cummings, Julian Holloway, Dave Workman, Joe Alaskey, Jack Angel, Jeff Bennett, Gregg Berger, Susan Blu, Carol Channing, Cam Clarke, Brian Cummings, Jennifer Darling, Jeanne Elias, Pat Fraley, Maurice LaMarche, Mary McDonald Lewis, Michele Mariana, John Mariano, Chuck McCann, Pat Musick, Alan Oppenheimer, Rob Paulsen, Jan Robson, Roger Rose, Susan Silo, Frank Welker

◎ WIDGET, THE WORLD WATCHER

An awesome, tiny flying extraterrestial with chameleonlike powers becomes the hero of the day, with the help of three young humans—eight-year-old Brian, his 16-year-old sister, Christine, and their older brother, Kevin—when he solves some of Earth's most pressing environmental and endangered species problems in this half-hour animated series syndicated in 1990. Initially produced as a weekly series, the program began airing daily in 1991. Peter Keefe, creator of the syndicated animated favorite *Denver, The Last Dinosaur,* created the series.

A Kroyer Films/Zodiac Entertainment/Calico Creations Production in association with Dinosaur Productions. Color. Half-hour. Premiered: 1990. Syndicated.

Voices
Widget: Russi Taylor; **Mega Brain/Elder #1:** Jim Cummings; **Brian/Christine:** Kath Soucie; **Kevin:** Dana Hill; **Elder #2:** Tress MacNeille

⊚ WILD C.A.T.S.
Two prehistoric alien races—the superheroic, good-guy C.A.T.S. (Covert Action Team) and the ever-evil Daemonites battle for galactic domination in this half-hour cartoon series based on Jim Lee's widely popular comic book. The series originally debuted on CBS and was rerun on USA Network.

A Nelvana Entertainment Production. Color. Half-hour. Premiered on CBS: September 17, 1994–September 2, 1995. Rebroadcast on USA: September 17, 1995.

Voices
Dockwell: Dennis Akiyama; **Zealot:** Roscoe Handford; **Void:** Janet-Laine Green; **Voodoo:** Ruth Marshall; **Marlowe:** Sean McCann; **Warblade:** Dean McDermott; **Maul:** Paul Mota; **Grifter:** Colin O'Meara; **Spartan:** Rod Wilson; **Helspont:** Maurice Dean Wint

⊚ WILDFIRE
This 13-episode half-hour adventure series, originally broadcast on CBS in 1986, tells the story of Princess Sara of the planet Dar-Shan who, as an infant, is spirited away from the clutches of an evil sorceress, Diabolyn, by the mystically powerful stallion Wildfire. Wildfire carries the baby princess to the safety of the mortal world where, now grown up, she reunites with the great stallion to defeat Diabolyn and rescue Dar-Shan for the forces of goodness. She is joined by a motley band of companions (Dorin, Brutus and Alvinar) who help her on every step of her perilous quest. Grammy Award–winning composer Jimmy Webb created the series' music.

A Hanna-Barbera Production. Color. Half-hour. Premiered on CBS: September 13, 1986–September 5, 1987. Rebroadcast on CAR: April 15, 1995–April 16, 1995 (Look What We Found!).

Voices
Princess Sara: Georgi Irene; **Wildfire, the stallion;** John Vernon; **Dorin, a young boy:** Bobby Jacoby; **Brutus, his clumsy horse:** Susan Blu; **Alvinar, a loyal farmer:** Rene Auberjoinois; **John, Sara's father:** David Ackroyd; **Ellen, John's best friend:** Lilly Moon; **Diabolyn, wicked sorceress:** Jessica Walter; **Dweedle, her hapless servant:** Billy Barty; **Mrs. Ashworth:** Vicky Carroll

⊚ THE WILD WEST C.O.W.-BOYS OF MOO MESA
In this weekly half-hour take-off of the Old West, a group of bovine cowboys led by Marshall Moe Montana and his deputies Tenderfoot, Dakota Dude and Cowlorado Kid, uphold the "Code of the West" (the meaning of the acronym, "C.O.W.-Boys") and protect the friendly residents of Cow Town from a pair of power-hungry, corrupt gangs bent on making trouble. *A Gunther-Wahl/Ruby-Spears/RC Bee/Greengrass Production in association with King World Productions. Color. Half-hour. Premiered on ABC: September 13, 1992–September 11, 1993; September 18, 1993–August 27, 1994.*

Voices
1992–93 and 1993–94 episodes: Troy Davidson, Pat Fraley, Bill Farmer, Michael Horse, Neil Ross. 1992–93 episodes: Robby Benson, Tim Curry, Michael Gough, Michael Greer, Kath Soucie, Sally Struthers, Russi Taylor. 1993–94 episodes: Charlie Adler, Jack Angel, Michael Bell, Corey Burton, Ruth Buzzi, Jodi Carlisle, Jim Cummings, David Doyle, Brad Garrett, Ellen Gerstell, Mark Hamill, Dorian Harewood, Kate Mulgrew, Rob Paulsen, Stu Rosen.

⊚ WILL THE REAL JERRY LEWIS PLEASE SIT DOWN?
Comedian Jerry Lewis created this half-hour series for ABC in 1970 in which his animated self, a bumbling janitor for the Odd Job Employment Agency, becomes a last-minute substitute and is reluctantly given several temporary assignments by the agency's owner, Mr. Blunderbuss. Lewis did not voice his own character in the series (David L. Lander, a.k.a. Squiggy on TV's *Laverne and Shirley*, provided the voice characterization), but he did contribute to several stories based on his roles in features including *The Caddy* (1958) and *The Errand Boy* (1962). Other series regulars included his girlfriend, Rhonda; his sister, Geraldine; and Spot, her pet frog.

A Filmation Associates Production. Color. Half-hour. Premiered on ABC: September 12, 1970–September 2, 1972.

Voices
Jerry Lewis: David L. Lander; **Geraldine Lewis/Rhonda:** Jane Webb; **Mr. Blunderbuss/Ralph Rotten Lewis/Won Ton Son/Professor Lewis/Hong Kong Lewis/Uncle Seadog:** Howard Morris

⊚ WING COMMANDER ACADEMY
This original half-hour cartoon series, spun off from the popular CD-ROM interactive game, features a team of futuristic rocket jockeys who earn their wings. Produced for USA Network, it features the voices of Mark Hamill, Tom Wilson, Malcolm McDowell and Dana Delany.

A Universal Cartoon Studios/Electronic Arts/Origin Systems Production. Color. Half-hour. Premiered on USA: September 21, 1996.

Voices
Christopher "Maverick" Blair: Mark Hamill; **Commodore Geoffrey Tolwyn:** Malcolm McDowell; **Todd "Maniac" Marshall:** Thomas F. Wilson; **Gwen "Archer" Bowman:** Dana Delany; **Alien:** Michael Dorn

⊚ WINKY DINK AND YOU

Children were given the chance to participate and solve problems in this unique series, featuring the adventures of Winky, a little boy, and his dog, Woofer. By attaching a transparent sheet to the television screen, kids were able to assist their cartoon friends in escaping from danger by drawing outlets and other imaginary pathways on the sheet with ordinary crayons. The program originally aired on CBS between 1953 and 1957, hosted by Jack Barry, who co-created the series with Dan Enright. (Barry and Enright later gained prominence as producers of such top-rated game shows as *The Joker's Wild*.) CBS Films syndicated the old black-and-white series through the mid-1960s before it was given a color revival in 1969.

An Ariel Productions in association with Barry and Enright Productions. Color. Half-hour. Premiered on CBS: October 10, 1953–April 27, 1957. Premiered (syndication): 1969. Syndicated.

Voices
Winky Dink: Mae Questel; **Woofer:** Dayton Allen

⊚ WISHKID STARRING MACAULAY CULKIN

Home Alone film star Macaulay Culkin plays a young kid, named Nick McClary, whose magic baseball glove grants him his every wish, in this half-hour cartoon series telecast on NBC. Culkin, who provided the voice of his character, also appeared at the beginning of each episode in a live-action segment. The series, which lasted one full season on NBC, began airing (in reruns) on The Family Channel in 1992. In the fall of 1994, 52 new original episodes were produced, also for The Family Channel.

A DIC Enterprises/Macaulay Culkin Production. Color. Half-hour. Premiered on NBC: September 14, 1991–September 7, 1992; FAM: Fall 1994 (new episodes). Rebroadcast on FAM: 1992–1996.

Voices
Macaulay Culkin, Quinn Culkin, Paul de la Rosa, Paul Haddad, Marilyn Lightstone, Judy Marshak, Andrew Sabiston, Stuart Stone, James Rankin, Harvey Atkin, Tara Charendoff, Joe Matheson, Benji Plener, Catherine Gallant, Susan Roman, Greg Swanson

⊚ THE WIZARD OF OZ

Spirited Kansas farm girl Dorothy and her spunky terrier, Toto, are summoned back to Oz to help her friends (the tenderhearted Tin Man, the resourceful Scarecrow and the timid Cowardly Lion) where the Wicked Witch of the West and her evil winged monkeys have taken over the Emerald City. There Dorothy struggles to learn the most valuable lesson of all: to believe in yourself. This half-hour animated series adaptation was loosely based on the 1939 MGM feature-film classic. Featuring story line variations and memorable music from the original movie, the series debuted on ABC in the fall of 1990. The characterizations and voices of the Scarecrow, the Tin Man, the Cowardly Lion, the Wizard and the Wicked Witch of the West—even the Munchkins—were all drawn and based on the characters in MGM's 1939 film version, except for Dorothy, who was redesigned to look more like Disney's Little Mermaid (not actress Judy Garland). The 26-episode series lasted one season on ABC and was rerun in syndication as part of the weekend cartoon block, *Amazin' Adventures*.

A DIC Enterprises Production in association with Turner Entertainment. Color. Half-hour. Premiered on ABC: September 8, 1990–September 6, 1991. Syndicated: 1992 (part of Amazin' Adventures).

Voices
Dorothy: Liz Georges; **Scarecrow:** David Lodge; **Tin Man:** Hal Rayle; **Cowardly Lion:** Charlie Adler; **Wizard:** Alan Oppenheimer; **Toto/Truckle:** Frank Welker; **Wicked Witch:** Tress MacNeille; **Glinda The Good Witch:** B.J. Ward; **Munchkin Mayor:** Susan Silo

⊚ WOLF ROCK TV

Famous radio disc jockey Wolfman Jack (alias Bob Smith) hires three teenagers, Sarah, Ricky and Sunny, to run his rock-and-roll television station. Along with their pet bird, Bopper, they keep the station manager, Mr. Morris, on the edge of his seat worrying about the next broadcast in this half-hour comedy series, first broadcast on ABC in 1984. The eight-episode series, produced in association with Dick Clark, was rerun in syndication, combined with another DIC Enterprises music-video series, *Kidd Video*, under the title of *Wolf Rock Power Hour*.

A DIC Enterprises Production in association with Dick Clark Productions. Color. Half-hour. Premiered on ABC: September 8, 1984–September 13, 1984. Syndicated: 1989 (as Wolf Rock Power Hour).

Voices
Wolfman Jack: Himself; **Sarah:** Siu Ming Carson; **Sunny:** Noelle North; **Bopper:** Frank Welker; **Mr. Morris:** Jason Bernard; **Ricardo:** Robert Vega

⊚ THE WONDERFUL STORIES OF PROFESSOR KITZEL

Historic and cultural events are related by Professor Kitzel, an electronic wizard, combining film clips, commentary and animation in this half-hour educational series produced by veteran animator James "Shamus" Culhane. The series, which was originally produced for classroom instruction, was syndicated between 1972 and 1976.

A.M.G. Animation Production. Color. Half-hour. Premiered: 1972. Syndicated.

⊚ THE WONDERFUL WIZARD OF OZ

The land of Oz is revisited in this half-hour animated series of adventures featuring Dorothy, the Scarecrow, the Tin Man, the Cowardly Lion and all the favorite Oz characters (Ozma, the Gnome King, Jack Pumpkinhead and General Ginger). The 26-episode series, first broadcast in Canada in 1987, then in the United States on HBO three years later, was narrated by actress Margot Kidder of *Superman* film fame.

A Cinar Films Production. Color. Half-hour. Premiered on HBO: May 6, 1990–June 30, 1992.

Voices
Dorothy: Morgan Hallett; **Tinman:** George Morris; **The Lion:** Neil Shee; **The Scarecrow:** Richard Dumont; **Narrator:** Margot Kidder

⊚ WOODY WOODPECKER AND HIS FRIENDS

Cartoon favorite Woody Woodpecker appeared in this syndicated series of popular cartoon shorts, combined with additional episodes of creator Walter Lantz's "Inspector Willoughby," "Chilly Willy," "Maw and Paw," "The Beary Family," and others in this half-hour weekday program for first-run syndication. In 1995 Woody joined USA Network's *Cartoon Express* in reruns and in 1997 on the Cartoon Network.

A Walter Lantz Production. Color. Half-hour. Premiered: 1958–1966, 1972. Syndicated. Rebroadcast on USA: May 29, 1995–February 26, 1996; Rebroadcast on CAR: June 23, 1997–December 26, 1997.

⊚ THE WOODY WOODPECKER SHOW

Walter Lantz's high-strung woodpecker, whose staccato laugh ("Ha-ha-ha-ha-ha!") was his trademark, headlined this series of theatrical one-reelers starring himself and other characters from Lantz's studio, namely Oswald the Rabbit, Wally Walrus, Andy Panda and Chilly Willy. The series was first broadcast on ABC in 1957. Creator Walter Lantz initially hosted the program in live-action wraparounds, introducing the cartoons. In 1970, the series shifted to NBC, which broadcast 26 additional half hours of episodes from Lantz's post-1948 cartoon classics, including "Foolish Fables," "Chilly Willy," "Inspector Willoughby," "Maw and Paw," "The Beary Family" and "Doc." The program was later syndicated, with additional episodes, as *Woody Woodpecker and Friends*.

A Walter Lantz Production. Black-and-white. Color. Premiered on ABC: October 3, 1957–September 25, 1958; Premierd on NBC: September 1970–September 1971 (new episodes). Rebroadcast on NBC: September 1971–September 1972; September 1976–September 3, 1977. Syndicated.

Voices
Woody Woodpecker: Mel Blanc, Ben Hardaway, Grace Stafford; **Andy Panda:** Bernice Hansen, Sarah Berner, Walter Tetley; **Wally Walrus:** Hans Conried, Paul Frees; **Buzz Buzzard/Hickory/Dickory/Inspector Willoughby:** Dal McKennon; **Maw and Paw:** Grace Stafford, Paul Frees; **Chilly Willy/Smedley/Windy/Gabby Gator:** Daws Butler; **Space Mouse:** Johnny Coons; **Doc:** Paul Frees; **The Beary Family:** Paul Frees, Grace Stafford

⊚ WORLD PREMIERE TOONS

Re-creating cartoons the way they were supposed to be made in the 1930s and 1940s—short, fast and furious—this 10-minute weekly series showcased the largest outpouring of original cartoon shorts in 50 years. The series debuted in February of 1995 under the title *World Premiere Toon-In*, as part of a half-hour simulcast on the Cartoon Network, TBS and TNT, hosted by Space Ghost, followed by the animated feature showcase *Mr. Spim's Cartoon Theatre*. The program was the brainchild of Hanna-Barbera president Fred Seibert and Cartoon Network president Betty Cohen, who developed the idea after contemplating one day the fate of "funny cartoons." The result was the initial production of 48 cutting-edge animated shorts produced and directed by well-known and independent animators, including Bill Hanna, Joe Barbera, Pat Ventura, Jerry Reynolds, Craig McCracken, Van Partible, Eugene Mattos, Meinert Hansen, Don Jurwich, Jerry Eisenberg, Butch Hartman and Jon and Chris McClenahan.

"Dexter's Laboratory" (by Tartakovsky), about a boy genius in pursuit of scientific greatness, debuted on the series opener (and was later spun off into its own series), followed by many other first-timers: "Short Orders" starring Yuckie Duck (directed by Ventura), the frenetic goings-on of a duck waiter in a chic restaurant; The PowerPuff Girls in "Meat Fuzzy Lumkins," the superhero adventures of barely-out-of-diapers crimefighting kindergarteners Blossom, Buttercup and Bubbles (directed by McCracken, who called them "Whoopass Girls" in a previous cartoon short that he produced and directed); "Stay Out" (directed by Barbera), the first of a proposed series starring the Flintstones' Dino; and "Johnny Bravo," about a womanizing, pompadour-wearing rocker out to win the affection of an attractive zookeeper (directed by Partible), also later turned into an animated series of its own.

Other new 'toons to debut included Slegehammer O'Possum in "Out and About" (directed by Ventura), about a dog who meets trouble in the form of a malevolent possum; "Look Out Below" (by Ventura), a new George and Junior cartoon (an updated version of Tex Avery's buffoonish bears) in which they confront a belligerent, hammer-wielding pigeon; and William Hanna's "Hard Luck Duck," the misadventures of a duck chased by a Cajun fox.

Also spotlighted on the show were animated "one shots," such as "Shake and Flick" (by Mattos), about a timid dog (Shake), who shudders at the sight of a terminator flea (Flick); "The Adventures of Captain Buzz Cheeply" (by Hansen), about a comical superhero who vows to rescue his friend after he takes care of his laundry; "Rat in a Hot Tin Can" (by Reynolds), the story of a skid-row denizen who happens to be a rat (O. Ratz) and his pet fly (David D. Fly), featuring the voices of Harvey Korman and Marvin Kaplan; "Short Pfuse" (by Hartman), in which a land shark (Phish) and a Scottish tabby cat (Chip) have the misfortune of working on a bomb squad; "Drip Dry Drips" (by the McClenahans), about two down-on-their-luck fat cats (Louie and Elmo) who undertake their latest "get-rich" scheme; and "Yoink of the Yukon" (by Jurwich and Eisenberg), about a grizzly fed up with hunters who steals uniforms off the wrong people—the Royal Canadian Mounties.

Subsequent broadcasts introduced other first-timers: "Mina and the Count," directed by Rob Renzetti; "Cow and Chicken," created by David Feiss (later spun off into a series of its own on the network); and the world television premiere of the 1996 Oscar-nominated animated short "The Chicken from Outer Space," about a cowardly dog named Courage who battles with a beady-eyed chicken from outer space, written and directed by John R. Dilworth. In late April of 1996 the series name was changed to *What a Cartoon! Show,* airing three times a week. The show mixed repeats with new animated shorts.

A Hanna-Barbera Cartoons/Cartoon Network Production. Color. Ten minutes. Premiered on CAR: February 20, 1995 (as half-hour World Premiere Toon-In); April 28, 1996 (as What a Cartoon! Show).

◎ THE WORLD OF DAVID THE GNOME
Based on the world-famous children's books *The Gnomes* and *The Secret of the Gnomes* by Rien Poortvliet and Wil Huygen, this half-hour series narrates the life and circumstances of a Gnome family, including their enemies, the Trolls. The 26-episode series, which aired weekdays in Nickelodeon beginning in 1988 and was later rebroadcast on The Learning Channel, is narrated by actor Christopher Plummer.

A Cinar Films Production in association with Miramax Films and B.R.B. Internacional, S.A. Color. Half-hour. Premiered on NIK: January 4, 1988. Rebroadcast on TLC: September 30, 1996–March 23, 1998.

Voices
David, the father: Tom Bosley; **Lisa, the mother:** Jane Woods; **Holler:** A.J. Henderson; **Susan:** Barbera Pogemiller; **King:** Richard Dumont; **Pit:** Adrian Knight; **Pat:** Rob Roy; **Pot:** Marc Denis; **Narrator:** Christopher Plummer

◎ THE WORLD OF PETER RABBIT AND FRIENDS
This series of six half-hour specials is based on nine of Beatrix Potter's popular Peter Rabbit storybooks in celebration of the popular character's 100th anniversary. Mischievous young Peter, the bad boy of the cabbage patch, creates trouble for his doting mother, his siblings—Flopsy, Mopsy and Cottontail—and other woodland creatures.

The Emmy Award–nominated British series made its American television debut on The Family Channel in March 1993 (the premiere episode: "The Tale of Peter Rabbit and Benjamin Bunny"), marking the first time that Potter's work was adapted as an animated series. Subsequent episodes—"The Tale of Samuel Whiskers," "The Tailor of Gloucester," "The Tale of Pigling Bland," "The Tale of Tom Kitten and Jemina Puddleduck" and "The Tale of Mrs. Tiggly-Winkle and Mr. Jeremy Fisher"—were broadcast in the summer, fall and winter of that year. Each episode opened with a beautiful live-action sequence, filmed in Potter's home, featuring Niamh Cusack as young Beatrix Potter, shown writing and painting, to introduce each story. The series was the most expensive animation project ever undertaken in the United Kingdom—costing an estimated $11 million to produce.

A TVC London Production for Frederick Warner and Company/BBC in association with Pony Canyon Inc. and Fuji Television Inc. Color. Half-hour. Premiered on FAM: March 29, 1993–November 13, 1995 (original broadcasts). Rebroadcast on FAM: April 4, 1993–December 19, 1997.

Cast (live action)
Beatrix Potter: Niamh Cusack

Voices
Niamh Cusack, Derek Jacobi, Prunella Scales, Rory Carry, Andrew Clitherne, Alan Bowe, Mary Jane Bowe, Jenny Moore, Rosemary Leach, Patricia Routledge, Sue Pollard, Dinsdale Landen, Enn Reitel, Selma Cadell, June Whitfield, Richard Wilson, June Watson, Sara Woolcock, Moir Lesley

THE WORLD'S GREATEST SUPER FRIENDS

The success of Hanna-Barbera's 1978 superheroes series *The All-New Super Friends* spurred network interest in another show based on the comic-book stories of the Justice League. The new series, comprised of eight half-hour episodes, featured, as did the earlier one, such popular superheroes as Superman and Wonder Woman in animated form.

A Hanna-Barbera Production. Color. One hour. Premiered on ABC: September 22, 1979–September 27, 1980.

Voices

Wonder Woman: Shannon Farnon; **Superman:** Danny Dark; **Batman:** Olan Soule; **Robin:** Casey Kasem; **Aquaman:** Bill Callaway; **Zan/Gleek:** Mike Bell; **Jayna:** Liberty Williams; **Narrator:** Bill Woodson

WOWSER

A large white sheepdog named Wowser acts as a guinea pig of sorts to try out a series of strange inventions created by his eccentric master, Professor Dinghy, in this half-hour series coproduced in Europe and Japan in 1988. The series was broadcast daily for 12 months in the United States on The Family Channel, beginning in September of 1989.

A Telecable Benelux/Saban Entertainment Production. Color. Half-hour. Premiered on FAM: September 4, 1989–September 14, 1990.

THE WUZZLES

The Wuzzles (Bumblelion, Eleroo, Hoppotamus, Moosel, Rhinokey and Butterbear) are two creatures in one (i.e., a duck/fox, a pig/chicken, etc.) who live on the island of Wuz. The furry creatures never leave the island, so they never encounter any being that is not born by Wuzzle convention, nor are they even aware of other such beings in this 13-episode fantasy/adventure series originally produced for CBS in 1985. Following its CBS run, the Saturday-morning series was rebroadcast on ABC for one full season and immediately thereafter on The Disney Channel.

A Walt Disney Television Animation Production. Color. Half-hour. Premiered on CBS: September 14, 1985–September 6, 1986. Rebroadcast on ABC: September 13, 1986–September 5, 1987; Rebroadcast on DIS: 1987.

Voices

Bumblelion/Flizard: Gregg Berger, Brian Cummings; **Eleroo/Girafbra:** Henry Gibson; **Hoppopotamus:** Frank Welker, Jo Anne Worley; **Moosel/Brat:** Will Ryan, Bill Scott; **Rhinokey/Croc/Pack-Cat:** Alan Oppenheimer; **Butterbear:** Kathleen Helppie; **Mrs. Pedigree:** Steve Kramer, Tress MacNeille; **Narrator:** Stan Freberg

X-MEN

With a telephatic therapist on their side (Professor Charlers Xavier), these crimefighting mutants (Cyclops, Wolverine, Jubilee, Storm, Rogue, Gambit, the Beast and Jean Grey), each bestowed with superhuman abilities, band together to fight for self-respect and overcome their enemies (Apocalypse, Magneto, Mr. Sinister, the Sentinels, Juggernaut, Proteus and others) in this half-hour Saturday-morning series, based on one of the largest-selling comic-book lines in history from Marvel Comics. The weekly half-hour adventure series debuted on the Fox Network in October 1992; it missed its original premiere date due to production delays. Finishing as the number-one rated show with children after only six weeks on the air, according to A.C. Nielsen, the success of *X-Men* not only bolstered Fox's ratings position on Saturday morning with young viewers but contributed to the erosion of kid viewers for ABC and CBS, the only major networks that still aired animated cartoons on Saturday.

A Marvel Films/Saban Entertainment/Graz Entertainment Production. Color. Half-hour. Premiered on FOX: October 24, 1992–September 20, 1997. Rebroadcast on FOX: September 27, 1997–January 24, 1998. Syndicated: 1998.

Voices

Scott Summers/Cyclops: Norm Spencer; **Logan/Wolverine:** Cal Dodd; **Ororo Munroe/Storm:** Alison Sealy-Smith, Iona Morris; **Gambit:** Chris Potter; **Jean Grey:** Catherine Disher; **Hank McCoy/The Beast:** George Buza; **Rogue:** Lenore Zann; **Jubilation Lee/Jubilee:** Alyson Court; **Professor Charles Xavier:** Cedric Smith

YOGI AND HIS FRIENDS

The picnic-basket–stealing Yogi and best friend, Boo-Boo, enjoyed new life in syndication via this half-hour series of old Hanna-Barbera favorites, costarring Hokey Wolf, Huckleberry Hound, Pixie and Dixie, Snagglepuss and Yakky Doodle.

A Hanna-Barbera Production. Color. Half-hour. Premiered: 1967. Rebroadcast on CAR: February 27, 1995–June 28, 1995 (weekdays).

THE YOGI BEAR SHOW

After making his debut on *The Huckleberry Hound Show* in 1958, shrewd Yogi ("Smarter than the average bear") and his shy sidekick, Boo-Boo, quickly rose to stardom and were given their own half-hour series two years later, sponsored by Kellogg's Cereals and syndicated by Screen Gems, a subsidiary of Columbia Pictures. The program contained madcap adventures of the picnic-stealing bars (one per show) who cause trouble for vacationers at Jellystone Park, plus individual episodes of two other Hanna-Barbera favorites: Snagglepuss, the calamity-stricken lion ("Exit stage left . . .") and Yakky Doodle, a dwarf duckling protected by his friend, Chopper the bulldog (who affectionately calls Yakky "little fella").

The series was kicked off in syndication in 1961 with 27 new Yogi Bear cartoons produced between 1960 and 1961, including 24 Snagglepuss and 24 Yakky Doodle cartoon shorts (one each per show), packaged as 30-minute programs. New episodes of each character were added to the mix, produced between 1961 and 1962, for broadcast, and the series remained in syndication through 1963.

In 1988 Hanna-Barbera resurrected the series, featuring Yogi and Boo-Boo in 65 all-new adventures (three per show), in a half-hour program for first-run syndication.

A Hanna-Barbera Production. Color. Half-hour. Premiered: January 30, 1961. Syndicated. Rebroadcast on CAR: September 20, 1993–January 7, 1994 (weekdays, Saturdays); January 9, 1994–October 2, 1994 (weekdays, weekends); May 5, 1997– (weekdays).

Voices
Yogi Bear/Snagglepuss/Fiber Fox/Alfy Gator: Daws Butler; **Boo-Boo, the bear club/John Smith, park ranger/Major Minor:** Don Messick; **Yakky Doodle:** Jimmy Weldon; **Chopper, the bulldog:** Vance Colvig

◎ YOGI'S GANG
Yogi Bear, Boo-Boo, Snagglepuss, Wally Gator and a host other cartoon pals traverse the world in a flying ark, battling environmental pollution and other hazards along the way, in this weekly Saturday-morning series produced for ABC in

Yogi Bear and his cartoon pals set forth in search of riches and adventure in Yogi's Treasure Hunt. *© Hanna-Barbera Productions*

1973. The series featured 17 half-hour episodes, broadcast during the 1973–74 season (then rebroadcast the following season), including a two-part episode "Yogi's Ark Lark."

A Hanna-Barbera Production. Color. Half-hour. Premiered on ABC: September 8, 1973–August 30, 1975. Rebroadcast on CAR: September 20, 1993–December 31, 1993 (weekdays under Yogi's Spin-Offs*).*

Voices
Yogi Bear/Huckleberry Hound/Snagglepuss/Quick Draw McGraw/Augie Doggie/Wally Gator/Peter Potamus: Daws Butler; **Boo-Boo/Touché Turtle/Squiddly Diddly/Ranger Smith/Atom Ant/So-So:** Don Messick; **Paw Rugg:** Henry Corden; **Doggie Daddy:** John Stephenson; **Magilla Gorilla:** Allan Melvin; **Secret Squirrel:** Mel Blanc

◎ YOGI'S SPACE RACE
The science-fiction classic *Star Wars* inspired this animated spoof teaming the irrepressible Yogi Bear and his pals in a space race to different galactic planetoids. Along the way they battle space guardian Captain Good, Clean Cat (alias Phantom Phink) and Sinister Sludge, who try to prevent Yogi and friends from crossing the finish line in this half-hour comedy/science-fiction series broadcast Saturday mornings on NBC.

Yogi's TV return was minus his longtime cherubic cub partner, Boo-Boo, who had starred in early television adventures. Instead, Hanna-Barbera's animators created a new sidekick, Scarebear (voiced by former Three Stooges member Joe Besser) for the "Space Race" and "The Galaxy Goof-Ups" segments.

In November 1978 NBC gave "The Galaxy Goof-Ups" its own half-hour time slot after shuffling the Saturday-morning kidvid network lineup. It was the most popular segment of the entire *Space Race* show, featuring Yogi Bear, Scarebear, Huckleberry Hound and Quack-Up (a modern version of Daffy Duck) as purveyors of justice—under the command of Captain Snerdley (a Joe Flynn prototype)—who find more time for disco dancing than completing missions.

Other weekly segments of *Yogi's Space Race* were: "The Buford Files," a crime-solving dog and his teenage companions, Woody and Cindy Mae; and "Galloping Ghost," the adventures of a wild and woolly cowboy ghost, Nugget Nose.

A Hanna-Barbera Productions. Color. Ninety minutes. Premiered on NBC: September 9, 1978–March 3, 1979. Rebroadcast on CAR: September 20, 1993–December 31, 1993 (weekdays under Yogi's Spin-Offs*).*

Voices
Yogi Bear/Huckleberry Hound: Daws Butler; **Scarebear:** Joe Besser; **Quack-Up:** Mel Blanc; **Captain Snerdley:** John Stephehson; **Jabberjaw/Buford, dog detective/Nugget Nose:** Frank Welker; **Woody:** Dave Landsburg;

Cindy Mae/Rita: Pat Parris; **Sheriff:** Henry Corden; **Goofer McGee, his deputy:** Roger Peltz; **Wendy:** Marilyn Schreffler; **Mr. Fuddy:** Hal Peary

ⓖ YOGI'S TREASURE HUNT
Yogi Bear captains a crew of classic Hanna-Barbera characters (Ranger Smith, Boo-Boo, Top Cat, Huckleberry Hound, Super Snooper, Blabbermouse, Snagglepuss, Augie Doggie and Doggie Daddy), who set sail aboard the magical S.S. Jelly Roger in search of treasures, which they donate to charitable causes. Episodes were produced for first-run syndication as part of *The Funtastic World of Hanna-Barbera*, then later rebroadcast on USA Network's *Cartoon Express* and on the Cartoon Network.

A Hanna-Barbera Production. Color. Half-hour. Premiered: September 1985. Syndicated. Rebroadcast on USA: September 18, 1989–September 10, 1992. Rebroadcast on CAR: October 1, 1992–January 9, 1993 (weekdays); June 28, 1993–September 18, 1993 (weekdays, Saturdays); October 31, 1994– (weekdays).

Voices
Yogi Bear/Huckleburry Hound/Quick Draw McGraw/Snooper/Blabbermouse/Augie Doggie/Snagglepuss: Daws Butler; **Boo-Boo/Ranger Smith/Muttley:** Don Messick; **Top Cat:** Arnold Stang; **Doggie Daddy:** John Stephenson; **Dastardly:** Paul Winchell

ⓖ YOUNG ROBIN HOOD
This preteen and teen version of Robin Hood and His Merrie Men (including Will Scarlet and "Brother" Tuck) and other well-known fictional characters (such as Maid Marian and Prince John) from legendary Sherwood Forest, in half-hour animated adventures tracing the origin of the Robin Hood legend was originally produced in Canada and France in 1989 and syndicated in the United States two years later (part of the weekend cartoon block *The Funtastic World of Hanna-Barbera*). Following the path of previous Hanna-Barbera "retro" cartoon series (*Flintstone Kids* and *A Pup Named Scooby-Doo*) of established properties, the series introduced several new characters—Mathilda, Marian's nurse/escort; Hagalah, a kindly sorceress and Robin Hood's surrogate mother; Gilbert of Griswold, assistant to the Sheriff of Nottingham; and Gertrude, Gilbert's jealous sister—in order to create additional subplots and story lines for each program. In 1994 the series was rebroadcast on the Cartoon Network.

A Hanna-Barbera/Cinar/France Animation/Antennae 2 Production in association with Crayon Animation/France Animation/Fils-Cartoons. Color. Half-hour. Premiered: September 1991 (part of The Funtastic World of Hanna-Barbera). Rebroadcast on CAR: October 2, 1994 (Sundays).

Voices
Robin Hood: Thor Bishopric; **Will Scarlet:** Sonja Ball; **Mathilda:** Kathleen Fee; **Gertrude of Griswold:** Jessalyn Gilsig; **Maid Marian:** Anik Matern; **Sheriff of Nottingham:** A.J. Henderson; **Hagalah:** Bronwen Mantel; **Alan-A-Dale:** Michael O'Reilly; **Prince John:** Michael Rudder; **Little John:** Terrence Scammell; **Brother Truck:** Harry Standjofsky

ⓖ THE YOUNG SENTINELS
Three young teenagers, who represent different races of the world, use their superhuman powers to frustrate evil on planet Earth in this weekly science-fiction/adventure series first broadcast on NBC in 1977. The 13-episode series was moved to a different time slot at midseason and subsequently retitled *Space Sentinels*.

A Filmation Associates Production. Color. Half-hour. Premiered on NBC: September 10, 1977–September 2, 1978.

Voices
Hercules/Sentinel One: George DiCenzo; **Astrea:** Dee Timberlake; **Mercury:** Evan Kim; **M.O.:** Ross Hagen

ⓖ YO, YOGI!
Yogi Bear, Boo Boo, Cindy Bear, Snagglepuss and Huckleberry Hound starred as crimebusting teens (each redesigned by Hanna-Barbera animators in the same vein as *A Pup Named Scooby-Doo*) who hang out at the Jellystone Mall and whose principal troublemakers are "retro" versions of Dastardly and Muttley in this half-hour Saturday-morning cartoon series that debuted on NBC in the fall of 1991. Starting with the January 25, 1992 broadcast, the series went entirely to 3-D (requiring special 3-D glasses offered inside Kellogg's Rice Krispies boxes) for 13 consecutive episodes, becoming the first TV show to be produced with 3-D effects in nearly every episode. NBC dumped the series—as well as all animated cartoons—from its fall 1992 Saturday-morning lineup, in favor of live-action programs. In the fall of 1992 the series was repeated in syndication on *The Funtastic World of Hanna-Barbera*.

A Hanna-Barbera Production. Color. Half-hour. Premiered on NBC: September 14, 1991–January 18, 1992; January 25, 1992–April 18, 1992 (in 3-D); April 25, 1992–July 25, 1992. Syndicated: 1992 (part of The Funtastic World of Hanna-Barbera).

Voices
Yogi Bear: Greg Burson; **Boo Boo:** Don Messick

ⓖ ZAZOO U
Created by children's author and illustrator Shane DeRolf, this half-hour animated series follows the misadventures of

an offbeat, fanciful and diverse menagerie of Americanimals, led by the cool, unflappable Boink, who attend an exceptionally zany institute of higher knowledge where anything can happen. Airing briefly on the Fox Network, episodes followed the school day of the series' characters through a series of short, funny and hip vignettes and feature transitions by rappers Rawld-O and Buck, rocking commentary by Boink and his bandmate—gross-out king Grizzle, a razorback hog with a ravenous appetite; Tess, the tough but sweet tomboy; and Bully, the gentle, giant, music-loving "moolly wammouth"—plus at least one poem reading per half-hour.

A Film Roman Production in association with Wang Film Productions/Cuckoo West Studios/Fox Children's Productions. Color. Half-hour. Premiered on FOX: September 8, 1990–January 19, 1991.

Voices
Boink: Michael Horton; **Grizzle:** Jerry Houser; **Logan/Chomper:** Neil Ross; **Ms. Devine:** Tress MacNeille; **Seymour:** Lee Thomas; **Bully:** Brian Cummings; **Rawld-O/Buck/Poem Reader:** Dorian Harewood; **Tess:** Susan Silo; **Rarf:** Danny Mann; **Dr. Russell:** Stu Rosen

⊚ ZORAN, SPACE BOY
Accompanied by his pet Space Squirrel, Zoran, a superhero from outer space, travels to Earth looking for his sister only to find action and adventure in this 96-episode, Japanese cartoon import for first-run syndication.

A Global Production. Color. Half-hour. Premiered: 1966. Syndicated.

⊚ ZORRO
A legendary figure with all the zest and zeal of a 1990s' hero, Zorro, an unmatched horseman and master of sword and whip (whose true identity, as Don Diego de la Vega, is a secret to all but his faithful companions Isabella and Bernardo), unnerves his opponents—notably the Spanish military force, headed by its cruel and ruthless commandant, Capitan Montecero, and aided by his overweight second-in-command, Sergeant Garcia—in his never-ending fight against injustices in this 26-episode half-hour series produced for weekend syndication.

A Fred Wolf Films, Dublin Production in association with Warner Bros. Productions, Warner Bros. International Television, Harvest Entertainment, Carring Productions International and Zorro Productions, Inc. Color. Half-hour. Premiered: (weekend of) September 20, 1997. Syndicated.

Voices
Diego/Zorro: Michael Gough; **Isabella:** Jeannie Elias; **Capitan Montecero:** Earl Boen; **Sergeant Garcia:** Tony Pope; **Don Alejandro:** Pat Fraley

AWARDS AND HONORS

⊙ ACADEMY AWARDS

The Academy of Motion Picture Arts and Science first began recognizing animated cartoons in its annual Oscars derby in the 1931–32 season. Initially the films were nominated under one category—Best Short Subject—along with live-action comedy and novelty short subjects. (The category underwent several changes throughout its history and is now called Best Short Films.) Over the years animated films have garnered nominations in other major categories, including Best Musical Score, Best Song and many others.

The following is a complete listing of the winners and runners-up in the respective categories for each year. Winners are preceded by an asterisk.

1931–32
Flowers and Trees, Walt Disney
Mickey's Orphans, Walt Disney
It's Got Me Again, Warner Bros.

1932–33
Building a Building, Walt Disney
The Merry Old Soul, Walter Lantz
**The Three Little Pigs*, Walt Disney

1934
Holiday Land, Charles Mintz/Columbia
Jolly Little Elves, Walter Lantz
**The Tortoise and the Hare*, Walt Disney

1935
The Calico Dragon, MGM
**Three Orphan Kittens*, Walt Disney
Who Killed Cock Robin? Walt Disney

1936
**Country Cousin*, Walt Disney
Old Mill Pond, MGM
Sinbad the Sailor, Max Fleischer

1937
Educated Fish, Max Fleischer
The Little Match Girl, Charles Mintz/Columbia
**The Old Mill*, Walt Disney

1938
Brave Little Tailor, Walt Disney
Mother Goose Goes Hollywood, Walt Disney
**Ferdinand the Bull*, Walt Disney
Good Scouts, Walt Disney
Hunky and Spunky, Max Fleischer

1939
Detouring America, Warner Bros.
Peace on Earth, MGM
The Pointer, Walt Disney
**The Ugly Duckling*, Walt Disney

1940
**Milky Way*, MGM

Puss Gets the Boot, MGM
A Wild Hare, Warner Bros.
*Best Original Score: *Pinocchio* (Leigh Harline, Paul J. Smith, Ned Washington)
*Best Song: "When You Wish Upon Star" from *Pinocchio* (Leigh Harline, Ned Washington)

1941
Boogie Woogie Bugle Boy of Company B, Walter Lantz
Hiawatha's Rabbit Hunt, Warner Bros.
How War Came, Columbia
Lend a Paw, Walt Disney
The Night Before Christmas, MGM
Rhapsody in Rivets, Warner Bros.
The Rookie Bear, MGM
Rhythm in the Ranks, George Pal Puppetoon
Superman No. 1, Max Fleischer
Truant Officer Donald, Walt Disney
*Best Scoring of a Musical Picture: *Dumbo* (Frank Churchill, Oliver Wallace)
Best Song: "Baby Mine" from *Dumbo* (Frank Churchill, Ned Washington)
*Special Award: Walt Disney, William Garity, John N.A. Hawkins, and the RCA Manufacturing Company for their outstanding contribution in the advancement of sound in motion pictures through the production of *Fantasia* (certificate)
*Special Award: Leopold Stokowski and his associates for their innovative achievement in the creation of a new form of visualized music in *Fantasia*
*Irving Thalberg National Award for Consistent High-Quality Production: Walt Disney

1942
All Out for V, Terrytoons
The Blitz Wolf, MGM
Der Fuehrer's Face, Walt Disney
Juke Box Jamboree, Walter Lantz
Pigs in a Polka, Warner Brothers
Tulips Shall Grow, George Pal Puppetoons
Best Documentary: *The New Spirit* (Donald Duck), Walt Disney
Best Documentary: *The Grain That Built a Hemisphere*, Walt Disney
Best Song: "Love Is a Song" from *Bambi* (Frank Churchill, Larry Morey), Walt Disney
Best Score: *Bambi* (Frank Churchill, Edward Plumb), Walt Disney
Best Sound Recording: *Bambi* (C.O. Slyfield), Walt Disney

1943
The Dizzy Acrobat, Walter Lantz
The Five Hundred Hats of Bartholomew Cubbins, George Pal Puppetoon

Greetings Bait, Warner Bros.
Imagination, Columbia
Reason and Emotion, Walt Disney
Yankee Doodle Mouse, MGM
Best Song: "Saludos Amigos" from *Saludos Amigos* (Charles Wolcott, Ned Washington), Walt Disney
Best Sound Recording: *Saludos Amigos* (C.O. Slyfield), Walt Disney
Best Scoring of a Musical Picture: *Saludos Amigos* (Edward H. Plumb, Paul J. Smith, Charles Wolcott), Walt Disney
Best Scoring of a Dramatic or Comedy Picture: *Victory Through Air Power* (Edward H. Plumb, Paul J. Smith, Oliver G. Wallace), Walt Disney
*Special Award: George Pal for the development of novel methods and technique in the production of short subjects known as *Puppetoons* (Plaque)

1944
And to Think I Saw It on Mulberry Street, George Pal Puppetoon
The Dog, Cat and Canary, Columbia
Fish Fry, Walter Lantz
How to Play Football, Walt Disney
Mouse Trouble, MGM
My Boy, Johnny, Terrytoons
Swooner Crooner, Warner Bros.

1945
Donald's Crime, Walt Disney
Jasper and the Beanstalk, George Pal Puppetoons
Life with Feathers, Warner Brothers
Mighty Mouse in Gypsy Life, Terrytoons
Poet and Peasant, Walter Lantz
Quiet Please, MGM
Rippling Romance, Columbia
Best Scoring of a Musical Picture: *The Three Caballeros* (Edward H. Plumb, Paul J. Smith, Charles Wolcott), Walt Disney
Best Sound Recording: *The Three Caballeros* (C.O. Slyfield), Walt Disney
Best Picture: *Anchors Aweigh*, MGM (has animated sequence with Jerry Mouse)
Best Song: "I Fall in Love Too Easily" from *Anchors Aweigh* (Jules Styne, Sammy Cahn), MGM
Best Scoring of a Musical Picture: *Anchors Aweigh* (Georgie Stoll), MGM

1946
The Cat Concerto, MGM
Chopin's Musical Moments, Walter Lantz
John Henry and the Inky Doo, George Pal Puppetoons
Squatter's Rights, Walt Disney

Walky Talky Hawky, Warner Bros.
*Special Scientific or Technical Award:** Arthur F. Blinn, Robert O. Cook, C.O. Slyfield and the Walt Disney Studio Sound Department for the design and development of an audio finder and track viewer for checking location noise in sound tracks (certificate)

1947
Chip 'an' Dale, Walt Disney
Dr. Jekyll and Mr. Mouse, MGM
Pluto's Blue Note, Walt Disney
Tubby the Tuba, George Pal Puppetoon
*Tweetie Pie, Warner Bros.
Best Scoring of a Musical Picture: *Song of the South* (Daniele Amfitheatrof, Paul J. Smith, Charles Wolcott), Walt Disney
*Best Song:** "Zip-A-Dee-Doo-Dah" from *Song of the South* (Allie Wrubel, Ray Gilbert), Walt Disney
*Special Award:** James Baskette for his able and heartwarming characterizations of Uncle Remus, friend and storyteller to the children of the world (statuette)

1948
*The Little Orphan, MGM
Mickey and the Seal, Walt Disney
Mouse Wreckers, Warner Bros.
Robin Hoodlum, UPA
Tea for Two Hundred, Walt Disney
*Best Two-Reel Subject:** *Seal Island*, Walt Disney
Best Song: "The Woody Woodpecker Song" from *Wet Blanket Policy* (Ramey Idriss, George Tibbles), Walter Lantz

1949
*For Scent-Imental Reasons, Warner Bros.
Hatch Up Your Troubles, MGM
MagicFluke, UPA
Toy Tinkers, Walt Disney
Best Song: "Lavender Blue" from *So Dear to My Heart* (Eliot Daniel, Larry Morey), Walt Disney (has animated sequence)
*Special Award:** Bobby Driscoll as the outstanding juvenile actor of 1949 for *So Dear to My Heart*, Walt Disney (miniature statuette)
*Best Documentary Short:** *So Much for So Little* (cartoon), Warner Bros.

1950
*Gerald McBoing-Boing, UPA
Jerry's Cousin, MGM
Trouble Indemnity, UPA
Best Scoring of a Musical Picture: *Cinderella* (Oliver Wallace, Paul J. Smith), Walt Disney
Best Song: "Bibbidy-Bobbidy-Boo" from *Cinderella* (Mack David, Al Hoffman, Jerry Livingston), Walt Disney

1951
Lambert, the Sheepish Lion, Walt Disney
Rooty Toot Toot, UPA
*Two Mouseketeers, MGM
Best Scoring of a Musical Picture: *Alice in Wonderland* (Oliver Wallace), Walt Disney

1952
*Johann Mouse, MGM
Little Johnny Jet, MGM
Madeline, UPA
Pink and Blue Blues, UPA
Romance of Transportation, National Film Board of Canada
Best One-Reel Subject: *Neighbors*, National Film Board of Canada/Norman McLaren
*Best Documentary Short:** *Neighbors*, National Film Board of Canada/Norman McLaren

1953
Christopher Crumpet, UPA
From A to Z-Z-Z-Z, Warner Bros.
Rugged Bear, Walt Disney
The Tell-Tale Heart, UPA
*Toot, Whistle, Plunk and Boom, Walt Disney
Best Two-Reel Subject: *Ben and Me*, Walt Disney

1954
Crazy Mixed-Up Pup, Walter Lantz
Pigs Is Pigs, Walt Disney
Sandy Claws, Warner Bros.
Touché, Pussy Cat, MGM
*When Magoo Flew, UPA

1955
Good Will to Men, MGM
The Legend of Rock-a-Bye Point, Walter Lantz
No Hunting, Walt Disney
*Speedy Gonzales, Warner Bros.

1956
Gerald McBoing Boing on Planet Moo, UPA
The Jaywalker, UPA
*Mr. Magoo's Puddle Jumper, UPA
Best Documentary Short: *Man in Space*, Walt Disney

1957
*Birds Anonymous, Warner Bros.
One Droopy Knight, MGM
Tabasco Road, Warner Bros.
Trees and Jamaica Daddy, UPA
The Truth About Mother Goose, Walt Disney

1958
Knighty Knight Bugs, Warner Bros.
Paul Bunyan, Walt Disney
Sidney's Family Tree, Terrytoons

1959
Mexicali Shmoes, Warner Bros.
Moonbird, Storyboard, Inc.
Noah's Ark, Walt Disney
The Violinist, Pintoff Productions
Best Documentary Short: *Donald in Mathemagic Land*, Walt Disney
*Special Scientific or Technical Award:** Ub Iwerks of Walt Disney Productions for the design of an improved optical printer for special effects and matte shots

1960
Goliath II, Walt Disney
High Note, Warner Bros.
Mouse and Garden, Warner Bros.
Munro, Rembrandt Films (released by Paramount)
A Place in the Sun, George K. Arthur-Go Pictures, Inc.

1961
Aquamania, Walt Disney
Beep Prepared, Warner Bros.
Ersatz (The Substitute), Zagreb Film
Nelly's Folly, Warner Bros.
The Pied Piper of Guadalupe, Warner Bros.

1962
The Hole, Storyboard, Inc.
Icarus Montgolfier Wright, Format Films
Now Hear This, Warner Bros.
Self Defense—for Cowards, Rembrandt Films
Symposium on Popular Songs, Walt Disney

1963
Automania 2000, Halas and Batchelor Productions
The Critic, Pintoff-Crossbow Productions
The Game, Zagreb Film
My Financial Career, National Film Board of Canada
Pianissimo, Cinema 16
Best Scoring of Music—Adaptation or Treatment: *The Sword in the Stone* (George Bruns), Walt Disney

1964
Christmas Cracker, National Film Board of Canada
How to Avoid Friendship, Rembrandt Films
Nudnik No. 2, Rembrandt Films
The Pink Phink, DePatie-Freleng

1965
Clay or the Origin of Species, Eliot Noyes

The Dot and the Line, MGM
The Thieving Magpie, Giulio Gianini-Emanuele Luzzati

1966
The Drag, National Film Board of Canada
Herb Alpert and the Tijuana Brass Double Feature, Hubley Studio (released by Paramount)
The Pink Blueprint, DePatie-Freleng

1967
The Box, Murakami-Wolf Films
Hypothese Beta, Films Orzeaux
What on Earth! National Film Board of Canada

1968
The House That Jack Built, National Film Board of Canada
The Magic Pear Tree, Murakami-Wolf Productions
Windy Day, Hubley Studio (released by Paramount)
Winnie the Pooh and the Blustery Day, Walt Disney

1969
It's Tough to Be a Bird, Walt Disney
Of Men and Demons, Hubley Studio (released by Paramount)
Walking, National Film Board of Canada

1970
The Further Adventures of Uncle Sam: Part Two, The Haboush Company
Is It Always Right to Be Right? Stephen Bosustow Productions
The Shepherd, Cameron Guess and Associates
Best Original Song Score: *A Boy Named Charlie Brown* (music by Rod McKuen and John Scott Trotter; lyrics by Rod McKuen, Bill Melendez and Al Shean; adapted by Vince Guaraldi)

1971
The Crunch Bird, Maxwell-Petok-Petrovich Productions
Evolution, National Film Board of Canada
The Selfish Giant, Potterton Productions

1972
The Christmas Carol, Richard Williams
Kama Sutra Rides Again, Bob Godfrey Films
Tup Tup, Zagreb Film

1973
Frank Film, Frank Mouris
The Legend of John Henry, Stephen Bosustow-Pyramid Film Production
Pulcinella, Luzzati-Gianini
Best Song: "Love" from *Robin Hood* (music by George Bruns; lyrics by Floyd Huddleston), Walt Disney

1974
Closed Mondays, Lighthouse Productions
The Family That Dwelt Apart, National Film Board of Canada
Hunger, National Film Board of Canada
Voyage to Next, Hubley Studio
Winnie the Pooh and Tigger Too, Walt Disney

1975
Great, British Lion Films, Ltd.
Kick Me, Swarthe Productions
Monsieur Pointu, National Film Board of Canada
Sisyphus, Hungarofilms

1976
Dedalo, Cineteam Realizzazioni
Leisure, Film Australia
The Street, National Film Board of Canada

1977
The Bead Game, National Film Board of Canada
The Doonesbury Special, Hubley Studio
Jimmy the C, Motionpicker Productions
Sand Castle, National Film Board of Canada

1978
Oh My Darling, Nico Crama Productions "Rip Van Winkle," Will Vinton/Billy Budd
Special Delivery, National Board of Canada
Honorary Award: Walter Lantz, for bringing joy and laughter to every part of the world through his unique animated motion pictures (statuette)

1979
Dream Doll, Godfrey Films/Zagreb Films/Halas and Batchelor
Every Child, National Film Board of Canada
It's So Nice to Have a Wolf Around the House, AR&T Productions for Learning Corporation of America

1980
All Nothing, National Film Board of Canada
The Fly, Pannonia Film
History of the World in Three Minutes, Michael Mills Productions, Ltd.

1981
Crac, Societ Radio-Canada
The Creation, Will Vinton Productions
The Tender Tale of Cinderella Penguin, National Film Board of Canada

1982
The Great Cognito, Will Vinton Productions
The Snowman, Snowman Enterprises, Ltd.
Tango, Film Polski

1983
Mickey's Christmas Carol, Walt Disney Productions
Sound of Sunshine—Sound of Rain, Hallinan Plus
Sundae in New York, Motionpicker Productions

1984
Charade, Sheridan College
Doctor Desoto, Sporn Animation
Paradise, National Film Board of Canada

1985
Anna & Bella, The Netherlands
The Big Snit, National Film Board of Canada
Second Class Mail, National Film & Television School

1986
The Frog, the Dog and the Devil, New Zealand National Film Unit
A Greek Tragedy, CineTe pvba
Luxo Jr., Pixar Productions
Best Song: *Somewhere Out There* (*An American Tail*, Universal; music by James Horner and Barry Mann, lyrics by Cynthia Well)

1987
George and Rosemary, National Film Board of Canada
The Man Who Planted Trees, Societe Radio-Canada
Your Face, Bill Plympton

1988
The Cat Came Back, National Film Board of Canada
Technological Threat, Kroyer Films, Inc.
Tin Toy, Pixar

1989
Balance, A Lauenstein Production
The Cow, The "Pilot" Co-op Animated Film Studio with VPTO Videofilm
The Hill Farm, National Film & Television School
Best Original Song: "Kiss the Girl" (*The Little Mermaid*, Walt Disney; music by Alan Menken; lyrics by Howard Ashman)
Best Original Song: "Under the Sea" (*The Little Mermaid*, Walt Disney; music and lyrics by Alan Menken and Howard Ashman)

1990
A Grand Day Out, National Film & Television School
Creature Comforts, Aardman Animations Ltd. Production
Grasshoppers (Cavallette), Bruno Bozetto Productions

1991
Blackfly, National Film Board of Canada

Manipulation, Tandem Films Production

Strings, National Film Board of Canada

Best Picture: *Beauty and the Beast*, Walt Disney

Best Original Song: "Belle" (*Beauty and the Beast*, Walt Disney; music and lyrics by Alan Menken and Howard Ashman)

Best Original Song: "Be Our Guest" (*Beauty and the Beast*, Walt Disney; music and lyrics by Alan Menken and Howard Ashman)

*Best Original Song:** "Beauty and the Beast" (*Beauty and Beast*, Walt Disney; music and lyrics by Alan Menken and Howard Ashman)

Best Sound: *Beauty and the Beast*, Walt Disney (David J. Hudson, Doc Kane, Mel Metcalfe and Terry Porter)

1992

Adam, Aardman Animations Ltd. Production

Mona Lisa Descending a Staircase, Joan C. Gratz Production

Reci, Reci, Reci . . . (Words, Words, Words), Kratky Film Production

Screen Play, Bare Boards Film Production

The Sandman, Batty Berry Mackinson Production

Best Original Song: "Friend Like Me" (*Aladdin*, Walt Disney; music and lyrics by Alan Menken and Howard Ashman)

*Best Original Song:** "A Whole New World" (*Aladdin*, Walt Disney, music and lyrics by Alan Menken and Howard Ashman)

Best Sound: *Aladdin*, Walt Disney (David J. Hudson, Doc Kane, Mel Metcalfe, Terry Porter)

Best Sound Effects Editing: *Aladdin*, Walt Disney (Mark Mangini)

1993

Blindscape, National Film & Television School

Small Talk, Bob Godfrey Films

The Mighty River, Canadian Broadcasting Corporation/ Societe Radio-Canada Production

The Wrong Trousers, Aardman Animations Ltd. Production

1994

Bob's Birthday, Snowden Fine Animation "The Big Story," Spitting Image Production

The Janitor, Vanessa Schwartz Production

The Monk and the Fish, Folimage Valence Production

Triangle, Gingco Ltd. Production

*Best Original Score:** *The Lion King*, Walt Disney (music and lyrics by Elton John and Tim Rice)

Best Original Song: "Hakuna Matata" (*The Lion King*, Walt Disney; music and lyrics by Elton John and Tim Rice)

Best Original Song: "Circle of Life" (*The Lion King*, Walt Disney; music and lyrics by Elton John and Tim Rice)

*Best Original Song:** "Can You Feel the Love Tonight" (*The Lion King*, Walt Disney; music and lyrics by Elton John and Tim Rice)

1995

A Close Shave, Aardman Animations Ltd. Production

Gagarin, Second Frog Animation Group Production

Runaway Brain, Walt Disney Pictures Production

The Chicken from Outer Space, Stretch Films/Hanna-Barbera/ Cartoon Network Production

The End, Alias/Wavefront Production

Best Original Music or Comedy Score: *Toy Story*, Walt Disney (music and lyrics by Randy Newman)

Best Original Song: "You've Got a Friend in Me" (*Toy Story*, Walt Disney; music and lyrics by Randy Newman)

Best Screenplay (Written Directly for the Screen): *Toy Story*, Walt Disney (Joel Cohen, Peter Docter, John Lasseter, Joe Ranft, Alec Sokolow, Andrew Stanton, Joss Whedon)

*Special Achievement Award:** John Lasseter, *Toy Story*, Walt Disney

1996

Canhead, Timothy Hittle Production

La Salla, National Film Board of Canada

Quest, Thomas Stellmach Animation Production

Wat's Pig, Aardman Animations Ltd. Production

Best Original Musical or Comedy Score: *The Hunchback of Notre Dame*, Walt Disney (music by Alan Menken and lyrics by Stephen Scwartz).

Best Original Musical or Comedy Score: *James and the Giant Peach*, Walt Disney (music and lyrics by Randy Newman).

1997

Famous Fred, TVC London Production

Geri's Game, Pixar Animation Production

La Vielle Dame et Les Pigeons (The Old Lady and the Pigeons), Production Pascal Blais

The Mermaid, Film Company DAGO/Alexander Pictures Production

Redux Riding Hood, Walt Disney Television Animation Production

Best Song: "Go the Distance" (*Hercules*, Walt Disney; music by Alan Menken and lyrics by David Zippel)

Best Song: "Journey to the Past" (*Anastasia*, 20th Century-Fox; music and lyrics by Diane Warren)

Best Original Musical or Comedy Score: *Anastasia*, 20th Century-Fox (music by Stephen Flaherty and lyrics by Lynn Ahrens)

1998

*Bunny, Blue Sky Studios
The Canterbury Tales, 54C-BBC Wales/HBO
Jolly Roger, Astley Baker-Silver Bird for Channel 4
More, Bad Clams Productions/Swell Productions/Flemington Productions
When Life Departs, A. Film Productions
Best Original Musical or Comedy Score: A Bug's Life, Buena Vista Pictures (music and lyrics by Randy Newman)
Best Original Musical or Comedy Score: Mulan, Walt Disney (music by Matthew Wilder and Jerry Goldsmith; lyrics by David Zipple)
Best Original Musical or Comedy Score: The Prince of Egypt, Dreamworks (music and lyrics by Stephen Schwartz and Hans Zimmer)
Best Original Song: "The Prayer" (Quest for Camelot, Warner Bros.; music and lyrics by Carol Bayer Sager, David Foster, Tony Renis and Alberto Testa)
Best Original Song: "When You Believe" (The Prince of Egypt, Dreamworks; music and lyrics by Stephen Schwartz)

⊚ EMMY AWARDS

In 1949, following the formation of the National Academy of Television Arts and Sciences, the annual presentation of the Emmy Awards was born. Local and national awards shows were organized to honor local television station programming and prime-time entertainment programming that aired on the three major networks. The awards presentation ceremony became an annual event in 1957. Animated cartoons have been the recipients of Emmys throughout the history of the awards. A complete listing of Emmy-nominated cartoon series and prime-time animated specials follows. Winners are preceded by an asterisk.

1959–60

Outstanding Achievement in the Field of Children's Programming:
*Huckleberry Hound (Syndicated)
Quick Draw McGraw (Syndicated)

1960–61

Outstanding Achievement in the Field of Children's Programming:
Huckleberry Hound (Syndicated)

1965–66

Outstanding Children's Program:
*A Charlie Brown Christmas (CBS)

1966–67

Outstanding Children's Program:
*Jack and the Beanstalk (NBC)

Charlie Brown's All-Stars (CBS)
It's the Great Pumpkin, Charlie Brown (CBS)

1973–74

Outstanding Children's Special:
A Charlie Brown Thanksgiving (CBS)

1974–75

Outstanding Children's Special:
*Yes, Virginia There Is a Santa Claus (CBS)
Be My Valentine, Charlie Brown (CBS)
Dr. Seuss' the Hoober-Bloob Highway (CBS)
It's the Easter Beagle, Charlie Brown (CBS)
Outstanding Entertainment Children's Series:
*Star Trek (NBC)
The Pink Panther (NBC)

1975–76

Outstanding Children's Special:
*You're a Good Sport, Charlie Brown (CBS)
Outstanding Informational Children's Special:
*Happy Anniversary, Charlie Brown (CBS)

1976–77

Outstanding Children's Special:
It's Arbor Day, Charlie Brown (CBS)
The Little Drummer Boy, Book II (NBC)

1977–78

Outstanding Children's Special:
*Halloween Is Grinch Night (ABC)
A Connecticut Yankee in King Arthur's Court (CBS)
The Fat Albert Christmas Special (CBS)

1978–79

Outstanding Animated Program:
*The Lion, the Witch and the Wardrobe (CBS)
You're the Greatest, Charlie Brown (CBS)
Happy Birthday, Charlie Brown (CBS)

1979–80

Outstanding Animated Program:
*Carlton Your Doorman (CBS)
Dr. Seuss' Pontoffel Rock, Where Are You? (ABC)
Pink Panther in Olym-Pinks (ABC)
She's a Good Skate, Charlie Brown (CBS)

1980–81

Outstanding Children's Program:
Paddington Bear (PBS)
Outstanding Animated Program:
*Life Is a Circus, Charlie Brown (CBS)
Bugs Bunny: All American Hero (CBS)

Faeries (CBS)
Gnomes (CBS)
It's Magic, Charlie Brown (CBS)

1981–82
Outstanding Animated Program:
*The Grinch Grinches the Cat in the Hat (ABC)
A Charlie Brown Celebration (CBS)
The Smurf Springtime Special (NBC)
Smurfs (NBC)
Someday You'll Find Her, Charlie Brown (CBS)

1982–83
Outstanding Animated Program:
*Ziggy's Gift (CBS)
Here Comes Garfield (CBS)
Is This Goodbye, Charlie Brown? (CBS)
The Smurfs Christmas Special (NBC)
What Have We Learned, Charlie Brown? (CBS)

1983–84
Outstanding Animated Program:
*Garfield on the Town (CBS)
A Disney Christmas Gift (NBC)
It's Flashbeagle, Charlie Brown (CBS)
The Smurfic Games (NBC)

1984–85
Outstanding Animated Program (Daytime):
*Jim Henson's Muppet Babies (CBS)
Alvin and the Chipmunks (NBC)
Fat Albert and the Cosby Kids (Syndicated)
Smurfs (NBC)
Outstanding Animated Program (Nighttime):
*Garfield in the Rough (CBS)
Donald Duck's 50th Birthday (CBS)
Snoopy's Getting Married (CBS)

1985–86
Outstanding Animated Program (Daytime):
*Jim Henson's Muppet Babies (CBS)
CBS Storybreak (CBS)
The Charlie Brown and Snoopy Show (CBS)
Fat Albert and the Cosby Kids (Syndicated)
The Smurfs (NBC)
Outstanding Animated Program (Nighttime):
*Garfield's Halloween Special (CBS)
Garfield in Paradise (CBS)

1987–87
Outstanding Animated Program (Daytime):
*Jim Henson's Muppet Babies (CBS)
Alvin and the Chipmunks (NBC)
Disney's Adventures Of The Gummi Bears (NBC)
Punky Brewster (NBC)
The Smurfs (NBC)

Outstanding Animated Program (Nighttime):
*Cathy (CBS)
Garfield Goes Hollywood (CBS)

1987–88
Outstanding Animated Program (Daytime):
*Jim Henson's Muppet Babies (CBS)
Alvin and the Chipmunks (NBC)
CBS Storybreak (CBS)
Disney's DuckTales (Syndicated)
The Smurfs (NBC)
Outstanding Animated Program (Nighttime):
*A Claymation Christmas Celebration (CBS)
Brave Little Toaster (Disney)
A Garfield Christmas Special (CBS)

1988–89
Outstanding Animated Program (Daytime):
*The New Adventures of Winnie the Pooh (ABC)
DuckTales (Syndicated)
Jim Henson's Muppet Babies (CBS)
A Pup Named Scooby-Doo (ABC)
The Smurfs (NBC)
Outstanding Animated Program—For Programming More Than One Hour (Nighttime):
*Disney's DuckTales: Super DuckTales (NBC)
Outstanding Animated Program—For Programming Less Than One Hour (Nighttime):
*Garfield: Babes and Bullets (CBS)
Abel's Island (PBS)
Garfield: His Nine Lives (CBS)
Madeline (HBO)
Meet the Raisins (CBS)

1989–90
Outstanding Animated Program (Daytime):
*The New Adventures of Winnie the Pooh (ABC)
*Beetlejuice (ABC)
Outstanding Animated Program—One Hour or Less (Nighttime):
*The Simpsons (Fox)
Garfield's Feline Fantasies (CBS)
Garfield's Thanksgiving (CBS)
Why, Charlie Brown, Why? (CBS)
The Simpsons Christmas Special (Fox)

1990–91
Outstanding Animated Program (Daytime):
Bobby's World (Fox)
Captain Planet and the Planeteers (TBS)
Garfield and Friends (CBS)
Slimer! and the Real Ghostbusters (ABC)
*Tiny Toon Adventures (Syndicated)
Outstanding Animated Program—One Hour or Less (Nighttime):
Garfield Gets a Life (CBS)

The Simpsons (Fox)
Tiny Toon Adventures: The Looney Beginning (CBS)
Will Vinton's Claymation Comedy of Horrors (CBS)

1991–92
Outstanding Animated Program (Daytime):
Darkwing Duck (ABC/Syndicated)
Doug (Nickelodeon)
The New Adventures of Winnie the Pooh (ABC)
*Rugrats (Nickelodeon)
Tiny Toon Adventures (Syndicated)
Outstanding Animated Program—One Hour or Less (Nighttime):
A Claymation Easter (CBS)
The Ren & Stimpy Show (Nickelodeon)
Shelly Duvall's Bedtime Stories (Showtime)
*The Simpsons (Fox)

1992–93
Outstanding Animated Program (Daytime):
*Tiny Toon Adventures (Syndicated)
Batman: The Animated Series (Fox)
Disney's Darkwing Duck (ABC)
Doug (Nickelodeon)
Rugrats (Nickelodeon)
Outstanding Animated Program—One Hour or Less (Nighttime):
*Batman: The Animated Series (Fox)
Inspector Gadget Saves Christmas (NBC)
Liquid Television (MTV)
The Ren & Stimpy Show (Nickelodeon)
The World of Peter Rabbit and Friends: The Tale of Peter Rabbit and Benjamin Bunny (The Family Channel)

1993–94
Outstanding Animated Program (Daytime):
*Rugrats (Nickelodeon)
Batman: The Animated Series (Fox)
The Halloween Tree (Syndicated)
Rugrats (Nickelodeon)
Animaniacs (Fox)
Outstanding Animated Program—One Hour or Less (Nighttime):
Duckman (USA)
Flintstones Family Christmas (ABC)
The Ren & Stimpy Show (Nickelodeon)
*The Roman City (PBS)
The Town Santa Forgot (NBC)

1994–95
Outstanding Animated Program (Daytime):
*Where on Earth Is Carmen Sandiego? (Fox)
Animaniacs (Fox)
Disney's Aladdin (CBS)

Disney's the Little Mermaid (CBS)
Rugrats (NIK)
Outstanding Animated Program—One Hour or Less (Nighttime): *Dexter's Laboratory* in "Changes" (The Cartoon Network)
Dr. Seuss' Daisy-Head Mayzie (TNT)
A Rugrats Passover (Nickelodeon)
*The Simpsons (Fox)
Steven Spielberg Presents Tiny Toons Night Ghoulery (Fox)

1995–96
Outstanding Animated Program (Daytime):
*Animaniacs (WB Network)
The New Adventures of Madeline (ABC)
Scholastic's The Magic School Bus (PBS)
Where on Earth Is Carmen Sandiego? (Fox)
Outstanding Animated Program—One Hour or Less (Nighttime):
Cow and Chicken in "No Smoking" (The Cartoon Network)
Dexter's Laboratory (The Cartoon Network)
Duckman (USA)
*A Pinky & the Brain Christmas Special (WB)
The Simpsons (Fox)

1996–97
Outstanding Children's Animated Program (Daytime):
*Animaniacs (WB Network)
Pinky & the Brain (WB Network)
Scholastic's The Magic School Bus (PBS)
Schoolhouse Rock (ABC)
Where on Earth Is Carmen Sandiego? (Fox)
Outstanding Animated Program—One Hour or Less (Nighttime):
Dexter's Laboratory (The Cartoon Network)
Duckman (USA)
King of the Hill (Fox)
Rugrats (Nickelodeon)
*The Simpsons (Fox)
The Willows in Winter (The Family Channel)

1997–98
Outstanding Children's Animated Program (Daytime):
*Arthur (PBS)
Steven Spielberg Presents Animaniacs (WB Network)
Disney's 101 Dalmations (ABC)
Steven Spielberg Presents Pinky, Elmyra & The Brain (WB Network)
Disney's Doug (ABC)
Outstanding Animated Program—One Hour or Less (Nighttime):
Cow and Chicken (Cartoon Network)
Dexter's Laboratory (Cartoon Network)
King of the Hill (Fox)
*The Simpsons (Fox)
South Park (Comedy Central)

SELECTED BIBLIOGRAPHY

Adamson, Joe. *Tex Avery: King of Cartoons*. New York: Popular Film Library, 1975.

———. *The Walter Lantz Story*. New York: Putnam, 1985.

Bakshi, Ralph. *The Animated Art of Ralph Bakshi*. Norfolk, Va.: Donning Company Publishers, 1989.

Beck, Jerry, and Friedwald, Will. *Looney Tunes and Merrie Melodies: A Complete Illustrated Guide to the Warner Bros. Cartoons*. New York: Henry Holt, 1989.

Blanc, Mel, and Bashe, Phillip. *That's Not All Folks!: My Life in the Golden Age of Cartoons and Radio*. New York: Warner Books, 1988.

Brooks, Tim, and Marsh, Earle. *The Complete Guide to Prime Time Network TV Shows: 1946–Present*. New York: Ballantine Books, 1988.

Cabarga, Leslie. *The Fleischer Story*. New York: DaCapo Press, 1988.

Canemaker, John. *Felix: The Twisted Tale of the World's Most Famous Cat*. New York: Pantheon Books, 1991.

———. *Winsor McCay: His Life & Art*. New York: Abbeville Press, 1987.

Crafton, Donald. *Before Mickey: The Animated Film 1898–1928*. Cambridge, Mass.: MIT Press, 1982.

Culhane, Shamus. *Animation from Script to Screen*. New York: St. Martin's Press, 1990.

———. *Talking Animals and Other People*. New York: St. Martin's Press, 1986.

Edera, Bruno. *Full Length Animated Feature Films*. New York: Hastings House, 1977.

Erickson, Hal. *Television Cartoon Shows, 1949–1993*. Jefferson, N.C.: McFarland & Company, 1995.

Fischer, Stuart. *Kids' TV: The First 25 Years*. New York: Facts On File, 1983.

Gifford, Denis. *American Animated Films: The Silent Era, 1897–1929*. New York: McFarland & Company, 1990.

Grant, John. *Walt Disney's Encyclopedia of Animated Characters*. New York: Harper & Row, 1987.

Grossman, Gary H. *Saturday Morning TV*. New York: Arlington House, 1987.

Jones, Chuck. *Chuck Amuck: The Life & Times of an Animated Cartoonist*. New York: Farrar Straus & Giroux, 1989.

Lenburg, Jeff. *The Great Cartoon Directors*. Jefferson, N.C.: McFarland & Company, 1983.

Maltin, Leonard. *Of Mice and Magic*. New York: McGraw-Hill, 1980.

McNeil, Alex. *Total Television: A Comprehensive Guide to Programming from 1948 to 1980*. New York: Penguin, 1980.

Peary, Danny, and Peary, Gerald. *The American Animated Cartoon: A Critical Anthology*. New York: E.P. Dutton, 1980.

Schneider, Steve. *That's All Folks!: The Art of Warner Bros. Animation*. New York: Henry Holt, 1988.

Sennett, Ted. *The Art of Hanna-Barbera: Fifty Years of Creativity*. New York: Viking, 1989.

Terrace, Vincent. *Encyclopedia of Television Series, Pilots and Specials: 1937–1973*. New York: New York Zoetrope.

———. *Encyclopedia of Television Series, Pilots and Specials: 1974–1984*. New York: New York Zoetrope.

Woolery, George. *Children's Television: The First Thirty-Five Years, 1946–1981*. (Part I: Animated Cartoon Series.) Metuchen, N.J.: Scarecrow Press, 1983.

INDEX

Boldface numbers indicate major treatment of a topic; *italic* numbers indicate illustrations.

493591

DH

791.
433
LEN

5000130236